圖書館學家文庫
Library of Library Scientists

李德竹文集
Collected Works of Lucy Te-Chu Lee

李德竹 著

中山大学出版社
SUN YAT-SEN UNIVERSITY PRESS

·广州·
·Guang Zhou·

版權所有　翻印必究

圖書在版編目（CIP）數據

李德竹文集/李德竹著.—廣州：中山大學出版社，2012.11
ISBN 978-7-306-04325-2

Ⅰ.①李…　Ⅱ.①李…　Ⅲ.①李德竹—文集 ②圖書館工作—咨詢服務—文集　Ⅳ.①G252.61-53

中國版本圖書館 CIP 數據核字（2012）第 233019 號

出 版 人：	祁　軍
策劃編輯：	王俊輝
責任編輯：	王俊輝
封面設計：	林綿華
責任校對：	曾育林
責任技編：	何雅濤
出版發行：	中山大學出版社
電　　話：	編輯部 020-84111996，84113349，84111997，84110779
	發行部 020-84111998，84111981，84111160
地　　址：	廣州市新港西路 135 號
郵　　編：	510275　　傳　真：020-84036565
網　　址：	http://www.zsup.com.cn　　E-mail：zdcbs@mail.sysu.edu.cn
印 刷 者：	广东省农垦总局印刷厂
規　　格：	787mm×960mm　1/16　52 印張　1250 千字
版次印次：	2012 年 11 月第 1 版　2012 年 11 月第 1 次印刷
定　　價：	238.00 元

如發現本書因印裝質量影響閱讀，請與出版社發行部聯繫調換

編委會成員

顧　問：周和平（文化部原副部長，中國圖書館學會名譽理事長，中國國家圖書館館長）

主　編：譚祥金

副主編：程煥文　吳　晞　劉洪輝　趙燕群

編輯委員會委員（按姓氏拼音順序排列）

　　　　程煥文　杜秦生　方家忠　李國新　劉洪輝　倪曉建　邱冠華
　　　　沈　津　譚祥金　吳建中　吳　晞　謝灼華　趙燕群

《圖書館學家文庫》總序

  圖書館是社會文明進步的標志，爲傳承歷史、延續文明、開拓未來提供着信息與知識保障；是建設學習型社會的重要陣地，承擔着提高公民學習能力與創新能力，滋養公民文明素質的重要責任；是通向知識之門，爲構建國家知識創新體系提供着知識與智力支撐；是公共文化服務體系的重要組成部分，對於彌合數字鴻溝，保障人民群衆的基本文化權益發揮着重要作用。

  新中國成立以來，尤其是改革開放以來，在黨和政府的高度重視下，在廣大圖書館理論與實踐者的共同努力下，我國圖書館事業得到了長足的發展。在這個發展歷程中，一代又一代圖書館學家作出了卓越貢獻。

  圖書館學，圖書館工作，是學術性和實踐性都很突出的一個領域。何爲圖書館學家？我以爲，既要有深厚的專業學術造詣，還要有勇於實踐、善於探索的精神。對於圖書館的學科發展和事業發展，更要有理論和實踐的雙重推動，兩者猶如雙翼：理論研究要總結實際工作、帶動實際工作；實際工作要注重正確理論的指引，還要不斷給學術研究帶來新的活力和突破。

  由中山大學圖書館、深圳公共圖書館研究院編撰、中山大學出版社出版的《圖書館學家文庫》，旨在薈萃一批優秀圖書館專業工作者在長期的圖書館學理論研究與工作實踐中積累的成果，將爲我們展現出一幅圖書館學研究和圖書館事業發展的絢麗畫卷，這些成果對於當今圖書館事業發展仍然具有指導和借鑒意義。

  《圖書館學家文庫》首批結集出版的是業界老一輩學人的成果。他們或身居學術研究前沿，或奮鬥於事業發展一綫，或身居海外關注中國圖書館事業，他們當中的很多人都是在極其艱苦的條件下，孜孜以求，不懈努力，取得了豐碩的成果，爲圖書館學和圖書館事業作出了不可磨滅的貢獻，他們對事業的熱愛在中國圖書館事業發展史上留下了令人感動的篇章。

  公共圖書館研究院是 2009 年在深圳成立，是國內第一家以公共圖書館爲研究對象的專業研究團體。公共圖書館研究院是一家非政府機構，由文化部社會文化司、中國圖書館學會和深圳市文體旅游局出任指導單位，深圳圖書館、深圳圖書情報學會主辦，匯聚了中國大陸、臺港澳及海外衆多的專業學者和圖書館管理者，爲公共圖書館事業發展提供了一個新的學術研究和交流平臺。

  《圖書館學家文庫》的編輯出版展現了廣東圖書館學界的眼光和實力，值得贊許。最后，還要感謝中山大學出版社，正是他們的遠見卓識和鼎力支持，才使《圖書館學家文庫》得以面世。

周和平
文化部原副部長
中國國家圖書館館長
中國圖書館學會名譽理事長
2011 年春於北京

序 言

　　李德竹教授為圖書館學與資訊科學領域前輩，學術卓越，桃李滿門。在時序推移、李教授辭世一年零九個月後，欣見《李德竹文集》得以出版，並收在深圳公共圖書館研究院編撰、廣州中山大學出版社出版之《圖書館學家文庫》中，十分可喜可賀。

　　筆者為李教授後進，在臺灣大學圖書資訊學系同事二十七載，期間李教授曾擔任第八屆系主任。筆者對李教授之學術成就甚為欽佩，亦一向作為個人專業生涯中之學習標竿。如今有幸被邀約撰寫序言，雖然愧不敢當，但基於同儕厚誼，也就誠惶誠恐的接下任務。

　　李教授早年留學美國，讀完大學部後，繼續進修，最後榮獲匹茲堡大學圖書館學與資訊科學研究院博士學位。回臺灣後，任教於淡江大學與臺灣大學，作育英才無數。李教授之學術專長以資訊科學為主，而筆者偏重圖書館學。學術上實不敢妄議其高深；因此，本文僅就李教授著作選集之內容作一簡介。

　　《李德竹文集》，共收"論述"60篇，"傳記及訪談"6篇，"書評"4篇，全書共達800餘頁，可謂卷帙厚重。其中所含"論述"，遍及資訊科學、資訊科學課程、圖書館學與資訊科學教育、圖書館自動化、科技資源、圖書館資訊標準、資訊素養、資訊倫理等議題。"傳記及訪談"，顯示出李教授實事求是之為學態度與開朗豁達之個人性情。本書附錄《李德竹教授主要著作目錄及學術貢獻》一文，長達五頁，洋洋灑灑，即使外行讀來，亦可一目了然，讚佩李教授之卓著學術成就。前已述及，筆者專長不在資訊科學；因此，本文僅作簡介，不能深入討論李教授之學術內容，尚祈資訊科學專家學者見諒。

　　本書收集李德竹教授一生辛勤耕耘之學術成果。作為圖書館學與資訊科學領域之一員，李教授之後進，筆者本人極力推薦本書《李德竹文集》給領域中之同行同儕與學生後輩。尤其期盼李教授生前之得意弟子與桃李門生，仔細研讀，俾能將李教授之學術思想與著述內容發揚光大，傳承李教授一生貢獻杏壇、作育英才、弘揚學術之崇高抱負與使命。

盧秀菊
臺灣大學圖書資訊學系榮退教授
2012 年 11 月於臺北

序　言

　　我們兄弟姊妹八人，家三姊李德竹教授行六，有三兄二姊二弟。家三姊一生以資訊科學研究教學與培育優秀人才服務國家社會為志業。她在教學方面是一絲不苟，但對學生則是愛護有加，視如家人，可稱得上是"望之儼然，即之也溫"。二〇一一年元月初，家三姊感覺身體不適，住院檢查並治療，因黃金治療時間已過，於一個月後安息主懷。

　　在家人整理家三姊遺物時，在她的已出版著作外，並發現家三姊尚有很多論文、專題報告及各種研究心得等，未曾對外發表過。我與家人對於圖書資訊科學全不瞭解，除將家三姊全部著作出版品捐贈"國家圖書館"外，並商請"國家圖書館"曾館長淑賢將上述論文、研究報告等全權處理。經盧教授秀菊、趙教授燕群、曾館長淑賢等諸賢研商討論，咸認應將家三姊主要著作暨研究成果彙整編印專集，提供各界人士研究參考。

　　現業經家三姊生前摯友譚教授祥金、趙教授燕群賢伉儷，盧教授秀菊、曾館長淑賢等諸賢彙整完成，並擬於近期內付梓。曾館長希望我代表家人作一序言，我雖服務公職四十餘年，但對圖書資訊科學從未涉獵，實不敢妄置一詞。我只能代表全體家人對譚教授祥金、趙教授燕群賢伉儷，盧教授秀菊、曾館長淑賢、謝教授寶煖、蔡主任佩玲、高主任鵬、廖主任秀滿等諸位女士先生付出的辛勞與心血，由衷地表示十二萬分的敬意、感謝與感恩。謝謝您們，祝福您們。

李德武敬上

李德竹
(1935—2011)

目　次

論述

1. EDUCATION AND TRAINING FOR ONLINE USE OF DATABASES IN TAIWAN ……………………………………………………………………（1）
2. ONLINE PUBLIC ACCESS CATALOG FORMATS ………………（18）
3. ON-LINE PUBLIC ACCESS CATALOG DISPLAY FORMATS ……（32）
4. WEBNET CIRCULATION SYSTEM：AN EARLY USE STUDY ……（46）
5. NON-BIBLIOGRAPHIC DATABASES ………………………………（57）
6. CHINESE MARC FORMAT AND BIBLIOGRAPHIC DATABASES ……（71）
7. CHINESE MARC FORMAT FOR BOOKS ……………………………（84）
8. CHINESE MARC：ITS PRESENT STATUS AND FUTURE DEVELOPMENT（99）
9. US MARC 21 社區資訊機讀格式…………………………………（111）
10. 圖書館資訊素養之培養方針與評量指標…………………………（122）
11. 臺灣圖書資訊學術語詞彙之參考資料……………………………（151）
12. 資訊素養的意義、內涵與演變……………………………………（153）
13. 海峽兩岸圖書資訊相關國家標準現況之研究……………………（179）
14. 從 VANNEVAR BUSH "AS WE MAY THINK" 談資訊科學與技術之演進與發展……………………………………………………（210）
15. 資訊巨人 VANNEVAR BUSH（1890—1974）……………………（225）
16. 臺灣圖書館相關 "國家標準"………………………………………（237）
17. 臺灣與美加地區圖書資訊學資訊科學課程之研究………………（260）
18. 圖書館學與資訊科學課程革新之探討……………………………（287）
19. 評析 "國立大學" 校院圖書館自動化系統線上公用目錄功能與介面特性……（297）
20. EDI 與圖書館應用…………………………………………………（322）
21. 大學圖書館資訊倫理認知與問題之研究…………………………（343）
22. 臺灣地區 "國立大學" 校院圖書館自動化之經驗與問題研究……（358）
23. "建構資訊高速公路圖書館應扮演的角色" 研討會紀要…………（369）
24. 資訊網路時代臺灣地區圖書資訊服務的新方向…………………（374）
25. 圖書館學教師研究趨勢及資訊需求………………………………（388）
26. 我對改進圖書資訊學教育的淺見…………………………………（413）
27. 美國書目計量學博士論文評析……………………………………（415）
28. "中華圖書資訊學教育學會"…………………………………………（427）
29. 圖書館自動化系統線上目錄及其顯示格式之研究………………（429）
30. 臺灣科技資訊網路…………………………………………………（487）
31. 加值與圖書館作業…………………………………………………（494）

32. 資訊與電腦 …………………………………………………………（497）
33. 圖書館自動化座談會紀錄 ……………………………………………（499）
34. 臺灣圖書館自動化資訊系統發展之探討 ……………………………（518）
35. 圖書館業務自動化基本注意事項 ……………………………………（531）
36. 學術研究圖書館館員對圖書館作業自動化認識與態度 ……………（534）
37. 第四十七屆國際圖書館協會聯盟年會紀實 …………………………（556）
38. "教育部"和本系新修訂之圖書館學系必修課程 …………………（560）
39. 美國資訊科學學會 ……………………………………………………（562）
40. 資料庫與線上檢索服務 ………………………………………………（577）
41. 技術報告的分析 ………………………………………………………（598）
42. 資訊科學課程：四年來發展報告 ……………………………………（623）
43. 資訊科學概論 …………………………………………………………（647）
44. 泛論資訊科學 …………………………………………………………（673）
45. 中美科學資料運用發展研討會 ………………………………………（675）
46. 簡介"行政院國家科學委員會"科學資料及儀器中心 ……………（679）
47. 美國報導科學 …………………………………………………………（683）
48. 中文圖書機讀編目格式研訂工作報告 ………………………………（690）
49. ERIC 索引典與索引典之結構 ………………………………………（691）
50. LIBRARY NETWORKS ……………………………………………（702）
51. INTRODUCTION TO LIBRARY AUTOMATION ………………（704）
52. PRESENT STATUS OF LIBRARY & INFORMATION SCIENCE EDUCATION IN TAIWAN AREA ……………………………………（706）
53. 圖書館自動化概論 ……………………………………………………（715）
54. PLANNING AN INTEGRATED LIBRARY INFORMATION NETWORK SYSTEM：THE TAIWAN EXPERIENCE ……………………………（730）
55. 專題演講：NII 對圖書館事業的衝擊（題綱）……………………（731）
56. 海峽兩岸第四屆圖書資訊學術研討會紀要 …………………………（732）
57. 圖書資訊學教育西文書目（1991—1997 年）………………………（735）
58. 臺灣地區圖書館自動化人才之教育與訓練 …………………………（737）
59. E 時代圖書館自動化、網路化之注意事項 …………………………（757）
60.《資訊科學先驅》序言 ………………………………………………（766）

傳記及訪談

61. DICTIONARY OF INTERNATIONAL BIOGRAPHY, LANDMARK, MILLENNIUM TWENTY-EIGHTH EDITION PUBLICATION：MARCH/APRIL 2000 …………（769）
62. 德竹論 …………………………………………………………………（772）
63. 實事求是，開朗豁達 …………………………………………………（779）
64. 李德竹：臺灣資訊科學教育的領導者 ………………………………（785）

65. 本會李德竹教授為資訊科學專家，親自主持"中文機讀編目格式"小組……（793）
66. 談圖書館發展趨勢 …………………………………………………（794）

書評

67. INTRODUCTION TO AUTOMATION FOR LIBRARIANS ……………（798）
68. EDITOR：SHIRLEY HAVENS ………………………………………（801）
69. "圖書館學暨資訊科學常用字彙"評介 …………………………………（803）
70. 評介"重要科技文獻指南"第一輯 ……………………………………（805）

附錄：李德竹教授主要著作目錄及學術貢獻 ……………………………（808）

論　　述

EDUCATION AND TRAINING FOR ONLINE USE OF DATABASES IN TAIWAN[*]

INTRODUCTION

We are living in the "information age". Information is a vast, dynamic, and inexhaustible resource that affects all disciplines as well as the lives of all people. In this information-rich and information-seeking era, information seekers are constantly striving to maximize the utility of graphic records. But unfortunately, we are facing a crisis—the rapidly growing cost of productions and processing of publications which many libraries neither have the budgets to purchase nor the place to house them. Traditional techniques and technologies used by many libraries cannot cope, and changes must take place in order to keep pace with the increasing volume of information.

Fortunately the timing is right; with the assistance of modern technological innovations and capabilities, the control and the demand for accessibility, speed, efficiency and effectiveness of information can be more easily fulfilled with online database searching. This refers to the use of computers to retrieve information online from databases. A database is a collection of data in machine readable form for the purpose of information storage and retrieval. Online computerized bibliographic databases have been here with us since the early 1970s; the number of publicly available bibliographic and non-bibliographic databases has grown to more than 2,000 in 1984,[1,2] and they are increasing at a rate of 20% ~ 30% per year.[3] At the same time, the number of online database searches performed each year has rapidly grown from 700,000 in 1974 to an estimated 10 million in 1984.[4]

Kent said, during the 1977 Pittsburgh Conference on the Online Revolution in Libraries, that online bibliographic searching gives us "a new kind of power" which can be used as an enhanced basis for selection and exploitative control of world information. He also cautioned us that as "with any kind of power, both evil as well as good can result."[5] That is, one must posses the appropriate knowledge and skill in order to use this powerful tool efficiently and effectively. Therefore, the education and training for use of online databases is of vital importance.

The purpose of this paper is to provide an overview of the present status of education and training for the use of online databases in Taiwan: the background development; the types of organizations that provide education and training; the types of persons to be trained; the problems involved with education and training and possible solutions to them; and the future planning for education and training in the use of online databases. In addition, a recent survey

---

[*] *Library and Information Science Education* (Scarecrow Press, 1987)

of online databases searchers/intermediaries in this country will also be reported here.

BACKGROUND DEVELOPMENT IN GENERAL

General Background

The beginning of database production was in the late 1960s. In view of the literature, one can easily recognize that the online database searching service originated in the United States, the country that also produces the world's largest quantity of databases.

In 1977, Williams identified four phases in the history of database generation in U.S.: in the first phase, computer-readable databases were generated as a by-product of hard-copy production of A & I (Abstracting and Indexing) Services; in the second phase, computer-readable databases were generated as a direct product of A & I Services production activities; in the third phase, computer-readable databases were generated as distributable tapes but with no hard-copy counterparts being published; and in the fourth phase, computer-readable databases were generated as direct product but with no physically distributable tapes—only electronic distributions are available.[6] Figure 1 shows the four phases of database generation and their characteristics.[7]

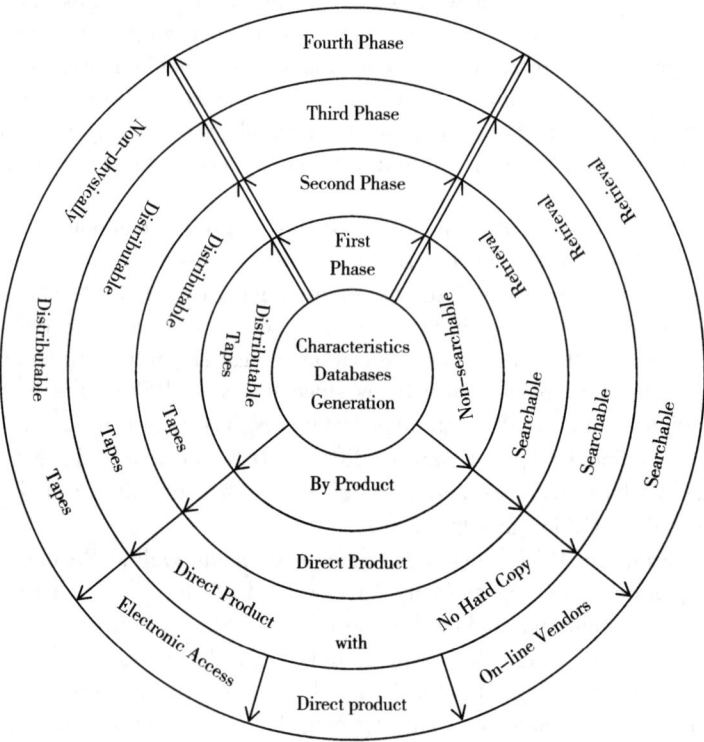

Figure 1 Databases Generation Phases and their Characteristics.

There are various types of databases existing today, and they have multifaceted characteristics. They are often called bibliographic, non-bibliographic, numeric, graphic, textual, or mixes type databases. The commonly used databases can also be classified in three categories: 1) by type of parent organization, such as profit, non-profit organizations, or governmental agencies; 2) by subject, such as multidisciplinary, science and technology, social sciences and humanities, news, business and finance, law and legal, and medical/biological sciences databases; and 3) by type of source materials, such as books, journals, patents, dissertations, current research, government reports and publications, newspapers, etc.

The Development of Online Database Searching Services

Online bibliographic searching was first investigated by Bagley in 1951, and it was several years before the first demonstration of bibliographic searching in 1954 in the form of batch searching, but the online bibliographic searching system was not shown until 1960: The delay was due largely to the absence of appropriate technology, such as computer time-sharing, remote terminal equipments, and communications capability. The first public demonstration of online bibliographic or text searching was conducted in the U. S. in 1960 using the System Development Corporation's interactive system known as Photosynthe. The second public demonstration was made by Lockheed online system known as CONVERSE in 1964, using an in-house library database. Two years later, in 1966, the first public use of a cathode ray tube (CRT) display for online searching was demonstrated with Lockheed system and also with SDC's Bibliographic Online Display (BOLD) system.[8] But the widespread online searching of bibliographic databases was not begun until the early 1970s. Christain pointed out that the development of online searching services was because:

1) The increasing number and cost books and journals publications; library staff and operating costs of libraries are rising each year; and user information demands.

2) The massive unclassification and declassification of government documents with important technical information.

3) The switch to photocomposition and computer-aided production technology in the part of publishers of conventional A & I Services.

4) Technological progress in computer processing, storage, terminal and communication.

5) The dramatic decreases in the cost of necessary equipment.

6) The increased acceptance and recognition by librarians of the power of online databases searching services.

7) The availability of sophisticated commercial online/services to provide efficient, nationwide access and worldwide access to various individual database.[9]

Database Producers and Online Service Vendors

According to the latest survey, there are more than 2,000 publicly available databases, 176 database producers, and nearly 400 online vendors. Among them, fifteen vendor services are the major distributors, they are

BRS — Bibliographic Retrieval Services
CAS — Chemical Abstracting Service, CAS Online
DIS — DIALOG Information Services
DJN — Dow Jones
INF — INFORM (now called Vu Text)
ISI — Institute for Scientific Information
LEG — Legislate
MDC — Mead Data Central
NLM — National Library of Medicine
NYT — New York Times (now on MDC)
PER — Pergamon Inforline
QUE — QUESTEL
SDC — System Development Corporation
SRC — The Source
WST — Westlaw

Of the fifteen online vendors included in the survey, seven of them account for all of the most used database vendors in terms of usage connect hours and user expenditures. The seven vendors are: BRS, DIALOG, Mead Data Central, National Library of Medicine, New York Times, SDC, and Westlaw.

Education and Training Methods

Online searching of bibliographic databases has been an integral and continually growing facet of librarianship. Education and training activities have been instrumental in the diffusion and adoption of online retrieval technology in order to maximize such a powerful searching mechanism.

It is not always easy to make a clear distinction between education and training; apparently they differ in functions, but educational objectives may sometimes well require training components and vise-versa. To quote Fenichel and Hogan's statement on education and training definitions, "education encompasses the basic principles and theories of information science and information retrieval systems. Its scope is much broader than training which focuses on the specific information and skills needed to operate the systems. In the context of these definitions almost all instruction for online searching has been 'training'. So far only library schools have attempted to educate."[12]

1. Who Are the Trainees?

A spectrum of audience can be identified as the potential trainees for online searching training programs, they are:
— Intermediaries/searcher/information broker
— Working librarians and library staff
— Library school students.
—End-user group: Researchers, faculty, graduate and undergraduate students, the general public, etc.

2. Who Are the Sponsoring Body/Trainers for Education and Training? Education and training, for online searching have been conducted by various types of organizations and professionals in U.S. and in other countries, they usually are:
— Database Producers/Search Services
— Database Processors/Online Vendors
— Schools of Library and Information Science
— Online Training Centers
— Continuing Education Extension Programs
— Professional Societies and Associations
— Consulting Firms
— Internal/In-house Training Programs
— Online Users Groups.

3. Methods of Instruction. The methods of instruction for education and training programs are of two types: the formal and the informal training programs.

(1) The Informal Training: The methods are used usually for self learning purposes. Online searchers teach themselves the searching techniques by:
— studying systems workbooks and manuals.
— practicing on practice files which are usually provided by online vendors, e.g. Lockheed's ONTAP (Online Training and Practice). Or using BRS/After Dark, DIALOG's Knowledge Index, the self-service method.
— Computer-assisted Instruction (CAI), such as "TRAINER" of the University of Pittsburgh, and "MEDLEARN" of the National Library of Medicine.

(2) The Formal Training Programs: Keenan identifies three types of formal training programs: ① Promotional activities for potential users; ② educational training for library students, working librarians and information specialists; ③ operational training for searchers/

intermediaries. In many countries, formal training in onlinesearching is offered by database producers, database processors, online vendors, schools of library and information science, continuing education extension programs, consulting firms, etc. [13]

1) Online Vendors/Database Processors Training Programs.

The contribution of online vendors and database processor to education and training of online users is extensive, especially in the U. S. In fact, most of the training of online searchers in the U. S. has been done by the online vendors, such as NLM, BRS, DIALOG, and SDC. The mode of instruction of BRS, SDC, and DIALOG is usually one to one and one half day training sessions aimed at either the beginners or advanced searchers, incorporating lectures, online demonstrations, and online student practice for a minimal fee. [14]

Wanger's "Survey of Users, 1974-1975" indicated 55% of searchers are learning to use systems through formal workshops given by online vendors/database processors; 45% of searchers learned the system informally. [15]

2) Database Producers/Suppliers Training Programs.

Some of the database producers support active educational programs; others have none. Some are free and some charge a fee. Today, the active database producers in U. S. in this area are Chemical Abstracts Service (CAS), Bio-Sciences Information Service of Biological Abstracts (BIOSIS), National Library of Medicine (NLM), and Educational Resources Information Center (ERIC).

3) School of Library and Information Science Education and Training Programs.

The emergence of online searching service as a powerful and useful tool has also been reflected in library school curriculums. In a 1977 survey, Harter found that at least two-thirds (42 of the 64) of ALA-accredited library schools were providing some sort of instruction in the use of online systems. [16] Again in 1981 Fenichel and Harter's *Survey of Online Searching Instruction in Schools of Library and Information Science*, 116 questionnaires were mailed; 72 returned. Sixty-eight of 72 responding schools (94%) indicated that they are providing some types of instruction in online searching as part of their regular curriculum. [17]

The level of instruction provided by library schools varies widely. Some give only introductory sessions and others devote an entire course to online searching, covering such topics as file organization and evaluation measures. Students who combine such a course with the courses of reference service, computer science, information science, and information analysis and retrieval systems offered by library schools should have a firm knowledge of both the principles and practice of online searching. Most of the schools are using either in-house systems or the commercial search systems, such as Lockheed's DIALOG, SDC's ORBIT, or BRS systems for instruction as well as for handson student use, the amount of connect time provided varying widely from school to school.

Perhaps the most extensive program of this kind undertaken by a school is at the Online Training Center of the School of Library and Information Science (SLIS) of the University of Pittsburgh. Software are developed to replicate the languages, formats and search capabilities of DIALOG, ORBIT and BRS—emulators of these systems which are operating on a dedicated DEC VAX computer and using samples from sixty commercially available databases. The students work at their own terminals, to gain a great deal of "hands-on" experience. Two types of programs are given at the Online Training Center: ① An Online Bibliographic Retrieval course for SLIS students, and ② A four-day training program for people of outside communities. Since April 1978, the Center has trained approximately 1,100 searchers, and over 800 of them are students. [18]

The financial support for this type of programs is always difficult to obtain. Although vendors provide the service to the library schools for educational use at much reduced rate of US

$15 per hour, the costs still mount up rapidly with many students using it. Because of this problem, some schools have designed in-house systems or other teaching aids for training students, such as audio and digital recording devices, audio-visual aids-overhead transparencies, slides, tape-slide programs, videotapes, films, have been developed and used also for education and training for online searching. [19]

4) Professional Associations and Societies, Consulting Firms, National and Research Organizations.

Professional associations and societies, consulting firms, national and research organizations usually conduct a one-day workshop or pre-conference seminars on online training for their members, such as Cuadra Associates, Inc., National and International Online Conferences, and national libraries.

(3) Online Training Materials.

Written materials are very important educational and training aids for online searching and for keeping up with the field. The publications are online database directories, online searching system manuals, database manuals and workbooks, thesaurus, word lists, and newsletters. Most of the online vendors are providing some training materials. for their customers for a fee.

(4) Evaluation and Assessment.

Little has been written on the evaluation analysis of education and training programs for online use of databases. A recent article by Swanson was a study primarily on the application of various instruction methodologies to teach the use of online databases of nine U.S. programs, and he identified two "must" elements of instruction programs: "printed manuals" and "handson" practice. [20] The criteria used for evaluation of this kind are often difficult to determine and formulate.

Survey of Online Professionals

The 1980 Online Users Survey reported that the average online searcher in the U.S. is a full-time person, spends 8.86 hours per week online, making $19,900 per year, is a female, and has a degree in chemistry and library science. [21] And also, Marquis, after surveying online professionals in 46 countries, published its *Marquis Who's Who Directory of Online Professionals* in 1984, which contains 6,100 names. The collected data indicated that a majority of online professionals work in the private sector and have between two and nine years of experience in the field; 32 per cent of them hold a master degree in library science; three-quarter (72 percent) of the online professionals are between the ages of 25 and 44, and fifty-eight per cent of them are women. DIALOG is the most frequently used system, and 69 per cent of the respondents still searched using dumb terminals; but the online industry has predicted that there will be a major shift in 1984 and 1985 using the micro-computers with 1,200 baud modems to conduct searches. [22]

Problems and Trends

Cost will still be the important constraint related to the education and training for online use of databases in many library schools; promoting and marketing of online services are continuously needed; the good, inexpensive, and easy to use training packages will still be in great demand; and also the standardized procedures for training and education of skilled professionals as well as end users must be developed. Now, it seems that the growth in number, size and diversity of databases is directly proportional to the increasing market demand for trained personnel in many organizations, and the training activities will definitely continue for some time to come. Thus, the library schools, database producers, online vendors, professional associations, and consulting firms will be more and more involved in the education and training for online use of databases than ever in the future.

EDUCATION AND TRAINING FOR ONLINE USE OF DATABASES IN TAIWAN

Background Development

Taiwan is a small and beautiful island, 13,892 sq. miles in size with a population of over 19 million. The economy of the Taiwan continues to grow in 1985 despite the slow recovery of the world economy. The national economic growth in 1984 was 4.92 per cent. Per capital income at market price reached NT $87,270 in 1981, NT $121,467, or the equivalent of US $3,067 in 1984.[23]

It has been realized that in order to maintain the growing speed of the economy and the advancement of scientific and technological development of the country, information and information services are the vital factors. For years, the greatest emphasis in Taiwan was on scientific, technological, and industrial research and development, and overlooking the importance of information and information services that are related to it; unfortunately, these have caused the repetition of research works, and wasted time, and money.

Information is power; one must be in control and in an active position with the most up-to-date news and information on hand in order to compete with others and survive. Also, the best and fastest way to introduce new technology and foreign know-how is through information and information services. Consequently, in 1978, the Taiwan government announced the Twelve New Construction Projects. The Twelfth Project is the Construction of Local Cultural Centers including libraries, museums, and music halls in each city and county at a cost of NT $1,500 million.[24]

In 1979, "the National Science and Technology Development Program" was initiated by the Taiwan Government, and in the same year, the Information Industry Institute (III) was established in Taipei with the miss of assisting, up-grading, and developing the nation-wide information industries, such as computer hardware, software, micro/mini-computers, Chinese computers, Chinese character sets for information interchange, databases management systems (DBMS), manpower training, etc. In 1980, the government announced that the second week of December, a week after Library Week, will be "the National Information Week". And at the same time, the Library Automation Planning Committee (LAPC) was established by the Library Association of Taiwan, in cooperation with "the National Central Library" of Taiwan with the purpose of improving information services and meeting the diverse needs of libraries in a local and international environment. The Committee has since drafted "the National Library Automation Project", which is to be implemented according to the following stages:

I. Automation Project for Taiwan Library Materials.
II. Automation Project for Western Language Materials.
III. Development of Library Operational Systems, and
IV. Planning and Implementation of a National Information Network.[25]

For the past five years, with the strong support from the government, the concepts and the importance of information find information services have been widely publicized throughout the Taiwan. People have realized that information and information services are not only of vital importance to support decision making, research and development, but also for the production of goods and services that touch all parts of our lives.

Libraries, Library Schools and Their Programs

In 1943, there were 95 libraries in Taiwan as whole. Now, according to a 1982 survey of libraries in Taiwan there are 4,094 libraries. The various types of libraries are listed in

Table 1. [26]

Table 1　Types of Libraries in Taiwan

Type of Library	Total Number
National	1
National Branch	1
Public	217
College & University	135
High School and Vocational School	1046
Elementary School	2474
Special	220
Total Libraries	4094

There are five colleges and universities in Taiwan with library science departments; they are: "National Taiwan University", "National Taiwan Normal University", Catholic Fu-jen University, Tamkang University, and the World College of Journalism. In addition, the Chinese Culture University is offering a graduate program in Taiwan bibliography. The only formal graduate institute of library science at present is at the "National Taiwan University". The Institute was established in 1980. The following Table 2 will provide the latest information on library schools and their programs in Taiwan.[27]

Table 2　Library Schools and Their Programs in Taiwan

Institution Name	Date of Est.	Admission Requirements	Duration of Study	Degree Conferred
"National Taiwan Univ".				
Graduate Institute of Libr. Science	1980	Bachelor Deg.	2 yr. +	MA
Dept. of Libr. Sci.	1961	High School Graduate	4 yr.	BA
"National Taiwan Normal Univ".				
Dept. of Social Ed.,				
Section of Libr. Science (Day)	1955	High School Graduate	4 yr. +	EDB
Night School	1980	Teachers of All Levels	4 yr.	EDB
Chinese Culture Univ.				
Graduate Institute of History,				
Libr. and Archives Section	1970	Bachelor Deg.	2 yr. +	MA
Catholic Fu-jen Univ.				
Dept. of Libr. Sci.				
(Day)	1970	High School	4 yr.	BA
(Night)		Graduate	5 yr.	
Tamkang University				
Dept of Educationa Media Sciences	1971	High School Graduate	4 yr.	BA

(續上表)

Institution Name	Date of Est.	Admission Requirements	Duration of Study	Degree Conferred
World College of Journalism				
Section of Libr. Sci.	1964	High School		
(Day)		Graduate	3 yr.	—
Section of Libr. Sci.	1965	High School		
(Night)		Graduate	4 yr.	—

The Development of Online Databases Searching Services

On December 28, 1979, National Telecommunication Day, the International Telecommunication Administration (ITA) of the Ministry of Transportation of the Taiwan announced the opening of the Universal Databases Access Service (UDAS) to academic, research, commercial, industrial, and governmental organizations in Taiwan. The purpose of UDAS is to provide domestic users via satellite with the accessibility to world coverage of online bibliographic and non-bibliographic information systems, such as Lockheed Information Systems (LIS), BRS (Bibliographic Retrieval Services), SDC's ORBIT system, Data Resources, Inc. (DRI), and public data network in other countries, to satisfy the needs of local information users and further help the social, economical, scientific; and technological improvement of the country.[28]

UDAS, How It Works?

The telephone and telecommunication systems in Taiwan are owned by the government. Therefore, ITA provides tile UDAS subscribers with all the international telecommunication connection facilities to foreign countries, such as international leased line, telex, telephone, terminal rentals, and the basic usage training of such facilities. The arrangement of UDAS service routing to other countries is shown in Figure 2.

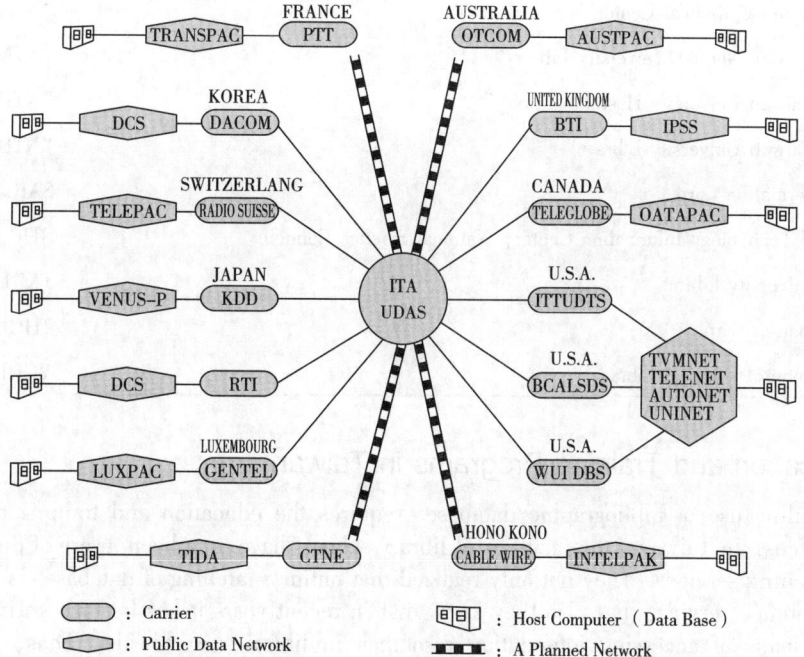

Figure 2. Arrangement of UDAS Service Routing to Other Countries

Present UDAS Subscribers, Who Are They?

After ITA announced the opening of UDAS to the public in 1979, the first subscriber requested to use the service was the Bank of America in March, 1980. By September the same year, the total of subscribers was 12. Total usage time from March to September in 1980 was 79,638 minutes: 29,244,000 words were transmitted.[29] Now, November, 1985, five years latter, the average monthly usage time is over forty thousand minutes and monthly transmitted words are averaging over 50 million. The total subseribers are 63, 33 are private companies. 14 banking and financial organizations. and 16 academic and research institutions. Among 63 UDAS subscribers 19 are using the service for information retrieval purposes. They are:

Name of Oranization	Abbreviation
Agricultural Science Information Center	ASIC
Chemical Industrial Research Laboratories	CIRL
Industrial Technology Research Institute	ITRI
"China Steel Corporation"	"CSC"
Chung-hua Institution for Economics Research	CHIER
Chung Shah Institute of Science & Technology	CSIST
Directorate General of Budget, Accounting & Statistics	DGBAS
Industrial Technology Research Institute	ITRI
(4 research labs: Materials, Mechanical, Electronics, Energy Research Labs.)	
Institute of Economics, Academic Sinica	IEAS
Legislative Yuan Library	LYL
"National Defense Medical Center"	"NDMC"
"National Taiwan Normal University Library"	"NTNUL"
"National Taiwan University Hospital Library"	"NTUHL"
"National Taiwan University Library"	"NTUL"
Satellite Information Corp	SAIC
Science and Technology Information Center, National Science Council	STIC
Tamkang University Library	TKUL
2100 Information Corp.	21IC
Veterans' General Hospital Library	VGHL

Education and Training Programs in Taiwan

The online use of bibliographic databases requires the education and training of users of online services. In Taiwan, the faculties of library schools have long been aware of the trends in online searching services. They not only realized that online searching of databases is a powerful tool for reference service, but also they knew that in recent years it has become an increasingly important means of accessing information resources in libraries worldwide. Thus, they have started to introduce the concepts of online databases and the search strategies in a number of related courses. (Shown in Table 3) And at the same time, they made suggestions to ITA and urged the government to support ITA to establish connections with various online databases vendors in the U. S. and in other countries. So the UDAS was inaugurated in 1979. [30]

Table 3   Library Science Courses Related to Teaching and
Education of Online Databases Concepts

Institution Name	Course Name	Searching Facility/Location/Systems
"National Taiwan Univ". Graduate Institute & Dept. of Libr. Sci.	* Online Searching Library Automation Library Trends * Information Analysis & Retrieval S. & T. Literature * Abstracting and Indexing Intn. to Info. Sci. Info. Sci. Seminar	"NTU" Library and Hosp. Library Online Facility/DIALOG Online Demo for Students
"National Taiwan Normal University" Dept. of Social Edu., Section of Libr. Sci.	* Information Searching Library Automation Reference Services Intn. to Info. Sci.	"NTNU" Library Online Facility/DIALOG, BRS 10 min. /student
Catholic Fu-jen Univ. Dept. of Libr. Sci.	* Information Ret'l Intn. to Info. Sci. S. & T. Literature	No Online Facility/ Demo 20 min. / DIALOG (STIC)
Tamkang University Dept. of Educational Media Science	* Information Centers & Services Library Automation Reference Services S. & T. Literature A & I Course Intn. to Info. Sci.	Tamkang Univ. Libr. Online Facility/ DIALOG Lab. Fee for Online practice
World College of Journalism	* Chinese Cat. & Class. Documentation	No Facility/No Demo.

At present time, there are no established training centers or training programs in the country. In the beginning, the training sessions were connected occasionaly by the vendor representatives who were in Taiwan marketing their products and services, or upon the requests of the customers in Taiwan to solve certain problems. At the same time, ITA and the vendor would schedule a short (two-day) training session for local subscribers and potential users, usually free of charge. Since then, the training sessions were handled by the subscribers themselves to train their searchers and users, and sometimes other libraries' personnel. In addition, the Science and Technology Library Network (SATLINE), an inter-library loan organization, and a few experienced subscribing institutions are also conducting workshops and seminars on online databases. Table 4 lists training sessions which were given from May, 1980 to the present.[31]

Table 4 Training Sessions Given From May, 1980 – Present

Training Institution	Trainer	Training Period	No. Trainee	Fee
"National Taiwan Univ".	DIALOG/ NTU Hosp. Searcher;	Regular Class	12	Free
	Libr. Auto. Workshop Instructor & "NTNU" Searcher	Aug. 29, 1980	42	Fee
		Aug. 18, 1981	42	Fee
"National Taiwan Normal Univ". Library	SDC/ "NTNU" Searcher	May 12 – 13, 1980	138	
		Nov. 28 – 30, 1980	40	Free
		May 10 – 11, 1980	15	
		Regular class	6 – 8	Fee
Science & Technology Information Center	DIALOG/	Aug. 26 – 27, 1980	12	NT $ 1000
		Aug. 28 – 29, 1980	12	NT $ 1000
	STIC. Searcher	Dec. 15 – 19, 1982 (half day)	37	Internal Training
ITA	DIALOG	May 16 – 17, 1982	40	Free
Tamkang University Library	DIALOG	Jan. 1982	Faculties	Free
	Searcher	July, 1982 (half day)	& Students L. S. Graduates (30)	Fee
	Class Instructor	Regular Class once/semester	Whole Class	Lab. Fee
21 Cent. Info. Co.	DIALOG	Two Days	50 +	?
SATLINE	Into of Major S. & T. Online DBs No online Training	Sept. 16 – 17, 1985	130	Free

The Graduate Institute and Department of Library Science of the "National Taiwan University" is now offering courses, such as "Online Searching" and "Information Storage and Retrieval" to train studens in online searching concepts and techniques. At the present time, both "NTU"

Library and its Hospital Library have subscribed to DIALOG Service, which will be used for the university community, online demonstration, and library students online hands-on searching practicce. In the future, if there is any indication of great demand for training or education in online use of databases in the country, the "National Taiwan University" would consider expanding its program to establish a National Training Center for the entire Taiwan region.

Survey of Online Users in Taiwan region

To understand the present status of online users, their problems and needs, a recent survey of online searchers was conducted. Questionnaires are mailed to 18 online subsribing organizations and ther searchers, and 16 (88.8%) subscribers returned the questionnaire. The survey results indicated that there are approximately 40 online searchers in 16 subscribing organizations, among them, 12 (30%) full-time searchers, 29 (72.5%) of them library science graduates, and the majority of them learned to search by themselves.

Their problems and needs are: the lack of subject background; difficulty in negotiating with users; not enough searching tools and lack of familiarity with the existing ones; problems in getting the original articles; lack of adequate online education and training programs; no one to solve searching problems; and some databases, such as economics, commercial databases are not relevent to the practical needs of industrial organizations in the country. All of them agreed that needs continuing education and training especially in the areas of online database structure, design principles, new search strategies, and functions. Major findings of online users, and frequently used databases are listed in Table 5.

Table 5 Major Findings of Online Users in Taiwan region

Orgn. Name	Av. Month Searches	No. of Searchers (fulltime)	Degree	Search Learn. Methods	Cont. Ed. & Train. Needs	System Name
ASIC	40	4 (1)	Marine & Agr. Sciences	Self-learn. In-house	yes	DIALOG BRS ORBIT
CIRI	26	2 (1)	Chem. Econom.	Self In-house ITA	yes	DIALOG BRSV ORBIT
CSC	20–30	1 (0)	Lib. Sci.	LS Class	yes	DIALOG
CHIER	5	1 (0)	Banking	In-house	yes	DRI
CSIST	38	2 (1)	Lib. Sci.	LS Class Others	yes	DIALOG
DGBAS	2	1 (0)	?	Self Vendor	yes	DRI
ITRI: ERL ERSO MRL MIRL	38	8 (0)	Lib. Sci. German Ind. Engr.	Self In-house Others Vendor ITA	yes	DIALOG
IEAS	3–5	1 (0)	Econom.	Self Vendor	yes	DRI

（續上表）

Orgn. Name	Av. Month Searches	No. of Searchers (fulltime)	Degree	Search Learn. Methods	Cont. Ed. & Train. Needs	System Name
LYL	7	5 (3)	Lib. Sci.	LS Class Self Others	yes	DIALOG
NDMC	30	3 (1)	Lib. Sci.	Self Others Seminar	yes	DIALOG
"NTNUL"	30	1 (1)	Lib. Sci.	Self Vendor	yes	DIALOG ORBIT
"NTUL"	?	6 (1)	Lib. Sci.	Self ITA	yes	DIALOG
"NTUHL"	40	1 (1)	Lib. Sci.	Self	yes	DIALOG
STIC	90	1 (1)	Lib. Sci.	Self Others Vendor ITA	yes	DIALOG BRS ORBIT
TKUL	?	1 (1)	Lib. Sci.	LS Class Self Others Vendor	yes	DIALOG
VACRS	80	2 (1)	Lib. Sci.	Self In-house Others Seminar	yes	BRS

Most Frequently Used Databases are: 1. CA Search
2. MEDLINE
3. BIOSIS
4. COMPENDEX
   INSPEC
   CLAIM
   PIS
5. WPI
6. NTIS
7. US Central
   DRI-CEI
   U. S. Patent
8. CAB
   IPAB
   ERIC
   LDC-ASIA
   LC

CIS
FSTA
Geoarchive
ISMEC
Magazine Index

Present Problems and Future Prospects

Online databases searching services. just began in the Taiwan Area, but there are many problems to be solved. Formal education and training programs for online use of databases must be established and formulated in the country to train skilled searchers. Fortunately, a number, of seminars, workshops, and training sessions have been conducted for online searchers and potential users by various organizations in the country. On November 8th, 1985, at the SATLINE Annual Meeting, a proposal to establish an "Online Users Groups" has been formally approved by its members. The Group will consist of online users in this area who will have formal and informal meetings to discuss and exchange experiences among themselves.

Another important problem is marketing of online searching services. Many authors, such as Williams, Keenan, and Tedd[32] have suggested strongly that marketing is important! Williams identifies that "Marketing is concerned with making various target groups aware of services and of the content, characteristics, features, advantages, and benefits that accure to specific searching databases. Marketing is also concerned with motivating or contracting for products and/or services."[33] Online searching is indeed a dynamic tool, but it is the duty and responsibility of librarians, information specialists, and library schools in the country to promote online searching services and make them known.

Another major problem of online searching is the cost. Cost of using the online services, cost of setting up an in-house searching system, cost of subscribing to the commercial searching services, and a minimum cost just to maintain it. It seems that the cost problem is the same in Taiwan Area as in other countries.

It has been realized by researchers in the area, that besides using UDAS service for locating foreign materials, another important factor also should be taken into consideration; that is the development of online databases of Chinese language materials. For years building databases of resources in Chinese language materials has long been an emphasized research area of various academic and research organizations in the Taiwan Area. And now, with advanced Chinese computer technology, many bibliographic and non-bibliographic Chinese language databases exist in the area. To name a few: the Chinese Database for Educational Resources Information System (CERIS), five databases of Agricultural Science and Technology Information Management System (ASTIMS), the Freedom Council Information Abstracts (FICA) database, and the "National Science Council" database etc.[34] Now, with modern computer and communication capabilities, and joint cooperative effors in research, the country is strongly urged to develop a national centralized online interactive bibliographic search service system in Taiwan Area.

CONCLUSIONS

In Taiwan Area, online service has just begun, and the tasks of developing the education and training programs for online use of databases will not be easy. Perhaps, with strong support of the government, the cooperative endeavor of local professionals and library schools, and also using other countries' experiences as a guide, the education and training for online use of databases in Taiwan Area will soon becomea reality.

I would like to conclude this paper with some thought of Lancaster,[35] who has once identified the goals of online education and training, especially in library schools, as train information services librarians who specilize in provision of information service from machine-readable databases. Such a librarian must be knowledgeable about databases, search systems, evaluation methodology, indexing techniques, vocabulary control procedures, and search strategies, and he felt that education programs should more than prepare individuals to work with the online systems. Moreover, he further said that many current technological applications are moving rapidly in a paperless direction, and eventually we will enter a paperless society. In this paperless environment, users will depend heavily on their online facilities, especially the terminals or their personal computers, and education and training in online searching will be more in demand than ever, not only to train the information professionals but also the end users a well. It seems to me that in the future society, paperless or not, one, any one must posses online searching skills in order to survive!

REFERENCES

1. Martha E. Williams, "Highlights of the Online Databases Filed— 'Statistics, Pricing and New Delivery Mechanism.'" *National Online Meeting 1984: Proceedings of the Fifth National Online Meeting*, New York, April 10 – 12, 1984. (Medford, N. J.: Learned Information, 1984), p. 1.
2. Emil H. Levine, "The National Online Meeting 1984," *ASIS Bulletin* 19 (April, 1984): 9.
3. Martha E. Williams, "Usage and Revenue Data for the Online Database Instry," *Online Review* 9 (September, 1985): 205 – 210.
4. C. H. Fenichel and Thomas H. Hogan, *Online Searching: A Primer*. 2nd ed. (Malton, N. J.: Learned Information, 1984), p. 3.
5. Allen Kent, "The Potential of Online Information Systems," *Online Revolution in Libraries* (New York: Marcell Dekker, 1978), pp. 28 – 29.
6. Martha E. Williams, "Education and Training for Online Use of Data Bases," *Journal of Library Automation* 10 (December, 1977): 326.
7. Lucy Te-Chu Lee, "Bibliographic Databases and Online Retrieval Services," *Journal of Library and Information Science* 5 (April, 1979): 79 – 103.
8. Charles P. Bourne, "Online Systems: History, Technology, and Economics," *Journal of ASIS* 31 (January, 1980): 155 – 160.
9. Roger Christain, "Bibliographic Data Bases," *The Professional Librarian*; *Reader in Library Automation and Technology* (White Plains, N. Y.: KIP, 1980), pp. 22 – 35.
10. Williams (1985), *op. cit.*, p. 1
11. Fenichel, *op. cit.*, p. 3.
12. Ibid.
13. Stella Keenan, "Promote, Educate or Train?" *Third International Online Information Meeting* (Malton, N. J.: Learned Information, 1979), pp. 342 – 349.
14. Charles Bourne and Jo Robinson, "Education and Training for Computer based Reference Services: Review of Training Efforts Todate," *Journal of ASIS* 31 (January, 1980): 25.
15. Judith Wanger, "Education and Training for Online System," *Annual Review of Information Science and Technology*. vol. 14 (White Plains, N. Y.: KIP, 1979), pp. 219 – 245.
16. S. P. Harter, "An Assessment of the Instruction Provided by Library Schools in Online Training," *Information Processing and Management* 15 (1979): 71 – 75
17. Carol H. Fenichel and S. P. Harter, *Survey of Online Searching Instruction in Schools of Library and Information Science* (Dublin, OH: OCLC, 1981), p. 8.

18. Conversation with Dr. E. Duncan, Director of the Online Training Center of the University of Pittsburgh School of Library and Information Science, August, 1985.
19. Lucy A. Tedd, "Teaching Aids Developed and Used for Education and Training for Online Searching," *Online Review* 4 (Spring, 1981): 205-216.
20. R. W. Swanson, "An Assessment of Online Instruction Methodologies," *Online* 6 (January, 1982): 38-55.
21. M. M. K. Hlava, "Online Users Survey 1980," *Online Review* 4 (June 1981): 294-299.
22. Carol Tenopir, "Online Professionals," *Library Journal* 110 (February 1985): 122-123.
23. Information supplied by the Directorate General of Budget, Accounting and Statistics, Taiwan, March, 1985.
24. *Central Daily News*, Taiwan, Feb. 15, 1985.
25. Library Association of China. "Library Automation Planning Program." *Library Association of China Newsletter* 22 (1980): 9-10.
26. National Central Library, Taiwan, A Survey of Libraries in Taiwan, *Taiwan* (Taipei: NCL, 1982), p. 28.
27. Chen-Ku Wang. "Libraries and Librarianship. in Taiwan, Taiwan" *The* 1980 *Library Development Seminar Proceedings* (Taipei: NCL, 1980), pp. 293-298.
28. S. F. Cheng. *Chao Tung Chieh Sheh.* (December, 1980), pp. 16-24.
29. Conversation with S. F. Cheng of ITA Office, March and November 1985.
30. Conversation with various organizations and library Schools in Taiwan, March and November, 1985.
31. A Survey on Online Searchers was conducted in November, 1985.
32. Lucy A. Tedd. "Education, Training and Marketing for Online Information Retrieval Systems." *Online Review* 3 (June, 1979): 205-212.
33. Williams (1977), *op. cit.*, p. 321.
34. T. S. Fung, "Chinese Data Processing Systems." The International *Workshop on Chinese Library Automation Proceedings* (Taipei: NCL. 1981), pp. Ⅰ-ⅩⅤⅢ.
35. F. W. Lancaster and L. C. Smith. "Online Systems in the Communication Processing: Projections." *Journal oF ASIS* 31 (September, 1980): 196-200.

ONLINE PUBLIC ACCESS CATALOG FORMATS*

Librarians for centuries have attempted to establish appropriate cataloguing rules for the preparation of quality catalogs in several physical formats (e. g., card, book, or microform). All are aiming at the same goal: to standardize catalog practice and prepare catalogs that provide the best possible access to library collections.

The catalog is an instrument of communication. For the past three quarters of a century, the card catalog has been the predominant model for the display of and access to library materials. The data elements for bibliographic description of records on the traditional 3 by 5 card are generally uniform in their layout, photography, content, sequencing, spacing, and arrangement from catalog to catalog. The card represents a display format of bibliographic data that has been familiar to all library users. [1]

With the emergence of the on-line catalog, both Salmon and Veaner observed the new and enhanced capabilities for bibliographic access; the flexible, changeable, and interactive characteristics of the online catalog; and the users' incredible excitement in experiencing the new form of library catalog. [2,3] When implementing the on-line catalog system, the bibliographic formats often have to be redesigned for CRT (cathode-ray tube) displays, but unfortunately, no standards have been established yet. As Matthews points out "format, or the manner in which the bibliographic information is displayed on the CRT screen is a vital yet frequently overlooked area of the human-computer interface." [4]

The main purpose of this paper is to study on-line catalog display formats, especially those of the on-line public access catalog (OPAC). Prior to analyzing the present status of on-line catalog display formats. one must fully understand the development of on-line catalogs: of which the display format is a part.

The increasing deficiencies and the existing costs of maintaining card catalogs have forced some libraries to seek and implement "alternative" catalogs. In addition, the adoption of the new cataloguing code. The Anglo-American Cataloguing Rules. Second Edition, and the closing of the card catalog of the Library of Congress (LC) in early 1981 have had an even greater impact on libraries worldwide. Some libraries, instead of waiting and observing the ongoing activities, are actively investigating potential alternatives to the card catalog. [5,6]

There are three commonly recognized alternatives to the card catalog: the book catalog, the COM (computer-output microform) catalog in fiche or film. and the on-line catalog. [7] Librarians believe that any catalog system considered or selected "must be at least as good as the card catalog it replaces"[8]; this is a considerable challenge requiring good judgment to make the decision, as record in the literature on comparative assessment of alternative catalogs: for example, the articles by Matthews,[6] Malinconico and Fasana,[9] and Marcum.[10]

Boss and Marcum state that the most important factors associated with the development of on-line catalogs are: "the improvements in computer technology, trends in library data development, and the availability of bibliographic records in machine-readable form from LC or one of the four North American utilities". [11] The four utilities are OCLC. RLIN. WLN. and ULTAS. Hildreth's 1982 book reported that the first on-line cataloguing system available for public use was the Online Computer Library Center (OCLC) system, which began as Ohio

---

* 本文選自李德竹教授所著之 Library Automation and Information Science: a Collection of Essays 一書。曾發表在《書府》6 期（1985 年 8 月），第 39—57 頁。

College Library Center in January 1974. The Research Library Information Network (RLIN) of Research Library Groups. Inc. (RLG) was available to the public in December 1974. and the Ohio State University Library Control System (LCS) was opened to public use in January 1975.[12] As of late 1981 the commercial vendor systems-CLSI. INC. with a newly developed "touch screen" terminal, and Universal Library Systems (ULISYS). with an authority control function were marketing their turnkey online catalog systems.[13] Excluding the three bibliographic utilities in 1982 Salmon identified seven commercial vendors among the 20 U. S. on-line public catalogs.[14]

Library automation is entering its third decade,[15] but the on-line catalog is in its early infancy.[16] And yet, the historical development of the on-line catalog is a part of the evolution of the traditional library catalog which is traced back to the beginning of the library catalog, perhaps to ancient Babylonian times.[17] The work of Norris, Strout, Pettee, Ruffin, Schley, and Corcoran provides a thorough overview of the history of the catalog and the emergence of the card catalog (see Tauber. Ref. 18).

The LC MARC II communications format was inaugurated in 1968,[19] and a series of conferences— "The Nature and Future of the Catalog," "The Catalog in the Age of Technological Change," "Closing the Catalog," etc. —sponsored by library associations began in the mid-1970s.[20,21] The themes of all of these programs were viewed as a "sign" that "the library profession has encountered its own 'future shock' in the wake of cybernetic and electronic revolutions that have been accelerating since the mid-fifties".[22]

In a recent development, CLR funded a survey among 125 CONDOC (Consortium to Develop an Online Catalog) member libraries which resulted in a ranked list of the 40 most important on-line catalog features for small and medium-sized libraries. One-fourth of the 40 features are display format related matters. With this list, CONDOC attempts to influence the direction of the offerings of vendors in the market place to develop a "library-driven" product of on-line catalog systems of interest to CONDOC members.[23]

Later, at the 1980 summer working session on on-line public catalogs at Dartmouth College, sponsored by the Bibliographic Services Development program of the Council on Library Resources (CLR), the 25 participants identified four priority areas for study and action:[24]

1. Analysis of user behavior and requirements
2. Examination of existing on-line public access systems
3. Development of methods for cost analysis and management
4. Development of distributed computing techniques and system-to-system links

After these recommendations, the council awarded OCLC a grant for the study "Online Public Access System: Data Collection Instruments for Patron and System Evaluation" (See Ref. 25). The results of this work were reported in Hildreth's book.[1] In early 1981 CLR funded LC, RLG, OCLC. J. Matthews and Associates, and the University of California to conduct a coordinated study of nationwide on-line public access catalogs using the questionnaire methodology.[26] Twenty-nine libraries having 16 different on-line catalog systems were surveyed. and 12,075 on-line users and nonusers completed their questionnaires.[27]

The preliminary reports on the study findings were reported at the 1982 ALA Annual Conference, and again at the American Society for Information Science (ASIS) 45th Annual Meeting.[28] Final reports were published in Using Online Catalogs: A Nationwide Survey,[27] Online Catalogs: Requirements. Characteristics and Costs,[29] and in a series of Online Catalog Project publications listed in CLR Research Developments.[30] Thus, it was declared that "1982 was the year of the online catalog".[31] and that the on-line catalog is the "first wave" of future catalogs.[32]

Gorman characterized an on-line catalog as an "integrationist" and defined it as

> a bibliographic control system that allows access by means of a number of access points (conventional and "unconventional"; single and in combination) to bibliographic data stored in machine-readable form. The data retrieved is displayed on a terminal screen or printed out on demand. Terminals are housed in the library or elsewhere. The user retrieves information about items held by the library and by other libraries.[33]

Stevens explained that the on-line catalog replaces nothing but the physical format of the traditional catalog, and that it will retain the standard bibliographic information. Ideally: the on-line catalog, in comparison with the traditional catalog, should possess greater accessibility, accuracy, up to dateness, flexibility, comprehensiveness, user-cordialness, and faster response; but there is no best or standard system as such yet.[34]

There have been discussions on whether or not Cutter's objectives of library catalogs are applicable to on-line catalogs. Kilgour, for instance, restricts the role of the on-line catalog to a "finding list".[35] On the contrary, Malinconico, Lubetzky, and others argue that Cutter's objectives are valid for all types of catalogs including on-line catalogs.[36-38] Similarly, the Ohio State University Library; based on Margaret Mann's seven functions of a catalog in the 1930s,[39] developed its Circulation System and now LCS.[40] Mann's functions were echoed again by Malinconico in his recent article.[41]

In the design and evaluation of an on-line catalog system. Kilgour identified seven important independent variables.[42] Boss and Marcum, in 1980, compiled a list of elements which they considered essential for designing and evaluating an on-line catalog.[43] In 1982 Horny suggested a number of points which she felt to be significant considerations that should be utilized for the assessment of an on-line catalog system.[44] These three lists are excellent and very similar in content. Based on these elements, the components for an on-line catalog system can be synthesized and developed.

The user, the task, the organizational interface (library), the on-line system, the data base/file, and the human-system interface/communication are the six components of the on-line catalog according to the CLR national on-line catalog survey.[45] On-line catalogs, as interactive man-computer systems, require a well-designed interface between man and the computer, also known as the human-system interface, user-system interface, or simply, user interface. This interface is the interaction undertaken between catalog users at a terminal and the computer system using a specific "language or protocol." Usually the interface has two distinct functions: "link" and "barrier." It is a user-oriented interface a newly, added dimension to catalog use, which occurs only in the interactive on-line catalog system. Consequently, to create a humaan-computer interface that is "user-cordial" is the sole objective for an on-line catalog. Unfortunately, system designers have often overlooked the characteristics and needs of current and potential users in their system designs.[46]

In Public Access Online Catalogs: The User Interface, the pioneer publication on on-line public catalogs, Hildreth presented a state-of-the-art review of the research and development efforts for improving the user-oriented interface and summarized guideline clusters for the interface design of on-line catalog systems as: easy to use friendly and cordial, protective and forgiving, reliable and responsive, and adaptive and flexible.[47]

The format of the display information on the CRT or "touch screen" terminal screen is crucial in the human-system interface. The fundamental requirement for formatting display is that language or communication from the computer should be organized and structured in a form appropriate to the task and frame of reference of the user. Stewart pointed out that "the way in which the material is organized and presented may determine the way in which the material is used or the conclusions that are drawn from it",[48] and that, the ergonomics and human factors are also to be considered. He identifies six factors that contribute to good format design; they are logical sequencing, spaciousness, relevance, consistency, grouping, and simplicity.[48] In addition, display formats of on-line catalog systems will be dependent on whether all or selected bibliographic elements were included in the data base, the on-Line system output display techniques, and the command capabilities. Therefore, the amount of information presented on a display screen is important. Research has revealed that information density loading for a printed journal page is 40% and for CRT display screens to be effective, the preferred amount of information density loading is only 15%.[49]

Galitz stated in the Handbook of Screen Format Design (1981) that "The format and content of a screen will be determined by where and how information is placed, and what information is included on the screen".[50] A lengthy technical review of electronic displays, display types, and display human factors was offered by Bylander,[51] and in 1981 turtle, Penniman, and Hickery explored the data entry-display devices for interactive information retrieval, for the past 15 years.[52]

According to Martin, 23 display techniques can be used for alphanumeric Keyboard displays of possible structure forms of a real-time screen conversation. It is common for a system to be able to employ a number of different display techniques at one time.[53] Finally, the system command capabilities of selection display are all important to display formats; these include "predefined" or "undefined" formats, specific record (s) /field (s), forward-backward movement of records on the screen, scrolling, sarting results, etc.[54]

Display formats are the direct user-system communication device which supplies the user's information needs. A well-designed screen or display format can increase human processing speed, reduce human errors, speed computer processing time, and increase productivity.[55]

What are the user's preferences and needs in display formats? Who are the decision makers concerning the number of display formats needed for on-line catalogs? What, how, and where are the information/data elements arranged on the screen? Little research has been conducted in these areas.[56-58] And little attention has been given to the display of bibliographic information on CRT terminal screens from the perspective of the user. Often people have taken them for granted and seldom inquired about who made the decisions on display formats and the reasons for their choices.[59]

Fortunately, in recent research on and surveys of on-line catalogs, display format data were also collected and analyzed: The CLR National Online Catalog Survey reports a nationwide survey of users and nonusers of 16 on-line catalog systems in 29 U. S. libraries in 1982. The major findings of the survey are (a) over 90% of users like the on-line catalog; (b) 75% of users prefer the on-line catalog over the card catalog; and (c) most of the users prefer subject, keyword, or term searching.[60] The first five topranked interface system problems in the survey are concerned with: (a) increasing the results, (b) finding the correct subject term, (c) knowing what is in the on-line catalog, (d) computer search by subject, and (e) scanning through a "long display".[61]

On display formats, the questions asked were related to "problems in coping with and understanding the initial instructions displayed on the screen, single record and multiple record displays, understanding explanations on the screen, and finding a specific element on the screen, e. g. the call number ...".[62] The user appeared to have no serious problem in understanding the information displays used. The most serious problem directly related to display formats was understanding "abbreviations".[63] The variations for display data on a CRT screen were vast and complex; with the on-line catalog there is more flexibility, capability, choice of technique, and space to arrange and display the data than there is on a catalog card.

The need for standardization of and consistency in display information on the screen and the use of codes and abbreviations is indicated. The survey revealed that this standardization is currently being considered by an ANSI Z39 committee under the directorship of P. A. Cochrane.[64] It is strongly felt that there is much to be learned about the display of bibliographic information on the screen, and about its users and their needs and preferences.[65-67]

The Hildreth study revealed the diversity and nonstandardization of every facet in the user-system interface in 10 existing OPACs, and the design issues of output control and display are both many and complex. There are 37 different display formats used for the same record among the 10 systems. The number of predefined display formats provided by the 10 systems range from two to seven, with different levels of bibliographic display such as the index/review, brief/short standard/medium, or full/MARC display formats. The various forms are assigned to similar formats. Six systems have MARC/MARC-oid formats and five systems offer a format that closely resembles the catalog card, but no two are alike.[68]

Should the on-line catalog display mimic the traditional catalog? Boss and Marcum, in their list of important "elements in the design of online catalogs," stated that "it should be possible to specify a format that resembles that of a card catalog".[69] The CONDOC specifications require bibliographic displays that "shall closely resemble or replicate the information display on existing 3 × 5 cards in the card catalog".[70] But Dwyer's question was "why tie COM and online catalogs to the format and jargon that have worked so poorly on cards?"[71]

Recently researchers have discovered that alternative display formats have a significant impact on user performance or preference. Tullis studied the subject's response to four different types of display formats and found that two graphic formats were superior to the narrative formats.[72] Fryer tested 347 college library users' responses to various display formats, and he concluded that most library users preferred the "labeled, underlined" and "table of contents" formats over the traditional ones[73] in addition. Marcus urged system designers to improve the legibility, and attractiveness of information display to users of computer system.[74]

Spacing, layout, sequencing, vocabulary and punctuation, data contents, and arrangement are the component variables for designing display formats, according to Hildreth.[1] The question is what are the most useful layouts, vocabulary, data contents, etc., for display formats? The present variations of OPAC display formats illustrate that there is a definite need for research on display formate and the on-line catalog, focusing on the user.[75]

In England, Reynolds attempted to establish the general principles for the presentation of bibliographic data in relation to the particular visual characteristics of PRESTEL displays. She began with this statement of principle:

> It is important that the visual presentation of bibliographic information should both reflect its logical structure and facilitate its use.[76]

From her study of experimental frames on PRESTEL displays, the major recommendations drawn were that "the layout should be kept as simple as possible, and the number of colours used should be restricted to two in most cases. Indention can be used to facilitate the scanning of alphabetically listed entry headings, while colour can be used to emphasize certain elements within the entry if necessary. Emphasis is placed on designing the information according to the way in which it will be used".[77]

Matthews's guide state that "for a 'public access' online catalog to be a tool that truly meets the needs of the public, the need of the user must dictate the format and amount of information that is displayed".[78] Ideally, on-line catalog systems should have various levels of display formats for various user types, but Matthews points out another aspect: According to the

Palmer study, "a brief record containing author, title, call number, date of publication, subject headings, add contents notes would satisfy more than ninety percent of patron needs"[79] —and at less cost. Perhaps the costly full-MARC display will be used only by scholars and librarians. Inevitably, Matthews believes, "the way in which the call number is identified and displayed is crucial to the success of a user-cordial online catalog ... Understanding the information seeking behavior of users is also crucial, in order to design an online catalog that truly complements the search strategy of users".[80] A collection of 34 public access on-line catalog profiles included in his book are valuable for further study, analysis, and evaluation of various catalog systems and their display formats.[81]

Salmon's study of the characteristics of 20 U. S. on-line public catalogs showed that there are a total of 43 display formats for record displays. The number of different display formats used in a single system ranges from one to five in four types of display formats: index, brief, full, and MARC formats. Most of the systems studied have a full bibliographic display with bibliographic information similar to that normally found in a card catalog, but most of the displays are in "tabular" form; only two systems have display formats resembling the card form for the user assistance display format. Salmon commented that "probably the most helpful means of assistance is the use of common English and the avoidance of jargon, computerese, symbols of the type commonly used by programmers, and what Neville has called 'biblish' ..."[82] His tentative recommendation on display formats was that the "index," "brief," and "full bibliographic" formats are desirable, but whether a MARC format is really needed is still an unanswered question.[83]

The CONDOC library survey of requirements for an on-line catalog for small and medium academic libraries indicates that multiple display formats are required: Indix, brief, and full record with/without MARC tags; and flexibility in formatting and arrangement or sequences of information on the screen are desired.[84]

The 1982 CLR Conference on Online Catalogs: Requirements, Characteristics and Costs concluded that "there is a need for a standard for display of bibliographic information. Such a standard should provide for brief display and the order of the elements in the display. Expanded display should also be standardized ... [there is a] need for research on user evaluation of the existing and potential display of bibliographic information with attention on the differences between display terminals that provide 80 × 24 character display versus those that provide 64 × 16. The issue of canned versus user-tailored displays needs review as part of this effort ...".[85]

In conclusion, the on-line public access catalog has arrived; there is no doubt that there are many on-line catalog projects presently under development, both in-house and commercially. The variation of display formats reviewed indicates that there are many problems concerning display formats that need further study. As Daily has pointed out, "the format of the catalog can (and should) depend upon the convenience of the users of a library, not on the formulation of theory to support one format over another".[86] Thus, the catalog users are the sole users of the design format, and the user should provide the principal input and feedback for the design principles and guidelines. In addition, more detailed research should be conducted on users' reactions to and preferences among the design formats of existing or potential on-line catalogs.

Fortunately, the attention of the library community is currently and actively involved in this. With support available from the Council on Library Resources, a number of research projects on display formats can be funded. Since no defacto standards exist at the present time, it is urgent that the ANSI Z39 committee collaborate with librarians and system experts to establish proper standards for OPACs display formats, and related matters. Workshops, meetings, and conferences are scheduled to introduce this new tool to the library community. Presently, the on-line catalog is still in its infancy; it will require years of hard work and research to achieve its refinement and adoption. Reviewing the forthcoming studies On display formats and OPAC development will be a fruitful and exciting experience.

REFERENCES

1. Charles Hildreth, Public Access Online Catalogs: The User interface, Ohio Computer Library Center, Dublin, Ohio, 1982, p. 144.
2. Steven R. Salmon, "Characteristics of Online Public Catalogs," Lib. Resources Tech. Serv., 27, 36 (January – March, 1983).
3. Allen B. Veaner, "Technical Services Research Needs for the 1990s," Lib. Resources Tech. Serv., 27, 203 (April – June, 1983).
4. Joseph R. Matthews, Public Access to Online Catalogs: A Planning Guide for Managers, Online, Weston, Conn., 1982, p. 36.
5. S. Michael Malinconico and Paul J. Fasana, The Future of The Catalogs: The Library's Choices, Knowledge industry Publications, White Plains, N.Y., 1979.
6. Joseph R. Matthews, "Online Public Access Catalogs: Assessing the Potential," Lib. J., 107, 1067 (June, 1982).
7. Norman D. Stevens, "The Catalogs of the Future: A Speculative Essay," J. Lib. Automation, 13, 190 (June, 1980).
8. Karen L. Horny, "Online Catalogs: Coping with the Choices," J. Acad. Librarianship, 8, 14 (March, 1982).
9. Malinconico and Fasana, Ref. 5, pp. 84 – 99.
10. Richard W. Boss and Deanna B, Marcum, "The Library Catalogs: COM and Online Options," Lib. Technol. Rep., 16, 446 – 448 (September – October, 1980).
11. Boss and Marcum, Ref. 10, p. 448.
12. Hildreth, Ref. 1, p. 3.
13. Matthews, Ref. 4, p. 23.
14. Salmon, Ref. 2, p. 37.
15. Richard De Gennaro, "Library Automation and Networking Perspectives on Three Decades," Lib. J., 108, 629 (April, 1983).
16. Matthews, Ref. 4. p. 108.
17. Dorothy May Norris, A History of Cataloguing and Cataloguing Methods 1100 – 1850: With an Introductory Survey of Ancient Times, Grafton, London, 1939, p. 1.
18. Maurice F. Tauber, Cataloguing and Classification, The State of the Library Art, Vol. 1, Pt. 1, Graduate School of Library Services, Rutgers The State University, New Brunswick, N.J., 1966, p. 10.
19. Henriette D. Avram, MARC: Its History and Implications, Library of Congress, Washington, D.C., 1975, pp. 1 – 4.
20. Maurice J. Freedman and S. Michael Malinconico, eds., The Nature and Future of the Catalog: Proceedings of the ALA's Information Science and Automation Division's 1975 and 1976 Institutes on the Catalog, Oryx Press, Phoenix. Ariz., 1979, pp. 1 – 290.
21. D. Kayo Gapen and Bonnie Juergens, eds., Closing the Catalogs' Proceedings of the 1978 and 1979 Library and Information Technology Association Institutes, Oryx Press, Phoenix, Ariz., 1980.
22. Richard J. Hymen, From Cutter to MARC: Access to the Unit Records, Queens College of the City University of New York, Flushing, N.Y., 1977, p. v.
23. Joseph R. Matthews, "Requirements for an Online Catalog," Technicalities, 1, 11 – 13 (October, 1981).
24. Neal K. Kaske and Douglas Ferguson, Online Public Access to Library Bibliographic Data

Bases: Development, Issues, and Priorities: Final Report, OCLC, Dublin, Ohio, 1980 (ED 195275).
25. Douglas Ferguson et al., "The TLR Public Catalog Study: An Overviews" Inf. Technol. Lib., 1, 85 (June, 1982).
26. Ferguson et al., Ref. 25, pp. 84–85.
27. Using Online Catalogs: A Nationwide Survey: A Report of a Study Sponsored by the Council on Library Resources (Joseph R. Matthews, Gary S. Lawrence, and Douglas K. Ferguson, ods.), Neal-Schuman, New York, 1983, pp. viii, 10.
28. "LAMA / LITA Program on the Public Online Catalog Project," Lib. Congress Bull., 41, 266–267 (August, 1982); and "Panel on the Online Public Access Catalog Project Findings," Reported at the 45th American Society for information Science Annual Meeting, Columbus, Ohio, October 17–21, 1982, (on tape).
29. Online Catalogs: Requirements, Characteristics and Costs: Report of a Conference Sponsored by the Council on Library Resources (David B. McCarn, comp. and ed.), Council on Library Resources, Washington, D. C., 1983.
30. "Online Catalog Project Publications." CLR Res. Devel., 11, 3–4 (June, 1983).
31. Online Catalogs: Requirement..., Ref. 29, p. v.
32. Using Online Catalogs, Ref. 27, p. vii.
33. Michael Gorman, "Thinking the Thinkable: A Synergetic Profession," Am. Lib., 13, 473–474 (July-August, 1982).
34. Norman D. Stevens, "Online Catalogs: What They Replace, What They Change," Lib. Issues, July, 1983, p. 3.
35. Frederick G. Kilgeur, "Design of Online Catalogs," in The Nature and Future of the Catalog, Ref. 20. pp. 34–40.
36. Michael S. Malinconico, "The Library Catalog in a Computerized Environment," in The Nature and Future of the Catalog, Ref. 20, pp. 47–49, 66.
37. Seymour Lubetzky, "The Traditional Ideals of Cataloguing and the New Revision," in The Nature and Future of the Catalog, Ref. 20, p. 156.
38. David R. McDonald and Susan E. Searing, "Bibliographic Instruction and the Development of Online Catalogs." Coll. Res. Lib., 44, 6 (January, 1983).
39. Margaret Mann, Introduction to Cataloguing and the Classification of Books, American Library Association, Chicago, 1930, p. 137.
40. Susan L. Miller, "The Changing Role of a Circulation System: OSU Experience," RQ, 20, 48 (Fall, 1980).
41. S. Michael Malinconico, "Circulation Control Systems as Online Catalogs," Lib. J., 108, 1207–1210 (June, 1983)
42. Kilgour, Ref. 35, pp. 34–35.
43. Boss and Marcum, Ref. 10, pp. 491–498.
44. Horny, Ref. 8. pp. 14–19.
45. Using Online Catalogs..., Ref. 27, p. 84.
46. Using Online Catalogs..., Ref. 27, pp. 2–5.
47. Hildreth, Ref. 1, p. 59.
48. T. F. M. Stewart, "Displays and the Software Interface," Appl. Ergonomics, 7, 142 (September, 1976).
49. M. M. Danchak, "CRT Displays for Power Plants," Instrum. Technol., 23, 33 (October, 1976).
50. Wilbert O. Galitz, Handbook of Screen Format Design, Q. E. D. Information Sciences, Wellesley, Mass., 1981, p. 13.
51. E. G. Bylander, Electronic Displays, McGraw-Hill, New York, 1979.

52. Howard Turtle, W. David Penniman, and Thomas B. Hickery, "Data Entry/Display Devices for Interactive Information Retrieval," in Annual Review of Information Science and Technology, Vol. 16 (Martha E. Williams, ed.), Knowledge Industry Publications, White Plains. N. Y., 1981, pp. 55 – 83.
53. James Martin, Design of Man-Computer Dialogues, Prentice-Hall. Englewood Cliffs, N. J., 1973, pp. 87 – 88.
54. Hildreth, Ref. 1, p. 139.
55. Galitz, Ref. 50, p. 1.
56. Stanley McElderry, "Alternatives to the Conventional Card Catalog from the User Point of View," IFLA J., 2, 235 (November, 1976)
57. Patrick Wilson, "The Catalog as Access Mechanism: Background and Concepts," Lib. Resources Tech. Serv., 27, 9 – 10 (January-March, 1983)
58. Alan Seal, "Experiments with Full and Short Entry Catalogues. A Study of Library Needs," Lib. Resources Tech. Serv., 27, 145 (April-June, 1983).
59. Hildreth, Ref. 1, pp. 137, 145.
60. Using Online Catalogs …, Ref. 27, p. 152.
61. Using Online Cacalogs …, Ref. 27. p. 124.
62. Using Online Catalogs …, Ref. 27. pp. 137 – 138.
63. Using Online Catalogs …, Ref 27. p. 138.
64. Using Online Catalogs …, Ref. 27, p. 139.
65. Pauline A. Cochrane. "Can a Standard for an Online Common Command Language Be Developed?" Online, 7, 36 – 37 (January, 1983).
66. Sue Pease and Mary Noel Gouke, "Patterns of Use in an Online Catalog and a Card Catalog," Coll. Res. Lib., 43. 279 – 291 (July, 1982).
67. Susan L. Miller, "The Library User Meets LCS," J. Acad. Librarianship, 64, 37 (January, 1982).
68. Hildreth, Ref. 1. p. 148.
69. Boss and Marcum, Ref. 10, p. 494.
70. Matthews. Ref. 23, pp. 11 – 13.
71. Jim Dwyer, "Libraries. Funding and Technological Change. Dinosaurs Face a New Ice Age," Technicalities, 1, 11 (December, 1980).
72. Thomas S. Tullis, "An Evaluation of Alphanumeric, Graphic, and Color Information Displays," Human Factors, 23, 541 – 550 (October, 1981).
73. Benjamin Scott Fryer. The Effects of Spatial Arrangement, Upper Lower Case Combinations, and Reverse Video on Patron Response to CRT Displayed Catalog Card, Brigham Young University, School of Library and Information Sciences, Provo, Utah. 1981.
74. Aaron Marcus. "Designing the Face of an Interface," IEEE Comput. Graphics Appl., 2, 23 – 29 (January, 1982).
75. Using Online Catalogs…, Ref. 27. pp. 123 – 124.
76. Linda Reynolds, The Presentation of Bibliographic Information on Prestel, The British Library, London, 1980, p. 4.
77. Reynold, Ref. 76, p. 2.
78. Matthews, Ref. 4, p. 35.
79. Richard P. Palmer, Computerizing the Card Catalog in the University Library, Libraries Unlimited, Littleton, Colo., 1972, pp. 85 – 86.
80. Matthews, Ref. 4, p. 42.
81. Matthews, Ref. 4. pp. 111 – 320.
82. Salmon, Ref. 2, p. 58.

83. Salmon, Ref. 2, p. 65.
84. Matthews, Ref. 23, pp. 11-13.
85. Online Catalogs: Requirements ..., Ref. 29, p. 36.
86. Jay E. Daily, "Format. Catalog," in Encyclopedia of Library and Information Science (A. Kent, H. Lancour, and J. E. Daily, eds.) Dekker, New York, 1973, Vol. 9, p. 23.

BIBLIOGRAPHY

Automated Cataloguing in ARL Libraries, Association of Research Libraries, Washington, D. C., 1978 (Kit 47 of the Systems and Procedures Exchange Center).
Avram, Henriette D., MARC: Its History and Implications, Library of Congress, Washington, D. C., 1975.
Besant, Larry, "Users of Public Online Catalogs Want Sophisticated Subject Access," Am. Lib., 14, 160 (March, 1982).
Bierman, Kenneth, "The Future of Catalogs in North American Libraries," in The Nature and Future of the Catalog, Proceedings of the ALA Information Science and Automation Division's 1975 and 1977 Institutes on the Catalog, Oryx Press, Phoenix, Ariz., 1979, pp. 114-119.
Boss, Richard W., and Deanna B. Marcum, "The Library Catalogs: COM and Online Options," Lib. Technol. Rep., 16, 445-698 (September-October, 1980).
Bylander, E. G., Electronic Displays, McGraw-Hill, New York, 1979.
Cakir, A., D. J. Hart, and T. F. M. Stewart, Visual Display Terminals: A Manual Covering Ergonomics, Workplace Design, Health and Safety, Task Organization, Wiley, New York, 1980.
Clinic on Library Applications of Data Processing, University of Illinois at Urbana-Champaign, April 20-23, 1980, Public Access to Library Automation, University of Illinois, Urbana-Champaign, 1980.
Cochrane, Pauline A., "Can a Standard for an Online Comman Command Language Be Developed" Online, 7, 36-37 (January, 1983).
Cochrane, Pauline A., "Where Do We Go from Here?" Online, 5, 30-42 (July, 1981).
Cole, George Watson, "An Early French General Catalog," Lib. J., 25, 329-331 (July, 1900).
Conference on Displays: Loughborough, September 1971, Institution of Electrical Engineers, London; 1971.
Conference Record of 1982 International Display Record Conference, Advisory Groups on Electronic Devices, IEEE, New York, 1982.
Corey, James F., Helen H. Spalding, and Jeanmarie Lang fraser, "Involving Faculty and Students in the Selection of Catalog Alternatives." J. Acad, Librarianship, 8, 328-333 (January, 1983).
"Council on Library Resources Bibliographic Service Development Program: The Evaluation of Online Public Access Catalogs," Crus News, November 1981, pp. 11-13.
Cramer. S. A., "The Computerised Catalogue in a University Library," Libri, 26. 38-53 (March, 1976).
Daily, Jay E., "Format, Catalog," in Encyclopedia of Library and Information Science (A. Kent, H. Lancour, and J. E. Daily, eds.), Dekker, New York, 1973, Vol. 9. p. 18-23.
Danchak, M. M., "CRT Display for Fower Plants." Instrum. Technol., 23, 29-36 (October, 1976).

Debons, Anthony, "Introduction to Display System," in Display System Engineering (H. R. Luxenberg and R. L. Kuehm, eds,), McGraw-Hill. New York, pp. 1 – 23.

DeGennaro, Richard. "Library Automation and Networking: Perspectives On Three Decades," Lib. J., 108, 629 – 635 (April, 1983).

Dwyer, Jim, "Libraries, Funding, and Technological Change: Dinosaurs Face a New Ice Age," Technicalities, 1, 10 – 11 (December, 1980).

Ferguson, Douglas. et al., "The CLR Public Catalog Study: An Overview," Inf. Technol. Lib., 1, 84 – 97 (June, 1982).

Freedman, Maurice J., and S. Michael Maiinconico, eds., The Nature and Future of the Catalog: Proceedings of the ALA's Information Science and Automation Division's 1975 and 1977 Institutes on the Catalog, Oryx Press, Phoenix, Ariz., 1979.

Friedman, Elaine S., "Patron Access to Online Cataloguing Systems: OCLC in the Public Service Environment," J. Acad. Librarianship, 6, 132 – 139 (July, 1980).

Fryer, Benjaman Scott, The Effects of Spatial Arrangement, Upper-Lower Case Combinations, and Reverse Video on Patron Response to CRT Displayed Catalog Card, Brigham Young University, School of Library and Information Sciences, Provo, Utah, 1981.

Galicz, Wilbert O., Handbook of Screen Format Design, Q. E. D. Information Sciences, Wellesley, Mass., 1981.

Galitz. Wilbert O., "Human Engineering in Screen Design," J. Syst. Manage., 34, 6 – 14 (May, 1983).

Gapen, D. Kaye, and Bonnie Juergens, eds., Closing the Catalogs: Proceedings of the 1978 and 1979 Library and Infolmation Technology Association Institutes, Oryx Press, Phoenix, Ariz., 1980.

Gorman, Michael, "The Prospective Catalog?" in Closing the Catalog Proceedings of the 1978 and 1979 Library and Information Technology Association Institutes, Oryx Press, Phoenix, ariz., 1980, pp. 85 – 96.

Gorman, Michael, "Thinking the Thinkable: A Synergetic Profession," Am Lib., 13, 473 – 474 (July-August, 1982)

Hildreth, Charles, Online Public Access Catalogs: The User Interface, OCLC. Dublin, Ohio, 1982.

Hitt, W. D., et al., "Development of Design Criteria for Intelligence Display Formats," Human Factors, 3, 86 – 92 (July, 1961).

Horny. Karen I. "Online Catalogs: Coping with the Choices," J. Acad. Librarianship, 8, 14 – 19 (March 1982).

Huchingson. R. D., et al., "Formatting, Message Load, Sequencing Method. and Presentation Rate for Computer-Generated Displays," Human Factors, 23, 551 – 559 (October, 1981).

Hyman, Richard J., From Cutter to MARC: Access to the Unit Record, Queens College of the University of New York, Flushing, N. Y., 1977.

Jones, C. LEE, and Nancy Gwinn, "Bibliographic Service Development: A New CLR Program," J. Lib. Automation, 12, 116 – 124 (June, 1979).

Kaske, Neal K., and Douglas Ferguson, Online Public Access to Library Bibliographic Data Bases: Develpment, Issues, and Priorities: Final Report, OCLC, Dublin, Ohio, 1980 (ED 195275).

Kilgour, Frederick G., "Design of Online Catalogs," in The Nature and Future of the Catalog: Proceedings of the ALA's Information Science and Automation Division's 1975 and 1977 Institutes on the Catalog (M. J. Freedman and S. M. Malinconico, eds.), Oryx Press, Phoenix, Ariz., 1979, pp. 34 – 41.

Krikelas, James, "Catalog Use Studies and Their Implications," in Advances in

Librarianship, Vol. 3, Seminar Press, New York, 1972. "LAMA/LITA Program on the Public Online Catalog Project" Lib. Congress Inf. Bull., 41, 266 – 267 (August, 1982).

Landcaster, F. W. The Measurement and Evaluation of Library Services, Information Resources Press, Washington, D. C., 1977.

Lees, Roger, "The Man/Display Relationship," in International Conference on Display for Man-Machine Systems April 4 – 7, 1977. University of Lancaster, Lancaster. 1977 CIEEE Conference Publications No. 150).

Loewe. Richard T., "System Design, Coding, Formats, and Programming," in Display Systems Engineering (H. R. Luxenberg and R. L. Kuehn, eds.), McGraw-Hill, New York, 1968, pp. 24 – 69.

Lubetzky, Seymour, "The Function of the Catalog," College Res. Lib., 17, 213 – 215 (May, 1956).

Lubetzky, Seymour, "The Traditional Ideals of Cataloguing and the New Revision." in The Nature and Future of the Catalog: Proceedings of the ALA's Information Science and Automation Division's 1975 and 1977 Institutes on the Catalog, Oryx. Press, Phoenix, Ariz., 1979. pp. 152 – 169.

McDonald. David R., and Susan E. Searing, "Bibliographic Instruction and the Development of Online Catalogs," College Res. Lib., 44. 5 – 11 (January, 1983).

McElderry, Stanley. "Alternatives to the Conventional Card Catalog from the User Point of View." IFLA J., 2. 232 – 236 (November, 1976).

Malinconico, S. Michael "Circulation Control Systems as Online Catalogs." Lib. J., 108. 1207 – 1210 (June, 1983).

Malinconico. S. Michael. "The Library Catalog in a Computerized Environment," in The Nature and Future of the Catalog, Proceedings of the ALA's Information Science and Automation Division's 1975 and 1977 Institutes on the Catalog, Oryx Press, Phoenix, Ariz., 1979, pp. 46 – 71.

Malinconico. S. Michael, and Paul J. Fasana, The Future of the Catalog: The Library's Choices, Knowledge Publication Industry, White Plains. N. Y., 1979.

Mann, Margaret, Introduction to Cataloguing and the Classification of Books. American Library Association. Chicago, 1930.

Marcus, Aavon. "Designing the Face of an Interface," IEEE Comput. Graphics Appl., 2. 23 – 29 (January, 1982).

Markey, Karen. Analytical Review of Catalog Use Studies. OCLC. Columbus, Ohio, 1980 (Report No. OCLC/OPR/RR – 80/2).

Martin, James, Design of Man-Computer Dialogues, Prentice-Hall. Englewood Cliffs, N. J., 1973.

Matthews, Joseph R., "The Automated Library System Marketplace, 1982: Change and More Change!" Lib. J., 108, 547 – 553 (March, 1983).

Matthews, Joseph R., "Online Public Access Catalog: Assessing the Potential," Lib. J., 107, 1070 – 1071 (June, 1982).

Matthews, Joseph R., Public Access to Online Catalogs: A Planning Guide for Managers, Online Weston, Conn., 1982.

Matthews, Joseph R., "Requirements for an Online Catalog," Technicalities, 1, 11 – 13 (October, 1981).

Mays, Tony, "Online Public Access Catalogues in North America," LASIE, May-June, 1982, pp. 5 – 11.

Miller, Susan L., "The Changing Role of a Circulation System: OSU Experience," RQ 20, 47 – 52 (Fall, 1980).

Miller, Susan L., "The Library User Meets LCS," J. Acad. Librarianship. 64, 31 – 38 (January 1980).

Moore, Carol Weiss, "User Reactions to Online Catalogs: An Exploration Study," College Res. Lib., 42, 295 – 302 (July, 1981).

Nordan, David J. and Gall Herndon Lawrence, "Public Terminal Use in an Online Catalog: Some Preliminary Results," College Res. Lib., 42, 308 – 316 (July, 1981).

Norris, Dorothy May, A History cf Cataloguing and Cataloguing Methods 1100 – 1850: With an Introductory Survey of Ancient Times, Grafton, London, 1939.

Online Catalogs: Requirements, Characterisitcs and Costs: Report of a Conference Sponsored by the Council on Library Resources, compiled and edited by David B. McCarn, The Council, Washington, D. C., 1983.

Palmer, Richard P., Computerizing the Card Catalog in the University Library, Libraries Unlimited, Littleton, Colo., 1972.

"Panel on the Online Public Access Catalog Project Findings." American Society for Information Science 45th Annual Meeting, Columbus. Ohio, October 17 – 21, 1982 (on tape).

Pease, Sue, and Mary Noel Gouke, "Patterns and Use in an Online Catalog and a Card Catalog." College Res. Lib., 43. 279 – 291 (July, 1982).

Ranz, Jim, The Printed Book Catalogue in American Libraries: 1723 – 1900. American Library Association. Chicago, 1964.

Reynolds, Linda, The Presentaion of Bibliographic Information on Prestel. British Library, London. 1980 (BL R&D Report 5536).

Seal, Alan, "Experiments with Full and Short Entry Catalogues: A Study of Library Needs," Lib. Resources Tech. Serv., 27. 144 – 155 (April-June, 1983).

Shurteff, Donald A., "Symbols. Abbreviations and Formats for CRDs," in The Power of Information. Proceedings of American Society for Information Science 1980 Mid-Year Meeting. ASIS. Washington, D. C., 1980, pp. 34 – 40.

Siegel, Elliot R., et al., "Research Strategy and Methods Used to Conduct a Comparative Evaluation of Two Prototype Online Catalog Systems," in The 4th National Online Meeting Proceedings, Learned Information, Medford. N. J., 1983. pp. 503 – 511.

Smith, Sidney, "Letter Size and Legibility." Human Factors, 21, 661 – 670 (December 1979).

Stevens, Norman D., "The Catalogs of the Future: A Speculative Essay," J. Lib. Automation, 13 (June, 1980).

Stevens, Norman D., "Online Catalogs: What They Replace, What They Change," Lib. Issues. 3 (July 1983).

Stevenson, Gordan. "Descriptive Cataloguing in 1982." Lib. Resources Tech. Serv., 27, 259 – 268 (July-September, 1983).

Stewart, T. F. M., "Communicating with Dialogues." Ergonomics, 23, 909 – 911 (September, 1980).

Stewart. T. F. M., "Displays and the Software Interface." Appl. Ergonomics. 7, 137 – 146 (September, 1976).

Tauber. Maurice F., Cataloguing and Classification, Graduate School of Library service. Rutgers-The State University, New Brunswick, N. J., 1966 (Vol., Pt. 1, The State of the Library Art).

Tinker, M. A., Legibility of Print, Iowa State University Press, Ames, 1963.

Tullis, Thomas S., "An Evaluation of Alphanumeric, Graphic, and Color Information Display." Human Factors. 23, 541 – 550 (October, 1981).

Turtle. Howard. W. David Penniman, and Thomas B. Hickery. "Data Entry/Display Devices for Interactive Information Retrieval." in Annual Review of Information Science and

Technology. vol. 16, (Martha E. Williams, ed.), Knowledge Industry Publication, White Plains, N. Y., 1981, pp. 55 –83.

User Instruction for Online Catalogs in ARL Libraries. Association of Research Libraries. Washington, D. C., 1983 (Kit 93 of the Systems and Procedures Exchange Center).

Using Online Catalogs: A Nationwide Survey: A Report of a Survey Sponsored by the Council on Library Resources (Joseph R. Matthews. Gary S. Lawrence, and Douglas Ferguson, eds.), Neal-Schuman, New York, 1983.

Veaner, Allen B., "Technical Services Research Needs for the 1990s," Lib. Resources Tech. Serv., 27, 199 –210 (April-June, 1983).

Vitz, Paul C., "Preference for Different Amounts of Visual Complexity," Behav. Sci., 11, 105 –111 (March, 1966).

Weintraub, D. Kathryn, "The Essentials or Desiderata of the Bibliographic Record as Discovered by Research," Lib. Resources Tech. Serv., 23, 391 –405 (Fall 1979).

Wiederkehr, Robert R. V., Alternative for Future Library Catalogs: A Cost Model: Final Report of the Library Catalog Cost Model Project Prepared for the Association of Research Libraries, King Research, Rockville, Md., 1980.

Williamson, Nancy J., "Is There a Catalog in Your Future? Access to Information in the Year 2006," Lib. Resources Tech. Serv., 26, 122 –135 (April-June, 1982).

Wilson, Patrick, "The Catalog as Access Mechanism: Background and Concepts," Lib. Resources Tech. Serv., 27, 4 –17 (January-March, 1983).

ON-LINE PUBLIC ACCESS
CATALOG DISPLAY FORMATS*

Librarians for centuries have attempted to establish appropriate cataloguing rules for the preparation of quality catalogs in several physical formats (e. g. , card, book, or microform). All are aiming at the same goal: to standardize catalog practice and prepare catalogs that provide the best possible access to library collections.

The catalog is an instrument of communication. For the past three-quarters, of a century, the card catalog has been the predominant model for the display of and access to library materials. The data elements for bibliographic description of records on the traditional 3 by 5 card are generally uniform in their layout, photography, content, sequencing, spacing, and arrangement from catalog to catalog. The card represents a display format of bibliographic data that has been familiar to all library users[1].

With the emergence of the on-line catalog, both Salmon and Veaner observed the new and enhanced capabilities to bibliographic access; the flexible, changeable, and interactive characteristics of the on-line catalog; and the users' incredible excitement in experiencing the new form of library catalog [2,3]. When implementing the on-line catalog system, the bibliographic formats often have to be redesigned for CRT (cathode-ray tube) displays, but unfortunately, no standards have been established yet. As Matthews points out "format, or the manner in which the bibliographic information is displayed on the CRT screen is a vital yet frequently overlooked area of the human-computer interface"[4].

The main purpose of this paper is to study on-line catalog display formats, especially those of the on-line public access catalog (OPAC). Prior to analyzing the present status of on-line catalog display formats, one must fully understand the development of on-line catalogs, of which the display format is a part.

The increasing deficiencies and the existing costs of maintaining card catalogs have forced some libraries to seek and implement "alternative" catalogs. In addition, the adoption of the new cataloguing code, *The Anglo-American Cataloguing Rules*, Second Edition, and the closing of the card catalog of the Library of Congress (LC) in early 1981 have had an even greater impact on libraries worldwide. Some libraries, instead of waiting and observing the ongoing activities, are actively investigating potential alternatives to the card catalog[5,6].

There are three commonly recognized alternatives to the card catalog: the book catalog, the COM (computer-output microform) catalog in fiche or film, and the online catalog[7]. Librarians believe that any catalog system considered or selected "must be at least as good as the card catalog it replaces"[8]: this is a considerable challenge requiring good judgment to make the decision, as recorded in the literature on comparative assessment of alternative catalogs, for example, the articles by Matthews[6], Malinconico and Fasana[9], and Boss and Marcum[10].

Boss and Marcum state that the most important factors associated with the development of on-line Catalogs are: "the improvements in computer technology. trends in library data development, and the availability of bibliographic records in machine-readable form from LC or one of the four North American utilities"[11]. The four utilities are OCLC, RLIN, WLN, and ULTAS. Hildreth's 1982 book reported that the first on-line cataloguing system available for public use was the Online Computer Library Center (OCLC) system, which began as the Ohio College Library Center in January 1974. The Research Library Information Network (RLIN) of

---

* *Encyclopedia of Library and Information Science* Vol. 38 Supplement 3 (1985): pp. 325 – 338.

Research Library Groups, Inc. (RLG) was available to the public in December 1974, and the Ohio State University Library. Control System (LCS) was opened to public use in January 1975[12]. As of late 1981 the commercial vendor systems-CLSI, Inc., with a newly developed "touch screen" terminal, and Universal Library Systems (ULISYS), with an authority control function were marketing their turnkey on-line catalog systems (13). Excluding the three bibliographic utilities, in 1982 Salmon identified seven commercial vendors among the 20 U. S. on-line public catalogs[14].

Library automation is entering its third decade[15], but the on-line catalog is in its early infancy[16]. And yet, the historical development of the on-line catalog is a part of the evolution of the traditional library catalog which is traced back to the beginning of the library catalog, perhaps to ancient Babylonian times[17]. The work of Norris, Strout, Pettee, Ruffin, Schley, and Corcoran provides a thorough overview of the history of the catalog and the emergence of the card catalog (see Tauber, Ref.[18]).

The LC MARC II communications format was inaugurated in 1968[19], and a series of conferences— "The Nature and Future of the Catalog," "The Catalog in the Age of Technological Change," "Closing the Catalog," etc. —sponsored by library associations began in the mid-1970s[20,21]. The themes of all of these programs were viewed as a "sign" that "the library profession has encountered its own 'future shock' in the wake of cybernetic and electronic revolutions that have been accelerating since the mid-fifties"[22,p. v].

In a recent development, CLR funded a survey among 125 CONDOC (Consortium to Develop an Online Catalog) member libraries which resulted in a ranked list of the 40 most important on-line catalog features for small and medium-sized libraries. One-fourth of the 40 features are display format related matters. With this list, CONDOC attempts to influence the direction of the offerings of vendors in the marketplace to develop a "library-driven" product of on-line catalog systems of interest to CONDOC members[23].

Later, at the 1980 summer working session on on-line public catalogs at Dartmouth College sponsored by the Bibliographic Services Development Program of the Council on Library Resources (CLR), the 25 participants identified four priority areas for study and action[24]:

1. Analysis of user behavior and requirements
2. Examination of existing on-line public access systems
3. Development of methods for cost analysis and management
4. Development of distributed computing techniques and system-to-system links

After these recommendations, the council awarded OCLC a grant for the study "Online Public Access System: Data Collection Instruments for Patron and System Evaluation"[25]. The results of this work were reported in Hildreth's book[1]. in early 1981 CLR funded LC, RLG, OCLC, J. Matthews and Associates, and the University of California to conduct a coordinated study of nationwide on-line public access catalogs using the questionnaire methodology[26]. Twenty-nine libraries having 16 different on-line catalog systems were surveyed, and 12, 075 on-line users and non-users completed their questionnaires[27].

The preliminary, reports on the study findings were presented at the 1982 ALA Annual Conference, and again at the American Society for Information Science (ASIS) 45th Annual Meeting[28]. Final reports were published in *Using Online Catalogs: A Nationwide Survey*[27], *Online Catalogs: Requirements, Characteristics and Costs*[29], and in a series of Online Catalog Project publications listed in *CLR Research Developments*[30]. Thus, it was declared that "1982 was the year of the online catalog"[31], and that the on-line catalog is the "first wave" of future catalogs[32].

Gorman characterized an on-line catalog as an "integrationist" and defined it as a bibliographic control system that allows access by means of a number of access points (conventional and "unconventional"; single and in combination) to bibliographic data stored in machine-readable form. The data retrieved is displayed on a terminal screen or printed out on demand. Terminals are housed in the library or elsewhere. The user retrieves information about items held by the library and by other libraries[33].

Stevens explained that the on-line catalog replaces nothing but the physical format of the traditional catalog, and that it will retain the standard bibliographic information. Ideally, the on-line catalog, in comparison with the traditional catalog, should possess greater accessibility, accuracy, up to dateness, flexibility, comprehensiveness, user-cordialness, and faster response; but there is no best or standard system as such yet[34].

There have been discussions on whether or not Cutter's objectives of library catalogs are applicable to on-line catalogs. Kilgour, for instance, restricts the role of the on-line catalog to a "finding list"[35]. On the contrary, Malinconico, Lubetzky, and others argue that Cutter's objectives are valid for all types of catalogs including on-line catalogs[36~38]. Similarly. the Ohio State University Library, based on Margaret Mann's seven functions of a catalog in the 1930s[39], developed its Circulation System and now LCS[40]. Mann's functions were echoed again by Malinconico in his recent article[41].

In the design and evaluation or an on-line catalog system, Kilgour identified seven important independent variables[42]. Boss and Marcum, in 1980, compiled a list of elements which they considered essential for designing and evaluating an online catalog[43]. In 1982 Horny suggested a number of points which she felt to be significant considerations that should be utilized for the assessment of an on-line catalog system[44]. These three lists are excellent and very similar in content. Based on these elements, the components for an on-line catalog system can be synthesized and developed.

The user, the task, the organizational interface (library), the online system, the data base/file, and the human system interface/comnunication are the six components of the on-line catalog according to the CLR national on-line catalog survey (45). Online catalogs, as interactive man-computer systems, require a welldesigned interface between man and the computer, also known as the humansystem interface, user-system interface, or simply, user interface. This interface is the interaction undertaken between catalog users at a terminal and the computer system using a specific "language or protocol." Usually the interface has two distinct functions: "link" and "barrier." It is a user-oriented interface, a newly added dimension to catalog use, which occurs only in the interactive on-line catalog system. Consequently, to create a human-computer interface that is "user-cordial" is the sole objective for an on-line catalog. Unfortunately, system designers have often overlooked the characteristics and needs of current and potential users in their system designs[46].

In Public Access Online Catalogs: The User Interface, the pioneer publication on on-line public catalogs, Hildreth presented a state-of-the-art review of the research and development efforts for improving the user-oriented interface and summarized guideline clusters for the interface design of on-line catalog systems as: easy to use, friendly and cordial, protective and forgiving, reliable and responsive, and adaptive and flexible[47].

The format of the display information on the CRT or "touch screen" terminal screen is crucial in the human-system interface. The fundamental requirement for formatting display is that language or communication from the computer should be organized and structured in a form appropriate to the task and frame of reference of the user. Stewart pointed out that "the way in which the material is organized and presented may determine the way in which the material is used or the conclusions that ard drawn from it"[48], and that the ergonomics and human factors are also to be considered. He identifies six factors that contribute to good format design; they are logical sequencing, spaciousness, relevance, consistency, grouping, and simplicity[48].

In addition, display formats of on-line catalog systems will be dependent or whether all or selected bibliographic elements were included in the database, the online system output display techniques, and the command capabilities. Therefore, the amount of information presented on a display screen is important. Research has revealed that information density loading for a printed journal page is 40%, and for CRT display screens to be effective, the preferred amount of information density loading is only 15%[49].

Galitz stated in the *Handbook of Screen Format Design* (1981) that "the format and content of a screen will be determined by where and how information is placed and what information is included on the screen"[50]. A lengthy technical review electronic displays, display types, and display human factors was offered by Bylander[51]; and in 1981 Turtle, Penniman, and Hickery explored the data entry-display devices for interactive information retrieval for the past 15 years[52].

According to Martin, 23 display techniques can be used for alphanumeric key board displays of possible structure forms of a real-time screen conversation. It's common for a system to be able to employ a number of different display technique at one time[53]. Finally, the system command capabilities of selection display are important to display formats; these include "predefined" or "undefined" format specific record (s) /field (s), forward-backward movement of records on the screen, scrolling, sorting results, etc.[54]

Display formats are tile direct user-system communication device which supplies the user's information needs. A well-designed screen or display format can increase human processing speed, reduce human errors, speed computer processing time, and increase productivity[55].

What are the user's preferences and needs in display formats? Who are the decision makers concerning the number of display formats needed for on-line catalogs? What, how, and where are the information/data elements arranged on the screen? Little research has been conducted in these areas[56~58], and little attention has been given to the display of bibliographic information on CRT terminal screens from the perspective of the user. Often people have taken them for granted and seldom inquired about who made the decisions on display formats and the reasons for their choices[59].

Fortunately in recent research on and surveys of on-line catalogs, display format data were also collected and analyzed: The CLR National Online Catalog Survey reports a nationwide survey of users and nonusers of 16 on-line catalog systems in 29 U. S. libraries in 1982. The major findings of the survey are: (a) over 90% of users like the on-line catalog; (b) 75% of users prefer the on-line catalog over the card catalog; and (c) most of the users prefer subject, keyword, or term searching[60]. The first five top-ranked interface system problems in the survey are concerned with: (a) increasing the results, (b) finding the correct subject term, (c) knowing what is in the on-line catalog, (d) computer search by subject, and (e) scanning through a "long display"[61].

On display formats, the questions asked were related to "problems in coping with and understanding the initial instructions displayed on the screen, single record and multiple record displays, understanding explanations on the screen, and finding a specific element on the screen, e. g. the call number ... "[62]. The user appeared to have no serious problem in understanding the information displays used. The most serious problem directly related to display formats was understanding "abbreviations"[63]. The variations for display data on a CRT screen were vast and complex; with the on-line catalog there is more flexibility, capability, choice of technique, and space to arrange and display the data than there is on a catalog card.

The need for standardization of and consistency in display information on the screen and the use of codes and abbreviations is indicated. The survey revealed that this standardization is currently being considered by an ANSI Z39 committee under the directorship of P. A. Cochrane[64]. It is strongly felt that there is much to be learned about the display of bibliographic information on the screen, and about its users and their needs and preferences[65~67].

The Hildreth study revealed the diversity and nonstandardization of every facet in the user-system interface in 10 existing OPACs. and the design issues of output control and display are both many and complex. There are 37 different display formats used for the same record among the 10 systems. "The number of predefined display formats previded by the 10 systems ranges from two to seven with different levels of bibliographic display such as the index/review, brief/short, standard/medium, or full/MARC display formats. The various terms are assigned to similar formats. Six systems have MARC/MARC-old formats and five systems offer a format that closely resembles the catalog card, but no two are alike[68].

Should the on-line catalog display mimic the traditional catalog? Boss and Marcum, in their list of important "elements in the design of online catalogs," stated that "it should be possible to specify a format that resembles that of a card catalog"[69]. The CONDOC specifications require bibliographic displays that "shall closely resemble or replicate the information display on existing 3×5 cards in the card catalog"[70]. But Dwyer's question was "why tie COM and online catalogs to the format and jargon that have worked so poorly on cards?"[71]

Recently researchers have discovered that alternative display formats have a significant impact on user performance or preference. Tullis studied the subject's response to four different types of display formats and found that two graphic formats were superior to the narrative formats[72]. Fryer tested 347 college library users' responses to various display formats, and he concluded that most library users preferred the "labeled, underlined" and "table of contents" formats over the traditional ones[73]. In addition, Marcus urged system designers to improve the legibility and attractiveness of information display to users of computer systems[74].

Spacing, layout, sequencing, vocabulary and punctuation, data contents, and arrangement are the component variables for designing display formats, according to Hildreth[1]. The question is: What are the most useful layouts, vocabulary, data contents, etc., for display formats? The present variations of OPAC display formats illustrate that there is a definite need for research on display formats and the on-line catalog, focusing on the user[75].

In England, Reynolds attempted to establish the general principles for the presentation of bibliographic data in relation to the particular visual characteristics of PRESTEL displays. She began with this statement of principle:

> It is important that the visual presentation of bibliographic information should both reflect its logical structure and facilitate its use[76].

From her study of experimental frames on PRESTEL displays, the major recommendations drawn were that "the layout should be kept as simple as possible, and the number of colours used should be restricted to two in most cases. Indention can be used to facilitate the scanning of alphabetically listed entry headings, while colour can be used to emphasize certain elements within the entry if necessary. Emphasis is placed on designing the information according to the way in which it will be used"[77].

Matthews's guide states that "for a 'public access' online catalog to be a tool that truly meets the needs of the public, the need of the user must dictate the format and amount of information that is displayed"[78]. Ideally, on-line catalog systems should have various levels of display formats for various user types, but Matthews points out another aspect: According to the Palmer study, "a brief record containing author, title, call number, date of publication, subject headings, and contents notes would satisfy more than ninety percent of patron needs"[79] and at less cost. Perhaps the costly full-MARC display will be used only by scholars and librarians. Inevitably, Matthews believes, "the way in which the call number is identified and displayed is crucial to the success of a user-cordial online catalog ... Understanding the information-seeking behavior of users is also crucial in order to design an online catalog that truly complements the search strategy of users"[80]. A collection of 34 public access on-line catalog profiles included in his book are valuable for further study, analysis, and evaluation of various catalog systems and their display formats[81].

Salmon's study of the characteristics of 20 U. S. on-line public catalogs showed that there are a total of 43 display formats for record displays. The number of different display formats used in a single system ranges from one to five in four types of display formats: index, brief, full, and MARC formats. Most of the systems studied have a Full bibliographic display with bibliographic information similar to that normally found in a card catalog, but most of the displays are in "tabular" form; only two systems have display formats resembling the card form for the user assistance display format. Salmon commented that "probably the most helpful means of assistance is the use of common English, and the avoidance of jargon, computerese, symbols of the type commonly used by programmers, and what Neville has called 'biblish' ..."[82]. His tentative recommendation on display formats was that the "index," "brief," and "full bibliographic" formats are desirable, but whether a MARC format is really needed is still an unanswered question[83].

The CONDOC library survey of requirements for an on-line catalog for small and medium academic libraries indicates that multiple display formats are required: Index, brief, and full record with/without MARC tags; and flexibility in formatting and arrangement or sequences of information on the screen are desired[84].

The 1982 CLR Conference on Online Catalogs: Requirements, Characteristics and Costs concluded that "there is a need for a standard for display of bibliographic information. Such a standard should provide for brief displayand the order of the elements in the display. Expanded display should also be standardized ... [there is a] need for research on user evaluation of the existing and potential display of bibliographic information with attention on the differences between display terminals that provide 80 × 24 character display versus those that provide 64 × 16. The issue of canned versus user-tailored displays needs review as part of this effort..."[85].

In conclusion, the on-line public access catalog has arrived: there is no doubt that there are many on-line catalog projects presently under development, both in-house and commercially. The variation of display formats reviewed indicates that there are many problems concerning display formats that need further study. As Daily has pointed out, "the format of the catalog can (and should) depend upon the convenience of the users of a library, not on the formulation of theory to support one format over another"[86]. Thus, the catalog users are the sole users of the design format and the users should provide the principal input and feedback for the design principles and guidelines. In addition, more detailed research should be conducted on users' reactions to and preferences among the design formats of existing or potential on-line catalogs.

Fortunately, the attention of the library community is currently and actively involved in this. With support available from the Council on Library Resources, a number of research projects on display formats can be funded. Since no standards exist at the present time, it is urgent that the ANSI Z39 committee collaborate with librarians and system experts to establish proper standards for OPACs, display formats, and related matters. Workshops, meetings, and conferences are scheduled to introduce this new tool to the library community. Presently, the online catalog is still in its infancy; it will require years of hard work and research to achieve its refinement and adoption. Reviewing the forthcoming studies on display formats and OPAC development will be a fruitful and exciting experience.

REFERENCES

1. Charles Hildreth, Public Access Online Catalogs: Tile User Interface, Ohio Computer Library Center, Dublin, Ohio, 1982, p. 144.
2. Steven R. Salmon, "Characteristics of Online Public Catalogs," Lib. Resources Tech. Serv., 27, 36 (January – March, 1983).
3. Allen B. Veaner, "Technical Services Research Needs for the 1990s." Lib. Resources Tech. Serv., 27, 203 (April – June, 1983).
4. Joseph R. Matthews, Public Access to Online Catalogs: A Planning Guide for Managers, Online, Weston, Conn., 1982, p. 36.
5. S. Michael Malinconico and Paul J. Fasana, The Future of the Catalogs: The Library's Choices. Knowledge Industry Publications, White Plains, N.Y., 1979.
6. Joseph R. Matthews, "Online Public Access Catalogs: Assessing the Potential," Lib. J., 107, 1067 (June, 1982).
7. Norman D. Stevens, "The Catalogs of the Future: A Speculative Essay," J. Lib. Automation, 13, 190 (June, 1980).
8. Karen L. Horny, "Online Catalogs: Coping with the Choices," J. Acad. Librarianship, 8, 14 (March, 1982).
9. Malinconico and Fasana, Ref. 5, pp. 84 – 99.
10. Richard W. Boss and Deanna B. Marcum, "The Library Catalogs: COM and Online Options," Lib. Technol. Rep., 16, 446 – 448 (September-October, 1980).
11. Boss and Marcum, Ref. 10, p. 448.
12. Hildreth, Ref. I, p. 3.
13. Matthews, Ref. 4, p. 23.
14. Salmon, Ref. 2, p. 37.
15. Richard De Gennaro, "Library Automation and Networking: Perspectives, on Three Decades," Lib. J., 108, 629 (April, 1983).
16. Matthews, Ref. 4, p. 108.
17. Dorothy May Norris, A History of Cataloguing and Cataloguing Methods 1100 – 1850: With an Introductory Survey of Ancient Times, Grafton, London, 1939. p. 1.
18. Maurice E. Tauber, Cataloguing and Classification, The State of the Library Art, Vol. 1. Pt. 1, Graduate School of Library Services, Rutgers The State University, New Brunswick, N. J., 1966, p. 10.
19. Henriette D. Avram, MARC: Its History and Implications, Library of Congress, Washington. D. C., 1975, pp. 1 – 4.
20. Maurice J. Freedman and S. Michael Malinconico, eds., The Nature and Future of the Catalog: Proceedings of the ALA's Information Science and Automation Division's 1975 and 1976 Institutes on the Catalog, Oryx Press, Phoenix. Ariz., 1979, pp. 1 – 290.
21. D. Kaye Gapen and Bonnie Juergens, eds., Closing the Catalogs: Proceedings of the 1978 and 1979 Library and Information Technology Association Institutes, Oryx Press. Phoenix. Ariz., 1980.
22. Richard J. Hyman, From Cutter to MARC: Access to the Unit Records, Queens College of the City University of New York, Flushing, N. Y., 1977, p. v.
23. Joseph R. Matthews, "Requirements for an Online Catalog," Technicalities, 1, 11 – 13 (Octoberk, 1981).
24. Neal K. Kaske and Douglas Ferguson, Online Public Access to Library Bibliographic Data

Bases: Development, Issues, and Priorities: Final Report, OCLC, Dublin, Ohio, 1980 (ED 195275).
25. Douglas Ferguson et al. , "The CLR Public Catalog Study: An Overview," Inf. Technol. Lib. , 1, 85 (June, 1982).
26. Ferguson et al. , Ref. 25, pp. 84 – 85.
27. Using Online Catalogs: A Nationwide Survey: A Report of a Study Sponsored by the Council on Library Resources (Joseph R. Matthews, Gary S. Lawrence, and Douglas K. Ferguson, eds.), Neal Schuman, New York, 1983, pp. viii, 10.
28. "LAMA/LITA Program on the Public Online Catalog Project," Lib. Congress Bull. , 41, 266 – 267 (August, 1982); and "Panel on the Online Public Access Catalog Project Findings," Reported at the 45th American Society for Information Science Annual Meeting, Columbus, Ohio, October 17 – 21, 1982 (on tape).
29. Online Catalogs: Requirements, Characteristics and Costs: Report of a Conference Sponsored by the Council on Library Resources (David B. McCarn, comp. and ed.), Council on Library Resources, Washington, D. C. , 1983.
30. "Online Catalog Project Publications," CLR Res. Devel. , 11, 3 – 4 (June, 1983).
31. Online Catalogs: Requirements ..., Ref. 29, p. v.
32. Using Online Catalogs, Ref. 27, p. vii.
33. Michael Gorman, "Thinking the Thinkable: A Synergetic Profession," Am. Lib. , 13, 473 – 474 (July-August, 1982).
34. Norman D. Stevens, "Online Catalogs: What They Replace, What They Change," Lib. Issues, July 1983, p. 3.
35. Frederick G. Kilgour, "Design of Online Catalogs," in The Nature and Future of the Catalog, Ref. 20, pp. 34 – 40.
36. Michael S. Malinconico, "The Library Catalog in a Computerized Environment," in The Nature and Future of the Catalog, Ref. 20, pp. 47 – 49, 66.
37. Seymour Lubetzky, "The Traditional Ideals of Cataloguing and the New Revision," in The Nature and Future of the Catalog, Ref. 20, p. 156.
38. David R. McDonald and Susan E. Searing, "Bibliographic Instruction and the Development of Online Catalogs," Coll. Res. Lib. , 44, 6 (January, 1983).
39. Margaret Mann, Introduction to Cataloguing and the Classification of Books, American Library Association, Chicago, 1930, p. 137.
40. Susan L. Miller, "The Changing Role of a Circulation System: OSU Experience," RQ, 20, 48 (Fall, 1980).
41. Michael S. Malinconico, "Circulation Control Systems as Online Catalogs," Lib. J. , 108, 1207 – 1210 (June 1983).
42. Kilgour, Ref. 35, pp. 34 – 35.
43. Boss and Marcum. Ref. 10, pp. 491 – 498.
44. Horny, Ref. 8, pp. 14 – 19.
45. Using Online Catalogs..., Ref. 27. p. 84.
46. Using Online Catalogs..., Ref. 27, pp. 2 – 5.
47. Hildreth, Ref. 1, p. 59.
48. T. E. M. Stewart, "Displays and the Software Interface." Appl. Ergonomics, 7, 142 (September, 1976).
49. M. M. Danchak, "CRT Displays for Power Plants," Instrum. Technol. , 23. 33 (October 1976).
50. Wilbert O. Galitz, Handbook of Screen Format Design, Q. E. D. Information Sciences. Wellesley. Mass. , 1981, p. 13.
51. E. G. Bylander, Electronic Displays, McGraw-Hill, New York, 1979.

52. Howard Turtle, W. David Penniman, and Thomas B. Hickery. "Data Entry/Display Devices for Interactive Information Retrieval," in Annual Review of Information Science and Technology. Vol. 16 (Martha E. Williams, ed.), Knowledge Industry Publications, White Plains, N. Y., 1981. pp. 55 – 83.
53. James Martin, Design of Man-Computer Dialogues, Prentice-Hall. Englewood Cliffs, N. J., 1973. pp. 87 – 88.
54. Hildreth, Ref. 1, p. 139.
55. Oalitz, Ref. 50, p. 1.
56. Stanley McElderry, "Alternatives to the Conventional Card Catalog from the User Point of View." IFLA J., 2, 235 (November, 1976).
57. Patrick Wilson, "The Catalog as Access Mechanism: Background and Concepts." Lib. Resources Tech. Serv., 27, 9 – 10 (January-March, 1983).
58. Alan Seal, "Experiments with Full and Short Entry Catalogues: A Study of Library Needs." Lib. Resources Tech. Serv., 27, 145 (April-June, 1983).
59. Hildreth, Ref. 1, pp. 137, 145.
60. Using Online Catalogs…, Ref. 27, p. 152.
61. Using Online Catalogs…, Ref. 27, p. 124.
62. Using Online Catalogs…, Ref. 27, pp. 137 – 138.
63. Using Online Catalogs…, Ref. 27, p. 138.
64. Using Online Catalogs…, Ref. 27, p. 139.
65. Pauline A. Cochrane, "Can a Standard for an Online Common Command Language Be Developed?" Online, 7, 36 – 37 (January, 1983).
66. Sue Pease and Mary Noel Gouke, "Patterns of Use in an Online Catalog and a Card Catalog." College Res. Lib., 43, 279 – 291 (July, 1982).
67. Susan L. Miller, "The Library User Meets LCS," J. Acad. Librarianship, 64, 37 (January, 1982).
68. Hildreth, Ref. 1, p. 148.
69. Boss and Marcum, Ref. 10, p. 494.
70. Matthews, Ref. 23, pp. 11 – 13.
71. Jim Dwyer, "Libraries, Funding and Technological Change: Dinosaurs Face a New Ice Age," Technicalities, 1, 11 (December, 1980).
72. Thomas S. Tullis, "An Evaluation of Alphanumeric, Graphic, and Color Information Displays," Human Factors, 23, 541 – 550 (October, 1981).
73. Benjamin Scott Fryer, The Effects of Spatial Arrangement, Upper-Lower Case Combinations, and Reverse Video on Patron Response to CRT Displayed Catalog Card, Brigham Young University School of Library and Information Sciences, Provo, Utah, 1981.
74. Aaron Marcus, "Designing the Face of an Interface," IEEE Comput. Graphics Appl., 2, 23 – 29 (January, 1982).
75. Using Online Catalogs…, Ref. 27, pp. 123 – 124.
76. Linda Reynolds, The Presentation of Bibliographic Information on Prestel, The British Library, London, 1980, p. 4.
77. Reynolds, Ref. 76, p. 2.
78. Matthews, Ref. 4, p. 35.
79. Richard P. Palmer, Computerizing the Card Catalog in the University Library, Libraries Unlimited, Littleton, Colo., 1972, pp. 85 – 86.
80. Matthews, Ref. 4, p. 42.
81. Matthews, Ref. 4, pp. 111 – 320.
82. Salmon, Ref. 2, p. 58.
83. Salmon, Ref. 2, p. 65.

84. Matthews, Ref. 23, pp. 11 – 13.
85. Online Catalogs: Requirements..., Ref. 29, p. 36.
86. Jay E. Daily, "Format, Catalog," in Encyclopedia of Library and Information Science (A. Kent. H. Lancour, and J. E. Daily, eds.), Dekker, New York. 1973, Vol. 9, p. 23.

BIBLIOGRAPHY

Automated Cataloguing in ARL Libraries, Association of Research Libraries, Washington, D. C., 1978 (Kit 47 of the Systems and Procedures Exchange Center).
Avram, Henriette D., MARC: Its History and Implications, Library of Congress, Washington. D. C., 1975.
Besant, Larry. "Users of Public Online Catalogs Want Sophisticated Subject Access," Am. Lib., 14, 160 (March, 1982).
Bierman, Kenneth, "The Future of Catalogs in North American Libraries," in The Nature and Future of the Catalog, Proceedings of the ALA Information Science and Automation Division's 1975 and 1977 Institutes on the Catalog, Oryx Press, Phoenix, Ariz., 1979, pp. 114 – 119.
Boss, Richard W., and Deanna B. Marcum, "The Library Catalogs: COM and Online Options," Lib. Technol. Rep., 16, 445 – 698 (September-October, 1980).
Bylander. E. G., Electronic Displays, McGraw-Hill, New York, 1979.
Cakir, A., D. J. Hart, and T. F. M. Stewart, Visual Display Terminals: A Manual Covering Ergonomics, Workplace Design, Health and Safety, Task Organization, Wiley, New York, 1980.
Clinic on Library Applications of Data Processing, University of Illinois at Urbana-Champaign, April 20 – 23, 1980, Public Access to Library Automation, University of Illinois, Urbana-Champaign, 1980.
Cochrane, Pauline A., "Can a Standard for an Online Common Command Language Be Developed?" Online, 7, 36 – 37 (January, 1983).
Cochrane, Pauline A., "Where Do We Go from Here?" Online, 5, 30 – 42 (July, 1981).
Cole, George Watson, "An Early French General Catalog," Lib. J., 25, 329 – 331 (July, 1900).
Conference on Displays: Loughborough, September 1971, Institution of Electrical Engineers, London, 1971.
Conference Record of 1982 International Display Record Conference, Advisory Groups on Electronic Devices, IEEE, New York, 1982.
Corey, James E, Helen H. Spalding, and Jeanmarie Lang Fraser, "Involving Faculty and Students in the Selection of Catalog Alternatives," J. Acad, Librarianship, 8, 328 – 333 (January, 1983).
"Council on Library Resources Bibliographic Service Development Program: The Evaluation of Online Public Access Catalogs," Crus News, November 1981, pp. 11 – 13.
Cramer, S. A., "The Computerised Catalogue in a University Library," Libri, 26, 38 – 53 (March, 1976).
Daily, Jay E., "Format, Catalog," in Encyclopedia of Library and Information Science (A. Kent, H. Lancour, and J. E. Daily, ers.), Dekker, New York, 1973, Vol. 9, pp. 18 – 23.
Danchak, M. M., "CRT Display for Power Plants," Instrum. Technol., 23, 29 – 36 (October, 1976).
Debons, Anthony, "Introduction to Display Systems," in Display System Engineering (H. R.

Luxenberg and R. L. Kuehn, ers.), McGraw-Hill, New York, 1968, pp. 1 – 23.

DeGennaro, Richard. "Library Automation and Networking: Perspectives on Three Decades," Lib. J., 108, 629 – 635 (April, 1983).

Dwyer, Jim. "Libraries, Funding, and Technological Change: Dinosaurs Face a New Ice Age," Technicalities, 1, 10 – 11 (December, 1980).

Ferguson, Douglas. et al., "The CLR Public Catalog Study: An Overview," Inf. Technol. Lib., 1, 84 – 97 (June, 1982).

Freedman, Maurice J., and S. Michael Malinconico, eds., The Nature and Future of the Catalog: Proceedings of the ALA's Information Science and Automation Division's 1975 and 1977 Institutes on the Catalog, Oryx Press, Phoenix, Ariz., 1979.

Friedman, Elaine S., "Patron Access to Online Cataloguing Systems: OCLC in the Public Service Environment," J. Acad. Librarianship, 6, 132 – 139 (July, 1980).

Fryer, Benjaman Scott, The Effects of Spatial Arrangement, Upper-Lower Case Combinations, and Reverse Video on Patron Response to CRT Displayed Catalog Card. Brigham Young University, School of Library and Information Sciences, Provo, Utah, 1981.

Galitz, Wilbert O., Handbook of Screen Format Design, Q. E. D. Information Sciences, Wellesley, Mass., 1981.

Galitz, Wilbert O., "Human Engineering in Screen Design," J. Syst. Manage., 34, 6 – 11 (May, 1983).

Gapen, D. Kaye, and Bonnie Juergens, eds., Closing the Catalogs: Proceedings of the 1978 and 1979 Library and Information Technology Association Institutes, Oryx Press, Phoenix, Ariz., 1980.

Gorman, Michael "The Prospective Catalog?" in Closing the Catalog: Proceedings of the 1978 and 1979 Library and Information Technology Association institutes, Oryx Press, Phoenix, Ariz., 1980, pp. 85 – 96.

Gorman, Michael, "Thinking the Thinkable: A Synergetic Profession," Am. Lib., 13, 473 – 474 (July-August, 1982).

Hildreth, Charles, Online Public Access Catalogs: The User Interface, OCLC, Dublin, Ohio, 1982.

Hitt, W. D., et al., "Development of Design Criteria for Intelligence Display Formats," Human Factors, 3, 86 – 92 (July, 1961).

Horny, Karen I., "Online Catalogs: Coping with the Choices," J. Acad. Librarianship, 8, 14 – 19 (March, 1982).

Huchingson, R. D., et al., "Formatting, Message Load, Sequencing Method, and Presentation Rate for Computer-Generated Displays," Human Factors, 23, 551 – 559 (October, 1981).

Hyman, Richard J., From Cutter to MARC: Access to the Unit Record, Queens College of the University of New York, Flushing, N. Y., 1977.

Jones, C. Lee, and Nancy Gwinn, "Bibliographic Service Development: A New CLR Program," J. Lib. Automation, 12, 116 – 124 (June, 1979).

Kaske, Neal K., and Douglas Ferguson, Online Public Access to Library Bibliographic Data Bases: Development. Issues. and Priorities: Final Report, OCLC, Dublin, Ohio. 1980 (ED 195275).

Kilgour, Frederick G., "Design of Online Catalogs," in The Nature and Future of the Catalog: Proceedings of the ALA's Information Science and Automation Division's 1975 and 1977 Institutes on the Catalog (M. J. Freedman and S. M. Malinconico, eds.), Oryx Press, Phoenix, Ariz., 1979. pp. 34 – 41.

Krikelas, James, "Catalog Use Studies and Their Implications," in Advances in Librarianship, Vol. 3, Seminar press, New York, 1972.

"LAMA/LITA Program on the Public Online Catalog Project," Lib. Congress Inf. Bull., 41, 266–267 (August, 1982).

Lancaster, F. W., The Measurement and Evaluation of Library Services, Information Resources Press, Washington, D. C., 1977.

Lees, Roger, "The Man/Display Relationship," in International Conference on Display for Man-Machine Systems: April 4–7, 1977, University of Lancaster, Lancaster, 1977 (IEEE Conference Publications No. 150).

Loewe, Richard T., "System Design, Coding, Formats, and Programming," in Display Systems Engineering (H. R. Luxenberg and R. L. Kuehn, eds.), McGraw-Hill, New York. 1968, pp. 24–69.

Lubetzky, Seymour, "The Function of the Catalog." College Res. Lib., 17. 213–215 (May, 1956).

Lubetzky, Seymour, "The Traditional Ideals of Cataloguing and the New Revision," in The Nature and Future of the Catalog. Proceedings of the ALA's Information Science and Automation Division's 1975 and 1977 Institutes on the Catalog, Oryx Press, Phoenix, Ariz., 1979, pp. 152–169.

McDonald, David R., and Susan E. Searing, "Bibliographic Instruction and the Development of Online Catalogs," College Res. Lib., 44, 5–11 (January, 1983).

McElderry Stanley, "Alternatives to the Conventional Card Catalog from the User Point of View." IFLA J., 2, 232–236 (November, 1976).

Malinconico, S. Michael, "Circulation Control Systems as Online Catalogs," Lib. J., 108, 1207–1210 (June, 1983).

Malinconico, S. Michael, "The Library Catalog in a Computerized Environment," in The Nature and Future of the Catalog. Proceedings of the ALA's Information Science and Automation Division's 1975 and 1977 Institutes on the Catalog, Oryx Press, Phoenix, Ariz., 1979, pp. 46–71.

Malinconico, S. Michael, and Paul J. Fasana, The Future of the Catalog: The Library's Choices. Knowledge Industry Publications, White Plains, N. Y., 1979.

Mann, Margaret, Introduction to Cataloguing and the Classification of Books, A Mericaa Library Association, Chicago, 1930.

Marcus, Aaron. "Designing the Face Oran Interface," IEEE Cornput. Graphics Appl., 2, 23–29 (January, 1982).

Markey, Karen, Analytical Review of Catalog Use Studies, OCLC, Columbus, Ohio. 1980 (Report No. OCLC/OPR/RR –80/2).

Martin, James, Design of Man-Computer Dialogues. Prentice-Hall, Englewood Cliffs, N. J., 1973.

Matthews, Joseph R., "The Automated Library System Marketplace, 1982: Change and More Change!" Lib. J., 108, 547–553 (March, 1983).

Matthews, Joseph R., "Online Public Access Catalogs: Assessing the Potential," Lib. J., 107, 1070–1071 (June, 1982).

Matthews, Joseph R., Public Access to Online Catalogs: A Planning Guide for Managers, Online, Weston. Conn., 1982.

Matthews, Joseph R., "Requirements for an Online Catalog," Technicalities, 1, 11–13 (October, 1981).

Mays, Tony, "Online Public Access Catalogues in North America," LASIE, May-June, 1982, pp. 5–11.

Miller, Susan L., "The Changing Role of a Circulation System: OSU Experience," RQ, 20, 47–52 (Fall, 1980).

Miller, Susan L., "The Library User Meets LCS." J. Acad. Librarianship, 64, 31–38

(January, 1980).

Moore, Carol Weiss, "User Reactions to Online Catalogs: An Exploration Study" College Res. Lib., 42, 295–302 (July, 1981).

Nordan, David J., and Gall Herndon Lawrence, "Public Terminal Use in an Online Catalog: Some Preliminary Results," College Res. Lib., 42. 308–316 (July, 1981).

Norris, Dorothy May, A History of Cataloguing and Cataloguing Methods 1100–1850: With an Introductory Survey of Ancient Times. Grafton, London, 1939.

"Online Catalog Project Publications," CLR Res. Devel., 11, 3–4 (June, 1983).

Online Catalogs: Requirements, Characteristics and Costs: Report of a Conference Sponsored by the Council on Library Resources, Compiled and edited by David B. McCarn, The Council, Washington, D. C., 1983.

Palmer, Richard P., Computerizing the Card Catalog in the University Library. Libraries Unlimited. Littleton, Colo., 1972.

"Panel on the Online Public Access Catalog Project Findings," American Society for Information Science 45th Annual Meeting. Columbus, Ohio, October 17–21. 1982 (on tape).

Pease, Sue, and Mary Noel Gouke, "Patterns and Use in an Online Catalog and a Card Catalog," College Res. Lib., 43, 279–291 (July, 1982).

Ranz, Jim, The Printed Book Catalogue in American Libraries: 1723–1900, American Library Association. Chicago, 1964.

Reynolds, Linda, The Presenation of Bibliographic Information Prestel, British Library, London, 1980

(BL R&D Report 5536).

Seal. Alan, "Experiments with Full and Short Entry Catalogues: A Study of Library Needs," Lib. Resources Tech. Serv., 27. 144–155 (April-June, 1983).

Shurteff, Donald A., "Symbols, Abbreviations and Formats for CIDs." in The Power of Information, Proceedings of American Society for Information Science 1980 Mid-Year Meeting, ASIS. Washington, D. C., 1980, pp. 34–40.

Siegel Elliot R., ct al., "Research. Strategy and Methods Used to Conduct a Comparative Evaluation of Two Prototype Online Catalog Systems," in The 4th National Online Meeting Proceedings, Learned Information, Medford, N. J., 1983, pp. 503–511.

Smith, Sidney, "Letter Size and Legibility," Human Factors, 21, 661–670 (December, 1979).

Stevens, Norman D., "The Catalogs of the Future: A Speculative Essay:" J. Lib. Automation, 13 (June, 1980).

Stevens, Norman D., "Online Catalogs: What They Replace, What They Change," Lib. Issues, 3 (July, 1983).

Stevenson, Gordan, "Descriptive Cataloguing in 1982," Lib. Resources Tech. Serv., 27, 259–268 (July-September, 1983).

Stewart, T. F. M., "Communicating with Dialogues," Ergonomics, 23, 909–911 (September, 1980).

Stewart, T. F. M., "Displays and the Software Interface," Appl. Ergonomics, 7, 137–146 (September, 1976).

Tauber, Maurice F., Cataloguing and Classification, The State of the Library Art, Vol. 1, Pt. 1, Graduate School of Library Service, Rutgers The State University, New Brunswick, N. J., 1966.

Tinker, M. A., Legibility of Print, Iowa State University Press, Ames. 1963.

Tullis, Thomas S., "An Evaluation of Alphanumeric. Graphic, and Color Information Displays." Human Factors, 23, 541–550 (October, 1981).

Turtle, Howard, W. David Penniman, and Thomas B. Hickery, "Data Entry/Display

Devices for Interactive Information Retrieval," in Annual Review of Information Science and Technology, Vol. 16 (Martha E. Williams, ed.), Knowledge Industry Publications, White Plains, N. Y., 1981, pp. 55 – 83.

User Instruction for Online Catalogs in ARL Libraries, Association of Research Libraries, Washington. D. C., 1983 (Kit 93 of the Systems and Procedures Exchange Center).

Using Online Catalogs: A Nationwide Survey: A Report of a Survey Sponsored by the Council on Library Resources (Joseph R. Matthews, Gary S. Lawrence, and Douglas Ferguson, eds.), Neal-Schuman, New York, 1983.

Veaner, Allen B., "Technical Services Research Needs for the 1990s," Lib. Resources Tech. Serv., 27, 199 – 210 (April-June, 1983).

Vita, Paul C., "Preference for Different Amounts of Visual Complexity," Behav. Sci., 11, 105 – 111 (March, 1966).

Weintraub, D. Kathryn, "The Essentials or Desiderata of the Bibliographic Record as Discovered by Research," Lib. Resources Tech. Serv., 23, 391 – 405 (Fall, 1979).

Wiederkehr, Robert R. V., Alternatives for Future Library Catalogs: A Cost Model Final Report of the Library Catalog Cost Model Project Prepared for the Association of Research Libraries, Kinf Research, Rockville, Md., 1980.

Willianson, Nancy J., "Is There a Catalog in Your Future? Access to Information in the Year 2006," Lib. Resources Tech. Serv., 26, 122 – 135 (April-June, 1982).

Wilson. Patrick, "The Catalog as Access Mechanism: Background and Concepts," Lib. Resources Tech. Serv, 27, 4 – 17 (January-March, 1983).

WEBNET CIRCULATION SYSTEM:
AN EARLY USE STUDY*

I. Introduction

There are "older" and "more recent" views of the circulation function stated by Barbara Markuson in her 1975 *Library Technology Reports* study of automated circulation control systems. The "older" view was that circulation control centered conservation of the collection and recordkeeping; the "more recent" view encompasses "all activities related to the use of library materials."[1] Circulation services, as described by Freedman, involve that function which is ultimately one of the most fundamental: "the satisfactory bringing together of the library user and the materials sought by that person."[2]

Over the years, the increase in library collections, workloads, and library services overwhelms traditional manual library systems, and causes libraries to turn to more efficient means-automated systems. Similarly, when the total number of annual circulation transactions reach/over 250,000, the manual circulation system must be replaced by other modern methods, computerized systems, in order to handle and manage them effectively. In addition, there are many libraries with manual circulation systems able to support their work loads, which also considered automation, often in the belief that it will result in cost savings.[3]

In 1978, the Association of Research Libraries (ARL) conducted a survey of more than one hundred of its members on using automated circulation systems. Of sixty-seven questionnaires returned, thirty-seven libraries use automated circuiation systems. Half of these systems were custom-developed in-house systems, and half of them were using commercial vendor systems. The majority of all the systems were batch processing, or partial online applications.[4]

With the advent of minicomputers in 1970s, the turnkey market of circulation systems, using the capabilities and special characteristics of the minicomputers, have increased remarkably. It was estimated the gross value between 1970 to 1976 was 10 million dollars. In the single year of 1977, sales totalled 10 M. dollars, the gross one-year revenue from July 1, 1980 to June 30, 1981 was in excess of $25,000,000. The number of turnkey circulation systems that are scheduled to be installed in 1981 was 75, and the total number of installed turnkey circulation systems is 301.[5]

Evidently, the present integrated library systems, library consortia, and networks have long shown an interest in automation of circulation. And also some of the integrated library systems were developed from the existed circulation systems such as the Library Control Circulation System (LCS) of Ohio State University. For an integrated library system, the "total system approach", information about the status of an item, from the time it is ordered, is processed by technical services, is put on the shelf, and has been checked out by a patron, is available to one and all in one central data base. For library cooperatives, a central circulation system provides a mechanism for resources sharing, especially when cooperating libraries are in geographic proximity. In addition, it has been reported that the greatest benefits from the automation of functions besides cataloguing have been those that have shared an automated circulation control system. This is particularly popular among the cooperated automated programs

---

* *Library and Information Science* (Taipei, Taiwan) Vol. 10 (Oct., 1984): pp. 163–183.

of public libraries, such as, the North Suburban Library System in Metropolitan Chicago, and several hundred public libraries in Illinois, Conneticut, and other states have installed similar shared automated circulation system. [6,7]

In the network environment, a network-supported circulation system will have the potential for integration of circulation with other shared network functions. Thus, many networks are pregently developing and planning their circulation subsystems, such as, OCLC, WLN, etc. Of course, there are also networks that have installed their automation circulation systems, such as the WEBNET (Western Pennsylvania Buhl Network) circulation subsystem. It is the intent of this paper to study the early use of WEBNET Circulation system.

II. Purpose of the Study

The intent of this study are threefold:
1) To study the early use of the WEBNET circulation system by the Carlow College library personnel.
2) To collect suggestions and comments from the library personnel for possible improvement of WEBNET circulation system, and
3) To learn the operations of WEBNET circulation system by the investigator.

III. Methodology

Two methods are used:
1) A questionnaire was administrated to the library personnel who have learned the use of WEBNET circulation system. (the instrument is included in the appendix)
2) To observe the circulation personnel at work and to discuss with them about the problems of the circulation system.

IV. WEBNET Circulation System Development

WEBNET was initially developed by the Office of Communication Programs (OCP) at the University of Pittsburgh in 1975, and it was planned as a demonstration-pilot operation of a full library service and resources sharing network in Western Pennsylvania by linking six libraries in the Pittsburgh area. They are California State College, Carlow College, Chatham College, Point Park College, University of Pittsburgh, and Westminster College.[8] Kent stated that "the chief objective of the WEBNET has been to develop a pilot project which would demonstrate how a full-service regional resource sharing network would operate and to make a close study of the costs..."[9] In the original proposal, the services provided by the network are acquisitions, cataloguing, inter-library loan, mail, reporting, and a public-access online catalog. It was lacking a circulation function in the network, and it was soon realized that "a regional network will not be considered economically viable without the [circulation] function." Therefore, a second proposal was proposed to the Buhl Foundation in 1980. There are two structural alternatives for automating circulation control in a networking environment, for WEBNET, it was decided the decentralized approach should be used. That is the storage of patron and item data at each library, accessible via terminals from any other libraries through the central computer.[10]

Two participating libraries are selected as the test sites for the circulation system. The first circulation system was installed at Carlow College library in late August 1982. The circulation system was officially opened to the public on October 12, 1982. The hardware installed at the

Carlow College library were: a microcomputer DEC PDP 11/23 (256 KB), a printer, a Bar Code Reader, Z19 Terminal, and a Modem. The data stored in the microcomputer are the Patron File, the Item Bar Code File, and the Temporary (Demo.) File. The total collection in the system for Carlow College library are 63,000 items.

V. An Idealized Circulation System

Boss in 1979 *Library Technology Reports* stated that an ideal circulation system should be able to do the following:
1. Permit the library staff to quickly determine that a patron is eligible for service, what his or her privileges are, and at what address he or she can be reached.
2. Permit the library's patrons and staff to quickly determine what titles are in the library's collection and where they are located.
3. Enable the staff to quickly and efficiently charge and discharge library materials, and to keep accurate and current records of these transactions.
4. Permit the library patrons or staff to quickly determine what is currently in circulation and when it is or was due back.
5. Produce overdue and recall notices, and permit the library staff to quickly determine what notices have been sent to patrons with materials charged out and what action is next to be taken.
6. Place holds on items, and permit library staff to quickly determine what titles are being held for patrons, for whom they are being held and after what date the materials are no longer wanted.
7. Provide management information on the utilization to aid in staff scheduling, collection weeding and storage, and acquisitions.
8. Accommodate dramatic increases in collection size, number of users, number of transactions, or number of locations without major system redesign.

Boss also developed a list of desirable circulation features, they are:
1. Response time averaging two seconds or less for charges and discharges.
2. Response time of five seconds or less for simple inquires by author or title.
3. Ability to sort three classification schemes (LC, DC, other).
4. Ability to sort in call number and display or print.
5. Maximum response time of eight seconds or less for subject inquires.
6. Ability to distinguish multiple volumes and multiple copies of the same call number to permit specific access.
7. Ability to handle up to twenty types of patron.
8. Ability to charge materials to specific carrells or offices for in-building use.
9. Ability to set variant-length loan periods and reset when necessary.
10. Ability to override loan period.
11. Identification of restricted or blocked borrowers during charge-out.
12. Immediate updating of the data base including immediate call number access and access to holds.
13. Ability to place holds on items and notify patrons of their availability, including the capability of producing a list of holds in call number.
14. Ability to produce a report on hold queues that exceed a specified number of copies.
15. Ability to adjust the hold queue.
16. Capability of easily posting holds against all circulating copies of a multicopy item or only against specific copies.
17. Easy, regular preparation of overdue notices, recall notices fine notices and replacement

bills in background rather than overnight.
18. Ability to produce a list (dummy run) in call-number order of all books for which overdue notices are schedules to be sent.
19. Access to information concerning materials charged to an individual borrower by the borrower's name.
20. Ability to access patron accounts for current and past fines.

Reserve Functions

1. Ability to charge book to linked course/faculty member.
2. Ability to circulate books for an hourly, overnight, daily, weekly, or other loan period from course/faculty member to other patrons.
3. Ability to place holds on reserve books.
4. Ability to fine books on an hourly basis.
5. Ability to generate overdue notices daily.
6. Ability to generate course/faculty directories.
7. Ability to trace book to course/faculty member through item query.
8. Circulation statistics for the number of times each item was borrowed, tied to course/faculty member.

Management Information Functions

1. The production of circulation statistics by time of day, week, month, or year—including ability to cumulate.
2. Ability to measure collection demand by classification number—including both loans and recall requests.
3. Identification of frequently demanded titles—including both loans and recall requests.
4. Identification of infrequently circulated titles.
5. Circulation statistics by borrower type.
6. Circulation statistics by location.
7. Circulation statistics by computer terminal.

Training Program

1. Designed to facilitate ease of operation so that up to 100 people can be trained to use the system.
2. Formal training program by vendor as a part of the standard contract.
3. Staff manual provided.
4. Patron-orientation materials provided.

Flexibility of System

1. Ability to increase the item file to 2,000,000 items without replacement of hardware or software at added cost.
2. Ability to increase the patron file to 500,000 without replacement of hardware or software at added cost.
3. Ability to increase the number of terminals to more than 100 without replacement of hardware or software at added cost.
4. Ability to extend to remote locations.
5. Ability to "network" with other circulation systems of same vendor.
6. Ability to "network" with other vendors' systems. [11]

The above lists are very useful references for libraries to plan, design, or purchase a circulation system.

VI. System Capabilities of WEBNET Circulation System

WEBNET circulation system is a very sophisticated system, which can perform many circulation functions that are normally can not or will take a long time to do it manually. The major functions of WEBNET circulation system are:
1. Lend/return items to legitimate patrons.
2. Add items to and remove items from the general circulating collection.
3. Transfer items from the general circulation collection to the reserve collection or transfer items back.
4. Add or remove personal copies and photocopies to/from the reserve collection.
5. Retrieve bibliographic information from the VAX concerning any item in the general collection and a skeleton bibliographic record from the circulation computer for any item in the reserve collection.
6. Determine who has a borrowed item, and put a reserve note, and notify the requested person when item returns.
7. Record lost items, if lost by a person be able to input the cost of replacement on the patron's record.
8. Record damaged item.
9. Return a "lost" item to the collection.
10. Retrieve information concerning any item in the collection whether in the library, in circulation, lost, damaged, etc.
11. Calculate fines on overdue items based on the length of time the items are overdue and the status of the patron.
12. Attach all fines on overdue items and/or lost items to the patron responsible for the violation.
13. Recall an item borrowed for reserve.
14. Establish limits for the number of items a patron can have in his/her possession, and the maximum amount of money that can be owed—a patron passing either of these automatically loses borrowing privileges.
15. Add and delete patrons both individually or in groups.
16. Create reports and send out overdue notices.
17. Waive fines for lost or overdue books.
18. Collect fines either in entirely or only in part.
19. Create a list of lost items.
20. Send periodic the follow-up notices.
21. Renew an item already on loan.
22. Detailed circulation statistics related to library usage by various types of patrons and materials can be generated from the WEBNET statistics package.
23. Other capabilities will add to the system when needed. [12]

VII. Questionnaire and Observation Results

Thirty-eight questionnaires were administered to the library personnel at the Carlow College library. Selection criteria were: all library staff and the circulation staff. There are nine library staff and their questionnaires were administered and collected by the Library Director. Twenty-nine student aide questionnaires were administered and collected by the Head of the Circulation Department. The results were analyzed and tabulated on p. 173 – 176. Major reactions to the use of WEBNET circulation system are the following:

1. 35, or 93%, out of 38 library personnel surveyed indicated the system is easy to use.
2. 71% of the library personnel prefer the automated system over the manual one.
3. 29 (76%) library personnel would like to recommend the circulation system to other libraries.
4. 70% of library personnel are capable of using most of the system commands.
5. All agreed that "hand-on" experience is very important.
6. Some of the commands take too many steps.
7. System downtime was mentioned in several questionnaires.
8. Sometimes it was difficult to wand the bar code.
9. Circulation Manual should be stated and explained in simple language terms. 17 of the personnel commented the manual was helpful to them, 6 indicated very helpful, and 7 indicated it has no help at all. Command steps should be more clearly stated and explained; too much computer jargon is used in the manual.
10. One person's comments on the manual "Burn it!". It seems that this is not a valid answer, because in her other answers to the manual, she said that the manual is clear, easy to use, and helpful!
11. An "English Language Index" for the manual was suggested by the Library Director.
12. A record of the problems of the system was kept (only for the first three weeks).
13. 4 of the library personnel indicated that they learned to use the system by the circulation manual, 11 learned it from others, and 22 learned the use of the system by the combination of above methods.

Library Personnel Statistics

	Library Staff (9)	Student Aides* (29)	Total Number of Personnel Surveyed (38)
Total Number Surveyed	9	29	38
Total Number Returned	9	29	38
Full Time	7	0	7
Part Time	2	29	31
Circulation Desk Personnel	2	29*	31
Taken Computer Related Courses Previously	3	7	10
Knowledge of Using Terminal	7	18	25
Using Terminal for Present Work	5	0	5

*Student Aides Works Schedule: 2-9 hours per week
27 or 90% of them came to the library to work at least twice a week.

Circulation System Manual Instruction

	Library Staff	Student Aides	Total Number
Clearly Stated	4	17	21
Not Clearly Stated	1	9	10
Easy to Use	3	15	18
Not Easy to Use	2	10	12
Very Helpful	3	3	6
Helpful	1	16	17
No Help at All	1	6	7

The Use of Automated Circulation System

	Library Staff (9)	Student Aides (29)	Total No. (38)
Learning Methods:			
Circulation Manual	3	1	4
Taught by Others	2	9	11
Both (Above) Methods	3	19	22
Use of Circulation System:			
Complicated	1	0	1
Easy to Use	7	28	35
No Comment	1	1	2
Prefer the Automated Circulation System over the Manual One:			
Yes	6	21	27
No	0	2	2
Not Sure	3	6	9
Recommend the System to Other Libraries:			
Yes	6 (66%)	23 (80%)	29 (76%)
No	0	0	0
Not Sure	3	6	9

Knowledge of Circulation System Major Commands

Commands	Library Staff (9)	Student Aides (29)	Total No. (38)
Checkout	7	29	36
Return	6	27	33
Renew	4	22	26
Fines	3	22	25

（續上表）

Commands	Library Staff (9)	Student Aides (29)	Total No. (38)
Display Patron (d p)	5	24	29
Display Item (d i)	5	20	25
Display Patron Items (d p i)	5	18	23
Display Item Owner (d i o)	4	10	14
Renew by Phone	2	7	9
Not Comment	1	0	1

Suggestions and Comments
(Direct quotes are taken from the returned questionnaires)

The System
— It is a very easy system.
— Get it (system) to work so it doesn't break down.
— It is often hard to wand the bar code for student I. D. and the book because it gets worn down and the scanner can not pick up the code.
— The computer goes down often and books can be checkout, they are written up but must be put into computer later, and they can not be returned either (books could be shelved must wait).

The Circulation Manual
— An "English language index"; for example: User's question: Who has this book out? Command: display item owner (d i o).
— It needs a clearer explanation.
— Use simple terms.
— Simplier terms the words and understanding are unclear and difficult.
— For individuals who only function to check books in and out etc. the procedures are too lengthy—it would be easier to have those required by this position specifically laid out.
— For command fines, it isn't cleared about waiving a fine and when it should appear on the screen.
— The steps could be stated in more simple terms.
— It is often difficult to undertand/steps are sometimes skipped/language not clear.
— You need to practice not just read a book.
— I think it is very explanatory.
— Burn it!

VIII. Suggestions and Conclusions

Perhaps it is too soon for this type of questionnaire survey, but because of the time limitation of the investigator, the survey had to be conducted at this time. It is strongly recommended by the investigator that there should be further studies and evaluations of this circulation system in the future. From the questionnaires and personal observations of the system, the following are recommended.
1. The system downtime should be recorded with the reasons for it in order to test the system reliability.
2. A record of the number of transactions during the system downtime should be kept. This is an

important factor to measure since a comparison of these transaction against the total transactions could be made if the data was available.
3. All the recommended changes to the system by the prsonnel should be recorded.
4. A list of "don'ts" should provided by the system person for the circulation system operators.
5. The command steps used to locate the desired information should be 1 ~ 2 steps and no more than 3 steps.
6. The present data in the patron file is inconsistent and incomplete; it should be thoroughly checked and updated especially the data which was used to print patron's address which was used for sending the overdue notices.
7. Circulation manual should be explained in simple language terms; more examples should be given and in regular size for easy reading.
8. It would be desirable to have more library staff members with a thorough knowledge of the system as backups.
9. The library should reconsider its policy concerning waiving fines since it cost more staff time to waive fines online.
10. A trainning program should be developed for the student aides and library staff; it would appropriate to have formal instruction in the new automated system.
11. Better communication is essential. Everyone in the library should be informed of any new changes and/or corrections made in the system.
12. It is felt desirable that the call number and author of an item should be made directly searchable in the circulation system. Now one has to switch to the Public Service Version of WEBNET in order to locate the information.
13. It is strongly recommended that the use of commands in the circulation system should be monitored by the system in order to establish the possible standard specifications for an ideal circulation system in a network environment.
14. The investigator also strongly recommends that further studies on this system should be conducted in the near future. To study not only the use of the circulation system but also the benefits and cost-effectiveness of the automated circulation system in comparison with the manual system.

In conclusions, this investigator believes that an ideal circulation system is related to the individual library's needs. There are three major variables in the circulation system: the specification requirements established to meet local needs, the system design factor (how easy is the system to use), and the human factor (staff acceptance of the system).

In the recent March - April 1982 issue of *Library Technology Reports* on "Automated Circulation Control Systems" Boss concludes "a system is only as good as the way in which it is implemented and controlled, ... the installation of an automated circulation system does not absolve the administrator of the responsibility to manage and monitor the performance of all resources—human, materials...machine [and money],"[13] and it should enhance the efficiency of library management.

Acknowledgements: The author is grateful for the cooperation of Mrs. Joan Mitchell, library director of Carlow College, as well as the library staff, without whose cooperation this research could not have been done.

References

1. Barbara Evan Markuson, "Automated Circulation Control Systems: An Overview of Commercial Vendor Systems," *Library Technology Reports* (July and Sept., 1975), p. 6.
2. Maurice J. Freedman, "Circulation Systems: Past and Present," *Journal of Library Automation* (Dec., 1981), p. 279.

3. Richard W. Boss and Judy McQueen, "Automated Circulation Control Systems," *Library Technology Reports* (March & April, 1982), p. 151.
4. Association of Research Libraries, Systems and Procedures Exchange Center *Automated Circulation*, *Kit 43* (Washington, D. C.: ARL, 1978), pp. 1-2.
5. Joseph R. Matthews, "The Automated Circulation System Marketplace: Active and Heating Up," *Library Journal* (Feb., 1982), pp. 233-234.
6. Boss, *op. cit.*, pp. 155-156.
7. Barbara Evan Markuson, "Granting Amnesty and Other Fascinating Aspects of Automated Circulation," *American Libraries* (April, 1978), p. 209.
8. Allen Kent, *A proposal on Resource Sharing in Libraries—A Pilot-Demonstration* (Pittsburgh, Pa.: University of Pittsburgh, 1974), p. 1.
9. Allen Kent, *Augmentation and Continuation of WEBNET, A Proposal to the BuM Foundation* (Pittsburgh, Pa.: University of Pittsburgh, 1980), pp. 1-6.
10. Kent (1974), *op. cit.*, pp. 1-5.
11. Richard W. Boss, "Circulation Systems: the Options," *Library Technology Reports* (Jan. & Feb., 1979), pp. 19-22.
12. E. E. Duncan and P. J. Klingensmith, *WEBNET Circulation System* (Pittsburgh, Pa.: University of Pittsburgh, 1982), pp. 3-4.
13. Boss (1982), op. cit., p. 231.

Appendix

The purpose of this questionnaire is to obtain general information about your newly installed automated circulation system in terms of its usage activities, such as how well the system was accepted by the partons and the library staff especially, what are the difficulties, and your suggestions for the system improvement. Please answer the questions as accurately and objectively as possible, if you can not answer some of the questions, please leave them blank.

1) Respondent's title: _____
2) Length of time in current position: _____
3) Length of time employed by library: _____
4) Do you work in the library: Full time _____ Part time _____
5) Do you work at the circulation desk: Yes _____ No _____
6) Are you aware of your library having an automated circulation system?
   Yes _____ No _____
7) If you work at the circulation desk, how many hours per week do you work there? _____ hrs.
   Which day(s) of the week, please circle: M. T. W. TH. F. S. Sun.
8) Have you taken any course relating to computers: Yes _____ No _____
9) Have you used a computer terminal before: Yes _____ No _____
10) Do you like machines: Yes _____ No _____
11) Are you using a terminal for your present work (please do not include the terminal at the circulation desk):
    Yes _____ No _____
12) Did you have any training on how to use the circulation system:
    Yes _____ No _____ How many hours of training _____ hrs.
13) How did you learn to use the circulation terminal:
    Self-learning _____ Taught by others _____ Not learned yet _____
14) Did you learn the use of circulation system by following the *Circulation Manual*?
    Yes _____ No _____ Or by others _____ Both _____

15) Do you think the *Circulation Manual* instructions on how to use the circulation system are clearly stated: Yes _____ No _____ and easy to use: Yes _____ No _____
16) Do you think the *Circulation Manual* is:
    Very helpful _____ Helpful _____ No help at all _____
17) Any suggestions for the *Circulation Manual* please:
    _____
    _____
18) Do you think the circulation system is easy to use: Yes _____ No _____
19) Do you like the automated circulation system better than the manual one:
    Yes _____ No _____ Not sure _____
20) Do you think "hand-on" experience is very important: Yes _____ No _____
21) Do you know how to use most of the commands of the circulation system:
    Yes _____ No _____
22) Do you know how to use the following commands:
    Checkout _____ Returns _____ Renew _____ Fines _____
    Display patron (d p) _____ Display item (d i) _____
    Display patron item (d p i) _____ Display item owner (d i o) _____ Renew by phone _____
23) Did you find some of the commands are not very easy to use:
    Yes _____ No _____ Which ones _____
24) Did you report or record the problems that you have with the system:
    Yes _____ No _____
25) Do you think this circulation system is too complicated for you:
    Yes _____ No _____ Not sure
26) Would you recommend this system to other libraries:
    Yes _____ No _____ Not sure _____
27) Any more suggestions and comments: _____
    _____

Many thanks for your kind cooperation and assistance.

NON-BIBLIOGRAPHIC DATABASES*

1. Introduction

The dial-up on line information retrieval service has been with us for over ten years since the inauguration of the first dial up online information retrieval service, the MEDLINE of the "National Library of Medicine" in 1971.[1] Increasing numbers of libraries all over the world are finding vital information rapidly through online infromation retrieval services, and online services of all kinds play an increasing role in the large, modern library today.

Online information retrieval services have been commercially available since the early 1970s.[2] Since that time, the online databases have grown in size, type, and number. It was estimated that by the end of 1980, the number of public available computer-readable databases would reach over 650 and would contain more than 75 million records.[3] There are various online database system vendors in the USA, Canada, and Europe who also provide online database services. Major vendors include the "National Library of Medicine (NLM)", Lockheed Information System (LIS), System Development Corporation (SDC), Bibliographic Retrieval Service (BRS), the Canada Institute for Scientific Information (CISTI), and the European Space Agency (ESA).[4]

In the beginning, these computer-readable databases were given a general name: bibliographic databases; but actually the majority of the computer-readable databases are non-bibliographic in nature.[5] Non-bibliographic databases (NBDBs) have existed among us for a long time, particular in the financial, economics, and technology areas. Because of their special characteristics, it is impossible to estimate the total number of them and locate them all.[6]

Online output examples of bibliographic and non-bibliographic databases are shown in the Appendix.

In recent years, there were many promotional activities on NBDBs conducted in the United States, such as the founding of the ASIS Special Interest Group on Numeric Databases (SIG/NDB) in 1975; the chapter on "Numeric Databases ancd Systems" in the 1977 volume of the *Annual Review of Information Science and Technology* (ARIST) by Luedke et al.;[7] Cuadra Associates' seminar team on NBDBs in this country and in four European countries which began in 1978;[8] the sessions on non-bibliographic online systems at the 1979 ASIS National Meeting;[9] a symposium on problems and techniques in retrieval of numerical data at the 178th National Meeting of the American Chemical Society in 1979;[10] and a list of non-bibliographic databases online also appears periodically in *Online Review*. All of these were aimed at creating awareness of the existence and the importance of NBDBs to the information community and to users as well.[11]

2. Definitions and Classifications

A *database* is an organized collection of bibliographic or non-bibliographic information/data in machine-readable form accessible by computer. Databases vary in subject, type, scope, format, currency, and chronological coverage.[12] Databases have been classified in various

---

* *Library of Information Science*, Vol. 9 No. 1, (April, 1983) pp. 74-91.

ways. Two major classifications are mentioned:

A. Bibliographic and Non-bibliographic Databases:

1. *Bibliographic*: This database refers or points to literature sources for information.

2. *Non-bibliographic*: This database contains facts and yields actual information which may be numeric, full-text, or directional in nature rather than bibliographic; and these databases stand alone as source information or raw data. Other names, such as "data fries", "data bank", "information bank", "facts bank" are used to indicate this type of database. The term "data bank" is usually used in European countries.[13]

B. Cuadra Associates' Classification Scheme: The recently adopted classification scheme for online databases by Cuadra Associates, Inc. (CA) used in its publication *Directory of Online Databases*.[14] It is very similar to the above classification scheme in categorizing the databases, but further subdivides them into the following groups:

1. *Reference Databases*: These contain references or secondary information that refer the users to primary sources (e.g., articles, patents, organizations, or individuals) for more complete information. It further divides into the following:

a. *Bibliographic*: This database contains bibliographic citations with/without abstracts of the printed materials.

b. *Referral*: This database refers users to organizations, experts, directories, and audio visual materials for information.

2. *Source Databases*: These databases contain the primary, complete, full-text, or source information/data for the answers. Source databases are further divided into the following:

a. *Numeric*: This database contains the numeric values of an original survey, or experimental data that has been analyzed, summarized, or statistically manipulated-typically the time series.

b. *Textual-numeric*: This database contains records with a combination of textual information and numerical data.

c. *Properties*: This database contains handbook or dictionary type of information/data, typically chemical and physical properties.

d. *Full-text*: This database contains records of a complete text of an item, e.g., a newspaper article, a court decision, or a patent specification.[15,16]

3. The Characteristics of Non-bibliographic Databases

The non-bibliographic database possesses a particular set of characteristics which are in marked contrast to the bibliographic databases. These characteristics, which have been identified by various authors, are synthesized as the following:

A. Access
B. Software
C. Use
D. Type of Information
E. Data Management
F. Production
G. Types of Systems[17,18,19]

A. Access to NBDBs is frequently restricted and limited to a specific user community, or to closed user groups, or to users of particular countries, or to persons with a "need-to-know" status, or to users of specific retrieval services. The reason for limited accessibility is data security/confidentiality, because many NBDBs are created by government agencies and private organizations only for their internal use. Furthermore, many of the NBDBs are not even online at this time.

B. Software configurations in the NBDB service systems are often more sophiticated than in the bibliographic systems. They permit the users to do retrieval, analysis, statistical manipulation, modeling, forecasting, and report generation with the databases, and also they are capable of displaying graphic presentation in various formats.

C. Use of non-bibliographic online services is governed by the system functions as determined by the sophisticated software packages. Due to system capability, the end-users are the primary users (e. g.: economists, lawyers, chemists, doctors, etc.) rather than librarians and information specialists. This is especially true in most cases in using numeric databases. The efficient use of the system may well require a knowledge of system protocols, programming ability, statistical analysis procedures and techniques, and subject expertise. This compares to bibliographic services, in which 79 per cent of the use is by the intermediaries (e. g.: librarians, information specialist).[20] According to Houghton and Wisdom's survey on the use of NBDBs in economics, finance, and business, 80 per cent of the users were analysts, economists, and planners, and 19 per cent of users were library or information personnel.[21] The NBDB users expressed their satisfaction with these databases, and said that they are versatile, convenient, time-saving, and easier to use than the bibliographic ones. They liked best of all, the unique feature of NBDB services in retrieving the "actual information" rather than references or citations to the information.[22,23]

D. Type of Information: Information/data are derived from the areas of business, economics, social science, science and technology. The majority of NBDBs are in the business area with numeric information in their content. The primary types of NBDBs contain social science survey data, statistics, demographic data, corporate financial information, stock market quotations, securities, current exchange rates, chemical and physical properties, chemical and structure, technology transfer information, grants/contracts/sources/awards, directory/handbook/dictionary/catalog type information, thesaurus, authority lists, news articles, charts and maps, laws and regulatory decisions.[24,25]

E. Database Management in NBDB services is more complex. Data are variable in character and can be represented and measured in many ways. The record structures are many and variable, unlike the record formats in bibliographic databases, which are basically uniform and have greater structural clarity. Some systems are required to store various conditions of search parameters for manipulation purposes. Update frequencies in some of the NBDBs are vitally important, especially in some of the business and legislative databases. Dow Jones News/ Retrieval Service and Stock Quote Reporter (DJNR) claims to update its database information in seconds.[26]

F. Production of NBDBs is said to be more costly than the production of the bibliographic databases.[27] Further investigation and studies are needed in this area. At the present time, NBDBs are provided by a far greater number of vendors. Because of minimal advertising and poor marketing, it is difficult to become aware of their existence. Most of the vendors are marketing their database services directly, to the end-users. The United States produces more NBDBs than the European countries. Also, government agencies produce more NBDBs than bibliographic databases. Numeric databases constitute some 75 per cent of all NBDBs. Luedke estimates that there are more than ten thousand numerical databases in existence, although most of these are private and out of the public domain. Currently there are over 150 publicly available non-bibliographic database.[28,29]

G. Types of Systems: Systems that support use of the majority of NBDBs are of four kinds, according to Wanger and Landau:[30]

1. *Generalized Systems*: The generalized information retrieval systems are found in major

bibliographic systems that usually provide access to a wide range of bibliographic and referal databases, such as DIALOG, BRS/STAIRS, and ORBIT systems. The design criteria for generalized systems are focused on "user-orientation", powerful functions, cost-effectiveness, and flexible command-structure interfaces, so that the users may very easily use various commands to conduct searches. In addition, many of the time-sharing firms offer online services through a database management system (DBMS) which has generalized capabilities for handling even numeric databases. At the present time, DIALOG has over 40 NBDBs in its system.

2. *Tailored Systems*: The design of this system type has been tailored to provide particular capabilities or to solve specific problems. These systems tend to be "prompt-oriented" in their interface languages. The system is less flexible but as powerful as a generalized system, e. g., the Business International Corporation's BI/DATA database.

3. *Retrieval and Display Systems*: These systems are designed to provide straight forward retrieval and display functions only, such as the Toxicology Data Bank (TDB) of the NLM, and the Computerized Resources Information Bank (CRIB). Both are bibliographic-like systems which can handle easily the textual/numerical type of databases.

4. *Modeling and Analysis Systems*: The idea of "doing something with the data" the heart for designing these sophisticated systems, which combine modeling and simulation capabilities with significant databases components and value-added facilities. These enable the users to do complicated searches, analysis, and statistical manipulations with the database. For example, the ManLab-NPL Materials Data Bank, and SANSS (Structure and Nomenclature Search System) of the NIH/EPA Chemical Information System (CIS). Because of the complexity of the analysis techniques of the searching procedures involved, it is believed that knowledge of the subject and the system operations is imperative. With SANSS, a subsystem of CIS, which contains 200,000 chemical compounds, the users can draw the structure of a molecule and have the system search for molecules of the same or similar structure, or retrieve nomenclature and structural information for all related substances. [31,32]

4. Problems in Non-bibliographic Databases

There are no "supermarket" NBDB systems. Also, there are certain problems in these systems relating to standardization, quality of data, data evaluation, government NBDBs, and costs.

A. No "supermarket" systems: There are no systems such as Lockheed, SDC, and BRS, which offer access to several databases in a wide variety of subjects for NBDB services, but there are many "specialty vendors" or "specialty online database suppliers'" who provide access to only one or a few databases or groups of databases of particular types or in certain subject areas for specific target customers, e. g., Data Resources, Inc., (DRI) the world's most successful online database company, handles one type of NBDB-numeric databases exclusively.[33] Users may need to subscribe to several online, services in order to meet their needs, and the searchers must learn the functions of each system in order to use them all. With constant changes in the systems, it is very inconvenient, time consuming, costly, and frustrating. Another problem is that since information concerning NBDB systems and services usually appears in various sources rather than professional journals, it is very difficult to learn of the existence of such services and to locate them.[34]

B. Standardization is a major problem in both bibliographic and non-bibliographic services. A user must learn the language and protocols peculiar to each service. In dealing with NBDBs, the more complex file structure and variety of each formats exacerbate this problem. In addition, the use of terminology, definitions, measurement units, codes, indexing techniques and search languages of various databases is not uniform. Incompatibility among databases and systems is a major obstacle to data exchange and inter-system communication. Development of a standardized format for machine-readable bibliographic and non-bibliographic databases is needed. At the present time, the U. S. Energy Research and Development Administration (ERDA) interlaboratory Working Group for Data Exchange is designing the format based on the American National Standard for Bibliographic Information Interchange on Magnetic Tape, ANSI Z39. 2 – 1971 Standard and the International Standard Documentation Format for Bibliographic Information Interchange on Magnetic Tape (ISO 2709 – 1973). [35]

C. Data evaluation and quality control: The accuracy and reliability of data in NBDBs are of great importance. In NBDBs, data evaluation is currently applied mostly to certain kinds of scientific and technical numeric data. Quality control of social and economic data is difficult, because many variable parameters are used with the data, and it is very complicated to evaluate the data accurately. [33] Data evaluation requires subject knowledge, and is very time consuming and very expensive. What is the trade-off between the dissemination of unevaluated current data and not so timely evaluated data? Research is needed here. As for quality control of the data, Nancy Norton once said that a lack of quality control could diminish the magic of online information service; search funds are wasted, end-users are disappointed, and intermediaries are embarrassed. [37] In NBDBs, some of the economic and financial databases with incorrect data and information errors are used for decision making which, could cause a tremendous financial disaster!

D. Government NBDBs: In the USA there are government agencies which provide databases relevant to their own operation for public online searching. In Canada, Statistics, through its CANSIM facilities, provides centralized online access to statistical data produced by Canadian federal agencies. And there are no comparable government databases available for public use in Europe. [38]

E. Costs: For most NBDBs an annual fee, or signing-on charge plus reduced annual subscription, are the normal means of handling costs. The charges will be higher or lower within the rates range of individual database depending upon the service package and combination of databases selected. In general, the NBDBs are more expensive to subscribe to, to use, and to produce in comparison with bibliographic databases. [39]

5. National and International Data Activities

The formation of NBDBs began with numeric databases. As previously mentioned in this paper, 75 per cent of NBDBs are numeric. Thousands of numerical databases are being compiled daily and stored in various places, but only a small fraction can be found easily. The need for better organization, accessibility, and utilization of all types of NBDBs has been recognized especially by national government agencies and various organizations. Both national and international data activities and centers have been established to deal with these matters. It has been estimated there are more than 5,000 national data centers in all fields of knowledge existing around the world. [40] One should be aware of the major ones:

A. CODATA (The Committee on Data for Science and Technology) was established by the International Council of Scientific Unions (ICSU) in 1966. The objective of CODATA is the improvement of all aspects of Scientific and technical data compilation and dissemination on a world wide basis. Subjects covered today by CODATA are physical, chemical, technological, biological, and geological data. [41]

B. NDAB (The Numerical Data Advisory Board) of the U. S. National Academy of Sciences-National Research Council was created in 1963. It was stated that the function of NDAB is to assess adequacy of, and stimulate improvement of the quality, reliability, availability, accessibility, dissemination, utilization, and management of numerical data. Subject coverage includes numerical data of the physical, chemical, biological, and geological sciences, and engineering and technology. [42]

C. NSRDS (National Standard Reference Data System) was established in 1963. It is operated by the Office of Standard Reference Data (OSRD) of the U. S. National Bureau of Standards. NSRDS is one of the largest data evaluation networks in the world. It consists of 15 decentralized data centers. Their program includes numerous data evaluation projects. These centers generate and disseminate critically evaluated scientific and technical data. [43]

Other important data center are: ICSU's WDCS (World Data Centers), CINDAS (Center for Information and Numerical Data Analysis and Synthesis of Purdue University), IASSIST (The International Association for Social Science, Information Service and Technology), etc.

6. Role of the Library, Information Center, and School of Library and Information Science

Regardless of the trend toward a predicted "paperless" or "less paper" society, there is no doubt that more NBDBs will be produced and used in the future. At the present time, the growth of numeric and modeling databases and systems is impressive. This is especially true for business-oriented and full-text data-bases which were high on the agenda of the National Online Meeting this year in New York City. Text line, a new "international" online business information service, covers foreign language materials. Full texts of the Harvard Business Review is available online now. In addition, the integration of online numeric data handling and manipulation capabilities with online text (e. g., Bibliographic reference) retrieval systems is of increasing interest to users, vendors, and system designers. It will link the bibliographic data to the non-bibliographic data. [44,45]

What is the role of libraries, information centers, and schools of library and information science in relation to NBDB services? It was suggested by authors from the information profession that both the library and the information center should become more interested in NBDB online services and explore their contextual relevance to both worlds. Some libraries and information centers, indeed, are already examining and using NBDB services. At the same time, librarians and information specialists, should prepare themselves for the tasks of furnishing this type of service by studying the characteristics of NBDBs and learning the searching skill. Now, there is urgent need for schools of library and information science to provide online teaching packages to include NBDB retrieval. There is a need for trained "data librarians" now and there will be greater demand in the future. [46,47]

7. Conclusion

With the rapid development of online access to NBDBs, the future of libraries and information centers as providers of electronic information services of all kinds probably depends more on NBDB services than it does on bibliographic ones, because it is predicted that "Everything You Always Wanted to Know May Soon be Online."[48] The economics of the online business indicates that about 80 per cent of revenues accrue from non-bibliographic services, with the remainder coming from bibliographic services.[49] So "the librarian and information workers should wake up to the implications of the databank phenomenon or surrender to traditional reference function to service suppliers and information brokers."[50] And also Blaise Croninsaid:

"... most databank users were specialists/professionals, but that does not mean that the information worker has no part to play. It is up to the profession to decide that it should become involved in the databank revolution and then to establisk areas in Which its particular expertise and experience can most profitably be developed..."[51]

In conclusion, the future is in our hands. Shall we do something about it?

References

1. Charles P. Bourne, "Online Systems: History, Technology, and Economics," *Journal of American Society for Information Science*, 31 (May, 1980): 157.
2. Donald T. Hawkins, "Online Information Retrieval Systems," in *Annual Review of Information Science and Technology* (White Plains, NY: Knowledge Industry Publications, 1981), p. 171.
3. Martha E. Williams, "Databases, Computer Readable," in *ALA Yearbook: A Review of Library Events 1980* (Chicago: ALA, 1981), p. 117.
4. Martha E. Williams, "Online Retrieval—Today and Tomorrow," *Online Review*, 2 (December, 1978): 335.
5. Martha E. Williams, *Computer-Readable Data Bases: A Directory and Data Sourcebook* (Washington: ASIS, 1979), p. vii.
6. Blaise Cronin, "Data Banks," *Aslib Proceedings*, 33 (June, 1981): 245 – 246.
7. James A. Luedke, "Numeric Databases and Systems," in *Annual Review of Information Science and Technology* (Washington: ASIS, 1977), pp. 119 – 181.
8. "Spreading the World on Non-bibliographic Databases: Caudra Associates Works to Close the Knowledge Gaps," *Information Manager*, 1 (May/June, 1979): 28 – 29.
9. Hawkins, *op. cit.*, p. 178.
10. W. V. Metanomski, "Symposium on Techniques and Problems in Retrieval of Numerical Data. Introductory Remarks," *Journal of Chemical Information and Computer Sciences*, 20 (August, 1980): 131.
11. Hawkins, *op. cit.*, pp. 176 – 179.
12. Williams, 1978 *op. cit.*, p. 357.
13. Mary Ellen Jacob, et al., "Special Libraries and Databases: A State of the Art Report," *Special Libraries*, 72 (April, 1981): 104 – 105.
14. Ruth Cuadra, et al., *Directory of Online Databases* (Santa Monica, CA: Cuadra Associates, Fall, 1981), pp. 7 – 8.
15. Ryan E. Hoover, ed. *The Library and Information Manager's Guide to Online Services* (White Plains, NY: Knowledge Industry Publications, Inc., 1980), pp. 4 – 18.
16. Ching-chih Chen and S. Schwerzer, *Online Bibliographic Searching: A Learning Manual* (New York: Neal-Schuman, 1981), pp. 1 – 2.
17. Nancy F. Hardy, "The World of Non-bibliographic Information," *Information Manager*, 1 (July/August, 1979): 20 – 22.
18. Cronin, *op. cit.*, p. 244.
19. A. Tomberg, "Data Banks: A Survey," in 1st International Online Information Meeting, *Proceedings* (Oxford: Learned Information, 1977), p. 157.
20. *Ibid.*, p. 163.
21. B. Houghton and C. Wisdom, "Non-bibliographic Online Databases: An Investigation into Their Uses within the Fields of Economics and Business Studies," in the 3rd. International Online Information Meeting, *Proceedings* (Oxford; Learned Information, 1979), pp. 214 – 215.

22. Allen Foster, "Non-bibliographic Online Databases: An Investigation into Their Uses within the Fields of Economics and Business Studies, An Review," *Crus News*, no. 13 (March, 1981): 14.
23. Cronin, *op. cit.*, p. 244.
24. C. H. Fenichel and T. H. Hogan, *Online Searching*: A Primer (Malton, NJ: Learned Information, 1981.), pp. 103 – 104.
25. *Directory of Non-bibliographic Database Services*, *A Seminar* (Santa Monica, CA: Cuadra Associates, 1979), pp. 133 – 140.
26. Cronin, *op. cit.*, p. 246.
27. Tomberg, *op. cit.*, p. 167.
28. Hawkins, *op. cit.*, p. 177.
29. Luedke, *op. cit.*, pp. 127 – 141.
30. Judith Wanger and R. N. Landau, Non-bibliographic Online Data Bases Services, "*Journal of American Society for Information Science*, 31 (May, 1980): 175 – 178.
31. Donald T. Hawkins, ManLab-NPL Materials Data Banks," *Online*, 3 (April, 1979): 40.
32. G. W. A. Milne, et al., "Environmental Uses of the NIH-EPA Chemical Information System," *Science*, 215 (January, 1982): 371 – 375.
33. Wanger, *op. cit.*, p. 173.
34. Spreading the World on…, *op. cit.*, p. 30.
35. James A. Luedke, "Numeric Data Bases Online," *Online Review*, 1 (September, 1977): 213.
36. Leudke, *op. cit.*, pp. 122 – 123.
37. Nancy Prothro Norton, "Dirty Data: A Call for Quality Control," *Online*, 1 (January, 1981): 40 – 41.
38. Houghton, *op. cit.*, p. 219.
39. Cronin, *op. cit.*, p. 245.
40. Judith A. Werdel, "International Programs/Issues," *Bulletin of American Society for Information Science*, 1 (Feb., 1975): 7.
41. G. C. Carter, "Numerical Data Retrieval in the U. S. and Abroad," *Journal of Chemical Information and Computer Sciences*, 20 (August, 1980): 146.
42. Hendrik van Olphen, "The Numerical Data Advisory Board," *Bulletin of American Society for Information Science*, 1 (Feb., 1975); 8 – 9.
43. Bettijoyce B. Molino, et al., "Activities of the Office of Standard Reference Data in Relation to the Online Distribution of Scientific Numeric Data," in the 3rd. National Online Meeting, *Proceedings* (Weston, CT: Online, Inc., 1982); p. 371.
44. Emil H. Levine, "Business and Full-Text Data Top Online Agenda," *Bulletin of the American Society for Information Science*, 8 (June, 1982): 31.
45. Richard C. Simon, "Combined Online Numeric/Text Analysis and Retrieval Systems," in ASIS National Meeting, *Proceedings* (Washington: ASIS, 1976), p. 71.
46. Judith S. Rowe and C. L. Geda, "Training the Professional Data Librarian," *Drexel Library Quarterly*, 13 (January, 1977): 100 – 108.
47. Claire Wisdom, "The Needs of Users of Non-bibliographic Databases Online," *CrusNews*, No. 9 (April, 1980): 15.
48. Walter Kiechel Ⅲ, "Everything You Always Wanted to Know May Soon Be Online," *Fortune* (May 1980): 226 – 228, 233, 236, 240.
49. Hoover, *op. cit.*, p. 251.
50. Houghton, *op. cit.*, p. 219.
51. Cronin, *op. cit.*, p. 249.

Appendix: Online Output Examples of Bibliographic and Non-bibligraphic Databases:

Bibliographic Databases:

1. SDC ORBIT system: ERIC Database

ss 5/c?
USER:
cultural and pluralism

PROG:
SS-5 PSTG (10)

SS 6/C?
USER:
prt fu indented

PROG:

– 1 –

ACCESSION NUMBER	EJ226749
CLEARINGHOUSE ACCESSION	UD507914
TITLE	Ideolosical-Electicism and Coherence among Black Soldiers: A Research Note.
AUTHORS	Weisert, Kathleen Maas
SOURCE	Journal of Nesro Education; v49 n2 p173 – 83 Spt., 1980
(1980)	
ISSUE	CIJNOV80
DOCUMENT TYPE	080; 143
LANGUAGE	English
INDEX TERMS	* Activism; * Black Attitudes; Black Power; * Cultural Pluralism; * Goal Orientation; * Political Attitudes
ABSTRACT	Data from a sample of Black soldiers are utilized to examine extent to which " electicism " (low interrelatedness between soal and means) rather than "coherence" (high interrelatedness between toal and means) characterizes the ideological Profiles of members of this minority group. (GC)

SS 7 /C?
JSER：
prt ss 5 Fu

PROG：

$-1-$

AN	—	ED187915
CHAN	—	CE025595
TI	—	Project CHOICE：#62. A Career Unit For Grades 5 and 6. Hospitals. (Health Occupations Career Cluster).
OS	—	Kern County Superintendent of Schools, Bakersfield, CaliF.
SPO	—	Office of Education (DHEW), Washington, D. C.
SO	—	Sep. , 1977；37pp
LO	—	U. S. ；California
IS	—	RIESONOV
AV	—	EDRS Price - MF01/PC02 Plus Postase. (1 MF).
NO	—	For related documents see CE 025 584 – 585, CE 025 587, CE 025 580 – 596, CE 025 599 – 600, CE 025 GO3, CE 025 605, CE 025 607, and CE 025 G09.
DT	—	052
LA	—	English
IT	—	* Allied Health Occupations；* Career Awareness；Career Development；* Career Education；Educational Resources；Grade 5；Grade G；* Hospital Personnel；Instructional Materials；Intermediate Grades；Learning Activities；Lesson Plans；Occupational Clusters；Occupations；Units of study
ST	—	Project CHOICE
AB	—	This teaching unit, Hospitals, is one in a series of curriculum guides developed by Project CHOICE (Children Have Options in Career Education) to provide the classroom teacher with a source of career-related activities linkins 5th and 6th grade elementary classroom experiences with the world of work. These eight lessons on hospitals cover the departments and Jobs found in a typical hospital and describe training and school skills necessary for various hospital related professions. An introductory section siues the rationale for the unit, scale, Performance objectives, entry-level assessment, and evaluation. A list of sussested instructional materials, such as films, filmstrips, books, community resources, and art supplies, is included in this section. Each lesson contains a statement of purpose, materials needed for the lesson, an introductory statement, class activities, and a summary activity. Written materials (such as worksheets, surveys, and task cards) are included where feasible. (MEN)

ss 7 /C?
USER：
research and development centers

PROG：
ss 7 PSTG (6)

ss 8 /C?
JSER：
infor $

2. DIALOG System: Art bibliographic Modern Database
? s stack options
      1   4 STOCK OPTIONS
? t 1/5/1
1/5/1
    80007206   ID No: 80007206
    The options Market
    Metzser, Irwin H. ; Diliberti, Barbara A.
    Executive vGn1 37-40 Fall 1979 Jrn Code: EXT
    Doc Type: JOURNAL PAPER

The remarkable growth of the stock options market is largely due to its versatility and flexibility. A call option is an option to purchase 100 shares of specific actively traded stock at a certain price any time during the life of a contract. The action revolves around the price movement of the underlying stock and its effect on the call's premium. The decision to be a buyer or seller reflects the investor's analysis of the market, the underlying stock, and his own financial objectives. Covered call writing is a popular option stratesy, as it can be tailored to suit and offers the potential for a higher investment return; selectively and timing are the keys to success. Naked or uncovered call writing, a very assressive option strategy, can offer very attractive leverase, but potential profit is limited, while potential loss is not. Buying a call may serum numerous investment objectives and offers excellent leverase and limited risk, but the buyer must be prepared to lose 100% of his investments. Put options, the mirror images of calls, allow investors to speculate on a stock decline and to accomplish conservative, long-term aims.

    Descriptors: Stock options; Options markets; Options trading; Put & call options; Investment; Speculation; Strategy.

Non-bibliographic Databases:

1. PTS/U. S. Forecats
? S POPULATIOH
      10   387 POPULATION
? S YR = 1999
      11   80 YR = 1999
? C 10-11
      12   1 10-11
? T 12/5/1
12/5/1
840272 AUTD NEWS 80/05/19 P32 UNITED STATES DRIVING AGE POPULATION.

YEAR	GROWTH/YR
1990	–
TO	–.7%
1999	–

GROWTH RATE = –.7%
SHILLING (A GARY)
CC = IUSA   PC = E12194

2. BI/Data Time Series
13/8/1
0104442
CC = 528   TAIWAN
IC = 60PC   TOTAL GROSS DOMESTIC PRODUCT (GDP), IN CONSTANT PRIOES
            PILLIONS OF 1971 NEW TAIWAN DOLLARS

1981	1,065.000	1980	1,004.322	1979
1978	872.854	1977	769.720	1976
1975	616.869	1974	588.654	1973
1972	515.724	1971	455.407	1970
1969	362.737	1968	333.119	1967
1966	276.179	1965	253.397	1964
1963	203.068	1962	185.648	1961
1960	155.501			

SOURCE：BUSINESS INTERNATIONAL CORP. DIALOG FILE 128

13/8/2
0104435
CC = 528   TAIWAN
IC = GDP   TOTAL GROSS DOMESTIC PRODUCT (GDP)
            BILLIONS DF NEW TAIWAN DOLLARS

1981	1,756.000	1980	1,442.870	1979
1978	970.269	1977	816.943	1976
1975	584.494	1974	545.024	1973
1972	314.301	1971	262.247	1970
1969	195.940	1968	169.153	1967
1966	125.672	1965	112.224	1964
1963	86.856	1962	76.744	1961
1960	62.814			

SOURCE：BUSINESS INTERNATIONAL CORP. DIALOG FILE 128

3. MILL-EPA Chemical Information System

A very simple way to find a chemical substance in the CIS is with the nomenclature search option of the Structure and Nomenclature Search System (SANSS). This option, NPROBE, takes either a complete name or some fragment of a name of a substance and finds all occurrences of the name in the data base. Upon request, these can be printed, using the option SSHOW. The SSHOW option will provide, amongst other things, the CAS Registry number of the compound, the key to other CIS components. The Registry number can then in turn be used to find the compound wherever it is cited in the CIS, permitting retrieval, for example, of its mass spectrum or its carbon-13 nmr spectrum, or its
toxicity data.

OPTION? NPROBF
FRAGMENT OR WHOLE NAME SEARCH (F/W) (F)?
SPECIFY FRAGMENT (CR TO EXIT):   BHT
FILE   1,   1 COMPOUNDS HAVING FRAGMENT: BHT
SPECIFY FRAGMENT (CR TO EXIT):

OPTION? SSHOW 1
STRUCTURE   1 CAS REGISTRY NUMBER 128 – 37 – 0
CIS Sources of Information
    2 -CIS, EI Mass Spectrometry
    3 - CIS, Carbon 13 NME Spectrometry: 128 – 37 – 0.01.
    6 - Cambridge Xray Crystal: 128 – 37 – 0.01
    32 - NIOSH/CIS, RTECS: G07875000
    71 - JCPDS/CIS, Powder Diffraction Patterns: 20133, 241580
    115 - EPA/CIS, WaterDROP
    124 - CIS, CZ Mass Spectrometry
    18 Non-CIS References Available

$C_{15}H_{24}O$

```
                    C
                    *
                    *
                    C
                  .   .
                .       .
        C   C           C   C
        *     .       .     *
        *       .   .       *
  C**C**C           C**C**C
        *       .   .       *
        *     .       .     *
        C   C           C
                    *
                    *
                    O
```

Phenol, 2, 6-bis (1, 1-dimethylethyl) -4-methyl – (9CI)
Cresol, 2, 6-di-tert-butyl – (8CI)

o-di-tert-Butyl-p-methylphenol
Avastab 401
Antioxldant DBPC
    69 more names available

CHINESE MARC FORMAT AND BIBLIOGRAPHIC DATABASES[*]

ABSTRACT

This paper reports the development of an integrated Chinese MARC format for book and non-book materials in Taipei. The structure of Chinese MARC format based on UNIMARC with modifications to accommodate the unique features of the Chinese library materials and library practices is discussed by using the portion for non-books as examples. The current status of the development of Chinese bibliographic databases is also presented.

INTRODUCTION

The impetus for developing Chinese MARC format has been caused by both domestic and international demands for more efficient bibliographic control thru the use of computers. The need to process Chinese vernacular library materials has become more evident since the announcements of 1) a nation-wide Chinese Cultural Development Program, 2) the closing of the card catalog at the United States Library of Congress.

The former which was announced in 1979 indicated a rapid growth of libraries throughout Taiwan with a possible establishment of two hundred local libraries within five years. Cultural centers, information centers, and libraries will become an emphasized portion of the Cultural Development Program. A national information network as such depends on standardization for the sharing of information and efficient management of information. The latter factor accelerated the need for processing vernacular East Asian materials in countries using other languages. Investigations and researches to solve this problem involved computer technology, linguistic expertise and library practices. Standardized Chinese MARC format is one of the necessities for data transferring, information sharing, and computerized library network. Information industry and computer technology for processing Chinese materials have received due attention and have been well-developed for all types of applications. Under these circumstances: the library automation advocators found it timely to form a Chinese MARC Format Working Group for the development of such standards.

THE STRUCTURE OF CHINESE MARC FORMAT

After careful evaluation of all the available MARC formats, the working Group decided to base the structure on a communication format which is issued for the purpose of universal bibliographic control. UNIMARC is therefore used as a basis for further development. UNIMARC, however, has not taken the special features of East Asian materials into consideration. Instead of building up a national MARC format, the Chinese MARC format incorporates the uniqueness of Chinese materials and the necessary aspects of handling Chinese materials in a non-Chinese speaking environment. LC MARC II format are consulted. Inter MARC of France, Canadian MARC & UK MARC etc. have also been studied and evaluated. In comparison with the UNIMARC major differences include: (Appendix 1)
1) Subfiled identifier " $ r" is added to Fields 200, 225 and 5xx for the purpose to get access

---

[*] Chinese MARC Working Group, Library Automation Planning Committee, LAC Taipei.

to the Romanized versions of title proper, and other variant titles.
2) Subfield identifier "$ u" is added to field 3xx for libraries using cataloguing rules other than CCR to record notes in Chinese, English and in Romanized forms.
3) Subfield identifier "$ s" is assigned to fields 600, 700, 701, and 702 for identification of a dynastic era during which a Chinese person lived.
4) New functions have been assigned to some undefined indicators in UNIMARC, e. g., indicators in Field 215 and Fields 010, Oil, 204, 225.
5) Fields 501 (Collective Uniform Title) and 503 (Uniform Conventional Headings) are not used in Chinese MARC because of CCR requirement.
6) Fields 432, 433, 442, 443 in UNIMARC are excluded by Chinese MARC because they are not compatible with ISBD (S) and AACR2.
7) Field 326 has been changed to read "... former frequency is first, followed by those pertaining to the current frequency in order to be in confirmity with ISBD (S) and AACR2."
8) Fields 770 – 792 added to record names in Roman alphabets and fields 700 – 722 are used for names in Chinese characters.
9) Subfield identifiers are added to Field 805 (local library holdings) to record detailed information on library holdings, e. g., Sa for agency code, Sb for location, and $ c for accession numbers, etc.
10) Additions for Chinese music compositions and Chinese music instruments are recorded in Field 125. (Appendix 2)
11) Addition of Tag 550 for titles of series.

Comparison between Chinese MARC and UNIMARC is listed on (Appendix, 3)

BIBLIOGRAPHIC DATABASES

The Chinese MARC is to facilitate the handling of Chinese materials with computers for the purpose of information exchange and sharing. The National Central Library wishes to reach this objective at the earliest possible date. Beginning 1981 the newly acquired titles of the National Central Library will be built into data bases for the purpose of bibliographic control. So far, Six thousand new books published in 1981 and acquired by seven participating academic libraries in Taipei Area have been input into the data base as national union list of book. The first magnetic tape for books will be distributed before December 1982. In addition, a national union list of eight thousand records of Chinese serial holdings which have been contributed by one hundred seventy different types of libraries in the country.

With the bibliographic data bases, one can perform the following operations:
1) Computer-produced MARC format proofsheet for editing or cataloguing reference (Appendix 4)
2) Computer-produced Cataloguing Cards. (Appendix 5, 6, 7)
3) Computer-produced National Bibliographies in book forms. (Appendix 8)
4) Computer-produced title index for the national bibliography. (Appendix 9)
5) Computer-produced author index for the national bibliography. (Appendix 10)
6) On-line display of Chinese bibliographic records in three forms.
   1 Chinese MARC Bibliographic record. (Appendix 11)
   2 Chinese MARC Bibliographic entries. (Appendix 12 & 13)
   3 Chinese MARC Card form (as mention above)
7) On-line update and search funitions: On-line input, On-line update, On-line delete, and modify and On-line searching bibliographic information by system ID. author, title, subject, corporate body, title/author, ISBN, ISSN. and CODEN. (Appendix 14)

Since July 1982, the National Central Library has been considering to adopt the LC MARC records as the basis of filing Western books, that is, to have LC MARC records converted into the Chinese MARC. This task is being studied and tested for implementation. Actually, we have succeeded in using Chinese MARC format to handle Western-language materials. The other words, when we see the Western-language bibliographic cards are produced by the Chinese MARC format we become more confidention it, universality. (Appendix 15)

At present time, we have published the Chinese MARC format for Books in Chinese & in English Versions and MARC Format for Books: the User's Manual (1981) and in the last month we completed Chinese MARC Format for Books & Non-books (comprehensive edition) which are also available in Chinese & English editions.

CONCLUSION AND FUTURE OUTLOOK

The design of Chinese MARC format is not only best suited for Chinese libraries in handling both Chinese and Western language materials but also for other libraries with East Asian collections. All angles involved with Western and Chinese materials handling either in Chinese libraries or Western libraries have duly been treated with careful deliberations. Continuous revisions will be made and updated by public announcements either in the Library Association of China Newsletter or itl the NCL Newsletter.

The next project for the Chinese MARC Working Group is the task of developing formats for rare books, authorities and thesaurus. With the advent of such formats, MARC records will have more comprehensive coverage and better quality control.

* Hsiu-ying Chiang
  Nancy Ou-Ian Chou (Chairperson)
  Margaret C. Fung
  Jack K. T. Huang
  Lucy T. C. Lee (Ex-chairperson)
  Liu-li Wu
  M. D. Wu

Appendix 1　List of Fields, Indicators, and Subfields being changed

Tag	Field		Indicator		Subfield Code	Subfield Comment	Name of Field, Indicator, or Subfield Code
	Length	Comment	1	2			
010	V	R			b	R	International Standard Book Number Qualification
			0				For library uses Chinese Cataloguing Rules
			1				For library uses other cataloguing rules
011	V	R					
			0				For library uses Chinese Cataloguing Rules
			1				For library uses other cataloguing rules
110	F	N					Coded Data Field Serials Frequency of Issue d = tenthly
125	F	N					Sound Recordings & Music Scores
					b	R	From of composition—Chinese music compositions are added
					d	R	Instruments or voices for soloists—Chinese music instrument are added
200	V	N					Title and Statement of Responsibility
					P	N	Number of Chuan
					r	N	Romanization of Title Proper
204	V	R					General Material Designation
			0				For library uses CCR
			1				For library uses other cataloguing rules

F = Fixed　　V = Variable　　R = Repeatable　　N = Not repeatable

CHINESE MARC FORMAT AND BIBLIOGRAPHIC DATABASES

Tag	Field Length	Field Comment	Indicator 1	Indicator 2	Subfield Code	Subfield Comment	Name of Field, Indicator, or Subfield Code
215	V	R					Physical Description
			0				For library uses Chinese Cataloguing Rules
			1				For library uses other cataloguing rules
225	V	R					Series
				0			Make added entry for series in Chinese
				1			Make added entry for series in Romanization
				2			No series added entry
				3			Make added entry for series in Chinese and Romanization
					r	N	Romanization of Series Title
300	V	R					General Note
					u	N	United Languages
301	V	R					Notes pertaining to Identification Numbers
					u	N	United Languages
302	V	R					Notes pertaining to Coded Information
					u	N	United Languages
304	V	R					Notes pertaining to Title and Statement of Responsibility
					u	N	United Languages
305	V	R					Notes pertaining to Edition and Bibliographic History
					u	N	United Languages
306	V	R					Notes pertaining to Publication, Distribution, Etc.
					u	N	United Languages
307	V	R					Notes pertaining to Physical Description
					u	N	United Languages
332	V	R					Copy Being Described and Library's Holdings
					u	N	United Languages
432	V	R					Excluded
433	V	R					Excluded
442	V	R					Excluded
443	V	R					Excluded

（續上表）

Tag	Field		Indicator		Subfield Code	Subfield Comment	Name of Field, Indicator, or Subfield Code
	Length	Comment	1	2			
500	V	R					Uniform Title
					P	N	Chuan
					S	N	Medium
					T	N	Serial, Opus, or Thematic
					W	N	Arranged Statement
					X	N	Key
510	V	R					Parallel Title Proper
					r	N	Romanization of Title
512	V	R					Cover Title
					r	N	Romanization of Title
					P	N	Chuan
513	V	R			r	N	Added Title-page Title Romanization of Title
514	V	R					Caption Title
					r	N	Romanization of Title
					P	N	Chuan
515	V	R					Running Title
					r	N	Romanization of Title
					P	N	Chuan
516	V	R					Spine Title
					r	N	Romanization of Title
					P	N	Chuan
517	V	R					Other Variant Titles
					r	N	Romanization of Title
					P	N	Chuan
541	V	R					Translated Title Supplied by Cataloger
					r	N	Romanization of Title
					P	N	Chuan

550	V	R	0				Series
							    Title is not significant
							    Title is significant

					a	N	Series titles
					e	N	Subseries
					h	N	Number of part
					i	N	Name of part
					r	N	Romanization of title
					z	N	Language of title

(續上表)

Tag	Field		Indicator		Subfield Code	Subfield Comment	Name of Field, Indicator, or Subfield Code
	Length	Comment	1	2			
600	V	R					Personal Name Used as Subject
					s	N	Dynasty
681	V	R					Chinese Classification Scheme
					a	N	Chinese Class Number
					b	N	Book Number
700	V	R					Personal Name-Primary Intellectual Responsibility
					s	N	Dynasty
701	V	R					Personal Name-Alternative Intellectual Responsibility
					s	N	Dynasty
702	V	R					Personal Name-Secondary Intellectual Responsibility
					s	N	Dynasty
710	V	N					Corporate Body Name-Primary Intellectual Responsibility
720	V	N					Family Name-Primary Intellectual Responsibility
770	V	N					Personal Name in Roman Alphabet –
771	V	R					Personal Name in Roman Alphabet –
772	V	R					Personal Name in Roman Alphabet –
780	V	N					Corporate Body Name in Roman Alphabet
781	V	R					Corporate Body Name in Roman Alphabet
782	V	R					Corporate Body Name in Roman Alphabet
790	V	N					Family Name in Roman Alphabet
791	V	R					Family Name in Roman Alphabet
792	V	R					Family Name in Roman Alphabet

（續上表）

Tag	Field		Indicator		Subfield Code	Subfield Comment	Name of Field, Indicator, or Subfield Code
	Length	Comment	1	2			
805	V	R					Local Library Holdings
					a	N	Agency Code
					b	R	Sublocation
					c	N	Accession Number
					d	N	Class Number
					e	N	Book Number
					f		Cataloger
					p		prefix
					g		Dfinition of Bibliographic Subdivision
805					1		
					2		
					3		
					4	R	Bibliographic Subdivision
					5		
					6		
					7		
					y	R	Date
					n	R	Remarks

Appendix 2

A LIST OF CHINESE MUSIC COMPOSTION FORMS ADDED IN FIELD 125

Subfield b—Form of Composition

Ya	宋朝雜劇	Sung chao tsa chü
Yb	元朝南曲	Yüan cháo nan chú
Yc	元朝北曲	Yüan cháo pei chú
Yd	明朝傳奇	Ming cháo chúan chí
Ye	平劇	Píng chü
Yf	昆曲	Kún chú
Yg	秦腔	Chín chíang
Yh	廣東戲（粵劇）	Kuang-tung hsi
Yi	梆子	Pang tzu
Yj	紹興戲	Shao-hsing hsi
Yk	滬劇	Hu chü
Yl	大鼓	Ta ku
Ym	評彈	Píng tán
Yn	潮州戲	cháo-chou hsi
Yo	歌仔戲	Ko tsai hsi
Yp	南管	Nan kuan
Yq	北管	Pei kuan
Yz	其他	

Subfield d—Instruments or Voices for Soloists

撥弦樂器		Strings, Plucked:
te	琴	Chín
tf	瑟	Se
tg	箏	Cheng
th	琵琶	pípá
ti	三弦	San hsien
tj	月琴	Yüeh chín
tk	揚琴	Yang chín
tl	阮弦	Juan hsien
擦弦樂器		Strings, Bowed:
sh	胡琴	Hu chín

si	二胡	Erh hu
sj	大胡	Ta hu
sk	低胡	Ti hu
sl	粵胡	Yüeh hu
sm	椰胡	Yeh hu
sn	京胡	Chíng hu
so	四胡	Sau hu
sp	板胡	Pan hu
sq	高胡	Kao hu

敲擊樂器		Percussion：
pe	中國鼓	Ku
pf	大鼓	Tq Ku
pg	建鼓	Chien Ku
ph	鐘	Chung
pi	鈴鐘	Ling chung
pj	磬	Chíng
pk	銅鈸	Túng pa
pl	雲鑼	Yün lo
pm	木魚	Mu yu
pn	拍板	Pái pan

木管樂器		Woodwinds：
wj	中國笛	Ti
wk	簫	Hsiao
wl	排簫	Pái hsiao
wm	笙	Sheng
wn	嗩吶	So na
wo	壎	Hsün
wp	竽	Yü
wq	箎（ㄔ）	Tzú（Chinese flute）
wr	籥（ㄝ）	Yüeh

Appendix 3

Comparison Between Chinese MARC and UNIMARC

Numbers of Tags, Indicators and Subfields in
UNIMARC being added to / modified for Chinese MARC

A = Added　　　　　　　　　M = Modified

Items Block	Tay (Field)		Indicator		Subfield	
	A	M	A	M	A	M
0 ——			2			
1 ——						
2 ——			3		3	
3 ——					23	
4 ——						
5 ——	1		2		21	4
6 ——		1			3	
7 ——	9		21		60	
8 ——		1			18	
Total	10	2	28		128	4

Appendix 4

Computer-produced MARC Format Proofsheet for Editing or Cataloging Reference

MK0020 SYSID： 81000001   CHINESE MARC DATA PROOF SHEET
        DATE： 82/08/20 PAGE： 1

MARK	TAG	IND	T-REP	LENG	1…5…10…5…20…5…30…5…40…5…50…5…60…5…70…5…80…5…90…5…100…5…110…5…120
	001		1	024	Rec-status = n Imp-code = aso Add-def = 21
	100		1	038	Enter-date = 19811228 pub = d Yri = 1981 Yr2 = Aud = Gov = y
					Mod = 0 Lan = Chi Trans = b Char = 09 Add = Title = e
	105		1	016	Ill = a Form = c Conf = 0 Fest = 0 Index = 1 Lit = y BLO = y
	101	1	01	012	Sachi sceng
	102		01	004	sacw
	801	G	01	018	Sacwsb 中國 Sc810925
	801	1	02	018	Sacwsb 中國 Sc811228
	805		01	034	Sa 中國 Sc611132sd448.878 Se845 sfH
	805		02	032	Sa 淡江 Sb 工 Sc159684sd448.63se8457
	681		01	016	Sa448.552 Sb845
	200	1	01	084	SaCOMOS 邏輯設計 SdCMOS databooksfwilliam L. Hunter 著 Sg 李明陸 SrCMOS lo chi she chiszeng
	210		01	030	Sa 臺南市 Sc 復文書局 Sd 民 70 ［1981］
	215	0	01	024	Sa ［10］, 259 面 ScESd21 公分
	215	1	02	029	Sa ［10］, 259 p. Scill. Sd21 cm.
	320		01	010	Sa 附：索引
	320		02	016	SuInciudes Index.
	010	0	01	018	Sb 平裝 Sd 新臺幣 96 元
	010	1	02	012	SbpbksdNTs96
	606		01	048	S21cSaMetal oxide semiconductors. Complementary.
	606		02	026	S21cSaIntegrated circuits.
	700	1	01	032	Sa 亨特 S4 著 Sc （Hunter, William L.）
	770	1	01	022	SaHunter, SbWilliam L.
	702	1	01	014	Sa 李 Sb 明 IS4 譯
	772	1	01	020	SaLi, SbMing-k'uel.
	676		01	018	Sv19Sa621.38195835
	680		01	018	SaTK7871.99Sb. M44

TOTAL   26   RECORDS.

Appendix 15

Western-language Catalog Card
processed by the Chinese MARC
(For libraries abroad)

BL820
.M55
1980
	Espeland, Pamela, 1951 –
	    The story of King Midas / Pamela
	Espeland; Pictures by George Dverlie.
	Minneapolis: Carolrhoda Books, 1980.
	    [32] p. : col. ill. ; 24 cm.
	    ISBN 0-87614-129-7 (lib. bdg): $5.95
	
	    1. Midas - Juvenile literature. I.
	Overlie, George. II. Title.

資訊提供力量
瞭解促進和平

INFORMATION: INFORMATION INTERFLOW
PROMOTES WORLD PEACE
THROUGH UNDERSTANDING

CHINESE MARC FORMAT FOR BOOKS*

Lucy Te-Chu Lee
Nancy Ou-lan Hu
Sophia Hong-Chu Huang
Ming-der Wu
Jack Kai-Tung Huang

ABSTRACT

The purpose of this paper is to report the principles, purposes & scopes of designing the Chinese MARC Format for books. With emphasis on the special features & characteristics of Chinese MARC Format structure & its major differences with UNIMARC. It also gives the detailed explanation on the present activities of applying Chinese MARC Format to process Chinese language materials for local libraries, and the plans for future development.

National Taiwan University
Tamkang University
Ming Chuang College

1. Introduction

The Library Automation Planning Committee (LAPC) was established by the "Library Association of China" in (Taipei), in cooperation with the "National Central Library" in 1980, to improve library and information services, and to keep in step with the needs of libraries in a local and international environment. By current demand, the National Library Automation Project "(NLAP)" was formed under the auspices of LAPC in May, 1980 to study related library problems and to carry out cooperative ventures with the purpose of accomplishing the following objectives:

1) to develop the Chinese MARC Format, within the constraint of international requirements, as the standard for cataloguing Chinese publications;

2) through joint efforts to organize a data processing system for improving technical and information services of Chinese language materials;

3) to create a data base for Chinese publications and to introduce data bases from overseas to meet local research needs; and

4) to establish a national information network to further the advancement of academic research and development.

Since the Chinese MARC format is the essence of library automation, the Chinese MARC Working Group (CMWG) was formed by the Committee in May 1980. The Group has been assigned the following tasks: 1) to design a Chinese MARC format which meets international requirements, in order to facilitate data processing of Chinese materials and 2) to promote international resource sharing and exchange.

In the course of designing a format structure to be acceptable internationally, attempts have been made to take into consideration every possible method for the data processing of Chinese materials in libraries. In addition, UNIMARC (Universal MARC Format, 1980 edition, IFLA) and the Library or Congress MARC Ⅱ Format have been thoroughly studied and compared. Through the cooperative endeavor of the Group, a desirable format for Chinese publications has now been worked out. The next phase of our task will be aimed at designing a format structure for non-book materials.

---

* IFLA Annual Meeting (Oct. 1981). (available ERIC ED 214508).

2. Principle, Purpose, and Scope

The guiding principle in developing a format for Chinese publications is to achieve a structure that would have a wide applicability to all types of bibliographic data written in the Chinese language. From the very beginning, the Group has agreed that the layout of the format has to be hospitable to all kinds of bibliographic information for all forms of Chinese imprints (books, serials, maps, music, etc.) and related records (name, subject, etc.). Meanwhile, the Group has considered it of the same priority to develop a format which could be utilized in a wide variety of computers to manipulate machine-readable cataloguing records. Regardless of the form of Chinese materials received in a given library, it is anticipated that Chinese MARC would be able to provide a format necessary for processing.

Inevitably the UNIMARC and Library of Congress MARC II Format have consulted from time to time. The UNIMARC format has been recommended as a medium for recording information in roman alphabet; nevertheless, the primary purpose of UNIMARC is to facilitate the international exchange of bibliographic data in machine-readable form between national bibliographic agencies. As a result of these considerations, the Group has opted to model Chinese MARC on the UNIMARC format, while incorporating certain modifications to adjust to the current local requirements. The ultimate objective of Chinese MARC is to facilitate the processing of Chinese language materials with computers for regional and international information exchange and sharing.

3. Characteristics

In order to achieve the goal for international information exchange, consideration has been given to various standards, such as ISO-2709 (Documentation—Format for Bibliographic Information Interchange on Magnetic Tape, 1973, and revised 1980) for record structure, ISO-3166 Codes for the Representation of Names of Countries, the Library of Congress Revised List of Languages and Language Codes for various languages and so on...

Special attention has also been given to the needs of a non-Chinese speaking environment: major fields are designed in such a way that could be recorded and searched in Chinese, English, or Wade-Giles transliteration. They are, for instance, title proper, statement of intellectual responsibility, physical description, series, subject, etc.

The character set used for the Chinese MARC is prescribed by the Chinese Character Code for Information Interchange (CCCII), which is formed with the 7-bit code and is based on ISO-646 (7-bit Coded Character Set for Information Processing Interchange) and ISO-2022 (Code Extension Techniques for use with the ISO - 7-bit Coded Character Set). Reservation of space for future expansion of encoded data has been prepared. There is sufficient coding room for more than at least 50 thousand Chinese characters in various forms. In addition, it provides many options for selecting a filing system for Chinese characters, with which data files may be arranged according to a predetermined sequence or method.

For full description of bibliographic records in the Chinese language, it is essential to follow the Chinese Cataloguing Rules (CCR), which has just been partially completed in 1981, and which conforms, to a large extent, to ISBDs (International Standard Bibliographic Descriptions) and AACR 2 (Anglo-American Cataloging Rules, Second edition, 1978) principles.

The Wade-Giles romanization is used in the Chinese MARC as the standard transliteration for its bibliographic records.

Special features and major characteristics of UNIMARC, such as the consistant meaning of coded data values, subfield identifiers, etc. are retained in Chinese MARC.

Also, Chinese MARC format is definitely machine independent.

4. Comparison Between Chinese MARC and UNIMARC

The CCR follows the basic framework of ISBDs; however, the characteristics of Chinese materials and the tradition of Chinese bibliography dictate the pattern for CCR, which in reality has departed to a certain degree from ISBDs. Consequently, additions and changes are necessary for Chinese MARC to reflect all these features.

Figure 1 shows the tag relationship between Chinese MARC and UNIMARC.

Figure 2 List of Tags, Indicators and Subfields being added to/modified for Chinese MARC.

In summary, the major modifications in Chinese MARC are as follows:
1) Add subfield indentifier " $ r" to fields 200,225 and 5xx. This identifier marks title proper, series title, variant titles, and related titles accessible by romanization. There is likely to be such a need in libraries located in the United States and Europe, whereas " $ r" may not be a necessity for local libraries where the likelihood of accessing a bibliographic record by transliteration would be at minimum.
2) Add subfield identifier " $ u" to fields 3xx for libraries which use cataloguing rules other than CCR to record notes in Chinese, English, or Romanization.
3) Subfield identifier "Ss" is assigned in fields 600,700,701, and 702 to identify the dynastic era during which a Chinese individual lived either in the Ch'ing dynasty or earlier. The association of a personal name with the name of a dynasty when he lived is a long observed tradition in Chinese scholarship.
4) Some undefined indicators employed in UNIMARC have been assigned new functions in Chinese MARC to offer flexibility in the format, e. g., indicators in Field 215 (Physical description) and Field 225 (Series).
5) To make them compatible with CCR, some fields found in UNIMARC are not used in Chinese MARC, e. g., Field 501 (Collective Uniform Title), Field 503 (Uniform Conventional Headings). However, they are reserved in Chinese MARC with an asterisk (*) for libraries adopting other cataloguing rules.
6) Field 770 – 792 are added to record names is roman alphabet and fields 700 – 722 are exclusively for names in Chinese characters. These changes make personal and corporated authors accesible both by Chinese and roman alphahets.
7) Add subfield identifiers to Field 805 (Local Accession Number and Call Number) to record detailed information related to individual libraries' holdings, e. g., $ a for Agency Code, $ b for sublocation, Sc for Accession Number in the library and so on.

5. Present Activities and Accomplishment

The Group set for itself the herculean task of completing within eight months (from May 1980 to January 1981) the design of Chinese MARC format for books and computer program requirements for testing and implementation purposes.

The Format and the publication of Chinese MARC Format for Books were announced during the First International Workshop on Chinese Library Automation (IWCLA) in Taipei in Feburary 1981, and drew wide attention in library and information circles, both domestic and foreign. Many valuable suggestions and opinions on the improvement of Chinese MARC were offered. Immediately after the workshop the Group began to revise and modify the format, and the second edition of Chinese MARC Format for Books was published in July, 1981.

At the present time, 1100 records have been carefully selected from the National Bibliography of NCL, the L. C. National Union Catalog, and the catalog of the "National Taiwan University" Library holdings, for input into the Chinese MARC data bases. With this data base one can perform the following operations:
1) Computer produced National Bibliography (Figure 3)
2) Computer produced catalog cards (Figure 4)
3) On-line display of Chinese bibliographic records in three forms: —
   a. Chinese MARC Bibliographic Record (Figure 5)
   b. Chinese MARC Bibliographic Entries (Figure 6)
   c. Chinese MARC Card Form
4) On-line update and search functions:
   a. On-line input
   b. On-line update
   c. On-line delete and modify
   d. On-line searching bibliographic information

6. Future Development

Although through cooperative efforts, the Chinese MARC format for books has finally materialized, its counter-part for non-book publications has yet to be fully developed. Nevertheless, it is anticipated that the Chinese MARC will be employed as the sole standard for Chinese language materials regardless of their type or format. As for the future development of Chinese MARC, it is expected to be carried out within the first two stages of the three phases in the "NLAP":

The first phase: Beginning from 1981, the Group has been inputting, in Chinese MARC format, the newly acquired titles of the NCL to a special file on computer with the anticipation that it will grow to be a data base for bibliographic control. Presently seven large academic and public libraries have agreed to participate in the same program by taking corresponding measures from April 1981. Each of them will utilize the records found in the Chinese MARC data base, add data information as required, evaluate the usefulness of all data obtained, and report to the Group their assessment, which may be considered as the basis for future improvement. This operation can also help to pave the way for further cooperation among libraries.

Meanwhile, the Group will be involved in implementing the goal for constructing Chinese MARC format for non-book materials. As reports come in from various participating libraries, further modification and improvement of the format will be executed.

The second phase: The first distribution of catalog cards based on the Chinese MARC format is to begin in Jan. 1982 by the Bibliographic Center of the NCL. The first test tape is scheduled to be mailed in 1982. In addition, more participants will be invited to cope with the complex goal of setting up a national library network. Also during this period, plans are being made to convert retrospective records.

Along with the setting up of the data base of Chinese materials, the computerization for materials in Western languages (including books and non-books) will be conducted. At the present time, the computerization of western books is now being experimented with by several local libraries. But the ultimate objective in this respect is nation-wide unification and standardization.

The third phase: Preparations for the establishment of the national information network will be made after the completion of the tasks in the first and second phases. Starting from 1983, all libraries and institutions in this country will be welcome to take part in this cooperative project for a national library automation system. Accordingly, the Committee will take the responsibility of selecting the most suitable systems for achieving the objectives of "NLAP".

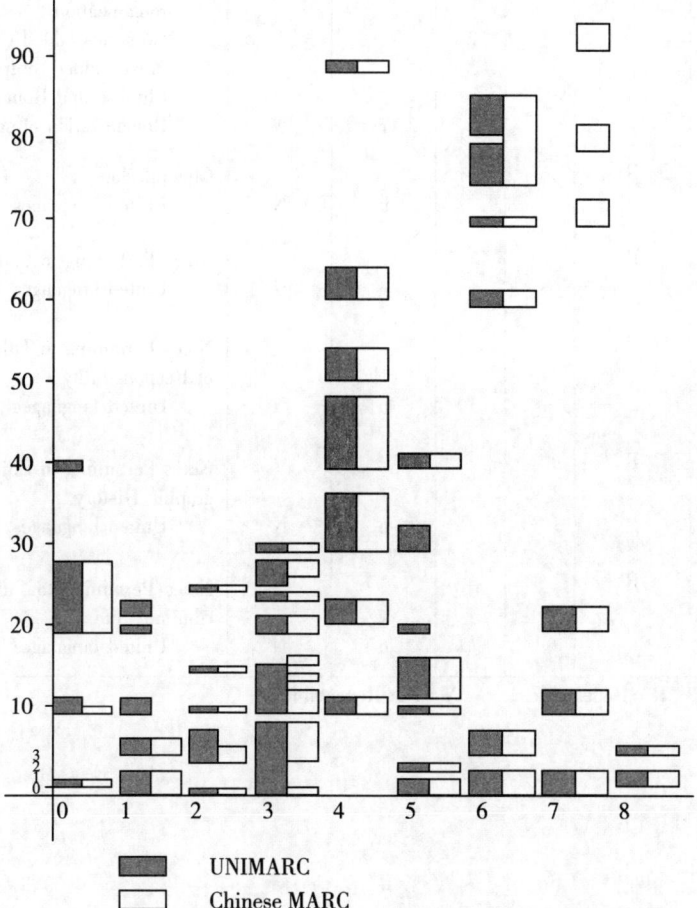

Figure 1. Tag Relationship between Chinese MARC and UNIMARC

IN CONCLUSION, the accomplishment of the Chinese MARC is not merely a success in providing a uniform standard for the processing of publications in the Chinese language, but also an achievement in enabling Chinese libraries to participate in the communication with information service systems world-wide.

Figure 2. List of Tages, Indicators, and Subfields being added to/modified for Chinese MARC

Tag	Field Length	Field Comment	Indicator 1	Indicator 2	Subfield Code	Subfield Comment	Name of Field, Indicator, or Subfield Code
200	V	N					Title and Statement of Responsibility
					P	N	Number of Chüan (卷)
					r	R	Romanization of title proper
215	V	R					Physical Description
			0				For Library uses Chinese Cataloging Rules
			1				For library uses other cataloguing rules
225	V	R					Series
				0			Make added entry for series in Chinese
				1			Make added entry for series in romanization
				2			No series added entry
				3			Make added entry for series in Chinese and Romanization
					r	N	Romanization of series title
300	V	R					General Note
					u	N	United languages
302	V	R					Notes Pertaining to Coded Information
					u	N	United languages
304	V	R					Notes Pertaining to Title and Statement of Responsibility
					u	N	United languages
305	V	R					Notes Pertaining to Edition and Bibliographic History
					u	N	United languages
306	V	R					Notes Pertaining to Publication, Distribution, etc.
					u	N	United languages

V = Vairable   R = Repeatable   N = Not Repeatable

(續上表)

Tag	Field		Indicator		Subfield Code	Subfield Comment	Name of Field, Indicator, or Subfield Code
	Length	Comment	1	2			
307	V	R					Notes Pertaining to Physical Description
					u	N	United languages
308	V	R					Notes Pertaining to Series
					u	N	United languages
310	V	R					Notes Pertaining to Binding and Availability
					u	N	United languages
311	V	R					Notes Pertaining to Linking Fields
					u	N	United languages
312	V	R					Notes Pertaining to Related Titles
					u	N	United languages
314	V	R					Notes Pertaining to Intellectual Responsibility
					u	N	United languages
316	V	R					Notes Pertaining to Number of Chüan
					u	N	United languages
320	V	R					Bibliography, Index, Appendix Note
					u	N	United languages
321	V	R					Availability of Indexes and Abstracts Note
					u	N	United languages
324	V	R					Facsimile Note
					u	N	United languages
327	V	R					Contents Note
				0			Chinese
				1			Other languages
328	V	R					Dissertation (Thesis) Note
					u	N	United languages
330	V	R					Summary or Abstract Note
					u	N	United languages
332	V	R					Copy Being Described and Library's Holdings
					u	N	United languages
500	V	R					Uniform Title
				2			Title is in Chinese but not used as a primary entry

(續上表)

Tag	Field		Indicator		Subfield Code	Subfield Comment	Name of Field, Indicator, or Subfield Code
	Length	Comment	1	2			
510	V	R					Parallel Title Proper
					r	N	Romanization of title
512	V	R					Cover Title
					r	N	Romanization of title
513	V	R					Added Title-page Title
					r	N	Romanization of title
514	V	R					Caption Title
					r	N	Romanization of title
515	V	R					Running Title
					r	N	Romanization of title
516	V	R					Spine Title
					r	N	Romanization of title
517	V	R					Other Variant Titles
					r	N	Romanization of title
541	V	R					Translated Title Supplied by Cataloger
					r	N	Romanization of translated title
600	V	R					Personal Name Used as Subject
					s	N	Dynasty
681	V	R					Chinese Classification Scheme
					a	N	Chinese class number
					b	N	Book number
700	V	N					Personal Name-Primary Intellectual Responsibility
					s	N	Dynasty
701	V	R					Personal Name-Alternative Intellectual Responsibility
					s	N	Dynasty
702	V	R					Personal Name-Secondary Intellectual Responsibility
					s	N	Dynasty

（續上表）

Tag	Field		Indicator		Subfield Code	Subfield Comment	Name of Field, Indicator, or Subfield Code
	Length	Comment	1	2			
770	V	N					Personal Name in Roman Alphabet. Primary Intellectual Responsibility
			0				Name entered under forename
			1				Name entered under surname
					a	N	Entry element
					b	N	Part of name other than entry
					c	R	Additions to name other than dates
					f	N	Dates
					3	N	Authority record number
					4	R	Designation of function
771	V	R					Personal Name in Roman Alphabet-Alternative Intellectual Responsibility
			0				Name entered under forename
			1				Name entered under surname
					a	N	Entry element
					b	N	Part of name other than entry
					c	R	Additions to name Other than dates
					f	N	Dates
					3	N	Authority record number
					4	R	Designation of function
772	V	R					Personal Name in Roman Alphabet-Secondary Intellectual Responsibility
			0				Name entered under forename
			1				Name entered under surname
					a	N	Entry element
					b	N	Part of name other than entry
					c	R	Additions to name other than dates
					f	N	Dates
					3	N	Authority record number
					4	R	Designation of function
780	V	N	0				Corporate Body Name in Roman Alphabet-Primary Intellectual Responsibility
			1				Corporate name
							Meeting
							Name in inverted form
				0			Name entered under place or jurisdiction
				1			Name entered under name in direct order
				2			
					a	N	Entry element
					b	R	Subdivision (or name if entered under place)
					c	R	Addition to name or qualifier
					d	N	Number of meeting
					e	N	Location of meeting

（续上表）

Tag	Field Length	Field Comment	Indicator 1	Indicator 2	Subfield Code	Subfield Comment	Name of Field, Indicator, or Subfield Code
					f	N	Date of meeting
					g	N	Inverted element
					h	R	Part of name other than entry element and inverted element
					3	N	Authority record number
					4	R	Designation of function
781	V	R					Corporate Body Name in Roman Alphabet-Alternative Intellectual Responsibility
			0				Corporate name
			1				Meeting
				0			Name in inverted form
				1			Name entered under place or jurisdiction
				2			Name entered under name in direct order
					a	N	Entry element
					b	R	Subdivision（or name if entered under place）
					c	R	Addition to name or qualifier
					d	N	Number of meeting
					e	N	Location of meeting
					f	N	Date of meeting
					g	N	Inverted element
					h	R	Part of name other than entry element and inverted element
					3	N	Authority record number
					4	R	Designation of function
782	V	R					Corporate Body Name in Roman Alphabet-Secondary Intellectual Responsibility
			0				Corporate name
			1				Meeting
				0			Name in inverted form
				1			Name entered under place or jurisdiction
				2			Name entered under name in direct order
					a	N	Entry element
					b	R	Subdivision（or name if entered under place）
					c	R	Addition to name or qualifier
					d	N	Number of meeting
					e	N	Location of meeting
					f	N	Date of meeting
					g	N	Inverted element
					h	R	Part of name other than entry element and inverted element
					3	N	Authority record number
					4	R	Designation of function

(續上表)

Tag	Field		Indicator		Subfield Code	Subfield Comment	Name of Field, Indicator, or Subfield Code
	Length	Comment	1	2			
790	V	N					Family Name in Roman Alphabet-Primary Intellectual Responsibility
					a	N	Entry element
					3	N	Authority record number
					4	R	Designation of function
791	V	R					Family Name in Roman Alphabet-Alternative Intellectual Responsibility
					a	N	Entry element
					3	N	Authority record number
					4	R	Designation of function
792	V	R					Family Name in Roman Alphabet-Secondary Intellectual Responsibility
					a	N	Entry element
					3	N	Authority record number
					4	R	Designation of function
805	V	R					Local Accession Number and Call Number
					a	N	Agency Code
					b	R	Sublocation
					C	R	Accession number
					d	N	Class number
					e	N	Book number
					f	N	Cataloger
					P	N	Prefix

Figure 3. Computer Produced Chinese National Bibliography

植物奇觀/何豐吉撰. ——宜蘭縣蘇澳鎮：華大出版社，〔1977〕
　54 面：彩圖版；21 公分. ——〈彩色植物叢書〉
　新臺幣 100 元
　　Ⅰ. 何豐吉

370/6754

人類遺傳學概論/武光東，王昇同撰. ——臺北市：臺灣商務印書館，〔1979〕
　〔6〕156 面：圖表；19 公分. ——〈國民醫藥衛生叢書〉
　新臺幣 34 元
　　Ⅰ. 武光東　Ⅱ. 王昇

391.7/8367

家庭護理/周照芳等撰. ——臺北市：健康世界雜誌社，〔1979〕
　174 面：圖表. ——〈健康世界叢書；17〉
　新臺幣 60 元
　　Ⅰ. 周照芳　Ⅱ. 叢書

410.8/8965 v. 17

生活與健康/惠施撰. ——臺北市：惠施出版社，〔1979〕
　〔8〕163 面：表；19 公分. ——〈惠施叢書；7〉
　新臺幣 55 元
　　Ⅰ. 惠施

411/834

心靈福至/練思忠編. ——高雄市：劉毅文，〔1979〕
　〔10〕196 面：圖表；19 公分
　新臺幣 50 元
　　Ⅰ. 練思忠

411.1/8944

臺灣省的防癆工作/臺灣省防癆局編. ——臺北市：該局，〔1977〕
　〔5〕82 面：圖表；21 公分
　防癆局十週年紀念〔1967—1976〕
　　Ⅰ. 臺灣省防癆局

412.44/8484

張氏醫通/〈清〉張璐撰. ——新竹市：金藏書局，〔1976〕
　2 冊：圖；22 公分
　張璐字路玉
　新臺幣 350 元〈精〉
　　Ⅰ. 張璐

413/744 85

藥用植物學 = Pharmacautical botany/甘偉松編. ——5 版，——臺北縣新店鎮："中國醫藥研究所"，〔1977〕
　〔14〕699 面：圖版，彩圖版 52 葉，圖表；21 公分
　新臺幣 500 元〈精〉
　　Ⅰ. 甘偉松

414.1/8473 88

復健醫學概要/陸以仁撰. ——臺北市：臺灣商務印書館，〔1979〕
　〔4〕，157 面：圖表；19 公分，——〈國民醫藥衛生叢書〉
　新臺幣 34 元
　　Ⅰ. 陸以仁

418.9/8448

團體膳食管理/蘇尚毅撰. ——臺北市：撰者，〔1979〕
　〔4〕157 面：圖表；27 公分
　新臺幣 160 元
　　Ⅰ. 蘇尚毅

427/8858

合作農業推廣學 = Co-operative extension work：簡稱農業推廣學/吳恪元撰. ——臺北市："中國農業推廣學會"，〔1960〕

Figure 4.   Computer Produced Catalog Card

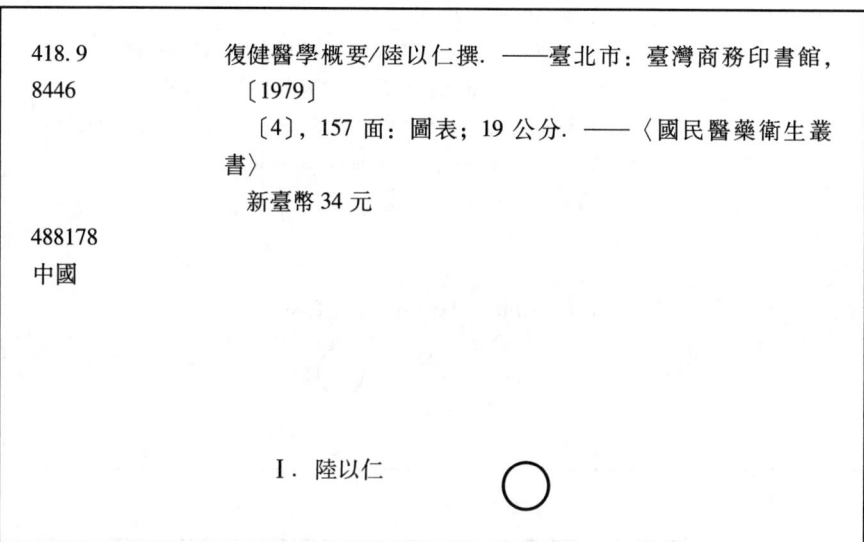

	欄號	分　　　　欄
Local Accession and Call Number →	805	＄a 中圖 ＄d418.9 ＄e8446 ＄c488178
Title and Statement of Responsibility →	200	＄a 復健醫學概要 ＄f 陸以仁撰
Imprint →	210	＄a 臺北市 ＄c 臺灣商務印書館 ＄d〔1979〕
Collation →	215	＄a〔4〕, 157 面 ＄c 圖書 ＄d19 公分
Series →	225	＄a 國民醫藥衛生叢書
Price →	010	＄d 新臺幣 34 元
Author →	700	＄a 陸 ＄b 以仁

```
QL556       Ch'an. Wei-sou.
.T29C493       (Ta tzu jan ti wu chi)
          大自然的舞姬：臺灣的蝴蝶世界/〔作者陳維壽〕. ——
          臺初版. ——臺北市：白雲文化事業公司,〔1977〕
            128 p.：ill.（some col.）；22 cm. ——〈錦繡系列；1〉
          Series romanized：Ch'in hsiu hsi lieh.
          新臺幣 200 元


            1. Butterflies—Taiwan  Ⅰ. Title.
```

	Tag	Subfield
Local Accession and Call Number →	805	$ dQL556. T29 $ eC493
Personal Name in Roman Alphabet-Primary Intellectual Responsibility →	770	$ aCh'en, $ bwei-sou.
Title and Statement of Responsibility →	200	$ rTa tzu jan ti wa chi
	200	$ a 大自然的舞姬 $ e 臺灣的蝴蝶世界 $ f〔作者陳維壽〕
Edition Statement →	205	$ a 臺初版
Imprint →	210	$ a 臺北市 $ c 白雲文化事業公司 $ d 民國66年〔1977〕
Collation →	215	$ a128p. $ cill.（some col.） $ d22 cm.
Series →	225	$ a 錦繡系列 $ v1
Notes Pertaining to series →	308	$ uSeries romanized：Chin hsiu hsi lieh.
Price →	010	$ d 新臺幣 200 元
Subject →	606	$ a Butterflies $ yTaiwan

Figure 5.   Chinese MARC Bibliographic Record

MENU OF SEARCHED BIBLIOGRAPHIC RECORD

Menu3 0015 0) NEXT 3) FIRST 7) PREV 8) LAST 18) EXIT SELECT **

1	001		Sysid:PRTI0069 Rec Status:n Tmp-cado:am0
2	100	$ a	Dt Ent:19801008 Type Pdate 1:d Date 1:1979 Lan:chi
3	105	$ a	Iil:a Conf:0 Fest:0 Lit code:y Bio codd:y
4	200 1	$ afr	$復健醫學概要 $陸以仁撰 $ Fu chien i hsueh kai yao
5	210	$ acd	$臺北市 $臺灣商務印書館 $〔1979〕
6	215 0	$ acd	$〔4〕,157 面 $圖表 $19 公分
7	215 1	$ acd	$〔4〕,157 p. $ ill. $19 cm.
8	225 22	$ a	$國民醫藥衛生叢書
9	308	$ u	$ Series romanized:Kuo min i yao wei cheng tsung shu.
10	010	$ d	$新臺幣 34 元

MENU OF SEARCHED BIBLIOGRAPHIC RECORD

Menu3 0015 0) NEXT 3) FIRST 7) PREV 8) LAST 18) EXIT SELECT **

11	700 1	$ a4	$陸以仁 $撰
12	700 1	$ ab	$ Lu, $ I – jen
13	681	$ ab	¥418.9 ¥8448
14	102	$ a	$ CW
15	805	$ acdeb	$中圖 $418.9 $8446 $4 $488178

Figure 6. Chinese MARC Bibliographic Entries

MENU OF SEARCHED BIBLIOGRAPHIC ENTRIES

TOTAL 0009 SELECT ****0）ENTER　3）FIRST　7）PREV　8）LAST　12）HOLD　18）EXIT

RPTI0060　370　8754
　　　Chih wu chi kuan　植物奇觀　何豐吉撰　宜蘭縣蘇澳鎮　華大出版社　〔1977〕

2　RPTI0062　391.7　8367
　　　Jen lei i ch'uan hsüeh kai lun　人類遺傳學概論　武光東，王昇同撰　臺北市　臺灣商務印書館　民國68年〔1979〕

3　RPTI0063　410.8　8965 v. 17
　　　Chia t'ing hu li　家庭護理　周照芳等撰　臺北市　健康世界雜誌社　〔1979〕

4　RPTI0064　411　834

CHINESE MARC: ITS PRESENT STATUS AND FUTURE DEVELOPMENT*

Lucy Te-Chu Lee[1]
Nancy Ou-lan Hu [2]
Sophia Hong-chu Huang[3]
Jack Kai-Tung Fiuang[4]
Ming-der Wu[5]

ABSTRACT

中文機讀編目格式（Chinese MARC Format）之現況及展望爲本文之主題：報告中文機讀編目格式之發展歷史及目的，並重點介紹本格式之特色，與國際機讀編目格式（UNIMARC）之比較，目前完成情況及其未來發展之計劃。

1. INTRODUCTION

The Library Automation Planning Committee (LAPC) was established by the "Library Association of China", in cooperation with the National Central Library in 1980, to improve library and information services, and to keep in step with the needs of libraries in local and international environment. By the present demand, the "National Library Automation Project (NLAP)" was formed under the auspices of LAPC in May, 1980 to study the related library problems and to carry out cooperative ventures with the purposes to accomplish the following objectives:

1) to develop the Chinese MARC Format within the constraint of international requirements, as the standard for cataloguing the Chinese publications;

2) through joint efforts to organize a data processing system for improving technical and information services of Chinese language materials;

3) to create a data base for Chinese publications and introducing data bases from overseas to meet the local research needs, and

4) to establish a national information network with the coordination of the "National Reconstruction Project and the advancement of academic research and development".

Since the Chinese MARC format is the essence of library automation, the Chinese MARC Working Group (CMWG) was formed by the Committee in May 1980. The Group has been assigned to the tasks of designing the Chinese MARC format which should meet the international requirements in order to facilitate data processing for Chinese materials and to promote international resources sharing and exchange.

In the course of designing a format structure to be acceptable internationally, attempts have been made to take into consideration of every possible way for data processing of Chinese materials in libraries. In addition. UNIMARC (Universal MARC Format; 1980 edition,

---

* Paper presented at the International Workshop on "Chinese Library Automation", Taipei, Feb. 14-19, 1981.
[1] Associate Professor, "National Taiwan University".
[2] Associate Professor, Tamkang University.
[3] Head, Dept. of Educational Media Sciences, Tamkang University.
[4] Professor, Ming Chung College.
[5] Head, Technical Services Dept., "National Taiwan University" Library.

IFLA) and the Library of Congress MARC II Format have been thoroughly studied and compared. With cooperative endeavor of the Group, a desirable format for the Chinese publications has been worked out, whereas the next phase of our task will be aimed at designing a format structure for non-book materials.

2. PRINCIPLE, PURPOSE, AND SCOPE

The guiding principle in developing a format for the Chinese publications is to achieve a structure that would have a wide applicability to all types of bibliographic data written in the Chinese language. The Group, at the very beginning, has agreed that the layout of the format has to be hospitable to all kinds of bibliographic information for all forms of Chinese imprints (books, serials, maps, music, etc.) and related records (name, subject, etc.). Meanwhile, the Group has considered it of the same priority to develop a format which could be utilized in a wide variety of computers to manipulate machine-readable cataloguing records. Regardless of the form of Chinese materials received in a given library it is anticipated that the Chinese MARC would be able to provide a format necessary for processing.

Inevitably the UNIMARC and Library of Congress MARC II Format have been consulted from time to time, the structure design for Chinese MARC format is essentially a cooperative achievement of the team. The UNIMARC format has been recommended as a medium for recording information in roman alphabet, nevertheless. The primary purpose of UNIMARC is to facilitate the international exchange of bibliographic data in machine-readable form between national bibliographic agencies. As a result of these considerations, the Group has opted to map out Chinese MARC as modeled on UNIMARC format incorporating with certain modifications to adjust to the current local requirements.

The bibliographic records in magnetic tapes are processed on the basis of ISO-2709 (Documentation—Format for Bibliographic Information Interchange on Magnetic Tape, 1973, and revised 1980).

The character set used for the Chinese MARC is prescribed by the Chinese Character Code for Information Interchange (CCCII) which is formed with the 7-bit code and is based on ISO-646 (7-bit Coded Character Set for Information Processing Interchange) and ISO-2022 (Code Extension Techniques for use with the ISO-7-bit Coded Character Set).

For full description of bibliographic records in the Chinese language, it is essential to follow the Chinese Cataloguing Rules (CCR) just partially completed in 1981, which conforms, to a large extent, to ISBDs (International Standard Bibliographic Descriptions) and AACR 2 (Anglo-American Cataloguing Rules, Second edition, 1978) principles.

The Wade-Giles romanization is used in the Chinese MARC as the standard transliteration for its bibliographic records.

The ultimate objective of the Chinese MARC is to facilitate the processing of Chinese language materials with computers for regional and international information exchange and sharing.

3. CHARACTERISTICS

In order to achieve the goal for internationl information exchange, consideration has been given to: ISO-2709 for record structure; ISO-3166 Codes for the Representation of Names of Countires, the Library of Congress Revised List of Languages and Language Codes for various languages and so on...

Special attention has also been given to the needs of non-Chinese speaking environment: major fields are designed in such a way that could be recorded and searched in Chinese, English, or Wade-Giles transliteration. They are, for instance, title proper, statement of responsibility, physical description, series, subject. etc.

Chinese Character Code for Information Interchange is employed for encoding data. Reservation of space for future expansion of encoded data has been prepared. There is sufficient coding room for more than at least 50 thousand Chinese characters in various forms. In addition, it provides many options selecting a filing system for Chinese characters, with which data file may be arranged according to a predetermined sequence or method.

Special features and major characteristics of UNIMARC, such as the consistant meaning of coded data values, subfield identifiers, etc. are retained in Chinese MARC.

And, Chinese MARC format is definitely machine independent.

4. COMPARISON BETWEEN CHINESE MARC AND UNIMARC

The CCR follows the basic framework of ISBDs, however, the characteristics of Chinese materials and tradition of Chinese bibliography dictate the pattern for CCR which in reality has departed to certain degree from ISBDs. Consequently, additions and changes are necessary for Chinese MARC to reflect all these features.

FIGURE 1 shows the tag relationship between Chinese MARC and UNIMARC:

FIGURE 2 List of Tags, Indicators and Subfields being added or modified to Chinese MARC:

In summary, the major modifications in Chinese MARC are as follows:

1) Add subfield indentifier "Sr" to fields 200, 225 and 5xx. This identifier marks title proper and series title accessible by romanization. Such need is likely to be in libraries located in the United States and Europe. Whereas "Sr" may not be a necessity for local libraries where the likelihood for accessing a bibliographic record by transliteration would be at minimum.

2) Add subfield identifier "Su" to fields 3xx for libraries which use cataloguing rules other than CCR to record notes in Chinese, English, or romanization.

3) Subfield identifier "Sg" is assigned in fields 600,700,701, and 702 to identify the dynastic era during which a Chinese individual lived either in the Ch'ing dynasty or earlier. The association of a personal name with the name of a dynasty when he lived is a long observed tradition in Chinese scholarship.

4) Some undefined indicators employed in UNIMARC have been assigned new functions in Chinese MARC to offer flexibility in the format, e. g., indicators in Field 215 (Physical description) and Field 225 (Series).

5) To make them compatible with CCR, some fields found in UNIMARC are not used in Chinese MARC, e. g., Field 501 (Collective Uniform Title), Field 503 (Uniform Conventional Headings). However, they are reserved in Chinese MARC with an asterisk (*) for libraries adopting other cataloguing rules.

5. PRESENT ACTIVITIES AND ACCOMPLISHMENT

The Group set for itself the herculean task of completing within eight months the design of Chinese MARC format for books and computer program requirements for testing and implimentating purposes. At present time, 1100 records were carefully selected from the "Chinese National Bibliography of National Central Library", the L. C. National Union Catalog, and the catalog of the National Taiwan University Library holdings, and input into the Chinese MARC data base. With this data base one can perfrom the following operations:

1) Computer produced Chinese National Bibliography (Figure 3)
2) Computer produced catalog cards (Figure 4)
3) Online display of Chinese bibliographic records in three forms: —
   a. Chinese MARC Bibliographic Record (Figure 5)
   b. Chinese MARC Bibliographic Entries (Figure 6)
   c. Chinese MARC Work From

4) Online query and search functions:
   a. Online input;
   b. Online update;
   c. Online delete and modify, and;
   d. Online seaching bibliographic information.

6. FUTURE DEVELOPMENT

Through cooperative efforts, the Chinese MARC format for monographs has been finally materialized, its counterpart for non-book publications has yet to be fully developed. Nevertheless, it is anticipated that the Chinese MARC will be employed as the sole standard for Chinese language materials regardless of their type or format. For future development of the Chinese MARC, it is expected to be carried out within the first two stages of the three phases in the NLAP:

The first phase: Beginning from 1981, the Group has been inputting, in Chinese MARC format, the newly acquired titles of the "National Central Library" to a special file on computer with the anticipation that it will grow to be a data base for bibliographic control. Presently seven large local libraries have agreed to participate in the same program by taking like measures from 1981. Each of them will utilize the records found in the Chinese MARC data base, add data information as required, evaluate the usefulness of all data obtained, and report to the Group of their assessment which may be considered as the basis for future improvement. This operation can also help to pave the way for further cooperation among libraries.

Meanwhile, the Group will be involved in implementing the goal for constructing Chinese MARC format for non-book materials. As reports come in from various participating libraries, further modification and improvement to the format will be executed.

The second phase: The first distribution of catalog cards based on the Chinese MARC format is to begin in October, 1981 by the Chinese MARC Distribution Office located at the "NCL". The first test tape is scheduled to be mailed in 1982. and also more participants will be invited to cope with the goal of setting up a national library network. During this period, the retrospective records are planning to be converted.

Along with the setting up of the data base of Chinese materials, the computerization for materials in western languages including books and non-books will be conducted. Since this will involve the domestic and international library cooperation, careful considerations will be made and unanimous support and valuable suggestions from all participants, will also be required for working out a better cooperation exchange program in this conference discussions. The computerization of western books is now being experimented by several local libraries. But the ultimate objective in this respect is the nation-wide unification and standardization.

The third phase: Preparations for the establishment for the national information network will be made after the completion of the tasks in the first and second phases. Starting from 1983, all libraries and institutions in this country will be welcome to take part in this cooperation project for national library automation system. Accordingly, the Committee will take the responsibility of selecting the most suitable systems for achieving the objectives of NLAP.

IN CONCLUSIONS, the accomplishment of the Chinese MARC is not merely a success in providing a uniformed standard for the processing of publications in the Chinese language but also an achievement in enabling Chinese libraries to participate in the communication with information service systems world-wide.

Figure 1. Tag Relationship between Chinese MARC and UNIMARC

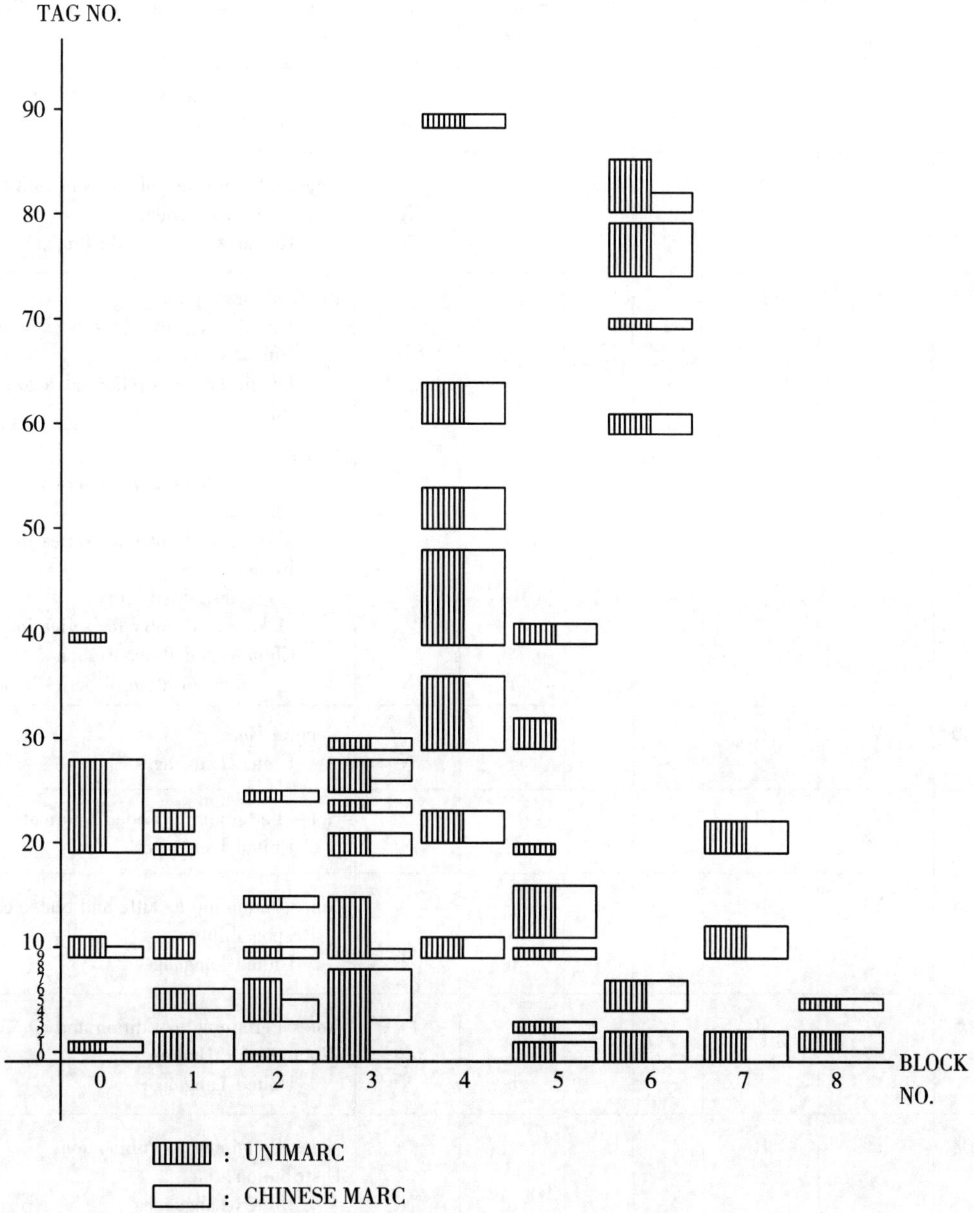

Figure 2. List of Tags, indicators, and subfields being added to Chinese MARC:

Tag	Field		Indicator		Subfield Code	Subfield Comment	Name of Field, Indicator, or Subfield Code
	Length	Comment	1	2			
010	V	R					International Standard Book Number
					b	R	Qualification
200	V	N					Title and Statement of Responsibility
					P	N	Number of Chüan
					r	N	Romanization of Title Proper
215	V	R					Physical Description
			0				For library uses Chinese Cataloging Rules
			1				For library uses other cataloguing rules
225	V	R					Series
				0			Make added entry for series in Chinese
				1			Make added entry for series in Romanization
				2			No series added entry
				3			Make added entry for series in Chinese and Romanization
					r	N	Romanization of Series Title
300	V	R					General Note
					r	N	United Languages
302	V	R					Notes Pertaining to Coded Information
					u	N	United Languages
304	V	R					Notes Pertaining to Title and Statement of Responsibility
					u	N	United Languages
305	V	R					Notes Pertaining to Edition and Bibliographic History
					u	N	United Language
306	V	R					Notes Pertaining to Publication, Distribution, etc.
					u	N	United Languages
307	V	R					Notes Pertaining to Physical Description
					u	N	United Languages
308	V	R					Notes Pertaining to Series
					u	N	United Languages

(續上表)

Tag	Field		Indicator		Subfield Code	Subfield Comment	Name of Field, Indicator, or Subfield Code
	Length	Comment	1	2			
310	V	R					Notes Pertaining to Binding and Availability
					u	N	United Languages
312	V	R					Notes Pertaining to Related Titles
					u	N	United Languages
314	V	R					Notes Pertaining to Intellectual Responsibility
					u	N	United Languages
316	V	R					Notes Pertaining to Number of Chüan
					u	N	United Languages
320	V	R					Bibliography, Index, Appendix Note
					u	N	United Languages
321	V	R					Availability of Indexes and Abstracts Note
					u	N	United Languages
324	V	N					Facsimile Note
					u	N	United Languages
328	V	R					Dissertation (Thesis) Note
					u	N	United Languages
330	V	R					Summary Note
					u	N	United Languages
332	V	R					Copy Being Described and Library's Holdings
					u	N	United Languages
510	V	R					Parallel Title Proper
					r	N	Romanization of title
512	V	R					Cover Title
					r	N	Romanization of title
513	V	R					Added Title-page Title
					r	N	Romanization of title
514	V	R					Caption Title
					r	N	Romanization of title
515	V	R					Running Title
					r	N	Romanization of title

(續上表)

Tag	Field		Indicator		Subfield Code	Subfield Comment	Name of Field, Indicator, or Subfield Code
	Length	Comment	1	2			
516	V	R			r	N	Spine Title 　　Romanization of title
517	V	R			r	N	Other Variant Titles 　　Romanization of title
600	V	R			g	N	Personal Name Used as Subject 　　Dynasty
681	V	R			a b	N N	Chinese Classification Scheme 　　Chinese Class Number 　　Book Number
700	V	R			g	N	Personal Name-Primary Intellectual Responsibility 　　Dynasty
701	V	R			g	N	Personal Name-Alternative Intellectual Responsibility 　　Dynasty
702	V	R			g	N	Personal Name-Secondary Intellectual Responsibility 　　Dynasty
710	V	R					Corporate Body Name-Primary Intellectual Responsibility
720	V	R					Family Name-Primary Intellectual Responsibility
850	V	R			a b c d e	N R N N N	Local Accession and Code Number 　　Agency Code 　　Accession Number 　　Class Number 　　Book Number 　　Cataloger

Figure 3. Computer produced Chinese National Bibliography

易一貫/（清）呂調陽撰. ——影印本. ——臺北市：新文豐出版公司,〔1979〕
〔1〕620 面：圖；22 公分
據觀象□叢書本影印
新臺幣 320 元（精）
Ⅰ.（清）呂調陽

121. 12/7536 68

易經精華　六卷，首末各一卷/（清）薛嘉穎編. ——臺北市：新文豐出版公司,〔1979〕
〔10〕476 面；22 公分
據清同治二年刻崇文堂藏版影印
新臺幣 250 元（精）
Ⅰ.（清）薛嘉穎

121. 12/7643 68

五峯山房易學　十卷，首一卷/武鈺撰. 臺北市：新文豐出版公司,〔1979〕
〔8〕564 面：圖；22 公分
據民國八年（己未）鄂垣□華林工業□習廠鉛印本影印
新臺幣 280 元（精）
Ⅰ. 武鈺

121. 12/835 68

周易□氏學　八卷，首末各一卷/馬其昶撰. ——臺北市：新文豐出版公司,〔1979〕
1 冊：圖；21 公分
據民國九年（庚申）抱潤軒藏版影印
新臺幣 360 元（精）
Ⅰ. 馬其昶

121. 17/8333 68

無爲的思想/森三樹三郎撰；姚百勤譯. ——高雄市：敦理出版社,〔1979〕
159 面：圖；19 公分. ——（敦理叢刊；16）
新臺幣 50 元
Ⅰ. 森三樹三郎　Ⅱ. 姚百勤

121. 3/8743

莊子天下篇校釋/譚戒甫校譯. ——影印本. ——臺北市：新文豐出版公司,〔1979〕
〔90〕面：圖；21 公分
據民國二十四年排印本影印
新臺幣 150 元（精）
Ⅰ. 譚戒甫

121. 335/8433 68

墨子析義/王企縈撰. ——臺中市：金氏圖書公司,〔1979〕
〔8〕135 面；21 公分
新臺幣 90 元
Ⅰ. 王企縈

121. 417/8462

心理學論集/饒兆平撰. ——臺北市：黎明文化公司,〔1979〕
〔4〕193 面：有表；21 公分. ——（大學叢書）
附錄：公民心理自覺測驗表
新臺幣 60 元
Ⅰ. 饒兆平

170. 7/8755

Figure 4.　Computer Produced Catalog Card

```
856.17            賢手札/〈清〉郭子瀞輯. ──臺北市：老古出版社，
7444              〔1979〕
483948            〔3，381〕面：19公分
中圖               收錄曾國藩、胡林翼、駱秉章、左宗棠、彭玉慶、曾國荃、
                  沈葆楨、李鴻章等八位手札
                    附錄：清史八賢列傳
                    新臺幣 100 元
                  Ⅰ.〈清〉郭子瀞
```

	TAGS	Subfields
Local Accession and Call Number ⟶	805	$ c856.17 $ d7444 $ b483948 $ a 中圖
Title and Statement of Responsibility ⟶	200	$ a 八賢手札 $ f（清）郭子瀞輯
Imprint ⟶	210	$ a 臺北市 $ c 老古出版社 $ d〔1979〕
Collation ⟶	215	$ a〔3，381〕面 $ d 19 公分
Note ⟶	300	$ a 收錄曾國藩、胡林翼、駱秉章、左宗棠、彭玉慶、曾國荃、沈葆楨、李鴻章等八位手札
Note ⟶	320	$ a 附錄：清史八賢列傳
Price ⟶	010	$ d 新臺幣 100 元
Author ⟶	700	$ g（清）$ a 郭 $ b 子瀞

Figure 5. Chinese MARC Bibliographic Record

```
           Chinese MARC Bibliographic Record
           Record Label：RS = n    IC = am0    ARD = 2i
001              ? 0 - 00003
100       ǂ a    1 = 19801004   2 = d   3 = 1979   4 =      5 =       6 = y
                 ? = 0   8 = Chi   9 = b   10 = 3c2i   11 = 3c2i   12 = e
105       ǂ a    1 = C    2 =     3 = 0    4 = 0    5 = 0    6 = y   7 = y
805   1   ǂ abcde   ǂ 中圖   ǂ 487864   ǂ 943.6   ǂ 8334   ǂ 12
200   1   ǂ afr    ǂ 澹廬一門師生作品集   ǂ 澹廬書會編   ǂ Tan lu i men shih
                   sheng tso p'ing chi
210       ǂ acd   ǂ 臺北市   ǂ 該會   ǂ〔1979〕
215   1   ǂ adad   ǂ 144 面   ǂ 28 公分   ǂ 144 P.   ǂ 28 cm.
712   02  ǂ a4a    ǂ 澹廬書會   ǂ 編   ǂ Tan lu shu hui
681       ǂ ab    ǂ 943.6   ǂ 8334
102       ǂ a     ǂ C W
```

Figure 6.　Chinese MARC Bibliographic Entries

```
                    Chinese MARC Bibliographic Entries
70 - 00082                673.23/8725
    臺灣堡圖集 = Atlas of the historic administrative pau division of Taiwan/張炳南、李汝和
    同修；洪敏麟等編. ——臺北市：臺灣文獻委員會，〔1969〕


70 - 00033                230.4/8328
    仙學辭典全集/載源長編；李樂俅校. ——臺北市：真善美出版社，〔1970〕


70 - 00031                830/5265
    標眉箋正正續文章軌範/（宋）謝枋得輯；（明）李延機評訓；原田由已標箋　七
        卷. ——臺市：廣文書局，〔1970〕


70 - 00017                673.2/
    臺灣省通志/張炳楠監修；李汝和等纂.　卷十，光復志　收復準備篇　光復紀盛篇
        日俘日僑遣送篇. ——臺北市：臺灣省文獻委員會，〔1970〕
```

US MARC 21 社區資訊機讀格式 *

【摘要　Abstract】

　　US MARC 21 社區資訊機讀格式是針對處理社會中多樣的非書目性資源而設計的格式，雖然始於1980 年代初期，至今仍甚少爲圖書館界重視而予以運用。本文目的在介紹社區資訊格式之設計理念、特質、應用、問題及實例，強調其重要性並呼籲圖書館界重視利用。

　　The US MARC 21 Community Information Format is a format for description of nonbibliographic resources that fulfills the information needs of a community. The Community Information Format allows libraries to include individuals (people), organizations, programs or services, events, and other resources that can help library users gain information they need, enrich their lives, solve problems and enhances their enjoyment of life. Although this format was initiated in the early 80's, first published in 1993, and it was recently included in MARC 21 family of formats, but it is the least used format. This paper attempts to introduce the US MARC 21 Community Information Format, its design concept, characteristics, applications, problems and examples. Finally, the author of this paper solicits the library community the importance of using of this format to handle nonbibliographic resources.

關鍵詞：美國機讀格式　美國社區資訊機讀格式　社區資訊
Keyword：US MARC 21 Format；US MARC Community Information Format；Community Information

壹、前　言

　　1999 年，美國國會圖書館和加拿大"國家圖書館"聯合對外公告將 US MARC 和 CAN MARC 兩格式合而爲單一格式，並命名爲 MARC 21，以達到未來廿一世紀和全世界使用之目的。MARC 21 格式涵蓋五種格式，是一個機讀格式家族模式（Family of formats），其中有書目（Bibliographic）、權威（Authority）、館藏（Holdings）、分類（Classification）和社區資訊（Community Information）五種格式。同時加拿大亦出版法文版的 MARC 21。（註1）本文旨在介紹鮮爲圖書館界認識而又少被應用的 US 21 MARC 社區資訊機讀格式（US MARC Community Information Format，簡稱 CIF）。MARC 社區資訊格式重要的特色是專爲描述社區需要的非書目性資源（Nonbibliographic resources）而設計的機讀格式。這些非書目性資源，如計劃/節目（Programs），服務（Services），組織/機構（Organizations）、個人（Individuals），事件（Events）或其他對社區有用的資源（Other resources），其目的是對社會中各方面多樣又不同的需求皆可以提供資訊服務。

---

　　* 本文曾發表在《圖書與資訊學》38 期（2001 年8 月），第1—13 頁。

（註2）1980年代初期，由於社區資訊多為非書目性的，更具有動態的、活潑的而又不斷發展的特性，其資料單元（Data elements）無法放入標準機讀格式中，另外又因無編目規則可循，美國圖書館界之解決方法當時則是另外為社區資訊設計格式，或修改已有的 MARC 格式以容納社區資訊的資料單元。（註3）

1985年至1993年間是社區資訊格式發展時期，其間經過美國公共圖書館協會技術委員會和已自行開發以機讀形式輸入館內的自動化系統之圖書館共同擬定"社區資訊標準化資料單"（詳見下表一），該委員會於1989年向美國國會圖書館網路發展（The Network Development and MARC Standards Office, the Library of Congress）和 MARC 顧問小組（US MARC Advising Group）提出要求，要求由國會圖書館為社區資訊設計機讀格式。美國國會圖書館於1992年4月核准 USMARC Community Information Format 為暫時性的格式，期許透過圖書館的使用，得到經驗而再予以修改。（註4）最後，美國社區資訊機讀格式終於1993年正式出版，是一個較新的而最少被使用的機讀格式，為融入 MARC 家族之一員，故其格式內容設計類似和/或仿用書目性格式（Bibliographic）所用之欄位和編碼，其設計理念與書目性格式相同，也可用於公共目錄中。（註5）MARC 21 Community Information Format 之 Field list 項目詳見表二。（註6）

表一：美國隊 MARC 社區資訊格式採用之標準資料單元項目表（1992）
(Standardized list of data elements for community information)

Accessibility	Licensing/Accreditation
Additional Address Locations	Meeting Room/Facilities/Equipment
Affiliation（membership; parent organization）	Meeting Times
Annual Budget	Mission Statement/Purpose
Application for Service（required documents）	Mutual Support Groups
Cataloging Record Source	Name of Public Contact Person
Child Care	Officer Names/Advisory Board Members/Peer Advisory Group
Classification Number	
Control Number	Primary Address
Date of Record（original entry date/date record updated）	Program Description/Description of Services
	Programs（titles）
Director's/Administrator's Name	Publication Titles
Eligibility Requirements	Size of Staff
Fee	Speakers Bureau
Former Name（s）/Acronym（s）	State
Funding Source	Subject Headings
Geographic Area/Location Served（in text and in coded form）	Target Group
	Telephone Number—including TTD, FAX, 800 number; electronic mail address
Handicapped Accessibility	
Hours of Operation	Title of Organization（program name/popular name）
Human Service Number	
Languages in which Services are Provided（in text and in coded form）	Volunteer Opportunities
	Waiting List
Languages Spoken by Staff（in text and in coded form）	Year Established/Founding Date
	Zip Code

表二：MARC 21 Format for Community Information：Field List
2000 English Edition
Update No. 1 (October, 2000)

Leader and Directory
　　見表三
Control Fields (001 – 008)
　　001 – CONTROL NUMBER (NR)
　　003 – CONTROL NUMBER IDENTIFIER (NR)
　　004 – CODED DATES FIXED FIELD (NR) [OBSOLETE]
　　005 – DATE AND TIME OF LATEST TRANSACTION (NR)
　　007 – PHYSICAL DESCRIPTION FIXED FIELD (NR)
　　008 – FIXED – LENGTH DATA ELEMENTS (NR
Number and Code Fields (01X – 08X)
　　010 – LIBRARY OF CONGRESS CONTROL NUMBER (NR)
　　016 – NATIONAL BIBLIOGRAPHIC AGENCY CONTROL NUMBER (R)
　　035 – SYSTEM CONTROL NUMBER (R)
　　040 – RECORD SOURCE (FIR)
　　041 – LANGUAGE CODE (FIR)
　　043 – GEOGRAPHIC AREA CODE (NR)
　　046 – SPECIAL CODED DATES (NR)
　　050 – LIBRARY OF CONGRESS CLASSIFICATION NUMBER (R)
　　052 – GEOGRAPHIC CLASSIFICATION (R)
　　058 – OTHER GEOGRAPHIC CLASSIFICATION CODE (R) [DELETED]
　　060 – NATIONAL LIBRARY OF MEDICINE CLASSIFICATION NUMBER (R)
　　066 – CHARACTER SETS PRESENT (NR)
　　070 – NATIONAL AGRICULTURAL LIBRARY CLASSIFICATION NUMBER (R)
　　072 – HUMAN SERVICES CODE (R)
　　073 – TYPE OF PROGRAM OR ORGANIZATION CODE (R)
　　080 – UNIVERSAL DECIMAL CLASSIFICATION NUMBER (NR)
　　082 – DEWEY DECIMAL CLASSIFICATION NUMBER (R)
　　084 – OTHER CLASSIFICATION NUMBER (R)
Primary Name Fields (1XX)
　　100 – PRIMARY NAME—PERSONAL (NR)
　　110 – PRIMARY NAME—CORPORATE (NR)
　　111 – PRIMARY NAME—MEETING (NR)
Title and Address Fields (2XX)
　　245 – TITLE (NR)
　　246 – VARYING FORM OF TITLE (R)

247 – FORMER TITLE (R)
270 – ADDRESS (R)
271 – ADDITIONAL ADDRESSES (R) [DELETED]
275 – ADDRESS ASSOCIATED WITH TITLE (R) [DELETED]

Physical Description, Hours, Etc. Fields (3**XX**)

301 – HOURS, ETC. (R) [DELETED]
303 – SUBORDINATE ENTITLES (R)
307 – HOURS, ETC. (R)
311 – MEETING ROOMS AND FACILITIES AVAILABLE (R)
312 – EQUIPMENT AVAILABLE (R)

Series Statement Fields (4**XX**)

440 – SERIES TITLE (R)

Note Fields (5**XX**)

500 – GENERAL NOTE (R)
501 – CURRENCY OF INFORMATION NOTE (R)
505 – PROGRAMS NOTE (R)
511 – PARTICIPANT OR PERFORMER NOTE (R)
520 – DESCRIPTION NOTE (R)
521 – TARGET GROUP NOTE (R)
522 – GEOGRAPHIC COVERAGE NOTE (NR)
531 – ELIGIBILITY, FEES, PROCEDURES NOTE (R)
536 – FUNDING SOURCE NOTE (R)
545 – BIOGRAPHICAL OR HISTORICAL NOTE (R)
546 – LANGUAGE NOTE (R)
551 – BUDGET NOTE (R)
570 – PERSONNEL NOTE (R)
571 – VOLUNTEERS NOTE (R)
572 – AFFILIATION AND OTHER RELATIONSHIPS NOTE (R)
573 – CREDENTIALS NOTE (R)
574 – TRANSPORTATION AND DIRECTIONS NOTE (R)
575 – ACCOMMODATIONS FOR THE DISABLED NOTE (R)
576 – SERVICES AVAILABLE NOTE (R)
581 – PUBLICATIONS NOTE (R)
587 – OTHER INFORMATION AVAILABLE NOTE (R)

Subject Access Fields (6**XX**)

600 – SUBJECT ADDED ENTRY—PERSONAL NAME (R)
610 – SUBJECT ADDED ENTRY – CORPORATE NAME (R)
611 – SUBJECT ADDED ENTRY—MEETING NAME (R)

630 - SUBJECT ADDED ENTRY—PUBLICATION TITLE（R）
650 - SUBJECT ADDED ENTRY—TOPICAL TERM（R）
651 - SUBJECT ADDED ENTRY—GEOGRAPHIC NAME（R）
653 - INDEX TERM—UNCONTROLLED（R）
654 - SUBJECT ADDED ENTRY—FACETED TOPICAL TERMS（R）
656 - INDEX TERM—OCCUPATION（R）
657 - INDEX TERM—FUNCTION（R）
658 - INDEX TERM—CURRICULUM OBJECTIVE（R）

Added Entry Fields（7XX）
700 - ADDED ENTRY - PERSONAL NAME（R）
710 - ADDED ENTRY - CORPORATE NAME（R）
711 - ADDED ENTRY—MEETING NAME（R）
720 - ADDED ENTRY—UNCONTROLLED NAME（R）
730 - ADDED ENTRY—PUBLICATION TITLE（R）
740 - ADDED ENTRY—SPECIFIC PROGRAM TITLE（R）

Location and Alternate Graphics Fields（8XX）
856 - ELECTRONIC LOCATION AND ACCESS（R）
880 - ALTERNATE GRAPHIC REPRESENTATION（R）

首先比較 US MARC 社區資訊格式與書目格式不同之處，詳見下表三：（註7）

表三：美國 MARC 社區資訊格式與書目格式欄位之比較

（一）記錄標示（Leader）

US MARC Community Information Field		US MARC Bibliographic Field	
00 - 04	Logical record length	00 - 04	Logical record length
05	Record status	05	Record status
	c　Corrected or revised		c　Corrected or revised
	f　Deleted		d　Deleted
	n　New		n　New
			a　Increase in encoding level
			p　Increase in encoding level from prepublication
06	Type of record	06	Type of record
	q　Community information		（codes a - g, i - k, m, o, r）
07	Kind of data	07	Bibliographic data
	n　Individual		（codes a - d, m, s）
	o　Organization		
	p　Program or service		
	q　Event		

(續上表)

US MARC Community Information Field		US MARC Bibliographic Field	
	z Other community information data		
08－16	(same as for the bibliographic format)		
17－19	Undefined	17	Encoding level
		18	Descriptive cataloguing form
		19	Linked record requirement
20－23	(same as for the bibliographic format)		

(二) 段 (Blocks)

US MARC Community Information Field		US MARC Bibliographic Field	
0XX	Control Information, Numbers, and Codes	0XX	Control Information, Numbers, and Codes
1XX	Primary Name	1XX	Main Entry
2XX	Titles, Addresses	2XX	Titles and Title Paragraph
3XX	Physical Information, Etc.	3XX	Physical Description, Etc.
4XX	Series Information	4XX	Series Statements
5XX	Notes	5XX	Notes
6XX	Subject Access Fields	6XX	Subject Access Fields
7XX	Added Entries Other than Subject	7XX	Names, Etc. Added Entries or Series; Linking Fields
8XX	Miscellaneous	8XX	Series Added Entries; Holdings and Locations
9XX	Reserved for Local Implementation	9XX	Reserved for Local Implementation

US MARC 社區資訊記錄之有別於其他 US MARC 記錄是在格式中記錄標示 (Leader) /06 (記錄種類) 位置上是以 "q" 代碼標示其爲社區資訊記錄，同時在 Leader/07 (資料種類) 位置以下列代碼標識之：(註8)

n (Individual)：代表 "個人" 方面之資訊；

o (Organizafion)：代表 "組織/機構" 相關之資訊；

p (Program or service)：代表某計劃或服務項目的資訊；

q (Event)：表示某事件之相關資訊；

z (Others)：表示除以上資源種類外，與社區相關之其他資源。

以下介紹 MARC 社區資訊格式記錄實例：(註9)

(一) 機構

COMMUNITY INFORMATION RECORD: AGENCY

This example can be identified as a record for an organization (including agencies) by code o in Leader/07. The record contains fields 110 (Primary Name-Corporate) and 270 (Address), two fields used with organizations.

Leader/06   q   [*community information*]

Leader/07	o	[organization]
001		< control number >
003		< control number identifier >
005		< date and time of latest transaction >
008		930917aaaaaaeng
040		##$a< MARC code > $c< MARC code >
041		0#$aengspa
110		2#$aHaven House.
270		1#$aP. O. Box 50007 $bPasadena $cCA $e91115 $j213－681－2626 (24 hour hotline)
307		##$a24 hours a day, 7days a week.
520		##$aA residential shelter for women and their children who have been abused by alcoholic partners.
531		##$aWomen (18－64) with their children (0－18) who need shelter from physical and emotional abuse due to alcohol in family member; $bfrom ＄1.50/day (Residential) to ＄20.00/month (Group CNSL); $ctelephone; no walk-ins.
546		##$aEnglish, Spanish.
574		##$aPublic transportation. Call RTD: 818－246－2593.
650		#0$aBattered women.
650		#0$aWomen's services.

(二) 計劃/節目

COMMUNITY INFORMATION RECORD: PROGRAM

The example can be identified as a record for a program or senvice by code p in leader/07. The record contains field 245 (Title), a field used with events and programs. A field 004 (Coded Dates Fixed Field) is also present.

Leader/06	q	[community information]
Leader/07	p	[program or service]
001		< control number >
003		< control number identifier >
005		< date and time of latest transaction >
008		921229aaaaaa ｜｜｜
040		##$a< MARC code > $c< MARC code >
046		##$f19931226 $g19931221 $h19931115 $i19931220
110		2#$aUnited States Marine Crops.
245		#0$aToys for Tots.
270		1#$aP. O. Box 223 $bBroken Arrow $cOK $e74012 $pSgt. Kathy Hibner

307	8# $ aBegins November 15, 1993.
500	## $ aAnnual toy drive.
500	## $ aCollection locations include: All fire stations in Tulsa, Broken Arrow; Tulsa National Bank, 71st and Yorktown; All Wendy's restaurants; Eastland Mall; All three American Shopping Channel Stores; Riverside Chevrolet; West Star Bank on Garnett; Scissors Hair and Body; Dresser Rand; Kindercare; Capelli's Hair Salon; All U-Haul locations and Bargain Time in Sand Springs.
501	8# $ aUpdated 6/93.
572	## $ aSponsored by the United States Marine Corps.
650	#0 $ aChristmas.

（三）組織

COMMUNITY INFORMATION RECORD: ORGANIZATION

This example can be identified as a record for an organized by code o in leader/07. The record contains field 110 (Primary Name – Corporate) and 270 (Address), two field used with organizations.

Leader/06	q	[community information]
Leader/07	o	[organization]
001		< control number >
003		< control number identifier >
005		< date and time of latest transaction >
008		930608aaaaaaeng
040		##Sa< MARC code > Sc< MARC code >
046		## $ f199311uu
110		2# $ aWasatch Front Road Runners.
270		1# $ aP. O. Box 8344 $ bSalt Lake City ScUT $ e84108 $ k467–4203 $ pRichard Barnum-Reece
308		##SaM–F, 8–5.
501		## $ aSERVICES: Runners organization.
502		8# $ aDate revised: 9/93.
531		## $ bFees for membership/newsletter.
581		8# $ aPublishes the newsletter The Utah Runner and Cyclist.
587		## $ aSPORTS ORGANIZATIONS: CIF pamphlet file.
650		#0 $ aRunning.
650		#0SaJogging.
730		0# $ aUtah Runner and Cyclist.

（四）事件

COMMUNITY INFORMATION RECORD: EVENT

This example can be identified as a record for an event by code q in leader/07. The record contains field 245 (Title), a field used with events and programs.

Leader/06	q	[*community information*]
Leader/07	q	[*event*]
001		< control number >
003		< control number identifier >
005		< date and time of latest transaction >
008		930816anannneng
040		##＄a< MARC code >＄c< MARC code >
046		##＄g19931002＄h19931001＄i19931001
245		#0＄aContemporary Music and Inter-disciplinary Music Theatre.
270		1#＄aRadcliffe Dance Center, Agazziz House＄k437-2247
307		8#＄aOct. 1, 1992, 2 p.m.
440		#0＄aLearning through Performers Program
511		##＄aA lecture/demonstration by Paul Dresher and Rinde Eckert, composers and members, Paul Dresher Ensemble.
520		8#＄a"About 'Pioneer', which examines the burden of the American frontier past and the uncertainty of the future through Dresher's innovative electronic score and Ekert's arrangement."
531		##＄bGeneral admission,＄6.00; free for Harvard and Northwestern faculty, staff, and students; half-price discount for seniors, students, and advance sales buyers.
650		#0＄aTheatre.

貳、US NARC 社區資訊格式應用上的問題

US MARC 社區資訊格式自公佈以來，一些自動化系統中亦有增列社區資訊記錄者，但也被一些大學和公共圖書館以及圖書館系統代理商所採用，社區資訊格式並不常被使用，似乎並未得到圖書館界之重視，其原因分析如下：（註10）

一、編目對象之選擇：由於社區資源甚廣，非書目性資料種類繁多，如何選擇適當的資源，根據何種編目規則，特質不易取捨，又圖書館如何訂定其館藏發展及採購非書目性資料之政策皆需要進一步的研究及規範。

二、編目規則：任何一種機讀格式之設計，除社區資訊格式外，皆是先有編目規則再訂定格式。對社區資訊而言，情況複雜，訂定編目規則並不容易，正因爲無適當之編目規則可依據，其標目形式和資料單元的款目以及統一用語之問題甚多。

三、資訊來源：社區資訊來源甚廣，難以掌握，如何確定和評估其來源之真實性，

皆需費時查詢確認。以個人記錄爲例，常由於介紹個人爲依據爲宣傳材料，是否適合選用列入記錄很有爭議。

　　四、記錄之更新：社區資訊多爲動態的，變化無窮，除一些已完成的事件外，組織機構之改變，服務項目之變更，個人資料等，常因更新太慢而使記錄失去真實性、正確性、有效性，故需要常常維護，時時更新記錄：又何況社區資訊記錄需要原始編目（Original cataloguing），所需人力時間甚多，以圖書館有限的人力而言，書目性的記錄已耗去甚多人力，已無力顧及非書目性的資料。

　　雖然，社區資訊格式在應用上有多種問題，但由於其活潑有彈性，而優點甚多，例如用社區資訊格式建立內部館員資料、各種活動節目，如內部訓練，會議，新知告知等。亦可將校園內之設備、活動、服務項目，利用此格式建置於線上目錄中，供讀者使用，對外可建立個人關係聯絡之資料網路，亦可增強對外界之公共關係。何況將社區內公園、游泳池、高爾夫球場和其他設施之資訊一併建置亦是很有意義的資訊！雖然這些資訊皆需原始編目，但大家一起來，正如書目性資料庫，亦是一筆筆建立起來的。（註11）

叁、結　論

　　當今圖書館界正在憂心如何處理那麼多的非書目性資源，如網路資源、機構團體、個人資料、服務項目或事件等等，臺灣外一窩蜂的設計各式各樣不統一規格之 Metadata 格式，如 Dublin Core，MICI 等，其實這些格式設計理念仍看到 MARC 之影子，爲何不考慮試用 MARC 社區資訊格式？而另創新格式，使大環境又掀起了春秋戰國時代之局面，各自挖空心思，各顯風騷，到頭來各做各的，各玩各的，製造亂局。MARC 社區資訊格式，其設計活潑、有彈性，並採用 ISO 2709 及 ANSl 39.2 之標準，是很容易融入現有 MARC 之資料庫中。因此，作者特撰文介紹 MARC 21 社區資訊機讀格式，並建議圖書館與資訊界不妨嘗試研究運用此格式，以解決所有資料資源處理上之問題，俾使世界上各類型資源記錄之標準統一。

（收稿日期：2001 年 5 月 28 日）

（後記：此文是爲慶祝 盧荷生教授七秩榮慶論文集而撰。匆忙中難免有疏漏之處，尚祈不吝指正。）

註　釋

註1：< http://lcweb.loc.gov >（Apr. 26, 2001）.

註2：Mary Engle, "Using the Community Information Format to Access Nonbibliographic Information, LITA Online Catalog Internet Group Meeting, American Library Association Conference, San Francisco, June, 1992," Technical Services Report 10：4（1993），pp. 57–63.

註3：同上註。

註4：Phyblis Burns, "The US MARC Community Information Format：A History and Brief

Description," Information Technology and Libraries 11：4（Dec. 1992）, pp. 387 – 392.

註5：同上註, pp. 392 – 401.

註6：< http://lcweb. loc. gov/marc/community/eccilist. html >（Jan. 8, 2001）.

註7：同上註；"The MARC 21 Formats：Background and Principles," Nov. 1996, < http://www. lcweb. loc. gov/marc/96principl. html >（Apr. 26, 2001）.

註8：Deborah J. Byme, Marc Manual：Understanding and Using MARC Records, 2nd ed., （Englewood, Colo.：Libraries Unlimited, 1998）, pp. 233 – 235.

"MARC 21 Concise Community Information：Introduction；" < http://www. loc. gov/marc/community/ecciintr. html >（Apr. 26, 2001）.

註9：MARC 21 Format for Community Information：Including Guidelines for Content Designation, 2000 ed., prepared by Network Development and MARC Standards Office, Library of Congress in Cooperation with Standards and Support. National Library of Canada. Appendix B. pp. 1 – 4.

註10：同註8。Deborah J. Byrne, pp. 237 – 239.

劉蘇雅，"US MARC 社區信息格式──圖書館自動化信息服務的新發展"，中國圖書館學報, 24：113（1998年1月），頁35—40。

註11：同上註。

圖書館資訊素養之培養方針與評量指標*

[摘要 Abstract]

　　本研究以問卷與座談會方式調查臺閩地區圖書館資訊服務之現況和臺灣學者專家及圖書館從業人員對資訊素養的認知與期望，研擬圖書館推展資訊素養計劃之具體行動，以及推廣資訊素養落實於圖書館資訊服務之觀念，並同時探討目前各類型圖書館推展資訊服務可能面臨的問題及其需求。

　　根據研究結果發現，目前臺灣各類型圖書館已普遍施行圖書館推廣教育與服務，然受限於館藏與設備之不足，使得資訊素養教育推廣並不普遍。學者專家的意見認為圖書館館員各種資訊素養能力應在中等能力以上，然館員實際能力只有初級能力。針對此一現況，本研究分別就圖書館、學校教師及政府教育單位研擬資訊素養培育方針，與圖書館資訊素養評量指標初稿，作為培育民眾及專業圖書館館員資訊素養的藍圖。本研究針對政府、"教育部"、圖書館、學校教師及電腦資訊業界等，提出十項建議，以全面推展資訊素養活動，迎接21世紀資訊社會的來臨。

　　The purpose of the research is to study the present status of information services in Taiwan libraries and information literacy knowledge of professional libraries in order to establish "the Guidelines and Evaluation Indicators of Information Literacy Education in Library Information Services." Three Questionnaires were used to survey：1. information services activities in library programs nationwide, 2. librarians' knowledge of information literacy, and 3. peers review of recognized information literacy skills for librarians. In addition, four meetings were conducted in order to further understand problems and needs of libraries and librarians with relation to information literacy education.

　　Based on the research findings, a draft of library information literacy education guidelines and evaluation indicators was formulated and ten suggested recommendations were included. It is hoped that Taiwan government, Ministry of Education, libraries of all kinds, computer and information community, educators, and librarians will use the indicators to develop the national information literacy education program for preparing citizen of the country the basic skills and abilities of information literacy for embracing the challenge of 21st century.

關鍵詞 Keyword
資訊素養　圖書館資訊服務　資訊素養評量指標　資訊素養培育方針
Information literacy；Library information services：Information literacy indicator

壹、前　言

　　21世紀資訊社會中，資訊已成為現代人生活中之必需品，無論在生活、工作或實現

＊ 本文曾發表在《圖書與資訊學》37期（2001年5月），第1—26頁。

個人計劃均需具備資訊管理技巧與資訊利用知識，此即為資訊素養。資訊素養係培育公民瞭解資訊的價值，在需要資訊時能有效率地查詢資訊、評估資訊、組織資訊與利用資訊。

資訊對個人的功能有：(1) 具備對資訊價值判斷力、成為獨立的學習者；(2) 養成利用資訊的習慣，成為終身學習者；(3) 具備資訊組織能力，成為知識的創造者。對於工商業資訊可發揮下列功能：(1) 對資訊價值的重視，可提昇企業決策的品質；(2) 有效的利用資訊，可降低決策的風險，增加成功機會；(3) 檢索資訊能力越好，則投資的選擇性越多；(4) 對資訊的重視，將帶動整體企業員工對知識的重視，間接鼓勵員工不斷追求新知，增加工商業永續經營的動力。資訊對社會方面之功能：(1) 全民對資訊價值的重視，促進社會多元發展與言論自由；(2) 全民有效的利用資訊，可提昇民主的素養；(3) 全民對資訊有效的蒐集與評估，可以促使民意有效的表達；(4) 全民資訊素養是造就資訊化社會與維護民主制度之基石。

2000 年美國圖書館學會會長 Nancy Kranich 女士 "American Libraries" 文稿中論及，應該為未來 21 世紀建構 "資訊智者的社區"（Information-Smart Communities），此社區需要有能力的圖書館館員和好的圖書館作為保障所有公民在民主社會中皆能公平的生活條件，同時又需要圖書館提供豐富多元化資源協助商界、家庭、學校、政府與社區團體業務成功的發展。在今年極力推動的 Presidential Committees on Advocacy and Information Literacy 的要點中宣告：（註1）

1. 社會有豐富的資訊，圖書館館員則是資訊智者，館員更是最基本的搜尋引擎（Search engines）協助資訊需要者；

2. 館員是資訊時代最前導重要的技術見識者（Techno-savvy），努力建立資訊智者的社區；

3. 學校和大學圖書館中館員是教導學生資訊素養技能的關鍵人物，不但使學生能在學業上和職場上成功發展，更進一步的使其成為終生有用的資訊見識者（Information-savvy）。

圖書館資訊服務之新模式以培養終生學習、獨立自導式學習之公民為目標，進而建構以增加公民具備下列五種資訊素養之能力之計劃綱領：(1) 知道什麼是有用資訊之能力；(2) 知道何處可以獲得資訊之能力；(3) 檢索資訊之能力；(4) 闡釋、評估與組織資訊之能力；(5) 使用與傳播資訊之能力。此新模式即以培養公民五種資訊素養能力，與圖書館擔任教育者、資訊供應者、圖書館三者一體之角色為模式之軸心原則，而應用到各類型圖書館資訊服務，如學校圖書館，大專院校圖書館、公共圖書館、與專門圖書館等作為模式軸心結構。為能真正落實這些理念與實際推廣資訊素養的概念，本研究以問卷、座談會及學者專家建議，研擬臺灣資訊素養培育方針、內容綱要與資訊素養評量指標，以作為發展臺灣圖書館資訊素養的參考。

貳、資訊素養意義與內容

美國自 1970 年代即倡導 "資訊素養" 之觀念，許多學者專家認為資訊素養是人類各種基本 "知識素養"（Literacy）之重要部份，不僅是學術環境從事的人們之需要，並且包括各行各業，是現代社會生活的要件。Paul Zurkowski 是最早定義與提出 "資訊素養"的學者,在1974年美國國家圖書資訊科學委員會(United States National Commission on Libraries and Information Science,簡稱NCLIS)中,建議美國應建立全國資訊素養計劃以培養公民的資訊能力。(註2)資訊素養不僅是爲特定需求而檢索及評估資訊的能力,而且是一種讓人得以尋求、蒐集、檢索、辨識、分析、評估及供應資訊解決問題的思考過程,是一種終生的技能。

根據美國圖書館學會和臺灣學者專家李德竹,Jones、McHenry and Wu、Olsen、Cuban、Rader、McCrank、McClure、Spitzer和Breirik (註3) 對資訊素養定義內涵之闡釋總結,所謂"資訊素養是培育公民具備瞭解資訊的價值,在需要資訊時能有效率地查詢資訊、評估資訊、組織資訊與利用資訊,資訊素養內容包含傳統素養、圖書館素養、電腦素養、媒體素養,網路和技學素養。"而資訊存在社會各個角落,若要培育公民具備資訊素養,必須從有系統的資訊環境開始去認識資訊的價值與結構,這些有組織有系統的資訊環境包括圖書館、博物館、資訊中心、檔案機構、各類資訊服務站、民衆服務中心、社教與文化中心、電話查詢中心、電腦網路、全球資訊網與線上資料庫等。透過瞭解與利用這些資訊系統,將可培育公民對於資訊價值的覺知與使用的習慣,從而使資訊成爲生活不可缺少的一部份。

叁、資訊素養教育

美國艾森柏格(Michael Eisenberg)在資訊素養活動中影響最多,主張學校圖書館媒體資源中心在教學方面應提供圖書館與資訊技能課程(Library and Information Skills Curriculum),並從教學/訓練歷程方面,發展圖書館與資訊技能課程的架構:六大資訊技能(Big Six Skills)。首先,艾森怕格依據布隆(Benjamin Bloom)六級人類認知目標:知識、理解、應用、分析、綜合、與評估,發展出下列資訊問題解決歷程的六大資訊技能:(註4)

1. 問題界定(Task definition):決定資訊問題與界定資訊查詢的目的;
2. 資訊查詢策略(Information seeking strategies):針對前已界定的資訊問題,選擇最適當的資訊資源種類與策略;
3. 找尋與查詢資訊(Location of and access to information):找到資訊資源並且從中檢索特定的資訊;
4. 利用資訊(Use of information):依據前已界定的資訊需求以運用查得的相關資訊;
5. 綜合(Synthesis):整合、組織、與重新組裝各種資訊以滿足前述問題的需要;
6. 評估(Evaluation):以效率與效能評估資訊問題解決歷程是否滿足資訊的需求。

Eisenberg 和 Robert E. Berkowitz 於1999年又出版 *The New Improved BIG6 Workshop Handbook*(註5),希望協助老師\館員\科技教師\行政人員\父母\社區人員千口學生能做到:

1. 學習 Big6;
2. 在各項活動中利用 Big6;
3. 實施 Big6 資訊和技術技能計劃或項目在課堂、圖書館和實驗室;在各校、各地區、各州,甚至於可將 Big6 融入國家和國際先導計劃中。(註6)

這六大技能課程係以系統式的結構表現教學目標，六大技能的每一技能領域中，均再列舉次目標說明所需的重要技能與協助獲得的完整能力。六大技能課程係幫助學生成為有效的資訊問題解決者，目的是訓練學生在找尋、使用、組織、表現、與評估資訊過程中運用系統性策略與批判式思考以有效地解決問題。

　　1994年科羅拉多州教育媒體學會（Colorado Education Media Association）制定"資訊素養指南"（*Infornaation Literacy Guidelines*），主張具備資訊素養的學生才是有競爭力與獨立的學習者，此資訊素養指南係課程中學習資訊素養的歷程，並從學術環境擴展至真實的生活中。該指南涵蓋了五項資訊素養教育的領域，各領域並詳細訂定培育的具體行動，依次說明如後：（註7）

1. 培育學生成為知識尋求者
（1）確定資訊需求；
（2）發展資訊尋求策略與找尋資訊；
（3）徵集資訊；
（4）依需求分析已檢得的資訊；
（5）組織資訊；
（6）處理資訊；
（7）根據資訊而展開行動；
（8）評估歷程與成果。

2. 培育學生成為優良產品的創造者
（1）區別品質與工匠技術之不同；
（2）規劃品質良好的產品；
（3）創造優良的產品；
（4）展現優良的產品；
（5）評估優良的產品。

3. 培育學生成為自我導向的學習者
　　幫助學生發現有些生活需求是課堂作業難以涵蓋的，對這些學術環境以外的事物，應抱存懷疑的看法。
（1）自動訂定明確的資訊目標與管理自己進度；
（2）自動為娛樂需要而參考各種媒體資源，閱讀、傾聽與廣徵意見；
（3）發掘個人興趣的主題；
（4）確認與發展個人成就標準。

4. 培育學生成為團體的貢獻者
（1）協助團體確認其資訊需求；
（2）分擔團體計劃與成品的規劃與制作責任；
（3）合作判斷相關資訊；
（4）認識各種不同的概念；
（5）提供團體有用的資訊；
（6）在呈現團體的成品時可以清楚地溝通意見；
（7）不斷地評估產品、團體歷程與個別的角色。

5. 培育學生成為負責的資訊使用者
(1) 符合倫理行為地利用資訊與資訊科技；
(2) 尊重智慧財產自由的原則；
(3) 遵循指南與禮儀以使用電子資訊資源；
(4) 維護資訊資源與設備實體的完整；
(5) 認識合理利用資料與資源的重要。

鑑於美國勞工部必備技能促進委員會（Secretary's Commission on Achieving Necessary Skills，簡稱 SCANS）的報告書中將資訊素養列為五種個人基本工作能力之一，同時美國前總統柯林頓之美國全國技術政策中也定其為重要的高技能工作能力，監督與課程發展學會（Association of Supervision and Curriculum Development）呼籲資訊素養是個人能掌握全球資訊社會機會的重要關鍵，1995 年美國學校圖書館員學會（American Association of School Librarians）針對資訊素養提出一份資訊問題解決技能課程基本培育計劃"資訊素養：資訊問題解決宣言"（Information Literacy：A Position Paper on Information Problem Solving），主張資訊素養是培養學生成為終身學習者的重要基礎，也是應用資訊問題解決技能（Information problem solving skills）的同義詞。此資訊素養宣言確認資訊素養要件，並提供將資訊素養培育與幼稚園及中小學課程整合的理論。該學會在該文件中界定資訊問題解決技能為個人在學校、工作與生活中具有查詢與使用資訊之能力。資訊素養課程基本要件詳細如次：（註8）

1. 界定資訊需要

使學生認識資訊的存在、界定需求，以及懂得：(1) 認識資訊不同的使用（如職業的、智識的、娛樂的）；(2) 將需要的資訊置於一關聯架構（誰、什麼、何時、何處、為什麼）；(3) 將需要的資訊與從前知識相關連；(4) 用各種詢問技能建構資訊問題。

2. 擬定查詢策略

使學生規劃查詢策略，以及懂得：(1) 透過一連串問題以決定需要什麼資訊；(2) 腦力激盪產生概念，從各種關係確認各種概念組織方法；(3) 依主題選擇與使用有組織工具；(4) 列出關鍵字、概念、主題標目、敘述詞；(5) 解釋使用多種資訊資源的重要性；(6) 確認潛在資訊資源；(7) 確認評估資訊資源標準。

3. 找尋資源

使學生從各種資源找到特定的資訊，以及懂得：(1) 在學校資源中心利用目錄或其他書目工具找尋書本式、視聽與電腦式資源；(2) 透過線上資料庫、館際互借、電話、傳真科技找尋學校資源中心以外之資源；(3) 確認與使用社區資訊機構；(4) 透過訪談、調查與詢問信，而將人視作一種資訊資源；(5) 向教師—圖書館員與教師尋求資訊資源之協助；(6) 利用資訊資源內部組織工具與電子查詢策略查找特定資訊。

4. 評估與瞭解資訊

使學生找到有用資訊，知道檢視與決定有用之資訊，以及懂得：(1) 依重要概念與關鍵字來檢視以找出相關資訊；(2) 區別第一資源與第二資源；(3) 決定資訊之權威、新穎性與可靠性；(4) 區別事實、意見，宣傳、各種觀點與偏見；(5) 找出邏輯錯誤；(6) 找出遺漏的資訊；(7) 將資訊分類、分組、與加標籤；(8) 確認概念中之相關性；(9) 區別原因與結果；(10) 從資訊資源找出同意與反對之觀點；(11) 依據學生學習類型選擇資訊。

5. 解釋資訊

使學生在評估資訊後，必須利用資訊解決特定資訊問題，以及懂得：（1）依學生自己的詞彙摘要資訊，視需要將重要事實與詳細資訊重新解釋或引用；（2）綜合新收集之資訊；（3）以新方法組織與分析資訊；（4）將收集資訊與原來問題作比較，調整策略，而找到額外資訊或依需要再檢視所獲資訊；（5）依收集資訊提出結論，而由學生詮釋。

6. 傳播資訊

學生必須將資訊問題解決之結果組織，並傳播資訊與他人分享，以及懂得：（1）使用查詢資訊以確認重要結論或解決方式以與其他人分享；（2）傳播資訊給意圖知曉的閱聽人；（3）依讀者與目的選擇傳播的形式；（4）創造產品，如演講、研究報告、錄影帶與戲劇；（5）提供適當與合於著作權法的文獻。

7. 評估產品與程序

使學生評估最後成品是否解決資訊問題與採用的步驟是否適當與有效，以及懂得：（1）評量結論與計劃是否符合原來界定之資訊需求與作業要求；（2）考慮所研討的問題、查詢策略、資源或解釋是否應該擴充、修改或修正；（3）重新評估學生對資訊問題解決歷程之瞭解與確認是否需要更進一步瞭解、發展技能與實務。

"教育部"之資訊教育計劃始於 1989 年，當時重點是推展電腦輔助教學計劃。至 1993 年，"行政院"核准"改善各級學校資訊教學計劃"（執行期限 1993 年 7 月至 1997 年 6 月），才正式推出資訊教育多項計劃，其中資訊教育基礎建設計劃、國家資訊通信基本建設 NII 人才培育計劃、資訊課程、師資、設備、在職教師資訊培訓等。（註 9）1997 年"教育部"為配合"行政院"提昇競爭力政策，決定整合資訊教育相關計劃，而推出"資訊教育基礎計劃"，目標是為配合資訊時代的需求，建置完善的資訊教學環境，"教育部"整合原有資訊相關計劃——改善各級學校資訊教學計劃、電腦輔助教學軟體發展及推廣計劃、TANet 到中小學計劃，匯總為"資訊教育基礎建設計劃"（1997 年 7 月至 2007 年 6 月），除延續與拓展既有的資訊教育重點工作外，長期目標為建置一個全方位的資訊教學環境，普及全民資訊教育。計劃目標分為短期（1997 年 7 月至 2001 年 6 月）與長期（2001 年 7 月至 2007 年 6 月），計劃內容共七項：

1. 充實資訊教學資源；
2. 改善教學模式；
3. 加強人才培訓；
4. 推動調整組織制度；
5. 提昇設備；
6. 延伸臺灣學術網路；
7. 普及資訊素養。

此計劃之影響是希望（1）透過資訊教育基礎建設計劃，提昇全民資訊素養，建置資訊化校園環境，為臺灣推動資訊基礎建設 NII、亞太營運中心等計劃奠定基石。（2）在各國競相投入資訊教育相關建設以厚植國力之際，臺灣亦可並駕齊驅，不致在資訊化時代中成為落後地區。（註 10）

最近，"教育部"又委託"國家圖書館"推動資訊素養至國中方案，撥款 980 萬元，希望在 2000 年 12 月完成三項事情：（1）針對 18 個縣市國中小校長舉辦"資訊素養：圖書館利用與學校政策之研習班"，培訓校長的資訊素養和圖書館利用與學校政策間之關係及重要性；（2）再印製"國家圖書館"編印之《圖書館與資訊素養叢書》多套，以備推廣資訊素養時之需；（3）製作資訊素養宣導短片。（註 11）令人憂心的是，民眾常對資訊與電腦兩者之認知上混淆不清，此將造成推動資訊素養之觀念上阻礙，值得重視。

肆、中國臺灣圖書館資訊服務之現況

圖書館之資訊服務由於其類別之不同、服務對象不同，而在其資訊服務之推廣方面亦有其差異性。以下依據各類型之圖書館功能，以及圖書館推廣資訊服務之現況分別介紹如下：

一、"國家圖書館"資訊服務

"國家圖書館"是由"中央政府"所設立的圖書館，臺閩地區僅有一所"國立國家圖書館"。"國家圖書館"負責徵集與典藏全國圖書文獻、調查編製國家書目、辦理出版品國際交換，並研究全國圖書館事業發展等事宜，對讀者提供的資訊服務主要包括（1）典藏與閱覽服務；（2）參考資訊服務；（3）讀者服務推廣與輔導活動；（4）國家書目中心等主要服務項目。（註 12）目前"國家圖書館"總館館舍面積爲 42,155.40 平方公尺，閱覽席次約 2,000 多席，正式編制工作人員 96 人。依據《2000 年圖書館年鑑》的調查顯示 1999 年"國立國家圖書館"館藏資料數爲 1,741,720 冊。（註 13）

二、公共圖書館資訊服務

公共圖書館是由政府或私人機構所設立、支援或管理的圖書館。主要目的爲配合地方特性和需求，蒐集、整理、保存及利用圖書資料與地方文獻，並提供諮詢服務推展文化和社教活動，以社區或地區民眾爲主要服務對象。根據《圖書館事業發展白皮書》1997 年的統計資料顯示，臺閩地區共有 548 所公共圖書館（含分館與民眾閱覽室）。其類型包括各地省縣市立圖書館、文化中心圖書館、鄉鎮市圖書館與社教館附設之圖書館等。各級公共圖書館之館藏總數爲 15,633,308 冊（註 14），館員人數 1,905 人。（註 15）

根據 2001 年 1 月最新公佈之《圖書館法》第四條第二款規定，公共圖書館由各級中央主管機關、鄉（鎮、市）公所、個人、法人或團體設立，以社會大眾爲主要服務對象，提供圖書資訊服務，推廣社會教育及辦理文化活動。（註 16）1949 年《聯合國教育科學文化組織的公共圖書館宣言》（Unesco Public Library Manifesto）與 1986 年國際圖書館學會聯盟的《公共圖書館指南》（Guidelines for Public Libraries）中，對於公共圖書館的服務提出下列原則：（1）提供終身全方位的教育；（2）增進民眾對人類知識與文化成就的鑑賞；（3）公共圖書館應成爲記錄人類思想、智慧和表達人類創造性與想象力的主要場所；（4）藉由提供圖書與其他媒體所帶來的娛樂與休閒，振奮民眾的精神；（5）公共圖書館應該協助學生讀者和（6）公共圖書館應該提供最新的技術性、科學性與社會性資訊。（註 17）1994 年，聯合國教育科學文化組織又提出新的"公共圖書館宣言"，

該宣言將公共圖書館定位為兼具教育文化、資訊意涵的民主政治機構。（註18）

1977年美國圖書館學會的公共圖書館學會在參考各種標準之後，也制定了《公共圖書館任務宣言》（Mission Statement for Public Library）。宣言內容說明了公共圖書館服務的目標包括：（1）公共圖書館透過本身的館藏與網路聯接各地區、各州、各國家與世界的圖書館館藏，檢索過去人類事實性、想像性、科技性與人文等記錄；（2）組織人類的記錄，以致於可從多方向檢索到事實與記錄中的智慧；（3）蒐集、翻譯、與組織任何印刷與非印刷的各種智慧層次的人類知識；（4）除了選擇、蒐集，組織與保存人類記錄外，也使用可行的程序讓全民可以靠自己以獨特方式被告知；（5）以最簡易的檢索方式組織與表現人類記錄，提供給失學、缺乏語言設備、不同種族或文化背景、年齡、肢體或心智障礙者使用。（註19）1987年美國圖書館學會出版之《公共圖書館規劃與角色定位》（Planning and Role Setting for Public Libraries：A Manual of Options and Procedures）書中，列出公共圖書館的八項角色，強調公共圖書館為社區活動中心、社區資訊中心、正式教育支援中心、個人獨力學習中心、通俗資料中心、學齡前兒童學習中心、參考圖書館、研究中心等，充分凸顯公共圖書館以全民為服務對象之特質。（註20）

1996年，Charles R. McClure等學者自國家資訊基礎建設之觀點檢視公共圖書館應具備之角色，認為在資訊高速公路，公共圖書館應扮演之角色為網路素養中心、全球電子化資訊中心、政府資訊連絡站、電子化終身教育中心、公共資訊檢索中心（Public Access Center）、社區資訊中心、經濟發展中心等。（註21）

2000年，"中國圖書館學會"為配合社會發展之資訊需求，研擬《圖書館事業發展白皮書》。白皮書中針對公共圖書館資訊服務體系，擬定主要發展目標：（1）建立適用的館藏，辦理各種推廣活動，使成為民眾的社區大學、文化活動中心、個人學習與心靈加油站；（2）蒐集並保存各地方文化資源，俾傳承並發揚鄉土文化；（3）結合各地相關資訊，建立"文化與社教資訊網"，便於民眾利用網際網路節點；（4）主動服務年長、幼童與肢體障礙讀者，以達成資訊為全民共享的目標；（5）與當地其他類型圖書館建立合作關係以及（6）結合當地教育文化機構、團體，倡導地方讀書風氣推展終身教育活動。（註22）

總之，公共圖書館的服務應包括社會教育、保存人類文化記錄、提供人民所需各種資訊與發揮休閒娛樂的功能等。

三、大專院校圖書館資訊服務

大專圖書館是由大專院校所設立之圖書館，主要目的為支援教學、配合研究與推廣學術。以該校師生及研究人員為主要服務對象；在不妨礙其設立宗旨下，應提供民眾利用。大學圖書館依現行學制可以區分成大學、學院、專科、軍警學校及比叙專科等五種。根據《圖書館事業發展白皮書》1997年的統計的調查顯示，臺閩地區共有158所大學院校圖書館，圖書總冊數為36,392,587冊，其中包含圖書冊數25,291,675冊，非書及其他資料約11,100,912冊。圖書館利用統計方面，登記的讀者總人數為12,500,798人，平均每月進館人數為17,645.31人。1997年度開館日數為273.80日，圖書開架率為94.9%，圖書資料借閱總人次為5,081,952人次、13,590,462冊。（註23）

大專圖書館由於具備支援教學、配合研究與推廣學術的功能，因此教導讀者明瞭圖書館的服務、設施、組織、圖書館資源與查詢資料方法等活動便成為大專圖書館資訊服務的重點。大專圖書館的資訊服務方式，除一般的圖書借閱與館際合作服務外，主要的服務尚包括：（1）認識圖書館環境：以介紹圖書館的設備、館藏、服務項目、閱覽規則等；（2）圖書館利用教育：教導讀者如何使用圖書館目錄、分類系統、各種資料排架規則、參考工具書等圖書資源；（3）書目利用指導：教導讀者如何有效利用書目工具，包括書本式書目、摘要、索引、與電腦資料庫等。（註24）近年來由於電腦技術的進步，大專圖書館已紛紛採用自動化系統，以協助加強各項服務的進行。在臺灣地區各類型圖書館之中，大專圖書館自動化進展的成效最為顯著，尤其近年來臺灣地區學術網路的建立，更促進大專圖書館邁向無國界的資訊服務發展。

四、學校圖書館資訊服務

學校圖書館是由大專以下各級學校所設立之圖書館，其主要目標為支援教學研究與輔導學生利用圖書館。以該校師生為主要的服務對象；在不妨礙其設立宗旨下，可提供民眾利用。根據《圖書館事業發展白皮書》1997年的統計資料，臺閩地區共有高中高職圖書館440所、公民中學圖書館719所及公民小學圖書館2,540所。閱覽總席次為244,691席。館藏資料方面，館藏總數量為28,293,067冊。圖書館利用方面，登記的讀者總人數為4,409,304人，1997年度為圖書資料借閱總計13,735,584人次、22,451,707冊。（註25）

學校圖書館又常稱之為教育資料中心、學習中心（Learning Center）或媒體中心（Media Center）等。當代學校圖書館的經營已逐漸擺脫單一閱覽的功能，在結合視聽資料中心與圖書館雙重性質，不但蒐集適合教學的各種資料，並且配合製作教材。具體而言，當代的學校圖書館包括以下的服務功能：（1）蒐集教學及個人閱讀研究所需的圖書資料，以充實學生的知能；（2）指導學生為適應其個人興趣與課程需要選擇圖書資料；（3）提高學生利用圖書和圖書館的能力，並培養其自學習慣；（4）鼓勵學生利用圖書館資料，從事自我教育；（5）幫助學生利用圖書資料，增廣其多方面的興趣；（6）培養學生良好的公民道德習慣，並增長其社會經驗。（註26）

過去學校圖書館在各類圖書館發展最不受重視，一方面導因於昇學主義的影響，另方面在高中小學課程或圖書館設施上均不完備，導致學校圖書館在整個學校的體制與教學環境中，沒有受到應有的重視與發展。近年來政府教育單位也開始重視學校圖書館的重要性，針對高中、中小學圖書館也開始一系列的補助發展與指導。1988年"教育部"奉"行政院"核定實施為期五年的"發展與改進高級中學教育中程計劃"，計劃中將"發揮圖書館功能計劃"列為其中一項，並逐年編列預算以推展高中圖書館業務。至1993年度將動用新臺幣二億六千多萬元經費，用於改善館舍、充實圖書館設備、健全組織編製、提高圖書館專業素質、提昇服務品質，以逐步發揮高級中學圖書館教育的功能。在發揮圖書館功能方面有以下重點措施：（1）規定各校圖書館每週至少應開放五十小時，假日、寒暑假、課餘時間應充份開放；（2）圖書館工作人員配合開放時間，採彈性上班；（3）圖書館應採開架式閱覽，並成立新書展示處；（4）編印圖書館手冊或製作視聽媒體，介紹圖書館使用方法與經營理念；以及（5）成立"高中圖書館館際合作組織"交換圖書資料等。（註27）計劃推行之後確使高中圖書館的發展有了生機，然而因長期沒有受到重視，因此多數圖書館仍在充實館藏的階段，各項推廣服務受限於人員編制與時間，發展不一。

五、專門圖書館與資訊中心資訊服務

專門圖書館或資訊中心是由政府機構、工商企業或其他專業團體所設立、支援或管理的圖書館。此類圖書館可由隸屬機構支援或爲獨立之機構，其主要目的爲提供專門性的圖書資源與服務，以機構內的人員、特定羣衆或一般民衆為主要服務對象。這些機構包括政府機構、工商企業以及非營利組織中附設圖書館，也包括專以蒐集專門性資料的圖書館，如商業、法律與醫學圖書館等。根據1964年的美國"專門圖書館標準"（Objectives and Standards of Special Libraries, 1964）第四章服務的標準規定，專門圖書館的服務方式包括參考、書目的服務、圖書資料出納彈性政策，及其他對資料具有生產價值與利用的各種服務。服務目標包括：（1）專門圖書館員應及時將讀者所需資料指出或說明其所在；（2）參考服務工作包括文獻資料之查索，書目之編製以及摘要索引工作；（3）除了參考資料及其他特殊規定之資料外，專門圖書館應準借出其資料；（4）專門圖書館應儘速提供翻譯服務；（5）讀者所需要的資料在本館中無法供應時，應設法向其他圖書館、機構或透過館際合作借用；（6）當期期刊雜誌之充份利用，亦爲整個專門圖書館服務措施中一個不可缺少的部份；（7）諮詢活動亦爲專門圖書館館員之職責；（8）專門圖書館應讓讀者瞭解館藏及網路資源。（註28）

根據（2000年圖書館年鑑）1999年的統計資料顯示，臺閩地區共有專門圖書館573所。依所隸屬的機關區分爲機關議會、研究機關、公營事業、民營事業、軍事單位、大衆傳播、醫院、民衆團體、宗教團體及其他等。閱覽總席次爲12,328席。館藏資料方面，館藏總冊數爲8,103,114冊，其中包含圖書6,024,041冊，非書及其他類型資料總件數爲2,079,073件。（註29）圖書館利用方面，登記的讀者總人數爲1,013,466人，平均每月進館人數爲1,004.97人。86年度開館日數爲276.14日，圖書開架率爲92.30%，圖書資料借閱總計708,711人次、1,632,038冊。（註30）由於專門圖書館主要功能是對隸屬機構提供服務，因此規模較小，蒐集較精，有固定的讀者與特殊的服務方式。根據許令華於1988年對臺灣155個專門圖書館對母機構關係研究中，服務項目的參考服務內容以人工查尋服務最高（95.2%），其次爲館際互借（91.3%），新知通告服務（82.7%），事實與研究性資料查尋（76.0%）。（註31）根據范豪英教授在1988年對於醫學圖書館現況調查的研究結果，有46.88%的醫學圖書館提供期刊目次通報服務。此外提供線上檢索與光碟資料庫檢索服務的醫學圖書館也有增加的趨勢（註32），顯見提供資訊是專門圖書館服務最大而又重要的特色。

面臨21世紀資訊社會新時代，圖書館資訊服務除一般基本功能外，將朝下列方向發展：（1）從以資訊爲中心轉變成以知識爲中心；（2）從存取資訊轉變爲選擇最相關的資訊；（3）從集中式資訊系統轉成分送式資訊系統；（4）從國家資訊網轉成全球資訊網路；（5）圖書館從保存資料的庫房變成重視資料內容的利用；（6）資訊科技之應用由輔助圖書館業務變成圖書館讀者利用的工具；（7）從個別技術之利用轉變成圖書館科技整合與資訊利用。（註33）

伍、資訊素養的評量

評量（Assessment）常被認為是標準化的測驗，如多選題或填充題式的測驗。早期的智力標準測驗是為了診治智力障礙者，而由松岱克（Thorndyke）與特爾曼（Terman）發展，及至20世紀初期，美國各地已普遍應用智力測驗於天才學生、學業資優、與低成就者的評量上。隨著教育的演變與資訊社會的形成，批判式思考/問題解決技能與資訊素養能力等資訊處理能力成為教育學習的新課題。針對這些新能力，舊有的評量方式無效，於是發展新的評量表，如：作業編組（Performance tasks），組套程序（Portfolio processes）與發展評量（Development Assessment）等。（註34）

從將學習視為一種歷程來看，評量應界定為依據目標的作業標準，可分析工作的特質，而運用各種標準評量從事評鑑。美國加州在標準參考技能評量之研究成果傑出，尤其是加州評量教學機構（California Assessment Program），以"學生學習所得即其測驗結果"的理念，主張教育者應遵循教學成績以評量的成果為準的原則，這些能力可成功應用於實際生活中，而經由各種複雜工作之執行獲得較高思考技能，評量將使學生保持高度興趣而使其更有成就。該機構也是課程架構發展之發啓者，強調課程必須將文獻基礎、文化模式、與價值觀念整合於課程領域中，評量之核心在學習的品質係取決於各項評量標準。（註35）

道爾（Christina S. Doyle）基於現代教育評量的理念，根據美國1990年全國教育目標（National Goals of 1990）發展資訊素養評量成就評量模式（Model of Information Literacy Outcome Measures）。採用德慧研究方法（Delphi Method），先界定資訊素養為具備從事各種資訊來源查詢、評估、與利用資訊之能力；而具備資訊素養的人應具有下列特質：（註36）

1. 瞭解資訊需求；
2. 瞭解正確與完整資訊是一個智慧決策的基礎；
3. 根據資訊需求以建構問題；
4. 確認潛在資訊來源；
5. 懂得發展成功之查詢策略；
6. 具備查詢各種資訊資源的能力，除了傳統形式的資訊資源，還包括電腦式系統與其他資訊科技形式的資源；
7. 具備評估資訊的能力；
8. 懂得組織資訊以實際運用；
9. 整合新資訊於現有的知識系統；
10. 以批判式思考與問題解決方式利用資訊。

1989年美國布希總統在全國州長會議（National Governors' Conference）上宣布美國"1990年教育目標"（National Education Goals of 1990），共有六項總體目標，其目的在個人方面，提昇每位學生的學習成就至更高的階段；在團體方面，使建立美國成為世界最具競爭性的強大國家。道爾以此六項教育目標詢問學者專家哪些目標與資訊素養的培育相關，結果大家認為目標一、三、五與資訊素養較相關。道爾並針對每一目標進一步分析學者專家的共同概念，並主張可根據這些共識發展資訊素養教育的評量模式，以下將與資訊素養相關的三項教育目標，以及學者專家的共同概念縱析如次：

教育目標一　公元 2000 年時，所有美國人均作好兒童入學準備。

學者專家對此目標的共識：

（1）父母是兒童的第一位教師，提供資訊對決策價值最重要的角色模式。此外，父母也是閱讀與利用資訊之最佳模範。

（2）兒童在開始入學時，應具備資訊有價值的觀念，以及主動/熱心的處事態度。

（3）父母必須在子女入學之前承擔起第一位教師的責任，以協助建立其資訊價值觀念。

教育目標三　公元 2000 年時，美國每一位四年級、八年級與十二年級的學生將具備英語、數學、科學、歷史與地理各學科的知識。而每個學校也將保證其學生善於運用智慧以成為負責之公民，具備終生學習能力，以及在現代經濟社會中成為高生產力的員工。

學者專家對此目標的共識：

（1）學生瞭解正確而完整的資訊是最佳決策的基礎；

（2）教師利用各種教學策略以培養學生成為主動的學習者；

（3）學生不斷地在學校與個人生活中運用問題解決技能；

（4）學生知道如何學習；

（5）學生將不斷運用批判性思考技能於學校與個人生活中；

（6）教師將運用資源基礎學習方式（Resource Based Learning）於課堂上；

（7）學生能夠運用充份的資訊作決策；

（8）教師將在團體與個人教學中提供充份的學習機會；

（9）圖書館媒體專家將與學校的教學計劃整合一體，與課堂教師共同工作以實踐其課程目標；

（10）學生將展現其資訊素養能力，以成為自我主動與獨立學習者；

（11）學生將自動建構假設命題，並且具有研究技能找尋答案；

（12）學生可從不同的觀點觀察與瞭解事物；

（13）課程目標之訂定涵蓋資訊素養的歷程，並將資訊素養基本原則納入各主題範圍；

（14）父母支持並參與學生之學習，使其更為完整；

（15）學生具備各年級應達到的閱讀能力。

教育目標五　公元 2000 年時，每位美國人將具備資訊素養與現代世界經濟的知識與技能，並且懂得運用其權利以成為負責之公民。

學者專家對此目標的共識：

（1）大專院校均應意識大學畢業生必須具備資訊素養技能之重要；

（2）所有美國人將能夠獲得尋找資訊以解決問題與具有作智慧決策之能力；

（3）社區推行終生學習的活動；

（4）所有的印刷與非印刷資源將提供全部美國人藉由公共圖書館、全國線上資訊網以及與商業及公共機構以低成本將資源分享給大眾；

（5）工商業界將致力於資訊素養技能的培育，保證員工的工作技能得以不斷的更新以配合經濟人力市場的需要，同時工商業界必須參與社會各種訓練計劃。

1991年美國康乃爾大學緬因圖書館（Cornell University Ithaca, NY. Albert R. Mann Library）從事一項兩年的研究計劃以評量該圖書館的資訊素養教學，調查凡接受過該校圖書館利用課程的畢業生以決定其畢業就業時最有用的技能。此外，還調查雇用該校畢業生的工商企業界，以決定初入社會的工作者需要的資訊技能。該研究根據調查結果設計未來的圖書館資訊素養教學課程的內涵與評量，並規劃資訊素養教學課程的目標，應培育學生具有下列重要的資訊素養的能力：（1）瞭解資訊在民主社會的角色與力量；（2）瞭解資訊各種內涵與形式；（3）瞭解資訊組織的標準系統；（4）發展從各類系統與各種形式資訊來源檢索資訊的能力；（5）發展各類查詢與檢索的資訊組織與利用能力。（註37）

鑑於未能提供適當的教學，美國中小學系統最近幾年從事於教育改造運動，其中以著重於學習者的"教學成就基礎式教育"（Outcome-Based Education，簡稱OBE）成為領導主流。其理念是基於所有學生均能學習，提供學生掌握學習的機會以及教師掌握學生教學成就。葛洛佛（Robert Gover）以"教學成就基礎式教育"發展資訊技能教學模式，包括資訊技能與評量技術兩部份，資訊技能係參考艾森柏格（Michael Eisenberg）的資訊六大技能，評量技術包括八種方式，其模式詳如下表：（註38）

表一：艾森柏格（Michael Eisenberg）的資訊技術及評量技術方式表

資　訊　技　能	評　量　技　術
1. 問題界定 　　1.1 定義問題 　　1.2 依據問題確認資訊 2. 資訊查詢策略 　　2.1 決定可能的資訊來源範圍 　　2.2 評估不同的資訊來源以決定優先順序 3. 找尋與查詢資訊 　　3.1 找尋資訊資源 　　3.2 在資訊資源中找尋資訊 4. 利用資訊 　　4.1 使用資訊（如：讀、聽、看） 　　4.2 從資訊資源摘錄資訊 5. 綜合 　　5.1 從各種資訊資源組織資訊	1. 觀察 　　觀察學生的行為與記錄筆記。 2. 訪談 　　與學生訪談以決定其資訊技能，並作筆記。 3. 日誌 　　要求學生解決資訊問題，擇要其想法與解決過程。 4. 計劃 　　要求學生運用資訊技能完成計劃。 5. 紙與筆的測驗 　　5.1 採用參照標準 　　5.2 採用模範標準 6. 自我評鑑 　　學生個別的記錄日誌，自我評估其成果，並採用6大資訊技能架構。

（續上表）

資　訊　技　能	評　量　技　術
5.2 展現資訊 6. 評估 　6.1 評估產品（的效率） 　6.2 評估資訊問題解決程序（的效能）	7. 同學評鑑 　　同學以2～5人一組相互以6大資訊技能的步驟評量其成果。 8. 學習檔案（Portfolio） 　　學生與圖書館媒體專家規劃與收集其資訊技術活動與評量的資料檔。

　　美國"中部區域的高等教育組織"（Commission on Higher Education, Middle States Association of College and Schools）聯合全國資訊素養論壇（National Forum on Information Literacy）以及大學院校與研究圖書館學會（Association of College and Research Libraries）於1995年舉行資訊素養研討會，會中皆認為各單位應致力於提昇資訊素養的活動，以及資訊素養將有助於終身教育的推行。此外，學校課程應重新改組，將資訊素養技能融入整合於課程中，列為核心課程，並在各教學組織的理論、任務與目標説明列入資訊素養的理念。在發展完成資訊素養的目標宣言之後，各教學機構必須建立特定的學習成果、確認學生應持續獲得的複雜技能以及如何在課程大綱中評量學生的學習成果。該研討會建議評量的學習成果可分為兩類：蒐集資訊與利用資訊，此兩類的學習成果為：（註39）
1. 蒐集資訊的學習成果
（1）提出正確的問題；
（2）檢查資訊來源的品質；
（3）學習如何找到權威的資訊來源；
（4）評估蒐集到的資訊；
（5）利用科技獲得便利。
2. 利用資訊的學習成果
（1）過濾大量的資訊；
（2）學習選擇與綜合資訊；
（3）批判式思考資訊的內涵；
（4）學習展現資訊；
（5）認識倫理問題。

　　1995年，美國米勒斯佛大學（Millersville University）開授了一門研究所課程，名為"資訊素養：創造主動的學習者"（Information Literacy: Creating Active Learners），特別針對小學與中學的教師與圖書館員，主張資訊素養非僅著重於課程的內涵而已，並重視結構基礎，如主動式、以學生為導向學習並輔以組套式作業以培養學生查找、分析、解釋與運用資訊的技能。該課程的教學法與評量法皆反映了近代的改良教育，並且小組教學也提供教師與圖書館員合作的良好模式。（註40）

陸、資訊素養研究設計與調查結果分析

　　本研究係利用問卷調查和座談會以瞭解臺灣各圖書館資訊服務之現況，以及圖書館

員與學者專家對於資訊素養的認知與期望。調查對象涵蓋各類型圖書館（"國家圖書館"、公共圖書館，國小圖書館、國中圖書館、高中職圖書館、大學院校圖書館與專門圖書館），圖書館員以及學者專家。

一、調查問卷

（一）研究對象

本研究以臺灣地區五大類圖書館的圖書館從業人員為主要調查對象。因此在問卷調查部份，問卷調查樣本的取得，乃根據"中國圖書館學會"會員名錄中（註41）各類型圖書館會員名單為調查的母體。本研究根據名單清冊349名中隨機抽樣出調查樣本147名。此外，為能瞭解學界對此一研究主題的看法，針對臺灣大學、政治大學、輔仁大學、淡江大學、臺灣師範大學及世界新聞傳播學院等六校的圖書資訊學相關系所的46位教授，施行問卷調查。

（二）問卷回溯情況

除"國家圖書館"1館之外，公共圖書館共發出111份問卷，回收64份有效問卷，問卷回收率57.66%。大專院校圖書館共發出49份問卷，回收37份有效問卷，問卷回收率75.51%。高中職圖書館共發出96份問卷，回收74份有效問卷，問卷回收率77.08%。國中圖書館共發出178份問卷，回收122份有效問卷，問卷回收率68.54%。國小圖書館共發出577份問卷，回收371份有效問卷，問卷回收率64.30%。專門圖書館共發出113份問卷，回收62份有效問卷，問卷回收率55.75%，各類型圖書館共發出問卷1,125份，共收回731份，有效問卷667份，回收率59.5%，所回收問卷利用SPSS套裝軟體統計分析。

（三）背景資料分析

背景資料含所屬分館，涵蓋圖書館藏、期刊館藏、視聽資料館藏、專職工作人數、服務讀者人數、參考館員人數、專職圖書館利用教育人數等七項。

二、座談會討論

本研究進行問卷調查後，根據問卷調查結果研擬十項議題，在臺灣北、中、南三地分別舉辦座談會邀請學者專家、圖書館從業同仁及研究所研究生進行面對面討論，以期更深入瞭解臺灣圖書館界對於資訊素養之意見，以彌補問卷調查之不足。

三、綜合討論

本文將綜合文獻分析、各項統計結果及座談會，針對臺灣圖書館資訊素養的培育與評量標準分別討論如下。

（一）圖書館資訊服務現況與困難

本研究為瞭解臺灣圖書館資訊服務之現況與問題，針對4,386所圖書館以問卷抽樣調查1,125所圖書館，共回收有效問卷667份，回收率59.5%。根據回收問卷統計分析結果如下：

1. 圖書館資源方面

整體而言，目前圖書館在圖書、期刊、視聽資料等館藏資源明顯不足。藏書十萬冊以下者，在公共圖書館高達73.6%，大專院校圖書館亦佔48.6%，高中圖書館亦佔

84.0%。國中圖書館藏書一萬冊以下者佔59.0%，小學圖書館則佔68.5%，專門圖書館53.2%。顯示目前圖書館的圖書資源有待大力充實，期刊視聽資料亦如此。

　2. 圖書館專職人員

　　臺灣各級圖書館專職人員數目相對也是偏低。公共圖書館專職人員2～4人佔51.6%，高中圖書館2～4人則有58.1%，國中小學圖書館及專門圖書館半數以上，均是一人圖書館。相較之下，以大專院校圖書館的人力較多，專職人員19人以下者佔64.8%。從事圖書館利用教育或參考服務的專職人員，以大專院校圖書館較為充裕。目前由於中小學圖書館專職人員人數不足，多數無法兼顧圖書館推廣教育的服務。

　3. 圖書館資訊服務現況

　　根據統計分析，目前圖書館流通服務項目，以借還書為圖書館最重要的服務項目，其他如館際互借與複印等，多數集中在大專院校圖書館或專門圖書館。而圖書館參考服務項目中，參考櫃臺諮詢服務為最重要的服務項目。目前大專院校圖書館及高中圖書館多已完成自動化作業，大專院校圖書館有91.9%、高中圖書館有60.8%提供線上公共目錄查詢服務。其他如提供光碟檢索、線上資料庫檢索、期刊目次服務、www首頁、Internet網路資源查詢等仍以大專院校圖書館為主。在參考服務的深度方面，仍以一般性問題回答居多。較為深入的參考服務，如協助讀者界定問題、研擬查詢策略、查詢電子資料庫、協助取得館內外資料等，皆以大專院校圖書館提供服務較多。至於專精的參考服務，如協助讀者組織分析資訊、評估資訊、協助報告的撰寫、建立讀者興趣檔等，其服務比率均偏低。各類型圖書館中，以大專院校提供專精的參考服務較高。圖書館推廣活動方面，大專院校圖書館多數以舉辦書展、演講為主，公共圖書館則以讀書會、舉辦演講及研習班等活動為中心，國中小學圖書館推廣活動較少，小學圖書館以講故事活動居多。

　4. 圖書館利用教育施行與內容

　　目前在圖書館利用教育實行方式中，各類型圖書館均以舉辦參觀圖書館頻率最高，其次是印發圖書館手冊資料。大專院校圖書館較其他類型圖書館在利用教育活動施行種類為多，較經常舉行的活動有利用網路傳播圖書館訊息資源、舉辦資訊檢索、網路資源利用研習班、個別指導利用圖書館、圖書館週演講展覽等。高中職圖書館在舉辦新進教師參觀圖書館及圖書館週活動較為頻繁。從圖書館利用教育內容分析顯示，目前各種圖書館利用教育內容以介紹圖書館使用規則為主，其次是參考工具書使用。圖書館公用目錄的利用與期刊電子文件介紹，則以大專院校及高中圖書館最常舉辦。資訊檢索、利用查詢及光碟線上資料庫或網路資源等課程，則以大專院校圖書館最常提供。

　5. 圖書館資訊服務系統與設備

　　圖書館服務系統與設備，因各類型圖書館服務方式不同所具設備有所差異。調查顯示，"國家圖書館"及半數以上的大專院校圖書館、高中圖書館，均有圖書館自動化系統。錄音機、錄放影機等視聽器材，在各類型圖書館多數已具備。光碟機、投影機與連接上網路等設備，又以大專院校圖書館最為齊全。

　6. 圖書館資訊服務的困難

　　目前圖書館資訊服務所遭遇的問題，在人力資源方面普遍缺乏，即使在專業人員較多的大專院校圖書館亦有此問題，其次則是圖書館館員電腦與通訊專業技能的欠缺。而高中職、中小學圖書館在人力資源問題上，除專業人員不足外，更欠缺在職進修管道。在館藏資源方面，多數圖書館均有館藏、視聽資料及電子媒體資源不足的問題。自動化、電腦及通訊設備方面，以高中職、中小學圖書館最為缺乏，同時大專院校圖書館有空間不足的問題。圖書館利用教育問題方面，國中小學圖書館最大障礙在於缺乏圖書館利用教育的知識與技能。而值得慶幸的是，上級主管或母機構不重視圖書館的問題在各類型圖書館的比例並不高，顯示多數母機構或主管相當支持圖書館，只因受限於環境、經費與人員等問題，而無法有效大力興革。圖書館最需解決問題中，各類型圖書館迫切希望解決人力資源的問題，其次高中職、中小學及專門圖書館亦希望儘速解決自動化系統及網路設備的問題。相對之下，館藏資源及利用教育雖然亦有待解決，但未如前二者來的迫切，只要具備充份的人力與設備，要建立館藏或推行利用教育將不是問題。

(二) 學者專家與圖書館從業人員對於資訊素養之認知與期望

1. 學者專家對於資訊素養認知與期望

圖書館學界學者專家的問卷調查，乃根據中華圖書資訊學教育學會會員名錄中，抽出 46 位專家學者予以調查。發出 46 份調查問卷，回收 34 份有效問卷，回收率 73.9%。教授有 14 位（佔 41.2%）；副教授 14 位（佔 41.2%）；講師 6 位（佔 17.6%）。85.3%的學者專家均認同資訊素養是指"具備瞭解資訊價值、查詢資訊、獲取資訊、利用資訊、組織整理資訊，與評估資訊的能力"的定義。90%以上的學者專家同意學校在培育公民資訊素養，應該"充實圖書館館藏"，"開設網路教學課程，包括如何上網、使用 E-mail，BBS，Internet 等"，"開設網路資源應用課程"，"加強圖書館利用教育"、"教導學生如何利用各種工具書"、"教導學生如何整理資料"、"教導學生如何操作各種資訊檢索工具"、"教導學生如何評估各種資訊"、"教導學生如何寫作報告"、"教導學生資訊倫理及網路禮節的概念"等。其中 82.4%的學者專家同意應"廣設電腦教室"，87.9%的學者專家同意"多開設電腦相關課程"，只有 67.7%的學者專家同意"多開設外語課程"。

91.0%以上的學者專家認同老師於培養公民具備資訊素養的措施中，是"老師應於課程中充份利用圖書館"、其次是"老師應將圖書館視為教室的延伸"，再次為"老師教導學生如何查檢使用圖書館的藏書"、"老師的教學應該充份結合學校社區中各種資訊資源"，"老師應該多介紹各式各樣的資訊媒體"、"老師教導學生如何使用網路資源與相關軟體"、"老師應該教導學生如何使用電腦軟體"等。79.4%的學者專家同意"老師應該多由百科全書中指定家庭作業"，與其他項目比較同意度較低。

90%以上的學者專家同意社會教育在培養公民具備資訊素養措施中，是"圖書館應該充份配合任課老師需要，提供所需的各種資訊資源與服務"，其次是"公民資訊素養建立與否將影響到未來臺灣競爭力的提昇與生活素質"，再次為"學校圖書館應該加強相關設備與服務"、"是終身教育課程設計的重要理念"、"終身學習有賴於公民資訊素養能力的養成"、"圖書館館員應負起資訊素養教育工作並提供相關服務"、"圖書館應針對民眾廣泛舉辦各種如何利用資訊的研習會"。有 87.9%的學者專家認同資訊素養"是全民教育的重要指標；85.3%的學者專家同意"應該廣設資訊服務中心、圖書館、博物館、社區學院、婦女學院、老人學院或公民學院等"；79.4%的學者專家同意"各類型圖書館應該通力支援成人教育資源中心的推廣與服務"；75.8%的學者專家同意"公共圖書館應廣設成人教育資源中心"；74.4%的學者專家同意"父母應該參與再教育"；僅有73.6%的學者專家則同意資訊素養教育"應該從幼教開始進行"。

2. 圖書館專業人員對於資訊素養認知與期望

為瞭解圖書館專業人員對於資訊素養的看法與期望，本研究從"中國圖書館學會"會員名錄中，抽出201位館員予以調查，有效回收問卷128份，回收率為63.7%。根據統計多數圖書館館員同意資訊素養的定義，並認同資訊素養的範圍包括使用圖書館的能力找尋與收集資訊資源的能力、瞭解資訊需求能力分析判斷資訊能力、使用電腦能力、使用網路能力、研擬資訊查詢策略能力、組織與綜合資訊能力、使用媒體能力及展現評估資訊能力等。

（1）圖書館從事資訊素養培育時，圖書館館員期望在繼續教育方面

96.1%的館員希望能加強圖書館與資訊服務的繼續教育；95.3%的館員則期望加強電子資源與網路利用教育；94.5%的圖書館館員則希望加強電腦技能教育；93.0%的圖書館館員期望能加強網路技能教育，顯示圖書館館員有非常強烈的學習動機。

（2）圖書館館員對於改善圖書館利用教育方面

96.1%的館員同意應積極推廣圖書館利用教育活動；94.5%的圖書館館員同意從資訊素養理念設計圖書館利用教育活動；93.8%的圖書館館員同意學校單位應加強與圖書館合作，以建立資源式的學習教學模式；93.7%的館員同意圖書館應利用網路科技提供圖書館利用教育；93.0%圖書館館員同意開設圖書館與資訊資源利用課程或研習訓練；90.7%館員同意圖書館應依據使用者需求設計圖書館利用教育活動；89.9%的圖書館館員同意對遠端使用者提供圖書館利用教育。整體而言，圖書館館員非常支持圖書館利用教育活動的推展。

（3）針對改善圖書館設備與環境方面

95.3%的圖書館館員認同應該加強圖書館網路設備；94.6%的館員認為應該加強電腦設備與光碟資料庫等資訊系統；94.5%圖書館館員認為應加強圖書館自動化設備；92.2%的館員同意加強圖書館館際合作與電子文件傳遞服務；90.7%的圖書館館員同意應推展圖書館行銷活動與公共關係；86.7%的館員認為應加強視聽設備。面對目前電子圖書館發展的趨勢，館員更認為應加強圖書館的設備，其中又以網路及電腦設備的充實最為殷切。

（4）館員對圖書館館員資訊素養程度自評方面

根據統計分析60.9%的圖書館館員認為館員資訊素養能力僅達到基本能力，30.5%的館員認為達到中級能力。顯示圖書館館員的資訊素養能力應再充實與提昇，以從事圖書館資訊素養服務。

（三）圖書館資訊素養培育方針與內容

綜合以上的資料分析結果，圖書館資訊素養培育方針與內容如下：

1. 圖書館方面：

圖書館從提供資訊服務而言，對資訊素養培育應有下列措施：

（1）各類型圖書館應持續推動圖書館推廣與利用教育活動。

（2）加強圖書館各種資源的充實，包括館藏資料、電腦網路基本配備、資料庫與網路資源等。

（3）圖書館從資訊素養的觀點，提供教學性的服務。以解決資訊問題的觀點，教導學生如何利用各類工具書、檢索光碟網路資料、評估與整理資料及撰寫報告等。圖書館可由舉辦演講、訓練課程，開授有學分的課程，或以個別指導方式進行。

（4）圖書館應與學校或社教機構合作舉辦資訊素養推廣教育課程或訓練，充份發揮圖書館社會教育功能，針對一般民衆定期舉辦資訊素養的教育訓練。包括各種不同年齡層的讀書會、電腦網路教學課程、語言訓練課程、利用資訊研習營等。

（5）針對資訊素養教育的推動，圖書館應適時成立"終身學習資源中心"與設立工作推動小組。有計劃蒐集成人繼續教育之相關資料及研究計劃，並推動相關活動或服務的進行。

2. 學校教師方面：

學校教師是培育公民資訊素養第一線的人員，其教學方法與教學內容直接影響到學生資訊素養的養成，針對老師從事資訊素養的培育有以下措施：

（1）學校教師於課程教學中，應充份利用圖書館資訊資源，以充實教學內容的廣度與深度。

（2）圖書館是教室的延伸，教師應與圖書館專業人員合作，訓練教導學生使用基本工具書（例如百科全書、字典、名錄等），熟悉資訊的檢索、組織，評估與利用過程，以完成家庭作業或寫作報告。

（3）教師也應鼓勵與教導學生使用電腦與網路相關軟體，以檢索網路資源及使用網路相關功能。

（4）教師教學中善用各種資訊媒體，如視聽媒體、電腦多媒體、光碟資料庫等，輔助教學工作的進行，培育學生認識各類資訊媒體的性質、資訊展現方式與操作方法。

（5）教師的教學應充份結合社區的各種資訊資源，包括臨近的公共圖書館、文化中心、博物館、政府資訊服務中心等，以擴展學生對資訊來源的認知。

3. 政府教育政策方面：

政府的教育政策影響到公民素質提昇，並間接影響國家整體的發展。因此政府教育政策的擬訂相當重要。從問卷統計顯示，學者專家非常同意公民資訊素養能力，將影響到國家競爭力與生活素質的提昇，因此資訊素養將是邁向21世紀資訊社會，公民應該具備的基本能力之一。根據"教育部"的教育白皮書《邁向二十一世紀的教育遠景》與學者專家意見匯整，政府資訊素養具體的教育政策如下：

（1）公民教育方面："推展資訊及科學教育，因應現代科技社會需求"。計劃在國中將電腦課程列爲必修，小學列爲選修，並逐年編列預算設立電腦教室。

（2）大學教育方面："配合'國家'建設需要，加強重點科技人才培育"。針對資訊基礎建設計劃人才的需要，"教育部"將協助學校改進教學環境，規劃校園網路以培育所需人才及發展遠距教學、遠距圖書服務及遠距醫療等。

（3）社會教育方面："規劃生涯學習體系，建立終身學習社會"。將終身教育制度化，研擬成人教育法、博物館法、圖書館法、公民體育法及"國立空中大學"設置等，並廣泛設立民衆學院、老人學院及社區學院等，以增加民衆參與成人教育的機會，同時"推動建立社會教育網路及輔導體系計劃，落實基層社會教育活動"，規劃鄉鎮圖書館成爲當地社會教育中心，加強資訊網路功能輔助學習，以於社區中落實終身學習的理想。

(4) 教育支援系統方面："加強各級學校資訊教育，普及全民資訊素養"；"教育部"將充實各級學校資訊相關軟硬設備，及要求學生畢業前應修滿一定時數的電腦課程，使之具備資訊素養，能活用資訊工具及具備資訊倫理的概念。

(四) 圖書館資訊素養評量指標初稿

為具體落實從圖書館資訊服務建立圖書館資訊素養的培育，本研究針對資訊素養各種能力，研擬學習及能力指標。本指標的建立乃匯集學者專家及圖書館專業人員的意見，經由統計結果整理所得。有關公民資訊素養能力指標，依據本研究分成三大類，即基本能力、中級能力及高級能力等三種。所謂基本能力是指該能力足以處理大部份工作，中級能力指具備純熟與精練的工作技巧，高級能力則是具備專業與權威的技術。由於"素養"一詞具有基礎的意思，因此每項能力指標都指公民應具備能力的最低標準。

近年來，由於各界正在積極推動終身學習觀念，其中並包含資訊素養，因此對資訊素養之意義、內涵及其重要性已有初步之認識。為求本指標之正確性、新穎性，於今 (2001) 年元月再發問卷 115 封，針對參與"中國圖書館學會"主辦之"知識管理—方法與系統研討會"與會之代表，選擇具代表性之學者專家、館員發出問卷，請其對 1997 年所訂定之資訊素養指標初稿之內容表示意見，回收有效問卷 85 份，回收率 73.9%。經整理後發現學者專家、館員對 1997 年之資訊素養能力指標有明顯的差異性，還證實圖書資訊界對公民資訊素養之認知觀念及資訊素養能力亦顯著地提昇。以下為 1997 年和 2001 年公民和圖書館員應具備之資訊素養能力指標之比較表：

表二：學者專家和圖書館員對公民資訊素養程度能力指標比較表

項目比較	1997 年 (n=34)		2001 年 (n=85)	
	問卷總數	能力等級	問卷總數	能力等級
1. 熟知獲取資訊管道的能力	33	中級	84	中級
2. 實際問題組織資訊的能力	34	中級	85	中級
3. 資訊準確性與完整性的判斷能力	34	中級	85	中級
4. 資訊運用於決策的能力	34	中級	85	中級
5. 評估資訊價值的能力	34	中級	85	中級
6. 檢索與使用各種資訊媒體能力	33	中級	85	中級
7. 依據資訊需求研擬問題	34	基本	85	中級*
8. 讀、寫、算的基本能力	34	基本	85	基本
9. 傳播資訊的能力，例如參加網路討論群	34	基本	85	基本
10. 電腦使用與操作能力	34	基本	85	基本
11. 使用網路的基本能力，例如 E-Mail, Netscape, Gopher 等	34	基本	85	基本
12. 使用電腦應用軟體能力	33	基本	85	基本
13. 具備網路基本概念，例如上網指令操作、網址的概念等	33	基本	85	基本

*代表 2001 年該項能力指標已變動。

表三：學者專家和圖書館員對圖書館員資訊素養能力指標比較表

項　　目　　　比　　較	1997 年（n = 126）		2001 年（n = 85）	
	問卷總數	能力等級	問卷總數	能力等級
1. 瞭解索引/資料庫的概念與範圍	125	中級	85	中級
2. 分析評估與辨識資訊的正確性、客觀性、權威性與適當性	126	中汲	85	中級
3. 列出待解決的問題並選定問題的主題	124	中級	85	中級
4. 認識各類資料來源並判斷使用優先順序	125	中級	85	中級
5. 懂得將需要資訊置於關係架構中考量	125	中級	84	中級
6. 組織與綜合資訊	124	中汲	85	中級
7. 使用社區其他資訊機構查找其他資源	124	中級	85	中級
8. 根據資訊作成推論，提出結論與預測結果	126	中級	84	中汲
9. 確定資訊智慧財產權與責任	125	中級	85	中級
10. 資訊儲存與建檔以供未來使用	124	中級	85	中級
11. 建立資訊產品評估標準	126	中級	84	中級
12. 建立評估資訊查詢與利用歷程的標準	124	中級	85	中級
13. 網路檔案傳輸處理的能力	125	中級	85	中級
14. 瞭解各種不同的資訊需求	125	中汲	85	中級
15. 認識圖書、電子文件等各種資訊媒體的結構	125	中級	85	中級
16. 電腦使用與操作能力	126	中級	85	中級
17. 撰寫書面報告	126	中級	85	中級
18. 使用電腦文書處理與應用軟體的能力	126	中級	85	中級
19. 使用視聽資料與多媒體資料	124	中級	85	中級
20. 欣賞、選擇與表達聽覺及視覺資料	126	基本	85	中級*
21. 使用視聽資料與多媒體等播放設備	124	基本	85	中級*
22. 設計網路首頁的能力	125	基本	85	中級*
23. 確定重要關鍵字/查詢用語/敘術語等字間的關系，并發展查詢策略	125	中級	85	高級*
24. 利用線上資料庫、網際網路、館際互借、電話、傳真等途徑查詢資料	125	中級	85	高級*
25. 利用圖書館目錄或書目工具書找尋印刷、視聽或電腦形式資源	124	中級	85	高級*
26. 使用圖書館各種參考資源與電子參考資源	125	中級	85	高級*
27. 選擇適合的資訊來源以收集資訊	126	中級	85	高級*

（續上表）

項　　　目　　　比　　較	1997 年（n＝126）		2001 年（n＝85）	
	問卷總數	能力等級	問卷總數	能力等級
28. 圖書館目錄的使用	126	中級	85	高級*
29. 認識圖書館與資訊服務機構的種類與功能	125	中級	85	高級*
30. 透過其他圖書館館員與學者專家尋求幫助找到資訊	125	中級	85	高級*
31. 使用電子信件，Internet 瀏覽器、電子佈告欄等網路工具能力	126	中級	85	高級*
32. 具備網路基本概念	124	中級	85	高級*
33. 電腦程式寫作能力	124	基本	85	基本

＊代表 2001 年該項能力指標已變動。

根據前兩項內容之比較，本研究研凝制定之公民資訊素養能力指標如下：
1. 公民資訊素養"中級能力"計有：
（1）熟知獲取資訊管道的能力；
（2）實際問題組織資訊的能力；
（3）資訊準確性與完整性的判斷能力；
（4）資訊運用於決策的能力；
（5）評估資訊價值的能力；
（6）檢索與使用各種資訊媒體能力；
（7）依據資訊需求研擬問題。
2. 公民資訊素養"基本能力"計有：
（1）讀、寫、算的基本能力；
（2）傳播資訊的能力，例如參加網路討論羣；
（3）電腦使用與操作能力；
（4）使用網路的基本能力，例如 E-mail、Netscape、Gopher 等；
（5）使用電腦應用軟體能力；
（6）具備網路基本概念，例如上網指令操作、網址的概念等。

圖書館館員資訊素養能力指標，依據本研究分成三大類，即基本能力、中級能力及高級能力等三種。所謂基本能力是指該能力足以處理大部份工作，中級能力指具備純熟與精練的工作技巧，高級能力則是具備專業與權威的技術。由於"素養"一詞具有基礎的意思，因此每項能力指標都指圖書館館員應具備能力的最低標準。根據本研究最新的調查，特擬定圖書館館員資訊素養能力指標如下：
1. 圖書館館員資訊素養"高級能力"計有：
（1）確定重要關鍵字/查詢用語/叙術語等字間的關係，並發展查詢策略；
（2）利用線上資料庫、網際網路、館際互借、電話、傳真等途徑查詢資料；
（3）利用圖書館目錄或書目工具書找尋印刷、視聽或電腦形式資源；
（4）使用圖書館各種參考資源與電子參考資源；

（5）選擇適合的資訊來源以收集資訊；
（6）圖書館目錄的使用；
（7）認識圖書館與資訊服務機構的種類與功能；
（8）透過其他圖書館館員與學者專家尋求幫助找到資訊；
（9）使用電子信件、Internet 瀏覽器、電子布告欄等網路工具能力；
（10）具備網路基本概念。
2. 圖書館館員資訊素養"中級能力"計有：
（1）瞭解索引/資料庫的概念與範圍；
（2）分析評估與辨識資訊的正確性、客觀性、權威性與適當性；
（3）列出待解決的問題並選定問題的主題；
（4）認識各類資料來源並判斷使用優先順序；
（5）懂得將需要資訊置於關係架構中考量；
（6）組織與綜合資訊；
（7）使用社區其他資訊機構查找其他資源；
（8）根據資訊作成推論，提出結論與預測結果；
（9）確定資訊智慧財產權與責任；
（10）資訊儲存與建檔以供未來使用；
（11）建立資訊產品評估標準；
（12）建立評估資訊查詢與利用歷程的標準；
（13）網路檔案傳輸處理的能力；
（14）瞭解各種不同的資訊需求；
（15）認識圖書、電子文件等各種資訊媒體的結構；
（16）電腦使用與操作能力；
（17）撰寫書面報告；
（18）使用電腦文書處理與應用軟體的能力；
（19）使用視聽資料與多媒體資料；
（20）欣賞、選擇與表達聽覺及視覺資料；
（21）使用視聽資料與多媒體等播放設備；
（22）設計網路首頁的能力。
3. 圖書館館員資訊素養基本能力計有：
（1）電腦程式寫作能力。
（五）臺灣圖書館資訊素養推行活動計劃
針對臺灣圖書館資訊素養推行活動的進行，根據學者專家座談會結論如下：
1. 學會方面：
"中國圖書館學會"和"中華圖書資訊學教育學會"，在資訊素養培育活動推行方面：
（1）學會設置具體的資訊素養指標，以建立館員應有的資訊素養能力及客觀的評估標準，同時依據館員專業知識的不同程度設計在職訓練課程，以規劃有系統的培訓管道。考量採用認證制度，要求館員接受再職進修，以提昇圖書館整體服務的素質。

（2）學會應有系統舉辦相關訓練課程。尤其應注意訓練的普及性，例如"中國圖書館學會"暑期舉辦的訓練課程，應考慮中南部圖書館館員的需要，增加中南部舉辦推廣訓練與活動。

（3）針對現今網路與推廣教育，學會應該設立相關網頁及成立圖書館利用教育小組，推展圖書館網路的專業討論羣，共享彼此的經驗。學會可將大家討論的資料製成網頁精華區，開放供專業人員參考使用。此外，以建議學會應依據實際需要從事訓練的問卷調查，作為重新設計與規劃圖書館館員網路教育課程，及提供各單位在職訓練課程的建議。

2. 圖書館學系所方面：

圖書館學校系所配合資訊素養活動推行，於教師教學、課程內容及在職進修等方面：

（1）教師教學方面：為使學生及圖書館從業人員具備終身學習能力，建議學校教師教學方式應逐步朝向自我學習的教學方法，教師授課應從單向的傳授方式改變為雙向溝通的教學方式，以培養學生具備自我導向學習的能力。

（2）課程內容方面：圖書館與資訊科學系所應配合資訊發展趨勢，加強開設資訊科學及資訊網路利用或教育課程。此外，更應充實學生學科背景或第二專長，以訓練學生教學與表達能力，例如開授教學設計課程，讓學生具備實際授課經驗，訓練表達及講授技巧等。類似"人際溝通"、"問題解決"、"教學法"、"課程設計"均可融入圖書館專業課程之中，以提昇學生資訊素養能力。

（3）在職進修方面：部份圖書館學研究所提供在職進修的管道，配合週休二日制的施行，館員可利用業餘時間至各大學教育推廣部進修，以取得修習學分或其他學科學位。

四、建議

（一）臺灣資訊基礎建設計劃中，除網路硬體建設推動外，應同時加強全民資訊素養教育

在政府積極推動"臺灣資訊基礎建設"與亞太營運中心下，臺灣地區電腦網路硬體建置工作不但已初具規模，且網路使用人口亦快速成長，但整體而言，能利用電腦網路從事終身學習的民眾仍是極為少數。因此，目前在建置推展資訊基礎建設電腦網路硬體之同時，更應加強資訊素養的教育工作，並雙管齊下才能提昇整體的效益與臺灣競爭力。

（二）"教育部"推動終身學習教育理念中，應從資訊素養教育做起

根據"教育部"1995年公佈《教育報告書：邁向二十一世紀的教育遠景》教育白皮書內容，明顯指出因應未來建設與規劃生涯學習體系等發展需要，將建立終身學習的社會。目前臺灣地區民眾壽命延長，社會老年化現象日趨明顯，加上國際化與自由化的壓力，民眾更需具備終身學習的能力。而終身學習能力的培育，則必須從資訊素養教育著手。因此，建議"教育部"應根據教育白皮書之計劃內容，提早推動全民資訊素養教育。

（三）建議"教育部"根據本研究所研擬的資訊素養指標，落實資訊素養教育與訓練

以圖書館資訊服務設計資訊素養培育方針與評量指標，其內容是參照海內外相關文

獻、學者專家及圖書館專業人員意見綜合所得。建議"教育部"依據本研究成果，提供相關單位參考與設計資訊素養教育課程及訓練內容，以全面提昇公民資訊素養的素質。

（四）持續加強圖書館軟硬體設備與充實館藏資源

根據本研究調查發現目前圖書館圖書數量普遍偏低，從電子化圖書館的服務需求而言，目前各級圖書館電腦軟硬體的設備急待加強。因此建議主管圖書館事業的機構，應充份瞭解資訊社會的來臨與終身學習發展的趨勢及重要性，大力充實各級圖書館的館藏資源與軟硬體設備。

（五）加強公共與鄉鎮圖書館推廣利用教育，以發揮社會教育功能，建立終身學習的基礎

目前臺灣各地區鄉鎮、公共圖書館及文化中心均已建置完成，除作爲當地民眾文化休憩場所外，亦是社區的學習教育中心。建議政府應充份利用既有的設施，聘任合格的圖書館專業人員，以加強鄉鎮、公共圖書館與文化中心的社教功能，並宣導民眾終身學習的信念，使鄉鎮、公共圖書館與文化中心成爲社區民眾終身學習的教室。

（六）加強圖書館專業人員教學服務的培訓與經驗交流

未來各級圖書館應加強圖書館利用與輔助教學的服務，尤其目前多數大學院校圖書館有計劃推行圖書館利用教育或開授有學分的利用課程教育。圖書館在未來若要提昇服務品質與輔助教學，則更應增強圖書館專業人員教學經驗與方法。因此，建議"中國圖書館學會"或"中華圖書資訊學教育學會"，研擬舉辦圖書館館員教學服務研習會或研討會，使館員能與學者專家相互研討教學經驗與心得。

（七）圖書資訊教育課程中，增設資訊素養相關課程與訓練

目前圖書資訊學系所課程中，對資訊素養教育的理論或講授並不普遍，僅在"中西文參考資料"、"參考服務"或"資訊與網路資源利用"等少數課程中提及，但內容不多。因此，一般學生或圖書館館員對於如何進行資訊素養教育或訓練，缺乏應有的觀念與能力。從本研究顯示圖書館館員資訊素養能力指標，應該具備中級能力，然依據館員自評統計，館員自認僅具基礎能力。爲因應未來圖書館終身學習的需要，建議圖書資訊學系所應於圖書資訊課程中，增設與資訊素養相關課程及內容，以準備學生將來能夠從事資訊素養的資訊服務工作。

（八）應從現有的各中小學師資中，培育資訊素養種子師資或學員，以協助資訊素養教育

資訊素養教育的推動是件長期性的全民教育工作，各類圖書館專業人員皆應積極參與外，中小學教師更應參與相關的訓練課程。建議"教育部"或教育廳局等，遴選國中小學優秀教師施與資訊素養專業訓練，以培訓各校資訊素養推動計劃的種子教師，再透過種子教師的領導與推動，落實資訊素養教育紮根的工作。

（九）針對不同學習階段學生，設計所需之資訊素養教學範本，以供學校教師與圖書館服務人員參考利用

雖然"國家圖書館"已編印"圖書館與資訊素養叢書"一套十冊，但仍嫌不足。爲有系統性推動資訊素養教育，建議"教育部"或國立編譯館召集學者專家，針對不同學習階段學生、授課教師或各類型圖書館研究撰寫資訊素養教育教學範本，以提供學校教師及圖書館館員參考使用。

（十）圖書館學界、電腦學界、教育學界與傳播學界相互合作，研究推廣資訊素養教育，以整體推動資訊素養教育的實現

資訊素養是識字教育、圖書館專業、電腦素養、視覺素養、媒體素養與網路與技學素養等能力的培育，因此建議圖書館學界應邀請電腦學界、教育學界、傳播學界的學者專家，同心合力研究探討與推動全民資訊素養教育工作，以加速實現臺灣資訊基礎建設及提昇臺灣整體的競爭力。

（收稿日期：2001 年 2 月 19 日）

註　釋

註 1：Nancy Kranich, "Building Information-Smart Communities," American Libraries 31：1（Dec., 2000），p. 5.

註 2：Kathy, L. Spitzer, Michael B. Eisenberg, and Carrie A. Lowe, Information Literacy：Essential Skills for the Information Age（Syracuse, NY：ERIC Clearinghouse in Information and Technology, 1998），p. 22.

註 3：American Library Association Presidential Committee on Information Literacy, Final Report（Chicago：American Library Association, 1989），p. 1.

李德竹，"資訊素養的意義、內涵與演變"，圖書與資訊學刊 35（2000 年 8 月），頁 1—25.

L. B. Jones, "Linking Undergraduate Education and Libraries：Minnesota's Approach," in Information Literacy：Developing Students as Independent Learners, ed. by D. W. Farmer and T. F.. Mech（San Francisco：Jossey-Bass, 1992），pp. 31－32.

K. E. McHenry, J. T. Stewart, and J. L. Wu, "Teaching Resource-Based Learning and Diversity," in Information Literacy：Developing Students as Independent Learners, ed. by D. W. Farmer and T. F. Mech（San Francisco：Jossey-Bass, 1992），pp. 55－56.

J. K. Olsen, "The Electronic Library and Literacy," in Information Literacy：Developing Students as Independent Learners, ed. by D. W. Farmer and T. F. Mech（San Francisco：Jossey-Bass, 1992），p. 94.

C. Curran, "Information Literacy and the Public Librarian," Public Libraries 29：6（Nov. /Dec., 1990），p. 349.

H. B. Rader, "Bibliographic Instruction or Information Literacy," College & Research Libraries News 51：1（Jan., 1990）p. 20.

──── "Information Literacy：A Revolution in the Library," RQ 31：1 (1991), p. 26.

L. J. McCrank, "Academic Programs for Information Literacy：Theory and Structure," RQ 31：4 (1992), pp. 485－487.

C. R. McClure, "Network Literacy：A Role for Libraries?" Information Technology and Libraries（June 1994），p. 117. 同註 2.

Patricia Senn Breivik, "Information Literacy Background Paper," in Information

Literacy: Advancing Opportunities for Learning in the Digital Age, ed. Richard P. Alder (Washington D C.: The Aspen Institution, 1999), p. 30.

註4：Michael B. Eisenberg and Robert Berkowitz, "Chapter 10 Library and Information Skills Curriculum Scope and Sequence: The Big Six Skills," in Current Initiative: An Agenda and Strategy for Library Media Programs (Norwood, NJ: Ablex Pub., 1988), pp. 99–119.

註5：Michael B. Eisenberg and Robert Berkowitz, The New Improved Big Workshop Handbook (Washington, Ohio: Linworth Pub., c1999).

註6：同前註, p. I。

註7：Colorado Educational Media Association, Information Literacy Guidelines. ERIC Document. Sep., 1994.

註8："Information Literacy: A Position Paper on Information Problem Solving," American Association of School Librarians Position Statement. Emergency Librarian 23: 2 (Nov. /Dec., 1995), pp. 20–23.

註9：資訊教育. < http://www.edu.tw/information/index.html > (30 Oct., 2000)

註10：資訊教育基礎建設簡介. < http://www.edu.tw/moecc/art/8609/8609a5.htm > (2 Nov., 2000).

註11："國家圖書館"提供。

註12：宋建成,《"國立中央圖書館"的讀者服務》,"國立中央圖書館"館刊26:1 (1993年), 頁134—136.

註13："國家圖書館"編.《2000年圖書館年鑑》(臺北：編者自印, 2000年), 頁106。

註14：同前註, 頁142.

註15：圖書館事業發展白皮書, 圖表。< http://lac.ncl.edu.tw/intb/ehart.htm > (20 Nov. 2000).

註16："國家圖書館",《圖書館法》"國家圖書館"編印（"行政院"華總一義字第9000009320號, 2001年1月17日公佈）。

註17：G. S. Hunter, "Public Libraries," in World Encyclopedia of Library and Information Services (Chicago: ALA, 1993), p. 675.

註18："The UNESCO Public Library Manifesto," Libri 44: 2 (Mar. 1994), pp. 171–173.

註19："中國圖書館學會"."圖書館事業發展白皮書"編輯委員會暨專案研究小組, 圖書館事業發展白皮書（臺北：圖書館學會, 2000年), 頁138—139。

註20：Charles R. McClure, Planning and Role Setting for Public Libraries: A Manual of Options and Procedures (Chicago: American Library Association, 1987), p. 28.

註21：Charles R. McClure, John Carol Bertot, and John C. Beachoard, "Enhancing the Role of Public Libraries in the Information Infrastructure," Public Libraries 35: 4 (1996), pp. 232–237.

註22：圖書館事業發展白皮書：公共圖書館。< http://lac.ncl.edu.tw/info/6-2.htm > (20 Nov., 2000).

註23：同註15。

註24：范豪英，《大學圖書館讀者利用教育現況調查研究》，"中國圖書館學會" 會報 48（1991 年 12 月），頁 58。
註25：同註 15。
註26：王振鵠，《現代圖書館的功能》，圖書館學論叢（臺北：學生，1990 年），頁 54—55。
註27：張世惠，《臺灣高級中學圖書館之推展現況》，"中國圖書館學會" 會訊 48（1991 年 12 月），頁 180。
註28：張樹三著，專門圖書館管理（臺北：曉園，1988 年），頁 131—134。
Mount, Ellis, and Renee Massoud, "The Nature of Special Libraries and Information Centers," in Special Libraries and information Centers（Washington, D. C., USA：Special Libraries Association, c1999), p. 8.
Mount, Ellis, and Renee Massoud, "Typical Special Libraries and Infomration Centers in Action," in Special Libraries and information Centers（Washington, D. C., USA：Special Libraries Association, c1999), pp. 21 – 22.
Cathy A. Porter, "What is a Special Library," in Special Libraries: A Guide for Management（Washington, D C.：Special Libraries Association, 1997), pp. 3 – 6.
Cathy A. Porter, "What does the Special Library Do," in Special Libraries: A Guide for Management（Washington, D. C.：Special Libraries Association, 1997), pp. 21 – 25.
註29：同註 13，頁 218。
註30：同註 16，頁 4—5。
註31：許令華著，臺灣科技性專門圖書館與其母機構關係之研究（臺北：漢美，1990 年），頁 134—135。
註32：范豪英，《七十七年度醫學圖書館現況調查》，"中國圖書館學會" 會報 43（1988 年 12 月），頁 128。
註33：Ching-chih Chen, "Technological Potentials for the Global Library: Realities and Challenges," International Conference on National Libraries Towards the 21st Century, Apr. 20 – 24, 1993（Taipei：National Central Library, 1993), pp. 2 – 3.
註34：Christina S. Doyle, Development of A Model of Information Literacy Outcome Measures Within National Goals of 1990（Unpublished Ph. D. diss., Northern Arizona University, 1992), pp. 20 – 24.
註35：同前註。
註36：同註 34，pp. 79 – 98。
註37：Mary Ochs, Assessing the Value of an Information Literacy Program（Comell Univ., Ithaca, NY Albert R. Mann Library, 1991）
註38：Robert Grover, "Assessing Information Skills Instruction," Reference Librarian 44（1994), pp. 173 – 189.
註39：Commission on Higher Education, Philadelphia, Middle States Association of College and Schools, Information Literacy: Lifelong Learning in the Middle States Region. A

Summary of Two Symposia, 1995.

註40: Marjorie M. Warmkessel and Joseph M. McCade, "Integrating Information Literacy into the Curriculum," Research Strategies 15: 2 (1997), pp. 80-88.

註41: 1994年臺閩地區圖書館暨資料單位名錄（臺北市："國立中央圖書館"，1995年）。

臺灣圖書資訊學術語詞彙之參考資料[*]

近年來，兩岸開放交流後，深感在很多方面出現了差異，特別是在學術研究方面，因為雙方使用的名詞術語不同，致使在兩岸合作交流上產生阻礙，造成基本認知上之差距，而影響成果，圖書資訊學亦不能例外。術語是學術上所用之名詞，每一門學科皆有其專用之術語，掌握最新的術語又是何其重要，走學術研究與知識普及的基礎工作，故每一學科必要蒐集整理和建立其專用術語詞彙，並力求其完整性、正確性及新穎性。兩岸在圖書資訊學術語上更應建立共識，力求統一，以增進兩岸交流合作的效果。

本次會議中討論"圖書資訊學術語規範資料庫"，本人深感兩岸應先瞭解現況，然後規劃合作進行之詳細步驟，訂定目標、範圍、時刻表、工作人員等事項，如兩岸皆能積極行動，建立"兩岸圖書資訊學術語規範資料庫"應不是件困難之事。

現在向諸位報告目前臺灣圖書資訊學術語詞彙相關之參考資料：

一、李德竹著。圖書館學暨資訊科學詞彙，第二版。臺北市：文華，[1997]。790頁。

　　全書共10,984項詞彙，是一本英中圖書館學與資訊科學詞彙對照表。其前身是1981、1985和1993年分別出版之《圖書館學暨資訊科學常用字彙》、《圖書館學暨資訊科學字彙》和《圖書館學暨資訊科學詞彙》第一版。

　　詞彙來源：1）蒐集臺灣學者專家發表文獻和書籍中詞目
　　　　　　　2）蒐集臺灣詞目，請教學科專家翻譯
　　　　　　　3）編者自譯

　　編者計劃2001年底出版第三版。

二、漢美編輯委員會編。圖書館學與資訊科學海峽兩岸名詞對照表。臺北市：漢美，[1993]，322頁。

　　全書共約7,245項名詞。本書條列方式足以英文名詞為經以兩岸之中文譯名為緯，分列兩側，相互對應；英文按字母順序排列。

三、胡述兆總編輯；李德竹、盧荷生副總編；王振鵠總校訂；朱則剛等各組主編。圖書館學與資訊科學大辭典。臺北市：漢美，[1995]，共三冊。

　　本大辭典之詞目共4,482條。其涵蓋範圍，除圖書館學與資訊科學外，尚包含目錄學與檔案學兩個相關學門，凡與這些學門有關的知識及人物，均擇要立目介紹。附錄五附有"圖書館學與資訊科學海峽兩岸名詞對照表"。

四、薛理桂、吳美美主持，圖書館學與資訊科學索引典，"國科會"計劃 NSC83-0301-H180-001-M2，[1996]。

　　本索引典編製之目的在提供圖書館學與資訊科學實務工作者與研究人員查檢資料或文獻分析時，可作為詞目選擇參考之依據。其涵蓋之範圍以圖書

---

[*] 本文發表於第二次中文文獻資源基建共享合作會議（臺北市"國家圖書館"，2001年4月23—24日）。

館學與資訊科學有關之術語爲主，選用之述詞約計1360個，非描述詞約870個。

五、盧震京撰。<u>圖書學大辭典</u>。臺北市：臺灣商務，［1971］。

　　本書編輯目的：在各節述各種圖書學說；並提示圖書館所用之術語；摘叙中外圖書制度之概要；旁徵博引，詳爲參證，以供圖書館學及學者之參考。本書在專門條目之詮釋，凡圖書之專門名詞，均詳爲羅列，並就專家校正，每條成一有組織之專篇。俾閱者得其者得其要領，對於普通條目有關圖書者，亦盡量列入。

六、楊若雲主編。<u>圖書館學辭典</u>。臺北市：五洲，［1988］。

　　本辭典蒐集圖書館學詞語約萬餘條，除附中文詞義的對譯外，並加詳明的註釋。選詞範圍廣泛，除圖書的分類、編目、管理外，舉凡與圖書館學有關的如：圖書的製作、裝潢、印刷、攝影、世界著名圖書館、出版社、情報蒐集機構、圖書館學者學會等機構、世界著名刊物等皆蒐集在內。

其他參考資料尚有：

1）陳福崇主編。<u>信息、資訊技術辭典</u>。臺北市：五洲，［1987］。
2）洪進德、李之爲編著。<u>圖書文獻資料辭典</u>。臺北市：五洲，［1988］。
3）<u>科技索引典</u>。臺北市："國科會"科學技術資料中心。［1992］。
4）<u>農業科技索引典</u>。臺北市：農業科學資料服務中心。［1988］。
5）"立法院"圖書館編。立法資訊系統索引典。臺北市："立法院"圖書館，［1989］，473頁。
6）吉村善太郎編。<u>圖書館用語辭典，日、漢、英對譯的圖書工作詞彙</u>。東京都：雄松堂，［1997］。

資訊素養的意義、內涵與演變*

[摘要 Abstract]

　　資訊時代中培育具有資訊素養之公民己為現代民主國家之必要條件，先進國家如美國早在七十年代已倡導資訊素養理念，並積極推動資訊素養教育活動，目的在教育公民成為終身學習者、獨立與自導式學習者。反觀臺灣地區不但遠落於後，又觀念混淆，故撰文試釋資訊素養的意義、內涵及其演變情形，並特別介紹海內外重要資訊素養教育活動之發展現況，期能協助人們對資訊素養觀念上有基本正確之認識。

　　The quality and quantity of information needed to function effectively in society and the workplace continues to increase. Individuals are faced with the escalating challenge of managing far more information, in increasingly diverse formats and locations. They must be able to master rapidly changing information technology and possess the information literacy skills to act independently in this information rich environment. Information literacy is common to all disciplines, to all learning environments, and to all levers of education. It forms the basis for lifelong learning. Thus, an information literate person is able to "recognize when information is needed and have the ability to locate, evaluate, and use effective the needed information." The present paper attempts to explore the definitions, contexts and developments of information literacy, and also to survey major information literacy activities and educational programs in U. S. other countries, and the present status of information literacy in Taiwan. is also investigated.

關鍵字 Keyword
資訊素養 資訊素養教育 終身學習
Information literacy; Information literacy education; Lifelong learning

壹、前　言

　　美國傑佛森總統（Thomas Jefferson）之名言："民主社會奠基於學識豐富與教養良好之公民。"（A democratic society depends upon informed and educated citizenry），一語道出資訊與教育對於個人與國家之重要。而歐文（Major R. Owens）對此有更具體之闡釋："資訊素養（Information Literacy）是對民主制度存在之保證。世界上所有人類均有追求同等利用社會資訊資源之權利，而資訊素養富有者遠較資訊素養缺乏者，無論在生活的表現或工作的決策上更為圓滿與智慧。在決策過程中充份運用資訊資源者，才能成為真正實踐現代公民責任的人，這也是構成民主社會之重要而必須的條件。"[1]

　　人類一直不斷追求生活的改善與超越，從早期以農林畜牧業為主之"農業社會"，

---

* 本文發表在《圖書與資訊學》35 期（2000 年 11 月），第 1—25 頁。

進化至以依賴機器之製造業為主之"工業社會",已為人類文明進步跨進一大步。而今更由於電腦與通信技術結合之推波助瀾,使人類又邁入"資訊社會"(Information Society)。新的資訊社會中,資訊是重要而豐沛之資源與智慧財產,資訊社會中處處有豐富之資料、事實、事件、問題、資訊等,於是又有人以"資訊爆炸"(Information Explosion)一詞形容這個時代資訊之豐富與普遍。

在這充滿豐沛資訊資源的社會中,具備資訊素養的人懂得如何在資訊社會中學習,瞭解知識是如何組織的,知道如何去找尋資訊,以及利用資訊俾助於其追求真善美的人生。資訊可以幫助人類改善生活的品質與內涵,並且可藉由各種專業資訊來滿足各式各樣的個人與工商企業之需求,這些需求更是引發個人之成長與提昇之原動力,也是促使整個社會環境中各種社會、政治、文化、經濟各層次、各方面迅速變遷之主因。資訊素養對於個人是生活之重要工具,對於工商企業則由於資訊取得與運用而改善工商企業,並且使國家與社會獲得改變與進步。

更由於富於資訊素養之優秀公民為國家締造現代化與健全的民主制度,俾使得全民獲得更大之福祉,因此資訊素養與知識是國家與人類社會最珍貴之寶藏。自 1980 年代以來美國等先進國家已在資訊素養活動之研究與推展方面投註相當多之努力,反觀臺灣在資訊素養之觀念與活動尚在萌芽起步階段。

貳、研究緣起

以科學為基礎的現代技術,改變人類的生活環境,促使社會結構快速變遷。臺灣的科學研究在"國科會"等有關機構的推動下,研究風氣逐漸形成,但技術科學教育之基礎研究則因研究羣尚未形成,影響技術科學教育(Technology Literacy)甚鉅。因此,有識之士遂於 1990 年第四次臺灣科學技術會議中第二中心議題:"提昇基礎研究水準"子題之二"基礎研究新領域之推展"提出議案,籲請"教育部"和"國科會"重視技術科學教育的基礎研究工作,落實技術科學教育之實施,藉以提昇全民技術科學涵養、加速培育專業技術人力以及促進臺灣科技之全面發展。[②]

技術科學教育的目的在於"使一般民眾具備技術科學素養(Technology Literacy),並培育優良技術人力,以促進科技之全面發展":技術科學教育兼具專門技術人力培育與全民技學素養之責,同時也隸屬於學校教育與社會教育的範疇內。"行政院"國家科學委員會本其推動科學研究之精神,執行第四次科學技術會議之決議,倡導技術科學教育的基礎研究,並將之區分為"技術科學素養教育"和"技術科學專業教育"兩大類,由"國科會"科學教育發展處統籌,分別委託學者組成規劃小組,進行研究規劃。

資訊素養對於現代公民為生活必備之條件,並且為技術科學素養教育之重要環節。圖書館在資訊資源與教育主體中,無論在傳播、學習與生活中均扮演重要角色;圖書館是社會資訊、知識與文化中心;更是培養民眾資訊素養之教育者與資訊供應者。因之本文即緣自"技術科學素養教育"研究,於資訊與傳播技術領域中,首先初步探討資訊素養與圖書館資訊素養之意義、內涵與演變。

叁、資訊素養之意義與內涵

一、素養的涵意

"素養"（Literacy）一詞在臺灣社教譯作為"識字"，是指十五歲以上的民眾，具有基本的讀、寫、算技能，可以應付日常生活所需者。③查閱 Random House 英文字典素養的意義有（1）受教育的狀況或品質，特別是指能讀與寫能力；（2）教育的內涵；（3）個人具備某一特殊主題或學科的知識。④從探究這個字的涵義，可以發現素養是個具變化性概念的用字。它的意思可從指個人最基本的讀寫能力，到某個人擁有某種程度學科的知識。可見"素養"一詞可隨著社會環境的變化，而賦予不同的定義與內涵。由於十九世紀工業革命以後，許多新興國家體認到公民要能生活在工業化的社會中，必需要有最基本的素養，其中最重要的便是基本讀寫能力。而各國政府也體認到公民識字能力的提昇，對於國家的經濟、工業、社會與政治發展都有重大的影響。⑤到了二十世紀，許多國家政府便開始展開一連串掃除文盲的計劃，有系統地推展全民識字運動。而"素養"一詞的內涵便成"識字"的意思。

素養可以分成兩類：一類是傳統所謂識字的意思，即個人具備讀、寫、算的能力，以適應生活的需要；另一類是功能性的素養（Functional Literacy），是指個人擁有某些特定的技能，並依自己設定的目標，以順應在家庭、工作、社區等社會生活的角色扮演。⑥因此，功能性的素養完全依照社會環境的需要，來決定素養的內涵，即隨著社會環境時間與空間的不同，一個公民所需具備的素養也將隨之不同。因此素養的定義與內涵，完全視整體社會環境的需要來決定。二十世末期由於電腦、通訊科技的快速進步，整個社會環境已經產生極大的改變。人們的生活方式、工作環境、思考形態、價值觀念、社會發展、政治理念等都在改變之中。所謂的"後工業化社會"或"資訊化社會"，均是預言一個嶄新社會的來臨。面對新的社會環境，人們應該賦予素養一個符合時代需求的新意義與新內涵。

二、資訊素養之意義

資訊素養根據美國圖書館學會（American Library Association，簡稱 ALA）的定義是指一個人具有能力覺知到何時需要資訊，且能有效地尋得、評估與使用所需要的資訊。⑦

鍾尼斯（L. B. Jones）認為資訊素養包括覺知到需要資訊、同時知道需求的內容、以致能有效地尋求資訊、評估資訊、組織資訊並使用資訊。⑧

麥克亨利（K. E. McHenry）引用葛來契（B. Gratch）的看法認為資訊素養有四個部份：第一是能體認資訊價值與力量的態度；第二是能覺知資訊形式與種類的多樣性；第三是能理解到資訊並非是知識，除非資訊已被分析、被探討、被整合到現存的知識體之中；第四是除檢索的過程外，要有效率且具有批判性的檢索資訊。⑨

奧爾森（J. K. Olsen）定義資訊素養是除了具備傳統能讀、說、寫的基本素養技巧外，還需要瞭解資訊的角色、力量與使用，知道資訊不同的內涵與種類，瞭解組織資訊的系統，具備檢索資訊的能力，且能評估、組織與操作資訊。⑩

肯浪（C. Curran）認為資訊素養是許多使用資訊能力的綜合，包括：（1）知道資訊具有輔助性的能力;(2)知道何處可獲得資訊的能力;(3)具有檢索資訊的能力;(4)有解釋、組織與綜合資訊的能力;(5)有能力使用與傳播資訊。⑪

瑞德(H. B. Rader)定義資訊素養為:⑫

瞭解獲取及時性與回溯性資訊的過程與系統,如資訊辨識與傳輸系統與服務;針對不同的資訊需求,有能力評估不同資訊管道與來源的效度及可靠性;以及熟悉許多徵集與儲存自己所擁有資訊的基本技巧,例如資料庫、試算表、文書處理與資訊處理系統等。

Rader更進一步定義資訊素養是具備有效檢索與評估資訊,以解決問題與決策的能力。簡言之,一個具備資訊素養的公民在資訊化社會中,知道如何成為一位終身學習者。具體而言有以下的特徵:⑬

1. 於資訊與技術環境下,不但適應得很好且能獲致成功;
2. 在民主社會中,過一種具生產性、健康且滿意的生活;
3. 對快速變化的環境,能有效的處理;
4. 對下一代的未來深具信心;
5. 對個人與專業性的問題解決,均可獲得適當的資訊;
6. 精通寫作與電腦操作。

麥克奎雷克(L. J. McCrank)認為資訊素養是一個抽象、理想化且涉及許多技巧與知識的能力或行為的術語,這個詞有時常成為圖書館技巧(Library Skills)、圖書館利用(Library Use)或書目利用指導(Bibliographic Instruction)的替代品。因此,資訊素養假若要成為圖書館教學計劃的一個大的架構,則資訊素養的各種內涵需要加以具體考量,同時革新範圍必需是擴及圖書館以外的範疇。⑭

綜合以上各家定義,所謂"資訊素養是培育公民具備瞭解資訊的價值,在需要資訊時能有效率地查詢資訊、評估資訊、組織資訊與利用資訊"。而資訊存在社會各個角落,若要培育公民具備資訊素養,必需從有系統的資訊環境開始去認識資訊的價值與結構,這些有組織有系統的資訊環境包括圖書館、博物館、資訊中心、檔案機構、各類資訊服務站、民眾服務中心、社教與文化中心、電話查詢中心、電腦網路與線上資料庫等。透過瞭解與利用這些資訊系統,將可培養民眾對於資訊價值的覺知與使用的習慣,從而使資訊成為生活不可缺少的一部份。

三、資訊素養的重要性與功能

資訊素養已成為在邁向資訊化中,民眾必需具備的基本素養之一。尤其在未來資訊基礎建設(National Information Infrastructure,簡稱 NII)完成之後,資訊將猶如今日家家戶戶所使用的自來水一般,人人在家中即可方便取得所需要的資訊。因此,培養民眾能解讀、評估與分析所獲得的資訊,將是今日資訊素養所要努力的方向。而民眾利用資訊能力的增加,將使民眾無論參與政治事務或日常生活決策事務時,均依據可信的資訊解決問題,因而間接地提高民眾的素質與增加社會的生產力。其重要性影響有以下列幾方面:

(一)民眾生活方面

臺灣近幾年來隨著報禁的解除、開放境外觀光、兩岸探親與廣播電視開放民營等政治開放措施,已使得海內外的資訊更加的暢通,進而促成社會多元化的發展。人民對於政府各項施政與要求,可以透過各種管道向政府表達。而人民對於生活品質與政治民主的追求,亦較以往更加迫切。然而由於今日生活的層面更加多樣化,及現今社會更依賴科技與資訊的應用,使得這些目標較以往更難達成。尤其在欠缺足夠的資訊下,每日生活中的許多問題將更難有效地決策。而根本的問題在於民眾沒有充份的養成利用資訊的習慣,以至於對於日常生活的食、衣、住、行、育、樂等決策,只能依靠個人過去的經驗或別人的口語相傳等被動式有限的資訊來源做決策,因而喪失許多可選擇的機會。

資訊素養是培育公民使用資訊力量的方法,使人民可以接受或拒絕專家的意見,成為可以獨立追求真理的個體。這種能力使得公民可以建立自己的意見,同時經驗到追求知識的熱誠,這不僅只為終身學習作準備,同時也是鼓動年輕學子追求終身學習的動力。藉由對知識查詢與交流的過程,不但深化公民對自我處身之社會團體時空地位的認識,進而認同自己的文化、歷史、藝術,同時能獨立地決定自己未來該走的方向。不幸的是,這些需要資訊以改善所處地位或環境的人,常常是最欠缺基本素養與資訊素養的。例如中途失學的年輕人、不識字的成年人、平地山胞、低收入民眾等。這些民眾較任何一般民眾,更需要利用資訊來改善自己的生活處境,但他們較任何人都更不知道資訊的用處,以致於喪失許多可能必要的協助機會。圖書館與各地的資訊服務站均是提供資訊最好的場所,這些場所均潛藏著眾多改善生活品質的訊息。如何培養每位公民能有效利用這些資訊資源,增進本身與社會的福祉,將是臺灣未來教育的重點。因此,資訊素養對於個人可以有以下的功能:

1. 具備對資訊價值判斷力,成為獨立的學習者;
2. 養成利用資訊的習慣,成為終身學習者;
3. 具備資訊組織能力,成為知識的創造者。

(二) 工商業企業方面

近幾年來臺灣在國際要求開放市場及貿易自由競爭的壓力下,已經大幅放寬各種貿易的限制與降低各項進口貿易關稅,使得臺灣各種商業活動更加活絡與有競爭力。而民眾可以公開的投資海內外的股票市場、境外的期貨、債券、貨幣與房地產等。這些多樣化的投資管道不但增加投資貿易的複雜性,也增加投資者決策的困難度。商場決策困難度的增加也意味著風險的提高,因此如何降低決策的風險程度,就有賴於可靠資訊的獲取。這些資訊的來源包括來自於政府單位發佈的公開性資訊。例如各項鼓勵民間投資獎勵條約、各種財經重要決策、每日境內外的市場行情、政府頒佈的優惠投資減免條約、專利商標、每日股市行情等。這些資訊的獲取對於投資者與公司都相當重要,尤其面對境外廣大的市場競爭,如何與外國公司合資生產,或併購境外的公司,甚至如何開發具有潛力的產品等,都需要蒐集大量的資訊以作為商業決策的參考。然而境內大多數的企業體仍然沿襲著過去傳統中國人作小本生意的經驗,依賴個人勤奮打拼的精神從事商業的競爭活動。這種精神雖為臺灣贏得經濟奇蹟的美譽,但面對越來越有競爭力的亞洲其他新興工業國家,也不得不重新調整經濟的體質。

一個具備有資訊素養的企業體在從事各項投資的同時,不但會評估本身的條件,也會考慮其他國家的競爭能力、技術條件、環境條件與市場潛力等。因此,企業體在從事一項投資案時,會收集各種決策所需要的資訊,包括市場調查報告、經貿專家發表的論文、各國經貿現況報導、當日或過去股市行情或指標、各國政府的貨幣政策、國際重大投資案、國際重大政治新聞事件等。經由這些資訊的綜合研判，才決定一項投資案。因此資訊的蒐集，可增加企業體投資策略多重選擇的機會；經由不同資訊的綜合分析，降低投資的風險；透過有效資訊的研判，減少不必要的錯誤與失敗，增加成功的機會。因此，資訊素養對企業體有以下的功能：

1. 企業體對於資訊價值的重視，可提昇企業決策的品質；
2. 企業體有效的利用資訊，可以降低決策的風險，增加成功機會；
3. 企業體對檢索資訊能力越好，則投資的選擇性越多；
4. 企業體對資訊的重視，將帶動整體企業員工對知識的重視，間接鼓勵員工不斷追求新知，增加企業體永續經營的動力。

（三）社會方面

臺灣近年來因為政治改革開放的關係，在政治民主上，要求更多元化的發展與重視民意。因此，社會各種團體在對政府各種施政上，也能以各種不同方式表達。包括陳情、訴怨、集會、遊行、靜坐絕食、召開記者會、登報、上廣播的電話熱線等。一時之間社會上充斥各種不同的政治主張、各種聲音與各種請求。每日的報章、雜誌、新聞媒體成了各種社會團體言論角力的方塊。對於政治人物而言，陳訴自我的主張與維護自我的形象，已成為爭取選票最佳策略。各種社會團體也經由媒體的報導與造勢，爭取社會對其主張與意見的支持與認同。政府機構也透過媒體表達政府的立場與施政決策，爭取全民的支持。這些政治人物、社會團體、政府機構均設法透過言論的表達，以影響公共政策、公共問題與公共的建設。這些社會公共事務的決策，在民主國家乃訴諸於民意。透過民主的表決程序，決定了多數人共同的意願。同樣一件社會問題，不同政治主張的團體有不同的看法，因而產生不同的結論。例如以蓋核電廠為例，環保團體以核電廠會破壞沿海海底生態為由，反對核電廠的興建；而政府以蓋核電廠對於未來經濟發展的重要性為由，力主核電廠要興建。當然更有學者專家主張不興建核電廠，改建火力發電廠。面對這些不同的主張，全民的意見該如何去作判斷？資訊素養便是使全民能具備解讀這些社會言論重要的能力。具有資訊素養的民眾面對媒體所報導的言論，可以接受與批判報導的公正性，對於可疑的報導會利用有效的資訊加以驗證。同時與民眾切身相關的各種資訊，包括醫療保健、社會福利、社區活動、環境衛生、教育制度、消費者權利等均會注意與蒐集。這些資訊的有效被利用與評估，將成為全民民主素養與品質的基礎。即全民擁有越多的資訊，越不易被不當的言論與媒體所蒙騙，也越能對於自己的主張作選擇。因此，資訊素養對於社會有以下的功能：

1. 全民對資訊價值的重視，促進社會多元發展與言論自由；
2. 全民有效地利用資訊，可提昇民主的素養；
3. 全民對資訊有效的蒐集與評估，可以促使民意有效地表達；
4. 全民資訊素養是維護民主制度的基石；
5. 全民資訊素養是造就資訊化社會與邁向未來資訊社會之資訊基礎建設的根本素養。

四、資訊素養相關名詞

與資訊素養相關的名詞有下列幾項：

(一)科學素養(Science Literacy):一個公民生活於今日社會所具備的科學基本知識與應用能力。

(二)技學素養(Technology Literacy):一個公民為適應現代團體/社會生活應具備的基本技術科學知識及應用的技能。[15]

(三)資訊服務素養(Information Services Literacy):指公民在需要資訊時,具備使用各種服務機構或資訊中心的各項資訊服務或尋找適切專家顧問諮詢的能力與知識,以解決其生活上的各種問題。

(四)圖書館素養(Library Literacy):圖書館素養是指一個人使用圖書館各種服務的能力,例如使用卡片目錄、參考工具書等。

(五)資訊素養(Information Literacy):培育公民具備瞭解資訊的價值,在需要資訊時能有效地查詢資訊、評估資訊、組織資訊與利用資訊。

(六)電腦素養(Computer Literacy):電腦素養指一個人對電腦軟硬體使用的能力。如軟體方面,例如文書處理軟體、電子試算表或資料庫系統軟體等。硬體包括電腦基本結構的認識、電話撥接通訊網路、通訊介面等知識。

(七)文化素養(Cultural Literacy):社會上每位公民對於該民族或世界文明史,及偉大的政治、哲學、宗教與科技通曉的程度,亦包括對於時事新聞與流行趨勢的知識。[16]

(八)家庭素養(Family Literacy):家庭是社會的基礎,透過父母親的親職教育,幼童可以習得說讀的能力,奠定幼童家庭教育的基礎。透過各種計劃教育父母親對於親職教育的知識與教育兒童的能力。

(九)人力素養(Workforce Literacy):執行某項工作或特殊工作,所需要的一組技巧。特別強調對於場所、工作特定的分析能力。由於工作內容變化的程度越來越快,工作素養也越加強調"如何學習"的能力。[17]

(十)媒體素養(Media Literacy):公民具有使用後印刷式媒體(Post-Print Media)的能力,即瞭解如何使用能產生影像、文字與聲音的媒介物,從事相關訊息的傳遞與溝通的能力。凡具備媒體素養的公民,能同時使用印刷與電子媒體,從事資訊的解讀、評估、分析與製作。[18]

(十一)網路素養(Network Literacy):公民具備網路的知識與技巧,而能在網路化環境下,順利操作網路系統與檢索網路上各種資訊資源,以解決問題。[19]

麥克庫勞爾(C. R. McClure)於1994年將傳統的識字、電腦素養、媒體素養、網路素養與資訊素養間的關係以下圖表示:[20]

肆、資訊素養相關活動的歷史發展

在"國科會"規劃技術科學素養教育研究開始探索資訊素養問題,以及近來臺灣各界開始推展資訊素養理念之際,美國與許多國家早已注意此一重要性,在過去廿餘年已進行許多重要活動與研究,並有具體豐碩的成果,由此資訊素養之重要可見一斑。本研究首先陳述這些海外的重要成就,可作為臺灣研究之參考借鑑,同時並審視相關研究之現況,以避免重複研究,並可累積他人的經驗以獲致較具體之成效。

一、美國資訊素養之活動與研究

美國自1970年代即倡導"資訊素養"之觀念,許多學者專家認為資訊素養是人類

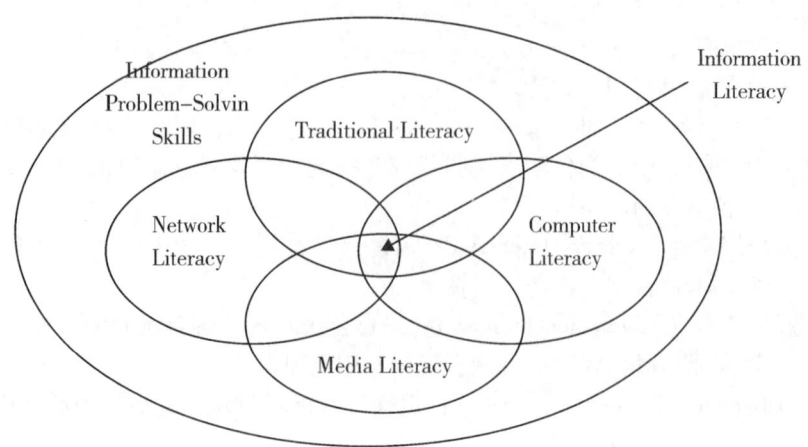

圖一：資訊素養概念示意圖

各種基本"知識素養"（Literacy）之重要部份，不僅是學術環境從事的人們之需要，并且包括各行各業，是現代社會生活的要件。在1979年美國召開之"白宮圖書館與資訊服務會議"（White House Conference on Library and Information Services，簡稱 WHCLIS）時，資訊素養被列爲八項主要討論議題之一[21]，爲首先提供資訊素養之概念，但是當時並未受到普遍之重視。

1983年美國"追求卓越教育全國委員會"（National Commission Excellence in Education）公佈的一份報告：《國家的危機：教育改革之必要》（A Nation at Risk：The Imperative for Education Reform），檢討美國全國教育問題並針對如何邁向一個"知書達禮"之社會提出各種建議，但是惟獨遺漏圖書館在教育改革中之角色。於是引起教育界與圖書館界人士重視，開始疾呼圖書館對於人類終生教育是一重要資源，也是資訊改革中最重要部份。[22]自此遂引發一連串探討資訊素養與圖書館角色之研究。

1986年"卡內基基金會教學改革計劃"（Carnegie Foundation for the Advancement of Teaching）所提改革報告指陳：一所優良學院可由學生使用校園學習資源情形，以及學生是否因此成爲獨立性、自導性之學習者作評量。然而根據調查統計，美國大學生每週利用圖書館紀錄，每四名即有一名不上圖書館，百分之六五之學生每週使用圖書館時間不及四小時。均充分顯示美國大專院校課堂教學與圖書館利用有很大之差距。[23]

卡內基這份報告立即引起美國高等教育注意到圖書館在學校教育中扮演之角色。科羅拉多大學（University of Colorado）與哥倫比亞大學圖書館服務學院（Columbia University School of Library Service），在1987年3月合作舉辦一項研討會："圖書館與追求學術卓越"（Libraries and the Search for Academic Excellence），會議中叙述美國教育改革報告，並認爲圖書館所扮演之角色應以達成學術目標爲定位，會中邀請許多教育者與圖書館員共同發表論文研討，該會最重要的成果係力促美國圖書館學會儘速成立"資訊素養委員會"之專門單位，以探討資訊素養相關問題。[24]

嗣後，美國圖書館學會在1989年提出一份重要之歷史文件："美國圖書館學會資訊素養委員會總結報告書"（The Final Report of the American Library Association Presidential Committee on Information Literacy），該報告內容具體而字字真知灼見。文中界定資訊素養意義，探討資訊素養對於人類的重要價值，無論對於個人、公司團體或國家全民福祉均大有助益。同時針對提昇資訊素養以促進教育改革提出許多具體建議，俾使學生主動瞭解與利用各種豐富之資訊資源。並且設計資訊素養發展之模式，以及在教師教學與研究之應用。這份報告最重要之貢獻在於其對資訊素養提出改革新方案之建議與訂定圖書館發展之新角色，並且受到其他非圖書館團體之普遍認同。[25]

同年"美國圖書館與資訊科學委員會"（U. S. National Commission on Libraries and Information Science，簡稱 NCLIS）與美國學校圖書館協會（American Association of School Libraries，簡稱 AASL）邀請全國教師、教育者、圖書館界參加此全國性會議："廿一世紀資訊素養與教育：行動綱領"（Information Literacy and Education for the 21st Century: Toward an Agenda for Action），會中提出許多資訊素養與教育之具體建議：包括（1）改變教育中小學教師之方式；（2）改變中小學教育之方式；（3）改變學校行政管理之方式；（4）改變學校經費分配之方式；（5）改變學校圖書館媒體課程。[26]

有關大學之資訊素養問題之研討亦十分積極，1989 年美國學院與研究圖書館協會（Association of College and Research Libraries，簡稱 ACRL）召開第五屆全國會議時，即以"廿一世紀之建設"（Building on the First Century）為會議主題，探討資訊素養與圖書館書目利用指導服務，內容包括圖書館如何與教員合作、整合課程之圖書館指導、課程評估、教學方法與學習類型等。[27]

美國又於 1989 年成立"全國資訊素養論壇"（National Forum on Information Literacy）聚集許多全國性組織共同致力於協助一般民眾成為有效的資訊使用者，其成員包羅廣泛，包含國家教育學會（National Education Association）、五十二個州立學校主管委員會（Council of Chief State School Officers）、美國報紙出版者協會（American Newspaper Publishers Association）、西班牙裔政策發展計劃（Hispanic Policy Development Project）、資訊工業協會（Information Industry Association）與全國黑人公共行政官員全國論壇（National Forum for Black Public Administrators）等會員。其中"幼稚園至 12 年級"（K-12）論壇，專門探討以資源基礎學習（Resources-Based Learning）作為課程改革之工具。[28]另有一成員"高等教育中部各州委員會"（Middle States Commission on Higher Education），亦協助教師於教學中培養學生資訊素養，並且支持許多資訊素養工作研習會，俾使教師達到資源基礎學習之教學方式。[29]

另外 1990 年 4 月由羅吉斯大學傳播資訊與圖書館研究學院召開第廿八屆畢業校友與教師會議（Proceedings of the Twenty-Eighth Annual Symposium of the Graduate Alumni and Faculty of the Rutgers School of Communication, Information and Library Studies），主題為"資訊素養：如何學習"（Information Literacy: Learning How to Learn），研討之內容涵蓋學生學習如何學習；如何幫助不懂資訊的人、圖書館及資料中心之使用；整合課堂之學習技巧與方法：將課程與圖書館結合一體；定義資訊素養為圖書館之外延角色；以及設計課程整合模式等。[30]

1991 年美國白宮圖書館與資訊服務會議（White House Conference on Library and Information Services）召開，聚集了全國圖書館界之精英，以"資訊 2000 年：廿一世紀

圖書館與資訊服務"（Information 2000：Library and Information Services for the 21st Century）為會議名稱，主要規劃未來美國圖書館與資訊服務應朝三方向發展：培養各種生活所需之素養、增進競爭力與提昇民主化，並再次呼籲資訊素養為美國圖書館資訊服務之主要方向。㉛

為檢視 1989 年美國圖書館學會發表之總結報告書（Final Report of the ALA Presidential Committee on Information Literacy, 1989）的執行成效與推展資訊素養的進展情形，美國全國資訊素養論壇（National Forum on Information Literacy）於 1998 年 3 月發表資訊素養進展報告書（A Progress Report on Information Literacy：An Update on the ALA Presidential Committee on Information Literacy：Final Report）此份報告根據1989年總結報告書中六項建議分別報告其進展情形及未來工作之建議㉜，此外美國資訊素養論壇之成員深思僅依賴科技本身並不能使美國在教育企業上發揮資訊時代的競爭優勢，唯有所有的美國公民具備完整的資訊素養技巧，方能實現美國邁向美好明天的夢想。為此，該論壇成員更努力積極推展資訊素養，共同決議在未來 2000 年優先列入實施的建議案如下：㉝

（一）推動學校資訊素養課程之認證
（二）教師養成教育與教學表現應涵蓋資訊素養技能的培養
（三）圖書館員養成教育與服務績效應涵蓋資訊素養層面的考量
（四）讓企業主管瞭解具備資訊素養能力工作者的優點及重要性
（五）推動更多相關研究計劃

如需詳盡瞭解美國十年來推動資訊素養之活動成果以及1998年報告內容對未來之建議，可查閱。http://www.ala.org//acrl/nili/nili/html。

除上述這些蓬勃的學術活動外，美國尚有幾個相關之團體主導資訊素養之研究，如美國高等教育協會（American Association for Higher Education，簡稱 AAHE）是第一個肯定圖書館對於提昇卓越學術貢獻之美國高等教育團體，並且出版充份利用圖書館（Making the Most of Libraries）著作，並建立"資訊素養行動社區"（Action Community on Information Literacy），專門從事此方面之研究與規劃。

二、其他國家之活動與研究

除美國大力倡導資訊素養外，尚有其他國家也重視這方面之研究。澳洲在1990年全國職業教育與訓練委員會（National Board of Employment Education and Training）報告中，提及圖書館亦是一種教育者，與探討資訊素養相關課題。並且在 1992 年 12 月又召開全國會議"資訊素養：澳洲的行動計劃"（Information Literacy：Australia's Agenda），聚集澳洲教育界、圖書館界、政府與企業界各方領導者共同探討資訊素養課題。㉞

英國於1980年由大英圖書館主導三項有關資訊技術訓練實務之研究。英國一般慣用"資訊技巧"（Information Skills）名詞，其內涵相當於資訊素養。這些研究涵蓋英格蘭與蘇格蘭各地之大學與理工學院在校園中從事各項資訊使用技巧實務訓練，例如：羅堡福大學（Loughborough University）教授以企業公司為對象，指導學生分析工業界如何利用資訊。㉟

荷蘭則為12至16歲年齡層之學生設計全國電腦與資訊素養計劃，討論有關電腦與資訊素養應用於課程發展,並強調教師與學生應相同對等參與課程。[36]而加拿大由昆斯大學布瑞昆公共衛生科學圖書館(Bracken Health Sciences Library Queen's University)引介資訊素養計劃以引導學生認識知識,培養其具備利用各種工具以檢索與管理資訊之能力,並發揮圖書館員之教育者角色。[37]其他如中國大陸與德國均也開始重視資訊素養之推行。

經過上述活動之灌溉,圖書館資訊服務以教育現代人具備資訊素養為服務目標之理念已逐漸在國際間傳播。1993年在巴塞隆納召開之國際圖書館學會聯盟(International Federation of Library Associations and Institutions,簡稱IFLA)會議,所標示之主題為,"寰宇圖書館:圖書館為供應寰宇資訊之中心",即表達圖書館將提供所有資訊,並藉由資訊媒體傳播全世界希望與需要資訊的人的服務理念,這充份顯示所有知識範疇之資訊將透過圖書館資訊服務供應全球上每一個人。

反觀臺灣雖然已有文章探討圖書館之社會教育功能與圖書館利用教育,但甚少真正觸及資訊素養與圖書館資訊服務之涵義,檢視臺灣有關這方面文獻相當貧乏,但近年來已大有進步。撰寫此文的目的,首先探究資訊素養之真意、內涵以及其演變情形,並希望能進一步探究由圖書館資訊服務整體性、系統性與全方位之規劃資訊素養之培育方針與評鑑指標,提供人們參考。

三、臺灣資訊素養活動與研究

近年臺灣地區教育改革的理念普遍受到重視,消除昇學壓力,提倡終身學習的觀念亦廣泛受到討論。而資訊素養並沒有很具體以活動方式開展出來,但在相關研討會中,許多專家學者發表的論文,逐漸地提出資訊素養相關具體的作法或理念。

李德竹教授於1994年國科會專案研究計劃"由資訊素養研究圖書館資訊服務之意義與內涵"中,探討海內外圖書館資訊服務之發展現況、資訊服務的定義與內涵,並研擬圖書館資訊服務之資訊素養發展模式。該計劃研究認為在未來資訊社會中,資訊已成為現代人生活中之必需品,因此無論在生活、工作或實現個人計劃時,公民均需具備資訊管理技巧與資訊利用知識,此即為資訊素養。賦於資訊素養之定義是:"資訊素養係培育公民瞭解資訊的價值,在需要資訊時能有效率地查詢資訊、評估資訊、組織資訊與利用資訊"。[38]

1997年,李德竹教授繼1994年之資訊素養之意義與內涵之研究後,發表"由圖書館資訊服務規劃臺灣圖書館資訊素養之培育方針與評量指標"之研究報告。該研究係根據1994年原計劃研究成果與教育白皮書──臺灣教育報告書,以問卷與座談會方式調查臺閩地區圖書館資訊服務之現況和學者專家及圖書館從業人員對資訊素養的認知與期望,研擬圖書館推展資訊素養計劃之具體行動,以及推廣資訊素養落實於圖書館資訊服務之觀念。研究結果發現,目前臺灣各類型圖書館以普遍施行圖書館推廣教育與服務,然受限於館藏與設備之不足,使得資訊素養教育推廣並不普遍。根據學者專家的意見認為圖書館館員各種資訊素養能力應在中等能力以上,然館員實際能力只有初級能力。針對此一現況,該研究分別就圖書館、學校教師及政府教育單位研擬資訊素養培育方針,與圖書館資訊素養評量指標初稿,以作為培育公民及專業圖書館員資訊素養的藍圖。最後,該研究針對政府、"教育部"、圖書館、學校教師及電腦資訊業界等,提出十項建

議，以全面推展資訊素養活動。㊴

《社教》雙月刊第 73 期（1996 年）曾以"資訊素養與終身學習"爲主題，作一系列專題探討。其中，王振鵠教授認爲所謂的資訊素養簡言之，即是資訊利用的基本能力。並認爲資訊素養的養成有兩個步驟，第一是教導民衆如何善於利用資訊，第二是保障資訊自由化。此外，圖書館館員素質的提昇，才能豐富使用者的學習機會。對於未來資訊素養與圖書館使用者教育的昇級，則有賴於建立資源充裕的圖書館，與聘請學有專精之士，而圖書館面臨的挑戰也大於從前。㊵

林美和教授認爲資訊素養與傳統圖書館技能有別，必需超越傳統圖書館利用範圍。因此，一個資訊素養者應該具備五項基本能力，包括知道哪些是有幫助的資訊能力；知道哪裡獲取資訊的能力；具備檢索資訊能力；具備解釋、評估及組織資訊的能力；以及具備利用及傳播資訊的能力。林教授並針對家庭教育、學校教育及社會與成人教育等三方面，對如何培育資訊素養之措施皆提出具體建議。㊶

李隆盛教授認爲資訊素養就廣義而言是指有目的性之資料蒐集與處理的基本能力；狹義的資訊素養則等同於電腦素養。定義的寬窄常因人看的角度不同而有差別，當前資訊素養大都被視爲電腦素養。提昇資訊素養必需從學校、家庭與社會三個管道，但目前的現況均不理想，有待努力。素養是生活中的萬能鑰匙，未來發展是可期許的。㊷

陳仲彥探討圖書館利用教育與資訊素養的關係。並利用 McClure 之資訊素養概念，認爲資訊素養是包括傳統素養、媒體素養、電腦素養及網路素養等四種素養的交集點。因此，若要培育公民具備資訊素養，應從此四方面逐漸加強。圖書館在利用教育方面亦可從此四種素養，設計合於使用者需要的課程。㊸吳美美教授則認爲在資訊時代，資訊素養是人人必備的一項能力。尤其政府自 1995 年推動 NII 資訊基礎建設後，資訊素養能力的具備也更加迫切。㊹

謝金菊館長從臺北市立圖書館利育教育活動推廣方面，看資訊素養發展的未來，認爲加強臺北市民對圖書館電腦的操作與正規課程中加入資訊素養學科是相當必要，並又建議政府在增進公民資訊素養的同時，也應詳細規劃臺灣資訊系統整合，以營造一個良好的資訊使用環境。㊺

莊道明教授以資訊素養爲基礎，設計圖書館利用教育課程，並實際運用於新生圖書館之旅、通識課程及推廣教育課程。根據實行結果建議：（1）資訊素養的提昇有賴於資訊利用習慣的培養；（2）從實作導引學生成爲獨立學習者；（3）以圖書館爲學習場所；（4）整合與利用各種資訊媒體；（5）倡導資訊倫理的概念。㊻

楊美華教授認爲圖書館利用教育課程，可從資訊素養的觀點出發，培養師生成爲資訊社會的資訊消費者。建議在圖書館內部成立圖書館利用教育工作小組、合作編製教材、成立圖書館利用資訊交換中心及實行讀者研究。㊼

近年來，臺灣相關單位積極推動多項與資訊基礎建設相關之計劃，如 NII、教育改革、終身學習等，並明訂政策、目標及執行辦法，分別由不同單位執行。全民資訊素養之培育，爲具重要項目之一，期能在資訊爆炸的社會中，如何提昇公民使用資訊技能，正確認識資訊知識，進而培養尊重資訊的態度，臺灣社會相關學術單位已紛紛回應，積極行動中。

1999 年"資訊素養與終身學習社會國際研討會"（International Conference on

Information Literacy and Lifelong Learning）召開，以資訊素養與學習社會、國小課程與資訊素養教育、國高中課程與資訊素養教育、資訊科技與資訊素養教育、成人資訊素養教育、教師與資訊素養教育、圖書館與資訊素養教育等主題發表論文，同時邀請海外資訊素養專家，如 M. Eisenberg, C. C. Kuhlthau, P. Breivik, D. Sonnenwald 與會作專題演講，參加與討論踴躍，但討論中，似乎不同學科背景與會人員、學者、政府官員等對資訊素養之認知，有其差異性，這代表大家對資訊素養之基本認知問題，這次會議正好是一次認識資訊素養的基礎教育。[48]

臺北市立圖書館於1999年爲推動資訊素養以培育公民終身學習之技能，而在該館網頁放置終身學習網。該網站之協辦單位包括國中小學、高中、高職、"國家圖書館"、政府機構、各類基金會及服務中心、醫院、教育館、美術館等228個機構，該網站內容豐富、資源廣闊，甚具參考價值。請參閱（http://lll.tprnl.edu.tw//legt.htm）。

"國家圖書館"爲推動終身學習，促進民衆認識及利用圖書館以及增進公民資訊素養能力，於1999年配合"邁向學習社會白皮書"第五案："結合圖書館推動讀書會活動專案"的推動而編印圖書館與資訊素養叢書。其內容涵蓋：圖書館的利用—公民小學篇、公民中學篇、高中高職篇和大專院校篇，另有公共圖書館利用、網路資源的利用、期刊資源的利用、視聽資源的利用、參考工具書的利用以及閱讀的愉悅等共十冊。該叢書爲配合不同使用對象而著，是利用圖書館即掌握資訊的入門書籍。[49]次年，"國家圖書館"爲配合"教育部"建立終身學習社會之政策，以及推動兒童及全民閱讀運動之計劃，擬結合"國家圖書館"、各級公共圖書館、師範校院及圖書資訊相關學系，共同培養各級學校校長、教師等具備圖書館利用及資訊素養教育之知能，俾成爲推動圖書館利用、資訊素養及閱讀指導之種子教師，以奠定學童終身學習之基本能力，進而提昇公民之人文素養，於2000年又提出"圖書館利用及資訊素養教育推廣活動計劃（草案）"執行期限爲2000年10月至2001年12月爲計劃，仍在進行中。同樣地，"國家圖書館"又於2000年在其"'國家圖書館'全球資訊網"網頁中設置"終身學習資訊網"（http://www.ncl.edu.tw/f8.htm），企能培養教育具有資訊素養之21世紀之公民。

2000年，由時報文教基金會、NII民間諮詢委員會、公共電視、"國科會"主辦"資訊人談資訊素養座談會"，共十三集。座談會主題包括：資訊素養的培養、資訊時代的溝通和知識的處理、作資訊的主人、資訊的窮人和富人、資訊時代的人權和隱私權、資訊政策、資訊犯罪等，邀請臺灣資訊知名專家學者主講和座談，對公民之資訊素養之培育，助益甚多。[50]

伍、圖書館資訊素養的演變

圖書館資訊素養是推廣資訊素養之主要動力，圖書館資訊素養的演變與圖書館成人教育（Library Adult Education）的發展有密不可分的關係，尤以美國爲然。所謂美國成人教育的意義常常與繼續教育（Continuous Education）、繼續學習（Continuous Learning）、成人學校（Adult School）、終身學習（Lifelong Learning）、夜校（NightSchool）及大學推廣課程（Extension Course）並無太大差異，這些教育方式也可以說是成人教育的同義詞。從此也可看出美國成人教育是一種多樣化的教育活動，這些教育活動包括正式與非正式的課程訓練，加上聯邦政府、地方政府、民間學術與公益團體的推動，使得美國成人教育在形式與方式上相當複雜且多樣性。[51]

美國早在 1830 年代便已經開始討論，公共圖書館對失學青年繼續教育與終身學習的問題所該扮演的角色。[52]美國公共圖書館在十九世紀中葉建立之初，主要的任務之一就是透過非正式的發展成人教育，使社會成人能有個自我學習與持續習得新事務的環境。識字教育的推展就是當時公共圖書館最重要的活動之一。其他如政治活動的參與、權利與義務的認識、健康與家庭教育的學習，也先後成為初期美國公共圖書館成人教育的內涵。1900 年至 1915 年之間美國擁入大量各國的移民，這股移民的風潮讓許多美國有識之士擔心，因為過多的移民人口使得美國的生活品質降低，因此紛紛要求對這些外來的移民施行教育，希望透過教育的方式使這些移民能瞭解美國的生活方式與說、寫、讀美式的英語，最後達成同化的目的。當時美國的公共圖書館針對移民的成人，就提供有關美國憲法、政府、公民訓練與風土人情的讀物，并開設免費的語言訓練班。[53]

1924 年美國圖書館學會在美國卡內基基金會（Carnegie Foundation）的贊助下，成立一個負責調查圖書館與成人教育的委員會。主要調查成人教育運動現況，及圖書館對失學成年人，可協助的活動方法與研究。根據這份研究報告對於成人教育概念的定義是：[54]

> 何謂成人教育？成人教育或許可以是對不識字者施以教導，使之具備閱讀能力。對某些人而言，成人教育意謂著對外來者美國化的活動；對其他人而言，成人教育代表職業訓練。然而成人教育絕對不止於此，根據對事實的明辨，教育是一種終身的過程，人在短暫的學校教育，即大學畢業後，更需要進一步的訓練、啟發與心智成長。學校教育因受制於基本教育的限制，使個人的真正發展必須完全仰賴畢業後獨自的努力。

歷經兩年對公共圖書館的調查工作之後，該委員會提出正式的報告。報告提出六項建議，其中有九個明確的需求，需要圖書館認真的予以考量，以達成對成人教育應負的責任。同時建議美國圖書館學會設立永久的成人教育委員會（Adult Education Board），以繼續這方面的努力。在 1926 年至 1937 年間，美國圖書館學會設置圖書館與成人教育理事會（Board on Library and Adult Education），在 1937 至 1955 年間改組成立美國圖書館學會教育理事會（American Library Association Education Board）。1920 年至 1940 年間，美國公共圖書館提供的成人教育服務主要目標包括個人發展、職業改善訓練與全民啟蒙教育等。根據這些目標，公共圖書館建立提供給個人與群體使用圖書館的圖書資源，作為個人教育與啟蒙的服務哲學。讀書會、展覽、演講活動、電影欣賞、與讀者的諮詢服務等，均是當時公共圖書館經常性的成人教育活動。在 1951 至 1955 年間，美國公共圖書館學會更推出一系列成人教育的計劃，以提昇民眾教育水準。[55]

至 1950 年代末期，由於美國聯邦政府積極的支援，美國公共圖書館開始步入黃金時期而快速發展。1956 年美國國會通過 "圖書館服務法案"（Library Services Act），使得美國公共圖書館在獲得聯邦政府財政支持下，發展各鄉鎮地區公共圖書館事業並建全圖書館的財源基礎。當時許多圖書巡迴車的購置與利用，對於偏遠地區的讀者，包括老年人、家庭婦女、殘障者，在提昇成人服務方面發揮了相當的作用，也使成人教育呈現另一種面貌。[56]在 1957 年的美國圖書館年會上，通過將成人教育理事會更名為成人服務部

（Adult Services Division，簡稱 ASD）。此時為了回應對於識字教育的需要，該部門與公共圖書館學會（Public Library Association，簡稱 PLA）合作成立了兩個委員會，一個是成人閱讀改善委員會（ASD Committee on Reading Improvement for Adults），及功能性文盲服務委員會（PLA Committee on Serving the Functionally Illiterate）。回顧美國此時期圖書館推展成人教育活動，所面臨的最大問題，則是缺乏適當教材來提供給初學的成人讀者。[57]

自 1967 年到 1985 年之間，在高等教育法案之圖書館研究與示範計劃（The Library Research and Demonstration Program, Title II-B of the Higher Education Act，簡稱 HEA Title II-B, Library R&D）與圖書館服務與建設法案的圖書館服務計劃（The Library Services Program, Title I of the Library Services and Construction Act，簡稱 LSCA Title I）兩計劃下，圖書館共獲得 140 萬美金的資助，用於支援八個識字教育的計劃上。由於這些計劃相繼在美國各地先後推展，使得圖書館成為美國成人識字教育的重要場所之一。[58]

美國圖書館在歷經如此長期的成人識字教育計劃之後，也漸漸開始重新評估各種活動的效益，及檢討圖書館往後在成人教育應該扮演的角色與功能。甚多學者也開始體認到由於資訊技術廣泛被應用於圖書館的各種服務，使得傳統僅將成人識字教育定位對紙本圖書的識字活動上，已經不能符合時代的需求。因此主張對於"識字"一詞應該採取更廣泛的解釋。諾理斯（M. S. Knowles）認為在一個知識爆炸、技術革新與講求教育均等的時代中，對教育目的的定義與對移轉知識力量的信念已經不適宜。面對未來的社會我們必須重新定義教育的任務，乃在於培育公民具備適應新環境的能力。這些公民在任何變動的情況下，均能夠運用本身的知識解決所面臨的問題。每位公民需所應具備之基本條件，是具備能夠參與任何終身自我導向學習（Lifelong Self-Directed Learning）之能力。[59]類似的討論也廣泛獲得許多圖書館界的回響，終於在 1987 年美國圖書館學會召開資訊素養主席委員會議（The American Library Association's Presidential Committee on Information Literacy），在主席克利思郝姆（M. Chrisholm）主持下，召集教育界與圖書館界的許多領袖針對三項議題作廣泛的討論。[60]

該委員會於 1989 年出版<u>美國圖書館學會資訊素養主席委員會總結報告</u>（American Library Association Presidential Committee on Information Literacy, Final Report）。在 1991 年美國圖書館與資訊服務全國委員會（National Commission on Library and Information Science，簡稱 NCLIS）在美國白宮圖書館與資訊服務會議（White House Conference on Library and Information Services，簡稱 WHCLIS）中，資訊素養成為重要的討論議題，並在其報告中正式將資訊素養列為未來重點工作。美國更將 1990 年定為素養年（Literacy Year）。美國聯邦政府在 1991 年透過國會立法通過"美國國家素養法案"（National Literacy Act）。法案中對"素養"一詞的定義已經予以擴大，其定義足以含蓋"成人教育法案"（Adult Education Act）與"圖書館服務與建設法案"（Library Services and Construction Act）中素養的定義。"美國國家素養法案"於素養的定義是：[61]

　　一個人能使用英語達到讀、寫、說的能力，且在工作與社會需求上，以具生產方式從事計算與解決問題，以達成個人的目標，發展個人的知識與潛能。

此定義已將素養定義內容予以擴充，考慮到整個人的需求，這個需求可隨著時間的不同而有所不同，且可由傳統教室外的方法獲得滿足。針對這個法案美國已經擬妥五個發展方向,同時成立國家素養局(National Institute for Literacy),希望與各地區、州與聯邦的素養機構攜手合作,設定需要達到計劃預期的效果。計有五個發展計劃包括:成立各州的素養資源中心(State Literacy Resource Centers);發展國家工作力素養策略(National Workforce Literacy Strategies);州與地方監獄犯人的功能性素養(Functional Literacy for State and Local Prisoners);州與地方監獄犯人的生活技巧訓練(Life Skills Training for State and Local Prisoners);家庭素養公共廣播計劃(Family Literacy Public Broadcasting Program)等。[62]美國各地方圖書館也積極配合這些計劃的目標,在獲得不同程度資助下提出各種發展計劃。1998年美國全國資訊素養論壇發表"資訊專業進展報告書",除針對"美國圖書館學會資訊素養委員會結案報告書"之六項建議逐項進行成果報告之外,並提出未來工作建議,更進一步的促使美國推展資訊素養之積極發展。[63]

從以上發展過程的演進,可以瞭解美國圖書館界配合社會發展的需要,努力積極回應成人教育活動的需求,推展成人素養教育。隨著科技的進步與整個資訊環境的改變,對於素養的定義與內涵也產生了變化。從早期將素養視為識字教育,到今日產生各種特定領域的素養,例如家庭素養、工作素養、電腦素養、資訊素養等,皆說明今日多元社會發展下,學校正規教育已經無法滿足人一生的需求。全民的終身教育已是時勢所趨,美國圖書館一本積極參與成人教育的初衷,適時提出資訊素養作為圖書館未來成人終身教育的發展方向,是值得圖書館界從業人員學習與借鏡。

陸、資訊素養教育活動

資訊素養教育的目的係培育人們從各種資訊資源學習,即透過課程學習或人力發展的機會而成為具有資訊素養特質的人。一般資訊素養教育涵蓋的內容如下:[64]
・瞭解資訊社會的本質;
・瞭解資訊查詢與利用的價值;
・能夠確認資訊需求;
・找尋、檢索、評估與綜合所需的資訊;
・發展高度的傳播技能,包括與同儕及資訊專家的溝通能力;
・發展重要的資訊資源知識,並包括網路資源與使用的策略;
・藉由電腦的使用以發展管理檢得資訊的能力,如文書處理、試算表、書目管理軟體等。

同時亦應培育資訊科技硬體與軟體、圖書、報紙、錄影帶、光碟、各種資訊媒體以及其他電腦設備的知識與技能。

大體而言,資訊素養教育方面,臺灣目前尚缺乏具體活動,海外則以美國最活躍,以下從美國地區、其他國家和臺灣分別陳述之。

一、美國資訊素養教育活動方面

艾森柏格(Michael Eisenberg)在資訊素養活動中影響最大,主張學校圖書館媒體資源中心在教學方面應提供圖書館與資訊技能課程(Library and Information Skills Curriculum),並從教學/訓練歷程方面,發展圖書館與資訊技能課程的架構:六大資訊技能(Big Six Skills)。首先,艾森柏格依據布隆(Benjamin Bloom)六級人類認知目標:

知識、理解、應用、分析、綜合與評估,發展出下列資訊問題解決歷程的六大資訊技能:[65]

（一）問題界定（Trask Definition）：決定資訊問題與界定資訊查詢的目的；

（二）資訊查詢策略（Information Seeking Strategies）：針對前已界定的資訊問題，決定找尋資訊資源的種類與策略；

（三）找尋與查詢資訊（Location of and Access to Information）：找到資訊資源並且從中檢索特定的資訊；

（四）利用資訊（Use or Information）：依據前已界定的資訊需求以運用查得的資訊；

（五）綜合（Synthesis）：整合、組織與重新組裝資訊以滿足前述問題的需要；

（六）評估（Evaluation）：評估資訊問題解決歷程是否滿足資訊的需求。

這六大技能課程係以系統式的結構表現教學目標，六大技能的每一技能領域中，均再列舉次目標說明所需的重要技能與協助獲得的完整能力。六大技能課程係幫助學生成為有效的資訊問題解決者，目的是訓練學生在找尋、使用、組織、表現、與評估資訊過程中運用系統性策略與批判式思考以有效地解決問題。

美國亞歷桑那州立大學（Arizona State University）為改善圖書館利用指導活動，支援學校教學，以及將資訊素養的概念推廣於學校課程發展中，該校組織任務小組並編製一份學校資訊素養能力清單，以圖書館為標誌，題名為"學生資訊素養能力"（Information Literacy Competencies for Students）。此清單分發給每一位圖書館員，作為各學科領域開授課程與訓練的大綱[66]，其內容主張資訊或圖書館素養須涵蓋三種能力：查詢資訊能力、評估資訊能力與綜合資訊能力。一旦學生具備這些能力則具備終生學習的潛能。學生將獲得下列的概念性資訊素養能力：

（一）瞭解能力；

（二）認識各種層級、種類與形式的資訊，以及其適當的運用。

（三）重視資訊查詢政策相關問題，如著作權、隱私、政府資訊之民營化、電子資訊查詢、與資訊指數成長等。

1990年資訊技能委員會（Information Skills Ad Hoc Committee）發表一份資訊技能清單提供新漢普夏（New Hampshire）地區的圖書館媒體專家，協助他們將資訊技能的培育整合於該區的學校教學中。其界定資訊技能（Information Skills）為有效的查詢、評估、組織、傳播與應用資訊的歷程。該委員會訂定中小學各年級資訊技能課程核心目標，列舉以下九項：（1）瞭解資訊在現代社會的功能；（2）利用圖書館與資訊系統作為資訊與娛樂的資源；（3）以負責任與合乎倫理的方式利用資訊科技；（4）認識資訊資源的優點、缺點與影響；（5）辨識資訊需求與發展查詢策略；（6）利用各種技能與策略以記錄與組織資訊；（7）建構資訊的意義；（8）利用各種途徑與形式以傳播資訊；（9）評估資訊查詢策略與資訊利用的成果。[67]

1991年柏札娜（Susan N. Bjorner）提出一份資訊素養課程模式，界定資訊素養應涵蓋下列能力：（1）確認資訊需求；（2）主動尋求滿足這些資訊需求；（3）發展找尋資訊的策略；（4）實施這些策略；（5）組織、評估與利用資訊。並參考州際職業技術教育聯盟（Vocational-Technical Education Consortium of States，簡稱V-TECS）所發展的教育訓練模式，係一種行為式與工作能力基礎式，專為職業教育訓練設計的課程。柏札娜根據州際職業技術教育聯盟課程發展技術參考手冊（V-TECS Product Development Technical Reference Handbook）發展其工作能力基礎模式（Competency-Based Model），將培育的資訊素養能力，細分八項行動（或職責），每一行動之下並詳列其特定的資訊管理行為，詳細臚列如次：[68]
（一）認識與接受資訊差距（Information gap）的存在
（二）積極回應研究的需求
（三）發展各種策略以減少資訊距離
（四）評估與選擇策略
（五）依據策略行動
（六）評估策略的效率
（七）利用資訊
（八）儲存資訊以供未來使用

1987—1988年蒙大那公共教育局（Montana Board of Public Education）從事一項"卓越計劃：規劃下一個世紀的教育"（Project Excellence：Designing Education for the Next Century）的活動，廣泛地檢視該州認可標準而制定一系列模式教育目標與評量以協助發展蒙大那中小學良好品質的教育。1992年由公共教學處組成的蒙大那教學者小組發展圖書館媒體教學計劃的模式課程以協助各區域的課程發展，其要件有：合作規劃、問題解決歷程、研究規劃指南、素養教學計劃、科技書面說明、評量策略。首先，該模式以文字說明圖書館與資訊技能的任務；其次，說明合作規劃的內容、程序與合作單元的評量；復次，界定問題解決歷程以及闡釋其六項主要技能：問題界定、資訊找尋策略、找尋與查詢資訊、資訊的利用、綜合以及評估。此外，還舉例與示範問題解決歷程的評量、提供研究規劃的指南、界定素養，以及討論素養教學計劃的要件與評量。最後，該模式尚提供豐富的文件指南，如具彈性的時程規劃、學校媒體中心人員安置。以及學校圖書館媒體教學計劃角色等。[69]

1994年科羅拉多州教育媒體學會（Colorado Education Media Association）制定"資訊素養指南"（Information Literacy Guidelines），主張具備資訊素養的學生才是有競爭力與獨立的學習者，此資訊素養指南係課程中學習資訊素養的歷程，並從學術環境擴展至真實的生活中。該指南並指導教師將資訊素養課程與其他課程標準（如社會科學、地理、閱讀、寫作、科學與數學等）整合，以培育學生成為具有資訊素養的人，而資訊素養的培育更應該是圖書館媒體專家、教師、學校行政主管與社會的共同責任。該指南涵蓋了五項資訊素養教育的領域，各領域並詳細訂定培育的具體行動，依次說明如后：[70]
（一）培育學生成為知識尋求者
（二）培育學生成為優良產品的創造者
（三）培育學生成為自我導向的學習者
（四）培育學生成為團體的貢獻者
（五）培育學生成為負責的資訊使用者

鑑於美國勞工部必備技能促進委員會（Secretary's Commission on Achieving Necessary Skills，簡稱SCANS）的報告書中將資訊素養列為五種個人基本工作能力之一，同時柯林頓總統在美國全國技術政策中也定其為重要的高技能工作能力，監督與課程發展學會

（Association of Supervision and Curriculum Development）呼籲資訊素養是個人能掌握全球資訊社會機會的重要關鍵，1995 年美國學校圖書館員學會（American Association of School Librarians）針對資訊素養提出一份資訊問題解決技能課程基本培育計劃 "資訊素養：資訊問題解決宣言"（Information Literacy: A Position Paper on Information Problem Solving），主張資訊素養是培養學生成為終生學習者的重要基礎，也是應用資訊問題解決技能（Information Problem Solving Skills）的同義詞。此資訊素養宣言確認資訊素養要件，並提供將資訊素養培育與幼稚園及中小學課程整合的理論。該學會在該文件中界定資訊問題解決技能為個人在學校、工作與生活中具有查詢與使用資訊之能力。資訊素養課程基本要件如次：[11]

（一）界定資訊需要：使學生認識資訊的存在、界定需求
（二）擬定查詢策略：使學生規劃查詢策略
（三）找尋資源：使學生從各種資源找到特定的資訊
（四）評估與瞭解資訊：使學生找到有用資訊，知道檢視與決定有用之資訊
（五）解釋資訊：使學生在評估資訊後，必須利用資訊解決特定資訊問題
（六）傳播資訊：學生必須將資訊問題解決之結果組織，並傳播資訊與他人分享
（七）評估產品與程序：使學生評估最後成品是否解決資訊問題與採用的步驟是否適當與有效

二、其他國家資訊素養教育活動方面

英國 Faculty of Information Services at the Cheltenham and Gloucester College of Higher Education 自 1990 年起利用研習會（Workshop）方式以協助資訊技能課程的教學，課程的目的係培育學生成為終生自我教育者，在任何時候均可有效處理資訊，其目標包括：圖書館導介、建立使用者信心、資訊資源的認識以及培養資訊技能。資訊技能學習手冊用以培育學生的資訊技能，其內容包括：(1) 文獻查詢程序綱領；(2) 各種資訊資源概介；(3) 依學系學科主題編製指南；(4) 參考與編製書目；(5) 著作權；(6) 學習中心的概介；(7) 評鑑問卷；(8) 詞彙；(9) 支援與加強上述課程之活動。此外，尚設計其他練習，如初步作業、從閱讀清單查找圖書與期刊、利用線上公共目錄從事主題檢索、期刊用作主題檢索以及使用各主題參考書。[12]

鑑於資訊素養的重要，澳洲在 1992 年舉行："資訊素養：澳洲的行動計劃"（Information Literacy: Australia's Agenda）研討會，從個人、各類圖書館、工商業從業人力以及政府等各角度分別探討資訊素養的重要性與其培養問題。其中哈里森（Chris Harrison）列舉現代人成為有效的工作者所必備的重要技能，包括：(1) 蒐集、分析與組織資訊；(2) 傳播概念與資訊；(3) 規劃與組織活動的能力；(4) 與他人以及在團體中共同工作的能力；(5) 使用數學概念與技能；(6) 解決問題之能力；(7) 利用科技的能力。[13]

哈里森更具體界定 "蒐集、分析與組織資訊的能力" 為找尋、汲取與分類資訊的能力，即依其需要以實用的方式選擇資訊，評估資訊與資訊資源，以及獲得資訊。此一定義是基於下列四種理念：(1) 反應各種資訊目的、資訊資源與讀者的特質；(2) 查詢與檢索技能與原則之應用；(3) 資訊之分析與組織；(4) 資訊品質與有效性之評估。為確

實培養蒐集、分析與組織資訊的能力,哈里森研定下列三等級的表現程度(Performance Level):[74]

第一級表現程度(Performance Level 1):此級的人懂得
·遵循資訊蒐集、分析與組織的指南;
·從特定資訊評估與記錄資訊;
·根據既有的資訊分類方式組織資訊;
·檢核資訊的完整與正確;
·並懂得其他蒐集、分析與組織資訊的應用,如:從電腦資料庫查詢人事資訊;使用檔案整理發票;從技術的需求來決定處理事物的限度;更新電話與地址索引;在團體活動會配合各成員的需求安排最佳的開會時間等。

第二級表現程度(Performance Level 2):此級的人懂得
·辨別讀者需求與資訊目的;
·從許多資訊資源中查詢與記錄資訊;
·根據資訊組織的方式選擇適當的資訊種類與結構;
·評估所獲得資訊的相關性、正確性與完整性;
·並懂得其他蒐集、分析與組織資訊的應用,如:根據成員的需求安排團體旅遊活動;準備工作訓練計劃;建立個人與機構的物料與設備的需求等。

第三級表現程度(Performance Level 3):此級的人懂得
·界定讀者需求與資訊目的;
·判斷研究資料以確認相關資訊;
·根據主要的組織類型與結構以確認資訊;
·評估資訊的品質與有效性;
·並懂得其他蒐集、分析與組織資訊的應用,如:建立決策資料庫、蒐集會議論文與委員會開會的記錄;懂得運用有關機構利潤、客戶需求、自助餐、與四季變化的記錄行事;建立海外的旅游資訊庫;從事澳州社會家庭型態之文獻查詢等。

另一方面,澳州布魯斯(Christine Susan Bruce)對於高等教育的資訊素養的教育也提出建議,發展"葛福斯大學資訊素養藍圖"(Griffith University's Information Literacy Blueprint),以道爾的博士論文資訊素養的定義與能力特質作爲理論架構,而建議高等教育應重視獨立與自主式的學習;運用資訊的處理;利用資訊科技;重視資訊價值;以及培育學生具備批判性資訊處理的能力。布魯斯更進一步提出資訊素養教育的內涵。教育責任、培育策略、學術課程的規劃、教育的評量以及在此活動中所有參與者應扮演的角色。[75]

三、臺灣資訊素養教育活動方面

臺灣在資訊素養教育方面缺乏具體活動,與此較爲相關者如"教育部"計劃推動的資訊教育活動,大分爲四個方向:(1)資訊普及教育;(2)資訊專業教育;(3)資訊應用教育;(4)整體教育資訊環境之建立。資訊普及教育係指在各級學校普遍實施資訊基礎課程,使學習者具備電腦基本素養,以培養其適應資訊社會的知能。資訊專業教育係指在資訊科系所及資訊相關科系所之資訊專業人才教育,培養從事資訊系統之研究、開發、管理及教學等工作。資訊應用教育係爲應用電腦各專業科目中,培養學生具有活用資訊工具的能力。教育資訊環境之建立即利用資訊科技發展教育與研究網路系統及電腦輔助教學軟體,以增進學習成效,提高教學品質,建立良好的教學與研究環境。[76]

"教育部"之資訊教育計劃始於 1989 年,當時重點是推展電腦輔助教學計劃。至 1993 年,"行政院"核准"改善各級學校資訊教學計劃"(執行期限 1993 年 7 月至 1997 年 6 月),才正式推出資訊教育多項計劃,其中資訊教育基礎建設計劃、資訊通信基本建設 NII 人才培育計劃、資訊課程、師資、設備、在職教師資訊培訓等。[77]1997 年"教育部"爲配合"行政院"提昇臺灣競争力政策,決定整合資訊教育相關計劃,而推出"資訊教育基礎計劃",目標是爲配合資訊時代的需求,建置完善的資訊教學環境,"教育部"整合原有資訊相關計劃——改善各級學校資訊教學計劃、電腦輔助教學軟體發展及推廣計劃、TANet 到中小學計劃,彙總爲"資訊教育基礎建設計劃"(1997 年 7 月至 2007 年 6 月),除延續與拓展既有的資訊教育重點工作外,長期目標爲建置一個全方位的資訊教學環境,普及全民資訊教育。計劃目標分爲短期(1997 年 7 月至 2001 年 6 月)與長期(2001 年 7 月至 2007 年 6 月),計劃內容共七項:

(一) 充實資訊教學資源
(二) 改善教學模式
(三) 加強人才培訓
(四) 推動調整組織制度
(五) 提昇設備
(六) 延伸臺灣學術網路
* (七) 普及資訊素養

計劃內容中,主要工作項目共 14 項;該計劃之預期效果如下:(1)資訊際遇向下紮根、普及全民資訊教育,使公民具基本資訊素養、輕鬆邁入資訊化社會。(2)資訊教育基礎環境之建置暨網路科技,將使各級學校共享教育資源,縮短城鄉教育差距。(3)資訊科技融入各學科,使教材、教法及教學媒體多元化,改善傳統教學模式與制度,建立啓發式、互動式學習環境,提昇學習效益。(4)以電腦資訊網路連結成開放式學習環境,延伸學習理念得以逐步落實。

此計劃之影響是希望(1)透過資訊教育基礎建設計劃,提昇全民資訊素養,建置資訊化校園環境,爲臺灣推動資訊基礎建設 NII、亞太營運中心等計劃奠定基石。(2)在各國競相投入資訊教育相關建設以厚植國力之際,臺灣亦可並駕齊驅,不致在資訊化時代中成爲落後地區。[78]

最後,"教育部"資訊教育計劃中,除資訊教育基礎建設計劃正進行中,另 NII 人才培育、在職教師資訊培訓、終身學習通網未來、社會教育資訊網計劃等皆同時進行。"'教育部'擴大内需方案"中已訂出"中小學教師資訊基本素養短期指標"。[79]由於"教育部"資訊教育一系列計劃偏向資訊基礎建設,多以電腦素養爲主,與真正的資訊素養之理念有其差異性,尚未觸及真正資訊素養教育的全部層面,因此愈加肯定了研究此主題的重要性與迫切性。資訊與電腦在公衆之認知上一直混淆的,基本認知不清,推動資訊素養理念將會偏頗,令人憂心!

柒、結 論

在資訊社會中，資訊已成為現代人生活中之必需品，無論在生活、工作或實現個人計劃均需要具備資訊管理技巧與資訊利用知識，此即為資訊素養，至為重要。本文已定義資訊素養係培育公民瞭解資訊，在需要資訊時能有效率地查詢資訊、評估資訊、組織資訊與利用資訊之能力。

今日正值資訊社會時代，或稱為後工業社會時代，或稱為知識經濟時代，其主要特徵以知識與資訊為重，將資訊和理論知識視為未來社會的策略資源。著名學者波拉之論述分析社會中[⑧]主要資訊部門為八大類，圖書館與資訊中心則歸類其中，足茲證明圖書館為社會主要資訊部門，而提供資訊服務為其職能。圖書館資訊服務之活動主要包括：圖書館資訊之選擇、徵集、組織與傳播及利用。

圖書館資訊服務新模式[⑧]，是以圖書館擔任教育者、資訊供應者、圖書館三位一體之角色為模式之軸心原則，而應用到各類型圖書館資訊服務，如學校圖書館、大專院校圖書館、公共圖書館與專門圖書館等作為模式軸心結構。圖書館資訊服務之新模式是以培養終身學習、獨立自導式學習之民眾為目標，以增加民眾具備下列五種資訊素養之能力：（1）知道什麼是有用資訊之能力；（2）知道何處可以獲得資訊之能力；（3）檢索資訊之能力；（4）闡釋、評估與組織資訊之能力；（5）使用與傳播資訊之能力。因此，培養資訊素養主要目標在教育人們成為終身學習者與獨立及自導式學習者，所以中小學教育與高等教育首應推動資訊素養教育，並且充分運用圖書館資源以發展新的學習模式，使學生接受批判性思考方式與主動學習之教學形式。

資訊時代中培養具有資訊素養之公民已為民主社會現代國家之必備條件。先進國家如美國已在七十年代倡導資訊素養觀念，並積極成立專門小組研究，舉行各種會議討論，廣徵各方意見，與四處宣傳執行。目前在學校圖書館、大專院校圖書館與公共圖書館均有建樹。反觀臺灣則遠落於後，雖已在起步階段，但觀念仍在懵懂之際。為迎接現代化美好的資訊人生，任何國家皆應以培植終身學習與富有資訊素養的公民為首先要務，此應是圖書館資訊機構當人不讓之職責與任務。

註 釋

註①：Major R. Owens, "State Government & Libraries," Library Journal 101 (I Jan. 1976), p. 27.

註②："國家科學委員會"，《技術科學素養教育重點研究規劃》，"國家科學委員會"研究報告 NSC81－0111－S－155－501（1992年3月1日至8月31日）。頁1。

註③：黃富順等，《成人識字教育之研究摘要》，在成人基本教育研究專集（臺北："教育部"社教司，1993年），頁5。

註④：The Random House Dictionary of the English Language 2nd. ed. (NJ: Random House, 1987), p. 1122.

註⑤：同註③，頁1。

註⑥：同註③，頁6。

註⑦：American Library Association Presidential Committee on Information Literacy, Final Report (Chicago: American Library Association, 1989), p. 1.

註⑧：L. B. Jones, "Linking Undergraduate Education and Libraries: Minnesota's Approach," in Information Literacy: Developing Students as Independent Learners, ed. by D. W. Farmer, T. F. Mech (San Francisco: Jossey-Bass, 1992), pp. 31-32.

註⑨：K. E. McHenry, J. T. Stewart, and J. L. Wu. "Teaching Resource-Based Learning and Diversity," in Information Literacy: Developing Students as Independent Learners, ed. by D. W. Farmer, T. F. Mech (San Francisco: Jossey-Bass, 1992), pp. 55-56.

註⑩：J. K. Olsen. "The Electronic Library and Literacy," in Information Literacy; Developing Students as Independent Learners, ed. by D. W. Farmer, T. F. Mech (San Francisco: Jossey-Bass, 1992), p. 94.

註⑪：C. Curran, "Information Literacy and the Public Librarian," Public Libraries (Nov. / Dec. 1990), p. 349.

註⑫：H. B. Rader, "Bibliographic Instruction or Information Literacy," College & Research Libraries News 51: 1 (1990), p. 20.

註⑬：── "Information Literacy: A Revolution in the Library." RQ 31: 1 (1991), p. 26.

註⑭：L. J. McCrank, "Academic Programs for Information Literacy: Theory and Structure," RQ 31: 4 (1992), pp. 485-487.

註⑮：此定義為謝清俊教授對技學素養所下的定義。引用自"國家科學委員會"研究報告, 技術科學素養教育重點研究規劃, (1992年8月31日)。

註⑯：E. D. Hirsch, Jr., Cultural Literacy: What Every American Needs to Know (New York: Random House, 1987).

註⑰：H. H. Lyman, "Libraries, Literacy and the Information Society," The Bookmark 48: 3 (Spring, 1990), p. 171.

註⑱：C. R. McClure, "Network Literacy: A Role for Libraries?" Information Technology and Libraries (June, 1994), p. 117.

註⑲：同註18。

註⑳：同註18, p. 118。

註㉑：Ling. Wey Jeng, "Information Literacy for Information Professionals," Managing Information and Technology. ASIS Proceedings of the 52nd Annual Meeting of the American Society for Information Science, October 30 November 2, 1989 (Washington, D. C.: American Society for Information Science, 1989), p. 188.

註㉒：Howard M. Dess, "Information Literacy: A Subject Source Survey and Annotated Bibliography," in Information Literacy: Learning How to Learn, ed. by Jana Varlejs (Jefferson, NC: McFarland & Company, 1990), p. 63.

註㉓：Patricia Senn Breivik, "Education for the Information Age," in Information Literacy: Developing Students as Independent Learners. eds. by D. W. Farmer, T. F. Mech

(San Francisco, CA: Jossey-Bass Publishers, 1992), p. 7.

註㉔: Patricia Senn Breivik and Robert Wedgeworth, <u>Libraries and the Search for Academic Excellence</u> (Metuchen, N. J.: Scarecrow Press, 1988).

註㉕: <u>American Library Association Presidential Committee on Information Literacy, Final Report</u> (Chicago: ALA, January 1989).

註㉖: U. S. National Commission on Libraries and Information Science. <u>Information Literacy and Education for the 21st Century: Toward the 21st Century</u> (Washington, D. C.: NCLIS, 1990).

註㉗: Janice Fennell, ed., <u>Building on the First Century Proceedings of the 5th National Conference of the Association of College and Research Libraries, Cincinnati. April 5－8, 1989</u> (Chicago: ACRL, 1989).

註㉘: 同註12。

註㉙: 同前註, pp. 11－12.

註㉚: Jana Varlejs, ed., <u>Information Literacy: Learning How to Learn</u> (Jefferson, NC: McFarland & Company, 1990).

註㉛: <u>Information 2000: Library and Information Services for the 21st Century. Final Report of the 1991 White House Conference on Library and Information Services.</u> (Washington, D C: U. S. National Commission on Libraries and Information Science, 1992).

註㉜: http://www. ala. org//acrl/nili/nili. html (30 Oct., 2000).
Patricia Senn Breivik, "Information Literacy: the 21st Century Literacy," <u>資訊素養與終身學習社會國際研討會會議論文集</u>, 1999年5月13—14日（臺北市："國立師範大學"社會教育學系, 1999年）。

註㉝: 同前註。

註㉞: 同註㉓, pp. 9－10.

註㉟: 同前註。

註㊱: Ard P. Hartsuijker, "Development of Computer and Information Literacy in the Netherlands," <u>Education and Computimg</u> 2 (1986), pp. 89－93.

註㊲: Suzanne Maranda, "Developing the Role of the End-User Librarian," <u>Bibliotheca Medica Canadian</u> 10 (1989), pp. 126－129.

註㊳: 李德竹,《由資訊素養研究圖書館資訊服務之意義與內涵》, <u>"國科會"專案研究計劃</u>（臺北市："國科會", 1994年）。

註㊴: 李德竹,《由圖書館資訊服務規劃臺灣圖書館資訊素養之培育方針與評量指標》, <u>"國科會"專案研究計劃</u>（臺北市："國科會", 1997年）。

註㊵: 陳靖儀採訪, "專訪王振鵠教授——談資訊素養與圖書館使用者教育", <u>社教</u> 73（1996年6月）, 頁22—23。

註㊶: 林美和,《資訊素養與終身學習的關系》, <u>社教</u> 73（1996年6月）, 頁7—12。

註㊷: 郭鍠莉採訪,《專訪李隆盛教授——談資訊素養教育》, <u>社教</u> 73（1996年6月）, 頁23—24。

註㊸: 陳仲彥,《資訊素養與圖書館利用教育》, <u>社教</u> 73（1996年6月）, 頁19—22。

註㊹：吳美美，《資訊時代人人需要資訊素養》，社教 73（1996 年 6 月），頁 4—5。
註㊺：馮嘉玉採訪，《專訪謝金菊館長——臺北市圖推展市民資訊素養的努力》，社教 73（1996 年 6 月），頁 25。
註㊻：莊道明，《以資訊素養為基礎的圖書館利用教育課程——世界新聞傳播學院圖書館實施方式》，資訊網絡時代圖書資訊利用教育研討會論文集（1997 年 3 月 6—7 日），頁 37—17。
註㊼：楊美華，《網路時代大學通識課程圖書資訊利用教育之實行》，資訊網路時代圖書資訊利用教育研討會論文集（1997 年 3 月 6—7 日），頁 159—163。
註㊽：資訊素養與終身學習社會國際研討會，"國立臺灣師範大學"，1999 年五月。（臺北市：1999 年）。
註㊾：《館務簡訊》，"國家圖書館"館訊 3（2000 年），頁 37。
註㊿：http://kids.yam.com/fresh.news/fresh.active/act-20000825.htm
註51：范承源，《美國的成人教育》，美國月刊 5：6（1990 年 10 月），頁 123—124。
註52：J. E. Coleman, "ALA's Role in Adult and Literacy Education," Library Trends 35：2（Fall 1986）, p. 207.
註53：賴麗珍，《美國公共圖書館的成人識字教育角色任務與策略》，成人教育 12（1993 年 3 月），頁 37。
註54：同註52, p. 208.
註55：同註52, p. 209.
註56：范承源，《美國公共圖書館與成人教育》，美國研究 17：4（1987 年 12 月），頁 47。
註57：同註52, P. 210.
註58：A. J. Mathews, A. Chute, and C. A. Cameron, "Meeting the Literacy Challenge：A Federal Perspective," Library Trends 35：2（Fall, 1986）, p. 219.
註 59：D. E. Weingand, "The Library-learner Dynamic in a Changing World," Library Trends 35：2（Fall, 1986）, p. 188.
註60：American Library Association Presidential Committee on Information Literacy, Final Report（Chicago：ALA, 1989）, p. 15.
註61：B. Humes, "The National Literacy Act：What Librarian should Know," The Bookmark 50：3（Spring, 1992）, p. 206.
註62：同註52, pp. 206-207.
註63：同註32。
註64：Christine Susan Bruce, "Information Literacy：a Framework for Higher Education," The Australian Library Journal 44：3（August 1995）, p. 163.
註65：Michael B. Eisenberg and Robert Berkowitz, "Library and Information Skills Curriculum Scope and Sequence：The Big Six Skills," in Current Initiative：An Agenda and Strategy for Library Media Programs（Norwood, NJ：Ablex Pub., 1988）, pp. 99-119.
註66：Dennis Isbell and Carol Hammond, "Information Literacy Competencies," College and

註⑯：　Research Libraries News 54：6（June 1993），pp. 325–327.
註⑰：　Information Skills：A Report from the Ad Hoc Committee（New Hampshire State Dept. of Education, Concord, 1992）.
註⑱：　Susan N. Bjorner, "The Information Literacy Curriculum—A Working Model," Iatul Quarterly 5：2（1991），pp. 150–160.
註⑲：　Nancy Keenan and Others, The Montana Library and Information Skills Model Curriculum Guide（Montana State Office of Public Instruction, Helena, Dept. of Vocational Education Services, 1994）.
註⑳：　Colorado Educational Media Association, Information Literacy Guidelines ERIC Document. Sep. 1994.
註㉑：　"Information Literacy：A Position Paper on Information Problem Solving," American Association of School Librarians Position Statement, Emergency Librarian 23：2（Nov./Dec. 1995），pp. 20–23.
註㉒：　Lynnette Bailey and Martin Jenkins, "Evolution of a Workbook as Part of an Information Skills Programme," Library Review 44：4（1995），pp. 13–20.
註㉓：　Chris Harrison, "Open and Flexible Learning：Information Literacy as a Key Competency," in Information Literacy：The Australian Agenda, ed. by Di Booker（Adelaide：University of South Australian Library, 1993），pp. 118–120.
註㉔：　同前註。
註㉕：　同註㉔, pp. 159–170.
註㉖：　"教育部", 資訊教育現況與展望（臺北："教育部", 1996年）。
註㉗：　資訊教育, < http://www.edu.tw/information/index.html >（30 Oct. 2000）.
註㉘：　資訊教育基礎建設簡介, < http://www.edu.tw/moecc/art/8609/8609a5.htm >（2 Nov. 2000）.
註㉙：　"教育部" 擴大內需方案, < http://www.edu.tw/information/expand/index.doc >（30 Oct. 2000）.
註㉚：　Marc Uri. Porat, The Information Economy：Definition and Measurement（Washington D.C.：Office of Telecommunications with Partial Support of National Science Foundation, 1997）.
註㉛：　同註 38。

海峽兩岸圖書資訊相關國家標準現況之研究*

摘　要

本文主要目的是蒐集、整理及分析比較兩岸圖書資訊相關國家標準制定之現況，同時簡介兩岸國家標準的主管單位、國家標準的制訂程序與分類系統，並依據兩岸圖書資訊相關國家標準主題內容之分析比較結果，提出合作之可行性建議。

一、前言

標準可以說與人類同在，如影隨形而不可分割。臺灣早在兩千年前即有標準和標準化的觀念，如《左傳》中之"車同軌，書同文"。標準種類很多，語言可能是所有標準中最古老的一種，早期的口述，經符號之演進至書寫文字，而成爲今日人類燦爛的文化記載。但標準並不局限於語言和文字，尤其工業革命和現代之資訊革命皆與"標準"關係密不可分，貢獻很大。標準廣泛涉及人類所有活動與事物，其對人類文明之進步，意義及影響至鉅。

標準爲一準則，是一種已訂的規範，其乃科學、技術、各項活動與經驗之結合，並經由各有關機構之合作與同意而制定。對工商業而言，適當的標準制定，以利產業之自動化、合理化作業，而達到生產力與產品品質的提昇，產業昇級、環境及勞力改善及邁向國際化等目標。對圖書資訊業而言，在強調資訊服務的現代社會裏，除硬體設備的發展列有規格標準外，軟體服務亦不容忽視，而圖書館爲正式提供資訊的主要機構之一。在歐美先進國家早已發展出諸多圖書館相關業務標準，而臺灣與大陸則進展較爲緩慢。

隨著電腦與網路科技的突飛猛進，兩岸各圖書館爲提昇其資訊的品質與效率，正積極進行各項館際合作及自動化作業；然而圖書館各項作業應儘速建立標準，並採取現代化、科學化的管理模式，以使海峽兩岸圖書館間及與海外圖書館之間，得以交換資訊，達到資源共享及服務品質提昇之境。然而海峽兩岸圖書館對於圖書資訊相關標準之制訂及內容是否相同或略有差異？目前海峽兩岸圖書資訊相關標準之制訂現況如何？二者是否能藉由彼此的合作，以加速圖書資訊相關標準之建立，將是本文探討的重點。惟因大陸資料蒐集不易，僅能就有限的資料進行研究，本研究恐有遺漏之處，尚請大家指正。

二、海峽兩岸國家標準主管單位

臺灣方面的"國家標準"主管機構，多年來經過數度制法的變革而略有變動：依1949 年政府頒佈之"標準法"及 1947 年"經濟部中央標準局"組織條例公佈，度量衡局及工業標準委員會合併成立"中央標準局"，1950 年"經濟部"授權"中央標準局"兼爲專利業務，1964 年增設計量檢定實驗室。1979 年"中央標準局"組織條例修正公佈，其業務含標準、度政、專利和商標四項。1998 年 10 月 21 日"經濟部"標準檢驗局

---

* 本文與臺灣大學圖書館視聽服務組組長童敏惠合作完成。發表於"海峽兩岸第五屆圖書資訊學學術研討會"（成都市 2000 年 8 月）。

組織法通過後，將"中央標準局"之標準和度政業務合併於標準檢驗局，而原"中央標準局"之專利、商標業務將另與著作權委員會和仿冒小組合併而成立一新單位——智慧財產局。"中央標準局"之標準和度政等業務將於 1999 年 1 月 26 日正式移入"經濟部"標準檢驗局。是以目前圖書館相關"國家標準"之主管機構爲"經濟部"標準檢驗局。（註1）

在大陸方面，依據 1988 年《中華人民共和國標準化法》第五條規定："國務院標準化行政主管部門統一管理全國標準化工作。……"目前由國家技術監督局負責發佈國家標準。另外，根據《國家標準管理辦法》規定，國家標準分爲強制性國家標準和推薦性國家標準，國家標準的代號由大寫漢語拼音字母構成，強制性國家標準的代號爲"GB"，推薦性國家標準的代號爲"GB/T"。國家標準的編號由國家標準代號、國家標準發佈的順序號，以及國家標準發佈的年號等三項組成。（註2）此外，依《中華人民共和國標準化法》規定，根據標準的適應領域和有效範圍，把標準分爲四級，即國家標準、行業標準、地方標準和企業標準。

國家標準：國家標準由各專業標準化技術委員會或國務院有關主管部門提出草案，由國家標準化主管機構批准發佈，是全國範圍內統一的標準。它主要包括：有關通用術語、互換配合等方面的標準；有關安全、衛生和環境保護方面的標準；有關廣大人民生活、跨部門生産的重要工農業産品標準；基本原料、材料標準；通用零部件、元器件、配件和工具、量具標準；通用的試驗方法和檢驗方法標準等。

行業標準由行業標準化主管部門或行業標準化組織批准、發佈，是某行業範圍內統一的標準。

地方標準是由省、自治區、直轄市標準化主管部門發佈，在當地範圍內統一的標準。

企業標準是由企業批准發佈的標準。

三、標準制訂作業程序

臺灣方面之"國家標準"編修不僅是制定而已，尚有修訂、廢止與確認等，其程序依《"國家標準"制定辦法》。該辦法於 1946 年首次公佈實施以來，至今已修正八次，最近一次修正爲 1998 年。現行"國家標準"制定程序有六項步驟：建議、起草，徵詢、審查、審定、核定公佈等。具體的制定程序流程説明如下：（註3）

（1）建議：由"中央"標準局或民間單位、機關團體等提出標準制定建議書。

（2）審查建議書：由審查委員會審核，決定可制定之標準後，委託相關單位進行起草。

（3）起草：由標準局專業人員或委託相關單位編擬。

（4）徵求意見：由標準局將標準草案分送有關委員、專家、機關、團體、廠商等以徵詢意見。

（5）審定：經"國家標準技術委員會"審查通過後，由"國家標準審查委員會"審定之。

（6）核定公佈：標準草案經審定後，由標準局報請"經濟部"核定公佈。

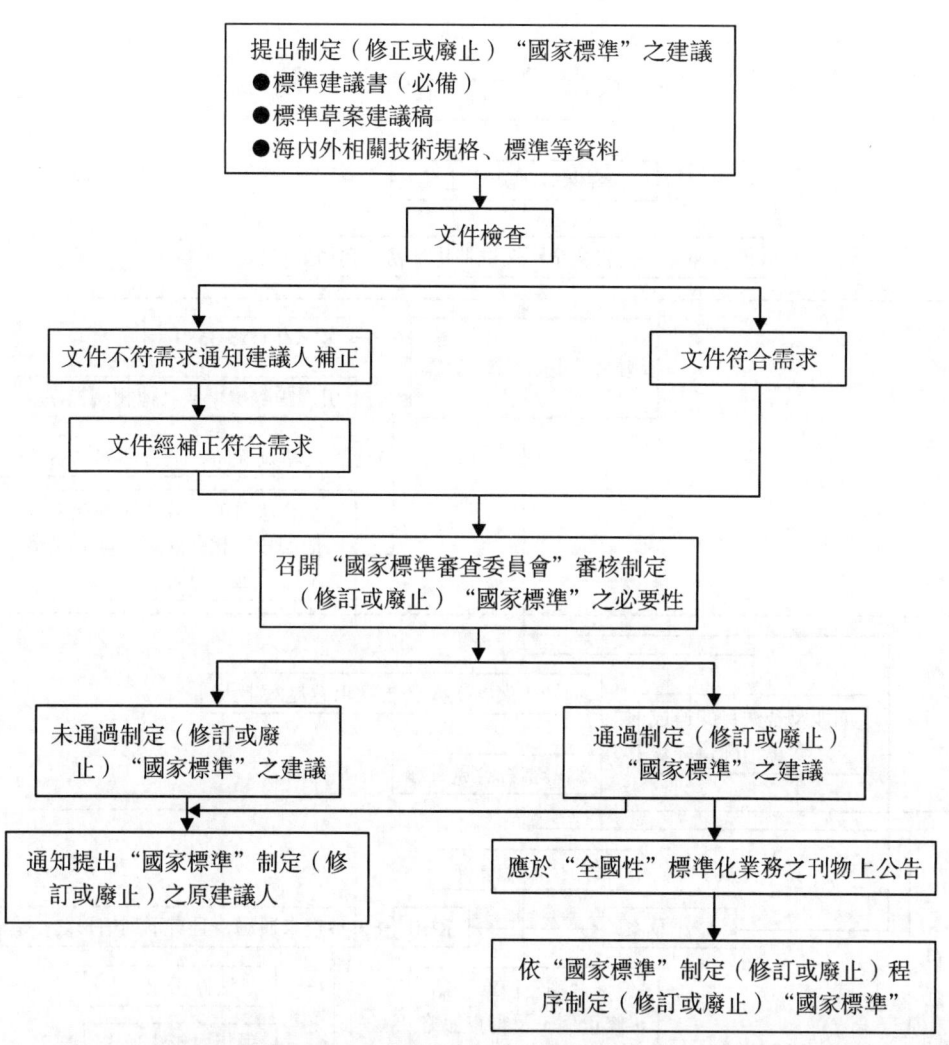

圖一：臺灣方面"國家標準"制定（修訂或廢止）建議之程序

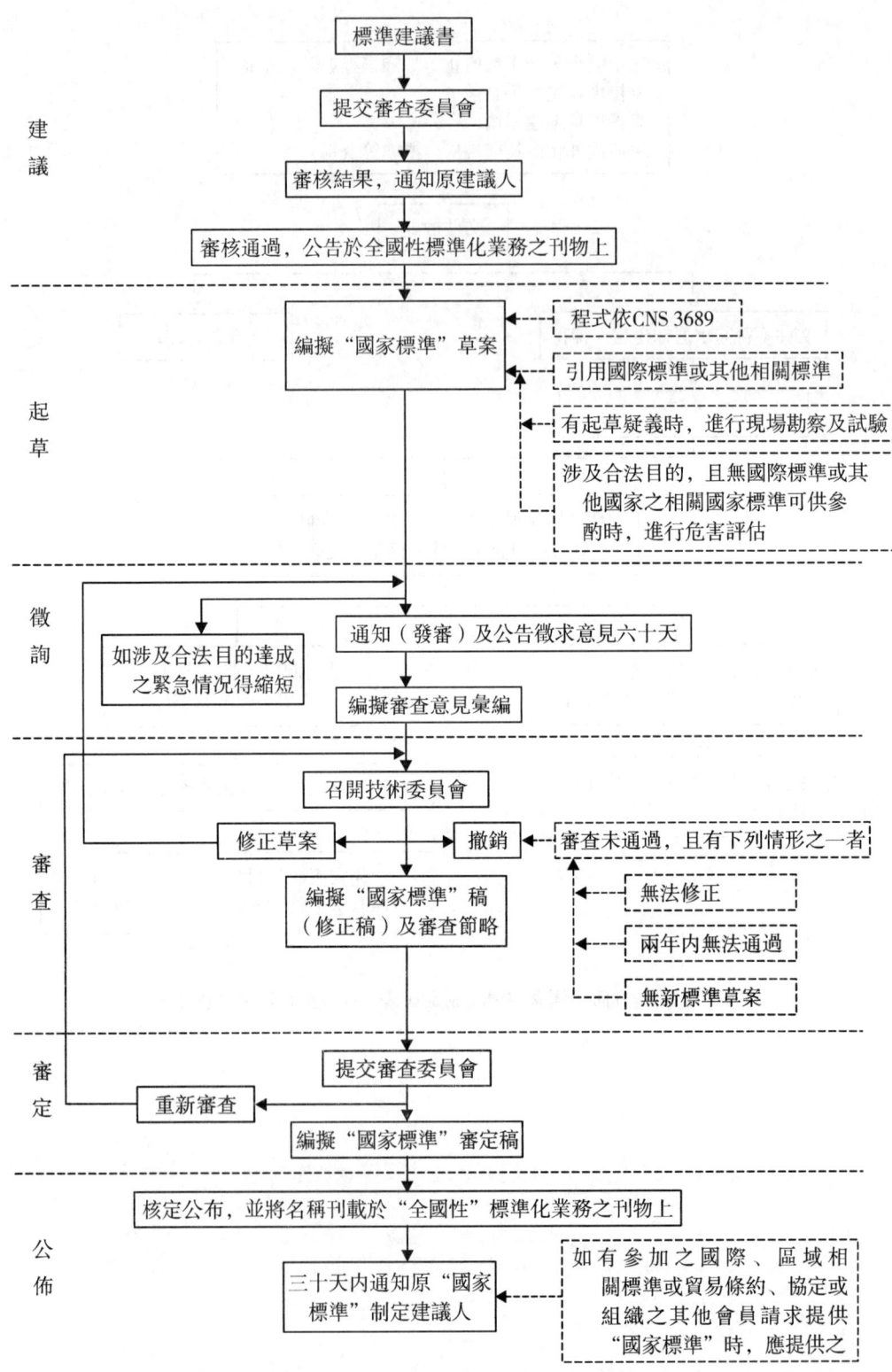

圖二：臺灣方面"國家標準"制定程序

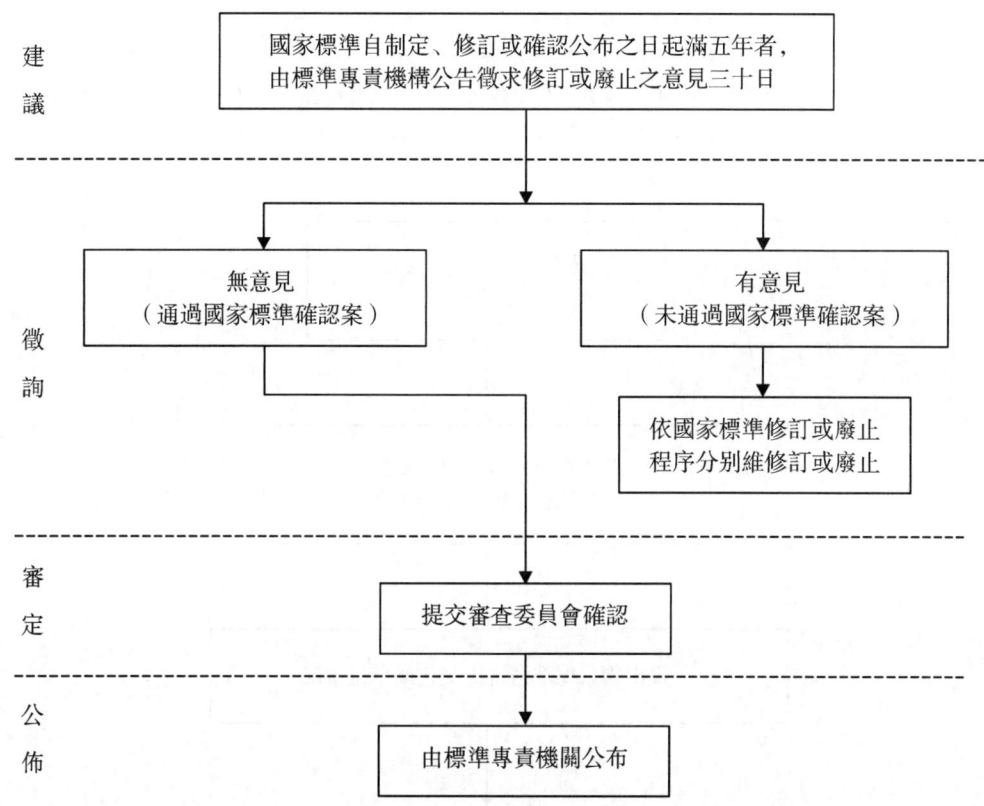

圖三：臺灣方面"國家標準"確認程序

大陸方面國家標準制定的作業程序，依《國家標準管理辦法》辦理，包括國家標準的制定、國家標準的審批、發佈，以及國家標準的複審。在國家標準的複審中將針對複審結果，進行標準的確認、修訂與廢止。其標準制定作業程序如下：

（1）起草國家標準徵求意見稿：負責起草的單位必須對所定國家標準全面負責，並按《GB1：標準化工作導則》的要求起草國家標準徵求意見稿，同時編寫"編製說明"及有關附件。

（2）徵求意見：送有關部門徵求意見，徵求意見的期限，一般為二個月。

（3）提出國家標準送審稿：由起草單位對徵集的意見進行歸納整理、分析研究和處理後，提出國家標準送審稿、"編製說明"及有關文件、"意見匯總處理表"等交技術委員會秘書處或技術歸口單位審閱。

（4）送審稿審查：由技術委員會進行國家標準送審稿之審查，其審查方式可依實際需求情況採用會議審查或函審。

（5）提出國家標準報批稿：由負責起草單位應審查意見提出國家標準報批稿。

（6）審批：國家標準報批稿由國務院有關行政主管部門或國務院標準化主管部門與管理的技術委員會，報國家標準審批部門審批。

（7）標準正式頒布：由國務院標準化行政主管部門統一審批、編號及發佈。

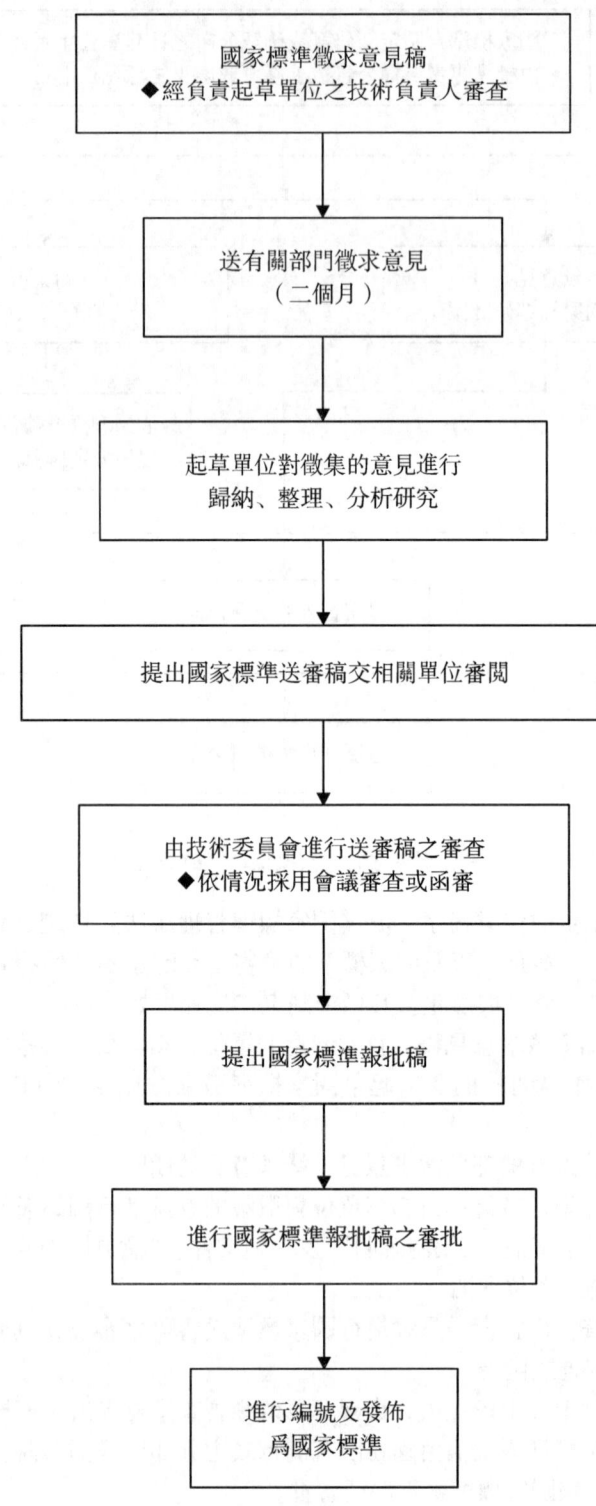

圖四：大陸方面國家標準制定之程序

四、分類系統

臺灣方面,在標準分類系統上,經過最近之修訂,目前標準類別共分為26類,其代號及類別如下表所示。圖書館相關標準被納入Z類下的一般及其他類之中,表一中標示※處之Z7:雜類,即是目前圖書資訊相關國家標準所在之類別。(註4、5)

表一:臺灣標準分類表

代用符號	標準類別(英文名稱)
A	土木工程及建築(Civil Engineering and Architecture)
B	機械工程(Mechanical Engineering)
C(C1–C4)	電機工程(Electrical Engineering)
C(C5–C7)	電子工程(Electronic Engineering)
D	機械車及航太工程(Automotive and Aircraft Engineering)
E	軌道工程(Railway Engineering)
F	造船工程(Shipbuilding)
G	鐵金屬冶煉(Ferrous Materials and Metallurgy)
H	非鐵金屬冶煉(Non-Ferrous and Metallurgy)
J	核子工程(Nuclear Engineering)
K	化學工程(Chemical Industry)
L	紡織工業(Textile Industry)
M	礦業(Mining)
N(N1–N4)	農業(Agriculture)
N(N5–N6)	食品(Foods)
O	木業(Wood Industry)
P	紙業(Pulp and Paper Industry)
Q	環境保護(Environmental Protection)
R	陶業(Ceramic Industry)
S(S1–S2)	日常用品(Domestic Wares)
T	衛生及醫療器材(Sanitation, and Medical Equipment)
X	資訊及通信(Information and Communication)
Z(Z1–Z3)	工業安全(Industrial Safety)
Z(Z4)	品質管制(Quality Control)
Z(Z5–Z6)	物流及包裝(Packing and Packaging)
Z(Z7–Z9)	一般及其他(General and Miscellaneous) ※Z7:雜類 　Z8:檢驗 　Z9:照相及電影

在大陸方面,《中國標準文獻分類法》是目前大陸專門用於標準文獻管理的一部大型檢索工具書。該分類法由24個一級大類目組成,用英文字母表示。每個一級類目下分100個二級類目。二級類目用兩位數字表示。一級類目如下表所示。表二為24個一級

大類之代號及類別。（註6）

表二：大陸標準分類表

專業分類	標準類別
A	綜合
B	農業、林業
C	醫藥、衛生、勞動保護
D	礦業
E	石油
F	能源、核技術
G	化工
H	冶金
J	機械
K	電工
L	電子元器件與信息技術
M	通信、廣播
N	儀器、儀表
P	工程建設
Q	建材
R	公路、水路運輸
S	鐵路
T	車輛
U	船舶
V	航空、航天
W	紡織
X	食品
Y	輕工、文化與生活用品
Z	環境

在 A 綜合類之下，又細分為許多小類，圖書資訊相關標準則納入 A14—圖書館、檔案、文獻與情報工作類中，A 類之詳細類別如下表所示，表三中標明※處即是圖書館、檔案、文獻與情報工作所屬之類別。

表三：A 類之二級類目表

分類號	類　名	分類號	類　名
00/09	標準化管理與一般規定	52	長度計量
00	標準化、質量管理	53	力學計量
01	技術管理	54	熱學計量
02	經濟管理	55	電磁計量
10/19	經濟、文化	56	無線電計量
10	商業、貿易、合同	57	時間、頻率計量

(續上表)

分類號	類　名	分類號	類　名
11	金融、保險	58	電離輻射計量
12	供應與使用關係	59	聲學計量
13	文件格式	60	光學計量
※14	圖書館、檔案、文獻與情報工作	61	化學計量
15	電影與攝影技術	65/74	標準物質
17	印刷技術	65	金屬化學成分標準物質
18	教育、學位、學銜	66	非金屬化學成分標準物質
20/39	基礎標準	67	物理特性標準物質
20	綜合技術	68	物理化學特性標準物質
21	環境條件與通用試驗方法	69	工程技術特性標準物質
22	術語、符號	75/79	測繪
24	分類編碼	75	測繪綜合
25	人類工效學	76	大地、海洋測繪
26	顏色	77	攝影與遙感測繪
28	篩分、篩板與篩網	78	精密工程與地質測繪
29	材料保護	79	地圖制印
31	爆破技術	80/89	標志、包裝、運輸、儲存
40/49	基礎學科	80	標志、包裝、運輸、儲存綜合
40	基礎學科綜合	82	包裝材料與容器
41	數學	83	包裝方法
42	物理學與力學	84	包裝工具
43	化學	85	集裝箱、託盤、貨架
44	地球科學	87	運輸、儲存
45	海洋學	88	包裝印包、鉛封、貼標
46	天文學	90/94	社會公共安全
47	氣象學	90	社會公共安全綜合
50/64	計量	91	安全防範報警系統
50	計量綜合	92	犯罪鑑定技術
51	量和單位	94	警用裝備與器械

　　兩岸之標準分類系統均以英文字母爲代號，在類別項目上則稍有差異，相同的類別在詞彙用語上亦略有不同。兩岸標準分類表之照對比較如表四所示：

表四：臺灣及大陸標準分類之對照

分類	臺灣地區標準類別	分類	大陸地區標準類別
A	土木工程及建築 A2：建材	P Q	工程建設 建材
B	機械工程	J	機械

(續上表)

分類	臺灣地區標準類別	分類	大陸地區標準類別
C1－C4	電機工程	K	電工
C5－C7	電子工程	L	電子元器件與信息技術
D	機械車及航太工程	T V	車輛 航空、航天
E	軌道工程	S	鐵路
F	造船工程	U	船舶
G	鐵金屬冶煉		
H	非鐵金屬冶煉	H	冶金
J	核子工程	F	能源、核技術
K	化學工程 　K5：油類	G E	化工 石油
L	紡織工業	W	紡織
M	礦業	D	礦業
N	農業	B	農業、林業
N	食品	X	食品
O	木業		
P	紙業		
Q	環境保護	Z	環境
R	陶業 　R4：儀器	N	儀器、儀表
S	日常用品	Y	輕工、文化與生活用品
T	衛生及醫療器材	C	醫藥、衛生、勞動保護
X	資訊及通信	M	通信、廣播
Z1－Z3	工業安全		
Z4	品質管制		
Z5－Z6	物流及包裝	R	公路、水路運輸
Z7－Z9	一般及其他 　Z7：雜類 　Z8：檢驗 　Z9：照相及電影	A	綜合

五、臺灣與大陸已制訂之圖書館相關標準數量與內容之比較

　　1991 年以前臺灣圖書館相關標準的制定實屬有限，直至 1991 年"中國圖書館學會"第三十八屆理監事聯合會議正式通過成立"圖書館標準委員會"，並聘請臺灣大學圖書館學系李德竹教授擔任該委員會主任委員後，始積極與"經濟部中央標準局"聯繫並自 1991 年 8 月開始接受該局委託進行圖書館相關"國家標準"起草工作，至今已完成 43 項標準。加上自 1969 年至 1999 年"中央標準局"公告之其他圖書資訊相關國家標準 53 項，共計 96 項。本研究對象之圖書館相關國家標準，以由"中國圖書館學會"圖書館標準委員會所負責起草之標準為主，不包括縮影學會等起草之微縮攝影等相關標準。根據"經濟部標準檢驗局"編印之《1999 年"中國國家標準"分類目錄》一書所載，目前已制定公佈之圖書館相關國家標準各項類別、CNS 總號及標準名稱如下表所列，其中標示＊號者為"中國圖書館學會"研訂之標準：

表五：臺灣圖書館相關"國家標準"類別一覽表
（註：＊代表為"中國圖書館學會"研訂之標準）

類別名稱	CNS 總號	標 準 名 稱
字符、字元、交換碼	CNS 5205	資訊技術—資訊交換用七位元碼元集
	CNS 7219	資訊處理—孔帶上碼字元集（組）之表示法（六與七數元）
	CNS 7223	資訊處理—七數元碼字元集（組）之控制字元圖示法
	CNS 7654	資訊技術—字元碼（結構及延伸技術）
	CNS 7656	資訊技術—資訊交換用八位元碼—實作結構及規則
	CNS 11643	中文標準交換碼
	CNS 11643—1	中文標準交換碼使用方法
	CNS 13246	資訊處理—8 位元單一位元組碼化圖形字元集（第 1 部：拉丁字母第一號）
	CNS 13247	資訊處理—8 位元單一位元組碼化圖形字元集（第 2 部：拉丁字母第二號）
	CNS 13325	資訊處理—8 位元單一位元組碼化圖形字元集（第 3 部：拉丁字母第三號）
	CNS 13326	資訊處理—8 位元單一位元組碼化圖形字元集（第 4 部：拉丁字母第四號）
	CNS 13327	資訊處理—8 位元單一位元組碼化圖形字元集（第 5 部：拉丁/斯拉夫字母）
	CNS 13328	資訊處理—8 位元單一位元組碼化圖形字元集（第 9 部：拉丁字母第五號）
	CNS 13384	資訊處理—8 位元單一位元組碼化圖形字元集（第 6 部：拉丁/阿拉伯字母）
	CNS 13385	資訊處理—8 位元單一位元組碼化圖形字元集（第 7 部：拉丁/希臘字母）
	CNS 13386	資訊處理—8 位元單一位元組碼化圖形字元集（第 8 部：拉丁/希伯來字母）
	＊CNS 13607	文獻處理—書目控制字元
編碼及代碼	CNS 89	"中國國家標準"之編號
	＊CNS 3927	校對符號

（續上表）

類別名稱	CNS 總號	標　準　名　稱
編碼及代碼	CNS 8381	資訊交換—人類性別表示法
	CNS 12842	國家名稱代碼表示法
	CNS 12864	"國家標準書號"
	*CNS 13153	"國家標準期刊號標準"
	CNS 13188	語言名稱代碼表示法
	CNS 13189	國際使用地方代碼
	CNS 13205	資訊交換—機構識別之結構
	*CNS 13773	技術報告標準號
	*CNS 13774	期刊與圖書之文章書目識別號
	*CNS 13947	國際標準錄音、錄影資料代碼
	*CNS 13948	國際標準樂譜號
	*CNS 17332	臺閩地區圖書館代碼編製原則
分類與著錄標準	CNS 88	"中國國家標準"之分類
	*CNS 13148	中國書目資訊交換格式—磁帶部份
	*CNS 13150	館際互借書目資料項目標準
	*CNS 13162	制定標準建議書格式
	*CNS 13222	書目排檢原則
	*CNS 13225	期刊館藏著錄標準
	*CNS 13226	機讀編目格式標準
	*CNS 13227	書目資料著錄總則
	*CNS 13463	圖書及其他出版品書背題名標準
	*CNS 13490	機關團體簡稱標準
	*CNS 13608	叢書題名展現標準
	*CNS 13609	圖書書名頁標準
	*CNS 13611	學術論著參考書目
	*CNS 13775	非期刊性質出版品著錄標準
文獻與資訊詞彙	CNS 3029	文獻報告
	CNS 9359	資料處理詞彙（第1部：基本術語）
	CNS 9360	資料處理詞彙（第2部：算術與邏輯運算）
	CNS 9361	資料處理系統—詞彙（第3部：設備技術）
	CNS 9362	資料處理系統—詞彙（第4部：資料之組織）

（續上表）

類別名稱	CNS 總號	標　準　名　稱
文獻與資訊詞彙	CNS 9691	資料處理系統—詞彙（第 5 部：資料之表示方法）
	CNS 9692	資料處理系統—詞彙（第 6 部：資料之準備與處理）
	CNS 9693	資料處理詞彙（第 7 部：數位計算機程式）
	CNS 10239	資料處理詞彙（第 10 部：作業技術及裝備）
	CNS 10240	資料處理—詞彙（第 11 部：處理單元）
	CNS 10241	資料處理系統—詞彙（第 12 部：週邊設備）
	CNS 10242	資料處理詞彙（第 14 部：可靠性，維護及可用度）
	CNS 10243	資料處理詞彙（第 16 部：資訊理論）
	CNS 10244	資料處理系統—詞彙（第 19 部：類比計算）
	CNS 11404	資料處理詞彙（第 9 部：數據通信）
	CNS 11405	資料處理詞彙（第 13 部：電腦圖形）
	CNS 12647	資料處理（計算機系統組態圖形符號及規定）
	CNS 12717	資料處理系統—詞彙（第 8 部：控制、完整、安全）
	CNS 12718	資料處理系統—詞彙（第 15 部：程式語言）
	CNS 12758	資料處理系統—詞彙（第 18 部：分散資料處理）
	CNS 12759	資料處理系統—詞彙（第 21 部：程序電腦系統與技術處理間之介面）
	CNS 12760	資料處理系統—詞彙（第 22 部：計算器）
	＊CNS 13771	文獻與資訊詞彙—第 1 部份：基本術語
	＊CNS 13946	文獻與資訊詞彙—第 2 部份：傳統文獻
	＊CNS 14307	文獻與資訊詞彙—第 3 部份：文獻資料採訪、辨識與分析
非書資料標準	＊CNS 3030	工程及科學之論文發表格式
	＊CNS 3031	科學期刊（篇幅）
	＊CNS 13503	學位論文撰寫格式標準
	＊CNS 13610	科學與技術報告撰寫格式
	＊CNS 13950	期刊目次格式
	＊CNS 14309	期刊及連續性出版品文章編排格式
資訊檢索	＊CNS 13461	資訊檢索服務與協定標準
	＊CNS 13462	共同指令語言
	＊CNS 13491	書面文獻章節層次編碼標準
	CNS 13228	電子資料交換—資料元索引
	CNS 13283	電子資料交換—語法規則

（續上表）

類別名稱	CNS 總號	標準名稱
索引與摘要	＊CNS 13149	西文資料審查文獻、訂定主題及選擇索引詞彙之方法
	＊CNS 13152	摘要撰寫標準
	＊CNS 13223	索引編制標準
	＊CNS 13224	西文單一語文索引典編制標準
	＊CNS 13949	文獻處理—期刊出版品摘要表
一般與其他	CNS 3689	"中國國家標準"之程式
	CNS 7648	資料元及交換格式—資訊交換—日期及時間的表示法
	CNS 10987	國際單位制
	＊CNS 13151	圖書館統計
	＊CNS 13612	公共圖書館建築設備
	＊CNS 13776	圖書館與檔案室典藏出版品與文件之紙質保存性標準
	＊CNS 13945	電子訂購圖書方式
	＊CNS 14308	圖書館之鋼製書架
	CNS 12408	商品條碼
	CNS 12409	商品配銷條碼

　　大陸方面，有關情報文獻工作標準化始於1979年，而其情報、圖書、檔案和出版界所使用的標準包括二部份：一部份是由情報工作標準化技術委員會制定的標準，另一部份是由其他技術委員會制定的有關信息管理方面的標準（註7）。此外，在科學技術信息系統標準方面，其標準範圍則包括了文獻工作（CSBTS/TC4）、信息技術（CSBTS/TC28）、文件格式及數據元表示（CSBTS/TC83）、縮微攝影技術（CSBTS/TC86）、印刷技術（CSBTS/TC170）、質量管理和質量保證（CSBTS/TC151）等標準化技術委員會負責起草之標準。本研究比較之對象乃是以情報文獻工作相關標準為主，不涉及縮微攝影技術、質量管理和質量保證，以及印刷技術等。截至1999年，根據《中華人民共和國國家標準目錄及信息總匯》一書所著錄共有18,467項國家標準，其中與圖書資訊相關之GB總號及標準名稱如下表所示，共計109項。表中註明★者為專業分類為A14（圖書館、檔案、文獻與情報）之國家標準（但不含縮微攝影方面之標準），共計有30項標準。

表六：大陸圖書資訊相關國家標準一覽表（註8）
（註：★代表專業分類為 A14—圖書館、檔案、文獻與情報之國家標準）

GB 總號	標準名稱
GB/T 1.1—11993	標準化工作導則　第1單元　標準的起草與表述規則　第一部份　標準編寫的基本規定（註：代替 GB 1.1—1987）
GB/T 1.2—1988	標準化工作導則　標準出版印刷的規定
GB/T 1.3—1987	標準化工作導則　產品標準編寫規定
GB/T 1.4—1988	標準化工作導則　化學分析方法標準編寫規定
GB/T 1.5—1988	標準化工作導則　符號、代號標準編寫規定
GB/T 1.6—1988	標準化工作導則　術語標準編寫規定
GB/T 1.22—1993	標準化工作導則　第2單元　標準內容的確定方法　第22部份　引用標準的規定
GB/T 788—1987	圖書、雜誌開本及其幅面尺寸
GB/T 826—1989	發文稿紙格式
GB/T 3935.1—1983	標準化基本術語　第一部份
GB/T 7026—1986	標準化工作導則　信息分類編碼標準的編寫規定
GB/T 7027—1986	標準化工作導則　信息分類編碼的基本原則和方法
GB/T 1988—1989	信息處理交換用的七位編碼字符集
GB/T 2260—1986	中華人民共和國行政區劃代碼
GB/T 2261—1980	人的性別代碼
GB/T 2311—1990	信息處理交換用七位編碼字符集的擴充方法
GB/T 2312—1980	信息交換用漢字編碼字符集　基本集
GB/T 2659—1994	世界各國和地區名稱代碼
GB/T 2901—1992	書目信息交換用磁帶格式
★GB/T 3179—1992	科學技術期刊編排格式（註：代替 GB 3179—82 科技學術期刊編排規則）
★GB/T 3259—1992	中文書刊名稱漢語拼音拼寫法（註：代替 GB 3259—82）
GB/T 3304—1991	中國各民族名稱羅馬字母拼寫法及代碼
★GB/T 3468—1983	檢索期刊編輯總則
★GB/T 3469—1983	文獻類型與文獻載體代碼
★GB/T 3792.1—1983	文獻著錄總則
★GB/T 3792.2—1985	普通圖書著錄規則
★GB/T 3792.3—1985	連續出版物著錄規則
★GB/T 3792.4—1985	非書資料著錄規則
★GB/T 3792.5—1985	檔案著錄規則

（續上表）

GB 總號	標準名稱
★GB/T 3792.6—1986	地圖資料著錄規則
★GB/T 3792.7—1987	古籍著錄規則
★GB/T 3793—1983	檢索期刊條目著錄規則
★GB/T 3860—1995	文獻敘詞標引規則（註：代替 GB 3869—83 文獻主題標引規則）
GB/T 4880—1991	世界語種代碼
GB/T 4881—1985	中國語種代碼
★GB/T 4894—1985	情報與文獻工作詞彙——基本術語
GB/T 5271.1—1985	數據處理詞匯：01 部份　基本術語
GB/T 5271.2—1988	數據處理詞匯：02 部份　算術和邏輯運算
GB/T 5271.3—1987	數據處理詞匯：03 部份　設備技術
GB/T 5271.4—1985	數據處理詞匯：04 部份　數據的組織
GB/T 5271.5—1985	數據處理詞匯：05 部份　數據的表示法
GB/T 5271.6—1985	數據處理詞匯：06 部份　數據的準備和處理
GB/T 5271.7—1986	數據處理詞匯：07 部份　計算機程序設計
GB/T 5271.8—1993	數據處理詞匯：08 部份　控制、完整性和安全性
GB/T 5271.9—1986	數據處理詞匯：09 部份　數據通信
GB/T 5271.10—1986	數據處理詞匯：10 部份　操作技術和設施
GB/T 5271.11—1985	數據處理詞匯：11 部份　控制器、運算器和輸入輸出設備
GB/T 5271.12—1985	數據處理詞匯：12 部份　數據媒體、存儲器和有關設備
GB/T 5271.13—1986	數據處理詞匯：13 部份　計算機圖形
GB/T 5271.14—1985	數據處理詞匯：14 部份　可靠性維修和可用性
GB/T 5271.15—1986	數據處理詞匯：15 部份　程序設計語言
GB/T 5271.16—1986	數據處理詞匯：16 部份　信息論
GB/T 5271.18—1993	數據處理詞匯：18 部份　分佈式數據處理
GB/T 5271.19—1986	數據處理詞匯：19 部份　模擬計算
GB/T 5271.20—1994	信息技術詞匯：20 部份　系統開發
GB/T 12118—1989	數據處理詞匯：21 部份　過程計算機系統和技術過程間的接口
GB/T 5271.22—1994	數據處理詞匯：22 部份　計算器
★GB/T 5795.1986	中國標準書號
GB/T 6447—1986	文摘編寫規則
GB/T 6513—1986	數學字符編碼字符集

（續上表）

GB 總號	標準名稱
GB/T 6864—1986	中華人民共和國學位代碼
★GB/T 7156—1987	文獻保密等級代碼
GB/T 7408—1994	數據元和交換格式　信息交換　日期和時間表示法
★GB/T 7713—1987	科學技術報告、學位論文和學術論文的編寫格式
★GB/T 7714—1987	文后參考文獻著錄規則
GB/T 8054—1987	信息處理交換用蒙古文七位和八位編碼圖形字符集
GB/T 8565—1988	信息處理　文本通信用編碼字符集
GB/T 9704—1988	國家機關公文格式
★GB/T 9705—1988	文書檔案案卷格式
★GB/T 9999—1988	中國標準刊號
GB/T 10112—1988	確立術語的一般原則與方法
GB/T 11383—89	信息處理　信息交換用八位代碼結構和編碼規則
★GB/T 11668—1989	圖書和其他出版的書脊規則
GB/T 11714—1995	全國組織機構代碼編制規則
★GB/T 11821—1989	照片檔案管理規範
★GB/T 11822—1989	科學技術檔案案卷構成的一般要求
GB/T 12050—1989	信息處理　信息交換用維吾爾文編碼圖形字符集
GB/T 12052—1989	信息交換用朝鮮文字編碼字符集
GB/T 12200.1—1990	漢語信息處理詞匯：01部份：基本術語
GB/T 13134—1991	信息交換用彝文編碼字符集
GB/T 12345—1990	信息交換用漢字編碼字符集　輔助集
★GB/T 12450—1990	圖書書名頁
★GB/T 12451—1990	圖書在版編目數據
GB/T 12904—1991	通用商品條碼
GB/T 12906—1991	中國標準書號（ISBN部份）條碼
GB/T 12907—1991	庫德巴條碼
GB/T 12908—91	三九條碼
GB/T 13000.1—1993	信息技術　通用多八位編碼字符集（UCS）　第一部份：體系結構與基本多文種平面
GB/T 13141—1991	書目信息交換用希臘字母編碼字符集
GB/T 13142—1991	書目信息交換拉丁字母代碼字符擴充集

（續上表）

GB 總號	標準名稱
★GB/T 13143—1991	情報與文獻工作詞彙——傳統文獻
★GB/T 13190—1991	漢語敘詞表編制規則
★GB/T 13191—1991	情報和文獻工作機構統計標準
★GB/T 13417—1992	科學技術期刊目次表
★GB/T 13418—1992	文字條目通用排序規則
GB/T 13396—1992	中國音像制品編碼
GB/T 13726—1992	術語與辭書條目的記錄交換用磁帶格式
GB/T 13745—1992	學科分類與代碼
GB/T 13959—1992	文件格式分類與代碼編制方法
GB/T 13968—1992	檔案交接文據格式
GB/T 14706—1993	校對符號及其用法
GB/T 14707—1993	圖像複製用校對符號
GB/T 14915—1994	電於數據交換術語
★GB/T 15416—1994	中國科學技術報告編號
★GB/T 15417—1994	文獻：多語種敘詞表編制規則
★GB/T 15418—1994	檔案分類標引規則
★GB/T 15693—1995	印刷型文獻價格指數標準
GB/T 15835—1995	出版物上數字用法的規定
GB/T 16159—1996	中文拼音正詞法基本規則

依表五、表六將兩岸圖書資訊相關國家標準加以歸類統計並比較，則兩岸已制定之圖書資訊相關國家標準類別數量統計如表七所示：

表七：兩岸圖書資訊相關國家標準類別數量統計

標準類別名稱	臺灣已制定之標準數量	大陸已制定之標準數量
字符、字元、交換碼	17	14
編碼及代碼	14	19
分類與著錄標準	14	17
文獻與資訊詞彙	25	26
非書資料標準	6	15
資訊檢索	5	1

(續上表)

標準類別名稱	臺灣已制定之標準數量	大陸已制定之標準數量
索引與摘要	5	2
一般及其他	10	15
總　　計	96 項	109 項

此外，依圖書資訊標準題名及內容加以對照比較（如附件一所示），發現兩岸均已制定的圖書資訊相關國家標準僅有 55 項，其表現在各類別上的情況為：字符、字元、交換碼方面有 6 項；編碼、代碼方面為 9 項；分類與著錄標準方面 8 項；文獻與資訊詞彙方面為 22 項；非書資料方面 3 項；資訊檢索方面為 1 項；索引與摘要方面 2 項；一般及其他方面 4 項，其統計分析詳見表八。以標準之迫切需要及選擇訂定的方向來看，發現兩岸對於圖書資訊相關國家標準之選擇制訂的方向有相當的差異。

表八：兩岸均已制定之圖書資訊標準數量統計

標準類別名稱 ＼ 項目	兩岸均已制定之標準數量	佔臺灣制定標準數量之百分比	佔大陸制定標準數量之百分比
字符、字元、交換碼	6	35%（6/17）	43%（6/14）
編碼及代碼	9	64%（9/14）	47%（9/19）
分類與著錄標準	8	57%（8/14）	47%（8/17）
文獻與資訊詞彙	22	88%（22/25）	85%（22/26）
非書資料標準	3	5%（3/6）	20%（3/15）
資訊檢索	1	20%（1/5）	100%（1/1）
索引與摘要	2	40%（2/5）	100%（2/2）
一般及其他	4	40%（4/10）	27%（4/15）
總　　計	55 項	57%（55/96 項）	50%（55/109 項）

六、兩岸圖書館相關標準擬訂之合作可行性建議

由前述兩岸圖書資訊相關標準制定的現況來看，可以瞭解臺灣地區開始積極進行各項圖書館相關國家標準之制定始於 1991 年，主要由臺灣的"中國圖書館學會"圖書館標準委員會主導並負責起草；大陸則開始於 1979 年，比臺灣早了 12 年，由多個相關的標準化技術委員會共同負責。根據上述各項之分析比較，茲有下列結論及建議：

（一）圖書資訊相關國家標準之數量尚嫌過低

臺灣方面，截至今年初"經濟部"標準檢驗局公佈之圖書館相關國家標準共計有 96 項，在"國家標準"總數 14,799 項中僅約佔千分之六點五（0.65%）。若以圖書館標準委員會所制訂的標準來看，僅有 43 項是由該委員會所草擬訂定者，其比率更低。

大陸方面，至1999年底公開發佈的國家標準共有18,467項，其中圖書資訊相關之標準計有109項標準，亦僅佔全部標準約千分之六（0.59%）。其中屬於A14—圖書館、檔案、文獻與情報工作之相關國家標準僅有30項，其比率亦是十分微少。由此可知圖書資訊相關標準在兩岸的國家標準比率上均明顯過低，因此，建議兩岸圖書資訊界應更積極重視和督促相關標準之制定，以利本專業之進步與發展。

（二）以ISO為基礎，朝向國際化發展

臺灣方面在制訂國家標準時，經常採用ISO相關標準為基礎，以進行翻譯或參考之用。近年來，因國際化政策之推行與實施，逐漸以ISO標準為基準，凡ISO標準可適用於臺灣使用者，不再另訂國家標準而以ISO標準內容為主而增修適用當地特別需求的部份，再訂為國家標準。

大陸的國家標準內容方面亦見到大量翻譯ISO標準的情況，應亦是朝向國際化之故，大陸因特殊情況之需但無適用之ISO標準者，將自行訂定，否則將以ISO為國家標準。因此，大陸已對ISO進行翻譯的成果將可供臺灣參考使用，惟在詞彙用語上必須統一。

以ISO為基礎，朝向國際化發展的趨勢上，臺灣方面也有直接翻譯ISO標準而給予CNS編號的情況，而大陸則直接採用ISO編號，可見兩岸在做法上的依據是相同的，且兩岸均有愈來愈多趨向於採行ISO標準的實際行動。

（三）互補不足，共同合作

根據前述研究發現兩岸目前已訂定之圖書資訊相關國家標準總數分別為96項及109項，其主題內容相同之圖書資訊標準僅有55項，各佔雙方圖書資訊相關標準之57%及50%。由此可見兩岸在選擇訂定的標準主題與內容的優先次序上有其差異性。

但從未來合作的角度來看，兩岸正可以互補不足，一方已經制定的標準正可以提供給另一方作為擬訂標準時的參考，以節省起草討論的時間以及人力。此外，經由分析兩岸已訂定標準的主題項目，可以作為雙方各自檢視已制訂或未來制訂標準的方向與重點，以加速圖書資訊相關標準的制訂。

因局限於資料蒐集上的困難，此篇報告僅做個初步的分析比較與探討，為使上述建議能確實進行，建議兩岸應推出一個負責的單位成為對口單位，密切聯繫合作，積極進行，以推動兩岸圖書資訊相關國家標準的制訂。

（四）詞彙用語，尚待統一

從標準主題內容的比較上，兩岸在文字詞彙的使用標準上有相當大的差異性，有時會造成使用上的誤解及困擾。如何促使兩岸合作，共同整理圖書資訊學科專業的用語詞彙，將是當務之急。

（五）共同研訂，分工合作

為加速圖書資訊相關國家標準的制訂，兩岸學者應共同研訂出圖書資訊相關國家標準未來之五年計劃，共同商討急需擬訂的相關標準主題項目並依其重要性排序，建議可依各自的專長分工合作，分別草擬標準初稿，並相互參考提供修訂意見，後再分別依各自的行政體系流程訂定標準。

註　釋

註1：李德竹，臺灣圖書館相關國家標準，圖書與資訊學刊，第 28 期（1992 年 2 月），頁 5—6。
註2：全國文獻工作標準化技術委員會編，科學技術信息系統標準與使用指南：第一卷 綜述（北京：中國標準出版社，1996），頁 9—13。
註3：同註 1，頁 6—9。
註4：同註 1，頁 11。
註5："經濟部"標準檢驗局編，"中國國家標準"分類目錄：1999 年（臺北市："經濟部"標準檢驗局，[1999]）。
註6：國家技術監督局標準化司編，中華人民共和國國家標準目錄及信息總匯（北京：中國標準出版社，1993 年）。
註7：沈玉蘭、張鳳樓、郭秀婷，信息化過程中情報文獻工作標準化的內容及對策初探，情報學報，第 13 卷第 4 期（1994 年 8 月），頁 311—319。
註8：表十係參考下列資料整理而成：
  (1) 國家技術監督局標準化司編，中華人民共和國國家標準目錄及信息總匯（北京：中國標準出版社，1996 年）。
  (2) 國家技術監督局標準化司編，中華人民共和國國家標準目錄及信息總匯（北京：中國標準出版社，1999 年）。
  (3) 沈玉蘭、張鳳樓、郭秀婷，"信息化過程中情報文獻工作標準化的內容及對策初探"，情報學報，第 13 卷第 4 期（1994 年 8 月），頁 311—319。
  (4) 中國標準出版社第四編輯室編，作者編輯出版常用國家標準（北京：中國標準出版社，1993 年）。
  (5) 科學技術信息系統標準與使用指南：第二卷　術語標準（北京：中國標準出版社，1996 年）。
  (6) 科學技術信息系統標準與使用指南：第三卷　信息分類與編碼標準（北京：中國標準出版社，1996 年）。
  (7) 科學技術信息系統標準與使用指南：第四卷　數據交換標準（北京：中國標準出版社，1996 年）。
  (8) 科學技術信息系統標準與使用指南：第五卷　情報文獻工作標準（北京：中國標準出版社，1996 年）。

附錄一：兩岸已制定之圖書館相關國家標準對照一覽表
（1999 年）

類別名稱	CNS 總號	中國臺灣 標準名稱	GB 編號	中國大陸 標準名稱
字符、字元、交換碼	CNS 5205	資訊技術—資訊交換用七位元碼元集	GB/T 6513—86	數學字符編碼字符集
			GB/T 1988—80	信息處理交換用的七位編碼字符集
	CNS 7219	資訊處理—孔帶上碼上碼字元集（組）之表示法（六與七數元）		
	CNS 7223	資訊處理七數元碼元字元集（組）之控制字元圖示法		
	CNS 7654	資訊技術—字元碼（結構及延伸技術）	GB/T 2311—80	信息處理交換用七位編碼字符集的擴充方法
	CNS 7656	資訊技術—資訊交換用八位元碼元—實作結構及規則	GB/T 11383—89	信息處理 信息交換用八位代碼結構和編碼規則
			GB/T 13000.1—1993	信息技術 通用多八位編碼字符集（UCS）第一部分：體系結構與基本多文種平面
			GB/T 13134—1991	信息交換用彝文編碼字符集
	CNS 13385	資訊處理—8位元單一位元組碼化圖形字元集（第7部：拉丁/希臘字母）	GB/T 13141—91	書目信息交換用希臘字母編碼字符集
	CNS 13246	資訊處理—8位元單一位元組碼化圖形字元集（第1部：拉丁字母第一號）	GB/T 13142—91	書目信息交換用拉丁字母擴展字符集
	CNS 13247	資訊處理—8位元單一位元組碼化圖形字元集（第2部：拉丁字母第二號）		
	CNS 13325	資訊處理—8位元單一位元組碼化圖形字元集（第3部：拉丁字母第三號）		

(續上表)

類別名稱	中國臺灣		中國大陸	
	CNS 總號	標準名稱	GB 編號	標準名稱
字元、字符、交換碼	CNS 13326	資訊處理—8位元單一位元組編碼化圖形字元集（第4部：拉丁字母第四號）		
	CNS 13327	資訊處理—8位元單一位元組編碼化圖形字元集（第5部：拉丁/斯拉夫字母）		
	CNS 13328	資訊處理—8位元單一位元組編碼化圖形字元集（第9部：拉丁字母第五號）		
	CNS 13384	資訊處理—8位元單一位元組編碼化圖形字元集（第6部：拉丁/阿拉伯字母）		
	CNS 13386	資訊處理—8位元單一位元組編碼化圖形字元集（第8部：拉丁/希伯來字母）		
	CNS 11643	中文標準交換碼	GB/T 2312—1980	信息交換用漢字編碼字符集 基本集
			GB/T 12345—1990	信息交換用漢字編碼字符集 輔助集
			GB/T 8054—1987	信息處理交換用蒙古文七位和八位編碼圖形字符集
			GB/T 12050—1989	信息交換用維吾爾文編碼圖形字符集
			GB/T 12052—1989	信息交換用朝鮮文字編碼字符集
			GB/T 8565—1988	信息處理 文本通信用編碼字符集
	CNS 11643—1	中文標準交換碼使用方法		
	*CNS 13607	文獻處理—書目控制字元		

（續上表）

類別名稱	中　國　臺　灣		中　國　大　陸	
	CNS 總號	標　準　名　稱	GB 編號	標　準　名　稱
編碼代碼	CNS 8381	資訊交換—人類性別表示法	GB/T 2260—86	中華人民共和國行政區劃代碼
			GB/T 2261—80	人的性別代碼
	CNS 12842	"國家" 名稱代碼表示法	GB/T 2659—86	世界各國和地區名稱代碼
	CNS 13189	國際使用地方代碼		
			GB/T 3304—91	中國各民族名稱羅馬字母拼寫法及代碼
			★GB/T 3469—83	文獻類型與文獻體載代碼
			GB/T 4881—85	中國語種代碼
			★GB/T 7156—87	文獻保密等級代碼
			GB/T 6864—1986	中華人民共和國學位代碼
	CNS 89	"中國國家標準" 之編號		
	*CNS 3927	校對符號	GB/T 14706—1993	校對符號及其用法
			GB/T 14707—1993	圖像複製用校對符號
	CNS 12864	"國家標準" 書號	★GB/T 5795—86	中國標準書號
	*CNS 13153	"國家標準" 期刊號標準	GB/T 12906—1991	中國標準書號（ISBN 部分）條碼
			★GB/T 9999—88	中國標準刊號
	CNS 13188	語言名稱代碼表示法	GB/T 4880—85	世界語種代碼
	CNS 13205	資訊交換—機構識別之結構		
	*CNS 13773	技術報告標準號	★GB/T15416—1994	中國科學技術報告編號

(續上表)

類別名稱	中　　國　　臺　　灣		中　　國　　大　　陸	
	CNS 總號	標　準　名　稱	GB 編號	標　準　名　稱
編碼、代碼	＊CNS 13774	期刊與圖書之文章書目識別號		
	＊CNS 13947	國際標準錄音、錄影資料代碼	GB/T 13396—92	中國音像製品編碼
	＊CNS 13948	國際標準樂譜號		
	＊CNS 17332	臺灣臺閩地區圖書館代碼編製原則	GB/T 11714—1995	全國組織機構代碼編制規則
			GB/T 13745—1992	學科分類與代碼
			GB/T 13959—1992	文件格式分類與代碼編制方法
			★GB/T 3259—1992	中文書刊名稱漢語拼音拼寫法
			★GB/T 3792.1—83	文獻著錄總則
分類與著錄標準			★GB/T 12451—90	圖書在版編目數據
	CNS 88	"中國國家標準"之分類	GB/T 7027—1986	標準化工作導則　信息分類編碼的基本原則和方法
	＊CNS 13148	"中國"書目資訊交換格式——磁帶部分	GB/T 2901—92	書目信息交換用磁帶格式
	＊CNS 13150	館際互借書目資料項目標準	GB/T 13726—1992	術語與辭書條目的記錄交換用磁帶格式
	＊CNS 13162	制定標準建議格式	GB/T 7026—1986	標準化工作導則　信息分類編碼標準的編寫規定
	＊CNS 13222	書目排檢原則	★GB/T 13418—92	文字條目通用排序規則
	＊CNS 13225	期刊館藏著錄標準		
	＊CNS 13226	機讀編目格式標準		

（續上表）

類別名稱	CNS 總號	中國臺灣標準名稱	GB 編號	中國大陸標準名稱
分類與著錄標準	＊CNS 13227	書目資料著錄總則	★GB/T 3792.2—85	普通圖書著錄規則
	＊CNS 13463	圖書及其他出版品書背題名標準	★GB/T 11668—89	圖書和其他出版物的書脊規則
	＊CNS 13490	機關團體簡稱標準		
	＊CNS 13608	叢書題名展現標準		
	＊CNS 13609	圖書書名葉標準	★GB/T 12450—90	圖書書名頁
	＊CNS 13611	學術論著參考書目	★GB/T 7714—87	文后參考文獻著錄規則
	＊CNS 13775	非期刊性質出版品著錄標準		
			★GB/T 15417—1994	文獻：多語種敘詞表編制規則
			GB/T 15835—1995	出版物上數字用法的規定
			GB/T 16159—1996	中文拼音正詞法基本規則
			★GB/T 15418—1994	檔案分類標引規則
			GB/T 13968—1992	檔案交接文據格式
			GB/T 10112—1988	確立術語的一般原則與方法
			GB/T 12200.1—1990	漢語信息處理詞匯：01 部分：基本術語
文獻與資訊詞彙	CNS 9359	資料處理詞彙（第 1 部：基本術語）	GB/T 5271.1—1985	數據處理詞匯：01 部分：基本術語
	CNS 9360	資料處理詞彙（第 2 部：算術與邏輯運算）	GB/T 5271.2—1988	數據處理詞匯：02 部分：算術和運輯運算
	CNS 9361	資料處理系統—詞彙（第 3 部：設備技術）	GB/T 5271.3—1987	數據處理詞匯：03 部分：設備技術
	CNS 9362	資料處理系統—詞彙（第 4 部：資料之組織）	GB/T 5271.4—1985	數據處理詞匯：04 部分：數據的組織

(續上表)

類別名稱	CNS總號	中國臺灣標準名稱	GB編號	中國大陸標準名稱
文獻與資訊詞彙	CNS 9691	資料處理系統—詞彙（第5部：資料之表示方法）	GB/T 5271.5—1985	數據處理詞匯：05 部分 數據的表示法
	CNS 9692	資料處理系統—詞彙（第6部：資料之準備與處理）	GB/T 5271.6—1985	數據處理詞匯：06 部分 數據的準備和處理
	CNS 9693	資料處理詞彙（第7部：數位計算機程式）	GB/T 5271.7—1986	數據處理詞匯：07 部分 計算機程序設計
	CNS 10239	資料處理詞彙（第10部：作業技術及裝備）	GB/T 5271.10—1986	數據處理詞匯：10 部分 操作技術和設施
	CNS 10240	資料處理—詞彙（第11部：處理單元）	GB/T 5271.11—1985	數據處理詞匯：11 部分 控制器、運算器和輸入輸出設備
	CNS 10241	資料處理系統—詞彙（第12部：週邊設備）	GB/T 5271.12—1985	數據處理詞匯：12 部分 數據媒體、存儲器和有關設備
	CNS 10242	資料處理系統—詞彙（第14部：可靠性，維護及可用度）	GB/T 5271.14—1985	數據處理詞匯：14 部分 可靠性維修和可用性
	CNS 10243	資料處理系統—詞彙（第16部：資訊理論）	GB/T 5271.16—1986	數據處理詞匯：16 部分 信息論
	CNS 10244	資料處理系統—詞彙（第19部：類比計算）	GB/T 5271.19—1986	數據處理詞匯：19 部分 模擬計算
	CNS 11404	資料處理詞彙（第9部：數據通信）	GB/T 5271.9—1986	數據處理詞匯：09 部分 數據通信
	CNS 11405	資料處理詞彙（第13部：電腦圖形）	GB/T 5271.13—1986	數據處理詞匯：13 部分 計算機圖形
	CNS 12647	資料處理（計算機系統組態圖形符號及規定）		
	CNS 12717	資料處理系統—詞彙（第8部：控制、完整、安全）	GB/T 5271.8—1993	數據處理詞匯：08 部分 控制、完整性和安全性
	CNS 12718	資料處理系統—詞彙（第15部：程式語言）	GB/T 5271.15—1986	數據處理詞匯：15 部分 程序設計語言
	CNS 12758	資料處理系統—詞彙（第18部：分散資料處理）	GB/T 5271.18—1993	數據處理詞匯：18 部分 分布式數據處理
			GB/T 5271.20—1994	信息技術詞匯：20 部分 系統開發

（續上表）

類別名稱	CNS 總號	中國臺灣標準名稱	GB 編號	中國大陸標準名稱
文獻與資訊詞彙	CNS 12759	資料處理系統—詞彙（第21部：程序宇電腦系統與技術處理間之介面）	GB/T 12118—1989	數據處理詞彙：21部分 過程計算機系統和技術過程間的接口
	CNS 12760	資料處理系統—詞彙（第22部：計算器）	GB/T 5271.22—1994	數據處理詞彙：22部分 計算器
	CNS 3029	文獻報告	★GB/T 13190—91	文獻：漢語敘詞表編制規則
	★CNS 13771	文獻與資訊詞彙—第1部份：基本術語	★GB/T 4894—85	情報與文獻工作詞彙—基本術語
	★CNS 13946	文獻與資訊詞彙—第2部份：傳統文獻	★GB/T 13143—91	情報與文獻工作詞彙—傳統文獻
	★CNS 14307	文獻與資訊詞彙—第3部份：文獻資料採訪、辨識與分析		
非書資料標準			★GB/T 3179—1992	科學技術期刊編排非格式
			★GB/T 3468—83	檢索期刊編輯總則
			★GB/T 3792.3—85	連續出版物著錄規則
			★GB/T 3792.4—85	非書資料著錄規則
			★GB/T 3792.5—85	檔案著錄規則
			★GB/T 3792.6—86	地圖資料著錄規則
			★GB/T 3792.7—87	古籍著錄規則
			★GB/T 11821—89	照片檔案管理規範
			★GB/T 11822—89	科學技術檔案卷構成的一般要求
	★CNS 3030	工程及科學之論文發表格式		

(續上表)

類別名稱	中華臺灣		中國大陸	
	CNS 總號	標準名稱	GB 編號	標準名稱
非書資料標準	* CNS 3031	科學期刊（篇幅）		
	* CNS 13503	學位論文撰寫格式標準		
	* CNS 13610	科學與技術報告撰寫格式	★ GB/T 7713—87	科學技術報告、學位論文和學術論文的編寫格式
	* CNS 13950	期刊目次格式	★ GB/T 13417—92	科學技術期刊目次表
	* CNS 14309	期刊及連續性出版文章編排格式	★ GB/T 3793—83	檢索期刊條目著錄規則
			GB/T 826—1989	發文稿紙格式
			GB/T 9704—1988	國家機關公文格式
			★ GB/T 9705—1988	文書檔案案卷格式
資訊檢索	CNS 13228	電子資料交換—資料元索引	GB/T 14915—1994	電子數據交換術語
	CNS 13283	電子資料交換—語法規則		
	* CNS 13461	資訊檢索服務與協定標準		
	* CNS 13462	共同指令語言		
	* CNS 13491	書面文章章節層次編碼標準		
索引與摘要	* CNS 13149	西文資料審查文獻、訂定主題及選擇索引詞彙之方法	★ GB/T 3860—1995	文獻敘詞標引規則
	* CNS 13152	摘要撰寫標準	GB/T 6447—86	文摘編寫規則
	* CNS 13223	索引編製標準		
	* CNS 13224	西文單一語—索引典編制標準		
	* CNS 13949	文獻處理—期刊出版品摘要表		

海峽兩岸圖書資訊相關國家標準現況之研究 207

(續上表)

類別名稱	中國臺灣		中國大陸	
	CNS 總號	標準名稱	GB 編號	標準名稱
一般及其他	CNS 3689	"中國國家標準"之程式	GB/T 3935.1—1983	標準化基本術語 第一部分
			GB/T 1.1—1993	標準化工作導則 第 1 單元 標準的起草與表述規則 第一部分 標準編寫的基本規定（註：代替 GB1.1—1987）
			GB/T 1.2—1988	標準化工作導則 標準出版印刷的規定
			GB/T 1.3—1987	標準化工作導則 產品標準編寫規定
			GB/T 1.4—1988	標準化工作導則 化學分析方法標準編寫規定
			GB/T 1.5—1988	標準化工作導則 符號、代號標準編寫規定
			GB/T 1.6—1988	標準化工作導則 術語標準編寫規定
			GB/T 1.22—1993	標準化工作導則 第 2 單元 標準內容的確定方法 第 22 部分 引用標準的規定
	CNS 7648	資料元及交換格式—資訊交換—日期及時間的表示法	GB/T 7408—1994	數據元和交換格式 信息交換 日期和時間表示法
	CNS 10987	國際單位制		
	*CNS 13151	圖書館統計	★GB/T 13191—91	情報和文獻工作機構統計標準
	*CNS 13612	公共圖書館建築設備		
	*CNS 13776	圖書館與檔案室典藏出版品與文件之紙質保存性標準		
	*CNS 13945	電子訂購圖書方式		
	*CNS 14308	圖書館之鋼製書架		

(續上表)

類別名稱	中國臺灣		中國大陸	
	CNS 總號	標準名稱	GB 編號	標準名稱
一般及其他	CNS 12408	商品條碼	GB/T 12904—1991	通用商品條碼
	CNS 12409	商品配銷條碼		
			GB/T 12907—1991	庫德巴條碼
			GB/T 12908—91	三九條碼
			GB/T 788—1987	圖書、雜誌開本及其幅面尺寸
			★GB/T 15693—1995	印刷型文獻(價格指數標準

從 VANNEVAR BUSH "AS WE MAY THINK"
談資訊科學與技術之演進與發展[*]

[摘要 Abstract]

　　Vannevar Bush 於 1945 年發表 "As We May Think" 一文，提出將電子計算機技術應用於處理個人文獻資訊之構想，也為其後資訊科學與技術之發展開創新境，並有學者視該文為現代資訊科學之濫觴。本文說明 "As We May Think" 一文中 "Memex" 之構思，及其所演化成的現代資訊科技產物，並詳列 1638 至 1999 年間資訊科學與技術發生之重要記事，期能提供後人對資訊科學與技術之演進與發展有更深刻之認識。

　　The origin of modern information science is often recognized to be Vannevar Bush's seminal paper "As We May Think", with its conceptual design of a desktop personal information machine called the "Memex", which was published in "Atlantic Monthly" in 1945. In order to understand the influences and contributions of Bush's "As We May Think" and the "Memex", its relations to the evolution of modern information science and technology, it is the purpose of this present research to study the effect of "As We May Think" and the "Memex" on the developments of information science and technology between 1638 to 1999. And as a result of this study, a list of related major events was investigated and also included.

關鍵字　Keyword

圖書館學；資訊科學；資訊技術
Vannevar Bush；Memex；Library Science；Information Science；Information Technology

　　資訊科學究竟源起何時？依研究者著眼的角度不同，而有不同的說法。Joseph C. Donohue 與 N. E. Karioth，Dorothy B. Lilley 與 Ronald W. Trice 以及 Saul Herner 等學者均主張 Vannevar Bush 於 1945 年所發表的 "As We May Think" 一文，可視為資訊科學發展之源起。

　　"As We May Think" 中所提出之 Memex 構想，首次將資訊儲存、檢索的觀念與當時電子計算機（電腦）的功能結合，使個人文獻資訊的處理邁入電腦化時代，Memex 並可依文獻的主題或其他屬性來儲存與檢索。"As We May Think" 被視為第一篇論及超文件基本觀念的文獻，啟發資訊科學家對資訊檢索技術之研究。Bush 的另一項設計──微分分析儀（Differential Analyzer）則為早期電腦之雛型，也帶動科學界對電子計算機技術與人工智慧的相關研究。Memex 之設計理念在現代資訊社會中，演化成為以下各項電腦科技與通訊網路產物：

1. 個人電腦

　　個人電腦之架構首先由 Bush 於 1945 年建立，對於其外型及可進行智慧型工作，供

---

[*] 本文與臺灣大學醫學院圖書館分館組員周利玲合作完成。曾發表在《圖書與資訊學》32 期（2000 年 2 月），第 1—15 頁。

個人操作之功能特色亦詳加說明。利用電腦輔助資訊之儲存與檢索在 As 一文中即已提出，電腦具有個人使用、快速且具彈性之特性，可作為輔助人類記憶之一項設備。

2. 資訊檢索與儲存（Information Retrieval and Storage）

"As We May Think" 一文為利用資訊技術以處理學術研究資訊之理想典範；說明電腦如何幫助科學家處理大量科學資訊，提出全域資料庫系統（Global database system）的構思，以使得科學家在任何地方皆可進行資訊檢索。但今日的科技，是否真能依照 Bush 之理念，設計出一個類似 Memex 功能強大的資訊檢索系統？

Memex 為一資訊檢索系統，可依使用者之需求檢索資訊，並著重在使用者與系統之間的互動。透過系統所建置的聯結路徑（trails）以串連相關資訊，此運作方式即為超文件之原型，根據超文件的概念進而發展成為後來之超媒體系統。

3. 超文件與超媒體

Memex 建立了超文件與超媒體之理念，闡明透過類似人腦記憶方式之設計，可連結大量資訊，以節省研究人員搜索資訊時間。超文件與超媒體之技術已普遍應用於各種學術研究與教育訓練上，如教育團體用以進行教學活動與教育訓練活動；人文學研究人員也應用其進行研究；臨床醫學研究以此技術設計互動式光碟自學軟體──The Virtual Practium。

4. 線上公用目錄（Online Public Access Catalog，簡稱 OPAC）

Don Swanson 在 1964 年所著的 "Dialogues with a Catalog" 一文中，提出 OPAC 的觀念，其所構想之工具──以縮影片的形式查尋目錄，和 Bush 所構思的 Memex 觀念是相近的。

5. 網際網路（Internet）

Internet 可以說是實現了 Memex 之夢想──整合功能強大之應用軟體、功能完善且價廉的桌上型電腦，以及高速的通訊網路等資訊科技於一體。

6. 全球資訊網（World Wide Web，簡稱 www）

全球資訊網達成 Bush 在二次大戰後，對資訊處理技術所提之構思，即能根據研究之需求建立個人化圖書館，對資料加註並可互相串連。

7. 數位圖書館（Digital Library）或虛擬圖書館（Virtual Library）

"As We May Think" 一文為第一篇探討數位圖書館之著作，Memex 可處理大量的資訊，為今日虛擬圖書館之雛型。Vannevar Bush 所勾勒之 Memex 構思，即為電子圖書館所追求之理想藍圖。建置於全球資訊網上之電子期刊，如全球醫療保健網路（Global Health Network，簡稱 GHN）亦為 Memex 構思之實現。為紀念 Vannevar Bush 於 "As We May think" 一文中的 Memex 機器理念，Dr. Edwin Brownrigg 資助成立 Memex Research Institute，網羅各方專家學者從事資訊技術的相關研究，以作為建構新一代全球性共用資訊系統的研發機構，尤其著重電子圖書館與電子館藏之開發，以實現 Bush 之 Memex 理想。

8. 數位神經系統（Digital Nervous System）

Memex 是一項結合個人電腦與網際網路概念的裝置；而 Bill Gates 於 1998 年所提出之數位神經系統係藉由網路連結不同之個人電腦，以掌握、分享、運用數位資訊，可說是一種數位資訊基礎建設。

綜合以上敘述，在 "As We May Think" 文中 Bush 所勾勒出的藍圖，為電子計算機科學、圖書館學、檔案管理、資訊科學、人工智慧、超文件等技術指引了未來的發展方向，也引領資訊科學與技術之發展邁入新的紀元。

茲將 1638 年美國哈佛大學圖書館成立至 1999 年間電腦與網路通訊科技、圖書館學與資訊科學之重要發展整理如下表，以瞭解三個多世紀來，資訊科學與技術之發展與演進。

1638 年至 1999 年資訊科學發展記要一覽表

年代	資訊科學發展記要
1638	美國哈佛大學圖書館（Harvard University Library）成立
1753	大英博物館圖書館（British Museum Library）成立
1800	美國國會圖書館（Library of Congress，簡稱 LC）成立
1822	Charles Babbage 列出 "Difference Engine" 功能大綱，為電腦的初步設計
1834	Charles Babbage 設計 "Analytical Engine"，第一代 General-Purpose Computer
1836	美國國家醫學圖書館（National Library of Medicine，簡稱 NLM）成立
1839	美國國家農業圖書館（National Agricultural Library，簡稱 NAL）成立
1854	美國波士頓公共圖書館（Boston Public Library）成立，第一個美國現代化公共圖書館
1858	美國 First Trans-Atlantic Cable 設置
1859	George Boole 發表有關符號語言（symbolic language）之論文集
1860	美國印務局（U. S. Government Printing Office，簡稱 GPO）成立
1868	第一臺打字機問世
1876	• 美國圖書館學會（American Library Association，簡稱 ALA）成立 • Melvil Dewey 設計出杜威十進位分類系統（Dewey Decimal Classification System） • Charles A. Cutter 出版字典式目錄之規則 • Alexander Graham Bell 發明電話
1880	范恩圖（Venn Diagram）問世，用在建立 relationship between sets，並運用於資訊檢索
1887	Melvil Dewey 在哥倫比亞大學（Columbia University）成立美國第一所圖書館學校
1890	歐洲開始研究文獻學（Documentation）
1895	Paul Otlet 與 Henri Fontaine 成立國際書目組織（International Institute of Bibliographie，簡稱 IIB）
1899	磁帶錄音機發明
1904	美國國會圖書館分類系統大綱出版
1905	國際十進分類系統（Universal Decimal Classification System，簡稱 UDC）出版
1908	國際文獻學會（International Federation of Documentation，簡稱 FID）於荷蘭海牙成立
1911	Computing Tabulating Recording Company 成立，即是 IBM 之前身
1924	首次使用傳真（Facsimile Transmission，簡稱 FAX）
1925	電視問世

(續上表)

年代	資訊科學發展記要
1930	Vannevar Bush 開發 Analog Machine
1935	美國德州大學圖書館推出用 IBM punched cards 之 Circulation System
1937	• 英美編目規則（Anglo-American Cataloging Rules）出版 • 文獻學傳至美國，Watson Davis 提倡成立美國文獻學學會（American Documentation Institute，簡稱 ADI），為美國資訊科學學會（American Society for Information Science，簡稱 ASIS）之前身
1938	ADI 出版其會刊 *Journal of Documentary Reproduction*（於 1943 年停止出刊）
1939—1943	哈佛大學在 IBM 公司 Howard Aiken 之指導下組成 MARK I 電腦
1945	• Vannevar Bush 撰"As We May Think"一文，提出 Memex 之構想；同年，*Science: the Endless Frontier* 一書出版；此二出版品對新式非傳統型之資訊系統、1950 年國家科學基金會（National Science Foundation，簡稱 NSF）之成立以及改善國家各型主要圖書館之館藏和設備均有所啟發 • Arthur C. Clarke 發表 *Extra-Terrestrial Relays* 一文，引起世人對其地球衛星（earth satellites）之構想加以注目
1946	• Bush 著作 *Endless Horizons* 出版 • 美國賓州大學（University of Pennsylvania）發明第一代電腦 ENIAC
1948	• S. C. Bradford 出版 *Documentation* • C. E. Shannon 與 W. Weaver 發表 *The Mathematical Theory of Communication* • Norbert Wiener 出版 *Cybernetics or Control and Communication in the Animal and the Machine* 和 *Human Use of Human Beings* • 英國 Royal Society Scientific Information Conference 在倫敦召開
1950	美國國家科學基金會（National Science Foundation，簡稱 NSF）正式成立
1951—1956	開發磁帶和磁碟（Magnetic tapes and disks），使其成為貯存記憶體媒介
1951	第一部商業電腦 UNIVAC1 問世
1952	• Mortimer Taube 建立文獻公司（Documentation, Inc） • Information Retrieval 由 C. N. Mooers 首次在"Information Retrieval Viewed as Temporal Signaling"提出
1953—1959	Mortimer Taube 及其他學者合著出版 *Studies in Coordinate Indexing*（共 5 冊）
1953	Hans Peter Luhn 出版 *A New Method of Recording and Searching Information* 一書
1955	• Eugene Garfield 發表"Citation Index for Science"一文 • James Perry 等人於 Western Reserve University（簡稱 WRU）建立文獻交流研究中心（Center for Documentation Communications Research）
1957	蘇聯發射第一顆人造衛星 Sputnik，促使美國國防部成立尖端研究企畫署（Advanced research Project Agency，簡稱 ARPA）

（續上表）

年代	資訊科學發展記要
1958	● Hans Peter Luhn 在美國科學研究院（National Academy of Sciences）、ADI、NSF 之贊助下，籌辦於華盛頓特區（Washington, D. C.）舉行之 International Conference for Scientific Information；同年又設計 Automatic Indexing and Abstracting 程式 ● 由美國 Air Force Office of Scientific Research（簡稱 AFOSR）贊助之 Taube-Wooster Conference on Information Strage and Retrieval 於華盛頓特區召開 ● NSF 所屬之科學資訊服務處（U. S. Office of Scientific Information Service，簡稱 OSIS）成立；Burton W. Adkinson 爲第一任主管
1960—1965	發展第二代電腦
1961	● King's Report（Red Book）出版，旨在探討美國國會圖書館自動化之可行性 ● 美國國家醫學圖書館之 MEDLARS（Medical Literature Analysis and Retrieval System）第一階段發展規格書撰寫完成 ● 美國圖書館資源委員會（The Council on Library Resources，簡稱 CLR）委託 J. C. R. Licklider 研究未來圖書館
1962	● GE 公司與 Photon Co. 合作發展 Medlars 之 GRACE（Graphic Arts Composing Equipment）計劃 ● Allen Kent 等完成 ERIC（Educational Research Information Center）之可行性研究，此計劃由美國教育部（U. S. Office of Education，簡稱 USOE）贊助 ● 美國與歐洲開始利用人造衛星現場廣播電視節目
1963	● 溫柏格報告（The Weinberg Report：Science, Government and Information）提出 ● 科學引用文獻索引（Science Citation Index，簡稱 SCI）首次出版 ● 美國伊利諾大學開始 Clinic in Library Application of Data Processing 年會
1964	● NLM 啟用 MEDLARS 系統 ● 美國科技資訊委員會（Committee on Scientific and Technical Information，簡稱 COSATI）成立 ● 按鈕電話（Touch-tone Telephone）啟用
1965—1971	倡議建立美國國家資訊網路
1965	● 發展第三代電腦 ● Ted Nelson 提出超文件（hypertext）資料庫系統的構想 ● Laurence G. Roberts 構思 ARPANET ● CLR 贊助 LC 研究發展機讀記錄之可行性 ● J. C. R. Licklider 發表 Libraries of the Future 一書，提出"電腦化圖書館（computer-based library）"的觀念 ● M. M. Kessler 的技術性資訊研究計劃（Technical Information Project，簡稱 TIP）於 MIT 進行。 ● 美國麻省理工學院（MIT）開始 INTREX（Information Transfer Experiment）計劃

（續上表）

年代	資訊科學發展記要
	• COMSAT（Communication Satellite Corp.）發射第一個人造衛星——晨鳥（Early Bird），Intelsat I
	• 提出 ARPANET（Advanced Research Project Agency Network）之構思
1966—1968	美國國會圖書館設計 MARC I 與 MARC II
1966	• Educational Research Information Center（簡稱 ERIC）成立，由 11 個 clearinghouse 組成
	• ALA-ISAD（ALA's Information Science and Automation Division）成立
	• Annual Review of Information Science and Technology（簡稱 ARIST）出版，Carlos A. Cuadra 擔任主編
	• 美國洛克希德公司（Lockheed Corporation）推出 DIALOG 線上資訊檢索系統
1967	• Andy Van Dam 等學者建立超文件編輯系統（Hypertext Editing System）
	• Fred Kilgour 進入 OCLC，並完成編目作業批次處理系統
	• 美國總統 Lyndon Johnson 提議建立"Knowledgy Network"
	• Interuniversity Communication Council（EDUCOM）出版"Summer Study of Information Networks"一文
	• Donald W. Davies 設計分封式線路交換（Packet Switching）
1968	• ALS-ISAD 出版 Journal of Library Automation（簡稱 JOLA）刊物，由 Fred Kilgour 任總編輯
	• Doug Engelbart 推出超文件系統 The On-Line System（簡稱 NLS）
	• ARPANET 測試分時（time-sharing）服務
	• 美國開始以資訊科學（Information Science）取代文獻學（Documentation），American Documentation Institute 改名為 American Society for Information Science（簡稱 ASIS）
	• 提出 EDUNET 構想
	• 美國國會圖書館發行 MARC II 格式之編目資料磁帶
1969	美國國防部（U. S. Department of Defense，簡稱 DOD）啟用 ARPANET
1970	• 第一個加值型網路（Value Added Telecommunications Network，簡稱 VAN）TYMNET 開始運作
	• 美國圖書館暨資訊科學委員會（National Commission for Library and Information Science，簡稱 NCLIS）成立
1971	• OCLC 開始線上服務
	• 美國國會圖書館採用"多用途機讀目錄系統（Multiple Use MARC System，簡稱 MUMS）"
	• 第一部微電腦（Intel 4004）開始運作
	• 美國國家醫學圖書館啟用 Medlars Online（簡稱 MEDLINE）開始提供線上即時服務

(續上表)

年代	資訊科學發展記要
	• ERIC 開始線上服務
	• 美國國家技術資訊服務中心系統（National Technical Information Service，簡稱 NTIS）線上作業開始
	• G. Salton 的 SMART 系統開始線上作業
	• C. Cuadra 提出 13 項改進"人與電腦交談"之建議
1972	• DARPA 開始進行 Internet 之相關研究
	• DIALOG 開始商業化作業
	• Jon Postel 及 Abhay Bhuuhan 提出檔案傳輸協定（File Transfer Protocol，簡稱 FTP）草案
	• 美國麻州 BBN（Bolt，Beranek & Newman）公司之 Ray Tomlinson 發表電子郵件軟體 SNDMSG 及 Readmail，以 @ 符號區隔使用者與主機的名稱
	• 光纖（Optical fibers）開始被認為是未來通訊系統之線路（wires）
	• M. Greenberger 報告認為 Sophisticated Information Networks 應包括通訊、電腦、資訊和人造衛星之運用
	• "中國圖書館學會"年會中首次討論"資訊科學"
1973	• Frederick Wilfred Lancaster 與 Emily Gallup Fayen 出版 *Information Retrieval On-line* 一書
	• System Development Corporation（簡稱 SDC）推出 ORBIT 系統對外開放檢索
	• 全錄實驗室（PARC）研究員 Robert Metcalfe 研究出以同軸電纜串聯的乙太網路（Ethernet），可供資料快速傳輸
1974	• 網際網路之父 Vinton Cerf 和 Robert Kahn 設計出 TCP（Transmission Control Protocol）通訊協定，使不同的電腦網路可互相連結
	• BBN 開放 Telnet，為第一個提供公共封包資料服務的機構
	• Ted Nelson 在其著作 Computer Library 中提出"超文件及其空間（Hypertext and Hyperspace）"名詞，并闡述兩者之概念
1975	• Carnegie-Mellon University 首度公開一分散式超媒體系統 ZOG（即 Knowledge Management System，簡稱 KMS）
	• Alan Kay 生產第一部個人電腦（Xerox PARC）
	• John Vittal 發展出第一個綜合性的電子郵件軟體 MSG
	• NCLIS 發表"Toward a National Program for Library and Information Services: Goals for Action"一文，闡述該委員會之設置宗旨
	• 華盛頓圖書館網（Washington Library Network，簡稱 WLN）成立，後又改為 Western Library Network
	• 美國國家農業圖書館將 CAIN（Cataloging and Indexing）服務擴大，改為 AGRICOLA（Agricultural Online Access）

（續上表）

年代	資訊科學發展記要
	• 美國國會圖書館發展"主題內容連線資訊檢索系統（Subject Content Oriented Retriever for Processing Information Online，簡稱 SCORPIO）"與 COMARC（Cooperative Machine-Readable Cataloging）
1976	• Martha E. Williams 擔任 ARIST（自 Volume 11 起）之第二任主編
	• *Computer-Readable Bibliographic Databases：Adirectory and Data source Book*，1st ed. 開始出版，Martha E. William 擔任總編輯
1977	• 書目檢索服務（Bibliographic Retrieval Services，簡稱 BRS）公司啟用線上資訊系統檢索服務
	• Martha E. Williams 主編 *Online Review* v. 1 至今
	• Apple 電腦推出全球第一臺個人電腦 Apple Ⅱ
	• OCLC 改爲 OCLC, Inc. 公司
1978	• MIT 之 Architecture Machine Group 展示第一套超媒體影碟（The Aspen Movie Map）
	• Ward Christensen 發明數據機（modem），讓電腦可以透過電話撥接連線電腦網路。
	• 史丹佛大學（Standford University）發展之大型圖書館書目自動化作業分時系統（Bibliographic Automation of Large Library Operations Using a Time Sharing，簡稱 BALLOTS）改稱爲研究圖書館資訊網（Research Libraries Information Network，簡稱 RLIN）
	• F. W. Lancaster 發表 *Toward Paperless Information System* 一書，提出"無紙社會（Paperless Society）"的觀點
1979	• Charles Goldfarb 設計 Standard Generalized Markup Language（簡稱 SGML）
	• Kent 與 Galvin 編撰之 *Structure and Governance of Library Networks* 一書，獲得 ASIS 最佳資訊科學論著獎（ASIS Award for Best Information Science Book）
	• NCLIS 於華盛頓特區召開美國白宮圖書館暨資訊服務會議（White House Conference on Library and Information Services，簡稱 WHCLIS）
	• Tom Truscott, Jim Ellis 及 Steve Bellovin 建立最早且是最大的合作式網路 Usenet，主要提供新聞討論羣組服務
	• 臺灣資訊工業策進會（Institute for Information Industry，簡稱 III）成立
1980	• *Harvard Business Review* 成爲第一個提供機讀式全文資料檢索的期刊，並可在 BRS 和 DIALOG 資訊服務系統上查詢
	• 第四代電腦（Very Large Scale Integrated Circuit，簡稱 VLSI）出現
	• 電子計算機漸漸趨於"User Friendly"
	• 美國國會圖書館於本年一月一日宣佈關閉其卡片目錄
	• 美國制訂《電子資料交換（Electronic Data Interchange，簡稱 EDI）國家標準（ANSI X12）》
	• 美國開始 Linked Systems Project（簡稱 LSP）之研究，即是 Z39.50 標準之前身
1981	• Ted Nelson 構思"Xanadu-Literary Machines"，爲集中式超文件資料庫系統

(續上表)

年代	資訊科學發展記要
	● 中國機讀編目格式（Chinese MARC Format）問世
1982	● 網際網路（Internet）名詞首次出現
	● 286 微處理器上市
	● C. R. Hildreth 發表 *Online Public Access Catalogs：the User Interface*，開始 OPAC 之設計構思
	● 美國資訊科學學會（ASIS）臺北分會成立
1983	● ARPANet 分裂爲二：ARPANet 和 MILNet，前者用於研發和學術界，後者專屬於國防資料傳遞用
	● Jon Postel、Paul Mockapetris 及 Craig Partridge 提出 "網域名稱制度（Domain Name System，簡稱 DNS）"
1984	● Telos 發表 Filevision，爲 Macintosh 之超媒體資料庫
	● Martha E. Williams 預示資訊系統將會對使用者更透明化（transparent）
	● William Gibson 在其科幻小說中創造 "Cyberspace" 一字
	● Steve Case 創辦美國線上公司（America Online，簡稱 AOL）
1985	● Brown University 的 Norman Meyrowitz 與其他學者共同提出超媒體系統 Intermedia 之構想
	● 386 處理器問市
1986	● 國際標準組織（International Organization for Standards，簡稱 ISO）制訂《標準通用標誌語言（Standard Generalized Markup Language，簡稱 SGML）國際標準（ISO8879：1986：Standard Generalized Markup Language）》
	● OWL 發表超媒體文件瀏覽器 GUIDE
1987	● 蘋果電腦（Apple Computer）公司推出第一套廣泛使用的個人超媒體系統 HyperCard
	● 1987 年超文件會議（Hypertext' 87 Workshop）於 North Carolina 召開
	● 歐洲量子物理實驗室（European Laboratory for Particle Physics，簡稱 CERN）與美國各大研究室利用 Internet 連線以交換資訊
1988	● RobertMorris Jr. 的網路蟲（Internet Worm）病毒程式造成約十分之一的網路主機暫時無法運作，始倡導成立網路安全議題的電腦危機處理小組
	● Jarkko Oikarinen 設計多人線上聊天系統（Internet RelayChat，簡稱 IRC）
1989	● 486 微處理器面世
	● Memex Research Institute 成立
	● 美國 Autodesk 公司進行發展 Xanadu 計劃
	● 第二屆 White House Conference on Library and Information Services 在華盛頓舉行
	● 臺灣 "教育部圖書館事業委員會" 成立，並開始整體規劃全臺圖書館資訊網路系統
1990	● 歐洲超文件會議（European Conference on Hypertext，簡稱 ECHT）召開

（續上表）

年代	資訊科學發展記要
	• 歐洲高能物理學家 Tim Berners-Lee 於量子物理實驗室（European Laboratory for Particle Physics，簡稱 CERN）提出全球資訊網（World Wide Web，簡稱 WWW）的概念；並創超文件標誌語言（Hypertext Markup Language，簡稱 HTML）
	• Peter Deutsch, Alan Emtage 和 Bill Heelan 發表 Archie 檔案搜尋軟體
	• The world（world. std. com）成為第一個提供電話撥接服務的公司
	• ARPANET 終止運作
	• 美國國會圖書館推行 American Memory 數位圖書館五年先導計劃（American Memory Pilot, 1990—1995）
	• "臺灣學術網路（Taiwan Academic Network，簡稱 TANet）"建立，係由"教育部"及"國立大學"共同建立，主要為教學研究用網路
1991	• 史丹佛線性加速器中心（Stanford Linear Accelerator Center，簡稱 SLAC）設置美國第一個 Web 伺服器
	• 美國明尼蘇達大學（University of Minnesota）的 Paul Lindner 和 Mark McCahill 發明分散式文件傳輸系統，以明尼蘇達大學的吉祥物小田鼠（Gopher）命名，但該系統不支援超連結功能
	• Brewster Kahle 發明廣域訊息伺服器（Wide Area Information Servers，簡稱 WAIS），為客戶瑞的資料搜尋引擎
	• 美國總統簽署《高效能計算法案（The High Performance Computing Act，簡稱 HPCC）》，其中規劃建立高速之"全國研究與教育網路（National Research and Education Networks，簡稱 NREN）"
1992	• Autodesk 放棄發展 Xanadu 計劃
	• CERN 正式發表全球資訊網，並公開 The portable browser 供免費利用
	• Jean Armour Polly 創造"Surfing the Internet"一詞
	• 美國參議員 Al Gore 提出《資訊基礎建設與科技法案（The Information Infrastructure and Technology Act of 1992）》，法案中首次出現"數位圖書館（Digital Library）"一詞
	• 臺灣成立國家高速電腦中心（National Center for High-Performance Computing，簡稱 NCHC）
1993	• 臺灣資策會 SEEDNet 提供企業界試用網路
	• 國際超媒體與超文件標準研討會（International Workshop on Hypermedia and Hypertext Standards）於 Amsterdam 召開
	• 美國國家超級電腦應用中心（National Center for Supercomputer Applications，簡稱 NCSA）發表 NCSA Mosaic 1.0 for X Windows 應用軟體第一屆全球資訊網開發者會議（World-Wide Web developers' conference）於美國麻州舉行
	• Ted Nelson 擔任於西雅圖（Seattle, Washington）召開之 Hypertext Conferencc 榮譽主講人

(續上表)

年代	資訊科學發展記要
	• 美國國家科學基金會、國防部與太空總署聯合發表《數位圖書館先道研究計劃 (Digital Libraries Initiative Research Project)》
	• A Hard Day's Night 成為第一部轉製成超文件格式的電影,且以碟片型式發行
	• 民間組織網際網路協會 (Internet Society, 簡稱 ISOC) 成立
	• Marc Andreessen 於美國伊利諾大學高速電腦中心研發出第一個圖像網頁瀏覽器 Mosaic (Navigator 的前身)
	• 美國柯林頓總統在矽谷宣佈美國資訊基礎建設 (National Information Infrastructure, 簡稱 NII) 開始,並發佈 NII 行動綱領
	• 美國國會 (U. S. Congress) 制訂國家資訊基礎建設法 (National Information Infrastructure Act)
	• 臺灣第一個搜尋引擎"蕃薯藤"成立,主要供學術研究使用
	• 臺灣經濟部工業局引進 EDI 技術,開始推廣 EDI 之應用
1994	• 美國國家科學委員會開始《數位圖書館先道計劃 (Digital Libraries Initiative)》,第一階段預計進行五年 (1994—1998)
	• World-Wide Web 在 Internet 上的使用量超越 Gopher
	• 網路書店亞馬遜 amazon. com 開張,為開啟電子商務的先驅
	• 第一屆國際全球資訊網會議 (First International World-Wide Web Conference) 於 Geneva 舉行;會後制訂虛擬實境模式語言 (Virtual Reality Modeling Language, 簡稱 VRML) 規格書
	• Jim Clark 與 Marc Andreessen 創立第一家瀏覽器公司"網景 (Netscape)"
	• 臺灣"行政院"成立"國家資訊基本建設 (National Information Infrastructure, 簡稱 NII) 推動小組"
	• 中華電信 HiNet 提供商業網際網路服務
1995	• 楊致遠和 David Filo 建立搜尋引擎站"雅虎"(Yahoo!)
	• Sun Microsystems 研發出 HotJava,為一種結合互動式物件的瀏覽器語言
	• Win 95 上市,結合網頁瀏覽噐和作業系統
	• Pentium (Intel 586) 專業處理器問世
	• 美國 OCLC/NCSA MetadataWorkshop 中提出 Dublin Core (Dublin Metadata Core Element Set),為描述網路電子資源之格式
	• 臺灣公佈施行《電腦處理個人資料保護法》
1996	• Dell 電腦公司創立,開辦線上銷售業務
	• Yair Goldfinger, Arik Vardi, Sefi Vigiser 和 Amnon Amir 創設 Mirabilis 公司,發展即時通訊免費軟體 ICQ (取自 I Seek You 之諧音)
	• 微軟 (Microsoft) 公司及網景 (Netscape) 公司引發瀏覽器 (Explorer 與 Navigator) 版本的對抗

(續上表)

年代	資訊科學發展記要
1997	• 全球資訊網聯盟（World-Wide Web Consortium，簡稱 W3C）於 SGML 96 Conference 中提出 XML（Extensible Markup Language）草案 • 美國柯林頓總統提出"新世代網際網路計劃（Next Generation Internet，簡稱 NGI）"構想，於 1998 年獲美國國會通過施行 • 美國 98 所大學宣佈成立 Internet 2 計劃，以供學術研究使用 • 美國政府宣示推動"全球資訊基礎建設（Global Information Infrastructure，簡稱 GII）" • 美國柯林頓總統發表《電子商務政策白皮書》 • 臺灣精誠資訊公司成立入口網站"奇摩"（Kimo），為臺灣第一個商業化的搜尋引擎 • 臺灣加入美國之"新世代網際網路計劃（Next Generation Internet，簡稱 NGI）"
1998	• 美國數位圖書館先道計劃進入第二階段（Digital Libraries Initiative Phase II） • 微軟公司併購 Hotmail 免費電子郵件網站 • 美國線上（America OnLine，簡稱 AOL）公司併購網景公司 • Intel 公司開始經營電子商務網站 • Pentium III 問世 • 臺灣 SEEDNet 從資策會獨立出來，成為數位聯合電信股份有限公司
1999	• 微軟公司發表 Internet Explorer 5，在瀏覽器版本的競爭上，首度領先網景公司 • Intel 公司推出 Pentium III 處理器，係針對網際網路應用而設計，擴充了影、音、動畫和 3D 影像的操作能力 • Bill Gates 出版《數位社經系統》（Business@ the speed of thought: using a digital nervous system）一書 • 美國麻省理工學院提出"活氧計劃（Oxygen Plan）" • 美國國會圖書館啟用新系統——Endeavor 公司之 Integrated Library System • 臺灣"經濟部"商業司公佈《電子商務政策綱領》，期能透過電子商務的應用，建構臺灣成為廿一世紀亞太地區商務中心

（收稿日期：1999 年 12 月 25 日）

　　作者多年從事資訊科學之教學研究，期望能整理資訊科學與技術發展之大事記，慶幸獲得"國家科學委員會"之研究獎助（計劃編號 NSC88－2413－H－002－029），始得完成，特此致謝。以上摘要記錄 1638 至 1999 年間資訊科學與技術之發展與演進，疏漏之處在所難免，尚請學者專家不吝指正，期能使此記要內容更為完臻。

註　釋

註：Joseph C. Donohue and N. E. Karioth, "Coming of Age in Academe Information Science at

21,"American Documentation 17（July, 1966）, p. 117.

註：Dorothy B. Lilley, Ronald W. Trice, A History of Information Science, 1945–1985（San Diego, Calif.：Academic Press, 1989）.

註：Saul Herner, "Brief History of Information Science," Journal of the American Society for Information Science 35（1984）, p. 157.

註：張新華著，資訊學概論（臺北市：臺灣商務，1991 年），頁 25—26。

註：A. Tepper, "Controlling Technology by Shaping Vision," Policy Sciences 29：1（1996）, pp. 29–44.

註：B. R. Schatz, "Information Retrieval in Digital Libraries：Bringing Search to the Net," Science 275：5298（1997）, pp. 327–334.

註：B. Shackel, "Human-Computer Interaction：Whence and Whither," Journal of the American Society for Information Science 48：11（1997）, pp. 970–986.

註：E. Meyer, N. F. Funkhouser, "A Brief History of Networking in the US," Journal of Chemical Information and Computer Sciences 38：6（1998）, pp. 951–955.

註：M. T. Day, "Transformational Discourse：Ideologies of Organizational Change in the Academic-Library and Information Science Literature," Library Trends 46：4（Spring, 1998）, pp. 635–667.

註：T. A. Finholt, G. M. Olson, "From Laboratories to Collaboratories：A New Organizational Form For Scientific Collaboration," Psychological Science 8：1（1997）, pp. 28–36.

註：N. V. Findler, S. Maini, A. F. M. Yuan, "Shrif, a General Purpose System for Heuristic Retrieval of Information and Facts, Applied to Medical Knowledge Processing," Information Processing & Management 28：2（1992）, pp. 219–240.

註：G. B. Newby, "An Invistigation of the Role of Navigation for Information Retrieval," Proceedings of the ASIS Annual Meeting 29（1992）, pp. 20–25.

註：N. J. Davis, R. Weeks, M. C. Revett, "Information Agents for the World Wide Web," BT Technology Journal 14：3（1996）, pp. 105–114.

註：D. H. Jonassen, S. Wang, "Acquiring Structural Knowledge from Semantically Structured Hypertext," Journal of Computer Based Instruction 20：1（1993）, pp. 1–8.

註：M. D. Dunlop, C. J. Vanrijsbergen, "Hypermedia and Free Text Retrieval," Information Processing & Management 29：3（1993）, pp. 287–298.

註：M. Frolick, N. K. Ramarapu, "Hypermedia：The Future of EIS," Journal of Systems Management 44：7（1993）, pp. 32–36.

註：A. Moulik, D. Lai, "Rebels in Search of Champions：Envisioning the Library of Future," Electronic Library 10：2（April, 1992）, pp. 97–102.

註：P. Skagestad, "Thinking with Machines：Intelligence Augmentation, Evolutionary Epistemology, and Semiotic," Journal of Social and Evolutionary Systems 16：2（1993）, pp. 157–180.

註：N. J. Davis, R. S. Stewart, R. Weeks, "Knowledge Sharing Agents over the World Wide Web," BT Technology Journal 16：3（1998）, pp. 104–109.

註：O. C. Park, "Instructional Applications of Hypermedia: Functional Features, Limitations, and Research Issues," Computers in Human Behavior 8: 2–3 (1992), pp. 259–272.

註：B. Cronin, E. Davenport, "Social Intelligence," Annual Review of Information Science and Technology 28 (1993), pp. 3–44.

註：J. J. Wellington, "The Role of New Technology in Teacher Education: A Case Study of Hypertext in a PGCE Course," Journal of Education for Teaching (1995), pp. 37–50.

註：E. K. Welsch, "Hypertext, Hypermedia, and the Humanities," Library Trends 40: 4 (Spring, 1992), pp. 614–646.

註：J. V. Henderson, "Comprehensive, Technology-Based Clinical Education: the Virtual Practicum," International Journal of Psychiatry in Medicine 28: 1 (1998), pp. 41–79.

註：S. F. Su, "Dialog With an OPAC: How Visionary Was Swanson in 1964," Library Quarterly 64: 2 (1994), pp. 130–161.

註：E. Perez, "Oregon Online: Automated Document Management of an Infobase," Database: the Magazine of Electronic Database Reviews 18: 6 (1995), p. 30.

註：E. S. Metcalfe, M. E. Frisse, S. W. Massan, etc., "Academic Networks: Mosaic and World Wide Web," Academic Medicine 69: 4 (1994), pp. 270–273.

註：A. J. Weiland, "Beyond Fear: Forging a New Path," Journal of Bone and Joint Surgery 80A: 7 (July, 1998), pp. 935–940.

註：B. Blansit, Elizabeth Connor, "Making Sense of the Electronic Resource Marketplace: Trends in Health-Related Electronic Resources," Bulletin of the Medical Library Association 87: 3 (July, 1999), pp. 243–250.

註：M. P. D'Alessandro, "Creating and Curating a Pediatric Radiology Digital Library to Make the Internet a Useful Reference Tool for the Radiologist," Pediatric Radiology 28: 1 (1998), pp. 890–5.

註：L. W. McClure, "From Brick Face to Cyberspace," Bulletin of the Medical Library Association 83: 3 (1995), pp. 311–314.

註：陳亞寧，另類圖書館：電子圖書館綜觀，資訊傳播與圖書館學 5 卷 3 期（1999 年 3 月），59—73。

註：D. Schoonbaert, "Biomedical Journals and the World-Wide-Web," Electronic Library 16: 2 (April, 1998), pp. 95–104.

註：李德竹，"以書目計量學方法探討資訊科學之父 Vannevar Bush 對資訊時代的重要影響和貢獻"，"行政院國家科學委員會"專題研究計劃成果報告（臺北市：臺大圖書資訊學系，1999）NSC88–2413–H–002–029。

註：比爾・蓋茲（Bill Gates）著，樂爲良譯，數位神經系統：與思考等快的明日世界（Business@ The Speed of Thought: Using a Digital Nervous System）（臺北市：商業周刊出版；城邦文化發行，1999 年）。

註：J. M. Pemberton, C. R. Nugent, "Information Studies: Emergent Field, Convergent Curriculum," Journal of Education for Library and Information Science 36: 2 (Spring, 1995), pp. 126–138.

註：Robert Cailliau,"A Short History of the Web," <u>Text of a speech delivered at the launching of the European branch of the W3 Consortium Paris, 2 November 1995</u>, < http：// www. inria. fr/Actualites/Cailliau-fra. html > （7 June 1999）.

註：Jean Paul Emard,"An Information science Chronology in Perspective," <u>Bulletin of the American Society for Information Science</u> 2：8（March, 1976）, pp. 51 – 56.

註：Kevin Hughes,"A Hypermedia Timeline," <u>Entering the World-Wide-Web：A Guide to Cyperspace</u>, May 1994, < http：//linux. cis. nctu. edu. tw/docs/woven/www-help/guide. 61/guide. 14. html > （8 June 1999）.

註：Karen Sparck Jones and Peter Willett, eds., <u>Readings in Information Retrieval</u>（San Francisco：Morgan Kaufman Pub., 1997）.

註：Dorothy B. Lilley and Ronald W. Trice., <u>A History of Information Science 1945 – 1985</u>. San Diego：Academic Press, c1989. Appendix B.

註："Timeline." <u>The Electronic Labyinth</u>, 1995, < http：//jefferson. village. virginia. edu/elab/hfl0267. html > （8 June 1999）.

註："A Brief History of Internet", <u>數位時代</u>, 創刊1號（1999年7月1日）, 頁149—154。

註：同註。

資訊巨人 VANNEVAR BUSH (1890—1974)*

[摘要 Abstract]

邁入資訊社會時代之今日,個人電腦、網路及多媒體已廣被人們使用,成為每個人生活與工作上不可或缺的重要工具;海內外圖書館亦已完成自動化作業,利用網路與電腦提供讀者各項線上資訊檢索服務。現代人每天經由電腦與網路設備所接收與處理之資訊更常以上億萬個字元來計算,故快速而有效掌握資訊,成為當前資訊社會的特色。現今資訊科學與技術的進步實非一蹴可及,其影響之源可追溯自西元 1945 年 Vannevar Bush (1890—1974) 所發表之文章"思維之際"(*As We May Think*) 及其 Memex 之設計理念,成為影響現代資訊科學與技術發展之關鍵。因此撰文介紹這位資訊巨人 Vannevar Bush 的生平、著作與記事,以及其對資訊社會之重要貢獻與影響。

Vannevar Bush (1890—1974), the Information Giant, during his lifetime, had made many great and influential contributions in science and engineering, in proposing the establishment of the National Science Foundation (NSF), and in re-shaping the institutions of research and development in America and the World. Yet it is in information science and technology that Bush has become a mythic hero. He was also hailed as "the father of information science". "the father of modern computer", and "the grandfather of hypertext", the beginning of which is often recognized to be 1945 when Bush's seminal paper "As We May Think", With its conceptual design of a desktop personal information machine called the "Memex". was published in Atlantic Monthly. This classical paper "As We May Think" and the "Memex", along with Bush's "Rapid Selectors" and "Comparators" machines, have had a highly inspirational and significantly impact on the important developments of modern information science and technology and the ernergence of the Information age. Thus, it is the purpose of this paper to introduce this outstanding information scientist, his biographical data, major publications, important contributions and lifetime events.

關鍵字:Vannevar Bush、Memex、資訊科學、資訊技術、資訊檢索、超文件

Keyword:Vannevar Bush, Memex, Information science, Information technology, Information retrieval, Hypertext

壹、前言

近五十餘年來,資訊科技的發展可謂一日千里,因 Vannevar Bush 對資訊社會的建

---

* 本文曾發表在《臺北市立圖書館館訊》17 卷 2 期 (1999 年 12 月),第 55—67 頁。

立居功厥偉，後人尊稱為"資訊科學之父"（註2）、"現代電腦之父"（註3）及"超文件之始祖"（註4）；且因 Bush 倡議建立美國國家科學基金會（National Science Foundation，簡稱 NSF），故又稱其為"NSF 之父"（註5），該基金會於 1980 年起設置 Vannevar Bush Award 以紀念之（註6）；而 Memex 設計之理念，則成為影響資訊技術發展方向之關鍵。綜觀言之，Bush 對資訊時代的影響與貢獻，實不容忽視，因而撰文介紹。

貳、生平

布希（Vannevar Bush）生於 1890 年 3 月 11 日美國麻省（Massachusetts）波士頓（Boston）鄰近的 Everett 鎮，父親是教會牧師，兄姊各一人。幼年深受父親個性堅毅及姊姊熱愛科學的影響，而養成追求事實及熱愛真理的人格特質。1913 年由塔福次學院（Tufts College）以優異成績先後獲得學士及碩士學位。妻 Phoebe Davis，育有二子 Richard Davis 和 JohnHathaway。（註7）

Bush 22 歲（1912 年）時已設計 profile tracer，並獲得專利，次年入通用電子公司（General Electric Company）任職，因為 Bush 深感自己較適合學術研究工作而返母校任教。1915 年，Bush 同時入麻省理工學院（Massachusetts Institute of Technology，簡稱 MIT）電機系和哈佛大學（Harvard University）二校攻讀博士學位，由於成績優異，次年即獲兩校學位，Bush 隨即應聘至麻省理工學院電機工程學系任教。為協助教學，Bush 於 1922 年出版專書 *Principles of Electrical Engneering*。任教麻省理工學院期間，深受該校校長 Karl Compton 之賞識，於 1932 年聘其為副校長兼電機學院院長，因而也開啟後來二人長期合作與政府研究計劃之關係。（註3）

1930 年代，Bush 專心於電子計算機械的各種設計工作，其中尤以 1934 年為麻省理工學院設計的微分分析儀（Differential Analyzer）最為有名。該分析儀則遠較機械加法機進步，是第一臺類比式電子計算機之雛型，曾用於第二次世界大戰期間協助解決原子物理方面問題，該機器實為數位電子計算機奠定基礎，故後人稱 Bush 為"電腦之父"。此外，Bush 協助美國聯邦調查局設計檢視指紋機器（Fingerprint Machine），並與美國海軍合作設計 Rapid Analytical Machines，以及比較器（Comparator）等工作。1939 年，Bush 除接任美國航空顧問委員會（National Advisory Committee for Aeronautics，簡稱 NACA）主席外，又被聘為華盛頓卡內基研究院（Carnegie Institute of Washington）院長，整頓該院財政及運作問題。同年，Bush 向美國聯邦調查局局長 J. Edgar Hoover 提出空戰武器計劃報告，建議使用雷達協助戰機偵測敵情。（註9）

1940 年，Busk 預測美國將會捲入第二次世界大戰，而向羅斯福總統建議將國家防衛研究委員會（National Defense Research Committee，簡稱 NDRC）更名為國防委員會（National Defense Committee，簡稱 NDC），該委員會應由軍事、科學、商業方面之專家組成，經費由政府提供，以研究武器設備為宗旨，協助戰爭及三軍間互相合作。總統接受其建議並任命 Bush 為該委員會主席，負責整合全國之科學研究，為未來參戰作準備。同年，Bush 又擔任鈾礦顧問委員會（Advisory Committee on Uranium）召集人，推動發展原子彈之曼哈頓計劃（Manhattan Project）。翌年，美國羅斯福總統為擴大國防委員會而成立科學研究發展處（Office of Scientific Research and Development，簡稱 OSRD），邀請

Bush擔任首長，負責結合工業界與學術界共同研究發展早期原子彈技術，其間Bush又成立雷達實驗室。1940年12月7日日本偷襲美國珍珠港，美國正式捲入第二次世界大戰。（註10）

第二次大戰期間，Bush從事軍事方面之研究，研究項目包含火箭、戰車、雷達、爆破和通訊等，對美國軍事上的協助甚大，使美國能克服德國的U-boat及V–1武器之威脅，Bush後被譽爲"縮短戰爭的關鍵人物"（註11）。1941年，Bush又積極尋求政府支援原子彈（Atomic Bomb）研究計劃，向美國總統羅斯福報告其重要性，獲其同意執行，使美國得以於日本東京及廣島投下原子彈而結束第二次世界大戰。1944年，時代雜誌讚頌Busk對大戰的貢獻而稱其爲"物理將軍"（General of Physics），以別於第二次大戰英雄Dwight D. Eisenhower與Douglas MacArthur將軍。（註12）同年，Bush出版 Science: The Endless Frontier，該書內容強調科學是沒有止境的，雖如此，但人類最終的成就並非科學而在提昇人文素質。

1945年Bush於《大西洋月刊》（Tne Atlantic Monthly）發表影響後世資訊科學技術最深切重要的經典之作《思維之際》（As We May Think）一文，二次大戰後，各學科之蓬勃發展，研究成果豐碩而致出版量急增，Bush認爲如能對人類的知識作適當的處理及掌控，以及如何有效的儲存、檢案，利用這些研究資料/訊，才是科學研究人員責任與任務。並提出Memex（memory & index）之設計構思，Memex爲一個人以機器判讀資料之資料庫系統，透過建立聯結路徑、蒐尋、處理及整合等技術，供研究人員蒐集、分析各類資科並加以應用，可說是後世個人電腦、超文件、超媒體等科技發展之濫觴。（註13）1946年艾森豪將軍深受Bush影響對全國發表《軍事備忘錄》，內容含1.陸軍應支援軍事計劃；2.政府應給予科學家及工業界最大之研究發展空間；3.查驗解密後之軍事成果應可用於工業技術；4.軍中應設置獨立之研究發展部門，以及5.政府武器製造部門應與軍隊計劃密切整合等五項原則。（註14）同年，Bush又出版 Endless Horizons 專書。（註15）1949年，美國杜魯門總統公開表揚Bush，並稱之爲自1940年來美國最重要的軍事及技術導師，同時，Bush之著作 Modern Arms and Free Men: A Discussion of the Role of Science in Preserving Democracy 亦成爲當年暢銷書，對美國政治及軍事政策影響甚巨。（註16）

Bush平時特別關心國家安全問題，而大力鼓吹美國切勿與蘇俄競相發展核子與氫彈武器，危害到人民的生命與福祉。（註17）1940年代，Bush積極推動人民安全及福祉之工作，建議美國政府成立國家科學基金會（National Science Foundation，簡稱NSF），政府應資助民間之科學研究，以廣泛支持戰後美國基礎研究及科學教育，同時又建議政府應成立健康與教育福利委員會（Health, Education Welfare Commission）。1955年，Bush因健康問題自華盛頓卡內基研究院（Carnegie Institution of Washington）退休返回麻省。退休後，Bush仍本其對週遭事物關懷之熱誠，除設計改良汽車引擎、觀察分析鳥翼行動、設計推動軍用船隻之螺旋葉（Hydrofoil）、研究適用腦部與心臟疾病的微小型醫療瓣膜（Valve）等外，並經常至各地演講。1957年蘇俄先美國而發射第一顆人造衛星Sputnik號，Bush認爲當時美國研究人造衛星落后蘇俄之主要因素，追究於美國陸海空三軍未能密切合作之故。（註18）

Bush之專書《科學貧乏》（Science is Not Enough）於1969年出版。1972年又出版

Pieces of the Action，該書集合 Bush 多年來所發表的文章、備忘錄及其生活和思想記錄，是 Bush 的自傳，文中 Bush 表示人生如能重來一次，他仍會做相同的事。Bush 於 1974 年 6 月 30 日去世，享年 84 歲。當時紐約時報及華盛頓郵報追悼並讚譽 Bush 在第二次世界大戰中的卓越貢獻。（註 19）歸納 Bush 對現代科技的貢獻如 Memex、資訊檢索、原子彈、飛彈發展、人造衛星、氫彈及登月計劃等，明顯的，Bush 是位成功的工程師、科學家、教師、發明家、作家、企業家及人道主義者，實為一位全方位的時代巨人。

叄、重要貢獻及影響

Bush 是第一位設計並使用電算機械解決數學與工程問題的美國學者。1945 年影響後世深遠的重要文獻"思維之際"（As We May Think）刊在《大西洋月刊》，該文認為人類所有之創造及發明，僅能增強和延伸人類體力面而非其心智面，所提出 Memex 系統之構想為個人儲存資料及與外界聯繫設計的機器，類似人腦，可幫助人類記憶和組合檔案。該文內涵除使 1950 年後資訊科學蓬勃發展外，進而促使超文件（Hypertext）及電腦輔助教學（CAI）技術的產生，文中並預言未來世界將出現乾式攝影（Dry Photography）技術，類似現今的拍立得技術、利用微捲（Microfilm）儲存大量資料、記錄人類語音之機器（Vocoder）、傳真技術（Facsimile）以及可自動進行邏輯運算的思想機器（Thinking Machine）等。（註 20）上述預言對學術貢獻、後世科學、超文件（Hypertext）、電子圖書館（Electronic Libraries）、資訊檢索（Information Retrieval）等之研究與發展有無限之啟發，以下詳述 Bush 的影響及貢獻。

一、一般科學技術影響及貢獻

Bush 於 1933 年發表 "The Inscrutable Past" 一文，該文以大學教授日常生活中使用各項自動化設施為研究對象，印證人類不需要瞭解所用機器的複雜結構方可使用，並預測人類未來生活之條件會更好。（註 21）1941 年，Bush 希望能改變人們對科學的認知，也就是科學並非僅應用於戰爭之觀念，其在傳輸、食物、衣著和其他方面，皆有其更重要之用途，遠較製造武器更能造福人類。同時並強調應用科學可以創造無數契機，善用科學可解決人類疾病問題、增進生活水準及品質、追求人類快樂幸福。（註 22）1945 年，Bush 答覆羅斯福總統之報告書 *Science: the Endless Frontier: A Report to the President*，其內容詳釋科學與政府之關係、戰爭期間疾病問題、科學和公共福利關係如國家安全、人民工作、基礎研究，以及培養美國青年人之科學研究等方面，並強調政府應延續二次大戰期間對醫藥和相關科學之研究以及協助公私立組織機構進行科學研究工作。（註 23）Bush 深感科學研究對國家重要性，於次年建議政府應長期提供研究環境及經費，以鼓勵年輕人培養其科技創造力，以及網羅各界學者專家組成基金管理委員會，以合約或獎助金方式贊助政府以外的組織進行研究，支援公私立學校之基礎研究並將研究成果呈報總統。此外，為發展和鼓勵國家科學研究及科學教育，建議成立國家科學基金會（National Science Foundation，簡稱 NSF），以支援基礎研究，同時並規劃該會之成員、組織、任期及功能，故 Bush 被稱為 "NSF 之父"。（註 24）1949 年，Bush 專書 *Modem Arms and Freemen* 出版，內容強調科學在民主政治國家所扮演的角色，呼籲美公民主政治和科學研究應不因世界局勢轉變而受影響。（註 25）Bush 於 1964 年闡述科學設計之各種機器，

但科學並非萬能,仍有其不足之處,認為人類應同時重視信仰和哲學以補其不足。(註26)

1992年,James M. Nyce 和 Paul Kahn 分析 Bush 1930年在 MIT 設計製造的 Rapid Selector 機器,推論其係依 Machine Intelligence 原理而製造,可檢索經編碼過之縮影資料,並具備複製和列印功能。同年,美國農業部圖書館館員 Ralph R. Shaw 修改 Bush 設計之 Rapid Selector 功能並使其能適用於圖書館之作業。(註27) 當時,Colin Burke 則認為 Bush 之 Memex 構想源自於 Rapid Selector,但因 Rapid Selector 組件過於龐大、處理速度慢、價格昂貴、未取得專利、市場導向不明及類碼表問題等皆尚未解決,而無法進一步發展。(註28) Bush 博學多聞,不僅在科學與技術方面為人類開啟新頁,其他如醫學、公共福利及軍事方面亦對美國及全人類貢獻良多。由於 Bush 認為醫學與科學具有密切關係,陸續發表此類文獻,期能影響政府運用既有的科學技術促進醫學研究。

二、Memex方面

Bush 的 Memex 是現代個人電腦的雛型,也是首次為協助人類思考和管理資訊而設計的理想機器。1939年在"Mechanization and the Record"中,BLuh 詳述 Memex 的功能,此理念於六年後才撰寫成"As We May Think",該文綜論 Memex 具有增強人類控制資訊環境、增加自行控制處理資訊能力、增進人類福祉與支援以及加強人類思想處理能力等四方面影響。當時 Memex 被 Bush 視為個人檔案和私人圖書館,強調其獨特性質,為一類似人腦的機器,其功能遠超越當時已發展之數位電腦(digital computer)。(註29) 1945年的 Memex 是為伸展人類體能而設計,並無法加強智慧能力,後世研究者於 Memex 加入索引及連接等功能,以擴增其為人類提供資訊相關服務之能力。1959年,Bush 提出 Memex II 理念,對首次提出之 Memex 設計概念作進一步解釋及修正。(註30)

Douglas C. Engelbart,美國加州史丹福研究所(Stanford Research Institute)高級研究員於1962年讚譽 Bush 學術成就,認為 Bush 的 Memex 與其本人所研究之人類智慧效能計劃相關,因此將該計劃函寄 Bush 並請其指導。(註31) 1967年,Bush 估計當時全世界每週產生之印刷資料,可以數噸計算,這些資料隨著時間的流逝,或遺失或內容重覆,因此需要對資料之製作、儲存和檢索採取革命性的改良措施,以經濟人類的資源,因此發表"Memex Revisited"一文以修正1945年所提出之 Memex 理念。(註32) 1970年,Bush 說明於1934年設計 Differential Analyzer 的架構及功能,同時分析其與 Memex 的設計理念之異同。(註33) Theodor H. Nelson 於1972年深入分析 Bush Memex 所具備之展現形式、全文編輯檔案以及數位式傳輸文件等功能,啟發 Nelson 發展超文件(hypertext)之理念,如設計全文編輯方式之接收與傳送資料等,因此,於1989年Nelson 稱 Bush 為"超文件始祖"(註34),而 Nelson 則被稱為"超文件之父"。

1981年,Linda C. Smith 曾研究學者文獻引用"As We May Think"一文對現代資訊科學之影響,將所蒐集之引用文獻內容整理成歷史背景、硬體、軟體、資訊儲存及個人資訊系統等五方面詳加分析,發現 Memex 具有縮小儲存空間、增快檢索速度、擴大記憶體等特性。(註35) 十年後 Linda Smith 再次與 Paul Kahn 研究1980年至1990年間引用"As We May Think"之情形,將引用文獻內容依硬體說明、資訊儲存、歷史背景、關聯與選擇及個人資訊系統等五方面影響分別討論,再次證實 Bush 的 Memex 對資訊檢索系統的貢獻,並建議對建立檢索、分享資訊及連結功能等做進一步研究。(註36) 1999年李德竹教授延續研究1991年至1998年間"As We May Think"被引用之情形,根據引用文獻之內容,分析結果顯示個人電腦、超文件與超媒體、線上公用目錄、網際網路、全球資訊網、數位圖書館及神經系統等技術,皆根據Memex之構思研發而成。(註37)

Larry Owens之博士論文詳細探討Bush之微分分析儀(Differential Analyzer)之設計理念及製造方式,認為微分分析儀實為美國戰後最重要的機械,可視為早期的電子計算機之雛型。(註38)綜合Bush之貢獻,Bush不但是一位具有工程師、發明家、教師、作家和行政管理專家等專長的偉大學者,其重要的經典之作"As We May Think"視為是應用機器處理資訊和知識的先驅,所提出的Memex設計理念影響後世超文件(Hypertext)、多媒體(Multimedia)、資訊檢索(Information Retrieval)、人工智慧(Artificial Intelligence)及電子圖書館(Electronic Library)等技術的演進與發展。

三、現代化影響與貢獻

Bush的Memex是模仿人腦細胞之結構,也就是非直線之特性,設計資訊儲存、處理及檢索之運作路徑(Trail),因此直接影響後世之超文件(Hypertext)、光碟技術(Optical Technology)之發展。但研發之技術似乎仍無法與人腦功能完全相同。以上三項技術中,超文件技術則有Theodor Nelson積極發展,而提出國際知名Xanadu Hypertext Systems;光學技術促使光學媒體之開發;而資訊儲存技術則朝向線上檢索及全文資料庫方面快速進展。(註39)

1989年,Noman Meyrowiz依據Memex設計構想討論超文件,認為當時超文件技術包含無線電網路、掃描器及儲存功能,以及處理圖片、聲音、手稿外,但未來尚須解決內容檢索、連結、查尋、影像、編輯與輸出入技術、展現品質、應用目標導向、超媒體資訊、著作權及作業標準化等方面技術及相關實務問題。(註40)為紀念並發揚Vannevar Bush於"As We May Think"一文中的Memex機器理念,Dr. Edwin Brownrigg資助成立Memex Research Institute,網羅各方專家學者從事資訊技術的相關研究,以作為建構新一代全球性共用資訊系統的研發機構,尤其著重電子圖書館與電子館藏之開發,以求實現Bush Memex之理想。(註41)

1992年,有學者認為Memex是個有機體,如能繼續研究延伸超文件特質,更具有創新發展。(註42)Randall H. Trigg認為利用Memex中路徑(Trailblazing)與連結(Linking)功能,建立有效的檢索路徑,可查尋大量資料及訊息記錄,但仍無法解決超文件易使人迷失的問題,因此建議超文件系統中設計指引(Guide)之必要性。(註43)同時又分析超文件功能之所以尚未實現的主要原因是因為安全保密、著作權問題、光學掃描暨儲存資訊媒體技術尚未成熟、多樣性的硬體環境及封閉性系統、編輯作業以及缺乏適切標準,而使得不同資訊來源不易整合。(註44)換言之,超文件技術仍有待繼續開發。美國麻省理工學院和布朗大學為"As We May Think"發表五十週年,於1995年舉辦紀念研討會,再次發揚Bush的Memex理想及影響,以激勵啟發後人。(註45) 1999年,麻省理工學院電腦科學實驗室推出之"活氧計劃"(Oxygen Plan),該計劃之目的與Bush於1945年所建構之Memex系統構思更是不謀而合。(註46) Memex的直接或間接影響方面,可由網際網路上設有無數的以Memex為名之網站證實,Memex之影響層面將繼續對未來資訊科學與技術之研發更是息息相關,永無止息。

肆、結語

總而言之,Bush 之 As We May Think 文獻及 Memex 之設計構思影響力久而彌新,雖然 Memex 之設計僅是一個理念並未實現,但已成爲科技研發所追求之理想境界,後世學者立其爲研究之目標,對不同學科産生不同内涵,追本溯源仍爲 Bush 當時所提出之創見而致。因此,相關研究及技術隨著時代演進不斷有新的創意及設計産生。明顯的,從豐富的 Bush 著作及學者專家引用文獻中(註47,註48,註49,註50,註51,註52),顯示其成就及貢獻並不因時間流逝而遞減;相反的,仍將會持續不斷的導引人類開創嶄新的技術境界和面向。這證實了牛頓之名言:"站在巨人的肩膀上,會看得更高、更遠!"

Bush 生平的重要記事及著作

一、重要記事

Vannervar Bush 生平重要記事一覽表

日期	生平重要記事
1890	出生
1912	設計 Profile Tracer 獲美國專利
1913	• 獲 Tufts College 學士與碩士學位。
	• 任職 General Electric 公司
1914	至 Tufts College 任教
1915	入美國麻省理工學院 Electrical Engineering Department 及哈佛大學攻讀博士學位
1916	• 獲得麻省理工學院及哈佛大學博士學位
	• 加入 AMARD(American Radio and Research Corp.)
1919	離開 Tufts College,轉入麻省理工學院任教
1922	出版 Principles of Electrical Engineering,爲麻省理工學院電機系教科書
1923	任麻省理工學院電子工程學系教授
1932	• 任職麻省理工學院電子工程學系主任
	• 參與麻省理工學院主持之計算機器 Differential Analyzer 的設計和製作計劃
1934	修正 Differential Analyzer 之設計,因造價昂貴麻省理工學院負擔不起,轉向洛克菲勒基金會尋求經費贊助,以持續該計劃
1936	• 協助美國聯邦調查局建立指紋檢視器
	• 與美國海軍(NAVY)合作設計 Rapid Analytical Machine
	• 開始設計 Comparator.
1938	開始擔任政府職務,聘爲美國航空顧問委員會(National Advisory Commitee for Aeronautics,NACA)委員

（續上表）

日期	生平重要記事
1939	● 任美國航空顧問委員會主席
	● 擔任華盛頓卡內基研究院（Carnegie Institute of Washington）院長
	● 向美國聯邦調查局局長胡佛（J. Edgon Hoover）提出空戰計劃武器報告
1940	● 任國家防衛委員會（National Defense Research Committee, NDRC）主席
	● 任鈾礦顧問委員會（Advisory Committee on Uranium）主席
	● 向美國政府推薦規劃 Manhattan Team 以發展原子彈
	● 與羅斯福總統見面，達成設立國家防衛部共識
1941	● 美國總統任命 Bush 為科學研究發展處（Office of Scientific Research and Development, OSRD）首長
	● 成立雷達實驗室
	● 發表第一份原子彈報告，提出鈾元素對原子彈的影響
	● 遊說政府支持原子彈發展計劃
1942	● 協助美國政府成立新武器研發部門
	● 向美國總統報告控制原子能力量之研究結果
1943	研發新武器，迫使德國 U-Boat 戰艦撤離北大西洋，維護歐洲安全
1944	● Time 雜誌撰文稱讚 Bush 為"物理將軍"，以表揚其對國家多方面之貢獻
	● 羅斯福總統針對美國國家研究科學之多項發展問題，向 Bush 請教
1945	● Bush 於 The Atlantic Monthly 發表 "As We May Think" 一文，提出 Memex 設計構思對後世資訊科學影響深遠
	● 發表論文 "Mechanization and the Record"
	● 出版 Science: the Endless Frontier 強調科學研究沒有止境，討論本質及冷戰期間科學與公共政策所引起問題，並分析科學對人類的貢獻及影響，以及科學與社會間之複雜關係，要求美國政府大力支持基礎研究，因而促使美國政府於 1950 年成立國家科學委員會（National Science Foundation，簡稱 NSF）
1946	● 艾森豪總統受其影響發表軍事備忘錄
	● Endless Horizons 出版，內容包含科學、Memex、軍事、公共利益及戰爭的主題
1947	擔任美國防部祕書處下設之研究發展委員會（Research Development Board，簡稱 RDB）的負責人
1948	Bush 因疑患帕金森病及腦瘤而離開 RDB
1949	● Modem Arms and Freemen 出版，論述科學在民主政治所應有之角色，影響美國政治及軍事甚鉅
	● 杜魯門總統公開表揚並稱 Bush 為美國 1940 年來最重要之軍事及技術的導師
1950	美國國家科學委員會（National Science Foundation，簡稱 NSF）成立
1952	● Coronet 雜誌專文報導 Bush 其人其事，並讚揚其人格特質

(續上表)

日期	生平重要記事
	• Bush 對美國政府建議已久之 Health, Education and Welfare 部門終於成立
1955	自 Carnegie Institute 退休返回故鄉麻省
1959	Bush 爲 Memex 再次作一更詳盡描述，而提出 Memex Ⅱ 草稿、但未正式發表
1964	出版 Science Pauses 闡明科學技術輔助人類設計各項機械設備而改善其生活；哲學是夢想，但科學則可實現夢想，二者關係相輔相成
1965	麻省理工學院爲紀念"As We May Think"一文發表二十年而舉辦研討會
1969	• 任麻省理工學院爲客座教授 • 出版 Science is not Enough
1970	美國原子能委員會（(U. S. Atomic Energy Commission）贊譽 Bush 爲原子能先驅者
1972	Pieces of the Action 出版爲 Bush 論文、備忘錄及其生活與思想之記錄論集
1974	Bush 於家中去世，享年 84 歲
1989	Memex Research Institute 成立
1995	麻省理工學院和布朗大學爲紀念"As We May Think"一文發表五十年而舉辦研討會
2000	Internet 中以 Memex 命名之網站甚多，可證實 V. Bush 對後世之影響

二、重要著作

（完整著作請參考李德竹教授之國科會研究報告 NSC88－2413－H－002－029，以書目計量學方法探討資訊科學之父 Vannevar Bush 對資訊時代的重要影響和貢獻）

1. Bush, V. and William Henry Timbie. Principles of Electrical Engineering. New York：Wiley, 1922. 513p.

2. Bush, V. The Differential Analyzer：A New Machine for Solving Differential Equations. [Philadelphia]：[n. p.], 1931.

3. Bush, V. and Karl Taylor Compton etc. Scientists Face the World of 1942. New Brunswick：Rutgers University Press, 1942. 80p.

4. Bush, V. "As We May Think." The Atlantic Monthly. 176：1（1945）：101.

5. Bush, V. Science, the Endless Frontier. North Stratford, N. H.：Ayer Company Publishers. 1945.

6. Bush, V. Endless Horizons. New York：Arno Press, 1946, 182p.

7. Bush, V. and etc. The Individual and Liberal Education. Paper Delivered at the Dedication of Johnston Hall, April 19－21, 1951. [Minneapolis]：University of Minnesota Press, [1952]. 102p.

8. Bush, V. Modern Arms and Free Men：A Discussion of the Role of Science in Preserving Democracy. London：Scientific Book Club, 1949.

9. Bush, V. Memex Ⅱ. MIT Archives, MC78, Box 22, 1959.

10. Bush, V. Man's Thinking Machines. MIT Archives, MC78, Box 21, 1963.

11. Bush, V. Science Pauses. MIT Archives, MC78, Box 22, 1964.

12. Bush, V. Project Intrex. MIT Archives, MC78, Box 20, 1965.

13. Bush, V. Science is Not Enough: Reflections for the Present and Future. Bombay: Vakils, Feffer, and Simons Private, Ltd., 1969.

14. Bush, V. Pieces of the Action. New York: Morrow, 1970. 366p.

15. Bush, V. and. etc. From Memex to Hypertext: Vannevar Bush and the Mind's Machine. Boston: Academic Press, 1991. 367p.

16. Bush, V. and etc. Vannevar Bush Ⅱ: Science for the 21st Century: Current and Future Challenges for Federal Support: A Report. Research Triangle Park, NC: Sigma Xi, The Scientific Research Society, 1995.

註 釋

註1：Vannevar Bush, "As We May Think," Atlantic Monthly 176：1（1945）：101－108.

註2：D. B. Lilley & R. W. Rice, A History of Information Science 1945－1985（San Diego, CA：Academic Press, 1989）.

註3：林富松，"評介'科學的貧乏'"，書評書目60期（1978年4月），頁126。

註4：<http://www.lei.dlo.nl/projects/MOOK/Knowledgebase/Artikelen/paradigm/Bush.html>.

註5：同註2。

註6：<http://www.nsf.gov/nsb/awards/bush/start.htm>.

註7：Emily J. Ncmurry, Jane Kelly Kosek, Roger M. Valade ed. Notable Twentieth Century Scientists, v. 1.（Detroit：Gale Research, 1995），285.

註8：G. Pascal Zachary. Endless Frontier: Vannevar Bush Engineer of the American Century.（New Yorrk：The Free Press, 1997），41.

註9：龐君豪主編，Our Times：20世紀史，（臺北市：貓頭鷹，1998年），頁222。

註10：同註7，頁287.

註11：同註8，頁149.

註12：同註8，頁183.

註13：Vannevar Bush. "As We May Think, " Atlantic Monthly 176：1（1945）：641－649.

註14：同註2，頁315—316。

註15：Vannevar Bush. Endless Horizons（Washington, D. C., 1933）.

註16：Vannevar Bush. Modern Arms and Free Men: A Disscussion of the Role of Science in Preserving Democracy.（London：Scientific Book Club, 1949）

註17：同註13。

註18：同註15，頁1—15。

註19：同註8，頁391—407。

註20：同註13。

註21：同註15，頁1—15。

註22：Vannevar Bush. "Memorandum Regarding MEMEX." in James M. Nyce and Paul Kahn ed. From MEMEX to Hypertext: Vannevar Bush and the Mind's Machine.（San Diego：

Academic Press, 1991), 81-84.

註23: Vannevar Bush. Science: the Endless Frontier: A Report to the President on a Program for Postwar Scientific Research. (Washington, D. C. : National Science Foundation, 1945), 220

註24: Vannevar Bush. Endless Horizons. (New York: Arno Press, 1946), 182

註25: Vannevar Bush. Modern Arms and Free Men: A Disscussion of the Role of Science in Preserving Democracy. (London: Scientific Book Club, 1949).

註26: Vannevar Bush, Science Pause. MIT Archives, MC78, Box 22, 1964.

註27: James M. Nyce and Paul Kahn, A Machine for the Mind: Vannevar Bush's MEMEX. (Boston: Academic Press, 1992).

註28: Colin Burke, "A Practical View of MEMEX: The Career of the Rapid Selector." in James M. Nyce and Paul Kahn eds. From MEMEX to Hypertext: Vannevar Bush and the Mind's Machine (San Diego: Academic Press, 1991), pp. 145-164.

註29: Bush, V. "Mechanization and the Record" [Vannevar Bush Papers Library of Congress], Box 138.

註30: Vannevar Bush. MEMEX II. MIT Archives, MC78, Box 22, 1959.

註31: Douglas C. Engelbart. "Letter to Vannevar Bush and Program on Human Effectiveness." In James M. Nyce and Paul Kahn ed. From MEMEX to Hypertext: Vannevar Bush and the Mind's Machine. (San Diego: Academic Press, 1991), 235-244.

註32: Vannevar Bush, "MEMEX Revisited." in Science Is Not Enough. (New York, 1967), 75-101.

註33: Vannevar Bush, "From of Inventions and Inventors" in Pieces of the Action. (New York, 1970): 181-195.

註34: Theodor H. Nelson, "As We Will Think" in James M. Nyce and Paul Kahn ed. From MEMEX to Hypertext: Vannevar Bush and the Mind's Machine. (San Diego: Academic Press, 1991), 245-260.

註35: Linda C. Smith, "MEMEX as an Image of Potentiality in Information Retrieval Research and Development" in R. N. Oddy et al. ed. Information Retrieval Research (London: Butteworth, 1981), 345-369.

註36: Linda C. Smith, "MEMEX As An Image of Potentiality Revisited." in James M. Nyce and Paul Kahn ed. From MEMEX to Hypertext: Vannevar Bush and the Mind's Machine. (San Diego: Academic Press, 1991), 261-286.

註37: 李德竹, 以書目記量學方法探討資訊科學之父 Vannevar Bush 對資訊時代的重要影響和貢獻, "行政院國家科學委員會" 專題研究計劃成果報告 (臺北: 臺大圖書資訊學系, 1999 年) NSC 88-2413-14-H-002-029

註38: Larry Owens, "Vannevar Bush and the Differential Analyzer: The Text and Context of and Early Computer." Technology and Culture 25: 1 (January, 1986): 63-95.

註39: Tim Oren, "MEMEX: Getting Back on the Trail," In James M. Nyce and Paul Kahn ed. From MEMEX to Hypertext: Vannevar Bush and the Mind's Machine. (San Diego:

Academic Press, 1991), 261–286.

註40: Noman Meyrowitz, "Hypertext: Does it Reduce Cholesterol, Too?" In James M. Nyce and Paul Kahn ed. From MEMEX to Hypertext: Vannevar Bush and the Mind's Machine. (San Diego: Academic Press, 1991), 287–318.

註41: Brett Butler, "The Electronic library Program: Developing networked Electronic Library Collections," Library Hi-Tech 9: 2 (1991): 21–30.

註42: Gregory, Crane, "Aristotle's Library: MEMEX as Vision and Hypertext As Reality," In James M. Nyce and Paul Kahn eds. From MEMEX to Hypertext: Vannevar Bush and the Mind's Machine. (San Diego: Academic Press, 1991), 339–352.

註43: Randall H. Trigg, "From Trail blazing to Guided Tours: The Legacy of Vannevar Bush's Vision of Hypertext Use," In James M. Nyce and Paul Kahn eds. From MEMEX to Hypertext: Vannevar Bush and the Mind's Machine. (San Diego: Academic Press, 1991), 353–367.

註44: Paul Kahn and James M. Nyce, "The Idea of Machine: the Later MEMEX Essays." in James M. Nyce and Paul Kahn eds. From MEMEX to Hypertext: Vannevar Bush and the Mind's Machine. (San Diego: Academic Press, 1991), 113–144.

註45: Memex and Beyond, <http://www.cs.brown.edu/memex/> (9 Jan. 1998).

註46: 王志仁,《活氧計劃》,數位時代創刊1號(1999年1月),頁232—236.

註47: H. Bornman and S. H. Vonsolms, "Hypermedia, Multimedia and Hypertext: Definitions and Overview." Electronic Library 11: 4–5 (August/October 1993): 259–268.

註48: R. P. C. Rodgers, "Automated Retrieval from Multiple Disparate Information Sources: the World Wide Web and the NLMs Sourcer Project." Journal of the American Society for Information Science 46: 1 (1995): 755–764.

註49: H. Schmondt, "Hyperfiction, the Romanticism of the Information Revolution." Southern Humanities Review 29: 4 (Fall 1995): 309–321.

註50: H. Baptist, H. Primas and H. Schadler, etc. " The Hypercatalog Graz: Budapest (HyperKGB)." Proceedings of the ASIS Annual Meeting 34 (1997): 196–201.

註51: N. J. Davis. R. S. Stewart and R. Weeks. "Knowledge sharing Agents over the World Wide Web." BT Technology Journal 16: 3 (1998): 104–109.

註52: Saracevic Tefko, "Information Science." Journal of the American Society for Information Science. 50th Anniversary 50: 12 (October, 1999): 1051–1063.

臺灣圖書館相關"國家標準"*

[摘要 Abstract]

　　本文主要目的是蒐集、整理及分析"經濟部中央標準局"1969 年至 1998 年間公佈之五十六項圖書館相關"國家標準"。同時並對標準的意義、種類及其重要性、海內外重要標準組織，以及中國臺灣相關標準制定程序作簡要介紹。

　　The purpose of this paper is to collect, organize and analyze fifty-six library-related "Chinese National Standards" (CNS) between 1969 – 1998 period. And also including a brief introduction of the meaning, types and importance of standards, major international and national standards organization, and "Chinese National Standards" developing procedures.

關鍵詞　keyword
圖書館相關"國家標準"　"國家標準"
Library-related national standards; "National standards"; "Chinese National Standards"; "CNS"

壹、前言

　　標準可以說與人類同在，如影隨形而不可分割。臺灣早在兩千年前即有標準和標準化的觀念，如《左傳》中之"車同軌，書同文"。標準種類很多，語言可能是所有標準中最古老的一種，早期的口述，經符號之演進至書寫文字，而成為今日人類燦爛的文化記載。但標準並不局限於語言和文字，尤其工業革命和現代之資訊革命皆與"標準"關係密不可分，貢獻很大。標準廣泛涉及人類所有活動與事物，其對人類文明之進步，意義及影響至鉅。[1]1841 年 Joseph Whit worth 曾提出螺紋（Screw-Threads）標準化之觀念，但未受重視而造成損失。[2]Eli Whitney 於 1978 年亦提出建議槍彈、口徑及螺絲標準化，俾便零件交換。[3]

貳、標準的意義及其重要性

一、標準的意義

　　根據《Webster Dictionary》，"標準（Standards）是經由權威所建立有關物理量、重量（力）、空間範圍（長度、面積、體積等）、價位及品質等之量度準則"。標準為一準則，是一種已訂的規範，其乃科學、技術、各項活動與經驗之結合，並經由各有關機構之合作與同意而制定。根據 1984 年"中央標準局"所下的定義，凡對產品的品質、尺寸、成分、厚度或式樣，或其製造過程、方式等訂定一連串準則，就是標準。根據"中

---

*　本文曾發表在《圖書與資訊學》28 期（1999 年 2 月），第 1—21 頁。

國國家標準"（"Chinese National Standard"，簡稱"CNS"）對"標準"的定義是："經由共識與某一公認的機構核准，提供一般或重複使用，以提供各項活動或其結果有關的規則、指導綱要或所建立之文件，期使在某種情況下秩序的最佳程度。"④

美國 John Gallard 根據多年從事標準化工作之經驗，於 1934 年提出標準的定義："標準爲一種有系統而明確的陳述，係以口頭方式、書面方式，或用其他圖示方式，或利用模型、樣本，或其他實物方法爲表徵，在某期間內，對某種單位（即計量的基礎）、物體、作用、製程、方法、實務、能量或機量、功能、義務、權利、責任、行爲、觀念或計劃，加以定義、命名或規範者。"此定義之內涵最爲廣泛。⑤

標準化（Standardization）依 ISO/STACO – 1961 之定義，標準化係"爲所有關係人員的方便和利益目的，針對某特定活動而制定有規律和正確的規則過程"。標準化對企業經營或日常生活，尤其是在確保均勻的品質與提高生產力、降低成本方面有很大效用，即使在日常生活中，標準化亦影響很大。⑥

二、標準的重要性

對工商業而言，適當的標準制定，以利產業之自動化、合理化作業，而達到生產力與產品品質的提昇，產業昇級、環境及勞力改善及邁向國際化等目標，故標準之重要性是：⑦

（一）標準爲工業水準之表現；
（二）標準爲發展自動化之基礎；
（三）標準爲強化產業體系之方法；
（四）標準可加速產業昇級；
（五）標準可激發廠商提高商品品質；
（六）標準有助於拓展國際貿易；
（七）標準有助於經濟發展；
（八）標準有助於環境保護；
（九）標準有助於公共安全；
（十）標準有助於消費者保護。

對圖書資訊業而言，在強調資訊服務社會，除硬體設備的發展類有規格標準外，軟體服務亦不容忽視，而圖書館正式提供資訊的主要機構之一。在歐美先進國家早已發展出諸多圖書館相關業務標準，而臺灣則進展緩慢。在臺灣即將邁入已開發地區之林，臺灣各圖書館爲提昇其資訊的品質與效率，正積極進行各項館際合作及自動化作業；然而圖書館各項作業應儘速建立標準，並採取現代化、科學化的管理模式，以使各圖書館間及與海外圖書館之間，得以交換資訊，達到資源共享及服務品質提昇之境。故標準對圖書資訊事業之重要性，可由下列幾點說明：

（一）加強圖書館資訊組織及服務工作之科學管理；
（二）建立並健全統一的資訊報導、檢索體系，開拓臺灣和國際間圖書資訊交流和資源利用；
（三）增進臺灣和國際間之合作服務關係；
（四）提昇圖書館服務品質與效率；

（五）奠定圖書館事業現代化、專業化的基礎。

叁、標準的種類及其階層體系

一、標準的種類

"標準"一詞因引用廣泛，界定其內涵常是模糊不清，產生困惑。又，標準的採用，可以是強制性的（Mandatory）或志願性的（Voluntary）。因此，標準的種類多而較難分析。如依形式尚可略分為：

（一）服務的"指引"（Guidelines）或模式（Models）：圖書館服務標準即屬此類，如參考服務項目、程度、各類型圖書館營運標準等。

（二）活動的"規則"（Rules）：此類標準之應用，重視其一致性，實際採用仍會產生差異，如圖書館的編目規則。

（三）"規格"（Specifications）或"技術"標準（Technical Standards）：此為嚴格遵循之標準，如：字元集（Character Sets）、格式架構（Format Structure）等。

工業標準（Industry Standards）多數可依其範疇分為：技術、產品、採購、生產、設備、安全和管理等類標準。

根據 Grogen[8]，Houghton[9]和 Spivak 及 Winsell[10]四位專家之文獻，標準可綜合分類為下列七種：

（一）尺度標準（Dimensional Standards）：即劃一的尺度或公差，與設計相關。

（二）材料標準（Material Standards）：設定各項材料採購之標準。

（三）品質標準（Performance or Quality Standards）：即確保產品之工作性能與品質標準。

（四）試驗標準（Standards Test Methods）：決定材料和產品是否符合指定的品質標準所作之操作。

（五）生產標準（Codes of Practice）：用於最佳的、正確的、製造過程、方法、裝置、維護和操作。

（六）術語標準（Terminology Standards）：決定專門名詞、符號、釋名等的意義與內涵之一致性，即採用標準的術語。

（七）物理及科學標準（Physical and Scientific Standards）：決定物理質量，為工商業之基本測量，如長度、時間、體積、溫度等。

臺灣制定之"國家標準"大致上亦分為三類：

（一）產品標準：規定產品之形狀、尺度、品質、機能、性能等。

（二）方法標準：規定作業方法，以及試驗、分析、檢查與測定之方法。

（三）基本標準：名詞、符號、單位及數列等標準。

二、標準體系階層架構

標準化系統存在五種階層。公司內部有公司的標準，團體或協會有團體/協會標準，國家有國家標準，地區亦有區域標準，國際間亦有共認的國家標準。從標準化而言，其目的相同，但隨著階層由公司（企業）擴展至團體/協會、國家、區域至國際，由於階層不同、立場不同、看法不同,其利害關係亦因不同而趨複雜化。五種標準階層間之關係是由上而下亦是由下而上,標準系統架構見圖一:

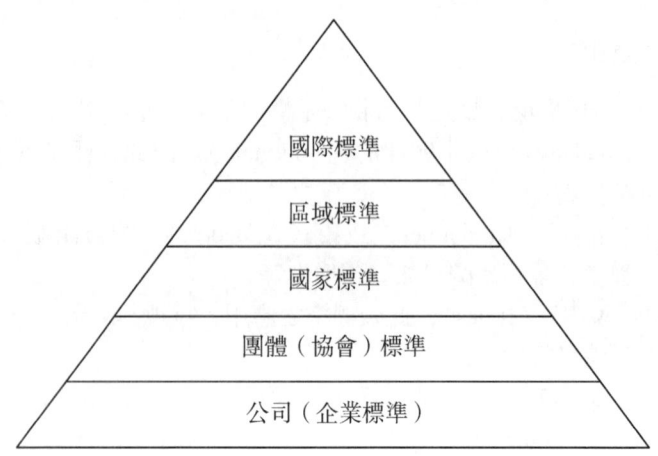

圖一:標準體系階層架構

標準體系架構中,臺灣較弱的是團體/協會與公司/企業標準,急待政府推動、加強與輔導。各階層之標準說明如下:[11]

(一) 公司/企業標準(Company Standards)

公司標準定位於標準階層系統中的底層。公司和企業界已很瞭解標準化的利益及重要性,重視標準工作,而訂定各種標準規範。故公司標準的定義為:"於公司或工廠,就材料、零件、製品、組織及採購、製造、檢查與管理等工作以作適當使用為目的所訂的標準"。

(二) 團體標準(Association Standards)

團體標準即是由各產業團體、學會、協會等所訂適合此一產業所使用之標準是之。

(三) 國家標準(National Standards)

各國皆有全國性標準。國家標準是以全國性的規模、意見而制定,並執行的標準。ISO 的定義是:"國家標準機構所採用的標準"。

(四) 區域標準(Regional Standards)

根據 ISO 的定義是:"限於特定國家之關連團體會員資格的標準化團體,亦即地區標準化團體所選用的標準"。區域標準是由數個國家或地區標準機構所制定。

(五) 國際標準(International Standards)

由國際制定而適用於國際上的標準,亦即國際標準化團體所選用的標準即是國際標準。

肆、海內外重要標準組織

全球各國皆有標準,而標準之制訂則有不同層級的組織機構負責。以下擬由國際間及臺灣重要標準組織,分別介紹如下:

一、國際標準組織（International Organizations for Standardization，簡稱 ISO）

國際標準組織是一個特殊而非政府的國際標準機構，於 1946 年成立，是爲輔助國際間物質與服務的交流及對全世界的知識、科學、技術與經濟活動的領域提供並發展所需的標準的相關活動，以增進國際間的協調爲目的。現約有 110 個國家，以正規會員國或通信會員國入會。上述兩種會員均須以政府機關名義加入，每一國家限一名，因大陸爲 ISO 會員，故臺灣無法成爲 ISO 會員。目前 ISO 所公佈之國際標準不含電機和電子（由 IEC 負責）、電報和電訊（由 CCITT 負責）和資訊技術（ISO/IEC JTCI 負責）。所有國際標準草案必須獲得會員國 75% 的投票同意通過而成爲正式國際標準，其制訂過程甚爲嚴謹。所有 ISO 標準雖爲志願性的（Voluntary），但深受各國重視及尊敬而被採用，甚至於變爲強制性質的國家標準，如臺灣"國家標準"多依據 ISO 標準而訂定之。[12][13]

二、美國國家標準機構（American National Standards Institute，簡稱 ANSI）

美國國家標準機構成立於 1918 年，爲美國標準全國性交換中心，並代表美國參與國際標準組織（ISO），是一個私人、非營利性的會員組織，爲官方及衆多民間組織所支持。ANSI 的主要目標在借由促進標準共識、整合及遵照一致的評估程序系統，以加強美國商業的全球競爭力，並提昇人民的生活品質。ANSI 並不制訂美國國家標準（American National Standards），而是由其合格的會員團體制訂之。ANSI 現代表約 1400 個美國機構團體和政府單位，總部設於紐約市。根據 1966 年之統計，美國國家標準量已達 13,056 項，其中多數已被 ISO 採用而成爲國際標準。目前 ANSI 是 ISO Council 中五位永久委員之一，ISO Technical Management Board 四位永久委員之一，同時也是 IEC 行動管理委員會 12 位委員之一，此可代表 ANSI 對世界標準之推動影響甚大。[14]

三、美國國家資訊標準組織（National Information Standards Organization，簡稱 NISO）

美國國家資訊標準組織（NISO）成立於 1984 年，目的在發展及推動有關資訊服務之相關技術標準。是美國國家標準組織（American in National Standards Institute，簡稱 ANSI）認可之標準制定組織，亦是 ANSI 會員之一。NISO 是一個非營利組織，有資訊專業使用者包括圖書館、出版業、政府機關和其他以資訊爲基礎商業界爲其支持者，NISO 標準名稱前皆冠予 ANSI、Z39…，是因其前身爲 American National Standard Committee Z39（ANSC Z39），故 NISO 是國際間資訊標準之領導者，NISO 代表美國參加 ISO/TC46 會議之討論，確定工作。多項 NISO 標準皆爲 ISO 和其他國家標準組織所採用。[15]

四、"經濟部中央標準局"（"Bureau Chinese National Standards, Ministry of Economics"，簡稱"CNS"）

1949 年，政府頒佈"標準法"，1947 年"經濟部中央標準局"組織條例公佈，度量衡局及工業標準委員會合併成立"中央標準局"，1950 年"經濟部"授權"中央標準局"兼爲專利業務，1964年增設計量檢定實驗室。1979年"中央標準局"組織條例修正公佈，其業務含標準，度政、專利和商標四項，均爲加強經濟建設之環節，亦爲促進現代化、國際化的將來，與社會大衆福祉之保障與增進息息相關。

"國家標準"的制定需經過"國家標準技術委員會"審查"國家標準"草案，再經"國家標準審查委員會"審定"國家標準"稿，審定通過後賦予 CNS 總號及類號，請經濟部核定公佈，並將新訂標準名稱透過全國性標準化刊物公告。[16][17]

根據1998年10月21日"經濟部"標準檢驗局組織法通過后，將"中央標準局"之標準和度政業務合併於標準檢驗局，而原"中央標準局"之專利、商標業務將另與著作權委員會和仿冒小組合併而成立一新單位——智慧財產局。"中央標準局"之標準和度政等業務將於1999年1月26日正式移入"經濟部"標準檢驗局。[18]

五、"中國圖書館學會"標準委員會

1991年"中國圖書館學會"第三十八屆理監事聯合會議正式通過成立圖書館標準委員會。聘請臺灣大學圖書館學系李德竹教授擔任該委員會主任委員。同年七月該委員會召開第一次會議，並擬定圖書館標準委員會任務及工作目標：[19]

（一）任務
1. 蒐集、整理圖書館標準；
2. 引進海外圖書館相關標準；
3. 研議圖書館急需之標準；
4. 建議有關單位擬訂及修訂圖書館有關之標準。

（二）工作目標：

同年八月開始接受"經濟部中央標準局"委託進行圖書館相關"國家標準"起草工作。

1. 近程目標
（1）蒐集整理臺灣圖書館標準及相關資料。
（2）聯同本學會法規委員會召開會議，研議圖書館標準及法令事宜，編輯出版《圖書館法令及標準》。
（3）研擬圖書館標準研究之專案計劃。

2. 中程目標
（1）根據實際需求，將現有之有關標準加以分類並排定優先順序，分組研議，以進行修訂。
（2）引進海外圖書館相關標準，選擇適合者，以研議修訂，由學會建議"經濟部中央標準局"修訂採用，成爲"國家標準"。

伍、臺灣"國家標準"制訂程序[20]

"國家標準"編修不僅是制定而已，尚有修訂、廢止與確認等，其程序依"'國家標準'制定辦法"。該辦法於1946年首次公佈實施以來，至今以修正八次，最近一次修正爲1998年。現行"國家標準"制定程序有六項步驟：建議、起草、徵詢、審查、審定、核定公佈等。具體的制定程序流程說明如下：

（一）建議：由"中央標準局"或民間單位、機關團體等提出標準制定建議書。
（二）審查建議書：由審查委員會審核，決定可制定之標準後，委託相關單位進行起草。
（三）起草：由標準局專業人員或委託相關單位編擬。
（四）徵求意見：由標準局將標準草案分送有關委員、專家、機關、團體、廠商等以徵詢意見。
（五）審定：經"國家標準技術委員會"審查通過後，由"國家標準審查委員會"審定之。
（六）核定公佈：標準草案經審定後，由標準局報請"經濟部"核定公佈。

（一）"國家標準"制定（修訂或廢止）建議之程序

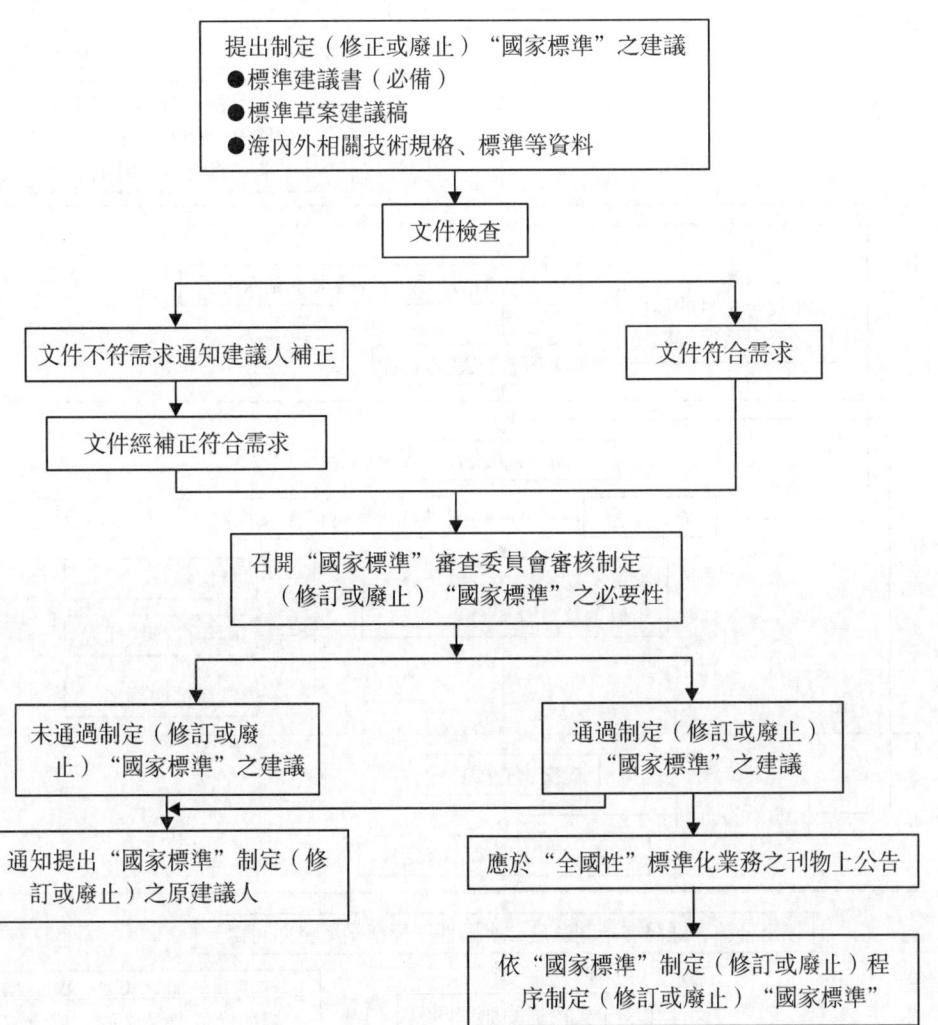

(二)"國家標準"制定程序

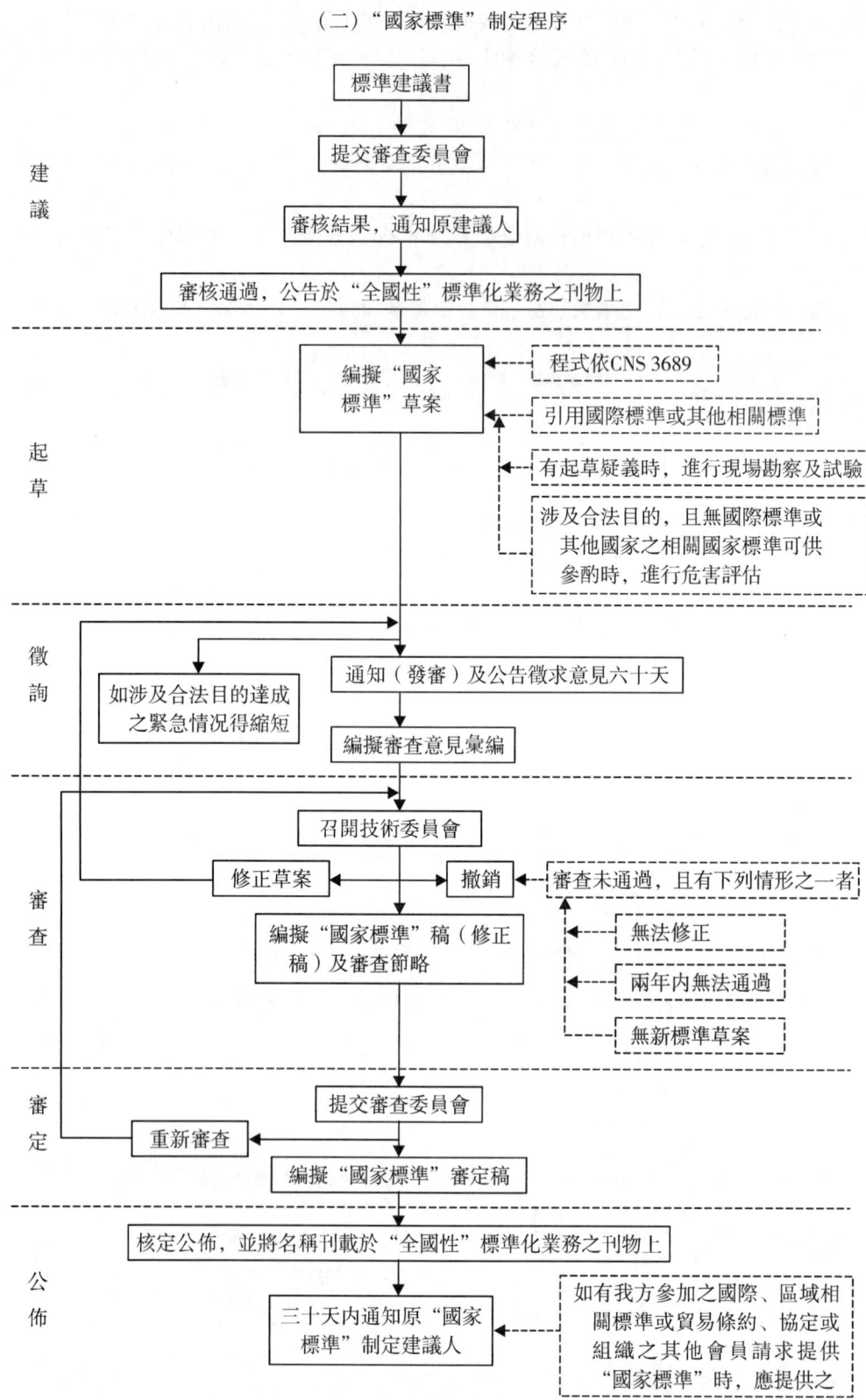

（三）"國家標準"確認程序

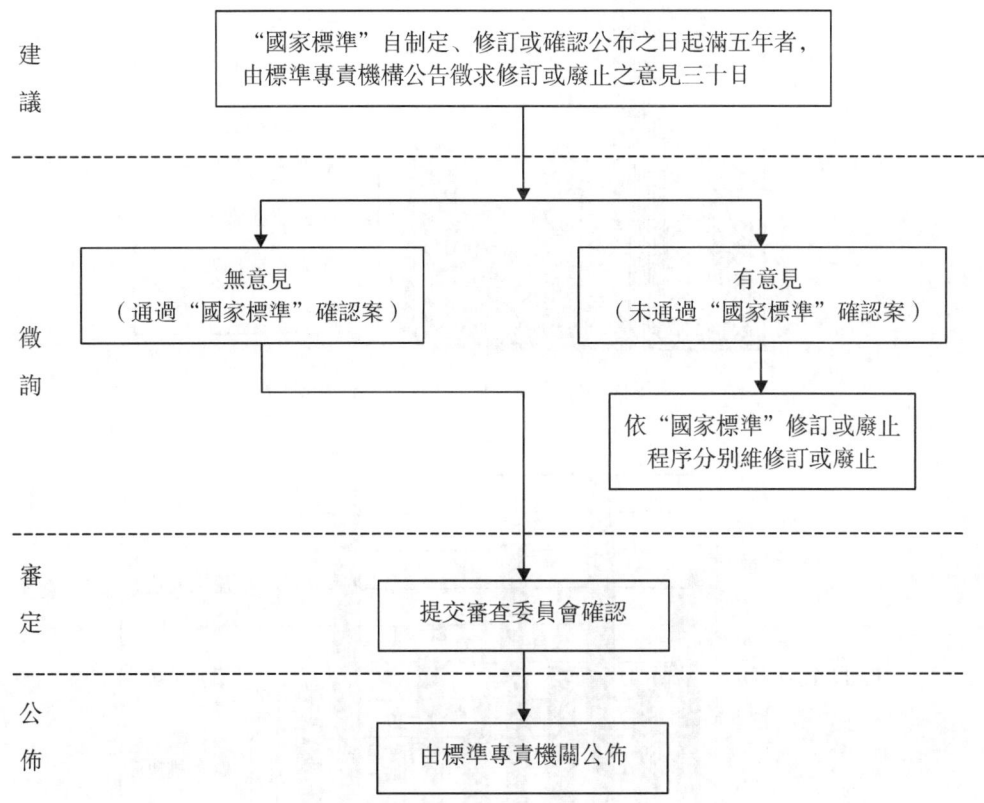

陸、臺灣圖書館相關"國家標準"

　　圖書館委員會自1991年成立以來至1997年5月間，先後共接受"經濟部中央標準局"六次委託標準起草計劃，完成40項圖書館相關"國家標準"起草工作，其中37項已公佈爲"國家標準"，三項標準草案正在審查中。由1994年至今，已舉辦五期北中南三地圖書館相關"國家標準"說明會。（詳見圖二、三、四）[21]

　　茲將圖書館相關"國家標準"項數、摘要內容、類別分別介紹並統計分析如下：

一、圖書館相關國家標準摘要（1969年—1998年）

　　（註：★代表非"中國圖書館學會"研訂之標準）

　　★1. CNS 88 "中國國家標準"之分類 Classification of "Chinese National Standards".（80.10.18.）

　　本標準規定"中國國家標準"（"Chinese National Standards"，簡稱"CNS"）之分類。

　　標準之類別、英文名稱及代用符號如下：

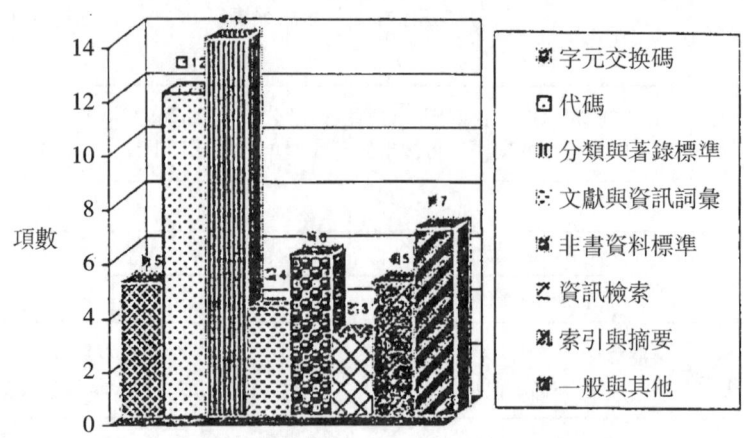

圖二：臺灣圖書館相關"國家標準"各類分佈圖

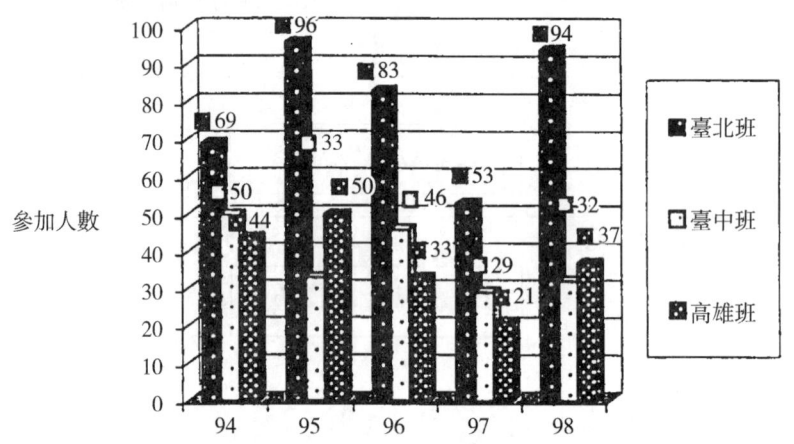

圖三：圖書館相關"國家標準"說明會北中南三區參加人數（1994－1998 會計年度）

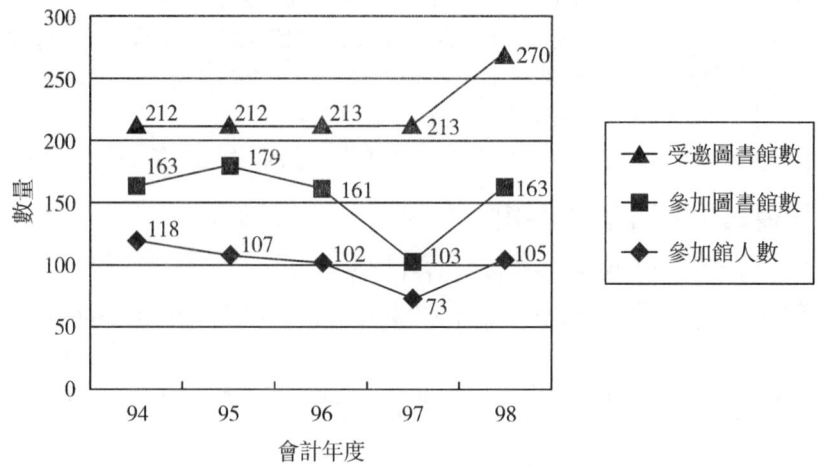

圖四：圖書館相關"國家標準"說明會歷年參加館數與人數（1994－1998 會計年度）

標準類別（英文名稱）（＊爲已改之類別名稱及新增類）	代用符號
土木工程及建築（Civil Engineering and Architecture）	A
機械工程（Mechanical Engineering）	B
電機工程（Electrical Engineering）	C
電子工程（Electronic Engineering）	C
機動車及航空器工程（Automotive and Aircraft Engineering）	D
＊（類名已改爲：機械車與航太工程）	
鐵道工程（Railway Engineering）	E
＊（類名已改爲：軌道工程）	
造船工程（Shipbuilding）	F
鐵金屬冶煉（Ferrous Materials and Metallurgy），	G
非鐵金屬冶煉（Non-Ferrous and Metallurgy）	H
核子工程（Nuclear Engineering）	J
化學工程（Chemical Industry）	K
紡織工業（Textile Industry）	L
礦業（Mining）	M
農業（Agriculture）	N
食品（Foods）	N
木業（Wood Industry）	O
紙業（Pulp and Paper Industry）	P
＊新增類：環境保護（Environmental Protection）	＊Q
陶業（Ceramic Industry）	R
日常用品（Domestic Wares）	S
衛生及醫療器材（Sanitation，and Medical Equipment）	T
資訊及通信（Information and Communication）	X
工業安全（Industrial Safety）	Z
品質管制（Quality Control）	Z
包裝（Packing and Packaging）	Z
（＊類名已改爲：物流及包裝）	
普通及雜業（General and Miscellaneous）	Z
（＊類名已改爲：一般及其他）	

★2. CNS89"中國國家標準"之編號 Codes of "Chinese National Standards"．(62.11.27.)

　　本標準規定"中國國家標準"（"Chinese National Standards"，簡稱"CNS"）之編號。標準之編號分別爲總號及類號，並加印萬國十進分類編號。（註：係"國家標準"目錄索引或目錄依萬國十進分類編訂後，類號即行停止使用。）

　　★3. CNS 3029 文獻報告（暫行標準）Literature Reports（Tentative）．(58.6.4.)

　　本標準適用於文獻報告，不限於一定之形式、內容及範圍，其方式可分爲標題、內容，討論等之類。本標準爲暫行標準。

★4. CNS 3030 工程及科學之論文發表格式（暫行標準）Format for Publications of Engineering and Scientific Reports. (58.7.26.)

本標準規定工程及科學之論文發表格式，使著者對論文及印刷品之寫作，具有標準之格式。在發表之過程中，由準備開始寫作至印刷資料，除具一定格式外，就編輯至印刷場所之程序，有相當之安排，以使該項論文能讓讀者充分利用。本標準規定之論文發表格式包括：（1）論文內容格式；（2）印刷資料格式；（3）著者與編輯人之聯繫等內容。

★5. CNS 3031 科學期刊（篇幅）（暫行標準）Format for Scientific Periodicals (Tentative). (58.6.4.)

本標準規定科學期刊雜誌之篇幅標準。規定之內容涵蓋：期刊名稱、出版之陳述、各期目錄、論文內容之概述、每欄之標題、頁數、表格、圖片及插頁、出版情形、卷（期）數編號、合訂本之封面、目錄及合訂本之登記、補充版以及特別印刷（續刊、附件等）等。

★6. CNS 3689 "中國國家標準"之程式 Rules for the Drafting and Presentation of "Chinese National Standards". (82.4.21.)

本標準規定"中國國家標準"（"Chinese National Standards"，簡稱"CNS"）之構成、表現形式及體裁。

7. CNS 3927 校對符號 Proof Corrections. (85.9.26.)

本標準規定之符號及用法適用於海內中外文資料出版工作，在進行各類校稿之核對時，所需使用之改正符號。

★8. CNS 5205 資訊技術—資訊交換用七位元碼元集 Information Technology-7-bit Coded Character Set for Information Interchange. (85.12.30.)

本標準適用於標準處理系統及數據通信系統之資訊交換。本標準規定包含 128 個字元之字元集（控制字元及圖形字元，如字母、數字、符號）及其編碼表示，亦規定一個七位元碼字元集及一些選項。並運用這些選項制定不同應用的指引，運用這些選項規定一個國際參考版本（IRV）。

★9. CNS 7654 資訊技術—字元碼（結構及延伸技術）Information Technology-Character Code Structure and Extension Techniques. (86.11.29.)

本標準規定用於字元集之八位元碼與七位元碼之結構及其延伸技術。本標準以八位元碼及七位元碼通用的碼元件來規定碼結構。編碼使用多種技術以延伸基本的八位元及七位元碼之能力。八位元碼及七位元碼結構中使用通用的元件，使任何特定符合八位元的碼可以用簡單又直接的方式，轉換成相當的七位元碼，反之亦同。

CNS 7656［資訊處理—資訊交換用八位元碼—實施結構及規則］符合本標準規定的八位元碼結構，且 CNS 5205［資訊處理—資訊交換用七位元碼字元集］符合本標準規定的七位元碼結構。

★10. CNS 10987 國際單位制（SI）The International System of Units（SI）. (73.8.15.)

國際單位制標準全名 International System of Units，簡稱 SI，適用於國際單位及其相關單位。國際單位制共有三類：1. 基本單位，2. 輔助單位，和 3. 導出單位。基本單位有七種，其單位名稱爲：公尺、公斤、秒、安培、克耳文、莫耳和坎德拉；輔助單位有弳和元弳；導出單位是以基本單位或輔助單位表示，其符號可由基本單位或輔助單位之符號以乘式或除式表示之，如速度單位爲公尺除以秒（m/s）等。

★11. CNS 11643 中文標準交換碼 Chinese Standard Interchange Code.（81. 5. 21.）

本標準，中文標準交換碼（Chinese Standard Interchange Code，簡稱 CSIC）適用於中文資訊之處理。本標準規定中文標準交換碼之編碼原則、字集編排原則及字碼表之使用方法與內容等，以求其依普遍推廣及實用性。本碼以"教育部"公佈的四個字體表之字極爲範圍，並涵蓋常用之外語字母及工商界與學校所使用之文字與符號，同時符合國際資訊傳輸上所用之 CNS 2505［資訊處理及交換用之數元碼字集（組）］及 CNS 7654［資訊處理—七位元及八位元碼字元集—延碼技術］標準通信定則。

★12. CNS 11643—1 中文標準交換碼使用方法 The Usage of Chinese Standard Interchange Code.（84. 1. 4.）

本標準規定 CNS 11643 中文標準交換碼之使用方法，並介紹 CNS 5205［資訊處理及交換用七位元碼字集（組）］、CNS 7654（資訊處理—七位元及八位元集—延碼技術］等相開標準以爲參考。

★13. CNS 12842 國家名稱代碼表示法 Codes for the Representations of Names of Countries.（80. 3. 1. 15.）

本標準規定表示國家、屬地或某特殊區域等實體（Entity）名稱的代碼，以達到國際交流的目的。但並不考慮有關國家合法地位、領土範圍、其主權所有或是國境的界限等因素。本標準提供二英文字母碼（英字—2 國家碼），特殊用途之英文字母碼（英字—3 國加碼）及由聯合國統計局所建立的三位數字碼。

★14. CNS 12864 國際標準書號 Documentation – International Standard Book Numbering（ISBN）．（80. 4. 23.）

本標準適用於境內出版者所出版或代理進口之出版品。國際標準書號係因應圖書出版、管理需要，並便於國際間出版品之交流與統計所發展之國際統一編號制度。由一組冠有"ISBN"代號之十位數碼組成，分爲羣體組別號、出版者識別號、書名識別號及檢查號四段，以識別出版品所屬國別地區（語言）、出版機構、書名、版本及裝訂方式。

15. CNS 13148 中國書目資訊交換格式——磁帶部份 Format for Chinese Bibliographic Information Interchange-Magnetic Tape.（82. 1. 28.）

本標準所稱之書目資訊交換格式，適用於圖書館及資料單位於整理館藏文獻時所產生的各種類型記錄，如書目記錄、權威記錄等。它不定義每一項記錄的長度或內容，亦不定義欄號、指標等特定意義，該部份由其他機讀編目格式詳細規範之。本標準係敘述圖書館自動化系統間資料交換之一般性結構和基本架構，而非專爲系統內部之處理格式。雖然本標準是爲磁帶而設計，但其結構亦可作爲其他記錄資料媒體之參考。

16. CNS 13149 西文資料審查文獻、訂定主題及選擇索引詞彙之方法 Documentation of Western Language – Method for Examining Documents, Determining Their Subjects, and Selecting Indexing Terms.（82. 1. 28.）

本標準旨在建議審查文獻、訂定主題及選擇適當索引詞彙的流程，無論採用前組合索引法或後組合索引法，均僅限於索引編製的預備階段，與任何一種特定的索引系統無關。它同時也敘述一般性文獻分析技巧,該技巧特別適用於控制語言的索引系統。本標準之目的在於提供文獻分析作業共同遵循之標準及便於書目資料之交換。此外亦做爲索引者在文獻分析及觀念確認階段的指引。對於讀者諮詢的分析及爲了檢索目的將讀者需求轉譯爲索引詞彙,並作爲摘要編寫依據等工作也可能有所助益。以人工分析文獻主題,並以索引詞彙表達主題的任何機構均可採用本標準中所敘述的技巧;然而採用自動化索引技術的機構則不適合採用本標準。

17. CNS 13150 館際互借書目資料項目標準 Bibliography Data Element Directory – Interloan Applications.（82. 1. 28.）

本標準旨在制訂一圖書館及資料單位在執行館際互借業務時所採行之書目項目的標準名稱;經由對書目項目加以界定說明並統一規定,使記載之項目能在館際互借作業流程中取得一致之標準,確實可提昇館際互借業務之效率。

18. CNS 13151 圖書館統計 Library Statistics.（82. 1. 28.）

本標準旨在定義圖書館統計的項目名稱,並闡釋其內容及範圍,以作爲圖書館記錄與報告圖書館統計數據之標準。其制定原則以符合臺灣實際情況,並與國際標準組織（ISO）公佈之 ISO 2789（1991）Information and Documentation—International, Library Statistics 相符,除使臺灣圖書館之統計數據易於合計與比較之外,亦能與其他國家之圖書館統計數據相互比較。

19. CNS 13152 摘要撰寫標準 Abstracts Writing.（82. 1. 28.）

本標準係編寫摘要時的指引,以規範原著者編寫摘要爲主,但亦適用於索引與摘要機構所製作之摘要。

20. CNS 13153 國際標準期刊號標準 International Standard Serial Number.（ISSN）（82. 1. 28.）

本標準旨在定義連續性出版品特定識別號——國際標準期刊號（ISSN）的結構及使用,並指定該標準號碼之管理機構。

★21. CNS 13162 制定標準建議書格式 Form of Proposals for the Establishment of Standards.（82. 2. 20.）

本標準規定標準制定建議書之格式,供各界人士或有關團體,向制定機關提出釐訂新標準建議時撰寫,以協助政府有關機關正確評估該建議,使其合理適切的運用資源人力,以遂行臺灣標準化政策爲目的。標準建議書內容包括:標題、範圍、目的及理由、工作計劃、相關文件資料以及可提供協助之單位與聯絡方法等基本項目,建議者可依實際情況,增加所需之項目。

★22. CNS 13188 語言名稱代碼表示法 Codes for the Representation or Names of Languages（82. 4. 21.）

本標準提供語言名稱代碼表示法,符號之設計主要是作爲使用在術語、字典編纂和語言學,但亦可用在任何需要以代碼形式表示的語言,在某些應用方面,它亦包含語言使用指南。

★23. CNS 13205 資訊交換—機構識別之結構 Data Interchange – Structure the Identification of Organizations.（82. 5. 19.）

本標準之規定資訊交換時機構識別的唯一機構;資料交換時國際指定碼

（International Code Designator，簡稱 ICD）指定機構識別之編碼系統時，其管理的必要規定。本標準認可一些存在的機構識別方法，並提供系統性的整合方法，將這些方法組合而成一種統一的結構，以供資料交換。本標準中，一個機構是可以使用一種以上的編碼方法以識別之。機構識別之結構與機構識別之管理的使用說明範例亦會於本標準中。

24. CNS 13222 書目排檢原則 Bibliographic Filling Principles.（82. 6. 25.）

本標準旨在規範圖書館與資料單位之館藏目錄，以及各種形式書目之排檢原則，適用於印刷式或線上顯示之書目資料，亦適用於以人工或機器排檢之書目記錄。

25. CNS 13223 索引編製標準 Index of a Publication.（82. 6. 25.）

本標準旨在訂定編製索引時之處理原則，供編輯者或出版者於編製索引時之參考。它適用於各種不同類型出版品的索引編製，亦適用於人工及機器索引法。關於各種不同索引之編製細節及技巧，則不在本標準討論範圍內。

26. CNS 13224 西文單一語文索引典編製標準 Guidelines for the Establishment and Development of Monolingual Thesauri in Western Language.（82. 6. 25.）

本標準旨在定義或說明西文單一語文索引典之編製技巧，例如詞彙選擇與控制、標點符號、索引典維護管理等技巧，以確保單一索引機構或不同索引機構間作業的一致性。本標準亦僅適用於以人工分析文獻並以控制語言表答主題概念的索引編製機構，而不適用於全盤運用自動化索引技巧的機構。

27. CNS 13225 期刊館藏著錄標準 Serial Holdings Statements.（82. 6. 25.）

本標準旨在研訂圖書館及資料單位之期刊館藏記錄的著錄規則與標點符號，藉以達成期刊館藏記錄與顯示方式之一致性與標準化。

28. CNS 13226 機讀編目格式標準 China MARC Format.（82. 6. 25.）

本標準旨在訂定機讀編目格式以利電腦處理各種語文及資料類型之書目記錄，進而達成資訊交換及分享的要求。本格式以各種欄號、指標、分欄識別、代碼等說明磁帶上書目記錄之內容。所適用之資料類型包括：圖書、連續性出版品、放映資料、錄音資料、微縮資料、音樂資料、圖片、地圖、電腦檔、善本書及拓片等。

29. CNS 13227 書目資料著錄總則 General Rules for Bibliographic Description.（82. 6. 25.）

本標準以國際標準書目著錄（ISBD）爲基礎，旨在制定各種類型出版品之書目資料著錄標準，以確保臺灣書目資料著錄之一致性，達成臺灣外書目資料之交換與分享。

30. CNS 13461 資訊檢索服務與協定標準 Information Retrieval Service and Protocol.（83. 12. 1.）

本標準爲開放系統互連（OSI）而制定，描述資訊檢索應用服務，並說明資訊檢索應用協定。本標準主要爲圖書館及資訊科學領域而制訂，說明利用電子通訊連接時，程式對程式之間的溝通方式，而不在闡述以終端機或其他實質媒體做資訊交換的狀況。

31. CNS 13462 共同指令語言 Common Command Language.（83. 12. 1.）

本標準旨在訂定線上交談式資訊檢索系統所使用之指令的辭彙、語法及意義，適用於書目資料、全文資料、數據資料、化學資料等線上交談式資訊檢索系統。本標準不限制或禁止共同指令語言與其他檢索介面並用，如：畫面驅動式、選單式、自然語言，或是自訂的非標準語言等；然而若本標準之共同指令語言與自訂指令或自然語言相矛盾，則須以本標準爲準。此外本標準不規定資訊檢索系統必備或應有的功能與指令。

32. CNS 13463 圖書及其他出版品書背題名標準 Spine Title on Books and Other Publications. (83.12.1.)

本標準旨在訂定書背題名的定義、內容與設計原則，促使出版界在書背題名的印刷方式與內容上取得統一，以利出版品排架時方便圖書館與讀者辨識。本標準適用於一般圖書、叢書、套書、期刊及其他資料類型的出版品。

33. CNS 13490 機關團體簡稱標準 Principles for Corporate Bodies Abbreviations. (84.1.26.)

本標準旨在訂定中文書目資料著錄時的機關團體簡稱原則，提供中文書目資料著錄及交換之用。適用於書目記錄中有關"出版者、經銷者敘述項"，以及權威記錄之各機關團體簡稱；亦可供社會大衆簡稱機關團體名稱時參考。

34. CNS 13491 書面文獻章節層次編碼標準 Numbering of Divisions and Subdivisions in Written Documents. (84.1.26.)

本標準定義中外文書面文獻中大類與次類之編碼原則。藉由層次編碼可廓清文獻內容之次序、重要性與相互關係，亦可簡化文獻篇章間的查尋檢索，及方便著作時的參考引用。

35. CNS 13503 學位論文撰寫格式標準 Presentation of Theses and Dissertations. (84.2.16.)

本標準訂定學位論文的撰寫格式、學位論文的組成單元及其順序，以及裝訂製作時的注意事項，適用於各級與各種資料類型的學位論文。

36. CNS 13607 文獻處理——書目控制字元 Documentation – Bibliographic Control Characters. (84.11.30.)

本標準係 CNS 5205（資訊處理及交換用七數元碼字元集（組）]基本控制字元的延伸，包含 15 個應用於編目規則、檔案排序規則及索引規則所使用的控制字元，旨在爲書目資訊交換之用。本標準說明該 15 個控制字元之名稱、英文代碼、意義，及其用法等。

37. CNS 13608 叢書題名展現標準 Presentation of Title Information of Series. (84.11.30.)

本標準旨在闡釋叢書及其分冊的識別要項，並將此要項在出版品中之位置及呈現方式予以定義，以便區別隸屬於叢書的出版品，並方便叢書採購、編目及利用。

38. CNS 13609 圖書書名頁標準 Title Leaves of Books. (84.11.30.)

本標準係說明圖書書名頁上應呈現的書目資料項目及其意義，以協助編輯者與出版者印製書名頁，並便利書商、圖書館員、文獻工作者、著者、索引人員、編目人員、資料庫製作人員等引用或辨識書名頁上的書目資料。至於圖書形式包括單行本、合集、教科書、畫冊、地圖集、學位論文、會議記錄、技術報告等；其印行方式可爲單冊出版、多冊出版或以叢書子冊之方式出版。

39. CNS 13610 科學與技術報告撰寫格式 Documentation – Presentation of Scientific and Technical Reports. (84.11.30.)

本標準適用於任何書本式的科學與技術報告，不論它被稱爲報告、備忘錄或筆記，此外本標準或部份條文亦適用於其他科學與技術文件的撰寫，例如年度報告或手冊。

40. CNS 13611 學術論著參考書目 Bibliographic References：Content, Form and

Structure. (84. 11. 30.)

本標準係針對圖書及其章節、期刊論文、學位論文、視聽資料、專利文件所成之參考書目與註釋，規定其應包含之資料項目、資料項目之順序，並建立書目資料來源相關資訊編寫與呈現之規則。本標準主要提供著者與編者從事編輯參考書目與正文中引用之註釋，不適用於圖書館員以及索引編製者等所從事之書目著錄工作。

41. CNS 13612 公共圖書館建築設備 Guidelines for Planning and Design of Public Library Building and Facilities. (84. 11. 30.)

本標準旨在擬定公共圖書館建築設備規劃設計之指導原則，以提供館長、建築師及其他建築小組之相關人員，作爲圖書館建築規劃設計或整建、擴建、改建時之參考。本標準係以公共圖書館爲主要適用對象，國立圖書館、大專院校圖書館、專門圖書館、中小學校圖書館等，得斟酌參考之。

42. CNS 13771 文獻與資訊詞彙—第 1 部份：基本術語 Documentation and Information – Vocabulary – Part 1：Basic Concepts. (85. 9. 26.)

文獻與資訊詞彙標準系列主要定義文獻與資訊的基本概念，這些表達基本概念的詞彙包括一般性介紹文獻與資訊的基本詞彙，以及一些在實際應用中最常見的衍生詞，所涉領域計有：圖書館學、檔案學、資訊科學、文獻與資訊中心、索引與摘要，以及出版事業所使用之一般標準詞彙均屬之。本標準爲該系列之第一部份，主要定義文獻與詞彙的基本概念。

43. CNS 13772 臺閩地區圖書館代碼編製原則 Principles for Library Code in Taiwan and Fuchien Area. (85. 9. 26.)

本標準旨在定義臺閩地區各級各類圖書館或資料單位之代碼編製原則，並整理現有之圖書館代碼一覽表於附錄，俾便編製圖書館名錄、統計之用。

44. CNS 13773 技術報告標準號 Standard Technical Report Number (STRN). (85. 9. 26.)

本標準適用於所有之技術報告，包括各種印刷和非印刷媒體資料，其目的在提供各技術報告之唯一且一致化之編碼格式，並顯示各技術報告間之關聯性。

45. CNS 13774 期刊與圖書之文章書目識別號 Bibliographic Identification (biblid) of Contributions in Serials and Books. (85. 9. 26.)

本標準旨在利用各篇惟一且一致化之書目識別號來識別期刊及圖書中之單篇文章，俾使記錄的比對、資訊檢索、抽印本的識別、文件訂購及傳遞等作業，在處理時更爲簡便正確。

46. CNS 13775 非期刊性質出版品館藏著錄標準 Holding Statements for Non-Serial Items. (85. 9. 26.)

本標準旨在訂定圖書館及資料單位之非期刊性質出版品館藏記錄的著錄規則與標點符號，藉以達成非期刊性質出版品館藏記錄與顯示方式之一致性與標準化。

47. CNS 13776 圖書館與檔案室典藏出版品與文件之紙質保存性標準 Permanence of Paper for Publications and Documents in Libraries and Archives. (85. 9. 26.)

本標準旨在建立塗佈紙與非塗佈紙高保存性之規範，並說明其特殊性質與檢驗方法，使得圖書館與檔案室所典藏出版品的紙張能在正常使用與保存之下，維持數百年之久而不致產生明顯的損害。此外藉由紙質永久保存性質之說明，本標準期能推廣保存性紙張之使用，及體認可記錄性知識須長久保存之重要；並建議凡出版品符合本標準所規範之紙張印製者，應印有明顯的標記與陳述，以利辨識。

48. CNS 13945 電子訂購圖書格式 Computerized Book Ordering. （86.10.1.）

本標準係參考美國圖書工業系統諮詢委員會（BISAC）之 ANSI/NISO Z39.49（1992）〔電子訂購圖書格式〕而設計，旨在提供已利用電腦存取資訊的買賣雙方，經由線上、磁帶、磁片等電子媒體傳遞並處理圖書訂購訊息。此外通訊雙方可以是下列任二者：批發商、經銷商、出版社、書店、圖書館。

49. CNS 13946 文獻與資訊詞彙—第 2 部份：傳統文獻 Documentation and Information – Vocabulary – Part 2：Traditional Documents. （86.10.1）

文獻與資訊詞彙標準系列主要定義文獻與資訊的基本概念，這些表達基本概念的詞彙包括一般性介紹文獻與資訊的基本詞彙，以及一些在實際應用中最常見的衍生詞，所涉領域計有：圖書館學、檔案學、資訊科學、文獻與資訊中心、索引與摘要，以及出版事業所使用之一般標準詞彙均屬之。本標準爲該系列之第二部份，主要定義傳統文獻之相關詞彙。

50. CNS 13947 國際標準錄音、錄影資料代碼 Documentation – International Standard Recording Code（ISRC）. （86.10.1.）

本標準旨在制定錄音、錄影資料之國際標準代碼，並促進該資料代碼之使用，俾使錄音資料及音樂性錄影資料有共通的辨識方式。本標準代碼可供有聲出版或影視製作廠商、著作權仲介團體、傳播界、媒體中心、圖書館等識別錄音、錄影資料用。

51. CNS 13948 國際標準樂譜號 Information and Documentation—International Standard Music Number（ISMN）. （86.10.1.）

本標準旨在制定印刷形式樂譜之國際標準代碼，俾使印刷式樂譜有共通且簡易的辨識方式。此外亦可適用於由錄音資料與印刷式樂譜共組之成套作品，但單獨發行之錄音、錄影資料則不適用。

52. CNS 13949 文獻處理—期刊出版品摘要表 Documentation—Abstract Sheets in Serial Publications. （86.10.1.）

本標準敘述期刊或其他連續性出版品之摘要表的製作與呈現原則。摘要表主要目的在對當期出版品的內容做詳盡的描述，以提供文獻處理工作所需的重要內容。摘要表包含標題和區段兩個部份，通常將期刊名稱作爲摘要表的標題，各區段則描述各單篇論文的相關資料，但摘要表仍無法取代期刊的目次頁。

53. CNS 13950 期刊目次格式 Contents List of Periodicals. （86.10.1.）

本標準旨在制定期刊中目次的編輯格式。

54. CNS XXXXX〔文獻與資訊詞彙—第 3 部份：文獻資料的採訪、書目辨識與分析〕〔審查中〕〔Documentation and Information – Vocabulary – Section 3（a）：Acquisition, Identification, and Analysis of Documents and Data.〕

文獻與資訊詞彙標準系列主要定義文獻與資訊的基本概念，這些表達基本概念的詞彙包括一般性介紹文獻與資訊的基本詞彙，以及一些在實際應用中最常見的衍生詞，所涉領域計有：圖書館學、檔案學、資訊科學、文獻與資訊中心、索引與摘要，以及出版事業所使用之一般標準詞彙均屬之。本標準爲該系列之第三部份，主要定義文獻資料的採訪、辨識與分析之相關詞彙。

55. CNS XXXXX［期刊及連續性出版品文章編排格式標準］［審查中］［Presentation of Contributions to Periodicals and Other Serials.］

本標準規範科技性期刊及連續出版品各單篇文章之編排格式，其旨在訂定共同遵守的格式及增進該類資料的被利用，俾便圖書館的文獻檢索及其他的讀者服務。［審查中］

56. CNS XXXXX［圖書館之鋼製書架］［審查中］［Single-Tier Steel Bracket Library Shelving.］

本標準僅規範臺灣地區各公共、學校、學術研究圖書館使用單面（自立式）鋼製書架典藏圖書資料時的最低性能要求；不在描述書架各部結構組件之重量、厚度、材料、尺寸或形狀，亦不闡述其成品之使用方法、組成或其厚度。［審查中］

二、圖書館相關國家標準起草中長程（1998至2002會計年度）計劃

□□目□（□□23□□□）

（一）1998會計年度：四項標準

1. *ISO 5127－6*（*1983*）：文獻語文詞彙標準（Vocabulary – Part6：Documentary Languages）

2. *ANSI Z39. 66*（*1992*）：圖書持久性封面裝訂標準（Durable Hardcover Binding for Books）

3. *ANSI Z39. 45*（*1983*）：遺失期刊之催缺標準（Claims for Missing Issues of Serials）

4. *ANSI Z39. 56*（*1991*）：期刊項目辨認標準（Serial Item and Contribution Identifier (SICI)）

（二）1999會計年度：五項標準

1. *ISO 5127－3*（*1988*）：圖示文獻詞彙標準（Vocabulary – Part3：Iconic Documents）

2. *ISO 5127－11*（*1987*）：視聽資料詞彙標準（Vocabulary – Part 11：Audiovisual Visual Documents）

3. *ISO 2788*（*1986*）：中文語文（單一語文）索引典製作標準（Guidelines for the Establishment and Development of Monolingual Thesauri）

4. *ISO 6716*（*1983*）：未剪裁之圖書及期刊尺寸標準（Text-books and Periodicals-Sizes of Untrimmed Sheets and Trimmed Pages）

5. *ANSI Z39. 52*（*1987*）：多書名之圖書資料訂購單格式標準（Standard Order Form for Multiple Titles of Library Materials）

（三）2000會計年度：四項標準

1. *ISO 4217*（*1990*）：經費代碼展現標準（Codes for the Representation of Currencies and Funds）

2. *ISO 8459－2*（*1992*）：採購用之名錄書目資料單元標準（Information and Documentation—Bibliographic Data Element Directory—Part 2：Acquisition Applications）

3. *ISO 9707*（*1991*）：圖書、報紙、期刊及電子出版品之製作及發行統計標準（Information and Documentation—Statistics on the Production and Distribution of Books,

Newspapers, Periodicals and Electronic Publication)

4. *ISO 9230*（*1991*）：圖書館採購之圖書及期刊價格索引標準（Information and Documentation – Determination of Price Indexes for Books and Serials Purchased by Libraries）

（四）2001會計年度：五項標準

1. *ANSI Z39. 54*（*199X*）：圖書館藏書環境標準（Conditions for Storage of Paper-based Library Materials）

2. *ANSI Z39. 69*（*199X*）：讀者資料單元標準（Patron Record Data Elements）

3. *ANSI Z39. 70*（*199X*）：流通動態記錄格式標準（Format for Circulation Transactions）

4. *ANSI Z39. 71*（*199X*）：書目資料館藏敘述標準（Holdings Statements for Bibliographic Items）

5. *ANSI Z39. 76*（*199X*）：圖書館裝訂資料著錄標準（Data Elements for Binding of Library Materials）

（五）2002會計年度：五項標準

1. *ISO 7098*（*1991*）：羅馬拼音標準（Romanization of Chinese）

2. *ISO 5964*（*1985*）：多種語文索引典製作標準（Guidelines for the Establishment and Development of Multilingual Thesauri）

3. *ISO 8439*（*1990*）：基本格式設計標準（Forms Design-Basic Layout）

4. *ISO 8440*（*1991*）：商業文獻之館藏地代碼標準

5. *ANSI Z39. 20*（*199X*）：圖書館館藏資料價格索引（Criteria for Price Indexes for Library Materials）

中國臺灣圖書館相關"國家標準"類別一覽表

類別名稱	CNS 總號	標準名稱
字元、交換碼	＊CNS 5205	資訊技術—資訊交換用七位元碼元集
	＊CNS 7654	資訊技術—字元碼（結構及延伸技術）
	＊CNS 11643	中文標準交換碼
	＊CNS 11643 – 1	中文標準交換碼使用方法
	CNS 13607	文獻處理—書目控制字元
代碼	＊CNS 89	中國國家標準之編號
	CNS 3927	校對符號
	＊CNS 12842	國家名稱代碼表示法
	＊CNS 12864	國家標準書號
	CNS 13153	國家標準期刊號標準
	＊CNS 13188	語言名稱代碼表示法
	＊CNS 13205	資訊交換—機構識別之結構

（續上表）

類別名稱	CNS 總號	標準名稱
代碼	CNS 13773	技術報告標準號
	CNS 13774	期刊與圖書之文章書目識別號
	CNS 13947	國際標準錄音、錄影資料代碼
	CNS 13948	國際標準樂譜號
	CNS 17332	臺閩地區圖書館代碼編製原則
分類與著錄標準	＊CNS 88	"中國國家標準"之分類
	CNS 13148	中國書目資訊交換格式—磁帶部份
	CNS 13150	館際互借書目資料項目標準
	CNS 13162	制定標準建議書格式
	CNS 13222	書目排檢原則
	CNS 13225	期刊館藏著錄標準
	CNS 13226	機讀編目格式標準
	CNS 13227	書目資料著錄總則
	CNS 13463	圖書及其他出版品書背題名標準
	CNS 13490	機關團體簡稱標準
	CNS 13608	叢書題名展現標準
	CNS 13609	圖書書名頁標準
	CNS 13611	學術論著參考書目
	CNS 13775	非期刊性質出版品著錄標準
文獻與資訊詞彙	＊CNS 3029	文獻報告
	CNS 13771	文獻與資訊詞彙—第 1 部份：基本術語
	CNS 13946	文獻與資訊詞彙—第 2 部份：傳統文獻
	＊CNS XXXXX［審查中］	［文獻與資訊詞彙—第 3 部份：文獻資料採訪、辨識與分析］
非書資料標準	CNS 3030	工程及科學之論文發表格式
	CNS 3031	科學期刊（篇幅）
	CNS 13503	學位論文撰寫格式標準
	CNS 13610	科學與技術報告撰寫格式
	CNS 13950	期刊目次格式
	＊CNS XXXX（審查中）	［期刊及連續性出版品文章編排格式標準］

（續上表）

類別名稱	CNS 總號	標準名稱
資訊檢索	CNS 13461	資訊檢索服務與協定標準
	CNS 13462	共同指令語言
	CNS 13491	書面文獻章節層次編碼標準
索引與摘要	CNS 13149	西文資料審查文獻、訂定主題及選擇索引詞彙之方法
	CNS 13152	摘要撰寫標準
	CNS 13223	索引編制標準
	CNS 13224	西文單一語文索引典編製標準
	CNS 13949	文獻處理—期刊出版品摘要表
一般與其他	＊CNS 3689	中國國家標準之程式
	＊CNS 10987	國際單位制
	CNS 13151	圖書館統計
	CNS 13612	公共圖書館建築設備
	CNS 13776	圖書館與檔案室典藏出版品與文件之紙質保存性標準
	CNS 13945	電子訂購圖書方式
	＊CNS XXXX（審查中）	［圖書館之鋼製書架］

柒、結　論

　　"中國圖書館學會"標準委員會自1991年成立以來，至今制定圖書館相關國家標準已有四十項，加上自1969年以來，"經濟部中央標準局"公佈之其他圖書館相關國家標準十六項，共計五十六項。此佔14,000多項國家標準總類之千分之四（0.4％），實在少之又少。標準之重要性無可置疑，各行各業更需積極重視和督促相關標準之制定，以利各專業之進步與發展，圖書館標準自不例外。因此，撰寫本文之主要目的除全面整理作者五年來負責制定之圖書館相關國家標準外，更希望圖書館界透過本文之介紹對圖書館相關標準現況有初步之瞭解與認識，並積極重視推動標準之制訂工作，其能使圖書館業務標準化、現代化和國際化，以因應21世紀資訊時代之挑戰。

（收稿日期：1999年1月11日）

註　釋

註①：宋光梁編著，工業標準概論（臺南：大名，1959年），頁1—6。
註②：Dennis Grogan, Science and Technology: An Introduction to the Literaturre, 4th ed., (London: Clive Bingley, 1982). pp. 315-323.
註③：Bernard Houghton. Technical Information Sources: A Guide to Patent. Specifications,

　　　　Standards and Technical Reports Literature, 2nd ed., （London：Bingley, 1972）, pp. 64 – 90.
註④："經濟部中央標準局"編，標準體系之現況與發展（臺北：編者，1997 年）. 頁 1。
註⑤：John Gailland, Industrial Standardization：Its Principles and Application（New York：H. W. Wilson, 1934）.
註④：同註④，頁 2—4。
註⑦："經濟部中央標準局"編，"序言"，國家標準作業手冊，（臺北：編者，1997 年）。
註⑧：同註②。
註⑨：同註③。
註⑩：Stephen M. Spivak and Keith A. Winsell, A Sourcebook of Standards Information：Education, Access and Dovlopment（Boston. G. K.：Hall. 1991）, pp. 319 – 323.
註⑪：同註④。
註⑫："經濟部"，臺灣標準度政會議，（臺北：國際會議中心，1996 年 2 月 27 日），頁 9—10。
註⑬：Walt Crawford, Technical Standards：An Introduction for Librarians.（Boston：GK Hall, 1991）, pp. 116 – 120.
註⑭：< http：//web. ansi. org/public/about. html >（1999/1/8 AM 11：04）
註⑮：< hrtp：//www. niso. org/ >（1999/1/8 AM 11：04）
註⑯："經濟部中央標準局"編，"國家標準"作業手冊（該局，1997 年）。
註⑰：同註⑪，頁 13—18。
註⑱："經濟部中央標準局"提供。
註⑲：李德竹，《圖書館相關"國家標準"介紹》87 年度圖書館相關"國家標準"說明會，圖書館相關國家標準簡介（臺北市："國家圖書館"，1998 年）
註⑳：同註⑯。
註㉑："經濟部中央標準局"編，圖書館相關"國家標準"彙編（該局，1998 年）；"經濟部中央標準局"編印，"中國國家標準"分類目錄（該局，1998 年）。

臺灣與美加地區圖書資訊學資訊科學課程之研究*

[摘要 Abstract]

　　本研究旨在探討臺灣七所圖書資訊學系所和美國 U. S. News 和 Gourman 報告中排行榜前十名之美國圖書資訊學學校共十二所,以及一所加拿大學校的資訊科學課程內容之特色與差異。研究發現:1. 美加地區之資訊科學課程之設計、課程項目多元化、內容深淺層次系統化;2. 八類資訊課程中,美加又以"資訊系統、設計與評估"和"圖書館自動化、網路與通訊"兩類課程最多,其次爲"資訊貯存與檢索"課程,而臺灣則以"圖書館自動化、網路與通訊"類課爲最多,但多是基礎性課程"資訊系統分析、設計與評估"課程數量嚴重缺乏。最後本研究參考美加地區資訊課程並配合我方所需,研擬適合我方圖書資訊學資訊科學課程名單,以供圖書資訊學界設計及改革資訊科學課程之參考。

關鍵詞　Keyword

資訊科學課程　課程設計　圖書資訊學

Information science curriculum, Information science course

Curriculum design, Library and information science

一、緒論

　　處於今日資訊爆發之資訊時代,資訊媒體多元化,網路資源更是豐富多變,網際網路開發了許多圖書館與資訊服務之新技術,爲電子資訊服務帶來新發展契機。如何因應社會的變遷及發展,培養適當的資訊人才以掌控最有效的電子資訊服務,乃圖書館與資訊科學教育之首要任務。資訊科學教育最直接的方式,莫過於資訊科學與技術相關課程的實施落實。本文擬從臺灣圖書資訊學系所和美國排行榜前十名之圖書資訊學研究所開設之資訊科學課程,進行研究,試圖分析其特色,並歸納比較兩者間資訊科學相關課程之異同,以供學人設計資訊科學教育課程時之參考,進而研擬適合我方之資訊科學相關課程表。

二、資訊科學的定義

　　論及資訊科學教育,首先需界定何謂"資訊科學"。其定義隨科技之進步、環境之異動而不斷變化。最常被引用如 1968 年 H. Borko 提出著名之資訊科學定義是[①]:

　　"資訊科學是研究資訊的特質及行爲,控制資訊流的力量,以及最佳的獲取使用和處理資訊的方法的學科。其關心的是資訊的產生、蒐藏、組織、檢索、解釋、傳遞、改

---

*　本文曾發表在《圖書與資訊學》26 期(1998 年 8 月),第 1—27 頁。

變及利用的知識本體。包括了在自然和人工系統中資訊表現的研究，有效訊息傳遞的符碼使用，以及資訊處理的設施和技術，如電腦和其程式系統的學問等。它也是一門由相關學科，如數學、邏輯學、語言學、心理學、電腦科學、作業研究、繪圖藝術、傳播、圖書館學、管理學及其他相關學科中，所粹取而成的綜合學科。它有因研究主題而要求應用的純科學成份；亦有爲發展服務和制作產品的應用科學成份。"

1991年G. A. Forgionne亦爲資訊科學定義："資訊科學即爲學習資訊本質，資訊傳輸與人類思想的連續過程，以及如何有效利用資訊的觀念、方法和技術。"並説明資訊科學的主要領域涵蓋：通訊、電腦工程、電腦科學、資訊系統和圖書館學。而其核心則包括六方面：1. 通訊和資訊理論；2. 電腦硬體、軟體和程式設計；3. 資料庫發展和管理；4. 模擬和解決問題；5. 科學研究設計和方式；6. 系統理論、分析和設計[2]。

1996年，Hon-Arild Johnnessen則認爲資訊科學是專門研究資訊與通信的結構、特性以及資訊傳輸、貯存、檢索、評估之理論與方法的科學。同時亦涵蓋以資訊科學理念之資訊系統、網路、功能、過程和活動。知識由其源頭傳達至讀者，並在不同之實用性系統和環境中利用資訊。因此，資訊科學具有結構化、功能化和行爲方面的兩種論點[3]。

三、資訊科學課程規劃

學科課程的規劃將會對學生所接受的教育產生重大影響，故規劃設計資訊科學課程時亦應考慮到學生對基礎理論的認識、應具備之專業能力，以及將來就業時對資訊科技的熟習程度。由於資訊科學是一門實用性較強的學科，故與資訊科技的進步息息相關，因此，資訊科學課程的規劃與修訂應是長期且持續性的工作。

F. M. Stieg認爲資訊科學課程可分爲必修課與選修課兩類[4]。必修課著重於各種資訊環境服務時，所必須具備之理論、原則、實務與價值之學習；而選修課則是依興趣并滿足畢業學分所修習者。因此，必修課應視爲基礎，爲專業知識的核心；而選修課則爲專業選項的組合，爲將來就業做準備。必修課通常爲十分基本的課程，如理論基礎課等。由於時勢所趨，目前已逐漸偏向資訊理論方面，如通訊理論與資訊移轉過程模式等之課程。另外，管理課程與資訊科技也形成一種趨勢，其目的在引導學生如何建立資料庫及資訊系統等並加以妥善經營管理。最後，實習課程亦爲資訊科學課程不可或缺的條件。總之，課程的選擇、取捨、規劃與設計雖較爲見仁見智而主觀。但在課程設計應以動態的方式設計，隨社會時代的脈動變遷而修訂，但仍應考量：1. 理論與實務並重；2. 社會的需求與要求；3. 資訊科技之發展趨勢；4. 職業與資訊市場；5. 研究與發展；6. 國際觀、世界觀等方面。課程設計除應按照學科課程設置目標與目外，更應訓練資訊專業工作者具有技巧（skills）、態度（attitudes）和知識（knowledge）的條件及高度能力（competencies）[5][6]。

四、臺灣圖書資訊學系所資訊科學課程

（一）臺灣圖書資訊學系所

臺灣圖書館事業自1949年後在穩定中發展，對圖書館事業人員的需求漸形迫切。目前已有七所大學院校開設圖書資訊學課程。師範大學社會教育系圖書館組成立於1955年，爲臺灣第一所圖書館學系。臺灣大學圖書館學系成立於1961年，1980年開始招收研究生，1989年成立博士班，於1998年系名改爲圖書資訊學系。1970年輔仁大學圖書

館學系成立，1992年更改系名為圖書資訊學系，並於1995年成立研究所。淡江大學教育資料科學系成立於1971年，1991年設立教育資料科學研究所。世界新聞專科學校圖書資料科成立於1964年，1991年該校改為世界新聞傳播學院，1995年改設圖書資訊學系。政治大學亦於1996年設立圖書資訊學研究所。中國文化大學於1964年成立歷史研究所並設置斷代史組、近代史組、圖書館文物組（原名圖書博物組）和美術組四組，該所原名中國文化研究所，於1964年成立，可授與史學博士學位。上述五所大學（臺大、淡江、輔大、政大、文化）之研究所，除臺大設有圖書資訊學博士班外，其餘皆為碩士班[7]。

（二）系所資訊科學相關課程

目前臺灣圖書資訊學系所資訊科學相關課程之設計特色，大學部的課程內容重點是基礎性介紹，而研究所的課程基本上仍以大學部的課程為骨幹，繼續賦予資訊科學更豐富深入的知識內涵。為使學生有更彈性的選擇空間，幾乎全部的資訊科學課程均為選修，部份與大學部課程相同或相似的課程名稱，則冠以"專題"、"研究"或"研討"等字樣，以區別其學習的層面較廣博精深。茲針對大學部和研究所資訊科學相關課程分八大類，並分析說明如下：（見表一、表二）

第一類"電腦與程式設計"，（Computers and Programming）

此類課程，以"電子計算機概論"、"程式語言"及"文書處理"三科目為核心，六所大學均列為大學部必修課程。現代化圖書資訊服務最重要的工具是電腦，"文書處理"主要學習中英文電腦文書處理，因此，基本的電腦知識是必備的根本。至於次要之外圍課程有"程式設計"、"資料結構"及"個人電腦與圖書館"等。

第二類"資訊需求與尋求行為"（Information Needs and Seeking Behavior）

"資訊需求與資訊尋求行為"是目前圖書館資訊服務中最重要的課題，強調對讀者需求與資訊尋求行為做深入探究與分析。島內有四所學校皆開授此課，惟名稱略有出入，同時亦開授"認知心理學"基礎課程。

第三類"資訊儲存與檢索"（Information Storage and Retrieval）

資料必須有系統的加以組織，方可有效的查尋而達到資訊傳輸的目的，無論是圖書館自動化系統或網際網路的資源。"資訊儲存與檢索"及"線上資訊檢索"乃此類課程之主軸，其次是"索引與摘要"。此類課程則另有"索引典結構"與"自動分類與索引"等相關課程。

第四類"資訊系統分析、設計與評估"（Information Systems Analysis, Design and Evaluation）

此類課程以"系統分析"為中心，"資料庫管理系統"與之平行並列，課程主旨著重採用適當方法和技術設計、分析和評估資訊系統。"作業系統"、"光碟資料庫系統"及"CAI系統之設計"亦屬此類課程，但較遠離核心。

第五類"資訊科學與技術"（Information Science and Technology）

毋庸置疑的，"資訊科學導論"乃此類課程之當然核心。名稱雖稍有差異，但島內圖書資訊學系均定為大學部必修課，課程之實質內容主要是對資訊科學有一初步全面性的認識。研究所方面則開授"資訊學研討"或"圖書資訊學研討"為必修課程，其餘次要課程則包括"資訊科技與圖書館學"、"資訊傳播學"、"資訊中心與服務"等。

第六類"圖書館自動化、網路與通訊"(Library Automation、Networks and Communication)

為因應網路時代社會之變遷及發展,各校特加強開設"圖書館自動化"、"網路與通訊"此類課程。主導此類課程為"圖書館自動化"、"網路與通訊"及"網路資源"。"圖書館自動化"為各校統一採用之名稱,但亦有稱之為"數位化圖書館"者。網路課程之名稱較多樣化,例如:"網路資源"、"網路資源與應用"、"電腦網路概論"、"學術網路資源應用"、"電腦網路與通訊"等。此外,由於多媒體之迅速發展,自動化系統和網路亦趨向多媒體走勢,各系所開授之課程有多媒體概論、製作和資源等,是未來發展趨勢。

第七類"資訊政策與管理"(Information Policy and Management)

設計此類課程的意義在學習認識資訊政策及資訊管理理論。"資訊政策"和"資訊管理"為多數學校開設,尤其是研究所階級。其次有"電腦中心管理"、"媒體中心管理"、"個人資訊管理"、"資訊科技與組織管理"和"圖書資訊標準"等相關課程。

第八類"資訊社會、倫理與其他"(Information Society、Ethics and Others)

各系所開授此類課程並不多,其中以"資訊社會"、"圖書資訊法規"和"智慧財產"方面之課程較多,而"圖書資訊倫理"之內容則融入相關課程中,並未單獨另設獨立課程。

綜觀前面所述可見在八類課程中,又以第一類電腦與程式設計、第三類資訊儲存與檢索、第五類資訊科學與技術及第六類圖書館自動化、網路與通訊等四類課程各校之重覆性較高,因而反應出彼此共同認定之重要性。其餘四類課程各校認定的同質性較低,因而課程呈現零星分佈的局面。

為透視課程之層級結構,圖一與圖二將更清楚描繪課程間的關係。圖一為同質性較高之第一、三、五、六四類課程,依其重要性,自圓心逐較向外圍擴散。圓心部份代表核心課程之所在,外圍部份則為邊緣課程的代表。圖二則是同質性較低之其餘四類課程的分佈情形。

表一:臺灣地區圖書資訊學系所資訊科學相關課程類別表
(A:臺大,B:師大,C:淡江,D:輔大,E:世新,F:政大,G:文化)
1. 電腦與程式設計

課程名稱	學校代碼(*):必修
電子計算機概論	A*, B*, D*, E*
電子計算機專題	A
電於計算機資料結構	A
電子計算機應用	E*
電子計算機程式寫作	C*
電子文件處理專題	C*
電腦文書處理	C
電腦與教學	B
文書處理	D*
資料結構	A

（續上表）

課程名稱	學校代碼（＊）：必修
中文電腦專題研討	A
中英文電腦輸入法	C＊
程式語言原理	D
程式設計	E＊
程式語言	B
模糊邏輯導論	C＊
個人電腦與圖書館	A
物件導向語言	D＊
總課數	18（9＊）

2. 資訊需求與尋求行爲

課程名稱	學校代碼（＊）：必修
資訊尋求行爲	A, D
資訊與認知	D
資訊心理學	A, B, C, D
認知心理學	D
總課數	4（0＊）

3. 資訊儲存與檢索

課程名稱	學校代碼（＊）：必修
資訊檢索	A＊, B＊
資訊檢索原理	A, D
資訊檢索系統專題	E
資訊儲存與檢索	A, C, E＊, F
資訊儲存與檢索專題	C
資訊組織與主題分析	F
資料庫檢索	D＊
資料庫檢索服務專題	D
索引及摘要	A, B, C＊, E＊
索引典結構	A
線上檢索	B
線上資訊檢索	A, C
自動分類與索引	A
自動文獻處理	D
中文電腦檢字	A, C
多媒體資訊檢索	D
元資料	D
總課數	17（4＊）

4. 資訊系統分析、設計與評估

課程名稱	學校代碼（＊）：必修
系統分析	A, D＊, F
系統分析與系統管理	B
管理資訊系統	A, C
光碟資料庫系統	A
資料庫管理	B
資料庫管理系統	A, E＊, F＊
資料庫系統	A
資料庫系統導論	D
資料庫結構	C
資訊管理系統	C
資訊系統發展評估	D
圖書館系統分析	C, F
各科資訊系統	E
作業系統	A, D
UNIX 導論	D
CAI 課程原理與設計	A
總課數	16（2＊）

5. 資訊科學與技術

課程名稱	學校代碼（＊）：必修
資訊科學導論	A＊, D＊
資訊科學專題研究	A, D
資訊科技概論	E＊
資訊組織	D＊
資訊與傳播原理	B
資訊傳播學	D
資訊科技與圖書館	B
資訊學研討	A＊
資訊中心與服務	C
資訊服務中心	C
資訊概論	C＊
圖書資訊學專題	E
圖書資訊學研究	F＊
圖書館史與資訊科學史研究	C
圖書館學與資訊科學研究課題	C
圖書館學與資訊科學理論	C
圖書館學與資訊科學導論	C＊
書目計量學	E
總課數	

6. 圖書館自動化，網路與通訊

課程名稱	學校代碼（＊）：必修
電腦輔助多媒體	A, B
電腦網路與通訊	A＊, B＊, E＊, F
電腦網路概論	D＊
電腦在圖書館的應用	C
電子傳播科技	C
自動化專題研究	C
圖書館自動化	A＊, B＊, C, E＊
圖書館自動化專題	C
圖書館自動化作業	C＊
圖書館資訊系統	D
圖書資訊系統專題	A
網路資源	A＊, D＊
網路與通訊	E＊
網路資源與應用	C＊
網路資源徵集與利用	B
網路資源與利用	D
網路資源管理研究	F
網路概論	C
網路專題	C
網路資源檢索與應用	E
開放系統應用協定	D
電子圖書館導論	D
資訊網路	C
學術網路與圖書館	C
線上目錄	C
檔案自動化專題	F
CAI/多媒體與讀者專題	D
媒體資源服務	D
多媒體技術與應用	E＊
多媒體概論	E＊
多媒體製作專題	E＊
多媒體資源研究	F
多媒體製作	B
總課數	(10＊)

7. 資訊政策與管理

課程名稱	學校代碼（＊）：必修
個人資訊管理	B
圖書資訊標準	A
電腦中心管理	A
資訊管理	A
資訊政策	A
資訊政策專題	C
資訊政策研究	F
資訊管理研討	A
資訊科技與組織管理	A
媒體中心管理	C
總課數	10（0＊）

8. 資訊社會、倫理與其他

課程名稱	學校代碼（＊）：必修
圖書館與資訊社會	A
圖書資訊法規	A
圖書資訊法學	D
媒體資訊法學	C
資訊自由化專題	D
智慧財產	A，C
總課數	6（0＊）

表二：臺灣地區圖書資訊學系所資訊科學課程類別課數之統計分析

課程類別 \ 學校代碼（課程數）	開課學校代碼							總計
	A	B	C	D	E	F	G	6
電腦與程式設計 18（9＊）	6	3	5	4	3	0	—	21
資訊需求與尋求行為 4（0＊）	2	1	1	4	—	—	—	8
資訊儲存與檢索 17（4＊）	8	3	5	6	2	2	—	26
資訊系統分析、設計與評估 16（2＊）	7	2	4	5	2	3	—	23
資訊科學與技術 18（7＊）	3	2	7	4	3	1	—	20

（續上表）

課程類別 / 學校代碼（課程數）	開課學校代碼							總計
	A	B	C	D	E	F	G	6
圖書館自動化、網路與通訊 33（10*）	5	5	11	8	7	4	—	40
資訊政策與管理 10（0*）	6	1	2	—	—	1	—	10
資訊社會，倫理與其他 6（0*）	3	—	2	2	—	—	—	7
Total	40	17	37	33	17	11	0	155

＊必：必修之學校總數

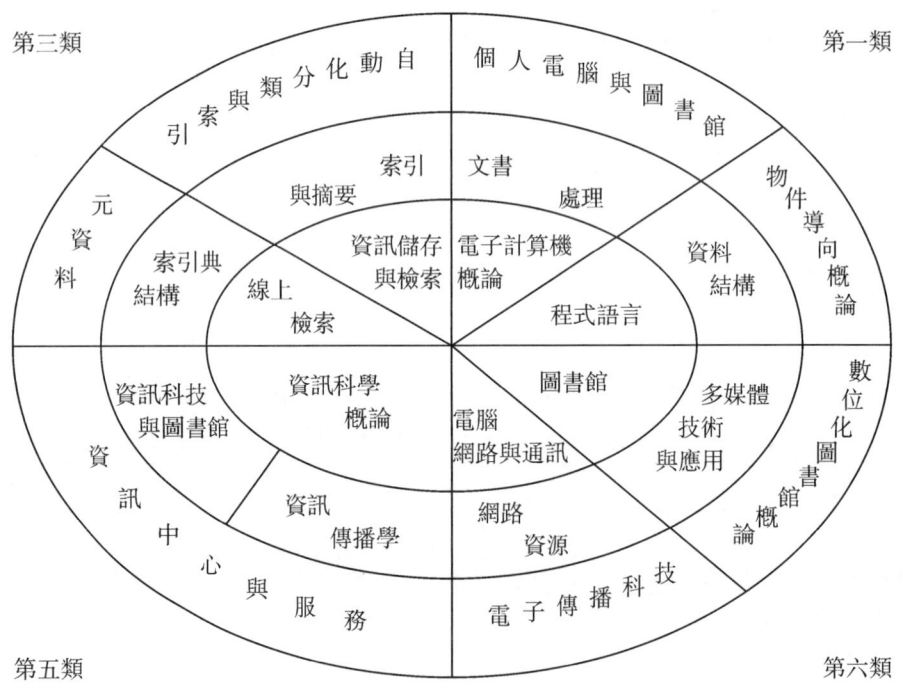

圖一：第一、三、五、六類資訊科學課程分佈

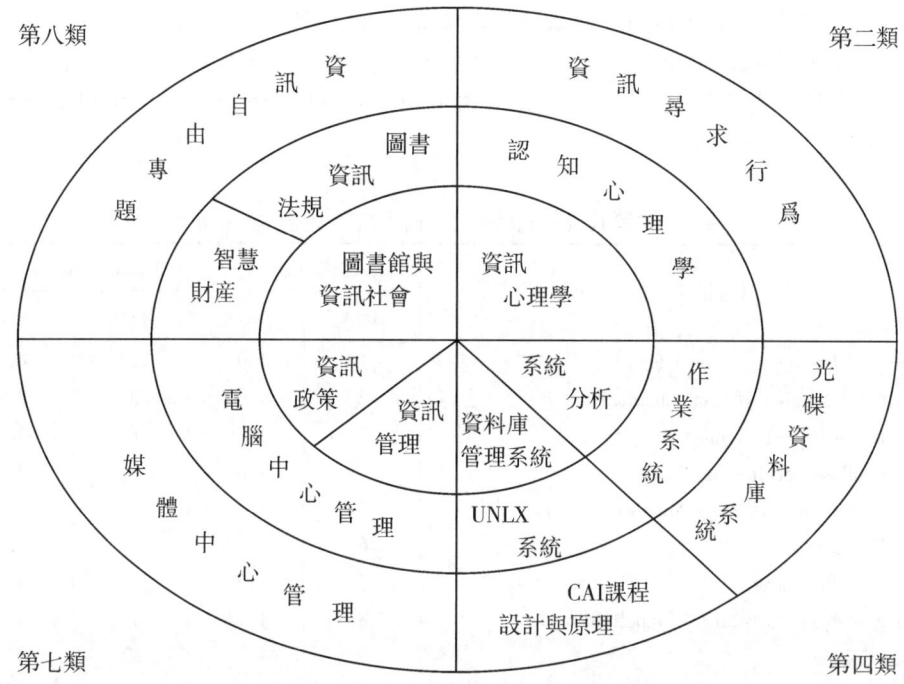

圖二：第二、四、七、八類資訊科學課程分佈

五、美國和加拿大圖書資訊學研究所資訊科學課程

(一) 美加地區圖書資訊學院

美國和加拿大為世界圖書資訊學教育最先進的國家，但同樣地受到資訊科技高度發展之衝擊與社會變遷之影響，積極地做出因應之改革。不幸的是，自1987年以來仍有十餘所美加圖書資訊學院因此遭到淘汰而關閉的命運[8]。這也證實了在1960年代Dr. Robert Hayes，前美國加州大學洛杉磯分校圖書館學與資訊科學院院長之警告："圖書館學的教育訓練，如不包括資訊科學課程，絕對無法適應當今（或未來）社會圖書館作業的要求…"因為資訊科學正是設法提供一個完整有實效的方法來處理多變複雜的圖書館問題[9]。因此，美加地區圖書資訊學研究所資訊科學之改變情形，值得深入研究。

根據《1996/97 美國圖書館名錄》（American Library Directory, 1996-97）之統計，美國自第一所圖書館學校1887年設立以來，至1996年先後共成立圖書資訊學院、所、系、科共約211所[10]。《1997/98 年美國圖書資訊學教育學會名錄》（1997/98 ALISE Directory）之調查列出，由美國圖書館學會認可之圖書資訊學院有57所，其中美國49所，波多黎各1所，加拿大7所，27所學校並授予博士學位[11]。

(二) 圖書資訊學院資訊科學課程

美加兩地目前與臺灣圖書資訊學教育制度上最大不同，是美加圖書資訊學教育多設置在研究所階段，而臺灣則始於大學部，大學部的核心與必修課程則多且是基礎性的。一般美加碩士班之核心與必修課程則約四至五門，如：資訊資源與服務、資訊組織與尋取、資訊管理、圖書館資訊與社會、研究方法等，各校課程名稱會有差異但其內容大同小異。其他皆選修課程，博士班課程多爲選修。

爲進一步瞭解美加地區圖書資訊課程之現況，蒐集1998 U. S. News[12]及1997年"The Gourman Report"[13]兩報告中調查所評估之美國大學圖書資訊學研究所前十名排行榜，共計十二所學院（表三）之課程，另加拿大 University of Toronto, Faculty of Information Studies，總計13所學校。

表三：美國圖書資訊學研究所前十名學校排行榜名單

Institutions	Gourman*		U. S. News**	
	Rank	Score	Rank	Score
University of Michigan—Ann Arbor	1	4.91	2	4.3
University of Illinois—Urbana-Champaign	2	4.90	1	4.4
Indiana University—Bloomington	3	4.86	6	3.9
University of Wisconsin—Madison	4	4.84	6	3.9
University of California—Los Angeles	5	4.82	11	3.6
Rutgers University	6	4.80	6	3.9
University of Pittsburgh	7	4.77	5	4.1
University of North Carolina—Chapel Hill	8	4.74	2	4.3
Simmons College	9	4.71	12	3.5
University of Texas—Austin	10	4.66	9	3.8
Drexel University	15	4.47	10	3.7
Syracuse University	14	4.51	4	4.2

資料來源：*The Gourman Report, Eighth revised ed.（Random House, 1997）

**U. S. News：(http://www.usnews.com/usnews/edu/beyond/gradrank/gbinfos.html 1998)

茲綜合說明美國和加拿大圖書資訊學研究所資訊科學相關課程如下[14]：（見表四、表五）

"電腦與程式設計"課程，美加以程式語言C與自然語言，資料結構課程爲多；與臺灣同類的課程層次上有差異。"資訊需求與尋求行爲"類課程則著重在認知科學和資訊使用者利用及行爲內容方面；"資訊貯存與檢索"類課程，13所學校設置47種不同深淺層面之資訊貯存與檢索課程，多而豐富。第四類"資訊系統分析、設計和評估"課程，共64門課，課程強調資訊系統分析設計與評估，資料庫理論、應用和管理，以及資訊使用者介面設計等，同時又添增知識基礎系統和視覺化資訊介面設計等新課；"資訊科學與技術"類課程，各校對此類課程之設置重點，在加深增廣資訊科學及技術之課程，如：多媒體資訊技術應用和系統、維護技術、技術基礎建設專題、資訊技術在非營利組織之應用等課程。"圖書館自動化、網路和通訊"是13所學校皆相當重視的課程類，爲八類中最多課目者，共65門課，其中網路及通訊課程則佔此類之83%（54門課）。"資訊政策和管理"課程方面，增多了國家資訊政策、光學技術與資訊管理、資訊環境管理等課程，皆爲迎合時代所需之課程。最後，"資訊社會、倫理與其他"類，爲近來海內外圖書資訊學系所開始重視之課題，爲八類中最少課程類。美加地區則設有圖書資訊科技使用之倫理與價值、組織/資訊倫理、資訊自動化與檢查制度、資訊與社會、圖書館與資訊素養等課程。

表四：美國和加拿大圖書資訊學研究所（博碩士班）
資訊科系相關課程表（各校代碼見附錄）

1. COMPUTERS AND PROGRAMMING

Course Name	學校代碼（＊）：必修
Applications of Natural Language Processing	R
Client-Server & Workstation	I
Compiler Design	I
Computing Methods in Information Science	J
Computer Programming	
—C Programming	A
—C programming in a Client/Server Environment	C
—Computer Programming for Information Processing	A
—Computer Programming for Non-Numerical Information Processing	C
Data Structures	I
Data Structures for Library and Information Science	F
Digital Transmission	I
Distributed Computing for Information Professionals	C
Generalized Programming and Data Structures	J
Introduction to C++	R
Introduction to Computing	A
Introduction to Computer Programming for Text Management	B
Language Processing	A
Natural Language Processing	C, I, R
Non-numeric Programming for Information Systems Applications	R
Programming Languages and Environment	I
Special Topics：Object-Oriented Design and Programming（Java）	H
Tools and Techniques for Information Engineering	C
總課數	22（0＊）

2. INFORMATION NEEDS AND SEEKING BEHAVIOR

Course Name	學校代碼（＊）：必修
Cognitive Engineeing	A
Cognitive Studies	K
Design of Library and Information Services	D
Doctoral Seminar: Information Seeking and Use	D
Foundations of Cognitive Science	I
Human/Computer Interaction	D
Human Behavior in Online Searching	L
Human Factors in Systems	I
Independent Study-Cognitive Science	I
Independent Study-Cognitive Systems	I
Information Use and Users	M
Information Seeking Behavior	D
The Use of Information	H
Use and Users of Information	F, R
User Education /Bibliographic Instruction: Theory and Technique	D
User Needs and Behavior in Theory and Practice	B ＊
User Perspectives in Information Systems and Services	R
總課數	17（1＊）

3. INFORMATION STORAGE AND RETRIEVAL

Course Name	學校代碼（＊）：必修
Abstracting and Indexing	A, F, K, R
Advanced Computerized Retrieval Systems	C
Advanced Database Searching	J
Advanced Online Searching	A
Artificial Intelligence for Information Retrieval	R
Basics of computerized Retrieval Systems	C
Bibliographic Access and Control	B ＊
Bibliographic Data and Information Processing	M
Biomedical Database Searching	A
Concepts of Information Retrieval	B
Cognition and Information Retrieval	A
Computer-Based Information Resources	D
Doctoral Seminar: Information Storage and Retrieval Systems	D
Information Graphics	C
Information Access	D
Implementation of Information Storage and Retrieval	F
Indexing	M

(續上表)

Course Name	學校代碼（*）：必修
Indexing and Abstracting Systems and Services	C
Indexing for Information Retrieval	P
Indexing and Thesaurus Construction	D
Information Interaction, Mediation, and Searching	J
Information Organization and Access	F
Information Organization and Retrieval	L
Information Retrieval	D, R
Information Retrieval Systems	L
Information Storage and Retrieval Theory	B, F
Information Systems Implementation	A
Information Usage and the Cognitive Artefact	B
Introduction to Human Computer Interaction	B*
Human Interaction with Computers	C
Knowledge Representation for Information Retrieval	J
Methods of Inquiry	J*
Online Bibliographic Searching	A
Online Information Retrieval	B, L
Online Information Services	P
Online Information Systems	F
Online Reference and Information Services	M
Organizing and Providing Access to Information	K
Organizing and Retrieving Information	R
Online Retrieval Services	C
Retrieval Information	I, J
Research in Information Retrieval	R
Search and Retrieval	H
Seminar: Information Access	D
Seminar in Information Retrieval	R
Seminar in Information Storage and Retrieval	M
Topics in Information Processing and Retrieval	M
總課數	47（3*）

4. INFORMATION SYSTEMS ANALYSIS, DESIGN AND EVALUATION

Courses	學校代碼（*）：必修
Advanced Topics in Information Systems	B, C
Analysis of Information Systems	L
Artificial Intelligence	A
Artificial Intelligence and Expert Systems	K
Community Information Systems	F
Data Administration Concepts and Database Management	C
Database Management Principles and Applications	K
Database Management	P
Database Management Ⅰ	A, I
Database Management Ⅱ	A
Database Management Systems	J
Database Structures for Bibliographic Inquiry	B
Database Systems Ⅰ	R
Database Systems Ⅱ	R
Image Databases	H
Database Design	L
Database Management Systems	D
Designing Information Systems	L
Distributed Systems	I
Evaluation of Information Retrieval	A
Evaluation of Information Retrieval Systems	R
Evaluation of Information Systems	B
Evaluation & Methods of Medical Informatics	I
Implementation of Distributed Information Systems	F
Independent Study in Information Systems	R
Independent Study-Systems & Tec-Systems Design	I
Independent Study-Systems and Tec-Computing Systems	I
Independent Study-Systems and Tec-Applications Information	I
Information Services Design and Evaluation	A
Information Systems	I, J*
Information Systems Analysis	A
Information Systems: Analysis and Design	P, R
Information Systems Analysis: Concepts and Practice	C
Information System Analysis and Management	F
Information Systems: Theory and Design	C
Information Systems Effectiveness	R
Interactive Graphics	I
Introduction to Information Systems	L
Introduction to Information Systems Analysis	A*
Knowledge Base Systems	A, R

(續上表)

Courses	學校代碼（*）：必修
Knowledge-Based Systems for Information Services	J
Management Information Systems	I, J
Managing in the Information Systems Organization	R
Managing in the Information Systems Projects	C
Measurement and Evaluation of Information Systems and Services	D
Principles of Information Systems Analysis and Design	D
Problem Solving Information Systems	C
Seminar in Information Systems Research	A, C
Seminar in Information Systems & Technology	I
Seminar in Information Science and Knowledge Systems	K
Strategic Intelligence	B*
System Analysis	R
System Analysis and Design	B*
System Analysis and Evaluation	K
Systems Analysis and Management	F
Systems Analysis in Information Services	P
Systems Implementation	R
Systems Theory	R
Users Interfaces Design	R
Users Interfaces for Information Systems	A
User-Centered Information System Development	L
User-System Interface Design	K
User-Centered Database Design	B*
Visualizaing Information：Interface Design for Human Computer	B
總課數	64（5*）

5. INFORMATION SCIENCE AND TECHNOLOGY

Course Name	學校代碼（*）：必修
Biomedical Informatics	K
Computer Graphics in Information Science	L
Emerging Technologies and the Library/Media Center	P
Enterprise Strategy and Information Technology	R
Foundations of Information Science	C
Information Models	R
Information Structures	D
Information Processing Standards	I
Information Technology for Libraries and Information Centers	C
Information Technology in Schools and Libraries	C
Information Technologies in Small Nonprofit Organization	H

（續上表）

Course Name	學校代碼（*）：必修
Information Technology Standardization	B*
Introduction to Information Science	I
Introduction to Information Technology	K, L
Library and Information Science: The Role of Research	P*
Management and Information Technology	J
Multimedia Information Technology Applications and Systems	P
Photographic Archives and Visual Information	P
Practical Engagement Workshop: Information Technologies in Small Non-Profit Organization	H
Preservation Technologies	P
Research in Information and Library Science	R
Seminar: Advanced Topics in Technological Infrastructures	C
Seminar: Special Topics in Information Science	D
Study in Information and Library Science	R
Scholarly Communication and Bibliometrics	D
Technology in Design: Methods and Means	H
Technology for Libraries and Information Agencies	J
The Social Impact of Information Technology	L
Understanding Information	I
總課數	29（2*）

6. LIBRARY AUTOMATION, NETWORKS AND COMMUNICATION

Course Name	學校代碼（*）：必修
Advanced Telecommunication and Information Network Management	C
Automation of Library Process	D
Automation of Library and Information Services	K
Automated Services and Systems for Library/Media Operations	P
Communication and Information Processes	J*
Communication in the Workplace	J*
Communication Processes	R
Computer-Mediated Communication	F
Computer-Media and the Information Professions	P
Computer Networks	I
Computer-Supported Cooperative Work	A
Critical Issues in Cyberspace	A
Current Issues: The Internet: Applications and Issues	L
Data Communication	R
Design of Library Automation Systems	B
Distributed Computing and Networking	A

(續上表)

Course Name	學校代碼（*）：必修
Development of Cultural Information Sources Using Digital Multimedia	D
Electronic Communications 1	I
Electronic Communications 2	I
Fundamentals of Telecommunications	I
History of Visual Communication	P
Impact of New Information Resources: Multimedia and Networks	H
Independent Study: Computer Communications	I
Independent Study in Communication Systems	I
Independent Study in Networking	I
Information in Cyberspace	K
Information Network	K
Information Networking	C
Information Services and the World Wide Web	P
Intelligent Networks	I
Internet Applications	R
Internet Resource Discovery, Organization, and Design	H
Introduction to Clinical Multimedia and Internet	I
Introduction to Communication Networks	R
Introduction to Computer Networking	C
Introduction to Internet Resources and Services	K
Introduction to Local Area Networks	R
Introduction to Telecommunications	I
Introduction to Telecommunications & Network Management	C
Library Automation	B*, R
Local Area Networks	I
Mediated Communication Processes	J*
Network Design	I
Network Management	I
OCLC Systems and Services	P
Practical Engagement Workshop: Review, Recommendations and Other Internet Metadata Applications	H
Protocols and Network Management	R
Seminar in Digital Libraries	H
Seminar in Internet Policy and Future Initiatives	R
Seminar in Information Science and Knowledge Systems: Advanced Internet Resources and Services	K
Seminar in Information Science and Knowledge Systems: Client Server Admnistration	K
Special Topics: Information Networking: Design & Management	I
Special Topics: Internet Interfaces	J

(續上表)

Course Name	學校代碼（*）：必修
TCP/IP Networking and Network Programming	R
Telecommunication	F
Telecommunications and Computer Networks in Libraries	P
Telecommunications and Information Network Technology	C
Telecommunication for Information Systems	K
Telecommunications Project	C
Telecommunications Policy and Regulation	C
Telecommunications Systems	R
The Internet	A
The Virtual Library	R
Visual Communications: Systems, Interfaces and Applications	H
Wireless Interactive Communications	C
總課數	65（4*）

7. INFORMATION POLICY AND MANAGEMENT

Course Name	學校代碼（*）：必修
Doctoral Seminar: Policies and Issues in Library and Information Science	D
Fiscal Management of Library and Information Systems	P
Information in Society	D
Information Management Tools	A*
Introduction to Information Management & Technology	C
Managing Information-Technology-Enabled Change	C
Management of Electronic Records	H
Management of Information Organizations	L*
Management of Information Technology	P
Management of Digital Records	D
National Information Policy	P
Organization of Information	R
Organization and Representation of Knowledge and Information	B*
Optical Technologies and Information Management	P
Records Management	P, K, C
Representing, Organizing and Storing Information	L*
Seminar in Information Policy in the Public Sector	R
The Management of Information Environments	B*
United States Government Information Policies, Resources, and Services	P
總課數	19（5*）

8. INFORMATION SOCIETY、ETHICS AND OTHERS

Course Name	學校代碼（＊）：必修
Ethics and Values：Dilemmas in Use of Information Technology	H
Information and its Social Contexts	B＊
Information and Society	L
Intellectual Freedom and Censorship	P
Legal Informatics	K
Libraries, Contemporary Society, and the Adolescent	P
Literacy：The Issue and the Library's Response	P
Organization/Information Ethics	P
Social Aspects of Information-Oriented Society	D
Seminar：Intellectual Freedom and Information Policy Issues	D
Seminar：Legal Informatics	D
The Electronic Information Environment	B
總課數	12（1＊）

表五：美國和加拿大圖書資訊學研究所（博碩士班）
資訊科系相關課程類別課數之統計分析

課程類別 \ 學校代碼（課程數）	開 課 學 校 代 碼												統計
	A	B	C	D	F	H	I	J	K	L	M	P	R	12
Computer and Programming （22/0＊）	4	1	5	—	1	1	6	2	—	—	—	—	4	24
Information Needs and Seeking Behavior （12/1＊）	1	1	—	5	1	1	4	—	1	1	1	—	1	17
Information Storage and Retrieval （42/3＊）	6	5	6	6	5	1	1	5	2	3	5	2	6	53
Information Systems Analysis, Design and Evaluation （61/5＊）	9	6	7	3	4	1	9	4	5	5	—	3	11	67
Information Science and Technology （27/2＊）	—	1	4	3	—	3	3	2	2	3	—	5	4	30

(續上表)

課程類別 / 學校代碼 (課程數)	開課學校代碼													統計
	A	B	C	D	F	H	I	J	K	L	M	P	R	12
Library Automation, Networks and Communication (63/4*)	4	2	8	2	2	5	14	4	7	1	—	6	11	66
Information Policy and Management (16/5*)	1	2	3	3	—	1	—	—	—	1	—	6	2	19
Information Society and Ethics (8/1*)	—	2	—	3	—	1	—	—	—	1	—	4	—	11
Total	25	20	33	25	13	14	37	17	17	15	6	26	39	287

六、臺灣與美加資訊科學相關課程之總數和種數之比較

明顯地，美加十三所資訊科學課程總數和種數皆遠較臺灣七所學校為多。邏輯上，此處課程總數之比較是不正確的，僅製表供參考之用；而資訊科學相關課程種類之比較則是為瞭解臺灣與美加地區圖書資訊學學校所設置課程內容之重視方向。根據課程類別之分析，美加資訊科學課程之八類中，著重"資訊系統分析、設計與評估"、"圖書館自動化、網路與通訊"和"資訊貯存與檢索"三大類課程設計深入而多層化，但臺灣雖積極加強此三方面課程，尤其在"資訊系統分析、設計與評估"課程之設置方面明顯的不足，"資訊貯存與檢索"課程亦不夠深度，應待加強。其他如資訊社會、資訊政策、倫理、資訊需求與尋求等方面之課程，臺灣與美加學校同樣的已開始重視，而"電腦與程式設計"課程，臺灣因為設在大學部，故課程多為基礎性，亦顯示此類課程之不足且欠缺深度，應考量在研究所部份增添課程。（見圖三、圖四）

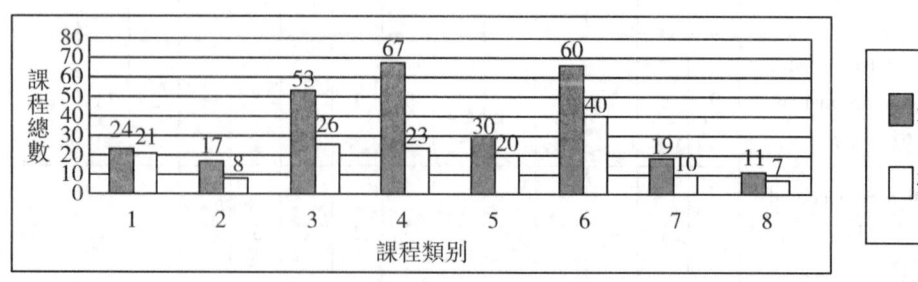

圖三：臺美加資訊科學相關課程總數比較

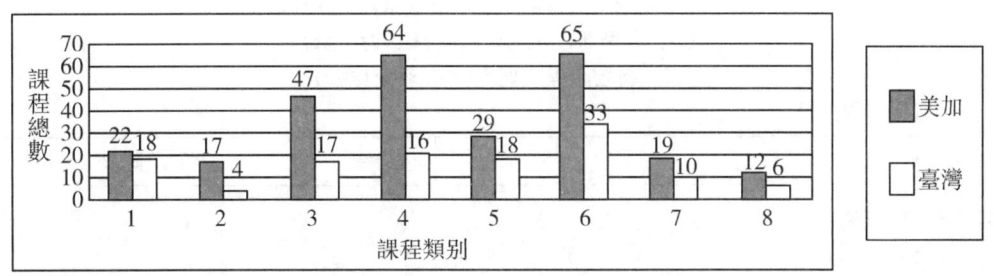

圖四：臺美加資訊科學相關課程種數比較

七、結論與建議

綜合研究分析結果，臺灣圖書資訊學系所資訊科學課程在設計理念上較趨一致。大學部電子計算機概論、電子文書處理、資訊科學導論均被認同是修習資訊科學的根基。根基穩固後，方可架設以資訊儲存與檢索、圖書館自動化及網路與通訊為核心的主幹；最後，再由主幹延伸多樣化的主題課程，以擴寬其深度與廣度。現況之分析，僅能反應"既有"，不能前瞻"未來"。作者曾於1994年完成"國科會"補助之"美國、大陸和臺灣地區圖書館學系所資訊科學課程之研究"計劃。該研究曾參酌美國、大陸及臺灣三地圖書館學校當時授課之清單，並參考海內外相關文獻對資訊科學課程之建議，同時又以問卷對三地圖書資訊學系所課程調查、訪談中美雙方教師及座談會結果予以綜合整理分析，最後，試圖嚴謹的、周詳的研擬"適用"於臺灣圖書資訊學系所之資訊科學課程清單[15]。又該份清單當時尚稱詳盡完整，但現已過時。因此，本研究再次蒐集臺灣及美加地區最新發展之資訊科學課程重新分類並修增新課，重新研擬適合臺灣資訊科學相關課程清單（見表六），期能提供臺灣圖書資訊學系所設計或改進資訊科學課程之參考。

表六所建議臺灣圖書資訊學系所資訊科學課程清單，與1994年研究之課程相較，增加甚多，除修改前表外，資訊科學課程總數已增至108項。八類中，除第一類"電腦與程式設計"外，其他七類，如"資訊需求與尋求行為"、"資訊儲存與檢索"、"資訊系統分析、設計與評估"、"資訊科學與技術"、"圖書館自動化與網路"、"資訊政策與管理"、"資訊社會、倫理與其他"中增加如：資訊政策、資訊自動化、智慧財產權、組織與資訊倫理、資訊環境研究、多媒體、傳播技術、視覺化系統、資訊與檢索自動化與維護研究、知識基礎系統、資訊與技術基礎建設專題研討，各類專題研究等主題方面，皆納入資訊科學新增課程之考量。表中有※號者，則代表新增課程，有47門，佔總課數50%。

表六：建議臺灣圖書資訊學系所資訊科學課程清單
（B：大學部，M：碩士班，D：博士班）
※：新增課程（與 1994 年研究比較）

1. 電腦與程式設計

課程名稱	必選修	開設階段
電子計算機概論	必	B
文書處理	必	B
資料與檔案結構	選	B
程式語言※	選	B
主從式架構概論※	選	B

2. 資訊需求與尋求行為

課程名稱	必選修	開設階段
認知心理學	必	B
資訊尋求行為	選	B
資訊需求與利用※	選	B/M
資訊服務與用戶研討※	選	M
人體工學※	選	M
讀者需求與行為理論與實務※	選	M
專題研究※	選	M/D

3. 資訊儲存與檢索

課程名稱	必選修	開設階段
線上資訊檢索	必	B
索引與摘要	選	B
資訊儲存與檢索	必	B/M
索引典結構與製作※	選	B/M
資訊組織與主題分析※	選	B/M
多媒體資料檢索※	選	B/M
自然語言處理	選	M
中文資訊處理專題研討	選	M/D
人機關係與介面研討	選	M/D
專題研究※	選	M/D

4. 資訊系統分析、設計與評估

課程名稱	必選修	開設階段
系統分析	選	B
作業系統※	選	B
光碟與多媒體系統	選	B
管理資訊系統	選	B
資料庫管理系統	選	B
系統設計與評估※	選	B/M
系統理論※	選	B/M
分散式系統※	選	B/M
CAI 課程原理與設計	選	B/M
物件導向資料庫（Object-Oriented dB）	選	B/M
影像處理系統	選	M
互動式系統（Interactive Systems）	選	M
資訊檢索系統評估※	選	M
平行與分散式系統	選	M
專家系統專題研討	選	M/D
人類資訊處理（Human Information Processing）	選	M/D
知識基礎系統※	選	M/D
視覺化資訊系統設計※	選	M/D
專題研究※	選	M/D

5. 資訊科學與技術

課程名稱	必選修	開設階段
資訊科學導論	必	B
資訊傳播學概論※	選	B
電子出版※	選	B
資訊技術與管理※	選	B
資訊處理標準※	選	B/M
資訊傳播技術※	選	B/M
資訊學研討	選	M
資訊與檔案維護技術※	必	M
多媒體專題研討	選	M
資訊科技與非營利機構※	選	M
資訊與知識專題研討※	選	M/D
書目計量學	選	M/D
圖書館與資訊工業	選	M/D
資訊經濟學	選	M/D
資訊與技術基礎建設專題研討※ (Information and Technological Infrastructures)	選	M/D
專題研究※	選	M/D

（續上表）

課程名稱	必選修	開設階段
資訊科學專題研討	選	D
資訊科學教育	選	D
資訊理論※	選	D
資訊專業研究※	選	D

6. 圖書館自動化、網路與通訊

課程名稱	必選修	開設階段
圖書館自動化	必	B
網路資源與利用※	選	B
電腦通訊與網路	選	B
多媒體概論	選	B
電子傳播科技※	選	B/M
圖書館自動化專題研究	選	B/M
多媒體技術與應用※	選	B/M
視覺通訊※	選	B/M
電子圖書館研討※	選	M
網路設計與管理※	選	M
資訊網路服務研討※	選	M
檔案自動化專題※	選	M
網路介面專題※	選	M
圖書資訊系統專題	選	M/D
專題研究※	選	M/D

7. 資訊政策與管理

課程名稱	必選修	開設階段
資訊管理	必	B
網路與介面管理※	選	B/M
資訊科技與組織管理※	選	B/M
政府資訊政策、資源與服務※	選	M
光電技術與資訊管理※	選	M
媒體中心管理	選	M
電腦中心管理	選	M
資訊資源管理（IRM）	選	M
資訊政策	選	M/D
資訊管理與分析研討	選	M/D
資訊環境管理※	選	M/D
資訊服務政策專題※	選	M/D
網路通訊政策與法規※	選	M/D
專題研究※	選	M/D

8. 資訊社會、倫理與其他

課程名稱	必選修	開設階段
資訊素養※	選	B
圖書資訊法規※	選	B
組織/資訊倫理※	選	B/M
媒體資訊學法規※	選	B/M
資訊倫理專題※	選	M/D
資訊自由化與檢查制度專題※	選	M/D
智慧財產※	選	M/D
圖書館與資訊社會	選	M/D
專題研究※	選	M/D

　　總之，根據臺灣與美加地區資訊科學課程比較分析結果顯示，臺灣資訊科學課程，無論在課程項目、內容的完整性及深廣度的設計方面皆明顯不足。特別是課程間之層次關係、先後順序皆少予區分，不如美加課程層次分明，課程除利用數字代號註明外，並在每門課程內容的描述中，明確訂出與其他課程間之關係及選修時應注意之事項，課程設計系統化而不易混淆。臺灣大學部的資訊科學課程之設計與規劃，因多是基礎課程，尚切合理適用，但研究所博碩士班的資訊科學課程方面，各校設計理念不同，欠缺嚴謹設計而突顯其零亂而無目標，課程似乎多因人而設。最明顯的是博士班資訊科學課程似乎少至又少，可說是沒有任何規劃設計。當然，設計理想而完整的課程不易，但在結束二十世紀前之今日，仍期望臺灣圖書資訊教育決策者運用他/她們的智慧、慎思而執著，並參考本研究所擬定之資訊科學課程名單，整合規劃圖書館學和資訊科學課程，為臺灣設計一套深淺層次有系統化的、適應性、前瞻性、多元化、適時而又具彈性的整體圖書資訊學課程，已因應並迎合二十一世紀資訊時代環境和快速變遷之挑戰。

（收稿日期：1998 年 8 月 14 日）

註　釋

註①：H. Borko, "Information Science：What is it?" <u>American Documentations</u>, 19（Jan. 1968）．pp. 3-5.

註②：G. A. Forgionne, "Providing Complete and Integrated Information Science Education," <u>Information Processing and Management</u>, 27（1991），pp. 575-590.

註③：Jon-Arild Johnnessen, "The Cognitive Authority of Information：Information Science, the Theory of Science and Ethics." In Johan Olaisen, Erland Munch-Petersen and Patarick Wilson, eds. <u>Information Science：From the Development of the Discipline to Social Interaction.</u> Boston：Scandinavian University Pr. 1996. pp. 113-134.

註④：M. F. Stieg, <u>Change and Challenges in Library and Information Science Education</u>（Chicago：ALA, 1992），pp. 106-127.

註⑤：Hose-Marie Griffiths and Donald W. King, <u>New Directions in Library and Information</u>

Science Education（Westport. Conn：Greenwood. 1985），p. 465

註⑥：李德竹，"我對改進圖書資訊學教育的淺見"，上海高校圖書情報季刊，13 期（1994），頁 7。

註⑦："中華圖書資訊學教育學會"編，圖書資訊學系所現況暨教育文獻書目（臺北：編者，1998 年），頁 1—4。

註⑧：Larry J. Ostler, Therrin C. Dahlin and H. D. Willardson, The Closing of American Library Schools（London：Greenwood. 1995）. pp. 1－5.

註⑨：李德竹教授之資訊科學概論課程講義。

註⑩："Library School and Training Courses," American Library Directory 1996－97. Vol 1, 49th ed.（New Providence, NJ：Bowker, 1997），pp. 2473－2491.

註⑪：1997/98 ALISE Directory, 28th ed. （Arlington, VA：ALISE, 1998），pp. 5, 21, 27－115.

註⑫：U. S News：（http//www. usnews. com/usnews/edu/beyond/gradrank/gbinfos. html 1998）

註⑬：Jack Gourman, The Gourman Report：a Rating of Graduate and Professional Programs in American and International Universities, Eight Revised Ed. （New York：Random House, 1997）.

註⑭：http：//www. cis. drexel. edu（1998，7）
http：//www. slis. lib. indiana. edu（1998，7）
http：//istweb. syr. edu（1998，7）
http：//www. lis. gesis. ucla. edu/LIS（1998，7）
http：//alexia. lis. uiuc. edu（1998，7）
http：//search. si. umich. edu（1998，7）
http：//www. sis. pitt. edu（1998，7）
http：//www. scils. rutgers. edu（1998，7）
http：//www. gslis. utexas. edu（1998，7）
http：//www. fis. utoronto. ca（1998，7）
http：//polyglot. lss. wisc. edu（1998，7）
http：//www. simmons. edu/gslis（1998，7）
http：//www. ils. unce. edu（1998，7）

註⑮：李德竹，美國、大陸和臺灣地區圖書館學系所資訊科學課程之研究（臺北："行政院國科會"，1994 年）。NSC 82－0301－H－002－093。

圖書館學與資訊科學課程革新之探討*

關鍵字（keywords）：課程改革（curiculum reformation），課程設計（course design），圖書館學史（library science history），資訊科學史（information science history）

[摘要] 面對二十一世紀的來臨，圖書館學與資訊科學課程的革新是必然的趨勢。本文將從圖書館學發展的歷程及圖書館社會環境的重要改變，探討圖書館學與資訊科學課程改革的趨勢與方向。課程革新有四個主要趨勢：一、資訊技術與資訊服務發展仍將主導課程設計，課程應時更新已成常態；二、核心課程的界定更爲困難，選修課程成爲發展主流；三、課程內容應強調理論及研究；四、終身學習教育成爲課程發展的核心。

[Abstract] In facing the coming of the 21st century, the reformation of library and information science curriculum have become a necessity. The purpose of this paper attempts to study and analyze, from the historical, social and environmental points of view, the directions and changes in the library and information science curriculum, It seems that four major trends related to curriculum reformations: 1. The development of information technology and information servies have great influenced on the course design; 2. The distinction between core courses and the electives becomes difficult, and the electives have tendency to be the predominant courses; 3. The content of these courses should emphasis on research and theoretical studies and, 4. Life-long learning will be the center of curriculum design.

一、前言

資訊技術的進步影響人類社會的發展與工作環境的變革，圖書館是社會機構的一份子，亦深受影響。近年來，無論美國、英國、中國臺灣地區或大陸地區的圖書館學系所，相繼更改系名或更改課程名稱及其內容。面對這一連串圖書館學課程重大的革新，已引發圖書館學界的關切與研討。面對二十一世紀的來臨，臺灣地區開始進行一系列教育的改革，大幅放寬高等教育的管制，鼓勵各校自主發展，對課程的限制亦大幅放鬆。在此教育開放政策下，臺灣地區圖書館學校在課程設計上，具備更彈性的發展空間，但相對也造成課程設計的難題。即使如此，面對跨越下一世紀資訊社會的來臨，若無法對教育提出前瞻性的看法，將影響學科未來的發展力。因此，改變是必要的，但如何改變，且能符合發展趨勢，將是今日課程改革的重點。本文將從圖書館學發展歷程及圖書館社會環境的重要改變兩方面，探討圖書館學與資訊科學課程改革的趨勢與方向。

二、圖書館學與資訊科學發展歷程

（一）美國圖書館學會的設立

近代圖書館學的興起，應該自1876年美國圖書館學會及1887年杜威（Melvil

---

* 本文與世新大學圖書資訊學系莊道明教授合作完成，曾發表在《資訊傳播與圖書館學》4卷1期（1997年9月），第17—25頁。

Dewey）在紐約哥倫比亞大學設立第一所圖書館學校（The School of Library Economy at Columbia University）開始。十九世紀末美國高等教育快速的興起，當時教師鼓勵學生不以教科書為知識的唯一的來源，要求學生多利用圖書館的藏書，以追求更廣泛的知識。此外，德國的研討式教學法也深深影響了美國的學者，而紛紛要求在圖書館設立研討資料專櫃（Seminar-Collections），同時也開啟了系圖書室的制度。[①] 此種教學方式的變革，引發對圖書館經營方式的改變。當時多數學校的圖書館每日只開放幾個小時，並無專門的管理人員，多由教師以輪職方式看管圖書館。面對教學改變的壓力，全時且專業的圖書館員就成為當時圖書館首要解決的問題。

為配合當時美國高等教育的興革、課程的擴充及研究上的需要。十九世紀末大學圖書館面臨改革的壓力，此種壓力促使圖書館事業必需走向專業化的道路。1876年10月4日在美國費城（Philadelphia）美國圖書館學會（American Library Association）正式成立，當時共有103位館員參加。創會的著名人物包括杜威（Melvil Dewey）、溫森（Justin Winsor）及普爾（William F. Poole），溫森當選首任的會長，杜威為首任學會的執行秘書。而整個學會的成立得歸功於杜威的推動。當時杜威年僅25歲，剛畢業於恩合斯特學院（Amherst College），充滿年輕朝氣，富有衝勁及活力。[②] 美國圖書館學會的成立，象徵圖書館事業已該開始邁向專業化及標準化的道路。透過學會的領導，美國學術圖書館的從業人員的專業地位開始獲得肯定，同時就業也獲得應有的保障。大學圖書館成為學校教育機構重要的一環，館員與教師同樣地必需擔負起學校教學的任務。

（二）圖書館學校的創建與發展

美國圖書館學會成功的經驗，再度鼓舞杜威從事另一個事業的開創。在杜威的想法中，認為正規的學校教育，才是真正回應圖書館事業及提昇圖書館服務的主要關鍵。當時圖書館的經營大多依賴個人的工作經驗、詢問他人、參考相關文獻或是參加學會活動。杜威認為圖書館從業人員也該如同醫生、律師或是教師一般，接受正規教育訓練的培育。鑒於當時欠缺一套足以訓練各類型圖書館工作的教材及訓練方法，因而促使杜威決心創辦圖書館學校的想法。杜威於1978年的學會年會，曾提議討論有關圖書館員訓練的問題，但未獲大會的接受。雖然其後又提出替代性的方案，建議由圖書館界較著名的館員，研擬一套有系統的教學方法，但仍未獲得當時會員的支持。直到1883年5月7日杜威接受哥倫比亞學院圖書館館長一職後，才有機會實現他第二個理想。當時杜威32歲。[③]

杜威在當時哥倫比亞學院院長巴爾納德（F. Barnard）的支持下，於1887年成立美國第一所圖書館學校，從此開啟了圖書館學正規教育的大門。當時杜威堅信圖書館學校必需依附在一個大的學術圖書館底下，這樣的信念使得早期圖書館學的發展偏向實務的教學，以致於當時的授課是採學徒制形式。課程內容包括編目、分類、書目學及圖書館經營等基本科目及專題演講。學生除了教室上課外，每天有三小時的圖書館實習，以使學生能獲得圖書館的實務工作。[④]

1891年杜威在學會年會上，針對圖書館教育的現代專業的要求，揭諸了以下幾個要點：[⑤]

1. 圖書館的榮譽：與醫生、律師及部長為社會所認可一樣。學生對其所選擇的事業必需有正確的認知及目標。

2. 使興趣能完全與所學相配合，並以正確的方法教育民眾，訓練與實務要結合。

3. 訓練學生具有現代化的管理方法與視野，同時也要多觀察其他圖書館的成就，以使學生具備有多方面的觀點。
　　4. 館員必須在其專業上不斷發展，才不致於落後於學校教育，使圖書館教育成爲館員晉昇的階梯。
　　5. 圖書館學校教育必需保證每位畢業生所受的訓練品質及服務水準，如此才能贏得別人對圖書館專業的尊重。
　　1919年紐約卡內基基金會（Carnegie Corporation of New York）委託威廉生（Charles C. Williamson）調查當時15所美國圖書館學校的教育狀況。依據調查報告，11個學校的專業圖書館課程共有26門。這些課程之中有5門特別的重視，即編目、圖書選擇、參考工作、分類及圖書館行政。由此看出在1920年以前，圖書館學的發展已屬於穩定的常態科學，其中核心課程已建立共識，課程內容多以實務工作爲主。⑥1926年美國圖書館學會因威廉生的報告，開始制定一套圖書館營運基本標準，分別制定四種不同圖書館教育計劃。1933年公佈《圖書館學校基本要件》（Minimun Requirements for Library School），這些標準的設立更奠定了圖書館學校專業的要求。⑦1930年美國芝加哥大學設立第一所圖書館博士班課程，開啟了圖書館學高等教師的培育。至此美國圖書館學教育體系發展大致完備。
　　1930年至1945年間爆發第二次世界大戰。美國本土並未遭受炮火波及，得以在戰後快速復元。1951至1969年間可稱爲美國圖書館發展的黃金歲月，主要歸功於戰後東西方冷戰，美國爲能趕上蘇聯的太空技術，而致力於科學教育的改革，因而帶動了圖書館教育的蓬勃發展，要求改革傳統圖書館教育，增加資訊科學課程的聲音也逐漸形成。此時圖書館學界開始討論圖書館學的教育制度及課程的內容，但多數仍然在原有的基礎上做修正。例如1951年美國圖書館學會公佈新標準，將專業館員的認定提昇到碩士學位，1953年芝加哥大學圖書館學研究所召開核心課程的研討會，建議擴大圖書館的社會責任，提昇傳播的功能，增加研究的方法，實務工作將不再列入課程之中。⑧
　　（三）資訊科學的興起
　　二次大戰結束後，無論歐洲或亞洲均忙著收拾殘破的家園，重整國家的內務。而唯獨美國在未受戰火的攻擊下，配合大量湧入各國高級人才，造成戰後一片繁榮的景象。二次大戰期間，許多德國著名的科學家爲躲避德國納粹的迫害，紛紛逃亡美國。間接也促進美國在國防工業及基礎科學的進步。戰後東西雙方進入冷戰時期，美蘇各自進行一場太空競賽，美國爲能趕上蘇聯的太空科技，大幅度的修正高等教育制度，投入大量經費於科學研究上。戰後1945年至1955年期間，這是各學科文獻快速增加的年代，許多科學家開始感受到資訊爆炸的危機，此種危機包括：⑨
　　1. 科技出版品快速的增加，在1910年有關化學及化工的期刊圖書也只不過13,000種，但到1975年已增加到413,000種，增加了31倍之多。
　　2. 科技期刊種數不斷的增加，將降低使用的效率。
　　3. 許多未出版的科技文獻，例如小冊子、研究報告、備忘錄等重要性日增。
　　4. 非傳統紙本的資料快速增加，例如磁帶、電子出版品、微縮資料等。
　　5. 科學家花在科技資訊的活動時間延長，包括找尋資料及閱讀文獻、準備報告或研討等。

6. 研究領域的窄化,使科學家在應付日益成長的科技資訊產生無力感。
7. 從日益增多的科技文獻中,找尋特定的科技文獻困難度增加。

面臨以上危機困難,首先想解決這些問題的往往是深受其苦的科學家。

在1945年布希(Vannevar Bush)在 Atlantic Monthly 期刊上發表一篇深具啓發性的文章,文章標題"As We may Think"。布希以其工程的背景描繪了一部他理想中的機器 Memex(取自 Memory + Index)。這部機器可以無限制的儲存圖書、期刊及各種資料。由於整部機器採用機械的原理,所以可以從事快速的運作、儲存及檢索資料。[10]雖然布希並沒製造這部機器,但確爲後來的資訊科學及電腦發明起了啓發作用。1940年代的末期,在賓州大學的幾位科學家已默默將第一代電腦 ENIAC(Electric Numerical Integrater and Calculator)創造出來。資訊系統的產生,輔助了資訊科學理論的發展,自此揭開了資訊科學發展的序頁。

回顧1945到1985年間,資訊科學發展的歷史,有24位先驅者(Pioneers)爲代表。這24位先驅者的學科背景均不相同,貢獻亦各不相同,大致可以區分成五個階段:[11]

第一階段資訊科學夢想家(visionary)時期:此一時期約從1945至1968年之間。包括資訊科學的思想啓發者與美國國家科學基金會的創始者的布希(V. Bush),亦是一位工程師;第一代電腦修改的啓發者亦是著名的數學家溫能(N. Wiener, 1894—1964);布萊福德定律的創立者,亦是科學家暨文獻學家的布萊福德(S. C. Bradford, 1878—1948);預見地球衛星的產生,本身是一位科幻作家的克拉克(A. C. Clarke, 1917—)及通訊數學基本公式創立者的雪儂(C. E. Shannon)。以上五位被稱之資訊科學的夢想家(Dreamers),他們重要的貢獻乃對今日資訊科學發展,提出創新性的想法。包括基礎理論的建立(如雪諾、布萊福德),基本工具架構的想像(如布希、溫能、克拉克)。由於他們大膽的想像與假設,爲後人留下嘗試的機會。

第二階段非傳統資訊系統的先驅者(1948—1968)時期:在1948年至1968年間,電腦已由第一代真空管進步到第三代積體電路。不但運算更快速、記憶體儲存量與可靠程度亦大幅提昇,關鍵是電腦價格降低。電腦程式語言廣泛使用,一部電腦可同時提供多人同時使用。由於電腦工具的成熟,資訊科學家開始嘗試利用電腦從事非數字運算的處理,包括文字自動索引摘要等研究。此一時期重要的資訊科學家,包括圖伯(M. Taube, 1910—1965)利用組合索引用法,製作資訊系統使資訊系統從事邏輯檢索儲存。發明家也是工程師的魯恩(H. P. Luhn, 1896—1964)發明 KWIC/KWOC 索引法及專題資訊選粹資訊系統(SDI System);化學家加菲德(E. Garfielld, 1925—)發明引用索引(Citation Index)法,運用於科學文獻分析工作,後又運用於社會科學、人文學的文獻處理,他同時是美國科學資訊研究所(Institute for Scientific Information, ISI)的創始人。以上三位非圖書館學領域的科學家,首度利用以電腦資料處理架構,嘗試爲處理文字,建立處理的方法,採取非傳統資料儲存方式及檢索法的開創者。當中除了圖伯曾於美國國會圖書館擔任過科技計劃主持人(Head of the Science and Technology Project)外,其餘二位均非圖書館本行。他們新創的概念及方法爲當時的圖書館界,造成相當的震撼與衝擊。許多館員最初抱持著排斥的心態,然而部份館員則附和而加入研究的行列,當然批叛的聲音也此起彼落。[12]隨著電腦技術發展日益成熟,改革創新的趨勢已非傳統圖書館學可以抵擋。1963年美國文獻學會(American Documentation Institute, ADI)

正式更名為美國資訊科學學會（American Society for Information Science，ASIS）。

　　第三階段資訊科學應用在圖書館（1958— ）時期：自 1961 年美國三個 "國家圖書館" 即美國國會圖書館（Library of Congress），美國國家醫學圖書館（National Library of Medicine）及美國國家農業圖書館（National Agricultural Library），已認識到資訊科學應用於圖書館，將漸漸具有領導性的地位，尤其資訊科學近 30 年發展的成就，已使圖書館認識到資訊科學的研究，不但有助於圖書館業務的發展，同時也有助於讀者服務。[13] 此一時期有三位重要的資訊專家，投入圖書館文獻資訊處理的研究行列。包括艾芬蓉（H. D. Avram）設計 MARC I, MARC Ⅱ, RECON，同時也是美國國家資訊網路的推動者。蓋雷諾（R. De Gennaro）是圖書館自動化與網路的研究者與監督者。蓋格爾（F. G. Kilgour）則創立全美第一個也是世界最大的書目共用中心 OCLC。以上三位資訊專家，結合圖書館學背景及電腦資訊系統，成功將資訊科學引進傳統圖書館的服務上。

　　第四階段線上資訊活動（1940—1985）時期：數學家戴維斯（R. M. Davis）首度提出人機交互作用理論之研究，隨之黎克賴德（J. C. Licklider）建立人機共生理論（Man-Computer Symbiosis）；夏米特（R. K. Summit）建立 Dialog 系統的管理及擴充；心理學家蔻卓拉（C. A. Cuadra）對圖書館網路，資訊網路，個人電腦及電子出版品有卓越的貢獻；威廉斯（M. E. Williams）在資料庫服務，研究及教授上貢獻良多；賀金斯（D. T. Hawkins）線上書目系統，貝爾實驗室之資訊服務，前端儀器的貢獻；布格曼（C. L. Borgman）人機交互作用；資訊學家坦挪波（C. Tenopir）全文資料庫檢索新技術；圖書館學者海德倫斯（C. R. Hildreth）對人機介面的研究與 OPACs 的研究等。在此階段資訊科學已漸漸脫離以圖書館為架構的服務，著重利用電腦資料庫及通訊網路的線上資訊服務系統。此時出現以資料庫服務為主的線上資料庫服務代理商，如 ORBIT, DIALOG, 及 BRS 等公司，圖書館亦成為這些資料庫公司的使用者。圖書館此時所關心的，是如何引介線上資料庫，以彌補本身資料之不足，及如何推廣線上服務與增強檢索的效率。從以上幾位先驅者的學科背景不難發現，多數均非圖書館學本科的專家。這一時期產生了新型態的專業領導者，新電子出版物增加，新型態的通訊與教育及新型態的資訊使用者。

　　第五階段網路發展（1965— ）時期：圖書館學者貝克（J. Becker）推動國家資訊網路的建立；伊文斯（G. T. Evans）發展紐約州圖書館網路；馬庫森（B. E. Markuson）推展印第安納州的圖書館網路系統；圖書館學馬丁（S. K. Martin）博士則從事網路系統管理的研究。此一時期可以說是圖書館面臨分裂的階段，面對資訊科學的興起及美國圖書館學會內部不合等因素，一些 "國家圖書館" 及資訊中心已不再認同美國圖書館學會，甚至學院及研究圖書館協會（Association of College and Research Libraries）於 1978 年亦想脫離美國圖書館學會。一些會員紛紛投效美國資訊科學學會或是國家線上會議（National Online Meeting）或國際線上會議（International Online Meeting）及美國計算機學會（Association for Computing Machine，ACM）、國際圖書館協會聯盟（International Federation of Library Associations，IFLA）及國際文獻聯盟（International Federation for Information and Documentation，FID）等。[14] 此時許多網路系統已廣泛運用在商業界、法律界、科學界及其他各種組織與學會。全文資料庫及數據資料庫，如雨後春筍般，廣泛被社會大眾所運用。資料庫使用者也開始自己上機檢索資料。

由資訊科學四十年發展史來分析，無論是初期夢想家或是後來的先驅者，從其學科背景可以發現，多數都不是圖書館學本科。面對這樣的發展趨勢，已註定資訊科學的發展是多學科（Interdiciplinary）型態，尤其因先驅者學科背景的差異，對問題的解決採取不同的切入點，造成典範不易形成，此對資訊科學進入常態科學的階段相當不利。資訊科學在欠缺有利的主導力量與學會的引導下，短期間內要進入常態科學的階段將不太容易，百家爭鳴的現況恐仍要持續一段時間。根據愛莎貝姬（I. A. Al-Sabbage）對資訊科學的研究發現，對資訊科學最有貢獻的八個學科領域，分別是電腦科學、圖書館學、一般科學、心理學、管理學、化學、數學及統計學。資訊科學對電腦科學引用的文獻分析，自 1970 年代的 6.02% 一直增加至 1980 年 17.43%，成長達 200%。而資訊科學引用圖書館學的文獻在 1970 年至 1975 年是 14.3%，1975 至 1979 年約 15.13%，但到 1980 至 1985 年則降低到 9.4%。此種現象減少顯示圖書館學與資訊科學的關係已越來越薄弱，但對與電腦科學的關係越來越密切。[15]此種關係在未來將繼續持續下去，但以目前資訊科學尚未形成一門獨立學科發展，對於其學科內容課程綱要尚未有定論。

三、課程變革幾個環境要素

（一）圖書館進入資訊傳播的時代

美國自柯林頓總統上臺以來，以高爾副總統為首宣佈與推動國家資訊基礎建設（National Information Infrastructure，簡稱 NII），已引發許多國家的仿效，紛紛開始研擬自己國家的資訊基礎建設，相繼已有新加坡的 IT2000 年智慧島計劃、菲律賓 2000 年國家資訊計劃、日本的資訊技術基礎建設新政策、歐體資訊基礎建設以及"臺灣臺灣地區建立亞太營運中心計劃下的國家資訊基礎建設計劃專案"等。一場國家與國家間的資訊競賽已正式起跑，在可見的未來將因 NII 計劃的完成，推向全球資訊基礎建設（Global Information Infrastructure，簡稱 GII），達到世界地球村的境界。NII 全球發展的趨勢，對圖書館事業發展將產生相當大的衝擊。由圖書館學發展歷程中不難發現，圖書館服務的內涵深受資訊技術發展的影響。現今也不例外，電腦與通訊的結合已為資訊社會開創新的資訊傳播環境，NII 的發展勢必為資訊社會奠立基礎。圖書館也應隨著環境的變遷繼續成長。面對 NII 的發展圖書館應該以大格局的心胸，努力接受並研擬相關的服務，將人類知識有效傳播給所有公民使用。以往圖書館受限於傳播工具與經費的限制，使得圖書館的推廣服務始終無法有效的向外傳播給全體公民。而在此限制下圖書館不得不設立分館，購買圖書巡迴車，或以郵寄借書方式推廣服務。如今透過網際網路，圖書館可以在網路上大張旗鼓的行銷圖書館各項的資訊服務，同時將圖書館終身學習的社會教育理念透過網路付諸實行。因此，圖書館在網際網路服務上，應從傳播訊息的角度，致力將紙本文獻與訊息轉成數位化資訊，透過網際網路將資訊傳遞到民眾的家中。將圖書館傳統有限的，"推廣"概念擴展到無遠弗屆的"傳播"理念。圖書館館員除從事數位化資料的管理之外，並應協助讀者分析處理各類資訊。指導讀者於網路上擷取資訊、解讀分析資訊，使圖書館成為民眾初入網際網路的大門，館員成為民眾通往網際網路的向導。未來圖書館將逐步邁向電子圖書館的新境界。

（二）圖書館與其他相關單位服務互競的開始

以往各服務機構有其特定的管道、提供特定的服務給特定對象。因此，服務的區隔相當的明顯。如今在網路上，就資訊消費者而言，所有的服務均集中於一個攤位上（電腦終端機）。因此要在網路上，明顯區隔出自己獨一無二的服務，將是一件不容易的事。現今因提供網路資訊服務的單位與內容更加多樣化，圖書館將不可避免會與其他資訊服務單位如電腦中心、資訊中心、商業資訊中心等，產生服務互競或重疊的問題。南西・希基肋（Nancy Schiller）針對美國大學的圖書館與電腦中心在 Internet 使用訓練與支援調查中，發現美國大學電腦中心無論在"告知網路使用者相關 Internet 的資源與工具"，"協助使用者上線使用網路資源"，或"教導使用者的服務工作"上，都比圖書館來的積極與頻繁。研究也發現圖書館館員對讀者的網路服務，主要仍以線上書目資料庫的查尋為主，但電腦中心的查尋服務的主題範圍則較為廣泛普遍。顯示圖書館在 Internet 資源的利用上，仍沒有跨出傳統書目利用服務的範疇。問卷的結果反應出，現今由於圖書館與電腦中心設立性質不同，因而二者在提供資訊服務上仍各有其特色，在服務的內涵上可以產生互補作用。目前許多美國大學的電腦中心與圖書館已共同合作推出一系列網路使用課程。許多尚未有具體行動的單位，也表示未來有意願彼此相互合作。雖然如此，但從回覆的問卷之中也發現，許多館員內心已感受到來自電腦中心服務的威脅；相對地，電腦中心的職員也擔憂圖書館的資訊服務會侵犯到電腦中心的服務功能。[16]面對網路快速的發展，許多商業機構在未來，勢必也會推出更多的資訊服務。屆時圖書館如何在眾多資訊服務之中，仍能保持獨特的圖書資訊服務與內涵，將是圖書館從業人員深思與規劃的主題。

（三）由資訊處理轉變為知識的整理

隨著科技快速的進步，各種記錄人類知識的媒體更多樣化。從傳統紙類的圖書及視聽資料，到近年快速崛起的光碟資料庫、多媒體、電子書、虛擬實體（Virtual Reality）、國際網際網路各種資訊站［如電子佈告欄（BBS）］、電子期刊（E-Journal）、電子報紙（E-Newspaper）、World Wide Web 等。已使資訊的種類與型態更多樣化與非規格化。面對資訊組織形式規格的解體，圖書館學對人類知識的徵集、處理、儲存與推廣工作進行，將不能只對裝載知識的媒體作處理，更重要的是針對媒體內容知識的整理與研究。尤其目前各國出版商大舉利用國際學術網路傳播資訊的現況下，部份文獻已停止紙本文獻的印刷出版，而改以電子方式在網路上傳遞。面對此種趨勢，圖書館必須面對如何處理電子文獻的問題。換言之，如何對電子文獻內容作有效的整理，使之具備可供檢索利用，將是未來圖書館學與資訊科學發展的主流。

（四）跨領域或國界研究合作需求的增加

圖書館學的發展始終不脫離以圖書館為經營目的的課程方針。而圖書館的經營亦不脫離人類知識的儲存與使用。然而在今日電腦通訊科技的進步下，許多學科領域的科學家也對人類知識產生的過程、使用能力、消費利用情況產生研究的興趣。例如，心理學家嘗試探究人類對於各種資訊認知的歷程、電腦專家探討人腦與電腦資訊處理或檢索的差異、社會學家探究知識傳播對於人類社會發展的影響。類似以人類知識為主題的研究也越來越多。此外，隨著網際網路的盛行，資訊已無分國界。面對資訊傳播所引發出的文化衝擊、資訊政策擬訂、商業行為規範，智慧產權的保護，已成為各國政府積極探討的議題。由資訊傳播所引發出的一連串問題，已不再只是一門學科或一個國家所要解決的主題，而是跨領域與跨國際間共同合作研究的學門。因此，面對此全球資訊發展的趨勢,圖書館學與資訊科學的發展,將面臨更大格局的環境變化。

四、課程革新的趨勢

(一) 資訊技術與資訊服務的發展仍將主導課程設計,課程應時更新已成常態

圖書館學與資訊科學課程的變革,最主要是仍是受到資訊技術進步的影響。從圖書館學發展的演變分析,杜威初期在設計課程時只有編目、分類、書目學及圖書館經營等課程。在1920年以前,圖書館學課程屬於穩定常態發展,對於核心課程有一定的共識,課程內容仍以實務工作爲主。從1951年起,受到美蘇科技競賽與電腦科技的蓬勃發展,影響所及是全面性的變革。1953年芝加哥大學召開的核心課程研討會中,已體認資訊科技將帶動圖書館學未來的發展,因此建議將實務性課程取消。自此以後,資訊科學的發展隨著電腦技術的進步,快速的成長。美國圖書館學校體認到資訊技術與服務的發展已成爲未來趨勢之下,紛紛更改課程內容,並於學系名稱加上資訊科學,以反應時代的需要。至今這種趨勢並沒有改變,只是隨著資訊技術進步的加速,圖書館學與資訊科學課程的變動與更新將更頻繁與不穩定。面對此現象,課程應時變革,應該視爲一種常態而非不尋常現象。因此,圖書館學校因應社會的需要與資訊技術的進步,應定期檢討課程整體的結構,評估課程的內容,調整師資陣容,更新學習設備,才能應付未來資訊社會的需求。

(二) 核心課程的界定更爲困難,選修課程成爲發展主流

1926年美國圖書館學會因威廉生的報告,開始著手研擬圖書館基本標準。1933年正式公佈《圖書館學校基本要件》(Minimun Requirements for Library School),標準要件的設立以確保專業訓練的品質及相關課程與設備的基本要求。此標準的公佈使得美國圖書館學校課程趨向標準模式發展。美國圖書館學會認可委員會(ALA's Committee on Accreditation)對於碩士課程訂立出四個基本發展方向。即課程應1. 闡明圖書館在教育與資訊機構的角色;2. 理解圖書資料蒐集、整理與組織的相關理論;3. 資訊媒體的知識與協助讀者尋得其所需資料,與闡釋資料內容之相關能力;4. 因提供服務所需之組織管理原則之知識。上述四個原則即成爲各校課程設計的核心宗旨。⑰許多學校依此分別設計出12至15學分的必修課程。第一個採取整體核心課程設計,是席拉(Jesse Shera)於1960年代任教於Case Western Reserve大學設計出來,至此許多學校乃延用之。某些學校整體核心課程的設計是以圖書館學基礎(Foundations of Librarianship)課程爲核心,每核心課程再輔以一些技術爲主的課程;另一種整體核心課程設計方式,是將9至12個學分的課程設計成一羣組的課程結構;或呈一系列前後相關的課程。此種核心課程設計通常以6個學分爲基礎,再配上3至6個其他學分。此整體核心課程設計的宗旨,強調對共通性專業知識的傳授,而非針對特定類型圖書館或資訊服務項目講授。採用整體核心課程的學校中,以美國Drexel大學實行時間最久,也最具成效。上述整體核心課程的內容仍不脫離參考、分類編目、行政與採訪等。圖書館學校強調核心課程設計,也顯示圖書館學校維護傳統圖書館服務企圖。但面對其他資訊學科或傳播技術課程的日趨重要,如何將這些學門融入核心課程,已是課程發展重要的問題。目前以臺灣地區而言,"教育部"在大學法施行之後,對於各校各學系課程的管理,採取開放政策由各校自主,對必選修學分的規定採彈性做法。減少必修課程,增加選修科目與通識課程的新教育政策,將可提供學生多樣化具選擇性的選課空間。此趨勢使學生可多方面涉獵廣泛各種知

識，以促成科際整合[13]。臺灣地區在各校自主的原則下，核心課程的規劃雖有其必要性，但往往因各校課程設計方式或教育理念的差異，對核心課程不易產生共識。因此，是否仍需維繫一個核心課程，以不變應萬變；或由各校自行設計課程，自行驗証課程效果之後，再改進檢討，也是值得考量的問題。

(三) 課程內容應強調理論與研究

圖書館學自冠上"科學"（Science）二字，即受到許多學者的質疑與引發爭議。究其爭議的重點仍在於圖書館學是否獨創出特有的知識理論，亦或掌握奧秘性知識，類似此類的質疑至今仍然存在。回顧圖書館學發展的歷程，不難發現圖書館學課程是一門特重實務的學科，欠缺理論的建立與探討。面對現今科技發展的挑戰、社會環境快速的變遷以及來自電腦學科互競的壓力下，圖書館的功能與角色，勢必作大幅度的變革。許多圖書館學與資訊科學的專家，已注意至NII所帶來的衝擊，將帶來社會工作環境全面的改觀，圖書館自然亦深受影響。館員的角色將改變提昇為資訊導航員。面對未來資訊化社會的衝擊，圖書館學與資訊科學的發展，已不能只停留在維繫傳統圖書館實務性的服務工作，必需加緊腳步研究資訊學的理論與學說。在圖書館學與資訊科學課程中，應強調研究與發展，並將理論與實務結合於教學中。[19]

(四) 終身學習教育成為課程發展的核心

二十一世紀是高齡化、資訊化、科技化的時代，屆時公民除了具備正規教育外，如何生活得更充實與健康，實有賴於資訊的獲取與利用。NII的發展是促成此發展的主要動力。面對二十一世紀電子化圖書館的發展趨勢，館員將是社區資訊的提供者、教育者、資訊專家。提昇全民的資訊素養，也將是館員重要的工作之一。因此，如何藉由課程的設計與安排，教育圖書館學系學生具備資訊素養，將是課程發展的重心。資訊素養課程的核心設計，應該含蓋圖書館素養、電腦素養、媒體素養與網路素養四大項。根據臺灣地區"教育部"公佈的《教育報告書：邁向二十一世紀的教育遠景》中，已明示配合推展終身教育體制與學習社會的來臨，將研擬或修訂社會教育法、成人教育法、圖書館法、博物館法等，使終身教育法制化。[20]因此，圖書館學與資訊科學教育課程的安排，為配合此教育政策的發展，勢必將終身教育作為未來課程設計的目標。以圖書館素養、電腦素養、媒體素養與網路素養為基礎設計相關課程。

五、結論

圖書館學是一個成長的有機體，隨著社會時代的改變及NII計劃的推展，圖書館學與資訊科學課程的革新是必然的趨勢。回顧圖書館學發展的歷史，核心課程隨資訊技術的進步與時代需要調整與改變。資訊科學的興起，更刺激與改變今日圖書館服務的內涵與方式。然而課程的改革，只是改變的第一步。如何將新課程以新教學法予以實現，則有賴於教師的努力。舉凡"換湯不換藥"的課程更名，都無助於課程的革新。因此，在研擬新課程發展時，不應忽略新師資的招募，鼓勵現任教師從事研究發展及教育訓練的相關工作。對於新課程也應切實施行並定期評估修訂。[21]二十一世紀即將來臨，"改變"是迎接新時代來臨重要的前兆。圖書館要跨越到二十一世紀，勢必要面臨一些改變與調整。今日圖書館學與資訊科學課程改革，將影響未來圖書館的發展與生存。迎接改變、接受改變、願意改變，將為學科發展創造新機。我們樂見二十一世紀的圖書館仍是一個充滿生機與活力的資訊通路。

註　釋

註①：M. A. Coffey, The Evolution of Libraianship into a Profession. (Ph. D. Dissertation), (Michigan：UMI, 1990)：pp. 30－37.

註②：同註①，頁45—46。

註③：同註①，頁66—67。

註④：C. M. White, A Historical Introduction to Library Education：Problem and Progress to 1951, (N. J.：Scarecrow, 1976)：53－55.

註⑤：同註①，頁87。

註⑥：胡述兆，"美國圖書館教育制度" 美國圖書館之教育功能研討會（臺北："中央研究院" 歐美研究所，1993年3月27日），頁1。

註⑦：王振鵠，"美國圖書館教育制度" 圖書館學論叢（臺北：學生，1984年）。

註⑧：同註⑥，頁2。

註⑨：A. I. Mikhailow, A. I. Chernyl, R. S. Galiarevskii, Scientific Communications and Informatics. (Virgina：IRP, 1984)：14－15.

註⑩：V. Bush, "As We may Think" Atlantic Monthly 176：1 (1945)：101－108.

註⑪：D. B. Lilley, R. W. Trice, A History of Information Science, 1945—1985. (New, York：Academic Press, 1989)：136－137.

註⑫：同註⑪，頁17。

註⑬：同註⑪，頁43—44。

註⑭：同註⑪，頁132—133。

註⑮：I. A. Al-Sabbagh, The Evolution of the Interdisciplinary of Information Science：A Bibliographic Study. (Ph. D. Dissertation) (Michigan：UMI, 1987)：130－148.

註⑯：N. Schiller, "Internet Training and Support Academic Libraries and Computer Centers：Who's Doing What?" Internet Research 4：2 (Summer, 1994)：43－44.

註⑰：J. Robbins-Carter, " Library Education ", in World Encyclopedia of Library and Information Services. (Chicago：ALA, 1993)：487.

註⑱："教育部"，教育報告書：邁向二十一世紀的教育遠景。（臺北："教育部"，1995年），頁88。

註⑲：P. Hernon and C. Schwartz, "Editorial：Regaining the Foundation of Understanding：the Role of LIS Education." LISR 17 (1995)：2.

註⑳：同註18，頁219。

註㉑：李德竹，美國、中國大陸和臺灣圖書館學系所資訊科學課程之研究。（臺北："行政院國家科學委員會" 專題研究計劃，1994年），頁129—130。

評析"國立大學"校院圖書館自動化系統線上公用目錄功能與介面特性*

摘　要

臺灣地區圖書館自動化已歷經二十年的緩慢發展，而"國立大學"校院圖書館自動化的發展歷程，在1990年之前則為各自發展的實驗性階段，早期系統多採用自行開發設計形式，其功能皆為單一性。自1991年6月後受到《整體規劃圖書資訊網路系統》研究報告的影響，和"教育部"大力支持"國立大學"校院圖書館自動化計劃，使得"國立大學"校院圖書館紛紛採購系統主機，並從整體規劃的觀點發展圖書館自動化系統。因此，"國立大學"校院圖書館進行自動化比例，在各類型圖書館中獨佔鰲頭。

本計劃主要研究"國立大學"校院圖書館自動化系統之線上公用目錄之檢索功能與介面特性，並以34所"國立大學"校院圖書館、170位讀者及12家圖書館自動化廠商為問卷調查對象，同時彙整館員座談會建議及實地使用經驗，期達成下列研究目的：

1. 調查、評估34所"國立大學"校院圖書館自動化系統之線上公用目錄所提供的各項檢索功能與介面特性。
2. 探討170位讀者（非館員）使用線上公用目錄之意見、評估及期望。
3. 探討圖書館自動化廠商對其線上公用目錄系統的設計及未來發展。
4. 分析目前自動化系統線上公用目錄的主要問題。
5. 建議線上公用目錄系統的基本需求項目及介面標準。
6. 研擬適合臺灣圖書館自動化之線上公用目錄查檢表。

關鍵詞彙：線上公用目錄，介面特性，圖書館自動化系統，公用目錄查檢表，線上目錄檢索功能

一、緒論

近年來由於電腦及網路技術的快速進展，各大學校院紛紛致力於圖書館的自動化工作，尤其自1991年起"教育部"以專案方式提供經費，協助各大學校院進行圖書館自動化，使得"國立大學"校院在短短的三年間不但完成圖書館自動化之主機硬體及圖書館自動化系統軟體的採購、安裝與測試，[1] 並且開放其線上公用目錄（Online Public Access Catalog，簡稱OPAC）於網路上供大眾使用。

圖書館進行自動化作業的目標，除節省圖書館各部門人員在處理資料上的人力、加速資料的處理並提昇對讀者的服務外，最重要的目標之一，是提供讀者方便、快速的書目資訊；而線上公用目錄則是讀者找尋圖書館資源、開啟圖書館寶藏的鑰匙。因此，圖書館自動化系統公用目錄查詢介面設計的好壞與功能的強弱，便成為讀者對圖書館自動化系統評價的依據，甚至於對圖書館館藏及服務良窳的最重要評鑑工具。

---

*　本文曾發表在"國科會"研究彙刊：《人文與社會科學》7卷3期（1997年7月），第334—351頁。

由於目前臺灣對於圖書館自動化系統之線上公用目錄功能與查詢介面，尚無一套可茲依據的設計標準，因而不論是引自海外或由臺灣專家自行設計的線上公用目錄子系統，皆是參照國外系統而設計的，致使系統設計較少考慮到公民使用資料的習慣和中文檢索的特性。隨著圖書館自動化的推展，線上公用目錄已逐漸取代卡片目錄，成為讀者利用圖書館館藏的必備工具；同時，由於電腦的普遍使用，讀者對線上公用目錄之檢索功能與介面的設計也隨著電腦軟體的革新而有更嚴格的要求。為使圖書館自動化系統之線上公用目錄能滿足讀者的期望，擬調查與評估現行"國立大學"校院圖書館自動化系統的線上公用目錄，藉以瞭解各系統的檢索功能與介面設計的特性，分析讀者對線上公用目錄的期望與需求，試研擬一套線上公用目錄系統之查檢表（Checklist），以提供圖書館未來在改進、設計或評估其線上公用目錄系統之參考。

二、文獻探討

自 1960 年代電腦開始應用在圖書館作業以來，為圖書館帶來服務型態及方式上的革命，隨著 1970 年代書目中心的發展，及 1980 年代各種自動化系統的興起，無一不是拜電腦之賜。[2]同時線上公用目錄亦在此時問世，廣為讀者利用及喜愛，近年來線上公用目錄之優劣已成為評斷圖書館自動化系統最重要的指標。

因此，有關線上公用目錄之研究文獻相當豐富，尤以美國發表論文數量為最多，內容也最豐富。根據 1990 年伊思米帝思（Efthimiadis）統計 1970 年至 1985 年線上公用目錄文獻每年平均成長 74.4％，其中以 1984 年達到最高峯。[3]有關線上公用目錄的研究文獻可歸納為檢索功能、螢幕格式、介面設計及讀者行為等四方面加以探討。

（一）檢索功能：尼柯森（Nickerson）於 1990 年提出設計易學易用的線上公用目錄功能，不但應融合圖書館學、電腦學、行為科學、心理學及應用技術等學科，並應由軟體專家、圖書館讀者服務人員及圖書館技術部門共同努力，才能設計出符合大多數讀者需求的線上公用目錄。[4]1991 年斯波爾（Spore）特別重視線上公用目錄中傾錄（downloading）功能，以克服線上公用目錄限於螢幕上閱讀的缺點。[5]1993 年希利（Sealy）亦針對傾錄時發生的雜訊（noise ines）問題提出解決辦法。[6]雀黎（Cherry）等人於 1994 年對加拿大十二個學術性圖書館的線上公用目錄進行調查，以其所研擬的評量表，逐一評估十二個系統的功能與介面特性。該研究結果發現，十個調查項目中，以"顯示格式"設計為最佳，"主題檢索輔助"為最弱功能，此研究成果有助於改善未來圖書館線上公用目錄系統的設計。[7]1994 年奇哥（Kilgour）強調線上公用目錄應以讀者使用為導向，並預測未來二十年圖書館的資料庫中將會涵蓋大量電子書，圖書館可利用網路上的電子書服務讀者，既節省圖書館經費又可增加圖書館館藏。[8]1995 年彼得森（Peterson）認為建置線上公用目錄應有各學科領域人員參與，同時亦應考量其建置及維護成本，並須經圖書館管理者、館內工作人員及讀者充分溝通才能建立適用的線上公用目錄系統。該研究又建議圖書館的書目資料庫應與線上公用目錄分開，其理由為：1. 線上公用目錄之讀者說明需要較清楚易懂之文字，而資料庫則不必；2. 線上公用目錄系統主機當機時讀者仍有資料庫可使用等優點。[9]

（二）螢幕格式：1990 年尼柯森（Nickerson）針對線上公用目錄之螢幕進行研究，結果顯示讀者認為觸摸式螢幕遠較傳統鍵入指令式更具親和力。[10]1992 年薛爾斯

（Shires）和奧賽克（Olszak）二位學者亦提出研究線上公用目錄螢幕格式時，應注意設計原則、選單及項目、指令，以及顯示給讀者之各種訊息等方面。[11]貝希思提（Beheshti）之研究則強調"瀏覽"（browsing）功能是讀者進行查詢資訊活動時一個很重要的功能，而且瀏覽功能應爲隨機式（random）或系統式（systematic）設計，使讀者能在螢幕上看到如書庫架上順序之資訊，以提供讀者一個虛擬型的資料庫。[12]

（三）介面設計：海德瑞斯（Hildreth）在1985年的"Annual Review of Information Science and Technology"，簡稱ARIST，中發表其探討美國地區自1980年至1985年間線上公用目錄的發展趨勢，並比較各種調查研究之內容，及其未來研究的發展方向之論文。其結論是讀者甚爲喜好使用線上公用目錄，但讀者仍有檢索失敗情形，而失敗的原因，多與介面設計有極大的關連性。例如線上公用目錄是否提供讀者適當的使用訊息、各種檢索符號有無說明與畫面的親和程度等之介面設計，這正說明各種功能介面之設計考量才是最重要的。[13]1991年亨利（Henry）研究人機介面和線上公用目錄的關係，認爲以人工智慧（artifical intelligence）設計之人機介面可增進線上公用目錄的功能，並應以使用者（end user）爲設計重點。1993年墨菲（Murphy）、波利特（Pollitt）和懷特（White）等學者亦認爲線上公用目錄應依讀者使用需求而設計。[14]1995年柏頓（Burton）認爲圖書館的線上公用目錄介面設計應朝向開放性系統發展，也就是系統不僅能提供當地的（local）讀者使用，亦能透過網路或其他傳播媒介供全球讀者檢索，正如網際網路（Internet）上的Gopher及Web OPAC中的線上公用目錄即是，除不須花費外，更可在資訊上進行超聯結（hyper link）、多媒體以及提供多樣化的服務特色，此將是未來線上公用目錄介面發展的主流。[15]

（四）讀者檢索行爲：1990年西蒙（Seymour）認爲目前很缺乏對圖書館讀者作研究及分析，未來的讀者研究（user study）應會愈來愈受重視。[16]1992年以加拿大渥太華等五所大學的2,916位讀者，進行關於對線上公用目錄滿意程度的學術研究，發現具有電腦素養（computer literacy）之讀者較常使用線上公用目錄；圖書館更應設計簡明清晰的讀者指示，以幫助讀者學習使用線上公用目錄。[17]1993年的一份調查報告指出：讀者檢索活動中，40%爲已知的資訊項目（known items），此種檢索稱爲問題檢索（query search）；60%的檢索則爲瀏覽檢索（browse search）。另外，亦指出第二代線上公用目錄應在題名和標題方面提供關鍵字檢索，並可使用布林邏輯運算元及線上輔助。[18]1994年在，"Redesign of Known-item Online Access Catalogs"文中，提到若以使用者的觀點設計，線上公用目錄應較傳統的卡片目錄更具備三項優點：1. 可於單一螢幕上顯示核心書目資料，即minicats；2. 讀者不必親至圖書館檢索，可在辦公室或家中檢索；3. 除題名及作者檢索外，還可用關鍵字檢索。[19]

各"國立大學"校院自1991年6月起因"教育部"定期召開"國立大學"校院圖書館自動化規劃研討會並受到政府財務和政策支持下，致使"國立大學"校院圖書館以整體規劃圖書館自動化方式，在短短兩三年間快速發展。但在線上公用目錄方面之研究和文獻卻不多。以下僅依線上公用目錄文獻發表年代略述於後。

李德竹教授在1985年《圖書館與資訊科學論文集》（Library Automated & Information Science: A Collection of Essays）中，曾就線上公用目錄相關的定義、發展歷史、設計評估、研究計劃與對圖書館未來發展，提出全面性的探討與研究。[20]1991年李德竹教授又針對讀者使用線上公用目錄的喜好程度，評估臺灣地區當時 18 個圖書館線上公用目錄顯示格式的特性與功能。研究結果依讀者的需求、檢索的習性與認知，對線上公用目錄的顯示格式設計提出建議。[21]同年，廖育珮以探討臺灣地區大學圖書館線上公用目錄使用者利用指導方式爲其碩士論文之研究重點，並建議圖書館應加強線上公用目錄的輔助功能。[22]

1992 年"教育部"委託"中國圖書館學會圖書館自動化規劃委員會"進行臺灣地區圖書館自動化之調查研究，並於 1993 年 6 月出版《臺灣地區圖書館自動化系統彙編》。根據調查結果，23 個已完成圖書館自動化系統中，18 個單位完成線上公用目錄子系統的運作。這些線上公用目錄子系統介面的設計與功能，有些是修改或仿自海外系統設計；有些則完全由臺灣專家設計。由於目前臺灣對於圖書館自動化系統之線上公用目錄功能與查詢介面設計，尚無一套可茲依據的標準，大部份系統都參照海外的系統設計，造成系統的設計較少考慮到大衆使用習慣與中文檢索的特性。

1994 年邱韻玲以清華大學圖書館線上公用目錄使用者爲研究對象，進行讀者利用指導方式之研究，發現讀者最常使用的檢索點爲關鍵字，而 50% 以上的使用者在檢索過程中只使用一個檢索點。[23]

近年來"國立大學"校院圖書館自動化系統多已完成，而過去多數的研究亦局限於讀者對線上公用目錄使用的研究，但對線上公用目錄尚缺乏有系統的整體評估與調查。本計劃針對"國立大學"各系統之線上公用目錄做全面性的研究，將有助於圖書館自動化系統更進一步改善。

三、研究方法與步驟

本研究採用文獻分析、問卷調查及實地訪問。根據本研究的調查目的及實際需要，利用 OCLC FirstSearch、LISA 光碟資料庫、期刊論文檢索系統等工具，查詢與線上公用目錄相關之研究文獻，並參考雀黎（Cherry）對加拿大 12 所圖書館所進行研究之調查問卷[24]與李德竹教授所著《圖書館自動化系統線上目錄及其顯示格式之研究》[25]之調查問卷，設計二種調查問卷，即"評析'國立大學'校院圖書館自動化系統線上公用目錄功能與介面特性：圖書館調查問卷"與"評析'國立大學'校院圖書館自動化系統線上公用目錄功能與介面特性：使用者調查問卷"，前者針對線上公用目錄功能進行評量，評估資料庫特性、操作控制功能、檢索與查詢、標題檢索輔助功能、檢索點、畫面顯示、輸出控制、指令、讀者輔助、遠程檢索等各項功能，該問卷由圖書館館員及圖書館自動化廠商填答。後者則對使用者進行調查，希望藉由使用者對使用線上公用目錄的滿意度及對線上公用目錄的期望，深入探討線上公用目錄功能應改進之處。

回收之問卷資料，將利用"統計分析系統"軟體進行分析工作。對於回覆問卷上不清楚之處，將實際透過網路連線至該圖書館系統進行查核。經由上述二種方法歸納設計擬定"線上公用目錄系統查檢表"，並至北、中、南三區舉行圖書館座談會，針對查檢表項目提供修正及建議，以使查檢表更能切合實際，以建立適合臺灣評鑑線上公用目錄功能之規範，期能作爲圖書館在改進、設計及評估線上公用目錄系統之參考。

本研究是以臺灣地區"國立大學"校院圖書館及其讀者爲研究對象，並對各"國立大學"校院圖書館目前所採用之圖書館自動化廠商進行問卷調查。根據"教育部"

《1994學年度公私立大學校院一覽表》[20]所列之34所"國立大學"校院圖書館爲實際進行調查之對象，每所圖書館寄發一份由圖書館填答之問卷，及五份由該圖書館轉發給讀者之使用者調查問卷。

對於圖書館自動化系統廠商之調查，則依據"中國圖書館學會圖書館自動化規劃委員會"編輯之《臺灣地區圖書館自動化系統彙編》[22]所列之12家廠商爲調查研究對象。

三種調查問卷於1995年11月15日寄發，經數次催索，34所圖書館回收32份（回收率94.1%）；170份讀者問卷回收146份（佔85.9%）；12家圖書館自動化系統廠商，僅回收3家，回收率25%（詳見表一）。

表一　各類型調查問卷回收率統計表

問卷類型 項目	發出份數	回收份數	回收率
大學校院圖書館	34	32	94.1%
圖書館讀者	170	146	85.9%
圖書館自動化系統廠商	12	3	25.0%
總計	216	181	83.8%

四、調查結果與分析

根據問卷結果，以圖書館填答率爲最高，其中廠商回覆過少，其調查結果未具代表性，故不予採計，其餘二項調查結果，茲分析討論如下：

（一）圖書館調查問卷結果分析

1. 採用系統軟體之情況

分析回收之32份圖書館調查問卷，各館採用之自動化系統十分複雜，32單位分別使用12種不同的系統，其中最多爲INNOPAC系統，有9個單位使用，其次爲傳技公司自行開發之TOTALS系統，有7所圖書館使用，再其次爲URICA系統與DYNIX系統，皆有4所圖書館使用，另有8個系統僅有1個單位使用，這些皆爲臺灣廠商自行開發者（詳見表二）。

各單位之圖書館自動化系統，採用海外系統者爲17單位，選用臺灣廠商修改海外軟體（如TAtIS系統）或臺灣廠商自行設計開發者爲15單位。整體而言，兩者差異不大，顯示"國立大學"校院圖書館在選擇自動化系統時，並不特別偏愛臺灣廠商或海外廠商。

2. 資料庫書目數量

資料庫爲自動化系統的核心，圖書館自動化早期的重要工作便是進行圖書館藏之書目資料建檔，以作爲自動化系統資料庫的基礎。倘若資料庫的資料未能及時並充分反應圖書館館藏，則讀者在利用線上公用目錄系統查詢資料時，則無法確實地掌握所需資料。

臺灣地區進行圖書館自動化的腳步較歐美國家緩慢，因此目前各圖書館仍面臨回溯建檔的壓力。根據調查問卷統計結果，系統資料庫之書目資料筆數以5萬至10萬筆之間者爲最多，計有12單位，佔37.5%；5萬筆以下有7單位，佔21.88%；40萬筆以上僅有1單位。顯示線上公用目錄尚無法充分反應各圖書館的實際館藏情況。

表二　各單位使用系統軟體統計

項目 系統/廠商名稱	使用單位數	百分比
*INNOPAC	9	28.1%
TOTALS（傳技）	7	21.9%
*DYNIX	4	12.5%
*URICA	4	12.5%
ROLIS	1	3.1%
TALIS（DOBIS）	1	3.1%
FORMOSA（大衆）	1	3.1%
永麒	1	3.1%
虹橋	1	3.1%
清江二號	1	3.1%
華興	1	3.1%
鉑特	1	3.1%
總　計	32	100%

＊海外系統

3. 資料庫特性及各項功能

資料庫特性及各項功能之問卷部份，計列出十大項目，以瞭解線上公用目錄所提供的各項檢索功能及介面特色，茲根據調查結果分析、討論如下：

（1）資料庫特性

本研究之問卷調查結果顯示，"國立大學"校院圖書館90%以上的單位均能於線上公用目錄之資料庫上提供索書號、著者、出版資料、題名、版本、標題、卷冊號、館藏地等基本書目資料供讀者參考。然而在線上公用目錄含蓋的內容與範圍方面，海德斯認爲線上公用目錄應是"所有館藏的檢索工具（full-collection access tool）"；[28]巴斯和海瑞森則認爲線上公用目錄之資料庫應是一個包含圖書館各類型資料的書目文獻資料庫。[29]另外，奇哥（Kilgour）強調線上公用目錄應以讀者使用爲導嚮，並預測未來二十年圖書館的資料庫中將會涵蓋大量的電子書。[30]而根據本研究調查結果顯示，目前僅有少數單位之線上公用目錄提供期刊目次、圖書目次以及網路文獻資源之資訊，但相信隨著網路資源的豐富化以及線上公用目錄系統功能的改進，將會逐漸增加網路資源與書目性以外的資料。

另外,本研究結果與雀黎等人在 1994 年針對加拿大 12 所學術圖書館之線上公用目錄的調查結果類似,其所調查的 12 所圖書館中大多數圖書館未能提供期刊文獻與手稿等資料,同時亦無任何圖書館能於線上公用目錄上提供圖書館所有的館藏資料。[31]

(2) 操作控制功能

尼柯森曾建議利用滑鼠來操作線上公用目錄,以改進傳統線上公用目錄操作方式的缺點。[32]隨著視窗軟體的普遍使用,線上公用目錄的設計,也逐漸開始採用 Windows 及 World Wide Web 介面,提供讀者更具親和力的查詢與操作環境。柏頓認為 WWW 型式的線上公用目錄具備資訊超連結(hyperlink)與多媒體之特色,將是未來線上公用目錄介面發展的主流。[33]然而根據調查結果,"國立大學"圖書館目前僅有 2 單位提供視窗介面、4 單位提供 WWW 之操作介面,及 1 單位提供連結網路文獻資源的功能,顯示臺灣圖書館在因應以滑鼠來協助操作查詢,以及提供 WWW 介面的發展潮流上,步調較為緩慢。

此外,依調查資料所示,線上公用目錄除具備卡片目錄提供讀者書目性資料的功能外,80% 以上的單位亦提供圖書館佈告欄、流通查詢、允許讀者自行預約等功能。將近 80% 的單位其系統採用選項式交談模式,較之指令式介面更易為初學者接受。

斯波爾的研究著重線上公用目錄的傾錄功能,強調該項功能將可解決線上公用目錄僅能於螢幕上閱讀的缺點;[34]而希利則針對傾錄時發生的雜訊問題進行研究。[35]"國立大學"圖書館線上公用目錄已有 11(34.4%)單位具備直接傾錄書目記錄至個人電腦的功能,3(9.4%)單位具備可透過電子郵件將檢索到之資料傳回的功能。隨著網路與個人電子郵件的推廣使用,未來該二項功能勢將成為線上公用目錄必備的功能之一。

(3) 檢索與查詢功能

檢索與查詢部份,以 20 個問題探討臺灣地區"國立大學"圖書館線上公用目錄檢索功能之強弱和讀者對查詢結果的使用是否方便。對讀者使用線上公用目錄時是否可以先針對某些事項設定預設值,以縮短查詢時間之功能,根據調查結果,提供查詢類型讓讀者設定預設值者有 18(56.3%)單位,在顯示格式上可先設定者有 16(50%)單位;提供關鍵字所在欄位及對話狀態可設預設值者僅分別為 8 單位及 6 單位。大體而言,多數單位皆不提供預設值功能。

另外,有 7(21.9%)單位之系統可在任何畫面下開始檢索,10(31.3%)單位可在輔助畫面下開始進行檢索;在檢索欄位方面,有 7(21.9%)單位提供全部欄位之檢索。該調查結果與雀黎在加拿大的研究結果略為不同,根據雀黎的研究,其調查的圖書館線上公用目錄系統均可提供讀者設定查詢類型(search type)與顯示格式(display format)之預設值功能;而約有半數的單位可允許讀者於任何畫面或於輔助畫面下開始或繼續檢索。[36]

對關鍵字檢索,本研究結果則與雀黎[37]的研究結果相同,兩者所調查的單位均提供關鍵字檢索,且 90% 以上的單位提供題名關鍵字檢索,該功能可幫助讀者對不明確或不記得完整的題名進行檢索。虛字(stop word)控制方面,雀黎之調查單位中僅 1 單位未具備該功能,而本研究之調查具備西文虛字控制者為 22(68.8%)單位,具備中文虛字控制者為 16(50%)單位,中文方面的發展尚待加強。

為方便讀者獲得較精確的資料,依調查結果顯示各單位皆提供布林邏輯運算功能,使讀者能進行較精確的檢索。另外,有 70% 以上的單位亦提供縮小範圍檢索功能,驗證了米爾塞和費特認為第二代線上公用目錄應使用布林邏輯運算元以協助讀者降低大量檢索結果的建議。[38]

瀏覽功能方面，1993年米爾塞和費特的調查報告指出讀者檢索活動中60%的檢索乃是瀏覽檢索；[39]貝希思提也認為瀏覽功能是讀者進行查詢時常使用的重要功能，線上公用目錄在設計上應能讓讀者在螢幕上看到圖書排列在書庫架上的位置。[40]根據本研究調查顯示，16（50%）單位提供相鄰字（word adjacency）排序（含中西文）功能，19（59.4%）單位可顯示相鄰近之排架位；而雀黎於1993年所進行的調查亦僅有一半的單位提供相鄰字排序功能，[41]顯示海內外系統對於此功能均應再加強。

窗字檢索功能方面，依調查結果所示，不論中文或西文皆以提供右邊窗字者較為主。中文方面，提供右邊窗字有20（62.5%）單位，左邊窗字為5（15.6%）單位，中間窗字6（18.8%）單位；西文方面，右邊窗字有24（75%）單位，左邊窗字為5（15.6%）單位，中間窗字6（18.8%）單位。較之雀黎的研究有10（83.3%）單位提供西文右邊窗字，但無任何單位提供左邊窗字功能，[42]似乎臺灣地區的系統在窗字方面的發展比海外略為進步。就實際情況而言，海內外對窗字的定義與認知有差異。

（4）標題檢索輔助功能

標題檢索輔助功能方面，亨利認為標題檢索對讀者查詢資料最有用，並主張線上公用目錄應增加線上標題表及標題權威檔；[43]斯樂特亦強調權威檔的重要性，指出其可使不同語文的資料相互連結，相互參考；[44]德拉貝斯特和威勒則針對標題檢索提出新設計理念，呼籲圖書館在設計線上公用目錄時，應擴大標題檢索的範圍。[45]根據本研究調查結果，有15（46.9%）單位具有主題權威控制功能，顯示島內部份"國立大學"圖書館已注意到主題檢索的重要性，惟因島內原本缺乏共同遵循的中文標題表，在中文標題檢索功能上尚需努力。另外，有11（34.4%）單位具備SEE參見功能，9（28.1%）單位提供SEE ALSO/BT/NT/RT參見功能，顯示權威控制功能方面，仍不夠完善。

（5）檢索點

檢索點方面，奇哥曾提到若以使用者觀點來設計線上公用目錄，則除提供傳統卡片目錄之題名、作者檢索外，還應提供關鍵字檢索；[46]邱韻玲於1994年針對清華大學線上公用目錄進行使用調查，也發現使用者最常使用的檢索點為關鍵字，且半數以上使用者在檢索過程中只使用一個檢索點。[47]根據本研究調查結果，有28（87.5%）單位提供題名關鍵字/詞檢索，25（78.1%）單位提供標題關鍵字/詞、22（68.8%）單位提供著者關鍵字/詞檢索，顯示島內多數系統已能配合讀者的需求提供關鍵字檢索功能。

馬休斯（Matthews）等人於1983年所進行的調查研究指出讀者對於改進圖書館服務、資料庫及自動化系統的前二項需求為檢索圖書目次及摘要之功能。[48]然而，本調查中僅1單位提供圖書目次之檢索，且無任何單位提供圖書/文獻引用書目之檢索；雖然早於1983年已有多數讀者對此提出需求，但事經10年之久，至今仍未被重視而予以發展。同樣地，雀黎的研究中亦無單位提供圖書目次、圖書索引及文獻引用書目之檢索。[49]顯示無論島內外，對於此方面之檢索功能均有待加強與改進。

（6）畫面顯示

由於線上公用目錄的主要使用者為一般讀者，因此在畫面顯示設計上應考慮讀者的觀點。薛爾斯和奧賽克二人認為線上公用目錄之畫面顯示應注意設計原則、選單及項目、指令,及給讀者閱讀的訊息等四方面,並應善用訊息以指導讀者進行查詢。根據調查結果,在畫面顯示方面,多數單位已考慮到中英文之雙語問題,26(81.3%)單位可讓讀者自行選擇以全中文或全英文畫面顯示;23(71.9%)單位提供中、英文畫面切換功能,而15(46.9%)單位則在畫面顯示上同時採用中文及英文。此外,有22(68.8%)單位之線上公用目錄系統會在畫面上經常顯示檢索用語及系統執行狀態,以協助讀者瞭解其所進行的查詢。

顯示格式方面,本調查結果指出有21(65.5%)單位提供簡略書目、14(43.8%)單位為部份書目顯示、20(62.5%)單位提供完整書目之顯示格式、10(31.3%)單位提供卡片格式之顯示格式;然而薛爾斯與奧賽克的研究卻發現線上公用目錄的使用者並不喜歡一長串的資訊及完整的書目記錄顯示型式。為滿足讀者的需求,薛爾斯與奧賽克的研究結果應可作為圖書館改進其線上公用目錄系統之參考。

(7) 輸出控制

輸出控制方面,本研究結果與雀黎的研究結果相似,各線上公用目錄系統在此方面的功能均較弱,對於檢索結果之資料顯示的格式及排序,多未具彈性設計。換言之,讀者無法任意選擇特別欄位的顯示或指定檢索結果的排序方式。根據調查結果,僅4(12.5%)單位提供讀者可選擇特別欄位之顯示,且不及25%的單位提供讀者指定檢索結果可依題名、作者、出版日期或索書號排序。另外僅3(9.4%)單位提供可將檢索所得資料依與檢索詞相關之密切程度,依次遞減排序之功能,而在雀黎的調查研究中,則無任何系統具備此功能。[50]

(8) 查詢指令用語

線上公用目錄之指令設計亦是重要人機介面之一,各種功能鍵的使用、指令定義的一致性,以及系統對查詢指令用語的處理等皆會影響讀者的查詢結果。薛爾斯和奧賽克認為採用標準字母寫法及標點符號應列為評估線上公用目錄的原則之一。根據本調查結果顯示,半數以上單位對其系統之功能鍵的定義一致、其每一指令在每處的作用一致、其指令皆採標準語法等各項查詢指令用語之功能均能達成。

(9) 讀者輔助功能

讀者輔助方面,依本調查結果有23(71.9%)單位提供一般線上輔助功能說明或利用指導、顯示錯誤訊息、清楚指導讀者如何檢索與輸入資料等三項功能,但系統所顯示之錯誤訊息清楚易懂者僅16(50%)單位,顯示各圖書館線上公用目錄之讀者輔助功能尚未令人滿意。

海德瑞斯在其研究中強調線上公用目錄是否提供讀者適當的使用訊息、各種檢索符號之說明及畫面的親和程度皆會影響讀者利用線上公用目錄進行檢索的成敗。[51]因此,圖書館在改進線上公用目錄時應特別加強讀者輔助功能的設計。此外,奇哥認為新一代即第三代線上公用目錄應具備自動偵錯功能,以避免讀者因打錯字而影響檢索結果。[52]然而,本調查結果中,僅2單位提供拼字檢查軟體,且由於中文方面並未具備拼字檢查軟體,顯示此調查結果局限於西文部份。

(10) 遠程檢索

柏頓(Burton)認為圖書館線上公用目錄應朝開放性系統發展,不但能提供當地讀者使用,亦應能開放於網路上供全球讀者使用;[53]另外,魯卡斯、[54]奇哥[55]及美國國會圖書館檢索計劃小組[50]亦皆提及線上公用目錄之遠程檢索功能的重要性。"國立大學"圖書館因校園網路及臺灣學術網路的普及，各校線上公用目錄多能開放於網路上，供眾使用。至於遠程檢索功能方面，根據調查結果顯示，68%以上單位提供之線上遠程檢索之公用目錄與館內供讀者使用者相同，畫面顯示亦十分清晰；50%以上單位之遠程檢索亦無使用時段的限制，並可連接網路上其他線上公用目錄。但是對於連線指導說明、系統內容與範圍介紹、鍵盤功能說明等讀者輔助功能之提供，則未超過半數，宜待加強。

(二) 讀者調查問卷結果分析與討論

(1) 滿足讀者資訊需求方面，根據調查結果顯示，133（91.1%）位讀者選擇書目資料為其第一需求，其次希望線上公用目錄能提供影像資料、期刊目次及全文資料。在線上公用目錄應包括之資料類型方面，80%以上讀者認為應包括期刊、圖書、網路文獻資源、電腦媒體資料及視聽資料。以服務讀者的角度來看，線上公用目錄資料庫的內容不應僅局限於圖書之書目資料，而應廣泛包涵各類型資料，其驗證了海德瑞斯、巴斯和海瑞森等人對線上公用目錄含蓋內容與範圍的看法。

(2) 線上公用目錄應提供之書目資訊項目方面，90%以上的讀者認為其應提供著者、館藏地、借閱狀態及標題；80%以上讀者認為應提供索書號、題名、當期期刊所在地及出版資料；另有50%以上的讀者認為版本、期刊目次、文獻摘要、圖書目次、網路文獻資源等資訊亦應提供。較之對圖書館之問卷調查結果，目前各"國立大學"圖書館線上公用目錄可提供期刊目次、圖書目次、文獻摘要及網路資源者皆未超過10%，顯然讀者對線上公用目錄應提供之資訊項目的期望與之實際情況有很大的差距。

(3) 除書目查詢外，約80%的讀者認為線上公用目錄尚須提供館際互借、流通查詢及圖書館佈告欄之訊息。本研究所調查的圖書館多數能提供後二項訊息，但對於館際互借之訊息，則僅3單位提供，顯示各線上公用目錄系統尚無法滿足讀者對館際互借的殷切需求。

(4) 關於查詢介面，除UNIX介面外，79%的讀者認為還應提供視窗介面、52%的讀者認為應提供World Wide Web介面；實際上，根據調查結果，僅2單位提供Window介面、4單位具備WWW介面，顯示讀者在應用新科技方面的速度比圖書館快許多。

(5) 除查詢資料外，線上公用目錄應提供之功能，依調查統計，131（89.7%）位讀者認為應提供連線至其他圖書館公用目錄或資料庫檢索系統。此項需求驗證了柏頓強調線上公用目錄應提供網路連結的主張。[57]此外，多數讀者認為尚應提供之功能如：讀者自行預約所需資料、薦購圖書資料、讀者自行續借資料、電子文件傳遞以及線上留言或建議等。

(6) 檢索點方面，調查結果顯示讀者最常使用的檢索點為題名關鍵字/詞，其與邱韻玲的研究[58]相符。讀者甚少使用的檢索點依調查統計分析，低於10%者為圖書目次、附註關鍵字/詞、中國圖書分類號、流通用條碼號、國際標準書號/期刊號、杜威十進分類號、國會圖書館索書號、國會圖書館卡片號等，多屬編碼式檢索點。此項結果，值得圖書館在規劃與設計公用目錄系統之檢索點時參考。

(7) 檢索功能方面，依調查統計，讀者未曾使用過布林邏輯運算功能者佔24%，使用AND運算元者為34.2%，使用OR者為22.6%，使用NOT者為6.8%；竄字功能方面，則從未使用過者為35.6%，使用中文右邊竄字者佔20.5%，西文右邊竄字者佔

17.8%。布林邏輯及寬字功能之使用率均不高,圖書館員在指導讀者使用線上公用目錄時,應多加介紹與推廣。

(8) 系統畫面顯示方面,約80%的讀者認為系統應提供中英文畫面切換功能,讓讀者能依其需求自行選擇;對螢幕上資料的呈現,則有68%的讀者喜好條列式,24%的讀者偏好卡片格式。根據對圖書館的調查結果,80%的單位可讓讀者自行選擇以全中文或全英文畫面,約78%的單位其完整書目之顯示係採條列式。大體而言,多數系統在此方面之功能設計已能符合讀者的需求。

(9) 讀者對使用過之線上公用目錄滿意程度方面,依調查統計結果,在整體看法上,勾選滿意者佔68.5%;另外,在操作、系統功能、螢幕用字、資料排列、輔助說明等項目,皆獲六至八成的讀者正面肯定,但對查詢結果滿意者約佔五成,系統可靠者為42.5%,系統反應速度快者只佔39.7%,而這些未獲多數讀者滿意的項目則正反應出各"國立大學"圖書館館藏尚未完全建檔的事實,及網路設備宜待加強。

(三) 圖書館自動化廠商對其線上公用目錄系統的設計及未來發展分析

由於回收廠商之問卷僅三份,樣本過少,無法反應出廠商對其線上公用目錄系統的未來發展方向。若從另一個角度來分析,因所調查之圖書館其所使用的系統係來自於廠商,各項功能的優缺點也正代表目前廠商對其線上公用目錄設計的良窳。對於網路文獻資源的掌握、WWW等網路新媒體的運用,以及網路連結功能的設計,部份系統已具備。在市場需求及競爭的環境下,廠商也應須時時配合新科技的發展及使用者的需求,改進其系統功能。

(四) 目前自動化系統線上公用目錄的主要問題探討

根據圖書館與讀者之調查問卷結果分析,目前"國立大學"圖書館線上公用目錄的主要問題有下列幾點:

1. 資料庫內容多為書目性資料,缺乏讀者所需之期刊目次、文獻目次、全文資料及網路資源。
2. 線上公用目錄除具備書目目錄、佈告欄、流通查詢外,缺乏館際互借功能。
3. 操作介面仍以DOS介面為主,在視窗及WWW介面之發展較緩慢。
4. 系統提供直接傾錄書目資料至個人電腦或經由電子郵件傳送之功能不足。
5. 檢索與查詢時,缺乏線上互動式交談功能,以指導讀者進行檢索。
6. 檢索策略及結果的保存功能較弱,且缺少進一步依檢索到之資料,直接檢索到該資料的引用文獻功能。
7. 檢索網路文獻資源後,缺乏直接可連結到該文獻所在之功能。
8. 標題檢索、權威控制、SEE與SEE ALSO參見等功能較弱。
9. 檢索結果之排序功能尚待改進。
10. 讀者輔助功能方面,缺少提供西文拼字檢查軟體,以幫助讀者減少輸入錯誤。
11. 缺乏連結其他網路線上資料庫及網路資源的遠程檢索功能。

五、結論與建議

本研究分析海內外圖書館自動化系統線上公用目錄相關文獻,以瞭解其功能與介面之特性,並彙整實際調查分析結果及座談會意見,試擬適合臺灣地區"大學圖書館線上公用目錄功能與介面項目查檢標準表"，作爲臺灣大學圖書館選擇自動化系統廠商暨評析其現有之線上公用目錄參考。就以上研究結果，歸納並建議如下：

（一）結論

根據 34 所大學校院圖書館自動化系統線上公用目錄的功能與介面特性之調查，其結論如下：

1. "國立大學"校院圖書館採用之圖書館自動化系統龐雜

32 所圖書館回覆中，採用 12 種不同自動化系統，雖然採用海外廠商設計之系統 15（46.9%）單位，採用島內廠商修改海外軟體或島內廠商自行設計開發者 17（53.1%）單位。根據調查，"國立大學"校院圖書館對島外或島內系統之偏好，並無差異。

2. 線上公用目錄資料庫多以傳統式資料爲主，不足代表各館全部館藏

各系統之書目資料以 5 萬冊至 10 萬冊爲最多，計 12（37.5%）單位，可見多數圖書館館藏尚未全部鍵入資料庫，故其線上公用目錄尚無法完全涵蓋實際館藏。各資料庫皆收錄圖書資料；收錄期刊資料有 26（81.25%）單位；收錄視聽媒體有 14（43.75%）單位。但僅有 3 單位之資料庫包含期刊目次；5 單位包含網路文獻資源。可見目前臺灣公用目錄資料庫資料類型未涵蓋圖書館全部資料類型。資料庫內容局限於書目性資料。90% 以上的單位提供索書號、著者、出版資料、題名、版本、標題、卷冊號、館藏地等書目基本資料供讀者參考查詢。但圖書目次、期刊目次、網路資源、文獻摘要、書評及引用書目等參考性資訊，則僅有極少數圖書館系統提供或甚至沒有提供。

3. 視窗介面及 WWW 發展步調緩慢

各圖書館自動化主機多採 UNIX 作業軟體，僅 2 單位提供視窗介面、4 單位提供 WWW 介面，顯示介面使用方面，未能與電腦科技發展潮流同步。且讀者認爲視窗爲最好介面，該項差距，有待圖書館在設備方面加以更新。

4. 引用文獻及全文資料功能尚待加強

由讀者調查得知，讀者偏好單純關鍵字檢索方式，對圖書館線上公用目錄所設計之相關功能，如虛字控制、布林邏輯、相鄰字排序、窽字檢索、縮小查詢範圍等，因而未有明顯的意見。但在直接檢索原件及引用文獻方面，僅 1 單位提供該項功能，且在讀者問卷及座談會中，館員皆同意應加強此項功能，俾便直接連接引用文獻或原件所在之處。

5. 標題檢索功能未臻理想

中文資料多未進行主題分析及著錄標題，故圖書館線上公用目錄多以西文標題爲主。然而，仍未達半數之圖書館能提供包含標題權威控制、參見、標題詞彙瀏覽功能，可見該項功能未臻完備。

6. 檢索點多而考量完整

各系統皆儘量將讀者可能用以查詢的書目項目列爲檢索點，包含著者、題名、標題、關鍵字、標準號碼、索書號、分類號等二十餘項。但讀者僅常用其中 2 至 3 項，圖書館系統是否須要設計如此多而完整的檢索點，值得進一步深入探討。

7. 畫面已考慮語文問題

由於臺灣大學校院圖書館館藏包括中西文書刊，讀者亦包括海內外讀者，多數圖書館在設計畫面時，已考量多種語文顯示之能力。調查證明 81% 單位提供中英文畫面選擇

功能。

8. 輸出控制之排序功能未具彈性設計

對於查詢結果的輸出，多數圖書館提供讀者在螢幕上前後翻頁及印表機列印結果，但在資料顯示的排序方面，僅有8（25%）單位可提供讀者指定檢索結果依序排列。

9. 以選項式（menu-driven）設計為主

臺灣有25所（78.1%）大學圖書館自動化系統採用選項式設計，少數（7單位，21.9%）提供指令式（command driven）。讀者亦偏好選項式之公用目錄交談方式，且建議其選項符號應具有助記功能，以協助初學者及不常使用線上公用目錄之讀者使用系統。

10. 讀者輔助功能仍需加強

有23（71.9%）單位提供一般線上輔助功能說明、利用指導、錯誤訊息顯示、檢索指引功能等，其他如功能鍵設計、文字輔助及檢索步驟之輔助說明等，僅一半圖書館系統具有，故該功能仍需加強。網路資訊迅速發展，讀者可經由所使用的檢索系統無限制地串連到其他的網路資源與線上公用目錄系統，遠程檢索功能設計更形重要。但依據調查所得，19（59.4%）單位提供連結網路與其他圖書館線上公用目錄；9（28.1%）單位連接其他線上資料庫；僅1（3.1%）單位連接網路其他資源，顯示圖書館尚未能充分掌握網路上圖書館書目資料以外的其他資源。

11. 讀者使用公用目錄之次數偏低，且多在圖書館使用

60%讀者每月使用次數為10次以內，可見"國立大學"校院圖書館讀者使用公用目錄次數偏低，各圖書館應探討其原因，並針對原因提出解決方案，以提昇線上公用目錄之使用率。而使用地點，約94%的讀者在圖書館，因此，圖書館應對在檢索地點、工作站數量、檢索開放時間、檢索介面等服務項目及設施等方面的加強，予以完善規劃。

12. 讀者常用關鍵字檢索資料，少用號碼式檢索點

讀者多以題名關鍵字、標題關鍵字及著者關鍵字為其檢索點，其中又以題名關鍵字使用比率最高，遠超過圖書館認為最重要的題名、著者及標題三大檢索點。此外，圖書館視為重要之索書號、登錄號、分類號、條碼及標準號碼等編碼式檢索點，則幾乎很少被讀者使用。

13. 讀者少用特殊之檢索功能

圖書館所設計而引以自豪之特殊檢索功能，如：縮小查詢範圍、布林邏輯運算及竄字等功能。讀者不僅不常使用，甚至多數讀者從未使用過，對讀者而言，較偏好簡單而易學的系統。

14. 讀者不理會圖書館使用之標題表及分類法

多數讀者雖表示知道中國圖書標題表及中國圖書分類法，但查詢時，讀者多以關鍵字或自由語彙進行檢索，而不去理會控制式的標題表與分類號。

15. 讀者對"國立大學"校院圖書館線上公用目錄檢索系統整體評價

目前"國立大學"校院圖書館線上公用目錄在軟體設計及硬體功能上仍有許多令讀者不滿意的地方，但整體而言，讀者給予中上程度之評價，即介於"非常好"與"尚可"之間。在操作、查詢結果、系統功能、螢幕上用字、螢幕上資料排列、系統反應速度、系統可靠性、指令名稱及其使用、輔助說明及提示訊息等方面皆給予滿意的正面

評價。

（二）建議

根據以上結論，提出下列建議：

1. 各系統間應建立互相連線介面，以加強合作及資源共享

臺灣地區大學院校圖書館目前所使用之公用目錄系統約有12種之多，造成讀者必須多方學習適應不同系統檢索方式，而館與館之間的資源亦因資料庫設計架構之不同，無法建立良好之合作關係。因此，爲達成資源共享，各系統應先設置資訊互通交換之介面（如遵循Z39.50、X.400及EDI標準等之通訊協定），使得資訊交流能透過日益發達普及的網路，而無遠弗屆。

2. 加速完成館藏全面自動化

目前各館書目資料庫並未涵蓋其全部館藏，致使讀者在利用上往往無法得到完整資訊而必須再藉助於卡片目錄，影響讀者使用公用目錄之意願及評價。建議各系統應加速進行全面館藏回溯作業。

3. 建立通用之中文標題

讀者使用線上公用目錄檢索時，利用標題當檢索點的機會遠大於其他檢索點，尤其是使用中文標題。但目前臺灣地區向無一通用之合適中文標題表，可供圖書館及讀者利用，僅能以關鍵字查詢方式代替之，故實有必要儘速建立一中文書刊資料通用標題表系統。

4. 圖書館於線上公用目錄功能完備後，可考量凍結卡片式目錄（或書本式目錄或縮影式目錄）

讀者於圖書館推出線上公用目錄後，繼續使用卡片式目錄、書本式目錄或縮影式目錄之比率不高，即使繼續使用亦僅是偶而爲之。因此，圖書館回溯建檔完畢後，可凍結或廢除卡片式目錄、書本式目錄或縮影式目錄等。

5. 重新考量檢索點之設計

讀者進行檢索時，往往拋棄圖書館專業上最引以自豪之編碼式檢索點，如分類號、作者號、登錄號或標準號碼等，而採用接近自然語彙的關鍵字、標題、題名及作者。建議線上公用目錄在設計檢索點時應避免難以記憶理解之號碼型式，而採接近自然語彙。圖書館認知檢索點應愈多愈詳盡，但根據調查，讀者多使用其中少數幾項，應再思考檢索點之設計理念。

6. 公用目錄應廣泛提供網路資源

在資訊流通、交換迅速的潮流衝擊下，僅提供所在圖書館之館藏書目訊息的系統已無法滿足讀者的需要。須廣泛蒐集全文資料、引用文獻及WWW上的網路資源，供讀者自行決定取捨。讀者對網路文獻資源、期刊目次及全文資料之需求程度高，不以查得所在圖書館之資訊爲滿足，除能提供所在圖書館的完整館藏訊息外，尚可直接與其他網路上的各種資料庫或資訊中心連線，查得其文獻資源及期刊目次，甚至得到全文資料，使所欲檢索的資訊更趨完備。

7. 圖書館自動化系統廠商應積極參與系統設計討論事宜

本次問卷調查針對廠商發出部份有12家，但僅有3家回覆問卷，此訊息透露出自動化廠商參與分析討論之誠意不足，自動化廠商多依據使用單位（即圖書館）所提需求設

計研發系統功能即可,本身無須多瞭解目前圖書館自動化發展趨勢,更不必負系統成敗之責,此種觀念造成圖書館與廠商互相不瞭解而難以溝通,甚而終止合作關係,殊為可惜。故建議島內廠商應提高其參與合作研究功能之意願,達到雙贏目的。

本研究參照問卷調查與實施方向及座談會建議等之分析結果,試擬適合臺灣"大學圖書館線上公用目錄功能與介面項目查檢標準表",作為大學圖書館選擇自動化系統廠商暨評析其現有之線上公用目錄之參考,查檢標準表詳列如下:

大學圖書館線上公用目錄功能與介面項目查檢標準表

第一部份:資料庫特性
(1) 系統提供下列資訊(含簡單記錄或完整記錄之顯示)
必備項:
①索書號
②著者
③題名
④標題
⑤版本
⑥出版資料(出版地、出版者、出版年)
⑦版權日期
⑧卷冊號
⑨當期期刊所在地
⑩館藏地
⑪借閱狀態
⑫關鍵字
⑬文獻摘要
⑭圖書目次
⑮網路文獻資源
⑯期刊目次
⑰系統應即時於主畫面上顯示異動資訊
⑱流通用條碼號
⑲處理狀態
選擇項:
①圖書/文獻的引用書目
②書評
③全文資料(full text)
第二部份:操作控制功能
(1) 系統除了提供書目查詢外,亦提供其他查詢如下
必備項:
①圖書館佈告欄
②流通查詢

③系統線上使用說明
④館際互借
⑤資料庫介紹
（2）讀者交談模式
必備項：
①選項式（menu-driven）與指令式（commanddriven）二者皆具備
②選項式（menu-driven）
選擇項：
①指令式（command-driven）
（3）提供不同的界面供讀者使用
必備項：
①視窗介面
②World Wide Web 介面
（4）提供直接查詢功能，如快速深入或跳出數個畫面
必備項
（5）終端機於定時不鍵入指令時，會自動回到起始之畫面
必備項
（6）關於功能選項方面
必備項：
①使用英文字母及數字
選擇項：
①以字母代替
②使用數字
（7）功能選項以有助記性質之字母代替，例如：Author 以 A 代表，Title 以 T 代表
必備項
（8）檢索指令方面
必備項：
①有指令使用範例
②有指令一覽表可供查用
（9）允許讀者自行預約/續借所需資料
必備項
（10）具備關於該系統、資料庫及圖書館方面訊息
必備項
（11）讀者可自行選擇閱讀詳細或簡短的系統訊息說明（system messages instruction）
如：錯誤訊息、輔助說明等
選擇項
（12）具有可隨時中斷檢索或取消查詢指令的功能鍵設計
必備項
（13）可隨時回到先前畫面以更改檢索指令

必備項
（14）可直接傾錄（download）書目記錄至自己的電腦上
必備項
（15）透過電子郵件（E-mail）將檢索到的資料傳回自己的電子郵件信箱中
必備項
（16）提供線上信箱供讀者留言
必備項
（17）讀者於 OPAC 上傳遞訊息或問題給某一特定館員或部門
選擇項
第三部份：檢索與查詢
（1）讀者可對下列項目設定預設值（default）
必備項：
①查詢類型（例：著者、題名、標題）
②顯示格式（display format）
選擇項：
①關鍵字所在的某個欄位
②對話狀態（指令或選項）
（2）讀者可在任何畫面下開始檢索
選擇項
（3）讀者可於輔助說明畫面下開始檢索
必備項
（4）全部欄位皆可進行檢索
選擇項
（5）具有關鍵字檢索，其範圍
必備項：
①題名關鍵字
②標題關鍵字
③著者關鍵字
選擇項：
①附註關鍵字
②摘要關鍵字
③圖書目次關鍵字
④網路文獻資源關鍵字
⑤期刊目次關鍵字
（6）虛字（stop word）控制
必備項：
①西文虛字控制
②中文虛字控制（例如：標點符號等）
（7）提供布林邏輯運算功能

必備項：
①AND
②OR
③NOT
(8) 可使用布林邏輯運算功能處
必備項：
①查詢關鍵字
②查詢題名
③查詢標題
④查詢著者
⑤混合查詢
(9) 單一檢索時，不限定布林邏輯運算元使用次數
必備項
(10) 具有相鄰字（word adjacency）排序功能
必備項
(11) 具有相鄰近排列顯示（例如：neighbor、expansion、shelf-position list 等）功能
必備項
(12) 檢索西文一個字以上時，中間空格具 AND 或 OR 意義
必備項
(13) 具有竄字（truncation）功能
必備項：
①西文右邊竄字，例：lib#
②中文右邊竄字，例：佛#
選擇項：
①西文中間竄字，例：WOM#N
②中文中間竄字，例：照#機
③西文左邊竄字（truncation），例：#ism
④中文左邊竄字，例：#星
⑤西文中間竄一個以上的字母，例：BEHAVI # R 可檢索到 BEHAVIOR 和 BEHAVIOUR
⑥中文中間竄一個以上的字母
(14) 能以下列欄位進行縮小範圍之檢索（limited search）
必備項：
①出版日期
②資料型態
③語文
選擇項：
①出版者
②館藏地

（15）讀者可利用已檢索之結果，繼續作進一步的檢索
必備項
（16）讀者可根據所檢索到的資料，直接檢索到該資料的引用文獻
選擇項
（17）系統可儲存讀者之檢索策略
選擇項
（18）系統具有保存讀者檢索結果之功能
選擇項
（19）讀者可以任意地轉換檢索類型，例：由原爲著者檢索轉成題名檢索等
必備項
（20）讀者檢索到網路文獻資源後，可以直接連接到該文獻之所在
必備項
第四部份：標題檢索輔助功能
（1）系統目前可以提供讀者瀏覽分類表大綱
選擇項
（2）系統目前可以提供讀者瀏覽分類細表
選擇項
（3）讀者可以查看第一層標題詞彙（例如：Library Automation-）
選擇項
（4）讀者可以查看全部之標題詞彙
選擇項
（5）系統具備 SEE 參見功能
必備項
（6）系統具備 SEE ALSO/BT/NT/RT 參見功能
必備項
（7）系統目前有主題權威控制功能
必備項
（8）將標題查詢結果爲零的檢索自動轉爲關鍵字檢索
選擇項
第五部份：檢索點
必備項：
①個人著者
②叢刊名
③團體著者
④題名
⑤中國圖書分類號
⑥標題
⑦題名關鍵字/詞
⑧著者/題名

⑨標題關鍵字/詞
⑩國際標準書號（ISBN）
⑪著者關鍵字/詞
⑫國際標準期刊號（ISSN）
⑬流通用條碼號
⑭國會圖書館索書號
⑮杜威十進分類號
⑯叢刊名詞關鍵字/詞

選擇項：
①政府出版品編號
②附註關鍵字/詞
③國會圖書館卡片號
④各類作品編號（如技術報告號、音樂作品號、CODEN…）

第六部份：畫面顯示

必備項：
①館藏的流通狀態與其索書號顯示在同一畫面
②能顯示出館藏的狀態，如：可流通、編目中、採購中…
③畫面顯示可讓讀者自行選擇全中文或全英文畫面
④查到之總筆數會先顯示出來，以便讀者使用縮小查詢範圍之功能，以縮小查詢結果
⑤完整書目（full record）之欄位顯示採用條列式（如：作者＝）
⑥簡單書目（brief record）之欄位顯示是否採用條列式（如：作者＝）
⑦提供中文及英文畫面之切換
⑧檢索用語常顯示在畫面上，以便讀者在查看檢索結果時隨時能知道自己所鍵入的用語
⑨查詢時會顯示系統執行狀態，如處理中，請稍候…
⑩提供"簡略書目"（AACR2 第一層著錄格式）
⑪提供"完整書目"（AACR2 第三層著錄格式）
⑫可顯示該查詢結果為第幾筆記錄（如：5 of 100）
⑬當館藏無法在一個畫面上顯示完畢時，則以一組連續號碼表示（如：1－8，9－18，等）
⑭檢索之結果筆數，有數量之限制
⑮提供 MARC 格式

選擇項：
①畫面顯示同時採用中文及英文字體
②提供"部份書目"（AACR2 第二層著錄格式）
③有檢索筆數數量顯示之限制
④提供"卡片格式"

第七部份：輸出控制功能

（1）輸出任何一筆資料（如：第12筆）必備項
（2）非依序輸出多筆資料（如：第2筆，第5筆等）
必備項
（3）輸出某一範圍之資料（如：第5筆至第9筆）
必備項
（4）選擇特別欄位之輸出
必備項
（5）合併顯示多次檢索的結果
必備項
（6）讀者能指定檢索結果依下列方式排序
必備項：
①題名
②作者
③出版日期
④索書號
⑤標題
（7）檢索所得之資料依與檢索詞相關之密切程度，并依次遞減排序（relevant ranking）
必備項
（8）可在螢幕上前後翻頁
必備項
（9）可用印表機直接印出查詢結果
必備項
第八部份：指令
必備項：
①檢索西文資料時可混用大、小寫字母
②每一指令在每一處的作用一致
③功能鍵的定義一致（如：F1 固定代表線上輔助）
④西文題名檢索時，系統會忽略冠詞
⑤所有指令皆採用標準語法（standardized syntax）
⑥中文題名檢索時，系統會忽略標點符號
⑦將字首字母之縮寫用作指令（如：A 代表 Author）
⑧讀者可忽略國會標題中主標題與複分標題之間的分隔符號"－"
⑨功能鍵作爲用以減少常用指令的按鍵次數
⑩按鍵次數維持最少（三次）
⑪系統具有不理會不必要之標點符號的功能
⑫系統可以接受以姓爲先或以名爲前的西文作者姓名排列（如：SmithA 或 A Smith）
選擇項：

①指令包含通用之標點符號
②多個指令可以先存在一起，再同時一次執行
第九部份：讀者輔助
必備項：
①系統具有一般線上輔助說明或利用指導
②系統會顯示錯誤訊息
③系統清楚指導讀者如何檢索和輸入資料
④進行檢索時，系統會例行出現檢索步驟之指示，以指示讀者下一步驟的指令
⑤當檢索時間過長時，會有訊息說明系統正在進行的事情
⑥可利用指令或功能鍵隨時叫出"HELP"
⑦當讀者檢索到某處時，有重點之文字輔助說明
⑧系統顯示之錯誤訊息清楚易懂
選擇項：
①系統提供其他可檢索之資料庫清單
②提供拼字檢查軟體
③系統會顯示使用時間
第十部份：遠程檢索
必備項：
（1）線上遠程讀者所檢索的公用目錄與在圖書館內所提供者相同
②線上遠程讀者所檢索的公用目錄與在圖書館內所提供者之畫面相同
③畫面顯示經常十分清晰
④遠程檢索沒有時段上的限制
⑤系統提供以網路連接方式查詢其他圖書館公用目錄
⑥有適當的離線說明
⑦有適當的連線說明（例如：所提供的終端機型態說明）
⑧系統提供以網路連接方式查詢其他線上資料庫
⑨當無任何輸入動作時，系統會發出即將自動斷線（disconnect）的警示訊息
⑩系統提供以網路連接方式查詢其他線上資源
⑪清楚地說明該線上公用目錄的內容及含蓋範圍
選擇項：
①系統明確告知遠程讀者能夠得到幫助之所在
②明確告知讀者系統鍵盤各鍵的功用
③遠程檢索若有時段上的限制時，系統會告知讀者

註　釋

① 李德竹、莊道明：《臺灣地區"國立大學"自動化之經驗與問題研究》，《資訊傳播與圖書館學》，1994，第1卷，第2期，頁24—33。
② Jamshid Beheshti, Browsing through public access catalogs, *Information Technology and Libraries*, 11：3（1992）：220-228.

③ Efthimios N. Efthimiadis, The growth of the OPAC literature, *Journal of the American Society for Information Science*, 41:5 (1990): 342.

④ Gord Nickerson, A mouse-based OPAC interface, *Computers in Libraries*. 10:8 (1990): 33.

⑤ Stuart Spore, Downloading from the OPAC: the innovative interfaces environment, *Library Hi Tech*. 9:2 (1991): 69-79.

⑥ Brian Sealy, Filtering out noise lines from OPAC downloads with sed, *Information Technology and Libraries*, 12:2 (1993): 270-276.

⑦ Joan M. Cherry. et al., OPACs in twelve Canadian academic libraries: an evaluation of functional capabilities and interface featufes, *Information Technology and Libraries*. 13:3 (1994): 174-191.

⑧ Frederick G. Kilgour, Redesign of known-item online access catalogs, *National Online Meeting*, (1994): 191-300.

⑨ Elaine Peterson, Management decisions: beyond the OPAC, *Journal of Academic Librarianship*, 21:1 (1995): 43-45.

⑩ Elaine Peterson, (1995): p. 33.

⑪ Nancy Lee Shires and Lydia P. Olszak. What our screens should look like: an introduction to effective OPAC screens, *RQ*, (1992): 357-369.

⑫ Jamshid Beheshti, (1992): pp. 220-228.

⑬ Charles R. Hildreth, Online public access catalogs, in *ARIST*, (1985): 233.

⑭ J. Murphy, A. S. Pollitt and P. R. White, Matching OPAC user interfaces to user needs, *Journal of Documentation*, 49:1 (1993): 72-73.

⑮ Jim Burton, OPAC: Freed by the Web, *Journal of Academic Librarianship*, 21:1 (1995): 46.

⑯ Sharon Seymour, Online public access catalog user studies: a review of research methodologies, March 1986-November 1989. *Library & Information Science Research*, 13:2 (1991): 89-102.

⑰ Joan M. Cherry and Marshall Clinton, OPACs at five Ontario universities: a profile of users & user satisfaction. *Canadian Library Journal*, 49:2 (1992): 123-124.

⑱ Larry Millsap and Terry Ellen Fert, Search patterns of remote users: an analysis of OPAC transaction logs, *Information Technology and Libraries*, 12:3 (1993): 321-343.

⑲ Frederick, G. Kilgour. (1994): 291-300.

⑳ 李德竹:《臺灣地區圖書館自動化系統線上目錄及其顯示格式之研究》,《圖書館學刊》, 1991, 第7期, 頁1—64。

㉑ 李德竹: 1991. p. 49。

㉒ 廖育佩:《臺灣地區大學圖書館線上公用目錄使用者利用指導方式之研究》, "國立臺灣大學" 圖書館學研究所碩士論文, 1991。

㉓ 邱韻玲:《 "國立清華大學" 線上公用目錄使用調查: 讀者查詢過程記錄 (transaction logs) 分析》, 1994, "國立臺灣大學" 圖書館學研究所碩士論文, 1991。

㉔ Joan M. Cherry. et al. , 13: 3 (1994): 174 - 195。
㉕ 李德竹:《圖書館自動化系統線上目録及其顯示格式之研究》,“國科會”計劃(NSC 79 - 0301 - H002 - 48),臺北市:“國立臺灣大學”圖書館研究所,1991 年。
㉖《一九九四學年度公私立大學校院一覽表》,臺北市:“教育部高等教育司”,1994 年。
㉗“中國圖書館學會圖書館自動化規劃委員會”編輯:《臺灣地區圖書館自動化系統彙編》,臺北市:“教育部”,1993 年。
㉘ Joan M. Cherry, ere. , 13: 3 (1994): 176.
㉙ Richard W. Boss and Susan B. Harrision, The online patron access catalog: the keystone in library automation, *Library Technology Reports*, 25: 5 (September/October, 1989): 635 - 723.
㉚ Frederick C. Kilgour, (1994): 291 - 300.
㉛ Joan M. Cherry, etc. , (1994): 176
㉜ Gord Nickerson, (1990): 33.
㉝ Jim Burton, (1995): 46.
㉞ Stuart Spore, (1991): 69 - 79.
㉟ Brian Sealy, (1993): 270 - 276.
㊱ Joan M. Cherry, et al. , (1994): 180.
㊲ Joan M. Cherry, et al. , (1994): 180.
㊳ Larry Millsap and Terry Ellen Fert, (1993): 321 - 343.
㊴ Larry Millsap and Terry Ellen Fert, (1993): 321 - 343.
㊵ Jamshid Beheshti, (1992): 220 - 228.
㊶ Joan M. Cherry, et al. , (1994): 180.
㊷ Joan M. Cherry, et al. , (1994): 180.
㊸ Helen K. Henry. Human-computer interfaces and OPACs: introductory thoughts related to INNOPAC, *Library Hi Tech*, 9: 2 (1991): 63 - 68.
㊹ Ron Slater, Authority control in a bilingal OPAC: multilis at Laurentian, *Library Resources & Technical Services*, 35: 4 (October 1991): 422 - 458.
㊺ Karen M. Drabenstott and Marjorie S. Weller, Testing a new design for subject searching in online catalogs, *Library Hi Tech*, 12: 1 (1994): 67 - 76, 86.
㊻ Frederick G. Kilgour, (1994): 291 - 330.
㊼ 邱韻玲: 1994 年.
㊽ Joseph R. Mattews, et al. , eds. *Using online catalogs: a nationwide survey*, New York: Neal-Schuman, 1983.
㊾ Joan M. Cherry, et al. , (1994): 185.
㊿ Joan M. Cherry, et al. , (1994): 185.
(51) Charles R. Hildreth, (1985): 233.
(52) Frederick G. Kilgour, (1994): 291 - 300.
(53) Frederick G. Kilgour. (1994): 291 - 300.
(54) Thomas A. Lucas, Research notes: time patterns in remote OPAC use, *College & Research*

Libraries, 54: 5 (September 1993): 439 - 445.
⑤⑤ Frederick G. Kilgour, (1994): 291 - 300.
⑤⑥ Library of Congress Access Project Team, access: new OPAC interfaces at the Library of Congress put a new face on software development, *CD-ROM Professional*, 4: 6 (November 1991): 83 - 86.
⑤⑦ Jim Burton, (1995): 46.
⑤⑧ 邱韻玲: 1994 年。

EDI 與圖書館應用*

前言

　　資訊社會的圖書館，如何經濟有效地購置及蒐集資料，以及如何讓讀者快速獲得所需之資料，是其兩大重要使命。圖書館為達上述任務，乃積極進行自動化，並透過網路連結各資訊自動化系統。近年來，雖然海內外圖書館自動化系統及網路連線進行得頗具成效，但在改善圖書館業務、節省人力時間成本、便於讀者能方便查詢各種連線資訊系統、並能快速獲得所需資訊等方面，尚待積極加強。目前海內外在商業上，尤其是貿易、通關、金融業、超市百貨、汽車零件業及圖書出版業等皆積極推動電子資料交換（Electronic Data Interchange，簡稱 EDI）技術之應用，正是提供圖書館界推動高度自動化，提昇作業效率之最佳參考及應用。

　　EDI 技術係以電腦通訊方式，在不同機構之電腦系統間傳遞具有標準格式資料文件之行為。採行 EDI 之產業有其共同特色，一為交易之商品或訊息種類繁多，一為交易對象繁多。在圖書館的業務中，則以書刊採購、館際資訊查詢以及館際互借複印同具有交易種類及對象繁多之特質，因此也是最適合採用 EDI 之作業項目。

　　政府於 1993 年 2 月 3 日公佈《公文程式條例部份條文修正案》第十二條之一中明定機關公文得以電子文件行之。"行政院"並責成研考會主辦擬具《機關公文電子交換作業辦法》，因此 EDI 有了法源依據。無論是企業間交易或圖書館間的館際互借以及圖書館與書商、書商與書商間的 EDI 交易行為也具有法律上的規範與保障（註1）：

　　EDI 在臺灣的發展只不過是近六年的事，臺灣幾個大型專案的推動，如通關自動化、商業加值型網路計劃、製造業 EDI 推廣計劃和最近積極研擬之圖書 EDI 計劃等推波助瀾之下，EDI 在臺灣已漸為一般企業與組織的重視，本文將就 EDI 的定義、EDI 的發展史，海內外 EDI 的應用作一基本的探討。

EDI 定義

　　海外 EDI 發展至今約有近三十年的歷史，因此對於 EDI 的定義，由於其使用目的或研究取材方向的差異，亦略有不同。以下是不同組織或學者對 EDI 的定義：

　　● 資訊工業策進會（1991）：EDI 乃指電子資料交換系統，是企業與企業之間的業務往來資料，以標準化的格式，無須人為的介入，不用紙張文件的傳送，而直接採用電子的型態，透過電腦通訊網路，在企業的電腦應用系統之間傳輸（註2）。

　　● Edward cannon（1993）：以電子傳輸的方式將標準的企業文件以預先設定的格式，由企業電腦應用系統傳送至交易夥伴之電腦系統（註3）。

　　● Margaret A. Emmelhainz（1993）：標準化且機器可以處理的商業資料格式，在跨組織間的電腦與電腦之間傳送（註4）。

＊ 本文摘錄自《圖書館與資訊研究論集：慶祝胡述兆教授七秩榮慶論文集》。（臺北市：漢美，1996 年 9 月。）

● Paula Tallim & J. C. Zeeman（1993）：在電腦與電腦間，以標準化資料格式交換企業資訊（註5）。

● Crowley（1993）：商業交易資訊，以標準化格式在電腦與電腦間進行傳送。（註6）

● Albert J. Marcella, Jr. and Sally Chan（1993）：在交易夥伴的電腦與電腦之間，傳送標準格式的企業資訊。（註7）

EDI 的特色及優點

一、EDI 特色

1. 企業與企業之間的交易資訊：

兩個以上的獨立組織或企業共同建立 EDI 體系，並且越多的交易廠商的加入，更是 EDI 關鍵成功因素之一。從影響產業結構的觀點，部份學者認為，EDI 應專指由兩個以上、目標獨立制訂的成員所建構的連線系統；而較廣義的說法，則垂直整合企業之事業單位的電子連線交易活動也含括在內；故在近幾年中，亦有人強調跨組織間（inter-organizational）的資料傳輸即可視為構成 EDI 的成分之一。

2. 電腦應用系統間的直接傳輸：

EDI 是發生在電腦之間的作業，而 EDI 的資料傳輸方式可有兩種型態：(1) 終端機與電腦連線 (2) 電腦與電腦連線。前者多見於組織內部的資訊網路建構，與初期的跨組織連線作業；後者需要兩個以上的單獨電腦應用系統的整合，不須人工介入，可發揮 EDI 的較大效益。因此，EDI 不僅可以省卻紙張的過度使用，亦可節省時間與資料的重複輸入，因為通常第一次由電腦產生的資料有 70% 將成為第二次接收企業的電腦輸入的資料。

3. 標準化格式：

EDI 的應用主要目的在於改善企業資訊的流程與管理效果。在參與 EDI 系統的各個通路，為了充份運用既有的資訊系統，又要達到資料傳輸暢通無阻的目的，必須建立交易雙方共同認可的通訊與訊息標準。此種 EDI 標準，主要可分為"專屬標準"與"公共標準"二種形式。前者為通路中的領導廠商所制之，後者則由業中的所有業者共同制定，以達成共識。甚至提昇至國家或國際層次，以整合不同產業或不同國家的通訊與訊息標準。此一標準化的格式應具結構化且必需要為電腦可以判讀的格式，方可避除在電腦之間傳遞過程的人為解讀。（註8）

EDI 系統間之轉換可以下圖示意（見下頁）：（註9）

二、EDI 的優點

當歐美各國的企業紛紛採用 EDI 且臺灣亦大力推動 EDI 的同時，對於 EDI 的應用，究竟有何優點是首先應該探討的課題。

對於 EDI 應用的效益首先直覺上的利益有下列幾點：

1. 減少紙張作業成本。
2. 資訊交換過程中較少錯誤。
3. 改善資料庫與資料庫、公司與公司間的資訊流。

4. 資料不需要重複輸入。

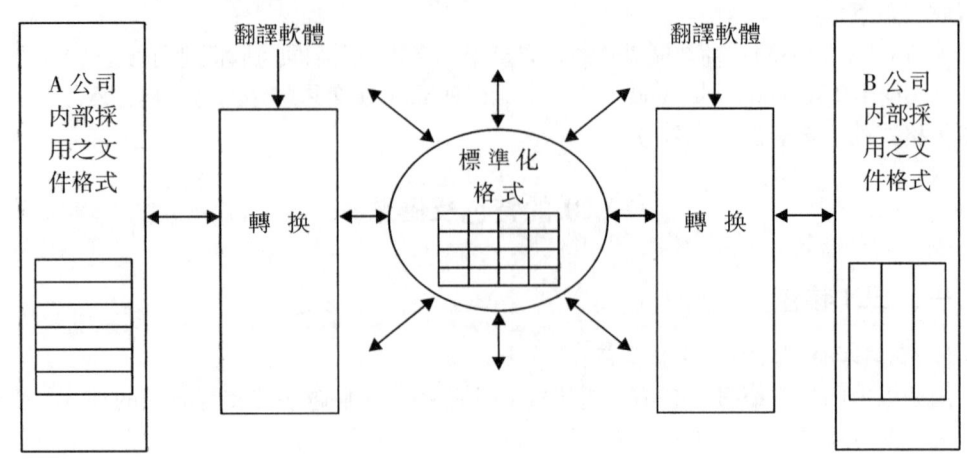

圖1　EDI系統間之轉接圖

（資料來源：資訊工業策進會EDI推廣中心）

5. 在通訊溝通上較少延遲。
6. 改善對賬、付款程序。

在企業經營的環境中，EDI的應用不僅是由電子資料傳輸來取代紙張的文件而已，其更重要的功能是將顧客的採購應用系統與供應商的訂單系統結合起來，故可以就下列三個企業經營的觀點來看EDI的效益（註10）：

1. 節省管理成本：

根據研究顯示，公司電腦系統的輸入有70%是來自於其他交易夥伴的電腦輸出，透過EDI的作業方式可由下列幾個方面來節省文件表單的處理成本：
- 重複輸入多於或重複的資訊。
- 從不同的表單中，由人工重作整理（如採購單、收料單、發票等）。
- 因不正確輸入所造成的錯誤。
- 文件的整理、散發與歸檔。
- 文件的郵寄或電話溝通資訊。

一般行業完成一筆交易所需要的文件，通常需要5至12種不同的文件，有些產業的特性，則可能需要達30種不同的文件。（註11）如使用EDI，不僅成本可由EDI而降低，且在工作的結構與流程上，都將因EDI的導入而引發甚多的變動，以至造成"企業重整"（Business Process Re-engineering）。此外，除節省成本外，交易的雙方也因此而彼此關係更為緊密，透過EDI的建置與應用過程，雙方溝通更頻繁，其重點將不在於交易上的問題，而是雙方如何以更緊密的作業流程，使彼此的交易更為順暢。

2. 效率的改善：

許多公司必需協調不同顧客與供應商之間的需求，以便將產品儘速地送至最終顧客的手上。例如製造公司必需與批發商、零售商、經銷商相互協調，以確保將產品送給客戶，使配銷通路（Distribution Channel）得以暢通，具良好的管理特性的公司總是想盡辦法，試圖改善本身的通路，所以公司多藉由降低通路的層級，使通路更具效益。為達此目的，資訊流通的速度與正確性，對於如何由更少的通路據點，獲取更完整的資訊需求而言，EDI 是協助達成此目標的工具。對 EDI 本身的特性而言，可由下列四個方向來協助企業改進動作效率：

- 資料正確性
- 完整的資訊
- 提供控制與時效的方法
- 提高交易夥伴的忠誠度

透過上述四個特性，企業將可提供更有效率的通路，而最後在通路上面的交易夥伴亦將更具忠誠度與承諾。故使用 EDI 不但可提供顧客更好的服務，且可使供應鏈的管理更為有效。

3. 改善內部流程：

如前所提，EDI 的應用可激發組織內部對工作與流程的重組，透過 EDI 的使用，改善內部的作業流程，可由三方面加以說明：

- 內部的重新評估：在電子資訊流完全取代紙張報表流程時，必需瞭解紙張報表流程。首先應評估現行作業流程，透過再評估的過程瞭解內部流程改善的空間或重新設計。
- EDI 整合系統：要提昇 EDI 的執行效益，如何與管理系統及技術結合，是關鍵之一，例如製造業的物料需求規劃與及時系統，便需要在交易夥伴間有快速與正確的資訊溝通技術，而 EDI 正好可以滿足此項需求。
- 改善人員生產力：EDI 可以消除許多準備與處理文件的管理活動，諸如錯誤的稽核、資訊的追蹤、文件的歸檔等，所需人力將因此減少許多，可以充分利用多餘的人力從事更有附加價值的活動，創造更高的生產力。

EDI 的實際運作過程及基本步驟

在 EDI 系統的實際運作過程中，大約可劃分為十項基本步驟，茲依序列示於下（註12）：

1. 首先在發送的公司系統中輸入資料（或原系統中的資料），當決定交易對象時，選定何種資料需要送給接收公司。

2. 送方的電腦程式將需傳送資料由系統取出，依送方電腦系統所實際使用的格式，排列成平坦檔（Flat File）或序列檔（Sequencc File）的格式。

3. 將此平坦檔載入"翻譯軟體"（Translator），加以轉換成適當的 EDI 訊息（message），或數個訊息以涵蓋交易之所需。

4. 該包含 EDI 訊息的檔案將交由通訊軟體，以便將該訊息由發送方的電腦系統送至接收方的電腦系統。

5. 傳送的方式可以藉由加值網路（Value Added Network，簡稱 VAN）來處理通訊工作，或者可以透過數據機（Modem）直接撥接對方的電話號碼傳送，但當發送的對象很多時，最好交由加值網路來處理通訊工作較為便利。

6. 當一個包含 EDI 訊息的檔案透過連線傳送完畢之後，即斷線回復原系統作業。若是直接連線者則可繼續連線，處理其他作業，如資料庫查詢；反之由加值網路服務者，則該 EDI 檔案由加值網路接收後，放置於接收者的電子郵箱（Mail Box）中，以備接收者連線由其郵箱取走相關的 EDI 檔案。

7. 接收方電腦系統由通訊網路上接收傳來的 EDI 檔案，將之存放於檔案儲存區中。

8. 將含 EDI 檔案轉入翻譯軟體中，轉換為接收端電腦所使用的平坦檔格式。

9. 翻譯軟體於此時建立一個 EDI 訊息稱之為功能回應（Functional Acknowledgement），透過通訊管道傳送給發送端，提供資料在技術層面的收訖指標，但其並非對交易的資料內容作一確認。

10. 收端之程式藉由翻譯軟體所轉換出來的平坦檔，將相關資料轉入接收端資料庫中的適當欄位，以供接收端應用系統的後續處理。

上述 EDI 的十項基本動作流程，可以圖2加以闡釋。

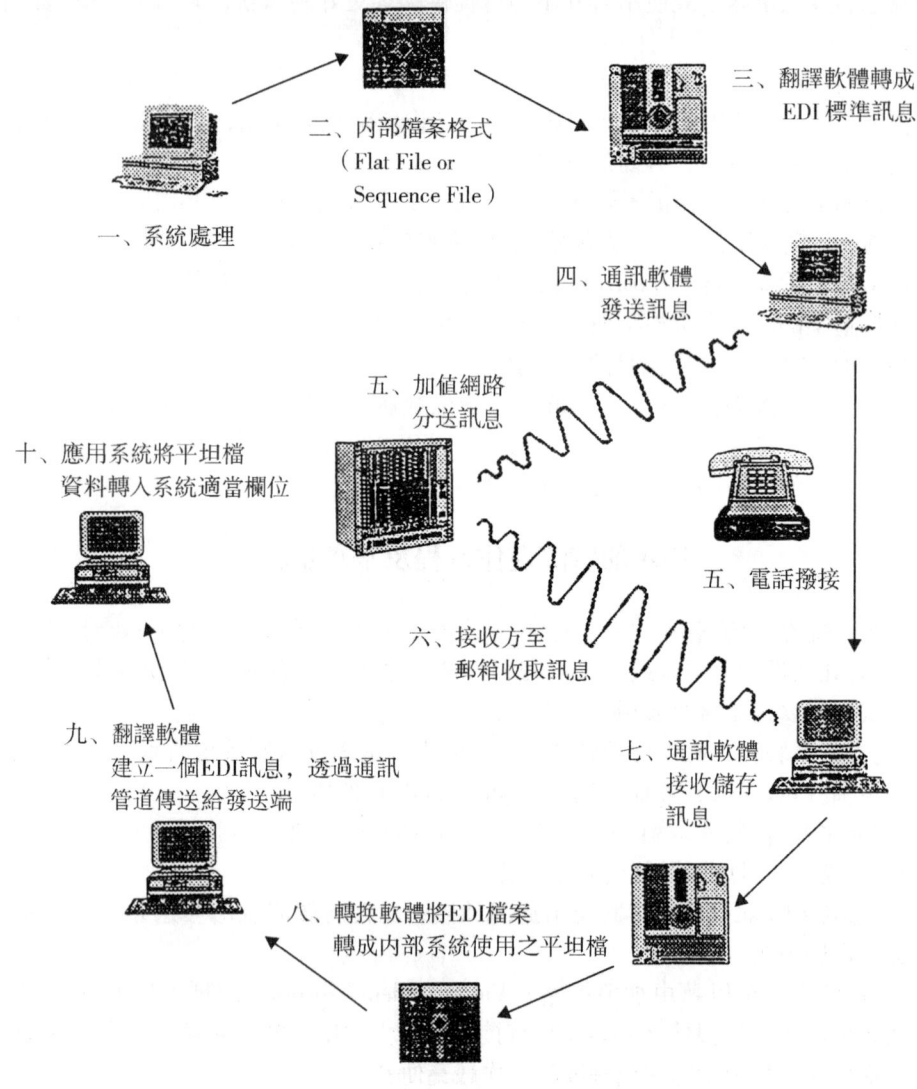

圖2　EDI 運作之基本步驟

（資料來源：R. T. Crowley）

EDI 標準之發展

　　正如 EDI 的定義所述，EDI 的標準對於使用 EDI 而言，它提供電腦可判讀、瞭解、處理企業文件的標準結構，因此標準扮演相當重要的角色，而 EDI 標準的發展與 EDI 應用的發展亦是密不可分的。

　　EDI 的應用肇始於約二十多年前，美國運輸業為解決因運輸所需的大量紙張表單使用上的困擾，提出 EDI 的觀念，以提昇不同運輸單位間資料交換效率。由企業間整合的產業標準，進而發展出跨產業的國家或區域標準，最後則形成國際上通用的 EDI 標準——UN/EDIFACT（United Nations/Electronic Data Interchange for Administration, Commerce and Transport）。以下就三個階段分述 UN/EDIFACT 的發展歷程（註13）：

一、產業標準階段：（1960—1980）

　　1960 年代末期，美國運輸業組織 TDCC（Transportation Data Coordinating Committee），在美國國防部的支持下，發展商業文件的電子傳輸格式，使運輸系統具有統一鐵路、公路、海運、空運的資料交換格式標準，並於 1975 年公佈了第一個 EDI 標準。歐洲方面，則於 1960 年初期，由聯合國歐洲經濟理事會 UN/ECE（United Nations/Economic Commission of Europe）開始集會探討貿易文件簡化及標準化的議題，是為 EDI 最早的研究。

　　產業標準的建立，引發更廣泛的使用需求，於是許多行業便依附其行業的特性與需求，發展出許多產業界的標準。在美國，諸如：運輸業 TDCC（Transportation Data Coordinating Committee）、汽車業 AIAG（Automative Industry Action Group）、零售業 VICS（Voluntary Inter-industry Communications Standard）、倉儲業 WINS（Warehouse Information Network Standards）等；在歐洲，則有零售業 TRADACOMS、汽車業 ODETTE（Organization for Data Exchange by Teletransmission in Europe）、海運業 DISH（Data Interchange for Shipping）等產業標準。在這些產業標準施行多年後，企業及產業界發現維繫日常運作，只有產業標準是不夠的，於是包容性更大的國家及區域性標準於焉產生。

二、國家（區域）標準階段：（1980—1985）

　　1980 年前後，EDI 的標準在歐美產生重大變化，也為通用性更高的 EDI 標準鋪路。首先在美國方面，1979 年，美國國家標準協會 ANSI（America National Standard Institute）授權 ASC X.12 委員會根據運輸業 TDCC 標準發展出更適合一般性行業均可適用的 EDI 標準，於是建立跨行業使用且具一般性的 EDI 國家標準 ANSI X12。

　　約在同時，早先聯合國歐洲經濟理事會負責簡化國際貿易程序事宜的 WP.4，已組成兩個分組委員會，分別就商業電子文件的資料結構模式與電子傳輸的標準語法進行研究，其成果於 1981 年正式發表。這成果分為兩大部份，一為資料結構成分模式的 TDED（Trade Data Element Directory）；另一則為包括語法及傳輸規則的 TDID（Trade Data Interchange Directory）。此外，UN/ECE 亦於 1980 年提出 GTDI（Guidelines for Trade Data Interchange）以供使用者瞭解如何使用 TDID，但除了應用的提示外，所欠缺的是訊息的標準,以致在實用性上並不高。

三、全球標準時代的肇始:(1985—)

1985年時,美國EDI專家學者及20餘國代表在紐約集會,以對建立世界性EDI標準的相關議題加以討論研究,會中對訊息結構(Message Syntax)及資料元(Data Element)進行比較,並協議產生國際性標準,而這些會議的成果則稱爲UNJEDI(United Nations Joint EDI)。各國代表要求在制訂國際性EDI標準時,應將現有各國EDI發展的現況納入考量,應以國際性標準爲重點,必須包括三個領域:行政(Administration)、商業(Commerce)、運輸(Transportation),這即是UN/EDIFACT(United Nations/Electronic Data Interchange for Administration, Commerce and Transport)名稱的由來。

聯合國歐洲經濟理事會第四工作小組(UN/ECE/WP.4),主要負責國際貿易程序簡化工作相關事務,爲聯合國授權整合EDI標準的任務,於1986年正式以"UN/EDIFACT"作爲國際間通用的EDI標準。另一方面,由於美國地區ANSI X.12的EDI標準制訂使用已有一段時間,透過美國企業向外的擴散效力,該標準的應用儼然已成爲建置EDI時,標準選用的重要考量。所幸在1992年時,ANSI ASC X12經投票決定在該標準第4版制訂(1997年)之後,將不再繼續發展與維護,全力投入與UN/EDIFACT的整合努力,而美國柯林頓總統亦下令所有美國採購案必須以電子化產業形式進行,並採X12及EDIFACT格式,應於1997年以前實施。因此一動作將可預期在1997年之後,全世界將趨於真正的統一。(註14)

UN/EDIFACT標準發展至今,使用的範圍愈益擴大,其標準的內容亦趨成熟,考慮的層面亦加擴大,更促進UN/EDIFACT之接受性與應用性。目前在全球已成立六大區域的委員會,綜理推動UN/EDIFACT標準相關事務,此六大區域爲泛美(Pan American)、西歐(Western Europe)、中歐及東歐(Central & Eastern Europe)、澳紐(Australia/New Zealand)、非洲(Africa)及亞洲(Asia)等。UN/EDIFACT標準係一相對成熟性的標準,除了已制訂的標準外,發展與維護亦針對實際應用的需求,不斷地更新與修正,故此標準之發行依其所制訂的需求時有修訂。

四、UN/EDIFACT相關標準

UN/EDIFACT標準主要分爲兩大部份:一爲語法規則及相關應用規則,另一爲訊息標準。在語法規則及相關規則方面,係用來規範UN/EDIFACT之訊息等資料規格標準的用法,而其主要內容含語法規則、語法建置指引、訊息設計指引等。

如同語法規則中所規定的,一個訊息規格係由各不同的資料段,依該訊息的功能及需求加以組合,形成訊息標準的規格,而一個訊息標準即是將表單文件中的資料項目,透過UN/EDIFACT語法及相關規則轉換成EDI電子資料的規格。訊息的發展是經過一系列的程序,並經審核通過成爲標準者即爲"聯合國標準訊息"UNSM(United Nations Standard Message)。依照UN/EDIFACT之訊息發展程序,每一個訊息發展將有三個階段的文件並由UN/ECE/WP.4對外發佈如下:

- 草案階段:Status 0(Draft)
- 試用階段:Status 1(Draft Recommendation)

● 建議使用階段：Status 2（Recommendation，登錄為 UNSM）

此三階段的訊息中，僅有將 Status 1 及 Status 2 編列為標準索引（Directory），而各年度之版本發展的過程如圖 3 所示。（註 15）

1994 年 9 月 UN/ECE/WP. 4 通過 D. 94B 共有 75 個標準訊息的發行，連同 Status 0 的訊息，共有約 180 個訊息涵蓋下列領域：貿易、運輸、海關、金融、營造、統計、會計、公衆行政管理等。

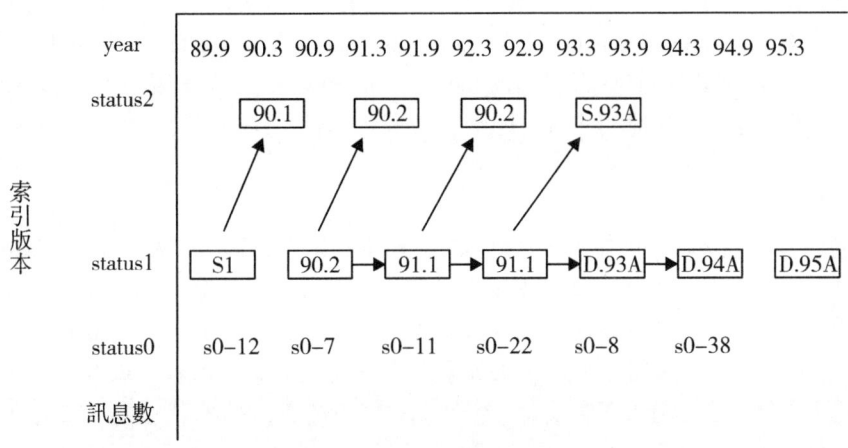

圖 3　UNSM 發佈的歷史過程

每一個訊息標準中，首先會針對該訊息的功能及應用領域作一訂定，使所有 UN/EDIFACT 的使用者都可以在相同功能與目的的資料交換過程中，使用同一訊息。其次將該訊息所有可能應用的資料段，依照該訊息之定義、功能及實際應用情形，依照訊息設計指引之相關規定加以排列組合，使訊息中的資料段排列及其重複次數得以符合實際需求。最後在訊息標準中會以資料段結構圖及資料段來表示訊息中資料段的使用狀況。

每一版本的 UN/EDIFACT 標準中（如 S. 93A、D. 93A、D. 94B、D. 95A），除了訊息標準的索引外，亦有相對應的資料段、資料元、代碼表等索引，透過這些不同的資料單元，建構出 UN/EDIFACT 標準的資料架構，使用者得以根據一定的規則與不同訊息規格，獲得判讀交換資料的能力，故使用 UN/EDIFACT 標準時，應同時參閱同版本內之各索引，方得取得其一致性。

EDI 在產業界的應用

EDI 的應用是否僅適於某些特定產業呢？其實不然，EDI 的應用是多方面的、廣泛的。只要兩個組織之間有資料交換的需求，即可以使用 EDI，且使用的對象亦不僅局限於大企業，許多中小企業、組織都可以加以運用，圖書館亦不例外。以下簡介 EDI 在海內外各產業的應用和圖書館的應用情形：

一、EDI 在歐美國家

歐美各國在不同產業間應用 EDI 的情形如下：

運輸業

運輸業可說是以整體產業觀點運用 EDI 的肇始。以美國而言，無論是鐵路、汽車貨運、海運、空運等運輸業目前皆已導入 EDI 的應用，應用的作業領域包含車輛調度資料、提單、託運單、貨運排程、訂位、管理、採購等資料，而在運輸業的日常運作中，溝通、聯繫對於貨物實際運輸過程中是最重要的。（註 16）

在英國，1986 年開始"運輸資料交換"（Data Interchange for Shipping，簡稱 DISH）先導計劃，結合 12 家主要出口商及陸、海、空運業者，DISH 更進一步結合的 DEDIST，荷蘭 INTIS（Internation Transport Information System）及比利時的 SEAGHA（system Electronic and Adapted Data Exchange in the Port of Antwerp）成為現今聯合國 EDI 標準 UN/EDIFACT 的前身。其他如法國、德國、西班牙、義大利等國的運輸業均已運用 EDI。（註 17）

零售業

美國雜貨業（Grocery）在 1978 年開始對 EDI 應用進行研究、根據估計 EDI 在雜貨業達到 50% 的使用率，因為降低錯誤及人員工作的直接節省效益每年可達八千四百萬美元，而每年的 EDI 操作費用僅需一千六百萬美元；在間接效益方面；由於資訊的正確性及生產力的運用，可帶來每年高達二億五千六百萬美元的成本節省。現今，在美國的雜貨業 EDI 體系中，已超過 250 個成員，包括 114 家製造商，96 家代理商，22 家批發商及 28 家雜貨商；在這 EDI 體系中，每年處理高達一億個訊息，以進行電子交易。

另一方面，美國幾家大型零售業，如 Sears、K-Mart、Walmart、JC Penney、Toys-R-us 等早在 60 年代已有專屬系統進行 EDI 之雛型。至今，EDI 在零售業的運用已是常態，且更進一步結合條碼系統（Bar-Coding）及銷售點系統（Point of Sale，POS），冀求獲得快速反應（Quick-Response）運作機能。（註 18）

英國方面，則以 TRADACOMS 的標準，在零售業及其供應商間進行 EDI 的交易。法國流通業協會（GENCOD）的專屬標準，德國零售業協會 CCG 的 SEDA 標準、義大利與荷蘭的零售業，採用 UN/EDIFACT 等，表示 EDI 在歐洲零售業已入 EDI 應用成長期。（註 19）

其他產業 EDI 應用

EDI 的應用正在許多產業擴展，且已經成為歐美先進國家在交易過程中不可或缺的資訊技術應用。除上述之運輸與零售業外，其他許多產業亦對於 EDI 的應用更是不遺餘力。

汽車業的應用，歐洲各大汽車廠於 1985 年成立 ODETTE（Organization for Data Exchange by Tele-Transmission in Europe），參與的廠商如"奧斯丁陸寶"、"通用"、"標緻"、"福特"等，配合英國汽車製造協會共同推動歐洲汽車業者間的 EDI 應用。美國汽車業間則有 AIAG（Automotive Industry Action Group）推動 EDI 在汽車業間的合作以抗拒外國汽車業的威脅，透過 EDI 的運用提供達成即時生產 JIT（Just in Time）的工具，並藉以評估收付款體系及整合製造管理系統。

此外在美國醫療保健方面，醫藥採購亦有利用 EDI 為之，其主要參與者為藥物的配送者及醫院的供應商，目前在此系統已包含採購及銷售作業的交易訊息，且正在擴大使用者的範圍。

美國政府亦於 1985 年公告《聯邦資訊資源管理辦法》（Management of Federal

Information Resource，A130），明確指出 EDI 的應用與否將成爲政府未來選擇標準之一，其中美國國防部更計劃於 1999 年前推動所有供應商使用 EDI，以期達到完全無紙化的交易環境。(註20)

在英國，除上述產業之應用外，政府部門亦大力推動 EDI 的應用，英國的港務、機場、海關、稅務局等皆已使用 EDI，而一般產業的應用亦廣泛使用。在化學業由 ICI 支持的先導計劃中，有 15 家化學業的公司加入；電子業則於 1986 年歐洲 EDIFICE 機構 (EDI For Companies with Interests in Computing & Electronics) 研究、提供 EDI 相關經驗後，開始應用 TRADACOMS 的標準進行 EDI 交易作業；醫療保健則於 1989 年開始開發 EDI 系統，結合大供應商，以期能提供完善的醫藥供應環節；保險業則利用 LIMNET、RINET、BROKERNET 等三個網路分別提供一般保險業務、再保險、汽車保險等保險業務的資料交換；建築業則是由 EDICON (EDI Construction Ltd.) 提供建築業者對於使用 EDI 的相關作業研究；旅遊業則推動 UNICORN (United Nations EDI for Cooperation in Research Networks) 計劃，推動訂位與售票 EDI 的作業等。(註21)

二、EDI 在臺灣之應用

臺灣地區各行業應用 EDI 的歷史並不長，早期少數幾個 EDI 的使用者，多係應海外交易伙伴或總公司之要求而實施 EDI 作業。而臺灣地區比較有計劃及有系統的應用 EDI 始自 1990 年，當時由"經濟部"委託資訊工業策進會進行 EDI 發展策略之規劃，乃開啓了各項 EDI 相關計劃之推動。(註22) 由於 EDI 已成爲先進國家從事經貿活動的重要工具，因此以外貿爲導向的臺灣地區，也以此爲開端，在 1990 年由"財政部"規劃貨物通關自動化，並於 1992 年完成空運貨物通關全面自動化。貨物通關自動化可說是島內第一個 EDI 應用計劃，自此，臺灣也正式邁入 EDI 應用的新紀元。1994 年資訊月活動主題是：加速臺灣資訊基礎建設—普及電子資料交換應用 (EDI)。主題館區展示 NII 及 EDI 之應用，可見 EDI 在臺灣的應用及發展已漸成氣候。

臺灣現有 EDI 使用者大多集中在報關貿易業、製造業及流通業等。通常資訊化程度較高，且業務範圍分佈較廣的行業，其使用 EDI 的意願及效益較佳。但近兩三年來，由於政府的大力推動及 EDI 服務業者提供越來越多的產品服務，使得某些資訊化程度並不高的行業亦投入 EDI 的應用世界裡（註23）。目前臺灣參與推動及建置 EDI 的單位可區分爲以下三類：

1. 政府機構："財政部"及"經濟部"爲主導 EDI 建置的兩個主要政府機構，其於近幾年主導了幾個成效頗著的大型 EDI 計劃。

2. 財團法人：資訊工業策進會及工業技術研究院兩個非營利性財團法人在推動 EDI 技術方面扮演著極重要的角色。

3. 民間企業：主要是 EDI 軟硬體廠商及企業界 EDI 使用者。(註24)

以下僅就臺灣各項 EDI 大型計劃發展的現況以及支援 EDI 軟硬體的廠商做一介紹：

EDI 大型計劃發展的現況：

1. 貨物通關自動化計劃：本計劃於 1990 年由"財政部"貨物通關自動化規劃推行小組負責執行，爲目前 EDI 計劃中進度較爲具體可見的計劃之一，自動化作業範圍涵蓋航空海運業、倉儲業、報關行及進出口業等。該計劃之目的乃在建置一個大型 EDI 網路中心,即關貿網路(TRADE-VAN),與整合海關資訊系統、串連貨物進出口、運輸及通關等相關單位,以達成貨物通關自動化,邁向無紙化通關放行的目標。(註25)該計劃已於1992年完成空運貨物報關自動化系統,並於1994年完成海運貨物報關自動化系統。

2. 汽車中心、衛星廠商EDI應用先導計劃:本計劃由"經濟部"工業局於1991年委託中心衛星廠發展中心與資策會共同規劃汽車中心衛星廠商EDI應用先導系統計劃。本計劃內容包括汽車業先導系統建置、汽車業訊息制定及人才培訓等。(註26)本計劃初期由四家中心廠,即裕隆、中華、福特及三陽,衛星廠則包括四個體系的14家零組件供應商,於1993年完成初步的測試工作,後續計劃正進行中。(註27)

3. 臺灣超市加值型網路先導計劃:計劃是由"經濟部"商業司於1991年委託資訊工業策進會系統工程處規劃,系統實施的對象包括一般超市、超市的批發商、貨運公司及銀行等,於1993年完成連線測試。(註28)

4. 金融EDI加值網路系統:"財政部"於1994年指示金融資訊中心擔任推動金融EDI的專責機構,並責成於1995年九月底前完成金融電子資料交換共用加值網路系統,未來將與商業EDI網路、關貿EDI網路、中衛EDI網路相連結,藉著結合金流、商流的自動化,創造電子商務的交易環境。

5. 電子EDI:近幾年來,由於政府大力推廣EDI之應用,民間企業也相繼投入,如宏碁電腦公司於1990年開始推動EDI的應用、臺灣國際標準電子公司於1991年底開始與其IC供應商(即德州儀器)進行電於資料交換,近半年電子業者已積極展開使用EDI。(註29)

6. 政府推廣商業EDI五年成效:1992年由"經濟部"商業司開始推廣"商業電子資料交換加值網路先導系統計劃",協助企業導入EDI技術,其成果矚目,於1994年獲頒"傑出資訊應用獎",亦成爲日本、新加坡仿效的對象。目前使用商業EDI的業者如前述之零售商、供應商、物價中心、貨運業、銀行業者等。至1996年5月底導入EDI的企業家有140家,2778個營業站,另有284家企業有意願導入EDI之列。新近推展的圖書業EDI亦頗有規模,有待開拓的領域有醫療健保作業、運輸、營建、保險、政府採購、政府統計等。由於政府大力推展,應用EDI的行業亦正持續擴散中。(註30)

7. 島內EDI廠商:EDI應用成功的關鍵除了參與者具有充分的認知、市場需求、資訊化程度及可用的訊息標準外,尚須仰賴技術支援的廠商。目前臺灣EDI廠商有三十餘家,如臺灣電訊、"中國嘉通"、高階資訊、電信局數據所、凌羣電腦、汎凌資訊、康大資訊等。其服務項目約可分爲EDI軟體開發、EDI系統整合、EDI諮詢服務,EDI教育訓練及EDI網路中心等。(註31)

EDI在海外圖書館界的應用

圖書館與出版商或代理商進行書刊交易之程序,包括報價、發訂單、催缺、發票處理及付款等,雖或可借助各自動化系統之協助,減少部份作業處理時間,但如雙方沒有約定之交易格式,雖透過網路相互傳遞交易訊息,則仍有許多缺點存在,諸如重複鍵入資料、郵遞費時、處理時間延遲以及因重複鍵人資料易生錯誤等,若能應用EDI技術於書刊交易上,則圖書館將來之書刊採購必可縮短處理時程、減少錯誤及節省人力時間。同樣地,目前館際間透過網路檢索各資訊自動化系統,及館際互借複印亦有傳統書刊交易之缺點,讀者除必須逐一查詢各種不同檢索指令之系統,或借助各類書目中心以查詢資料。

1. CTA(Canadian Telebook Agency)& CBISAC(Canadian Book Industry System Advisory Committee)

CTA 成立於 1981 年,爲一非營利機構,其職責在於簡化加拿大圖書發行與配送之搜尋與訂購,目前提供兩項採購相關服務:電子圖書訂購網路(Telebook Ordering Network)及加拿大資源資料庫(Canadian Sourcing Database)。自 1991 年開始推動與協調加拿大圖書業 EDI 的應用,目前 CTA 的圖書訂購網路已可提供符合 ANSI X12 標準的採購單。CBISAC 則成立於 1989 年,其性質與美國 BISAC 類似,並提供加拿大圖書業在建置 EDI 相關問題的協助,在 1992 年時,CBISAC 受政府資助,以合理的價格,提供相關軟體給圖書業界的每一個單位,使圖書業界儘可能皆利用 ANSI X12 的格式執行相關作業。(註 34)

2. SISAC(Serial Industry System Advisory Committee)

SISAC 主要有三項工作:

• 自 1982 年開始發展期刊業者間的電腦與電腦間的標準格式,該類標準並成爲美國國家標準。

• 透過機器可判讀的標準化代碼識別期刊的相關資料,以利圖書館對期刊的自動化查核與控制。

• 利用期刊的標準代碼(SICI,Serial Item and Contribution Identifier)可以簡化版稅的給付及在全文與目錄資料庫中識別、擷取相關文章。(註 35)

3. CSISAC(Canadian SISAC)

加拿大 CSISAC 成立於 1991 年,並以期刊爲對象發展 ANSI X12 的標準訊息,並與 CBISAC、SISAC 共同整合書籍與期刊的格式,以提供圖書館對書籍與期刊的共同需求(註 36)。

4. OCLC PromCat Service

美國 OCLC 書目中心於 1995 年 4 月推出新的 PromCat Service 服務項目,此服務含採購與編目兩種功能。書商用 ANSI X.12 format 通知 OCLC 哪些書已送至某採購圖書館,然後 OCLC 將此採購單查尋 OCLC 資料單中相關的 MARC 書目記錄,並以電子傳輸方式(FTP)送至該購書圖書館。(註 37)

5. OhioLINK(INNOPAC)圖書館 EDI 應用

美國 INNOPAC 圖書館自動化系統公司之 Ohio-LINK 網路圖書館使用 EDI X.12Protocol 做電子採購(Electronic Ordering)和期刊催缺(Serials Claim),限用於書刊 Vendors 與 INNOPAC 圖書館之間。(註 38)此作法係根據早期 Dartmouth College Library, Faxon 公司和 Innopace Interface 公司共同研究之期刊催缺先導計劃(Dartmouth + Faxon + Innopace + SISAC + X12 Serials Claims Pilot Project)。(註 39)

歐洲地區

1. BEDIS(Book Trade Electronic Data Interchange Standards)

BEDIS 爲英國圖書業於 1986 年結合出版商、書商及圖書館成立的組織,該協會的目標主要任務在於建立出版業界維護的書目資料庫,BEDIS 致力於以 MARC(Machine Readable Cataloging)爲基礎的書目資料加以配合 TRADACOMS 的標準,以圖書業的需求提供 EDI 的應用、實施、電子訂購系統，並在 1990 年以 JANET（Joint Academic Network）連結書商與大學圖書館。

由於歐洲地區多採用 UN/EDIFACT 標準，BEDIS 故發展 TRADACOMS 與美國 BISAC 及加拿大 CBISAC 所使用的 ANSI Xl2 之間的轉換機制，其後於 1991 年與 BIC 合併。

2. BIC（Book Indusrty Communication）

BIC 於 1991 年 3 月由出版商協會、書商協會、圖書館協會及大英圖書館贊助成立，其任務為"簡化圖書業間資訊型式與溝通，發展及推廣書目資訊的標準格式與傳輸，設計商業訊息或其他資訊以提昇產業間交易與供應的效率與效果"。經過兩年的運作，BIC 建立工作組與 BISAC、CBISAC 協調建立 EDI 的標準，並以 UN/EDIFACT 為基礎。

3. EDItEUR（Pan-European Book Sector EDI Group）

EDItEUR 係 BIC 協調發展泛歐洲圖書業 EDI 標準所建立的工作組織，以採用 UN/EDIFACT 為圖書業的 EDI 基礎，並以 UN/EDIFACT 標準架構下的歐洲商品編碼標準 EAN 版本（EANCOM, European Article Numbering）為標準，發展出配合圖書業界所需的專屬格式。

4. IPA（International Publishers Association）

IPA 在 1992 年一月的會議中，超過 50 個國家的出版業、書商、圖書館等協會的參與代表，提議使用 UN/EDIFACT 的格式并與 BIC 或其他組織的標準工作相互協調，期以此為基礎發展 EDI 的訊息（註 40）。

5. EDI 在英國圖書館應用現況

根據 Brian Green 之報導約 55% 英國的學術及公共圖書館已使用 EDI，多用在發訂單（Orders）、收付（acknowledgement）或發票（invoice）方面。在英國所有主要的圖書館書商、批發商、出版商皆提供 EDI links。（註 41）

國際性的計劃

EDILIBE（EDI for Libraries and Book in Europe）計劃係歐洲經濟社會理事會（ECE）對圖書館業的行動計劃，參加的國家包括德國、義大利、荷蘭、英國、西班牙等，該計劃的第一階段為以 UN/EDIFACT 為基礎發展資料格式，透過 X.400 將這一格式加以傳送。EDILIBE 的計劃共分為兩階段：

第一階段：如上所述，已於 1991 年底由德國 Stadtund University in Frankfurt, Germany 完成。

第二階段：計劃在參與者端建立 UN/EDIFACT 與 X.400 之軟體，並加以測試不同系統之間的相互運作狀況，此階段參與者包括圖書書商：Blackwell、Harrossowitz、Casalini；系統供應：BLCMP、PICA；圖書館：Gottingen、Madrid、Florence 等單位。（註 42）於 1995 年 9 月成立 EDILIBEII 計劃，由五個國家 10 個單位參加。（註 43）

二、EDI 與圖書館館際合作

1988 年，Millson 在"Interlibrary Loan Protocols"（註 44）一文中介紹館際互借自動化系統間交換訊息的通信協定。此通信協定使得各圖書館間的不同自動化系統得以交換訊息，從而使得館際互借的流程得以自動化。此通信協定即后來的 ISO 10160 及 ISO 10161 標準。

1989 年，Fay Turner 在 "Interlibrary Loan Protocol Implementation Issues"（註45）文中認爲館際互借通信協定雖然已將成爲 ISO 標準，但仍有許多實作上的問題 (Implementation Issues) 必須討論與克服。爲此 IFLA 成立了 Universal Dataflow and Telecommunications（UDT）ILL Feasibility Study 計劃。

本計劃之目標如下：
- 規劃成立先導計劃
- 探討技術關鍵問題，並定出統一的作業程序
- 評估實施館際互借計劃的時機

該文簡介該計劃實施的經過及結果，此外，其重點在整理出館際互借通信協定在實作上所面臨的問題及選擇，如：
- Functional profile
- Protocol features
- Interworking scenarios
- Application context
- Communication modes
- Transfer syntax
- Information retrieval
- Conformance testing

1990 年，Turner 首先探討現有館際（書目）網路無法提供全域性的館際互借服務的原因，一爲網路間的不互通，另一爲資料格式的不統一。後又介紹 ISO 標準訂定中的 ILL Protocol。ILL Protocol 可由以下四個層面明確規範館際互借的應用協定：
- 館際互借的交易中所使用的訊息種類（Message Types）
- 訊息中的資料元（Data Elements）
- 訊息傳遞的正確順序（Sequence of Messages）
- 傳輸的資料格式（Transfer Syntax）

文中亦介紹加拿大 "國家圖書館"（National Library of Canada，簡稱 NLC）對於 ILL Protocol 的支援措施，例如：實做計劃，應用協定測試，與其他書目網路系統間的橋接（Bridging Mechanism）等（註46）。

Swain 及 Tallim 於 1992 年發表之論文 "The Interlibrary, Loan (ILL) Protocol: Progress and Projects"（註47）除部份介紹 ILL Protocol 外，亦介紹近幾年來國際間使用此通信協定的一些活動，如：
- 自 1987 年開始，加拿大的圖書館即開始採用 ILL Protocol，National Library of Canada 並開始找系統廠商提供軟硬體。到了 1992 年這些系統都已陸續完成。
- 在加拿大，許多橋接系統已經完成，用來與非使用 ILL Protocol 的網路連接。
- NLC 開發 ILL Protocol 的相容性測試軟體。
- NLC、British Library Document Supply Centre（BLDSC）及 US Library of Congress 共同成立 The Interlibrary Loan Access Demonstration（ILIAD）Proiect，其目的在推廣 ILL Protocol 的使用，並從中獲得經驗。可惜這個計劃只進行到規劃階段，並未能持續下去。其最主要因素是此三個機構間之館際互借量太少，並未能達到合理的經濟規模。

● 英國 London and South Eastern Library Region（LASER）、荷蘭 Pica Centrum voor Bibliotheek Automatisering（Pica）及法國 Ministere de l' Education National, Direction de la Programmation et du Developement Universitaire, Sous-Direction Des Bibliotheques（SBD/SUNIST）三國共同成立 Projection-the OSI Pilot/Demonstration Project between Library Services in Europe for interlending services 計劃。其主要目標在建立機構間的連線以改善館際互借的效率並展示 ILL Protocol 的效能。本計劃共分爲三階段：第一階段爲需求的確認，第二階段爲系統的建置，第三階段則爲系統的使用與效能的評估。

● 美、加與歐洲的大型書目組織亦組成一個 International Forum on Open Internatioanl Standardized Profiles（ISPs）。ISP 的目的在於根據各地區的需求，將標準中的彈性選擇部份予以明確規定，以保證各通信伙伴間之相容性。

1988 年 ISO 發佈 ISO 8459 Bibliography Data Element Directory-Interloan Applications（註 48）標準，1993 年，臺灣地區根據 ISO 8459 制定 CNS 13150 館際互借書目資料項目標準。本標準制訂各圖書館、資料中心在執行館際互借業務時可採行的書目項目標準名稱。其中規定：申請號、資料敘述、書目查證、讀者識別、互借業務參與者、所需服務、申請情況、傳遞情形、付款方式、核准借閱、最高費用、賬號、借閱情形、日期形態及執行現況等。本標準對於館際互借的資料項目規定極爲詳細，但是對於各參與者之間的互動關係，則未觸及（註 49）。

1993 年，由 ISO 發佈 ISO/DIS 10160（註 50）標準，其中對館際互借作業作一個清楚的定義，其包括所牽涉的對象及角色、作業的內容、流程中的狀態等。爲清楚的描述 ILL Protocol，先在 ISO 10160 Interlibrary Loan Application Service Definition 中，將館際互借交易（ILL Transaction）的形態、角色及服務內容予以定義。同年，ISO 又發佈 ISO 10161（註 51），此標準規定了兩個以上的個體進行館際互借交易時，所需遵守的行爲規則，它規定以下事項：

● 當接到服務使用者的服務需求時，所需採行的動作
● 當接到對方傳來的通信協定訊息（Application Protocol Data Units, APDUs）時，所需採取的動作
● 己方系統的事件（Event）發生時，所需採行的動作
● APDU 的詳細內容格式

1989 年蘇倫伸的碩士論文（註 52）爲島內第一個對館際互借自動化作有系統的研究。文中以臺灣地區八個圖書館作基礎，分析其現行的館際互借作業流程及交換的資訊流。然後再提出一個建議，建立一個正規而統一的館際互借系統。本文的可貴處在於實際考慮臺灣目前的人工作業狀況，除館際互借外，尚考慮到與館合組織的通信以及賬目處理的問題。由於資訊科技的日新月異與作業流程的簡化與合理化，自動化後的作業流程勢必與人工作業有很大的不同，但本文並未提及。且本文的撰寫是在 ISO 10160 與 ISO 10161 訂定之前，館際互借的作業及通信協定應逐步朝向國際標準化，這也是當年所無法考慮到之原因。

EDI 在臺灣圖書館界的應用

EDI 應用之推廣在臺灣雖已有六年之久，但對圖書館界而言，EDI 僅是一個商業名

詞；關係遙遠，這也證實 EDI 在圖書館應用之現況。雖如此，但有心人士仍試擬計劃以期對圖書館界推銷 EDI 之觀念。1993 年，"中國圖書館學會"暑期委託臺灣大學圖書館學系舉辦的"圖書館自動化及網路專題研習會"中曾介紹"EDI 技術"給與會學員，其內容重點則是 EDI 觀念及標準，並未談及 EDI 在圖書館之應用。（註 53）

同年，由"國立中央圖書館"、"教育部"電算中心、"交通部"數據通信所、"行政院"研究發展考核委員會、"行政院"新聞局、"經濟部"商業司、臺北市出版商同業公會、圖書出版事業協會與"國立臺灣大學"及"國立中央大學"共同研擬建教合作計劃，定名為"圖書出版資訊網及其應用之規劃與建立"，其主要目的是基於"交通部"電信局數據通信所之網路及電子資料交換中心與"教育部"電算中心之學術網路，規劃建立一圖書出版與採購資訊網，藉由 ISBN 資料庫之建置與電子資料交換之作業方式，加速提供圖書館、出版業、書商、學校老師學生及社會上一般大眾對圖書出版與購買所需之資訊服務。同時也可提供政府相關單位對圖書出版業界及圖書出版品之瞭解、掌握、輔導、記錄與管理等所需之資訊服務。此資訊網之最終目的是加速塑造書香社會的未來美景，全面提昇文化建設。本計劃由"國立中央大學"資訊管理研究所郭更生擔任計劃主持人、"國立臺灣大學"圖書館研究所李德竹教授擔任共同主持人，實際負責計劃之執行工作，計劃召集人為"中國圖書館學會"王振鵠理事長擔任。遺憾的是，此計劃雖歷經八個月之協調溝通，但未能建立相關單位間之共識與認同，而未竟其功。（註 54）

近年來，資策會亦多次不定期舉辦 EDI 推廣說明會，重點多偏最新商業 EDI 方面之一般介紹。目前臺灣地區已制定 EDI "國家標準"有：CNS 13228 電子資料交換—資料之索引；CNS 13283 電子資料交換—語法規則；CNS 13323 電子資料交換—合成資料元索引和 CNS 13224 電子資料交換—資料段索引。有關圖書和館際合作方面之"國家標準"可供參考制定 EDI 標準者，目前僅有 CNS 13150 館際互借書目資料項目標準，和 1996 年擬定之"圖書電子訂購標準草案"。（註 55）

1995 年"圖書出版事業電子資料交換計劃"在"行政院"新聞局的大力推動下，於元月間成立圖書 EDI 使用者組織大會，同時委託資訊工業策進會對圖書 EDI 進行初步規劃，出版業界反映甚好，並積極參與。該案預計於當年六月底年度計劃結束時，完成採購清單、出貨單、收貨驗收單、退貨單、商品通告等五項表單之制定工作。金石堂、新學友等二十餘家出版業者進行密集工作會議建立共識。資策會根據出版商提出之交易項目、流程等需求，目前已完成了採購清單等各項標準表單的制定，同時資策會亦擬定"圖書 EDI 訊息建置指引"草稿，已交新聞局審查中，經正式公佈後，可作為圖書業者上、中、下游導入 EDI 應用之依據。（註 56）

資策會規劃之圖書事業電子資料交換計劃案中已擬定三年計劃，其工作項目及時程詳見下表：

圖書事業電子資料交換計劃工作項目及時程表

工作項目 \ 時程 月份	1996年度 10 11 12 1 2 3 4 5 6	1997年度 7 8 9 10 11 12 1 2 3 4 5 6	1998年度 7 8 9 10 11 12 1 2 3 4 5 6
1. 成立使用者組織	▬		
2. 研訂標準表單及EDI訊息優先順序	▬		
3. 研訂標準表單	▬▬	▬▬▬	▬▬▬
4. 辦理標準表單說明會	▬		
5. 設計EDI訊息	▬▬	▬▬▬	▬▬▬
6. VAN評選協調與測試		▬▬▬	
7. 輔導業者導入EDI		▬▬▬▬▬▬▬▬	▬▬▬▬▬▬▬▬
8. 協助提供EDI系統驗證		▬▬▬▬▬▬▬▬	▬▬▬▬▬▬▬▬
9. 辦理EDI推廣業務		▬▬▬▬▬▬▬▬	▬▬▬▬▬▬▬▬
10. 維護標準表單與EDI訊息		▬▬▬▬▬▬▬▬	▬▬▬▬▬▬▬▬
11. 圖書商品資料庫可行性分析		▬▬▬	
12. VAN與資料庫整合應用		▬▬▬▬	▬▬▬▬▬▬▬▬
13. 輔導資訊業者對小型業者提供服務		▬▬▬▬▬▬	▬▬▬▬▬▬▬▬

資策會提供（註57）

雖已積極推展圖書 EDI，目前計劃僅限於出版業界，尚未與圖書館界結合。館際合作方面 EDI 應用更是無人關懷與推廣。可慶幸的是，臺灣大學李德竹教授於 1995 年 7 月已完成"國科會"補助之"電子資料交換（EDI）應用與圖書館之研究報告"，已為圖書採購 EDI 及館際合作 EDI 做了初步之探討，圖書交易和館際合作 EDI 訊息，可供圖書館界參考。（註58）

結　論

近年來圖書館界已將圖書館自動化業務視為提昇服務品質及工作效率的不二法門。

然而各館的自動化業務多半著重於館內業務的自動化，如編目、流通、期刊、線上目錄等。對於各個圖書館之間或是與外界的聯繫，則限於以透過 Internet 為主的資訊查詢。而對於有交易往來的業務，如館際合作、圖書採購等仍限於人工作業的狀態。電子資料交換（EDI）經商業界採用多年，對於多重對象間的頻繁交易的自動化，已有卓著的成效，值得圖書館界參考採用。

根據海內外使用 EDI 之現況，同時為促進 EDI 應用於島內圖書館間的館際互借及圖書採購交易業務，提出以下建議：

1. 儘速訂定館際互借及圖書交易 EDI "國家標準"

EDI 之實施，首重標準之建立。茲建議以李德竹教授研究所擬定之館際合作和圖書採購訊息為參考應儘速建立館際互借和圖書採購相關的 "國家標準"，以作為實行之依據。

2. 積極建立館際互借 EDI 體系

臺灣圖書館界很早已對圖書館館際合作和互借有非常正確的觀念，故在1968年開始已訂定各類型圖書館館際圖書互借辦法。目前，正式成立的圖書館館際合作組織有 "財團法人科技圖書館及資料單位館際合作組織研究及發展基金會" 和 "人文社會科學圖書館合作組織"。其提供服務方式有：信件、電話、傳真、親自前往、電子郵件等多種，其中以使用信件方式為最多，約佔50%使用率，其次為電話方式21%（註59）。為求更能儘速提供讀者服務，建議館際合作組織應積極根據李德竹教授之 "電子資料交換（EDI）應用在圖書館之研究報告" 定義之館際互借應用協定及訊息，建立圖書館館際互借 EDI 體系，透過網路迅速提供圖書館讀者所需之服務及資料。（註60）

3. 主管機關協助圖書業建立全面性 EDI 交易體系

根據李教授研究報告對圖書業者對圖書交易 EDI 的認知分析，業者普遍認為 EDI 的應用可以提高效率，降低成本以強化企業競爭力，但也認為缺乏標準與交易伙伴配合度是實行 EDI 的障礙。且由於民眾缺乏同業合作的經驗、商業競爭等因素，業界的共識建立十分緩慢。此時實有賴主管機關如 "經濟部" 商業司出面安排，並廣為推廣說明，以早日促成標準的訂定及整體交易體系的建立。雖經 "行政院" 新聞局、"經濟部" 商業司、資策會等大力宣導，並提出 "圖書出版事業電子資料交換計劃"，圖書業者已有二十多家意願加入，但此計劃仍局限於 EDI 圖書出版業者，實應考慮整體性圖書 EDI 交易體系，除含圖書業者，亦應考量書商與圖書館間全部交易行為，建立一個完整的圖書 EDI 體系。

4. 建立圖書館及書商資訊資料庫

EDI 的實施可簡化許多作業程序，進而鼓勵大量的交易，活絡各種資源的流通。在此之前，其首當應健全資訊之整理及查詢功能。其中如聯合目錄、各種館藏資料庫，出版商圖書資料庫等，皆應及早整理開放，俾便透過網路提供各地讀者及交易伙伴查詢。

5. 加強圖書館學系有關 EDI 方面之內容及課程

EDI 常被視為僅限於商業方面的文件交換行為，實際上 EDI 可更廣泛地應用於各行各業的文件交換作業上。雖在資策會、新聞局，甚至於83年資訊月廣為 EDI 大肆宣傳，但圖書館界似乎對 EDI 的認知仍嫌不足，更遑論 EDI 利用。故建議將 EDI 觀念納入圖書館學系相關課程中，以加強學生對 EDI 之認識和瞭解，同時更應透過圖書館學會繼續教育或以研討會方式向全臺圖書館及資訊單位積極推廣介紹。

註 釋

1. 1993年2月,"交通部"電信總局發佈821營08119(一)號函"電子文件交換業務";"行政院"於1994年1月25日發佈"機關公文電子交換作業辦法總說明"。
2. 資訊工業策進會,EDI 發展策略研究計劃之研究報告,臺北市:資訊工業策進會,1991年。
3. Edward Cannon, EDI GUIDE: A Step by Step Approach, New York: Van Nostrand Reinhold, 1993, p. 2.
4. Margaret A. Emmelhainz, EDI: A Total Management Guide, New York: Van Nostrand Reinhold, 1993, p. 4.
5. Paula Tallim & J. C. Zeeman, "UDT Series on Data Communication Technologies and Standards for Libraries-Report #4" EDI: An Overview of EDI Standards for Libraries, Ottawa: IFLA International Office for Universal Dataflow and Telecommunication, p. 1.
6. Robert T. Crowley, EDI: Charting A Course to the Future: a guide to understanding and using electronic data interchange, Cary: Research Triangle Consultants, 1993, p. 2.
7. Albert J. Marcella, Jr. and Sally Chan, EDI Audit & Control, Norwood: Artech House Inc., 1993, p. 1.
8. 同註3,頁3—4。
9. 資訊工業策進會EDI推廣中心,企業致勝的最新配備—EDI,臺北市:該中心,頁4。
10. 同註8,頁13。
11. 同註4,頁21。
12. 同註6,頁18。
13. 同註5,頁54。
14. Sandra K. Paul, "EDI/EDIFACT", Library Resources & Technical Services, 39 (2) (April 1995): 180 – 183.
15. Kenzi Itoh, The Minutes of 9th ASEB Meeting, Taipei, 1994.
16. 同註4,頁37。
17. 徐熊健譯,電子資料交換-EDI實用導引。(臺北:財團法人資訊工業策進會,1994年),頁40。
18. 同註4,頁37—38,43—44。
19. 同註17,頁37—38。
20. 同註4,頁41—46。
21. 同註17,頁37—43。
22. 資訊工業策進會編,EDI應用總覽,第二冊,(臺北:該會,1993年)。
23. 同上註,頁4。
24. 陳寶珍著,"電子交易(Electronic Commerce)在臺灣雛形初現",EDI簡訊,第9期(1995年3月):17。
25. 同註22。

26. 同上註。
27. 程嘉君著,《抽絲剝繭談臺灣 EDI 發展現況與展望》,<u>網路通訊雜誌</u>(1992 年 11 月),頁 30。
28. 同註 26。
29. 同註 26。
30. "經濟部"編,《商業 EDI 推廣五年成效斐然》,<u>商業 EDIVAN 簡訊</u> 16 期(1996 年 6 月):1。
31. 王金土著,《從供給面看臺灣 EDI 服務經營狀況》,<u>網路通訊雜誌</u>(1992 年 11 月):35。
32. Susan Davis, "EDI and the Library: A Preconference on Electronic Data Interchange Standards for the Acquisitions of Library Materials", <u>Serials Review</u>, 19(1)(Spring, 1993):92–94.
33. 同註 5,頁 53—56。
34. 同註,頁 55—56。
35. 同註,頁 56—57。
36. 同註,頁 60—61。
37. 與 OCLC Asia Pacific Service 王行仁經理信件。
38. Innopac Interface Inc., <u>INNOPAC System Description</u>, 1995, pp. 1–86.
39. Joan C. Griffith, "Why Not EDI? One Librarian's Perspective." <u>Library Administration and Management</u> 10(Summer, 1996):147–150.
40. 同上註,頁 61—64。
41. Brian Green, "News From Access the Pond: The U. K. Experience." <u>Library Administration and Management</u> 10(Summer 1996):151–154.
42. 同上註,頁 64—65。
43. Margot Wiesner, "The Impact of EDI on the Acquisition Process." <u>Library Administration and Management</u> 10(Summer, 1996):155–160.
44. David, Millson "Interlibrary Loan Protocols: an Introduction and Review of Problem Areas", <u>Interlending and Document Supply</u>, 16(2),(1988):51–57.
45. Fay Turner, "Interlibrary Loan Protocol Implementation Issues", <u>Interlending and Document Supply</u>, 17(3),(1989):77–83.
46. Fay Turner, "The Interlibrary Loan Protocol: An OSI Solution to ILL Messaging", <u>Library Hi Tech</u>, 8(4), 1990.
47. Leigh Swain and Paula Tallim, "The Interlibrary Loan(ILL)Protocol: Progress and Projects" <u>IFLA Journal</u>, 18(1992):325–331.
48. ISO 8459–1 <u>Bibliography Data Element Directory-interloan Applications</u>, 1988.
49. CNS 13150 <u>館際互借書目資料項目標準</u>, 1993.
50. 46 ISO/DIS 10160 <u>Information and Documentation Open Systems Interconnection-Interlibrary Loan Application Service Definition</u>, 1993.
51. ISO 10161, <u>Information and Documentation Open Systems Inter-connection(OSI)-</u>

Interlibrary Loan Application Protocol Specification, 1993.

52. 蘇倫伸，圖書資訊網館際互借應用層通訊作業模式建構之研究（"國立臺灣大學"圖書館學研究所，碩士論文），1989年6月。
53. 尤克強，"EDI Technology"，圖書館自動化及網路專題研習會綱要，"國立臺灣大學"圖書館學系，1993年，頁201—248。
54. 郭更生、李德竹，圖書出版資訊網及其應用之規劃與建立計劃書，1993年，頁2，4。
55. "經濟部中央標準局"，中國國家標準分類目錄，"經濟部中央標準局"，1995年。
56. "經濟部"，"圖書業EDI完成商用標準表單制定"，商業EDI VAN 簡訊12期（1995，04，27）。
57. 資策會網路工程小組吳廷瑜小姐提供。
58. 李德竹，電子資料交換EDI應用在圖書館之研究，"國科會"研究報告，1995年。
59. 薛理桂，中英圖書館事業比較研究，臺北市：文華，1995，頁281。
60. 同註58。

大學圖書館資訊倫理認知與問題之研究*

[摘要 Abstract]

本研究針對大學圖書館館員的專業倫理素養加以調查，以研究臺灣圖書館專業倫理守則初稿。本研究採用文獻分析法、問卷調查法，並舉辦座談會深入探討大學圖書館中相關的倫理問題。研究結果發現：①各國國情不同或學會組織成員的差異，使各國專業倫理守則內容與條文表達形式有所差異。②90％以上被調查的圖書館界學者教授肯定制訂圖書館專業倫理守則之必要性。③80％以上被調查的大學圖書館館員對於圖書館專業倫理守則的制訂與功能持贊同的態度，91.3％的館員認為"目前圖書館員符合專業倫理行為"適當。本研究參考海外專業學會之專業倫理守則內容，及島內專家學者與圖書館從業人員之意見，研究出適合"圖書館之專業倫理理守則初稿"，並提出十項建議。

Abstract：The purpose of this research is to study the present status of professional ethical issues in university libraries, and to propose a draft of code of ethics for Chinese librarians. For this project, the questionnaire survey method and discussion meetings are employed. The major results and suggestions of the research are as following：（1）The differences in cultural background and professional organizations, the codes of ethics tends to be different in their contents and formats；（2）Over 90% of library peers are approved the importance of the codes of ethics for librarians in Taiwan；（3）Over 80% of university librarians also agreed with the necessity of formulating code of ethics for Chinese librarians; and（4）A proposed draft of code of ethics for Chinese librarians has completed.

關鍵詞：資訊倫理、道德判斷、專業倫理、大學圖書館。
Keywords：Information Ethics、Morality Judgement、Professional Ethics、University Libraries.

壹、前 言

本世紀以來，由於社會專業團體與職業的出現，為了維繫其共同利益、專業水準，並為獲取社會大衆對其職業的信賴與專業技能認定，進而要求會員做到自我約束與管理的目地，因此逐步發展出專業倫理。所謂專業倫理（Professional Ethics）是一套系統性的行為規範，其所規範的行為與專業服務密切相關，除一般的社會道德外，更包含與專業相關的職業道德。廣義而言，專業倫理是探討專業環境下，專業倫理的價值、專業服務的行為規範、專業服務的目的、專業人員與客戶間的倫理關係、專業服務對社會大衆造成的影響（尤其客戶利用專業服務對社會大衆造成傷害的問題）、專業人員在公司的地位與角色問題等。

---

* 本文與世界新聞傳播學院圖書資訊學系莊道明先生合作撰寫，曾發表在《臺北市立圖書館館訊》14卷1期（1996年9月），第1—17頁。

美國梅爾菲・杜威（Melvil Dewey）於 1887 年在紐約哥倫比亞大學（Columbia University）設立圖書館學院（School of Library Economy）後，正式開啟圖書館學專屬教育大門。圖書館學在歷經一百多年後，已形成專屬圖書館學的專業理論與實務。英、美、日的圖書館學會爲顯示對社會服務的責任與專業信念，紛紛制訂出圖書館館員的專業倫理。例如美國圖書館學會曾於 1938、1973、1975、1981 年公佈圖書館專業倫理守則（Statement on Professional Ethics）；英國圖書館學會（the Library Association of UK）在 1983 年公佈英國圖書館學會專業行爲守則（The Library Association, Code of Professional Conduct）；日本圖書館學會於 1980 年公佈圖書館員倫理綱領。以上三個國家的圖書館專業學會已都意識到專業倫理對專業服務的重要性，因而在匯聚各方意見之後，擬出屬於該學會的專業倫理守則。從英美日各國專業倫理守則中可以發現，隨着資訊化社會的來臨，圖書館專業倫理更加重視資訊自由的流通、隱私安全的保護、禁止個人不當利益、禁止對讀者的差別待遇、鼓勵提昇專業水準、鼓勵館員提供最好的服務等內容。反觀臺灣地區圖書館學會尚未發展出屬於臺灣地區圖書館的資訊倫理，一般館員無論在學校養成教育或工作環境之中，均缺乏對於專業倫理的認識，造成館員的服務缺乏專業素養與社會服務的責任感。有鑑於此，本研究針對大學圖書館館員的專業倫理素養予以調查，調查結果擬提供"中國圖書館學會"，研擬一份合乎社會現況需要的倫理守則。

貳、文獻分析

有關圖書館專業倫理的研究文獻，仍以英文期刊居多。芬克斯（Finks, L. W.）及修可菲爾德（Soekfeld, F.）、布立爾（Preer, J.）、藍尼爾（Lanier, D.）、賀歇伍德（Usherwood, B.）、葛林伍德（Greenwood, T.）等，分別探討英、美國圖書館學會圖書館專業倫理守則發展的歷史、意義、內涵、價值、評價等。碧兒苞恩（Bierbaum, E. G.）探討圖書館技術服務應注意的專業倫理原則。包伊桑納（Boissonnas, C. M.）、普雷斯里（Presley, R. L.）、得夫林（Devlin, M.）、柯菲（Coffey, J. R.）、葛賀那（Goehner, D.）、馬斯（Marsh, C.）研究圖書館資料徵集業務與代理商間專業倫理的內涵。巴若吉安（Bazirjian, R.）與艾立克生（Ericson, R. L.）探討圖書註銷作業應注意的專業倫理問題。

布朗（Brown, Y.）、卡芮（Caren, L.）及尚蒙米爾（Someville, A.）、高登（Golden, F. A.）、格梅爾（Gremmels, G. S.）、哈蒂（Hardy, G. J.）及羅賓森（Robinson, J. S.）、傑森（Jansen, L. M.）、波蒂（Protti, M. E.）、雷根（Regan, M.）、卡斯特（Koster, G. E.）探討圖書館參考服務應注意的專業倫理問題。史托佛（Stover, M.）、迪凡奇諾（DelVecchio, R. A.）、伍德（Wood, M. S.）探討參考服務中，讀者隱私保密的問題。愛倫・金（Alan King）、史密施（Smith, M. M.）、雪佛（Shaver, D. B.）、佛羅林契（Froehlich, T. J.）就圖書館線上資訊服務所面臨的專業倫理予以探討。謝清俊教授、盧荷生教授、羅格斯（Rogers, S. L.）等就專業倫理教育施行的必要性、課程設計及現況分別提出看法及調查報告。

李高美娜及張保隆教授、朱柏松教授、海芙納（Hafner, K.）及馬可夫（Markoff, J.）、道斯（Doss, E.）及勞依（Loui, M. C.）、巴須金（Bashkin, A. A.）、郝伯門（Hauptman, R.）與摩汀（Motin, S.）、蘇佛蘭（Szofran, N.）、撒佛妮（Saftner, D.）

及雪根哈納森（Raghunathan, B.）、李德（Reed, P.）鐘斯（Jones, R. A.）、歐季（Oz, E.）等對於現今網路資訊倫理問題予以探討。

有關圖書館專業倫理的專書方面，霍特曼（Hauptman, R.）從圖書館各服務層面探討圖書館專業倫理問題並輔以許多個案實例，以加強讀者對圖書館專業倫理的認知。林賽（Lindsey, J. A.）及普倫帝斯（Prentice, A. E.）從英美國家專業倫理發展歷程，逐步探索美國圖書館學會專業倫理的發展與演變的過程，是欲瞭解美國圖書館學會專業倫理守則發展史不可缺少的專著。明特支（Mintz, A. P.）編著的資訊倫理會議論文集中，收錄許多圖書館館員應該注意的資訊倫理相關議題，書中附有詳盡的參考書目。莫瑞（B. J. Murray）碩士論文探討美國圖書館學會專業倫理守則發展與演變史，是一本瞭解今日美國圖書館學會專業服務演變相當好的著作。

由於專業倫理發展始於英美國家，因而圖書館專業倫理文獻的相關著作仍以外文居多。近年來由於臺灣各行業逐步邁向專業化服務與認證制度，因此如何加強專業人員的專業技能與倫理，亦引發其他專業組織的關切，使得專業倫理論著亦逐漸增多之中。

叁、研究目的、方法與實施

本研究針對大學圖書館館員為主，採用問卷訪問調查法達到下列研究目的：
一、探究各國重要圖書資訊學會的倫理守則精神與內涵；
二、比較各圖書資訊學會專業倫理的異同；
三、分析專業倫理對於圖書館各項作業的影響層面；
四、調查大學圖書館館員的專業倫理認知程度與專業道德判斷能力；
五、研擬出圖書館資訊倫理守則初稿。

本計劃採用文獻分析法、問卷訪問調查法與座談會並行。採用文獻分析法蒐集各國圖書館和資訊科學學會的專業倫理，以瞭解其專業倫理的內涵與主題。依據文獻分析結果設計館員問卷調查表，以探究目前大學圖書館館員對專業倫理的認知程度與服務的道德判斷力。根據研究調查需要，本研究從中國圖書館會員名錄內之大學圖書館館員清冊中，抽出147個樣本，並實施大學圖書館專業人員專業倫理的調查。共回收有效問卷129份，回收率87.76%。此外，針對六校圖書資訊學相關系所任教教授的問卷普查，共回收有效問卷13份，問卷回收率81.25%。此外，本研究為進一步瞭解與釐清問卷有爭議的問題，分別於北中南各舉辦一次訪問座談，以廣徵各方建議。

肆、調查結果與分析

本研究首先蒐集海內外相關文獻，作初步的文獻探討，建立本研究的基礎背景。其次，分別邀請圖書館界的學者教授及樣選大學圖書館館員，就圖書館專業倫理問題實施問卷調查。根據問卷調查結果，分別於北、中、南三區舉辦座談與訪談，以進一步瞭解問題。以下針對本研究調查之結果逐一說明：

一、各國重要圖書館學會專業倫理守則

專業倫理守則乃根據專業精神與道德所訂立的書面文件。其內容均是原則性的專業

行為規範，文字清晰簡短具鼓勵性，不若法律條文講求週密嚴謹，為專業學會針對專業人員所制訂的服務行為準則。本研究為瞭解海外圖書館學會已建立的專業服務行為規範之內容，分別蒐集美國圖書館學會、美國資訊科學學會、英國圖書館學會及日本圖書館學會四個國外重要的圖書館專業學會的專業倫理守則，就其內容加以比較與分析。根據比較分析的結果，發現此四個專業學會的專業倫理守則，有四項是共同具備的內容，包括"專業服務的誠實、客觀與能力"、"熱誠提供大眾所需要的服務"、"維護專業的榮譽與尊嚴"、"尊重自主性、個人隱私保密與業務機密"。此四項專業倫理精神均是針對圖書館專業人員，服務社會大眾所需具備的基本態度而制訂。換言之，圖書館的專業館員在從事各種服務工作時，應憑藉專業的訓練與技能，在誠實客觀的判斷下，以熱誠的態度服務社會大眾，如此方能維護圖書館專業服務的榮譽與尊嚴。圖書館館員於服務社會大眾時，應注意對讀者隱私的保密與業務機密的維護。由於圖書館或資訊中心的服務內涵，均是以資訊的蒐集、整理、儲存、檢索及利用為主。因此，對於機構內部或讀者資訊的保密及隱私的維護，就成為圖書館學會專業倫理所關心的議題。

　　圖書館專業倫理中，隱私權保護的概念源自西方文化的思想，隱私權本身與人權有密切的關係。在民主國家中，隱私權亦屬於人權的一部份。當前由於個人的隱私權，常受到大眾媒體、商業機構、情治單位不當的侵犯，造成個人生活安寧上的困擾。因此，隱私權的維護即成為讀者利用資訊服務上，一個關切且重視的問題。英美的圖書館為建立社會大眾對其所提供之各項資訊服務的信任關係，在專業倫理守則中，明顯表示對讀者隱私權應有的保護。日本圖書館的發展，由於深受美國圖書館發展的影響，故在日本圖書館學會的圖書館員倫理綱領中，亦將讀者隱私權的保護列入其中。

　　從比較各國專業倫理守則之中，也可明顯看出各學會由於服務對象及國情不同，其倫理守則各有其特色。美國圖書館學會由於組成會員的份子眾多，為使其倫理守則能廣泛被會員接受與遵循，在不斷修改下逐步簡化，故其倫理守則的內容與條文，至今僅有八個條文。美國資訊科學學會的會員包括圖書館界、營利與非營利的資訊中心，電腦資訊界等從業人員。因此，守則制訂對象皆以資訊專家概稱之，並明訂營利性資訊專業服務，對贊助者、顧客或雇主等應注意的專業倫理守則。英國圖書館學會對會員有極高的控制權力，類似工會的性質，因此，其專業倫理守則之制訂相當嚴謹與嚴格。如守則內有明文規定處分的條款及方式，是四種專業倫理守則之中，唯一具備處分條款的倫理守則。日本圖書館學會的圖書館員倫理綱領中，極大部份乃沿用英美"國家圖書館"專業倫理守則的內容，但因應日本文化的傳統及特色，其倫理守則亦加入日本民族"羣"性與文化的條文，包括"強調服務合作性的重要"、"對自我努力的期許"、"參與文化發展與創造"等。這些均是英美圖書館學會專業倫理守則，所沒有的專業倫理的內涵。

　　根據上述四個海外專業倫理守則內容的比較，發現圖書館專業倫理守則中，具備一套基本共同專業倫理的價值觀。此價值觀不因國別不同而有所差異，其中如"專業服務的誠實、客觀與能力"、"熱誠提供大眾所需要的服務"、"維護專業的榮譽與尊嚴"、"尊重自主性、個人隱私保密與業務機密"等。此外，由於各國國情不同或學會組織成員的差異，致使各國專業倫理守則內容與條文表達形式有所差異。因此，任一學會有意制訂專業倫理守則時，除考量圖書館服務的基本專業倫理價值觀外，也應該將會員的屬性與本國文化傳統，適度的表達於專業倫理守則項目中。

二、圖書館專業倫理對圖書館各項作業的影響

圖書館專業倫理對於圖書館各項作業的影響相當廣泛。根據文獻的整理及研究結果，可分成五大類，包括"圖書館行政管理之專業倫理"、"技術服務與館藏發展之專業倫理"、"讀者與資訊服務之專業倫理"、"圖書館專業倫理教育"及"資訊倫理"等。

圖書館行政管理的專業倫理，亦是館員的"工作倫理"，其所關切的問題在雇主與雇員間應有之行為規範。雇主與雇員之關係中，由於身份職位的差異，產生對待行為上的差別，其中包括所屬機構主管與館員、館長與館員、主任與館員、館長與主任等。上述不同職位間之行為與對待關係應如何維繫，即成為圖書館行政管理倫理所關切的問題。在本研究中，就館員處理"業務機密"、"兼差"、"公出請假"、"公器私用"、"對外發表論著"、"場地外借"、"兼課或公假進修"等工作倫理進行調查研究。

技術服務與館藏發展之專業倫理所涉及的問題，乃是對"經費"及"資料"處理的方法及態度。圖書館經費與資料的來源，來自單位購買、交換及捐助等途徑。由於圖書館必須向外採購圖書等各種資料，其採購過程的公平性便成為專業倫理所關切的主題。而在資料處理方面，所關切的主題除館藏發展的客觀性外，對於捐贈資料處理的公私性亦是另一關注的焦點。本研究針對館員如何處理"書商的餐會"、"館藏發展的客觀性"、"贈款或贈書的公私處理"等問題加以調查。

讀者與資訊服務專業倫理是圖書館專業倫理問題中，最複雜也最具爭議的項目。圖書館的設立與提供服務，乃在於提供讀者利用，以促進社會發展及國家進步。上述圖書館服務的目標是一個至為崇高的理想，但就實際而言，圖書館服務讀者是否能夠促進社會大眾的福祉，決定權並非由圖書館單方面決定，其關鍵仍在讀者本身。根據文獻的研究發現，海外圖書館在讀者與資訊服務專業倫理的探討上，都是針對如何維護與保障讀者的基本權利，如隱私權、不可差別待遇、知的權利等。然而在實際問題的討論上，往往集中在讀者誤用資訊的專業倫理處理上。因此，圖書館館員在處理此問題時，常常陷入兩難的局面。一方面圖書館保障讀者的基本權利是基於專業理想與社會信託，但當讀者可能將此權利運用於非正途時，館員則必須在專業理想與可能發生不幸後果下面臨抉擇。因此，讀者與資訊服務專業倫理是圖書館專業倫理中，最為複雜且富爭議問題的主題。本研究中，針對"提供讀者潛在性危險的資訊"、"讀者違規使用設備"、"提供藥物、法律的知識"、"讀者隱私保護"、"智慧財產權保護"等議題亦加以探究。

圖書館專業倫理教育方面所涉及的議題，在探究專業倫理教育的有效性，及專業倫理教育應該如何實行？該採何種教學方式？教授的師資為何？根據海內外文獻的探討，某些專家學者認為倫理是無法教導的，亦認為倫理是一種生活方式與習慣，教師若將倫理當作一種知識傳遞給學生，將無助於學生倫理行為的產生，必需透過老師及家長的身教、社會風氣的推動，才能促進學生倫理行為的產生。因此，專業倫理教育若以一門專業課程方式教授，其效果將極為有限，猶如被開罰單的學生，都知道"闖紅燈是違規"一樣。在另一方面，亦有學者認為，專業倫理教育可協助專業人員對從事專業倫理問題的決策。由於現行專業環境日趨複雜，專業人員面對許多兩難的專業問題時，往往不知如何解決，專業倫理教育至少可以提供專業人員一個思考的方向。因此，專業倫理教育雖無法瞬間改變一個人的行為，但確可為專業人員提供解決倫理難題思考角度。本研究

針對專業倫理教育的"有效性"、"課程施行方式"、"必修或選修"等加以調查。

資訊倫理是探究人類使用資訊解決行為對錯的主題。該主題亦有利用電腦從事資訊的蒐集、整理、儲存與使用等。由於目前圖書館運用電腦極為普及，加上網路應用已成為趨勢，因此，資訊倫理的議題亦已涵蓋圖書館的各種服務。本研究針對"電腦軟體複製"予以探討。

由以上的探討，發現圖書館專業倫理遍佈於圖書館各種服務中。因此，如何根據圖書館專業倫理的理想，有效規範圖書館所提供的各種服務是一項極為重要的課題。

三、圖書館學者教授意見

本研究針對臺灣大學、政治大學、輔仁大學、淡江大學、臺灣師範大學及世界新聞傳播學院等六校的圖書資訊學相關系所的17位教授，施行問卷調查。根據回收有效問卷13份的統計結果發現：

（一）學者教授對專業倫理守則態度方面

90.0%以上的學者教授肯定應制訂"圖書館專業倫理守則"，並肯定專業倫理守則有助於"圖書館專業形象的建立"、"專業服務的提昇"、"圖書館系所學生對於專業服務的認知"及"館員對於從事專業服務的決定"等。其中"對專業倫理守則中是否應該制訂具處分性內容"中，有61.6%表示贊成，有15.4%不表示意見，另有23.1%表示反對。顯示在處分內容方面學者教授的意見較為分散。

（二）學者教授對於專業倫理守則內容方面

本研究依據海內外文獻及重要學會的倫理守則，共列出十六項專業倫理守則的內容，請學者教授勾選表示意見並選出五項最重要的項次。根據問卷統計結果，90%以上的學者教授都贊同十六項倫理守則的內容。而依據其選出五項最重要的項目統計結果，十六項中有七項是較重要的，其重要性分別是"熱誠提供大眾所需要的服務"、"避免任何利益的衝突與貪污"、"專業服務的誠實、客觀與能力"、"尊重自主性、個人隱私保密與業務機密"、"維護專業的榮譽與尊嚴"、"向大眾宣揚圖書館專業服務的優點"、"不能有任何服務的差別待遇"、"尊重智慧財產權"等。

四、大學圖書館館員專業倫理認知與道德判斷能力

本研究以大學圖書館專業圖書館員為主要調查對象。因此，在問卷調查部份乃依據"中國圖書館學會"會員名錄內，349名大學圖書館會員名單清冊中隨機抽樣出調查樣本147名加以調查。根據回收的有效問卷129份（問卷回收率87.76%）統計，獲得以下的結論：

（一）專業倫理問題處理方面

1. 圖書館行政管理倫理問題處理

多數館員對於行政管理倫理問題的解決，表現出相當高的一致性。對於"兼差"問題的處理上，多數的館員會採取徵求主管的同意，其次則選擇拒絕。對於"公出請假"及"業務機密"問題上，絕大多數館員表現出誠實的態度。在"公器私用"的問題中，多數館員表示不可為的態度。"對外發表論著"方面，館員的表現則較為分歧。由於對外發表論著問題上，涉及論著內容是否與職務相關？是否引用館內資料？引用資料內容是否涉及館內敏感或機密性問題等？加上發表者使用的身份與職稱。因此，館員對於此

問題的處理上較為分歧。對"場地外借"處理方面，絕大多數館員表示需按照性質來決定，因此是依個案來處理。"兼課或公假進修"問題處理方面，館員的態度亦較分散。其中多數館員認為應該利用非上班時間彌補公務，部份館員認為應視業務積壓情況而定，顯示館員對公務與進修兼課價值觀的選擇，有其不同的判斷。

2. 圖書館技術服務與館藏發展專業倫理問題

圖書館技術服務主要以採訪業務及編目業務為主。採訪業務的專業倫理常涉及特殊利益的問題，其中又以書商餐會邀請最為常見。"書商餐會"項目中，半數以上的館員選擇拒絕邀請，但在"其他"選項中，24.2%的館員表示，在某些狀況下是可以接受邀請，包括事先向主管報備並獲核准、依餐會性質而定等。圖書館館藏發展的專業倫理問題，在於"是否有館藏政策及執行客觀性"、"贈款或贈書的公私處理"兩大問題處理上。在"是否有館藏政策及執行客觀性"問題處理上，目前由於多數圖書館欠缺書面的館藏發展政策，因而圖書館館藏發展不免陷於人為主觀的判定。尤其當館藏發展受到人事命令干擾時，館員常會不知如何是從。本研究中假定當館藏發展與主管命令（主任）發生衝突時，館員會作何選擇？結果顯示18.3%的館員仍以館藏發展政策為主，37.3%的館員會尋求更上一層主管（館長）的意見。顯現當館藏發展政策不明確時，館員的態度較偏向從人事溝通方面尋求支持與解決難題。對"贈款或贈書的公私處理"議題上，館員處理的態度傾向於公私分明。例如對於"捐款更改用途"，85.3%的館員認為當捐款變更用途時，應通知捐贈者並徵得其同意。在"不符合館藏的贈書"處理上，48.1%的館員認為贈書可供讀者自由取閱，館員並不認為"館員可以隨己喜好收為己有"，顯示出館員對於公私問題的認知上，相當良好。

3. 圖書館參考及流通服務專業倫理問題

圖書館參考及流通服務是透過館員提供讀者所需要的各種資訊服務。因而館員所面臨的專業倫理問題可分為資料提供與讀者服務兩方面。在資料提供方面包括"潛在性危險的資訊"、"藥物、法律的知識"及"智慧財產權保護"；讀者服務方面則包括"違規使用設備"、"讀者隱私的保護"等。

在提供讀者"潛在性危險的資訊"問題處理上，館員回答相當分歧。館員對於提供讀者製作炸彈、毒品等資料時，由於擔心讀者誤用情況的發生，造成對問題回答上產生相當大的不確定性。本研究中高達45%的館員，在"其他"選項中表達其看法。多數館員表示對類似參考服務問題處理上，應該進一步瞭解讀者的使用企圖後，才決定是否要提供讀者資料，而有11.8%的館員認為應該無條件提供讀者所需要的資訊。為確保讀者正確使用資訊，是否可依據個人主觀的看法，來檢查讀者利用資訊的企圖，是一個相當受到爭議的問題。在英美圖書館專業倫理中，認為館員應以準確無偏見的做法，提供讀者所需要的服務。至於讀者對獲取的資訊作何種運用，則非館員應該考慮甚至檢查的事情。在英美國家文化體系，認為圖書館是提供人民資訊的重要單位，也是人民獲取知識與資訊的重要場所，民眾向圖書館查詢或索閱資料是人民的基本權利，因而圖書館有責任維護人民知的權利。凡有害於人民知的權利的任何舉動，圖書館都應該加以排除，其中亦包括對讀者不當的檢查行為。因此，館員是否應該基於任何安全的考量，對讀者的參考問題加以檢查？此外，館員是否應該發揮如偵探或警察的功能，對於讀者的參考問題偵察後，確定無安全顧慮才決定是否提供服務？但另方面館員是否可以全不考慮任何社會安全或責任,提供讀者所需的任何服務?將人民知的權利置於社會安全之上的專業服務精神,是否可為社會大眾所接受?這些爭議是否與國情、民情不同有關?皆是值得深入探討的專業倫理主題。

對"提供藥物、法律的知識"處理方面,如詢問安眠藥的使用方法,64.1%的館員主張請讀者找專業醫師或藥劑師洽詢,其次是詢問讀者需要此資料的目的,顯示館員對法律及醫藥等相關專業知識的處理方式,認知相當清楚。對"智慧財產權保護"方面,因館員對於智慧財產權認識程度不同,而有所差異。本研究中,以館際複印為例,結果顯示45.2%的館員會拒絕讀者不當的複印申請,21.4%的館員會允許分數次申請,顯示部份館員仍應加強智慧財產權的觀念。

讀者"違規使用設備"的處理,半數以上(54.7%)的館員會依館內規定處理,並無館員允許讀者違規使用圖書館的設備。在"讀者隱私保護"方面,本研究中,以保護讀者流通記錄為主。針對情治單位要求查閱讀者借閱資料的問題,有78.1%的館員選擇向主管請示。此顯示館員對於情治單位的要求,會尋求上級主管的支持,但亦顯示館員對讀者隱私的保護缺乏自主性。在查詢讀者已外借書籍方面,86.0%的館員選擇告知查詢讀者到期日並辦理預約,沒有館員選擇告知借閱者為何人。顯示館員對於讀者流通記錄的保護認知相當清楚。

4. 電腦倫理問題

島內圖書館在施行自動化及網路化後,圖書館許多服務的推展均有賴電腦的使用才能完成,對於電腦軟硬體的管理也成為圖書館管理工作的項目之一,電腦倫理的問題也成為圖書館專業服務所關切的一部份。本研究針對"電腦軟體複製"問題予以探究,結果顯示84.5%的館員認為應該遵守著作權之規定,合理使用電腦軟體,有11.6%的館員表示不同意也不禁止的態度,顯示多數館員對於電腦倫理的認知相當清楚。

(二)館員專業倫理工作守則內容方面

本研究為瞭解館員對工作環境中,專業倫理守則內容的認同程度,分別依"圖書館行政管理倫理問題"、"圖書館技術服務與館藏發展專業倫理"、"圖書館參考及流通服務專業倫理"、"電腦倫理"等四方面的專業倫理守則內容予以調查。所獲結論如下:

1. 圖書館行政管理倫理守則方面

55.1%的館員贊同"館員下班後不可任意使用辦公室的電腦設備,從事私人工作",不贊同者有12.5%。對館員發表著作方面,24.9%館員贊同"圖書館對館員欲對外發表之文章,不論其是否與其工作相關,應明文規定需先經主管審閱",然而卻有高達53.5%的館員不予認同。顯示圖書館對館員向外發表著作,應該訂立更明確的辦法,而不適合於專業倫理守則中來規範。對"圖書館應制訂相關之規則(如:閱覽規則、館藏發展政策等),以利專業服務之進行"的內容,有98.4%的館員表贊同,顯示館員認同圖書館規章的訂定,有助於專業服務的推展。

2. 圖書館技術服務與館藏發展專業倫理守則方面

80.0%以上的館員贊同下列專業倫理守則內容,包括"圖書館採訪館員應儘量避免參加代理商或書商所招待之商業餐會"、"圖書館採訪館員不應利用採購職務之便,為個人獲取特殊的利益"、"圖書館採訪館員對於書商或代理商所邀約之餐會,應主動告知主管。若獲得主管授權參與,應將與會過程內容告知"、"對於所有書商應該給予公平同等的服務機會，不應該對書商有差別待遇，但應依照圖書館採購的需求，選擇適合的書商"、"圖書館對於不符合館藏性質的贈書，應表示拒絕接受"、"贈書作業中應禁止館員私自將贈書據爲己有，不適合入藏的圖書也應透過正常行政程序淘汰後，才可讓館員選取擁有"、"編目館員從事分編作業時，除應依照專業技能外，更需秉持著公正無偏見的態度，從事資料的處理"、"編目館員應選擇適當而正確的主題表詞彙與分類號，以免影響讀者的價值觀及對知識結構的認知"、"會員圖書館應維持聯合書目資料庫內書目的品質"、"圖書館的館藏政策或採訪館員對於具爭議性主題的圖書（如：宣揚性或暴力之書刊），仍應秉持專業的精神，依據圖書館服務的宗旨從事選書的工作"。

較具爭議或贊同度偏低的守則內容有"圖書館基於保存文化遺產的責任，對於私人捐贈的圖書有接受的義務"（47.6%的館員表示反對，僅有40.6%的館員贊同）；及"圖書館爲維持館藏學術地位的形象，仍應接受不符合館藏需要但爲某一知名人士所捐贈的圖書"（65.1%的館員反對，9.5%的館員贊同）兩項。顯示館員對於社會人士捐贈的圖書具有選擇的自主權。

3. 圖書館參考及流通服務專業倫理方面

80.0%以上的館員贊同下列專業倫理守則內容，包括"圖書館對於讀者逾期還書的情況，得以罰款或停止借閱等方式加以處罰，以維護資訊之公平利用"、"圖書館流通館員對於讀者個人的隱私資料，應予保密"、"若讀者誤用自圖書館所獲取的資訊，而準備從事傷害自己或別人生命安全的事務時，圖書館得以向法律治安單位報告"、"圖書館的流通服務，館員之服務態度不得因讀者之身分地位或年齡等不同而有差別待遇"、"參考館員面對醫藥、法律、財務管理及消費等主題的參考問題時，應視情況與內容，適度地調整服務的層級或拒絕提供服務"、"參考館員從讀者之問題中察覺讀者可能誤用資訊，作出危及個人生命、權益或社會安全之情事時，得以拒絕回答讀者之參考問題"、"參考館員對於讀者有關毒品、性知識、槍砲等具危險性知識的提供，應適度地採取保留態度"、"檢索館員應避免因個人之喜好、習慣或熟悉程度，影響到對資料庫及資訊系統的選擇或檢索策略的應用，因而妨礙了讀者利用線上檢索的公平性"、"對於打字錯誤、通訊突然中斷、檢索結果儲存錯誤等不可避免的非人爲疏失所產生之誤失，館員應主動告知讀者，並不收取該次檢索所需之費用"、"線上檢索服務對讀者查詢資料的內容應予以保密，包括其檢索申請單、檢索策略、指令與其問題等"。

較具爭議或贊同率偏低者，包括"提供線上檢索服務時，若因館員檢索能力不足，造成檢索成果不佳，則該次檢索所需之費用應由圖書館自行吸收"（61.1%贊同）、"線上檢索館員不應利用爲讀者進行檢索的時候，藉機練習個人的檢索技巧"（76.5%贊同）、"線上檢索館員不應將爲讀者檢索所得結果，提供給亦需此類資料的其他讀者使用"（54.2%贊同）。由於線上檢索涉及變數多，造成館員對問題處理的認同度偏低，就專業倫理守則而言，並不適合統一規範，宜另訂處理辦法。

4. 電腦倫理方面

84.6%的館員贊同"若圖書館已採購具有智慧財產權的電腦軟體，不可讓館員複製以供個人或家庭使用"。對於"館員不可複製有版權的電腦軟體資料先予以試用，以作爲將來採購的依據"有76.0%贊同。

（三）館員對圖書館專業倫理守則看法方面

本研究調查館員對圖書館專業倫理守則的制訂與功能的看法。根據統計分析80.0%

以上的館員贊同"圖書館界應該制訂專業的倫理守則"、"圖書館專業倫理守則，有助於圖書館專業形象的建立"、"圖書館專業倫理守則，有助於圖書館專業服務的提昇"、"圖書館專業倫理守則，有助於圖書館學系所學生對於圖書館專業服務的認知"、"圖書館專業倫理守則，有助於館員對於從事專業服務的決策"。其中館員對"專業倫理守則中，應制定具有處分性的內容"看法較爲分歧，但仍有超過半數（51.5％）的館員贊同專業倫理守則中，應制定處分性的內容，而有21.1％的館員反對。在"對目前圖書館員符合專業倫理行爲之看法"意見中，有91.3％的館員表示尚可或好，僅有8.5％的館員認爲差。

伍、圖書館專業倫理守則初稿

（一）文獻分析比較

庫特真（Kultgen, J.）對美國八個專業學會專業倫理守則加以比較及分析，以"客觀誠實"、"對客戶、雇員及機構的忠誠與避免利益衝突"、"尊重同仁的工作空間、信任及公平的競爭"、"監督同仁、主動檢舉違反專業倫理的行爲"等四項爲上述八個學會共享的專業倫理守則內容。此外，根據美國圖書館學會、美國資訊科學學會、英國圖書館學會、日本圖書館學會正式頒佈的專業倫理守則內容比較分析，發現"專業服務的誠實、客觀與能力"、"熱誠提供大衆所需要的服務"、"維護專業的榮譽與尊嚴"、"尊重自主性、個人隱私保密與業務機密"等四項是上述四個學會共享的專業倫理，值得作爲擬訂專業倫理初稿的參考。（莊道明）

（二）問卷調查結果

本研究對臺灣圖書館學系所教授專家的問卷統計分析顯示，絕大多數的學者專家均肯定專業倫理對專業的影響與重要性。針對臺灣圖書館專業倫理守則內容調查統計發現，學者專家認爲下列圖書館專業倫理規範是較重要的：

(1) 熱誠提供大衆所需要的服務；
(2) 避免任何利益的衝突與貪污；
(3) 專業服務的誠實、客觀與能力；
(4) 尊重自主性、個人隱私保密與業務機密；
(5) 維護專業的榮譽與尊嚴，向大衆宣揚圖書館專業服務的優點；
(6) 不能有任何服務的差別待遇；
(7) 尊重智慧財産權。

此外在本研究座談會方面，王振鵠教授認爲圖書館專業倫理的宗旨應是發揮"敬業樂羣"的精神，具體的內容應包括"行政倫理"、"服務規範"、"人際關係"及"社會責任"等四方面。

依據文獻分析所得及調查問卷統計結果綜合整理，研擬"圖書館專業倫理守則初稿"如下：

(1) 圖書館專業人員基於社會大衆的託負，在公正客觀的前提下，應以熱誠的態度，提供讀者所需的服務；
(2) 館員有責任保護讀者的隱私權，即對讀者在圖書館查尋、檢索、利用的各種資訊，都應加以保密；

(3) 圖書館應尊重智慧財產權；
(4) 在維護讀者知的權利下，抗拒不當的檢查制度，以善盡告知的責任；
(5) 圖書館對讀者不應有服務或態度上的差別待遇；
(6) 館員應秉持誠實的態度，避免不當的利益及貪污行為；
(7) 館員為維護專業的榮譽與尊嚴，應隨時充實自己的專業知識及技能，並向大眾宣揚圖書館專業服務的優點；
(8) 館員應以公平及真誠的態度，維繫主管、同事及所屬機構間的關係。

陸、研究建議

根據本研究的調查與分析結果，針對臺灣圖書館專業倫理的發展與需要，提出以下幾項建議：

一、建議"中國圖書館學會"及早擬訂圖書館專業倫理守則

英美日等先進"國家圖書館"學會已訂該學會的專業倫理守則，作為館員從事各項服務工作的行為準則。由本研究分析亦發現，專業倫理遍佈於圖書館各項服務工作中。如何有效提昇館員專業服務的工作倫理與精神，避免不當的利益，實有賴"中國圖書館學會"及早擬訂臺灣圖書館館員專業倫理守則。根據本研究已擬訂之圖書館專業倫理守則初稿，建議"中國圖書館學會"可參考本初稿，廣徵會員意見，儘速公告圖書館館員專業倫理守則，以取信於社會大眾。

二、建議"中國圖書館學會"法規委員會下設立專業倫理小組

為促進專業倫理能持續受到館員的重視，並有效提昇圖書館專業服務水準，建議"中國圖書館學會"法規委員會下設立專業倫理小組，以教育館員如何有效解決所面臨的專業倫理難題；監督與裁決違反專業倫理守則的情事；對社會大眾表達圖書館客觀及專業的立場；持續研究圖書館專業倫理問題，以因應時代的變遷與需要，並隨時更新專業倫理守則的內容等。

三、建立圖書館專業倫理個案資料庫

由於專業倫理問題的解決需要經驗及分析能力，學會應該建立圖書館專業倫理個案資料庫，以提昇館員解決倫理問題之能力及提供專業倫理教育之參考。資料庫除蒐集專業倫理個案外，並應將決策及思考方法逐一說明與解析。資料庫除了提供館員參考使用外，亦應開放給圖書館學系所師生教學使用。

四、推動圖書館專業倫理教育課程

專業倫理的推動應始於教育，因此圖書館專業倫理應從學校教育著手。根據本研究調查發現，絕大多數的專家學者及館員均肯定專業倫理教育的重要性，並認為應納入學校教育課程之中。至於應採單獨課程教授或融入於各課程中，則應該視該校的師資與課程結構而定。至於專業倫理課程講授的方法，應有別於知識性課程講授的方式，力求課程生動活潑與生活實際化，教授方法包括倫理個案分析、機會教育、教師主導個案分析

或角色扮演等,逐一進行教學研討,以使專業倫理教育能落實於學生生活及未來專業服務工作中。

五、增進圖書館館員專業倫理問題處理與決策能力

面對日益複雜及多變的專業工作環境,館員所處理的專業倫理問題亦逐漸複雜。由本研究發現,館員對專業倫理問題的認知甚佳,但面對較複雜的難題時(如讀者誤用資訊的問題),其解決策略均尋求主管的意見或請求主管的同意,顯見館員面對較複雜的專業倫理決策時,缺乏獨立解決的技巧與行政上的自主性。因而如何透過在職教育與個案研討,加強館員對專業倫理問題處理的能力,應是館員專業倫理教育重點之一。

六、加強對網路資訊倫理問題的探討

現今由於各國推廣全球資訊基礎的建設,使得網路應用是大勢所趨。網路已成為各行各業必然應用的趨勢,圖書館亦復如是。面對網路應用日廣,如何加強網路用戶網路倫理的觀念,維護網路通道及使用的安全,已成為網路應用的重要課題。因此,圖書館身為網路資訊的提供者與使用者,應加強對網路資訊倫理問題的探討,並於網路服務推廣教育中,加強讀者網路倫理的教育,使讀者成為網路世界中的好公民。

七、加強館員對智慧財產權的觀念

從本研究中發現不少館員對電腦軟體使用及館際複印的問題,缺乏智慧財產權應有的觀念。因此,圖書館應該加強館員智慧財產權的觀念,並將具體的做法結合於各種服務工作項目之中。

八、促進工作場所專業倫理環境的建立

由於臺灣尚未制訂圖書館專業倫理守則,加上專業倫理缺乏有效的教育與提倡,使得臺灣圖書館的服務內涵中,欠缺專業倫理工作的環境。因此,圖書館除該加強專業倫理概念外,應鼓勵館員秉持敬業樂羣的工作態度,在不斷創新的努力下,積極提昇圖書館各項服務,建立圖書館專業倫理的工作環境。

九、加強館員專業倫理問題處理的自主性

從本研究個案中發現,館員對難以處理之問題時,均會選擇徵求主管的同意。此種必需訴諸更高主管的決策模式,顯示館員對於服務問題難題上,缺乏獨立判斷及自主的能力,如同未成年的兒童行事,都必需事先徵得父母認可一般。以專業技能而言,顯現專業館員欠缺獨立判斷能力。如何透過適當的在職訓練與教育,加強館員專業倫理問題處理能力,是提昇圖書館專業必要的一部份。

十、教師主管均應以身作則推動圖書館專業倫理

任何倫理教育或倫理環境要成功的建立,實有賴教師及主管以身作則。學校教師需以身教與言教並立,才能為學生樹立良好倫理行為的典範;同理,單位主管也必須以身作則,為部屬建立良好行事規範。任何倫理行為與教育的失敗,均導因於言行不一。因此,專業倫理若僅止於知識的傳授或言談,將無助專業服務與環境的改善,必須於實際

工作中落實。因此,教師與主管均應以身作則,爲學生及館員樹立專業倫理的典範。

以上建議提供相關單位參考施行,使圖書館專業倫理能早日落實於圖書館專業服務工作中,以提昇圖書館專業服務的形象與獲取社會大衆的認同。

誌　謝

感謝"國科會"資助研究經費,使得本研究得以順利完成。本研究計劃案爲"國科會"編號 NSC84-2421-H-002-008M2"大學圖書館資訊倫理認知與問題之研究"。

參考書目

朱柏松,"資訊時代、資訊問題及資訊法的範疇",法學叢刊,137,頁57—77。

李高美娜;張保隆,"大陸、香港及臺灣大學生對資訊倫理看法之比較研究",Hong Kong Journal of Business Management,七,1994,頁17—35。

海芙納（Katie Hafner）；馬可夫（John Markoff）,電腦叛客,（臺北：天下,1994）。

陳曉理,"圖書館專業道德規範之探討",政大圖資通訊,3,1991,頁41—44。

莊道明,圖書館專業倫理,（臺北：文華圖書館管理,1996）。

廖又生,"圖書館行政倫理初探","中國圖書館學會"會報,55,1995.12,頁7—12。

謝清俊,"資訊社會與倫理",新聞學研究,46,1992.9,頁1—15。

盧荷生,"規劃圖書館學校倫理課程的構思","中國圖書館學會"會報,55,1995.12,頁1—6。

Bashkin, A. A., "Behind netiquette", Conference on Ethical, Legal and Technological Aspects of Network Use and Abuse, American Association for the Advancement of Science, October 7-9, 1994.

Bazirjian, R.; Ericson, R. L., "The Ethics of library discard practices", The Acquisitions Librarian, 4, 1990, p. 135-145.

Bierbaum, Esther Green, "Searching for the human good: some suggestions for a code of ethics for technical service", Technical Services Quarterly, 11 (3), 1994, p. 1-18.

Boissonnas, C. M., "The cost is more than elegant dinner: your ethics are at steak," Library Acquisitions: Practice & Theory, 11, 1987, p. 143-152.

Brown, Y., "From the reference desk to the jail house: unauthorized practice of law and librarians", Legal Reference Services Quarterly, 13 (4), 1994, pp. 31-45.

Caren, L.; Somerville, A., "Issues facing private academic libraries considering feebased program", Reference Librarian, 22, 1988, pp. 37-49.

Coffey, James R., "Contracts and ethics in library acquisitions: The expressed and the implied". The Acquisitions Librarian, 3, 1990, pp. 95-110.

Del Vecchio, R. A., "Privacy and accountability at the reference desk", Reference Librarian, 38, 1992, pp. 133-140.

Devlin, Mary, Workshop Leader; Miller, Heather, Recorder, "Ethics in action: the vendor's Perspective". The Serials Librarian, 25 (3/4), 1995, pp. 295 – 300.

Doss, E.; Loui, M. C.. "Ethics and the privacy of electronic mail", The Informaiton Society, 11, 1995, pp. 223 – 235.

Froehlich, T. J., "Ethical considerations in enduser searching and training end users to be self searchers of CD-ROM and online databases", National Online Meeting, 1991, pp. 93 – 98.

Goehner, D., "Vendor-library relations: the ethics of working with vendors", in Karen A. Schmidt ed. Understanding the Business of Library Acquisitions, (Chicago: ALA, 1990), pp. 137 – 151.

Golden, F, A.. "The ethics of reference services for the public librarian", "Reference Librarian". 30, 1990, pp. 157 – 166.

Gremmels, G. S., "Reference in the public interest: an examination of ethics," RO, 30 (1), 1990, pp. 82 – 87.

Finks, Lee W. "Librarianship needs a new code of professional ethics". American Libraries, 22 (1). Jan., 1991, pp. 84 – 88, 90, 92.

Greenwood, Terry, Library Association Working Party on Ethics Draft Code, "Professional ethics", New Library World, 82 (1973), July, 1981, pp. 123 – 125.

Hardy, G. J.; Robinson, J. S., "Reference services to students: a crucible for ethical inquiry", RO, 30 (1), 1990, pp. 82 – 87.

Hauptman, R.; Motin, Susan, "TheInternet, cyberethics, and virtual morality", Online, March, 1994, pp. 8 – 9.

——Ethical challenges in librarianship, (New York: Oryx Press, 1988).

Jansen, L. M., "Welcome or not, here they come: unaffiliated users of academic libraries", Reference Services Review, (Spring, 1993), pp. 7 – 14.

Jones, A., "The ethics of research in cyberspace", Internet Research, 4 (3), Fall 1994, pp. 30 – 35.

King, A., "The seven deadly sins of online microcomputing", Online, July 1989, pp. 40 – 45.

Koster, G. E., "Ethics in reference service: codes, case studies, or values?", Reference Services Review, 20 (1), 1992, pp. 71 – 80.

Kultgen, J., Ethics and professionalism, (Philadelphia: University of Pennsylvania, 1988).

Lanier, D.; Boice, D., "The statement on professional ethics: implications and applications", The Serials Librarian, 8 (2) 1983, pp. 85 – 93.

Lindsey, J. A.; Prentice, A. E., Professional ethics and librarians, (Arizona: Oryx, 1985).

Marsh, C., "The business of library acquisitions: a consumer action model", "Library Acquisition: Practice & Theory", 11, 1987, pp. 161 – 163.

Mintz, A. P. ed., Information ethics: concerns for librarianship and the information industry, (North Carolina: McFarland & Company, 1990).

Murray, Barbara June., A historical look at the ALA code of ethics. (Ann Arbor, MI: UMI, 1990. Thesis of San Jose State University, 1990).

Oz, E., Ethics for the information age, (USA: Times Mirror, 1994).

Preer, Jean., "Special ethics for special librarians?", Special Libraries, 18 (1), winter, 1991, pp. 12-18.

Presley, R. L., "Firing an old friend, painful decisions: the ethics between librarians and vendors", Library Acquisition: Practice & Theory, 17, 1993, pp. 53-59.

Protti, M., "Dispensing law at the front lines: ethical dilemmas in law librarianship", Library Trends, 40 (2), 1991, pp. 234-243.

Reed, P., "Moral dilemma", Internet World, 6 (9), Sep., 1995, pp. 90-92.

Regan, M., "Library consulting: challenge, autonomy and risk", Reference Librarian, 22, 1988, pp. 217-232.

Rogers, S. L., "Accredited library school education in ethics", Journal of Educaiton for Library and Information Science, 35 (1), Win., 1994, pp. 52-54.

Saftner, D.; Raghunathan, B., "Privacy in the computer age", Journal of Information Ethics, 4 (2), Fall, 1995, pp. 43-51.

Shaver, D. B., "Ethics for online searchers", National Online Meeting, 1985, pp. 409-414.

Smith, M. M., "Educating for information ethics: assumptions and definitions", Journal of Information Ethics, 2 (1), Spring, 1993, pp. 5-9.

Stover, M., "Confidentiality and privacy in reference service", RO, 27 (2), 1989, pp. 240-244.

Szofran, Nancy, "Internet etiquette and ethics", Online and CD-ROM, Jan. 1994, pp. 66-68.

Usherwood, Bob., "Towards a code of professional ethics", Aslib Proceedings, 33 (6), June 1981, pp. 232-242.

Wood, M. S., "Public service ethics in health science libraries", Library Trends, 40 (2), 1991, pp. 244-257.

臺灣地區"國立大學"校院圖書館自動化之經驗與問題研究[*]

[摘要 Abstract]

臺灣地區"國立大學"院校的圖書館自動化在歷經二十年緩慢發展後,從1991年起有突破性的進展。"國立大學"圖書館不但以整體方式規劃圖書館自動化,且已有82%的圖書館完成自動化系統的採購安裝與測試。本文將以臺灣地區"國立大學"校院圖書館爲主,探討其自動化快速發展的原因與成就,並就現在與未來發展所面臨的問題進一步研討。

Abstract: After two decades of slow developing in library automation, the "national university" and college libraries in Taiwan area, started in 1991, have taken a major breakthrough in the advancement of their automating library programs. Since then, 82% of national university and college libraries have acquired and implemented their planned integrated library systems. The purpose of this paper attempts to study reasons and causes involved in such great changes, their encountered problems, and the future development of these national automated library projects.

關鍵字(Keywords): 圖書館自動化(library automation), 圖書館資訊系統(library information system), 臺灣地區(Taiwan area)

一、前言

臺灣地區圖書館於1974年由中山科學院圖書館,首先引進美國機讀編目磁帶印製西文圖書目錄卡片開始,揭開了臺灣地區圖書館自動化的序幕,至今已歷經了二十年圖書館自動化發展歷程。這二十年的圖書館自動化發展過程,由早期的各館自我摸索、引進與修改國外系統、自行設計自動化系統、以至現今整體規劃圖書館自動化系統爲止,臺灣地區圖書館自動化發展已從試誤的嬰兒階段,成長到壯年期。這過程中圖書館不但已經克服對自動化的陌生與恐懼,同時也累積了相當多寶貴的實務經驗。在臺灣地區各類型圖書館自動化發展歷程中,"國立大學"院校受到政府財務與政策的支持,加上由"教育部"定期召開"國立大學"校院圖書館自動化規劃研討會,致使"國立大學"校院圖書館自動化在短短兩三年間快速的發展,同時是以整體規劃方式進行。本文將以二十年來臺灣地區"國立大學"校院圖書館自動化進行歷程所累積的經驗探討其自動化成就與問題。

二、臺灣地區"國立大學"院校圖書館自動化發展歷程

臺灣地區圖書館自動化發展歷程可分成主要的三階段:[①]

第一階段 萌芽時期(1972—1977)

此階段臺灣地區的電腦系統,多爲租用國外大型電腦系統,並以從事科學的計算處理爲主,欠缺中文資訊處理的能力。此時電腦僅能處理西文資料,當時有中山科學研究院圖書館

---

[*] 本文與世界新聞傳播學院圖書資訊管理學系莊道明先生合作撰寫,曾發表在《資訊傳播與圖書館學》1卷2期(1994年12月),第24—33頁。

引進美國國會圖書館的機讀編目磁帶，進行西文圖書編目工作。淡江大學在 IBM370-138 電腦上，測試西文館藏目錄列印的作業。[2]這時期的圖書館自動化受限於電腦系統處理資料能力，自動化作業推展以實驗性質居多，且大都是單項自動化作業。"國立大學"校院圖書館自動化在此階段並無顯著的進展，反而是私立淡江大學在這方面積極投入研究。

第二階段　基礎時期（1978—1984）

此時期在電腦技術上有些重大的進展。臺灣地區不但推出八位元的個人電腦，同時也相繼推出可以處理中文資料的電腦。由於這些電腦硬體架構日趨成熟，帶給圖書館界相當的希望。1978 年"國立師範大學"圖書館利用神能電腦建立中文教育資料檔，並於 1980 年利用所鍵的資料檔直接列印出版第三期"教育論文摘要"。同年五月並引進海外 ORBIT 與 DIALOG 線上資料庫系統。[3]1979 年"國立清華大學"在 CDC CYBER 840 大型電腦上自型設計發展西文期刊編目系統，並利用該系統編印該館西文期刊聯合目錄。1981 年"國立臺灣大學"圖書館在 UNIVAC1100 電腦系統上，自行設計發展期刊控制系統，並列印紙本的臺大西文期刊聯合目錄。1982 年"國立政治大學"中正圖書館在 Perkin Elmer 32202 電腦系統上，自行設計發展圖書出納控制系統。1984 年"國立交通大學"圖書館在王安電腦 WANG VS-90 電腦上，設計西文期刊自動化系統。[4]從以上的發展可以看出，這時期的幾個"國立大學"在圖書館自動化作業上，除師範大學已開始著手利用中文電腦系統從事資料庫的鍵檔處理外，其他的圖書館仍在各自設計與發展自動化系統的嘗試階段。當時"國立大學"圖書館自動化作業的項目，較偏重於簡單的期刊管理自動化系統。至於自動化編目方面，1981 年"中國圖書館學會"已公佈中國機讀編目格式（Chinese MARC）第一版。"國立中央圖書館"於 1983 年於王安電腦 WANG VS-100 上，一方面開始進行中文圖書資料鍵檔工作，另方面也向美國 OCLC 購買 LC MARC 磁帶進行西文資料轉換作業。[5]此階段的"國立大學"圖書館在編目自動化作業方面，可說是處於觀望階段。1983 年"教育部"在發展"大事院校行政電腦化"工作中，決議在發展的六個子系統中，將包括圖書資訊子系統。該子系統由臺灣大學圖書館擔任召集人，並邀請各"國立院校"圖書館、"國立中央圖書館"、科資中心、農資中心、"文建會"、康大電腦公司等單位研商發展，最後根據十五所"國立大學"院校圖書館提出的報表，研擬出"圖書資訊管理系統報表需求草案"，於 1983 年 8 月報"教育部"核定，並委由康大電腦公司到各"國立大學"圖書館進行系統分析。後來因為需求書內容不佳等種種因素，該合約始終未曾簽訂，此案最後沒有具體進展。[6]

第三階段　整體圖書館自動化與網路發展時期（1985—）

從 1985 年起在短短的一兩年間，臺灣地區電腦技術發展可說是突飛猛進。電腦公司不但如雨後春筍般的設立，同時中文電腦處理的功能亦大幅提昇，許多海外自動化系統亦相繼被引進臺灣，使得圖書館自動化系統上有了更多的選擇。在這階段圖書館自動化的特色，是趨向整合性的圖書館自動化觀念設計與直接引用海外現成的套裝軟體。因此，圖書館自動化的腳步不但較以往迅速，同時自動化的成效也較以往更加顯著。1988 年私立淡江大學圖書館以 TALIS（Tamkang Automated Library Integrated System）系統，首先完成圖書館整體自動化系統，具備採購、中西編目、出納、期刊管理、參考服務、行政管理、線上公用目錄查詢等功能。這階段初期"國立大學"院校圖書館自動化發展在觀念與作業上，並沒有產生太大的改變，各館仍延續以往的情況在原有系統上僅作修正或增添一些功能，基本上並沒有太大的突破。根據李德竹教授在 1985 年的調查與"中國圖書館學會"圖書館自動化規劃委員會在 1988

年對圖書館自動化的調查問卷中，發現當時圖書館自動化最主要的困難有幾項，包括經費不足、缺乏負責自動化工作小組或人力、自動化經驗與技術的缺乏、上級的支持與觀念、電腦設備問題、自動化目標不明確與缺乏全盤規劃等。[7]在這些問題中，經費不足是當時"國立大學"校院圖書館發展自動化最大的阻力，尤其主機系統與軟體的採購動則需百萬臺幣，以及後續每一期資料建檔與書目轉換作業經費，爲當時的"國立大學"校院確是一個負擔。此外，爲發展自動化作業所需要的人員培訓與自動化規劃等相關作業，皆非當時圖書館及其有限人員能獨立負擔。因此，"國立大學"校院圖書館自動化發展在此階段初期，可說是慘淡經營。

1989年2月在"國立中央圖書館"召開"臺灣圖書館會議"，此次會議結論中建請"教育部"籌設專責機構，以統一規劃圖書館事業等相關事宜。在同年12月"教育部"成立"'教育部'圖書館事業委員會"，邀請專家學者、教育行政主管與圖書館界代表等，共同規劃圖書館事業。該委員會定期召開委員會議，除研擬與研訂各種圖書館相關法規與標準外，也進行各項專題研究。根據專題研究的結果與建議，提報委員會討論，最後建議"教育部"各相關單位研擬辦理。在該委員會決議進行的七項專題研究計劃中，包括"整體規劃圖書館資訊網路系統"專題研究計劃案，由臺灣大學李德竹教授與淡江大學黃世雄教授共同召集。[8]此研究計劃進行除邀約圖書館專家參與研究外，尚有電腦、資訊及通信界之專家學者共同研擬。該計劃小組定期召開會議數十次，設計問卷廣徵各界意見，並邀請全國圖書館界及電腦、電信界之主管人員舉行座談。該計劃於1991年6月完成，最後整份報告提交"教育部"參考辦理。報告建議"教育部"應設置"圖書館資訊網路推動小組"進行研議具體中長程發展計劃、審查及評估各級各類圖書館自動化計劃，以謀計劃性整合發展的提議；並建議"教育部"電算中心主導全國圖書館自勳化網路計劃與推廣"'國立大學'校院圖書館自動化系統整合暫行規範"。[9]在各"國立大學"圖書館強烈的要求與圖書館界全力支持下，"教育部"最後根據這份報告的內容與建議，作爲推展"國立大學"校院圖書館自動化之依據，使得各"國立大學"院校推展自動化上具備最基本的需求與方向。在1991至1993年間"國立大學"校院圖書館自動化發展，有了突破性的進展。一方面是"教育部"在政策與經費大力支持各"國立大學"圖書館發展自動化，另方面則是"教育部"電算中心開始與各"國立大學"圖書館合作共同推展圖書館自動化工作。在短短三年時間各館紛紛進行自動化系統之採購，一時之間"國立大學"校院圖書館自動化如火如荼快速進展。

歸結以上"國立大學"校院圖書館自動化的發展歷程，在1990年之前是各自發展的實驗性階段，早期系統發展都採行自行開發設計居多，功能也都是單一性。自1991年6月後受到整體規劃圖書館資訊網路系統研究報告的影響，使得"教育部"大力支持"國立大學"院校圖書館自動化計劃，而在短短三年內各圖書館紛紛採購系統主機，並從整體規劃的觀點發展圖書館自動化。這些發展使得"國立大學"校院圖書館自動化比率，在各類圖書館中獨佔鰲頭。

三、臺灣地區"國立大學"院校圖書館自動化現況

臺灣地區目前共有28所"國立大學"校院，其中有14所綜合大學（包括空中大學）、6所獨立學院、8所師範學院。根據1993年6月由"教育部"委託"中國圖書館學會"圖書館自動化規劃委員會所作的調查報告臺灣地區圖書館自動化系統彙編調查資料統計顯示，"國立大學"院校圖書館已有23所完成自動化系統的採購與安裝，佔所有"國立校院"的82%。

其他尚未自動化的"國立"校院圖書館也將陸續加速自動化的腳步。以下即是該調查資料中，23個已完成自動化系統採購與安裝的圖書館統計資料。⑩

由表（一）可以看出"國立大學"校院幾乎都在1991年至1993年之間，採購自動化系統。其中有8個單位採用臺灣地區開發的自動化系統，有15個單位則使用引進的自動化系統。

採用臺灣地區開發自動化系統中，以使用傳技TOTALS五個單位最多。引進的自動化系統中，以使用INNOPAC系統的九個單位最高。這兩個自動化的硬體系統都是採MainFrame架構，都具備開放式系統的結構，可直接連上臺灣學術網路系統。並可同時支援CCCII與BIG-5碼，且與多種編目系統或資料庫銜接，以從事線上書目資料轉換作業。例如BiblioFile，OCLC CD450，WLN，RLIN，CatssCD，OCLC與臺灣地區書目資訊網路等。

表一 "國立大學"院校圖書館自動化系統統計表

使用單位	系統名稱	日期	書目資料量	讀者檔筆數	主機	作業系統	系統功能
交通大學 ★	虹橋系統	1991	250,000	21,000	NCR 3345	UNIX	1, 2, 3, 4, 5, 6, 7, 8
花蓮師院 ★	清江一號	1990	-----	3,000	80386 CPU	清江一號	3, 5, 7
新竹師院 ★	鈊特系統	1991	70,004	5,728	80386 CPU	NETW ARE V2.1	2, 3, 5, 6
清華大學 ★	傳技 TOTALS	1991	183,500	-----	MOTOROLA M3840	UNIX	1, 2, 3, 4, 5, 6, 7, 8
工業技術學院 ★	傳技 TOTALS	1990	93,600	5,900	MOTOROLA M3840	UNIX	1, 2, 3, 5, 6, 7, 8
中興大學 ★	傳技 TOTALS	1993	83,478	0	-----	-----	全部
體育學院 ★	傳技 TOTALS	-----	15,896	0	中華一號工作站	UNIX	2, 3
海洋大學 ★	傳技 TOTALS	1993	8,000	0	-----	-----	3
臺北師院	DOBIS	-----	66,777	4,264	IBM 9373	VSE/SP	1, 2, 3, 4, 5, 7, 8, 9
臺灣大學	INNOPAC	1991	180,000	26,000	DEC 5900	ULTRIX RSX	全部
政治大學	INNOPAC	1992	27,000	0	DEC 5900	ULTRIX RSX	1, 2, 3, 4, 5, 6, 7, 8
師範大學	INNOPAC	1992	120,000	6,000	DEC 5/240	ULTRIX	全部
中正大學	INNOPAC	1992	56,000	463	DEC 5/240	ULTRIX	1, 2, 3, 5, 6, 7, 8
屏東師院	INNOPAC	1992	6,500	0	DEC 5/240	DEC UNIX 4.2	2, 3, 5, 7
中山大學	INNOPAC	1993	-----	-----	DEC 5/240	-----	1, 2, 3, 6, 7
高雄師大	INNOPAC	1993	25,446	4,477	DEC 5/240	ULTRIX 4.2	全部
陽明學院	INNOPAC	1992	34,000	0	DEC 5/240	UNIX	1, 2, 3, 4, 5, 6, 7, 8
彰化師大	INNOPAC	1993	20,000	2,000	DEC 5/240	-----	全部
空中大學	鼎盛 URICA	1993	10,000	0	SUN SPARC W/S 10	UNIX	全部
中央大學	鼎盛 URICA	1993	-----	-----	IBM RS6000	-----	-----
臺南師院	DYNIX	-----	-----	-----	IBM RS6000	-----	1, 2, 3, 5, 7
藝術學院	DYNIX	1993	-----	-----	IBM RS6000	-----	1, 2, 3, 5, 6
成功大學	凌羣 UTLAS	1991	220,000	13,000	TANDEM CLX 840	GUARDIAN 90	全部

◎ 系統功能代碼表：1. 採訪子系統 2. 中編子系統 3. 西編子系統 4. 權威檔控制子系統 5. 流通子系統 6. 期刊管理子系統 7. 書目查詢子系統 8. 參考子系統 9. 館際合作子系統。

★ 此符號代表採用自行開發的自動化系統。

四、臺灣地區"國立大學"院校圖書館自動化經驗

臺灣地區的"國立大學"院校圖書館在自動化發展歷程中，雖然不是領先發展，但在各類圖書館中，"國立大學"圖書館確是最先完成採購、安裝與測試自動化系統的圖書館。而各"國立大學"校院圖書館願意放棄早期各自開發系統，改採整體規劃方式，以至在短短時間內有如此成就主要受到以下幾個主要因素的影響：

（一）"國立大學"院校圖書館自動化發展，主要受到"教育部"圖書館事業發展委員會"整體規劃圖書館資訊網路系統"研究計劃之影響

根據"整體規劃圖書館資訊網路系統"研究報告結果，該計劃建議"教育部"應該推廣該計劃中，所研訂的"'國立大學'校院圖書館自動化系統整合暫行規範"。由於"教育部"接受了這個建議，使得這份暫行規範成了整份報告中具效力的地方。這份規範內容規定了採購自動化軟硬體系統的基本需求，致使"教育部"電算中心依據這份規範內容，函請各"國立大學"院校圖書館發展自動化時必須參照，使得這份暫行規範成了"國立大學"圖書館發展自動化系統的共同基本需求。

此份暫行規範共有六點：[⑪]

第一點：規訂新建立的中文圖書書目資料需符合 ISO 2709、Chinese MARC（第三版）及中文編目規則第二層的格式；

第二點：要求自動化系統需能提供中文查詢且具備 CCCII 交換碼從事書目交換工作；

第三點：規定圖書館自動化系統應納入各校校園網路系統，而網路系統宜採開放式架構；

第四點：請各館注意電腦廠商長期維護能力與系統軟體的彈性；

第五點：要求圖書館自動化作業應邀請各校相關教授專家的協助與咨詢；

第六點：要求各校圖書館自動化作業，應主動聯合性質相同學校共同辦理。

這六點成了"國立大學"院校圖書館自動化發展的基本需求，也是整份報告具有相當貢獻與影響力的地方。

（二）"國立大學"院校圖書館自動化的發展，受"教育部"電算中心協調與催化作業的影響

臺灣學術路網路（TANet）於 1989 年由"教育部"電子計算機中心提出，由"教育部"專案推動施行而建立，以作爲提供學術及教學研究之基本傳輸通道，並透過網路整合校園圖書館自動化系統、教學研究系統及行政資訊系統等。該網路初步雖以學術研究爲主，但逐步擴展至教學、圖書館自動化及行政業務上。在"教育部"電算中心的規劃中，初步是希望各"國立大學"圖書館自動化系統能連接上臺灣學術網路。但鑒於各"國立大學"院校圖書館在自動化發展的程度不一，加上所使用的系統不符合網路通信的標準，更由於書目格式也都不一致，造成書目交換的困難。因此，若要使各"國立大學"院校圖書館能夠順利連接上臺灣學術網路，同時能夠發揮書目共享的功能，勢必需從各館最基本的自動化作業重新規劃起。在這些考量下，"教育部"電算中心於是扮演著各圖書館自動化協調與催化的角色，積極協助推動"國立大學"校院圖書館自動化的發展。

"教育部"電算中心於 1991 年 6 月爲了使各"國立院校"圖書館自動化系統逐步朝向統一與密切合作發展，曾函各"國立大專院校"購置圖書館自動化系統時需參考

《"國立大學"校院圖書館自動化系統整合暫行規範》辦理。此外，爲促進圖書館自動化業務經驗的交流，該中心於1991年7月起每季委託各大學輪流舉辦"'國立大學'校院圖書館自動化規劃研討會"，至1994年3月止已經舉辦了九次的研討會。同時該中心爲促進中文書目資料共享於1993年3月邀集"國立大學"校院圖書館召開"研商加速推動圖書館促進書目共享會議"，除了就行政與技術方面的問題進行討論外，決議成立"書目共享工作小組"，該小組每月開會一次，研商各種書目交換的問題。[12]由於"教育部"電算中心在"國立大學"校院圖書館自動化發展中，發揮了積極協調與催化的功能，使得某些在原處觀望的"國立大學"校院圖書館，也不得不開始有所行動，加上因"教育部"經費大力支援政策誘導下，導致"國立大學"院校圖書館產生骨牌效應，在短短三年內紛紛採購自動化系統。

（三）"國立大學"院校圖書館自動化迅速發展，得力於"'國立大學'校院圖書館自動化規劃研討會"定期召開與"教育部"經費的支源

由"教育部"電算中心負責推動的"'國立大學'校院圖書館自動化規劃研討會"於1991年7月在國立交通大學圖書館召開第一次會議後，爾後由其他"國立大學"圖書館每季輪流辦理。該研討會除了凝聚各館發展圖書館自動化的力量外，也針對發展的困難共商解決的方案。此外，藉由固定的研討可多瞭解各館發展自動化的經驗與相關問題。由於增加這些共同研討的機會，使得"國立大學"院校圖書館在面對自動化發展相關的問題時，如主機的選擇、自動化系統的市場現況、自動化系統代理商的信譽等，都獲得相當多的資訊。該研討會對於圖書館自動化發展而言，好處是讓有發展圖書館自動化經驗的圖書館透過不斷研討，帶領尚未發展自動化的圖書館邁向自動化的途徑；但從另方面而言，這些尚不很清楚如何發展自動化的圖書館，可能會因爲先入爲主的觀念，導致在不很清楚或未瞭解自己圖書館需求時，便尾隨其他已發展的圖書館，採購了相同的主機或系統，而後衍生一些問題。但總體而言，"國立大學"校院圖書館自動化規劃研討會所發揮正面功能多於負面。

此外，在"教育部"政策與經費支持下，許多早期各館發展的自動化系統因不符合網路系統基本需求或是無法符合未來發展需求，也趁此機會另行採購合適的主機與軟體，然後設法將原先的書目資料轉換到新系統上，因而造成"國立大學"院校圖書館從1991年起，紛紛展開系統選機的工作，使得"國立大學"院校圖書館在短短兩三年內，幾乎多數都已完成自動化系統的採購與安裝測試。因此，"國立大學"院校圖書館自動化發展之所以如此迅速，可說是一方面拜"教育部"政策與經費之賜，另方面則得力於"'國立大學'校院圖書館自動化規劃研討會"定期的召開。

（四）"國立大學"院校圖書館自動化推展與自動化教育與訓練息息相關

根據李德竹教授於1986年的"學術研究圖書館員對圖書館作業自動化認識與態度"的調查研究發現，館長與館員共同認爲自動化最大癥結是缺少能負起自動化責任的工作小組等數項。歸結這些問題的關鍵，在於館員對於自動化方面背景不足所導致。因此，缺乏有自動化技術訓練的館員是推展自動化最大的瓶頸。在自動化重要性的認知統計上，館長與館員並無顯著差異，均認爲圖書館自動化是勢在必行。該報告結論認爲"館長、副館長、資料單位負責人和館員對圖書館業務自動化之意願很高，但缺乏實際對自動化作業之詳細作法與瞭解，以致於意願與行動脫節。近幾年來，常聽到圖書館要自動

化的熱門話題，但很少看到成果即說明了一切！"⑬

根據交通大學圖書館朱淑卿在 1989 年對五所 "大學圖書館自動化發展途徑之差異對館員知識與能力的影響研究" 發現，館員對電腦知識與能力實有繼續加強再職教育的需要。就當時五所大學圖書館館員參與圖書館自動化的心態上，館員在對於自動化發展方式的選擇與希望發展的方式有相當的矛盾。一方面館員理想上希望藉由實際的參與自動化系統開發，獲取自動化發展的實務經驗並使系統更完美，但另方面因限於電腦等相關背景的不足，希望能使用套裝軟體，以能在很短時間內建立自動化系統。⑭在當時多數大學圖書館自行開發自動化系統下，館員的心態一方面是很積極參與各種系統的開發工作，但另方面確也必須不斷的吸收自動化的新知與參加各種自動化再職進修訓練課程。"中國圖書館學會" 有鑒於此，於每年暑假委請臺灣大學圖書館學系辦理圖書館自動化研習會。此外，各種自動化的研討會也如雨後春筍般的在各地召開，許多 "國立大學" 圖書館更是利用暑假期間，派遣館員遠赴美國各重要圖書館或資訊中心，參觀與研習各種自動化系統與業務。經由自動化理論知識與各館實際發展自動化經驗的累積與交流，才能促使 "國立大學" 院校圖書館在短短幾年內全面推展自動化。各館在歷經過相當的準備階段，不但是館長對於自動化的認知更加深入，館員對於自動化的相關知識與經驗也具備，時機一旦成熟圖書館自動化的發展自然是水到渠成。

（五）"國立大學" 校院圖書館自動化的發展，促成各種自動化系統使用小組的產生

由於 "國立大學" 院校圖書館自動化推展工作中，經常會面臨各種自動化共通的問題。這些問題在過去各館只能獨立面對、默默的承受、靜靜的解決。如今由於 "教育部" 相關單位的領導，加上各 "國立圖書館" 館長與館員的互相激勵與合作，面對這些自動化問題已組織成不同層次及範圍的圖書館自動化工作小組。其中有 "中央圖書館" 負責的 "書目中心合作館館長會議"、"教育部" 電算中心與 "中央圖書館" 共同推動的 "書目共享工作小組"、"教育部" 推動的 "'國立大學' 圖書館館長聯席會"、由 "中央研究院" 召集的 "INNOPAC 自動化系統使用小組"、臺北市立圖書館召集的 "URICA 自動化系統使用小組" 及清華大學召集的 "傳技 TOTALS 自動化系統使用小組"。⑮由這些小組的成立，可以發現臺灣地區 "國立大學" 校院圖書館自動化的發展，已經摒棄過去閉門造車的觀念，以合作方式共同解決自動化所面臨的難題。尤其採用相同自動化系統所成立的使用小組，不但可以就自動化系統發展分享經驗，同時可對電腦廠商產生更大的約束力。這些不同層次與範圍的自動化工作小組，對 "國立大學" 校院圖書館自動化發展有相當的貢獻。由於這成功的經驗，目前 "教育部" 也逐漸採相同的模式，推動其他學校圖書館自動化的發展。

綜合以上五點促成 "國立大學" 校院圖書館自動化發展的因素，可以發現隨著電腦與通訊技術發展的日趨成熟，加上圖書館自動化系統的多樣化與整合性發展，使得圖書館自動化較之以往更加便利。誠如李德竹教授在圖書館業務自動化基本注意事項中所提的 "圖書館業務自動化並不難"，重要的是要 "瞭解自己（圖書館）、瞭解自己的需求、瞭解自動化的目的"。

而 "國立大學" 校院圖書館自動化之所以能在短期間快速的進展，"單位主管（'教育部'）之支持、態度及魄力是推展自動化成功重要關鍵"，尤其是政策與經費的支援。而由 "教育部" 電算中心負責推動的 "'國立大學' 校院圖書館自動化規劃研討

會"，給各"國立大學"校院圖書館自動化推動的館員及館長一個"多學、多聽、多讀、多看、多問"的機會，使各館逐漸摒棄"閉門造車"的觀念，同時也加強國立大學校院圖書館"自動化計劃負責人"的責任感與觀念，造成各館都相繼"成立圖書館自動化工作小組"，開始自動化需求書的研擬、系統的選機等相關業務。各種自動化研習會與研討會的舉辦，"加強館員自動化觀念及練習"。隨著各種不同層次與範圍的自動化工作小組的成立，持續加速"國立大學"校院圖書館自動化出推展。[16]以上這些因素都是促成"國立大學"校院圖書館自動化發展重要的經驗與成就。

五、目前"國立大學"校院圖書館自動化的問題

"國立大學"校院圖書館自動化推展至今，雖然已有82%的圖書館已完成自動化主機與軟體採購與安裝的作業，但各館確也面臨不同程度的自動化問題。以下針對幾項主要的問題加以探討：

（一）書目標準與轉檔的問題

根據歷次的"國立大學"校院圖書館自動化規劃研討會的正式提案統計，可以發現對於書目標準相關問題提案最多。其中包括自動化中文字集選擇的問題（CCCII，Big-5）字集的轉換、機讀書目 US MARC 與 Chinese MARC 轉換問題等。由於這些問題涉及未來在網路架構上，書目共享與書目轉換的問題。因此，在歷次的研討會上，一再被提案出來共同討論。而由這個問題的一再被提出，可以反應出"國立大學"院校圖書館自動化的發展模式，基本上已經預設在網路架構上，各館自動化的目標已不再只是館內作業的自動化而已，而是要更進一步達到資訊共享。目前中文字集的選擇上，各館的共識是利用 CCCII 作為館際間書目轉檔的基礎，至於各館內部作業仍以 Big-5 碼為主。目前多數自動化系統均具備由 Big-5 自動轉 CCCII 碼的功能。至於 US MARC 與 Chinese MARC 轉檔的問題，發生在一些早期自行發展自動化的圖書館。由於早期這些圖書館自動化書目鍵檔均採用 US MARC，如今在配合整體發展規範要求下新系統均以 Chinese MARC 為主，使得轉檔工作成了這些館的問題。"教育部"社教司委託"中國圖書館學會"邀請政治大學胡歐蘭館長研訂 US MARC 與 Chinese MARC 格式之對照表。現今"中國圖書館學會"已將中國機讀編目格式第三版與美國機讀編目格式對照表研訂出來，可提供給電腦公司發展轉檔程式之用，此轉換問題在未來將可迎刃而解。此外，"教育部"為協助解決這些問題，已於1993年3月成立"書目共享工作小組"以解決書目交換所產生的技術相關問題。[17]

（二）系統整合的問題

目前"國立大學"校院圖書館採用的自動化系統，基本上是集中於幾個主要的系統，例如 INNOPAC 有九個學校圖書館採用、TOTALS 有五個單位等。這些系統在網路上具備相同的功能與資料結構，但是讀者若要在臺灣學術網路上查詢各館資料，仍然是必需要多次分別載入各校系統，而無法一次查詢到各館館藏的全貌。因此，若能夠將相同自動化系統相互整合，仿照美國 OhioLink 方式，不但方便讀者利用，同時可建立各館館際合作的基礎。有關的提案與問題已獲得各"國立大學"院校圖書館初步的共識，目前位於中壢與新竹地區的交大、清華與中央大學三校，願意先行嘗試圖書館地區自動化系統整合的工作。未來可由試行的經驗提供"教育部"相關單位參考，並經由技術層面、人力與制度相關問題的解決，逐步擴展整合的區域與系統。

(三) 其他各館自動化發展個別的問題

多數"國立大學"院校圖書館自動化系統，雖已完成了主機的安裝與運作，但後續發展所發生的問題，依各館狀況有所不同，仍有待各館自行解決。以成功大學圖書館自動化為例，該館自動化所遭遇的困難則有中文字集不足、系統穩定性不足、資料轉檔不順、電力不足等。[18]臺灣大學圖書館對於 INNOPAC 的評鑑認為該系統在各功能的歸類與編排次序上不够清楚，此外各種統計報表中文化、中文關鍵字查詢、檢索人次統計、權威檔與書目的聯結都未臻理想。[19]清華大學圖書館使用傳技的 TOTALS 系統有待解決的問題，包括系統跳項功能尚不靈活、權威檔控制功能尚未完整、統計功能仍有缺失、報表處理速度緩慢、特殊字碼轉檔問題等。[20]從各館採購自動化系統與安裝運作之後，各館都會陸續發現這些套裝軟體系統實際上並非十全十美。針對各館不同的業務需求，也都需要作或多或少的修正。因此，同一系統中某項功能，對某館是很好的設計，對另一個館可能是不需要的功能。由各館自動化經驗的分享中，也可發現館員也漸漸能體會出，天下沒有一個十全十美的圖書館自動化系統，重要的是系統能夠滿足圖書館業務自動化的程度，然而更重要的是隨著科技的進步與讀者需要的增加，圖書館資訊系統也必須不斷地昇級。[21]此外，電腦公司的後續服務與合作也是圖書館自動化成功與否的關鍵之一，因此，在選擇圖書館自動化系統的同時，也該慎察電腦公司的技術能力與後續服務的熱誠。

六、結論

臺灣地區圖書館自動化發展已經歷經過二十餘年。在這發展過程中，"國立大學"院校圖書館並非是首先全力投入自動化行列的圖書館。早期雖有部份"國立大學"圖書館投入發展的隊伍，但多數終究是屬於實驗性質，由於初期沒有專用的電腦設備，使得此時的自動化系統到最後終需放棄。1991 年對"國立大學"校院圖書館自動化發展是一個關鍵性的開始。當時海外圖書館自動化系統不但大量被引進臺灣，同時系統中文化的程度也日趨成熟。此外，圖書館界對發展自動化的要求與聲音，也逐漸獲得主管單位"教育部"的重視與支持，使得"國立大學"校院圖書館在發展自動化系統上，一方面可獲得"教育部"政策與經費的支持，另方面也受到"整體規劃圖書館資訊網路系統"研究報告雙重影響下，各"國立大學"圖書館開始以整體規劃方式，重新發展圖書館自動化。此外，"教育部"電算中心也積極從事相關業務工作的推展，協調與催化各"國立大學"院校圖書館自動化的規劃與相關問題的解決，協助各種工作小組的成立與舉辦自動化的教育訓練等，這些因素均間接促成"國立大學"校院圖書館自動化在短短三年之間快速發展。自動化系統的採購安裝與運轉並非是圖書館自動化的結束，而是真正自動化的開始。因此，許多關於書目資料轉換，系統整合與各館面對系統不完美的地方，仍有待各館未來妥善的加以規劃解決。目前為進一步統整各自動化系統，"教育部"電算中心已決定，將原先"圖書館資訊網路推動小組"更改為"圖書館自動化及網路系統整合小組"，以因應圖書館事業未來發展之趨勢。總之，圖書館自動化並不難，只要多學、多聽、多讀、多看、多問、廣蒐資料，不要閉門造車，善用人際關係，保持幽默感，自動化真的不難。而"國立大學"校院圖書館正是以這樣的精神，以具體自動化規劃研討會與自動化推動工作小組的方式，發展出互相合作與經驗分享的模式。從"國立大學"校院圖書館自動化發展的成功經驗與模式，相信可提供給其他有意發展自動化作業務類型圖書館進一步參考。

附　註

①李德竹，"圖書館自動化資訊系統發展之探討"，"中國圖書館學會"會報43期（1988年12月），頁120。

②胡歐蘭，"臺灣地區圖書館資訊服務系統之發展"，圖書館與資訊科學教育研討會（臺北：臺大圖書館學系，1993），頁104。

③同註2，頁105。

④同註1，頁112—115。

⑤同註1，頁115。

⑥"國立大學"校院圖書館發展推動小組，"國立大學"校院圖書館發展計劃報告書，（臺北："教育部"高教司，1989年），頁1。

⑦同註1，頁121。

⑧宋美珍，"三年有成——'教育部'圖書館事業委員會"，"中國圖書館學會"會訊：1卷5期（1993年10月），頁1—2。

⑨李德竹，黃世雄，整體規劃圖書館資訊網路系統（臺北："教育部"圖書館事業委員會，1991年），頁233—234。

⑩"中國圖書館學會"圖書館自動化規劃委員會編輯，臺灣地區圖書館自動化系統彙編（臺北："教育部"，1993年6月），頁25—67。

⑪同註10，頁271。

⑫"各級圖書館自動化辦理情形"，"教育部"圖書事業委員會會訊11期（1993年10月），頁3—4。

⑬李德竹，"學術研究圖書館館員對圖書館作業自動化認識與態度"，圖書館學刊5期（1987年11月），頁32—33。

⑭朱淑卿，"大學圖書館自動化發展途徑之差異對館員知識與能力的影響研究"，"中國圖書館學會"會報44期（1989年6月），頁76。

⑮陳文生，"從學術網路談圖書館資訊網路之挑戰"，在圖書館自動化系統及機讀格式轉換研討會會議論文集（臺北：政治大學圖書館，1994年5月），頁168。

⑯李德竹，"圖書館業務自動化基本注意事項"，書府8期（1987年6月），頁16—17。

⑰"爲加速推動圖書館自動化，'教育部'成立書目共享工作小組"，"教育部"圖書事業委員會會訊9期（1993年4月），頁1。

⑱王元興，"'國立成功大學'圖書館自動化作業經驗與問題"，在"國立大學"校院圖書館自動化規劃第九次研討會會議資料（臺北："教育部"，1994年3月），頁25。

⑲童敏惠，"從系統館員看INNOPAC系統"，在圖書館自動化系統及機讀格式轉換研討會會議論文集（臺北：政治大學圖書館，1994年5月），頁90—91。

⑳陳美雲，"清華大學圖書館使用TOTALS系統的經驗及檢討"，在圖書館自動化系統及機讀格式轉換研討會會議論文集（臺北：政治大學圖書館，1994年5月），頁116—125。

㉑ R. De. Gennaro. "Integrated Online library Systems: Perspective, Perceptions, & Praticaties." Library Journal 110：22（Feb. 1985）：37-40.

"建構資訊高速公路圖書館應扮演的角色"研討會紀要[*]

一、前 言

面對資訊時代的來臨，爲加速建立資訊社會的腳步，期使不同的使用者可以很快速地獲得必要的資訊及服務，"資訊高速公路"已成爲世界的潮流，身處其中的圖書館，其做法應以宏觀的態度，將重要的圖書資訊經由快速的資訊網路，提供給最需要的人。本館曾濟羣館長指出，"中央圖書館"近年來一直致力於圖書館自動化作業的研發與推廣，希望將豐富的圖書資訊透過網路傳輸出去，也希望需要資訊的人，能以最快的速度取得，好讓新資訊的傳播深入每個人的家庭，就像家中的自來水一樣方便。他並期許圖書館不只是借還書的地方，而是重要的資訊傳播站，希望資訊界和圖書館界要加強合作，讓圖書館的資訊網路成爲知識的貨櫃車。

本館爲加速國家資訊基礎建設的推展，並配合"資訊網路系統"啓用，特於1994年10月1日於文教區國際會議廳舉辦"建構資訊高速公路圖書館應扮演的角色"學術研討會。有來自各大學圖書館館長、圖書館學科系教授、全臺灣地區圖書資訊網路合作館館長與書目網路業務負責人、縣（市）立文化中心暨縣（市）立圖書館負責人、資訊界電腦界專家、"行政院"研考會、新聞局、資訊工業策進會、"國立教育資料館"及本館業務相關同人共250人參加。期望透過"中央圖書館"的經驗，加速圖書館資訊網路化的腳步，以提昇大衆生活上的便利。

二、籌備與編印參考資料

爲籌辦是項研討會，曾館長於8月12日召集採訪組辜瑞蘭主任、編目組鄭恒雄主任、閱覽組宋建成主任、總務組劉興儀主任及電腦室歐陽崇榮編輯等共同研議。會中決定整個研討會進行方式、主持人主講人聘請名單、邀請對象及編印參考資料等，隨即緊鑼密鼓地展開各項作業。

爲便與會者對研討會主題——資訊高速公路，增加瞭解與認識，閱覽組特編印該研討會參考資料一册，其內容包括兩方面：（一）全文資料部份：1."行政院"資訊發展推動小組夏主任委員漢民於今年6月14日向"行政院"連院長簡報"推動資訊高速公路策略"資料摘要；2."資訊應用發展策略——教育研究與科技研發"，摘自第四次電子、資訊與電信策略會議（SRB會議）會議資料（1994年8月9日至13日）；3.美國國會圖書館館長比林頓博士"在建構資訊高速公路時圖書館應扮演重要的角色"全文譯稿；4.美國參議院公聽會上圖書館員尋求在資訊公路上的定位，本篇文章原文摘自美國圖書館學會華府辦公室提供的證詞，係全文譯稿。（二）書目部份：1.中文書目部份，收錄1994年1月至8月間，臺灣地區出版之報紙及資訊類雜誌所載有關"資訊基礎建設（NII）"及"資訊高速公路"之相關報導及論文，共計126篇；2.英文書目部份，收錄1989年以後至1994年6月間，檢索ABI/INFORM, ERIC, MARCHIVE CD-ROM, LISA,

---

[*] 本文曾發表在《"國立中央圖書館"館訊》16卷第4期（1994年11月），第4—7頁，由簡家幸整理。

Library Literature，以及 Readers' Guide Abstracts 等光碟系統，主題為 Information Superhigh-wav、National Information Infrastructure（NII）及 National Research and Education Network；（NREN）等之相關論文及政府出版品共計124篇；三是日文書目部份：由資策會提供圖書及期刊書目12種。該手冊共40頁。

另外，本館也向資策會推廣服務處索取遠瞻小冊系列：美國NII效益說帖、美國NII的行動方案、日本的資訊技術基礎建設新政策（IND）——野村綜合研究所的建議、新加坡的發展遠景——智慧島（IT2000研究報告）等各220冊，分送與會人員參考，頗受歡迎。

三、研討過程

（一）第一場研討會

曾濟羣館長主講："建構資訊高速公路圖書館應扮演的角色——'中央圖書館'的經驗"

曾館長首先指出本館舉辦這項研討會，主要目的是希望圖書館界與資訊界今後更密切合作，使得圖書館的資料能迅速傳給社會上所需要的人。同時，資訊界也因為圖書館界的投入、參與，使得資訊網路上所流通的資訊，有助於提昇全體公民的教育文化水準。

隨後曾館長就本主題從四個方面進行報告：

1. 撰寫此份報告的動機，主要是受到美國國會圖書館館長比林頓（Dr. James Billington）報告的影響。比林頓認為，面對建構資訊高速公路，圖書館應扮演的角色相當重要，即如何將圖書資料電子化輸入網路，使知識貨櫃車能迅速開上高速公路。另方面，去年美國柯林頓總統在矽谷作資訊高科技演講時，相當重視"建構資訊高速公路"，特別是對教育的重視，遺憾的是卻未將圖書館界的想法納入。

2. "中央圖書館"的角色定位：（1）"中央圖書館"為圖書館中的圖書館，對圖書館界應充分提供服務的功能；（2）"中央圖書館"應定位在學術研究圖書館，藉由豐富的館藏，提供社會大眾進行學術研究；（3）提供一般性社教功能的服務；（4）國際交換處扮演重要的功能，即代表政治實體從事圖書資訊的交流，並促進文化輸出；（5）兼辦漢學中心業務，提供圖書與資訊，以提昇漢學研究的水準；（6）積極推動國際標準書號與圖書預行編目制度。

由於本館兼具上述六項功能，因此圖書館自動化須朝著兩個方向進行：一是採開放性的系統；二是為展現本館多角化的功能，必須整合館內各種功能於一個系統，如此才能相互支援。

3. "中央圖書館"自動化的方向：面對資訊化的社會，圖書館的角色相當重要。圖書館員應瞭解資訊、掌握資訊、提供資訊：透過網路傳輸資料，利用光碟儲存資料。換言之，圖書館員應謹記以下之服務守則"What do you serve"、"How to serve"、"How to get more things to serve"。

4. 展望：就經驗理論主義（Experimentalism Theory）來看，無論是（1）自變數（Independent Variable）——實驗變數（Experimental Variable）；2. 他變數（Dependent Variable）——反應變數（Response Variable）；（3）外擾變數（Extraneous Variable）——如人員訓練；（4）中介變數（Intervening Variable）——涉及個人的動機，都非常樂觀。就經驗而言，自動化的推動，設備的充足應配合人員的訓練，因此唯有將

自變數與他變數結合在一起，減少外擾因素，提昇中介變數，方能有效地推動圖書館的自動化。

最後曾館長引用美國參議員 Paul Simon 在公聽會上所說，如果在建構資訊高速公路的同時，不能將圖書館納爲一體，那麼高速公路將自絕於大多數的美國人。聽了這些話，似乎我們大家的責任更重大了。

(二) 第二場研討會

資訊工業策進會果芸執行長主持並主講："資訊高速公路與資訊服務"，"中央研究院"資訊研究所謝清俊研究員主講："公共資訊系統"。

果執行長首先指出，由於資訊科技進步神速，對未來圖書與教學所造成的影響最大且最深遠。就資訊與電信基礎建設遠景來說有二：

(1) 資訊技術的進步，無論文字、圖形、聲音、影像皆可以 0 與 1 表達，以開放性文件結構（ODA）標準，可儲存及快速傳遞、處理資料；(2) 通信技術進步，大量資料可傳輸，遠端也可取得資料，將來對圖書館作業方式及方向會產生相當大的影響。

他接著介紹資訊建設基本因素有四：(1) 網路；(2) 使用者；(3) 資訊供應者；(4) 電腦設備等。可預見的未來是知識重於自然資源的資財，成爲社會建設的重要基礎。

果執行長指出新的圖書館扮演的角色爲圖書服務與知識領航（Library Services & Knowledge Navigation），包括資料庫服務（Database Service）、新知服務（information Alerting Services）、電子期刊傳遞（Electronic Journal Delivery）、公告和瀏覽（Alerting & Browsing）、影帶檢索服務（Video Retrieval Services）、文獻檢索服務（Document Retrieval Services）。並介紹支援教育作業模式及遠距教學與電傳訓練等內容。

謝清俊教授的演講，主要包括公共資訊、公共資訊系統，及資訊公用事業等三部份，茲簡述如下：

1. 公共資訊（Public Information）：美、日推行甚力。凡屬政府出版品、公立研究成果等，信託給政府管理，除了法令規定以外的都開放給全民查詢利用，即爲公共資訊；它爲全民所有，無版權。

2. 公共資訊系統（Public Information System）：係設計給一般大衆使用的，譬如教育，傳播，出版，政府提供的如財經、氣象、交易……，圖書館如公共圖書館，以及第四臺等皆是。由系統的管理行政上來看，包括：(1) 資料處理系統（Information Packaging System）：提供給有特殊需求的特定對象，如航空訂票系統、領款系統、自動查號系統、圖書館出納系統等。(2) Information Retrieval Systems：如新聞系統，其資料量較大，使用者涵蓋各行各業，應用面相當廣，有索引，其特點在提供瀏覽及檢索功能，可將相關資訊找出。另外，如公共教育系統，它提供電腦輔助教學（CAI）及其他服務，如學生互相討論學習、實驗等相關資訊。(3) Information Processing Systems：即資料與程式的分享，此種系統的設計需考慮使用者的能力、態度、背景知識及宗教信仰等，如公共醫療系統即是。

3. 資訊公用事業（Public Information Utilities）：謝教授引用日本未來學家增田米二所著"資訊地球村"的看法指出，資訊公用事業是一種公共資訊設施，並結合電腦與網路組合成各種資訊處理和服務設備，如 NII 即是；同時，任何人不分時間、地點，都能以簡單、便捷、廉價的方式取得所需的資訊如社區資訊系統之發展、視訊系統之發展。

至於資訊公用事業的特點有三：

（1）建立在一種社會基本設施的基礎上，所謂基礎，除基本的硬體外，包括基本的服務，以充分發揮設備的特性。

（2）協力生產，共同使用，認為資訊界使用資訊就是在生產資訊，需要有進步的技術支持，即所謂滾雪球之效應。相信有一天會進步到資訊為全民所共享，並沒有所謂智慧財產權的問題。

（3）全民參與，認為真正的資訊社會，知識擁有及傳播結構會改變，相信所有人都有公平機會、公平方法、公平結果分享資訊。

謝教授在總結時，提出下列幾點看法：

（1）公共資訊，廣義地說，可認為是：為公民應該有權享用的"免費"資訊，是在社會中生存，食、衣、住、行、育、樂、就業、醫療、生涯規劃……各方面可利用的信息。也是維持基本水準的生活，和在變遷迅速的社會中，得到人性尊嚴的保障。

（2）社會上，知識的公平分配（擁有、散播、擷取等）有賴公共資訊系統的建立。

（3）有了健全的公衆資訊系統，才能有公平合理的智慧財產權制度。

（4）公衆資訊系統的基本理念是充分的資訊共享。資訊共享含有道德情操：惜物、惜福；充分利用自然資源達到人盡其才、地盡其利、物盡其用、貨暢其流。（資訊是控制資源的資源）

（5）以往，資訊之所以無法充分共享，是因受制於物質，而電子媒體使它脫離束縛，成為享之不盡用之不竭之資源，若不能充分共享，則全屬人為因素。

（6）NII 不僅是工程建設，更是社會的"改造——長期持續的改造，而圖書館和網路的結合是必然的方向，未來如何？難以預料；機動地瞭解公衆的需求而因事制宜，並多在理論中探索，應是良策。

（7）注意 Information Disclosure 所帶來的衝擊，這需要智慧和教育。

（8）資訊倫理的研究和落實是成敗的關鍵。

謝教授認為，圖書館本來就有許多公共資訊系統的業務，如資料查詢、資料庫服務、公共圖書館、館外服務等。其實，整個圖書館事業就是人類公共資訊系統中重要的一環。

（三）第三場研討會

"中國圖書館學會"理事長王振鵠教授主持，臺大圖書館學系李德竹教授主講："資訊高速公路——邁向二十一世紀圖書館服務的契機"。

王振鵠教授首先指出，目前圖書館界能得到資訊界、社會各方面的關注，在"建構資訊高速公路"的計劃中，將圖書館納入，值得慶幸。

隨後李德竹教授介紹 NII（National Information Infrastructure）背景。她說 NII 為 1994 年資訊界最熱門的話題，實際上是國家為了創造競爭優勢，並為資訊化社會奠定基礎而推動的基礎建設，包括四項工作：①建立四通八達無遠弗屆的高速資訊網；②發展新型的資訊設備；③建立資訊資源；④研發資訊技術等。

1. 美國的 NII

由柯林頓總統召集成立跨部會的"資訊基礎建設任務小組"，負責協調國會及民間企業，研提加速 NII 發展所需要的政策和工作計劃。另成立 NII 民間諮詢委員會，由商務部邀請，並由民間主導，政府提供必要的輔導，因此政府只擔任催化帶動的角色。而在1993年9月提出9項行動綱領，24項行動方案，根據這些原則和目標推動，將使美國的企業在全球經濟體系中具備競爭力並獲得勝利，也將為美國民眾創造就業機會，從而使國家的經濟健全成長。

2. 新加坡的發展遠景——智慧島（IT2000研究報告）

IT2000的研究工作，其目的在探討如何運用資訊技術來開創國家的新競爭優勢，進而提昇新加坡的生活品質。在我們描繪智慧島遠景當中，新加坡在未來15年將成為世界具有頂尖資訊基礎建設的國家之一。每個家庭、辦公室、學校和工廠均透過電腦網路連結在一起。無論是文字、聲音、圖形、影像、文件等形式的媒體，均可透過光纖網路或無線網路傳送到家庭和辦公室中。另外，為全面發展圖書館，提出"公元2000年圖書館事業發展計劃"，成立5所區域圖書館、全國18所社區圖書館、100多所迷你圖書館、參考圖書館、商業圖書館，約有500所學術圖書館、專門圖書館與網路連線；使新加坡成為東南亞的資訊中心。

3. 日本的資訊技術基礎建設新政策（IND）

日本推動NⅡ，其目的在使資訊普及，為日本各地的使用者所利用。由於日本資訊環境不如美國，初期投資十分龐大，廠商力量有限，除靠民間企業獲利動機外，需要日本政府大量投資。因此，由日本首相徵得國會同意後，成立一個專責推動政府部門資訊新政的特別委員會，包括三個領域：（1）政府部門資訊新政，用以改善中央政府的資訊技術基礎建設；（2）區域資訊化新政，用以協助一般民眾能更容易取得更多資訊；（3）資訊技術研發新政，希望政府擴大投入及鼓勵資訊技術的研發工作。

接著李教授也特別就歐體國家如德國、法國資訊化社會的計劃方面，及臺灣推動的"資訊基礎建設"作精闢的介紹。

李教授特別提到圖書館界為因應21世紀資訊社會的來臨，亟需制定圖書館白皮書。至於NⅡ對圖書館的衝擊，圖書館員應扮演什麼角色？未來圖書館應更加重視資訊的存取和知識的管理，而圖書館員就如同知識的導航員，導引協助使用者利用資訊。可預見未來資訊服務內容是偏向知識性的，因此館員需具備學科背景，並從事組織管理資料，及教導使用資訊等工作。

四、結語

隨著電腦、通訊與傳播科技躍進和普及，臺灣建立"資訊高速公路"網路，以加速經濟、科技、教育、民生各方面的發展是必然的趨勢。在政府大力推動NII計劃時，相信現有圖書館的服務也將隨之轉型為電子圖書館的服務方式，也就是圖書館所擁有大量的圖書及資訊，結合資訊界共同發展資料庫的服務，提供讀者查檢利用。

目前世界各國都在推動"資訊高速公路"概念，透過資訊網路，把"知識貨櫃車"開上網路，達到快速傳輸大量數據的效果。美國、日本、新加坡現在都投資龐大經費於建構"資訊高速公路"。在未來，"資訊高速公路"的發展成果，將成為我們一般生活上的基礎，並會為我們的衣食住行等生活習慣，帶來全新的改變。

由本館主辦的這項研討會，在臺灣來說為首次，集合了圖書館界與資訊界的專家學者，共同研討與交換經驗，相信對加速建立"資訊高速公路"的理念，實具有深遠的意義。

資訊網路時代臺灣地區圖書資訊服務的新方向[＊]

[摘要 Abstract]

臺灣地區自 1987 年開始進入資訊網路發展的階段。至今已建立了臺灣學術網路（TANet）、臺灣地區書目資訊網路（NBINET）、科技性資訊網路（STICNET）、資訊軟體發展環境建立網路（SEEDNET）及加值網路系統（VAN）。網路系統上均擁有相當多的資訊資源，圖書館應善用網路的功能，並將網路的資訊源納入整體圖書館資源的一部份，以進一步提昇各項服務功能，建立符合資訊化社會需求的資訊服務。本文將探討資訊網路對臺灣地區圖書館的影響，並就未來發展的方向提出建議。

Abstract: There have been established many information networks, TANet, NBINET, STICNET, SEEDNET, and VAN, in Taiwan area since 1988. Lots of information resources in information networks can be retrieved and used by end users. Not only should libraries integrate the different types of networked information, but also gradually develop networked information services in library environment. This paper is to discuss how information networks influence library services and to recommend the future developments for libraries.

一、前言

隨著科學技術的進步，電腦與通訊的結合，正將人類的歷史帶往一個資訊網路的時代。人與人的溝通、地區與地區的通訊，將較以往更加便利與快捷，人們生活的方式與習慣也將隨之改變。舉凡食、衣、住、行、育、樂的方式，也因通訊的便利而更多樣化。因應資訊網路時代的來臨，圖書館的服務形態勢必要做適當的調整。近來，虛擬圖書館（Virtual Library）及無墻的圖書館（Library without Wall）兩個名詞的出現，正說明圖書館界已注意到網路的重要性。本文擬就臺灣地區資訊網路的發展現況予以介紹，並就此一趨勢探討對圖書館界的影響及未來的發展方向。

二、臺灣地區資訊網路的發展概況

所謂"資訊網路"是指組織間用以建立及共享資訊的一種網路，較圖書館網路廣泛，不僅局限於圖書館，更涵蓋了可提供及分享資訊的各種組織與機構。網路服務的方式以線上資訊檢索為主，並包括資料的傳輸、查詢及通訊等（註1）。

因此，資訊網路不僅是一種通訊的工具而已，更重要的是在網路上存在著極為豐富的各種資訊資源。圖書館除可利用此通訊管道建立各種合作性的服務（例如，館際合作、聯臺發展館藏及聯合編目等），更可藉此擴充圖書館的資源。

臺灣地區自 1988 年起在政府的政策推動下，開始實施一連串資訊網路建立的計劃。至今已有相當的成果，以下就具代表性者逐一介紹。

＊ 本文與莊道明先生合作撰寫，曾發表在《"中國圖書館學會"會報》52 期（1994 年 6 月），第 51—62 頁。

臺灣地區資訊網路的建立，可以分成以下幾種：
(一) 臺灣學術網路（TANet）

臺灣學術網路（Taiwan Academic Network，簡稱 TANet）是 1989 年由"教育部"電子計算機中心提出的計劃，該計劃採行當時廣為學術界使用的 Internet 網路的 TCP/IP 設計與經驗，使臺灣學術網路成為國際學術網路的一環。

因此，臺灣學術網路上的位址命名法皆採用國際性的標準及規範（註2）。

臺灣學術網路長期計劃的考量有以下四點：

1. 初步以學術研究為主，但將逐步擴展至教學、圖書館自動化及行政業務上。
2. 初步網路連接的範圍只有大學及獨立學院，以後逐步推廣至專科、高中及中小學。
3. 短期採用可行的軟硬體技術作為基本網路技術，然後逐漸發展出具備中文環境的地區性應用技術。
4. 臺灣學術網路發展的經驗，將提供其他單位發展網路系統的參考，並進一步與其他相關的科技網路相結合。

整個臺灣學術網路基本架構可分成三個層次，即校園網路、校際網路及國際網路。校園網路是整個臺灣學術網路的基礎，由"教育部"專案推動施行，以作為提供學術及教學研究之基本傳輸通道，並透過網路整合校園的圖書館系統、教學研究系統及行政資訊系統等。各校園網路之規劃及佈設則由各校自行負責執行。校際網路則是各大學於 1986 年起，自行利用電信局之數據線路將各校相同廠牌的電腦主機串接的網路系統，基本上是採用主機對主機的連線方式。目前均將這些區域性網路連接到各地區的區域網路中心，再連接上學術網路的主要骨幹上（見圖一）。最後整條網路的骨幹經由"教育部"電算中心，連接上美國本土的 Internet 及 BITNET，而完成整個網路系統。整個臺灣學術網路上連接單位及遠景可見圖二及圖三（註3）。

未來臺灣學術網路的發展將朝以下七點進行（註4）：

1. 推廣網路初學者的訓練及教育課程；
2. 擴展各區域網路中心的服務至鄰近學校；
3. 繼續提昇圖書館自動化系統間的連線工作；
4. 繼續發展中文環境的網路應用；
5. 協助各種電子資料庫的發展；
6. 進一步提昇高級網路的應用；
7. 加強連接寬頻的國際線路。

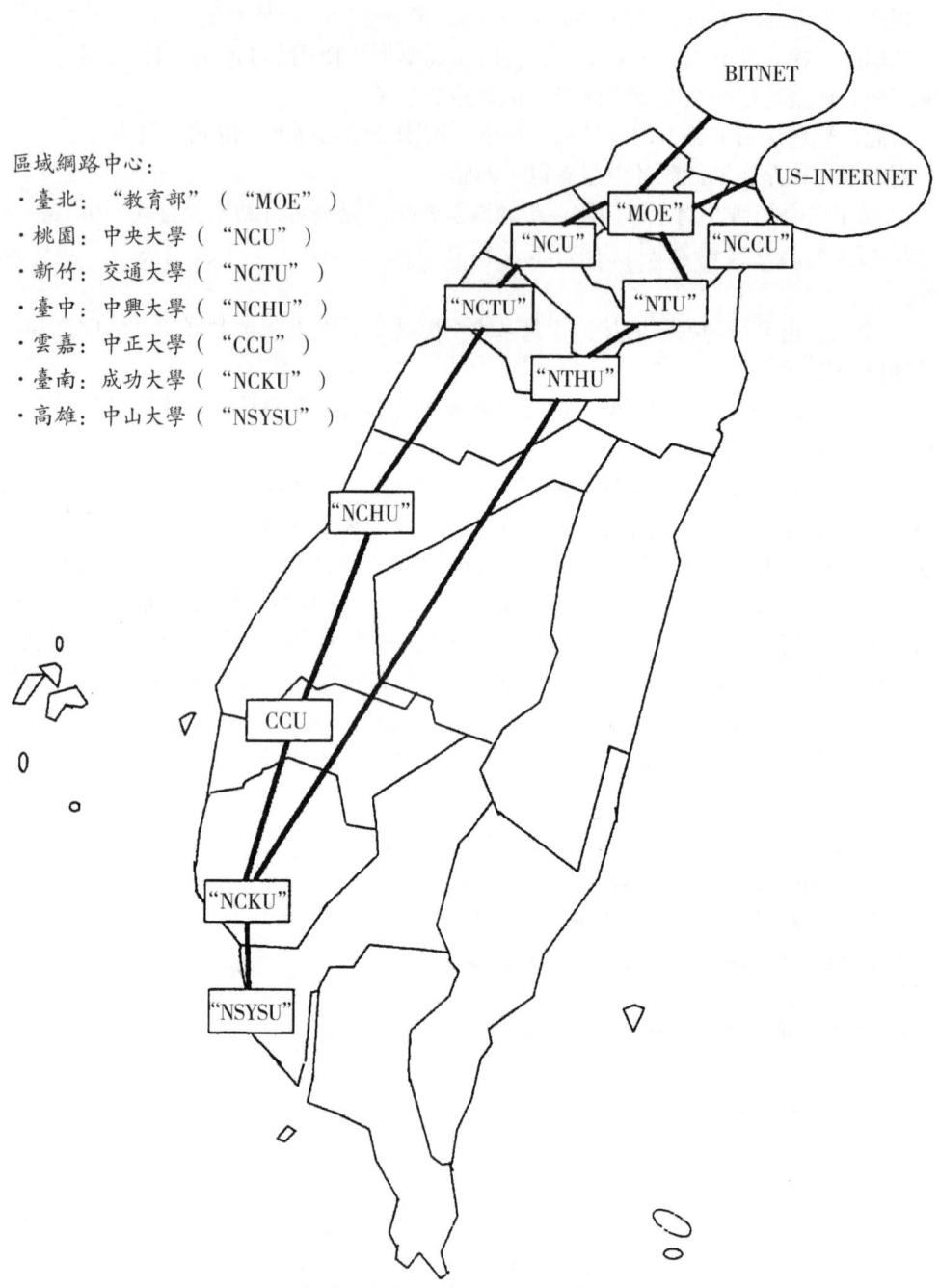

圖一　臺灣學術網路骨幹架構圖

資訊網路時代臺灣地區圖書資訊服務的新方向   377

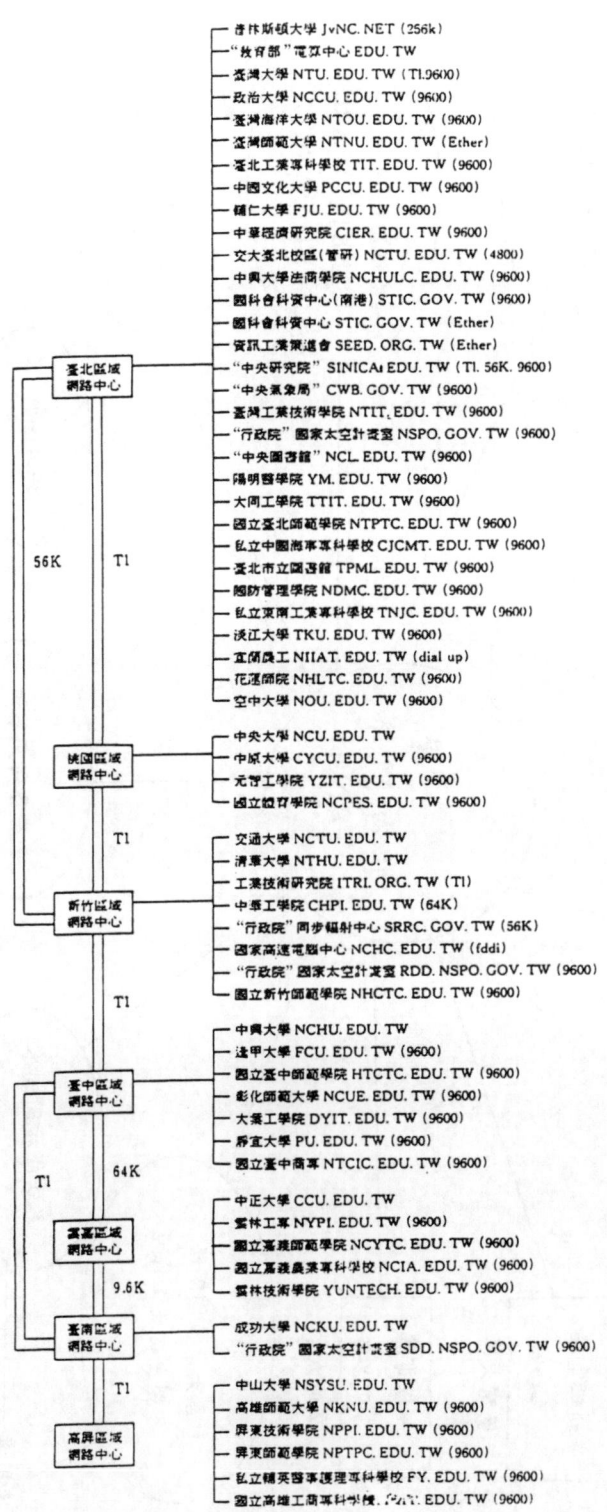

圖二　臺灣學術網路（TANet）連接單位一覽表（1993年5月）

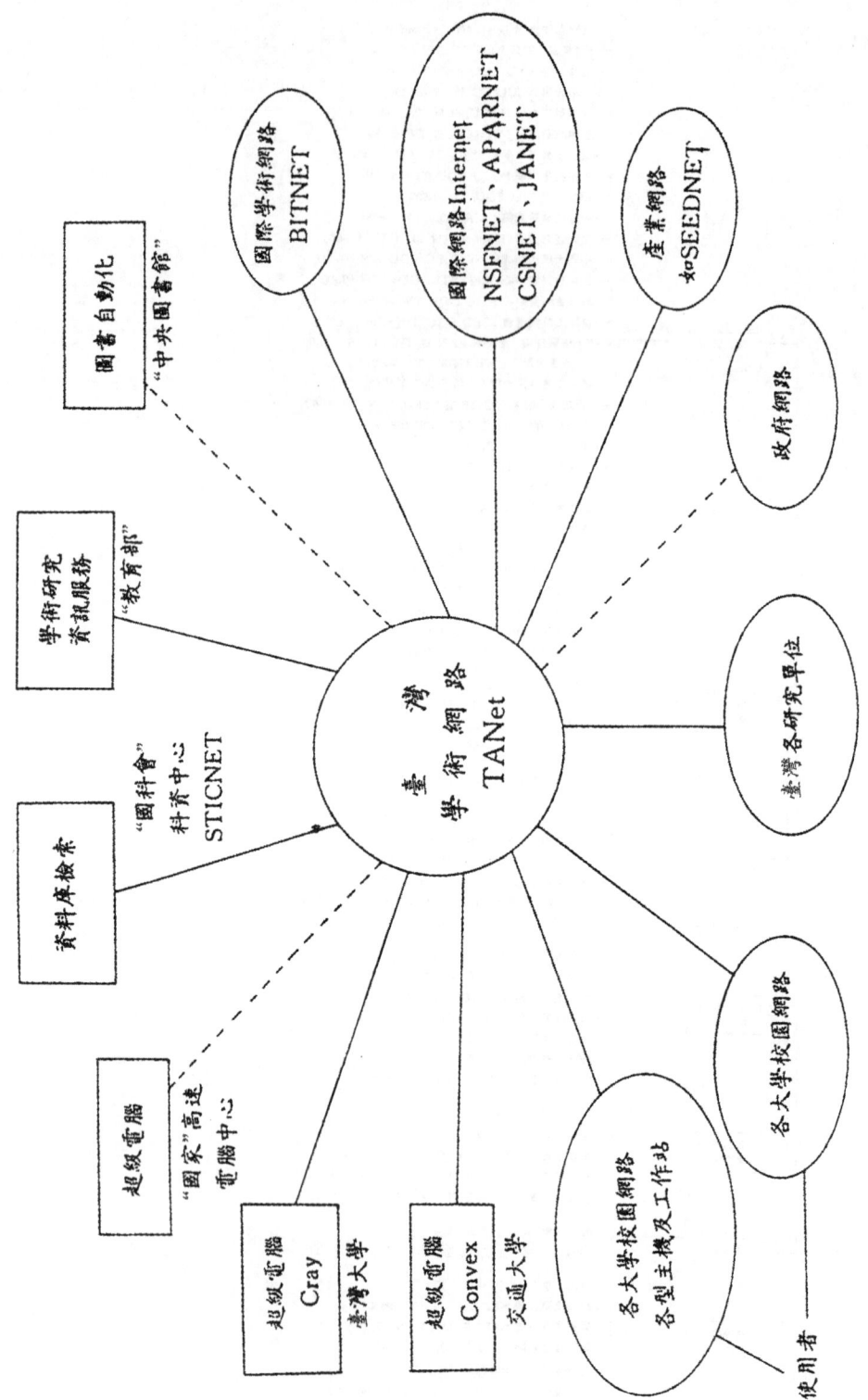

圖三 臺灣學術網路之遠景

(二) 臺灣地區書目資訊網路 (National Bibliographic Information Network，簡稱 NBINET)

"國立中央圖書館"於1988年奉準負責推動"全國圖書資訊網路系統"計劃。該計劃主要在建立國家書目資訊網，進而推展至臺灣圖書館館際網路乃至國際網路，以能互通訊息及交換書目資料，推行合作編目、合作採訪、合作流通以達到館際互借的資訊服務。1991年10月"中央圖書館"正式推出圖書資訊網路系統線上聯合編目。目前該系統可提供各個合作館以下的服務（註5）：

1. 提供線上合作編目：已有19所"國立大學"及獨立學院圖書館與省立臺中圖書館，以點對點連線方式，參與合作編目建檔工作。至1993年八月底已建檔書目達441,758筆，隨著機讀格式轉換及網路傳輸問題解決後，書目資料庫將可快速成長（註6）。

2. 提供權威檔控制處理系統：以一個標準書目資料檔，維護標目的一致性，並且提供美國國會圖書館的權威記錄，以作為各合作館建立權威檔之參考。

3. 提供編目批次作業處理系統：各合作館可使用自己的電腦設備，列印書目中心的書目卡片、書標、書後卡；或轉錄書目資料於磁碟、磁帶及軟碟等。

(三) 科技性全國資訊網路 (Science and Technology of Information Center Network，簡稱 STICNET)

STICNET由"行政院"科學委員會科學技術資料中心（簡稱科資中心）負責開發推動。於1988年底啓用，次年四月對外開放。該中心有鑑於科技性資料庫對於研究人員的重要性，於是在參考美國各個重要的線上資料庫系統，如 DIALOG、ORBIT、BRS 公司，及日本科技情報中心的 JICSTNET 後，建立此書目性資料庫網路系統。其目的主要有三項：

1. 整合處理科技研究資料；
2. 配合島內需要，引進海外高參考價值的書目性資料庫；
3. 提供民眾現代化的資訊服務業。

目前該網路可透過數據專線、分封式網路及電話撥接方式線上查詢資料庫。該網路現有海內外線上資料庫計有26種，範圍除了科技性資料庫外，亦逐步增加人文社會類資料庫。內容如下（註7）：

1. "國科會"科資中心自行建立資料庫15種：
・西文科技期刊聯合目錄資料庫（臺灣地區）
・西文科技圖書聯合目錄資料庫（臺灣地區）
・科技期刊論文資料庫
・人文社會期刊論文資料庫
・進行中科技及人文社會研究計劃摘要資料庫
・科技及人文社會研究報告摘要資料庫
・學術會議論文資料庫
・博碩士論文資料庫
・"國科會"研究獎助論文摘要資料庫
・科技簡訊與政策報導資料庫
・歐體文獻聯合目錄資料庫
・歐洲科技發展報導資料庫

・研究機構名錄資料庫
・科技分類典檔
・學術研討會訊息報導資料庫
2. 其他單位資料庫 1 種：
・工研院技術資料庫
3. 海外引進資料庫 10 種，收錄年代自 1984 年起：
・ABI/INFORM（行政商業資料庫）
・BIOSIS PREVIEWS（生物科學資料庫）
・CA SEARCH（化學摘要資料庫）
・COMPENDEX（工程資料庫）
・DAO（博士論文摘要）
・ERIC（教育研究資料庫）
・INSPEC（物理電子電機電腦資料庫）
・MICROCOMPUTER Index（微電腦資料庫）
・NTIS（美國政府科技研究報告資料庫）
・SPORT（體育資料庫）

（四）資訊軟體發展環境建立網路（Software Engineering Environment Development，簡稱 SEEDNET）

SEEDNET 由資訊工業策進會於 1988 年在"經濟部"支持下，聯合臺灣地區的資訊界及學術研究單位，著手"資訊軟體發展環境建立"開發計劃。希望透過良好的軟體開發環境，以提昇電腦軟體開發及應用的品質。爲落實計劃成果及資源共享，在該計劃下利用現有的公眾數據通訊設備，建立一個開放性電腦網路 SEETNET。該網路是一個非營利性的電腦網路，主要的目標有下列四項（註 8）：

1. 藉由傳播 SEED 計劃研究成果，促進企業間研發與資訊交流；
2. 連接國際的 Internet 網路，引進國際網路的資源；
3. 推動網路及資料庫服務的應用；
4. 建立整合性的資訊網路，提供臺灣各行業研發所需要的方法、標準、工具與各種市場資訊服務，以降低研發與維護的成本，並且提高生產力及品質。

SEEDNET 服務對象以從事研究開發的公私營企業或公司爲主，包括非營利的法人及採公司會員制的廠商。整個網路的骨幹由設置於臺北、新竹、臺中、高雄、花蓮等五個服務中心，分別負責運作管理。目前該網路提供的服務主要有以下三項：

1. 基本網路服務：包括電子郵件傳遞服務（E-Mail），檔案傳輸服務（File Transfer Services），及遠程終端服務（TELNET）等。
2. 資訊服務：該服務主要可區分成三種：

（1）文件擷取服務：透過網路的電子郵遞方式，可提供用戶取得政府科技專案研究報告摘要，公用電腦軟體程式資料庫，電腦與通訊技術文件，SEED 工作站規格與技術文件等。

（2）電子佈告欄服務：用戶可透過網路的電子佈告欄隨時獲取全球最新的資訊產品通告、市場行情專題通告、電腦專利程式著作權通告、海外會議展覽及訓練課程消息、新書期刊通告、資訊電腦類博碩士論文通告、島內研討會及訓練課程通告、SEED 計劃執行成果通告，及臺北市電腦公會產銷回報等。

（3）資料庫服務：用戶可經由資料庫管理系統取得電腦軟體產品資料庫與臺北市電腦公會會員及產品資料庫等。

3. 國際 Internet 連線服務：由於該網路也透過臺灣學術網路連接上國際 Internet 網路，因此透過 SEEDNET 亦可使用並檢索到 Internet 網路上所有的資訊。

（五）加值網路系統（Value-Added Network，簡稱 VAN）

"交通部"於 1989 年開放民間經營加值網路。所謂的加值網路是指利用電信總局提供的機線設備及附加電腦等，提供資訊之儲存、檢索及處理等電信服務。至 1992 年共有 41 家已取得核發審定。較著名的系統介紹如下（註9）：

1. 臺灣電訊網路（Taiwan Telecommunication Network，簡稱 TTN）：臺灣電信網路成立於 1990 年 2 月，又稱為龍門網。該網路的目標是希望能將資訊本土化。目前透過該網路可以連接使用美國 CompuServe 的各類型生活化資訊。該網路可提供以下的網路加值服務（註10）：

（1）全球電子交易服務：可提供用戶四種連線方式，取得資訊及數據傳輸服務。

（2）商業通訊服務：透過該網路用戶可與網路上任何公司行號，從事商業文件的電子郵遞，或傳真文件存送服務等。

（3）個人電腦資訊網路服務（TTN-Serve）：

在網路上可以查詢到以下各種海內外的資訊：

・服務介紹　　　　　・教育/文化
・電子郵遞　　　　　・商業/金融
・佈告欄　　　　　　・工商服務
・線上交談　　　　　・旅游資訊
・論壇　　　　　　　・生活資訊
・氣象/新聞　　　　・政府公告/法律

2. 時報資訊的電子即時新聞系統：由時報資訊公司於 1989 年 12 月推出，1991 年 4 月正式上線提供服務。第一階段所提供的資訊內容包括以下幾種（註11）：

（1）即時新聞：涵蓋海內外重大政經新聞、產業界動態、股市匯率市場、市場新聞與公司新聞等。

（2）資料庫檢索：提供 30 天內的新聞資料檢索服務。

（3）金融報價與分析：海外股市、匯率市場、期貨市況資訊、並設計有 10 餘種盤中、盤後即時分析系統、資產管理系統，以供專業投資人選擇運用。

該系統初期每天發稿 30 至 50 則，未來將朝向每天發稿 80 至 100 則的目標。

3. 電傳視訊（Chinese Videotex Service，簡稱 CVS）：電傳視訊是一種互動多功能的通訊系統。用戶可透過個人電腦、電傳視訊卡及數據機接收到資訊。由"交通部"數據通訊所於 1988 年開始對外營運。所提供的服務包括工商交易、電傳軟體、羣內服務、訊息交換及資訊檢索服務。資訊服務的內容包括：電子號簿、農產品行情、股市行情、商情、觀光旅游、交通時刻表、法規、圖書資訊、消費者資訊、英文資訊、昇學考試資訊及商品資訊等（註12）。

三、資訊網路對圖書館的影響

臺灣地區的資訊環境,隨著通訊網路的架設及通訊功能的完備,已正式進入了資訊化的環境。但任何資訊技術的改變,對於圖書館均會產生一定的影響力。以下就資訊網路對於圖書館環境、館藏、館員及讀者的影響予以探討。

(一) 對圖書館環境的影響

1. 提供第一手資訊的管道:圖書館在以紙本媒體為主的環境下,作者的作品必須透過出版商的出版印刷之後,才有可能被圖書館收藏。因此,基本上資料的內容已經過出版商過濾一次,可以說凡符出合出版商出版政策或利益的資料才有可能被出版,也才有可能被圖書館收錄。少數作者自行出版的圖書,也有可能因為印刷品質不佳,或因內容不妥而被圖書館拒絕收錄。所以在整個資訊環境中,圖書館所扮演的角色往往是二手資料 (正式的出版品) 的獲取與保存。至於第一手的訊息 (如研究人員之間的通訊、討論等),因圖書館沒有適當的管道,而無法有效的徵集及提供服務。如今資訊網路上,都俱備了電子論壇 (Electronic Forum) 的功能,即針對某一個特定主題,經由電腦網路,傳遞彼此言論,相互交換信息與心得等事宜 (註13)。電子論壇無疑將所謂的隱形學院 (Invisiable College) 的隱形外衣給顯形了。電子論壇不但將討論的內容具體的記錄下來,同時也使參與討論的層面擴大。每位使用者均可透過網路,參加各種主題的討論。此外,各式各樣的電子佈告欄,也隨時公告最新的訊息。因此,圖書館透過資訊網路系統,獲取的資料以資訊製造者第一手的資訊為多,其間並不需要出版者的介入。對圖書館在掌握資訊上,多提供了另一種管道。

2. 虛擬圖書館時代的來臨:美國著名的圖書館學家德簡涅格 (De Gennaro) 將圖書館自動化與網路的發展分成三個階段,即整體區域系統時代 (1960 年代),集中網路時代 (1970 年代) 及多重選擇時代 (1980 年代) (註14)。第四階段將是資訊網路時代,也是虛擬圖書館的時代。所謂虛擬圖書館是指經由網路化的資訊,讀者可以擁有一座類似傳統圖書館資料的私人圖書館 (註15),因資料相當的龐大且無法觸及,且在概念上具備了圖書館的性質而稱之。虛擬圖書館概念的形成,雖是屬於未來的一種概念,但卻也造成對傳統圖書館服務的挑戰與壓力。尤其許多館員深怕將來因服務功能減少而喪失職業。因此,如同隨著圖書館功能的轉型,調整服務的內涵與角色,將是面對虛擬圖書館來臨的一個重要的課題。

3. 圖書館地位與重要性的提昇:今天資訊網路的建立,象徵了一個國家社會對於資訊需求的層次已進入資訊化社會的境界。因此,能連接上資訊網路的圖書館,除了表示已經進行圖書館自動化外,也象徵有能力提供資源給其他圖書館分享,同時也願意將服務開放給不特定的使用者使用。目前在臺灣學術網路上的圖書館,大都採用開放式的鍵入 (即不須要特定的使用賬號),提供線上公用目錄 (OPAC) 供大眾查詢。無形中能上資訊網路的圖書館,象徵是一個現代化的圖書館,也是一個進步的圖書館,這對圖書館形象的提昇,有著相當正面的影響。此外,在資訊網路的資源需求上,使用者除了傳輸資料外,也希望從各個資訊站獲取更多可供決策的資訊。而圖書館在網路上,無疑的將扮演著資訊提供者的角色。這個角色也將因使用者資訊需求及使用量的增加,而越加的重要。

(二) 對圖書館館藏的影響

1. 館藏發展觀念的改變：過去圖書館館藏發展的觀念重心，是以一館館藏資料的徵集為重心。如何有效的獲取資料實體，成了館藏發展研究的主題。現今由於資訊網路通訊的便利，獲取資訊的管道相當的暢通。圖書館一旦連接上資訊網路，便可無限次的獲取網路上各個資訊站的資訊，且各資訊站的資料量亦不因為使用次數增多而減少。因此，圖書館對館藏發展的概念上，應該漸由一館館藏的發展轉變成對全球資訊資源的管理與控制。即在觀念上，必須跳脫對一個館資料蒐集的範圍，而轉變成對全球資訊的掌握與選擇。

2. 使用權比擁有更重要：傳統圖書館的資料媒體型式均以紙質的書籍為主，所以圖書的擁有象徵資料使用權的獲取。因此，圖書的徵集成為圖書館重要的業務，也是館藏發展過程中極為重要的程序。然而現今透過網路的通訊，圖書館仍可以獲取所需要的資訊，但所獲得的不再是資料的本體，而只是獲得網路資源的使用權。所以在資訊網路上，圖書館所要努力的是取得每個重要網路資源的使用權。目前在 Internet 國際網路上的資訊站上，對於資料的查詢及使用，會按資料的性質設定不同的使用權限。往往較特殊或具有智慧財產權限制的資料庫，必需先取得授權與賬號才可進入使用，有些甚至必須先付費取得使用賬號，才可進入檢索（註16）。

3. 館藏特色及特藏的發展將更加重要：透過網路系統的使用，使用者可以同時獲取數個不同資訊站的資訊。每個資訊站基本上均可視為相同的點，所以從豐富資訊網路的資源來考慮，每個資訊站應就本身的資訊特色及特藏，發展出具有獨特性的資料庫，以傳播提供給廣大的使用者利用。雷同性過高的資料庫應儘量避免重覆的建立，以免造成人力資源的浪費。

4. 館際合作的可行性增加：資訊網路上的遠端虛擬終端機、檔案傳輸及電子郵件功能，可提供館際合作館線上資料查詢、資料擷取及郵件通訊等即時性的服務。對圖書館推展合作館藏發展、合作編目及合作參考提供了更便捷的通訊聯絡管道（註17）。換言之，資訊網路具備了資源共享的架構，而該網路的架設有助於圖書館館際合作業務的推展。

(三) 對館員的影響

1. 資訊檢索中間人（Intermediary）的檢索服務將漸趨減少：資訊網路上各種資訊站的服務，均可由使用者自行上線檢索資料，與傳統圖書館必需透過檢索中間人線上查詢資料庫相較，前者給使用者較多的自主權及選擇權。加上使用者對線上檢索結果的信賴程度往往採較保留的現況下，使用者往往寧願透過資訊網路去檢索資料。近年來，許多網路資訊站提供了書目型的資料庫（例如，"國科會"的 STICNET），加上光碟資料庫的競爭下，未來圖書館透過檢索中間人的線上檢索服務將會面臨推廣的困難。將來檢索館員的服務角色，可由檢索服務轉變成指導檢索，也就是指導使用者如何作更有效率的檢索資料庫，而非代替使用者上線輸入檢索指令及操作電腦。

2. 館員角色的改變：傳統圖書館館員的角色單純是館內的服務工作。然而資訊時代的來臨也開啓了自我學習的時代。資訊網路的建構，使得館員的工作將不再只是局限於館內的服務，更重要的任務是必須開始從事決策性的資訊服務及教育性的資訊利用指導。決策性的資訊服務是資訊專家的任務，教育性的資訊利用指導則是資訊教師的職責。也就是館員將須同時具備有圖書館館員、資訊專家及資訊教育家三種角色（註18）。這三種角色將可達成服務讀者、指導讀者及教育讀者三項服務目標。面對這樣的需求，館員只有不斷的自我學習及教育方能跟上時代的需要。

3. 館員決策的複雜程度增加：資訊網路上的資訊日日更新，每個資訊站的資訊內容與種類也各具特色。面對一個每日均在變化的資訊網路，館員要選擇出適當的資訊站及使用適當的檢索方法，找出適當的資料提供給適當的讀者，將是一項挑戰。網路資訊的多樣性，相對也帶來複雜性，館員勢必要花費更多的時間，去瞭解每個資訊站的內容與特色。因此，資訊網路選擇性的增多，相對地館員的決策能力必需提昇。

（四）對讀者的影響

1. 隔空教育（Distance Education）盛行：現行美國地區有越來越多的學校，利用傳播媒體及網路系統進行學校教育。例如美國挪法大學（Nova University）的國際資訊管理學院（International School for Information Management）利用電子郵件及電子會議（E-conference）教學方式，訓練商業及工業界的資訊專家。而美國密西根州學院體系的學校也於1992年開始，利用電傳（Telecommunications）教學，提供兩年制的學位，給圖書館技術助理館員進修（註19）。由於目前資訊網路系統對於動畫影像的傳輸，尚未能達到應用的階段，因此，課堂老師的講解畫面仍需要透過電視廣播系統傳送，而許多講義或課後作業則可透過資訊網路傳送。往往老師也會將作業習題存放於校園網路上，讓學生透過網路的檔案傳輸功能（FTP）抓取作業。作業完成後，學生可將作業再傳回給老師批改。類似這種隔空教育的模式，未來也可利用於圖書館的指導教育上，例如，公共圖書館直接透過資訊網路，對網路使用者進行社會教育或終身教育的課程。

2. 讀者對傳統圖書館的依賴降低：當讀者漸漸習慣利用資訊網路之後，讀者的資訊需求將可由資訊網路來滿足。而政府及商業機構也會針對人民的需求及市場的需要，開發適當的資料庫供大眾使用。屆時讀者對傳統圖書館的使用將日趨減少。最明顯的例子是，當電腦的文書處理軟體功能增強之後，傳統的中英文打字機市場急速的萎縮。學校的英文打字課程也紛紛調整為電腦文書處理。這個現況將來也可能會反應於圖書館的利用上。一旦資訊網路內的功能，可滿足大多數使用者的需求後，使用者利用圖書館的意願將會大幅降低。尤其資訊網路終年無休的服務及不受地理位置與空間限制的特點，是傳統圖書館很難與之抗衡的地方。

3. 資訊素養的重要性：所謂的資訊素養是指一個人知道何時需要資訊，並且具備找到資訊、評估資訊及有效利用資訊能力的人，其目的是學習成為一位知道如何學習的人（註20）。要具備上述資訊素養的人，必須要能瞭解知識的組織，學習如何尋找資訊，以及如何使用資訊，以達成終身學習的境界。面對資訊網路化的趨勢，教導大眾如何使用網路找尋、評估及利用資訊，將是資訊化社會一個重要的課題。在現今傳統圖書館與資訊網路並行發展的時代中，如何借助傳統圖書館發展的經驗，幫助讀者逐步去使用資訊網路，培養出具備資訊素養的公民，將是一個值得深入研究探討的主題。未來圖書館也可針對網路的特點及民眾的資訊需求，設計出新的資訊服務方式。

四、未來圖書館資訊服務的發展方向

針對資訊網路的特性與影響，臺灣地區圖書館未來的發展方向，應可朝下列幾點進行：

(一) 加速全國圖書館連線的腳步，採用標準的規格，享受資訊共享的優點及提昇圖書館的地位

目前電腦通訊的技術已達到相當成熟的地步，同時軟硬體的價格亦相當便宜，而臺灣地區的網路系統，在政府的政策下已逐步完成，加上政府正有計劃的推動圖書館資訊網路系統下，目前臺灣地區發展圖書館自動化的條件，較之前幾年大有進展。圖書館應該配合這些優勢，儘速發展各館的自動化業務，並採行已公佈的"國家標準"，加速連接上資訊網路。目前"經濟部中央標準局"委託"中國圖書館學會"，已經分別制定出館際互借書目資料項目標準（CNS 13150）、機讀編目格式標準（CNS 13226）、期刊館藏著錄標準（CNS 13225）、中國書目資訊交換格式：磁帶部份（CNS 13148）、圖書館統計（CNS 13151）標準等。這些標準的相繼建立，對於圖書館資訊的交換與傳輸將有關鍵性的影響。未來希望能繼續朝向國際化，建立可資訊交換的國際性標準，以達到國際性的資訊交流與共享。

(二) 掌握全球資訊網路的資訊內容與發展趨勢，善用國際性資源

臺灣地區的資訊網路已達到全球資訊一線牽的境界。在網路上的任一點均可透過終端機連接上任何處的電腦（包括超級電腦）或區域性網路。由於目前整個網路的經營政策採開放及自由使用的原則，因此，任何使用者皆可利用網路，在不需用特定的賬號下，即可擷取到許多不設限的開放性資訊。因此，各區域性的圖書館應該掌握這項優勢，瞭解這些資訊的特性、結構、內容及功能，即時提供有用的資訊給適當的讀者，並將這些國際性的訊息傳播出去，進而改善並加強圖書館即時性的資訊服務。

(三) 發展具有特色的中文電子資料庫

在資訊網路上，圖書館將扮演著資訊提供者及出版者的角色。目前在臺灣地區的資訊網路服務中，圖書館佔著極為重要的地位。現今在臺灣地區的資訊網路上，以圖書館提供的資訊服務佔多數。由於圖書館一向以資料的收集、處理、儲存與檢索為服務宗旨，和圖書館擁有多數且完整的資料館藏，因此資訊網路上資訊資源的增加，有賴圖書館有計劃的建立與充實。未來圖書館可依據自己館藏特色，配合中文光學字形辨識（Optical Character Recognition，簡稱OCR）系統的輔助，加速建立中文電子資料庫（註21）。有了這些資料庫的建立，未來圖書館的資訊服務將更加便利。

(四) 加強資訊網路教育課程並納入學校課程，提昇館員對資訊網路的認知和資訊素養

資訊化社會下的館員將具有圖書館館員、資訊專家及資訊教師三種角色。要培訓出具有這三種能力與技術的館員，必須由學校教育著手。將資訊網路的相關課程，有系統的納入圖書館與資訊科學的課程裡，以漸進的方式培養學生對資訊網路的知識與技術。尤其是面對未來虛擬圖書館的來臨，應該及早重新設計資訊服務方面的課程及訓練計劃，藉由正規教育的訓練及課程安排，教育出具備資訊素養的資訊教師與資訊專家。目前服務於各圖書館的館員，也應該利用各種管道與在職訓練，加強對資訊網路的知識與服務技術。藉由此種實際利用資訊網路的經驗，可增強館員對資訊的掌握，並且增加對資訊選擇的決斷能力。

(五) 瞭解讀者在網路上的資訊需求，研擬具體的服務方式

隨著資訊網路的建立及讀者資訊素養的提昇，讀者對傳統圖書館的依賴度日漸降

低，圖書館應該加強對讀者資訊需求的研究。尤其在網路系統下，讀者將較以往更加不可見。並且由於讀者並不需要透過館員的服務才可接觸到資訊。因此，館員在網路系統中的角色將逐漸由傳統的館員轉型成資訊網路系統中的資訊專家。在網路系統中，資訊專家的任務將是指引與解答網路使用者各種的問題。在此種情況下，如何透過網路的溝通方式，瞭解與分析使用者的問題及需要，將是網路上虛擬參考服務重要的課題。

(六) 重視讀者教育及訓練

讀者利用資訊可分成對資訊內容的瞭解與對媒體運用的技術兩種。由於傳統圖書館的媒體多屬於靜態性的資訊，圖書館利用教育的內容也較偏向於對整體知識結構的介紹，例如工具書的使用介紹等。隨著線上資料庫、光碟資料庫及資訊網路系統的相繼引進成為圖書館的服務項目後，動態性的資訊亦日益增多。圖書館的讀者面對這些新型的電子媒體，不但感覺陌生且操作有困難。因此，圖書館利用教育的課程必須針對實際的現況做適當的調整與設計。在課程的內容上，必須兼顧對線上資料庫、光碟資料庫及資訊網路資源的介紹及使用技巧的講解。

四、結論

資訊網路時代的來臨，是科技進步及社會需求改變之下必然的結果。面對一個新時代的來臨，圖書館的功能雖未必會改變，但服務的方式及形態卻必須要能切合使用者的使用習慣及需求。在圖書館的角色及服務方式逐漸轉型的過程中，現行圖書館的從業人員將扮演著承先啟後的任務。如何從過去圖書館學發展經驗中，擷取出寶貴的經驗，研發出符合時代需要的資訊服務，將是一個重要的使命。可預期的將來因各國資訊網路逐步的建立，使得 21 世紀成為一個更加合作與發展的資訊時代。在這樣一個創新及挑戰的時代中，圖書館資訊事業的發展將充滿著生機與熱力。

附　　註

註1：李德竹、黃世雄主持，整體規劃臺灣圖書館資訊網路系統（臺北市："教育部"圖書館事業委員會，1991年），頁5。

註2：陳文生，《TANet 與圖書館資訊網路》，私立大學院校圖書館自動化規劃及學術網路發展知能研習會會議資料（1992年6月21－23日），頁37—38。

註3：同註2，頁51—54。

註4：同註2，頁50。

註5：同註1，頁63—66。

註6：研擬加速圖書館自動化促進書目共享第二次會議記錄（臺北："中央圖書館"，1993年9月14日）。

註7：徐玉梅，《科技性臺灣資訊網路之現況與發展》，"中國圖書館學會"會報，49期（1992年12月），頁139—142。

註8：陳家俊，*Internet* 入門導航（臺北：資訊與電腦，1992年），頁58—65。

註9：羅澤生，《網路服務業的現況與前瞻》，資訊傳真，152期（1992年7月5日），頁112。

註10：《臺訊的加值電訊服務》，資訊傳真，152期（1992年7月5日），頁121—123。

註11:《時報資訊電子即時新聞系統》,資訊傳真,152期(1992年7月5日),頁124—125。

註12:同註9,頁112。

註13:黃鴻珠,《圖書館界的電子論壇》,"中國圖書館學會"會報,49期(1992年12月),頁96—99。

註14:同註1,頁13。

註15:楊美華,《虛擬圖書館與資訊網路化》,"中國圖書館學會"會報,49期(1992年12月),頁110。

註16:同註15,頁112。

註17:吳明德,館藏發展(臺北市:漢美,1991年),頁290。

註18:L. M. Saurder, "The Virtual Library, Revisited," *Computers in Libraries*, 12:10 (Nov. 1992), pp. 54.

註19:D. Barron, "The Library and Information Science Distance Education Consortium: The Profession's Virtual Classroom," *Wilson Library Bulletin*, 66:2 (1991), pp. 41-43.

註20:*American Library Association Presidential Committee on Information Literacy: Final Report* (Chicago: ALA, 1989), pp. 1.

註21:沈蓓芬,《臺灣電子資料庫服務發展動向》,網路通訊,22期(1993年5月),頁25—27。

圖書館學教師研究趨勢及資訊需求[*]

前　言

　　臺灣圖書館學教育歷經數十寒暑，在圖書館學界教師及研究人員努力耕耘下，進步卓著。在教學內容方面，除了引進歐美各先進國家之新知與新技術外，更致力於本土性之研究發展，以加強圖書館專業訓練；在學術研究方面，更是著作豐富，貢獻良多。唯截至目前為止，尚未有專文對臺灣圖書館學教師研究趨勢及資訊需求（information needs）方面的問題進行分析研究。有鑑於此，本研究擬從圖書館學教育方面來探討目前之資訊需求、研究方向與教學內容，並提供圖書館學研究方面之核心館藏，作為圖書館學教學研究之參考。

　　目前海內外文獻尚無與本研究類似或直接相關者，因此，本研究採用之研究方法除問卷調查方式外，同時亦使用書目計量方法分析研究資料。以1988年唐秀珠所撰之碩士論文"以書目計量學方法探討專題選粹服務的發展"[①]，與1984年劉瑞蘭刊載於期刊上之"書目計量學在採選之應用"兩文中所述之書目計量學部份作為本研究之部份參考。海外1987年著有以書目計量學來評鑒資訊科學之博士論文[②]；另1988年之博士論文以書目計量學來調查化工技術報告；1990年著有專書討論如何以書目計量學來量化圖書館學與資訊科學之文件等[③]。

　　本研究是以臺灣圖書館學系教師之研究著作文獻為調查對象，由文獻中探討分析圖書館學系：一、教師研究概況；二、教師教學內容與研究著作相關性；三、教師著作的分佈狀況；四、教師著作中引用文獻的特性和利用的核心資料；五、專任教師與任職圖書館的兼任教師其研究著作之差異；六、教師研究主題與興趣的變動以預測未來臺灣圖書館學發展趨勢。

　　本研究以1990學年度在五所圖書館學科系任教之教師為調查範圍，蒐集的研究著作則以近十年（即1980—1900年）為限，以避免取樣數量太大，造成資料查對時因年代久遠而無法檢索。而教師的研究著作清單，由教師自行提供，不但能精確掌握各個教師著作，並可使教師個人著作有其完整性。

　　本研究採用問卷調查與書目計量學相關的研究方法，以五所圖書館學系所提供之現任專、兼任教師91人為對象，進行教師文獻資料來源，及研究時所遭遇問題的調查，並蒐集五所圖書館學校課程內容，以期能求得進一步的研究與引證。同時，本研究並利用"社會科學統計套裝軟體"（Software Package for Social Sciences，簡稱SPSS）詳加分析問卷調查資料。

　　本研究之最終目的是藉由圖書館學教育方面來探討目前臺灣圖書館學之研究趨勢及圖書館學教師教學與研究之相關程度，以瞭解圖書館學教師對資訊的需求程度、研究方向與教學內容，進而作為發展臺灣地區圖書館學研究所需的期刊核心館藏，俾便提供圖書館學

---

[*] 本文摘自《當代圖書館事業論集：慶祝王振鵠教授七秩榮慶論文集》，臺北市正中書局1994年版，第627—663頁。

研究教學時之參考,亦使圖書館學研究人員在研究資料擇取上,收事半功倍之效。

研究設計與實施

本研究之調查對象主要以五所圖書館學及相關科系所,1990學年度之圖書館學系教師為普查範圍。此五所圖書館學校包括:"國立臺灣大學"圖書館學系(所)、"國立師範大學"社會教育系圖書館組、私立輔仁大學圖書館學系、私立淡江大學教育資料科學系、私立世界新聞學院圖書資料科。研究過程中擬由問卷調查,得知教師的研究著作與利用資料的特性,研究範圍內各校專兼任教師,剔除重覆者共計91名。

教師著作的分析,則以教師個人十年內(1980—1990年)所有的著作為對象,其中所授課程非圖書館學課程之圖書館學系教師的著作,則不在研究範圍內,符合此研究範圍內的著作文獻,共計895筆。

本研究採用兩種研究工具:

(一) 問卷方面

調查問卷是依據本研究目的並參酌海內外相關文獻擬定,經多次修改而於1991年9月底定稿,內容分為十三項:

第一至三題旨在瞭解教師與本研究目的的相關背景資料。

第四至七題調查教師著作數量、著作動機及著作與教學相關度之資料。

第八、九題探討環境滿足教師研究或教學資訊需求的程度。

第十至十二題探詢各教師研究過程最大問題,其解決途徑以及最常使用的資料類型與資料庫。

第十三題是請各教師詳列個人至少近十年內所有著作,俾便本研究進行相關文獻分析用。

(二) 文獻分析方面

根據問卷每位教師所提之著作為主,依研究目的分析文獻的特性,其中主題分析歸類方式,係參照圖書館文獻目錄[4]與圖書館年鑑[5]所採用的分類表,若引用文獻為非圖書館學領域者,則依非圖書館學主題分類表分類,該表是依據Peritz的研究[6],參酌實際文獻主題分佈情況而擬定。

(三) 研究實施

1. 問卷調查

問卷調查的對象為五所大專院校圖書館學系1990學年度的專兼任教師。調查之前先蒐集各校1990學年度授課的教師名單及課程表,若教師任職不只一校者,則以專任的學校為主,共計91名教師。調查問卷於1991年10月1日寄出,繼以電話催詢未回收者,最終回收問卷共達68份,回收率74.5%。

按各校發出及收回情況如下:

(1) 臺灣大學25位教師,回收22位,回收率88%。
(2) 師範大學5位教師,回收4位,回收率80%。
(3) 輔仁大學7位教師,回收11位,回收率64.7%。
(4) 淡江大學27位教師,回收17位,回收率62.9%。
(5) 世新專校17位教師,回收14位,回收率82.4%。

2. 教師著作的建檔與整理

根據 68 份有效問卷中,以教師自行檢附的著作表為主,進行教師著作的類型資料、主題、年代以及語文的分析。68 位教師著作總數,共計 895 筆;分別進行著作文獻的建檔,其中著作類型分為:①圖書;②研究報告;③期刊論文;④其他等四類。主題建檔則根據主題類表賦予相當的類號,主要的分類原則為:

(1) 一篇文章以給一個主題為主。
(2) 主題的取決以題名為準,若無法確定再依文獻內容為主。
(3) 一篇文章包括兩個或兩個以上的主題,則以份量較多的主題為主。
(4) 一篇文章若具有兩個份量相同的主題,則以在書名或篇名先出現的主題為準。
(5) 文章若是圖書館的自動化,則放在自動化之類目下。如:採訪自動化歸於自動化而非採訪。
(6) 各類型圖書館的作業,則歸在各類型的圖書館之主題下。如:大學圖書館的利用指導,歸於大學圖書館。
(7) "中央圖書館"的作業則歸於"國家圖書館"類目下。
(8) 各主題之工具書,分別歸於各所屬之主題。如:資訊科學字彙歸於資訊科學。各筆資料依所屬名項特性,逐一編碼,以完成統計處理的準備。

3. 引用文獻的建檔與整理

教師 895 篇著作中,以間隔抽樣方式,取 1/3 的著作進行引用文獻分析,依隨機抽樣決定第一筆所取的編號,然後每隔三篇抽樣一篇,至抽選所有的著作為止,共計抽選 228 篇樣本。然後以選取的樣本為對象,至各館確實找出該篇資料予以影印。既經選取的樣本,每一樣本資料以分析八篇引用文獻為主,以隨機抽樣方式各類資料取樣 8 篇,若引用文獻總數不足 8 篇者,則取全部的引用文獻進行分析。共計取樣 1661 篇。引用文獻取樣過程的處理原則為:

(1) 期刊資料的取樣對象以附註文獻為主;圖書取樣則以書後的總參考書目為主。
(2) 期刊文獻若僅有參考書目而無附註者,則採用參考書目。
(3) 圖書資料若無參考書目,而以各章附註的形態出現,則匯集各章的附註,剔除重複者,再予以抽樣。

下一步驟是,進行各文獻的引用文獻總數、引用形態、引用文獻類型、主題、年代、語文等項分析。

(1) 引用形態的編碼,分別是:①著作有附註;②著作有參考書目;③著作有附註,亦有參考書目;④無任何參考來源。
(2) 引用文獻的類型,分為:①圖書;②研究報告;③期刊論文;④會議論文;⑤博碩士論文;⑥其他。
(3) 文獻主題方面,先分為:①圖書館學;②非圖書館學兩大類,以下再細分。

(四)資料處理與分析

所有填答問卷以及各文獻的建檔資料,則以社會科學統計套裝軟體(The Statistical Package for Social Science,簡稱 SPSS)進行統計分析。採用之分析法包括:

1. 次數分配(frequency distribution)[7]

計算本研究調查問卷中,每一題項的分佈情況,以及文獻的資料形態、主題、年代、語文、引用文獻的總數、引用形態、引用文獻類型等特性之次數分佈,以作為本次研究描述統計之依據。

2. 卡方檢定（chi-square test）[8]

利用卡方檢定本研究教師授課主題及其著作主題、行政職務及其著作主題、教師年齡及著作數量等三方面是否具有顯著差異,以檢定各變項之間的相關程度。

研究結果與分析

本研究主要的目的在於探討臺灣圖書館學教師的資訊需求,及其研究文獻、引用資料的特性。根據所得資料,分別列出三項分析結果：一、資訊需求的調查結果分析,包括分析問卷調查；反映圖書館學教師資訊需求的特性與意見；探討教師背景、研究著作特性及著作數量；以及教師授課類別之分析等。二、教師著作文獻分析,探討教師著作的類型、主題、年代、語文、各年代的主題分佈。三、引用文獻分析,主要統計引用文獻的總數、引用形態、主題、年代、語文及所引用之核心期刊。

（一）資訊需求問卷調查結果分析

問卷中第一至第十二個項所得資料如,教師的最高學位、性別、年齡、職稱、行政職務類別、專任兼任比例、授課主題、著作數量、著作及研究動機、資訊需求滿意程度、遭遇問題及使用參考資料類型情況等,分別統計分析,其結果如下：

1. 個人背景

（1）教師學位。

分析68位回答問卷的圖書館學教師學歷其中以具有碩士學位為最多,有44人,佔64.7%；其次是博士學位,有17人,佔25%；具學士學位者,有7人,佔10.3%。

（2）職稱。

68位圖書館學教師職稱之統計結果：專任教師中具有教授資格者稍高,有16人,佔總數68人中23.9%；其次為專任副教授,有14人,佔20.6%；專任講師12人,佔17.6%。兼任教師方面,以兼任講師為最多,有15人,佔11.8%；最少為兼任教授,僅2人,整體來看,專任教師不同職稱間人數差別有限。專任教師共42人,佔61.7%,兼任教師總共26人,佔總教師人數38.3%。

（3）年齡。

關於教師出生年代,見表一圖書館學教師出生年代統計表,人數最多為1951年至1960年出生的教師,即年齡為33歲至42歲者,有22人,佔32.4%；其次為1941年至1950年出生的教師,即年齡為43歲至52歲者,有20人；佔29.4%；1921年前出生的教師,即年齡72歲以上者,僅2人,佔3.0%。由此可見,圖書館學教師年齡分佈於33歲至52歲,佔了61.8%。

表一　圖書館學教師出生年代統計

出生年　　　　　（年齡）	數量	百分比%	累計數量	累計百分比%
1921年以前　　　（72歲以上）	2	2.9	2	2.9
1921年—1930年（63歲~72歲）	7	10.3	9	13.2
1931年—1940年（53歲~62歲）	11	16.2	20	29.4
1941年—1950年（43歲~52歲）	20	29.4	40	58.8
1951年—1960年（33歲~42歲）	22	32.4	62	91.2
1961年—1970年（23歲~32歲）	6	8.8	68	100.0

（4）擔任圖書館行政職務。

圖書館學教師是否擔任圖書館行政職務？擔任何種行政職務？依據統計所得，以表二示之。得知大部份圖書館學教師未在圖書館擔任行政職務，有45人，佔66.2%。而如果目前仍擔任圖書館行政職務的教師，最多為任行政主管，有14人，佔20.6%；在編目、視聽、閱覽及特藏四部門任職者共9人。

表二　圖書館學教師行政職務分析

單　位　別	數量	百分比%	累計數量	累計百分比%
未擔任行政職務	45	66.2	45	66.2
行政	14	20.6	59	86.8
編目	4	5.9	63	92.6
視聽	2	2.9	65	95.6
特藏	2	2.9	67	98.5
期刊	1	1.5	68	100.0
其他	0	0	0	100.0

2. 任教課程分析

根據本研究擬定之主題分析表，統計分析68位圖書館學教師於1989、1990、1991學年度所擔任之課程與主題，其結果詳見表三。由表中得知教師授課主題以資訊科學與圖書館自動化課程最多，有12人，佔19.7%；其次為讀者服務與參考服務課程，有11人，佔18.0%；館際合作因屬讀者服務與參考服務課程中的一部份，所以而無人勾選。此外，目錄學與版本學、出版事業及圖書館法規與標準三課程，可能因學校未開該課程，或是教授該課程的教師未填答問卷，而無人勾選，有關課程分析部份有7人未填答。

由表三所得的任教課程主題分佈情形中，依該課程之任教教師為專任或是兼任者作統計，結果是任教課程教師以專任為多數，42人，佔61.7%；兼任26人，佔38.3%。

表三　圖書館學教師任教課程主題分析

課程名稱	數量	百分比%	累計數量	累計百分比%
資訊科學與圖書館自動化	12	19.4	12	19.7
讀者服務與參考服務	11	18.0	23	37.7
各類型圖書館	10	16.4	33	54.1
技術服務	9	14.8	42	68.9
特殊資料處理	8	13.1	50	82.0
圖書館學與圖書館事業	7	11.5	57	93.4
圖書館行政與管理	2	3.3	59	96.7
圖書館與資訊科學教育	2	3.3	61	100.0
館際合作	0	0	61	100.0
目錄學與版本學	0	0	61	100.0
出版事業	0	0	61	100.0
圖書館法規與標準	0	0	61	100.0
未填答	7	10.3	68	100.0

3. 教師發表著作數量分析

關於臺灣地區 68 位圖書館學教師每年著作數量分析，分三部份探討。第一部份擬由教師填答認爲理想的每年發表著作數量，統計結果教師認爲每年發表應 2 篇著作爲最多，有 25 人，佔 36.8%；其次爲 3 篇，有 14 人，佔 20.6%；1 篇者，有 13 人，佔 19.12%。另外有 7 人未填答此項。

第二部份得知實際上教師每年發表著作數量分佈情形，發現實際每年發表著作數量以 1 篇爲最多，有 18 人，佔 26.5%；其次爲未填答該題者，有 16 人，佔 23.5%，再其次爲發表 2 篇者有 14 人佔 20.6%，此部份未填答的比率偏高。

第三部份是探討圖書館學教師發表著作及從事研究的動機，統計發現其中以"外界委託"佔最大多數，有 27 人，佔 39.7%；其次爲"保持不落伍"有 16 人，佔 23.5%而"校方鼓勵"與"輔助教學"皆無人勾選。

第四部份探討 68 位圖書館學教師對自己發表著作數量的滿意情形，依據統計所得結果爲：教師對其著作數量以"不滿意"爲最多，有 23 人，佔 33.8%；其次爲"尚可"有 19 人，佔 27.9%；再其次爲"滿意"，有 9 人，佔 13.2%；最少爲 2 人認爲"非常滿意"佔 2.9%。

4. 教師在研究教學上對資訊需求程度之分析

(1) 教師研究著作與教學相關程度：

68 位圖書館學教師認爲自己的研究著作與教學相關程度，以認爲"極相關"爲最多，有 23 人，佔 33.8%；其次爲"相關"，有 21 人，佔 30.9%；認爲"極不相關"則無人勾選。另外，有 4 人勾選"不相關"，佔 5.9%。

(2) 教師任教單位滿足其研究方面資訊需求程度：

教師認為在研究上，其所在任教單位能滿足資訊需求程度之統計分析，由表中得知以"部份滿足"為最多，有43人；佔63.2%；其次為"很少滿足"，12人，佔17.6%；無人填"全部滿足"。

（3）研究環境滿足教師研究方面資訊需求程度：

教師認為在研究方面，整個研究環境能滿足資訊需求程度，以填答為"部份滿足"者最多，有51人，佔75.0%；其次為未填答該題者，有8人，佔11.8%；另外勾選"全部滿足"與"未曾滿足"二項，皆各有1人，佔1.5%。

（4）任教單位滿足教師教學方面資訊需求程度：

68位圖書館學教師對任教單位滿足教學方面三項資訊需求的程度，認為"部份滿足"的最多，有45人，佔66.2%；其次為"很少滿足"，有11人，佔16.2%；最少為"全部滿足"，有1人，佔1.5%。

（5）研究環境滿足教學方面資訊需求程度：

教師認為在教學方面，整個研究環境滿足資訊需求程度，與上述任教單位滿足教師教學方面資訊需求程度完全相同，統計結果認為"部份滿足"者為最多，其次為"很少滿足"，最少為"全部滿足"。

5. 教師研究過程中相關問題之分析

探討教師研究過程中，所遭遇的問題、解決途徑、使用的檢索系統及利用資料類型等四部份，分別說明如下：

（1）教師研究過程中最常遭遇到的問題：

教師在研究過程中，最常遇到影響研究的問題為"沒有時間去尋找或閱讀資料"，有31人，佔45.6%；其次為"缺乏最新的資料"有15人，佔22.1%；而"無法迅速獲得所需資料"者僅有2人。

（2）資料問題解決途徑分析：

對上述得知圖書館學教師在研究過程中所遭遇到的困擾，教師所採取的解決途徑，第一優先選擇"自己購買"有46人，佔67.6%；與教師發表著作及研究動機分析中，"外界委託"排名第一，有很密切的關係。第一優先選擇"放棄"途徑的人數為零，可見圖書館學教師對研究的執著態度。

（3）教師於利用電腦檢索資料特性分析：

將教師是否利用電腦檢索相關資料庫情形，並更一步探討利用何種檢索系統，發現圖書館學教師曾利用電腦檢索資料庫的人數佔大多數，有47人，相當於69.1%；其中以利用"光碟"檢索系統為最多，有37人，佔54.4%。

（4）教師使用資料類型分析：

教師於研究教學過程中，最常利用何種類型資料，作為教學和研究之參考依據。發現第一優先選擇使用"參考工具書"（如字典、百科全書等）為絕大多數，有45人，佔66.2%；而第一優先選擇利用"會議論文集"者5人、"學術性期刊"者3人，"請教同行"者2人，及"視聽資料"者5人。值得注意的是沒有人第一優先選擇利用"圖書"及"研究報告"二類。

6. 圖書館學教師任教課程與著作主題相關程度分析

以68位圖書館學教師著作與任教課程做交叉統計分析，其結果詳見表四。自表中

表四 教師任教課程與著作主題之關係統計表

著作主題\授課類型	圖書館學與圖書館事業	圖書館行政與管理	技術服務	讀者服務與參考服務	館際合作	特殊資料處理	資訊科學與圖書館自動化	圖書館與資訊科學教育	各類型圖書館	目錄學與版本學	出版事業	圖書館法規與標準	合計
圖書館學與圖書館事業	28	15	8	32	5	1	44	21	57	5	1	0	217
圖書館行政	13	21	8	16	4	15	9	7	36	0	1	0	130
技術服務	15	18	27	20	2	18	25	5	44	5	1	2	182
讀者服務與參考服務	29	10	17	38	4	18	37	10	74	5	12	1	255
館際合作	3	1	0	1	2	1	13	2	4	1	0	1	29
特殊資料處理	2	3	3	8	1	93	21	0	12	0	0	0	143
資訊科學與圖書館自動化	14	4	9	24	5	13	158	6	25	1	6	3	268
圖書館與資訊科學教育	14	2	1	3	1	0	2	13	7	0	0	0	43
各類型圖書館	11	11	6	37	0	4	19	4	60	5	3	1	163
目錄學與版本學	2	0	3	0	0	1	8	0	1	29	0	0	44
出版事業	0	0	0	2	0	0	0	0	2	0	0	0	4
圖書館法規與標準	1	0	0	0	0	0	0	0	0	0	0	2	3
合計	132	85	84	181	24	164	336	68	322	51	24	10	1481

可以發現教師任教課程與著作主題有很大相關程度。除"館際合作"、"圖書館學與資訊科學教育"、"出版事業"與"圖書館法規與標準"四類中,著作主題與任教課程沒有明顯的集中分佈外,其他各類其著作主題篇數皆爲同類任教課程中最多者,具有明顯差異。

此外,就著作篇數之統計來看以"資訊科學與圖書館自動化"爲最多,有336篇;其次爲"各類型圖書館"有322篇;再爲"讀者服務與參考服務"有181篇;最少爲"圖書館法規與標準"。

(二) 教師著作文獻分析

由1990學年度五所圖書館學教師的著作中,選取1980年至1990年的所有著作,共得895篇文獻,其中可資分析的有效樣本884篇,各項特性分析結果如下:

1. 著作類型

著作類型分爲期刊、圖書、研究報告、其他等四大類。其中期刊762篇,佔86%。顯示圖書館學教師的著作,係以期刊型式爲主,圖書資料名列第二,佔10.1%的比例。

2. 著作語文

圖書館學教師的著作多以中文發表,884篇教師著作中,僅105篇文章(11.9%)以英文發表。778篇文章(88.1%)以中文發表;其餘的一篇以日文發表。

3. 著作之主題

分析學科領域的研究主題,可瞭解此學科領域的研究重點及研究興趣的變化趨勢。本研究將圖書館文獻的研究主題,分成十二大類,六十八小類,各大類、小類研究主題的文章篇數,分佈情形,如表五所示。

表五 各研究主題類型的文章數量

研究主題類型	文章篇數 (N=884)	佔全部著作的百分比%	累計篇數	累計百分比%
圖書館學與圖書館事業	73	8.3	73	8.3
圖書館行政與管理	45	5.1	118	13.4
技術服務	49	5.5	167	18.9
讀者服務與參考服務	112	12.7	279	31.6
館際合作	11	1.2	290	32.8
特殊資料處理	126	14.3	416	47.1
資訊科學與圖館自動化	214	24.2	630	71.3
圖書館與資訊科學教育	32	3.6	662	74.9
各類型圖書館	164	18.5	826	93.4
目錄學與版本學	35	4.0	861	97.4
出版事業	16	1.8	877	99.2
圖書館法規與標準	7	0.8	884	100.0

以大類研究主題而言，資訊科學與圖書館自動化是教師們主要的研究主題，共有214篇文章（24.2%），其次各類型圖書館，共有164篇。文章篇數最少的主題是圖書館法規與標準，僅有7篇（0.8%）；館際合作方面論文11篇（1.2%）。

　　十二大類主題下，除目錄學與版本學和出版事業兩大類未再有複分小類外，其他十大類皆有小類，各小類的文獻分佈情形。（參見表六）

表六　教師著作文獻於各主題的文章數量分佈

研　究　主　題	文章篇數（N＝884）
（一）圖書館學與圖書館事業	78（8.3%）
1. 通論	20
2. 圖書館與文化建設	10
3. 圖書館與資訊社會	13
4. 圖書館史	6
5. "中國圖書館學會"	3
6. 圖書館員	4
7. 海外圖書館及其相關組織	11
8. 圖書館週	0
9. 大陸圖書館事業	6
（二）圖書館行政與管理	45（5.1%）
1. 通論	12
2. 組織	3
3. 人事	6
4. 法令規章	1
5. 經費	4
6. 建築	4
7. 業務統計	2
8. 評鑑與館藏發展	13
（三）技術服務	49（5.5%）
1. 通論	1
2. 徵集	10
3. 分類	11
4. 編目	25
5. 典藏	2
（四）讀者服務與參考服務	112（12.7%）
1. 通論	1

（續上表）

研　究　主　題	文章篇數（N = 884）
2. 閱覽	1
3. 流通	1
4. 推廣	10
5. 參考服務	11
6. 參考資料	26
7. 利用指導	24
8. 特殊讀者服務	18
9. 讀者分析	1
10. 書評	19
（五）館際合作	11（1.2%）
1. 通論	6
2. 合作採訪	4
3. 合作編目	1
4. 合作典藏	0
5. 館際互借	0
6. 互惠閱覽	0
（六）特殊資料處理	126（14.3%）
1. 期刊	11
2. 視聽資料	105
3. 報紙、剪輯、小冊子	1
4. 特藏資料	4
5. 其他	5
（七）資訊科學與圖書館自動化	214（24.2%）
1. 資訊科學理論	12
2. 圖書館自動化通論	25
3. 圖書館自動化系統（OPAC…）	23
4. 資訊系統與資訊網	24
5. 資訊媒體與技術	36
6. 機讀目錄	17
7. 資訊貯存與檢索	23
8. 資料庫	16
9. 中文資訊處理（CCCII…）	38

（續上表）

研　究　主　題	文章篇數（N = 884）
（八）圖書館與資訊科學教育	32（3.6%）
1. 通論	0
2. 海內外圖書館教育	13
3. 圖書館學系（所）課程	8
4. 繼續教育	11
（九）各類型圖書館	164（18.5%）
1. "國家圖書館"	16
2. 文化中心	4
3. 大學圖書館	42
4. 專門圖書館	11
5. 公共圖書館	31
6. 學校圖書館	25
7. 兒童圖書館	30
8. 鄉鎮圖書館	3
9. 其他（如：博物館……）	2
（十）目錄學與版本學	34（4.0%）
（十一）出版事業	16（1.8%）
（十二）圖書館法規與標準	70（0.8%）
1. 圖書館法	0
2. 著作權法	2
3. 圖書館標準	5

　　（1）圖書館學與圖書館事業類：此類之小類的文獻分佈中，以"通論類"有20篇文章（27.4%）最多，其次爲"圖書館與資訊社會"13篇（17.8%）。

　　（2）圖書館行政與管理類：此類之小類中文章篇數最多的小主題，以"評鑑"13篇（28.9%）爲最多，其次爲"通論"12篇（26.7%）。

　　（3）技術服務類：其中"編目"小類有25篇文獻（51%）爲最多，次爲"分類"11篇，"徵集"10篇。"讀者服務與參考服務"類：以"參考資料"26篇，佔有23.4%的比例爲最高。次爲"利用指導24篇，篇數最少的主題，分別是"通論"、"閱覽"、"流通"、"讀者分析"等各僅有一篇文獻。

　　（4）館際合作類：其中以"通論"有6篇爲最多（54.5%），次爲合作採訪，至於"探討館際互借"、"合作典藏"、"互惠閱覽"的文獻則闕如，顯示學者在館際合作的努力上，較傾向館際合作觀念的介紹與推廣，但對實際進行"合作典藏"，"館際互借"的實例則不多。

(5) 特殊資料處理類：以"視聽資料"105篇（84.0%）爲最多，次爲"期刊"，至於探討"報紙"、"剪輯"、"小冊子"的文獻只有一篇。

(6) 資訊科學與圖書館自動化類：以探討中文電腦及中文資訊交換碼的"中文資料處理"，共有38篇（17.8%），佔最多比例。次爲"資訊媒體與技術"，共有36篇（16.9%）。

(7) 圖書館與資訊科學教育類：以海內外"圖書館教育"13篇（40.6%）最多，次爲"繼續教育"11篇。各類型圖書館類：以"大學圖書館"之著作42篇（25.9%）爲最多，次爲"公共圖書館"31篇，"兒童圖書館"30篇。探討"文化中心圖書館"及"鄉鎮圖書館"的文獻則相當缺乏，分別是4篇與3篇。目錄學與版本學類：計有35篇文獻，佔所有研究文獻的4%，其下未再復分小類。出版事業類：計有16篇文獻，由於文獻篇數過少，故未再復分小小類。圖書館法規與標準類，以"圖書館標準"發表之文章共有5篇最多（71.4%），但缺乏探討"圖書館法"的著作。

4. 著作年代

爲瞭解68位圖書館學教師著作的每個年度發表數量分佈及其成長情形。研究1980年至1990年的教師研究文獻，依年度區分，1989年發表的著作數量128篇，佔總篇數（884篇）最高的比例（14.5%），其次爲1986年計有112篇（12.7%）。但大致而言，顯示每年文獻發表的數量是呈現逐年增加的趨勢。

5. 著作年代與研究主題的關係

以下探討大類研究主題於歷年的數量分佈情形、成長趨勢以及各年度的主要研究主題，以及各大類研究主題於各年度的文章數量分佈。其中"館際合作"、"出版事業及圖書館法規與標準"三類主題，並與其他主題的文獻分佈比較，此三類研究文獻是在1986年以後才有教師撰寫，顯示此三類主題近幾年來才被學者重視。歷年圖書館學文獻主要的大類主題，除1981年、1990年以"各類型圖書館"皆爲排名第一的主題外，其他九個年度，均以"資訊科學與圖書館自動化"佔最多刊出的文獻篇數。但整體而言，近年發表的文獻數量普遍較早年文獻數量爲多。

6. 專任教師與兼任教師著作數量之差異

根據受訪之68位圖書館學教師中，有42位爲專任教師，佔總教師人數61.7%；有26位爲兼任教師，佔總教師人數38.3%，此68位教師之所有著作，可資分析者，共計884篇，其中專任教師的著作有659篇；兼任教師的著作有225篇。平均每一位專任教師發表的著作數量爲15.7篇；兼任教師8.7篇。可知，專任教師的著作數量普遍較兼任教師的著作數量高。

(三) 引用文獻分析

引用文獻分析係藉由分析每篇文獻之索引、摘要或期刊等資料來源，以探討學科所使用或產生的文獻特性。因此，本研究由884篇圖書館學教師的著作中，抽樣228篇做引用文獻之分析。

1. 引用文獻的數量分佈

228篇著作中，其引用文獻共1587篇，每篇著作引用數量的分佈，最少是0篇，最多453篇。若以資料類型加以區別，則以引用圖書資料文獻數量爲最多。此外，228篇抽樣著作中，有74篇完全沒有引用文獻，佔所有抽樣比例的32.5%。由此顯示約有1/3

的抽樣著作沒有引用文獻,如此為數甚多著作缺乏引用文獻的現象,值得圖書館學者加以注意及深思。而228篇著作中,平均每篇著作有7篇引用文獻,與海外相關的研究列表比較,平均一篇文章的引用文獻篇數,臺灣圖書館學教師著作之每篇引用文獻之平均量較多,結果如表七所示。

表七　平均一篇文章引用文獻篇數之相關研究

相關研究	研究年代	平均每篇文章引用文獻篇數
Peritz[9]	1950	3.9
	1960	6.9
	1965	7.2
	1970	7.1
	1975	8.7
Nur[10]	1980	12.6
Frohmann[11]	1969—80	9.5
本研究	1980—90	7.0

2. 著作的引用形態

Cline曾利用沒有參考書目的文章所佔的比例,及每篇文章平均的參考書目筆數為標準,衡量期刊的學術性。[12]由此可見,學者皆相當重視文章是否有附註或參考書目,並將其視為衡量文獻學術性的標準。

本研究分別以:(1)僅有附註;(2)僅有參考書目;(3)兩者皆有;(4)兩者皆無等四種類型,探討228篇著作中引用文獻的特性。其中以僅有附註的引用形態比例最高,佔全部著作的36.8%,無任何引用文獻的著作,則佔32.5%。

3. 引用文獻的語文

1587篇引用文獻中,中文的引用文獻共計526篇(33.1%),英文的引用文獻1059篇(66.7%),另有2篇(0.1%)以日文發表。顯示臺灣地區圖書館學者進行研究時,以使用英文文獻最多,其次才是中文文獻。

4. 引用文獻的資料類型

分析68位教師著作引用文獻各類型資料的數量分佈及其百分比。發現圖書是臺灣地區圖書館學研究最常引用的資料類型,共有引用文獻834篇(52.6%),其次為期刊601篇(37.8%)。此兩類資料共佔引用文獻的90.4%。除圖書、期刊外,其他引用頻率較高的資料,依序為會議論文(3.8%)、研究報告(2.2%)、博碩士論文(2.1%)。

海外的相關研究,Peritz對圖書館學的核心期刊進行引用文獻分析,Schrader針對一種圖書館學期刊進行分析[13],而Frohmann則對圖書館學有關分類編目的文獻進行分析[14],各研究結果顯示最常引用的資料類型,均為期刊。只有LaBorie分析186篇圖書館學博碩士論文的引用文獻[15],其結果顯示最常引用的資料類型為圖書,與本研究相符。本研究結果以引用圖書比例較高,此乃導因於為數甚多的"同註×"的附註形式,此附註形式所引用者多半為圖書資料,一旦經系統抽樣選取為分析樣本,將導致圖書型式的引用率偏高。

5. 引用文獻的年代

分析引用文獻的年代,以瞭解此學科進行研究所需資料的新穎程度,以十年為一階段,分析圖書館學引用文獻於各階段的資源分配情形。由表八顯示,1982年至1990年的引用文獻筆數最多,總計707篇(44.5%),其次為1972至1981年計有653篇(41.1%)。顯示圖書館學文獻引用資料的年代,仍以近十年左右的文獻為主。此外,根據計算顯示教師著作引用文獻之半衰期(Half-life)為11.19年,使用文獻年限分佈與前項結果吻合。

Peritz的研究指出近六年內的引用資料;將佔整體引用文獻數目的73%。Schrader的研究亦認為引用近五年資料佔全部研究文獻的50%。整體而言,國外的相關研究與本研究均認為引用文獻的年代相似,多半分佈於近年的時段內。

6. 引用文獻的學科領域

分析引用文獻所隸屬的學科領域,除可瞭解此學科自我引用(self-citation)的情形外,亦可探討此學科與其他學科領域的互動關係。1587筆引用文獻經統計分析後,屬於圖書館學相關領域的引用文獻有1355筆,共佔85.4%。其他學科僅有232筆,佔14.6%的比例,結果顯示臺灣圖書館學領域自我引用率相當高,引用其他學科領域資料的情形,並不普遍。其他學科領域的引用文獻,在九大類學科中的分佈情形,其中以"教育"71篇(30.6%)佔最多的比例,其次為"電腦"、"通訊",計有49篇(21.1%)。

表八 引用文獻年代的次數分配表

年 代	文章篇數 (N = 1587)	佔全部著作 的百分比	累計篇數	累計百分比
1912—1921	1	0.1	1	0.1
1922—1931	10	0.6	11	0.7
1932—1941	15	0.9	26	1.6
1942—1951	12	0.8	38	2.4
1952—1961	33	2.1	71	4.5
1962—1971	141	8.9	212	13.4
1972—1981	653	41.1	865	54.5
*1982—1990	709	44.6	1574	99.2
民國前	13	0.8	1587	100.0

說明:*表示引用文獻篇數最高的年代

7. 引用文獻的主題分佈

1355筆的圖書館學引用文獻,依十二大類加以類別,其中以"資訊科學與圖書館自動化"一類。計有329篇(24.3%),擁有最高的比例,次之為"各類型圖書館",共有220篇(16.2%)。最少的是"出版事業"、"目錄學與版本學"、"圖書館法規與標準"

等三類。此結果顯示引用文獻的主題分佈與前述教師著作的主題分佈情況極爲吻合。而十二大類中,各小類的主題分佈情況如下:

(1) 圖書館學與圖書館事業類:以"通論性"的文章爲首,計有35篇(25.7%),次爲"國外圖書館及其相關組織",有27篇(19.9%)。

(2) 圖書館行政與管理類:"以探討評鑑與館藏發展"的44篇(33.196)爲最多,次爲"通論"31篇,比較不受研究重視的主題是法令規章與業務統計。

(3) 技術服務類:以"編目"最多,共有49篇,其他主題的引用文獻數目多寡,依序爲"徵集"、"分類"、"典藏"。

(4) 讀者服務與參考服務類:以探討"參考資料"的文獻最多,計有52篇(32.7%),其次爲"利用指導"42篇(26.4%)。

(5) 館際合作類:以"通論性"文獻爲主,共有24篇(64.9%),最少的是"合作典藏"與"互惠閱覽",均各爲1篇。

(6) 特殊資料處理類:以"視聽資料"90篇最多,次爲"期刊",共有19篇。探討"剪輯"、"小册子"、"特藏資料"的文獻則闕如。

(7) 資訊科學與圖書館自動化類:大部份的文獻探討"資訊貯存與檢索",計有71篇(21.6%),次爲"資訊系統與資訊網"60篇(18.2%),顯示有關資訊檢索的問題已普遍受到島內學者的注意。

(8) 圖書館與資訊科學教育類:以分析海內外"圖書館教育"的文獻最多,計有23篇(59%),其次爲"繼續教育"10篇(25.6%)。

(9) 各類型圖書館類:以探討"學校圖書館"最多,共有27篇,其他"各類型圖書館"引用文獻的多寡順序,依次爲:"大學圖書館"(45篇)、公共圖書館"(38篇)、"兒童圖書館"(36篇)、"專門圖書館"(14篇)、"鄉鎮圖書館"(5篇)、"國家圖書館"(3篇)、"文化中心"(2篇)。

(10) 目錄學與版本學類:共計有18篇引用文獻,佔全部引用文獻的1.3%,其下未再複分。

(11) 出版事業類:共計有8篇引用文獻,只佔全部引用文獻的0.6%,故其下未再複分小類。

(12) 圖書館法規與標準類:以探討圖書館標準的文獻較多,可見標準的問題已逐漸受到重視,但最少的則是圖書館法,只有1篇文獻。

8. 最常被引用的核心期刊

本研究中1587篇引用文獻,資料類型屬於期刊的引用文獻,共計601篇。此601篇引用文獻分佈於177種不同的期刊之中。依期刊被引用次數的多寡,由上往下排列,各期刊被引用次數的累積次數分配情形,其中半數以上(52.2%)期刊只被引用一次。

與布拉福定律比較,將期刊分成三區,各區含有等量的引用文獻筆數。根據表九顯示,第一區共計有九種期刊,包含約三分之一的引用文獻,即所謂的核心期刊區;第二區有29種期刊,第三區有139種期刊。各區期刊種數的比例爲1:3.2:15.4,與布拉福定律的$1:k:k^2$大致吻合。(參見下圖及表九)

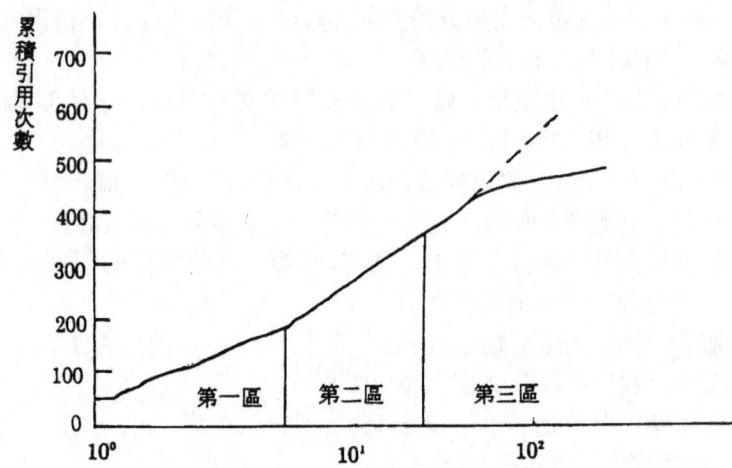

期刊種數與其被引用次數的累積次數分佈圖

表九　期刊被引用次數的累積次數分配表（布拉福定律）

期刊數（A）	累積期刊數	每一期刊被引用次數（B）	A×B	累計引用次數	
1	1（0.6%）	38	38	38	
1	2（1.1%）	33	33	71	第
1	3（1.7%）	28	28	99	
1	4（2.3%）	24	24	123	一
1	5（2.8%）	17	17	140	
1	6（3.4%）	16	16	156	
1	7（4.0%）	14	14	170	區
2	9（5.1%）	13	26	196	
1	10（5.6%）	12	12	208	
1	11（6.2%）	11	11	219	第
1	12（6.8%）	10	10	229	
3	15（8.5%）	9	27	256	二
4	19（10.7%）	8	32	288	
5	24（13.6%）	7	35	323	
3	27（15.3%）	6	18	341	區
11	38（21.5%）	5	55	396	
4	42（23.7%）	4	16	412	
12	54（30.5%）	3	36	448	第
30	84（47.5%）	2	60	508	三
93	177（100%）	1	93	601	區

核心期刊部份，Library Journal 被引用 38 次為最多，是臺灣學者最常引用之期刊，其次為"中國圖書館學會"會報，共引用 33 次。

綜述的分析與討論，可歸納研究結果如下：

（1）臺灣圖書館學者引用文獻的數量，平均每篇著作有 7 篇引用文獻，無引用文獻者，佔全部著作 32.5%。著作的引用形態，大部份是採用只有附註的方式。引用文獻的語文多以英文為主，擁有高達 66.7% 的比例。

（2）期刊及圖書是臺灣圖書館學者最常引用的資料類型，52.6% 的引用出自圖書，37.8% 的引用出自期刊，此二類資料佔引用文獻總數的 90.4%。

引用文獻的年代，以近年（1982—1990 年）的資料佔最高的比例，有將近 80% 的引用文獻是近二十年內的資料，顯示圖書館學研究引用的資料尚為新穎，對於最新資料的需求較高。

（3）引用文獻的學科領域，85.4% 屬於圖書館學，14.6% 屬於非圖書館學。圖書館學中，以資訊科學與圖書館自動化，佔 24.3%，引用非圖書館學的文獻，則以教育類最高（30.6%）。

（4）68 位教師著作的引用文獻，共引用 177 種期刊，利用布拉福定律獲得 9 種核心期刊，其中 3 種為中文，6 種為西文期刊。Library Journal 是最常被引用的期刊，其次則為"中國圖書館學會"會報，被引用次數均在 30 次以上，詳見表十。

表十　圖書館學引用文獻的核心期刊

排名	刊　名	引用次數
1	Library Journal	38
2	"中國圖書館學會"會報	33
3	College and Research Libraries	28
4	Library Trends	24
5	臺北市立圖書館館訊	17
6	Special Libraries	16
7	Library Resources & Technical Services	14
8	Journal of ASIS	13
9	教育資料科學月刊	13

結論與建議

本研究主要以問卷及書目計量方法，探討臺灣圖書館學教師的資訊需求，及其研究文獻、引用資料的特性。利用問卷調查可瞭解臺灣圖書館學教師對資訊需求的意見，及其個人近十年來（1980—1990 年）發表的著作狀況。此外，藉由分析 68 位（實際教師數91人）圖書館學教師的著作，可瞭解圖書館學研究的著作類型、著作語文、研究主題、著作年代等特性，並進一步分析教師著作的引用文獻。茲將本研究所得的結論及建議歸納如下，希望藉由這些研究結果，能使圖書館學界對本身所屬學科領域的文獻特性及其未來發展，有更充分的瞭解，進而可促進未來的圖書館學研究。

依資料分析的結果，所得的結論可分三部份說明。

（一）臺灣地區圖書館學教師資訊需求之調查分析

1. 臺灣地區圖書館學教師大部份為擁有碩士學位者

68位圖書館學教師學歷，以碩士學位為最多，有44人，佔64.7%。其次為博士學位17人，佔25%；具學士位者7人，佔10.3%。

2. 教師職稱的分佈，以專任教授資格佔最多數

根據實際填答的68位教師資料中，專任教師共42人，佔61.7%，兼任教師26人，佔總教師人數的38.3%。若以專兼任教師計算，兼任教師中，以兼任講師的身份最多，共計15人。專任教師中，以專任教授最多16人，佔全體教師總人數的23.5%。

3. 臺灣地區圖書館學教師的年齡分佈，以33歲至42歲者居多

以1951年至1960年的教師，即年齡33歲至42歲者居多有22人，佔32.4%，若將1941年至1960年出生（33歲52歲）的教師人數統計，則佔一半以上（61.8%）的比例。

4. 臺灣地區圖書館學教師有一半以上未擔任行政職務，而擔任行政職務者中，又以擔任主管級的行政工作者為最多

根據統計所得，圖書館學教師未在圖書館擔任行政職務者有45人，佔66.2%。目前有兼任圖書館行政職務者，多擔任行政主管（20.6%）；其他則分佈於編目、視聽、閱覽及特藏四個部門工作。

5. 1989—1991學年度臺灣地區圖書館學教師的任教課程，以教授資訊科學與圖書館自動化方面課程為最多

根據問卷中各教師填答的資料顯示，1989—1991學年度圖書館學教師所教授的課程，與本研究所擬的研究主題類表對照可歸納此三年中，68位教師授課主題以資訊科學與圖書館自動化的課程最多（19.7%），其次為讀者服務與參考服務（18.0%），館際合作、目錄學與版本學、出版事業、圖書館法規與標準等四門學科則無人填答。顯示此四個主題之課程於圖書館學界教授此課程較少，其中目錄學和出版事業皆在臺大開授，尤其目錄學為圖館系必修課，不應是無人教授，可能是老師漏填此項資料。

6. 68位教師發表著作及從事研究方面，以"外界委託"佔大多數

由問卷調查結果，可知大部份圖書館學教師發表著作及從事研究；以"外界委託"佔最多數（39.7%），其次為"保持不落伍"（23.5%），而"校方鼓勵"與"輔助教學"則完全無人勾選。

7. 教師認為每年發表的著作數量應以兩篇最適當，而實際上教師每年發表的著作數量多為一篇

問卷中教師們自己填答認為每年發表著作理想的數量，以兩篇著作為最適切者，佔最多數（36.8%）。其次是認為應有三篇（20.6%）。若實際統計每年發表的著作數量，多為一篇（26.5%）。顯示教師們每年著作數量，其理想與實際之間仍有差距。

8. 臺灣圖書館學教師對自己發表著作數量的滿意程度，以"不滿意"者居多

依據問卷統計結果，佔33.8%比例的教師對其每年發表的著作數量，皆表示"不滿意"此結果正印證前項結論，理想是兩篇，但僅發表一篇之差異。認爲"尚可"者，有27.9%比例。"滿意"者佔13.2%；"非常不滿意"者佔11.8%，只有少數學者認爲"非常滿意"，佔2.9%。

9. 大部份的教師認爲其研究著作與其教授課程"相關"

問卷統計結果顯示，圖書館教師普遍認爲自己的研究著作與教學之相關程度爲"極相關"（33.8%），認爲相關者有30.9%的比例，即是64.7%之教師認爲研究與教授課題"相關"。認爲"極不相關"者則無。

10. 臺灣圖書館學教師普遍認爲，不論其任教單位或是整體研究環境，均只能滿足部份的研究及教學資訊需求

在任教單位滿足教師研究需求面，多數學者認爲能"部份滿足"（63.2%）；若以臺灣整體研究環境而言，亦是"部份滿足"（75.0%）。關於滿足教師教學的資訊需求方面，無論是任教單位或是整體研究環境，均有66.2%的學者認爲只能"部份滿足"。

11. 臺灣圖書館學教師認爲研究過程中，最常遭遇的問題是"沒有時間去尋找或閱讀資料"，若所需資料無法尋獲時，則優先考慮"自己購買"

分析教師在研究過程中，最常遭遇的問題是"沒時間找尋或閱讀資料"（45.6%），其次爲"缺乏資料"（22.1%）。若無法取得所需資料時，大部份的教師將採取"自己購買"方式。選擇"放棄"途徑爲零，可知圖書館教師對其研究的執著態度。

12. 在研究過程中，多數的教師曾利用電腦檢索資料庫，其中又以利用"光碟"從事檢索者最多

臺灣圖書館學教師6.9%是利用電腦檢索資料庫者，其中利用檢索系統者，則以光碟進行檢索最多（54.4%），利用國際百科或科技網路者，則分別有10.3%及4.4%的比例。

13. 教師使用的資料類型，最常利用參考工具書

在各種資料類型中，教師們認爲最常利用的是參考工具書（66.2%），僅有少數教師使用會議論文、博士論文、學術期刊者，分別有7.4%、5.9%、4.4%。但並無優先選擇圖書及研究報告者。

(二) 以下歸納臺灣圖書館學教師著作文獻的特性分析

圖書館學教師的著作類型多半是以期刊發表佔86.2%，其次爲圖書，佔10.1%。圖書館學教師的著作多以中文發表，約88%，另約11.9%的著作則以英文發表。教師著作的研究主題，以"資訊科學與圖書館自動化"爲主，佔24.2%比例。其次爲各類型圖書館，佔18.5%。篇數較少的研究主題爲：出版事業（1.8%）、館際合作（1.2%）、圖書館法規與標準（0.8%）。自1980年至1990年間，圖書館學教師的著作數量大致呈現逐年增加的趨勢，其中以1989年發表著作數量最多（14.5%）。1980年至1990年間，除1981、1990兩年教師發表之文獻是以"各類型圖書館"佔最多的文獻篇數外，其他九個年度均以"資訊科學與圖書館自動化"佔有最多的著作篇數。另外如"館際合作"、"出版事業"、"圖書館法規與標準與其他主題的文獻分佈比較，在1986年以後此三類研究文獻才逐漸出現，可知此三主題直到近年才爲學者所注意。受訪之68位圖書館學教

師中，61.7%爲專任教師，38.3%爲兼任教師，其中專任教師的著作有69篇，兼任教師著作有275篇，平均每一位專任教師發表的著作數爲15.7篇，比兼任教師8.7篇，將近多出2倍，顯示專任教師的著作數量普遍較兼任教師多。

（三）歸納分析臺灣圖書館學教師著作中引用文獻的特性

1. 臺灣68位圖書館學教師著作的引用文獻數量偏低

228篇教師著作中，其引用文獻共1587篇，引用數量的分佈，最少是0篇，最多453篇，平均每篇著作爲7篇引用文獻。其中有32.5%的著作完全沒有引用文獻，此將近1/3的著作缺乏引用文獻的現象，值得臺灣學者加以注意。

2. 教師著作的引用類型，多半僅有附註的形式

228篇教師著作中，有36.8%是僅有附註的引用形態，僅附有參考書目者，佔10.1%。著作中有附註亦有參考書目者，佔20.6%。皆無任何引用文獻者，佔32.5%。

3. 教師著作的引用文獻以英文資料最多，其次爲中文資料

著作中的引用文獻約66.7%是引用英文資料，33.1%是引用中文資料，顯示臺灣圖書館學者相當借助海外的資料進行研究，亦說明臺灣圖書館學與資訊科學方面出版文獻不足。

4. 圖書及期刊是臺灣圖書館學教師最常引用的資料類型

關於引用文獻的資料類型，有52.6%是引用圖書資料；有37.8%是引用期刊資料，此兩類型資料共佔引用文獻數量的90.4%，爲進行圖書館學研究的主要來源。

5. 臺灣圖書館學教師著作以引用近十年內的資料居多

引用文獻的年代分佈，以1982年至1991年的篇數最多，佔44.5%，其次爲1972至1981年，佔41.1%。顯示圖書館學教師的引用文獻，仍以近年的資料爲主，這也是與研究主題有關之故，根據計算引用文獻之半衰期爲11.19年。

6. 圖書館學文獻自我引用的比例偏高

臺灣圖書館學教師著作引用圖書館學及圖書館學相關領域資料的百分比爲85.4%，引用其他學科領域資料的百分比爲14.6%。其他學科領域的引用文獻，以教育類的主題最多（30.6%），其次爲電腦與通訊（21.1%）。由此可知圖書館學文獻自我引用的比例相當高。

7. 引用文獻的主題以"資訊科學與圖書館自動化"最多

1355筆引用文獻中，以"資訊科學與圖書館自動化"佔有最高的比例（24.3%），其次爲各類型圖書館（16.2%），最少的是出版事業、目錄學與版本學、圖書館法規與標準。此項結果顯示引用文獻的主題分佈，與前述教師著作的主題分佈情況，極爲吻合。

8. 臺灣圖書館學教師最常引用的期刊是 Library Journal

利用布拉福定律進行引用期刊的分析結果，獲得9種圖書館學領域的核心期刊，此9種核心期刊中，有3種爲中文，6種爲英文期刊。"Library Journal"及"中國圖書館學會"會報分別是引用次數最多的英、中文期刊。綜觀上述的研究結論，有幾點特別值得注意之結果：

（1）教師授課的主題與其著作主題的相關程度上，大部份教師認爲自己的研究著作與其教學之相關程度爲"極相關"，以教師著作與任教課程進行統計分析，除了少數主題沒

有明顯的集中分佈外，大部份的主題皆與著作者授課之間具有明顯相關性。可知無論是教師們的意見或是文獻實際分析結果，皆可支持教師授課的主題與其著作主題相關。

（2）無論是教師授課的主題，或是教師著作的主題，引用文獻的主題，皆以"資訊科學與圖書館自動化"居多。由於授課主題與著作主題之間具有相關性，故兩者的主題類型，皆以"資訊科學與圖書館自動化"最多，亦代表目前圖書館學之發展趨勢，因而此特性亦反映在著作的引用文獻上。

（3）根據問卷統計結果，教師們認為最常使用的資料類型是各種參考工具書，而分析其著作引用文獻的資料類型，卻以引用圖書資料最多。兩者之間的差異在於教師研究過程中，固然須藉助許多參考工具書，但實際著述文獻時，引用工具書情況並不多。

上述的研究結果，主要是幫助圖書館界人士瞭解本身所屬學科領域著作及引用資料的特性，其核心期刊及研究主題的變動，可供圖書館徵集圖書館學資料的參考。根據本研究臺灣圖書館學教師研究趨勢及資訊需求之結論和分析海外相關文獻，提出下列數點建議：

1. 增加師資並鼓勵臺灣圖書館學教師多做研究

根據本調查，臺灣五個圖書館系所現有及兼任圖書館系教師共九十一人，而五校中圖書館學系所學生總數約1,650人，老師與學生之比例是1：18，與"教育部"之專任師生比例標準1：12相較偏低，如依專任教師對學生之比例計算則更低。又因教師授課時數負擔多而重，無時間從事研究和撰寫論文。雖教師們表示每人每年應發表兩篇文章，對每年發表著作數量現況，平均每人每年僅發表一篇論文不滿意，但似乎已分身乏術。反看大陸相同學系的教師，有專任研究教師，而教學教師之負擔課程時數不多，故每位授課教師皆有時間撰寫教課書和發表研究論著，故建議"教育部"和各學校研議增多師資，或減少其授課數，能使教師在教學之餘，從事相關研究及發表論文，達到教學和研究並重的目標。

2. 充實臺灣圖書館學及資訊科學資源

研究與教學是一體的兩面，課程內容之新穎性與教師研究有密切關係，研究和教學所需的資源，更是課程內容的重要元素。根據本研究結果，教師對臺灣整體及自己單位能滿足其資訊需求多表示"部份滿足"，可見臺灣這方面之資源不足，仍待充實，故建議相關單位資助經費，採購相關資源以滿足所需，提供更佳的研究環境。

3. 編製《全臺圖書館學與資訊科學資源聯合目錄》

聯合五所被調查的臺灣圖書館學系所，提出各圖書館有關圖書館學和資訊科學的圖書期刊及其他媒體資料清單，建立線上檔案並編製聯合目錄以增擴研究教學所需的資源和建立圖書館領域未來專業學術研究管道。

4. 加強正確之研究方法的訓練和教育

根據研究之抽樣教師著作中，約1/3（32.5%）著作完全無引用文獻，令人驚訝。此代表部份教師撰寫文章方法不正確，老式的寫作方式應改變，尤其身為圖書館學系教師更應使用標準正確的研究方法，根據瞭解目前臺灣各學科對研究方法認識缺乏，應加強訓練和教育。改善之道，則是應以教育著手，臺灣圖書館學系所應加強研究方法的課程與訓練，並建議各學系皆應開設研究方法課程，訓練學生正確的運用各研究方法，學習研究問題及評估研究結果的能力。必要時由學校協同圖書館學會辦理短期研習會，並訓練相關人員對研究方法認識，培養其正確的研究方式。

　　5. 引用其他學科領域的文獻

　　臺灣圖書館系教師著作與引用圖書館學及圖書館相關領域的資料，佔85.4%之多，以圖書館學與資訊科學課程而言，其涉及的學科應是多而廣，特別是電子計算機、通訊、統計學、心理學、管理學、社會學等方面，教師們的研究應是廣泛的、多面的，應多鼓勵教師們加強其各層面之研究，尤其在資訊社會中，圖書館問題之研究應是科際性的！

　　6. 鼓勵臺灣圖書館學教師多以英文發表論著

　　根據抽樣調查得知臺灣圖書館學教師著作有88.1%以中文發表，僅12%以英文發表，有關單位應鼓勵教師們多以英文寫作，並發表在國際刊物中，以提昇圖書館界在國際上的地位與形象。

　　7. 增加"圖書館法規與標準"及"出版事業"課程

　　目前，法規和標準在社會中日趨重要，但公民對法規和標準方面認識較差，對各專業之相關法規及標準更是貧乏，圖書館界亦不例外。本研究發現，圖書館界對相關法規與標準的認識甚為缺乏，建議圖書館系所設法開授這方面的課程。臺灣出版事業雖然很發達，但其作業方式及程序似乎各自為政，致使並未有完整的臺灣出版品目錄，如美國Bowker公司之 Book-sin-Print（BIP）目錄，無法一窺其全貌，更遑論書目控制。故圖書館學系所亦應設立"出版事業"課程。訓練教育學生正確出版程序與技術，以增進臺灣出版事業之正規化、系統化。

註　　釋

① 唐秀珠，"以書目計量學方法探討專題選粹服務的發展"，（"國立臺灣"大學圖書館學研究所，碩士論文，1985年5月）。

② I. A. Al-Sabbagh, "The Evaluation of the Interdisciplinarity of Information Science: A Bibliometric Study." UMI, 1990.

③ L. Egghe, and Rousseau R., "Introduction to Informetrics: Quantitative Methods in Library Documentaion and Information Science." (Elexevier, 1990.)

④ 圖書館學文獻目錄（臺北市："國立中央圖書館"，1986年），頁3—4。

⑤ 中華民國圖書館年鑑（臺北市："國立中央圖書館"，1981年），頁284—285。

⑥ Bluma C. Perite, "Citation Characteristics in Library Science Research: Some Further Results from a Bibliometric Survey," *Library Research 3* (1981): 48.

⑦ 林清山，心理與教育統計學（臺北：東華，1986年），頁16—19。

⑧ 同上註，頁244—268。

⑨ Bluma C. Peritz, "Citation Characteristics in Library Science Research: Some Further Results from a Bibliometric Survey," *Library Research* 3 (1981), pp. 47 – 65.

⑩ M. M. Nour, and B. C. Pertiz, "A Quantitative Analysis of the Research Articles Published in Core Library Journals of 1980," *Library and Information Science Research* 7 (July-Sept., 1985), pp. 261 – 273.

⑪ Bernd Frohmann, "A Bibliometric Analysis of the Literature of Cataloguing and

Classification," *Library Research* 4 (4) (1982), pp. 355-373.

⑫ Gloria S. Cline, "College & Research Libraries: Its First Forty years," *College and Research Libraries* 43 (1982), pp. 208-232.

⑬ A. M. Schrader, "The First Fine Years of PLQ, 1979-1984: A Bibliometric Analysis," *Public Library Quarterly* 9 (2) (1989), pp. 3-23.

⑭ Frohmann, op. cit., pp. 355-373.

⑮ T. LaBorie, and M. Halperin, "Citation Patterns in Library Science Dissertation," *Journal of Education for Librarianship* 16 (Spring, 1976), pp. 271-283.

參考書目

一、圖書

中文部份

圖書館年鑑。臺北市:"國立中央圖書館",1981年。

圖書館學文獻目錄。臺北市:"國立中央圖書館",1986年。

西文部份

Al-Sabbagn, I. A. *The Evoluation of the Interdisciplinarity of Information Science: A Bibliometric study.* UMI, 1987.

Apted, Sheila. *The University Library User and His Information Needs*, M. A. Thesis. London: University of London, 1970.

Cannon, P. A. *Interdisciplinary Citation Practices of Library Education Faculty.* UMI, 1988.

Egghe, L. and Rousseau R. eds. *Informetrics 87/88.* Amsterdam: Elsevier Science Publishes, 1988.

Park, Betsy. *Information Needs; Implications for the Academic Library.* Bethesda, M. D.: ERIC Document Reproduction Service, ED 288526, 1986.

Thompson, C. E. *Hard Science or Soft Science: A Bibliometric Analysis of Selected Library Science/Information Science Journals.* UMI, 1989.

二、期刊論文

中文部份

王振鵠、王錫璋:"二十五年來的圖書館事業"。"中國圖書館學會"會報43期 (1988年12月),頁3—15。

胡述兆。"圖書館學的界說"。"中國圖書館學會"會報41期 (1987年12月),頁47—64。

唐秀珠。"以書目計量學方法探討專題選粹服務的發展"。"國立臺灣"大學圖書館學研究所,碩士論文,1988年7月。

顧敏。"圖書館自動化有關文獻的剖析"。現代圖書館學探討,頁269—276。臺北:學生書局,1988年。

西文部份

Atkins, S. E. "Subject Trends in Library and Information Science Research, 1975-1984."

Library Trends 36 (Spring, 1988): 633 – 658.

Auld, L. W. S. "Library Trends Past and Present: A Descriptive Study." *Library Trends* 36 (Spring, 1988): 853 – 868.

Bloomfield. M. "The Writing Habits of Librarians." *College and Research Libraries* 27 (March, 1966): 109 – 119.

David, H. G., L. Piip; and A. R. Haly. "The Examination of Research Trends by Analysis of Publication Numbers." *Journal of Information Science 3* (1981): 283 – 288.

Frohmann, Bernd "A Bibliometric Analysis of Literature of cataloguing and Classification." *Library Research 4* (4) (1982): 355 – 373.

Kobayashi, Michiko. "User Needs and Library Services." *Library and Information Science* 20 (1982): 1 – 25.

Laborie, T. and M. Halperin. "Citation Patterns in Library Science Dissertation." *Journal of Education for Librarianship* 16 (Spring, 1976): 271 – 283.

Nour, Martyvonne M. and B. C. Pertiz. "A Quantitative Analysis of the Research Articles Published in Core Library Journals of 1980." *Library and Information Science Research* 7 (July, 1985): 261 – 273.

Peritz, Bluma C. "The Methods of Library Science Research: Some Results from a Bibliometric Survey." *Library Research* 2 (Fall, 1980): 251 – 268.

Wilson, Kathryn B. and J. D. Eustis. "The Impact of User Frustration on Humanities Research." *College and Research Libraries* 42 (July, 1981): 361 – 365.

我對改進圖書資訊學教育的淺見[*]

正規圖書館學教育自 1920 年創始以來已走過 70 多年的歷程。爲迎接 21 世紀即將來臨的今日，圖書資訊教育工作者應積極考量如何因應社會的變遷及資訊科技之衝擊所帶來之多樣化資訊需求，必須研究並擴大更新圖書資訊教育的目標及內容。以下就改進臺灣圖書資訊教育提出一些淺見。

一、課程方面

課程是教育的目標、教學計劃之具體化，而課程內容則應配合時代需要，以"動態"的課程形式，不斷的、定時的予以評估及修訂，同時設計適時的新課程。

1. 課程教材內容之設計：①設置基礎課程及多元化、多層次、多形式之課程內容。②整合圖書館學與資訊科學。③兼顧理論與實務。④加強並增多資訊科學與技術課程。⑤重視學科背景、管理、語文、溝通能力之培育。⑥配合圖書館與資訊中心作業及服務之需求。⑦體察社會環境轉變之資訊需求及導向。⑧強調增加資訊心理學、系統論、控制論及資訊理論等課程。⑨培育理想之圖書資訊專業人員。⑩設計圖書資訊課程之內容應具備國際觀、世界觀之視野觀點。

2. 實習課程之完整規劃：①充實實習課程之內容，並謀求改進，以配合印證圖書資訊之理論。②與各類圖書館、資訊單位聯繫，設置有實質意義的實習項目。③自建"實習圖書館"，使學生能體驗理論與實務並重之意義。④以個案研究（Case Study）形式做爲實習工作之項目，使學生對圖書館問題能有較深入的瞭解，培育其解決圖書館工作困難之能力。

3. 全民圖書資訊素養之培育：全面徹底研究，在資訊社會中一般民眾所需具備的圖書資訊知識，然後將圖書資訊課程按步就班、循序漸進，分層安排於小學、國中、高中及大學課程中。將圖書資訊教育發展成全民圖書資訊教育體系，以提昇全民對圖書資訊之素養及認知。同時建議行政教育制度予以配合實施，並擬定提昇全民圖書資訊素養之整體資訊服務政策。

4. 圖書館員在職教育之規劃：針對各類型、各層次的圖書館員作全面性的研究規劃——持續而健全的圖書館員在職教育計劃，擬請行政教育單位提供經費支援，並委託圖書館學會、圖書館學系所、專業機構分擔圖書館員之相關在職教育訓練事宜。

二、師資方面

教師是教育活動的組織者及主導者。教師的學養及態度更是直接決定教育內容及教學方法，更重要的是影響學生的成長及發展之關鍵因素，師資素質的重要性可想而知。師資的培養可由幾方面着手：

（1）鼓勵教師、學生赴海內外圖書資訊學相關研究所進修或攻讀學位。

（2）政府有計劃保送教師、學生赴海內外圖書資訊學研究所進修或攻讀學位。

---

* 本文曾發表在《上海高校圖書情報學》1994 年第 1 期，第 7 頁。

(3) 教師亦應不斷自我吸收新知，充實精進技術，以完成自我教育，方能開出新穎而適時的現代化課程。

三、海峽兩岸圖書資訊教育之交流

瞭解海峽兩岸圖書資訊教育之現況，並進一步求同存異，以尋求雙方圖書資訊教育之合作途徑。

美國書目計量學博士論文評析*

[摘要 Abstract]

  美國圖書館與資訊科學的博士論文中,以書目計量學為主題者約佔百分之五。本文以 UMI 博士論文資料庫所檢索到的 73 筆美國圖書館與資訊科學研究所書目計量學博士論文摘要為研究對象,評析論文的主題傾向、研究方法、出版年代、發表學校,及其影響與貢獻。涵蓋範圍自 1970 年起,至 1992 年 6 月止。其中以引用文獻分析的論文篇數最多(56.16%),1984 年和 1985 年達到論文量之高峯,而篇數最多的學校依次為 Case Western Reserve、Illinois,與 IRutgers 三所大學。這些論文大抵在驗證書目計量學的法則,未能提出新的定律。

一、問題陳述

  自從 Alan Pritchard 於 1969 年首創"書目計量學(Bibliometrics)"一詞(註1),至今已有二十多年的歷史。書目計量學是利用數學、邏輯和統計的方法,對各類型文獻做量的分析,以瞭解某知識領域的歷史發展,及其作者、出版和使用的情況。它是一種研究方法,也是一個具有理論的新興學門。其重要研究內容包括 Bradford、Lotka 與 Zipf 三大定律,引用文獻分析(Citation Analysis)、文獻退化(Obsolescence)、數學模式(Mathematical Models),以及科學家之間的溝通(Scientific Communication)等,引起圖書館學家、資訊科學家、數學家、統計學家和電腦專家很大的興趣。圖書館學一向被批評為偏重實際問題的解決,缺少理論的基礎。Charles Busha 批評圖書館學研究者在使用實驗方法及量化研究方面,遠落後於行為科學家、物理學家及社會學家(註2)。自從資訊科學整合到圖書館學後,愈來愈多研究採用所謂硬科學的研究方法,而書目計量學是資訊科學的一門學科,具有許多定律和數學模式,將整個學科領域以量化及科學化的風貌呈現,為圖書館學和資訊科學建立起研究的另一典範。

  根據 1990 年一項調查,在圖書館與資訊科學之論文中,以歷史法和調查法為研究方法者最多,使用書目計量法者僅佔 4.2%,最盛時期係 1980 年,達到 11%(註:3)。雖然運用書目計量學的技術來從事圖書館學與資訊科學的研究有許多問題,但它仍不失為一種客觀量化的研究工具。利用書目計量的方法探討一學科領域的發展及其文獻的特性,目前已運用得相當普遍,但何光國教授指出"從已發表的有關文獻計量學的論著中,不僅看不出它們的研究成果,也無法窺探這門學科今後發展的動向。主要的原因是現有論著中,還未見有對文獻計量學論著本身作解剖性的計量研究和分析。"(註4)學科領域的自我分析是深入瞭解一學科領域的重要方法,藉由學科領域的自我分析,可使研究者瞭解該領域的研究特性,觀察其由過去至現在的演進,並判斷需進一步研究的主題及可研究的方法與技術,以預測該領域未來的發展方向。何光國教授之"文獻計量學

---

* 本文與傅雅秀合作撰寫,曾發表在《"中國圖書館學會"會報》51 期(1993),第 7 頁。

論著樣本之計量分析"一文,以期刊為主佔90.9%,其餘9.1%為會議紀錄、專題報告和學位論文等(註5)。博士學位論文是學術期刊論文以外最重要的文獻,它代表了一學門的研究趨勢,由UMI博士論文摘要資料庫所檢索到的1970年以來美國圖書館學會(American Library Association, ALA)立案之美國圖書館與資訊科學研究所的書目計量學博士論文計有七十三篇。雖然過去有許多分析圖書館學博士論文之研究,但至目前為止,尚未有針對書目計量學博士論文作質與量的探討者,留下一知識累積的縫隙。

二、文獻分析

書目計量學的文獻很多,Pritchard收集1874年至1959年有關書目計量法之書目,共有700款目。1965年以後,書目計量之文獻大增,Hjerppe所編的1960至1980二十年間之書目共列出2,032條款目(註6)。

Khurshid和Sahai參考 *Statistical Theory and Methods Abstracts*、*Current Index to Statistics* 以及 *Library and Information Science Abstracts*,亦整理出最新書目(註7)。

在1977年之資訊科學與技術年度評論(*Annual Review of Information Science and Technology*)一書中,Narin和Moll對書目計量學做概括性介紹,是當時一篇較完整的書目性評論論文(註8)。White和McCain又於1989年之資訊科學與技術年度評論中,繼續介紹有關最新書目計量學文獻(註9)。以下為歷年來較重要之書目計量學論文。

(一)海外文獻

根據Broadus在 *Journal of American Society for Information Science* 的一篇文章中指出,書目計量學的方法始自亞歷山大圖書館之館藏計算(註10),而在書目計量法被引進科學領域以前,早已在法律學科中被應用。由於美國不成文法系規定,法官必須根據判例來定罪,因此早在1743年即有引用判例之索引表。之後,Shepard於1873年將伊利諾州最高法院判例之引用文獻印成法律引用文獻索引,即 *Shepard's Citation* (註11)。

1917年,Cole和Eales收集自1543年至1860年之比較解剖學文獻,依年代及國別來統計該主題出版文獻之分佈情形,發表了第一篇書目計量學的文章(註12)。

1923年,英國專利局前任圖書館館長Hulme分析1901年至1913年 *International Catalog of Scientific Literature* 中著者與期刊款目,於劍橋大學兩次演講中,首次用統計書目學(Statistical Bibliography)這個名詞來表示以計算文獻說明科技進展的研究方法,這是書目計量學(Bbliometrics)一詞的前身(註13)。

化學家Lotka於1926年發表"The Frequency Distribution of Scientific Productivity",一文,將1907年至1916年刊於 *Chemical Abstracts* 之1,891名作者以及刊於 *Auerbach's Geschichtstafelnder Physik* 之1,325名作者,以最小平方差值的方法研究作者與發表論文篇數的關係,發現發表n篇論文的作者總數是僅發表一篇論文的作者總數之 $1/n^2$。此理論稱為Lotka's Law,又稱為倒數平方定律(Inverse Square Law)(註14)。

1927年,Gross首先將引用文獻分析(Citation Analysis)應用到圖書館學,依據期刊論文被引用的次數多寡來鑑定期刊的價值,計算 *Journal of the American Chemical Society* 之引用文獻,將化學期刊依引用次數來排名(註15)。

1934年,英國圖書館員Bradford提出期刊眾多導致論文分散的概念,但是直到1948年出版 *Documentation* 一書時,其分散定律(Law of Scattering)才廣被注意,為日後書目計量學之研究提供了理論的架構。該定律之解釋是：以某學科在各種期刊所含相關論文篇數的多寡，依遞減次序排列，則這些期刊將可分爲一個核心區（第一區）及連接的數區，若每一區包含大約相同篇數的論文，則各區期刊種數的比例將呈現 $1: n: n^2$ 的關係，n 是 Bradford 的乘數 （multiplier），大約爲 5 或 6（註 16）。

　　哈佛大學德文教授 Zipf 在其 1949 年出版的 *Human Behavior and the Principle of Least Effort* 一書中介紹了一個法則，稱爲 Zipf's Law。此定律是說，一般人比較容易選擇並使用熟悉的字，因此熟悉的字之出現機率較高。因此 Zipf 比較希臘史詩 Ulysses 中出現的 29,899 個字，依其出現的次數排名，得到一結論：假如一篇文章中所出現的字，依照其出現的次數排名，則排名第 n 個字的出現頻率爲 k/n 次，k 是常數（註 17）。

　　1949 年，Fussler 研究美國化學家與物理學家之研究文獻的特徵，首次利用期刊之參考文獻來發展出一學科的核心期刊（註 18）。

　　1955 年，Garfield 首度使用被引用之"影響係數（Impact Factor）"這個名詞，並將 Shepard 之引用文獻原則應用到醫學文獻之索引技術上，將之發揚光大，於 1963 年創製 *Science Citation Index*，成爲書目計量法之基石（註 19）。

　　半衰期（Half Life）這個物理及核能工程師最熟悉的名詞，原來是用來描述輻射物質之退化，但 1960 年則被 Burton 和 Kebler 用來形容文獻之老化（註 20）。

　　1961 年，de Solla Price 提出 Price's Law，該定律認爲一半的科學論文篇數係由該主題所有著作人數之平方根所發表，並認爲書目計量分配特徵有成功培育成功（Success Breeds Success）之現象。Price 的著作中，*Science Since Babylon* 和 *Little Science, Big Science*：本書對書目計量法有很大的影響（註 21）。

　　1963 年，Kessler 首度介紹書目連結（Bibliographic Coupling）之概念，若二個文獻之參考書目中，列有一個或一個以上相同的參考文獻，則此二個文獻就是書目連結之關係。由共同參考文獻之多寡，可決定這二個文獻之相關程度（註 22）。

　　1964 年，Goffman 和 Newill 將醫學方面傳染的理論（Epidemic Theory）應用到資訊傳播和文獻成長方面（註 23）。在傳染病流行理論中，感染就是相似的結果，而資訊的傳播，即因思想相似所引起的共鳴。

　　由於統計書目學（Statistical Bibliography）極易和統計學之書目（Bibliography on Statistics）混淆，因此，1969 年 Pritchard 將之改名爲 Bibliometrics，首創書目計量學一詞（註 24）。

　　1973 年，Small 介紹了共同引用（Cocitation）之觀念，係指二個文獻被後來出版的文獻共同引用，由共同被引用次數的多寡，可決定這二個文獻之相關程度（註 25）。由引用、共同引用，以及書目連結，可以瞭解科學溝通（Scientific Communication）的情形。

　　自 1973 年後，似乎再無新的基礎理論出現，以後發表之論著多著重在假說、定律和技術之修改、擴展與應用而已，書目計量學主題的發展產生了停頓的現象。

　　幾乎所有書目計量學的數學模式，均是有關變數之間的關係，以簡單的函數型式呈現。1981 年，Hubert 在 Library Trends 中，對書目評量學的模式有詳盡的介紹（註 26）。

　　Brookes 認爲我們主要之興趣在於評量使用圖書和期刊之資訊過程，科技已使知識以非文獻的型式呈現，我們的評量亦應順應潮流。因此，他於 1988 年建議以 Informetrics

這個字取代 Bibliometrics（註27）。

二、臺灣文獻

在臺灣，有關書目計量學的文章屈指可數，除了蔡明月、施孟雅、劉瑞蘭之三篇文章曾介紹書目計量學這個方法以外（註28—30），其餘均是應用書目計量法來做研究。藍乾章先生是最早對圖書館學研究文獻進行有系統、大規模分析的學者，他將臺灣圖書館學研究的發展分成五個階段，分別探討每一階段的文獻出版數量及研究主題（註31）。鄭恒雄先生繼續探討1979年至1987年6月間，臺灣圖書館學研究的發展情況（註32）。徐小鳳女士蒐集1917年至1985年有關圖書館分類的文獻加以分析，以探討民國成立以來圖書分類的發展（註33）。吳明德教授分析公立大學研究生博碩士論文之引用文獻，以瞭解"國立大學"圖書館支援研究所學術研究的情形（註34）。顧敏先生曾針對圖書館自動化的文獻進行書目的剖析（註35）。筆者亦曾利用科學引用文獻索引（*Science Citation Index*）之期刊引用文獻報導（*Journal Citation Reports*）中的引用文獻分析資料，評估十七種海洋學的核心期刊（註36）。而最新的二篇研究性文章則是何光國教授對書目計量學西文期刊文章之解剖性的定量分析（註37），與李德竹教授對圖書館學教師研究趨勢及資訊需求之調查研究（註38）。"國立臺灣大學"圖書館學研究所亦不乏以書目計量法為研究方法之碩士論文，例如王梅玲應用 Bradford's Law 來研究臺大工學院聯合圖書室期刊使用情形（註39）；郭堯斌探討摩斯—馬可夫模式應用於臺大圖書館學系實習圖書室的有效程度，並預測系館的流通狀況（註40）；唐秀珠利用索引來探討專題選粹服務文獻的發展（註41）；施孟雅從專業期刊文獻分析中國臺灣地區之近十年來的圖書館學研究等（註42）。此外，在最近一次研討會中，中國大陸武漢大學圖書情報學院彭斐章教授亦提出了以現代書目計量學來詮釋中國目錄學的新見解（註43）。

三、研究目的、範圍與方法

本文試以美國二十多年來的書目計量學博士論文為研究對象，擬以內容分析法從質與量兩方面具體探討它們的主題傾向、研究方法、出版年代分佈、發表之學校，以及對書目計量學與圖書館學之影響與貢獻。

然因論文取得不易，本研究只限於由博士論文光碟（Dissertation Abstracts on Disc，簡稱DAO）所檢索到之 ALA 立案之美國圖書館與資訊科學研究所書目計量學博士論文摘要，計有73筆。"書目計量學"一詞始於1969年，因此本研究涵蓋範圍自1970年起，至1992年6月止。由於 UMI 光碟資料庫中1980年以前之博士論文未收錄摘要，故此期間之相關論文只能從書目紀錄去研判。

四、結果與討論

經分析73筆美國書目計量學博士論文摘要，結果顯示如下：

（一）主題傾向

書目計量學的重要研究範圍包括 Bradford、Lotka 與 Zipf 三大定律、引用分析（Citation Analysis）、文獻退化（Obsolescence）、數學模式（Mathematical Models），以及科學家之間的溝通（Scientific Communication）等，茲將73筆資料粗分如表一。

表一　書目計量學博士論文出版時期與主題傾向

	書目計量	引文分析	文獻成長	文獻老化	希萊德福律	齊夫普律	數學模式	科學溝通	合計	%
1970									0	0
1971									0	0
1972	2								2	2.74
1973									0	0
1974		1			1	1			3	4.11
1975	1	1							2	2.74
1976	1								1	1.37
1977	1								1	1.37
1978	1								1	1.37
1979	1	2							3	4.11
1980		1			1	1			3	4.11
1981	1	3		1	1		1		7	9.59
1982	1			1					2	2.74
1983	1	5				1			7	9.59
1984	1	2		1	2			2	8	10.96
1985	2	5		1					8	10.96
1986		5						1	6	8.22
1987		4		1					5	6.85
1988		4	1						5	6.85
1989		3							3	4.11
1990		2						1	3	4.11
1991		3							3	4.11
1992									0	0
合計	13	41	1	5	5	3	1	4	73	100.00
%	17.81	56.16	1.37	6.85	6.85	4.11	1.37	5.48	100.00	

"書目計量"類除了指書目（Bibliography）計算外，由於一筆資料只能置一處，只好將包含多種書目計量法之論文歸此總類。Cronin 曾說："Citations are frozen footprints on the landscape of scholarly achievement."（註 44），從引用文獻可看出資料被利用的情況，73 篇論文中超過一半的篇數以引用文獻分析的方法來研究各學科的引用文獻。原因之一大概是有美國科學資訊研究所（Institute for Scientific Information）提供現成的資料來源，即科學引用文獻索引（*Science Citation Index*）、社會科學引用文獻索引（*Social Sciences Citation Index*）與期刊引用文獻報導（*Journal Citation Reports*）；原因之二是因所

用的數學與統計較易，較能被圖書館學的研究者接受及運用。文獻成長與老化的研究在 1981 年至 1987 年間呈持續性、穩定的情況。研究 Bradford's Law 和 Zipf's Law 者，均只是驗證了其文獻分佈，極少能提出新的修正定律。至於純屬數學模式之論文雖只有一篇，但是用到數學模式的論文卻有 6 篇之多，表示圖書館學研究所不乏具有數理背景的學生。此外，研究合著者（Co-author）及科學家之間正式與非正式的溝通的論文有 4 篇。

上述各類論文中，一篇曾提及 Lotka's Law，二篇提到資訊傳染理論，二篇曾驗證了 Price's Index，另有二篇述及科學政策的問題。

書目計量學研究的資料來源為書目資料，不必依賴研究對象的合作。此 73 篇論文所採用的書目資料之學科範圍有音樂、藝術、宗教、文學、人類學、教育、會計、社會學、圖書館學、資訊科學、電子計算機、物理、農業、化學、生物及工程等，涵蓋了人文學、社會科學與自然應用科學。其中有少數非美國籍的學生，以自己國家的某一學科文獻為研究對象。美國書目計量學博士論文有此學科整合的現象，原因應歸諸於美國圖書館學研究所的學生具有不同的大學學科背景，不若臺灣圖書館學研究較自限於圖書館學範圍內。

（二）研究方法

73 篇論文中，除了採用書目計量法以外，亦有各種描述、推論統計以及數學模式，計有卡方（Chi Square）、相關（Correlation）、回歸分析（Regression）、各種檢驗方法（F Test、T Test、Kolmogorov-Smirnov Test、Goodness of Fit Test）、Brilloouin Information；Measure、Leavitt's Centrality Index、Goffman's Digraph Measure、Markov Chain Model、Nicholas Mullin's Model 以及 Dalziel、Kendall-Yule Models。此外尚有 Kernel Graph Theory、Discipline Information Score，與 Murugesan & Moravcsik Reference Typology 等技術。由於未能閱讀論文本身，無法研判所用之統計技術是否適當。

由於書目計量學是一種量的研究方法，缺乏對質的方面的探討，為其最大的缺陷，以致未能深入瞭解研究主題的內容。且由樣本推論全體，含有一種不確定性（Uncertainty），容易導致錯誤的結論，因此曾有人批評書目計量法只是一種數字的魔術遊戲。為了彌補量的研究方法之缺失，佐以質的研究方法，例如觀察法、訪問法與內容分析法等，亦可能是一可行之道（註 45）。例如 73 篇論文中有四篇論文將質與量的方法並用，有一篇論文以引用文獻分析列出期刊排名清單後，再用訪問法去調查同行專家之意見（Peer Review），再作圖書館使用調查，三者加以比較，可以驗證書目計量法之有效度。又一篇論文則將引用文獻和文章內容對照分析，發現有些因錯誤而回收之文章卻仍被正面地引用，引用者顯然未覺察文章已被宣佈收回，無效的資訊仍經由引用文獻深入在以後的文章中。雖然量的研究較為科學，資料客觀可靠，引用文獻是圖書館使用者真正發表研究結果之明鏡，也是真正使用圖書館之證明，但是引用文獻的問題很多（註 46），不可不小心。。

73 篇論文所分析的資料以期刊為最多。其他則取材自圖書、專刊，博碩士論文、技術報告、摘要，甚至 OCLC 的資料庫。以正確完整的研究而言，書目計量研究應以能代表研究主題之書目為依據，而不是只選一些期刊。但由於書目資料之收集極費功夫，使得許多篇論文只限制於少數幾種期刊之少數幾期，影響研究的完整性和代表性。例如，一種美國資訊科學學會的期刊 *Journal of the American Society for Information Science* (*JASIS*) 就被用來作為分析資訊科學發展的樣本，是不具代表性的，而另一種美國兒童期刊 *Horn Book* 和 *JASIS* 二種性質不同的期刊更是不可拿來相比，作為軟科學與硬科學之區分。

(三) 出版年代

由表一可見書目計量學博士論文在開始的前十年數量不多，1980年代開始發展，1984年和1985年達到論文量之高峯。1986年由於出版最多書目計量學博士論文之Case Western Reserve University 宣佈關閉圖書館研究所（註47），此後書目計量學之研究便開始走下坡。

最近三年來，書目計量學方面之論文篇數極少，未知係因DAO書目資料庫收錄論文較慢，抑或書目計量學走入死胡同（Dead End）之故，不得而知。若係後者，則希望只是一知識暫留的現象，注後仍會有所突破。根據何光國教授的研究，書目計量學之期刊文章生產量曾於1990年達到最高峯（註48），應可樂觀地認定書目計量學是一成長的資訊科學學科才是。

由於DAO書目資料庫之不完整，以及檢索策略的限制，使得樣本數太小，由表一很難看出各主題知識發展的趨勢。

(四) 所屬學校

生產書目計量學博士論文最多的學校係Case Western Reserve University，在1986年關門之前二、三年，每年有三、四篇書目計量學博士論文，不可謂不多，似可研判必有書目計量學大師當指導教授，且開設有這方面課程。其次為University of Illinois at Urbana-Champaign，而Rutgers, the State University of New Jersey則排名第三。Texas Woman's University近年來才急起直追，想必新聘有這方面的師資。至於其他設有博士班之ALA立案的圖書館學研究所，例如University of Michigan、University of California at Berkeley、Syracuse University以及University of Alabama等，何以未發表此類博士論文？究竟係因缺乏師資？抑或認為不重要？值得另文作進一步的研究。詳見表二。

經向設有博士班之美國ALA立案之圖書館與資訊科學研究所索取1992年至1993年之研究所簡介，發現目前只有下列三所學校（表三）開設書目計量學課程。

表二　書目計量學博士論文出版學校

校　　名	篇數	出　版　年
1. Case Western Reserve U.	22	72（2）*、74、75、76、77、79、81（2）、82、844（3）、85（4）、86（4）、87
2. U. of Ill. at Urbana-Champaign	10	81、84（3）、85（2）、87（2）、89、90
3. Rutgers	8	79、80、83（2）、86、87、88（2）
4. Drexel U.	5	78、82、84（2）、85
5. Texas Woman's U.	4	88、89、90、91
6. U. of Southern Calif.	4	79、83（3）
7. U. of Wisconsin-Madison	4	74、81、86、90
8. Indiana U.	4	81、83（2）、88
9. Florida State U.	3	74、80、87
10. U. of Pittsburgh	3	75、80、81
11. Columbia U.	1	81
12. U. of North Texas	1	89
13. U. of North Carolina	1	85
14. U. of Calif., LA	1	88
15. Simmons College	1	91
16. U. of Maryland	1	91

＊註：括號內之數字係指篇數。

表三　開設書目計量學課程之學校

校　　名	課程名稱
Univ. of Illinois	Bibliometrics
Rutgers	Bibliometrics & Information Structure
UCLA	Scholarly Communication & Bibliometrics

(五) 影響與貢獻

　　73篇論文中有研究科學史者，亦有研究科學社會學者，包括用引用文獻來評估個人著作的品質，找出尖端研究者（Research Front），以及由作者人數來調查科學溝通，研究的合作性，以利大型研究計劃之進行。有二篇論文並由瞭解某一學科之發展和文獻形態來建議科技政策之訂定，作爲研究獎助評審依據之一。

　　書目計量學博士論文也許可在學術的科學與社會學裡找到地位，但只有6篇實際應用到圖書館選擇核心期刊與文獻老化之淘汰，很少探究真正應用書目計量的方法之問題，大部份只是統計，而未把定律變成實用的館藏管理工具。只能驗證統計的模式，未見有新的定律出現。也許館藏管理技術本就以經驗為依據，這些應用在圖書館學的論文大都缺乏理論的背景。雖然未能提出一套可實際應用的公式，但是由多篇引用，共同引用，及共同作者之研究，應可用來設計自動化索引，可以檢索到更多相關的文獻。根據字的出現頻率，亦可設計資訊系統之檢索用字。例如，有一篇論文就是由書目連結和共同的索引詞來研究文獻之聚集。總之，只要能填補一點知識的空隙，這些論文就可説是有所貢獻。

五、結語

今日的圖書館管理，就像商業和服務業，需要客觀的資料來做管理決策之依據，而書目計量學可謂圖書館中最具理論基礎的研究方法之一。書目計量學的發展，可說是文獻遽增的結果。瞭解某一學科發展與各作者發表論著的情況，有助於圖書館之管理與利用。但是圖書館學有人為因素之複雜性，因此定量化的進行常遇障礙，無法與經濟計量（Econometrics）、生物計量（Biometrics）以及科學計量（Scientometrics）相類比（註49）。近年來，由於線上資料庫增加，書目計量之研究比較方便。未來，書目計量學有使用更多數學模式與電腦資料庫之趨勢。美國圖書館與資訊科學研究所提出73篇書目計量學博士論文，數量不多，其中以引用文獻分析的論文篇數最多，佔56.16%，而以1984年和1985年各發表8篇為最多。這些論文所採用的統計方法與數學模式雖多，但大抵在驗證書目計量學的法則，未能提出新的定律。發表書目計量學博士論文篇數最多的學校依次為 Case Western Reserve、Illinois 與 Rutgers 三所大學。目前開設書目計量學課程的 ALA 立案之美國圖書館與資訊科學研究所只有 Illinois、Rutgers 與 UCLA 三所。至於島內，則因缺少這方面的師資，過去僅於研究方法與資訊學兩門課程中論及書目計量法，唯有"國立臺灣大學"圖書館研究所於1992學年度第二學期聘請客座教授何光國教授講解書目計量學，使島內學子獲益良多。吾人應繼續開發此領域，試以質的方法彌補量的方法之不足，期能提出新見解。

附 註

註 1：Alan Pritchard, "Statistical Bibliography or Bibliometrics?", *Journal of Documentation* 2525 (Dec., 1969): pp. 348–349.

註 2：Charles H. Busha, "Library Science Research: the Path to Progress," in *A Library Science Research Reader and Bibliographic Guide*, ed. Charles H. Busha (Littleton, Colo: Libraries Unlimited, 1981), p. 12.

註 3：K. Jarvelin and P. Vakkari, "Content Analysis of Research Articles," in *Library and Information Science Research*, 12 (Oct.–Dec., 1990): p. 409.

註 4：何光國. 文獻計量學論著樣本之計量分析. 圖書館學與資訊科學，18卷1期（1992年4月），頁51。

註 5：同上註，頁60。

註 6：R. Hjerppe, *A Bibliography of Bibliometrics and Citation Indexing and Analysis*

(Stockhom, Sweden: Royal Institute of Technology Library, 1980), p. 163

註 7: A. Khurshid and H. Sahai, "Bibliometric, Scientometric and Informetric Distributions and Laws: A Selected Bibliography," *International Forum on Information and Documentation* 16 (April, 1991): pp. 18 – 29.

註 8: F. Narin and J. K. Moll, "Bibliometrics," in *Annual Review of Information Science and Technolgy*, ed. M. E. Williams (White Plains, N. Y.: Knowledge Industry Publications, 1977), v. 12, pp. 35 – 58.

註 9: H. D. White and K. W. McCain, "Bibliometrics," in *Annual Review of Information Science and Technology*. ed. M. E. Williams (Amsterdam: Elsevier, 1989): pp. 119 – 186.

註 10: Robert N. Broadus, "Early Approaches to Bibliometrics," *Journal of the American Society for Information Science 38* (March, 1987): pp. 127 – 129.

註 11: F. R. Shapiro, "Origins of Bibliometrics, Citation Indexing, and Citation Analysis; the Neglected Legal Literature," *Journal of the American Society for Information Science* 43 (June, 1992): pp. 337 – 339.

註 12: F. J. Cole and N. B. Eales, "The History of Comparative Anatomy. Pt. I. A Statistical Analysis of the Literature," *Science Progress* 11 (1917): pp. 578 – 596.

註 13: W. E. Hulme, *Statistical Bibliography in Relation to the Growth of Modern Civilization* (London: Grafton, 1923), p. 9.

註 14: W. G. Potter, "Lotka's Law Revisited," *Library Trends 30* (Summer 1981): p. 26.

註 15: P. L. K. Gross and E. M. Gross, "College Libraries and Chemical Education," *Science 66* (October, 1927): pp. 1229 – 1234.

註 16: S. C. Bradford, "Sources of Information on Specific Subjects," *Engineering 137* (January, 1934): pp. 85 – 86.

註 17: 施孟雅. 書目計量學──基本法則、擴展法則及應用. 美國資訊科學學會臺北學生分會會訊, 3 期（1990 年 6 月）, 頁 38。

註 18: H. H. Fussler, "Characteristics of the Research Literature Used by Chemists and Physicists in the United States," *Library Quarterly* 19 (January 1949): pp. 19 – 35.

註 19: R. Hjerppe, *An Outline of Bibliometrics and Citation Analysis* (Stockholm: Royal Institute of Technology, 1978), pp. 34 – 35.

註 20: R. E. Burton and R. W. Keble, "The Half-Life of Some Scientific and Technical Literature," *American Documentation* 11 (Jan. – Oct., 1960): p. 18.

註 21: Hjerppe, op. cit., p. 35.

註 22: M. M. Kessler, "Bibliographic Coupling Between Scientific Papers," *American Documentation 14* (January, 1964): pp. 10 – 25.

註 23: Allen Kent, ed. *Encyclopedia of Library and Information Science* (New York: Marcel Delker, 1987), v. 42, supp. 7, s. v. "Bibliometrics, History of the Development of Ideas in...", by D. H. Hertzel.

註 24: Pritchard, loc. cit.

註 25：H. G. Small, "Co-Citation in the Scientific Literature: a New Measure of the Relationship between Two Documents," *Journal of the American Society for Information Science 24* (July-August, 1973): pp. 265–269.

註 26：John J. Hubert, "General Bibliometric Models," *Library Trends 30* (Summer 1981): pp. 65–81.

註 27：B. C Brookes, "Biblio-, Sciento-, Informetrics?" "What Are We Talking About?" In *Informetrics 89/90*, ed. Leo Egghe and R. Rousseau (Amsterdam: Elsevier, 1990), p. 31.

註 28：蔡明月. 書目計量學. 教育資料與圖書館學, 24 期（1987 年 3 月）, 頁 261—269。

註 29：同註 13, 頁 31—51。

註 30：劉瑞蘭. 書目計量學及其在選採之應用. 書府, 5 期（1984 年 6 月）, 頁 79—84。

註 31：藍乾章. 圖書館學研究. "中華民國"圖書館年鑑（臺北市："國立中央圖書館", 1981 年）, 頁 263—285。

註 32：鄭恒雄. 圖書館學研究. "中華民國"圖書館年鑑・第二次（臺北市："國立中央圖書館", 1988 年）, 頁 67—80。

註 33：徐小鳳. 圖書分類研究文獻分析. "中國圖書館學會"會報, 39 期（1986 年 12 月）, 頁 107—117。

註 34：吳明德. 公立大學圖書館支援研究所學術研究之探討（"行政院國家科學委員會", 專題研究報告, 1987 年）。

註 35：顧敏. 圖書館自動化有關文獻的書目剖析. 現代圖書館學探討. 臺北市：臺灣學生, 1988 年, 頁 269—276。

註 36：傅雅秀. 以文獻引用分析評估海洋學期刊. 教育資料與圖書館學, 27 卷 3 期（1990 年）, 頁 311—322。

註 37：同註 4, 頁 48—82。

註 38：李德竹. 臺灣圖書館學教師研究趨勢及資訊需求之調查研究（"國立臺灣大學"圖書館學系暨研究所, "行政院國科會"專題研究計劃成果報告, 1992 年 7 月）, 頁 ix, 131。

註 39：王梅玲. "國立臺灣大學"工學院聯合國圖書室期刊使用研究（"國立臺灣大學"圖書館學研究所, 碩士論文, 1985 年 6 月）, 頁 143。

註 40：郭堯斌, 摩斯. 馬可夫模式的研究："國立臺灣大學"圖書館學系暨研究所實習圖書室流通之個案調查（"國立臺灣大學"圖書館學研究所, 碩士論文, 1986 年 6 月）, 頁 89。

註 41：唐秀珠. 以書目計量學方法探討專題選粹服務的發展（"國立臺灣大學"圖書館學研究所, 碩士論文, 1988 年 6 月）, 頁 107。

註 42：施孟雅. 從專業期刊文獻分析臺灣臺灣地區的圖書館學研究（"國立臺灣大學"圖書館學研究所, 碩士論文, 1992 年 6 月）, 頁 167。

註 43：彭斐章. 中國目錄學的今天和明天（"國立臺灣大學", 圖書館學與資訊科學教育研討會, 1993 年 2 月 28 日）, 頁 14。

註44：Blaise Cronin, "The Need for a Theory of Citing," *Journal of Documentation* 37 March, 1981）：p. 16.

註45：J. D. Glazier and R. R. Powell, *Qualitative Research in Information Management* (Englewood, Co.：Libraries Unlimited, 1992), p. 209.

註46：M. H. MacRoberts and B. R. MacRoberts, "Problems of Citation Analysis：A Critical Review," *Journal of American Society for Information Science 40*（September, 1989）：pp. 342 – 349.

註47：Richard Hyman, "Library Schools in Crisis：Stemming the Tide," *Wilson Library Bulletin 65*（January, 1991）：p. 49.

註48：同註4，頁70。

註49：王崇德. 情報科學原理臺北市：農業科學資料服務中心，1991年，頁128。

"中華圖書資訊學教育學會"*

"中華圖書資訊學教育學會"（英文名稱是"Chinese Association of Library & Information Science Education"，簡稱"CALISE"）於今年 5 月 30 日正式成立，現有團體會員 9 個和個人會員 88 人，該會仍在廣徵志同道合的伙伴，會員人數仍繼續成長中。

"中華圖書資訊學教育學會"發起是原由留美學人李志鍾教授於 1991 年在臺灣大學圖書館學系暨研究所客座時，有鑑於圖書資訊教育研究發展之重要性，望能成立專門學會加以推動、探討圖書館學與資訊科學教育之相關問題。並多次與圖書館界沈寶環教授、王振鵠教授、胡述兆教授和李德竹教授等開會商議交換意見，深獲圖書館學界之認同。此後李教授開始親自奔走邀請相關人士做該會發起人，同時由李教授初擬"中華圖書資訊學會章程草案"並至"內政部"蒐集有關申請成立民間團體之規定及程序。

由於圖書館界之熱烈響應，由來自全國 12 個縣市的 48 位圖書館界人士為本會發起人。後因李教授客座期滿返回美國，後續工作則交由"國立臺灣大學"圖書館學系李德竹所長辦理正式申請事宜，該會於 1991 年 9 月 7 日向"內政部"提出申請，同年 10 月 7 日獲內政部 8006465 號函通過，隨即於 12 月 7 日召開發起人會議，會中決定成立籌備會，並選出九位籌備委員進行學會成立大會之籌備工作。

大會籌備會委員有沈寶環教授、王振鵠教授、胡述兆教授、張鼎鍾教授、胡歐蘭教授、高錦雪教授、朱則剛教授、吳明德教授，並推選李德竹教授為籌備會主任委員，前後經過四次正式會議及多次會外諮商，同時亦時時得到"內政部社會司"王肇發視察及"中國圖書館學會"汪雁秋秘書長在各項法規事務方面的熱心協助下，就學會章程、徵收會員、準備成立大會及下年度工作計劃和歲入出預算表等，皆加以規劃擬訂。

成立大會在"國立臺灣大學"文學院會議室舉行，大會特別邀請臺大文學院黃啓方院長和"內政部"長官王視察肇發先生蒞臨指導，李志鍾教授亦特由海外趕來參加此盛會，當天參與成立大會之貴賓及會員約 80 人，場面熱鬧溫馨，會中選出理事九人，後補理事三人，監事三人，後補監事一人，並通過學會章程草案、下年度工作計劃、歲出入預算和追認籌備會間之開支費用等。

"中華圖書資訊學教育學會"成立之目的，在學會章程中第二條款有所說明，主要宗旨乃以研究、發揚、促進圖書資訊學教育為宗旨，具體的任務包括：
一、研究與推廣圖書資訊學教育。
二、研討圖書資訊學學制與課程。
三、促進圖書資訊學教育方法與經驗之交流。
四、推動學用合一，以及專才專用制度。
五、增進圖書資訊學教育之國際合作。
六、其他符合本會宗旨之事宜。
學會會員分三種：
一、個人會員（普通會員、永久會員及學生會員）

---

* 本文曾發表在《書府》13 期（1992 年 6 月），第 4—6 頁。

凡贊同本會宗旨、年滿二十歲、具有下列資格者，填具入會申請書，經理事會通過，並繳納會費後，爲個人會員。
（一）圖書資訊學教育人員
（二）對圖書資訊學及其相關學術有研究或有興趣者
（三）對圖書資訊學教育有貢獻者
（四）修習圖書資訊學及相關學科之在校學生。
二、團體會員
凡上列機構或團體，贊同本會宗旨，填具入會申請書，經理事會通過，並繳納會費後，爲團體會員，團體會員推派代表一人，以行使權利。
（一）圖書資訊學系所及研究機構
（二）圖書館及資訊單位
（三）文化機構及學術團體
三、贊助會員：熱心圖書資訊教育贊助本會活動之個人或團體。

學會成立後，於本年 6 月 11 日召開"中華圖書資訊學教育學會"第一次理監事會議，會中選出常務理事三人，常務監事一人，又在常務理事中選出學會理事長，選舉結果由"國立臺灣大學"圖書館學系暨研究所教授胡述兆博士爲第一任"中華圖書資訊學教育學會"理事長，沈寶環教授爲常務監事。會中籌備會將籌備會印章、檔案、財務及會員名冊移交理事長，決定會址設於臺灣大學圖書館學系，理事長提議先成立圖書資訊教育學術活動推展委員會和圖書資訊教育學術合作交流委員會，並委任賴鼎銘教授和薛理桂教授分別爲前列委員會主任委員，各委員會之組織章程由各委員會制訂，提下次會議討論。

圖書資訊教育應該是整個圖書館事業的火車頭，唯有方向正確，廣博精深的教育工作與學術研究，才能訓練出具有真才實學，實踐圖書資訊理念的專業人員，也才能落實各種圖書資訊的服務業務；可以説：若要健全圖書館事務，必先健全專業教育。目前又適逢科技日益精進，知識日益專深，資訊需求日益多元化的時代，如果吾人不能隨時調整自己的腳步，將很容易爲時代所淘汰，此時，"中華圖書資訊學教育學會"之成立正是時候，更敬佩的是能見圖書館人士踴躍加入，也正代表大家對圖書資訊學教育的研究發展之重視。希望將來大家能在各任的理事長領導下，捐棄門戶之見，開誠佈公的共同來解決我們這個學界首要的教育問題。

參考資料

1. "中華圖書資訊學教育學會"成立大會手冊. 該學會，1992 年 5 月.
2. "中華圖書資訊學教育學會"第一次理監事會議記錄，該學會，1992 年 6 月.
3. "內政部"編：申請組織全國性社會團體須知（臺北市："內政部"，1992 年）

圖書館自動化系統線上目錄及其顯示格式之研究[*]

［摘要 Abstract］

　　本研究乃針對目前臺灣現有 18 個圖書館自動化系統之線上公用目錄加以分析比較，以瞭解臺灣線上公用目錄之發展現況及讀者對線上公用目錄及其顯示格式的看法與評估建議，做為現有線上目錄改進之依據；並調查使用者之意見，作為設計圖書館自動化系統，特別是線上目錄之設計時的參考。

　　本研究方法採訪問觀察法和問卷調查法。調查結果顯示，臺灣所發展的線上公用目錄系統是以第二代線上公用目錄為主，即提供關鍵語、布林邏輯、切截、題名、著者、分類號與各種標準號碼等查詢功能，而且檢索項目亦較多，同時書目記錄可以不同的格式顯示或列印。大多數的系統均採用選項式（Menu driven）查詢；而系統畫面以欄位顯示格式為最，並不採用傳統的卡片格式；欄位的名稱及排列方式多由各系統自行設計訂定，並無標準模式或共通的原則。在使用者方面，多數使用者對系統的滿意程度多給予肯定的評價，但建議在"提供線上逐步使用指導"、"查知各種資料的館藏地"兩項應加以改善。使用者多以查詢特定的圖書或期刊，或者是某主題的期刊圖書為其主要之檢索目的；常用的檢索點為"部份書名"或"關鍵語"；但大多數使用者仍無法有效利用布林邏輯或切截查詢。以上所得的調查結果及使用者檢索行為值得圖書館界特別重視。

　　根據本研究結果，提出下列建議：一、系統設計應以使用者為主要考量，而非全以館內作業為導向；二、重視線上目錄顯示格式之美觀；三、改進並強化線上公用目錄之檢索方式與功能；四、圖書館應積極對讀者推廣線上目錄之功能及利用；五、加強中文輸入法之訓練；六、擴大線上目錄之範圍與內容，銜接其他各館內外之資料庫，以拓寬資源利用的層面。為配合臺灣圖書館資訊網路之建立，提出幾項進一步研究之建議：(1) 研究線上目錄格式統一化或標準化之可行性；(2) 研訂適用臺灣圖書資訊檢索之通用指令語言（Common Command Language）；(3) 繼續研究使用者利用線上目錄的情況，以瞭解其檢索行為，做為未來改進之參考。

壹、前　言

　　現代資訊社會中，以自動化方式處理業務已成為必然和必需的發展趨勢，圖書館業務自動化也不例外。歐美國家早在 1940 年代即已領先研究發展圖書館業務自動化系統；又在 1960 年代開始設計資訊網路，1974 年又啟用了線上目錄；自動化作業不僅提昇了圖書館工作效率、加強圖書館對讀者的服務，也使得資訊的傳播更為廣闊、迅速、正確。臺灣圖書館界於 1970 年代初期開始探討圖書館業務自動化之可行性，雖較歐美各國為遲，但興趣濃厚。經過多年之努力和近年來政府之大力推展及支持；雖進步遲緩，但

---

[*] 本文曾發表在《臺灣大學圖書館學刊》1991 年 11 月第 7 期，第 1—64 頁。

根據最近"教育部"之"整體規劃圖書館資訊網路系統研究小組"之調查，已有約 45 個大小各類型圖書館已初步完成整體或部份業務自動化設計工作，約 75 個圖書館正在進行中，其中已有值得贊賀之成果。（註 1）

早期的圖書館自動化作業是針對館員之需求而設計，其重點是解決圖書館內部作業自動化問題。至 70 年代中期才開始考慮讀者之需求，因而設計以"User-Friendly"為導向之線上公用目錄（Online Public Access Catalogs，簡稱 OPACs），其功能更是遠超傳統式目錄。"讀者至上"是圖書館奉為圭臬的座右銘，無論是人工或自動化作業時代，目標均一致。圖書館目錄不僅是開啟圖書館館藏資源之鑰，與讀者接觸的第一線；而圖書館線上公用目錄則更能提供讀者一個快速、便利的檢索工具。使用以來，根據美國 Salmon（註 2）、Matthews（註 3）等之全國調查，線上公用目錄廣受讀者的歡迎及喜愛是肯定的；因此，線上公用目錄之內容和顯示格式之設計更為重要。

島內對圖書館自動化問題的研究，大抵偏重於自動化硬體與軟體的選擇與設計、圖書館員與自動化之認識和態度，甚少探討線上公用目錄與其顯示格式。故作者決定在島內僅有部份自動化系統推出之時，儘速研究此問題，研究之結果將會對臺灣圖書館發展自動化系統之參考有所幫助；因此，本研究的重要性甚為明顯。

研究目的與範圍限制

本研究的目的是以整合性圖書館系統（Integrated Library Automation System）的觀點：

1. 探討臺灣地區 18 個單位之圖書館自動化系統之線上公用目錄及其顯示格式之設計及編排。
2. 瞭解 211 位讀者（館員及非館員）使用線上目錄之評估及意見。
3. 探討線上目錄檢索方式和指令、系統反應時速、顯示畫面種類及問題等。

研究方法與步驟

本研究採用訪問觀察和問卷調查法：

1. 訪問觀察並實際操作各系統以瞭解各線上目錄及其顯示格式之設計和內容是否好用、恰當，畫面是否美觀和容易被使用者接受等。
2. 以問卷調查各單位使用者對線上目錄及其格式之評估意見。實際操作線上目錄研究評估其①檢索步驟及檢索項目之繁簡；②系統反應時速；③檢索指令之種類；④線上畫面之種類；⑤顯示畫面格式之設計及編排；⑥顯示格式與傳統目錄格式之區別；⑦線上目錄與其他子系統間之相關性等。調查資料，用"統計分析系統"（Statistical Analysis System，簡稱 SAS）套裝軟體，進行統計分析工作。

相關名詞解釋

為便於研究和瞭解，特將本研究涉及重要名詞解釋如下：

1. 線上公用目錄（Online Public Access Catalogs，簡稱 OPACs）：線上公用目錄又稱線上目錄（Online Catalog），是一種圖書館資訊檢索系統，允許使用者以即時（Online real time）和交互（Interactive）方式查詢圖書館資料庫中之書目資料。
2. 目錄顯示格式（Catalog Display Formats）：顯示在螢幕上之各種書目格式，這些格式是由各系統自行設計，並無一定標準規格。

3. 顯示資料密度（Display Density）：螢幕上書目資料所佔之數元組（Character/Byte）與每一螢幕可顯示之總數元組數之比例，計算方式見下公式：

$$D = \frac{設定顯示之總數元組數（每行數元組（Byte）數 \times 行數）}{每一螢幕可顯示之總數元組數（每行總數元組 \times 總行數）}$$

4. 簡略格式（Brief display）：最簡單之書目顯示格式，島內用不同之名稱稱之，如簡目、簡明或部份資料格式等。

5. 基本資料格式（Medium display）：顯示任何書目記錄之基本資料，顯現格式較簡略格式為多，如增加館藏狀況或叢書項等。

6. 檢索款目（Access Point）：指標目、代碼等用以檢索書目記錄者。

研究架構及對象

本研究架構可分成三部份，第一部份是閱覽並分析海內外重要的文獻資料，以瞭解目前線上公用目錄的發展及使用情形。第二部份是問卷資料，根據本研究的目的，設計兩種問卷："線上公用目錄系統調查問卷"與"線上公用目錄使用者調查問卷"以蒐集所需之資料。第三部份為實地訪問，經由實際操作系統，以判斷各系統線上目錄及其顯示格式設計及內容是否好用，並當面瞭解使用者檢索線上目錄的情形。

本研究之對象為臺灣地區圖書館自動化系統之線上公用目錄及其使用者（包括館員及讀者）。目前已發展出線上公用目錄的圖書館，參考"教育部"圖書館事業委員會正進行中之"整體規劃圖書館資訊網路系統"調查研究，得知已有21個單位。後經電話洽談參觀訪問事宜時，確定桃園縣立文化中心的線上公用目錄系統當時尚未完成，而明道中學則因館內人事調動問題不便參觀以及臺灣省立新竹師範學院因系統更新亦不便參觀等因素，未進行實地訪問；故實際進行調查的對象為18個圖書館及資料單位。

調查實施

本研究問卷於1990年4月底開始設計並於同年5月24日以國防醫學院及臺大工學院的學生進行預試（Pretest）並加以修改。正式問卷於1990年6月底開始寄發至9月底止，僅4個單位的問卷回收；並於10月初再進行催索，至11月23日各單位問卷回收完畢。"線上公用目錄使用者調查問卷"之回收率詳見表1。

總計發出問卷285份，回收211份，回收率達74.04％。其中電信訓練所圖書室只填答1份是因為其讀者並不固定，故不易掌握。

至於實地訪問的單位則有：臺大工圖、師大、北一女、國防醫學院、中研院生醫所、臺灣神學院、淡大、經建會、電訓所、榮工處、交大、工研院、省立美術館、自然科學博物館、成大、亞蔬。而中國鋼鐵公司及澎湖文化中心則因地理位置及時間上之限制未能實地參觀訪問，僅郵寄調查問卷，委請館員代為進行。

表1：調查問卷回收率統計表

代碼	單位　　　　　　狀況	發出份數	回收份數	回收率
A	"國立臺灣大學"工學院聯合圖書館	15	11	73.33%
B	"國立臺灣師範大學"圖書館	15	14	93.33%
C	臺北市立第一女中圖書館	15	15	100.00%
D	"國防醫學院"致德醫學圖書館	15	15	100.00%
E	"中央研究院"生物醫學科學研究所圖書室	15	12	80.00%
F	臺灣神學院圖書館	15	15	100.00%
G	私立淡江大學圖書館	15	15	100.00%
H	"行政院經濟建設委員會"圖書室	15	8	53.33%
I	"交通部"電信訓練所圖書室	15	1	6.67%
J	"行政院國軍退除役官兵輔導委員會"榮民工程事業管理處圖書室	15	4	26.67%
K	"國立臺灣交通大學"圖書館	15	15	100.00%
L	工業技術研究院	30	19	63.33%
M	臺灣省立美術館資料中心	15	7	46.67%
N	"國立臺灣自然科學博物館"資訊組圖書室	15	7	46.67%
O	"國立成功大學"圖書館	15	15	100.00%
P	亞洲蔬菜研究發展中心圖書館	15	10	66.67%
Q	"中國鋼鐵公司"技術資料組圖書館	15	13	86.67%
R	澎湖縣立文化中心中正圖書館	15	15	100.00%
	總　　計	285	211	74.04%

表2：使用者現職統計表

現職	人數百分比單位	A	B	C	D	E	F	G	H	I	J	K	L	M	N	O	P	Q	R	總人數百分比
教師		0	0	0	1 6.7	1 8.3	0	0	1 12.5	1 100.0	0	0	0	0	0	1 6.7	0	0	0	5 2.4
研究生		6 54.5	3 21.4	0	5 33.3	4 33.3	10 66.7	0	0	0	0	4 26.7	1 5.3	0	0	2 13.3	2 20.0	0	1 6.7	38 18.0
大學生		3 27.3	10 71.4	0	6 40.0	2 16.7	3 20.0	12 80.0	1 12.5	0	0	7 46.7	0	0	2 28.6	9 60.0	0	0	0	55 26.1
中學生		0	0	15 100.0	0	0	0	0	0	0	0	0	0	0	0	0	0	0	0	20 9.5
職員		0	0	0	0	3 25.0	0	0	6 75.0	0	3 75.0	1 6.7	2 10.5	3 42.9	3 42.9	0	4 40.0	6 46.2	5 33.3	33 15.6
其他		0	0	0	0	2 16.7	0	3 20.0	0	0	0	0	12 63.2	2 28.6	2 28.6	0	3 30.0	4 30.8	2 13.3	28 13.3
館員		2 18.2	1 7.1	0	3 20.0	0	2 13.3	0	0	0	1 25.0	3 20.0	4 21.1	2 28.6	0	3 20.0	1 10.0	2 15.4	3 20.0	31 14.7
未填		0	0	0	0	0	0	0	0	0	0	0	0	0	0	0	0	1 7.7	0	1 0.5

資料處理

本研究是以訪問觀察法和問卷調查法來蒐集資料。問卷調查法所使用的問卷有兩種,其中"線上公用目錄系統調查問卷"的內容,以敘述性資料為主,因此直接以人工整理分析再編製成表。至於"線上公用目錄使用者調查問卷"的資料處理,則利用統計分析套裝軟體 SAS (Statistical Analysis System) 執行統計運算的工作。全部統計工作於1991年1月底完成。

貳、調查結果之分析與討論

調查對象基本分析

線上公用目錄使用者對線上公用目錄及其顯示格式的看法和意見,有助於改進現有的線上目錄,並可作為未來設計時之參考,相當值得重視。本節依回收所得的 211 份使用者的問卷資料中,將個人背景資料統計分析說明如下:

使用者的個人背景資料:

1. 現職:在本調查中,以大學生人數為最多,共 55 人,佔 26.1%;其次是研究生 38 人,佔 18.0%;職員 33 人,佔 15.6%;館員 31 人,佔 14.7%;"其他" 28 人,佔 13.3%;中學生 20 人,佔 9.5%;教師 5 人,佔 2.4%。填寫"其他"項者包括:軍人、助理研究員、研究人員、專門圖書館的使用者及研究助理。(參見表 2)

2. 系所別:經過統計,本調查的對象學科背景範圍涵蓋文、法、商、理、工、農、醫等系所。

3. 年齡:在 211 個樣本中,以 21～25 歲之間的人數最多,共 61 人,佔 28.9%;其次是 26～30 歲之間,共 45 人,佔 21.3%;20 歲以下者有 27 人,佔 12.8%;31～35 歲之間者有 22 人,佔 10.4%;35 歲以上者有 15 人,佔 7.1%。

4. 性別:女性填答者有 77 人,佔 36.5%;男性填答者有 96 人,佔 45.5%;其餘有 3 人未填。

5. 使用線上目錄的次數:

各單位使用者使用線上目錄的次數以 1～5 次者為最多,共 87 人,佔 41.2%;其次依序為 20 次以上者有 56 人,佔 26.5%;6～10 次者有 49 人,佔 23.2%;11～20 次者有 17 人,佔 8.1%。

6. 是否使用過其他電腦式的圖書館目錄:

有 48 人(佔 22.7%)表示曾使用過;而有 162 人(佔 76.8%)表示未使用過其他電腦式圖書館目錄。

7. 得知有線上目錄的方式:

以填答"參觀圖書館"者為最多,共 56 人,佔 26.5%;其次依序為"圖書館自動化系統通告"47 人,佔 22.3%;"圖書館館員"43 人,佔 20.4%;"其他"18 人,佔 8.5%;"朋友、同學"16 人,佔 7.6%;"新生訓練"13 人,佔 6.2%;"系統展示時得知"10 人,佔 4.7%;"教師"4 人,佔 1.9%;"校園刊物"2 人,佔 0.9%。"其他"項包括:自己發現、工作上必須使用、曾參與系統設計等方式。

8. 學會使用線上目錄的方式：

以"自我學習（嘗試錯誤）"者為最多，共 105 人，佔 49.8%；其次依序為"圖書館員" 81 人，佔 38.4%；"線上輔助說明" 61 人，佔 28.9%；"印刷式說明書" 51 人，佔 24.2%；"朋友、同學" 30 人，佔 14.2%；只有 20 人是填答"圖書館訓練課程"，佔 9.5%；另有 14 人填答"其他"項，包括：同事、由系統設計人員指導及館員在職訓練等方式。

9. 曾使用過的電腦產品：

曾用過"電子郵件"者有 36 人，佔 17.1%；"電子佈告欄"者有 18 人，佔 8.5；"套裝軟體"者有 146 人，佔 69.2%；"自動提款機"者有 173 人，佔 82.0%；"商業性線上資料庫"者有 50 人，佔 23.7%；"電腦遊戲"者有 158 人，佔 74.9%。

10. 個人是否擁有電腦：

填答"是"者有 77 人，佔 36.5%；填答"否"者有 133 人，佔 63.0%。

11. 曾使用過多少種文書處理或文書編輯軟體：

以填答會 1 種者為最多，有 51 人，佔 24.2%；其次為 2 種者有 46 人，佔 21.8%；3 種者 30 人，佔 14.2%；4 種者有 9 人，佔 4.3%；5 種者有 3 人，佔 1.4%；6 種者有 3 人，佔 1.4%；9 種者 3 人，佔 1.4%；而仍有 66 人（佔 31.3%）未曾用過任何一種軟體。

12. 會使用哪些語言撰寫程式：

有 89 人（佔 42.2%）不會使用電腦語言撰寫程式；而有 48 人，22.7%會用 1 種語言；31 人（佔 14.7%）會 2 種語言；會 3 種語言者有 31 人（佔 14.7%）；會 4 種語言者有 7 人，佔 3.3%；只有 5 人（佔 2.4%）會 5 種語言。

13. 曾使用過什麼作業系統：

有 37 人（17.5%）未曾用過任何一種作業系統；而有 123 人（佔 58.3%）曾用過 1 種；3 人（佔 16.1%）用過 2 種；14 人（佔 6.6%）用過 3 種；2 人（佔 0.9%）用過 4 種；1 人（佔 0.5%）曾用過 5 種。

14. 平均每週約花多少小時使用個人電腦或終端機工作：

每週平均花 1～10 小時利用個人電腦或終端機工作者有 107 人，佔 50.7%；花 11～20 小時者有 29 人，佔 13.7%；花 21～30 小時者有 11 人，佔 5.2%；31 小時以上者有 9 人，佔 4.3%；另外有 55 人（佔 26.1%）並不使用個人電腦或終端機工作。

15. 圖書館線上目錄推出後，是否繼續使用卡片目錄或書本式目錄：

有 104 人（佔 49.3%）在線上目錄推出後，仍偶而使用卡片目錄或書本式目錄；而有 28 人（佔 13.3%）則仍經常使用。但是有 74 人（佔 35.1%）在線上目錄推出後就不再使用卡片目錄或書本式目錄。

臺灣圖書館自動化系統線上公用目錄現況分析

本研究共調查臺灣十八個已發展完成線上公用目錄系統的圖書館暨資料單位。本節依"線上公用目錄系統調查問卷"（以下簡稱系統問卷）與"線上公用目錄使用者問卷"（以下簡稱使用者問卷）的調查結果，分為系統資料、系統操作控制、檢索控制、顯示功能及系統輔助功能五部份列表分析，並做重點性說明：

一、系統資料

各單位自動化系統名稱、線上公用目錄查詢子系統名稱及其啟用日期。（參見表 3）

表3：系統資料統計表

項目	單位代碼	A	B	C	D	E	F	G	H	I	J	K	L	M	N	O	P	Q	R
1. 自動化系統軟體名稱		出納查詢自動化系統（CIR-CIRAS）	師大線上公用目錄	URICA	（URICA）致德醫學圖書館自動化系統	URICA	（URICA）圖書館自動化系統	圖書館自動化系統	圖書館管理系統	圖書查詢資訊管理系統	圖書連線查詢作業	交通大學圖書館自動化系統	工業技術研究院圖書出納管理系統	國立中央圖書館臺灣省立臺中圖書館上查詢子系統	圖書館作業系統查詢子系統	"國立成功圖書館"合作自動化作業系統	MINSIS	中國圖書館自動化系統	三邊整合性圖書館電腦化系統
2. 線上公用目錄查詢子系統名稱			師大線上公用目錄	線上公用目錄查詢（OPAC）	線上公用查詢目錄（OPAC）	OPAC	LOCOPAC	線上公用目錄系統				國立交通大學圖書館線上查詢系統	圖書主檔查詢系統	線上查詢子系統	查詢子系統	公用目錄查詢	AVLIB	圖書館自動化公用目錄查詢系統	
3. OPAC啟用日期		77.2	78.11.9	79.9.16	78.11	78.2	78.9.15	75.9	76.7.1		77.7		74.7	77.9	79.1.1	75.8	75.8	78.5	78.2.26
4. 公用查詢終端機 (1) 一般型 (2) PC		(1) 2	(1) 7 (2) 3	(1) 1 (2) 1	(1) 4	(1) 1	(1) 2	(1) 23	(2) 2	(未填)	(未填)	(1) 5 (2) 1	(1) 1（能資所）	(1) 1	(1) 2 (2) 共23部	(1) 6 (2) 共6部	(1) 2 共9部	(1) (2) = 1（其他外部=400）	
5. 資料量（以種類數計）		50200 (79.11)	88159 (79.10.23)	(未填)	64115 (79.9.24)	52680 (79.9.24)	24023 (79.9.5)	(未填)	期刊640 3500 期刊論文 7500 (79.7)	(未填)	14385 (79.7.31)	63415 47079 1866 661 (79.10.16)	140000 (79.6.30)	10819 (79.8.24)	8618 (79.8.30)	256515 (79.6.27)	20000 (79.6)	39706 (79.11.9)	56214 (79.10.1)
6. 資料類型 (1) 圖書		×	×	×	×	×	×	×	×	×	×	×	×	×	×	×	×	×	×
(2) 資料			×	×	×	×	×	×		×	×	×	×	×	×			×	×
(3) 期刊		×	×	×	×	×	×	×	×	×	×	×	×	×	×	×	×		
(4) 其他		× (地圖,光碟資料)		× (地圖)													×（微片,微捲）	×（技術報告,專刊文獻）	
7. 中文輸入法																			
(1) 倉頡		×	×	×	×	×	×	×	×	×	×	×	×	×	×	×	×	×	×
(2) 簡易		×（漢易）	×	×	×	×	×												
(3) 注音			×	×	×	×	×												
(4) 碼				×（全漢碼）	×（全漢碼）	×（內碼）						×（三角）	×（三角）			×（內碼電信碼）			
(5) 片語					×	×（全漢）													

表 4：系統操作控制統計表

項目 \ 單位代碼	A	B	C	D	E	F	G	H	I	J	K	L	M	N	O	P	Q	R
1. 提供讀者中文或英文查詢方式。	X							X	X	X	X		X	X	X	X	X	X
2. 可選項查詢（如書目查詢、流通、館際互借等）。		X	X	X	X	X	X	X	X	X	X	X	X	X	X	X	X	
3. 可選擇交談模式 (1) 選項式 (menu driven)	X	X	X	X	X	X	X	X		X	X		X	X	X	X	X	X
(2) 指令式 (command directly)	X															X		
4. 有參數設定之功能。	X		X	X	X		X					X						
5. 可設定系統訊息長度。	X	X		X	X													
6. 可中斷或取消查詢指令。	X		X	X		X	X	X		X	X	X	X	X	X		X	X
7. 允許一次輸入多項指令 (stack command)。	X			X		X	X											
8. 系統有保護功能，禁止越權使用。	X	X	X	X	X			X		X	X	X	X	X	X		X	X
9. 螢幕可前後查看。		X		X			X			X	X	X		X	X	X	X	X
10. 系統有選頁功能	X																	
11. 可做部份字串修改，不須全部重打。	X						X				X			X		X	X	X
12. 提供直接查詢功能，可快速測入或跳出數個書面。（如從書目查詢直接跳到流通查詢）						X				X		X						
13. 可用列印機印出查結果。		X			X	X	X	X				X	X	X	X	X	X	X
14. 終端機於定時內不鍵入指令，則自動回到起始螢幕				X										X		X	X	

十八個單位中有六個單位提供一般終端機與個人電腦（PC）作為公用查詢終端機；而有七個單位是以一般終端機作爲查詢用終端機；二個單位是利用 PC 當做公用查詢終端機。（參見表3）

在中文輸入法方面，十四個單位提供倉頡輸入法；十二個單位提供簡易輸入法；十五個單位提供注音輸入法。根據使用者問卷的調查結果，在 211 個樣本中，有 163 人（佔77.3%）較常用注音輸入法，因此線上公用目錄中似乎應將注音輸入法列為必要的中文輸入法之一。各系統之其他基本資料統計，尚包含系統資料量，資料種類等。（參見表3）

二、系統操作控制

線上公用目錄的功能多寡及操作方法是否簡易是吸引讀者利用線上公用目錄的要件之一，根據系統問卷統計，列出各系統的操作控制功能統計（參見表4）。

三、檢索控制

系統提供的檢索方法和檢索點的數量是影響檢索是否成功的重要因素。根據問卷調查，統計各系統的檢索控制功能如下：在十八個單位中，有十三個單位提供布林邏輯查詢功能，但根據使用者問卷調查所得，有 52.6% 的使用者不會利用此項功能進行檢索。在切截（Truncation）查詢方面，有十二個單位可進行中文及西文的後切截查詢，但使用者問卷資料中有 69.2% 的使用者不會使用切截查詢。由以上可知，各單位有必要加強這兩項功能的指導，以確使使用者能有效地應用各種檢索方法。

各系統提供的檢索點中，以個人作者及書名較普遍，都有十五個單位提供此二種檢索點，而只有二個單位提供政府出版品編號作為檢索點。此一結果和使用者問卷的調查結果吻合：各系統使用者利用"部份書名"進行檢索者最多，佔65.9%；僅有 1.9% 的使用者以"政府出版品編號"進行檢索。有十個系統可提供其他檢索點，包括：叢書名、分類號、出版項、請購者及 CODEN 等。

四、顯示功能

系統顯示功能的統計資料可作為顯示格式設計時的參考。顯示畫面是否美觀及是否易被讀者接受是設計線上公用目錄時非常重要的一環。本研究之各系統的顯示功能經統計繪製成表。

五、系統輔助功能

線上公用目錄所提供的系統輔助功能是指導使用者進行檢索的方式之一。在十八個單位中，有十一個單位可利用指令隨時叫出"HELP"輔助說明；有八個單位提供線上使用指導。

臺灣地區圖書館自動化系統線上公用目錄使用者之調查分析

根據問卷調查所得之 211 位線上目錄使用者之資料，經使用 SAS 統計分析後，所得結果如下：

一、使用者背景分析

（一）現職/年齡性別之分佈，調查對象中以 21～25 歲之大學生最多（18.48%）；性別以男性研究生（13.74%）及大學生（14.22%）較多，女性則以館員（10.43%）或大學生（9.48%）分佈較多。

（二）是否使用過其他電腦式圖書館目錄？經卡方檢定有顯著差異，其中各組多半未曾使用過其他電腦式圖書館目錄，而館員中有51.61%曾使用過，其因是各館在選擇系統過程中曾接觸不少其他自動化系統；教師部份有40%曾使用過其他系統。

　　（三）個人是否擁有電腦？經卡方檢定有顯著差異，其中教師全擁有電腦，而職員及館員則僅少數人有電腦。

　　（四）是否繼續使用卡片目錄或書本式目錄？經卡方檢定有顯著差異，多數使用者仍會繼續使用傳統式目錄，但中學生則有30%仍使用卡片目錄，70%不再使用卡片目錄。

　　（五）由何處得知有線上目錄：從分佈中發現使用者主要得知線上目錄的方法為：圖書館自動化系統通告，參觀圖書館及圖書館員。

　　（六）如何學會使用線上目錄系統？各職稱的使用者學會使用系統的方法大致相似，其中僅有自我學習及圖書館館員二項有顯著差異。換言之，大學生中有72.73%是從嘗試錯誤中學會的；而80%的教師表示是經由館員學會使用系統的。

　　（七）曾使用過其他電腦產品：各種電腦系統中，以下幾項的使用經驗有顯著差異：

　　1. 套裝軟體：大部份人都曾使用過套裝軟體，但中學生中只有25%的人使用過，這表示中學課程中電腦課程仍未普及。

　　2. 自動提款機：大部份人都曾使用過，但中學生只有50%的人使用過。

　　3. 商業性線上資料庫：中學生無人使用過，其他使用百分比較高者為教師、館員及其他。

　　4. 電腦遊戲：玩過的人居多數，職員中未玩過的百分比稍高一點（48.48%）。

二、使用者檢索情形

　　（一）利用線上目錄是為查詢？不同職稱使用者查詢上有顯著差異，其說明如下：

　　1. 特定圖書、期刊或雜誌：中學生或許對資料類型較不熟悉，所以僅有45%是利用線上目錄查詢特定圖書、期刊或雜誌；而館員則高達93.55%。

　　2. 某主題或學科的圖書期刊：研究生因常撰寫報告，所以以此查詢的比率相當高（97.37%）。

　　3. 出版商、出版日期等資料：大部份使用者很少為查出版商資料進行檢索；而館員之比率（38.71%）較其他各組為高。

　　4. 某書之借閱狀況：館員中有80.65%是查詢借閱狀況，比率較高之原因可能是出納館員或參考館員為讀者查看之故。

　　（二）常用哪些檢索點：不同職稱使用者，查詢時所採用的檢索點有差異，包括：

　　1. 完整作者姓名：教師（80%）及中學生（85%）百分比較高，其他則只有25%常用作者姓名查詢。

　　2. 團體作者：大半讀者對團體作者不甚清楚，而館員則有51.61%用此檢索點。

　　3. 完整書名：教師80%常用此檢索點，或許他們較清楚要找的書就是那些特定的書；職員則僅有27.27%常用書名查詢。

　　4. 部份書名：館員經常用部份書名查詢（90.32%）；而中學生僅有40%。

　　5. 關鍵字：中學生或許不瞭解關鍵字之選擇，所以僅有30%用此檢索點。

　　6. 部份索書號：館員（58.06%）常用此檢索點，可見一般人對分類系統仍不甚清楚。

7. ISBN：讀者中僅2人曾使用過此檢索點，仍以館員使用頻率較高（19.35%）。

8. ISSN：讀者中僅3人曾使用過此檢索點，仍以館員使用頻率較高（19.35%）。

（三）檢索目的：不同職稱與檢索目的有很大的關係，所有選項均有顯著差異，說明如下：

1. 作研究報告：教師（80%）、研究生（94.74%）居多數；館員僅6.45%是為研究報告進行檢索。

2. 蒐集工作或教學資料：教師100%為此目的。

3. 個人進修：大學生（76.36%）為此目的，而中學生（25.00%）及館員（32.26%）則偏低。

4. 瀏覽：較少人會無目的的查詢，但中學生中有65.00%會進行瀏覽。

5. 消遣用：中學生百分比較高（45.00%），但多數使用者不是為消遣而做檢索。

6. 其他：館員中有51.61%是為其他目的，如：協助讀者查詢資料，工作需要或展示講解等。

（四）線上查詢結果：大多數使用者僅能查得部份資料（佔48.34%）；而館員能查得所需資料甚高，這可能是因館員熟悉檢索方法及策略，所以結果較佳。

（五）遇到困難時，解決的方法：各職稱的使用者解決問題的方法中，在以下幾項有差異：

1. 請教圖書館館員：教師、研究生、職員及其他使用者會詢問館員，反而年齡較小之中學生（30%）及大學生（41.82%）較少採用此方法；

2. 問旁邊的人：上述之中學生（45%）及大學生（38.18%）採用此方法者較其他組為多；

3. 放棄檢索：教師放棄之比例（40%）較其他組高。

（六）各職稱之使用者對檢索結果的滿意程度與利用關鍵詞查詢、減少查詢結果方面並無差異，但在下列幾項則有差異：

1. 是否找到其他相關資料？大部份都能找到相關資料，中學生找不到相關資料者較高（30%）。

2. 會用切截方式檢索：只有較多數的館員（67.74%）會利用切截方式。

3. 會利用布林邏輯檢索：館員90.32%會使用，而中學生卻只有5%知道如何使用。

（七）喜歡哪一種檢索：中、英文檢索方面，使用者間有顯著差異，只有大學生及中學生較喜歡以中文檢索，而教師、研究生、職員、館員及其他使用者較喜歡英文檢索方式。

（八）中文輸入法：中文輸入法中注音輸入法有顯著差異，其中教師（40%）及館員（58.06%）使用注音輸入之比率較低。

三、使用者滿意程度

（一）不同現職使用者滿意程度之分析

1. 整體看法：對系統的整體看法中，只有操作一項有顯著差異，多數使用者都認為操作容易。職員及其他的使用者亦不認為有困難。

2. 螢幕：對螢幕的滿意程度，在螢幕上的用字及亮度兩項有顯著差異：

(1) 螢幕上用字：多數使用者認為清晰易懂。
　　(2) 亮度：大學生及中學生中表示刺眼，多數使用者認為無意見或表示螢幕亮度柔和。
　3. 系統功能：對系統功能的滿意程度的差異程度，說明如下：
　　(1) 系統可靠性：多數人表示可靠；
　　(2) 錯誤的更正：職員認為容易者較高（60.61%），研究生及中學生則表示非常困難；
　　(3) 代碼和縮寫字的使用：教師有60%認為難懂；中學生有1人表示非常難懂，館員則多半認為易懂（54.84%）；
　　(4) 中西文系統的切換：大部份為無意見或容易，職員則表示無困難，但館員有1人認為非常困難。
　4. 在學習方面，以下幾項有差異：
　　(1) 提供直接而快速的檢索方式：大部份使用者認為多數能提供，但教師則覺得完全不能提供（40%）或少數能提供（40%）的百分比較多。
　　(2) 螢幕上的輔助說明：多數使用者覺得有用，但仍有使用者認為沒用。
　　(3) 書面式參考資料：多數使用者表示無意見或易懂，中學生認為易懂者人數百分比遠較其他各組者為低。
　5. 對於專門名詞及系統資訊的滿意程度：在採用辭彙一項上有顯著差異，大部份使用者表示尚可，但中學生表示難懂（15%）。
　（二）各系統之使用者對其系統滿意程度之分析
　　各系統之使用者對其系統滿意程度是否有差異，經由變異數分析（ANOVA）結果，說明如下：
　1. 在對系統整體看法方面：其中整體看法有差異，但無負面的看法；查詢結果有差異，美術館平均而言為無意見，其他則偏向滿意；而對系統功能方面，多半是正面意見，但有六系統平均偏負面看法。
　2. 螢幕設計方面：各系統之使用者滿意程度皆無差異。
　3. 系統功能方面：在系統反應速度方面，有9個系統偏向緩慢的看法，中研院生醫所平均值僅1.83，而臺神（3.60）及澎湖文化中心（3.67）則接近快速的看法。
　　以查詢功能而言，六系統使用者認為不足，臺神（3.80）以及榮工處（3.75）則偏向功能很強的意見；使用者對中西文系統切換功能，工研院偏向切換困難的看法，淡江（4.07）及澎湖文化中心（4.07）則表示容易。
　4. 學習方面：提供直接而快速的檢索方式，電訊所及科學博物館偏向少數提供的意見；螢幕上的輔助說明——平均而言均認為是有用的；同樣地，對館員所提供的指導的看法，均認為有用。
　5. 專門名詞及系統資訊：對系統顯示進行步驟，美術館平均認為只有少數提供；錯誤訊息之顯示——生醫所偏向沒用（2.92）的意見。
　（三）館員與讀者滿意程度之分析
　　館員與讀者對系統之滿意程度方面，其分析結果如下：
　　在螢幕上之字體與亮度、系統功能之中西文系統的切換、學習方面之螢幕上之輔助說明與書面式之參考資料有差異，整體而言，館員給予系統的評價較讀者高。

四、建議改善項目

根據統計分析，使用者之各項建議的差異，說明如下：

（一）使用者對於線上目錄終端機的使用上，並無顯著差異。

（二）線上目錄應增加功能，使用者在下列兩點上有顯著差異：

1. 提供逐步使用指導：80%教師及60%中學生認為需要，而館員只有19.35%認為需要。

2. 查知各種資料的館藏地：60.71%之其他使用者，如軍人、研究助理等及57.89的研究生認為需要，其他各組使用者則多認為不需要。

3. 經ANOVA之統計分析，以上兩項中館員與讀者的看法亦有差異。

畫面顯示格式分析

本節就線上目錄顯示格式加以分析說明。調查之18個系統中，因電訓所圖書館無法列印畫面及生醫所與澎湖文化中心不便提供畫面，故畫面顯示格式部份僅蒐集15個單位之畫面，各系統顯示格式之畫面如後：

各系統顯示格式之畫面：

A. "國立臺灣大學"工學院聯合圖書館

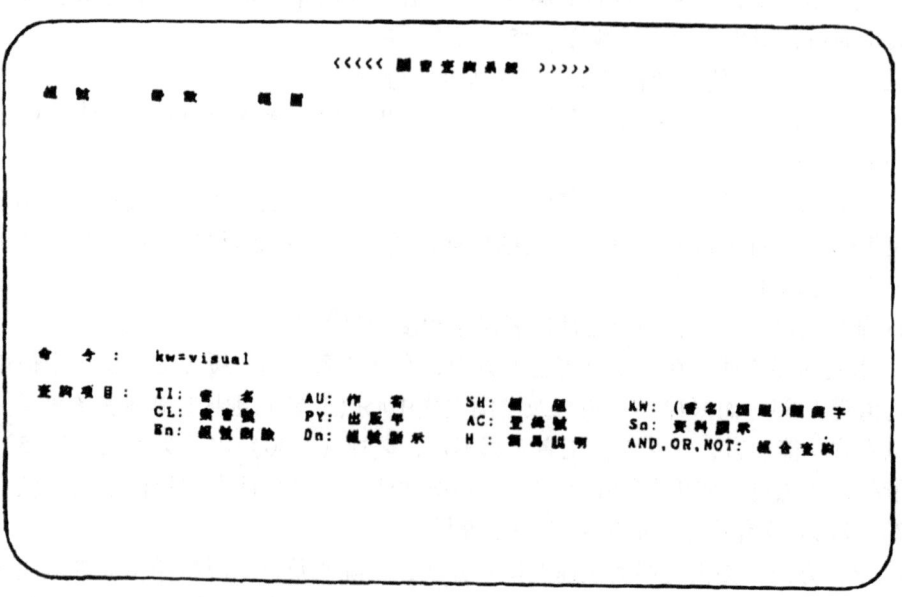

畫面（一）

```
                    \\<<< 圖書查詢系統 >>>>

        組號         筆數         範圍

        S1           19          kw=visual              --- KW書名部份
        S2           13          kw=visual              --- KW標題部份




        命  令 :  s1
        查詢項目:   Tl: 書 名      AU: 作 者      SH: 標 題      KW: (書名,標題)關鍵字
                   CL: 索書號      PY: 出版年      AC: 登錄號      Sn: 資料顯示
                   En: 組號刪除    Dn: 組號顯示    H : 簡易說明    AND,OR,NOT: 聯合查詢
```

畫面（二）

```
                        簡明資料      (共  2頁)    1頁
        項目 作者                    書名

         1 Baker, Charles A.        Visual capabilities in the space environment..
         2 Shu, Nan C.              Visual programming
         3 Sheppard, S. R. J. (StephenVisual simulation : a user's guide for archi..
         4 Srinivasan, B. (Bala, etc. Visual edting on unix
         5 Sheppard, S. R. J. (StephenVisual simulation : a user's guide for archi..
         6 Jakle, John A.           The visual elements of landscape
         7 Higuchi, Tadahiko, 1944- The visual and spatial structure of landscap
         8 Higuchi, Tadahiko, 1944- The visual and spatial structure of landscap
         9 Higuchi, Tadahiko, 1944- The visual and spatial structure of landscap
        10 Rutledge, Albert J.      A visual approach to park design
        11 Moraveo, Hans P          Robert rover visual navigation
        12 Eboch, Sidney C.         Operating audio visual equipment
        13 Eboch, Sidney C.         Operating audio visual equipment
        14 Smardon, Richard C., etc. Foundations for visual project analysis
        15 Moneo, Rafael, etc.      Wexner Center for the Visual Arts, the Ohio ..
        16 IEEE Computer Society. Tech1984 IEEE Computer Society Workshop on Visua..
        ================================================================
        底 第:3
                 按數字n,詳細說明       N: 下一頁       P: 上一頁
                 J: 直接跳頁           Q: 結束顯示      H : 簡易說明
```

畫面（三）

```
           詳細資料    （共   2 頁）  1 頁  3本
登錄號：1566364    單位：建城所   語文：西文   類別：普通書
索書號：NA2750 S54
作  者：a. Sheppard, S. R. J. (Stephen Richard John
          b.
          c.
書  名：Visual simulation : a user's guide for architects, engineers
        , and planners
出版項：New York : Van Nostrand Reinhold         出版年：1989
版  次：             複本：2    頁數：222     價格：1349
標  題：a. LANDSCAPE ARCHITECTURE--SIMULATION METHODS
          b. ARCHITECTURE--SIMULATION METHODS
          c. CITY PLANNING--SIMULATION METHODS
附  註：1.館內資料：    2.指定參考書：    3.參考書：

書  況：已借出  （歸還期：80年 1月16日）  借者：L120549366
預約者：
==================================================================
選  擇：
          N：下一本書    P：前一本書    J：直接跳頁
          Q：結束顯示    C：個別資料    H：簡易說明
```

畫面（四）

B. "國立臺灣師範大學" 圖書館

```
14:50 09 DEC 90              書名查詢              URICA 85/2
------------------------ 作品顯示格式 - BRIEF ----------------------
1. 中國語言學名詞匯編一九二五---一九七五 = Chinese linguistic usage 1925-197
     5 / 鄭知新，德福編編. - 台北市：台灣學生，民73 (BRN: 1006600)
        館藏地   索書號/書號 .......... 複本 .. 預約
        A1       R R R 420.4 489          2
        M        R R R 420.4 489          2
        MC       R R R 420.4 489          1
        RS       R R R 420.4 489          1

2. 語言學概論 / 謝國平著. - 初版. - 台北市：三民，民74 (BRN: 1006739)
        館藏地   索書號/書號 .......... 複本 .. 預約
        M        400 844                  4
        RS       400 844                  1



請按 <RETURN> 查看其他作品，或按 <.> 離開
B(國略)，M(標準)，F(詳細)，R(重選)，或輸入欲預約的行號
  ---- ---- ------ - -------- ----- ---------------- 續見次頁 ----
  選入選擇項，或按V(?)顯示說明
```

畫面（一）

```
14:51 09 DEC 90              書名查詢                    URICA SS/2
------------------------ 作品顯示格式 - MEDIUM ------------------------
1. 中國語言學名詞匯編--一九二五---一九七五 = Chinese linguistic usage 1925-197
   5 / 溫知新, 楊福綿編. - 台北市 : 台灣學生, 民73 (BRN: 1006600)

   館藏地 登錄號 .. 書號/索書號 ........ 圖書說明 .... 圖書狀況 ...
   A1    B10411615   R R R 420.4 489
   A1    B10473689   R R R 420.4 489
   M     B10408135   R R R 420.4 489
   M     B10408136   R R R 420.4 489            (R)
   MC    B10428777   R R R 420.4 489
   RS    B10413499   R R R 420.4 489

2. 語言學概論 / 謝國平著. - 初版. - 台北市 : 三民, 民74 (BRN: 1006739)

   館藏地 登錄號 .. 書號/索書號 ........ 圖書說明 .... 圖書狀況 ...
   M     B0004933    400 844                              借閱中 (Due 17 DEC)

請按 (RETURN) 查看其他作品，或按 (.) 離開
B(簡略), M(標準), F(詳細), R(重選)， 或鍵入欲預約的行數
                                                        ------ 側見大頁 ----
鍵入選擇項，或按V(?)顯示說明
```

畫面（二）

```
14:52 09 DEC 90              書名查詢                    URICA SS/2
------------------------ 作品顯示格式 - FULL ------------------------
1. 中國語言學名詞匯編--一九二五---一九七五 = Chinese linguistic usage 1925-197
   5 / 溫知新, 楊福綿編

   出版項 ....... 台北市 : 台灣學生, 民73

   稽核項 ..     [8], 409 面 ; 冠偉 : 26 公分

   個人著者 .....  溫, 知新
                  楊, 福綿

   書目資料編號(BRN) :1006600

   館藏地 登錄號 .. 書號/索書號 ........ 圖書說明 .... 圖書狀況 ...

請按 (RETURN) 查看其他作品，或按 (.) 離開
B(簡略), M(標準), F(詳細), R(重選)， 或鍵入欲預約的行數
                                                        ------ 側見大頁 ----
鍵入選擇項，或按V(?)顯示說明
```

畫面（三）

```
14:52 09 DEC 90                    書名查詢                    URICA S3/2
------------------------------作品顯示格式 - FULL------------------------------
  A1    B10411615  R R R 420.4 489
  A1    B10473639  R R R 420.4 489
  M     B10408135  R R R 420.4 489
  M     B10408136  R R R 420.4 489           (R)
  MC    B10428777  R R R 420.4 489
  RS    B10413499  R R R 420.4 489
```

請按〈RETURN〉查看其他作品，或按〈.〉離開
B(簡略)，M(標準)，F(詳細)，R(重選)，或鍵入欲預約的行號   翻見次頁

鍵入選擇項，或按v〈?〉顯示說明

畫面（四）

C. 臺北市立第一女中圖書館

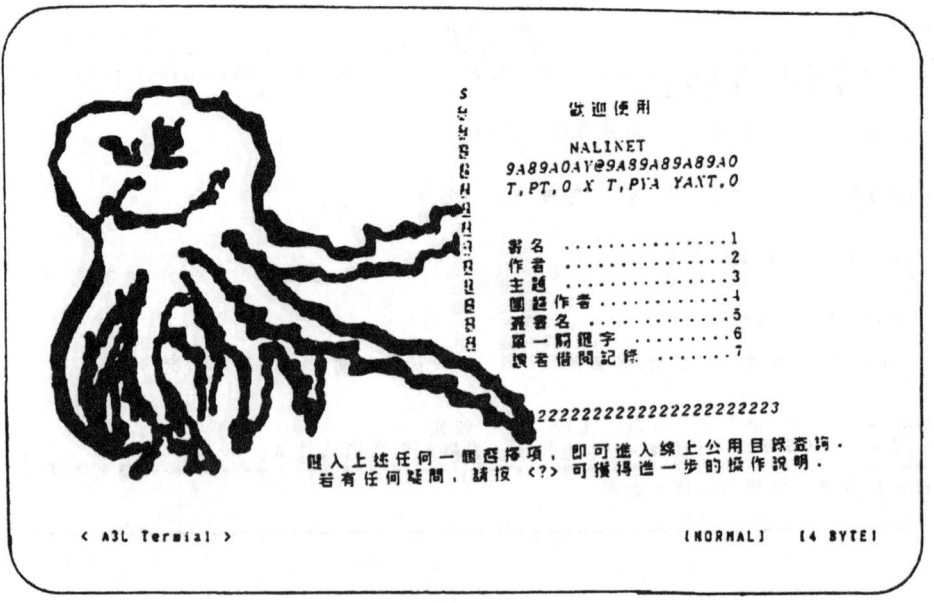

畫面（一）

```
15:57 19 NOV 90              書錄號查物                          北一
------------------------- 作品顯示格式 - BRIEF -----------------------
1. 國際政治學 / Fred I. Greenstein, Nelson W. Polsby 主編 ; 幼獅文化公司編譯
   . - 再版. - 台北市 : 幼獅, 民73 (BRN: 1004688)

    館藏地  索書號 ............     複本 .. 預約
    TFML    570 8475 v.8             l




B(簡略), M(標準), F(詳細), C(機讀格式), P(列印)
---------------------------------------------------------- 最後一頁 ----
鍵入選擇項 :
```

畫面（二）

```
15:58 19 NOV 90              書錄號查物                          北一
------------------------- 作品顯示格式 - MEDII ----------------------
國際政治學 / Fred I. Greenstein, Nelson V. Polsby 主編 ; 幼獅文化公司編譯.
 - 再版. - 台北市 : 幼獅, 民73 (政治科學大□ : 8)(書目資料編號 :1004688)

    館藏地  登錄號 .. 索書號 ........   圖書狀況 .... 圖書狀況 ...
    TFML    1003335   570 8475 v.8




B(簡略), M(標準), F(詳細), C(機讀格式), P(列印)
---------------------------------------------------------- 最後一頁 ----
鍵入選擇項 :
< A3L Termial >                                  [NORMAL]  14 BYTE]
```

畫面（三）

```
15:59 19 NOV 90              登錄號查詢                          之一
----------------------  作品顯示格式 - FULL  ----------------------
 1. 國際政治學 / Fred I. Greenstein, Nelson V. Polsby 主編 : 幼獅文化公司編譯

      版本項.......再版

      出版項.......台北市 : 幼獅, 民73

      稽核項.......32, 558面 : 22公分

      叢書名.......(政治科學大全 ; 8)

      個人著者.....格林斯坦
                  波子斯比

      團體著者.....幼獅文化公司

   B(回跳), M(顯示), F(瀏覽), C(換檢格式), P(列印)    --------- 續見次頁 ----
   個人追蹤項 :
      < A3L Terminal >                              (NORMAL)  (4 BYTE)
```

畫面（四）－1

```
16:00 19 NOV 90              登錄號查詢                          之一
----------------------  作品顯示格式 - FULL  ----------------------
   書目資料編號(BRN) :1004688

      館藏地  登錄號   ..  索書號 .............  圖書及冊 ....  圖書狀況 ...
      TFNL    1003335       570 8475 v.8
```

畫面（四）－2

```
-------------------作品顯示格式  NAEC------------------
       日期        CBF  07 JUN 89--JEN 01 OC 90--LEU
LDR  Leader     am p
BRN  001        1004688
FFD  008        890517s1984    ch         0  10 chi d
CAS  040        $a TFCHL $c TFCHL
LAN  041 1      $a chi
OOC  082 0      $a 570
TIL  245 00     $a 國際政治學 $c / Fred I. Greenstein, Nelson W. Polsby 主編 :
                   幼獅文化公司編譯
EDN  250        $a 再版
IMP  260 0      $a 台北市 $b : 幼獅 $c , 民73
COL  300        $a 12, 558面 $c : 22公分
PRI  350        $a 基價 6.62元 $b (精裝)
SET  440  0     $a 政治科學大全 $v : 8
NOG  500        $a 譯自: International politics
AEP  700 10     $a 格林斯坦 $q (Greenstein, Fred I.) $e 主編
AEP  700 10     $a 迫子斯比 $q (Polsby, Nelsor W.) $e 主編

B(簡略), N(標準), F(詳細), C(過讀格式), P(列印)
-------------------------------------------------- 項見次頁 ----
鍵入選擇項 :
  < A3L Termial >                            [NORMAL]  (4 BYTE)
```

畫面（五）-1

```
16:00 19 NOV 90          登錄號查詢                        北 一
-------------------作品顯示格式 · NAEC------------------
AEC  710 20  $a 幼獅文化公司 $e 編譯
AED  740 00  $a International politics

     館藏地  登錄號 .. 索書號 ..............  書況明 ....  圖書狀況 ...
     TFNL   1003335   570 8475 v.8




B(簡略), N(標準), F(詳細), C(過讀格式), P(列印)
-------------------------------------------------- 最後一頁 ----
鍵入選擇項 :
  < A3L Termial >                            [NORMAL]  (4 BYTE)
```

畫面（五）-2

```
13:38 08 JAN 90              組源名：詢                              左一
--------------------------------------------------------------------------
查得筆數太多，全部列出需花許多時間。
查得的資料筆數若少於"150"時，您可以按 RETURN> 列出所有資料：
或者，利用<設定範圍查尋>，縮小查尋的結果。

查得筆數................. 234           查得筆數......

--------------------------------------------------------------------------
如何使用設定範圍查詢：
    利用"設定範圍查詢"的方式，是利用"布林邏輯"方式來設定查詢範圍，以便查
    詢到更合乎您需要的資料。
    例如：1976年以後出版的書         DATE > "1976"
          作者的姓名為"王"且為
          1980年以後出版的書：       AUTHOR "王|" AND DATE > "1980"

使用"設定範圍查詢"時，可選擇納入書名(TITLE)，個人作者(AUTHOR)，出版年
(DATE)，標題(SUBJECT)，團體作者(CO P)，叢書名(SERIES)，資料撰寫標示

請按 <RETURN> 繼續
```

畫面（六）

D. "國防醫學院"致德醫學圖書館

```
14:01 2° NOV 87                   等名：詢                         男兒
------------- WORKS 0[S? BY - 9A:2F -------------
1. 精神醫學 / 徐靜著。- 四版。- 台北市 ：水牛，民 61 [1972] (BRN: 1008710)

    館藏地  登錄號 .. 書號/冊書號 .....  ... 圖書說明 ....  圖書狀況 ...
    ML    M002151   WM100 M87 1972




請按 <RETURN> 查看其它作品，或按 <.> 1詢
B(書給)，M(題涉)，F(第詢)，R(登錄)，   輸入索買的符號
                                                            ------- 最後一頁
輸入選擇項，或按<?>顯示說明。
```

畫面（一）

```
14:34 04 DEC 89              書名查        [MEDIUM]                    國圖
------------------------- WORKS DISPLAY -------------------------
1. 精神醫學 / 塗汝祥著. - 四版. - 台北市：水牛，民 61 [1972] (水牛大學叢書；
       25) (BRN: 1008710)

      館藏地 登錄號 .. 普通/不普通 ........ 圖書說明 .... 圖書狀況 ...
   NL   M002151   WM100 M87 1972




   請按 <RETURN> 查看其他作品，或按 <.> 回 !
   B(回到)，M(濃選)，F(詳細)，R(重選)，或鍵入欲選的行號
-----------------------------------------------------------------
   鍵入您希項，或按 <?> 顯示說明
```

畫面（二）

```
14:34 04 DEC 89              書名查     [FULL]                       國圖
------------------------- WORKS DISPLAY -------------------------
1. 精神醫學

      個人作者 ... .塗，汝祥
      題名項 ....... 精神
      出版項 ....... 台北市：水牛，民 61 [197:
      稽核項 ....... [9], 320 面；21 公分
      叢書名 ....... 水牛大學叢書；25
      一般註 ....... 英文題名：Psychiatry
      檢索題名 ..... Psychiatry
      ISBN ......... ( 平裝 ) NT$60.00
   BRN: 1008710

      館藏地 登錄號 .. 普通/不普通 ........ 圖書說明 .... 圖書狀況 ...
   NL   M002151   WM100 M87 1972

      請按 <RETURN> 查看其他作品，或按 <.> 回 !
   B(回到)，M(濃選)，F(詳細)，R(重選)，或鍵入欲選的行號        最後一頁
-----------------------------------------------------------------
   鍵入您希項，或按 <?> 顯示說明
```

畫面（三）

F. 臺灣神學院圖書館

```
10:41 12 OCT 90                      書名查詢                              台神
------------------------------- 選擇項目 -------------------------------
查詢到的資料有：

行號    作品數
 1.       6      The New Testament
 2.       1      The New Testament ; a guide to its writings
 3.       1      The New Testament: a translation in the language of the people
 4.       1      The New Testament: a new translation
 5.       1      The New Testament: revised Standard Version and Japanese
                 colloquial Version Bilingual edition
 6.       1      The New Testament the history of the investigation of its
                 problems
 7.       1      The New Testament: an introduction for the general reader
 8.       1      The New Testament: an introduction
 9.       1      The New Testament: an historical and analytic survey


A(全部顯示),B(回到上一頁),D(顯示作品)  K(關鍵字查詢)
                                                        ---- Last page ---
鍵入選擇項，或按▼(?)顯示說明
```

畫面（一）

```
10:42 12 OCT 90                      書名查詢                              台神
------------------------------- WORKS DISPLAY - BRIEF -------------------
1. Bible.N.T. The New Testament / a new translation by James Moffatt. - New
     edition, revised. - London : Hodder and Stoughton, 1950? (BRN:13541)

     館藏地  登錄號 .. 索書號/未書號 .......  圖書說明 .... 圖書狀況 ...
     TTC    B10017834   R BS2095 M5 1950

2. Bible.N.T.English.Moffatt.1935. The New Testament / a new translation by
     James Moffatt. - London : Hodder and Stoughton, 1935? (BRN:13545)

     館藏地  登錄號 .. 索書號/未書號 .......  圖書說明 .... 圖書狀況 ...
     TTC    B00013539    BS2095 M7 1935

3. Metzger, Bruce Manning. 新約導論 / Bruce Manning Metzger著 ; 陳慧如譯
     - 香港 : 基督教文藝, 1976 (BRN:14 6)


請按 <RETURN> 查看其他作品，或按 (.) 查閱
B(開始), M(標準), F(詳細), R(重選), 或鍵入欲預約的行號
                                                       ---- More pages --
鍵入選擇項，或按▼(?)顯示說明
```

畫面（二）

```
10:50 12 OCT 90                    書名查詢                        台神
------------------------ WORKS DISPLAY - FULL ------------------------
1. 新園 / 曹開欣譯
   出版項.......台灣省：大同教出版譯述委員會, 1965

   稽核項.......300 p. ; 19 cm.

   主題........Bahaism.

   附註........English title : The new g  den.

   個人著者.....Fathea'Zam, Hooshmand.

   書目資料編號(BRN) :4183


請按 <RETURN> 查看其他作品，或按 <.> 離開
B(簡略), M(標準), F(詳細), R(重返), 或鍵入欲預約的行號
--------------------------------------------------- More pages --
鍵入選擇項，或按▼<?>顯示說明
```

畫面（三）－1

```
10:50 12 OCT 90                    書名查詢                        台神
------------------------ WORKS DISPLAY - FULL ------------------------
館藏地 登錄號  .. 書號/索書號 .........  著者說明 ....  圖書狀況 ...
TTC  B00005056  BP 330 F312




請按 <RETURN> 查看其他作品，或按 <.> 離開
B(簡略), M(標準), F(詳細), R(重返), 或鍵入欲預約的行號
--------------------------------------------------- Last page ---
鍵入選擇項，或按▼<?>顯示說明
```

畫面（三）－2

G. 私立淡江大學圖書館

```
DOBIS/LIBIS/TALIS
         ///////////     ///     |      \\\\\\\\    \\\\\\\
         000000000000;  000.//   0      \00000000  \\\0000000\
         00/ 00/ 00/    00/00//  0      \00        \00      \00
歡迎使用   00/            00/ 00// 0      \00        \00\\\\\\
Welcome to 00/           00000000000/ 0   \00        \0000000\
         00/            00/ 00/ 0    ||   \00        \       \00
         00./           00/ 00/ 0  |||!00 \\\\00\   \00\\\\\\00
         0000/         00/ 00/ 0  000000  \00000000 \0000000

         (Tamkang Automated Library Integrated System)
              淡 江 圖 書 館 自 動 化 系 統

請選擇功能代號                    Enter the number
  1 查詢館藏目錄                    4 to change the dialog language to English
  2 查看你本人的借閱記錄
  3 傳送訊息給圖書館員

鍵入代號或代碼，按執行鍵
1
                 f 次頁
```

畫面（一）

```
目錄查尋           DBSSE02
著者              XSE020

 1            賽恩 (Shain, Merle)
 2 /          莎士比亞 (Shakespeare, William) :15
 3 /    文 (Gawain, Shakti
 4 /          山姆斯 (Shames, Irving Herman) :1
 5    --- 郭氏 (Kuo, Shan S ) --------------------
 6            向娜 (Shanne, William)
 7            夏匹洛 (Shaper, Albert)
 8            夏皮洛 (Shapiro, Ascher H.)
 9            夏皮洛 (Shapiro, B. P.)
10  ---------- 夏皮洛 (Shapiro, Edward) :1920- ----
11            夏竹麗 (Shapiro, Judith)
12            夏皮洛 (Shapiro, Linda G.)
13            夏普黎 (Shapley, Harlow) :1885-
14            謝拉夫 (Sharaf, Hussein A.)

鍵入代號或代碼，按執行鍵

t 換檢索語       f 次頁
i 換索引檔       b 前頁
                              e 結束
```

畫面（二）

```
目錄查尋            DBSSE03
著者              TSE030
簡略書目

莎士比亞(Shakespeare, William). 15    11〕 筆資料

   1  金言                                     民國 53
   2  暴風雨                                        日期
   3  莎士比亞全集                              民國 56
   4  終成眷屬                                   民國 43
   5  暴風雨                                     民國 48
   6  諧謔的喜劇                                民國 43
   7  過失記                                     民國 45
   8  羅密歐與朱麗葉                           民國 44
   9  量罪記                                     民國 43
  10  無事煩惱                                   民國 42
  11  溫莎的風流娘兒們                        民國 45
  12  馴悍記                                     民國 43

選入代號或代碼，按執行鍵

  t 換檢索語      f 次頁
  i 換索引檔
  v 顯示檢索檔   x 參照              e 結束
```

畫面（三）

```
目錄查尋            DBSSE11
著者              TCA130
完整書目          書目主檔號  509412

  著者：  莎士比亞(Shakespeare, Wiliiam). 1564-16
              16 /朱生豪 （譯者）
  題名：  馴悍記
  出版者： 世界書局 臺北市 ，民國 45

  集叢：  莎士比亞戲劇

  分類號： 873.43344

  包含：  82面；18公分

  館藏：  城  873.43344 /8966

選入k或其它代碼

  t 換檢索語         k 館藏情況   s 開端資料
  i 換索引檔
  ˙顯示檢索檔                          e 結束
```

畫面（四）

H. "行政院經濟建設委員會"圖書館

```
========================================
             查 詢 子 系 統
========================================

    1. 書名查詢              8. 圖書組合查詢
    2. 作者查詢              9. 期刊資料查詢
    3. 標題查詢             10. 論文檔查詢
    4. 分類號查詢           11. 新到圖書查詢
    5. 叢書名查詢           12. 新到期刊查詢
    6. 叢書作者查詢         13. 新編論文查詢
    7. 關鍵語查詢

                0. 結束


         請選擇作業代號：
```

畫面（一）

```
(LB3160)       *** 圖書組合查詢作業 ***     日期：73年 07月 25日

條 件：

步驟-總數-內容 ------------------------------------------------




  1    0   K1=#OECD# AND K5=#INFLATION#
  2    0   K1=#OECD# AND K6=#ECONOMICS#
  3  1113  K1=#OECD# OR K6=#ECONOMICS#
----------------------------------------------------------------
K1=作者 K2=書名 K3=分類號 K4=標題 K5=叢書名 K6=關鍵語 K7=出版年 Sx x=步驟
     <F1>:顯示詳細資料      <F7>:上一頁    <F10>:結束    <F3>:RECALL   <PF4>:執行
     <F2>:顯示書名作者      <F8>:下一頁    <F11>:取消    <F6>:HELP     <F9>:列印
----------------------------------------------------------------
<<C-3-00>> 作業完成                              ：圖書資料查詢作業
```

畫面（二）

```
(LS3161)         ××× 顯示部份資料作業 ×××      日期：77年 03月
流水號  作     者                         書    名
 00001  World Bank                 Economic and social analysis of projec
 00002  World Bank                 Economic Fluctuations and Speed of
                                   Urbanization: A Case Study of
                                   Korea.1955-1975
 00003  World Bank                 Economic growth and human resources.
 00004  World Bank                 Economics of supplemental feeding of
                                   malnourished children: leakages, costs
                                   and
 00005  World Bank                 Economic return to investment in
                                   irrigation in India.
 00006  World Bank                 Economics and the Politics of
                                   Protection-Some Case Studies of
                                   Industries.
 00007  World Bank                 Economic reform in socialist countries
 00008   World Bank                Economic Decisionmaking Structures and
                                   Processes in Hungary
 00009  World Bank                 Economic Appraisal of Rural Roads
 00010  World Bank                 Economic Aspects of Historical Desert

<F2>:顯示詳細資料   <F8>:下一頁    <F10>:結束
```

畫面（三）

```
< LS3100 >             << 書名查詢 >>           日期： 77年 03月
書名 : ECONOMIC THEORY?
-----------------------------------------------------------------
流水號  書     名                              作     者
 0001  Economic theory and method.            Zeuthen, F
 0002  Economic theory and operations analysis. Baumol, William J
       Maruzen Asian edition.
 0003  Economic theory and operations analysis. Baumol, William J
       Maruzen Asian edition.
 0004  Economic theory and operations analysis. Baumol, William J.
 0005  Economic Theory and the Construction    Hillebrandt, Patricia M.
       Industry.
 0006  Economic theory of fiscal policy.       Hansen, A H.
 0007  Economic theory of public enterprise    Bos, Dieter
 0008  Economic theory of the industry         Waterson, Michael
 0009  Economic theory of the industry         Waterson, Michael
 0010  Economic Theory, Intermediate           Mckenna, Joseph P
-----------------------------------------------------------------
<F1>:詳細資料   <F8>:下頁   <F10>:結束   <F11>:取消   <PF4>:執行
<< 請選擇欲顯示流水號：178              <CR>
```

畫面（四）

```
<LEBKDE>            ×××  書目詳細資料  ×××
圖書登錄號 : 0022289                  財產號 : 000000
編目日期 : 76 / 07 / 08     書類代號 : 單書      資料型態 :
分 類 號 : 330.1/Zeu                語文別 : E
國際書號 :              官書號 :         價 格 : 00000.00    等
作 者 (1) : Zeuthen, F
作 者 (2) :
作 者 (3) :
叢書作者 :
書    名 : Economic theory and method.
並列書名 :
副 書 名 :
出版年 : 1955                          版 次 :
出版地 : Cambridge,
出版者 : Mass., Harvard University Press.
稽核項 : xii, 364p.

叢書名 :
標題 :1             .2               3
附 註 :
借閱日期 :  / /      在館否 : 在館    借閱次數 :      報銷日期 : 00/ 00
       <F7>:上查            <F8>:下查           <F10>:結束
```

畫面（五）

```
(L33170)             ×××  期刊資料查詢  ×××           日  期 : 77年 03月
--------------------------------------------------------------
期刊代號 :0C001              分類號 :572
期刊名稱 :人事月刊
出 版 商 :人事月刊編輯委員會
出 版 地 :台北市復興街109號
附   註 :
刊期別 :M              卷期比 :12          電話 :(02)3146094
創刊日 :74 年 09 月 00 日    國際叢書號 :
來   源 :P              代理商號 :0002
訂購起始日 :76 年 09 月 01 日   訂購迄日 :77 年 08 月 31 日
--------------------------------------------------------------
<F10>:結束
```

畫面（六）

J. "行政院國軍退除役官兵輔導委員會"榮民工程事業管理處圖書室

畫面（一）

畫面（二）

畫面（三）

畫面（四）

```
          ==============================
          =   書 名 關 鍵 字 查 詢   =
          ==============================
  說  明 :
          請輸入一個或多個關鍵字
          (1) 完整關鍵字. 如:MANAGEMENT
          (2) 部分關鍵字. 如:MANA?(字尾須加'?'
          (3) 兩者可混合使用
           如 : MANAGEMENT AND 2.SCI?
          請輸入刊名關鍵字:(每一欄位只能輸入一個關鍵字)

          1._____ AND 2. _PROCESS?_____ AND
          3._____ AND 4. _____ AND
          5._____ AND 6. _____
          如再輸入書名第一個字母,可以減少出現筆數:
              __ OR __ OR __

----------------------------------------------------
          <TAB>:按/TAB鍵/跳至下一個輸入欄位
          ENTER:執行  /PF15:返回查詢總畫面   /PF16:返回前幕
```

畫面（二）

```
                                        總  數 = 43
--------------------- 簡  明  目  錄 ---------------------
1.Algoritgms for graphics and image processing
  :Pavlidis,Theo
2.Architectures and design techniques for real time image
  processing Ics :Ruetz, Peter Alexander
3.Advances in Digital Image Processing : theory, appl.
  implementation :Stucki, Petered. ;1978
4.Advances in computer vision and image processing.
5.Computer vision, image processing and communications
  systems and applications
  :wang,patrick S-P ed.
  :1985
6.Computer techniques in image processing
  :Andrews, Harry C. & Pratt, William K. & Caspari, Kenneth
7.Computer image processing and recognition
  :Hall, Ernest L.
8.Computing structures for image processing
  :Duff, M. J. B. ed.
----------------------------------------------------
 ENTER:輸入所需書目序號  4 即得基本資料
 PF2:首頁    /PF3:末頁     /PF4:上一頁
 PF5:下一頁  /PF15:返回查詢總畫面   /PF16:返回前幕
```

畫面（三）

```
------------------- 基 本 資 料 -------------------
書名：
  Image enhancement and restoration
作者：Huang, Thomas S. ed.
                                    索書號：TA1632
                                            Ad 95
出 版 年      ：1986                  V.2

   登錄號        館藏地           流通狀況
-------------------------------------------------
   0054322     博愛圖書館
```

```
PF1:詳細資料    /PF2:首頁      /PF3:末頁      /PF4:上 -- 頁
PF5:下 一 頁    /PF15:查詢總畫面      /PF16:前幕
```

畫面（四）

```
------------------- 詳 細 資 料 -------------------
版大：
頁數：378      價錢：1620
出版者：JAI Press
出版地：Greenwich, Connecticut
翻版者：
翻版地：
標題：1.Image processing--Digital techniques--Periodicals. 2
     .Computer vision--Periodicals. 3. Image processing--Pe
     riodicals. 4. Optical data processing--Periodicals.
叢書名：
  Advances in computer vision and image processing
會議名稱：


附 註：
-------------------------------------------------
   PF1:返回前幕      /PF15:返回查詢總畫面
   PF16:返回說明目錄畫面
```

畫面（五）

二、中文資料畫面：

```
::::::::::::::::::::::::::::::::::::
: 國立交通大學圖書館中文圖書查詢系統 :
::::::::::::::::::::::::::::::::::::

  此系統供查詢本館中文圖書資料包括：
  書名，作者，關鍵詞..........
       查詢途徑：
   PF1：書名關鍵詞查詢
   PF2：書名，作者，登錄號查詢
   PF16：結束

   (    請 按 適 當 PF 鍵    )
```

畫面（一）

```
   ::::::::::::::::::::::::::::::::
   :     書 名 關 鍵 詞 查 詢      :
   ::::::::::::::::::::::::::::::::
說明：
    請輸入一個或兩個關鍵詞
   (1)完整關鍵詞，如經濟學
   (2)部份關鍵詞，如經濟？（字尾須加？）
   (3)兩者混合使用．
       如：1總統 AND 2經濟？
    ．或：1中國？AND 2台灣

1. COBOL_____ AND 2. 程式？_____

------------------------------------------
<TAB>：跳至下一個輸入欄位
PF15：中文輸入法說明
ENTER：執行                    PF16：返回前幕
```

畫面（二）

```
                                                        阿目
0001 商用程式語言COBOL/鍾英明,陳秋發著
0002 COBOL程式設計範例/鍾英明編
0003 COBOL程式語言/許性敬著
0004 結構化COBOL程式語言：STRUCTURED COBOL PROGRAMMING/林家鵬
0005 高等結構化程式設計 ＣＯＢＯＬ：Advanced Structrued C
0006 結構化COBOL程式設計 /李昌平著
0007 MICROSOFT COBOL工具程式 / 邱志良譯
0008 PC RM COBOL程式設計 /陳守良著
0009 電子計算機程式設計COBOL/張豆雄著
0010 高等結構化程式設計 COBOL/陳能保
0011 結構化程式設計COBOL/STERN,ROBERT A.著;陳
0012 結構化RM/COBOL程式設計與應用/貢慶嗣著

-------------------------------------------
ENTER=第  1  項詳細資料
共    12  筆   PF9=按書名筆劃排序        PF16=返回前幕
```

畫面（三）

```
                                                        詳細書目
索書號：
(排架號)312.92
         8246

書  名：商用程式語言COBOL
作  者：鍾英明.陳秋發著
出  版：台北市：田野：民66
頁  數：294面


登錄號  /館藏地  /館藏狀況  /還期  /預約人數/
-------------------------------------------
01  19105  光  復       可    借


-------------------------------------------
                    PF14=說明        PF16=返回前幕
```

畫面（四）

L、工業技術研究院

畫面（一）

畫面（二）

畫面（三）

M、臺灣省立美術館資料中心

畫面（一）

```
┌─────────────────────────────────────────────┐
│  ・查詢子系統─功能選擇畫面・    臺灣省立美術館  │
│                                美術資料整合系統│
│ ─────────────────────────────────────────── │
│  01.書目查詢─題名         31.檢索點控制檔維護 │
│  02.書目查詢─著者         32.查詢畫面控制檔維護│
│  03.書目查詢─登錄號                          │
│  04.書目查詢─密碼         41.建立查詢檔      │
│                           42.更新查詢檔      │
│                                              │
│  21.書目查詢─其它檢索點   00.離開查詢系統    │
│ ─────────────────────────────────────────── │
│  功能選擇：01                                │
└─────────────────────────────────────────────┘
```

畫面（二）

```
┌─────────────────────────────────────────────┐
│                           查詢編號.....01    │
│  ・查詢子系統─書目查詢─題名・  紀錄識別號...   │
│                           書名.........中國美術史│
│ ─────────────────────────────────────────── │
│                                              │
│                                              │
│                                              │
│                                              │
│                                              │
│                                              │
│                                              │
│  輸入項次查詢詳細書目：_                     │
└─────────────────────────────────────────────┘
```

畫面（三）

```
┌─────────────────────────────────────────────────────┐
│                                    查詢編號.....01   │
│  • 查詢子系統─書目查詢─題名 •       記數識別號...    │
│                                    書名........中國美術史 │
│                                                     │
│  1. 中國美術史／鄭昶編／                            │
│  2. 中國美術史／張光福編著／                        │
│  3. 中國美術史略／閻麗川著／丹青藝術叢書            │
│  4. 中國美術史稿／李裕著／                          │
│  5. 中國美術史論集／金琳著者／                      │
│  6. 中國美術史導論／（英）鳥爾阿著／王德昭譯／      │
│  7. 中國美術年表／鄭昶編／                          │
│  8. 中國美術年表／閻抱石編／                        │
│  9. 中國美術家人名辭典／文史哲出版社編／            │
│                                                     │
│  輸入項次查詢詳細書目：1                            │
└─────────────────────────────────────────────────────┘

                    畫面（四）

┌─────────────────────────────────────────────────────┐
│                                    查詢編號.....01   │
│  • 查詢子系統─書目查詢─題名 •       記數識別號...607 │
│                                    書名........中國美術史 │
│                                                     │
│  正題名（書名）..........中國美術史                 │
│  主要著者..............鄭昶編                       │
│  版本敘述..............五版                         │
│  出版地、經銷地........臺北市                       │
│  出版者、經銷者名稱....臺灣中華                     │
│  出版、經銷日期........民71〔1982〕                 │
│  裝訂及其它識別字樣....平裝                         │
│  分類號................909.8                        │
│  書號..................8736                         │
│                                                     │
│  要查看館藏狀況嗎？                                 │
└─────────────────────────────────────────────────────┘

                    畫面（五）
```

N、"國立自然科學博物館"資訊組圖書室

```
┌─────────────────────────────────────────────┐
│   ┌- - - - - - - - - - - - - - - - - -┐     │
│   ╎   ◉       查詢子系統       ☺    ╎     │
│   └- - - - - - - - - - - - - - - - - -┘     │
│ ═══════════════════════════════════════════  │
│                                              │
│       〔1〕依題名查詢                         │
│       〔2〕依著者查詢                         │
│       〔3〕依標題查詢                         │
│       〔4〕依分類號查詢                       │
│       〔5〕庭擇與限制查詢                     │
│       〔0〕結束                               │
│                                              │
│ ═══════════════════════════════════════════  │
│  功能選擇 ：〔 _ 〕                           │
└─────────────────────────────────────────────┘
```

畫面（一）

```
┌─────────────────────────────────────────────┐
│   ┌- - - - - - - - - - - - - - - - - - - -┐ │
│   ╎ ◉  查詢子系統 ---- 依題名查詢  ◉ ╎ │
│   └- - - - - - - - - - - - - - - - - - - -┘ │
│ ═══════════════════════════════════════════  │
│                                              │
│       〔1〕依前幾個字查詢                     │
│       〔2〕依關鍵字查詢                       │
│       〔3〕依 2.3.3.2 查詢                    │
│       〔0〕結束                               │
│                                              │
│ ═══════════════════════════════════════════  │
│  功能選擇 ：〔 _ 〕                           │
└─────────────────────────────────────────────┘
```

畫面（二）

```
┌─────────────────────────────────────────────────────────────┐
│    ┌─ ─ ─ ─ ─ ─ ─ ─ ─ ─ ─ ─ ─ ─ ─ ─ ─ ─ ─ ─ ┐                │
│    │ ◎ 查詢子系統--題名查詢--依前幾個字 ◎ │        總共有    │
│    └─ ─ ─ ─ ─ ─ ─ ─ ─ ─ ─ ─ ─ ─ ─ ─ ─ ─ ─ ─ ┘                │
│    請輸入題名的前幾個字 : [ 教育社會學          ]            │
│    ═══════════════════════════════════════════════════════  │
│    題            名              著      者   出版年  分 類  │
│     1 教育社會學理論          布列克里局(David Blac- 1987 520.13│
│                               kledge), 杭特(Barry H-         │
│                               unt)著                         │
│                                                              │
│                                                              │
│                                                              │
│    ═══════════════════════════════════════════════════════  │
│    欲查詢詳細書目請輸入該書項次 : [    ] 〈註 : [↑↓]捲閱上下個 [Return]確定│
│    欲查詢某著者之相關作品請輸入著者名稱 : [              ]   │
│    欲查詢相關類號請輸入該類號 : [              ]             │
│                                                              │
│    功能鍵:( F17:結束  PF1:列印  PF2:上頁  PF3:下頁  PF4:暫存  Help:操作指引 )│
└─────────────────────────────────────────────────────────────┘
```

畫面（三）

```
┌─────────────────────────────────────────────────────────────┐
│    ┌─ ─ ─ ─ ─ ─ ─ ─ ─ ─ ─ ─ ─ ─ ─ ─ ─ ─ ┐                    │
│    │ ◎ 查詢子系統--------完整書目 ◎ │                        │
│    └─ ─ ─ ─ ─ ─ ─ ─ ─ ─ ─ ─ ─ ─ ─ ─ ─ ─ ┘                    │
│                                                              │
│    題名及著者 ...  教育社會學理論 / 布列克里局(David Blackledge), 杭特(Barry Hunt│
│    版本 ........   初版                                      │
│    出版 ........   臺北市 ; 桂冠圖書, 民76[1987]             │
│    稽核 ........   [6], 460面 ; 21公分                       │
│    集叢 ........   桂冠社會學叢書 ; 4                        │
│    特/分類/書...   520.1354 / 4084                           │
│    資料現況 ....   0003708: 已移送                           │
│    附錄等註 ....   附: 參考書目及索引                        │
│    內容註 ......   第一部份, 該用幹與功能論的傳統            │
│                    第二部份, 馬克思主義的觀點                │
│                    第三部份, 解釋取向.                       │
│                                                              │
│    ═══════════════════════════════════════════════════════  │
│    功能鍵:( F17:結束  PF1:列印  PF2:上頁  PF3:下頁  Help:操作指引 )│
└─────────────────────────────────────────────────────────────┘
```

畫面（四）

O、"國立成功大學"圖書室

```
80/01/14                                              QRY023
         *********************************
         *         你    好  !              *
         *     歡 迎 到 成 大 總 圖 書 館      *
         *********************************

         本公眾目錄查詢系統可查詢下列事項:

           F1 Key.  查詢你個人借閱狀況.
           F2 Key.  查詢書的流通狀況.
           F3 Key.  查詢本館(館藏,編目,採購)之書目資料.
           F4 Key.  查詢本館期刊資料.

         請選擇查詢之Function Key
```

畫面（一）

```
        圖 書 查 詢 功 能 三               QRY023
                                          80/01/15
   本功能提供本館(館藏,書目,採購)之書目資料
   提供你下列十種不同的檢索方式,輸入時不需考慮大小寫,並可忽略空白字元.
   另提供寬字(Truncation)功能,依序顯示(館藏,書目,採購)中之十二筆資料.

           1. 登錄號  ( ACC-NO )     *6. 叢刊項  ( SERIES )
           2. 書名    ( TITLE  )      7. I.S.B.N
           3. 作者    ( AUTHOR )     *8. I.S.S.N
          *4. 索書號  ( CALL-NO)      9. 出版者  ( PUBLISHER )
          *5. 標題    ( SUBJECT)    *10. L.C.C.N (請按 L Or l)
                                      E. 結束    ( EXIT )

   ※注意:採購檔資料無法以查詢項(*)者獲得資料.
         請選擇檢索方式 ( 1-10,E ) 空一格,再鍵入檢索字串.
         例:輸入方式 ->3 金屬

   Prev Page -上一頁;Next Page - 下一頁;Roll Down - 下一行;Roll Up - 上一行

   選 擇 ->
```

畫面（二）

```
請選擇檢索方式（1-10,E）空一格,再鍵入檢索字串.
例：輸入方式 ->3 金屬

Prev Page -上一頁;Next Page - 下一頁;Roll Down - 下一行;Roll Up - 上一行

選  擇 -> 3 朱天心
No.  登錄號      *作 者*（館藏）
---  ---------  ----------------
01   409333     朱天心          昨日當我年輕時
02   409336     朱天心          擊壤歌：北一女三年記
03   409340     朱天心          臺大女學生關琳的日記
04   505757     朱天心          大學生關琳的日記
05   619391     朱天心          方舟上的日子
06   627334     朱天心          未了
07   631550     朱天心          想我眷村的兄弟們
08   632292     朱天心          我記得
09   638866     朱天心          昨日當我年輕時
10   409317     朱天文          炎夏之都
11   409319     朱天文          淡江記
12   409335     朱天文          最想念的季節

詳細內容查詢請選？(1-12) 0
```

畫面（三）

```
80/01/15        << 國立成功大學 總圖書館 書目查詢 >>        GRY023

+登 錄 號：640120      +索 書 號：      855              7163c
+書    名：江湖人物
                                       LC NO：
+作    者：亮軒                                        裝訂別：平
+叢 刊 項：詩文之美，54.                              館藏處：總館
+標    題：                                            資料類別：
                                                      頁  數：153
                                                      高  廣： ×
+出 版 者：漢藝色研發行，錦德總經銷
 出 版 年：民79      版  次：                部冊號：c.2
 出 版 地：臺北市                           語文別：C       翻版書註：
+I.S.B.N                                    +I.S.S.N：     -
+L.C.C.N：                                  建檔日期：     列印通報否：N
 到館日期：891002   售價(NT$)：104           書  商：       報廢註：
<<請按 F2 至 F16 任何一鍵回主畫面>>            PF4 KEY -- 列印畫面
 F1 請取下一筆資料

讀取->( 00640120 ) 細項資料
```

畫面（四）

畫面（五）

P、亞洲蔬菜研究發展中心圖書館

系統畫面

```
••••••••••••••••••••••••••••••••••••••••••••••••••••••••
•                    AVAILABLE DATABASES                •
• (1) AVRDC WEATHER STATION RECORD   ( from 75/01/01 )  •
• (2) Available MINISIS Databases                       •
•        DB Name        Contents        Provided by  Records
•        --------       --------        -----------  -------
•     LIBRARY.LIBRARY   bibliography      LIBRARY    16,500
•     HOLDING.LIBRARY   holding of serials LIBRARY    2,850
•     MAIL.DIS          mailing list       DIS        7,000
•                                                       •
••••••••••••••••••••••••••••••••••••••••••••••••••••••••
                    Select(1-2) or 0 to EXIT :2
QUERY/MINISIS G.01.00 FRI, DEC 21, 1990, 2:08 PM
ENTER DATA BASE NAME OR EXIT - LIBRARY.LIBRARY
TYPE 'HELP' FOR VALID COMMANDS
```

畫面（一）

```
> FILES
   DB: LIBRARY.LIBRARY
     KEYWORD                   C210 (Default Query Field)
     PERSONAL AUTHOR           B210
     TITLE                     A230
     COUNTRY/REGION CODE       C100
     AVRDC GERMPLASM           C220
     YEAR OF PUBLICATION       B630
   DB: HOLDING.LIBRARY
     SERIAL TITLE              H100 (Default Query Field)
     SUBJECT HEADING           H210
     COUNTRY CODE              H400
```

畫面（二）

```
> = RT HEAT STRESS
    HEAT STRESS         P=20
    HEAT RESISTANCE     P=3
    HEAT SHOCK          P=15
    HEAT TOLERANCE      P=102
    HIGH TEMPERATURE    P=71
    TEMPERATURE RESISTANCE   P=11
      1 :    P=184   T=184
```

畫面（三）

```
Q> B

ISN= 272
CALL NUMBER     : REP.TM-476
AUTHOR          : Taianova, V.V. ; Titov, A.F. ; Drozdov, S.N. ; Akimova, T.V.
TITLE           : Effect of temperature on the thermoresistance and respiration
                  of tomato leaves (Lycopersicon esculentum Mill.)
SOURCE          : BIOCHEMIE UND PHYSIOLOGIE DER PFLANZEN  v.178(8):601-605, 1983
LANGUAGE        : En ; En [Abst]
KEY WORDS       : COLD RESISTANCE / DEHYDROGENASES / HEAT TOLERANCE / LEAVES /
                  LYCOPERSICON ESCULENTUM / PLANT PHYSIOLOGY / RESPIRATION /
                  TEMPERATURE RESISTANCE / TOMATOES
ABSTRACT        : The effect of temperature in the 4-45 degree C range on the
                  thermoresistance and respiratory activity of tomato leaves was
                  studied. It was shown that a change in temperature from 15 to
                  26 degree C (a back-ground range) does not affect the
                  resistance of tomato leaves, temperatures from 6 to 14 degree
                  C and those from 27 to 42 degree C induce an increase in
                  resistance to cold and heat, respectively; at temperatures
                  below 5 degree C and above 43 degree C a drop in
                  thermoresistance is observed. Hardening was accompanied by a
                  change in the oxygen uptake (by a decrease - when hardened by
                  cold and by an increase- when hardened by heat), by a rise in
                  the respiratory quotient (when hardened by cold), and by
                  increase in dehydrogenase activity. Cold dehardening resulted
                  in a sharp rise in respiratory activity (after 3 h at 25
                  degree C). Upon dehardening (25 degree C) the activity of
                  oxygen uptake, the respiratory quotient, and dehydrogenase
                  activity returned to the initial level after 5-6 d. Injurious
                  temperatures led to a drop in respiratory activity and in
                  dehydrogenase activity. [AS]

MORE (Y/N) -
```

畫面（四）

```
Q> B,SORT=8630
** 182 KEYS EXTRACTED

ISN= 8436
CALL NUMBER     : SB211.R3REP.E1
AUTHOR          : El Murabaa, A.I.M.
TITLE           : Effect of high temperature on incompatibility in radish
SOURCE          : EUPHYTICA  v.6:263-270, 1957
LANGUAGE        : En ; En [Abst]
KEY WORDS       : HIGH TEMPERATURE / INCOMPATIBILITY / RADISHES / SEED
                  PRODUCTION
ABSTRACT        : Clones of radish plants were cross-pollinated or selfed at 17
                  and 25 C. In cross-compatible plants the fruit; the average
                  number of seeds per fruit and the total seed yield were
                  decreased at 25 C. In incompatible plants the fruit set and
                  the total seed yield were increased when selfing was done at
                  the higher temperature. It is concluded that while high
                  temperature has an unfavourable effect on seed set of radish
                  plants, it also weakens the incompatibility reaction between
                  pollen and style, so that the result is a small increase in
                  yield. [AS]

MORE (Y/N) -
```

畫面（五）

```
ISN= 6714
CALL NUMBER      : REP.PP-009
AUTHOR           : Peterson, P.A.
TITLE            : Cytoplasmically inherited male sterility in Capsicum
SOURCE           : AMERICAN NATURALIST  v.92(863):111-119, 1958.
LANGUAGE         : En ; En [Abst]
KEY WORDS        : ALLELES / CAPSICUM / CYTOPLASM / CYTOPLASMIC INHERITANCE /
                   HIGH TEMPERATURE / MALE STERILITY / PEPPERS
ABSTRACT         : A cytoplasmic male sterile in peppers has been found, the
                   expression of which is dependent upon a sterile cytoplasm and
                   a nuclear non-restorer gene (ms). Six accessions and six
                   commercial varieties carry the restorer allele, Ms, and two
                   accessions and four commercial varieties carry the
                   nonrestorer, ms. The expression of sterility is affected by
                   modifiers and temperature. Higher temperatures accentuate the
                   sterile expression. Seed set is reduced by approximately
                   one-half in fruit of sterile plants. The significance of
                   temperature influence upon sterility expression is discussed
                   in relation to genic action. The relative infrequency of the
                   ms allele in wild populations and its survival among
                   commercial varieties is discussed. [AS]
MORE (Y/N) -
```

畫面（六）

Q、"中國鋼鐵公司"技術資料組圖書館

畫面（一）

畫面（二）

畫面（三）

畫面（四）

畫面（五）

```
·E864·           === 元智大學館藏目錄 ===
書　名： CICS/VS TASK PROCESSING : TEXT.

作　者： MAYBERRY-STEWART, MELODIE I. · NONA C. STRONG
版　本：
出版地： CHICAGO, ILL.
出版者： SCIENCE RESEARCH ASSOCIATES
出版年： INC. C1983.
稽核項： 1 V. (LOOSE-LEAF) : ILL. ; 29 CM. · PERSONAL REFERENCE GUIDE
附註項：
ISBN　：
索書號：   QA 76.8      /M467C
登錄號：   008214
館藏單位： T411

借閱者：           卡號：        單位：        電話：        到期日：

操作代碼： S
(書目顯示作業  S 顯略書目資料  1 左舉清示引表  2 詳細  訊息：  歡迎指教！
```

畫面（六）

根據畫面分析結果顯示：

（1）畫面顯示格式部份：16 個系統並無傳統卡片格式之顯示方式，其中 URICA 系統之顯示格式是由卡片式與欄位混合組成，其他的系統則完全採用欄位顯示格式。

（2）欄位名稱及其放置位置：欄位名稱各系統之間並不一致，例如有用"書名"者，亦有用"題名"者，欄位若置於左邊者，採左邊對齊或左右對齊方式，但若欄位不在左邊時，其排列便無一定次序。欄位名稱與內容之間以"："或"……"做為分隔符號。

（3）資料顯示層次及內容：調查結果系統中最多為提供 4 種不同層次與格式之畫面（如北一女系統），然而各系統所採用之顯示名稱有所出入，例如第一層之名稱有簡略（BRIEF）、簡明資料，簡略書目，部份資料、簡明目錄、簡目、簡略書目資料等；而各系統第一層所顯示之資料內容亦不盡相同，有些系統顯示之資料內容僅書名、作者，有的系統則尚包括登錄號、分類號、索書號、特藏號、主要款目、登錄日期，借閱狀態等（例如工研院系統）；有些系統為了將所有資訊放置在同一畫面（如經建會，工研院、成大等），便將所有系統設定的欄位放置於同一畫面上，資料顯示時往往有許多欄位之值是空白，又因欄位過多而易造成畫面混亂。

（4）螢幕顯示之字體，中文為兩個位元組數（byte），英文為一個位元組數，但淡江大學之系統在中文資料中，無論中、英文字均為兩個位元組數，此時之英文字體有欠美觀。

（5）交談模式：臺大工圖及亞蔬採用指令型式，工研院為格式化輸入，其餘則為選項式。目前各系統皆僅提供一種固定的交談模式。

各系統之交談模式、顯示格式及顯示層次與名稱可參見表5。

表5：各系統畫面顯示格式之比較

單位代碼 \ 項目	交談模式	顯示格式	顯示層次及其名稱
A	指令式	欄位顯示 欄位名稱大部份左右對齊型式，以：為分隔符號	1. 簡明資料 2. 詳細資料
B	選項式	卡片式與欄位顯示之混合，欄位名稱及內容靠左對齊，以…為分隔符號	1. BRIEF（簡略） 2. MEDIUM（標準） 3. FULL（詳細）
C	選項式	同 B	1. BRIEF（簡略） 2. MEDIUM（標準） 3. FULL（詳細） 4. MARC（機讀格式）
D	選項式	BRIEF 與 B、C 同，但 FULL 為欄位顯示格式，以……為分隔符號	1. BRIEF（簡略） 2. MEDIUM（標準） 3. FULL（詳細）
F	選項式	同 B、C	1. BRIEF（簡略） 2. FULL（詳細）
G	選項式	欄位顯示，欄位名稱左邊對齊，且有一行空白	1. Short Information（簡略書目） 2. Full Information（完整書目）
H	選項式	欄位顯示，左邊之欄位名稱左右對齊，但非所有欄位都置於左邊，畫面上無資料之欄位亦顯示出來；以：為分隔符號	1. 部份資料 2. 詳細資料
J	選項式	欄位顯示，欄位名稱設計型式有的加"："與內容分隔，有些不加，亦有欄位名稱置於內容之上面一行	不同檢索點得不同之顯示熒幕，且只顯示與該查詢項有關之資料及語言類序號
K	選項式	欄位顯示，中文欄位名稱左右對齊，英文僅左邊對齊；但中英文資料庫採用之欄位名稱及位置有部份不同；均以：為分隔符號	中文資料：1. 簡目　2. 詳細書目 英文資料：1. 簡明目錄　2. 基本資料　3. 詳細資料
L	格式化輸入	欄位顯示，欄位部份靠左對齊，部份靠右對齊，資料顯示時無內容之欄位亦出現，以：為分隔符號	1. List 2. Display
M	選項式	欄位顯示，欄位名稱及內容均靠左對齊，中間加……為分隔符號	1.（書名/作者） 2. 詳細書目
N	選項式	同 M	1.（題名，著者，出版年，分類） 2. 完整書目
O	選項式	欄位顯示，欄位名稱左右對齊，靠左及靠右均有：以為分隔符號，畫面中亦顯示採購訊息	1. 查詢結果 2. 細項資料
P	指令式	欄位顯示，欄位名稱內容靠左對齊，以：為分隔符號	只有一種格式（內容含 ISN, CALL Number, Author, Title, Source Language, key words 及 Abstract
Q	選項式	欄位顯示，欄位名稱左右對齊，但非全部置於左邊，以：為分隔符號	1. 簡略書目資料 2. 完整書目資料

叁、結論與建議

本研究根據海內外相關文獻之分析及實際調查結果，歸納出下列結論與建議，作為臺灣地區圖書館暨資料單位發展線上公用目錄之參考。

結 論

經調查統計分析後，茲將18個圖書館自動化系統線上公用目錄的系統功能、使用者調查分析與畫面顯示格式總結如下：

一、系統功能

（一）系統操作控制：

1. 在查詢方式方面：北一女及省立美術館之系統皆不能同時提供中文或英文查詢，其他則可。

2. 選項查詢功能：18個系統中有14個系統可供讀者選擇所需的查詢項目，如：書目查詢，流通記錄、館際互借等。

3. 交談模式方面：在18個系統中僅臺大工圖和亞蔬可採指令查詢方式，其餘則採選項查詢方式。

4. 中斷或取消查詢功能：若遇到檢索結果過多的情形時，系統提供中斷或取消查詢指令的功能就相當重要；在18個系統中，有10個系統提供此功能。

5. 錯誤修改功能：若查詢字彙在輸入時產生錯誤，則需加以修正；有8個系統提供部份字串修改的功能，而不須全部重新鍵入。

6. 提供印表機方面：可以線上列印檢索所得的資料是線上目錄的優點之一；目前有14個系統提供列印機以印出查詢結果。

7. 自動回復起始螢幕功能："國防醫學院"是唯一提供"終端機於定時內不鍵入指令，則自動回到起始螢幕"功能的系統。

（二）檢索控制：

1. 全文檢索功能：臺大工圖、"國防醫學院"和亞蔬三個系統可進行全文檢索；此外，有12個系統僅某些特定欄位適合進行全文檢索。

2. 布林邏輯和切截查詢功能：大部份系統均提供此項檢索功能。

3. 檢索點方面：各系統之檢索點不一，最多者有12個檢索點，最少者為4個，其中以個人作者，團體作者與書名為最普遍。

（三）顯示功能：

1. 顯示格式方面：多數系統提供2至3種查詢結果的顯示格式，包括：簡略，部份及完整書目等。

2. 檢索結果排序方面：有13個系統可依使用者所採用的檢索點，來排列檢索結果的顯示順序。

3. 螢幕密度方面：多數系統皆充分利用螢幕上可顯示資料的空間，故螢幕密度均相當高。

（四）系統輔助功能：

線上目錄所提供的輔助功能，對讀者使用線上目錄的吸引力及幫助相當大。

所調查的18個系統中，8個系統具提供線上使用指導的功能，可見這方面的設計尚待加強。

二、使用者調查分析

(一) 使用者檢索情形:

1. 查詢資料項目:利用線上目錄查詢資料時,研究生以查詢某主題或學科之圖書、期刊爲主;大部份使用者很少以出版商、出版日期等資料作爲查詢項目;而館員之查詢項目則不局限於某一項。

2. 檢索點方面:教師及中學生常用的檢索點是完整之作者姓名或書名;館員則常利用部份書名進行檢索。

3. 檢索目的:教師之檢索目的以作研究報告及蒐集教學資料爲主;研究生以作研究報告爲目的;大學生主要以個人進修爲檢索目的;館員之檢索目的則不定。

4. 檢索結果:大多數使用者反應僅能查得部份資料,而館員較能找到所需資料。

5. 解決問題方面:遇到困難時,教師、研究生、職員及其他使用者會詢問館員,而中學生與大學生以問旁邊的線上目錄使用者居多。

6. 布林邏輯及切截查詢功能:檢索時多數使用者都能找到相關資料;利用切截或布林邏輯檢索功能,除館員外,其他使用者較不熟悉。

7. 中西文檢索方式:大學生及中學生喜歡以中文進行檢索,而教師、研究生、職員、館員及其他之使用者則較喜歡英文檢索方式。

8. 中文輸入法:使用者多以注音輸入法爲主,而教師及館員使用注音輸入法比率偏低;其他輸入法較少用。

(二) 使用者滿意程度:

1. 根據統計分析結果顯示,不同職稱之使用者對系統之整體看法中,僅有操作一項有顯著差異。螢幕方面,在用字及亮度兩項有顯著差異。系統功能方面,多數使用者表示系統可靠;但錯誤之更正,代碼及縮寫字的使用及中西文系統切換方面,館員較不認爲有困難,而一般使用者則否。學習使用系統方面,不同職稱之使用者在提供直接而快速的檢索方式、螢幕上的輔助說明及書面式參考資料三項有顯著差異。至於書面上所用之專有名詞及系統資訊之滿意程度方面,以系統所採用辭彙一項上有顯著差異。

2. 各系統使用者對其系統滿意程度:

經由變異數分析結果發現:

(1) 系統整體看法雖有差異,但無負面的看法;查詢結果多數表示滿意;而系統功能方面有6個系統之平均值則稍偏負面意見(比較差)。

(2) 系統功能方面,有9個系統之使用者認爲反應速度緩慢;6個系統使用者認爲查詢功能不足;對中西文系統切換之滿意程度,以工研院系統使用者對該系統之切換功能感到不易使用。

(3) 學習方面:所有系統中,有2系統之使用者對系統提供之直接而快速的檢索方式表示不足;至於螢幕上的輔助說明及館員對使用者提供的指導則表示有用。

(4) 系統資訊方面:系統顯示進行之步驟項目中,省立美術館之使用者認爲僅有少數提供;"中研院"生醫所之使用者則認爲系統之錯誤訊息顯示"沒用"。

3. 館員與讀者滿意程度之分析:

其中以螢幕之字體與亮度、系統功能之中西文系統切換、學習之螢幕上輔助說明與書面式之參考資料等項有差異；而館員給予系統的評價較讀者高。

（三）建議改善項目方面：

各系統之使用者對線上目錄終端機的使用上之建議並無顯著差異；建議增加功能方面，教師及中學生多數認為需要提供線上逐步使用指導，大學生、研究生等認為應增加可查知各種資料館藏地之功能，而館員對此兩項建議的比例並不高。

三、畫面顯示格式

調查結果顯示線上公用目錄系統之畫面大多採用欄位顯示格式，而無傳統之卡片格式。資料顯示層次，有1至4層者，但各層之名稱及顯示之資料項均由各單位自行設定，故差異頗大。交談模式方面，目前多數採用選項式，僅有臺大工圖及亞蔬為指令式，且均設計成一種固定模式。畫面欄位名稱多數採左右對齊方式，並以":"或"……"做分隔符號，然而欄位之排列並無一定之次序及位置，有些顯得疏鬆，有的則又過於擁擠。

建　議

根據研究臺灣線上目錄及其顯示格式之調查結論及分析海外相關文獻，提出下列數項建議以供參考：

一、系統設計應以使用者為主要考量：圖書館自動化系統設計之考慮，應力求以使用者（讀者）為考量重點，而非全以館內作業方式為導向，尤其 OPAC 畫面之設計，讀者之習慣、好惡、畫面格式之美觀活潑、好用及親和力、查詢方式、步驟以及指令用語皆應注意，並做週詳之設計考慮。

二、重視線上目錄顯示格式之美觀：由調查中顯示島內圖書館自動化系統之線上目錄之顯格各式多採常用之欄位顯示格式，呆板而欠活潑，畫面上所採用之字體及其顯示亮度、項目間距離位置之安排及排序，資料顯示之加強重點等皆未顧及，更遑論美化。其中有些欄位為採購資料，也列為 OPAC 之欄位，造成畫面內容之混淆零亂無序，有些系統為充份利用螢幕上之空間，致使螢幕上之資料密度甚高。此外，最主要的卡片式 OPAC 畫面格式，也是讀者熟悉之查尋格式；島內系統中多未考慮此畫面，雖然海外圖書館對使用卡片式格式頗有爭論，但在轉換目錄形式之過渡時期，卡片格式亦有其存在之價值，此點也是出人意外之發現。由此可知人們對 OPAC 畫面格式之認識及經驗之欠缺，只求能查尋即可，故建議加強這方面觀念及重視。

三、改進強化 OPAC 檢索方式與功能：調查之臺灣18個系統中，少數一、二個系統可用指令（Command）查尋資料多數皆採選項之檢索方式。選項式一般對初學者使用較佳，但在熟悉系統後，讀者將會感到選項式較費時，慢、累贅且欠活潑。在檢索功能方面，中西文系統切換仍待改善，使其易用。以目前臺灣圖書館自動化系統情形而言，應考慮統一設計標準之查詢指令，可建議"中國圖書館學會"之圖書館標準委員會邀請相關專家學者研訂之。

四、圖書館對讀者之推廣宜導及訓練：整體而言，被調查之使用者對系統及線上目錄皆認為滿意，但一般讀者仍較館員多需利用指導。以18個系統而言，調查結果顯示利用指導皆不夠週詳，急需設計各式之使用者利用指導，除應定期舉辦使用者訓練講習外，系統應加添線上利用輔助功能和多種書面式之系統介紹和操作說明，以利使用者自我學習之用。

又根據最近"國立臺灣大學"圖書館學研究所之碩士論文"大學圖書館線上公用目錄使用者利用指導方式之研究"中所調查之八所大學圖書館負責線上目錄使用者利用指導業務之人員之結果發現：已啓用線上目錄的大學圖書館，尚未設計使用者利用指導教學模式，推廣方式亦較爲靜態消極。目前大學圖書館所採用的使用者利用指導多以館員實地協助爲主，而系統輔助功能和書面操作手冊皆未盡完善及新穎，與本研究之結果不謀而合。（註4）

　　五、積極推廣及訓練中文輸入法：中文輸入法是讀者使用線上目錄之先決條件，根據調查之對象表示多使用注音符號輸入；但由於臺灣較遲推廣使用電腦，多數讀者尤其是一般民衆皆不懂中文輸入法，這也是利用線上目錄之最大瓶頸，建議各級學校，或圖書館設置短期訓練班教導大衆多種中文輸入法，以提高對圖書館自動化及網路系統之利用。

　　六、擴大線上目錄之功能：線上目錄之內容不應局限於圖書館書目資料，應可利用同一終端機銜接其他館內外各種資料庫，拓寬利用資源及檢索之層面，以達到海內外是一個大系統的境地。

　　進一步研究的建議——爲配合臺灣圖書館資訊網路之建立，建議進一步進行下列各項：

（1）研究線上目錄格式統一化或標準化之可行性，以期能設計標準統一的線上目錄顯示格式；

（2）研訂適用於臺灣圖書資訊檢索之通用指令語言（Common Command Language），以利檢索；

（3）繼續調查研究使用者利用線上目錄的情況，以瞭解其檢索行爲，作爲未來改進開發 OPAC 之參考。

註　釋

註1：李德竹等"整體規劃圖書館資訊網路系統研究報告"，"教育部"1991年。

註2：Stephen R. Salmon, "Characteristics of Online Public Catalogs," <u>Library Resources and Technical Services.</u> 27（Jan. -March, 1983）：36–67.

註3：J. R. Matthews, <u>Public Access to Catalogs.</u> 2nd Ed.（New York：Neal Schuman, 1985）.

註4：廖育珮，"大學圖書館線上公用目錄使用者利用指導方式之研究"（"國立臺灣大學"圖書館學研究所，碩士論文，1991年6月）。

參考書目

1. 圖書：

Bylander, E. G. <u>Electronic Displays.</u> New York：McGraw-Hill, 1979.

Cochrane, Pauline A. <u>Improving LCSH for Use in Online Catalogs.</u> Littleton, Co.：Librarie Unlimited, 1986.

Crawford, W. Bibliographic Displays in the Online Catalog. New York: Knowledge Industry Publisher, 1986.

Fayen, Emily Gallup. The Online Catalog: Improving Public Access to Library Materials. White Plains, NY: Knowledge Industry, 1983.

Fryer, Benjamin Scott. The Effects of Spatial Arrangement, Upper-Lower Case Combinations, and Reverse Video on Patron Response to CRT Displayed Catalog Card. Provo. Utah: Brigham Young Univ., School of Library and Information Sciences, 1981.

Galitz, Wilbert O. Handbook of Screen Format Design. 3rd Ed. Ma.: QED Information Sciences, 1989.

Hildreth, Charles R. Online Public Access Catalogs: The User Interface. Dublin, Oh.: OCLC, 1982.

Hildreth, Charles R., ed. The Online Catalogue: Developments and Directions. London: The Library Association, 1989.

James, Martin. Design of Man-Computer Dialogues. Englewood Cliffs, NJ: Prentice-Hall, 1973.

Kesselman, Martin and Watstein, S. B. End-User Searching: Service and Providers. Chicago: ALA, 1988.

Lee, Lucy Te-Chu. Library Automation & Information Science: A Collection of Essays. Taipei, Taiwan: Sino-American Publishing Co., 1985.

Matthews, Joseph R. Public Access to Online Catalogs. New York: Neal-Schuman Publisher, 1985.

McCue, J. H. Online Searching in Public Libraries: A Comparative Study of Performance. Scarecrow, 1988.

Matthews, Joseph R. ed. The Impact of Online Catalogs New York: Neal-Schuman Publishers, 1986.

Williams, Joan Fryed ed. Online Catalog Screen Displays. Council on Library resources, 1986.

2. 期刊論文:

Akeroyd, John. "Information Seeking in Online Catalogues." Journal of Documentation 46 (1990): 33-52.

Beiley, Charles W. "Public-Access Computer Systems: The Next Generation of Library Automation Systems." Information Technology and Libraries 8 (June, 1989): 178-185.

Drabenstott, Karen Markey and Vizine-Goetz, Diane. "Search Trees for Subject Searching in Online Catalogs." Library Hi Tech 8 (1990): 7-20.

Drewett, Bill. "Report on the LITA Screen Design Preconference.: Information Technology and Libraries 7 (Dec. 1988): 430-438.

Efthimiadis, Efthimios N. "The Growth of the OPAC Literature." Journal of the American Society for Information Science 41 (July, 1990): 342-347.

Fokker, Dirk W. "Requirements for a User-friendly OPAC." The Electronic Library 7

(Feb., 1989): 4-10.

Kaplan, Denise ed. "Online User Assistance: a Symposium." Library Hi Tech 8 (1990): 65-84.

Kilgour, Federick G. "Design of Online Catalogs." in The Nature and Future of the Catalog: Proceedings of the ALA's Information Science and Automation Division's 1975 and 1976 Institutes on the Catalog. eds. Maurice J. Freedman and S. Michael Malinconico (Phoenix, Ariz.: Oryx Press, 1979), pp. 34-35.

Nielsen, Brian, and Baker, Betsy. "Educating the Online Catalog User: A Model Evaluation Study." Library Trends 35 (Spring, 1987): 571-586.

Stewart, T. F. M. "Displays and the Software Interface." Application Ergonomics 7 (Sep., 1976): 137-148.

Tullis, Thomas S. "An Evaluation of Alphanumeric, Graphic, and Color Information Displays." Human Factors 23 (Oct., 1981). 541-550.

Yee, Martha M. "System Design and Cataloguing Meet the User: User Interfaces to Online Public Access Catalogs." Journal of the American Society for Information Science 42 (March, 1991): 78-98.

Davis, Jinnie Y. 原著；聶克讓譯。"線上公用目錄對北卡諾來納州立大學圖書館之技術服務部門的影響"。圖書館學與資訊科學 15 卷（1989 年），頁 114—128。

吳明德。"線上目錄的分類號檢索" 書府 9 期（1988 年），頁 13—17。

張惠美。"各大學圖書館線上公用查詢系統的特色"。臺北市立圖書館館訊 8 卷 3 期（1991 年 3 月），頁 65—71。

臺灣科技資訊網路[*]

科技研究發展是任何國家皆重視的一環，不但代表一國之強弱與進步，尤爲國家經濟發展的重要關鍵。美蘇兩國長久以來之科技相較，更是稱雄世界之爭，故科技研究發展之重要性，實不容忽視的，臺灣當然亦不例外。近年來，政府投資之研究發展經費亦高達 150 億元，以"國科會"爲例，平均每年補助之科技研究計劃約 2,500 個。相對的，科技資源更是支援研究發展之主動力，更不可缺，極爲重要！

對研究者而言，無論何時何地皆可得到最新所需的資訊是必要的。1957 年蘇俄人造衛星之首次發射，對美國的教訓乃是科技資訊之不通暢，全國資訊網路之未建立等，因而急急迎頭趕上。透過政府大力支援及電腦與通訊技術之逐漸成熟，美國紛紛發展各種資訊網路及自動化系統，如美國之 DIALOG BRS ORBIT OCLC 等全國性資訊網路，自 1972 年先後成立以來，現已是國際性網路。另於 1980 年設立之歐洲共同市場國家 EURONET 資訊網路和日本 JOIS 系統，皆由地區性網路積極擴展成國際性網路。

近年來，臺灣學術研究機構與大型事業單位亦紛紛建立自己的資料庫或自動化資料處理系統，和蒐集與之專業有關之參考資料。這些散布各處之專門性資料庫及參考資料，極具研究之參考價值，應重視而予以整合處理，便於更多學者專家分享與利用，故興起建立科技網路之構思。有關單位先後曾計劃設立網路者有三：科資中心的"科技性資訊網路"、農資中心之"農業科技資訊服務系統網路"和醫學圖書館界之"生物醫學資訊中心網路系統"等。以下各分別簡介之：

壹、科技性臺灣資訊網路

爲配合臺灣科技發展政策，"行政院國家科學委員會"科學技術資料中心於 1986 年初擬建立科技性全國資訊網路計劃，以期能對研究人員提供現代化資訊服務，改善島內研究環境，加速研究工作之進行。建立科技性全國資訊網路之目的是：（一）整合處理臺灣科技研究資料；（二）配合需要，引進海外高參考價值資料庫；（三）提供大衆現代化之資訊服務業，網路定名爲"科技性資訊網路"（Science & Technology Information Center Network，簡稱 STICNET。該網路歷經選機、系統轉換、各種資料庫之引進及建立等作業，已於 1988 年 12 月 28 日正式啓用。其網路系統連線情形及網路架構女如圖一、圖二：

---

[*] 本文曾發表在《書府》1991 年 6 月第 12 期，第 4—10 頁。

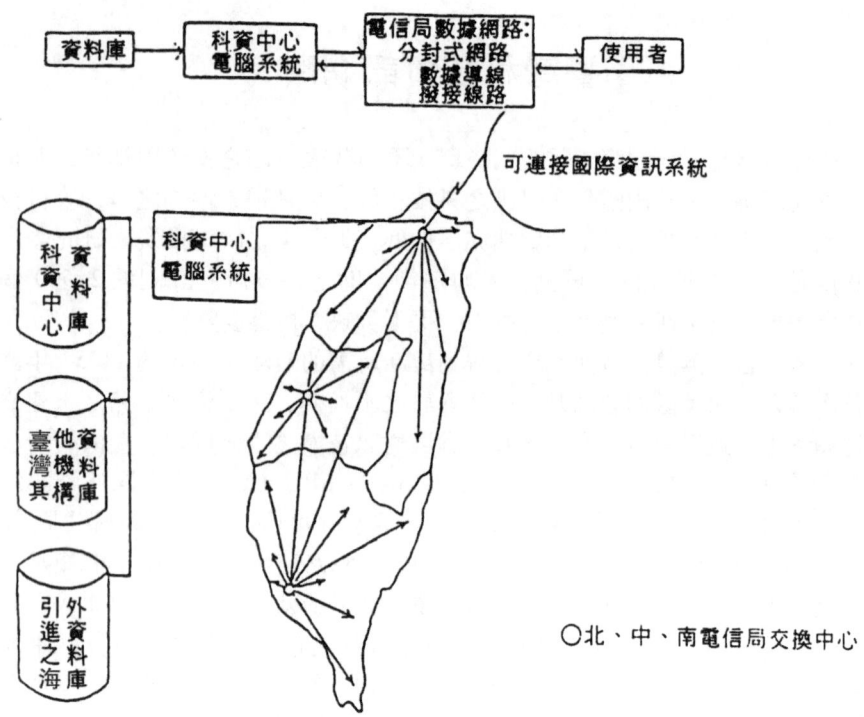

圖一　STICNET 系統連線圖

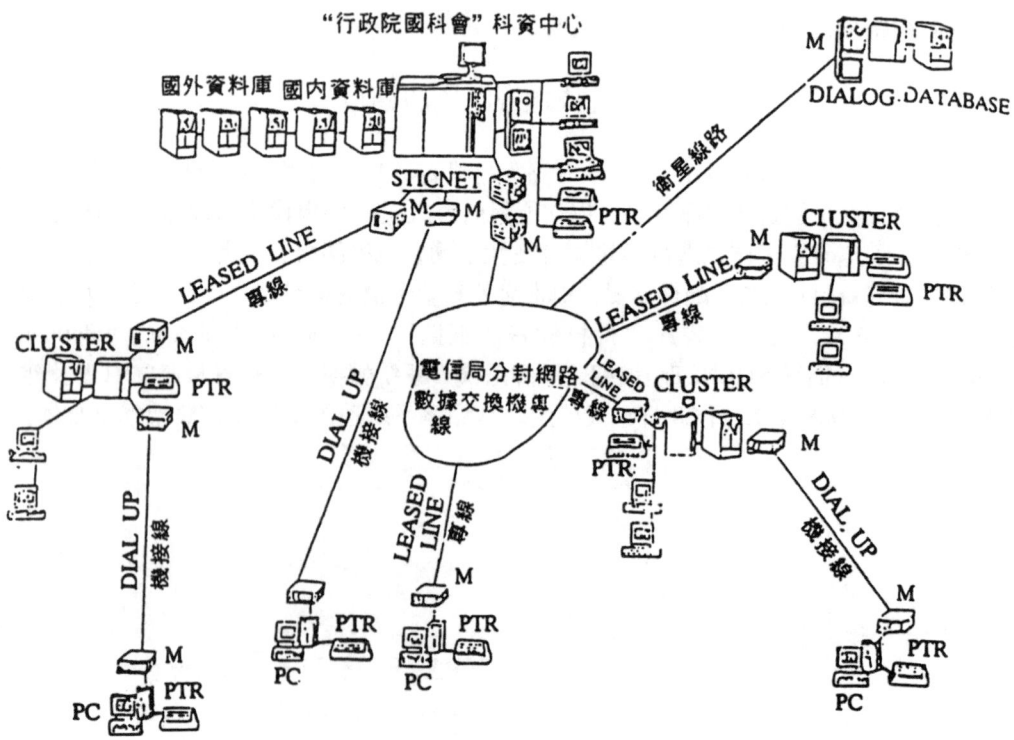

圖二　科技性資訊網路網路架構圖

該計劃預計分三階段約需時五年全部完成。現已完成第一階段之網路連線測試，進入第二階段，加強資料庫之引進，同時邀請臺灣各單位申請使用。第三階段將是加入國際資訊網路，尋求國際間之合作。該網路中可提供查詢之資料庫如下表：

表一 網路中可供查詢資料一覽表
（至 1990 年 4 月止）

資料庫名稱	收錄年代	現有資料量	年增加量
〈海外資料庫〉			
BIOSIS PREVIEWS（生物科學資料庫）	1988—1989	1046	520
CA SEARCH（化學摘要資料庫）	1987—1989	1213	500
COMPENDEX（工程資料庫）	1985—1990	600	125
ERIC（教育研究資料庫）	1985—1990	160	30
INSPEC（物理/電子電機/電腦資料庫）	1985—1990	1.223	250
NTIS（美國政府科技研究報告資料庫）	1985—1989	260	70
MEDLINE（醫學資料庫）	（正商洽中）		
〈臺灣實料庫〉			
臺灣西文科技期刊聯合目錄資料庫	每年更新	19	1
臺灣西文科技圖書聯合目錄資料庫	1975—1989	100	60
"國科會"研究獎助費論文摘要資料庫	1984—1987	7	2
臺灣科技期刊論文資料庫	1988—1989	11	15
進行中科技研究計劃摘要資料庫	1986—	8	3
臺灣科技研究報告摘要資料庫	1985—1987	5	2
科技簡訊與政策報導資料庫	1986—	45	10

STICNET 未來發展是：（一）網路系統之軟硬體之擴充及改進；（二）資料庫及量之增加；（三）其他附加系統之發展，如"中英文書目性資料庫線上更新系統"、"電子郵遞系統"、"專題選粹服務（SDI）系統"等之建立，提高其附加價值，以充份發揮網路功能。

貳、農業科技資訊服務系統網路

"農業科技資訊服務系統網路"是由農業科學資料服務中心（簡稱農資中心）負責規劃與設計，並以該中心已發展設置之各種農業科技資訊庫為網路之核心，現已積極規劃中。

農資中心於 1978 年成立，其目的是：（一）配合農業發展支援農業研究；（二）有效利用農業科技資訊；（三）促進海內外農業科技資訊交流；（四）建立有效的農業科技資訊服務系統。自 1979 年，該中心依據"行政院"科學技術發展方案進行建立農業科技資訊服務系統，以便能處理生產之農業科技資訊，同時自海外引進適合農業研究發展所需之各種資訊。

農資中心於 1982 和 1983 年間，先後完成農業科技資訊服務系統各資訊庫之設置工作，系統資料庫現有：（一）農業科技人才資訊庫，收錄臺灣農業專家資料，約 14,500 人；（二）農業科技文獻資訊庫，以收錄臺灣生產的農業科技文獻為主，資料類型含期刊、圖書、研究報告、期刊論文、學位論文及學術會議記錄等；（三）農業科技研究計劃資訊庫，專門收錄農發會（現農委會）自 1973 年以來，補助臺灣各單位執行之研究發展計劃，該中心並制定農業科技索引典，做為以上三種資訊庫之索引製作及檢索工具，該索引典之功能如圖三。1987 年農委會開始與該中心系統連線作業（見圖三）。

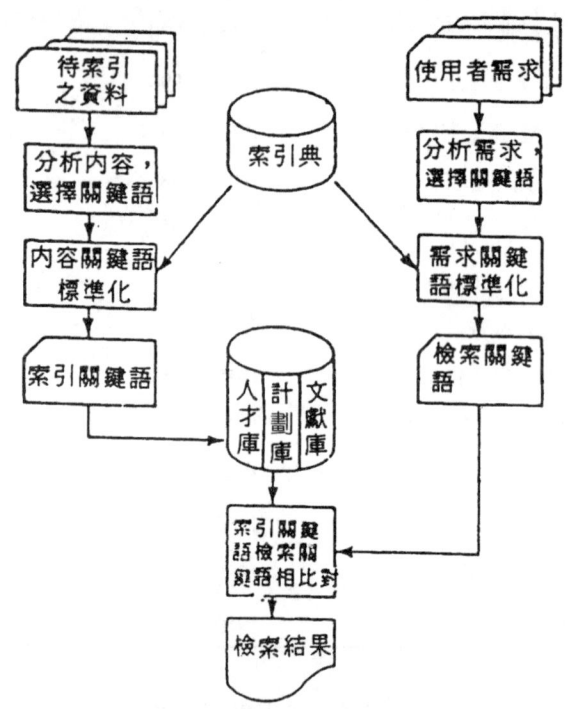

圖三　農業科技索引典功能

此外，該中心自 1982 年以來，對外提供國際百科資訊檢索服務，透過人造衛星通訊網路及電腦系統直接檢索海外 DLALOG、BRS、ORBIT、ESA-IRS、STN DIMDI 及 FOODLINE 等系統中約 600 多種資訊庫的資料並取得原件。

為能使更多的農業單位分享該中心之成果與資源，農資中心於 1989 年開始推廣發展臺灣農業資訊網路之觀念，期能儘速的達到建立農業科技資訊系統網路之日，但由於近三年來該中心更換新的硬體而為之延後，最近已初步擬定"參與農業科學資料服務中心連線作業網路各農業單位所需之配合條件"說明書及"農業科學資料服務中心連線網路系統基本架構"，見圖（四）。預測在近期內，臺灣的"農業科技資訊服務系統網路"即將誕生。

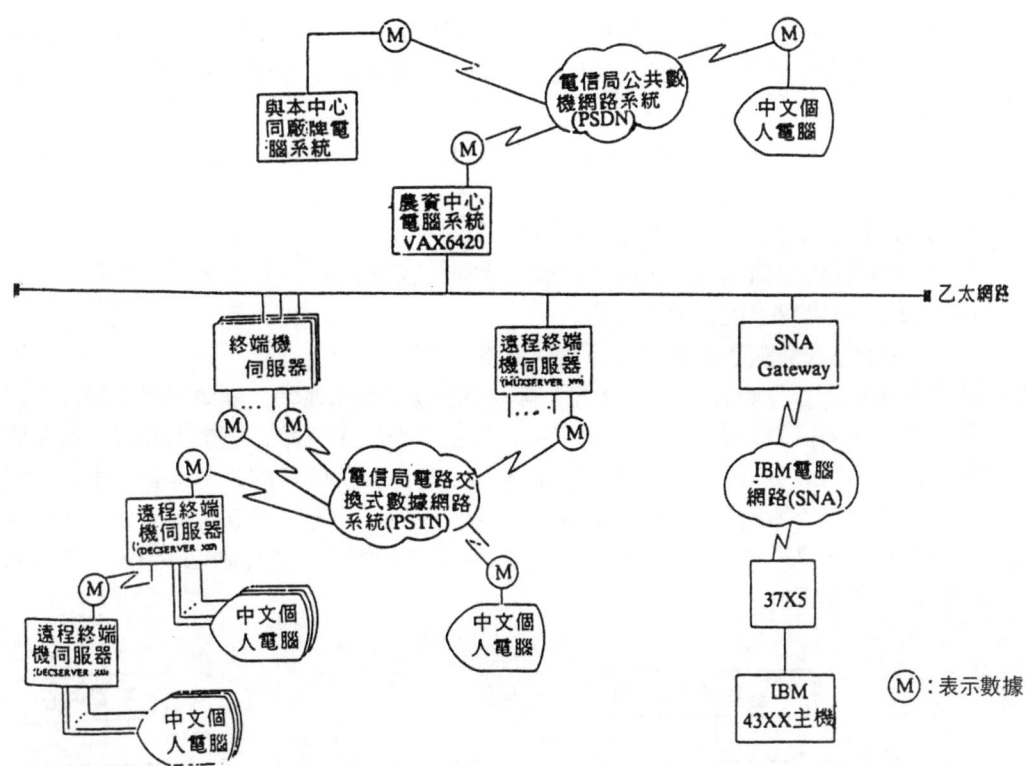

圖四　臺灣農業科技服務系統網路架構圖

叁、國家生物醫學資訊中心網路系統

　　1983 年，前美國國家醫學圖書館（National Library of Medicine）館長康明博士（Martin M. Cummings, M. D.）應"國立成功大學"醫學院之邀請來臺訪問後，向臺灣有關單位建議成立臺灣地區醫學資訊網路系統之必要性，以促進臺灣醫學專業之服務、教學與研究。有鑑於此，有關單位自 1984 年起曾多次召開會議研商，終於於 1988 年完成"研設醫學資訊中心計劃書"提陳"行政院"科技顧問研判，但由於涉及龐大經費，而未能獲得政府具體結果。

　　同年，"國科會"科學技術資料中心爲配合科技網路（Science & Technology Information Center Network，簡稱 STIC-NET）之建立，而引進美國國家醫學圖書館的"醫學文獻資料庫"（Medical Literature Analysis & Retrieval System，簡稱 MEDLARS）供人們檢索使用。"國立臺灣大學"醫學院有鑑於此，特邀請其他醫學單位進行研議多次，決定爲配合科資中心所提供之"醫學資料庫"，將"研設醫學資料中心計劃書"予以修訂，因而建議成立"臺灣生物醫學資訊中心"以對臺灣生物醫學專業人員提供最有效的資訊服務。

　　成立"國家生物醫學資訊中心"之目的。依該計劃之解說："擴充生物醫學資訊之蒐集並建立資源共享網路，採最有效、最經濟、最迅速之方法，提供資訊服務，以促進全民健康為最終目的"以臺灣地區所有與生物醫學有關的學者及專家人員為其服務對象。諸如：基礎與臨床醫學、衛生、保健、護理、生物技術、醫學工程學等學科。該計劃之工作要項是：

（一）配合臺灣生物醫學研究發展所需，有計劃的蒐集採購生物醫學相關資料充實資源。
（二）健全海內外合作資源共享制度及關係。
（三）加強改進臺灣醫學圖書館的功能、管理及服務方式。
（四）積極推動醫學圖書館自動化。
（五）規劃及建立醫學圖書館資源共享網路系統等。

該中心之組織（見圖五）形態分三級制。中心設於臺北地區，臺灣大學醫學院及成功大學醫學院之圖書館為南北一級資源中心，其他醫學院圖書館、醫學中心圖書館及區域醫校圖書館為二級資源中心，醫事專校圖書館及地區醫院圖書館為基本資源中心，以建立臺灣生物醫學資訊網路系統。全計劃分三階段進行，預定三至五年內完成，所需經費預估約需新臺幣 25,401 萬元，即兩億伍仟肆佰零壹萬元，該計劃已於 1989 年呈報"教育部"，仍在審核中。

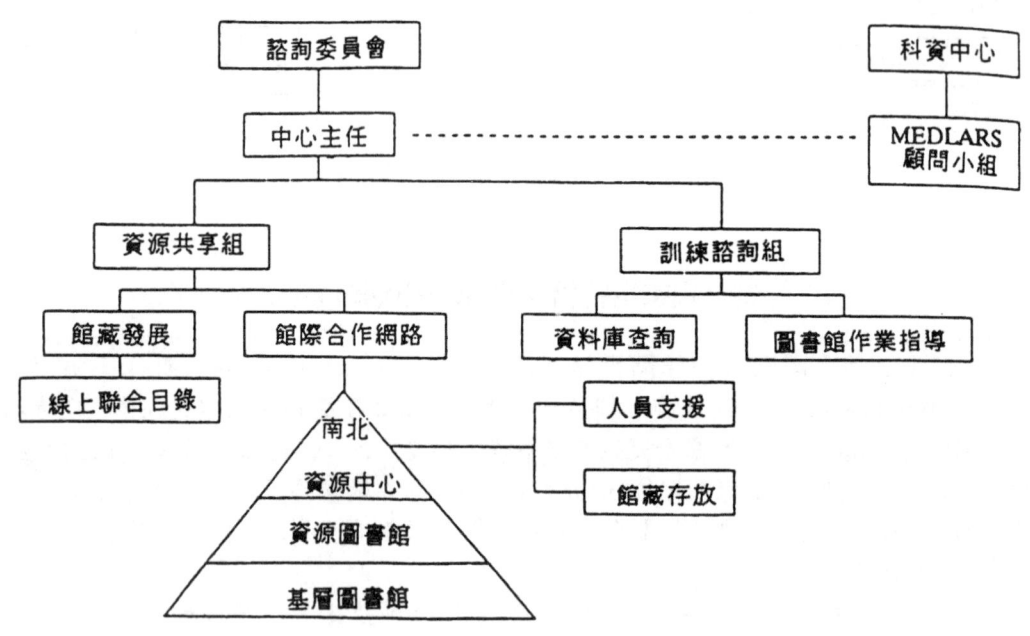

圖五　臺灣地區生物醫學資訊中心組織圖

以上簡單介紹臺灣地區三個科技資訊網路，其中除科資中心之"科技性資訊網路"已建立實施中，其他如"農業科技資訊服務系統網路"和"生物醫學資訊中心網路系統"仍在規劃推廣中，看來要多多爭取政府之重視及支持，故仍需臺灣之資訊界人士更多努力！

參考資料

（一）科技資訊網路：

1. 科技性資訊網路簡介，臺大閱覽組，臺北市，1990年。

2. 科學技術資料中心簡訊，"國科會"科技中心，臺北市。

3. 馬道行，臺灣"科技資訊網路"之建立，"中國圖書館學會"第三十七屆會員大會專題討論，臺北市，1989年，頁30—43。

（二）農業科技資訊服務系統網路：

1. 農業科技資訊服務系統簡介，農業科學資料服務中心，臺北市。

2. "參與農業科學資料服務中心連線作業網路各農業單位所需之配合條件"說明書，農資中心，臺北市，1990年。

3. 電話訪問農資中心相關人員。

（三）生物醫學資訊中心網路系統：

1. Dr. Martin M. Cummings 之信件。

2. 生物醫學資訊中心之規劃研究報告，"國立臺灣大學"醫學院圖書館，臺北市，1989年。

3. 電話訪問計劃主持人張慧銖主任。

加值與圖書館作業[*]

"加值"作用,對圖書館從業人士而言,似乎較為陌生的觀念,但實際而言,加值和圖書館作業有密切的關係。因為圖書館自創始以來是一直在做"加值"的工作。"加值"也可以說是圖書館作業的目的!

"加值"英文是 Value-Added,其意義,簡單的說,即是"增加價值"之意。它是一種作業方法,這種做法是對某產品、服務項目或系統等增加其利用價值及功能,加值之最重要決定則是以"使用者"之利益為導向的,同時以權衡考量做法帶來之好處與所耗時間、金錢和精力程度等為依據。

對資訊工業界而言,"加值"此名稱卻常被應用在資訊處理之各方面,因此也造成"加值"的含義很多而觀念反而不夠明顯。由文獻中看到"加值"常常應用在資料庫利用方面,它的重點是指利用人的智慧對基本書目性或全文性資料庫記錄中資訊增添一些"東西",這些"東西"可增加資料庫之利用價值及功能。這些"東西"即是"加值"作用,它代表很多作業方法,產生加值產品,如資料庫用的各種主題描述語(Subject Descriptors)、編碼(Codes)、分類表(Classification Scheme)、摘要(Abstracts)、索引(Indexes)等皆是。

最近常聽到的"加值網路"(Value Added Networks,簡稱 VANs)又是什麼?網路為何又稱之"加值網路"?這是指在一個大型網路由很多不同電腦系統相連,這些電腦公司依公共網路(Public Network)之規定外,另依該電腦公司所提供之其他特性而增強網路的功能,能使網路做更多的事,更好用,因而稱為"加值網路"。

"加值"名詞對一般人而言雖陌生,但由於用在資訊界較多,而誤導"加值"是資訊界之專有用語。對圖書館館員而言,對資訊產品和資訊服務加以價值處理實是常有之事,例如館員利用館藏規劃標準尋購最適切有價值的資料,編目人員提供查詢線索和資訊以便讀者很易檢索到所需之書目資料,和參考館員亦提增對讀者指導和解釋一些有價值的服務等,這些皆是"加值"處理後之結果。由於圖書館"加值"工作,讀者可在短短幾分鐘內由一百萬甚至二百萬館藏中找到所需資料及其所在地,或可借用書目網路立即查得所需資料在他館或他國之何地?多麼神奇!圖書館事業是資訊業中最資深者、資格者,因此思想作風較為傳統,而跟不上時代,對於新的名詞及觀念亦較為落伍!

雖然圖書館是從事資訊"加值"工作最早者,但最大的缺點是作業與管理皆不夠科學化,不但忽視衡量資訊之價值與價格,亦輕視圖書館作業之評估與權衡作用之重要性。一九八六年泰勒先生(Robert S. Taylor)研究"資訊生命週期之加值過程"(Value-Added Process in the Information Cycle),此加值做法,使資訊會因此更有利用價值,特別是用在決策過程和讀者各種活動中,他定出二十三種加值過程,同時提供一個結構式做法用來評估圖書館資訊管理系統(Management Information System),資訊分析中心(Information Analysis Center)和索引及摘要服務業等之實際作業狀況,特別強調以讀者為導向,並以實務為重點之作法,對資訊生命週期中各階段加值。以下介紹泰勒先生之資

---

[*] 本文曾發表在《書府》1990 年 6 月第 11 期,第 4—6 頁。

訊週期全貌:

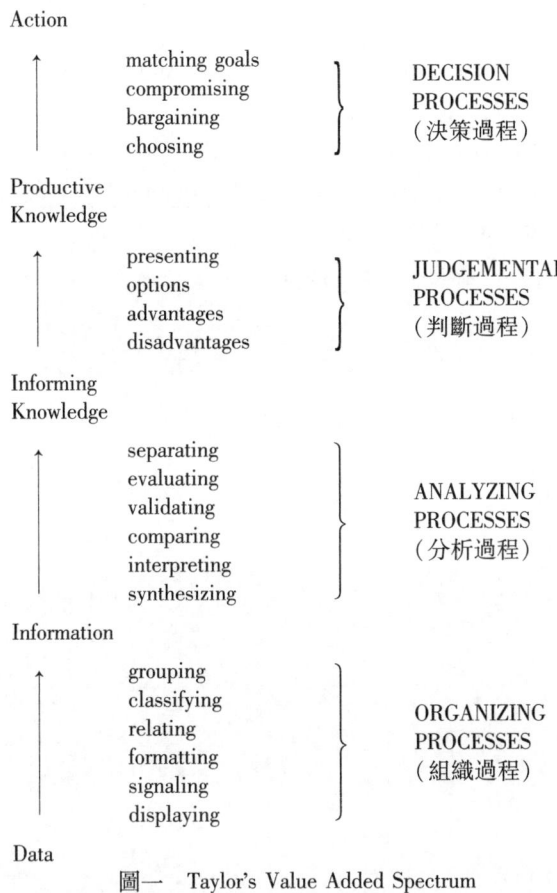

圖一　Taylor's Value Added Spectrum

　　由圖中資訊加值過程全貌中看出，它將各項加值活動，由初期蒐集、處理、支援決策到最後產生行動等，不難看出來，此加值方式與圖書館作業之類同之處。但根據泰勒先生之研究方向，是針對 "資訊資源管理" (Information Resources Management，簡稱IRM) 之加值處理而言，資訊資源管理是一九八○年興起的一種新資源管理制度，它是由行政部門運用規劃、預算、組織、指導、訓練及控制等管理方法、管理資訊及其相關資源以達到資源整合之目的，圖書館若能採用此管理制度，配合加值作業，當可使圖書館的運作更趨健全及現代化，這也是吾圖書館界積極共同努力之目標！

參考書目

1. Richard H. Lythe. "Information Resource Management: 1981 – 1986", in Annual Review of Information Science & Technology, v. 21, 1986, pp. 309 – 336.

2. Carol Tenopir, "Value-Added Searching," Library Journal 115 (6) (April, 1990)：79 – 80.

3. Robert S. Taylor, "Value-Added Processes in the Information Cycle," JASIS 33 (6)

(Sept, 1982): 341 – 346.

4. ——. Value-Added Processes in Information Systems (Norwood, NJ: Ablex, 1986), P. 6.

5. Aatto J. Repo, "Economics of Information", In Annual Review of Information Science and Technology, v. 22, 1987, pp. 3 – 35.

6. D. R. Worlock, "Value-Added Networks and the Professions: Changing the Rules for Information Access in the Late 1980s," in 10th International Online Information Meeting, London, 2 – 4 Dec., 1986, pp. 247 – 252.

7. 梁培華. 資訊詞彙. 臺北市：松崗, 1984 年。

資訊與電腦[*]

在目前的資訊社會中,"資訊"和"電腦"兩名詞被用得相當廣泛,但人們由於對之觀念混淆不清,常常誤將兩者混為一談,分不清兩者間之關係、區別。本文旨在指出兩者之關連、不同之處,以期能對"資訊"和"電腦"有一明確的瞭解,辨別兩者之不同。

首先,由兩者之英文名詞,很明顯的辨識其間之不同。"資訊"英文字是"Information",電腦是"Computer"。"資訊"一詞從1950年代即開始風行,是一個難以捉摸而又相當複雜的概念,資訊(Information)的字源為拉丁文"Informatis",意指溝通、傳播或通訊之過程或事物。由於研究者從各領域與觀念對其有不同之看法,至今資訊的定義分歧已是不爭之事實。據統計,資訊定義已超過400種。

早期,在海外,Information意指的是訊息(Messages)、消息(News)、資料(Data)、知識(Knowledge)、文件(Documents)、文獻(Literature)、智慧(Intelligence)、符號(Symbols)等;在臺灣,該名詞的中文譯名亦曾有"資料","情報"、"消息"、"報導"、"訊息"等,直到"中央研究院"之資訊科學研究所之籌備成立時,Information才被正式譯為"資訊",其意義涵蓋"資料"和"訊息"。

由於"資訊"的功能和成效愈來愈大,尤其在此資訊時代中,資訊已被認為是時代的主流,更趨重要性。資訊是什麼呢?資訊家如偉納爾(Wiener)說:"資訊就是資訊,不是事物也不是能源",可見資訊實際上是"抽象"的觀念。布魯克斯(Brooks)亦認為"資訊是知識(Knowledge)結構之一部份,其能修改這個結構,正如資訊對需要者而言,它是有意義、有用的資料接受的資訊,可增加需要者的知識,減少對某事之不確定性(Reduction of Uncertainty),修改了需要者的知識結構及範圍。

資訊亦是一種"商品"(Commodity)。由於人類對於資訊的強烈需求,對資訊標以價錢,獲得它,必須付費,可見資訊已從傳統的資訊本身(即知識)變成"商品"。資訊產品被生產、發展、引進市場、促銷、販賣,這即是資訊的商品性質。

資訊可以說是有用的資料,可輔助決策,導致行動,其價值亦因人因時而異。由哲理上探討資訊的本質、原因和本能,資訊可以說是物質和內容(Objects and Contents)之間的互動,關連的傳遞者(Carrier)。

根據資策會出版的"迎向資訊化社會"一書中,對資訊定義又有廣義和狹義的兩種說法:廣義的"資訊"是指"所有資料和訊息的總稱,包括文字、數據、聲訊與視訊",而狹義的"資訊"乃是指"電腦處理後的資料和訊息"。因此由狹義方面而言"資料"(Data)和"資訊"(Information)在現代化的資訊社會中,甚多仰賴電腦來處理它。

根據21世紀高度資訊化社會一書中所列,資訊具有下列六種特色:
1. 資訊是一種無形帶有意義的訊息
2. 資訊能用各種方式傳遞
3. 資訊可供多人同時使用

---

[*] 本文曾發表在《書府》1989年6月第10期,第8—9頁。

4. 資訊能被儲存、修改、消除
5. 資訊為重要資源之一
6. 資訊能重覆使用而不變質

"電腦"（Computer）是什麼？電腦又稱電子計算機，它是一種接受資料並接受人為指示的方法將之處理，並產生有用的結果的裝置謂之。電腦通常由輸入部門、輸出部門、中央處理單元、主記憶及算術邏輯單元五大部門組成，所以電腦是一種機器設備，是一種資料運算的工具（Tools），也是一種處理資料的系統，但它絕不是"資訊"！！

總合以上所述，"資訊"（Information）和資料（Data）、電腦（Computer）有密切的關係。但"資訊"絕不是"電腦"或"資料"，便於讀者更明確瞭解三者間之關係，以下圖示之。

原始資料→ 資料處理系統 →資　訊
（Data）　　　Computer　　　Information
　　　　　　或其他方法

參考資料

1. Wellish, Hans, "From Information Science to Informatics: a Terminological Investigation", <u>Journal of Librarianship</u> 4 (July 1972): 178–179.

2. Yuexiao, Zhang, "Definitions and Sciences of Information", <u>Information Processing Management</u> 24 (1988): 479–491.

3. 資訊工業策進會編. <u>迎向資訊化社會</u>. 臺北市：編者，1987年.

4. 汪靜君. "21世紀高度資訊化社會" <u>自動化科技</u> 51（4. 1988），頁11.

5. 黃嘉懋編. <u>電腦大辭典</u>. 臺北市：松崗，1987年。

圖書館自動化座談會紀錄[*]

議題一：臺灣圖書館進行自動化時所遭遇的問題
議題二：標準的必要性
議題三：圖書館資訊網路
議題四：圖書館自動化的教育與訓練

時　　間：一九八八年十一月十七日下午二時至五時
地　　點："國立臺灣大學"文學院會議室
座談內容：探討臺灣圖書館自動化發展現況、問題與建議
主 持 人：李德竹　"國立臺灣大學"圖書館學系暨研究所教授兼系主任
主 講 人：王振鵠　"國立中央圖書館"館長
　　　　　王逸如　"國立工業技術學院"圖書館館長
　　　　　宋　玉　"國科會"國際合作處處長、資策會顧問
　　　　　沈寶環　"國立臺灣大學"圖書館學系暨研究所教授
　　　　　吳明德　"國立臺灣大學"圖書館學系暨研究所副教授
　　　　　吳萬鈞　農業科學資料服務中心主任
　　　　　周誠寬　資策會副執行長
　　　　　胡述兆　"國立臺灣大學"圖書館學系暨研究所教授
　　　　　張鼎鍾　"國立臺灣大學"圖書館學系暨研究所教授
　　　　　陳國瓊　"國立藝術學院"圖書館採編組主任
　　　　　陳興夏　"國立臺灣大學"圖書館館長
　　　　　黃大偉　銘傳商業專科學校圖書館代館長
　　　　　黃世雄　淡江大學圖書館館長
　　　　　賈玉輝　"交通部"數據通訊所所長
　　　　　盧秀菊　"國立臺灣大學"圖書館學系暨研究所副教授
　　　　　顧　敏　"立法院"圖書館暨法律資訊中心主任
（依姓名筆劃序）

主席：
　　各位專家學者、各位貴賓、各位老師、各位同學，"圖書館自動化座談會是本系爲慶祝本校四十三週年校慶暨創校六十週年而舉辦的，感謝各位百忙之中，抽空參加。現在爲各位介紹主講人（略）。
　　本次座談會主要討論四項議題：

---

[*] 本文曾發表在《書府》1989 年 6 月第 10 期，第 35—54 頁。由謝寶煖整理。

議題一：臺灣圖書館進行自動化時所遭遇的問題

主席：
　　請各位專家學者踴躍發言。
宋玉處長：
　　請王振鵠館長和黃世雄館長就其經驗說明其進行自動化時所遭遇的問題。
王振鵠館長：
　　"中央圖書館"推動自動化已經有很多年了，與其說是"中央圖書館"推動自動化不如說是"中央圖書館"和"中國圖書館學會"以及圖書館界共同合作所推動的自動化。

　　"中央圖書館"自動化作業從1980年開始，到現在已有七年多快八年的時間了，我們回顧起來，好像覺得進度相當的慢，同時在這八年裏也走了很多重複的路、冤枉的路，所以宋顧問剛剛說"經驗"，我可以說發展自動化是非常痛苦的經驗，也可以說是從沒有經驗累積到有經驗，而也可以說是在各種不同的壓力下所發展的一項工作。

　　"中央圖書館"自動化的發展大致上可以分成三個階段，這三個階段在其他圖書館發展自動化時，可能也是同樣的情形，第一個階段是規劃，紙面作業，訂定各項的標準，第二個階段才真正開始建檔作業，而到第三個階段則可能步入另一個新的資訊網路的發展。

　　在這三階段裏，第一個階段可以說是圖書館界合作的一個階段，完成了中國機讀編目格式，也修訂了中國編目規則，同時也有了標題目錄的初稿（中文圖書標題總目初稿），這些都是在第一個階段兩年之內大家投入了相當大的心力所完成的。

　　第二個階段是"中央圖書館"在有限的經費之下所開始的建檔工作，從1982年底開始，買了王安的機器，開始做建檔，在建檔期間可以說一切都是在摸索之中，進度並不能按我們的預期，不過到現在已經建檔完成了差不多23萬筆資料，資料庫包括一般圖書的書目資料、善本書、期刊論文索引、政府公報和一般文獻資料；這些資料的建檔，現在很穩定的在發展，不過我們檢討起來，速度還是比較慢，慢的原因不是在自動化作業的程序或者是人力缺乏，而在其他作業的配合上。

　　"中央圖書館"從今年開始進入第三個階段，奉"行政院"的核定，增加經費，重新擴大機器，同時規劃網路系統，"中央圖書館"所規劃的網路系統主要是書目資訊服務系統，這個工作一方面考慮到聯合編目、合作目錄的需要，和資料解釋上的要求，一方面也考慮到海外和國際合作上的要求；在規劃上，機器，設備、經費已經確定，目前投注很多人力做程式的轉換和設計工作，預計明年底可先和十六所大學做連線作業，主要所做的還是合作編目工作，另外一點關於西文資料方面，現在"中央圖書館"和美國的OCLC已經有很密切的合作關係，雙方資料交換測試，甚至程式的轉換都正在進行當中，同時技術上的問題也都已經克服。

　　我們現在所遭遇的問題可以說是來自海內外兩方面，也可以說我們的困難也就是在此。在臺灣方面，怎麼更充實人力，同時把規格標準訂定明確，使發展更能順暢，這是我們感覺到的第一個困難；假如將來網路系統建立，而很多規格標準沒有建立，譬如說分類系統、檢索系統、標題或者詞語表等等這些工作沒有做好，可能即使連線之後，還是有若干的困難,這也是我們在技術方面感覺最大困難的地方,也就是在將過去傳統人工作業轉換成自動化作業上,因為過去的基礎並不穩固,所以轉換之後,連帶的我們要如何同時並進,把分類目錄所需要的基本技術要求,先要給予定位,給予標準化,這是非常迫切的問題。我也時常和宋顧問請教,是不是能夠把有關自動化的作業標準研究一下,分析一下,究竟有那些標準是必須訂定的,而我們如何來訂定,這可能勢必要集思廣益大家共同來努力的。

另外,我感覺臺灣各方面的壓力,主要還是在編目問題方面,過去"中央圖書館"也試行過合作編目一個階段,編目組的同仁也都全力投入,因為實在是人員不勝負荷,影響到我們內部的很多作業,所以不得不暫時叫停,我們覺得還是要整個規劃好後再做比較妥當。那麼現在各方面反應,不管是向"中央圖書館"或向有關單位等等,最迫切的還是要解決編目的問題,而"中央圖書館"現在雖然建檔了23萬筆資料,但一大部份是期刊論文索引,而圖書方面只有10萬多筆,目前這些資料還不能完全給大家使用的原因,是因為我們的 MARC FORMAT 修訂了好幾次,從過去到現在目錄本身的編目款目,還需花一段時間,重新的統一化,這也是需要相當大的人力的。

另外一點在來自海外方面給我們的督促,也可以說是壓力,第一個就是美國的二個大系統,一個是 OCLC,一個是 RLIN,這兩個系統都在發展 CJK(中日韓文)系統,OCLC 已經和"中央圖書館"合作,我們開始交換雙方面編目的資料,同時 RLIN 也一再要求"中央圖書館"把善本書建檔的資料提供給他們,但善本資料的處理是相當花時間精力的工作,進度也不是很快,雖然只輸進去了一萬多筆"中央圖書館"現有的善本書的資料,但是這方面的資料受到美國漢學界相當的重視,OCLC 和 RLIN 二個資訊系統都在爭取這方面的資料,都認為這方面的資料對漢學研究幫助很大,能更充實他們的資料庫,到現在我們在政策上還未完全確定。總而言之,我們願意和海外的各資訊系統合作,但我們不願只保障某一資訊系統,因為這裏面涉及的問題非常複雜,也涉及美國國會圖書館的基本態度,涉及各東亞圖書館的態度,這些問題可能是其他圖書館發展自動化所沒有遭遇到的,而"中央圖書館"發展上遭遇到也是有些個決定上的困難。至於一般的問題,我們在檢討過去發展的過程中,我覺得固然有些困難也有很多值得安慰的事情,第一個我們是圖書館界的合作努力才有今天的成果,假如沒有第一個階段大家心力的投入,我想也不會有第二個階段的成果,所以不能不在這方面向參與我們自動化作業的老師甚至各位圖書館界的同道表示謝意。

另外在一般的困難方面,在"中央圖書館"方面感受到最大的困難還是在技術標準的缺乏,第二是人力的短缺,人力的短缺不是一般圖書館的人力,而是指受過電腦訓練而兼具圖書館背景的人力的缺乏,所以有很多設計方面我們不得不仰賴軟體公司,或者是其他單位,那麼在設計上,往往為了程式的設計反覆討論研究,而設計出來並不一定完全符合我們的需求,時間上浪費很多,這個主要是由於人力缺乏的關係。不過我們從沒有經驗而逐漸滙聚成經驗,現在"中央圖書館"在自動化作業發展上已經比以前更成熟了一些,我們的各方面考慮也更週全了一些。

黃世雄館長:

王館長所報告的事情,大部份在我們圖書館電腦化的過程當中也都有遭遇到或考慮過,但我們也有"中央圖書館"所沒有碰到的問題,我來補充一下:

圖書館自動化嚴格說起來可以分為兩個大類：一個是 House Keeping，一個是 Information Retrieval，我們現在談的是 House Keeping 的工作，包括圖書館的採訪、編目、出納等等，在我們圖書館自動化過程當中，所碰到的問題是這樣的，因為我們的電腦是屬於全校性的，並不是圖書館自己擁有的電腦，雖然現在我們用的主機有80%是歸圖書館使用，20%交給其他教學單位來利用，但是也是屬於學校專責單位管理，因此我們必須要和學校資訊中心的電腦人員密切連繫，畢竟他們是屬於電腦方面的專家，電腦又是由他們控制的，所以整個發展過程中，我們必須要和他們建立很密切的關係。

要設計一個 House Keeping 的 Computer-based Library System，不能夠忽略兩種人的角色，一個是圖書館館員，一個是電腦專家，在我們發展過程當中，起初深深的感受到資訊中心的同仁並不是那麼容易和圖書館合作，而事實上在我們圖書館本身也有蠻多同仁對電腦頗有認識，但因為電腦是他們的，所以我們要尊重他們，那麼這兩方面人員的配合就很重要，圖書館員和電腦專家這兩種人的結合一定要突破，好在我們在發展初期雖意見相左，但逐漸地資訊中心的人發現這並不是如他們所想像的那麼容易，而把重心放在圖書館館員上，所以在很短的時間內就由圖書館扮演主要的角色，這點是當初我們所遭遇到的問題。

第二個問題是很多單位都會遭遇到的，主管人員他們對系統的開發都相當熱心相當支持，但總是有一種觀念，也是一般人所擁有的觀念，無法突破，都認為要圖書館自動化，我把機器買來給你們，好像這樣圖書館就可以自動化了，這一點必須在設計過程當中給上級主管一個認識，電腦硬體的價格由電腦公司報價，一目了然，看不出來的是軟體的成本，還有資料轉換（Data Conversion）的成本相當大，所以當時有關西文資料我們決定要和 OCLC 和國會圖書館做資料轉換時，提出計劃申請經費時，學校嚇一跳，為什麼要花這麼多錢，但事實上就是如此，所以一定要設法與主管人員就這一點取得共識。

軟體的設計方面，淡江大學的 TALIS 系統，事實上是利用 DOBIS 系統加以解剖增刪，變成中文版，但因為 DOBIS 軟體本身所用的語言不同，在這種情況下，我們把它轉換過來，花了相當多的人力，也運用了相當的智慧，有很多西方的習慣和東方的習慣不一樣的地方，而且我們當初設計這套系統時，不只考慮到淡江大學圖書館的使用問題，也考慮到其他圖書館的使用和習慣的作業方式，所以雖然不是從零開始，但是整個 TALIS 系統的設計是從相當的基本著眼，也花了相當多的時間，這些時間成本和軟體成本，以及資料轉換所需要的經費，當時我花了相當大的功夫去和主管人員說明爭取；所以要讓主管人員和圖書館建立共識，這一點一定要突破。

另外，我深深感覺到設計圖書館自動化的過程當中，最重要的是參與人員的士氣（morale），要讓他們有一種感受——我雖然很辛苦，但我可以學到很多；因為在整個過程當中，我所感受到的是，我們的同仁工作到晚上八點，圖書館的預算裏沒有加班費，而他們也沒有來向我要求加班費，整個投入工作，也沒有休息時間，事實上這種狀況到目前還是這樣，已經變成習慣了，因為這些同仁或是工讀生，他們雖然很辛苦，但他們都全力投入，他們認為收獲很大，可以學到很多很多東西，有很好的學習機會，諸此，以我的立場，我的感受是相當深刻的。所以在初期發展時，所要花的人力和心血是沒辦法用金錢來衡量的，好在大家辛苦了兩年多，到今年夏天已經完成了。

TALIS 是一個整合性的網路系統,在一個架構下可以完成採購、編目、出納流通、參考服務、館際互借和電子郵件等功能,以及各種報表輸出,非常方便快速。因為電腦在淡江大學用得很久而且頻率很高,很多主管人員包括董事長,他們有一個觀念認為圖書館自動化後應該有一些好處,所以我在今年八月提出成立參考資訊組,學校說你要成立一個組要用多少人,我說一個人都不增加,你只要給我一個名稱,讓我成立一個組,了不起我找個人出來當主任給他一份主任津貼,如此而已,學校說你不增加一個人那可以,因此我們從推廣組、編目組裏把剩餘的人力調出來,組成一個參考資訊組,這就是自動化以後剩餘的人力,這些人力,我們總不能請他們走路,而且這些人過去做的是相當 routine 的工作,比如分類編目、做書後卡、打字等等,這些都是專業人員在做,他們覺得很枯燥乏味,把這些人抽出來做比較高智慧的參考資訊服務,對他們來講也較有成就感,所以我們在八月一日在不增加人力情況下成立了參考資訊組,這個例子告訴我們,就長遠構想來說圖書館自動化是值得推薦的,也應該重視。

另外,將來建立全域性網路系統時,必要條件是每個圖書館都要自動化,而自動化的目標是建立全域資訊網路,甚至包括國際性的網路,這點也值得圖書館界的同仁和同學們大家共同來努力。

主席:

謝謝兩位館長,在座除了圖書館館長外,還有資訊中心主任,現在就請農業科學資料中心主任和"立法院"資訊服務中心主任為我們說明一下:

吳萬鈞主任:

農資中心的環境較單純,我們碰到的問題,情形可能不一樣,我先把我們的背景說明一下,農資中心從1978年開始發展自動化,政策方面非常支持,所以並沒有政策方面的問題,在人員設備各方面都得到充分的支援,在這種情形下很多問題可能都不會發生,而農資中心發展自動化過程當中最感困擾的問題是電腦人員的配合,而如何讓電腦人員能夠接受你的要求,讓電腦人員沒有藉口不做他應該做的事情,我想這是非常重要的,為什麼會有這種感受,因為農資中心完全是從零開始,而且我們所處理的資料完全是我們自己所產生的資料,我們自己的研究報告、研究計劃、期刊雜誌的論文、會議紀錄,不處理海外的任何資料,所以這個環境是有點不一樣,在剛開始的時候,我們也發展過所謂的 MARC,我們也參考了"中央圖書館"的 MARC,但是站在農資中心的立場,因為不是一個公共圖書館,也不是一個全科技的圖書館,而只是一個農業的資料中心,所以我們的第二個問題就是 MARC 的問題,就農資中心而言,UNIMARC 對我們來說太多了,太複雜了,而且裏頭有些資料實在是沒有必要,是不是可以考慮不需要,例如我們就不做作者的權威檔,不做作者的控制,我們只注重關鍵字,所謂索引典(thesaurus)裏面的字彙控制,這是一問題。

第二個問題,多年來資料陸陸續續將近十萬筆紀錄,那麼如果自動化以後我最擔心的問題是資料量很龐大時,如何找得到你所需要的東西,這就牽涉到分類索引的問題,農資中心今天最擔心的是主題內容的問題,因為五萬筆十萬筆資料存進去以後,如何能夠找到,那分類系統的精細就非常重要,意思是說可能有一個 subject 的 posting number 非常高,就表示分類系統太粗,不夠細,諸如此類的問題總是困擾著我們,我們也一直想辦法解決之中。

另外一個問題就是,雖然農資中心得到農委會的全力支援,但是我認為資料處理不純粹是事務性的工作,可是上級單位往往把你當成行政性的工作,我始終感覺這是研究發展同時並進的工作,農資中心也一直希望朝著研究發展的方向努力。
顧敏主任:
我所負責的單位,在性質上和農資中心比較接近,因為我們所發展的系統也是以資訊檢索方面為主,我也先向大家簡單的報告一下我們的背景,"立法院"有一圖書館、一法律資訊中心和一電腦中心。

在過去三年裏,我們也是從零開始,我們的電腦化工作,不光只是圖書館的工作,主要還要支援全立法院的電腦化工作,所以我們要做行政支援的工作,要做立法院辦公室自動化工作,目前我們整個大計劃的名稱為"法律資訊系統",英文簡稱 LEGISIS,本系統共分為六大部份,除了一部份是引進海外的資訊服務之外,其他的五種都是要靠我們自己來發展,換句話說都是中文系統,在發展中文線上檢索系統方面也是有許多困難。目前我們的計劃是在過去兩年發展兩個系統,在未來的三年我們繼續再開發三個系統,也就是三個資料庫,已經完成的兩個系統是:"立法委員質詢系統",從 1984 年到現在,有將近五年的資料,在這方面我們還同時支援議事組,因此這個系統不只是檢索,還有統計及各種事務報表;第二個系統是最近才完成的法律系統,將過去所通過的法律放到資料庫裏,現在系統已運作得很正常,是在十一月才正式開放,這是這兩年做的兩件事情。

未來我們也希望做三件事情,第三個系統我們可能嘗試以 MARC 來處理期刊文獻,第四個要做新聞資料系統,第五個我們將做整合,就技術上來講可以說是第一個階段的總結,在這五個系統完成之後,我們就要發展第二個階段,這是我們的大概規劃情形。

在發展的過程當中有一個問題可以提出來向各位報告的是,我們所發展的立法資訊系統有一個特色,我們要用自然語言和控制語言兩種並行的方式來發展的,在控制語言方面,我們引進美國國會圖書館國會服務處的索引典,做控制語言工具和標準,另外自然語言方面我們是用斷詞的方法,我們的系統特色,是關於主題方面我們是從自然語言、控制語言和分類三方面來處理,當然這中間所遇到的問題還是很多,可是我們抱持著一個簡單的理念,也是我們解決問題的一個觀念,任何問題都是可以實驗的,實驗結果如果是好的就留下來,不好的就不要,就一個管理者來講,我們也遇到了農資中心所講電腦人員、圖書館人員和資料處理人員配合的問題,我們的做法是使電腦人員變成資訊分子(Information Literacy),也使得圖書館人員成為電腦分子(Computer Literacy),讓大家在本科專長之外成為另一個領域的份子、熟知者的話,就比較容易溝通,計劃推行上可能也比較方便一點。

我的結論是,簡單的講最大的問題還是觀念問題,如果大家在觀念上能夠取得共識,這觀念包括:行政支援、讀者、不同背景的工作人員,如果大家都可以溝通的話,我想問題都可以解決;不能溝通的話,這個問題可能就會一直存在下去。
主席:
聽了了館長和主任的意見之後,我們再聽聽顧問的意見,宋處長擔任多所圖書館的顧問,如"中央圖書館"、"中央研究院"圖書館和農資中心等,我們現在請他來談他在擔任圖書館自動化顧問時所遭遇到的問題。

宋玉處長：

　　圖書館自動化在臺灣已有十多年的歷史，到今天來說圖書館自動化已經和十年前大不一樣了，現在提到自動化的話，我相信沒有人會反對，頂多是有困難而已，所以大家都有共識，認爲電腦和圖書館作業應該結合在一起，這是好的一面；還有一個好的一面就是電腦的價錢拚命在掉，尤其是小型電腦，這對自動化也是一個非常大的好處，但並不是沒有負的影響，剛剛聽到真正在做圖書館自動化的館長、主任的報告也有一大堆的問題，困難很多，進度很慢，錢多半是不夠，硬體的錢現在來講比較起來還是差得比較少的，軟體的錢則常常是不夠的，因爲大家總覺得軟體是看不見的東西，順理成章，學校裏要是有電腦作業人員，請他們寫兩個程式就可以上電腦了，就是買的話也不覺得需要花那麼大的錢，軟體公司，也覺得他們不應該花那麼大的時間來做事，至於軟體價錢的評估，我覺得還是偏低，偏低實際上是一個壞處，因爲一分錢一分貨，商家不會吃虧，做出來的產品就不無問題。另外還有幾方面的錢也常常被忽略，剛剛黃館長也講到 data conversion data keying 這一類資料準備工作所需要的錢；還有一項是大家不太注意，而我覺得蠻重要的，就是研究的錢，你需要做很多研究工作，頭一個就是分析圖書館的需求，第一步是調查人工作業的方式，有些統計資料把它整理出來，實際上還有一些是真正自動化系統已經完成了以後，業務又跟以前不一樣了，所以多少要往前看將來的問題，還有很多時候，對於甲館適用的東西不一定對於乙館也適用，所以我覺得應該花功夫和圖書館自動化人員、電腦人員，大家研究研究，甚至做點實驗測量的事情，這些都是應該做的，這些事情做了以後相信對以後的系統設計會方便一些。另外一項就是維護，假如整個系統都設計好了，硬體軟體都開張了，可以作業了，還有一筆錢是大家不知道的，因爲實際上作業時會發現很多問題，這時候就需要一些維護的錢，發展的錢，諸如此類，總之錢多半是不夠的。

　　以下就個人經驗提出若干問題，就教諸位專家學者：

　　1. 研究發展誰來做？前面我提到的是某一個單位要擁有一個自動化系統的話要做研究發展，實際上整體來說，我覺得我們圖書館自動化整個事情更需要有一個研究發展的單位，而且要研究發展的項目很多，現在的做法多半是在一個學校裏找幾位先生研究，當然這也是研究啦，但是這種情況下研究所包括的層面就不容易廣，有的時候是整個軟體工作交給軟體公司來做，軟體公司實際上來講對圖書館作業不是那麼瞭解，甚至你把你的要求告訴他，他多半也是不能瞭解，多半還拿一些技術上的理由來搪塞，告訴你不能做，事實上是因爲一方面他們不瞭解，二方面他們沒做過這類的東西，所以沒辦法照我們的要求做，這樣的話，就整個區域來講，因爲中文有他特別的地方，不能夠把海外成功的系統直接移植過來，淡江花了很多的時間，得到了一部份的解答，但是不是還有其他方面的問題，是不是還有其他的解答方式，這些都是很值得研究的問題。

　　還有一個問題是沒有數據，專家們問起時，回答都是感覺怎樣，感覺應這樣做或感覺應那樣做，但是沒有真正的數據；有數據的話比較好，要省時間要省到什麼程度，速度要快，快到什麼程度，才有明確的標準可循。

　　另外，大家剛剛也談得不少，電腦的人要和圖書館的人一起合作，我補充一下，通訊的人也很重要，因爲將來電腦連線的話是通訊方面的事，所以這是一個問題，很可惜的是圖書館學和資訊科學方面的研究發展的工作沒有一個主管機關負責。

　　2. 標準：假如一個圖書館做自動化，將也不預備和別人溝通，當然沒有問題；但是如果你要跟人家連線，要跟人家溝通，要跟人家交換資料，那就非得有一套標準；另外還有一個附帶的好處，標準不只是互相溝通，對你自己作業也有好處，館內作業也需要制定一套標準，若有現成標準可省卻很多麻煩。

　　3. 小型圖書館的自動化：臺灣小型圖書館館數目很多，規模不大，館員也不多，不可能有一個很複雜很大的系統，但他們也很需要自動化，怎樣的系統可以適合他們的需要，而又能與較大型較完整的系統，如"中央圖書館"的系統溝通，應是值得重視的問題。

主席：

　　接下來請銘傳商專和工技學院圖書館的兩位館長來談談他們所遭遇的問題。

黃大偉館長：

　　首先提出我們圖書館自動化所遭遇的問題，我們圖書館正如宋顧問所說是一個小館，我們所遭遇到問題正是圖書館進行自動化時可能遭遇到的問題，缺人、缺錢，而業務量日增，這是一個非常傳統而且非常實際的問題，我想從"中央圖書館"到我們這種小館，甚至更小的館都有這樣的問題，舉例來說如 ISBN 雖已核定由"中央圖書館"來主管，可是"中央圖書館"編制是變了，但是和淡江大學一樣，沒有增加人，試問在這樣有限的人力下，要做額外的工作，怎麼可能做得好呢？我們這種小館還面臨另外一個問題就是缺少權，不知"中央圖書館"在做 ISBN 時是不是常會有一種無力感，我想一定會的，因為"中央圖書館"對那些出版商沒有什麼約束能力，這種情況我們可以說已經到了癌症末期了；另外我前面提到缺人缺錢，他的原因在那裏，就在缺乏主管單位的重視；為什麼缺乏主管單位的重視呢，因為他們覺得投資報酬率很低；為什麼投資報酬率低呢，因為缺乏讀者的回饋；為什麼缺乏讀者回饋呢，因為服務品質低落；為什麼服務品質低落呢，還是因為缺人缺錢，如此惡性循環下去，是很多圖書館的行政人員都會唱的一首悲歌；雖然如此，我還是勉勵各位同學要有知其不可而為之的精神，雖然我們的資源很貧乏，還是要秉持著克難精神，突破當前的困難，畢竟圖書館的前途也就是各位的前途。

　　另外，我很贊成吳主任所提圖書館應有專職的電腦人員，不是工讀生，也不是電腦中心借調支援人員，更不是電腦公司的支援人員，為什麼呢？因為圖書館是一個成長的有機體，圖書館自動化系統更是成長的有機體，你不能說今年我們做圖書館自動化，花一筆錢，投入一些人，明年經費少了，對不起，請你暫時停止呼吸一學期，那就完了，以上這些是圖書館自動化當前所遭遇的困難及面臨的問題。

　　以下是我要提出來的一些問題，主要是請教賈所長：

　　1. 賈所長在三、四年前曾極力倡導分封交換，現在已完成了 PACNET，不知道 PACNET 和圖書館以前所慣用的 UDAS 業務上有沒有衝突，它所屬的單位不一樣？是否 PACNET 可能更經濟可行？

　　2. PACNET 對圖書館資訊網路有沒有實質上的助益，是否可以"財政部"的金融資訊小組為例，來說明一下資訊網路應如何與電信事業相結合？

　　3. PACNET 定義了 ISO 標準的下三層，那麼上面的四、五、六、七是不是該由圖書館界和電腦界的人來努力；現在圖書館館與館之間在交換書目資料時已有 MARC 標準，來作爲通訊協定，可是線上通訊標準目前還沒有訂定。

4. "中央圖書館"和淡江大學圖書館的資料不知可否提供給電信局，作爲電傳視訊的 information provider？

5. 臺灣電信事業有走向自由化、民營化趨勢，是否會對圖書館資訊網路造成什麼樣的衝擊？

王逸如館長：

首先就經驗回答黃館長有關 PACNET 和 UDAS 的問題，我們目前利用 PACNET 接 Dialog 一直都很順利，如果以後有圖書館要接國際網路的話，我覺得接 PACNET 較方便，因爲 PACNET 可以接海外也可以接島內。

接下來提供若干本館進行自動化時遭遇的問題，就教各位專家學者，也提出我們的錯誤以爲殷鑑。首先將我們圖書館自動化的情況分成三個階段簡單介紹一下，第一階段是從 1980 年到 1982 年，由本校的電腦專家主動來爲圖書館設計流通系統，但他們低估了圖書館，也不瞭解圖書館自動化的複雜性，而圖書館人員卻坐等成果，結果是完全失敗；第二期是由 1984 年到 1986 年，由圖書館人員與電腦中心人員合作開發，學校方面當時的政策是希望利用電腦中心資源，由電腦中心的人員來支援圖書館，而我們也毫無選擇，因爲十年來我們發展自動化都沒有額外的經費，沒有額外的人力，都要靠圖書館自己來做，別無選擇之下，也就只好做了；當時由電腦中心人員在 VAX 780 上建立期刊檔，應用程式則由圖書館的人自己來寫，到目前爲止還可以維持下去。後來也請電腦中心的人爲我們設計了一個 Chinese MARC 的檔，但不久中心的人走了，系統也沒有辦法維持下去，這階段我們的結論是圖書館需要有一獨立的電腦，同時圖書館人員不能完全依賴電腦人員，不僅需要參與規劃更要參與應用程式設計，這樣萬一電腦人員離職或有變動，圖書館還可以維持系統運作；第三期是從 1987 年起至現在，這個階段我們是一邊在等待救援，一邊在做準備工作，因爲經費有限，所以我們一直到目前爲止都沒有一個完整的系統，都是陸陸續續的在現有經費下發展；我們冀望的是"教育部"的"國立大學"圖書館自動化發展計劃，本館已寫了需求書，至今雖未定案，但總有一天會有決定，所以我們一直在等；可是我們也不能一直等下去，還要想辦法做點事，所以目前除了期刊建檔外，西文圖書已利用 Bibliofile 將舊資料轉錄到磁片上，除了排卡外，其餘如印製新書目錄、卡片目錄等均利用此系統，爲將來做準備工作；另外，除了我們館員認爲不能再等以外，學生也認爲不能再等了，所以已有學生做專題研究，預計明年可完成出納自動化。

同時也計劃中文圖書的 MARC 建檔，所以目前我們所做的都是爲將來的自動化做準備工作，雖然沒有一個完整的系統，只是做建檔工作，但我們的館員也可以感受到圖書館已開始進行自動化，對自動化的知識也不斷在充實，以下乃就未來的計劃提出若干問題。

(1) 以 PC 爲主的網絡系統適不適合中型獨立學院圖書館，假如"教育部"撥下經費的話，我們到底是要選擇以 PC 爲主的網路系統，還是至少要有 Supermicro 以上的系統，但因爲學校單位資料量增加迅速，我認爲走 PC 網路系統不太適合，不知專家們的看法如何？

(2)機器選擇問題,如果我們不走 PC 網路系統,而走另一途徑的話,以目前臺灣 Turnkey System 的市場來看,像我們這種經費不是很寬裕的圖書館,能選擇的系統好像不是很多,這是一個問題;另外如果我們要選擇硬體,選擇機器的話,爲了將來維護方便,必須要考慮到學校電算中心的廠牌,還有將來各大學會建立網路系統,那選擇硬體是否也要考慮到網路系統?

主席:

第一個議題到此告一段落,總結如下:我們討論的問題多半是人力的問題,經費的問題、硬體、軟體、網路,還有標準問題,和我 1985 年所做的調查結果差不多,我們有一個最好的現象,就是館員方面都沒有阻力,都願意自動化,上個月在美國 ASIS 年會中曾討論到圖書館自動化未來發展的方向及應注意的事項,便特別強調圖書館自動化系統的設計要考慮到使用者的需求(user needs)。

議題二:標準的必要性

主席:

首先請資訊科學專家張鼎鍾教授來談談標準問題。

張鼎鍾教授:

臺灣早期在推展圖書館自動化時就非常強調標準的重要性,也做出了很多標準,在"中央圖書館"王館長和同道的領導下,也完成了很多工作,例如 MARC 和 Character Set 方面標準,但圖書館自動化所需要的標準相當多,剛剛很多圖書館館長也都呼籲是不是應多做一些,所以我就提出幾個標準可能走的方向,提出來就教諸位。

1. Authority 方面的標準:很多中心都在做索引典(Thesaurus),這些索引典是不是有些可以共同來做,是不是有些是重複的;圖書館自動化最終目的是希望能夠資源分享(resource sharing),假如不同的索引典在同樣的範疇內有一些不同的名詞會不會造成問題,所以在 authority 方面是不是可以考慮到索引典及其他各種不同索引方法的統一性。

2. 關於 Command 方面:現在發展的系統都是用不同的硬體或軟體,也設計不同的Command,以後也必須針對不同的系統來訓練館員或教育使用者;所以是不是在Command 或 protocol 方面應該考慮到統一性。

3. 現在所有圖書館自動化時都是以所屬的單位爲依據,而圖書館之間的相通反而比較困難,因爲不是圖書館與圖書館之間 horizontal development,而是圖書館與所屬單位之間的 vertical development,所以溝通上就會發生問題;目前已有所謂 Transparency Program 可以解決這些硬體和軟體問題,是不是我們也可以發展一些 Transparency Program 來解決圖書館系統之間溝通的問題。

主席:

謝謝張教授。提到標準,宋顧問最近主持了一個終端機規格小組,可不可以簡單地向大家報告一下。

宋玉顧問:

我先來報告一下我所知道的標準,舉個例子來做比較,音響因爲有完善的硬體標準,所以不同的零件可以任意組合,但是各位使用光碟(CD-ROM)時會發現,某些光碟在某些機器上不能使用,這也是標準的緣故使之不能互通;因此,標準如果推行得好,產品利用就可既多樣化又廣泛,標準的重要性也就在此。

至於圖書館自動化時我們應該做哪些標準工作呢?剛剛張教授也提到了圖書館界已經做了一些標準工作,如中國機讀編目格式、中國機讀編目權威記錄格式等,另外 CCCII 也是為圖書館界所發展的,現在已為圖書館界所廣泛採用,這些都是已經完成的,但是還有一些標準亟待制定,一是次序問題,目前圖書館常用的排列方法是五筆檢字法,但其參考資料以現在的標準來看,一來字數不夠,二來當中也有錯誤,且其方法若以電腦來處理雖不是不可以做到,但是做起來非常佔儲存空間,因此在次序方面如果還要照原來的方法做的話,資料要加以更新,或許我們也可以研究另一套更適當的次序標準。

還有一項迫切需要研究制定的標準,就是中文標題(subject heading),臺灣到目前為止還沒有一套中文的標題,到底要用什麼樣的方法來做中文標題,是一項亟待研究也亟需制定標準的問題。

此外,在電腦和電信方面,我們還有相當多的標準要做,"中國圖書館學會"先後在王館長和李主任的領導之下成立圖書館自動化作業規劃委員會,其下組成了一圖書館終端機規格研訂小組,其計劃是做圖書館用的中文終端機規格的研究,希望訂出規格後電腦廠商能照我們訂的規格來製造終端機,以後圖書館界就有比較方便比較適用的終端機可以用了。目前這個規格已經制定完成,正在出版當中(註:已刊登在"中國圖書館學會"會報第 43 期),同時我們也把這個標準給了電腦公司,希望電腦公司能夠響應。

除此之外,實際上還有很多工作應該做,例如圖書館與圖書館之間要連線的話,這是一個問題,因為圖書館不是用同一系統或同一廠牌的電腦,所以要把它們連接起來就需要一些特別的技術;目前電信方面 ISO 雖定有 OSI(open system interconnection)的標準,可以讓不同的電腦連接,但是圖書館方面還必須做一些應用程式(application program)方面的努力,譬如查詢時應該用什麼樣的方法,Command 的型式等等都需要加以統一化。

主席:

謝謝宋顧問。標題在圖書館自動化方面的重要性是無庸置疑的,胡教授一直極力倡導臺灣應該建立中文標題,我們現在就請胡教授來為我們說明一下。

胡述兆教授:

談到這個問題就感慨萬千,我回來五年,這五年裏我無時無刻不想到這個問題,也希望能在這方面盡一點力量,過去幾年裏我和王館長、沈教授、李主任努力了三年多沒有結果,問題在什麼地方呢?在我們的長官、我們的主管部門對這個問題沒有瞭解,也不重視,而且是中國人的老毛病,你推我,我推你,結果是通通推掉了。我向國科會洽談,"國科會"說:"這你恐怕要和'教育部'接洽";向"教育部"申請,"教育部"說暫時沒有預算;向文建會申請,文建會說不歸我管也不便管;我們這幾年裏,開了好多次會,研擬計劃,計劃擬妥了,送到有關單位去申請經費,三年計劃共列一千多萬塊錢,一千萬在現在外匯七百多億的政府來說實在是少得可憐,而且還是不肯拿出來,那要怪誰呢!?恐怕只能怪我們沒有權位,人家不聽我們這一套;另外也是我們的主管單位眼光不夠,這樣一件重要的事,我們提出這樣的說明,竟然沒有一個單位知道它的重要性,現在我們的工作已經做完了,計劃已經擬出來了,可是沒人家買,你說怎麼辦呢？我不知道，只冀望"中央圖書館"方面能把這項工作承擔過去，我們請王館長來報告一下。

王振鵠館長：

關於中文標題的經過情形，我大致都瞭解，也經過很長時間的努力和溝通，但是還沒有具體的結果，"教育部"曾發函"中央圖書館"，要"中央圖書館"評估其價值，若確有必要請"中央圖書館"再向"教育部"提出報告，我們已經和"教育部"有關單位有過溝通，癥結在預算，他們一看到一千多萬的預算，會計單位就有點遲疑，因為照正常編列預算的方式，每年有一定的範圍，增加預算必須要有專案計劃，所以"教育部"認為假如超過一千萬最好報到"教育部"變成專案計劃，因此我們只好報專案計劃，因為"教育部"的預算可能不能容納；但這件事情，經過胡教授的努力，已引起重視。

另外，剛才黃先生也提到有關ISBN、CIP的情形，這個問題很複雜，大家都認為理所當然一定要做，"中央圖書館"差不多在九年前就取得了ISBN的編號——957，當時就試探實施，第一步我們先向出版社做了問卷調查，因為ISBN的編號必須先要掌握出版界出版的情況，假如出版界不支持，就沒有辦法給他編號；當時發出一千七、八百份的問卷，收回了四百多份，其中百分之六十是贊成，百分之四十是不贊成，他們的反應第一個是使用這個號碼對我的出版品的銷售有什麼好處，第二個是這樣做是不是會增加我們的困難，會不會影響出書速度，第三個是"中央圖書館"是不是授權的單位，政府有沒有給你權來做這件事；這三個問題的確是擊中我們的要害，我們的確是沒有權做這件事情，"中央圖書館"是基於我們的瞭解，我們認為必要，但是沒有人授權給我們做；因此我們把這個問題報到"教育部"，而"教育部"也開過幾次會，但基於出版品的主管單位還是在"新聞局"，所以"教育部"又把這件事轉到"新聞局"，"新聞局"非常同意，也非常支持，所以把這件事報到"行政院"，"行政院"在今年六月核定授權"中央圖書館"推行，這期間在與行政單位的溝通上的確花了很多時間，ISBN號碼涉及的單位差不多有五、六個——第一個是"教育部"，"中央圖書館"的上級單位；第二個是"行政院"研考會，他們也推行一個政府出版品的編號，所以與他們有關；第三個是"中央標準局"，其規定要成為"國家標準"就要依照申請、登記、核定；第四個是"文建會"，甚至第五個涉及出版協會等等；"中央圖書館"在今年十月把他們再度邀請來，告訴他們我們已獲得授權，請各單位給我們支持，大家提到的第一個問題就是應該做一份手冊，先做個調查，詳細地把步驟做好以便推行，但是涉及誰來做，經費哪來的問題，最後雖然是四、五十萬的經費，結果由四個單位分攤，所以剛才胡教授提到一千多萬，這個很困難，四十幾萬的預算為什麼還是由"新聞局"、文建會、臺北市政府、"教育部"幾個單位分擔？不是沒有錢，而是沒有預算的項目，如果要擬定預算，沒有這個科目，你一分錢也不能動，現在總算經費有著落了，所以我們計劃在半年內把他規劃完成，我們的規劃包括三點，第一點是ISBN的問題，第二點是CIP的問題，我們希望連帶把預行編目也做好，第三點和出版界有關的是做條碼制度，各位都知道商品都有國際條碼，而ISBN現在也在條碼化，ISBN中心和條碼中心正合作研究一套可推行的書籍條碼，我們也希望把條碼化的制度一併研究，這樣對書籍的銷售發行，甚至對圖書館的管理可能都有點幫助，所以這裏頭不只是單純ISBN的問題，我們希望在半年內做好規劃工作,然後再推行。不過最重要的一點是人力,做這個工作如果沒有適當的人力支援,以"中央圖書館"目前人力是不太容易配合;還有個問題大家也許會問,ISSN(叢刊號碼)怎麼辦?我們也連繫過,始終沒有得到國際 ISSN 中心的同意,這受到的壓力很大,國際 ISSN 中心的答覆是如果要申請的話,請向北京去申請,因為中國只有一個,不可能再給你一個代表國家的區域號碼,可是現在各位看到還是有很多雜誌上面有 ISSN 的號碼,是怎麼來的呢?這有兩個途徑,第一個是美國 Bowker 公司給的,因為比較重要的學術性期刊都納入 Bowker 的 Periodical Directory 中,所以都編了 ISSN 號碼,由 Bowker 公司統一向 ISSN 總部申請;第二個途徑是直接向巴黎的中心申請,但有困難,因其規定申請的中文期刊一定要用大陸的漢語羅馬拼音,不能用韋傑士拼音,這是我們遭遇到的問題,所以有些期刊為了避免羅馬拼音問題,就乾脆以英譯刊名申請,這也是我們不得已的做法,到目前為止已經有一百四十多份雜誌利用這種方法取得 ISSN 號碼,但問題還是無法突破,這是我所瞭解的情形,向各位報告。

主席:

謝謝王館長,請沈教授提供一些意見。

沈寶環教授:

講到自動化,西方國家自從打孔機發明以來,已經有九十八年,美國國會圖書館利用打孔機做聯合目錄也有三十八年歷史,而臺灣這十幾年之內也卓然有成,我說十幾年是因為十七年前我曾寫了一篇圖書館自動化的文章,而三年後張鼎鍾教授在師大開風氣之先利用國際百科展開自動化工作,從那時以後圖書館自動化的工作就以"中央圖書館"為中心轟轟烈烈地展開,我們有這樣的成就,我覺得非常欣慰,欣慰之餘就想到大家好像都有一種自動化熱,都在一窩蜂的搞自動化,究竟我們最終的目的是什麼?我想自動化最終的目的是資源共享,自動化只是一個手段(means),而不是目的(ends),這點關係我們應始終牢記在心裏,我覺得大家都努力做是很好,但是不是應該有一個通盤的整體計劃,我們應該以"中央圖書館"為中心來建一個全域的資訊網路。

剛剛大家提到很多問題,我現在把我的感想說一下,我們現在辦自動化研習會,在座很多圖書館的青年才俊都曾參與過,那是不是將來可以把方向轉移一下,為我們的長官、主管等決策者(decision maker)辦個兩三天的自動化講習,請在座的專家學者來上課,我想這未嘗不是一個可行的辦法。現在的阻力確是莫名其妙,剛才胡教授的苦處我是非常之清楚,我就想到是不是把計劃重新寫一下,和"中央圖書館"合作,集合人才來編定中文標題目錄,事實上我們的分類法也有問題,要做的事情還是很多。另外圖書館自動化發展到今天這個階段,是圖書館學、資訊科學和通訊的一種自然結合,但是我們系要求更改系名為"圖書館學與資訊科學學系"居然被駁回,我一直心裏很不愉快,胡教授恐怕就氣病了,現在就冀望我們李主任來爭取。換句話說,現在發生問題的不是你們青年這一代,也不在圖書館館員,而在上級單位,在有權的主管,這就有待各位專家學者來溝通。

主席:

現在請兩位編目專家吳教授、盧教授就這個主題來發表一下意見。

吳明德教授:

我們大家都知道標準的重要性,我非常贊成張教授提到有關檢索指令(Command)

的標準,大家不知道有沒有發現一個問題,以前我們使用人工目錄的時候,我們到任何一個圖書館使用他們的目錄都沒有問題,反而現在自動化了以後,很多圖書館都有線上目錄,我們到每一個圖書館使用線上目錄的時候都要重新學習;從這裏可以知道自動化以後,標準的問題確實是值得我們注意的。

另外剛才很多專家也提到我們所需要的很多標準,比如分類或標題等標準,現在很多圖書館已經有了線上目錄,但是這些線上目錄所提供的檢索項目和以前傳統的人工目錄比較起來好像沒有很大的差別,其實我個人覺得在自動化以後,線上目錄能夠提供給讀者比較多的或者是能夠讓讀者感受到線上目錄能夠幫助他們檢索的應該是主題檢索,所以在分類表、標題表,或者是主題辭彙表方面,我們還需要再繼續努力。

另外是中國機讀編目格式(MARC)的問題,很多圖書館都在使用MARC,而很多圖書館也都反應中國機讀編目格式太複雜,這個原因當然很多,其中一個原因可能是因爲中國機讀編目格式在設計的時候,圖書館界對於線上目錄的經驗並不是很多,所以當初所設計的機讀編目格式在線上目錄來說並不是十分的恰當,所以我覺得也許我們圖書館界需要再進一步地去努力,以使中國機讀編目格式能夠更適合線上目錄的需要。

盧秀菊教授:

關於標準這一項很多專家學者都已經談到了,我簡單地談一下這幾年教分類編目的感想,當然談到分類編目,前面很多專家也都提到目前最缺乏的就是中文標題,希望大家共同努力早日編訂中文標題目錄。

另外關於分類表的問題,臺灣的分類表也是非常的鬆散,另外我還感受到另一個牽涉到教育的問題,就是常常在學習的過程當中,往往無法讓同學很透徹的瞭解分類表等等有關標準的問題。

主席:

我有個建議談到中國機讀編目格式的問題,不知道"中央圖書館"的MARC小組可否研擬一套MINIMARC,這個問題有勞王館長加以研究。

另外談到檢索指令(Command)的問題,我想請資訊檢索專家,資策會副執行長周誠寬博士來爲我們說明一下Command標準化的問題。

周誠寬博士:

我覺得標準順應電腦科技的進步和自動化的腳步,有些標準立刻重要起來,有些要五年十年以後才重要;從前用卡片的話通通會用,現在用自動化的系統反而都不會用,這就牽涉到教育的問題,如果Command有一定標準的話,可能訓練起來比較方便,圖書館員之間,使用者之間,還有資料交換方面都比較方便,這是標準比較重要的原因。

另外,我對第一個議題有一些意見,今天已有多位專家提到,目前圖書館界的問題是怎樣讓更高層次的上級主管瞭解我們的問題,所以我覺得圖書館界可能需要成立一個強有力的小組,將重要的標準擬定通過後,鼓勵幾個重要的圖書館採用,假如迫切地需要政府支持的話,可由此小組共同出面溝通,衆志成城,比較容易成功。

另外是有關教育的問題,我覺得年輕的圖書館員,應該教育他們怎樣使部門或組織中的主管階層知道圖書館的用處,從前圖書館很重要的原因是因爲書很貴買不起,現在書很便宜,假如我覺得這本書重要的話我會去買一本,這本雜誌重要的話我會去訂一份,所以圖書館只靠書籍和雜誌是生存不下去的,那要如何才能生存下去呢?應該變成資訊供應者(information provider; IP),讀者在書或雜誌上找不到的資料,我們可以幫他找出來,而且不只供應技術性的資料(technical information),而且還可以供應經營管理的資料,協助研究工作,市場調查工作的進行,我們一定要和組織的目標結合起來,扮演資訊供應者的角色,所以我覺得年輕圖書館館員的訓練,可能重點在怎樣說服其主管,讓主管人員瞭解圖書館的重要性,讓他們知道如果沒有圖書館企業就無法生存,所以我認為推銷學是非常重要的。還有一點我覺得非常重要的,就是圖書館裏一定要有專門的程式設計師,這一點我不贊成,假如圖書館自動化要成功的話,非要圖書館員本身對自動化有深入的瞭解,這樣圖書館自動化才能成功,唯有圖書館員能夠掌握能夠瞭解科技在圖書館的利用才是比較重要的。

另外我非常贊成舉辦高級主管的圖書館自動化講習會。

議題三、圖書館資訊網路

主席:

現在進行第三個議題,請通訊專家賈所長來發表一下意見。

賈玉輝所長:

今天很高興有這個機會來說明一下有關於圖書館界目前如何利用最新的科技產品來達到更好的服務效果,大家都曉得圖書館事實上是非常非常重要的,譬如在美國的德州大學,我們最高的建築就是圖書館,最豪華設備一定在圖書館,圖書館內都是沙發椅,其他教室可以沒有空調設備,圖書館裏一定要有空調設備,讓大家能夠有最好的環境,把圖書館的效果發揮到淋漓透徹的地步,所以真正說起來圖書館實在是非常重要的,可是為什麼我剛剛聽來聽去好像都有志難伸,原因到底何在呢?基本上我個人倒是認為社會在變遷,整個環境在變,圖書館可能有些做法或許也可以小小的變一變,如果小小變一變或許耳目就可以一新;我隨便舉個例子,剛剛周博士也提到要行銷,這確實是非常重要的,工商業社會不管哪一行哪一業都要行銷,另外一方面我也忽然想到好比說廣告也很重要,我們幾乎沒有看到過圖書館有任何廣告,可是在現在的社會裏,如果沒有廣告的話,你的商品再好,好像也不太好賣,那如果大家都不知道有這麼好的商品,那麼你孤芳自賞,這也是人間的一大憾事;所以在這種情況下怎樣用新的媒體來做新的廣告,這可能是圖書館應該追求的近期目標,但媒體很多,譬如打電視廣告,登報紙,不過這些都貴得不得了,圖書館已經窮了,如果再這樣就更窮了。那怎麼辦呢?可能就要想想有沒有什麼新的媒體可以來用一用,我的建議是電傳視訊,新的通訊科技,譬如說市立圖書館,到底有哪些書呢?現在的人都懶得很,時間寶貴得很,他們不可能經常跑圖書館,因為你上班他也上班,你下班或許他也下班了,可是到底圖書館有些什麼資料,有些什麼圖書,新到了什麼雜誌,這些資訊對於讀者非常重要,如果這些資訊能夠在適當的媒體上表現出來,讓大家都知道,這樣的話效果就不一樣了。我只要舉一個例子諸位就可以瞭解,例如美國文化中心圖書館,我大概一兩個月就可以收到它們的通訊,告訴我新到了哪些書,我發現這本書正是我想要看的,立刻撥個電話預約就可以借到了,這樣圖書館的利用率就提高了;但它是用寄的,用寄的還要打字,還要花郵費,如果更進一步,圖書館可以把新書的廣告,甚至整個的圖書目錄,能夠在電子媒體如電傳視訊上,讓大家在家就可以知道圖書館有什麼資料可以利用,這樣圖書館會由靜態的搖身一變成為動態的圖書館，大家就會發現圖書館是和社會在同步，是跟生活打成一片，這種感受就會不一樣；這也是為什麼今天圖書館用得最多的還是學生的原因，因為學生在學校，環境本身和圖書館息息相關，可是一離開學校，有時候就會脫節，為什麼呢？因為缺乏環境，如果利用電子媒體顯然就可以繼續與之保持關係，這是我的一個看法。

另外，網路方面我必須稍加說明，事實上 PACNET 分封網路目前已和世界上三十個國家的八十個網路結合在一起，所有重要的國家都可以四通八達，這些網路也都很重要。至於 Dialog 臺灣在早期確實是採用 UDAS（國際百科），其基本功能是做資料庫的檢索服務，目前也已擴充成雙向溝通的方式，但發展速度還是沒有那麼快，而 PACNET 目前除了 PACNET I 以外，還有 PACNET II 明年春天即可推出，屆時網路上的功能就更完整，就可提供更多樣化的服務，更可以應付自動化社會的各種需要。而和圖書館的關係也更加密切，這也就是為什麼"國科會"這兩天舉辦"中日資訊交流研討會"的目的，"國科會"所開發的 STICNET 將於年底推出，明年初就可以和各大學連線，這就是利用 PACNET，連線單位利用分封交換網路可以立刻線上查詢科資中心的所有資料庫，如此一來科資中心的資料馬上就可被所有學術界的朋友來利用，而且因為觸角延伸出去了，就不會被孤立，立刻就可以和客觀的環境連成網路，還可以和國際間合作，個人覺得這是今後必然要發展的趨勢，因為世界到底是越來越小了，尤其是資料的流通更是無遠弗屆，在這種客觀環境下利用分封交換網路可以說是眼前最價美物廉的方式，再也找不到第二種，不管是海內外，皆然。

至於整體發展趨勢方面，目前我們正引進衛星通訊技術，今天屋頂上已經有很多小耳朵，我也希望以後圖書館也有很多小耳朵，圖書館的讀者也有很多小耳朵，事實上可以利用衛星通訊把讀者希望看到的資訊立刻送到每個讀者的眼前，這絕對不是做夢，絕對是可以行得通的，目前只是稍微貴一點，不過價格降得很快，各位想想看電腦以前多貴，現在多便宜，衛星通訊服務也是一樣，現在當然稍微貴一點，但是現在就可以開始著"眼"，著"手"大概還早了一點，可以開始著眼，學生就應該從這方面新的環境來著眼，到底怎樣來利用非常好的工具把圖書館的功能徹底地發揮。

一方面，圖書館本身的效率也需要全面的提高，效率在工商業可說一日千里，例如辦公室自動化、工廠自動化等等，圖書館的效率如果也能提高的話，大家會發現又跟以前不一樣了，簡單舉個例子來說，圖書館從採購一本書開始，到書到館，然後編目，所有的過程一定要電腦化，這種電腦化一般都當做資料處理來看待，不過我個人覺得現在應該走向標準化，目前有一個非常重要的世界標準 EDI（Electronic Data Interchange）電子資料交換，圖書館現在如果有機會的話，不妨可以考慮採用新的標準，可以一方面和圖書館界如書商、代理商、印刷廠等整體配合做電子採購，可以立刻用電子的方式來下訂單，將訂單傳送到世界各地方，這樣效率就可以提高了；更進一步，讀者如果希望留言給圖書館，有時打電話講不清楚，有時晚上圖書館關門了，圖書館也不妨採用電子信箱（Electronic Mailbox）或甚至 Voice Mailbox，像這些都可以加強效率，提高服務層面，這是從通信的角度來看我認為比較重要的地方。

另外談到 OSI 標準，就客觀環境而言全世界都朝這個方向走，所以當然圖書館必然也要朝著這個方面走，圖書館如果採用 OSI 標準當可事半功倍，且時機非常適當。

主席：

目前，臺灣發展的網路系統有"國科會"科資中心的STICNET、"中央圖書館"的全國資訊網路，和"教育部"的大專院校圖書館網路，這三個網路如果要連接的話會不會有問題，我們來請教一下賈所長。

賈玉輝所長：

基本上這些網路如果要互通的話，應該在一開始規劃的時候就要考慮進去，這樣就會比較簡單；就好像三個房間要通來通去的話，一開始就做個門，立刻就可以互通，否則規劃的時候本來是沒有門的，你硬要它通，那就只好打個門了，而在牆壁上打個門是很累的；所以最好是一開始整體規劃的時候就把這些互通性列為系統的基本需求，在這種需求下發展出來的成果，我相信互通就不會有問題，因為在國際間這種互通的例子可以說是屢見不鮮，不過最重要的還是規劃，比如說衣服上如果本來沒有口袋，現在要個口袋，那就難了，但不是不能做，非不能也，只是頭痛也。

議題四、圖書館自動化的教育與訓練

主席：

在座有幾位是圖書館自動化的老師，我們先請陳主任來發表一下教圖書館自動化的感想。

陳國瓊主任：

事實上我教圖書館自動化只有一年半，可是我是一個老員工，所以我對圖書館自動化不管在教書方面或是在與同學同道討論方面，我覺得最大的問題是在我們對人工系統瞭解得不夠透徹，這也是我們走很多冤枉路的原因；其次在教書方面，在評估系統的時候，同學們常常因為不瞭解人工系統，因此也就無法去評估自動化的系統，我曾經到一些已經自動化的圖書館去參觀，我的感覺是那些都是土法煉鋼的結果，很適合他們自己用，但將來要達到我們最終的目標——資源分享就會有很大的問題，當然讀者用得都很高興，因為他們對圖書館也都不太瞭解，只要能解決他們的現有問題就可以了，但在將來合作方面就有很大的問題。

另外在教書的時候也常發現文獻資料非常缺乏，尤其是中文資料方面非常少，外文資料對同學來講也有問題，因為不容易取得，這一點可能無論是同學或同道都可能有的問題。

另外是課程方面無法整合，教圖書館自動化時常常發現要講解人工系統的情況，可是那些內容好像又不屬於自動化課程的範圍，但若不講的話，同學又不容易瞭解，其次是有關電腦方面的概念問題，譬如資料庫管理系統（Data Base Management System, DBMS），如果不介紹的話，將來作為一個圖書館館員就會發生無法與電腦人員溝通的問題。

另外是在職訓練方面的問題，很多館員以前在學校時沒有接觸過電腦，而目前又沒有機會讓這些圖書館員接受長期正規的電腦訓練，希望資策會能夠提供這樣的在職進修機會。

主席：

淡江大學的圖書館自動化課程是由黃館長來講授，我們請他來說明一下。

黃世雄館長：

我們講課時理論與實際都能互相配合，因為如果涉及單一子系統，無論是採訪、編目或者流通的設計，都可以到圖書館去實際瞭解，而且圖書館的設備不錯，也有國際百科，也和OCLC連線，所以同學們都有實際驗證的機會，而圖書館裏的主任或館員對每個子系統都有深入的瞭解，當講授到某一功能時即由該部門之主任或負責的館員來現身說法，也可以減少我在教學方面負擔，所以幾年來我在教授圖書館自動化課程時並沒有很大的困難。

胡述兆教授：

我雖然不教圖書館自動化，但我想圖書館自動化應該從圖書館教育根本解決，我兩三年前就構想把圖書館學系改名為圖書館學與資訊科學系，可惜沒通過，議者曰資訊時代（information age）每一個系都可以，Library and Information Science 可以，Logic and Information Science 也可以，Politic and Information Science 都可以，簡直是對 Information 的濫用！結果這個提案就被擱置了。現在我有一個構想，改名不成，是不是可以把我們系分成兩組——資訊組和圖書館組，參考匹茲堡大學的模式，其在 School of Library and Information Science 下分兩系：Dept. of Library Science 和 Dept. of Information Science，兩年前我就有這個構想，為了加強師資陣容，就到青輔會去登求才廣告，條件是圖書館學的碩士加上電腦的博士，或者是電腦碩士加上圖書館學博士，但兩年來沒有一個人申請，找不到教員就無法分組，所以今天圖書館自動化的問題在教育，很多專家也都提到了，假如我們自己瞭解電腦，又瞭解圖書館的話，那麼圖書館自動化不必外求，自己就可以解決問題，這才是根本的辦法。現在我有兩個補充意見，第一個請李主任想辦法把我們系分為圖書館和資訊兩個組，第二個鼓勵同學修雙學位，以補學科背景之不足，如果圖書館學系的同學能夠到資訊系修雙學位，那麼圖書館自動化的問題就解決了，這是一個管道，另一個管道就是修輔系，我拼命鼓勵同學修資訊為輔系，但到目前為止還沒有同學選修，希望李主任能鼓勵同學朝這個方向發展，唯有我們自己懂圖書館也懂電腦，圖書館自動化才有希望，我想這是圖書館教育現階段最根本的問題。

主席：

胡教授為本系奮鬥了五年，以在很多方面我做起來都還算順利，而剛剛胡教授提到的問題，我也一直朝這個方向在努力，目標是加強資訊和自動化方面的課程。

至於在教圖書館自動化方面，我的感想和剛剛胡教授講的一樣，有很多基本教育的問題值得商榷，我上自動化課程時常常告訴同學圖書館自動化等於是再一次的 review 你四年所學的各項課程，但是很遺憾的是同學對圖書館的各項作業有時不是很瞭解，誠如陳主任所言，例如流通系統，以前課程裏沒有教過流通出納的各項工作，所以要他們畫流程圖他們就畫不來，這中間就有 gap 存在，應該想辦法加以彌補。另外在臺大教圖書館自動化有點像紙上談兵，因為沒有實際的系統可以讓同學們實地驗證所學，目前這幾年已經有瞭解決辦法，讓同學們分組去研究探討海內外現有的系統，藉此可以瞭解整個系統的功能及完整性，而且同學們在做口頭報告的時候也都能運用所學的各項知識，如視聽教育的理論和方法等，將他們的研究成果盡善盡美的表達出來，因此同學們都表示雖然很辛苦，但是收獲很多。

顧敏主任：
　　我們今天談到標準的問題，也談到教育的問題，當然圖書館自動化和圖書館教育有很大關係，而標準也可以把它分為兩方面，一方面是處理的標準，一方面是品質的標準，處理的標準可以說是行政的問題，也可以說是外標準，譬如標題表，資料傳輸標準，中文畫面的標準等等，另外一個是內標準，是品質的問題，尤其在教育方面訓練同學重視品質上的要求是非常重要的，因為假使今天我們有一個很好的分類表，並不表示我們有一個很好分類法，並不表示我們的分類問題就解決了，因為各館還要有各館的分類政策；假如我們有一套很好的編目規則，並不表示我們的編目問題就解決了，各館都要有各館的編目政策，那麼編目政策和分類政策是做什麼的呢？這就是一個內標準，所以，我想在教育上訓練同學這方面的觀念是非常重要的，因為這是一個品質的問題。
主席：
　　那麼本次座談會就到此結束，謝謝各位專家學者撥冗賜教，也謝謝大家能夠出席，謝謝。

臺灣圖書館自動化資訊系統發展之探討*

[摘要 Abstract]

本文主要研究目的是探討臺灣圖書館自動化資訊系統之發展情形,並特別分析其在發展中所遭遇的問題及困難,以瞭解臺灣圖書館自動化資訊系統之癥結及阻力。本文分三部份探討:(一)臺灣圖書館自動化資訊系統有關之文獻;(二)臺灣圖書館自動化資訊系統之發展情形;(三)臺灣圖書館自動化資訊系統之困難和問題因素。最後試提出個人的看法與建議。

Abstract: The purpose of this study is to investigate the development of automated library information systems in this country. The study has explored from (1) the related literature (2) the development of various library information systems and (3) the problems encountered when developing the automated systems, and finally some conclusions, comments, and suggestions.

在整個人類知識成長過程中,圖書館所負的任務是:人類文化遺產的蒐集和保存,促進文化的成長,以及為社會與人類福祉挑負起知識傳播的職責,因此,圖書館的功能就是"傳播資訊與推廣知識"。回顧近三十年來,科技發展日新月異,知識領域急劇擴增,使人類深覺知識爆炸的壓力。面對此挑戰:圖書館勢必更要加速其執行知識傳播的工作,儘快使讀者享受到知識成長的利益。為達成此項任務,圖書館必需借重現代化的資訊技術和設備,以協助拓廣控制知識的環境,加強人類快速完整的資訊連繫。因此,圖書館引用電子計算機來處理資料,將圖書館的業務自動化,借助通訊技術來建立館際間、地區性和國際間網路系統已是時勢所趨,迨無可避免。

自動化目的是追求效率和效益的工作,即提高工作效率而獲取效益。圖書館自動化之目的則在利用現代化科技和設備,來提昇圖書館工作效率,改善讀者服務品質,擴增資源互惠,致使圖書館資訊之傳播與運用更為遼闊、迅速、正確、直接協助政府推行之各項研究計劃及經濟的持續發展。

圖書館自動化的發展,已隨科技的進步,從最早1936年美國德州大學的孔卡流通系統(註一)至今日的線上分時網路整合性系統,歷經半世紀之久。用以推動自動化的技術與設備,從笨重昂貴的真空管電腦,改良成為晶片式的微處理機,而擁有人工智慧、語音系統和平行處理功能的第五代電腦,以及各種遠近距離資訊傳輸的通訊技術,價廉而功能多,致使圖書館有能力且必須運用這些技術和設備全面進行作業的自動化。因此美國圖書館自動化專家包斯(Richard W. Boss)先生則估計,在半世紀末,全美除學校圖書館之外的各類型圖書館將已全面自動化(註二)。

1983年美國圖書館學家笛加納瑞(Richard De Gennaro)探討美國圖書館自動化

---

* 本文曾發表在《"中國圖書館學會"會報》43期(1988年12月),第107—123頁。

和網路 1960—1980 三十年來之發展情況,以十年為一單元詳述其間之發展重點及特色,顯然地看出電子計算機進步與通訊技術是影響圖書館自動化發展的主要因素:(註三)

一、1960年代為整體區域自動化時代:此為美國圖書館自動化萌芽時期,雖新資訊科技尚不成熟,但人們卻是雄心萬丈,寄與無限希望。但由於費用及負擔困難,僅限於大型圖書館方能負擔。此時期是以發展館內系統(In-house Development Local System)為主。於是,多所圖書館即轉向共同合作的網路系統(Network System),促使70年代的網路系統和書目中心(Bibliographic Utilities)之興起,OCLC(Ohio College Library Center,後改為 Online Computer Library Center)即於1967年成立。

二、1970年代為集中網路時代:由於迷你電子計算機(Mini Computer)問世,價廉、功能強,又線上系統(Online System)設計成功,和通訊技術(Tele-communication)之發展,使網路系統成為70年代圖書館自動化主流,在合作而節省經費之觀念下,建立圖書網路和書目供應中心,致使1970年代成為圖書館合作之黃金時代。除 OCLC 外,在此時完成的書目中心有 RLIN(Research Library Information Network – 1974),WLN(Washington Library Network,現已改為 Western Library Network – 1976)和 UTLAS(University of Toronto Library Automated System – 1973)。

三、1980年代為多種選擇時代:多種自動化軟體(如 Turnkey System),電子計算機更進步、多功能、價廉、好用,微電腦在此時問世等,書商以設計期刊和圖書採購系統,給圖書館自動化帶來更多選擇。書目中心亦加強其功能設計 local system 以迎合圖書館之需求。

貝廷(P. Battin)將圖書館電腦化分成三個時代:第一代是圖書館的內部作業(Internal Functions)的自動化時代,第二代是整合圖書館自動化系統,含線上公用目錄之發展和裝置時代,第三代是利用區域網路(LAN)之通訊和計算功能設置個人工作站(Workstation)時代,第三階段將代表一主要的挑戰,它將是電算中心和圖書館功能之合併,而圖書館和館員所面臨的則是接受"科技"和"改變"(註四)。

很顯然地,歐美國家早已開發圖書館自動化系統,迄今已有相當成就,甚至於1983年解決了處理中、日、韓文的問題(註五)。根據瓦頓(Walton)和佈瑞吉(Bridge)1988年4月1日圖書館自動化工業之調查統計的報導(註六),現有1339個圖書館裝置自動化系統,這些系統多數是美國電腦公司和美國圖書館自行開發的系統。1987年一年即裝置302個系統,成長率則是前年的56%,裝置的圖書館則以美國為主。由此可看出美國圖書館界目前的積極推展圖書館自動化,同時這種情形亦代表美國圖書館事業之發展趨勢。

反觀臺灣圖書館自動化作業之發展情形,雖然臺灣在這方面起步稍遲,但實際上早在1971年代初開始探討圖書館自動化之可能性,由於客觀之條件和主觀意識的限制發展遲緩。本文主要研究目的是探討臺灣圖書館自動化資訊系統之發展情形,並特別分析其在發展中所遇的問題及困難,以瞭解臺灣圖書館自動化之癥結及阻力。本文分三部份探討:(一)臺灣圖書館自動化系統之文獻;(二)臺灣圖書館自動化資訊系統之發展情形;(三)臺灣圖書館自動化資訊系統之困難和問題因素。最後提出個人的看法與建議。

文獻是知識的記錄，書目則是知識精華的累積，由文獻目錄中可瞭解某學科的發展情形，更可發掘某學科或主題的歷史淵源。圖書館自動化資訊系統在歐美國家早已不再是熱門話題，而已視爲圖書館業務之正規之發展方向。故經過這麼多年，這方面的文獻多而豐富，如一九八三年美國出版的 *The Automation in Libraries : A LITA Bibliography* 之書目已超出 2500 項（註七）；*The Library and Information Science Abstracts* （LISA） 資料庫中有關圖書館自動化的文獻，1969—1988 年間有 8226 篇（註八），ERIC（Education Research Information Center）資料庫在 1966—1988 年間圖書館自動化亦有 1872 篇之多（註九）。

臺灣圖書館自動化資訊系統方面之文獻不多，因此，不難瞭解臺灣圖書館自動化系統之發展情形。尤其早期的圖書館學論文目錄中，這方面的文獻更是無一篇存在的！下列臺灣十一種圖書館學文獻目錄即可求證：1963 年"國立臺灣師範大學"社會教育系編印出版的"圖書館學論文索引"2100 餘篇論文中，並無一篇有關圖書館自動化方面的文章（註十）；王征和杜瑞青先於 1968 年合編"圖書館學論著資料總目"（含光緒十五年至 1968 年間之文獻）共 6500 項款目中，亦無圖書館自動化資訊系統類之文章列入（註十一）；1971 年，方仁先生編印"中文圖書館學及目錄學論文索引"（含 1945 年至 1975 年共有三十年間之文獻）6050 篇，其中僅有 35 篇談及圖書館自動化系統（註十二）；1984 年，由宋建成先生主編的"圖書館學期刊索引"（含 1975 年至 1983 年間文獻）中自動化系統之文獻共 78 篇；其中 20% 之論文在介紹國外自動化情形（註十三）；1987 年，"國立中央圖書館"爲配合國際書展，編印"圖書館學文獻目錄"（含 1980 年至 1986 年間文獻）3174 篇，有 328 篇是圖書館自動化書目，經總目錄篇數 10%，在其中僅 153（4.7%）篇是關於圖書館自動化情形（註十四）。1986 年以後，尚未有圖書館學文獻目錄出版，爲瞭解 1986 年以後，圖書館自動化系統之發展情形爲一個完整觀念，故詳查 1987 年的"國立中央圖書館"出版之"期刊論文索引"共 186 篇，41 篇是談圖書館自動化方面之文獻，佔 22%。（註十五）。由此 11 種文獻目錄很易透視臺灣圖書館自動化資訊系統發展現況之全貌！

臺灣圖書館作業自動化起步稍遲，遠較歐美國家慢了十年之久。1972 年"國立清華大學"物理圖書館首先利用電子計算機處理該館圖書目錄作業（註十六），雖設計較爲簡單而鮮爲人知，但此舉正式開啓了臺灣圖書館自動化作業時代，真正引起各界注目的則是 1974 年，由"國家科學委員會"科學技術資料中心利用電子計算機編排印製出版"科學期刊聯合目錄"，該目錄包括各大專院校圖書館和公私立學術研究機構所藏之西文科技期刊館藏，約六千餘種，和中山科學研究院圖書館購買美國國會圖書館 MARC Tape 書目磁帶，又自行設計系統印製西文圖書、技術報告等編目卡片（註十七）。此後，對圖書館作業嘗試者並不多，直到 1978 年。在此之前，圖書館作業自動化系統多以處理西文爲主的單功能系統，至此才開始處理中文圖書資料。如"國立師範大學"圖書館建立教育資料庫，以出版中文版教育論文摘要。次（1979）年，"國立中央圖書館"也以電子計算機編製中文期刊聯合目錄，以及農業資料中心設計成功農業科學管理系統，用以處理中西文農業文獻資料，是臺灣圖書館自動化作業重要的未來的轉戾點（註十八）。

一九七九年是臺灣圖書館自動化資訊系統發展史上最重要的一年，除以上重要系統開發外，臺灣國際電信局宣佈開放國際百科服務（Universal Database Access Service，簡稱 UDAS），民眾接電信局再傳人造衛星與國際間各種資料庫連線查尋各科資訊，目前臺灣圖書館界使用此項服務者約 19 單位（註十九）。此項服務增強資訊自動化（Information Automation）之功能，使圖書館界可迅速的查尋到圖書館以外的資訊，爲讀者服務擴展資源的範圍和層面。同年，由國學整理小組草擬完成中文資訊交換碼（Chinese Character Codes Information Interchange，簡稱 CCCII），爲電子計算機處理中文資料提供一項有用的工具（註二十），同時亦建立了中文資訊交換碼之標準。

同年，"中國圖書館學會"與"國立中央圖書館"爲加強海內外資訊管理與服務，合作組織"圖書館自動化作業規劃委員會"研訂"圖書館自動化作業計劃"，分三期完成，對臺灣圖書館自動化發展有甚大的影響（註二十一）。

此外，1981 年中國機讀編目格式（Chinese MARC Farmat）設計成功，同時期在國際中文圖書館自動化研討會中向世界各國發佈消息，爲臺灣建立電子計算機處理中文及其他語文書目資料之標準格式，同時也提昇臺灣在國際上的地位（註二十二）。因而更激起圖書館界積極推動自動化的熱潮。一些圖書館開始著手計劃設計軟體及系統。進行的方式很多，有自行設計，與電腦公司合作發展，與電腦中心合作開發，或採用現成軟體等。成功的，失敗的皆有，經費充裕者，系統設計修改數次，也有圖書館採觀望態度。所用硬體亦不同，有大型的主機，迷你型的，和個人電腦型的皆有。根據作者本人近年來數次問卷調查和電話訪問：1985 年調查臺灣兩大館際合作組織，科技圖書館暨資料單位和人文社會館際合作組織，149 份收問卷中 52 個單位，已有或籌劃中圖書館自動化作業佔 35%（註二十三）；同年又調查學術研究圖書館自動化現況有 31 個單位（43%，91 單位），（註二十四）最近一次調查是圖書館學會自動化規劃委員會調查自動化系統現況，發 67 份問卷，回件 44 件，其中 29 個單位（66%）已在做自動化（註二十五）。綜合近年蒐集資料加以編排，以年代爲序列表，介紹圖書館自動化資訊系統 1972—1988 年發展情況，表分六項："始年"代表該系統對外展示或宣佈或在該單位使用日期；"單位名稱"、"系統名稱/硬體名稱"，系統的"功能"和"進行方式"等分別列出。圖書館自動化系統發展情形詳見表一，因問卷並未全部收回，故資料可能有遺漏的地方。

表一　臺灣圖書館自動化資訊系統發展情形（1972—1988）

始年	單位名稱	系統名稱/硬體名稱	功　能	進行方式
1972	"國立清華大學"物理圖書室	·物理圖書系統/IBM 1130	圖書目錄	×
1973	中山科學研究院圖書館		購買 LCMARC 磁帶	

（續上表）

始年	單位名稱	系統名稱/硬體名稱	功　能	進行方式
1974	"國家科學委員會"科學技術資料中心	·期刊資訊服務系統（PISS）/IBM 370/135	西文科技期刊聯合目錄	×
	"國立臺灣大學"圖書館學系	·資訊檢索系統（展示）/Wang MVP 2200	中文書目資訊	×
	中山科學研究院圖書館	·中山科學研究院圖書資訊系統（CLIS）/IBM 370/135	期刊控制	×
		·圖書編目系統/CYBER 815	技術報告、研究文件之編目及制卡、新書通告	×
1977	私立淡江大學圖書館	·期刊控制與採購系統/IBM 370/148	西文期刊控制與採購	×
1978	"國立師範大學"	·中文教育論文摘要檔系統（CERIS）/Perkin Elmer 8-32（現改用 Prime 750）	中文教育論文摘要之出版	×
	中山科學研究院圖書館	·中山圖書資訊系統（CLIS）/IBM 370/138	西文期刊控制與採購	×
1979	"國家科學委員會"科技資料中心	·聯合採購系統/IBM 370/147（已改用 VS 7110）	西文期刊之採購（"國科會"補助單位）	×
	"中央研究院"資訊科學研究所	·Browsing MARC Ⅲ Database Generation System/DEC PDP 11/34	書目資料庫	×
	"國立清華大學"圖書館	·西文期刊編目系統/CDC CYBER 840	期刊聯合目錄（西文）	×
	"國立中央圖書館"	·期刊系統/Wang MVP 2200	中文期刊聯合目錄編製和出版	×
	農業資料中心	·農業科學技術管理系統（MISAST）FASTET, FASTEP, FASTER, FASTEL/Perkin Elmer 3220	農業技術人員名錄研究計劃、報告及文獻（中文）	×

（續上表）

始年	單位名稱	系統名稱/硬體名稱	功　　能	進行方式
1980	農業資料中心	・FASTEL /Perkin Elmer 3220	農業科學技術文獻檔案（英文）	×
	自由基金會資料中心	・自由基金會資訊摘要資料庫 /WANG MVP 2200	"自由中國"資訊摘要（中英文）	×
	"國家科學委員會"科技資料中心	・管理資訊系統（MIS） /IBM 370/135	科技人員、研究計劃之管理與編輯	×
	中山科學研究院圖書館	・中山圖書館資訊系統 /IBM 370/138	採購、出納	×
	"國立中央圖書館"	・中文期刊論文索引 /WANG VS–100	中文期刊論文索引	×
	"國立師範大學"圖書館	・DIALOG，ORBIT	*連接國際百科資料庫	×
1981	"中國圖書館學會"	・Chinese MARC 中國機讀編目格式推出	中文書目	×
	"中國圖書館學會"	・Chinese MARC 中文書目資料庫 /WANG MVP 2200		
	農業資料中心	・農業科學與技術資訊管理系統（ASTIMS） /Prime 750	農業人名檔、研究報告計劃、文獻及農業索引典（AGRI-Thesaurus）、中西編目，期刊，線上檢索	×
	"國立臺灣大學"圖書館	・期刊控制系統 /UNIVAC 1100	臺大西文期刊聯合目錄	×
	"國立中央圖書館"	・"國立中央圖書館"書目資料庫 /WANG VS–100	圖書、期刊、政府公報、善本書等書目資料	×
	"中國石油公司"煉製研究中心	・圖書館系統管理計劃（SLMP） /ALTOS 80150	書目查詢、採購、出納、編目、聯合目錄	×
	私立東吳大學經濟系圖書館	・經濟資料檢索系統 /IBM 370	經濟學圖書、期刊、論文資料	×

（續上表）

始年	單位名稱	系統名稱/硬體名稱	功　　能	進行方式
1982	"國立政治大學"中正圖書館	·圖書出納系統/Perkin Elmer 3220（1984年改用Prime 750）	出納	×
	"國家科學委員會"科學技術資料中心	·Domestic Science Technology System/HP 3000	聯合期刊目錄、研究報告、科學人員及技術專家檔、進行中之研究計劃	×
	工業技術研究所材料所	·書目資料系統/WANG VS－65	圖書、期刊、會議記錄、專利報告等資料	×
	"國立清華大學"圖書館	·期刊控制系統/CDC CYBER－172	期刊控制	×
1983	"國立中央圖書館"	·"國立中央圖書館"自動化資訊服務系統（NCLAIS）/WANG VS－100	Chinese MARC 資料庫；購買 LCMARC 磁帶進行西文資料之轉換	×
	"行政院"研究發展考核委員會	·"國家"管理資訊系統/IBM 370/148	決策支援系統含：國家現況、政策概況、科技資料、經濟發展情形、通訊狀況、國家安全資料	×
1984	"國立交通大學"圖書館	·交通大學圖書館系統/WANG VS－90	西文期刊自動化系統	×
	"中國圖書館用品供應中心"	·出納控制系統（CCS－100）/IBM 5550	出納	×
	工業技術研究所機械所	·自動化圖書館系統（ALS或MIRLALS）/IBM 5550	出納、提供技術資訊查詢	×
	"中央研究院"資訊所	·圖書館系統/PC－XT	西編、線上檢索製卡	×
	"中國鋼鐵公司"技術資料組	·圖書館資訊系統/IBM 4381	書目資料、出版商資料、期刊控制、出納及查詢	×
	"國立中央圖書館"	·"國立中央圖書館"自動化資訊服務系統（NCLAIS）/WANG VS－100	卡片服務、國家聯合書目、中文期刊論文索引、中文期刊聯合目錄、"中文政府"公報索引、線上公共檢索查詢目錄、行政業務、中文資料回溯性轉換等	

（續上表）

始年	單位名稱	系統名稱/硬體名稱	功　能	進行方式
1985	"國立臺灣大學"圖書館	・"國立臺灣大學"自動化圖書館資訊系統（NATALIS）/DEC PDP 11/73	編目、出納及線上公共目錄查詢（展示）	×
	"中央研究院"歷史語言研究所	中國古籍全文查詢系統/IBM 5550	古籍文獻之查詢檢索	×
	"國立交通大學"圖書館	・交通大學圖書館系統/WANG VS-90	西文圖書、西文期刊查詢、編目、校區網路	×
	"國立臺灣大學"工學院聯合圖書館	・出納及資訊檢索自動化系統（CIRAS）/VAX 785	出納、資訊檢索	×
	私立逢甲大學圖書館	・出納、期刊系統/WANG VS-80	出納、期刊	×
	"國立清華大學"圖書館	・編目子系統/CDC CYBER-172	西文編目	×
	亞洲蔬菜研究發展中心	・MINISIS/AVLIB/HP 3000/42	採購、編目、期刊、專題選粹	××
	臺灣傳技公司	・CLSI/VAX 系列	研究發展 CLSI 系統與傳技 CJK 終端機相連	××
	"國立成功大學"圖書館	・圖書出納系統/TI 990/10	出納	×
1986	私立淡江大學圖書館	淡江自動化圖書館資訊系統（TALIS-大力士）/IBM 4381/Mll	出納、編目、線上公共檢索查詢目錄	××
	"中國圖書館用品供應中心"	・介購系統（CAS-200）/IBM 5550	採購	×
	"國立交通大學"圖書館	・交通大學圖書館線上查詢系統/WANG VS-90	出納、採購、期刊、中西編目	×
	"國立成功大學"圖書館	・"國立成功大學"自動化圖書館系統/TI 990/10, /IBM PC/AT, /AppleⅡ	採購、出納、新書通報、期刊控制、查詢、館際合作、經費控制等	×

（續上表）

始年	單位名稱	系統名稱/硬體名稱	功　能	進行方式
1987	"中國鋼鐵公司"技術資料組	·圖書館資訊系統/IBM 3090	採購、中西編目、出納、參考、線上查詢、行政（皆部份完成）	×
	"國立中央圖書館"	·學術圖書館合作編目建檔（Batch）/Wang VS-100；·中文 Bibliofile CD-ROM 計劃	聯合編目（中文）	×
	"中國圖書館用品供應中心"	·編目控制系統（CCS-300）/IBM 5550	編目、檢索	×
1988	中鼎工程公司圖書館	·AUTOLIB/VAX 系列	西編；部份完成中編線上檢索、行政	×
	"國立教育資料館"	·視聽媒體管理系統/Honywell Bull X-40	行政	×
	長庚紀念醫院圖書館	·西文編目系統/IBM 5550	西文編目（部份完成）	×
	"國立臺灣工業技術學院"圖書館	·西編和期刊系統/VAX 780；Master 32	部份完成西編和期刊	×
	"國立清華大學"圖書館	·出納系統/IBM PC	出納	×
	私立淡江大學圖書館	·TALIS/IBM 4381/Mll	採購、中西編目、出納、期刊、參考服務、行政管理，線上公共檢索查詢目錄等	××
	"國立中央圖書館"	·OCLC	線上連接 OCLC System 可查詢和輸入資料	××
	"立法院"圖書資料室	·LEGISIS/VAX 8530	部份完成委員質詢與答覆系統，法規文獻全文系統、辦公室自動化、期刊控制、參考服務、行政管理、線上檢索等	×
	"國家科學委員會"科技資料中心	·"全國科學技術資訊網路"/WANG VS 542SI	Domestic Database 及 6～7 種海外的科技資料庫	××
	"國防醫學院"圖書館	·出納系統（CCS-100）/IBM 5550	出納、西編、線上檢索	××
		·將採用 URICA 軟體做圖書館整體自動化/Douglas 6400		××

×自行設計　　××購/使用現成軟體　　＊目前臺灣地區已有十九個單位連接國際百科資料庫

根據臺灣地區圖書館自動化資訊系統展情形，亦可劃分爲三個時代（Three Generations）：

第一代：1972—1977 年，圖書館自動化資訊系統萌芽時期：情形與西方國家情形相似，早期是單功能局部自動化作業，學用歐美國家處理的方式來實驗學習，圖書館各自摸索設計，以處理西文爲主，尤其偏愛先設計期刊系統。

第二代：1978—1984 年，圖書館自動化資訊系統基礎時期：建立標準，如 CCCII, Chinese MARC Format，中國編目規則等，各種基礎觀念漸漸建立，此時已有成功的系統推出，如交通大學圖書館系統，"國立中央圖書館"自動化資訊服務系統（NCLAIS），農資中心的農業科技的管理系統（MISAST），工研院機械所和"中國圖書用品供應中心"共同設計完成的 CCS，"國科會"科技中心的管理資訊系統等。

第三代：從 1985 年起—，整合圖書館自動化資訊系統和網路時期：1985 年以來，有更多的系統推出，趨向整合性的圖書館自動化系統觀念之設計，或採用現成套裝軟體，如淡江大學圖書館的 TALIS，亞洲蔬菜發展中心的 MINISIS 軟體等。此間亦開始設計中文全文檢索系統，如"立法院"法律資訊中心的法規文獻全文系統和委員質詢系統，"中央研究院"之史籍資料庫等，系統之設計愈來愈完整，考慮亦週密，以求更完美。此時最常爲主管們討論的主題——建立全域網路，目前臺灣三個網路計劃最令人注目是："國立中央圖書館"的書目網路，（註二十六）"教育部"的"國立大學校院圖書館發展計劃"中含大學校、院圖書館網路，另一個是"國科會"科技資料中心的科技資訊服務網路，最後目標則是臺灣資訊網路（註二十七）與國際間網路連接。

表面上看來臺灣圖書館自動化資訊系統發展很熱鬧，很積極，但根據三項調查，發現仍有很多問題存在。作者在 1985 年曾對臺灣科技和人文社會圖書館館際合作組織的館長和館員進行調查（註二十八），同年又對臺灣學術研究圖書館館長和館員調查，他們認爲圖書館自動化問題甚多（註二十九），最近今（1988）年又再次發問卷調查 67 個圖書館自動化現況及問題（註三十），結果這三次問卷有關自動化問題的答案，非常相同，這證實了三年前的自動化問題，並未改善很多。三次問卷結果比較如表二、表三：

表二　圖書館/資料單位業務自動化問題比較統計表（1985 年）

自動化問題項目	館際合作組織		學術研究圖書館	
	館長 N = 123	館員 N = 533	館長 N = 80	館員 N = 340
・經費不足	70②*	245①	39①	136②
・缺乏能負責自動化的工作小組	75①	289②	38②	158①
・自動化進行中，工作量增加，館員無法負擔	52④	124⑥	28③	78⑥
・機器設備問題（優先秩序）	54③	140⑤	27④	85④
・自動化目標不明確，缺乏全盤計劃	48⑤	179③	22⑤	107③
・館員與系統分析師、電腦人員無法溝通	36⑥	120⑦	19⑥	80⑤
・上級主管不重視	31⑦	89⑪	16⑦	46⑨
・傳統人工作業流程問題	25⑧	115⑩	16⑦	58⑦
・館員無法提供明確作業需求	21⑦	66⑫	11⑧	39⑩
・館員排斥自動化	44⑨	17⑬	2⑩	8⑪
・館員對自動化瞭解不多	36⑥	157④	19⑥	53⑧

*代表問題的重要性　◆15

表三 "中國圖書館學會"圖書館自動化規劃委員會調查圖書館自動化問題統計表（1988年）

自動化問題項目	數量（N=44）
經費不足	12
缺乏人力	11
自動化之經驗與技術缺乏	11
上級支持及觀念	6
等待全域網路之建立	4
館員與電腦人員不能溝通	2

由以上三種不同調查統計結果之比較，臺灣圖書館自動化所面臨的問題是經費不足，缺少人力，自動化方面的經驗與技術之不足，館員對自動化的排斥已微不足道，很容易看出館員在自動化方面訓練教育欠缺，對推進自動化有很大的阻力。

總而言之，臺灣圖書館自動化資訊系統之發展已有二十年之歷史，雖然我們也設計了些系統，但好用的系統又有幾個？我們到處可以聽到自動化的聲音，但其步調卻相當緩慢！研究發現其中最大的阻力，就圖書館自動化而言，則是缺乏自動化方面有經驗和技術的人員，也就是說圖書館員缺乏自動化方面的專門技術和經驗。而人們發展自動化系統，又非常偏愛"自行設計"，即使設計成功，也只是簡陋而不完整，還可能不合標準。

作者建議當前人們在推行自動化時應加強下面幾個事項：

一、圖書館自動化基礎方面：雖然以目前自動化現況來看，已是本末倒置，但仍有亡羊補牢之機會，由下列幾點做起

（一）圖書館自動化教育待加強

（二）從速訂定處理資料之統一規格與標準，例如編目規則，權威檔等。

（三）從速編定圖書統一"分類法"和"中文標準"總目。

（四）成立圖書館自動化系統專家顧問小組

二、自動化作業技術方面：可採下列三方式：

（一）使用現成軟體，現成的套裝軟體稍加修改即可使用，長遠看來，這種方式是較省錢、省事、省力、省時！

（二）委託有經驗的電腦公司或機構設計。

（三）觀摩他館系統，交換心得和經驗。

三、館員之自動化訓練：應主動擬定長期計劃，分層分批的訓練和再教育，唯有我們自己才能解決我們自己的問題！

附　　註

註一：Reynolds, Dennis, *Library Automation: Issues of Applications*, New York: Boroker, 1985, pp. 14–15.

註二：Boss, Richard W., "Technology and the Modern Library," *Library Journal* 108 (June 1984): 1989.

註三：De Gennaro, R., "Library Automation Network Perspectives on Three Decades," *Library Journal* 108（April 1983）：629-635.

註四：Battin Patricis, "National and International Perspectives," pesented at the Library and Information Resources for the Northwest（LIRN）Advisory Committee Meeting of July 31, 1984, and appearing in minutes of the meeting dated October 2, 1984, p. 3.

註五：Fisher, Russell, "The Computer Revolution Comes to East Asian Collections," *Wilson Library Bulletin* 58（June 1984）：398-405.

Roland Brown, OCLC Director 至臺灣大學之演講.

註六：Walton, Robert A & Frank R. Bridge, "Automated System marketplace 1987 maturity & Competition", *Libray Journal* 113（April 1988）：33-44.

註七：Adler, Ann G. et al. *Automation in Libraries: A LITA Bibliography, 1978-1982.* Ann Arbor, MI：Pierian Press, 1983.

註八：Library and Information Science Abstract,（LISA）Database London：AsLib, 1969-1988.

註九：ERIC Online Searching, 1966-1988, DIALOG System.

註十：圖書館學論文索引，"國立臺灣師範大學"社會教育學系編，1963年。

註一一：王征和杜瑞青，圖書館學論著資料總目，臺中：文宗出版社，1969年。

註一二：方仁，中文圖書館學及目錄學論文索引，1971年。

註一三：宋建成主編，圖書館學期刊論文索引，臺北，藍星，1984年，頁41—43，53—55。

註一四：圖書館學文獻目錄，"國立中央圖書館"編，1986年。

註一五：期刊論文索引，"國立中央圖書館"編，1987年一、二期。

註一六：Yu, Sung, "Cooperation & Computerization of Science and Technology Oriented Libraries in Taiwan", in Proceedings of the 1st Conference on Asian Library Cooperation, 1974, August, Tamsui, Taiwan, pp. 558-574。

註一七：王振鵠著，圖書館自動化作業之現況及展望 "國立中央圖書館" 刊 新十五卷，第一、二期 1982年，頁一——二。

註一八：Fung, Margaret C., "State of the Art: Library Automation in Taipei." Paper presented at IFLA Conference 1980, Manils.

註一九：Lee, Lung Te-Chu, "Education Training for Online Use of Databases in the Taiwan," in *Library & Information Science Education: An Internation Symposium.* Taipei, Taiwan, Nov. 29-30 1985. pp. 192-195.

註二十：同註十七 頁二。

註二一：Wang, Chen-ku, "Libraries & Librarianship in Taiwan," *National Central Library Newsletter*, 13（August 1981）：173-174。

註二二：中國機讀編目格式，第二版，圖書館自動化作業規劃委員會，中國機讀編目格式工作小組編，1984年。

註二三：李德竹"學術研究圖書館館員作業自動化認識與態度"，臺大圖書學刊第五期 1987年。

註二四：李德竹"圖書館作業自動化及資訊網路建立因素之探討研究計劃報告" "行政院文化建設委員會" 1986 年。

註二五：資料來源"自中國圖書館學會"自動化規劃委員會。

註二六：Chou, Nancy Ou-Lan, "The National Bibliographic Database & Its Network Development", Seminar in Library Automation & Information Network 1988, June 9 – 10, 1988. Taipei.

註二七：Lee, Luy T., "Library Automation of Network Systems, in R. O. C Sino-American Conference in Information Technology 1988, August, 1988, Taipei.

註二八：同註二十三　頁 596—597。

註二九：同註二十四　頁 88。

註三十：同註二十五。

圖書館業務自動化基本注意事項[*]

80年代早期，由於多功能整合圖書館系統之出現，無論系統之設計和費用方面，與60和70年代相比，圖書館作業自動化系統，顯然地，已邁入成熟階段。而圖書館業務自動化之原因，已不再是"爲什麼"？或"要不要"自動化問題，而是"如何進行"？"何時進行"？"多快"？圖書館自動化不但爲潮流趨勢，並且已視爲圖書館業務之正規之發展方向。海內外圖書館皆有此共識。

圖書館自動化最終目的是追求圖書館作業效率之提高，服務品質及層面之改善。進一步的，建立館間之連線及網路，以期擴增圖書資源之互惠互享。

據最近調查臺灣館際合作組織149所會員圖書館和資料單位，其中54個圖書館已在自動化，有些圖書館完成部份作業自動化或考慮/計劃中。但單位中尚無全部作業自動化之圖書館。近年來，臺灣"教育部"已開始計劃大專院校之行政管理系統之設置，圖書館行政管理自動化爲其中之一環。今年（1987），該部正式著手探討公立大學圖書館現況與未來發展，以及各圖書館對自動化系統之需求提出報告，做爲設計公立大學圖書館自動化系統及網路之依據。此外，"國立中央圖書館"亦在進行圖書館聯合編目建檔計劃。私立學校之圖書館方面亦不落後，各自發展圖書館自動化系統，同時也在進行建立地域性的圖書館網路。由此可見，臺灣目前對圖書館自動化之積極擴展及重視。

設計一個理想而實用的圖書館自動化系統是非常重要的，這也是圖書館所追求的目標。但在此之前，一些基本圖書館業務自動化之觀念及注意要點應事先建立是必要的。本文選重要者簡要提出下列幾點，以資參考：

（一）圖書館業務自動化並不"難"／一般人對圖書館自動化想像中那麼"難"與"可怕"，這由於對不知道或不熟悉的事，人人都會產生恐慌感而排斥它，實際圖書館作業自動化不難！

（二）瞭解自己，瞭解自己的需求，瞭解自動化的目的／這樣才可衡量到自動化爲我們帶來什麼好處，又能爲我們做些什麼？

（三）單位主管之支持、態度及魄力是推展自動化成功之重要關鍵／單位主管，無論是館長或館長的上司都是重要的決策者。但兩者間，前者最爲重要。他／她們的支持、積極態度、以及做事的魄力及決心將是圖書館業務自動化成功與否之關鍵。

（四）嚴忌將自動化計劃視爲圖書館行政部門之"最高機密"，而限少數人參與／相反的，圖書館自動化計劃開始即應讓全體同仁知曉與參與，並時常告知大家進展的情形。這樣讓大家知道有參與感，在推展作業上將會得到同仁們之支持與協助。

（五）切勿"閉門造車"／要不得，也行不通，應廣蒐意見。

（六）多學、多聽、多讀，多看、多問／島內對圖書館自動化方面有研究和專長者不多。大家都在摸索，何不相互切磋，交換意見與心得，集思廣益，以求有利於圖書館自動化業務之順利推展。

（七）溝通（Communications）與同心合作／意見和消息之傳播與交換溝通是必要的。

---

[*] 本文曾發表在《"中國圖書館學會"會務通訊》63期（1988年7月），第3—5頁。

共同合作努力、目標一致才是更重要的成功要素。

（八）成立圖書館自動化工作小組／一般情形，小組的成員多由各部門主管組成的。而多數主管，年齡較長，對自動化的知識方面較弱。但他們的態度多是積極的。不妨選用館內對自動化知識較強，有經驗的、有研究的館員加入小組。近年來，由於圖書館學系已將電子計算機概論和程式設計，以及圖書館自動化等課目列為必修課程。故年輕新進之館員接受自動化教育和機會多，也比較具有自動化之知識與興趣，也不妨借助於他們對自動化之新知與幹勁共同為自動化業務效力。

（九）加強館員自動化觀念及訓練／多給予館員機會學習和熟悉自動化作業之各種知識與技術，並不斷的讓他／她們知道最新自動化方面的發展趨勢，健全館員的心理準備！"Keep Current is important, and must!"可添購自動化方面之書籍及期刊，參加自動化研討會及演講、參觀、訪問等。

（十）自動化計劃負責人／此人非常重要，計劃推展以利或成功皆繫於此人。他／她應具有圖書館作業自動化之知識與經驗，頭腦清晰，科學管理之技術，更應具有豁達開朗的胸懷，易於接受他人之建議與批評。更應主動的廣徵意見，立即糾正系統之錯誤不當之處，以求協助達到自動化系統設計之完美與實用。

（十一）自動化的早期，館員工作是會增加／因為很多業務將會是雙軌進行方式。應對館員多加疏導、鼓勵、溝通此階段之重要性，僅是一過渡時期，希大家應有共識、合作和意願。這方面也是館員主要排斥自動化的原因之一。

（十二）圖書館自動化所用時間常常超出預定計劃的時間／圖書館自動化系統是一個龐大複雜的長程工作，過程中不易控制進度。

（十三）圖書館自動化所需費用常常超出預定之費用／無論計算的如何週密，費用也一定會超出的，根據多人經驗而言。

（十四）錢的問題（Costly）／自動化是很花費金錢的事，費用項目很多，應考慮：軟體費、硬體費、資料轉換費、訓練費、裝置費、維護費、繼續開發費等。

（十五）訂定各種標準／如編目規則、標題、MARC Formats、各種編碼（codes）等是非常重要的。決定採用時應考慮本館同時亦應考慮到未來建立網路，與他館連線之問題。

（十六）資料轉換與品質控制（Data Conversion and Quality Control）／事先考慮對館藏做清點（查）（inventory）工作，然後註銷（Weeding）。在自動化過程中，資料轉換（Data/Retrospective Conversion）所花費的時間、金錢和精力是相當大的。所以圖書館必須儘量在自動化前袪除一些不需要的資料。至於 Weeding Policy 則隨圖書館之大小和種類而不同，通常80%館藏可利用一般的註銷原則，20%則須要專業館員來判斷。

（十七）廣蒐資料／無論由文獻中，或蒐集他館自動化系統之需求書（Requirements for Automated System），RFP（Request for Proposal），系統手冊（System Manuals）等等。切記只能參考，不能照單全抄。先問一問這些與自己圖書館的需求相同否？

（十八）軟體較硬體重要／瞭解自己的需求，知道所要的軟體是什麼！先決定軟體再考慮硬體，軟體之選擇要考慮：好用（User Friendliness），適用性（Adaptability），活潑，有彈性（Flexibility），控光性（Expandability）等。

（十九）踏踏實實的整體規劃／紮實的計劃（Solid Planning）是自動化最重要的步

驟,系統之成敗關鍵。正如 Boss 說:"Planning is time consuming, but more time spent on planning the better!"切記!整體規劃,找出並建立系統之各種功能及其間關係,整體考慮週密,建立整體觀念,對自動化業務推展將更可得心應手而系統化。

(二十)切忌將圖書館業務自動化系統當作"研究計劃"/圖書館業務自動化系統是長期的繼續發展計劃,要不斷發展和改進,而"研究計劃"則多是"短期",也是很冒險的做法,由於研究者缺乏圖書館業務自動化方向的經驗,又非專職,時間與進度很難掌握,其結果與做法更不易控制,更重要的是研究結束後誰來收攤?又如何繼續?多考慮!

(二十一)聘請顧問(Conultant)(library Auomation)/圖書館自動化進行中可聘請顧問,亦可不聘請顧問,如聘請請教導他/她們,請他/她們參與所有活動,千萬不要當他/她們是裝飾品,如聘對了適當的顧問,他/她們是無儘的寶藏,對圖書館自動化之擴展,受益無窮!

(二十二)善用人際關係/廣交朋友,與館內外有關人,尤其決策者,保持良好關係,請他們支持,協調事情應助益良多!

(二十三)保持幽默感/自動化過程中,問題很多,館員應保持適切的幽默態度來解決問題,不致使問題更僵化而導致更大的危機。

以上圖書館自動化注意事項中,以"人的問題"為最多。顯然的,圖書館業務自動化雖工程浩大,費時費錢驚人,但並不如想像中那麼難做,最大的問題則是如何處理"人的問題"和您"要不要"做的問題。因此,館長、館員對圖書館業務自動化之推展之認識、態度、合作、同心、魄力、決心和共識才是最重要的!

1. Joseph R. Matthews and I. F. Williams. "Oh, If I'd only known", Library Journal June, 1983, pp. 408 – 412.

2. Susan B. Epstein. "Implementation of an Automated system", Library Journal, Sept. 1983. pp. 1771 – 1772.

3. Susan B. Epstein. "Automation Takes longer than you Planned", Library Journal, pp. 48 – 49.

4. Russeld T. Clement. "Cost is not Everything", Library Journal, Oct. 1985, pp. 52 – 55.

5. Richand Boss. The Library Managers Guide to Automation, 2nd ed. (White plains, N. Y. : KIP. Inc., 1984) 1968.

6. 李德竹、圖書館作業自動化及資訊網路建立因素之探討、"行政院文化建設委員會",1986年。

學術研究圖書館館員對圖書館作業自動化認識與態度[*]

前　　言

　　近三十年來，科技發展日新月異，知識領域急劇擴增，使人類深覺知識爆炸之壓力。面對此挑戰，圖書館勢必要加速其執行知識傳佈的工作，儘快使讀者享受到知識成長的利益。爲達成此項任務，圖書館必需借重現代化的資訊科技和設備來協助拓廣控制知識的環境，加強人類快速完整的資訊連繫。因此，圖書館引用電子計算機來處理資料，將圖書館的業務自動化，借助通訊技術來建立館際間網路系統已是時勢所趨，迨無可避免。

　　歐美國家早在一九四〇年代已領先研究開發圖書館業務自動化系統，又在一九六〇年代開始了圖書資訊網路之設計，迄今已有相當成就。環顧臺灣圖書館業務自動化情形，起步稍遲。臺灣圖書館界在七十年代初期開始探討圖書館業務自動化之可行性，但由於客觀環境與主觀意識的限制，至今僅有少數圖書館實施部份業務自務化，遑論"整體"自動化作業系統。

　　1980年，"中國圖書館學會"與"國立中央圖書館"合作組織了臺灣"圖書館自動化作業規劃委員會"，策劃發展臺灣圖書館自動化作業之各項規範及技術，分三期完成，並以建立全臺圖書館資訊網路爲最終目標（註1），但審諸目前實情，雖有少數圖書館對外發表他們的自動化系統，但就整體而論，圖書館自動化的工作仍在摸索階段，步調遲緩。

　　以臺灣圖書館自動化條件來說，硬體部份似乎問題較少，而軟體部份如能匯集圖書館界及電腦界的專才，並參考海外現有圖書館自動化系統，合力設計發展，亦不難獲得解決。因此，硬體與軟體均非臺灣圖書館自動化緩慢的主要因素，要解決圖書館自動化目前所遭遇的問題，不妨從另一角度來探討，那即是去瞭解與圖書館自動化業務的設計、支持與執行有密切關係的重要關鍵者──圖書館館員。

　　臺灣對自動化問題的研究，大抵偏重於自動化硬體與軟體的設計及選擇，而較少探討"人"的因素。在圖書館界全力發展自動化的過程中，圖書館員對自動化業務的認識與態度是否會影響此項業務之推展？因此，本文研究主要的目的是探討學術研究圖書館專業館員（含館長及副館長）對圖書館自動化業務的"認識"程度，以及他們對圖書館自動化所持的"態度"，並且研究圖書館員的背景及他們對自動化的認識與態度間之關係，更進一步分析影響"認識"及"態度"的因素，同時，調查學術圖書館自動化作業系統之現況及癥結所在。歸納研究結果提出建議爲圖書館及決策當局對圖書館作業自動化現況之認識，瞭解在發展自動化的過程中，除硬、軟體外，"人"的因素是不可忽視的一環，並可作制訂因應政策之參考和依據。

---

[*] 本文曾發表在《臺灣大學圖書館學刊》第5期（1987年11月），第13—36頁。

研究範圍、方法與術語解釋

本研究僅以臺灣學術和研究圖書館（包含大學院校圖書館及研究機構圖書館）專業人員為調查對象；以問卷及參觀訪問方式，調查九十一個學術研究圖書館的現況及其九十七位館長、六十八位主任和三百六十二位館員（主任和館員共四百三十人）。其中大學院校圖書館二十八個；醫學院圖書館八個；研究機構圖書館五十五個單位。

研究範圍僅就對所列圖書館及資料單位之業務自動化現況、問題，以及圖書館館長、副館長和專業人員對自動化之認識和態度進行分析討論，至於其他方面將不在本研究之列。資料的統計分析採用"社會科學統計軟體系統"（Statistical Programs for Social Sciences—SPSS）（註2）。

本研究所探討的問題，涉及一些專門術語，其定義由本研究內容予以詮釋，以資明確：

一、學術圖書館：指大學院校及研究機構之圖書館及資料單位。

二、圖書館業務自動化：指用電子計算機來處理和管理圖書館和資料單位的各項作業，如出納、編目、採購、期刊、參考、行政、公用目錄等業務。

三、圖書館專業人員：此定義參照"大學及獨立學院圖書館標準"（註3），圖書館專業人員應具備下列資格之一：

(1) 海內外圖書館學系、組及研究所畢業者。
(2) 資訊科學或教育資料科學系畢業者。
(3) 其他學系畢業曾經選修圖書館或資訊科學二十學分以上者。
(4) 其他學系圖書資料科畢業者，在圖書館服務兩年以上者。
(5) 圖書館人員高等考試及格者。
(6) 圖書館人員普通考試及格者，在圖書館服務兩年以上者。

四、認識：是指館長、副館長所受圖書館自動化教育與訓練之程度。

五、態度：是指館長、副館長和館員對自動化之看法及反應。

海內外圖書館自動化及網路之重要文獻

歐美各國由於圖書館業務自動化及網路建立之起步較臺灣地區為早，對館員自動化認識與態度之研究亦甚為重視，故文獻相當豐富。例如美國資訊科學學會（American Society for Information Science 簡稱 ASIS）由一九六六年開始每年出版一卷 *Annual Review of Information Science & Technology*（註4），評論近年來資訊科學與技術主題方面的文獻，至一九八六年已出版了二十一卷，其中有十六卷中皆有一章"圖書館自動化現況"文獻之評述，同時其中有十卷亦刊出"圖書館資訊網路"發展有關之文章。該書又在一九八三年卷中特別評述了臺灣和日本之資訊服務與系統之發展情形（註5），每章並附有約 300～400 項參考書目，詳盡而富參考價值。

美國圖書館協會（American Library Association）於一九六七年也開始編製出版圖書館自動化書目，書名是：*The Automation in Libraries：A LITA Bibliography*。該書一九六七年版自動化書目是 377 條，而一九八三年第六版則已超出 2500 項書目。蒐集資料以美國為主,此外亦選擇性的蒐集了英、加、奧、德等國自動化書目(註6)。此外,屬於世界性的重要自動化書目之總集應是 *Library Literature*(註7)和 *Library & Information Science Abstracts*(LISA)(註8),兩者皆可用線上或人工檢索相關文獻。

臺灣圖書館自動化作業及網路方面之文獻不多,而館員對圖書館自動化認識與態度之研究,由於臺灣自動化作業起步甚晚,迄今圖書館自動化仍在計劃設計階段,尚無人探討館員對圖書館認識與態度之問題。下列圖書館學文獻目錄中即可求證:早在1963年由"國立臺灣師範大學"社會教育學系所編的"圖書館學論文索引"中2100餘篇文章中,圖書館自動化方面之文章則無一篇(註9);1969年王征和杜瑞青先生編製的"圖書館學論著資料總目"(含光緒十五年至1968年間之文獻)6500項款目中,亦無圖書館自動化此類論文列入(註10);1982年,方仁先生編印"中文圖書館學及目錄學論文索引"(含1945年至1975年間之文獻)中查得三十年間6050篇圖書館學論文中,圖書館自動化及網路相關文獻共三十五篇(註11);另由宋建成先生主編的"圖書館學期刊索引"(1975至1983年)中查得有關自動化之文獻僅七十八篇,其中20%之論文在介紹海外自動化及網路系統(註12);最近由"國立中央圖書館"編印之"圖書館學文獻目錄"(含1980年至1986年之文獻)共3174篇,其中有關圖書館自動化書目328(佔10%)篇,僅153(佔47%)篇中談及圖書館自動化現況(註13),以上十種目錄中,皆無館員對自動化認識與態度之研究論文。由此文獻中很易透視圖書館自動化作業及網路系統發展現況之全貌!

館員對圖書館作業自動化之認識與態度之重要研究

由以上書目中知臺灣圖書館自動化文獻內容多偏重於圖書館自動化作業及網路系統之發展歷史、現況及未來計劃之描述,甚少涉及其發展問題及癥結之探討,更不談館員對自動化認識與態度方面之研究。

不可忽視的,現代科技設備是圖書館和資料單位作業自動化和網路系統建立的重要工具,資訊專家似乎常常着重於技術方面,希望如何把系統設計得更好更有效率,因而忽略了人——使用者和館員對現代資訊工具的認識、看法和態度,以及他們對接受這些新工具的意願或阻力。系統的成敗和其順利的發展執行,"人的因素"也是同樣地不可忽視的重要關鍵。在圖書館運用新科技促使作業自動化之際,重視館員對此問題的心理反應與態度,當更甚於技術本身(註14)。因此,近年來,圖書館學與資訊科學教育課程中增添"行為"(Behavior)方面的課程,同時亦有很多學者從事於圖書館與資料單位中人為因素(Human Factors)之各種研究(註15)。

在海外,尤其是美國,圖書館自動化及網路系統種類形態不一,這方面之調查研究甚多,至於館員對圖書館自動化之看法亦遠在七〇年代初期即已開始探討研究。

蒲瑞斯達斯(Presthus)於一九七〇年和范(Fine)於一九七九年分別調查館員對科技(Technology)而造成改變之反應,特別是圖書館自動化作業,發現館員對之有阻力(Resistance)(註16, 17)。范(Fine)又於一九八五年由伊利諾大學主辦的第二十二屆電子計算機在圖書館之應用年會中以"Terminal Paralysis or Showdown at the Interface"題目發表演講說:科技(Technology)已滲透我們生活中的每一部份,但阻力(Resistance)亦同時存在我們的四週。圖書館員對科技而導致的"改變"有阻力,而非

"科技"本身,但這些科技改變會繼續存在、增強,而絕不會因阻力而消失的,館員又該如何適應與選擇呢(註18)?!

一九八一年,斯杜歲(Stussy)以問卷方式調查美國館藏在300000以下105個天主教大學圖書館自動化實情,結果是除極少數館長認為圖書館太小可不必自動外,其他皆願意圖書館自動化的。他們認為加入圖書館資訊網路系統——如OCLC,做會員和參加館際合作組織對中小型圖書館作業自動化的成功幫助很大。而最大的問題則是經費不足和缺乏對自動化有經驗的館員(註19)。

一九八二年,麥卡瑟(McCarthy)博士論文探討"巴西圖書館自動化及圖書資訊系統"之現況及問題,研究資料蒐集方式是問卷調查和訪問兩種,對象是圖書館和高級館員。巴西現有八十五個自動化作業系統,其中以編目自動化系統為最多,其次為出納控制、資料庫、索引和專題選粹等。自動化主要問題是缺乏有自動化經驗的人員,其次是無經費,無官方督導和政府政策的支持,缺少圖書館資訊網路系統和館際間合作,另外則是人工作業有很多問題存在(註20)。

斯瑞爾(Schraml)(註21)的建議是:成功的圖書館自動化系統設計與設置一定要考慮到人、系統工作者和使用者的心理需求。她認為自動化系統亦成為一種發展趨勢,無論在圖書館或辦公室,它將執行重要的任務,正如皮塞爾(Pizer)所說:"它(自動化系統)的問題是很多,但它的好處卻是更多!"(註22)

烏滋(Woods)指出大部份的英國大學圖書館館員對圖書館自動化均表歡迎(註23)。魯克爾(Luquire)於一九七六年對使用OCLC之美國研究圖書館協會(American Research Library Association—ARL)會員圖書館的技術部門館員所作的對自動化態度調查研究,結果發現受試者大多承認自動化系統的價值。同時發現,以態度和心理上之準備而言,愈早熟悉系統者之館員,如事先強調館員工作的安全和保障,教育程度愈高和具有電子計算機方面訓練之館員,則與接受自動化系統之可能性有關;但使用OCLC愈久的圖書館員反而對OCLC之評估則愈低,顯然地看來,OCLC系統在當時有問題存在(註24)。

尤瑟(Yother)曾於一九八三年以抽樣方式調查全美國一七五個獨立學院,以館藏100000冊為限之圖書館之館長為對象,研究館長的自動化方面之教育訓練背景是否與他/她們對發展圖書館自動化之態度有關?其他因素如館的大小,公、私立和館員的自動化背景是否會影響自動化作業的發展?同時亦調查各館自動化現況等。調查分析結果是:館長們都贊成自動化;館長的自動化背景與對發展自動化的態度無關;公私立學校對發展自動化無何區別;有無經費皆不影響到館長們要自動化的意願與看法;圖書館館藏與該館自動化發展的程度有關;唯一的是館長們似乎對自動化軟體系統的價格毫無概念(註25)!

達新納馬提(Dakshinamurti)以加拿大各類型圖書館館員為研究對象的調查中顯示:大部份的館員都贊成圖書館使用新的科技——電子計算機進行圖書館作業自動化(註26)。

以"面談"方式探討美國密西根州立大學圖書館七十五位專業圖書館館員對電子計算機應用在圖書館的認知和看法,派克(Park)將館員之答案分成三大類:第一類的館員認為唯有自動化才能快速地提供更多的服務;第二類館員反對積極自動化,認為會帶來更多的問題；第三類館員自動化態度不明，他們反對同時又贊成。館員一般認爲自動化是必要的，但自動化時，必要慎重週密的策劃，避免產生某些困難（註27）。

鐵利（Daily）一九八五年出版 *Staff Personality Problems in the Library Automation Process: A Case in Point* 中，列出五個個案探討館員的個性與行爲問題在圖書館作業自動化過程中之影響，由這些問題可說明人與人間關係的三種事實：（1）人與人間之關係不是固定不變的，人的行爲之改變並不需要任何操縱才變的；（2）好的管理行政人員抓住問題的重點；（3）人與人間之關係非常複雜，以至於不能分析得很完整！除此之外，作者認爲溝通（Communication）是很重要的，在人際關係方面它具傷害性，亦具幫助性（註28）。

臺灣學術研究圖書館及資料單位館員對自動化認識與態度調查研究結果

本研究以臺灣學術研究機構之圖書館和資料單位九十一個作爲調查對象，以瞭解：（一）各單位之圖書館的一般概況及自動化現況與問題；（二）圖書館長、副館長及資料單位負責人和專業館員對圖書館的自動化的認識與態度。這些學術圖書館屬於教育機構單位者二十八個；醫學和醫藥學院者八個單位；研究機構者五十五個單位，總共九十一個單位。因館長、副館長人數不多，故全部調查，館員共八五一人，採抽樣法，因此館員被調查者人數是四三〇人，九十一個學術研究圖書館全部調查。

本研究對象遍佈臺灣各地，故所有問卷以郵寄方式進行。館和館長及資料單位負責人的問卷同一封信發出；副館長和館員的問卷個別單獨寄出。所有問卷先後寄發四次：第一次寄發問卷及回收日期是一九八五年六月十二日至六月二十六日；第二次寄發問卷及回收日期是一九八五年七月八日至七月十八日；第三次寄發問卷後回收日期是一九八五年七月二十五日至八月五日；最後一次，第四次發出和回收問卷日期是一九八六年二月十七日至二月二十六日。各種問卷的回收率是館及資料單位共發九十一個單位，回收七十五件（82.4%）；館長、副館長及負責人共發九十七（含六位副館長）件，回收七十四件（76.29%）；館員問卷發出四三〇件，回收三五〇件（81.37%）。館員四三〇中五十一位是主任級，回收四十四件（86.27%），館員三六二中回收二九一件（80.39%）（見表一至四）。所有收回問卷中，僅有兩件廢卷，先予以剔除，不列入統計計算。本研究所有問卷寄發情況由下列統計表中詳細說明：

表一　學術研究圖書館問卷調查情況統計表

圖書館類型	發出問卷	回收份數	尚未回收份數	回收率	備注
大　學	28	26	2	92.86%	寄發問卷及回收日期： 第一次：一九八五年六月十二日至六月二十六日 第二次：一九八五年七月八日至七月十八日 第三次：一九八五年七月二十五日至八月五日 第四次：一九八六年二月十七日至二月二十六日
醫學院	8	6	2	75.00%	
研究機構	55	43	12	78.18%	
總　計	91	75	16	82.42%	

表二　學術研究圖書館館員問卷調查情況統計表

圖書館類型	發出問卷	回收份數	尚未回收份數	回收率	備注
大　學	271	217	54	80.07%	同表一
醫學院	16	12	4	75.00%	
研究機構	143	107	36	74.82%	
總　計	430	350	80	81.39%	

表三　學術研究圖書館主任、館員問卷寄收情況統計表（一）

圖書館類型	寄收問卷數	未回收份數				回收份數			
		單位數	人數			單位數	人數		
			主任	館員	小計		主任	館員	小計
大　學		28	51	220	271	26	44	173	217
醫學院		8	2	14	16	6	1	11	12
研究機構		55	15	128	143	43	14	93	107
總　計		91	68	362	430	75	59	277	336

表三　學術研究圖書館主任、館員問卷寄收情況統計表（二）

圖書館類型 \ 項目	寄收問卷數	未回收份數			回收份數			
		單位數	人數		單位數	人數		
			主任	館員	小計		主任	館員	小計
大　學	2	7	47	54	92.86	86.27	78.64	80.07
醫學院	2	1	3	4	75.0	50.00	78.57	75.00
研究機構	12	1	35	36	78.2	93.33	72.66	74.82
總　計	16	9	85	4	82.2	86.76	76.52	78.14

表四　學術研究圖書館館長、副館長、負責人問卷調查情況統計表

圖書館類型 \ 數量（館長）\ 調查情況	發出問卷	回收份數	尚未回收份數	回收率	備　注
大　學	28	28	0	100%	
醫學院	8	8	0	100%	
研究機構	55	44	11	80%	寄發日期同表一
總　計	91	80	11	87.91%	

　　本研究是以問卷調查蒐集資料爲主，此外並選擇圖書館/資料單位訪問參觀，目的在證實所填資料內容並澄清問卷中填寫不完整和不清楚之處，借此面談亦可深入地交換意見，以彌補問卷中遺漏的地方。因時間有限，僅選五個地區：臺北市、臺中市、臺南市、高雄市和新竹市，訪問參觀的單位共二十四個。

　　問卷調查和參觀訪問蒐集的資料，使用"國立臺灣大學"電算中心之 CDC CYBER 170/805 之 SPSS Programs 做資料的各項統計分析，結果如下。

一、學術圖書館的一般概況

　　（一）所屬機構形態：七十五個樣本中，公立機構佔四十九個，佔總樣本的65.33%；私人機構則十四個，佔18.66%；另十二個單位填其他欄，並說明所屬機構形態是財團法人或國際機構，佔總樣本16%。

　　（二）圖書館/資料單位類型：在七十五個樣本中，大學和學院的圖書館二十六所（34.7%）；醫學院圖書館六所（佔8%）；研究機構圖書館四十三所（佔57.3%）（見表五）。

表五　學術研究圖書館/資料單位的背景資料統計表

圖書館背景資料 項目、館數、百分比	項　目	館　數	百分比
所屬機構形態	公	49	65.33%
	私	14	18.66%
	其他	12	16.00%
圖書館類型	大學、學院	26	34.70%
	醫學院	6	8.00%
	研究機構	43	57.30%

（三）館藏：七十三個單位填寫了館藏數。圖書冊數最多者是"國立臺灣大學"1584052冊，最少者僅600冊。其中有七個單位之館藏在三十萬冊以上者是："國立臺灣大學"、"國立師範大學"、私立文化大學、政治大學社會科學資料中心、政大中正圖書館、私立淡江大學和"國立成功大學"等。（見表六）

表六　學術研究圖書館/資料單位現有圖書總數統計分析表

現有圖書總數 館數	館　數	百分比	備　注
六〇〇～二〇、〇〇〇	38	52.0%	
二〇、〇〇一～四〇、〇〇〇	5	6.8%	
四〇、〇〇一～六〇、〇〇〇	3	4.1%	七個單位館藏在三十萬冊以上
六〇、〇〇一～八〇、〇〇〇	4	5.5%	
八〇、〇〇一～一〇〇、〇〇〇	4	5.5%	
一〇〇、〇〇一～二〇〇、〇〇〇	8	10.9%	
二〇〇、〇〇一～三〇〇、〇〇〇	4	5.5%	
三〇〇、〇〇〇以上	7	9.6%	
總館數	73		

（四）服務對象人數：有五十八個樣本中填寫了服務對象的人數。服務對象人數最少的僅30人，18000以上者有三個單位，他們是"國立臺灣大學"、"文化大學"和"中央研究院"民族所。

（五）實際使用人數：九十一樣本中僅五十九個單位列出他們圖書館之實際使用人數。平均每月使用最少者三十人，12000使用者有三家，他們是私立淡江大學、文化大學和"中央研究院"民族研究所。

（六）工作人員：57.57%，三十八所館的工作人員人數是在20人以下，而僅有五所，他們的工作人員是在40人以上，他們是"國立臺灣大學"、"國立師範大學"、"國科會"科資中心、中山科學院和私立淡江大學等。

二、學術圖書館/資料單位自動化作業之現況及困難問題因素

近年來,圖書館作業自動化已不再是引起爭論的事了,而且是非常熱門而時髦的話題了,海外如此,臺灣亦不例外。就調查中顯示,回答的七十五個單位中,三十一個單位,佔總樣本的42.5%,有或正在籌備中,三十個單位,佔41.1%,亦在考慮中;僅有十二個單位,佔16.4%,不考慮自動化;兩個單位未作答,一般看來,對自動化意願甚高。各單位作業自動化現況統計分析見表七,詳細統計分析資料將分別列表予以討論。

表七 圖書館/資料單位業務自動化現況統計分析表

圖書館類型 \ 自動化現況數量	有/籌備中	考慮中	不考慮	未答	合計
大學、學院	12	12	2	0	26
醫學院	3	3	1	0	7
研究機構	16	15	9	0	40
總計(百分比)	31 (42.5%)	30 (41.1%)	12 (16.4%)	0	73

(一) 圖書館/資料單位業務自動化實施項目之概況

由七十五所圖書資料單位中,已經完成自動化項目有採購,中、西文編目,出納,期刊,參考和行政業務等。(詳見表八)其中有八個單位已完成參考服務自動化,實際情形則是這些單位多數與"百科資料庫"連線,用之做參考服務工作。其中其他最多單位完成的項目是期刊,有六個單位。說來這也是臺灣自動化作業之特色之一,因為早期臺灣自動化作業較偏愛由期刊開始,為的是解決印製期刊聯合目錄和控制問題。西文編目完成者有五所,採購和出納系統各有四所,一般來說,出納系統是比較容易做而又討好的項目,圖書館多願由此部門開始;另完成中文編目作業自動化者僅有一所,據研究者本人之推測分析其因,可歸納兩點來說明:(1) 由於中國編目規則和中文機讀編目格式仍在試用和推廣階段;(2) 由於"國立中央圖書館"正在建立中文資料機讀編目檔,其他的館可能考慮將來可使用"中央圖書館"的磁帶,故目前暫不考慮自己發展中文編目自動化作業。在調查中,部份完成的自動化業務之單位則以採購為最多,其次是期刊控制和出納系統。各圖書館業務自動化項目及現況名單詳見表九。

表八　圖書館/資料單位業務自動化項目現況統計分析表

自動化項目 \ 自動化現況、館藏、百分比	已經完成	部份完成	計劃中	未　定	未　答	總　數
採　　購	4（5%）	7（9%）	8（10%）	2（3%）	54（72%）	75
西文編目	5（6%）	3（4%）	5（6%）	2（3%）	60（80%）	75
中文編目	1（1%）	2（3%）	5（6%）	2（3%）	65（86%）	75
出　　納	4（5%）	4（5%）	9（12%）	2（3%）	56（75%）	75
期　　刊	6（8%）	5（6%）	6（8%）	2（3%）	56（75%）	75
參考（含線上檢索）	8（10%）	4（5%）	2（3%）	3（4%）	58（77%）	75
行政業務	0（0%）	2（3%）	1（1%）	3（4%）	69（92%）	75
其　　他	2（3%）	0（0%）	2（3%）	1（1%）	70（93%）	75

＊其他項：・館際合作　　・工程設計　　・發行刊物　　・論文報告等

表九　圖書館/資料單位業務自動化現況名單

圖書館名稱 \ 自動化現況 \ 自動化項目	編目 中編	編目 西編	採購	出納	期刊	＊參考（含線上檢索）	行政業務	其他	備　注
"國立臺灣大學"	部完	計中	部完	部完	部完	部完	部完		
"國立政治大學"				已完					
"國立清華大學"		部完	計中		部完				
"國立交通大學"	部完	已完	部完	已完	已完	部完			
"國立成功大學"			已完	已完	部完	部完			
工業技術學院				計中		部完			
私立淡江大學					已完				
私立逢甲大學				計中	部完				
私立東海大學							部完		經費控制
私立輔仁大學社會科學圖書館				部完					
私立東吳大學	計中	計中	計中	計中	計中	計中	計中		
"國立成功大學"醫學院圖書館				部完					
"中國石油公司"高雄廠	計中	計中	計中	計中	計中		計中		
私立中山醫學院				部完		部完			
中山科學研究院	計中	計中	計中	計中	計中	計中	計中		
食品工業發展研究所				計中	計中	計中			
"行政院國科會"精密儀器發展中心	未定	未定	未定	未定	未定	未定	未定	未定	
"中央研究院"生物化學研究所	未定	未定	未定	未定	未定	未定	未定	未定	

(續上表)

自動化現況＼自動化項目＼圖書館名稱	中編	西編	採購	出納	期刊	*參考(含線上檢索)	行政業務	其他	備注
臺灣水產試驗所東港分所	未定	未定	未定	未定	未定	未定	未定	未定	
亞洲蔬菜研究發展中心		已完	已完		部完				
"中國石油公司"煉製研究中心		部完	部完		部完				根據資訊週所展示之資料
"國科會"科學技術資料中心			已完		已完	已完		部完	
農業科學資料服務中心	已完	已完	部完		已完	已完			其他：發行刊物之管理
工業技術研究院化學工業研究所		已完	計中			已完			
工業技術研究院機械工業研究所			計中	已完					
工業技術研究院電子工業研究所				計中	計中	計中	部完	部完	
工業技術研究院材料工業研究所								部完	
工業技術研究院工業經濟研究中心			部完			已完			
"中央研究院"資訊科學研究所		已完	已完			已完			其他：館際合作
"中央研究院"地球科學研究所			部完						
"中央研究院"統計學研究所		已完	計中	計中	部完	已完	部完		其他：館際合作
"中華經濟研究院"					已完	已完			
航空發展研究中心				計中		部完			
觸媒研究中心	部完	部完							
臺灣養猪科學研究所			部完	計中					

代碼：部完：部份完成　　計中：計劃中　　＊多數單位是指接百科資料庫而言
　　　已完：已經完成　　未定：未定中

部份學術圖書資料單位已將使用國際百科資料庫系統列入參考自動化項目中。由一九八〇年臺灣開始接用"國際百科"以來，臺灣現已有約十六個單位使用，而有增多的趨勢，其中有十四個使用單位是學術圖書館。

(二) 圖書館/資料單位業務自動化進行方式

根據統計資料中顯示六十六所圖書館/資料單位對業務自動化所採取的進行方式是：二十五所圖書館/資料單位是圖書館與單位之計算機中心或其他研究人員合作設計；十二個單位擬購買現成軟體；另十一個單位委託電腦公司；另有六個單位是自行開發；另有六個單位使用他館自動化軟體；三所圖書館願與他館連線；三個館採用其他方式進行業務自動化，但未說明何種方式。

(三) 圖書館/資料單位業務自動化問題及癥結

學術研究圖書館及資料單位業務自動化問題與癥結由調查所得之結果，歸納結果見

表十：一般認為最主要的問題是經費問題；其次則是缺乏能負責自動化的工作小組，成立小組固然重要，但小組成員具有自動化方面的訓練和經驗則更重要，否則不會發揮任何作用的！

再其次則是自動化進行中，工作量增加，館員無法負責；機器設備問題；目標不明確更缺乏全盤計劃；館員的自動化背景及訓練缺乏；上級主管支持不夠；傳統人工作業問題等。調查顯示，館員對自動化似乎無顯著的阻力，但館員對自己的工作無法提出明確需求做自動化的依據，這是較嚴重的問題。很顯然地，臺灣圖書館作業缺乏科學化的管理方法（Scientific Management），對自動化效益更是無法判斷和評估，這對推展圖書館作業自動化有很大的阻力！

三、圖書館／資料單位館長、副館長及負責人和館員對圖書館作業自動化的認識與態度

臺灣地區對自動化問題的研究，大抵偏重於自動化的硬體與軟體的設計，而較少探討"人"的因素，本研究除探討臺灣地區圖書館／資料單位自動化作業的一般問題外，深感館長、副館長、負責人，和館員對自動化業務的認識與態度必將影響這項業務的推展，因此，將之列為本研究目的之主要重點，以期瞭解臺灣地區圖書館自動化發展遲緩之癥結問題所在。茲將問卷調查此項資料分析結果歸納如下：

（一）館長和館員的一般資料（見表十、十一）

表十　圖書館／資料單位館長和館員一般資料統計分析表

項　目	職　稱	館　長（％）	館　員（％）
問卷寄收	寄 收	97 80（82.47％）	430 346（80.45％）
性　別	男 女	38（47.5％） 42（52.5％）	70（20.59％） 270（79.41％）

表十一　館長、副館長、負責人和館員年齡比較統計分析表

年　齡	職　稱	館　長（％）	館　員（％）
二〇歲以下		16（2.3％）	23（6.8％）
二〇～三〇歲		31（39.2％）	118（34.9％）
三一～四〇歲		17（21.5％）	139（41.1％）
四一～五〇歲		12（15.2％）	30（8.9％）
五一～六〇歲		3（3.8％）	25（7.4％）
六〇歲以上		0	3（0.9％）
總　計		79	338

1. 問卷收發：館長等問卷發九十七人，收回八十人，佔82.47%。館員（含主任等）問卷發四三〇人，收回三四六人，佔80.45%。

2. 性別：館長男性三十八人，佔47.5%；女性館長四十二人，佔52.5%。館員女性二七〇人，佔79.41%；男性七十人，佔20.59%。結論是臺灣學術圖書館工作人員以女性館員較多。

3. 年齡：以年齡比較，館長以二十～三十歲間者為最多，三十一人，佔39.2%，館長四十一歲以上者十五人，佔19%；館員年齡最多者為三十一～四十歲之間，一三九人，佔41.1%，六十歲以上者三人；館長六十歲以上者無；館員四十歲以上者五十八人，佔館員總人數17.2%。兩者相較，館長和館員在年齡上無甚差異。

4. 學歷：由調查資料歸納的統計表十二內顯示，尚無圖書館學博士館長和館員；圖書館系碩士館長十一人，圖書館學士館長有二十人，兩者佔總數44%；其他五六%的館長和資料單位負責人是非圖書館學系畢業者，其中三位館長學歷出人意料的是在專科以下程度。館員中有圖書館學碩士者十二人，圖書館學士或專科畢業者一七八人，兩者佔館員總人數55%，非圖書館學系館員有45%。有關館長、館員是否為圖書館相關科系畢業之統計，可參考表十二。

表十二　館長、副館長、負責人和館員學歷統計表

學歷＼職稱	館長（%）	館員（%）
圖書館學博士	1	0
圖書館學碩士	11（15.5%）	12（3.6%）
圖書館學學士	20（28.2%）	178（52.7%）
其他學科博士、碩士	20（28.2%）	13（3.8%）
其他學科學士、專科畢業	17（23.4%）	94（27.8%）
專科以下	3（4.2%）	37（10.9%）
其他	0	4（1.2%）
總　計	72	338

（二）對自動化作業的認識

"認識"意思是指館長或館員在自動化方面所接受的教育與訓練而言。為了探求圖書館自動化作業問題及癥結因素，調查研究學術圖書館館長和館員的自動化背景也正是本計劃研究的主要目的之一。以館長和館員問卷調查之資料，分析、統計列表和比較如下：

表十三　館長、副館長及資料單位負責人對圖書館自動化及網路建立的認識統計分析表

項　目	認識	是		否		總人數
		人數	%	人數	%	
在學校修過圖書館自動化的課程		29	37.2	49	62.8	78
參加過"中國圖書館學會"舉辦之暑期自動化專題研習會		17	22.4	59	77.6	76
修過電腦、系統分析或程式設計等課程		36	46.8	41	53.2	77
使用過電腦		54	68.4	25	31.6	79
撰寫過程式		30	38.5	48	61.5	78
閱讀有關圖書館自動化方面的書刊		59	74.7	20	25.3	79
閱讀有關電腦、程式設計或系統分析方面的書刊		53	67.9	25	32.1	78
參觀或訪問過其他圖書館自動化系統		59	75.6	19	24.4	78
參加圖書館自動化的演講或研討會		48	61.5	30	38.5	78
舉辦過圖書館自動化的演講或研討會		7	9.0	71	91.0	78
擔任有關圖書館自動化之工作		24	31.2	53	68.8	77
大概知道圖書館自動化能幫助圖書館做哪些工作		72	92.3	6	7.7	78
必要建立全臺圖書館資訊網？		79	100	0	0	79
平均數（總）		567	55.97	446	44.03	1,013

表十四　館員（含主任）對自動化的認識統計分析表

項　目	認識	是		否		總人數
		人數	%	人數	%	
在學校是否修過圖書館自動化方面的課程		128	37.6	212	62.4	340
是否參加過"中國圖書館學會"舉辦之暑期自動化專題研習會		87	25.9	249	74.1	336
是否修過電腦、系統分析或程式設計等課程		225	65.8	117	34.2	342
使用過電腦		261	76.5	80	23.5	341
撰寫過程式		170	50.4	167	49.6	337
閱讀有關圖書館自動化方面的書刊資料		254	74.9	85	25.1	339
閱讀有關電腦程式設計或系統分析等方面的書刊		236	69.6	103	30.4	339
參觀訪問他館自動化系統		222	65.0	120	35.0	342
參加館內外有關圖書館自動化的研討會或演講		168	50.5	165	49.5	333
目前參與圖書館自動化工作		70	21.4	257	78.6	327
大概知道圖書館自動化能幫助圖書館做哪些工作		320	95.5	15	4.5	335
總（平均數）計		2,142	57.70	1,572	42.30	3,712

（三）圖書館自動化問題

　　館的方面自動化問題分析前節已曾提過，由於館的問卷是發給館長的，故該問卷所列自動化問題是代表館長的看法。館員問卷亦問及此問題，兩者比較詳見表十五，以求

證兩者在觀念上、看法上是否一致？

表十五　圖書館/資料單位業務自動化問題館長館員看法比較分析表

自動化問題項目	館/館長數 (N＝80)%	館員數 (N＝340)%	備 注
經費不足	39	② 136	
缺乏能負責自動化的工作小組	38	① 158	
自動化進行中，工作量增加，館員無法負擔	28	⑥ 78	
機器設備問題（含優先權，及使用機器不便等問題）	27	④ 83	
自動化目標不明確，缺乏全盤計劃	22	③ 107	
館員在自動化方面之訓練和瞭解不夠，致使工作協調上的困難	19	④ 53	
館員和系統分析及程式設計師彼此溝通協調的問題	19	⑤ 80	
上級主管不重視	16	⑧ 46	
傳統人工作業流程問題	16	⑦ 58	
館員無法提出明確的作業需求	11	⑨ 39	
館員排斥自動化	2	⑪ 8	
其他	2	⑩ 11	館小不考慮、優先順序、館長問題

　　根據比較結果，兩者看法非常相近。舉例來說，兩者皆認為自動化最大問題是"經費不足"和"缺乏能負責圖書館自動化工作小組"，"館員排斥自動化"已微不足道，非常少數人而已，這是非常樂觀的發現。同時很明顯的看出來，館員在自動化方面的訓練不夠而產生的問題；機器設備，自動化目標不明確和缺乏全面計劃，以及傳統人工作業等問題很多。也有館員提及圖書館標準問題等。要解決這些問題，必要再深入研究及探討了！

　　此外，圖書館業務自動化被重視及支持的程度亦會對推展自動化有很大的影響！調查結果，館員及館長支持自動化意願很高，其所屬單位之上司對圖書館之支持及重視和對自動化之支持的程度尚可，但有47%的上司認為自動化後工作人員應減少，這些上司主管們需要進一步觀念上的疏通。

（四）館長、館員對自動化作業的態度

　　前節探討了館長和館員在自動化作業的認識及背景，這些因素是否影響他們對自動化作業的態度？這正是本節要深入瞭解的重點。根據調查所獲的資料，歸類以 Likert 量

表式詳述如下：（見表十六、十七）

表十六　館長、副館長及資料單位負責人對圖書館業務自動化及網路的態度統計分析表

項目＼態度人數	非常同意	很同意	同意	不太同意	不同意	總人數	贊同 %
1. 圖書館自動化是一種必然的趨勢。	42	17	21	0	0	80	100
2. 圖書館傳統的人工作業及服務方式已不足以應付日益增多的資料和滿足讀者的需要。	25	23	29	2	0	79	97.47
3. 圖書館自動化的作業方式應該優於傳統的人工作業。	22	17	33	6	0	78	92.31
4. 圖書館自動化可以節省時間和金錢，減少事務性的工作，提高工作效率。	21	23	28	7	0	79	91.14
5. 圖書館自動化初期，雖然需要用去很多的金錢與人力，但仍是值得做的。	28	18	32	2	0	80	97.50
6. 圖書館自動化後，館員會有更多的時間充實自己，從事更有意義的工作，提供讀者更好的服務。	26	21	26	7	0	80	96.25
7. 圖書館自動化有助於圖書館和館員地位的提高。	22	17	29	12	0	80	85.00
8. 圖書館自動化需要上級主管的支持。	52	14	14	0	0	80	100
9. 圖書館自動化需要每位館員的參與與支持。	37	21	20	1	0	79	98.73
10. 圖書館自動化需要充裕的經費。	45	15	20	0	0	80	100
11. 負責圖書館自動化規劃及設計的館員必須具備電腦及資訊科學的背景。	34	23	21	0	0	78	100

（續上表）

項目＼態度／人數	非常同意	很同意	同意	不太同意	不同意	總人數	贊同 %
12. 館員對自動化的看法與接受與否，對圖書館自動化有很大的影響。	28	23	23	5	1	80	92.50
13. 圖書館自動化將會威脅到館長的職務。	0	0	1	31	48	80	1.25
14. 無論圖書館自動化是否造成部份館員的失業問題，圖書館仍需要自動化。	17	14	40	2	3	76	92.11
*15. 自動化進行階段，圖書館工作量增加，是館員對自動化產生排斥感的原因之一。	1	11	32	25	9	78	56.41
16. 學習操作電腦不難。	23	21	35	0	0	79	100
17. 希望圖書館最好不要自動化。	0	0	0	14	66	80	0

表十七　圖書館／資料單位館員對自動化態度統計表

項目＼態度／人數	非常同意	很同意	同意	不太同意	不同意	總人數	贊同 %
1. 圖書館作業自動化是一必然趨勢。	142	56	139	3	0	340	98.82
2. 圖書館傳統的人工作業及服務方式已不足以應付日益增多的資料和滿足讀者的需求。	108	65	155	8	3	339	96.75
3. 圖書館自動化的作業方式應該優於傳統的人工作業。	71	73	172	19	1	336	94.05
4. 圖書館自動化後，可以節省處理資料的時間，減少事務性的工作，提高效率。	102	79	140	16	1	338	94.97
5. 圖書館自動化後，館員會有更多的時間充實自己，從事更有意義的工作，提供讀者更好的服務。	100	71	124	38	2	335	88.06

(續上表)

項 目 \ 態度 人數	非常同意	很同意	同 意	不太同意	不同意	總人數	贊同 %
6. 圖書館自動化有助於圖書館和館員地位的提高。	81	74	136	37	6	334	87.13
7. 圖書館自動化需要上級主管的支持。	200	55	83	1	1	340	99.41
8. 圖書館自動化需要充裕的經費。	191	54	92	2	0	339	99.41
9. 圖書館自動化需要每位館員的參與和支持。	166	75	97	2	0	340	99.41
10. 負責圖書館自動化規劃及設計的館員必須具備電腦及資訊科學的背景。	115	89	125	9	0	338	97.34
11. 館員對自動化的看法與接受與否，對圖書館推展自動化有很大的影響。	103	85	143	6	2	339	97.64
*12. 自動化進行階段，圖書館工作量的增加是館員對自動化產生排斥感的原因之一。	19	49	153	82	30	339	66.96
13. 圖書館自動化後，館員可能因爲電腦取代其工作，而對自動化產生排斥感。	3	8	72	162	89	334	24.85
14. 無論圖書館自動化是否造成部份館員的失業問題，但圖書館仍需要自動化。	62	65	180	18	8	333	92.19
15. 學習操作電腦不難。	76	76	177	7	0	336	97.9
16. 希望圖書館最好不要自動化。	1	1	1	63	269	335	0.89

綜合統計分析，館長和館員幾乎百分之百認同"圖書館自動化是必然趨勢"，贊同圖書館應該自動化作業即是會造成部份館員失業！兩者都認爲自動化需要館員與上級主管的支持；充裕的經費；和館員的自動化背景、知識、經驗和"Technology Know-How"！兩者同時認爲唯一造成館員對自動化產生排斥的原因是"自動化進行階段，圖書館工作量的增加是館員對自動化產生排斥感的原因之一！"（見表十六、十七中之有星號項目）館長贊同者56.4%，館員是67%。這答案按其他的答案的推測應該是不以爲然，即不贊

同的應該高反而低,這也是研究者驚奇的!推測是由於目前已有部份圖書館已實施或正在進行自動化,館長和館員深深體會到在進行自動化階段工作量增加所顯示其被影響後的態度!

(五) 認識與態度之關係

根據統計分析顯示,認識和態度之相關係數(Correlation Co-efficient)是"正"關,但相關很弱,即館長和館員對自動化的認識與館長和館員對自動化的態度之影響不大!態度都很積極,亦代表圖書館自動化時期已到,吾人對自動化方面的認識與否,圖書館業務自動化是必然的!

結 論

本研究,根據資料分析結果,歸納下列幾點結論:

臺灣學術圖書館/資料單位分佈在醫學院、大學、學院和研究機構中。館藏情形是600～1500000冊之間,工作人員是1人或120人,有65%圖書館機構是公立的!

有三十一個單位(42.5%)已實施或正在籌備自動化中,83%調查單位皆在推展自動化作業。現臺灣尚無完全自動化的圖書館/資料中心;自動化的項目以參考和期刊自動化為最多,自動化方式為採用圖書館與電子計算機中心合作,其次購買現成套裝軟體,委託電腦公司,使用或連線他館系統,館內自行設計等……顯然的,由此可知,臺灣圖書館缺乏有電子計算機和圖書館自動化經驗和訓練的館員和技術人員。因此,一些圖書館對自動化持觀望和等待的態度。

館長和館員共同認為自動化最大癥結是:缺少能負起自動化責任的工作小組和經費問題,其次是機器使用優先權和方便問題,上級主管不重視圖書館和自動化,以及傳統人工作業問題多和館員缺乏自動化及電子計算機之知識與訓練,而造成無法與系統人員溝通,和明確的提出作業自動化需求等……顯然的,又是館員的對自動化方面背景之不足而產生的問題!訪問中,有位館長曾說:如能爭取到經費,聘請自動化有經驗的人是理所當然的事,也是最困難的!因此,缺乏有技術訓練之館員是推展自動化最大瓶頸!

館長和館員對自動化認識與態度上幾乎百分之百的相同而無差異,而館長和館員對自動化之認識都不甚高,都需要加強!但在態度方面,兩者卻非常積極!都認為圖書館自動化是一必然趨勢,不贊同"圖書館不要自動化"的看法;館長和館員對自動化的意願甚高,已無阻力可言。總而言之,雖然館長們和館員對圖書館作業自動化的認識並不深入,但他們對自動化則幾乎是全力支持的!

綜合以上結論:臺灣學術研究圖書館/資料單位有80%已開始進行作業自動化,但僅限於局部作業自動化,尚無完整的圖書館自動化作業系統,但似乎也缺乏圖書館"整合"作業自動化之認識。最大問題是館員自動化"技術能力"不夠和自動化"經費"缺乏,致使臺灣學術圖書館業務自動化緩慢進展。館長、副館長、資料單位負責人和館員對圖書館業務自動化之意願很高,但缺乏實際對自動化作業之詳細做法與瞭解,以致於意願與行動脫節。近幾年來,常聽到圖書館要自動化的熱門話題,但很少看到成果即說明了一切!館長和館員雖欠缺自動化的知識與背景,但不影響他們對自動化的極力的支持,因為圖書館業務自動化已是當今圖書館發展趨勢,而又勢在必行也!

建　議

　　根據本研究結果結論，試提下列建議，以使學術研究圖書館/資料單位及決策者在推展自動化業務時，作為制訂因應政策之參考和依據。分別就圖書館自動化基礎方面；圖書館作業自動化問題；和館員訓練方面予以說明：

　　一、圖書館自動化基礎方面： 任何事情的推展，事先應將基礎打好，準備工作做好，圖書館自動化亦不例外。雖然以目前臺灣自動化現況來看，已是本末倒置，但仍有亡羊補牢之機會。

　　（一）圖書館自動化教育：教育方面，可由海內外圖書館學與資訊科學系及研究所負責，加強自動化和相關之課程，以建立及培植學生對圖書館自動化業務之認識。

　　（二）從速訂定處理資料之統一規格與標準：制定統一規格和標準，不但可作為各圖書館自動化作業時之依據，更便於未來網路建立的資料之分享與交換。這些標準，例如：編目規則、機讀編目格式、權威檔、各種代碼、資訊交換碼等。此事項可委託 "中國圖書館學會" 邀請專家成立專案辦理。

　　（三）從速編定圖書館統一 "分類法" 和 "中文標題" 總目：臺灣地區圖書館現採用不同的圖書分類法，有待統一之必要，此事可委託 "國立中央圖書館" 邀同有關專家研究辦理。無 "中文標題" 之設置是臺灣圖書資料處理及應用上最大缺陷。歐美各國統計是讀者最喜愛用主題（Subject）和標題（Subject Headings）來查尋和檢索資料，尤其利用自動化系統時，而臺灣地區竟無中文標題的存在，這將對臺灣地區圖書館自動化系統使用上有很大的阻礙和限制。因此，編訂臺灣地區 "中文標題總目" 及細節是必要的，而且迫切的，這方面可委託 "國立臺灣大學" 圖書館研究所負責編製。

　　（四）成立圖書館自動化系統專家顧問小組：此小組之成立，目的在幫助解決有關推展自動化時所遭遇之問題。此小組成員約十人，由圖書館自動化專家三人、電子計算機專家三人、通訊系統專家三人和一位負責人組成。這些專家和負責人可由 "國科會" 聘請或委託 "中國圖書館學會" 聘請之。

　　二、自動化作業問題方面： 由本研究中發現圖書館推展自動化最大的阻力是缺乏自動化方面有經驗的人員，換句話說，就是圖書館員缺乏自動化方面的專門技術和經驗，這種專才之短缺亦非一時即可訓練而成的。因此，圖書館自動化應考慮其他解決方法，此建議如下：

　　（一）使用現成軟體：根據一九八五年 Matthews 的統計，美國圖書館自動化系統75%是公司設計的啓鑰系統（Turnkey Systems）；25%則由圖書館自己發展的；在已自動化的圖書館中，88.9%是用啓鑰系統的（註29）；由於臺灣地區目前尚未有一套適合圖書館的自動化系統，但去年在美國，CLSI, Inc. 和 RLIN 的 CJK Terminal（中、日、韓文終端機）已相連接，也許可解決自動化問題（註30）；最近有澳大利亞的 URICA 系統在臺推銷，該系統也在發展中文系統與之銜接，這也是針對臺灣地區圖書館自動化之需求而設計的（註31）。軟體公司不但可解決圖書館自己在無經驗的狀態下摸索發展的痛苦，同時訓練人員亦是公司的職員。長遠看來，使用現成軟體則較省錢、省事、省時！據最近發展趨勢，很多系統供應者（Systems Provider/Vender）原依照圖書館的需求，連接圖書館與其他系統相連（註32）。近來，電腦界已逐漸有興趣引進海外自動化套裝軟體，為圖書館自動化提供服務！

（二）委託有經驗的電腦公司或機構設計：這種做法是為瞭解決電子計算機技術人員欠缺的問題，雖非最佳的解決途徑，但如能配合的好，成功的可行性則遠較圖書館自己開發來得高！

（三）觀摩他館系統交換心得和經驗：請教專家，觀摩已自動化作業的圖書館系統，因臺灣尚無全部完成的圖書館自動化系統，不妨由政府資助組團至海外參觀自動化系統，但臺灣現有之部份自動化作業，仍具參觀參考價值。

三、館員之自動化訓練： 由於館員缺乏自動化方面的背景和訓練，在職圖書館工作人員迫切需要再教育，特別加強對"圖書館自動化"，"電子計算機概論"，"資訊技術"，"資訊網路"，"通訊技術"，"系統分析"，"資訊貯存與檢索"等方面之介紹，期能建立館員對自動化之基本觀念，以配合圖書館業務自動化發展的工作。建議擬定五年在職圖書館自動化訓練計劃，分批分時接受訓練。可由"國科會"或"教育部"委託"中國圖書館學會"會同資訊策進會共同主持訓練，每期可訂六個月，並發結業證書。

綜合上述，是本研究計劃所提出對圖書館自動化問題及館員對自動化認識之培養訓練之建議，望有關單位及決策者能接納及參考使用。本研究在十三個月內（1985年3月至1986年4月）匆忙中完成，疏漏之處尚請學者專家多多批評指教！

附　註

註1：王振鵠，"圖書館自動化作業之現況及展望"，"國立中央圖書館"館刊，第新十五卷，第一、二期，1982年，第一——五頁。

註2：1983 SPSS—Statistical Programs for Social Sciences.

註3："大學及獨立學院圖書館標準"，圖書館年鑑，"國立中央圖書館"，1981年，第四三九—四四二頁。

註4：*Annual Review of Information Science & Technology*, V. 1 – 21（New York：Knowledge Industry Publications, 1966 – 1986）.

註5：*Annual Review of Information Science & Technology*, V. 18（New York：Knowledge Industry Publications, 1983）, pp. 307 – 354.

註6：Anne G. Adler, et al, *Automation in Libraries*：*A LITA Bibliography* 1978 – 1982.（Ann Arbor, MI：Pierian Press, 1983）.

註7：*Library Literature*（Bronx, NY：H. W. Wilson, 1972 –　）.

註8：*Library & Information Science Abstracts*（LISA）（London：ASLIB, 1969 – 1986）.

註9：圖書館學論文索引，"國立臺灣師範大學"社會教育學系編，1963年。

註10：王征和杜瑞青，圖書館學論著資料總目，臺中：文宗出版社，1969年。

註11：方仁，中文圖書館學及目錄學論文索引，1971年。

註12：宋建成主編，圖書館學期刊論文索引（臺北：藍星，1984年），頁41—43，53—55。

註13：圖書館學文獻目錄，"國立中央圖書館"編，1986年。

註14：Luquire, Wilson "Attitude Toward Automation Innovation in Academic Libraries," *Journal of Academic Librarianship*, 8（Jan. 1983）, p. 344.

註15：張鼎鍾編譯，資訊科學導論，臺北：學生書局，1984年，第五—十五頁。

註16：Presthus, Robert. *Technological Change & Occupational Responses: A Study of Librarians.* Final Report. Washington, D. C.：Office of Education, 1970.

註17：Fine, Sara. *Resistance to Technological Innovation in Libraries.* Washington, D. C.：U. S. Dept. of Health Education & Welfare, 1979.

註18：Fine, Sara. "Terminal Paralysis or Showdown at the Interface," The 22nd Annual Clinic on Library Applications of Data Processing, April 14 - 16, 1985.

註19：Stussy, S. A. "Automation in Catholic College Libraries," *Catholic Library World.* 53 (Oct., 1981), pp. 109 - 111.

註20：McCarthy, C. M. *The Automation of Libraries & Bibliographic Information Systems in Brazil.* Loughborough University of Technology (Great Britain) Ph. D. Dissertation, 1983.

註21：Schraml, Mary L. "The Psychological Impact of Automations on Library & Office Workers." *Special Libraries* 72. (April, 1981), pp. 149 - 156.

註22：Pizer, I. H. "Automation-Plianning to Implementations, the Problems on Route." *Bulletin of the Medical Library Association.* 64 (Jan, 1976), pp. 1 - 14.

註23：Woods, Rollo G. "Library Automation in British Libraries." *Programs* 20 (Oct., 1986), p. 375.

註24：Liquire, Wilson C. *Selected Factors Affecting Library Staff Perceptions of an Innovative System: A Study of ARL Libraries in OCLC.* Indiana University Ph. D. Dissertation, 1976.

註25：Yother, L. W. *A Study of the Extent of Automations in Small College Libraries & the Relationships of Attitudes of Library Directors Toward It.* University of Connecticut Ph. D. Dissertations, 1984.

註26：Dakshinamurti, Ganga. "Automation Effect on Library Personnel." *Canadian Library Journal* 42 (Dec., 1985), p. 343.

註27：Park, Hyung-Ji. *A Study of Perceptions of Library Personnel Concerning Computer Applications at the Michigan State University Library.* Michigan State University Ph. D. Dissertation, 1984.

註28：Daily, Jay E. *Staff Personality Problems in this Library Automation Process: A Case in Point.* Littleton, Colo.：Libraries Unlimited, 1985.

註29：Matthews, J. R. "Unrelenting Change the 1984 Automated Library System Marketplace." *Library Journal* 110 (April, 1985), p. 31.

註30：IFLA 1985 Annual Conference Exhibition, Chicago, 1985.

註31：URICA Taipei 展示 1987.

註32：Sloan, B. G. "The New Age of Linked Systems." *American Libraries* 16 (Sept., 1985), pp. 652 - 653.

第四十七屆國際圖書館協會聯盟年會紀實*

一、前言

　　國際圖書館協會聯盟（International Federation of Library Associations and Institutions—IFLA）創立於一九二七年，其目的為促進圖書館事業與書目控制方面之合作，特別是研究提倡有關圖書館，圖書館學會，書目學家，以及其他組織機構間之國際聯繫關係。會員分為兩種：（一）正會員：正會員有投票權，必須由執行委員會認可，有圖書館學會，國家及國際性學會，或相類似的機構；（二）副會員：副會員無投票權，由秘書處認可，有圖書館、書目機構及其他類似之單位。

　　臺灣於一九七一年退出聯合國後，因限於規定，失去了正會員之會籍，目前以副會員入會者有："國立中央圖書館"，"國立臺灣大學"圖書館學系，"國立臺灣師範大學"圖書館，以及淡江大學圖書館等。近年來，因受到國際政治的影響，該聯盟對我方會員的會籍與名稱問題，屢持偏見，對我會員名稱凡冠有"國立"，"中央"等字樣者，特別表示異議，遭此橫流，我圖書館界當不能退縮。一年來，我圖書館界及電腦界人士在中文資料電腦化作業之研究，已具有相當的成果，如中文圖書機讀編目格式及中文資訊交換碼之設計等，不但在臺灣發展推廣，亦應藉此年會宣讀我研究論文，公諸於世。同時有關我方會籍及排名等問題，均需與大會有關人士面商，因此，在"中央圖書館"之安排及"教育部"之資助之下，推派機讀編目工作小組的成員：臺大李德竹教授，銘傳商專黃克東教授，淡江大學黃鴻珠教授及胡鷗蘭教授等四位組團前往參加本年大會。

二、年會地點、時間及與會人士

　　該聯盟每年約在八月間輪流在世界各國舉行會員大會，如去年於菲律賓，明年將在加拿大，後年將在西德，大後年將在肯亞等，藉此觀摩與聯誼。今年在德國萊比錫的馬克斯大學（Karl-Marx Iniversity）圖書館學院舉行。

　　會議自一九八一年八月十七日至廿二日。大會出席者有七十餘國家的代表一千二百人，中國大陸派有代表六人。

　　大會開幕式是在萊比錫歌劇院舉行，典禮開始與結束都由萊比錫交響樂團演奏巴哈作品，儀式隆重別致，典禮由東德圖書館學會會長 Gotthard Rückel 主持，東德文化部長 Hans-Joachim Hoffmann，FLA 會長 Mrs. Else Granheim 及聯合國科技文教組織代表 Dr. Müller Karl-Heing 皆在會中致詞。

三、大會主題與分組討論

　　今年大會為加強各國圖書館間的聯繫與合作，將以"國家圖書館機構及專業組織"為主題，在第一天全體會員大會中，由美、俄、東、西德國等代表，就"國家圖書館之發展與國際間合作問題"為題，進行報告與討論，接著六天共舉行了 226 次分組會議。

---

*　本文與黃鴻珠、胡鷗蘭、黃克東合作撰寫。曾發表在《"中國圖書館學會"會報》33 期（1981 年 12 月），第 132—136 頁。

分組會議係依圖書館學科目，圖書館類型與業務分組，如生物與醫學圖書館組，科學與應用科學組，社會科學圖書館組，圖書館理論與研究組，圖書館統計組，圖書館史組，視聽資料組，學校圖書館組，大學圖書館組，公共圖書館組，資訊科學組，編目組，交換與採購組等等，每一組再按發表論文之多寡與性質，復分數次分會議，分別於不同時間舉行，每天經常在同一時間內，在各不同的會場分別進行各種不同性質的會議。與會代表可根據自己的興趣與需要選擇參加，茲將我代表分別參與之各種不同會議，選述如下，俾供參考：

（一）編目會議組：討論國際標準編目與英美編目規則第二版的問題，美國 Free Library or Philadelphia, Pensylvauia 的 Mrs. F. Hintou 在"AACR 2 and International Standards"一文中報告 AACR2 修訂的經過與現況，並強調其與國際標準之關係，對於英美編目規則第二版的採用，與會人士咸認過於繁雜。

（二）科學及應用科學會議組：主要討論國際機讀編目與資訊網等問題，加拿大"國家圖書館"的 Mr. H. Clemeut 宣讀論文"International MARC Network"談國際性資訊網建立的現況與展望，他希望各國能使用 UNIMARC 建立圖書資料庫及測試工作，他報告 IFLA 將著手進行 CCF（Common Communication Format）及權威檔（Authority File）之設計等工作。西德 Mrs. C. Bossmeyer (German Library, Frankfurt) 宣讀論文"Library Networks in the Federal Republic of Germany"，她在極力爭取 International MARC Network 之設計及測試機會，故我方代表會後向其詢問其測試現況，她說有些國家已將 MARC Format 舉列，她目前只作 MARC Format 之比較工作（人工的），並言稱國際間尚無任何國家使用 UNIMARC Format 建立圖書資料庫，我方代表糾正其說法，告知我方已根據 UNIMARC 建立資料庫，並贈送 *Chinese MARC Format for Books* 一書及論文一篇請其參考。由此深感我方設計之 *Chinese MARC Format for Books* 之宣傳不夠，有待加強。

（三）大學圖書館會議組：以大學圖書館標準為主題，討論熱烈，各國代表反應大學圖書館所訂定最低標準往往公佈後，成為一般圖書館的高標準，代表們一致認為大學圖書館標準之訂定應由圖書館從業人員修訂，較能符合實際需要。

（四）國會圖書館會議組：以國會圖書館線上資訊系統與資訊服務為主題進行報告與討論，根據美國代表的報告，國會圖書館使用電腦檢索者以國會議員最多，其服務與接受服務者的態度，值得為我方之借鏡。

（五）資訊科學會議組：討論電腦在圖書館之應用以及圖書館與資訊中心的發展，宣讀論文除了西德 Mr. R. Brudler 與利比亞 Mr. A. M. El-Hush 外，我方準備的二篇論文："Chinese MARC Format for Books"（由李德竹，胡歐蘭，黃鴻珠，吳明德與黃克東等著）和 The Design and Its Application of the CCCII in Library Automation（由黃克東，謝清俊，張仲陶與楊鍵樵等著）亦在此會中宣讀，很遺憾沒有充裕時間進行討論，雖然會中有些小差誤，但會後各方的反應良好，紛紛向我方索取資料者甚多。

因為會議類別繁多，往往時間衝突無法一一參與，在此也因篇幅所限，難以將參與之每種會議一一列出，敬祈見諒。

此外，由於今年為"國際殘障年"，故大會議程中亦特別配合此項活動，邀請有關此方面之論文宣讀，並辦理參觀盲人圖書館，以及各種殘障資料及儀器設備之展覽與宣傳，參加之殘障代表很多，可謂本屆年會之一大特色。

四、聯誼參觀與活動

在開會期間，地主國文化部長 Hans-Joachim Hoffmann 於八月十七日晚在萊比錫市賓館舉行酒會及餐會，歡迎全體代表，八月十九、二十兩日分別在聖多馬斯大教堂舉行巴哈教堂風琴演奏會及於富地演奏廳由來比錫交響樂團演奏貝多芬及柴可夫斯基作品。大會每日另安排有參觀節目，分別參觀藝術圖書館，圖書館學系，盲人圖書館、醫院圖書館、兒童及學校圖書館等，八月二十一日舉行全日郊游並參觀圖書館及各名勝古蹟，我代表四人一起參加赴波茨坦（Potsdam）文化城，參觀德國最大的研究中心圖書館，游歷國立故宮及十八世紀腓特烈大帝所建之無憂宮與花園。

此外，爲配合此次會議，當地一些圖書館和博物館辦理書展，在會議期間，特別展出：（1）"Most Beautiful Books From All Over The World"；（2）"Books Design in Leipzig in the 20th Century"；（3）"Rarities of the University Library in Leipzig"。

五、會後參觀訪問

會後我四人順道參觀訪問歐洲幾個國家，獲益良多，簡述數項以供參考：

赴西德參觀設於西柏林的"國家圖書館"Stract Biblioteket，並訪問設於該館的國際標準圖書館編號中心（International Standard Book Number Agency—ISBN Agency），我方代表與該中心負責人 Mr. Wawarsig 研商我方地區出版品代號問題，Mr. Wawarsig 熱心接待，態度非常友善，他很高興我方對標準書號之重視，根據 ISO-3166 號標準給予臺灣地區出版品代號，並建議我方應積極建立 ISBN 中心，最好是設在"國立中央圖書館"內，由該中心召開出版商、書商會議，向出版界解釋國際書號之目的及其重要性。然後由中心建立出版商代號，編出版商地區、代號、名稱等名錄。將此名錄提供國際標準圖書編號中心，以便列入國際標準圖書編號名錄中及分配我方國際書號。

Mr. Wawarsig 又陪同我方代表參觀 Struad Biblioteket，據他說此圖書館爲現在歐洲最大之圖書館，裝潢設計大方美觀，在該館東方資料部門，承 Mr. Wawarsig 的介紹認識留德學人王文田博士，由王博士帶引我們參觀東方書籍部份，該館約有三十萬冊東方資料，大陸資料很多，但其排架方式按登錄號排，對讀者使用不甚方便。

英國一行，由留英學人林麗惠小姐陪同參觀倫敦大學（University of London）與大英圖書館（British Library）。與倫敦大學亞非研究院代理館長 Mr. Stephen Goddard 及圖書館電腦作業系統分析師 Ms. Leevse 見面，對方急於瞭解我方 Chinese MARC Format 及 CCCII 進展情形，其時 Ms. Leevse 正在爲倫敦大學圖書館作電腦處理東方語文資料之系統分析，並向我方提出甚多問題，我方解答所提問題外，並贈送 Chinese MARC Format for Books 及 CCCII V.2 各一册以助其發展東方資料自動化之參考。

在大英圖書館首先參觀該館之 BLAISE 系統（British Library Automated Information Service），該系統設計週詳，爲一整體自動化系統，內含英國的 UKMARC File 之 BNB 資料，另交換而來的 LCMARC File，同時又涵蓋 MEDLINE，SDILINE，TOXILINE，CHEMLINE，RTECS，HISTLINE，BIOETHICS，HEALTH 和 MeSH 詞彙等檔，最近又發展 AVMARC（非書資料之機讀編目格式）由 Ms. Patricia Chapman 接待並做簡報及線上操作示範，後由 Ms. S. Woodhouse 陪同參觀 British Library，之 BNB 之整個處理情況。

接着由大英圖書館，東方圖書部負責人 Kenneth B. Gardner 與副館長 H. Nelson 二位先生接待及座談交換意見，對我近年來在中文資料電腦化處理甚爲驚奇與佩服，另提出讀字拼音問題，並由我方贈劉達人教授所著之 *A Comparative Study of Romanization Systems*（曾在一九八一年國際中文圖書館自動化研討會中發表），*Chinese MARC Format for Book* 及 CCCII V. 2 各一冊供其參考。

赴日內瓦國際標準組織，將我方之 Chinese MARC Format for Books 及 CCCII 之論文及書籍贈送給該組織秘書處之 Information Officer, Mr. Simeon Simeonov，並洽購組織之出版品及各種刊物之長期訂户等事宜。同時會見該組織副秘書長 Dr. L. D. Encher，商談有關臺灣會籍等問題，藉此將我方在電子、塑膠、紡織工業及中文圖書館資料自動化及中文電腦近年來之成就情況相告，以期在國際上訂定國際標準時，參與意見並提供經驗，與世界各國共享經驗。

六、感想與建議

在短短的半個月中，所見所聞很多，空間的變化很大，讓人深深體驗到"行萬里路勝讀萬卷書"之道理，對我等而言，正是將我方所作的成果公諸於世之好時機，又可由觀摩他人之成果，取其之長補己之短，其意義與效果頗鉅。此次參與會議後之感想與建議列舉數項就教於圖書館與資訊界同道：

（一）注意歐洲、非洲圖書館等的發展：我方圖書館研究的方向，一向以美國爲圭臬，但此次會議中各小組會議主持者，大多數爲歐洲人，而且此次會議由非洲地區出席人數之眾來看，可瞭解其對圖書館事業的重視，今後我方圖書館的研究方向，應以美、歐、非、亞及其他地區並重，以便争取廣大的國際友誼及支持。

（二）建議與大英圖書館東方圖書部及倫敦大學加強合作關係：大英圖書館 Howard Nelson 副館長再三表示對我方之 *Chinese MARC Format for Books* 與 CCCII 極感興趣並希望今後多多交換有關資料，該館研究成果享譽世界可加強聯繫，建立合作關係。

（三）重視國家書目控制：參觀英國圖書館時，由 Mr. S. Woodhouse 介紹中，發現他們有專職人員七十人專門處理 BNB 之編製工作，由其龐大的工作人員可看出其對國家書目控制的重視，此點甚值我方借鏡。

（四）密切注意國際間機讀編目格式資料交換工作：此項工作由加拿大負責，並成立 Inter MARC 專研小組，此小組的工作與動向，我應注意與聯繫，與其配合，與我機讀編目格式建立關係。

（五）重視第二外國語文的教育：爲達成與歐、非等國的合作關係，圖書館與資訊界對歐洲等語文人才之培養是刻不容緩。圖書館學系應將歐洲語文列爲必修或必選，有計劃地培養人才。

（六）加強資料之蒐集：對於資訊的掌握與資料之蒐集同等重要，尤其對那些與我方無邦交的國家資料應廣爲蒐集，而對其發展情況亦不可掉以輕心。

（七）此項國際會議年年舉行，不但有機關團體會員而且有個人會員，我圖書館與資訊界應多多參與，藉以瞭解世界圖書館與資訊事業發展情勢，將我各方之成就帶到世界各角落，達成學術文化之交流。

"教育部"和本系新修訂之圖書館學系必修課程[*]

"教育部"爲配合學術思潮，符合政策及社會需求，每五年按期修訂各大學學系必修課程。本系亦應時代需要，不定期而隨時修改或增加必修課程。本文就最近"教育部"和本系新修訂之必修課程分別介紹如下，以供老師和同學們參考：

壹、"教育部"新修訂圖書館學系必修課程

本系經一九八八年六月廿二日，公私立大學"文學院必修科目修訂委員會"第一次會議，推定爲"圖書館學系修訂小組"召集學系。本系依規定辦理程序，於同年八月廿六日和九月十日邀請相關校系主任，輔仁大學圖書館學系盧荷生主任和淡江大學教育資料科學系朱則剛主任，和兩位專家："國立中央圖書館"王振鵠館長和本系胡述兆教授共同參與。先後召開兩次圖書館學系必修科目修訂小組會議，討論修改圖書館學系必修課程有關事宜。依"教育部"規定，必修科目以三十～五十學分爲原則。修訂項目是：課程名稱、學分數及時間安排三部份，最後訂定圖書館學系共同遵循的標準必修課程，呈報"教育部"。"教育部"通過後，並於本（一九九〇）年三月五日函送公私立大學文學院各學系必修科目表，自一九九〇學年度入學新生起實施。必修科目表詳見下表：

科目名稱	學分	第一學年 上	第一學年 下	第二學年 上	第二學年 下	第三學年 上	第三學年 下	第四學年 上	第四學年 下	備註
圖書館學導論 Introduction to Library Science	2	2								
中文參考資料 Chinese Reference Sources	4			2	2					
資訊科學導論 Introduction to Information Science	2		2							
西文參考資料 Western Reference Sources	4			2	2					
分類編目學 I Cataloging and Classification I	4			2	2					
分類編目學 II Cataloging and Classification II	6					3	3			
計算機概論 Introduction to Computer Science	4	2	2							
書目學 Bibliography	4					2	2			
圖書館資料選擇與採訪 Selection & Acquisition of Library Materials	4					2	2			
圖書館管理 Library Management	4							2	2	
非書資料 Non-book Materials	4					2	2			
圖書館實習 Library Field Work	0							0	0	
圖書館自動化 Library Automation	4							2	2	
計	46									

注：一、教育部規定：修習本系課程須依其先修順序選課。

此次修訂課程中改變一九八三年之必修科目有下列：

---

[*] 本文曾發表在《書府》1期（1991年6月），第7—8頁。

一、"中文圖書分類編目"和"西文圖書分類編目"合併爲"圖書分類編目"(一)及(二)。

二、"非書資料"和"視聽資料管理"合併，取消"視聽資料管理"，以"非書資料"稱之，並在備註欄內加含"視聽資料管理"。

三、"圖書資料徵集"名稱改爲"圖書資料採訪"。

四、"電子計算機概論"和"中文參考資料"兩科，皆改在一年級教授。

五、"西文參考資料"由三年級改在二年級教授。

六、全部必修課程合計之學分由五十改爲四十八學分。

貳、系新訂必修課程

本系經多次討論，於一九八八學年度第一次系務會議討論事項第二條，決議本系定必修科目修訂如下，並報教務處備查：

新訂系必修科目對照表如左：

	普通心理學	理則學	社會學	傳播學概論	研究方法與論文	第二外國語(法西日任一)(免)	三民主義之一(大學、公民、專門等)	名著選讀之一(人文、社會)	圖書館統計學	圖書館學專題	英文打字	合計
90學年度實施 新訂學分	3	3	3	2	4	12	2	3	3	2	1	38

	普通心理學	理則學	大眾傳播	研究方法與論文	第二外國語(法西日任一)(免)	三民主義之一(大學、公民、專門等)	名著選讀之一(人文、社會)	圖書館學專題	英文打字	圖書館史	圖書館作業評估	合計
89學年度前實施 原訂學分	3	3	2	4	12	2	3	2	1	2	2	36
備註		新增							改爲選修	改爲選修	改爲選修	

系必修課程中，由對照表可看出：

一、本系新增"社會學"、"圖書館統計學"兩科各三學分。

二、"圖書館史"、"圖書館作業評估"改爲選修。

三、各型圖書館之一"學校圖書館"改爲"兒童圖書館"，"學校圖書館"改爲選修。

四、"大眾傳播"改爲"傳播學概論"。

新增修之系必修科目合計三十八學分，較以前增兩個學分；此外，原訂之四年實習也改爲兩年，實習將由三年級開始，以上修訂科目亦將於一九九〇學年度第一學期起實施。

根據新增必修科目，本系同學必須修滿149學分，方能畢業。

美國資訊科學學會[*]

一、前言

一九七四年四月筆者赴美參加"中美科技資料處理與運用研討會"時拜訪了美國資訊科學學會（American Society for Information Science 簡稱 ASIS）。由該會主席 Mr. Joshua I. Smith 接待，他說很高興能見到我這臺灣唯一的美國資訊科學學會會員。他曾建議在我方發起徵收新會員及設立美國資訊科學學會臺灣分會事，因當時深思人們對資訊科學之認識與瞭解問題，答允回臺灣後試收新會員，然後再考慮其他。回來後曾發寄介紹美國資訊科學學會小冊子給有關之機關及個人，但收獲甚少，五年來也只吸收了一位會員。現教育界和圖書館界已開始重視資訊科學之介紹、教育與研究，圖書館學系也增設這方面之課程，工商學院也增設有關資訊之學系或另外分設資訊組，甚至於工業界也於今年成立資訊工業財團法人組織等，可見對此方面之重視。因此，在此僅借中央圖書館館刊之篇幅，再一次的介紹美國資訊科學學會，它成立之歷史，宗旨，組織形態，出版品及各種服務項目等，以期增進大家對此學會之認識，並瞭解這個組織對從事於資訊科學研究和發展的人員之關係及重要性。

二、學會歷史

美國資訊科學學會是一非營利的專業學會機構，以科學、文學、教育為目的並致力於有關資訊及其傳遞知識之創意、組織、傳播和應用之研討，現已有四十三年之歷史，早期名稱 American Documentation Institute（簡稱 ADI）於一九三七年以德拉威州法（Laws of the State of Delaware）成立。此機構的起源可溯自一九二六年美國農業部所屬 Bibliofilm Service 縮影服務之 Science Service 部門，該部門負責人是 Walson Davis（第一任 ADI 會長），為文件資料（Documentation）之各種問題之改善而努力。由化學基金會（Chemical Fondation）資助 Science Service 成立 Documentation Institute 以製做科技書目，發展縮小攝影術和多種複製資料方法及探求各種對紀錄資料之有效通訊方法為目的。

依據 ADI 一九三七年成立之形式，組成會員是由與 Science Service 有密切聯繫關係之學會和學術或事業機構團體之代表所組成，當時僅六十八位，無需繳納會費，不收個人會員。初期 ADI 有卓越顯著之表現，完成事項甚多：如發展並研究微粒影片閱讀機、照相機和服務；Bibliofilm Service 首創將少用之期刊製成微片儲存備用：在第二次大戰時設立 Oriental Science Service 以保存提供亞洲科技資料之服務；又成立補助性出版品服務（Auxiliary Publication Service），以解決期刊編輯出版者對過長之文章資料表、附錄等處理問題；ADI 又透過 Science Service 介紹國際間使用 Interlingua（An International Language——國際語言）以便科學在國際間通訊交流；並又擔任召開 1958 International Conference on Scientific Information 會議之合作主持者等。

很顯然的，至一九五〇年，已有更多的人從事於多方面文件資料新學理和新技術之

---

[*] 本文曾發表在《"國立中央圖書館"館刊》新 12 卷第 1 期（1979 年 6 月），第 21—32 頁。

研究和發展，資訊服務也顯著增加，ADI 不再能僅限於機構團體會員而繼續存在下去，必要予以擴大，故在會長 Dr. Luther Evans 領導下，研討新的計劃及發展趨勢，結果於一九五二年修改其組織法，決定除團體會員外，增加個人會員。ADI 即成爲一國家性文件資料方面之專業學會。

一九五〇年代，由於察覺到自動化設備已開始用於文獻查尋和資訊貯存及檢索之趨勢，此觀念之成長快速，專業之興趣更擴至各方面，又因"資訊爆發"問題已成爲國家之憂慮，致使一九六〇年代會員增至原會員數之七倍以上。由於全部活動之改變和資訊科學之初現之反映，會員們投票決定更換學會名稱，認爲美國資訊科學學會（American Society for Information Science，簡稱 ASIS）較更爲適合現況，乃於一九六八年一月一日正式更名。該學會之獨特着重點是有關資訊處理之全面問題。現 ASIS 已成爲美國全國性最具領導性和代表性之專業組織，特別是對設計、管理和利用資訊系統和技術方面而言。其會員已遍及世界三十七個國家，並與其他國家和國際性協會組織保持密切連繫，目前，ASIS 已成爲一國際性之資訊科學學會了。

三、學會宗旨

該學會之宗旨在由研究發展應用及教育各方面促進資訊傳遞程序（Information Transfer Process）之改進，並特別着重於資訊之產生、蒐集、組成、詮釋、貯存、檢索、傳播、轉換和運用，並強調在此範疇內引用現代技術方法。同時致力於建立和構成資訊傳播有關之科學、技術及有系統之知識體系。該學會又充任各種資訊傳遞（Information Transfer）發展研究及需求之橋梁。該學會定期出版刊物，並召開有關資訊之傳達、交流通訊、作業之分析與理論及實用等各方面之研討會以期達成其目的。

四、學會組織

美國資訊科學學會之組織內容，如會員制度、學會會長，各部門負責主管人員，工作人員、學會會議和各種委員會、分會、會費、專門興趣團體、學會作業及選舉程序，以及學會之法規修訂等皆依據其組織法和其附則（ASIS Constitutions and Bylaws）。其重要組織詳介如下：

（一）學會行政組織

行政組織方面設有重要行政會議（Council），各種委員會及各種行政人員。行政人員中，一些是經會員選舉的，一些是任命的。在行政會議（Council）中重要人員有：President, Past President, President-Elect, Treasurer, Chapter Assembley Councilor, Councilorsat-large, Cabinet Councilor 等爲選擇的，其中另有 Managing Director 是由學會會長任命的。除 Council 以外之其他行政人員如 Deputy Assembley Chairman 是選舉外，學會總辦公室之 Executive Director, Council and Liaison Representative, Society Parliamentarlan, Special Consultant for Society Development 等皆由學會會長任命的。

此外，仍成立各種委員會：如 Standing Council Committees, Ad Hoc Committees, Standing Society Committees 等，這些委員會亦包括很多小型委員會，同時在學會總辦公處設有各部門辦理各種會務。學會行政組織結構見下圖：

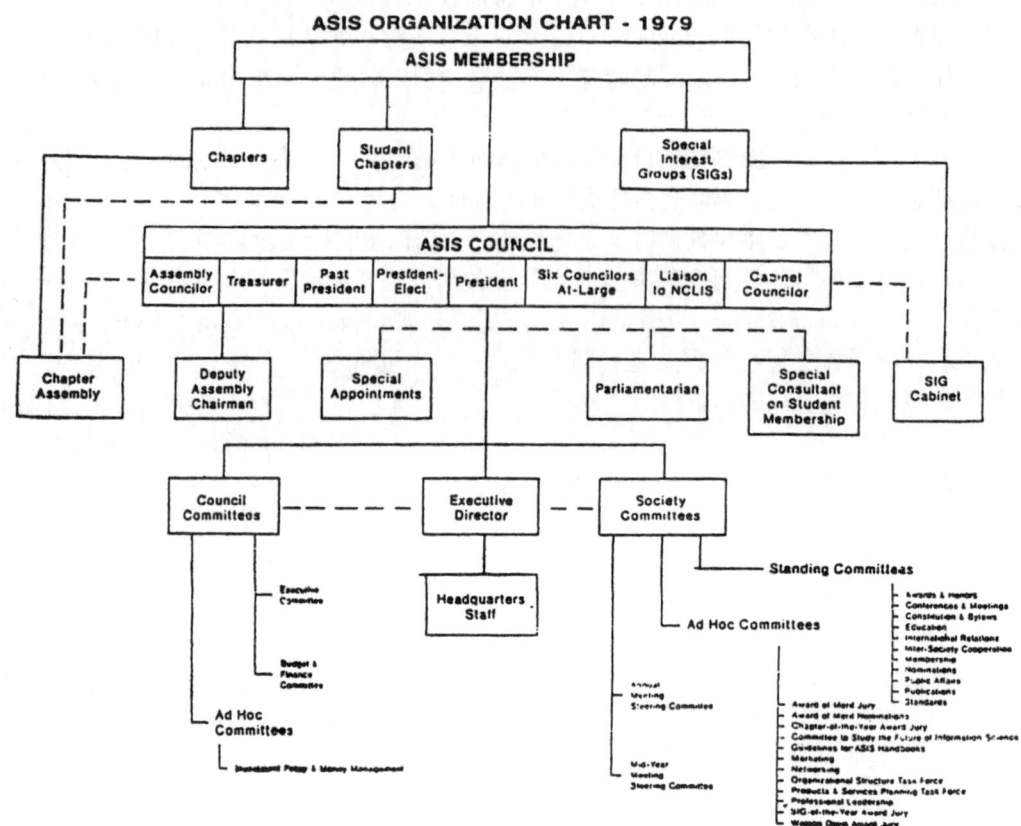

圖1　美國資訊科學會組織圖

(二) 會員制度

公開申請會員，有興趣者皆可申請加入。會員種類分個人會員（Individual Members）和團體會員（Institutional Members）兩大類。個人會員又分有一般會員（Regular Membership），學生會員（Student Membership）和退休會員（Retired Membership）三種。團體會員限團體、學會、機構等申請之。

會員們的背景真是多彩多姿，他們來自各種不同行業中之資訊專家，如圖書館學、電子計算機科學、工程學、化學、管理科學、作業研究、語言學、心理學、邏輯學、資料處理、通訊學、出版業、數學、經濟學、教育學等。

會員人數增加甚快，一九七九年約四千人（其中包括學生會員）現有八十七個機構加入團體會員。會員人數歷年來增加之情況見下圖：

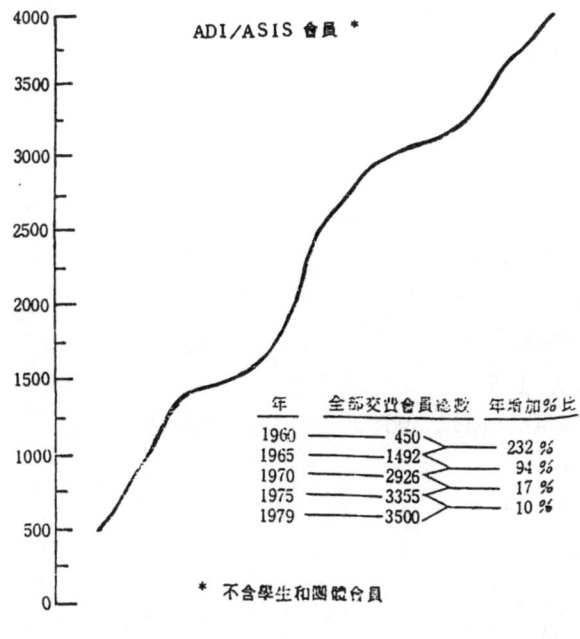

圖2

(三) 會費

個人會員申請無需任何資格條件限制，凡有興趣者皆可加入。繳納會費時間算法是——每年十月一日起至第二年九月卅日止為一年，繳費則應在十月一日之前，一九七九年會費是：一般會員費是美金四十五元，學生會員費十五元一年，退休會員每年會費是二十二元五角美金。

團體會員分兩類：企業團體會員（Corporate Sponsor），會費每年美金二百五十元，另一種是贊助團體會員（Sustaining Sponsor）會費是美金四百五十元。

(四) 學會分會

學會共分有廿六個分會和廿二個學生分會（Student Chapters）。學會分會（Chapters）多以地區劃分，學生分會則以學校為單位。茲表列其名稱，地區代號及成立年代於下：

Chapters and Student Chapters

Chapters

Carolinas (24) 1973
Central New Jersey (30) 1975
Central Ohio (12) 1961
Chesapeake Bay (19) 1968
Chicago (15) 1961
Delaware Valley (8) 1960
East Tennessee (29) 1975
Indiana (14) 1961
Los Angeles (18) 1961

Metropolitan New York (7) 1960
Michagan (21) 1969
Minnesota (16) 1968
Missouri (27) 1974
New England (5) 1961
North European (28) 1974
Northern Ohio (11) 1963
Pacific Northwest (22) 1971
Pittsburgh (10) 1961
Potomac Valley (9) 1960
San Francisco Bay Area (17) 1961
Southern (32) 1976
Southern Ohio (13) 1962
Texas (26) 1974
Upstate New York (6) 1962
Western Canada (20) 1969
Wisconsin (25) 1974

Student Chapters
Alberta, University of (1977)
Capital Area (Washington, D. C.) (1967)
Case Western Reserve University (1966)
Central New York (Syracuse) (1976)
Columbia University (1964)
Drexel University (1964)
East Texas State University (1977)
Illinois, University of, at Urbana-Champaign (1977)
Indiana University
Kent State University (1975)
Long Island Univerity (1977)
Los Angeles Area (1976)
Michigan. University of (1972)
Nashvill University Center (1970)
Pittsburgh, University of (1966)
Pratt Institute of Technology (1970)
Rutgers University (1964)
St. John's University (Jamaica, N. Y,) (1972)
Simmons College (1975)
South Carolina (1975)

State University of New York at Albany (1974)

Texas, University of, at Austin (1977)

(五) 專門興趣團體

(Speial Interest Groups-SIGs)

　　爲了會員們對資訊科學之研究興趣與範圍之不同，學會於一九六六年開始設立各種專門興趣團體（Special Interest Groups），便於各類相同專業會員加入，有機會互相切磋，交換意見。到目前（一九七九年）已成了二十二個專門興趣團體，繳付美金兩元即可加入一團體，會員可按自己興趣自由加入，加入數量不限制。這些專門興趣團體名稱及其名稱縮寫和成立年代見下表：

Special Interest Groups (SIGs)

Arts and Humanities (AH) 1967

Automated Language Processing (ALP) 1966

Behavioral and Social Sciences (BSS) 1966

Biological and Chemical Information Systems (BC) 1966

Classification Research (CR) 1966, Change to Content Reprsentation, 1978.

Community Information Services (CIS) 1976

Computerized Retrieval Services (CRS) 1969

Costs, Budgeting, and Economics (CBE) 1970

Education for Information Science (ED) 1966

Foundations of Information Science (FIS) 1972

Information Analysis Centers (IAC) 1966

Information Publishing (IP) 1975

Information Services to Education (ISE) 1974

Law and Information Technology (LAW) 1975

Library Automation and Networks (LAN) 1966

Management of Information Activities (MGT) 1975

Medical Records (MR) 1975

Non-print Media (NPM) 1970

Numeric Data Bases (NDB) 1975

Public-private Interface (PPI) 1974

Technology, Information, and Society (TIS) 1971

User On-line Interaction (UOI) 1971

(六) 學會與其他專業學會團體之關係

　　學會與其他專業學會團體建立非常密切之連繫關係，美國資訊科學學會是下列三學會之會員：

American Federation of Information Processing Societies (AFIPS)

Association of Special Libraries and Information Buresux (ASLIB)

National Federation of Abstracting and Indexing Services (NFAIS)

又是 Federation for Documentation (FID) 之 Institutional Affiliate, 和 American Library

Association（ALA）之 Affiliate。並又設有專門連絡代表人與下列學會協會團體等：

 American Association for the Advancement of Science（AAAS）
 American Chemical Society/Division of Chemical Information（ACS/DCI）
 American Association of Law Libraries（AALL）
 American Federation of Information of Processing Societies/Education Committee（AFIPS/EC）
 American Institute of Industrial Engineers（AIIE）
 American Library Association（ALA）
 American Society of Indexers（ASI）
 Association for Computational Linguistics（ACL）
 Association for Educational Communications and Technology（AECT）
 Association of American Library Schools（AALS）
 Association of Information and Dissemination Centers（ASIDIC）
 Association of Records Managers and Administrators（ARMA）
 Association of Research Libraries（ARL）
 Canadian Association for Information Science（CAIS）
 Computers and the Humanities Advisory Board（CHum）
 Council of Biology Editors（CBE）
 Drug Information Association（DIA）
 Federal Library Committee（FLC）
 Geoscience Information Society（GIS）
 Health Sciences Communication Association（HSCA）
 Information Industry Association（IIA）
 Institute of Mangement Sciences（IMS）
 International Communications Association（ICA）
 International Word Processing Association（IWPA）
 Medical Micrographics Association（MMA）
 National Translations Center（NTC）
 Society for Technical Communication（STC）
 Society of American Archivists（SAA）
 Special Libraries Association（ALS）

另設有 Standards Representative 標準代表人，與美國國家標準局中兩個有關資訊標準之委員會連繫：

 American National Standards Institute（ANSI）Committee Z39 on Library Work, Documentation, and Related Publishing Practices

 American National Standards Institute（ANSI）Committee PH5 on Micrographic Reproduction

學會亦派代表出席 American Federation of Information Processing Society（AFIPS），Documentation Abstracts, Inc., National Federation of Abstracting and Indexing Services（NFAIS）之重要行政會議。

(七) 其他組織

行政組織方面，另有 Rules of Procedure 學會方面根據最新版 Robert's Rules of Order 而執行。在修訂學會法則（Amendment of Bylaws）方面，必要全體會員三分之二選票才能通過任何改增。

五、活動和服務項目

為了達成學會成立目的及宗旨，以期能有效的建立專業人間連繫及提供適當之服務，該會設有各種活動及服務項目：

(一) 學會會議

該學會每年召開各種會議，有年會（ASIS Annual Meeting），年中會議（Mid-year Meeting），區域會議（Regionl Meetings），研討會（Seminars, Workshops），專門興趣團體（SIGs）會議和專題研討會等等：

1. 學會年會（Annual Meeting）：每年召開一次全體大會，時間是每年最後三個月（十、十一、十二月）間，地點每年不同。最近和未來幾年來年會地點是：

1975：Boston
1976：San Francisco
1977：Chicago
1978：New York City
1979：Minneapolis, Minn.
1980：Anaheim, California
1981：Washington, D. C.
1982：Columbus, Ohio
1983：Dallas, Texas

2. 年中會議（Mid-year Meeting）：一九七二年開始召開年中會議，由各地學會分會（Chapters）或 SIGs 主持。會議亦包括 Technical Sessions, Business Meetings of Council, Committees, Chapter Assembly, SIG Cabinet 和學會所屬其他單位聚會等。召開會議地點每年亦不同，如：

1978, May 22–24：Rice University, Houston, Texas.
1979, May 16–20：Banff Springs Hotel, Banff, Alberta.
1980, May Pittsburgh, Pa. Area.

3. 其他會議：每年召開各種地區性會議，研究討論會、研習會等。這些會議內容針對某些專題而召開的。各專門興趣團體（SIGs）每年借年會開會時亦聚會一次。近年來，學會亦常常在其他會議中如 Special Libraries Association, Medical Library Association, American Association for the Advancement of Science, and National Computer Conference 等召開會議中主持 Technical Sessions。

4. 歷年來學會會長：

1937–1943	Watson Davis	1964	Hans Peter Luhn
1944	Keyes D. Metcalf	1964–1965	Laurence B. Heilprin
1945	Waldo G. Leland	1966	Harold Borko

1946	Wats on Davis	1967	Bernard M. Fry
1947	Waldo G. Leland	1968	Robert S. Taylor
1948－1949	Vernon D. Tate	1969	Joseph Becket
1950－1952	Luther H. Evans	1970	Charles P. Bourne
1953	E. Eugene Miller	1971	Pauline A. Atherton
1954	Milton O. Lee	1972	Robert J. Kyle
1955	Scott Adams	1973	John Sherrod
1956	Joseph Hilsenrath	1974	Herbert S. White
1957	James W. Perry	1975	Dale B. Baker
1958	Herman H. Henkle	1976	Melvin S. Day
1959	Karl F. Heumann	1977	Margaret T. Fischer
1960	Cloyd Dake Gull	1978	Audrey N. Grosch
1961	Gerald J. Sophar	1979	James M. Cretsos
1962	Claire K. Schultz	1980	Herbert B. Landau
1963	Robert M. Hayes		（President-elect，1979）

（二）出版品項目

出版各種刊物的目的在於鼓勵和助長對資訊科學及其相關學科之學術與實用方面之研究及興趣，借出版方式提供給會員們、資訊科學家和有興趣者參考。該會出版品種類頗多，可分：

1. 連續性出版品

1－1 *Journal of the American Society for Information Science*（JASIS）.（Editor：Charles T. Meadow）. 1970－Bimonthly.（Formerly：*American Documentation.* Quarterly. 1950－1970）

25－years Collective Index to JASIS（1950－1974）.

內容包括世界性資訊科學技術和相關學科研究發展方面之學術報告、論文、書評等。免費贈送會員。

JASIS 訂購地址：

John Wiley & Sons, Inc.

605 Third Ave,

New York N. Y. 10016

U. S. A.

1－2 *Bulletin of the American Society for Information Science.*（BAISI）（Editor：Lois F. Lunin）1974－Bimonthly. 一報導性刊物，設各種資訊專欄，定期報導最新發展研究情況，對資訊專家，會員們每期皆有最新最快有關重要資訊事件、觀念、消息、意見等之報導。同時刊出學會方面對會員們之各種正式通告等。免費贈送會員。

1－3 *ASIS Handbook & Directory.* Annual

學會會員手冊，內含學會歷史、組織形態、活動、服務等資料。並列出全體會員名單及地址。

1－4 *Annual Review of Information Science of Technology*（ARIST）（Editor：Carlos A. Cuadra，1966－1975，V. 1－10. Martha E. Williams，1976－. V. 11－ ）1966－ v. 1－ Annual.
Cumulative Index to ARIST. Volume 1－7.（1966－1972）1972.
廣泛徹底的綜合及批判評論當年資訊科學技術專門研究之發展趨勢，由世界著名資訊科學家執筆。
ARIST 訂購地址：
Knowledge Industry Publications, Inc.
2 Corparate Park Drive
hte Plains, N. Y. 10604
U. S. A.

1－5 *Proceedings of the ASIS Annual Meeting.* 1963－Annual.
學會年會之會議記錄論文，參加年會者皆可在開會時獲得。由 Knowledge Industry Publications, Inc. 出版者有：
Volume 15（1978）：The Information Age in Perspective
Volume 14（1977）：Information Management in title 1980's
Volume 13（1976）：Information Politics
Volume 12（1975）：Information Revolution
Volume 11（1974）：Information Utilites
Volume 10（1973）：Innovative Developments in Information Systems：Their Benefits and Costs
Volume 9（1972）：A World of Information
Volume 8（1971）：Communication for Decisionmakers
Volume 7（1970）：The Information Conscious Society
Volume 6（1969）：Co-operating Information Societies
Volume 5（1968）：Information Transfer
卷一至卷四則由其他出版機構出版：
Volume 4（1967）：Levels of Interaction Between Man and Information
Volume 3（1966）：Progress in Information Science and Technology
Volume 2（1965）：Proceedings of the 1965 FID Congress
Volume 1（1964）：Parameters of Information Science
（1963）：Automation and Scientific Communication：The ASIS 1963 Annual proceedings.

1－6 *ASIS Newsletter* 1968－1974. Monthly（Formerly：*ADI Newsletter.* 1961－1968）已停刊，免費贈送會員。

2. 非連續性出版品：

該會經常出版各種資訊科學技術學科方面單行本：如 State of the Art Reviews, reprinted (Key) Papers Volumes, Reference Tools (Directories, Indexes, Bibliographies, Surveys); Conference Proceedings 等。同時與他機構合作出版資訊方面書籍等。重要的單

行本如下：

2-1　*H. P. Luhn：Pioneer of Information Science.* Edited by Claire K. Schutz. 1968.

2-2　*Survey of Commercially Available Computer-Readable Bibliographic Data Bases.* Edited by John H. Schneider. 1973.

2-3　*Key Papers in Information Science.* Edited by Arthur W. Elias. 1971.

2-4　*Proceedings of the ASIS Workshop on Computer Composition.* Edited by Robert M. Landau. 1971.

2-5　*Directory of Educational Programs in Information Science, 1971-1972*, Edition with Supplement for 1972-1973.

2-6　*Key Papers on the use of Computer-Based Biliographic Services.* Edited by Stella Keenan. 1973.

2-7　*Cost Reduction for Special Libraries & Information Centers.* Edited by Frank Slater. 1973.

2-8　*Omnibus Copyright Revision-Comparative Analysis of the Issue.* Cambridge Research Institute.

2-9　*Changing Patterns in Information Retrieval：Proceedings of the 10th Annual National Information Retrieval Colloquim.* Edited by Carol Fenichel.

2-10　*Librarians and Online Services.* Pauline Atherton and Roger Christian. 1977.

2-11　*The Electronic Library：Bibliographic Data Bases 1978-1979.* 2nd. Ed. Roger W. Christian.

2-12　*Minicomputers in Libraries, 1979-1980.* Audrey N. Grosch, 1979.

2-13　*Library Networks, 1978-1979.* 3rd. Ed. Susan K. Martin, 1978.

2-14　*Microforms：The Librarians, View, 1978-1979.* 2nd. Ed. Alice Harrison Bahr. 1978.

2-15　*Videotext：The Coming Revolution in Home/Office Information Retrieval.* Edited by Efrem Sigel. 1979. 單行本甚多，不能全部列出，可函 Knowledge Industry Publications, Inc. 提供書單參考。

3. 特種出版品服務項目：

3-1　*Computer-readable Bibliographic Data Bases：A Directory and Data Sourcebook.* Edited by Martha E. Willians. 1976 — With loose-leaf update Sheets.

3-2　*Audio-Cassette Tapes of ASIS Annual Meetings (1972-1978).*

3-3　*Information Science Abstracts* (Editor：Ben-AmiLipetz), 1969 – Bimonthly. Published by Documentation Abstracts, Inc. (Formerly：Documentation Abstracts. 1966-1969).

3-4　*Library and Information Servies for Special Groups.* 與 Science Associates/International, Inc. 23 East 26. St., New York. N. Y. 10010 合作出版。

3-5　*ASIS National Auxiliary Publications Service*（NAPS）. 一九三七年開始成立此全國性輔助出版品資料貯存服務（A Central Depository of Reproduction Service），所謂輔助出版品資料是指一些刊在期刊中文章之附屬資料，如

tables, maps, charts, appendices, bibliographies, experimental details, mathematical derivations, computer printouts, etc.（太長太佔篇幅而無法同文章同時刊在期刊中）這些輔助資料送至 NAPS 寄存備用。讀者可購得影印本或 Microfiche，訂購地址是：

ASIS/NAPS, C/O Microfiche Publications, 440 Park Avenue South, New York, N. Y. 10016.

（三）學會獎狀

學會於每年年會中頒發很多獎狀，得獎人由會員推薦提名的，再由學會適當的審核委員會選決之。獎狀種類很多，有：

1. Award of Merit：始於一九六四年，此獎頒給對資訊科學方面有顯著貢獻的個人，不論國籍，性別等，得獎人有：

1964	Hans Peter Luhn (Posthumously)
1965	Charles P. Bourne
1966	Mortimer Taube (Posthumously)
1967	Robert A. Fairthorne
1968	Carlos A. Cuadra
1969	（缺授）
1970	Cyril W. Cleverdon
1971	Jerrold Orne
1972	Phyllis Richmond
1973	Jesse H. Shera
1974	Manfred Kochen
1975	Eugene Garfield
1976	Laurence B. Heilprin
1977	Allen Kent
1978	Calvin N. Mooers.

2. 最佳資訊科學書籍獎（Best Information Science Book Award）：

1969	Carlos A. Cuadra: Annual, Review of Information Science and Technology, Volume 3
1970	F. Wilfrid Lancaster: Information Retrieval Systems: Characteristics, Testing, and Evaluation
1971	Joseph Becker & Robert M. Hayes: Handbook of Data Processing for Libraries
1972	Robert S. Taylor: The Making of a Library
1973	Michael A. Arbib: The Metaphorical Brain
1974	F. Wilfrid Lancastor and E. G. Fayen: Information Retrieval Online
1975	Gerard Salton: Dynamic Information and Library Processing
1976	Bernard M. Fry and Herbert S. White: Publishers and Libraries: A study of Scholarly and Research Journals
1977	Eugene Garfield: Essays of an Information Scientist, Volumes 1-2
1978	Award to be Given in 1979.

3. 最佳資訊科學論文獎（Best JASIS Paper Award）：
1969　F. Wilfrid Lancaster："MEDLARS: Report on the Evaluation of its Operating Efficiency"（April issue）
1970　Gerard Salton："Automatic Processing of Foreign Language Documents"（May-June. issus）
1971　James E. Rush, R. Salvador, and A. Zamora："Automatic Abstracting and Indexing. II. Production of Indicative Abstracts by Application of Contextual Inference and Syntactic Coherence Criteria"（July – Aug. issue）
1972　Christine Montgomery："Linguistics and Information Science"（May-June. issue）
1973　William S. Cooper："On Selecting a Measure of Retrieval Effectiveness"（March-April issue）
1974　Victor Rosenberg："The Scientific Premises of Information Science"（July-August. issue）
1975　Rowena Weiss Swanson："Performing Evaluation Studies in Information Science"（May-June. issue）
1976　Derek de Solla Price："A General Theory of Bibliometric and Other Cumulative Advantage Processes"（Sept. – October. issue）
1977　Michael F. Lynch："Variety Generation-A Reinterpretation of Shannon's Mathematical Theory of Communication, and its Implications for Information Science"（January issue）
1978　Award to be given in 1979.

4. 傑出之資訊科學非書媒介獎（Outstanding Information Science Non-print Media Award. Known 1969 – 1976 as the Outstanding Information Science Movie Award）
1969　Battelle Memorial Institute：*The COSATI Data Base*（George W. Tressel）
1970　Stanford University：*SPIRES/BALLOTS Report*（D. B. Jones, S. Longstreth, E. B. Baker, and A. B. Veaner）
1971　Battelle Memorial Institute：*Paper Blizzard*（George W. Tressel）
1972　No award given
1973　Hobel-Leiterman Productions, Toronto：*Challenging Men's Supremacy*
1974　American Telephone and Telegraph Company：*Hello, I Need to Tell You Something*
1975　NSF Office of Science Information Service：*Communication Medium in Conference*（Joseph Becker and Joseph Brunon）
1976　NASA Scientific and Technical Information Office：*Access*
1977　Pyramid Films：*The Electronic Rainbow：Television*（Sheldon Renan）
1978　Argonne National Laboratory：*Where Do We Go From Here?* and Oregon Legislative Information System：*Could It Be?*

5. 專門興趣團體或學會分會最佳出版品獎（Best Publication by An ASIS Chapter or Special Interest Group Award）
1969　SIG/Selective Dissemination of Information：*Survey of Current Systems for Selective*

　　　　　Dissmnination of Information（*SDI*）
1970　Chesapeake Bay and Potomac Valley Chapters：*Proceedings of Innovations in Communications Conference*, April 9 & 10, 1970。
1971　SIG/Education for Information Science：*Audiovisional materials in Support of Information Science Curricula*
1972　SIG/Antomated Language Processing：*Newsletter*
1973　SIG/Technology, Information, and Society：Newsletter
1974　Pacific Northwest Chapter：*Points Northwest*（*Newsletter*）
1975－1977　No award given
1978　SIG/Public-Private Interface：*White House Conference in Perspective*：*Where Are the Information Servies*?

6. 特別獎（Special Award）
1954　Atherton Seidell
1968　Isaac Asimov（Distinguishd Service Award）
1978　Hubert H. Humphrey

7. 卓越服務獎（Distinguished Service Award）
1968　Isaac Asimov

8. 最佳美國資訊科學學會學生會員論文獎（Best ASIS Student Member Paper Award）
始於一九七二年每年頒給學生會員論文獎。

（四）其他活動和服務項目
除以上活動及服務項目外，學會另設：
1. 會員保險計劃（ASIS Insurance Program）
包括人壽、意外、殘傷、醫療等保險、會員可自由參加。
2. 會員職業介紹服務（Placement Service）
會員可向學會登記尋找工作或事求人。此名單將在年會和年中會議時展出，供會員求事和機構求才之參考。平時設有電話專線，二十四小時皆可撥號查詢，此專線號碼是：（202－659－8132）。
3. 會員貸款計劃（ASIS Member Loan Program）
學會代爲辦理會員貸款事項，以書信保密方式進行。可貸款額是美金 2600～10000 元之間，僅付少數利息，付還期限是三年到五年間。學會不經手，直接由會員與指定之商業信用機構（Commercial Credit Corpration）交涉。

六、結語
以上簡略介紹美國資訊科學學會之概況，供大家參考。希望借此能激起島內人士之對資訊科學興趣及重視，進而協助支持推動資訊科學方面之研究及發展。

參考書目

1. "ASIS Awards Presentation for 1978". Bulletin of the Ameican Society for Information Science. V. 3. No. 3, pp. 43－46, 1979.

2. *ASIS Handbook of Directory*, *1979 Edition*. ASIS. 1979.

3. "Organization File: American Society for Information Science". Information: News, Sources, Profiles. V. 3. No. 3, pp. 177 – 180, 1971.

4. Schultz, Claire K & Paul L. Garwig "History of the American Documentation Institute-A Sketch". American Documentation. V, 20, No. 2, pp. 152 – 160.

5. Schultz, Claire K, "ASIS: Notes on Its Foundating & Development". Bulletin of the American Society for Information Science. V 2, No. 8, pp. 49 – 51, 1976.

6. Taylor, Robert S. & Harold Borko, American Society for Information Science. In: Lancour, Harold & Allen Kent, Comps. Encyclopedia of Library & Information Science: Volume 1, pp. 303 – 307, 1968.

中美科技資料處理及運用研討會報告。"中央研究院中美科學合作委員會"與"行政院國家科學委員會"科技資料中心編印。1974年。

資料庫與線上檢索服務*

[摘要 Abstract]

This article explores the growth, origins, technological development, and current activities of bibliographic data bases and on-line retrieval services in foreign countries, especially in the United States. Special emphasis is given to the analysis and evaluations of data bases and on-line searching systems, problems and the cost involved in the data bases and on-line retrieval services, the current research and development programs, and its future trends.

前 言

資料庫（Data Bases）很多，種類亦很多。它們發展成長於不同環境中，如銀行界，航空公司，食品市場，學術團體，研究或政府機構等，因而它們的形態是多面的，有書目式的（Bibliographic），非書目式的（Non-bibliographic），圖表式的（Graphic），數據式的（Numeric），全文式的（Full-text），各種混合式的（Mixed）不等。資料庫作業方面一般又可分為分批（Batch）和線上（On-line）作業兩方面。本文所研討的是以書目資料庫（Bibliographic Data Bases）及其線上檢索服務系統（On-line Retrieval Services Systems）為主。這些系統可用來協助科學家，研究人員，行政人員，圖書館員，資訊科學家或資訊檢索者儘速的，精確的以線上作業方式，由貯存在大型電子計算機的多種資料庫（Data Bases/Files）中檢索出所需的資訊。由於臺灣線上檢索系統之建立仍在起步時期。故此文之研討對象是以海外尤其以歐美各國近年來線上檢索服務系統現況，針對其發展趨勢，特性，線上作業問題，目前正在進行之各種研究以及未來發展等方面作詳盡的分析和探討。

定 義

資料庫（Data Base）：可釋為有組織的收集含有書目和或文件相關之機器可讀之記錄資料，此種資料庫亦稱為書目資料庫（Bibliographic Data Bases）。不同角度來看，資料庫可為某特殊企業機構中一些應用系統所用而儲存的一羣作業資料（Operational Data），是資料庫管理系統（Data Base Management System—簡稱 DBMS）中各種資料庫，是"一羣有用而最少重覆之資料單元，於適當之結構狀況下存儲，透過資料管理系統，可提供各種需要資料。"簡言之為"一羣適當存儲而便於選用之管理系統之單元資料。"設計資料庫之目的在於使大量有用資料"利於存儲，便於檢索"。①

線上資訊檢索系統（On-line Information Retrival Systems）：是一系統，使用者透過電

---

* 本文曾發表在《圖書館學與資訊科學》5 卷 1 期（1979 年 4 月），第 79—103 頁。

子計算機，可直接查詢一些機器可讀的書目資料庫中之資訊。

線上檢索服務（On-line Retrival Services）：是由公營或民營的代理商（Vendors）或出版商（Publishers）選擇或租得各種書目資料庫，設計線上資訊檢索系統，以便提供使用者線上查詢之一種服務。

資料庫發展成長階段

六十年代末期以來，機器可讀之資料庫生產甚多，爲什麼？一般資料庫的產生理由不外乎下列三種理由：(1)爲建立電子計算機印刷系統，用以出版期刊，索引，或其他第二手來源資料書本式出版品，原有資料必要轉換成機器可讀的資料庫（Machine-Readable Data Bases）；(2)採用電子計算機排印作業（Computerized Typesetting）；(3)爲了資訊檢索。由此可知資料庫製做可能成爲出版紙本出版品的副產品（By Products），或是主要產品（Direct Products）之一種。近年來，資料庫的增長，無論在數量、學科範圍，及類別方面皆發展得快速驚人，使用者人數亦隨之增多，尤其利用線上資料庫檢索作業以來，發展急速的程度幾乎不能被一般人適應與接受，似乎它突然的出現在我們的面前，有一種壓迫和被迫接受之感！

海外資料庫發展成長階段及在該階段中具有特色之處可暫分爲四階段。以圖示之並分別討論說明如下：

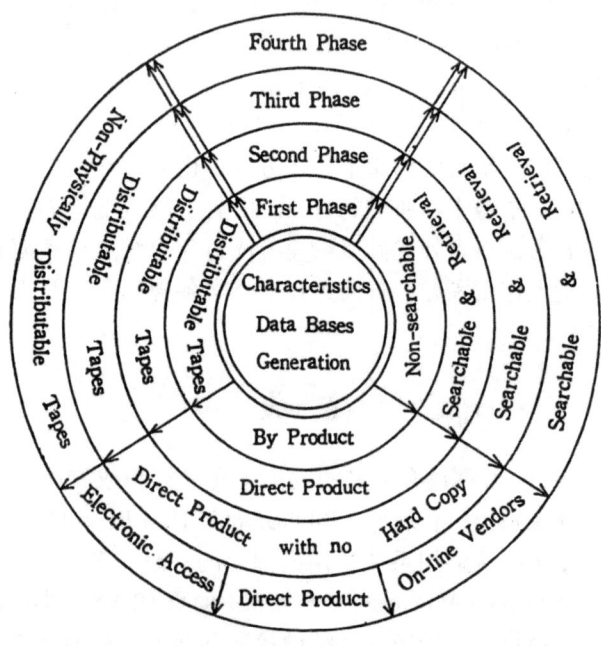

資料庫發展成長階段及其特色圖

第一階段：副產品（By Product）時期。此間製做電子機算機閱讀的資料庫之主要目的在出版一些摘要和索引服務社（Indexing Services）的書本式刊物。將原來出版方式轉換為照相排字印製（Photo Composition）的原因。製出之磁帶不過是附帶的副產品，設計方式非為檢索用的。

第二階段：為主要產品（Direct Product）之一。這些磁帶不再是副產品，與出版書本式刊物和製做磁帶是同樣的重要。而這些磁帶亦可用來查尋和檢索。第一二階段所製之磁帶皆可分銷購得。

第三階段：建立資料庫，是主要銷售性的產品而無相等書本式出版品（Direct product with no hard copy counterparts）。主要重點在製作各種資料庫磁帶銷售。

第四階段：為線上檢索服務代理機構（On-line Venders）和出版代理商（Publishers as Service Venders）提供線上服務階段。使用者可直接（Electronic Access）線上檢索服務代理商提供之各種資料庫資料。資料庫建立為提供線上服務並無實際資料庫磁帶推出銷售的，同時也沒有這種必要，使用者可直接線上使用這些資料庫，非常方便省事，資訊已成為營利商品（Commodety）出售。[2]

由以上資料庫發展成長階段來推測，目前似乎已邁進第四階段之中期，當然這些是針對海外情況而言。實際地來分析，現在正進入一變換過渡時間：是由書本式資訊記錄形態轉換為磁帶形態再轉換為電子形態之混合性變換過渡時期。也許不久的將來，新的技術和更完善的處理大量資訊貯存和檢索方法，資料傳遞費用減低於郵寄價格，資料庫的使用更普及予每一個家庭時，這將象徵著另一新的階段之來臨！

書目資料庫數量和種類

1965年，外界可利用的資訊檢索資料庫尚不到二十種，但1979年的今天，資料庫數量已達到三百多種。根據 Williams 和 Rouse 1976 年出版之 *Computer-Readable/Bibliographic Data Bases—A Directory and Data Sourcebooks* 統計大約已知的有 277 種書目資料庫見表一至表三，[3] 1978 年之統計見表四[4]。

表一　美國和其他國家之資料庫量和資料記錄量（Records）—1976

來源	資料庫數量	資料庫%	資料記錄數量（Records）（以百萬單位計）	資料記錄量%
美　國	160	58	46.3	89
其他國家	117	42	5.7	11
總　計	277	100	52.0	100

表二　資料庫和資料記錄（Records）數量和類別（Subject）

類別（Subject）	資料庫數量	資料庫%	資料記錄量（以百萬單位計）	記錄量%
科學和技術	161	58	25.6	49
醫學和生命科學	28	10	6.6	13
非科學和技術	42	15	4.3	8
科技相關	46	17	15.5	30
總計	277	100	52.0	100

表三　資料庫和資料記錄（Records）線上（On-line）和分批（Batch）作業

作業類別	資料庫數量	資料記錄（以百萬單位計）
線上作業	107	33
分批作業	170	19
總計	277	52

表四　美國和其他國家之資料庫量和資料記錄（Records）數量—1978

來源（Subject）	資料庫數量	資料庫%	資料記錄量（以百萬單位計）	記錄量%
美國	208	57	58	82
其他國家	154	43	13	18
總計	362	100	71	100

表四中23%美國資料庫中資料記錄（Records）來源於美國政府機構，77%來自私營機構。七千一百萬項記錄（Records）中5,200萬之資料記錄可線上檢索（On-line Search）！

另外據 M. E. Williams 1977年預估，1976年約有3,300萬書目項可供線上查尋，1977年將會增至5,000萬，更進一步，她又預測線上檢索數量是：

1974年　　　700,000　　　　　　On-line Searches
1975年　　　1,000,000　　　　　On-line Searches
1976年　　　1,200,000　　　　　On-line Searches
1977年　　　2,000,000　　　　　On-line Searches

這些估計和實際增長情況相當接近。由以上之統計資料分析結論：資料庫學科內容以科技和科學相關的資料為最多，佔總數的75%，資料庫數量之成長每年約20%，線上檢索量每年則以40%之速度增加！（這裏尚不包括分類和編目方面之線上作業量）。[5] 從另一角度由提供線上檢索服務系統來看，Lockheed Dialog System 近年來資料庫數量之增加情況是：

1974 年　　　　18 種資料庫
1976 年　　　　36 種資料庫
1977 年　　　　60 種資料庫
1978 年　　　　75 種資料庫

美國所有資料庫中被檢索使用最多的資料庫是：

① Medline
② ERIC
③ CA Condensates
④ Psychological Abstracts
⑤ BIOSIS Previews
⑥ NTIS
⑦ The Information Bank（The New York Times）
⑨ MARC Files（Machine Readable Catalog of the Library Congress，用在編目分類方面）[6]

總之，資料庫之數量、種類、使用量等將不停地繼續地快速地增加擴大。接受它，使用它是必定之事，更將不能避免的！

資料庫製作者是誰

資料庫製作者（Data Base Producers）很多，其中尤以出版機構爲主，以摘要和索引服務社爲最多。由基本上而言，資料庫製作者可分三大類；一種是以營利（For Profits）爲目的而製作資料庫者，如 Institute for Scientific Information（ISI），Derwent，Data Curier，Predicast 等。這些製作者依正規企業原理投資金錢製作資料庫營利。另一種資料庫製作者純粹是爲了興趣（For Funs）而爲之，他們並不必要製作爲營利，更不受任何法律或職責之約縛一定製作的，如 CAS, BIOSIS 是。再另一種製作者則是爲職責所在（From Duties）而爲。這些資料庫製作者多由政府機構設立的，或是因爲受某些國際立法制定下應盡供應資料庫之責而必製作它，如 MEDLARS, INIS, AGRIS 之資料庫是也。

製作資料庫的費用，無論是哪一類資料庫製作者都面對同樣基本製作費用問題，如發展，市場，人員設備，資料收集及處理等問題。其中以營利爲目的之資料庫製作者所需費用較高。平均一種資料庫一年製作全部費用約在美金三百五十萬左右。[7]

總之，資料庫製作者包括：政府和政府相關的機構、出版界、摘要和索引服務社，資訊工業界、視聽工業界、工商界的專門圖書館等，同時這些資料製作者有的亦可能是資料庫使用者。

使用者與使用機構

誰是資料庫使用者？哪些機構使用這些資料庫？由於資料庫本身發展演變而使用者和使用機構亦時時有所變化。一般來看有兩類資料庫使用者：資訊檢索中間人

（Intermediary），他們是圖書館員、資訊專家、學科專家等，這些中間人是受需要資料者之委託代他們檢索查尋資料庫之資訊。另一類使用者為需要資料者（End users），如科學家、研究人員、行政決策者等真正需要資料的人，直接利用資料庫自己檢索者。但由於種種因素，這些 End users 常委託中間人代為檢索。近年來，資料庫使用者又出現了第三者，可稱之為資訊經紀人（Information-Brokers of Search Service）或機構。他們非資訊需要者，而是為資訊需要者服務，為他們尋找所需資訊答案解決問題。他們常常使用 SDC，DIALOG，NLM 等資料庫查尋資料，是一種營利為目的資訊服務。[7]

早期，美國方面的資料庫製作者多由政府或與政府有合約的機構，故使用資料庫的機構也限與這些機構及其內部工作人員為使用者。後來由於政府機構支持這方面經費減少，同時外界設立資料處理中心和各種資料處理機構，政府資料庫製作者開始供銷資料庫給這些機構使用，民營的資料庫製作者增設，繼而美國和其他國家以電子計算機處理資料已成為一種新興的商業景象，商業性線上檢索服務（Commercially Funded On-line Retrieval Search Services）即時成立如 SDC，DIALOG 等即是。資料庫使用機構由最初的政府和其相關之機構使用，推廣至工業界，研究機構，學術機構，專門和大學圖書館，現已伸延其服務至公共圖書館，將來亦可能遍及每個家庭。

資料庫及檢索方法之分析與評鑑

Williams 將機器可讀之書目資料庫分為四大類：1. 專門學科類（Disciplinary）：如 COMPENDEX, BIOSIS Previews, CACON 等，是以某特殊學科的資料為主的資料庫；2. 以任務為主類（Mission-Oriented）：如美太空總署 NASA 和 ERDA 所製之資料庫；3. 以問題為主類（Problem-Oriented）：如 Pollution Abstracts, TRISNET 等資料庫；4. 綜合一般類（Multi-disciplinary）：如 Institute for Scientific Information 所製之資料庫等。[9] 無論任何一類資料庫，在選擇使用之前後，皆應加以分析（Analysis）與評鑑（Evaluation）。下列類點可為分析與評鑑資料庫及檢索方法之依據而予以判斷之：

（1）資料庫內容是否完整？學科內容範圍方面？資料來源是否涵蓋所有此門學科各種類型出版品之資料？全部採用或部份資料被採用？

（2）資料庫中項目，刊出在第一手資料（如期刊）時，刊出在第二手資料（如摘要，索引等）時，和製成資料庫時中間之時間差距是多少（lapse time）？

（3）資料庫的索引製作方法，代碼應用情況和字彙控制如何？控制或不控制？採用自然語言（Natural Language）？要字（Keywords）？索引的品質（Quality）和一致性（Consistency）？

（4）摘要、摘錄和文件全文是否包括在資料庫中？可供檢索或顯示？

（5）資料庫涵蓋資料內容和印製書本式出版品之內容是否完全相同？

（6）資料庫每年成長率多少？

（7）資料庫資料更新頻率？多久推出新的資料？每週？每兩週？每月一次……？

（8）資料庫本身錯誤率多少？可與書本式相比較之。

（9）使用資料庫，檢索所得結果不但要正確而且可靠性高。

（10）檢索方法應加以評鑑和分析。檢索方法是否容易接受，瞭解和使用？線上檢索時，是否附上線上解說檢索方法，說明如何使用？所用檢索指令（Commands）是否大衆化，易於使用等。

（11）檢索時，查尋點有多少項（Number of Access Points）？哪些項目（Terms in titles, abstracts, extracts, digest, phrases, controlled or uncontrolled index terms, keywords and codes....）可以檢索？皆直接影響檢索結果之回現率（Recall Ratio）和精確性（Precision Ratio）甚大。

（12）檢索時，有哪些查尋特色（Search Features）可利用？哪些 BooleanLogic？AND, OR, NOT？其他 Logic Operator？可用 Weighting？Arithmetic Operators？Left or Right Hand Truncation 性能嗎？這些對檢索結果之精確程度非常重要！

（13）資料庫之價格亦應考慮予以評鑑。[10]

以上僅舉數點作為對資料庫分析和評鑑準則，同時對資料庫檢索系統之檢索方法也一起評鑑分析之。

線上作業及檢索服務之特色與優點

1958 年，第二代電子計算機問世，如 IBM 709，同年 Norbert Wiener UCLA 演講中，預測不久的將來，人與機器（Computer）之間將會很快發展到一種相互受益的聯合（Mutually beneficial association）關係。顯然的說明了發展人與機器間線上直接交互作用系統之可能性。而 J. C. R. Licklider（麻省理工學院教授）又早先強調分享（Time-sharing）及人與機器間線上直接"合作"（Cooperation）之重要性。他早期在麻省理工學院（M. I. T.）開始 Project MAC（Machine-Aided Cognition/Multi-Access Computer）之研究，利用大型第三代計算機 CPU 連接如電視的終端機，用簡單的線上程式語言建立分享（Time-Sharing）制度。Project MAC 是幫助學生們用已貯存的或自己設計的程式解決他們自己數學上問題的實驗，甚爲學生們歡迎使用的。因此後來 Project MAC 方法由麻省理工學院圖書館 M. Kessler 採用而做線上書目系統（On-line Bibliographic System）之研究，亦即是 M. I. T. 的 Project TIP（Technical Information Project）。[11]現線上作業已廣爲大家使用，爲什麼？什麼是線上作業？其特色？線上作業：使用者利用輸入/輸出裝置如電報打字機（Teletype Writer）或陰極射線管（Cathode Ray Tube）或終端機透過通信系統如電話線（用 Acoustic Couplers）與電子計算機互接"交談"，查尋其所貯存各種資料庫中之資訊，各種結果立即由終端機顯示出來，這種線上作業附有下列數種特性：

（一）使用者與電子計算機之聯繫是雙軌的，人與機器間交接（Man/Machine Interaction）作用。

（二）輸入/輸出資料地點（Location）可在不同的任何地方處理。

（三）具有分時（Time-sharing），即時（Real-time），多種程式設計（Multi-programming）及多重處理（Multi-processing）等特性。

線上作業已久，利用在資訊檢索系統方面只不過是 1970 年以後的事。現在使用線上檢索和提供線上檢索服務的系統甚多，在歐美各國尤廣爲大衆所採用，而這方面之發展更是神速，究竟原因何在？採用線上作業和使用線上檢索服務之優點又何在？研究分析結果，重要的因素可歸納下列數點：[12][13]

（一）作業快速而收獲高（Fast and Productive）：利用線上檢索處理一項查尋（One Search Term），快的從始至終所需完成時間約 15～20 秒。同項查尋由人工作業，所需完成時間可能數小時，甚至以數日之久。兩者相較，線上檢索不僅快而且能於短時間內檢索大量的各種資料庫/檔（Multiple Sources）中資料，而且所獲得結果是豐富的。

（二）立即的答覆（Instant Answers）：使用者利用線上檢索不但直接而且立即得到結果，幫助解決疑難。

（三）費用低（Inexpensive）：目前線上檢索 1,000,000 項資料記錄（Records）中資訊所需的費用只不過是美金 10～50 元而已。又根據 1978 年 8 月 *Bulletin of American Society for Information Science* 之報道，108 種線上檢索服務（On-line Retrieval Services）資訊檢索收費由最低 8 美元一小時到 200 美元一小時不等，（這裏所列費用價格不包括電子機租費，接線費等）。歐洲方面私營線上服務平均收費每小時約 80 美元，（包括所有費用）。表面上看來似乎很貴，但分析下來，以其每小時內能檢索資料量來看是太便宜太經濟了。同時，由於採用線上檢索服務，可減少自己機構購買同樣書本式資料的開支。

（四）多面的，活潑的（Versatility）：線上檢索的另一優點是適於處理複雜和深入的問題（Complex Searches），這也是由於所輸入使用資料庫資料本身之內容分析，設計及結構之特性，才便於如此檢索。查尋策略（Search Stratigies）方面可依據初步獲得之結果予以立即修改而再進一步檢索之，問題磋商（Question Negotiation）方便。此外並可用 Logic Operators，如 AND, OR, NOT, ADJ, WITH 等查尋功能，作特殊深入之檢索，解決複雜問題之查尋，並能提高結果之精確度（Degree of Precision）。

（五）提供快速的資訊服務（Speed of Information Services）：利用線上作業，可儘速提供及時新訊通知服務（如 Current Awareness and SDI），並對既往舊資料的查尋（Retrospective Searches）亦可採用線上作業提供快速的服務。

（六）方便的（Convenience）：使用者可在任何有電話線或電源的地點，如辦公室，實驗室等，以終端機差不多隨時可查尋所需資料答案，不必到資訊中心，電腦中心或圖書館去查。

（七）透視性的（Transparent）：線上作業趨向於以使用者爲主（User-oriented）的。對使用者來說，線上作業易於接受瞭解透視整個系統的複雜性和其活動情況，如直接使用某些資料庫，某一代理商（如 SDC, Dialog 等）的某種資料庫，使用者爲誰？Password 是什麼？等等皆一目瞭然的可直接獲得，故線上作業愈是增加其透視特色，亦愈是更趨向於以使用者爲重點！

（八）線上貯存（On-line Store Searched Questions）：有些系統具有線上貯存保留使用者已檢索之問題答案之性能，爲使用者備用參考，再檢索時可不必從頭開始，節省時間與不必要之重覆檢索費用。

（九）線上通訊（News On-line）：可線上提供使用者最新有關檢索服務之消息，如資料庫內容方面之變更，增添新的功能，系統方面有關之改變情況等。

（十）資料統計研究性（Bibliometric Studies）：利用各種線上作業作各種資料統計方面之研究，如期刊統計、期刊學科範圍統計、索引項目統計業，皆可以線上作業方式製出而研究之。

（十一）便於示教（Ease of Demonstration & Training）：採用線上作業以示范教授讀者，圖書館員或圖書館系學生等如何使用線上檢索之方法，易於瞭解而被接受，更便於學習。歐美各國人士已在高中時授電子計算機知識,另一方面由於日常生中對電子計算機已有相當之認識,故接受這種使用方法更爲方便。

(十二) 平民大眾化(Democratic):線上檢索服務是大眾化、平民化!這種資源分享系統,是不重視使用個人,機構中心,圖書館,城市鄉鎮,甚至於國家他們自己擁有的資源的多寡,豐富與否,線上檢索服務是大家皆可共同地、平等地享用的資訊檢索服務。

由線上作業和線上檢索服務之特色及優點,不難看出它之被大眾所歡迎的原因,線上檢索是那麼完善無缺嗎?目前,資料庫在量和種類方面皆在增多,提供線上和分批檢索服務系統亦不斷地增多,雖然線上檢索解決了一些我們的資訊問題,同樣的,也帶來各種問題和困擾,這些將在下面予以分析。

線上檢索服務及其供應情況

前面已列出國際間現有書目資料庫類號大約爲 362 種,而數量似在繼續增多。對任何需要資訊的機構而言,卻無能爲力,根本不可能購得或選擇性購得這大量的資料庫,俾以提供資訊服務給他們的讀者,經費、設備、人員等各方面都是困難的。因此,由新興不久的資訊工業(Information Industry)中產生了一種行業——線上檢索服務(On-line Retrieval Services)——這種服務由出版商(Publishers)或代理商(Vendors)收買租用選擇性資料庫,集中處理設計線上資訊檢索系統,提供線上檢索服務給需要資訊的機構和個人。這種作業方式是以終端機(Terminals),透過電子計算機直接線上查尋系統中各種資料庫中資訊,所得答案顯示在終端機上。並且依照其連接使用時間(Connect time),查尋件數(Searches),書目或頁類印製量(Print Charge)等項目計費。各服務機構收費方式和價格不一,各種資料庫由於製作者有民營公營之別,和來源資料(Source Materials)本身價格等問題而收費相差很多。此外,使用者不同,如學生和研究人員收費不同:使用時間亦影響收費之多少等等。以每小時連線(Connect time)來算,各種資料庫間收費懸殊之差是美金 10 ～ 200 元不等,Print Charge 方面是美金 0.05 ～ 0.50 元/citation,美金 0.12 ～ 3.75 元/page,以上根據由 Bulletin of ASIS 1978 年 8 月之調查統計。近年來之大約收費情況,可見美國主要線上檢索服務收費概略表。[14]

表五　主要美國線上檢索服務[15]

檢索服務名稱	檢索系統	資料庫數量 (1978 年)
National Library of Medicine (NLM)	ELHILL	11
Lockheed Information System	DIALOG	75
System Development Corporation (SDC) Search System	ORBIT	46
Bibliographic Retrieval Services (BRS)	STAIRS	17
The Information Bank	—	1
Battelle Memorial Institute TRISNET (National Network of Transportation Research Information Service)	BASIS	1

(另外尚有 INFORMATICS, MEAD CORP., OCLC 等)

表六　主要美國線上檢索服務收費概略表①②

檢索服務名稱	1975年調查	1976年調查	1977年調查		1978年調查		
			(INFORM)	(ERIC)	Connect hour	*Citation	*Pages
BRS	—	—	$10.24/search	$5.27 – 11.63/search	$10 – 55/hr	—	$0.10 – 0.15/pages
Information Bank	—	$99.32/hr	—	—	$90/hr	0.30/cit	—
Dialog Lockheed Information System	$19.96/search	—	$25.82/search	$7.43 – 13.64/search	$25 – 150/hr	0.15 – 0.50/cit	—
NLM	$7.33/search	—	—	—	$15/hr	—	$0.12/pages
SDC	$25.72/search	$97.949/hr	$25.91/search	$5.84 – 20.47/search	$35 – 200/hr	0.06 – 0.35/cit	—
TRISNET	—	—	—	—	$45/hr	—	$3.75/pages

* Print Charge

目前，世界各國現有線上檢索服務系統很多，國際性特色者約有十五個之多，其中十二個是屬於美國方面的。所謂國際性特色是指這些系統，他們的內容種類，範圍以及服務對象等是國際性的，並且為各國所採用的。

以美國而言，主要的線上檢查服務及其收費情況見上兩表。

其他國家如加拿大的 Canadian On-line Enquiry（CAN/OLE），英國的 British Library Automated Information Services（BLAISE）等皆是主要的線上檢索服務。

歐美各國提供線上檢索服務機構/代理商或出版商各有獨特之處。歐洲國家之線上檢索服務是全部或部份多由政府機構支持下作業，但美國方面則相反，這些服務多由私營商業機構組織而成的。上表中除 NLM 為公營外其他皆為民營的，這也是美國傳統風格，主張自由企業（Free Enterprise）之特色。故他們間要競爭而不能壟斷情況下，對使用者則是有益的。他們不但對使用者的要求非常敏感，重視，而且反應很快。因此必要時時注意改進檢索系統之缺點，增加新的特別服務之項目等，以號召爭取及保留僱主。下列幾點是近年來在這種競爭情況下，而產生的一些重要改進發展及特別服務項目：

（1）服務時間之延長（美國主要檢索服務每天已開放 15 小時以上）
（2）為使用者線上保留已查得之資料（Search Saving）
（3）建立左邊截割（Left-hand Truncation）之能力（除附有 Right-Hand Truncation 外）。
（4）資料庫數量增多（如 Lockheed 1974 年 18 種資料庫，1978 年則增至 75 種）
（5）線上檢索收費價格降低
（6）原始文件訂購服務之提供
（7）提供當天快速線外資料印出服務

這些特別項目，非每種檢索服務皆全有的，僅有約一兩項而已。檢索收費價格方面，收費的目的是為了支付使用電子計算機，磁碟貯存機，和通訊設備之費用，每年資料庫本身的資料量一直是不斷的增加，貯存所需面積和電子計算機處理時間則因之增多，但零件設備方面價格近年來皆無減少，故一般來說檢索價格是保持不變或實際地已稍在降低。

回頭再看對使用者需求問題之重視下，時時改進，設計新程式，並增加更完善的檢索性能等等……使用者之 Feedback 和 System Redevelopment 是繼續的永無停止的。為了力求迎合使用者心理，必需不停的研究，不停的發展改進，這些對提供線上檢索服務界而言，線上檢索服務工作是多彩多姿的，而具有挑戰性和刺激性，同時亦常常是疲於奔命的。[13]

資料庫和線上檢索的一些問題

資料庫增多，使用線上檢索服務者增多，這並不代表解決所有一切資訊需求的問題，同樣的跟隨而來的是因他們而產生的各種不同的問題。這些問題技術方面的較少，而是由於資料庫和線上檢索服務市場之擴展而產生衝擊的結果，這些問題是多方面的，將逐項列出並試尋求可行解決辦法：

1. 資料庫本身問題：資料檔形式（File Format），資料記錄形式（Record Format），代碼（Codes），索引字彙（Indexing Vocabulary）等組成資料庫之要素缺乏標準的規格及統一一致性形式，造成種種形態不同的資料庫，對使用者非常不便，增加使用困擾。雖然已有 American National Standard Institute（ANSI Z39.2 – 1971）訂定 ANSI Standard for Bibliographic Information Exchange on Magnetic Tapes 和 MARC 建議的 Federal Information Processing Standards（FIPS），僅解決部份問題，仍待進一步的研究這方面的問題。

2. 經濟問題：目前趨向利用線上檢索服務和資料庫分享，是否會影響圖書館或資料單位對書本式的出版品訂購之減少？尤其書本式的摘要和索引方面之出版品？一種資料能透過資訊網可供應給很多讀者使用，甚至於全國？

3. 資料庫學科範圍偏差問題：據前面統計，資料庫學科方面75%為科技和科技相關的資料，為求其服務能更大眾化，並擴展至各學科，例如人類日常所需的各科問題方面資料庫：如消費、辯論、法律援助、兒童、娛樂、藥物、保健和社會服務等方面和其他實用方面的資料。

4. 法律上的問題：使用線上檢索者愈多因而擴大其使用範圍，將產生了許多法律上的問題，如資料版權、版稅及進出入口關稅（Copyright, Dataright, Royalties, Export-import Tariff）之考慮。如何計算？如何監督使用情形等？

5. 原始文件獲得問題：使用線上檢索之最大優點是立即能查尋到切題資料的文獻書目。如讀者需要進一步研究，希望立即能獲得原始文件，一般文獻書目僅限於列出文獻刊在某期刊的某年的那一卷那一期那一頁上，並未列出何處存有這種期刊，讀者將無法獲得。能解決這方面的問題的方法很多：

（1）由資料庫製作者貯存所有資料庫中的書目的原始文件，如 ISI, NTIS, ERIC 資料庫已建立這種制度，透過 Lockheed 或 SDC 服務可線上直接訂購原始文件，24 小時內送到。

（2）線上檢索系統中附有相關聯合目錄，供線上查得這些原始文件之所在地以便獲得。如 CAN/OLE 已附有 On-line Union List of Serials。

（3）成立全國期刊等資源中心，具有文件交換貯存中心之功能，提供原始文件服務。

（4）線上 facsimile Transmission，但費用很高。

（5）製作 Full-Text 資料庫以提供 Full-Text Service。目前已有此種資料庫，但限於法律圖書館和法律和立法機構之有關法律方面的資料庫。

6. 外界對此缺乏認識：在美國線上檢索服務已普及很廣，但仍有很多讀者對之不認識尚不知其存在。曾對一少部份（58位）生物科學家調查，84%回答在他們研究方面會用到電子計算機，86%科學家服務單位設有線上書目檢索服務，僅37%科學家利用它做資訊檢索，這都是缺乏宣傳與推廣的原因。

7. 資料庫內容重覆問題：資料庫間之資料內容重複，造成不必要的浪費，應由資料庫製作者商討解決之。

8. 民營與公營機構間之競爭問題：資料庫中的製作可能是公營政府相關機構或民營機構，同樣的線上檢索服務亦如此，但公營機構所提供之服務收費很低或甚至於不予收費，造成民營機構無法與之相競爭。

9. 誰是檢索者（Searcher）問題：誰是最恰當的檢索者？很難回答的問題。根據前面分析結果，判斷使用線上檢索者可能是兩種人：一種是受資料需要者之委託代為檢索資料的中間人（Intermediary），一種是資料需要者本人（End users）。資料中間人可能是圖書館員，資訊專家，或學科專家，而資料需要者是科學家，研究人員，或行政決策者。一般使用線上檢索可依三種形式進行：

（1）圖書館員或資訊中間人，討論瞭解讀者所需之檢索資料條件後，由中間人單獨檢索，將結果提供給讀者。

（2）由讀者和中間人共同合作磋商，同時使用終端機檢索之。

（3）讀者自己使用終端機檢索，隨時要求資訊專家協助之。

美國方面的調查結果，多採用第一種方式，由圖書館員或資訊中間人代為檢索之，而英國方面則偏向採用第二種方式。可能未來趨勢將會是走向第三種方式。[19][20][21]一般需要資料者，委託中間人代為檢索之原因多是：資料庫本身問題，種類多，內容複雜，索引之製作及結構卻不同，對檢索方法不熟悉等，時間上不允許自己去檢索資料種種原因下委託中間人代為查尋。

中間人之職掌是：①為讀者的問題選擇適當的系統和資料庫。②與讀者磋商檢索問題。③為讀者的諮詢或興趣需要建立有效的查尋策略。④檢索資料。⑤可能做查尋結果的評鑑。

由上推測可知，資訊中間人最好應具備的條件是：①受過線上檢索之特殊訓練。②對線上檢索系統功能及各種資料庫內容非常熟悉和瞭解。③對線上系統及資料庫之各種變化情況更是瞭如指掌。④中間人應是資訊專家同時亦是有專門學科的知識以便能作學科方面深入檢索。

總之，檢索方式仍以第二種型式為最恰當。

10. 教育與訓練問題：訓練和教育線上檢索使用者是當前非常重要而迫切的事。為了配合目前線上檢索服務之迅速擴展，不論檢索者是資料檢索中間人或是需要資料的讀者本人，皆急需接受適當的訓練，以便充分利用這些大量的資料庫中資料。據前面統計調查之結果，資料檢索工作多由中間人執行，因此無形中對圖書館學系和圖書館專業人員又多了一項新的職業名稱——資訊傳遞專家（Information Transfer Specialist）。圖書館學系的課程亦為之增添改變，除增設相關課程外，特別的設有線上檢索訓練設備供學生學習。線上檢索訓練和教育方式很多，如：

（1）由圖書館學系增設線上檢索方面之專門正式課程，教育訓練圖書館系學生和訓練外界已工作的圖書館專業人員。1977 年 Harter 曾對美國圖書館學系調查有關線上檢索訓練情況。調查美國圖書館學會認可的 64 所圖書館學系，收到 46 所之回答，其中 42 所圖書館學系提供這方面訓練，調查結果見下表：

表七　美國圖書館學系使用線上服務情況（46所學校）

主要書目服務	學校使用數
Lockheed	35
OCLC	25
MEDLINE	23
SDC	21

最多被使用之資料庫是 ERIC, OCLC, NTIS, MEDLINE, AGRICOLA 平均每位學生每年使用兩小時。[22]

（2）透過 Continuing Education Programs 成立研討會或講習班作短期的訓練。

（3）線上檢索服務機構如 Lockheed 等亦提供訓練。

（4）利用電子計算機輔助教學（Computer-Aided Instruction—CAI）方式訓練使用者。

（5）製作各種檢索手冊，使用者手冊等工具書幫助檢索者學習。

（6）製作各種 Multimedia Package（如 Audiotape, Slides, 或 Digital Display on a Terminal）示範介紹給使用者有關線上檢索是怎麼一回事？

尚有其他訓練方式，不久將會設有更多這種方面的訓練的節目的。[23]

無論那種形式的訓練，內容皆應包括：

（1）各種資料庫之介紹

（2）電子計算機，資料檔和通訊系統之基本概念

（3）重要專門術語之解釋

（4）線上和分批系統之介紹，他們不同處何在？

（5）查尋技巧

（6）檢索磋商和檢索方法

（7）線上檢索，人工檢索和分批檢索之基本理論

（8）線上作業之優缺點

（9）輸出媒體之認識等[24]

11. 收費問題：使用線上檢索查尋資料要收費的，研究人員較習慣這種方式，對一般人甚難接受！尤其公共圖書館之讀者，學生們覺得很有用但無能力付支。不過趨勢亦如此，將不能避免的。但如何收法？收多少很是問題？！

線上檢索問題重重，它發展得奇速，而缺乏週密的計劃，目前已有研究計劃針對這些問題來研究之。

資料庫及線上檢索方面之書目及參考文獻

每年約有 500 篇報導資料庫方面之期刊論文和報告列出。The Bulletin of the American Society for Information Science（ASIS）並設有報導資料庫專欄。1977年美國方面又出版了一種新的期刊 On-line（A Trade Journal），而英國方面也同時出版了 On-line Reviews（England）期刊。此兩種刊物內容以線上資料庫方面之介紹為主，前者偏重於美國方面，

後者則着重於英國及歐洲方面，此外 ACM（Association of Computing Machinery）於 1975 年夏季開始出版 Data Bases 期刊。機構方面如 ASIDIC（Association of Information and Dissemination Centers），EUSIDIC（European Scientific Information Dissemination Centers），NFAIS（National Federation of Abstracting & Indexing Services），ASIS SIG/SDI（1975 年改爲 SIG/CRS，CRS 是 Computerized Retrieval Services，SIG 是 Special Interest Group）和資料庫製作機構等常以簡訊 Newsletters 方式發佈關於資料庫方面之問題。

　　近年來，有關書目資料庫及其設計和管理等方面之論著及參考書籍等也紛紛不斷地問世，重要出版品有：

一、美國方面出版品：

1. American Society for Information Science 出版：

1－1　John. Schneider（ed.）*A Survey of Commercially Available Data Bases*. 1973.

1－2　R. W. Christian. *The Electronic Library: Bibliographic Data Bases 1975－76*.

1－3　R. W. Christian. *The Electronic Library: Bibliographic Data Bases 1978－79*.

1－4　M. E. Williams & E. J. Dunator. *Computer-Readable Bibliographic Data Bases: A Survey & Sourcebook*. 1976.

1－5　*Annual Review of Informatioin Science & Technology*（ARIST）V. 1－ 1966－（V. 1－10. 1966－75 Editor：C. A. Cuadra；V. 11－ 1976－ Editor：M. E. Williams）此評論性的年刊，由 V.9，1974 年開始，對資料庫方面之發展每年皆有專章詳盡的評述並附有相當份量的最新重要資料庫書目文獻。

2. National Federation of Abstracting & Indexing Services（NFAIS）出版：

2－1　Stella Keenan（ed.）*Key Papers on the Use of Computer-Based Bibliographic Services*. 1973.

3. Association of Research Libraries（ARL）出版：

3－1　D. M. Wax. *A Handbook for the Introducion of On-line Bibliographic Search Services into Academic Libraries* Washington D. C.：*ARC*, Office of University Library Management Studies.（Occessional Papers, No. 4）1976.

4. University of Michigan, Ann Arbor 出版：

4－1　A. Kruzar（ed.）*Encyclopedia of Information Systems & Services*. 2nd International edition. 1974；3rd. edition, 1978.

5. Illinois Institute of Technology Research Institute（IITRI）出版：

5－1　M. E. Williams & A. K. Stewart（eds.）*ASIDIC Survey of Information Center Servics*. Chicago, II：IITRI 1972.

6. Association of Infomation & Dissemination Centers, Athens, Georgia 出版：

6－1　M. E. Williams et. al.（eds.）*ASIDIC Survey of Information Centers Using Machine-Readable Data Bases*. 1976.

7. American Library Assoication 出版：

7－1　*ALA Yearbook*.

8. Linnet Books 出版：

8–1　B. Houghton, John Convey. *On-line Information Retrieval*: *An Introductory Manual to Principles and Practice.* 1977.

二、歐洲方面（以英國爲主）出版品：

1. 英國 Aslib 出版：

1–1　J. L. Hall（ed.）*On-line Information Retrieval 1965–1976*: *A Bibliography with a Guide to On-line Data Bases & Systems.*（Aslib Bibliography No. 8）1977.

1–2　J. L. Hall. *On-line Information Retrieval Sourcebook.* 1977.

1–3　J. L. Hall. *On-line Bibliographic Data Bases–1979 Directory.*

1–4　G. Prath & S. Harvey（eds）. *The On-line Age.* 1976.

1–5　G. Prath（ed.）*Data Bases in Europe.* EUSIDIC/Aslib. 1975.

2. Learned Information（Europe）Ltd. London 出版：

2–1　*Proceedings of the 1st. International On-line Information Meeting*: *1977, Dec. 13–15*; London, England. 1977.

其他期刊經常刊出資料庫方面之論文和相關報導者有：

ALA：Journal of Library Automation.

ASIS：Journal of American Society for Information Science.

Bulletin of Anurican Soiuty for Information science

Aslib：Aslib Proceedings.

ACS：Journal of Chemical Information & Computer Science.

FID：FID News Bulletin.

Learned Information：On-line reniews Online, Inc. Onlinc

SLA：Special Libraries.

Documentation Abstracts Inc.：Information Science Abstraccts.

Pergamon Press：Information Processing & Management. [25]

研究與發展趨勢

　　資料庫和線上檢索系統面臨很多問題待以解決處理是不可否認的。目前各界，如學校、研究機構、資訊服務機構等也正在不停地研究和發展解決這方面的各種問題，進而改進與之相關的困難，以求達到盡善盡美之境界。現在已在進行中之研究計劃甚多。尤其美國方面，甚爲政府方面重視而予以相當的經費支援研究尋找問題的答案。如美國科學基金會 Office of Scientific Information Service of the National Science Foundation（OSIS/NSF）。重要特殊資料和線上檢索的研究計劃及當今此方面之發展趨勢列述如下：

　　（1）OSIS/NSF 資助下，發展對各種資料庫的分析，使用和評鑑的方法與技術之研究，研究計劃有：

　　1）EDUCOM（Interuniversity Communication Council）利用 Networking 分享各種資源（如 Hardware, Software, Data Bases, Communication）。

　　2）爲了更容易使用各種資料庫和線上檢索系統，麻省理工學院（Massachusetts Institute of Technology M. I. T.）由 Professon Francis Reintjes 爲研究計劃主持人，正積極研

究發展一種共同使用指令語言便於檢索各種線上系統（A Common Command Language for Accessing Multiple On-line Systems），是一種通用的查詢語言（A Common Query Language），可用以檢索各種資料庫。

3）同時 Reintjes 等另外研究測試為 Congressional Informations Service 國會資訊服務能將來使用 Digital Full-Text Transmission。

4）University of Illinois 由 Martha Williams 主持研究兩項計劃：Data Base Selector 和 Data Base Mapping Model & Search Scheme 之研究。

由於資料庫本身問題很多，如學科範圍，原始資料形態種類，資料檔形式，資料記錄形式，所採用索引字彙等等之不同，對任何使用者而言，直接操作檢索使用諸多不便，而產生困擾。例如檢索某類（Subject）資料，使用哪種資料檔較為適合？很難確定。Data Base Selector 之作用即在解決這方面之問題的 Data Base Selector 允許使用者檢索某類資料時所用之 Query Terms 由 Data Base Selector 助其選擇適當的資料庫及其查尋次序，由終端機印出或顯示所需主題的資料庫之名稱。然後使用 Data Base Mapping Scheme 尋出資料庫的位置，這對使用者幫助甚大。

5）化學摘要服務社 Chemical Abstracts Service（CAS）研究 Chemical Structures Searching 問題。

6）OSIS/NSF 為了減少資料庫製作者間不必要之重覆資料和處理工作，資助並鼓勵他們彼此相關之機構合作協力研究採用標準的，統一的方法來處理資料庫組成內容項目。已在合作研究的有 CAS 和 BIOSIS，及 EI 和 AIP 等。

7）System Development Corporation（SDC）正在研究線上檢索服務之衝擊（Impact）情況。

8）Lockheed Missiles & Space Co. 之 DIALIB Project：透過公共圖書館，一般讀者可試用線上檢索服務，這是一種試驗，其目的是利用這些試用結果，研究分析一般讀者對資料庫及線上作業之反應，能否接受？及其他等等問題。

9）OSIS/NSF 聯合 American National Standard Institute（ANSI）Committee Z29（Library Work，Documentation & Related Publishing Practices）研究資料處理之標準化問題。已訂定 ANSI Z39.2－1971 Standard for Bibliographic Information Exchange on Magnetic Tapes 這種標準僅解決部份資料標準化問題，其他仍待進一步的研究。

（2）Salton G. 仍繼續研究 Automatic Indexing。

（3）University of Pittsburgh 由 Professor S. Tress 進行 Man/Machine Interface 方面之研究。

（4）Battelle Columbus Laboratory 由 D. Penniman 主持從事解決有關線上檢索活動與 Man/Terminal Interactions 間及資料庫詞彙間交互變換（Synonym translation）可能性。

（5）美國 National Commission on Librarics and Information Science（NCLIS）建議之 National Program for Library & Information Services 全國圖書館及資訊服務計劃，對美國全國圖書館及資訊服務做一通盤的計劃其中研討機器可讀資料之重要性，應加強重視之要項，特別強調對資訊網狀分享（Network Resource Sharing）之研究與發展。

（6）書目式資料庫之發展極速，另一種類型之資料庫之發展亦是不可避免的，那即是數據資料庫（Numeric Data Bases/Banks）之產生。工商研究組織尤其需要這種數據式的資料。可能將來另一線上大改革（On-line Revolution）是：讀者需要的是直接回答各種問題之答案而非一些相關的書目式文獻，這種提供檢索的系統，不但包括書目式資料庫和數據式資料檔，更廣泛地涵蓋所有其他各種類型的資料庫，將是一個整體的料庫管理系統（An Integrated Data Bases Management System-DBMS）。[27]

其他仍有更多有意義，特殊的研究計劃正在進行中，這些研究發展不但爲積極地解決當今現有疑難問題，同時預防將來可能產生的問題，同時也解答了一些資訊科學的基本問題。

結 論

線上作業技術始於50年代末期，而線上資訊檢索服務則在60年代末期才起步，但發展極速，這是由於電子計算機驚人儲蓄高速運算功能，傳輸設備和通訊線路之結合運用，自然語言之研究（Natural Language Research）成果，以及龐大的機器可讀之書目資料庫之產生等因素而致。線上資訊檢索服務正進入初期階段，它成長也不過數年左右，這不是一件流行時尚的事，它將會有更多的變化，但由於資訊和資料之"過產"，致使管理者和決策者使用線上檢索成爲當然之事，它將與我們長期在一起的。

分析討論海外的資料庫與線上檢索服務現況，但其影響確是國際性的。回顧在這方面之發展？亦計劃去做，但存在之問題甚多，如"書目本身"，"人員"，以及"觀念"三大關鍵問題，尤其對"資訊"觀念方面認識不夠不重視它，"資訊"是一切決策之基本要素，更難接受"資訊"是"商品"這種想法了！假如我們計劃去做，應參照研究他人的優缺點之處，設計精密的通盤計劃，由政府全力支援下進行。

五年十年以後，海外線上檢索服務將發展至何境地？我們將看到更多的資料庫，更多的系統及新的系統性能將會有更多的使用者，服務時間將更延長，價錢更低，印製更快速，系統更容易使用，將會更努力專心發展資訊檢索技巧，更加強重視研究，人與機器間之交結作用之研究等。對資訊服務者，未來充滿着刺激性，挑戰性的機會待以改進與努力！

附 註

①劉石若．管理資訊系統．臺北市．嘉德圖書公司．1978年．417—418頁。

② Williams, M. E. "On-line Problems-Research Today, Solutions Tomorrow." *Bulletin of American Society for Information Science.* 1977. April, p. 14.

③ Williams, M. E. & Sandra H. Rouse. *Computer-Readable Bibliographic Data Bases—A Directory and Data Sourcebook.* Washington, D. C.：American Society for Information Science, 1976, p. 817

④ Mccarn, David B. "On-line Systems Techniques & Services," In：Williams, M. E. ed. *Annual Review of Information Science & Technology.* Vol. 13 Washington, D. C.：ASIS. 1978, p. 88.

⑤ Ibid., p. 85.

⑥ Ibid., p. 89.

⑦ Collier, H. R. "Long-term Economies of On-line Services and their Relationship to Conventional Publishers Seen from the Data Base Producers, View Point." *Aslib Proceedings.* Jan. 1978, pp. 17–22.

⑧ "The Information Brokers: Can They Succeed?" *Bulletin of Amceican Society for Information Science.* Feb. 1976, pp. 11–20.

⑨ Williams, M. E. "Criteria for Evaluation and Selection of Data Bases and Data Base Services." *Special Libraries*, Dec. 1975, p. 562.

⑩ Ibid., pp. 563–567.

⑪ Becker, Joseph. "A Brief History of On-line Bibliographic Systems." In: Sherrod, J. ed. *Information Systems & Networks.* London: Greenwood Press, 1975, pp. 3–4.

⑫ Atherton, P. & Roger W. Christian. *Librarians & On-line Services.* White Plains, N. Y.: Knowledge Industry Publications. 1977, pp. 3–4.

⑬ Cuadra, Carlos A. "Commercialy Funded On-line Retrieval Services — Past, Present, Future." *Aslib Proceedings.* Jan. 1978, pp. 4–7.

⑭ Williams, M. E. & J. Brandhorst. "Data Bases On-line in 1978." *Bulletion of ASIS.* Aug. 1978, pp. 20–26.

⑮ Mccarn, *op. cit.*, p. 90.

⑯ Williams & Brandhorst, op. *cit.*, pp. 20–26.

⑰ Mccarn, *op. cit.*, pp. 102–104.

⑱ Cuadra, *op. cit.*, pp. 7–11.

⑲ Williams, *op. cit.*, pp. 15–16:

⑳ Mccarn, *op. cit.*, pp. 95–100.

㉑ Matron, B. & Dennis Fife. "On-line Systems Techniques & Services," In: Williams, M. E. ed. *Annual of Information Science & Technology*, Vol. 11. Washington, D. C.: ASIS. 1976, pp. 183–192.

㉒ Mccarn, *op. cit.*, p. 100–102.

㉓ Williams, M. E. "Education and Training for On-line Use of Data Bases." *Journal of Library, Automation.* Dec. 1977, pp. 320–334.

㉔ Marron & Fife, *op. cit.*, pp. 182–185.

㉕ Williams, M. E. "Data Bases—A History of Developments & Trends from 1966 through 1975." *Journal of American Society for Information Science.* Dec. 1975, pp. 561–569.

㉖ Williams, M. E. "The Impact of Machine-Readable Data Bases on Library & Information Services." *Information Processing & Management.* 1977. Vol. 13, p. 103.

㉗ Mccarn, *op. cit.*, pp. 94–95.

參考資料

1. *Annual Review for Information Science and Technology.* v. 1–13. Washington, D. C. ASIS. 1966–1978.

2. Atherton, Pauline and Roger W. Christian. *Librarians and On-line Services.* White

Plains, NY: Knowledge Industry Publications, Inc. 1977, p. 124

3. Brandli, M. J. "Current Awareness Services in Observations of the Past and Present and Implications for the Future." *Special Libraries.* 67 (1): 10–44, Jan. 1976.

4. Collier, H, R. "Long-term Economics of Online Services and Their Relationship to Conventional Publishers Seen from the Data Base Producers' View Point." *Aslib Proceedings.* 30 (1): 16–24, Jan. 1978.

5. Cuadra, Carlos A. "Commercially Funded Online Retrieval Services — Past, Present, Future." *Aslib Proceedings.* 30 (1): 2–15, Jan. 1978.

6. Gardner, J. J. & Wax, David M. "Online Bibliographic Services." *Library Journal.* 15; 101 (16): 1827–1832, Sept. 1976.

7. Holmes, P. L. "The British Library Automated Information Services." *Aslib Proceedings.* 29 (6): 214–220, June. 1977.

8. Hoover, Ryan E. "Patron Appraisal of Computer-Aided Online Bibliographic Retrieval Services." *Journal of Library Automation.* 9 (4): 335–350, Dec. 1976.

9. Kidd, J. S. "Online Bibliographic Services: Selected British Experiences." *College & Research Libraries.* 38 (4): 285–290, July. 1977.

10. Kidd, J. S. "Toward Cost-Effective Producers in Online Bibliographic Searches." *College & Research Libraries.* 38 (2): 153–159, March. 1977.

11. Lancaster, F. W. & Fayen, E. G. *Information Retrieval On-Line.* Los Angeles, CA: Melvalle Publishing Co., 1973. 597p.

12. Marcus, Richard S. "Network Access for the Information Retrieval Application," Panel on Access to Computer Networks, *1975 IEEE Intercon: Conference Record.* April, 1975. 25/4.

13. Marron, B. & Fife, D. "Online Systems Techniques & Services." In: Williams M. E. ed, *Annual Review of Information Science and Technology.* vol. 11. Washington, D. C.: ASIS, 1976: 163–210.

14. Mccarn, David B. "Online Systems-Techniques & Services." In: Williams, M. E. ed. *Annual Review of Information Science and Technology.* vol. 13. Washington, D. C.: ASIS; 1978: 83–124.

15. Nugent, William R. & Knodson, D. R. "A page Image Transmission & Display System for Congressional Information Retrieval." *Proceedings ASIS*, 1978 Annual Meeting. vol. 15. pp. 252–255.

16. Nyren, Karl. "The Online Revelution in Libraries." *Library Journal.* Feb. 1978, 15: 439–441.

17. Smith, S. W. Venn. "Diagramming for Online Searching." *Special Libraries.* 1975 Nov., 67 (11): 410–417.

18. Wilde, Daniel U. "Generation and Use of Machine-readable Data Bases." In: Williams M. E. ed. *Annual Review of Information Science and Technology*, vol. 11. Washington, D. C.: ASIS. 1976: 267–298.

19. Williams M. E. "Criteria for Evaluation and Selection of Data Bases and Data Bases Services." *Special Libraries.* 1975 Dec. , 66：561 – 469.

20. Williams M. E. "Data Bases—A History of Developments and Trends form 1966 Through 1975." *Journal of American Society for Information Science.* 1977, March, 28（2）：71 – 78.

21. Williams M. E. "Data Bases and Online Statistics—1977." *Bulletin of the American Society for Information Science.* Dec. 1977；4（2）：21 – 23.

22. Williams M. E. "Education and Training for Online Use of Data Bases." *Journal of Library Automation.* 1977 Dec. , 10（4）：320 – 334.

23. Williams M. E. "The Impact of Machine-readable Data Bases on Library Information Services." *Information Processing and Management.* 1977, 13：95 – 107.

24. Williams M. E. "Networks for Online Data Bases Access." *Journal of the Society for Information Science.* 1977 Sept. , 28（5）：247 – 243.

25. Williams M. E. "Online Problems Research Today, Solutions Tomorrow." *Bulletin of ASIS.* 1977 April, 3（4）：14 – 16.

26. Williams M. E. Use of Machine-readable Data Bases. In：*Annual Review of Information Science and Technology.* Vol. 9. Carlos A. Cuadra, ed. Washington, D. C. ：ASIS, 1974. 221 – 284.

27. Williams M. E. & Brandhorst, J. "Data Bases Online at LIS, SDC, & BRS." *Bulletin of ASIS.* 1977 June, 3（5）：18 – 24.

28. Williams M. E. & Brandhorst, J. "Data Bases Online in 1978." *Bulletin of ASIS* 1978 Aug. , 4（6）：20 – 26.

29. 張鼎鍾. 資料庫與資訊的利用. "中國圖書館學會"年報. 臺北市. 1978 年. 48—65 頁

30. 劉石若. 管理資訊系統. 嘉德圖書公司. 臺北市. 1978 年. 417—429 頁

31. 電子計算機處理科技資訊參考資料. "國家科學委員會科學技術資料中心". 臺北市. 1978 年. 資訊系統研討會會議實錄

技術報告的分析[*]

一、前言
二、技術報告的獨特性質
三、技術報告的重要性
四、技術報告獲得及採購途徑
五、編目及索引製作檢索問題
六、排列貯存及保留問題
七、縮影本式的技術報告
八、技術報告書目控制及重要工具書
九、重要技術報告貯存機構
十、如何發揮技術報告最大使用價值
十一、結論
十二、附註、參考資料

一、前言

第二次世界大戰使技術報告之發展邁進另一階段——大量生產。技術報告的萌芽時期是在二十世紀初。世界最早的技術報告是英國 1909 年開始發行的 Aeronautical Research Council R & M（Reports & Memoranda）Series'。而美國也於 1915 年開始由 National Advisory Committee for Aeronautics（NACA）出刊各種技術報告叢刊，這些報告內容偏重於航空工程，原子能工程和國防方面之研究。二次大戰中美國政府和其他國家大量投資致力於新工業方面之發展研究，於 1941 年美國政府又成立了 O.S.R.D.（Office of Scentific & Research Development）協助一切。研究結果的報告成為技術上最迅速的通訊之媒體。這些報告記錄研究的進展或最後結果交給補助機構，因安全問題這些報告不能公開發表，只很謹慎地傳遞給其他科學家或官方參考。英德兩國亦同樣地在進行相同的研究計劃。二次大戰後，獲得大量的德日兩國有關的技術報告，經整理後即是所謂的 BIOS（British Intelligence Objectives Sub-Committee），CIOS（Combined Intelligence Objectives Sub-Committee），JIOS（Joint Intelligence Objectives Agency）和 FIAT（Field Intelligence Ageny, Technical）等報告，現存在美國華盛頓軍方機構。（註1）

二次大戰後美國 DOD（Department of Defense）內部擴大，和 Atomic Energy Commission（AEC）和 National Aeronautics & Space Administration（NASA）等機構之成立，產生了更多的技術報告，技術報告增長情況更蔓延至整個科技界。1945 年美國政府成立 Publication Board（PB），其任務是蒐集、處理及分發有關非機密和已撤銷機密的技術報告，後改為 Office of Technical Service（OTS），後又改為 Clearinghouse for Scientific & Technical Information（CFSTI），又於 1970 年再度改為現在的 NTIS（National Technical Information Service），是現在世界最大科技資料機構。此機構用之報告號碼皆給一 PB Number。同時亦成立其他類似機構如 ASTIA（Armed Services of Technical Informatin Agency）是 DDC（DOD 的 Defense Documentation Center）之前身，該處用之報告號碼皆以 AD（ASTIA Document）為代號（其他主要機構將在後面詳細介紹）。

甚麼是技術報告（Technical Report）？技術報告有時亦稱為 Research Report 研究報告。技術報告即是政府、工商和學術研究機構報告其研究的出版品，多為科學和技術方

---

[*] 本文分上、下兩部分發表在《教育資料科學月刊》11 卷第 4 期和 12 卷第 1 期。

面之研究。這些研究和報告多為政府補助的，亦有非政府補助的。技術報告亦可說是記述科學，技術或實驗方面之研究報告包括私人工業機構之對內技術報告（Internal Report）等。

這些技術報告生產機構是分：

（一）政府機構：報告的安全等級在此很重要，一般可分為 Top Secret, Secret（這兩種報告是絕對拿不到的），Classified（機密性）可申請使用，資料可按照研究需要（Need to know）而準予使用。Unclassified（不機密的）和 Declassified（撤銷機密的）任何人皆可以使用。

（二）學術及研究機構：有政府補助的和不補助的。這些報告多是不機密的，多數會在正式期刊中發表，較容易獲得。

（三）工業研究機構：可能政府補助或不補助。有些是工業機構的內部研究報告（Internal Research Reports）資料可分 Confidential（保密的），Not for Publication（不能出版）Restricted（限閱）等，內部研究報告很難拿到。

臺灣地區技術報告的來源情況，技術報告真正的起步是 1959 年以後，政府當時為長期發展科學，於 1959 年訂頒"長期發展科學計劃綱領"，成立"長期發展科學委員會"簡稱（長科會）主持其事（後於 1967 年改為"國家科學委員會"隸屬"行政院"）。當時一面設置研究補助費，研究講座，研究設備費出國進修及設置客座教授辦法等。在研究補助費項下之條件即如美國和其他國家政府補助的條件一樣，即是一定要交寫研究報告。故由 1959 年即開始在每年年終時收集這些研究技術報告，直到現在。每年約 1,000 位左右接受補助的，從 1959 年到 1976 年總共約一萬篇報告，為臺灣技術報告之最大生產單位。（註：2）報告存在"國科會"有關單位，另外收集"國家科學委員會"（National Science Council—NSC）之技術研究報告最全的機構是——"國立政治大學"人文社會資料中心。

以下就技術報告之各種特質重要性採購，編目的排列貯存等分項分析介紹之。

二、技術報告的獨特性質

技術報告因和一般圖書館資料不同，處理及收藏情況亦因之而異，下列說明技術報告的獨特性質：

（一）報告文獻數量很大，根據 1963 年 Weinberg 報告（註3），美國每年出版約 10,000 件，現存在技術報告約有一百萬件，現每年美國技術報告出版品已增至約 60,000 件（註4）。又出版機構和分發機構不同，很易混亂。實際出版份數很少，50～100 本左右。

（二）這些報告的形式及內容不同而龐雜，報告可能由幾頁或數頁也可能是一套幾卷不等，報告內容可能是暫時受時間限制性的或是組織完善內容詳細有永久使用價值的報告等。

（三）報告有安全等級（Security Classification）之分，有的受政治因素之限制分發。不是每個人皆可閱讀使用所有報告。由於報告本身之特性需要保護故分別註明其安全等級機密的（Classified）和非機密性（Unclassified）的；細分為：Top Secret, Secret, Restricted, Confidential, not for Publication, Proprietary 等，如由於研究工作之需要是

"Need to know"，可申請使用 Classified Reports，圖書館員應特別注意處理機密性報告之規則予以適當控制並記錄報告使用之動向。

（四）報告印刷方式不一，多為打字油印非正式印出或散裝本式的尺寸大小不同。現已製成微影形式報告出售多採用微片單卡（Microfiche）亦有縮影片（Microfilm）和微卡（Microcard）等。

（五）報告號碼（Report Number）或稱連續性號碼（Serial Number）這是技術報告另一獨特性，每一報告皆有一號碼，美國圖書館皆稱之為 "Report Series Code"。號碼是由字母和數字組合而成，字母多代表機構名稱或計劃名稱之首字母，例如 AERE – R4932 報告號碼是指英國，Atomic Energy Research Establishment Report Number 4932 而言此簡單獨特的報告號碼對書目控制幫助很大。

下列介紹幾種較著名的 Report Series 報告叢刊（註5）

AD numbers（ASITIA Document number）：此報告號碼由 U. S. Defense Documentation Center）美國國防部 DDC 使用，此機構之前身是 Armed Services Technical Information Agency）

PB numbers（Puhlication Board numbers）：此報告叢刊號碼代表 U. S. National Technical Information Service-NTIS 機構之報告前身是 U. S. Clearinghouse for Federal Sceintific & Technical Information-CFSTI，再以前是 Publication Board

TID numbers（Technical Information Division numbers）：號碼用在 U. S. Atomic Energy Commission 所資助的研究報告該機構已改為 U. S. Energy Research Development Administration 簡稱 ERDA

NP numbers（Non-Proiect number）：非 AEC 資助有合約的而為 AEC 所蒐集的報告號碼 N numbers（NASA number）：美國太空總署合約資助的報告號碼 National Aeronautics & Space Administration-NASA）

RAND numbers（美國 RAND Corporation 報告號碼）

NSTIC }
ACSIL } numbers：美國 Naval Scientific & Technical Information Centre 的報告號碼前身是 Admiralty Centre for Scientific Information & Liaison

這些報告叢刊之字首（Prefixes）很多，詳細資料可由 H. F. Redman & L. E. Godfrey *Dictionary of Report Series Codes*（2nd ed. SLA，（1973 年）（註6）中查出，該字典包括約 22，500 以上報告號碼代號，英國 Atomic Energy Authority 之 Repnor Series 可查 J. Roland Smith，*Guide to UKAEA Decuments*（5th，ed. UKAEA，1973）（註7）

（六）報告編號：一般來說，報告編號可能包含下列數種標記：

(1) 出版機構名稱用機構名稱之首字母或代號

　如　AD：ASTIA Documents（DDC 報告）

　　　AFOSR：Airforce Office of Scientifre Resarch

　　　MIT：Masschusetts Institute of Technology

(2) 出版形式：

　如　TN：Technical Notes

　　　TM：Technical Memoranda

　　　　PR：Progress Report
（3）計劃名稱：
　　如　SHARP：Ships Analysis & Retrieval Program
（4）機密性質：
　　如　C = Classified；S = Secret；unclassified
（5）出版日期：
　　如　5-28-77　1977年5月28日
（6）主題內容：
　　如　LS（Literature Search）；C（Chemistry）

　　（七）技術報告文獻不包括在一般圖書出版商目錄中，一般書店出版商處買不到，必要向特殊政府機構如技術報告資料交換處，或資料中心購買，常常要經過軍方機構購得。出版機構免費贈閱給"合格的人"，非機密性可售的報告賣給一般圖書館及使用者，必須先付款尚能獲得報告。

　　（八）一般書目控制單上不包括技術報告，圖書管員必要熟悉有關可利用的查詢工具書。

　　（九）一般皆無技術報告聯合目錄可參考使用，查詢資料不便，不過可試向 NTIS, L. C., DDC, AEC, NASA 等機構或有關他們的 Depository Libraries 查詢。

　　（十）處理這些報告很不容易，因其出版方式及內容複雜，尺寸大小不一，出版形式有紙本和微卡本 Microfiche 等，報告號碼可能一篇有多個，不同的書名頁作者有或無等等問題致增加處理困難。

　　（十一）另一獨特性是報告內容新穎特殊出版快速，對科技專門圖書館收藏很重要。

　　（十二）技術報告來源是政府機構，工業研究機構和學術研究機構。這些技術報告或是由政府補助或非是政府補助的，而私人機構的技術報告則多是其內部研究報告（Internal Research Reports）更不易獲得。

三、技術報告的重要性

　　二十年前曾有位學者預言："技術報告文獻將會很快地取代科技期刊和學會期刊，而成爲最重要的科技通訊的媒體，特別是有關國防安全的科技方面"。又 Bedsole 亦說（註8）："At one time distribution of technical report was not considered only an interim step preceding publication in the open literatures, but in many fields today, the technical report is the final step. Any scientist or engineer who ignores the report literature does so at his own peril, since in large sigments of R. & D. the technical report is the primary means for written communication, with books and journals being of secondary importance."由此可見技術報告之地位之日趨重要而不可忽視！又因報告在科技文獻方面佔量很大，根據一九六三年匈牙利自然科學及醫學研究工作出版品統計，其中23%爲技術報告，美國科技研究出版品中其中20%爲技術報告。再看 U. S. AEC 出版之 Nuclear Science Abstracts（NSA）約30%之資料爲報告形式（註9），在原子能及太空方面技術報告所佔的百分比更高。

　　近年來專門圖書館和資訊服務單位深深體會到和經驗到，多數科技問題之解答可由技術報告中尋出之答案之百分比相當高，有時甚至於唯有在技術報告中才能得到解答，某些科目依賴技術報告文獻之答案更甚於他種資料,如原子能,太空等方面。一般來說技術報告具有兩點最大特性的是:出版迅速和主題新穎非一般期刊所能相比美的。

根據 U. S. Air Force Office of Scientific Research (AFDSR) 和 NASA 兩機構之推測估計,約 50%～60% AFDSR 和 NASA 出版之機密報告將會在正式期刊中發表的(註10)。但部份技術報告資料,不會在期刊中發表的,理由是:

(一)技術報告數量大,需要報告機構出錢才能在正式期刊中發表(國外著名的期刊由著作者付錢並經過期刊審核合格方予以發表)。

(二)技術報告內容太過新穎和專門性,無適當期刊可刊發,也非為一般人之興趣所在。

(三)很多技術報告零亂未經整理,作者無時間再予以整理發表之。

(四)技術報告寫作方式,不夠正式(Informal)不符合發表期刊論文之標準。

(五)某些資料是機密性或政治性,不宜出版。

(六)某些報告篇幅過長達 50 面以上,一般期刊論文每篇八面左右。

(七)報告缺乏內容或完整性,無發表價值。

(八)有些期刊編輯者拒絕刊登技術報告,認為它已出版被閱讀過,已不再是 Primary Original Article,已減少了利用價值(註11)。

四、技術報告獲得及採購途徑

技術報告之採購與一般圖書和期刊不相同,並無普通一般性的書目工具書可以參考或向書商直接購得那麼容易,因此技術報告的採購是非常複雜和困擾的問題,技術報告採購除公司,工商機構之出版品外,可有下列幾種途徑可行:

(一)與其他機構建立資料交換—這可能是非常重要的報告資料來源。

(二)訂購方式—可向報告資料服務機構訂購,如政府資料交換所或供應處(如 Clearinghouse, Documentation Centers 等如美國之 NTIS,英國 HMSO 即是。

(三)直接向報告生產機構購買或要求按期贈送。

(四)檢查閱看定期出版有關技術報告的 Abstracts, Indexes Announcents 等(如 NASA 的 STAR, AEC 的 NSA, HMSO 的 Daily List 等)選購所需的報告(有關重要的幾種技術報告書目文獻將在後面詳細介紹)。

(五)可向作者本人索取。

(六)如以上途徑皆有問題可向技術報告資料出借服務處(Lending Services)或技術報告的 Deposity Libraries 借閱或影印。

(七)工業研究機構之技術研究報告較不易購得,因這些報告關係到機構內部科學技術研究發展問題,尤其這些營刊為目的工業機構的 Interorel Reports 一般很少公開出版和外借的,不過有的報告仍可能以後會在期刊上出現的。另外大的工業機構亦印出機構報告 Reprint List 來,贈送到人參考如 General Electric Co.,可要求將自己機構名稱列在分發名單上。

下列為 U. S. Air Force Office of Aerospace Research Newsletter, STINFO Report 中列出 Technical Reports 可由下列機構獲得及各機構地址(註12):

1. U. S: Government Printing Office, Washington, D. C. 20402

2. Defense Documentation Center (DDC), Cameron, Station Alexandria, Va 22314

3. Federal Supply Service, Naval Weapons Plant, Washington, D. C. 20407

4. Director Naval Publications and Printing Office, Bidg 4, Section D, 700 Robbin Avenue, Philadelpnia, Pa. 19111

5. Naval Supply Depot, 5801 Tabor Ave., Philadelphia, Pa. 19120

6. Selected Public or University Libraries

7. Scientific and Technical Information Division, Code ATSS, NASA, Washington, D. C. 20546

8. National Technical Information Service, 5285 Port Royal Road, Springfield, Va. 22151

9. USAEC, Division of Technical Information, P. O. Box 62, Oak Ridge, Tenn. 37830 (USAEC, now U. S. Energy Research and Development Administration ERDA)

10. Science Information Exchange (SIE), 1730 M Street NW, Washington, D. C. 22036

五、編目及索引製作檢索問題

（一）編目問題：編目技術報告是很麻煩困難的，由於報告本身所含資料多而複雜，一般圖書館所使用之編目規則很難應用上，因此很多機構為了處理所有大量的技術報告而編製詳細自用的編目規則指南，如（註13, 14, 15, 16）

（A）Standard for descriptive Cataloguing of Government Scientific & Technical Reports, Springfield, Va, Clearinghouse for Federal Scientific & Technical Information, December 1963 PB 181605, vi, 21pp. (AD641092)

（B）Corporate Author Entries Used by th Atomic Energy Commission in Cataloguing Reports. Springfield, Va. CFSTI（現 NTIS）, 1964, TID 5059（6th, ed.）pp. 150

（C）Report Number Series Used by Dept of Technical Information Catalogers, Springfield, Va, CFSTI, Sept 1964, TID 85（4th, rev. ed.）, pp. 143

（D）Descriptive Cataloguing Guide: U. S. Atomic Energy Commission, Springfield, Va., CFSTI, Jan. 1966. TID 4577（rev. 1）. i, 77pp 等。

技術報告書名頁（Title page）上往往會包括各項資料複雜而多，如個人作者（有時作者不詳），報告號碼（可能不祇一個），作者服務單位，出版機構，亦辦單位（可能一個以上），出版日期，安全等級等，使編目者很難確定選擇主要款目（Main Entry）。

依照美國技術報告編目標準之規定，辨識技術報告項目應否有下列款目：

(1) 登錄號（Access no.）

(2) 報告號碼（Report Serial no.）

(3) 團體作者（Corporate Author）

(4) 書名（Title）

(5) 個人作者（Personal Author）

(6) 出版日期（Date of Publication）

(7) 頁數（Pagination）

(8) 合約號碼（Contract or Grant no.）

(9) 獲得出售機構（Availability）

（10）副款目（Added Entry）
（11）安全等級（Security Classification）

由各機構自己決定取捨上列款目為其標準編目款式。一般採用報告號碼/登錄號和安全等級列在報告卡上端，很多圖書館技術報告不予編目，因為有價值的報告將會刊在某些摘要期刊（Abstract Journals）中，故僅為期刊目錄卡編製簡單的報告號碼卡而已。如蒐集量很少可詳細分類如 Instrumentation Laboratory, Inc, Lexington, Mass. 量為三百按 COSATI Subject Category List 編目分類，平均每一報告做七張卡片（註17）。但自己機構出版之報告不論如何皆應予以詳細編目（Full Cataloguing）處理之。

一般技術報告編目皆採用出版機構名稱為主要款目（Main Entry），原因是：

（A）技術報告為集體研究工作而成的結果。

（B）團體機構名稱較個人作者顯著，同一出版團體機構之報告集中一起便於查詢使用。

（C）研究計劃之進行不因研究者之變更而受影響，否則即會造成同一報告而不同作者，編目查詢皆受影響。

（D）報告個人作者姓名有時含機密性，不易公開。

（E）如採用團體作者為 Main Entry，困擾之處是如何取捨那一團體為主要機構和機構層次部屬問題，如 "Great Britain, Ministry of Technology, Radio Research Station"，或 "Radio Research Station, Great Britain"？或 "Pittsburgh University, Mellon Institute" 或 "Mellon Institute"？這些規則可參考 Committee on Scientific & Technical Informatin（COSATI）'s *Standard for Descriptive Cataloguing of Covernment Scientific and Technical Reports*, AD641092, 此書為最詳細的技術報告編目指南。

另一編目問題是選擇書名（Choice of Title），很多報告中含數面書名頁或無書名頁將如何編目。不同形式的書名，如 Memoranda 報告，Final Report 或 Progress Report 之書名等，解決辦法是可將書名倒列，置重要字在前，如 *Metal fatigue in Aluminum Track Rods*, *Final Report on*。

（二）索引製作及檢索：多數圖書館檢索技術報告按報告號碼查尋，但實在需要檢索各類報告內容，故有些機構針對此需要將技術報告內容做成 Subject Index，索引法系統很多如 U. D. C, Uniterm Systemof Coordinate Indexing Alphabetical Subiect Index, Faceted Classification, Punched-Card Indexing, Peek-a-boo Indexing System 等皆已為各機構採用做處理技術報告 Lockheed Missiles & Space Company（LMSC）的 Atomated Self-Service Retrieval System for Science & Technology Report Collection（註18）和美國海軍 U. S. Dept of Navy 的 Scientific Documentation Div, Naval Ships Systems Command 的 SHARP（Ship's Analysis & Retrieval System）（註16），可以 Subject Term 來檢索報告資料，為專門圖書館查詢檢索資料之趨勢。但貯存大量報告的公共圖書館而言，不做 Subject Indexes，多仰賴出版之工具書來查詢技術報告，如 STAR, NSA（Nuclear Sciencce Abstracts 現已改為 ERA）等。

六、排列貯存及保留問題

（一）排列方式：視報告量多寡而決定。如報告量很少則可以小冊子或書來處理，數量很多即要分別排列貯存。特別要考慮到機密性的報告是否與其他非機密性的排列在一起，最好處理的方法是可與其他報告號碼或登錄號相連，但應分開貯存之。

一般排列方式有下列幾種，各有優缺點分別說明之：

（A）按報告號碼排列：優點是一般使用者多習慣以報告號碼找報告，容易查尋，使用方便，不容易混亂，並可很容易地查得同一機構之報告。缺點是換舊淘汰不易，Report Series 間需保留空間備同一叢刊新報告貯存用，很佔空間，無法以類別和作者查得資料。

（B）按圖書館登錄號碼排列：優點是可做緊密排列，節省空間，淘汰容易並可採用 Uuiterm Card System 檢索系統。缺點是無法以報告號碼查得報告，必要做報告號碼見片，登錄號報告，號碼太多易使用者辨識不清。

（C）按分類排列：優點是可以類查尋，缺點是難以找到適當的分類表，一般圖書館所用的分類表皆不能配合此種科技資料分類，編排維持皆不易。並需做報告號碼和登錄號碼見片等很浪費人力物力財力。

（D）按作者名稱排列：優點是可以作者姓名查尋報告，缺點是同一報告常會中途換人，必要做作者見片，亦需做報告號碼等見片。

以上四種排列方式，以採用（A）式者為最多。中山科學研究院處理技術報告方式是先將報告依該館標題分類法分為 22 大類（分類採用 Thesaurus of Engineering and Scientific Terms）做成標題卡片（該館稱技術報告為技術資料），排架方式得依原出版單位的報告編號排列不予另加分類號。如果原出版單位未列編號，則依出版者之國別、機構名稱、縮寫、代號、年份、出版順序等資料編排。（註20）每月由電腦印出每類新編報告及其報告號碼及登錄號，即可很容易而迅速地找到所需報告。

（二）貯存方式：視報告之機密性而定。一般工業機構貯存自己機構內部報告（Internal Reports）是和其他報告分開。這些 Internal Reports 是代表機構重要技術研究發展歷史的記錄，非常重要，對外絕不公開，對內也限於高階層主管參考使用，故採閉架式（Closed Access）。按重要性分三類貯存之（1）Top Security，（2）Documents Containing Information of Vital Importance to the Organisation，（3）Other Reports，機密性報告鎖在檔案櫃內，其他報告採開架式。

（三）保留期限：報告增加長速很佔空間，管理員應注意時常換舊更新及除出不用之報告，這是管理員最難決定的問題。幾點應注意的是：參考實際使用報告之統計記錄，這些被淘汰的報告是否很易在別圖書館或資料單位找到或製成縮影形式？雖然有些報告永遠都用不到，但以何種安全方法來決定將之淘汰應考慮之（註21）。

七、縮影本式的技術報告

由於技術報告貯存空間問題而應考慮使用縮影本（Microcopies）。很多發售出版報告機構已發行縮影本和紙印本兩種形式的報告。如 AEC，NTIS 等。雖可節省空間但亦產生其他問題。一般縮影本分兩種：

（一）不透明縮影本（Micro-opaques，Microcard），尺寸有：

(A) 5 by 3 inches Microcard（一般採用此種）

(B) $8\frac{1}{2}$ by $6\frac{1}{2}$ inches Microlex

（C）9 by 6 inches Microprint
保留縮影片上端部份記錄報告號碼，題目等資料每卡平均可存 36 面資料。
（二）透明縮影單卡 Transparencies，Microfiche 尺吋有：
（A）6 by 4 inches（一般採用此格式爲標準尺吋）
（B）5 by 3 inches
（C）8 by 5 inches
保留上端肉眼可看的部份，記錄辨識報告有關之資料等。一般 6 by 4 inches Microfiche 可存 60 面縮小報告資料。
縮影本優點與缺點之比較：
優點：省錢費用少，容易處理，節省空間 98%，分發寄送容易，採用標準尺吋便於貯存。
缺點：需用機器方可閱讀，一般使用者不喜用，不如印刷本容易翻閱瀏覽。另縮影本需有適當之潮濕度之調節控制的。

八、技術報告書目控制及重要工具書

一般圖書可由 BIP，Whitaker 等工具書上找到資料，但技術報告沒有一般普通工具書可以參考，造成很多不便之處。近年來，由於使用者和資料服務人員深感技術報告之重要性，但由於技術報告索引及摘要製作欠缺完善，再加上技術報告本身獨特的風格，使用者獲得和使用報告之不易，而要求政府予以適當的處理與改善。各國政府方面已開始注重此事而予以改進，故在近年來加強和增加正式的資料交換處和資料中心（Clearinghouse 和 Documentation Centers）之擴大與業務，以期來解決有關技術報告之問題。不但加強這些資料交換處和中心對技術報告之收集貯存處理分發的業務，更特別積極地展開鼓勵研究人員和科學家去利用這些重要的技術資料。

下列爲各國重要的技術報告書目工具參考指南書目，可幫助圖書館員資訊工作人員和科學家們查尋有關新舊技術報告之用：（註 22）

（一）美國方面：

（1）*Government Report Announcement and Index*（GRA）. V. 75, no. 7 –. Washington, National Technical Information Services, April 4. 1975 –. Semimonthly, Annual Cumulation.

刊名變遷：1946—Bibliography of Scientific & Industrial Reports Bibliography of Technical Reports.

1954—U. S. Government Research Reports（USGRR）

1965—U. S. Government Research & Development Reports（USGRDR）

1971—Government Reports Announcement（GRA）; Government Reports Index（GRl）

1975—Government Reports Announcement & Index（GRA）

自一九四六年開始發行，每月十號和廿五號刊出，爲一半月刊。此刊物係美國 NTIS（National Technical Information Service）所出版。NTIS（美國國家科技資料服務中心）是蒐集和發售美國政府資助的研究發展計劃報告的中心。收集內容以美國官方性的研究報告與美國政府有合約關係者的資料爲範圍，如 DOD（Department of Defense），AEC

(Atomic Energy Commission) NASA (National Aeronautics and Space Administration) 和其他政府機構公告之技術報告。在創刊時的內容僅收集第二次大戰時非機密性及撤銷機密性的研究報告，後加收集來自民間與軍事機構有關的技術報告及譯文，後又增加國防與軍方研究之資料，單獨成爲 TAB (Technical Abstract Bulletion)。(GRA) 係美國官方研究文獻的綜合性刊物。此刊物按 COSATI (Committee on Scientific and Technical Information) 學科分類順序排列，學科分十二大類，每大類下又分小類共 178 個小類，見下列分類表：

01. Aeronautics
02. Agriculture
03. Astronomy & Astrophysics
04. Atomspheric Sciences
05. Behavioral & Social Sciences
06. Biological & Medical Sciences
07. Chemistry
08. Earth Sciences & Oceanography
09. Electronics & Electrical Engineering
10. Energy Conversion (Non-Propulsive)
11. Materials
12. Mathematical Sciences
13. Mechanical, Industrial, Civil & Marine Engineering
14. Methods & Equipment
15. Military Sciences
16. Missile Technology
17. Navigation, Communications, Detection & Countermeasures
18. Nuclear Science & Technology
19. Ordance
20. Physics
21. Propulsion a Fuels
22. Space Technology

每篇摘要均刊有書名、團體或個人作者、合約號、登錄號或報告號、出版日期和頁數、紙裝本與微片之售價、主題叙述語 (Descriptor) 識別語 (Identifier)、摘要等資料，介紹內容，簡明扼要。此外，每期有完整的索引，每年彙集一次，包括團體作者索引 (Corporate Author Index)、個人作者索引 (Personal Author Index)、主題索引 (Subject Index)、合約號碼索引 (Contract Number Index) 和報告編號/登錄號索引 (Accession Report Number Index) 五種，查詢檢索方便。

所有報告可向 NTIS 購買，紙裝本或微片皆可，地址是：Customer Services Division, National Technical Information Service, Department of Commerce, 5285 Port Royal Road, Spring field, Va, 22151 U. S. A.

(2) *Scientific & Technical Aerospace Reports* (STAR) V. -. Washington, D. C. National Aeronautics & Space Administration, 1963 -. Semimonthly.

刊名變遷：1958—1963 Technical Publication Announcement (2v.)

自一九六三年開始發行，每月八號和二十三號列出，爲一半月刊，係美國太空總署 National Aeronautics & Space Administration (NASA) 資訊中心蒐集提供的科技文獻摘要，由美國政府出版處 (U. S. Government Printing Office) 印行出版。範圍包括全世界的太空及航空科學與技術的研究發展報告文獻。主要彙集 NASA 所屬機構及其有合約關係者，和美國其他大學研究組織等所出版以研究報告方式提供的資料、論文、譯文、NASA 專利及其他專利等，皆摘錄在內。本刊物內容按標題排列，標題由 NASA 訂爲三十四個大類，見下列分類表：

01 Aerodynamics	18 Materials, Nonmetallic
02 Aircraft	19 Mathematics
03 Auxiliary Systems	20 Meteorology
04 Biosciences	21 Navigation
05 Biotechnology	22 Nuclear Engineering
06 Chemistry	23 Physics, General
07 Communication	24 Physics-Atomic, Molecular, & Nuclear
08 Computers	25 Physics, Plasma
09 Electronic Equipment	26 Physics, Solid State
10 Electronics	27 Propellants
11 Facilities, Research & Support	28 Propulsion Systems
12 Fluid Mechanics	29 Space Radiation
13 Geophysics	30 Space Sciences
14 Instrumentation & Photography	31 Space Vehicles
15 Machine Elements & Processes	32 Structural Mechanics
16 Masers	33 Thermodynamics & Combustion
17 Materials, Metallic	34 General

每一摘要款目皆詳列該文獻重點，列有作者、書名、出版者、出版時間、頁數、價格及購買機構等參考資料。每期有主題（Subject）、個人作者（Personal Author）、團體作者（Corporate Author）、合約號（Contract No.）、登記號（Report Accession Number）及報告號（Accession Report Number）等索引。Accession/Report Number Index 在一九七一年第九卷時停出。由一九七二年第十卷開始，所有摘要按報告登錄號排列。每期有索引，每季有累積索引，並有年刊索引。利用 Annual Index 檢索最爲方便。NASA 又出版了 *The NASA Scientific and Technical Information System*，NASA，Washington，D. C.，20546. 1969. 可用做查詢有關 NASA 科技資訊系統之指南。

（3）*Classified STAR* V, 1 –. 1963 –. Semimonthly.

贈閱給合格的人，內包括40% STAR 內的資料，使用者一定要經過安全調查。

（4）*Index of NACA Technical Publication*，1915 – Sept.，1958. 8v. Washington D. C.，National Advisory Committee for Aeronautics（NACA）1949 – 1959

此爲 NASA 之前身，內容按大類分列文獻名單而無摘要，附有主題類別的字母順序索引和個人作者索引。便於查尋早期 NASA 之技術報告之用。

（5）*International Aerospace Abstracts*（IAA）. New York, American Institute of Aeronautics and Astronautics under Contract with the National Aeronautics and Space Administration，1961 –. Semimonthly.

自一九六一年開始發行，每月一號和十五號定期刊出，爲一半月刊。其範圍包括世界各國有關航空、太空科學及技術的文獻資料，由 Amcrican Institute of Aeronautics & Astronautics（美國航空太空學會）爲 NASA（美國太空總署）就期刊、圖書、會議報告論文等有關航空太空的非研究報告文獻，彙集摘要而成。本刊物分爲摘要和索引兩大部份，其分類排列程序，摘要內容與 STAR 相同，是分三十四類，每期索引部份包括五種索引，並出季和年彙積索引。所出摘要原文可向 Technical Information Service, American Institute of Aeronautics and Astronautics, 750 Third Ave., New York, N.Y. 10017, U.S.A. 詢問購買。

(6) *Nuclear Science Abstracts*（NSA）V. 1 – 33. Washington D. C. Energy Research and Development Administration. （ERDA）1948 – 1976. Semimonthly.

一九七五年二月十五日以前，此刊物發行機構爲 U. S. Atomic Energy Commission（美國原子能委員會）。NSA 雖自一九四八年七月開始發行，但真正的創始是起自 *The Abstracts of Declassified Documents*（(July, 1947 to June 1948) 爲 NSA 的第一卷。本刊物每月出版二次，廣泛蒐集世界各國核子科學技術文獻，資料來自美國原子能委員會（AEC）和與它有合約關係機構之研究報告，以及世界各國政府，民間機構，工業機構，大學及研究單位等各類出版物中，有關核能的文獻報告，彙編摘要而成。所收錄的資料形態有期刊論文技術報告，科技實驗報告、書籍、專論、博士論文、專利、譯文、繼續性出版品等。內容編排以主題排列，共分二十一個大類，每大類下另細分。每一摘要款目包括：摘要號碼（次序號）、報告號碼、書名、作者、出版機構及日期、刊載原文的期刊名稱、卷期年及頁碼、原文頁數及購買處和價格，使用文字的註明及摘要等。每一期有個人及團體作者，主題和報告號碼索引，累積本索引有：Vol. 1 – 4, and 5 – 10, Subject & Authors Index. Vol. 11 – 15 and 16 – 20, Subiect, Personal & Corporate Authors Index; Vol. 1 – 15, 16 – 20, and 21 – 28, Report Number Index. 其中又以 Cumulative Report Number Index 包含年份更廣，檢索快而方便。下列爲本刊物之二十一分類表：

Chemistry.	Physics（Atmospheric）
Controlled Thermonuclear Research.	Physics（Atomic & Molecular）
Engineering.	Physics（Electrofluid & Magnetofluid）
Environmental and Earth Sciences.	Physics（High-Energy）
Instrumentation.	Physics（Low-Temperature）
Isotope and Radiation Source Technology.	Physics（Nuclear）
Life Sciences.	Physics（Radiation & Shielding）
Materials.	Physics（Theoretical）
Nuclear Materials & Waste Management.	Reactor Technology & Regulation
Particle Accelerators.	General & Miscellaneous
Physics（Astrophysics & Cosmology）	

NSA 等於一九七六年六月停刊，另由 ERDA 改出一套 Energy Research Abstracts 简稱 ERA。下面介紹之。

(7) *ERDA Energy Research Abstracts*（ERA）V. 1 –. Washington D. C, Energy Research and Development Administration（ERDA）1976 –. Semimonthly.

刊名變遷：1976 年 1 月 – 2 月（vol. 1, no. 1 – 2）*ERDA Research Abstracts*, Monthly.
　　　　　1976 年 3 月（vol. 1 No. 3）*ERDA Energy Research Abstracts*（ERA）Semimonthly.

自一九七六年一月開始發行，已由月刊改爲半月刊。本刊蒐集的範圍，依美國機構技術報告爲主，以 ERDA 及其國際合作機構產生的研究報告爲限；內容已由核能擴展到非核能方面，凡屬能源有關的文獻，皆採集之。排列方式按類排，其分類表如下：

Coal and Coal Products.	Advanced Automotive Propulsion Systems
Petroleum.	Materials.
Natural Gas.	Chemistry.
Oil Shales & Tar Sands.	Engineering.
Fission Fuels.	Particle Accelerators.
Isotope & Radiation Source Technology.	Instrumentation.
Hydrogen.	Explosions & Explosives.
Other Synthetic & Natural Fuels.	Environmental Sciences, Atmospheric.
Hydro Energy.	Environmental Sciences, Terrestrial.
Solar Energy.	Environmental Sciences, Aguatic.
Geothermal Energy.	Environmental-Social Aspects or
Tidal Power.	Energy Technologies.
Wind Energy.	Biomedical Sciences, Basic Studies.
Electric Power Engineering.	Biomedical Sciences, Applied Studies.
Nuclear Power Plants.	Health & Safety.
Nucler Reactor Technology.	Geosciences.
Energy Storage.	Physics Research.
Energy Management & Policy.	Nuclear Physics.
Energy Conversion.	Controlled Thermonuclear Research.
Energy Conversion.	General & Miscellaneous.
Energy Conservation, Consumption & Utilization.	

NSA 的收錄範圍及資料來源已由核能擴展到非核能方面，範圍較 NSA 及 INIS Atomindex 更廣。其資料來源"核能"部份僅限於美國本國有關核子科學的技術報告。"非核能"部份則提供其他國家與其有合約關係的合作機構所產生的報告文獻。ERA 所收錄的資料形態有：科學技術報告、期刊論文、會議報告及記錄、書籍、專利、論文、專論等。其摘要內容編排方法與檢索方法皆與 NSA 相同。

（8）*Technical Abstract Bulletin*（*TAB*） Vol. 1 – . Washington D. C, U. S. Defense Documentation Center, Defense Supply Agency. 1944 – . Free to Qualified Users. Semimonthly.

刊名變遷：1944—*Technical Information Pilot*
1953—*Title Announcement Bulletin*
1956—*Technical Abstract Bulletin*

此刊物列出與國防有關之資料，只有在這方面研究和有合約的人可閱看。由美國國防部（Dept. of Defense）國防科學技術資料中心（Defense Documentation Center for Scientific & Technical Information（DDC））出版。一九六三年前之名稱是 Armed Services Technical Information Agency（ASTIA）。TAB 發行的報告號碼前皆有字母"AD"，這即是最初為了識別 ASTIA/Documents 而用的。最初機密和非機密報告和 Progress Reports on Going R. & D. Projects 皆包括在 TAB，現僅限於機密資料。內容按二十二大類排列每期並無索引，另外單獨出版 *TAB Indexes* 半月刊，一九五三年開始發行並有年累積索引，合格的讀者可免費收到此索引。

（9）*Selected Rand Abstracts*. Vol. 1 –. Santa Monica, Calif., Rand Corporation. 1963 –. Quarterly.

自一九六三年開始發行，爲一季刊。Rand Corporation 於一九四八年成立，是一獨立非營利科技研究分析的機構，研究有關美國安全和社會福利問題，這些研究有的是美國空軍總部或其他政府機構資助，和或有他自己 Rand Corporation 來資助。免費贈送政府團體，學術研究機構，公共圖書館，和非營利的研究機構。

內容分爲五大類：Science, Technology and Methodology-System Application-Economics & Foreign Affairs Defence Policy & Strategy General & Miscellaneous。Selected Rand Abstracts 是出版 Rand 最新而非機密性產品的最完整的指南。每期分成摘要和索引兩部份，索引部份包括主題和著者索引，摘要部份分四部份——圖書，報告，Rand Memoranda（RM）和論文及譯文。圖書按著者姓名字母順序排列，另三部份皆以出版品的 Serial Number 來排列。

另出版 *Index of Selected Publication of the Rand Corporation*. Volume 1: 1946 – 1962. Santa Monica, Calif., Rand Corporation, 1962 和 "*A Bibliography of Selected Rand Publicaions, June 1963 through 1971*"（1971）。

（10）*Monthly Catalog of United States Government Publications*. Vol. 1 –. 1895 –. GPO. Monthly.

此刊物內亦包括部份技術報告可查尋。

（11）Special Libraries Council of Philadelphia and Vicinity. *Correlation Index: Documenteries and PB Reports*. New York, Special Library Association, 1953.

這是依字母數字順序排列的技術報告號碼對照 PB（Publication Board）報告登錄號碼的索引。利用 PB 號碼可查到早期在 *U. S. Government Research & Development Reports*, *Bibliography of Tchnical Reports*（此刊物現名爲 *Government Report Announcement and Index*）。中的技術報告摘要。

（12）Godfrey, L. E., and H. F. Redman, eds. *Dictionary of Report Series Codes*. 2nd ed. New York, Special Library Association, 1973.

這本字典包括約 22,500 技術報告叢刊號碼，按其首字字母順序排列，可指出叢刊的出版單位。這些技術報告出版單位包括 AEC，DOD 和其有和約的機構，及少部份其他政府機構技術報告號碼。這本字典內容包括三部份：①參考資料，解說許多技術報告號碼之設計使用問題。②技術報告叢刊號碼名單，按號碼第一個字母順序排列及其使用機構名稱。③團體機構有關的技術報告叢刊號碼。例如 Bell Telephone Labs. Inc., N. Y. C.：BTL-（Number），（Letter）。這本書對使用技術報告者而言，是不可缺少的工具書。

（13）U. S. Atomic Energy Commission, Division of Technical Information. *Science Information Available from the Atomic Energy Commission*. Oak Ridge, Tenn., U. S. AEC, 12th. ed. 1971. TID 4550.

這本由美國原子能委員會技術資料組出版有關核能科學技術方面主要資料之介紹參考書，包括圖書、小册子、報告、譯文、參考工具及服務、教育影片及展覽等方面書單及內容。並附有提供服務機構之地址與名稱,這本參考資料書時時更新。

(二) 英國方面:

(1) *NLL Announcement Bulletin*: *A Guide to British Reports*, *Translations and Theses.* Boston Spa, Yorkshire, N. L. L., 1971 – . Vol. 1, No. 1 – . Monthly.

刊名變遷: 1966 – 1970: *British Research and Development Reports.*

本刊包括不僅限於英國技術報告文獻,同時列出英國政府機構,工業機構,學術及研究機構出版的譯文,和英國各大學的博士論文。內容按二十二個大類順序排列,*A – Z* (*Aeronautics ... Space Technology*),Plus "*Miscellaneous*"。並在 *British Research and Development Reports* 出版時蒐集大量美國所有 Clearinghouse for Federal Scientific and Technical Informtion (現 NTIS) Reports,有紙印本和微片本。

(2) *R & D Abstracts*: A Semimonthly bulletin of abstracts of research and development reports issued by the Ministry of Technology Reports Centre (Now Technology Research Centre-TRC) St. Mary Cray, Orpington, Kent, the Centre, [1948?] Vol. 1, No. 1 – . Semimonthly.

每期列出 TRC 新近收到的英國和其他國家的研究發展報告摘要,以科學及技術方面為主。內容按主題大類排列 (1. Aeronautics...8. Earth Sciences & Oceanography...22. Space technology)。

同時又出版 "*R & D Abstracts Selected Editions*", "Aerospace Engineering Edition", "Physics Edition" 等可分別按興趣購買。

此刊物有 "Quarterly Indexes" (Subject Index; Author Index; Corporate Author Index; Report/Accession Number Index; Contract Number Index; Title Index)

(3) *British Intelligence Objectives Sub-Committee. B. I. O. S. Surveys. Reports.* London H. M. Statinsery Office, 1947 – 52. 33V.

根據 B. I. O. S. (British Intelligence Objectives Sub-Committee) C. I. O. S. (Combined Intelligence Objectives Sub-Committee) F. I. A. T. (Field Intelligence Agency, Technical) 和 J. I. O. A. (Joint Intelligence Objective Agency) 報告和其他未出版而現存在 National Lending Library, Boston Spa, England 資料彙編此有關在一九三九──四五年間德國科技方面調查報告。已出版三十五項重要工業方面的調查報告。

(4) *Office of Military Government for Germany. Field Information Agencies Technical, British, French, U. S. F. I. A. T. Review of German Science*, 1939 – 1946. Berlin, the Office, 1947 – 1949. 86v.

六種重要有價值有關德國二次大戰時文獻的指南,內容包括物理、化學、數學、醫學、生物和土壤科學等。

(5) *Report on German and Japanese Industry, Classified List No.* 18. London, H. M. S. O. 1948.

(6) *Report on German and Japanese Industry, Classified List No.* 19. London, H. M. S. O. 1948.

(7) *Report on German and Japanese Industry, Classified List No.* 20. London, H. M. S. O. 1951.

(8) *Report on German and Japanese Industry, Reports on German Engineering Industry*:

B. I. O. S.，*C. I. O. S. & F. I. A. T. Series Published between 1946 and 1949*，London. H. M. S. O. 1954.

以上 3～8 六種文獻工具書爲第二次世界大戰，德、日工業的科技發展報告。

（9） *Smith*，*J. Rolanc ed. Guide to U. K. A. E. A. Documents.* United Kingdom Atomic Energy Authority（U. K. A. . E. A）5th ed. London，H. M. S. O. 1973.

內容包括三部份：1. U. K. A. E. A. Information & Its Availability 2. U. K. A. E. A. Document Series. 3. U. K. A. E. A. Unclassified Bibliographies. 並附有三種附錄和參考資料。此書對查詢有關 U. K. A. E. A. Report Series 特別有用之工具書。

（10）United Kingdom Atomic Energy Authority，*U. K. A. E. A. List of Publications Available to the Public.* Harwell，Atomic Energy Research Establishment（A. E. R. E.）1955 - Monthly，Annual Cumulation.

自一九五五年開始發行，爲一月刊。內容包括報告、譯文、圖書和期刊論文等文獻之通告。

（三）國際方面：

1）*INIS Atomindex*（*INIS A*） Vol. 1—International Atomic Energy Agency（IAEA），Vienna，Austria 1959—Semimonthly.

刊名變遷：1959 - *Atomindex*
　　　　　1970 - *INIS Atomindex*

本刊物是國際原子能總署所編的索引，INIS 是 International Nuclear Information System 之簡稱，性質與 NSA，ERA 相同。收集世界各國有關核能方面的文獻，其資料來源，一九七〇年以前由聯合國會員國提供各國核能方面的文獻彙編而成索引形式出版。當時篇幅甚小，每項款目內容僅用 Descriptors 敍述字而無摘要。摘要另製成微片發售。一九七〇年以後美國原子能委員會予以協助並將有關摘要整理出版，故漸上軌道，現內容已能與 NSA，ERA 相比美。

INIS Atomindex 收錄世界各國語言的核能資料，其摘要以英文刊出。資料形式包括：書籍、研究報告、期刊論文、會議報告、論文、專利、標準、技術報告等。內容排列按主題類排，其分類是：

A00—Physical Science.

B00—Chemistry，Materials & Earth Science.

C00—Life Science.

D00—Isotopes，Isotope & Radiation Applications.

E00—Engineering & Technology.

F00—Other Aspects of Nuclear Energy.

每期附有 Personal Author Index，Corporate Entry Index，Report，Standard & Patent Number Index，Subject Index，Conference Index. 亦出版彙積索引（Cumulative Indexes）

（四）臺灣地區方面（註 23）

（1）"國家科學委員會"年報 1967 年—年刊，"行政院國家科學委員會"出版

刊名變遷：1959 年—"國家長期發展科學委員會"年報
　　　　　1967 年—"國家科學委員會"年報

內容包括會務概況，當年度"國立研究機構"講座教授報告摘要，研究機構研究補助費受補助人研究報告摘要，研究講座及客座教授名單，歷年經費來源及用途分析統計等，並有姓名索引及受補助人研究報告索引等資料。

(2) "行政院國家科學委員會"研究報告目錄 (*Bibliography of Scientific Research Reports Sponsored by National Science Council, Taiwan, 1960 - 1973.*) "行政院"國家科學委員會科學技術資料中心 (Science & Technology Information Center, National Science Council) Taipei. 1974.

本目錄彙編了自1959年至1973年度十四年之由"國家科學委員會"補助的個人研究報告專題，共七千三百零二篇。共分研究報告專題題目及著者索引兩大部份：（一）報告專題目錄部份：按自然科學及數學、工程及應用科學、農學、生物及醫學四大類分類，每大類再按下列順序排列：學科別細分類、著者中英文姓名、次序編號、中文研究報告專題、英文研究報告專題及發表年份等。（二）著者索引部份：爲便於查閱，以著者中文索引，著者西文索引，研究單位名稱及著者服務單位索引四種方式編排。分類表見下列：

一、自然科學及數學
  1. 數學 3. 物理學
  2. 天文學及氣象學 4. 化學
  5. 地質學及地理學 6. 心理學

二、工程及應用科學
  1. 土木工程 6. 機械工程
  2. 水利工程 7. 電子電機工程
  3. 市政及衛生工程 8. 核子工程
  4. 航空工程 9. 化學工程
  5. 礦冶工程及材料科學

三、農學
  1. 農藝學 5. 水產及漁業學
  2. 園藝學 6. 農業化學
  3. 森林學 7. 農業機械學
  4. 畜牧學及獸醫學 8. 農業災害

四、醫學
  1. 植物學 7. 藥學及治療學
  2. 動物學 8. 疾病
  3. 生物學 9. 外科醫學及相關學科
  4. 人類解剖學 10. 婦產科學
  5. 生理學 11. 實驗醫學
  6. 衛生學及公共衛生

(3) 進行中之研究專題報導 (*On-Going Research Projects*) V. 1 - . 1973 - . 雙月刊，每年合訂本，"行政院國家科學委員會"科學及技術資料中心出版，臺北市，南港區，臺灣省。

此刊自 1973 年 10 月創刊，蒐集正在進行中研究計劃資料類似美國 SSIE Smithsonian Science Information Exchange）機構之作業，分數理及自然科學，工程及應用科學，生物及醫農科學三大類分別雙月刊出。每一大類再細分，以類按姓筆劃排列，並編年份類別順序號，每一款目包括：研究人姓名、服務機構名稱、計劃名稱、補助機構名稱及期限和摘要等。每年並分別列出不定期 List of Titles 不附摘要。另每年刊出年合訂本，已刊行 64～65 年之合訂本。每年約蒐集一千項研究計劃資料，對象包括政府機構，學術及研究機構，工商業研究機構，其研究計劃有政府補助或其他機構補助或無任何補助的不等，其中 85% 爲"國家科學委員會"補助的計劃，近年來由於"國家科學委員會"補助研究費規定變更，故現收到之進行中之研究專題計劃"中國科學委員會"補助的只佔 60%。其中以農業及生物醫學方面研究計劃較多。每年出版合訂本，分類表見下列：

　　一、數理及自然科學
　　　　數學　　　　　　　　　地理學及地質學
　　　　物理學　　　　　　　　心理學
　　　　化學　　　　　　　　　大氣科學
　　二、工程及應用科學
　　　　土木工程　　　　　　　材料科學
　　　　水利工程　　　　　　　電機及電子工程
　　　　市政及衛生工程　　　　電子計算機
　　　　交通工程　　　　　　　核子工程
　　　　航空及太空工程　　　　化學工程
　　　　礦冶工程　　　　　　　食品學
　　　　機械工程　　　　　　　管理科學
　　三、生物及醫農科學
　　　　生物學　　　　　　　　婦科及產科醫學
　　　　生物化學　　　　　　　小兒科醫學
　　　　生理學　　　　　　　　牙科醫學
　　　　細菌學　　　　　　　　皮膚科醫學
　　　　公共衛生學　　　　　　藥學及治療學
　　　　中國醫學　　　　　　　農藝學
　　　　病理學　　　　　　　　園藝學
　　　　內科醫學　　　　　　　森林學
　　　　外科醫學　　　　　　　畜牧學
　　　　眼科醫學　　　　　　　水產及漁獵
　　　　耳鼻喉科醫學

　　(4) *N. S. C. Abstracts.* （中英文版分開出版）1971 - 75, 1975 - 76. The Science & Technology Information Center, "National Science Council", 1976, 1977.

　　此摘要以"行政院國家科學委員會"補助的研究報告爲主，已出英文版二本：一九七一～七五年約一千篇以上；一九七五年～七六年約四百篇。內容按三大類排列：（一）自然科學及數學，（二）生物及醫農科學，（三）工程及應用科學，然後再細分。並附有作者索引,篇名索引及主題索引等便於查詢。同時亦出版中文版兩本,此摘要名稱爲:"行政院國家科學委員會"專題研究摘要,與英文版內容編排皆相同。

(5) 臺灣省各研究機構個人專題研究計劃索引 (*Index of the Individual Research Programs of the Research Institutes in Taiwan*) 1964 - ."中央研究院中美科學合作委員會"工作計劃小組出版。年刊蒐集各研究機構個人專題研究計劃資料,按類彙編成索引,每類下按著者英文姓氏字母排列、篇名、編號等以中英文對照方式編排,後附有機關縮寫表。與"國家科學委員會"出版之 *Bibliography* 部份重復。此索引除包括理、工、農、醫科、專題研究外,亦蒐有人文社會科學方面之研究計劃。

(6) 中文報章雜誌科學論文索引 (*Index to Selected Science & Technical Articles in Chinese Periodicals*) V.1 -. 1968 -. 臺北市 臺灣省"行政院國家科學技術資料中心出版"年刊。

V.1 第一輯 (1962 - 1967) 1968 年出版
V.2 第二輯 (1968 - 1969) 1970 年出版 ⎫
V.3 第三輯 (1969 - 1971) 1972 年出版 ⎬ 二年一版
V.4 第四輯 (1972 - 1973) 1974 年出版 ⎭
V.5 第五輯 (1974 - 1975) 1975 年出版 ⎫ 年刊
V.6 第六輯 (1976 - 1977) 1976 年出版 ⎭

最初每二年一版,由 v.5. 第五輯改爲年刊,蒐集重要科學研究報告、期刊論文、譯文等資料,以索引方式刊列。內容按自然科學和應用科學二大類分類排列,每類再細分,分類表參考《中國圖書分類法》,*Dewey Decimal Classification* 和《日本科學技術文獻速報分類表》而定,後附有中英文著譯者索引及期刊一覽表。可在此索引查到部份臺灣各政府學術研究及工業界之技術報告。

九、重要的技術報告收藏機構

由於技術報告的重要性,各國政府成立或加強技術報告之收藏機構,以解決技術報告之收集、分發和服務等問題,以下分別介紹美、英、臺灣地區重要的技術報告收藏機構。(註24)

美國方面:

(一) *National Technical Information Service* (*NTIS*) - NTIS 成立於 1970 年,其名稱變遷是:1954 年稱 Office of Technical Service (OTS), 1965 年稱 Clearinghouse for Federal Scientific Information (CFSTI), 附屬於美國經濟部。NTIS 之成立目的是做對商業部和政府機構之技術資訊活動連繫工作。它收集通告和傳播技術報告,這些報告由聯邦政府資助約 150 個單位之研究工作結果。目前 NTIS 已成爲世上最大的科技資料中心之一。

NTIS 它收集了來自 DDC, NASA, ERDA 以及其他與政府有合約關係的技術報告。其主要的工作有:

1. 通告服務 (Announcement Services):因此它擁有一些重要期刊如:

(1) Government Reports Announcements & Index (GRA & Index) 半月刊

(2) FAST Announcement Services 分 57 類,報導各種新資訊

(3) Government Reports Topical Announcement (GRTA) 半月刊,分 36 類可按類選購

（4）SCIM（Selected Categories in Microfiche）：可按學科選購，每月2次發行

（5）Weekly Government Abstracts（WGA）將最新收到之技術報告做成摘要以通訊方式出版分26大類可按類購買

2. NTIS Search：電腦化檢索系統

NTIS蒐集有關商業，科學技術方面的報告與資料，資料範圍已分為321類，採用電子計算機search約50,000篇報告。

3. 商務部資料服務

（二）*U. S. Atomic Energt, Commission*：美國原子能委員會成立於1946年，1974改為ERDA Energy Research & Development Administration和Nuclear Regulatory Commission收集海內外核子物理，材料科學，同位表等資料，與之合約與否皆收集，改ERDA後，服務範圍由核能擴充到非核能之資料。最主要的刊物為Nuclear Science Abstracts（NSA）和ERDA Energy Research Abstracts（ERA）半月刊。

（三）*U. S. National Aeronautics & Space Administration*（NASA）：蒐集美國航空及太空總署所產生的研究報告等技術資料，將書目及索引資料用電子計算機儲存起來，設置一系統稱NASA/RECON，便於查詢其主要刊物是Scientific & Technical Aerospace Reports（STAR）半月刊，內容以世界有關航空及太空方面之資料。

（四）*Defense Documentation Center. Dept. of Defense*（DDC）、主管國防部之科學及工程兩方面技術報告文獻收藏管理公佈，檢索及供應工作。刊物有Tehnical Abstracts Bulletin（TAB）多為機密資料，該中心服務對象，軍中約1,800單位，450個聯邦機構以及2,000個登記在案的教育、工業單位。技術資料已採用電腦作業。DDC前身稱Armed Services Technical Information Agency（ASTIA）。所有DDC出版之報告，皆採用AD Number。

（五）Smithsonian Science Information Exchange-SSIE或SIE

史密斯松氏科學資料交換處，簡稱SSIE或SIE。如於1948年，其主要目的是收集各地政府補助（80%）或私人機構20%正在進行中研究專題（On-Going Research Projects）方面之資料，並不斷加入最新資料以供外界查詢，並可避免不必要之重覆研究，以節省人力物力。SSIE（1949-1967 Total Master File）資料數據為50萬件，每年增加85,000～100,000件。資料內容包括：研究名稱，研究主持人姓名，地址、服務機構、補助機構名稱及其代號、補助期限等項目。有關資料可用電子計算機查詢。該處發行SSIE Newsletter內容包括Subject Areas, Most Popular Subject Areas NTIS或NTI Search之有關資料和N. R. P.（Notice of Research Project）等。此處為查詢以往和現在正在進行之研究計劃之機構。

英國方面：

（一）National Lending Library for Science & Technology（NLL）。

蒐集英國Research Reports, American AD & PB Series及其他國家科技研究發表報告，皆為"Unclassified"報告，亦蒐集NASA方面資料。NLL有完整的BIOS, CIOS, FIAT, and JIOA Report Series. NLL重要刊物British Research & Development Reports 1966-V. 1-月刊。

（二）Her Majesty Stationery's Office（HMSO）。

如美國NTIS和GPO一樣的情況，所有政府出版報告皆由HMSO出售。

蒐集有世界最早的報告叢刊 Aeronautical Research Council Reports & Memoranda Series（1909 年開始）重要刊物有：
Monthly List of Government Publications
Monthly BLLD Announment Bulletin—A Current Awareness Service.
（三）*Department of Industry Technology Reports Centre*（*TRC*）
包括 80% 政府資助合約的 R & D 報告，重要刊物有
a）R & D Abstracts Twice Monthly
b）Techlink—A Fast Anoncement Service 分 52 類。
（四）*U. K. Atomic Energy Authority*（*U. K. A. E. A*），*Ministry of Defense.* 最著名的是 AERE Collection 約十萬以上。蒐集英國及世界各國有關原子能方面技術報告，特別是與化學物理和冶金方面。
a）List of Publication Available to Public Monthly Publication。
（五）*Technical Information & Library Services*（*TIL*），Ministry of Aviation. 蒐集 U. K R & D Reports，美國 STAR，AD Series，AGARD Reports（Advisory Group for Aerospace Research & Development of NATO）等。

臺灣方面：
海外技術報告：
（一）中山科學研究院：蒐集美國 STAR，DOD，NTIS，AEC（ERA）等 Reports，現有 80,000 件。
（二）"國立清華大學"圖書館：是 U. S. AEC Depositary Library 存有關核工技術報告資料，如 NSA（ERA）
（三）"國家科學委員會"存有"國科會"補助之研究所有報告，但分散存在有關單位。
（四）"國立政治大學"人文社會科學資料中心：蒐集全部"國科會"補助之報告。
（五）"中央圖書館"和"國科報資料中心"存有少數報告，但有關其他機構之報告以"國家科學委員"科學技術資料中心最多。

十、如何發揮技術報告最大的使用價值

對許多專門圖書館來說，技術報告是很有價值而有用的資料。蒐集報告固然重要，如何積極地讓使用者知道使用是更為重要的。如何能發揮技術報告最大的使用價值呢？！有幾種方法可予以考慮，儘量介紹技術報告給使用者，尤其新的研究人員或研究生。當新的報告到來，立刻使使用者知道。是否應如新書和期刊一樣的陳列或做通告？！（臺灣中山科學研究院圖書館亦做到，每月到約 2,000 件，該館現有 80,000 件技術報告）。一般圖書館限於人力物力無法做通告的，可建立"Users Profiles"，可做 Selective Dissemination of Reports（SDR）之服務，美國政府為了使"技術報告"能充分利用，積極地鼓勵科學家，研究人員多多利用，特於 1962 年在美國各地共設有 12 個區域性的"技術報告中心"，各中心包括 NASA，DOD，AEC，ONR（Office of Naval Research）和其他很多機構之技術報告，這十二個"技術報告中心"地址如下：（註 25）

U. S. Federal System of Regional Technical Report Centers
Location of Centers and the Area Served by Each

1. Atlanta, Ga., Georgia Institute of Technology (Serving Alabama, Florida, Georgia, Mississippi, South Carolina, and Tennessee.)

2. Cambridge, Mass., Massachusetts Institute of Technology (Serving Maine, Massachusetts, Rhode Island, and Vermont.).

3. Chicago, Ill., John Crerar Library (serving Illinois, Indiana, Michigan, Minnesota, and Wisconsin.).

4. Dallas, Tex., Southern Methodist University (serving Louisiana, Oklahoma, and Texas.).

5. Boulder, Colo., University of Colorado (serving Colorado, New Mexico, North Dakota, South Dakota, Utah, and Wyoming).

6. Kansas City, Mo., Linda Hall Library (serving Arkansas, Lowa, Kansas, Missouri, and Nebraska.).

7. Los Angeles, Calif., University of California (Los Angeles Campus) (serving Arizona and Southern California.).

8. New York, N.Y., Columbia University (serving Connecticut, New Jersey, and New York.).

9. Pittsburgh, Pa., Carnegie Library of Pittsburgh (serving Kentucky, Ohio, Pennsylvania, and West Virginia.).

10. San Francisco, Calif., University of California (Berkeley campus) (serving Hawaii, Nevada, and Northern California.).

11. Seattle, Wash., University of Washington D. C. (serving Alaska, Idaho, Montana, Oregon, and Washington, D. C.).

12. Washington, D. C., Library of Congress (serving Delaware, District of Columbia, Maryland, North Carolina, and Virginia.).

在歐洲爲了鼓勵使用技術報告而建立特種資料庫和資訊中心，如使用德國 Darmstadt 城之 ESRO (European Space Research Organization) Computer 做 Space Documentation Service 之服務，其包括 NASA 和 European Space Programmes 之技術研究資料，可用 Remote Access, Terminals 接 ESRO Computer 以便查詢（註26）

臺灣地區近年來亦開始漸對技術報告注意，亦在開始整理分散的報告集中處理之，以備大家使用參考。

十一、結論

技術報告，這種技術資料很多人對之很是陌生，甚至於不知道它的存在。雖它本身甚爲特殊，有很多問題如經指點解釋一切問題將會迎刃而解了，故在此簡單分析介紹給大家認識技術報告是什麼和它有關之文獻工具書。特別是對正在就讀於各大專院校教育資料科學系和圖書館系的同學們，希望你們能進而有興趣再深入探討它研究它，瞭解此種資料之重要性，以備將來在圖書館或資料單位服務時參考之用。

十二、附註

1. Malinowshy, H. R. Science & Engineering Literature: A Guide to Reference Sources. 2d. Ed. Littleton, Colo.: Libraries Unlimited, Inc., 1976. p. 368

2. Science Development in Taiwan. N. S. C. 1972.

3. Weinberg, A. M. Science, Government, & Information. The White House, Jan. 10, 1963.

4. Matarazzo, James M. Library Problems in Science & Technology, New York: Bowker, 1971. 99–102.

5. Hall, J. L. "Technical Report Literature" W. E. Batten, Handbook of Special Librarianship & Information Work (Aslib, 4th.: ed. 1975) 102–123.

6. Redman, H. F. & L. E. Goelfrey, Dictionary of Report Series Codes, New York: SLA, 1973.

7. Smith J. R. Guide to UKAEA Documents, 5th ed. London: UKAEA, 1973.

8. Bedsole, D. T. "Technical Reports". In Isabel H. Jackson, ed. Acquisition of Special Meterials, San Francisco: SLA, 1966. p. 73.

9. Schneider, J. H. et al. ed. Survey of Commercially Available Computer in Readable Bibliographic Data Bases, Washington: ASIS. 1973. p. 111.

10. Herner, M. and Herner, S. Unesco Bulletin for Libraries. 13: 191 (Aug.–Sept. 1959).

11. Grogen, D. Science & Technology: An Introduction to the Literature. 3rd. ed. Hamden, Conn: Linnet, 1976.

12. U. S. Air Force Office of Aerospace Research Newsletter. STINFO Report.

13. Standard for Descriptive Cataloging of Government Scientific & Technical Reports, Springfield, V. A. CFSTI, Dec. 1963. PB 181605, Vi, 21pp. (AD 641092)

14. Corporate Auther Entries Used by the AEC in Cataloging Reports, Springfield, VA. CFSTI, 1964. TID5059 (6th ed.) pp. 150

15. Report Number Series Used by Dept. of Technical Information Catalogers, Springfield, VA. CFSTI, 1964. TID 85.

16. Descriptive Cataloging Guide: U. S. AEC, Springfield, VA. CFSTI. Jan. 1966 TID 4577.

17. Kates, J. R. "Cataloging Government Technical Reports" Special Libraries 65: 121–23 (Mar., 1974).

18. Drew, D. L. An On-line Technical Library Reference Retrieval System. American Documentation 17: 3–7 (Jan., 1966)

19. Smith, R. C. "SHARP: Experiences Library Automation". Special Libraries 65: 61–5 (Feb., 1974).

20. 陳炳昭：中山科學研究簡介。"中國圖書館學會"年報25期62年17–19

21. Wilson, C. W. J. Obsolescence of Report Literature Aslib Proceedings, Vol. 16,

No. 6. 1964; pp. 200 – 201.

22. Walford, A. J. Ed. Guide to Reference Materials; V. 1, Science & Technology 3rd. ed. The Library Association, 1973.

23. "行政院國家科學委員會"簡介及所屬科學技術資料中心出版品簡介

24. Houghton, B. Technical Information Sources. 2nd. ed. Hamden, Conn; Linnet, 1972; p. 119

25. "Federal System of 12 Centers to Collect Technical Reports", Library Journal. 87; 1870 (May 15, 1962).

26. Grogen, D. Science & Technology; An Introduction to the Literature. 2nd. ed. Hamden, Conn; Linnet. 1973; pp. 183 – 184.

參考資料

1. Boylan, Nancy "Technical Reports; Identification & Acquisition". RQ 10; 18 – 21 (Fall, 1970).

2. English, E. W. "Hits & Misses". Special Libraries 66; 237; 40 (May/June, 1975)

3. Ford, Stephen. The Acquisition of Library Materials, Chicago; ALA, 1973, p. 237.

4. Grogen, D. Science & Technology; An Introduction to the Literature. 3d. ed. Hamden, Conn; Linnet, 1976. p. 343.

5. Hanson, C. W. Introduction to Science Information Work. London; Aslib, 1971. p. 199.

6. Houghton, B. Technical Information Sources. 2d. ed. Handen, Conn; Linnet, 1972. p. 119.

7. Kaiser, F. E. ed. Handling Special Materials in Libraries. New York; SLA. 1974. p. 164.

8. Kates, J. R. "Cataloging Government Technical Reports". Special Libraries 65; 121 – 23 (Mar. 1974).

9. Leonar. J. C. "Report Literature & Source of Information" Special Libraries 59; 84 – 85 (Feb. 1968).

10. Malinowsky, H. R. Science & Technology Literature; A Guide to Reference Sources. 3d. ed. Littleton, Colo. ; Libraries Unlimited, Inc. , 1976, p. 368.

11. Miles, H. W. & J. L. Sweeney. "Diaog With Defense Documentation Center" Special Libraries 67; 498 – 503 (Nov. , 1976).

12. Owen, D. B. & M. M. Hanchery. Abstracts & Indexes in Science & Technology, A Descriptive Guide. Metuchen, N. J. ; Scarecrow. 1974. p. 154.

13. Scbemeckeier, L. F. R. B. Eastin. Government Publications & Their Use. 2d. ed. Washington, D. C. ; The Brookings Institution. 1969. p. 502.

14. Strauss, L. J. & et al. Scientific & Technical Libraries; The Organizations & Administration. 2d. ed. New York; Becker & Hayes. 1972. p. 450.

15. Smith, R. C. "SHARP: Experience in Library Automation". Special Libraries. 65: 61–65 (Feb. 1974).

16. 中美科技資料處理及運用研討會報告. "中央研究院中美科學合作委員會"工作計劃小組及"行政院國家科學委員會"科學技術資料中心編印. 1974年出版.

資訊科學課程：四年來發展報告[*]

[摘要 Abstract]

　　本文為第二次資訊科學課程的調查研究。以此次 1972 年調查與 1968 年第一次資訊科學課程的調查相互比較，當可觀察出資訊科學教育系統之發展趨勢。由於此次調查研究，係請求各學校就三種不同的教育階段（學士，碩士，博士）的資訊科學教學課程提供資料，並各加以統計列表敍述之；惟有關學科內容的比較方面則僅限碩士課程而已，因為 1968 年之調查範圍限於碩士階段之故。由分析調查結果看來，資訊科學已由傳統式圖書館學課程轉換為電腦化和自動化方面課程之強調和加強。此一趨勢顯然的不但包含理論方面同時亦包含工藝技術方面。

　　最常為各學校開授的資訊科學科目是"資訊科學概論"，以新的方式解說並啓發學生對圖書館和資訊問題的看法。並增多程式寫作，資訊內容辨認理論，圖書館自動化和基本數學原理等等課程之教授。如繼續這樣發展下去。圖書館可能將轉變為社區資訊中心（Community Information Center）利用通訊系統處理供應各界對資訊的需求。

　　如前幾次的研究一樣。並召開第三研討會，邀請院長，教授，專業學會和工業界代表參加審閱調查問卷分析其結果及並對三種不同階段（學士，碩士，博士）資訊科學學科教育目的和其課程提出適當的建議。

一、前　言

　　瞭解資訊科學的現況是重要的，同樣重要地是知道它的發展趨勢和方向。假若教育與社會的需求和職業機會連繫一起，教育的目標即受其委託而定向。

　　為求得以上問題的答案，用調查 1968 年資訊科學課程同樣問卷再一次請求各大學提供有關開設教授資訊科學課程情況，此次調查限於 1972—1973 年間之課程。調查的比較，反映出這四年重要的發展中資訊科學課程之變化。由於擴大調查範圍之故，此次發出的問卷的對象亦增多。資訊科學調查範圍包括學士，碩士和博士班的課程，而以前 1968 年調查僅限於碩士階段而已。

　　課程內容的比較，僅限於 1968 年、1972 兩項調查皆提供資料的學校，因此也僅限於碩士階段之課程。在此報告中，對學士和博士階段的課程祇做現況之說明而已。很多資訊科學課程學科，特別是大學階段中，與電子計算機科學有非常密切相連關係，甚至於有時幾乎是相同的，不同的是用資訊科學名稱代之。似乎很難劃一清晰的界限而區分資訊科學和電子計算機科學這兩門學科。然而，這次的調查研究儘量地要做到不因此而受到影響而有偏見！

---

　　[*] 譯自 Jack Belzer, James Williams, John Kronebusch and A. B. Gupta. "Curricula in Information Science: Four Year Progress Report", *Journal of the American Society for Information Science* 26（No. 1）: 17－32（1975）.

二、調查問卷統計

調查問卷分寄與 138 所大學，71 所寄回問卷。內包括總共約 566 項資訊科學科目。其中一些學校未回覆的原因是他們認為資訊科學即是電子計算機科學。寄回問卷的學校中 44 所是 1968 年調查過的學校，其中 University of Dayton, 和 University of Portland 已停止資訊科學課程，另七所未回覆。故剩下 35 所學校在兩項調查中皆授予碩士學位的。正如前次的調查研究，主要的重心是分析課程的每組科目的要目。有關課程計劃的一般性統計亦是很重要的。特別如此的是因為 1968 年與 1972 年調查之比較象徵着四年來資訊科學課程的變化。

表 1a 列出各大學設資訊科學課程最常教授的科目名稱。

表 1a

課 程 名 稱		1968 No.	1972 No.
資訊科學概論	Introduction to Information Science	18	51
系統分析，設計，評量	Systems Analysis, Design, Evaluation	12	47
資訊貯存和檢索	Information Storage & Retrieval	36	43
資料處理	Data Processing	7	33
電子計算機程式寫作	Computer Programming	6	29
分類理論，索引法，摘要法等	Theory of Classification, Indexing, Abstracting, etc.	—	23
通訊系統	Communication	—	22
圖書館自動化	Library Automation	15	19
數學	Mathematics	9	18
資訊科學研究方法	Research Methods in Information Science	10	11
資料結構（檔案處理）	Data Structures (File Organization)	—	11
交互系統和網路	Interactive Systems and Networks	—	11
語言學	Language & Linguistics	9	—

最值得注意的是"資訊科學概論"在 1972 調查中領先了；"資訊貯存和檢索（IS & R)"。其他變化的是理論和結構方面的科目被應用方式科目代替之。以我們的觀點來看，這正表示資訊科學這門學科在漸漸的成長擴展。

下列資料皆以百分比計算來比較 1968 年和 1972 年碩士班課程情形。

表 1b 中看出主要課程的變化和強調的情形。資訊科學的主要課程已由圖書館學改變強調電子計算機科學的程度是 10%。資訊科學的趨向將是更多的利用電子計算機來處理傳統式的圖書館功能問題。

表 1b

主要課程	1968 %	1972 %
電子計算機科學	20	30
圖書館學	42	30
行為科學	6	5
數學和邏輯學	9	7
統計學	2	2
作業研究	6	5
語言學	4	5
工程學	1	5
其他	10	11

教學的方式（見表 1c）和使用教科書（見表 1d）的情形是令人失望的。我們覺得在研究所階段課程應有比這些調查報告內的更多以研究討論和實驗為主的課程。講授方式對研究生是不應該的！同樣地應考慮到參考書和期刊論文資料比使用教科書來教研究生更為適當。評量學生表現成績應以他們處理長遠計劃和有深度報告寫作能力為準。考試方式（見表 1e），並不能夠真正衡量如此進展情況。

表 1c

授課方式	1968 %	1972 %
講授式	58	57
研究討論式	19	20
做實驗	18	14
實習	5	9

表 1d

使用教科書情形	1968 %	1972 %
使用	49	53
不使用	48	13
未回答	3	34

表 1e

評量成績表現方式	1968 %	1972 %
考試	45	48
寫報告	40	35
做計劃	15	17

表1f 表示在研究所階段的資訊科學課程大多是選修的，這本應如此。這由於此門學科之科際特性（Interdisciplinary nature）準許研究生去追求各種不同興趣方面的知識之故。

表1f

必修或選修	1968 %	1972 %
必　修	30	33
選　修	56	61
未回答	14	6

表1g 顯示60%的所存科目是約每年開課1次的。

表1g

每年開課的次數	1968 %	1972 %
少於一年一次	6	9
一次	40	51
兩次	32	26
兩次以上	22	14

在過去4～5年中，資訊科學學術研究計劃的穩定情形已很明顯看出其變更方面是採用"科學方法"。由此，我們可注意到以往使用人工做法而現在採用自動化處理之傾向。在學術研究環境下之所以如此，其最大的因素是課堂上用的教科書和全面教育程序問題。最常被提起的而被17種科目採用的書是 *Handbook of Data Processing for Libraries*（R. Hayes & J. Becker）。表1h 列出被採用的教科書名稱及其被採用之次數由17—5次。其他教科書使用在5次以下者從略。

表1h

下列教科書使用的次數由15次至5次	
Hayes, R. and J. Becker, *Handbook of Data Processing for Libraries*, New York：John Wiley (1970).	＊（17）
Artandi, S., *An Introduction to Computers in Information Science*（2nd ed.），Metuchen, NJ：Scarecrow Press（1972）.	（9）
Salton, G., *Automatic Information Organization and Retrieval*, New York：McGraw-Hill（1968）.	（9）
Hopcroft, J. E. and J. D. Ullman, *Formal Languages and the Relation to Automarta*, Reading, MA：Addison—Wesley（1969）.	（8）

Knuth, D. E., *Art of Computer Programming*, Vol. I: *Fundamental Algorithms*, Reading, MA: Addison—Wesley (1968). (8)

Lancaster, F. W., *Information Retrieval Systems*, New York: Wiley (1968). (7)

McCracken, D. D. and U. Garbassi, *A Guide to COBOL Programming* (2nd ed.), New York: Wiley (1970). (7)

Griswald, R., *et al.*, *The SNOBOL-Four Programming Language* (2nd ed.), Englewood Cliffs, NJ: Prentice-Hall (1971). (6)

Bell, C. G. and A. Newell, *Computer Structures Reading and Examples*, New York: McGraw-Hill (1971). (5)

Chapman, E. A., *Library Systems Analysis Guidelines*. New York: John Wiley, (n. d.) (5)

Foskett, A. C., *The Subject Approach to Information* (2nd ed.), Hamden CN: Shoestring Press (1971). (5)

Cries, D., *Compiler Construction for Digital Computing*, New York: John Wiley (1971). (5)

* 代表此書在問卷中曾被提起之次數

　　下列表中各組科目分析的主要重點是包括在這次研究中每一科目內容主題。所有科目題目包括其結構內容資料，只要能適合資訊科學這門學科皆編入科目組內以便分析。

三、碩士班課程內容

　　1972 年調查碩士班課程中有七組科目，與 1968 年調查的六組相比較：無論如何，其間差別甚大！1968 年調查，每組科目內容包括題目遠較 1972 年為多（見表 2a – 2g）。其所減少的原因是由於各校間共同同意決定減少的。最有意思的是"數學"和"研究方法"兩科在第二次調查中已不存在，代替的科目是："圖書館自動化"，"電子計算機作業系統"和"計算理論"。此次調查很明顯地看出來資訊科學教育已開始注意到哪些科目才能符合此門學科的問題。

表 2a

組 1：資訊科學概論	(Introduction to Information Science)
寫碼	(Coding)
通訊	(Communication)
攝控學或心靈交控學說	(Cybernetics)
決策程序	(Decision processes)
資訊服務	(Information services)
資訊系統環境	(Information systems environment)
資訊理論	(Information theory)
語言文字	(Languages-linguistics)

表 2b

組 2：系統評量	(Systems Evaluation)
評量方法論	(Evaluation methodology)
資訊系統評量	(Evaluation of information systems)
有效的測量	(Measures of effectiveness)
系統分析	(Systems analysis)
系統設計	(System design)

表 2c

組 3：電子計算機概論	(Introduction to Computers)
電子計算機程式設計	(Computer programming)
電子計算機	(Computers)
資料處理	(Data processing)
資料處理設備	(Data processing equipment)
流程圖製作	(Flowcharting)
硬體	(Hardware)
一般語言	(Languages-general)
軟體	(Software)

表 2d

組 4：電子計算機作業系統	(Computer Operating Systems)
編譯程式	(Compilers)
機器語言	(Machine languages)
多元程式規劃	(Multiprogramming)
作業系統	(Operating systems)
分時系統	(Time-sharing)

表 2e

組 5：資訊貯存和檢索	(Information Storage and Retrieval)
摘要法	(Abstracting)
自動資訊貯存和檢索	(Automatic information storage and retrieval)
分類法	(Classification)
事實檢索	(Fact retrieval)
檔案組織	(File organization)
索引法	(Indexing)
檢索理論	(Role of theory in retrieval)
查詢策略	(Search strategy)
查詢技巧	(Search techniques)
辭庫	(Thesaurus)

表 2f

組 6：計算理論	（Theory of Computing）
演算法	（Algorithms）
自動化理論	（Automata theory）
有限狀機器	（Finite state machines）
回歸函數理論	（Recursive function theory）
侗瑞機器	（Turing machines）

表 2g

組 7：圖書館自動化	（Library Automation）
出納系統	（Circulation systems）
圖書館自動化	（Library automation）
圖書館和資訊網	（Library and information networks）
圖書館標準	（Library standards）
MARC 系統	（MARC system）
圖書館自動化計劃，人員和實施	（Planning, staffing, and implementation of library automation）

四、1972 年調查問卷統計：學士、碩士、博士班

本文中其他的表分別列出 1972—1973 年間學士、碩士和博士班資訊科學課程的現況。

表 3a 中看出學士階級課程最重視的科目是"電子計算機科學"和"圖書館學"，其次是"工程學"和"數學"，主要強調的是"工藝技術"。碩士班課程，畢業生即是圖書館專業人員和資訊科學家，其課程重點是圖書館學。博士班階段，電子計算機科學學科又佔據重要的地位。看來資訊科學教育的階段愈高，而其強調的課程愈偏重於"行為科學"和"數學"和"邏輯學"，這和工科課程的情形正好相反。

表 3a

主要課程	1972			
	學士班 %	碩士班 %	博士班 %	全部 %
電子計算機科學	56	31	43	37
圖書館學	10	31	10	25
行為科學	2	7	10	7
數學和邏輯學	7	6	9	7
統計學	1	3	4	2
作業研究	2	5	3	4
語言	2	4	5	3
工程學	8	4	4	5
其他	12	9	12	0

表 3b 中令人失望的是博士階段課程的教學仍採用講授式的佔百分比是那麼高。滿意的地方是高階段課程用研究討論式的百分比亦很高。講授式教學對高階段思想成熟的學生來說不僅不恰當而且對其學習亦難以有所助益。

最好學習途徑是教導他人，可在研究討論中做到的。雖缺少理論概念但實驗室和實習經驗與實際情況中獲得經驗相關的。由此原因，教育程度愈高實驗室和實習經驗的訓練反而減少。同樣地，表 3c 中顯示出教科書使用情形，教育程度愈高使用教科書反較大學階段愈少。當然參考資料和專業期刊的閱讀應是博士階段中主要獲得知識的來源，因為這些才是包含此門學科之主要精華本質。

表 3b

教學方式	1972			
	學士班%	碩士班%	博士班%	全部%
講授式	57	52	68	54
研究討論式	10	22	16	19
做實驗	27	17	10	19
實習	6	9	6	8

表 3c

使用教科書情形	1972			
	學士班%	碩士班%	博士班%	全部%
使用	75	53	58	57
不使用	6	8	5	8
未回答	19	39	37	38

表 3d 說明課程每年開課次數

表 3d

每年開課次數	1972			
	學士班%	碩士班%	博士班%	全部%
不到一次	2	11	15	8
一次	34	52	55	49
兩次	31	21	20	23
兩次以上	33	16	10	20

表 3e

必修或選修課程	1972			
	學士班%	碩士班%	博士班%	全部%
必修	49	30	29	35
選修	46	63	66	58
未回答	5	7	5	7

評量學生成績表現方法（見表 3f）應不強調在考試和作業方面，而應重視強調長遠的表現和將各教育階段所學綜合為一的能力。學生能準備、組織和發表研究討論，和/或按指定題目撰寫報告等能力才是最好的學生，這遠較考試更為恰當！

表 3f

評量成績表現的方法	1972			
	學士班 %	碩士班 %	博士班 %	全部 %
考試	66	47	52	51
寫報告	12	34	38	30
做計劃	22	10	10	19

五、分析 1972 年調查大學各階段資訊科學課程內容

課程內容的分析是很有意義的，雖然資訊科學擴散地滲入大學教育的各階段，但由於各階段程度的差異而強調的重點不一。舉例言之，大學課程中"知識結構理論"一科在碩士課程中即被並入"資訊貯存和檢索"科目中，但在博士班資訊科學課程中（見表 5a－5k）"知識結構理論"這門課又採用另一新的範圍內容。同樣地可觀察到，學士班學生可學到很多以電子計算機為中心的學科而建立良好的基礎，碩士班學生進而利用所知電子計算機方面的知識進而學習"圖書館自動化作業"學科，而博士班階段"圖書館系統和高級電子計算機"科目代替了碩士班的以應用為重點的課程。各階段皆一致認為"數學"學科在學習資訊科學中重要性；然而在博士班課程中，由於着重於資訊科學的研究而又特別強調"統計學"和"研究方法"這兩門學科。

下列表 4a—4h 列出調查收集的學士班課程中各組科目的內容，表 5a—5k 是博士班課程內容，表 6a—6K 是綜合以上學士、碩士和博士三班的課程內容：

一九七二年學士班課程中各組科目內容
表 4a

組 1：資訊科學概論	（Introduction to Information Science）
寫碼	（Coding）
通訊	（Communication）
資訊需求	（Information needs）
資訊貯存和檢索	（IS & R）
資訊理論	（Information theory）
管理資訊系統	（MIS）
查詢技巧	（Search techniques）

表 4b

組 2：知識的組織理論	（Theory of Organization of Knowledge）
摘要法	（Abstracting）
編目法	（Cataloguing）
分類法	（Classification）
索引法	（Indexing）

表 4c

組 3：語言文字	（Linguistics）
記述文法	（Descriptive grammar）
衍生文法	（Generative grammar）
語言與資訊處理	（Linguistics & information processing）
自然語言分析	（Natural language analysis）
語音學	（Phonology）
統計語言	（Statistical linguistics）

表 4d

組 4：系統和評量	（System and Evaluation）
評量方法論	（Evaluation methodology）
有效的方策量計	（Measure of effectiveness）
模型建築	（Model building）
系統分析	（Systems analysis）
系統設計	（Systems design）

表 4e

組 5：數學	（Mathematics）
微積分	（Calculus）
微分方程	（Differential equations）
拉格蘭吉倍加器	（Lagrange's multipliers）
直線性方程式	（Linear programming）
數學和邏輯學	（Mathematics & logic）
非直線程式製作	（Non-linear programming）
組論	（Set theory）
向量與距陣	（Vectors & matrices）

表 4f

組 6：電子計算機概論	（Introduction to Computers）
電子計算機程式寫作	（Computer programming）
電子計算機概論	（Computers）
資料處理	（Data processing）
流程圖製作	（Flowcharting）
硬體	（Hardware）
一般計算機語言	（Languages-general）
軟體	（Software）

表 4g

組 7：電子計算機作業系統	（Computer Operating Systems）
電子計算機	（Computers）
機器語言	（Machine language）
多元程式規劃	（Multiprogramming）
作業系統	（Operating systems）
分時系統	（Time sharing）

表 4h

組 8：資料庫結構	（Data Base Stuctures）
檔案結構	（File organization）
資訊結構	（Information structures）
相關連名單	（Linked lists）
樹狀結構	（Tree stuctures）

一九七二年博士班課程中各組科目內容

表 5a

組 1：資訊系統	（Information Systems）
寫碼	（Coding）
檔案結構	（File organization）
科學史	（History of science）
資訊構造	（Information structures）
資訊理論	（Information theory）
資訊系統	（Information systems）
管理資訊系統	（Management information systems）
查詢策略	（Search strategy）
樹狀結構	（Tree stuctures）

表 5b

組 2：圖書館系統	(Library Systems)
出納系統	(Circulation systems)
圖書館自動化	(Library automation)
圖書館標準	(Library standards)
MARC 標準	(MARC standards)
圖書館自動化的策劃，人員和實施	(Planning, staffing & implementation of library automation project)

表 5c

組 3：知識的組織理論	(Theory of Organization of Knowledge)
摘要法	(Abstracting)
分類法	(Classification)
索引法	(Indexing)
資訊貯存和檢索	(Information storage & retrieval)
辭庫	(Thesaurus)

表 5d

組 4：語言文字	(Linguistics)
非關聯語言	(Context-free languages)
衍生文法	(Generative grammar)
一般語言文字	(Languages-general)
語言和資訊處理	(Linguistics & information processing)

表 5e

組 5：系統評論	(Evaluation of Systems)
評量方法論	(Evaluation methodology)
資訊貯存和檢索的評量	(Evaluation of IS & R systems)
有效的測量	(Measures of effectiveness)
系統分析	(Systems analysis)
系統設計	(Systems design)

表 5f

組 6：研究方法	（Research Methods）
通訊	（Communication）
實驗設計	（Design of experiments）
資訊中心和大眾傳播	（Information center & mass communication）
資訊媒介	（Media）
心理學	（Psychology）
研究技巧	（Research techniques）

表 5g

組 7：數學	（Mathematics）
微積分	（Calculus）
微分方程	（Differential equations）
記述統計	（Descriptive statistics）
數學和邏輯學	（Mathematics & logic）
向量與矩陣	（Vectors & matrices）

表 5h

組 8：統計學	（Statistics）
決策程序	（Decision process）
分配或然率	（Probability distribution）
佇列論	（Queueing）
樣品試驗法	（Sampling）
統計分析	（Statistical analysis）
統計決策理論	（Statistical decision theory）

表 5i

組 9：電子計算機程式寫作	（Computer Programming）
計算機程式寫作	（Programming）
電子計算機概論	（Computers）
資料處理	（Data processing）
硬體	（Hardware）
機器語言	（Machine language）
軟體	（Software）

表 5j

組 10：電子計算機作業系統	（Computer Operating Systems）
編譯程式	（Compilers）
多元程式規劃	（Multiprogramming）
作業系統	（Operating systems）
分時系統	（Time-sharing）

表 5k

組 11：計算理論	（Theory of Computing）
演算法	（Algorithms）
自動化理論	（Automata theory）
有限狀機器	（Finite state machines）
回歸函數理論	（Recursive function theory）
組論	（Set theory）
侗瑞機器	（Turing machines）

表 6a—6k 各組科目的內容是三種階段課程的綜合物，闡釋目前產生的資訊科學學科。下列 11 組內容特別強調資訊科學學科具有科際性（Interdisciplinary nature）。

1. 資訊科學基本概論　（Foundation of Information Science）
2. 知識結構理論　　　（Theory of Organization of Knowledge）
3. 計算理論　　　　　（Theory of Computing）
4. 電子計算機方法　　（Computer Methods）
5. 資料處理　　　　　（Data Processing）
6. 圖書館系統自動化　（Automation of Library systems）
7. 圖書館管理　　　　（Management in Libraries）
8. 系統評量　　　　　（Systems Evaluation）
9. 行為因素　　　　　（Behavioral Aspects）
10. 統計學　　　　　　（Statistics）
11. 數學　　　　　　　（Mathematics）

一九七二年綜合（學士、碩士、博士）課程的科目內容

表 6a

組1：資訊科學基本原理	（Foundations of Information Science）
資訊理論	（Information theory）
通訊概論	（Communication）
科學史	（History of science）
寫碼	（Coding）
資訊媒介	（Media）
語言和資訊處理	（Linguistics & information processing）
資訊展示	（Information displays）
資訊爆發	（Information explosion）
圖書館及傳播	（Libraries & communication）
資訊科學	（Information sciences）
資訊貯存和檢索	（Information storage & retrieval）
查詢策略	（Search strategy）
社會因素	（Sociological aspects）

表 6b

組2：知識的組織理論	（Theory of Organization of Knowledge）
摘要法	（Abstracting）
索引法	（Indexing）
摘錄法	（Extracting）
分類法	（Classification）
編目法	（Cataloguing）
內容分析	（Content analysis）
目錄控制	（Bibliographic control）

表 6b

組3：計算理論	（Theory of Computing）
資訊結構	（Information structure）
演算法	（Algorithms）
計算法	（Countability）
連續網	（Sequential nets）
交換理論	（Switching theory）
自動化理論	（Automata theory）
伺瑞機器	（Turing machines）
有限狀機器	（Finite state machines）
理論數學	（Meta-mathematics）
回歸函數理論	（Recursive function theory）

表 6d

組 4：計算機方法	（Computer Methods）
電子計算機	（Computers）
作業系統	（Operating systems）
編譯程式	（Compilers）
機器語言	（Machine language）
分時系統	（Time sharing）
多元程式規劃	（Multiprogramming）
電子計算機設備	（Computer utility）
相關連名單	（Linked list）
樹狀結構	（Tree structure）
檔案結構	（File organization）

表 6e

組 5：資料處理	（Data Processing）
電子計算機程式寫作	（Computer programming）
軟體	（Software）
硬體	（Hardware）
流程圖製作	（Flowcharting）
打卡	（Punched cards）
資料蒐集方法	（Data collection methods）
資料處理設備	（Data processing equipment）
記錄媒介	（Recording media）
自動撥號使用資訊	（Dial-up access）
通信	（Telecommunication）
資訊網	（Networks）

表 6f

組 6：圖書館系統自動化	（Automation of Library Systems）
圖書館自動化策劃，人員和實施	（Planning, staffing & implementation of library automation）
出納系統	（Circulation system）
微粒縮影	（Microforms）
期刊自動化	（Automation of serials）
MARC 系統	（MARC system）
醫學文獻分析檢索系統	（MEDLARS）
編目機械化	（Mechanized cataloguing）
圖書預借系統自動化	（Automation of book reservation system）

表 6g

組 7：圖書館管理	(Management in Libraries)
圖書館和資訊網	(Library & information networks)
圖書館機能	(Library functions)
圖書館標準	(Library standards)
經營的目標	(Managerial objectives)
未來的圖書館	(Future of libraries)
專業的觀點	(Professional aspects)
圖書館協會	(Library associations)
大學圖書館	(University libraries)

表 6h

組 8：系統評量	(System Evaluation)
評量方法論	(Evaluation methodology)
評量資訊檢索系統	(Evaluation of information retrieval systems)
有效的測量	(Measures of effectiveness)
策劃、安排和預算	(Planning, programming & budgeting (PPB))
作業研究和資訊系統	(Operations research & information systems)
系統設計	(Systems design)
系統分析	(Systems analysis)
決策程序	(Decision processes)
模型建築	(Model building)
工作量度	(Work measurement)
系統綜合法	(Systems synthesis)
佇列論	(Queueing)

表 6i

組 9：行爲觀點論	(Behavioral Aspects)
心理學	(Psychology)
人工資訊處理	(Human information processing)
概念形成	(Concept formation)
思考	(Thinking)
反饋和控制	(Feedback and control)

表 6j

組 10：統計學	(Statistics)
研究技巧	(Research techniques)
科學方法	(Scientific method)
實驗設計	(Design of experiments)
統計結果的解釋	(Interpretation of statistical results)
統計的決策理論	(Statistical decision theory)
因素分析	(Factor analysis)
方差分析	(Analysis of variance)
測驗假定	(Tests of hypotheses)
記述統計	(Descriptive statistics)
分配或然率	(Probability distribution)
樣品試驗法	(Sampling)
退縮和關聯	(Regression & correlation)
統計的分析	(Statistical analysis)

表 6k

組 11：數學	(Mathematics)
數學邏輯學	(Mathematical logic)
微積分	(Calculus)
向量與距陣	(Vectors & matrices)
微分方程	(Differential equations)
代數	(Algebra)
直線性方程式	(Linear programming)
非直線性方程式	(Non-linear programming)
動態程式規劃	(Dynamic programming)
拉格蘭吉倍加器	(Lagrange's multipliers)
拓撲學	(Topology)
組論	(Set theory)
畫圖理論	(Graph theory)

六、第三研討會

依據以前的研究（1—3）一樣召開研討會，邀請學術界、工業界、政府和專業學會專家人士代表出席。召開研討會的目的是，共同研究並提供建議各階段（學士、碩士、博士）資訊科學課程內容問題。兩天研討會，出席代表人員共 23 名（名單見 Appendix A）。

第一天會議中，首先由 Jack Belzer 報告調查問卷統計和有關事項，繼由資訊和教育研究中心（Center for the Study of Information and Education）教育研究部份負責人 C. Walter Stone 提出論文報告"圖書館與資訊科學課程的改進"（Curricula Reform of Library and Information Science），該中心主任 Donald P. Ely 報告"資訊系統和新境界"（Information Systems and New Towns），最後由西安大略大學（University of Western Ortario）圖書館和資訊科學研究所所長 William J. Cameron 報告該所使用研究討論方式教學方法的情況。接下是討論此四篇報告。然後將研討會分爲三小組，分別就學士班、碩士班和博士班資訊科學教學課程研討。學士班課程由 Vivian S. Sessions（The City University of New York Graduate School）主持，碩士班課程討論由 Pauline Atherton（Syracuse University School of Information Studies）主持，博士班課程由 Margaret Chisholm（Dean of the University of Maryland, College of Library and Information Studies）負責主持。

第二天下午，每小組對其負責討論的課程提出推薦建議。再由碩士班研討小組就所有三階段之研究另做一籠統總結論。並鑑定研究學問所需的四種方式之着重加強程度分三種階段列表說明之（見表7）

表7

	理論 (Theory)	概念 (Concepts)	工具 (Tools)	應用 (Application)
博士班	××××	××	×	×××
碩士班	×	××	×××	××××
學士班	×	×××	××××	××

（× = 加強的程度）

七、大學班課程建議

從資訊工作者眼光看來，大學資訊科學學士是非專業學位的。並把它看成是文理學院的學位輔系是資訊科系而已。由於此門學科之科際（Interdisciplinary）特性的原因，認爲此科之組成有七方面。學生可根據自己的興趣和導師之指導下，可專攻任何一方面。如學生學習階段以此爲終止，他必須學習相關的技術以幫助其未來事業。構成此學科之七方面是：

- 工藝
- 組織理論
- 數學
- 語言和語文學
- 基本科學
- 管理理論

工藝包括電子計算機，傳播和縮影學。組織理論包括項目有檔案結構，索引法和人類知識組織哲理。數學方面是用做協助學生定量分析的工具並瞭解數學的特性——如限度觀念，收斂率，反覆程序等。語言和語文包含自然和人工語言。

學生不可能全部讀完這七方面學科的。因爲文理學科教育學科的分配不同，學生只需概括瞭解這七方面的內容即可，可選修有關的輔系，如數學，電子計算機科學，管理科學或其他方面。另外，學生學習兩或三方面合併的學科作爲主修科目以期求得深入的知識。這種課程計劃下而畢業的學生各不相同，這是應該的！每人以追求其興趣爲目的。在此階段的課程計劃其主修科的重點是"工具"方面之瞭解認識，其次強調的是"概念"方面。(見表7)

研究小組已辨認出大學階段應含的學科方面是什麼，但令人奇怪的是在調查的科目分析中並未存在，研究小組建議管理理論應包括在大學階段的資訊科學課程內。

八、碩士班課程建議

碩士班課程特別強調的是應用和工具方面，而對概念和理論則比較次要（見表7）。下面是建議課程內容：──

A. 應用學科方面：
　　1. 系統作業
　　　　a. 圖書館和資訊中心
　　　　b. 資訊/通訊綱建立
　　2. 媒介物工藝和傳輸
　　　　a. 印刷與非印刷工藝技術
　　　　b. 媒介物散發
　　　　c. 有線電纜電視
　　3. 使用者環境問題
　　　　a. 不同用者和服務的需求
　　　　b. 社會問題和公共政策
　　　　c. 需求分析
　　　　d. 人的通訊程序
　　　　e. 答案分析和設計
　　　　f. 不同用者設置不同媒介物和系統的能力和效果之研究
B. 工具學科方面：
　　兩種工具，一種直接與資訊科學有關，另一種是輔助的工具。
　　1. 資訊貯存和檢索
　　　　a. 內容分析
　　　　b. 摘要法和索引法
　　　　c. 分類法
　　　　d. 辭庫結構
　　　　e. 查詢策略
　　2. 管理方面
　　　　a. 效果的估計
　　　　b. 系統分析和設計

3. 輔助範圍方面
      a. 數學和統計學
      b. 語言學
      c. 資料處理
      d. 管理計劃
         財務和預算
         市場調查
         人員資料
C. 理論與概念方面
   1. 資訊科學概論
   2. 哲學
   3. 資訊系統
      a. 字彙控制
      b. 索引法和分類法
      c. 檔案結構
   4. 輔助範圍方面
      a. 傳播和資訊理論
      b. 羣力學
      c. 決策理論
      d. 計算理論
      e. 語言學

　　輔助課程方面不屬於資訊科學課程內。最好是申請入碩士班時先修科目。由於申請碩士班的背景不一（BA/BS），故不能苛求學生具有同樣的技術。此地建議資訊科學碩士階段課程對輔助課程方面做相當適應性的處理。

　　研討小組並未明顯建議碩士班課程組分析中任何有關媒介物工藝技術的科目是哪些，也未提起哪些科目應合理屬於此方面。但資訊科學專業工作人員亦應具有媒介物工藝技術方面的知識的。

九、博士班課程建議

　　博士班課程的研究小組認爲資訊科學博士階段學科應包括的功能（Functions）是：研究、教學、行政、發展和諮詢顧問等五方面。研究學習一種或一種以上功能的混合科目即可，很少能包括全面的課程的。個人爲了有相當的適應性，以便運用以上列出任何一種功能，他必需是一學者。他能由一方貫連（應用知識和經驗）至另一面。研究方法理論和其效果應帶入課室研討，由此進而導致實驗室內新方法產生。基本理論基本工具的供給對現有存在現象的概念認識和進一步瞭解。由實際瞭解和研究某種現象"爲甚麼"發生而"創造的結果"遠較瞭解某現象"如何"發生或已發生了而得的結果更好，有從事研究的能力是一種能力形式，它是與學識相並進的。一個人可能有傑出的研究能力，但很可能並不適合做一個從業者的大有人在。雖然如此，具有特殊能力如：——研究方法和技術，技術的應用，研究人員工作環境之認識，和有關資訊系統的工作的社會因素等方面——皆與研究能力有密切關係。總而言之，這種研究能力和方式在博士階段學習中是必要的！

參考資料

1. **Belzer**, **J.** (ed.), "Information Science Education: Curriculum Development and Evaluation," *American Documentation* 20 (No. 4): 327-376 (1969).

2. ——, "Education in Information Science" *Journal of the American Society for Information Science* 21 (No. 4): 269-273 (1970).

3. ——, **A. Isaac**, *et al.*, "Curricula in Infomation Science Analysis and Development" *Journal of the American Society for Information Science* 22 (No. 3): 193-223 (1971).

4. **Stone**, **C. W.**, **J. Belzer** and **J. W. Brown**, *Needs for Improvement of Professional Education in Library and Information Science*, Center for the Study of Information and Education, Syracuse University, Syracuse, NY (1973).

5. **Belzer**, **J.**, "Curriculum Trends for Information Science Professionals" *Educational Media Yearbook* 1974, **J. W. Brown** [ed.], New York: R. R. Bowker Co., 28-30 (1974).

Appendix A:
寄回調查問卷的學校名單

調查學校名稱	第一次調查 1968	第二次調查 1972
Auburn University		×
Arizons State University		×
Bowling Green State University		×
California State University		×
Case Western Reserve University	×	×
Chattanooga State Technical Institute		×
City University of New York		×
Clarion State College	×	×
Cornell University		×
Dalhousie University		×
Drexel University	×	×
East Carolina University		
East Tennessee State University	×	×
Emory University		×
Florida Atlantic University		×
Florida State University	×	×
George Peabody College of Teachers	×	×
Georgia Institute of Technology	×	×

Harvard University		×
Illinois Institute of Technology		×
Indiana University	×	×
Iowa State University		×
Kent State University		×
Lehigh University	×	
McGill University		×
Northern Illinois University		×
Ohio State University		×
Point Park College		×
Pratt Institute	×	×
Queens College (CUNY)		×
Rosary College	×	×
Rutgers University	×	×
St. Cloud State College	×	×
San Jose State College	×	
Simmons College		×
Southern Connecticut State College	×	×
State University of New York (Albany)	×	×
State University of New York (Buffalo)	×	×
Stanford University		×
Syracuse University	×	×
Texas Woman's University	×	
University of Alberta		×
University of British Columbia	×	×
University of California (Berkeley)	×	×
University of Californaia (L. A.)	×	×
University of Chicago	×	×
University of Colorado	×	×
University of Dayton	×	Discontinued
University of Denver	×	×
University of Guam		×
University of Illinois	×	×
University of Iowa		×
University of Kentucky		×
University of Maine	×	
University of Maryland	×	×
University of Michigan	×	×
University of Minnesota		×

University of Missouri (Columbia)	×		×
University of Missouri (Rolla)	×		×
University of Montreal	×		×
University of North Carolina			×
University of Oklahoma	×		
University of Oregon	×		×
University of Portland	×		
University of Pittsburgh	×		×
University of Rhode Island	×		
University of Southern California	×		×
University of Southern Mississippi			×
University of Tennessee			×
University of Texas			×
University of Toronto			×
University of Washington	×		
University of Western Ontario	×		×
University of Wisconsin (Madison)	×		×
University of Wisconsin (Milwaukee)	×		×
Washington State University	×		
Washington University			×
Western Illinois University			×
Western Kentucky University			×
Western Michigan University	×		×
Total	80	45	70

There were 35 schools in both studies

資訊科學概論[*]

> **・譯者的話・**
>
> 　　資訊科學爲一新興學科，人們對此較爲陌生。《資訊科學概論》（*The First Book of Information Science*）是一九七四年出版，內容簡明扼要，容易瞭解。譯者覺得有譯成中文本介紹給業內人士認識之必要，即着手向著者 Mr. Joseph Backer 和該書發行者美國原子能委員會（U. S. Atomic Energy Commission）聯繫商量，很快即得到對方的回音，表示甚爲高興此書能譯成中文版，並自動寄來有關圖片，以備譯文出版之用，非常熱心幫忙。
>
> 　　此書譯文將分次連續刊出，以後將出版單行本。譯者翻譯此書最大的願望是想借此能"抛磚引玉"，不但想引起人們對此學科之探討研究興趣，同時更期望能激起海內外資訊科學專家們的熱誠，對此學科多做更深入的介紹，以增多人們對此學科之認識。

壹　前　言

　　數年前，紐約市的電子計算機首次與倫敦的電子計算機"通話交談"了。雖然電子計算機間之"交談"並不如人與人間之"交談"一樣方便，但這些機器亦能做到對很複雜的數學問題互相交換意見的。隔洋電子計算機之所以能聯繫如此，是由於經過一個叫做"晨鳥"人造衛星（Early Bird Satellite）所致，該人造衛星即是設在大西洋上空繞行地球軌道的一個如電冰箱大小的小型無線電中繼傳播站（Radio Relay Station）。

　　當數年前，一個大型火箭（Rocket）將晨鳥人造衛星送至太空軌道上，目的是利用此人造衛星將接受由美國無線廣播電臺送來之訊息轉遞到歐洲的廣播電臺去。因爲人造衛星可與電子計算機通訊，而電子計算機又可處理大量的資訊（Information）快如光速（Speed of light），均利用人造衛星往返傳遞資訊快於任何種傳遞方式。

　　電子計算機除能計算外，亦可處理字母、字和句子等，這叫做語文處理（Language Processing）、電子計算機利用人造衛星可以做上述工作，無形中電子計算機加增予我們一種新的力量——"資訊力量"（Information Power），此資訊力量對世界上任何人將來的生活是非常重要的。

　　資訊科學是一門富有刺激性的學科，一旦你能領悟它，你可能亦如其他的人一樣，願成爲資訊科學家在同一興趣陣線上，來共同爲關啓資訊奧妙的將來而努力。

貳　資訊（Information）是什麼？

　　當初生嬰兒首次睜開他的雙目時，他的腦子即開始收藏記憶四週看到的事物印象，

＊ 譯自 Joseph Becker "The First Book of Information Science". 分上、中、下三部份分別發表在《教育資料科學月刊》8 卷 5—6 期（1975 年 12 月）、9 卷 1 期（1976 年 1 月）、9 卷 2 期（1976 年 3 月）。

這是他第一資訊來源。待他再長大些,除視覺外,他亦感受到聽覺、觸覺、嗅覺,和味覺發育,所接受的資訊就更新穎了!無論如何,每一片的資訊都經過腦部記錄在記憶裏(Memory),漸漸地,由於閱讀和體驗,孩童開始將新舊資訊參合而用——我們稱此爲學習(Learning)。

到如今,科學家們仍不能全部瞭解人腦如何能做此奇妙的機能,但他們知道資訊和學習可賦予我們思考和創造的力量。當您閱讀此書時,您同時將讀過的資訊吸收並貯存入一個有組織的通訊中心裏——那就是您的腦中。

任何人都可將自己的腦當做個人的資訊中心,因爲它存有自己個人所知的並幫助每日工作的資訊。假使可以看到人腦內部的圖片,它看來像一束複雜摺疊的體素組織(Tissuefolds)。人腦是奇妙的工具,每一部門有它獨一的工作功能和複雜的連合皆有某種特殊作用幫助我們思考。

回憶的能力是從記憶中召回某些資訊,巧妙地將各種資訊混合用以創造新觀念,這就是人類最珍貴的特質。

雖然人腦的貯存量很大,如與世人現有的資訊總量相比,人腦的容量就顯太少了。一個人一生中所能學到的東西有限得很,然而,一生中人腦的利用只不過佔其總容量的七分之一而已。此外,大家皆知,一個人僅僅能記憶很多資訊,並不能使他成爲博學的或聰明人的!

知識和智慧得自能對資訊的瞭解和運用。一個博學的人,他能將各種資訊適當地連接湊合成有組織思想及觀念,進而產生敏捷才智的作爲,而一個聰明的人,他能有計劃引用這些思想及觀念到人生的問題上。

一、書寫(Writing)的歷史

到現在爲止,我們已經討論過人們如何吸收資訊。然而能使資訊充份利用,必須傳至他人。在書寫(Writing)發明以前,主要的資訊傳遞方法是由人口頭傳遞。這些通訊方式只便於交談和討論,這些受到聲音傳播距離的限制,而無他法可記錄人類以前曾說寫什麼?

很明顯的,人類需要記錄資訊的方法,能將過去人類的思想和作爲供給下一代參考。爲了達到此目的,人類發明了書寫(Writing)和其他種記錄知識的方法。

最初是畫圖記事法(Picture writing),繼而字母(Alphabet),再爲符號(Script),最後印刷(Printing)。每一新的記錄方法的發明皆較舊的更爲方便有用。數千年前,書寫被記錄在黏土碑(Claytablets)、乾動物皮(Dried animal skins)、紙草紙(Papyrus)和其他材料上。

中國人發明紙張以後,人們多採用紙來書寫和記錄資訊。第一本書之出現是"捲軸型"(Scroll)的,閱讀時必須"捲"和"轉"才能看。事實上,"卷"字,英文字"Volume",意思是書(Book),起源於拉丁文之"Volare",意思是"轉"(to turn)。這些古時的書籍被稱爲手抄本(Manuscript),是由手抄寫的。這些記錄和傳佈資訊的方法是非常慢的!

中國人也是第一個發明活動式的商業印刷機的,Johannes Gutenberg,第一位歐洲人在紀元後一四四〇年即開始用此印刷機,我們應特別地感謝他。因此,很多書籍可便宜且大量印出很多本，和現在我們所使用的印刷方法相同。

二、圖書和圖書館

圖書館員的工作是將所有的手抄本和圖書集中保存在一個地方。最初，只有少數圖書館存在，大家皆認為是學者的寶藏！數百年前，很少人識字，識字的人求知心切，不惜長途跋涉學習學問找尋資料。圖書和圖書館對人類文化有不可磨滅的貢獻，否則人類的文明無疑的不會進步如此神速。

三、資訊適用化

由於印刷機能將一本書印出很多本來，致能將這些書分送至不同地方的人去閱讀。書信和郵政系統開始建立了，幫助分寄圖書至各城市去，這樣沒多久，郵寄成為人們最常用的資訊交換的通訊方式。後來，輪船、火車、飛機等亦開始輸送郵件，更增強了郵政服務的容量和速度。如今，郵寄將成噸成噸的資料訊息移送至世界各地去，已成為每日例行業務了！

"電"（Electricity）供給另一資訊傳佈方法，如電話和電信能將人與人、地方與地方聯繫起來，這些新型通訊線網利用"電"能往返運送資訊，快如光速（Speed of light）。目前，全美國擁有約一億具電話，世界各地亦大約設置有百萬具電話，電話已成為個人通訊聯繫的必需部份。

另外一種資訊通訊方法是無線電收音機（Radio）。電話僅能允許一個人與遠方的另一個人通話，但是無線電收音機則不然，它可將訊息同時廣播給很多的人。電視就更進步了，它不但如收音機一樣可廣播很多訊息，同時人們亦可"看"到訊息的實況，故每種新通訊技術發展皆較以往方法更有效，更能廣泛的將資訊傳遞給更多的人。

叁　資訊的貯存及檢索

很多世紀以來，圖書館一直是主要貯存知識的寶庫。它積聚圖書、期刊和報章，將之整理便於他人使用，並提供多種幫助他人找尋資料的服務。圖書館種類很多——學校圖書館、公共圖書館、大學圖書館和專門圖書館等。專門圖書館是只包括某一專門科目資料的圖書館，如醫學或法律圖書館。圖書館執行多種功能：（一）選購讀者所需資訊，（二）資訊分類編目便於讀者查尋，（三）出借圖書資料給讀者帶回家閱讀，（四）解答讀者提出各類科目任何問題。專門研究圖書館功能的學科我們稱之為圖書館學。

圖書館是屬於大眾的！它免費供應研究、教育、娛樂等各方面的資訊，因而，多數的公共圖書館就成為市鎮上主要的資訊中心。

現代化圖書館不但蒐集圖書和雜誌等資料，同時亦蒐購視聽資料（Audio-visual materials），如微縮影片（Films）、膠片（Filmstrips）、卡式錄音帶（Audio cassettes）、電視錄音帶（TV tapes）、L. P. 唱片（Longplaying records）、幻燈片（Slides）、卡式影像錄影帶（Video cassettes）和其他種形式的視聽資料。圖書館愈大，蒐購的視聽資料也就愈多，圖書館更要能對讀者提出複雜的資訊要求有滿足的服務。它們發覺電子機算計和他種技術可能是提供加強圖書館資訊貯存和檢索能力的新方法，這種利用電子計算機和技術來處理圖書館各種業務機能上現象叫做圖書館自動化（Library automation）。

一、資訊爆發

人類自有歷史記錄以來,從未有這麼多的人居住在地球上——我們稱此爲"人口爆發"(Population explosion),在今日社會中,人們日常相處生活需要多方面的資料和訊息,由於世界人口大增,就更迫切地需要更好的方法來傳發需要的資訊。人口爆發造成更多的人產生更多的資訊,另外還有新科目亦不斷地增多。因此就釀成所謂的"資訊爆發"(Information explosion)。

資訊(Information),兩字已不再僅僅指代表印刷品資料而言。它也廣泛的包括其他如:影片、幻燈片、電視磁帶和電子計算機磁帶等含有資訊的東西。"資訊科學"(Information science)是研究人如何與他人通訊的學科。它的重點在於研討探尋完善最佳的方法,能將圖書館和資訊中心貯存的資訊正確快速地傳送給需要的人。

二、資訊科學（Information science）

"資訊科學"是一新興學科。到處的人皆關心資訊爆發,而不知如何處理此問題。舉例而言,一個醫生無疑的需要最新的、更有效的醫學治療方法的資訊報導,用來醫治他的病人。一個律師無疑的需要最新的法院法規方面的資訊,爲他的訴訟委託人案件申訴。一個工程師無疑的需要最新的資訊使他不致於浪費精力財力去研究已發明的東西上。一個生意人無疑的需要最新的商業資訊,使他的公司能經營妥善賺大錢。一個農人無疑的需要最新的農業資訊,使他能有最大的收成。其他各行各業的人同樣需要最新的各種資料,便利他們從事各種業務的推展。資訊科學是"研究"這些各類的人如何利用資訊在他們的工作和業務上,及研究如何提供對這些人工作業務上所需要最有用的資訊的有效供應方法。

任何資訊系統（Information system）能將知識和資訊分送給各個人,必須具備下列三個條件:(1)它能告知用者資訊能在何處找到;(2)當用者決定要某些資料時它必須能遞送過去;(3)對用者需要的資料,它必須能在用者要求之期限內回覆。所以,資訊科學是研究有關各類資訊的產生、索引製作、整理、貯存、查尋、分析、傳佈、取得和利用等情況的學科。

資訊科學的發展與很多科目有關:如數學（Mathematics）、邏輯學（Logic）、語言學（Language arts）、心理學（Psychology）、電子計算機技術（Computer technology）、通訊（Communications）、縮影學（Micrographics）、圖書館科學（Library science）、管理科學（Business management）等。不過,對資訊科學家而言,他必須學習應用和深入瞭解三種基本工具:(1)他必須對電子計算機有相當的認識,因此機器能處理資訊如計算數字樣的迅速。(2)他必須對通訊方面（Communication）很懂,通訊技術亦能快速地將圖片和文學等各種資訊傳佈到各處去,(3)他也必須懂得將資料縮小攝影的縮影學（Micrographics）這門學問,因縮影技術可使很多的資料縮小體積而佔很少的貯存空間。

下面幾章的介紹,爲使大家熟悉認識這些新資訊技術,瞭解它如何作業和它可能將改變大家資訊習慣。今日之圖書館和資訊中心似乎早已受到此新的電子發明的影響啦!

肆　將資訊存入電子計算機

一、打孔卡片（Punched cards）及紙帶（Paper tape）

當資訊成印刷品形式出現時，你我都能閱讀瞭解其內容。然而，資訊若用機器，如電子計算機來處理時，那麼勢必要建立其他的處理方法，將相同文字存入此機器中。當然，電子計算機未具有人類的肉眼，但其構造含有電子感應設備（Electrical sensing equipment），差不多亦同樣地能達成與人眼相同的功能。

舉例而言，我們大都去過超級市場（Supermarkets），其大門會自動開關。這些大門就是由一電子感應設備叫光電池（Photoelectric cells）的來控制，它的作用如同肉眼。每一扇門由兩個彼此通光電柱（Beams）的光電池來控制，當人入門時，此光柱即被切斷，光電池或"電眼"（Electric eyes）則感覺有人通行有如同人眼，同時電眼立即輸送大量的電能至門的機械樞紐上，而門則自動打開。

此光電池感應原理同樣地可以應用檢測卡片或紙帶上孔的存在，因此，如果以紙帶或卡片打孔來代表某些字母或文字的話，則很可能利用機器以電感應原理閱讀此卡片或紙帶上的資料。

一八八〇年，美國何樂禮氏（Herman Hollerith of Buffalo, New York）發明一種利用卡片打孔的方式來代表資訊的方法。當時，何樂禮氏在美國戶口調查局工作，處理全國人口的統計，他的職務是將手寫的各地人口數目總和起來，這種工作自然需要很多時間來計算。因之，他設計了一套機器幫助很快地處理這些工作，同時他亦想到一方法，藉打孔於卡片上的方式來記錄人口資料，使人口資料成為機器可閱讀的形式。

今日，卡片打孔和紙帶打孔成為電子計算機處理資料時，將資料轉換成機器可閱讀形式的兩種普通常用的方法。圖一是典型打孔卡片。

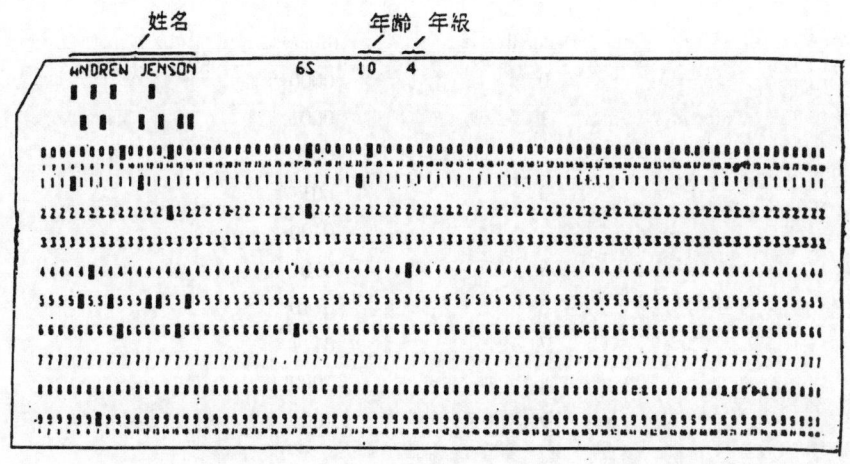

圖一　典型之打孔卡片，包含小學生的姓名、年齡和年級的資料

何樂氏於一八八〇年選用一元美鈔之大小為其卡片之尺寸標準，雖然目前一元美鈔

格式已經較小，但何樂氏所用卡片的尺寸並未改變。每張卡片分成行（Columns）與列（Rows），行上下，列左右，共八十行，十二列。如數字"六"，可用在任何行上第六列上打孔來代表，注意前圖所示第二十七行數字"六"。字母"S"，可在任何行上打兩個孔代表之，注意前圖所示字母"S"是打在第二十八行的十列及二列打孔組合而成。同樣的，用同一學生的資料（如前圖）由打孔紙帶來代表（見圖二），不同組合的孔代表不同的意思。請注意字母"J"和"R"在孔的組成的不同處。

由以上兩圖顯示出學生資料卡片如何準備的。然而，爲其他目的和用處，資訊可記錄在機器可閱讀的形式上。當今，亦有很多資訊已製成機器可閱讀的形式。許多機器附有打字機的鍵盤，可以很容易將一頁打字的資料自動製成打孔卡或紙帶。出版圖書、雜誌、報紙印刷界，也充分利用電子計算機及其他電子印刷機器方便製出很多機器可閱讀的資訊。

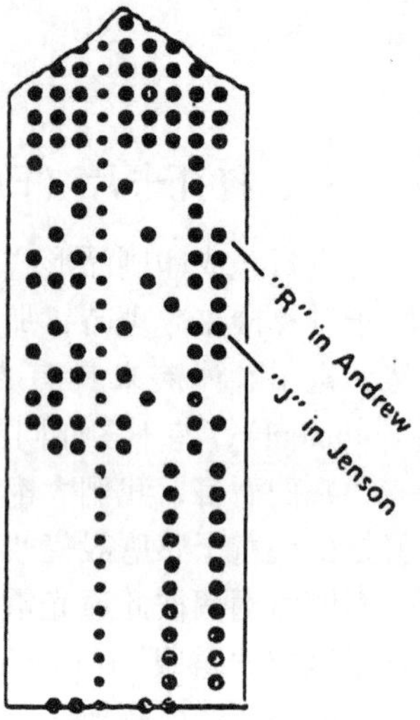

圖二　用前圖同樣的文字資料打在紙帶上，請注意字母"J"和"R"各用不同的孔組合而成

二、電子計算機語言（The Computer's Language）

電子計算機是基本的電子儀器，像其他電器一樣對電信號（Electrical signals）有所感應。利用這些電信號來代表資訊，並需電碼（Code）代替數字或字母。目前最適於一般電子計算機採用的電碼是二進位數字系統（The Binary number system）。此二進位數字系統只用兩個符號——0和1——來代表數字和文字。每一符號稱爲一"元位"（Bit）。藉著0和1兩個符號，我們可以編排任何數字或文字。

由圖三可以看到如何利用二進位數字0、1代替十進位數字1至9的例子。

Decimal	Binary
0	0000
1	0001
2	0010
3	0011
4	0100
5	0101
6	0110
7	0111
8	1000
9	1001

圖三

下列廿六個字母表，是由二進位符號1至9數字前面另加兩個0或1而組成的。

A = 110001	N = 100101
B = 110010	O = 100110
C = 110011	P = 100111
D = 110100	Q = 101000
E = 110101	R = 101001
F = 110110	S = 010010
G = 110111	T = 010011
H = 111000	U = 010100
I = 111001	V = 010101
J = 100001	W = 010110
K = 100010	X = 010111
L = 100011	Y = 011000
M = 100100	Z = 011001

利用下列的六元位（Bit）二進位的碼號，可以拼出 RADNOR ELEMENTARY SCHOOL 如圖四。

RADNOR	ELEMENTARY	SCHOOL
1 1 1 1 1 1	1 1 1 1 1 1 0 1 1 0	0 1 1 1 1 1
0 1 1 0 0 0	1 0 1 0 1 0 1 1 0 1	1 1 1 0 0 0
1 0 0 0 0 1	0 0 0 0 0 0 0 0 1 1	0 0 1 0 0 0
0 0 1 1 1 0	1 0 1 1 1 1 0 0 0 0	0 0 0 1 1 0
0 0 0 0 1 0	0 1 0 0 0 0 1 0 0 0	1 1 0 1 1 1
1 1 0 1 0 1	1 1 1 0 1 1 1 1 1 0	0 1 0 0 0 1

圖四

三、磁帶和磁碟（Magnetic Tapes & Disks）

適用於電腦的另一紀錄資訊方法，是把資訊互接存入磁帶（Magnetic tapes）中。當然，這不像將資訊打在紙上的做法。為了要瞭解資訊如何存入磁帶中，首先必須解釋一下磁帶是什麼？

由磁帶之橫斷面（Cross section）來看其結構似三明治。最下面一層是層透明塑膠（Plastics），上面塗上一層叫做氧化亞鐵（Ferrous oxide）的棕色物質，最上一層則包上另一層透明塑膠。圖三即是一小段磁帶的放大圖，磁帶很薄，由於每層都很緊的密合在一起，故看起來像一條緞帶。在三明治中間那層棕色的氧化亞鐵化學物，它含有鐵微粒（Grains of iron），在被電流撞擊時可重新排列而指向同一方向，這稱為磁化（Magnetizing）作用。如果電流只直接撞擊某一小點，則只有此點被磁化，這就是資訊如何被寫入或記錄於磁帶中做法。如果稱電流在已磁化點使之反向逆流，這磁點代表的資訊即被去磁（Demagnetized）或又稱被洗掉（Erase）。

所以，磁帶是用電（Electricity）將資訊寫入磁帶上，或將其已存入的資訊洗掉。然而，磁帶的特色是將資料記錄在非常細小的磁點上，而不必以打孔在卡片上來代替數字或文字的。這些細小磁點緊密地排聚在一起，肉眼很難看到的。

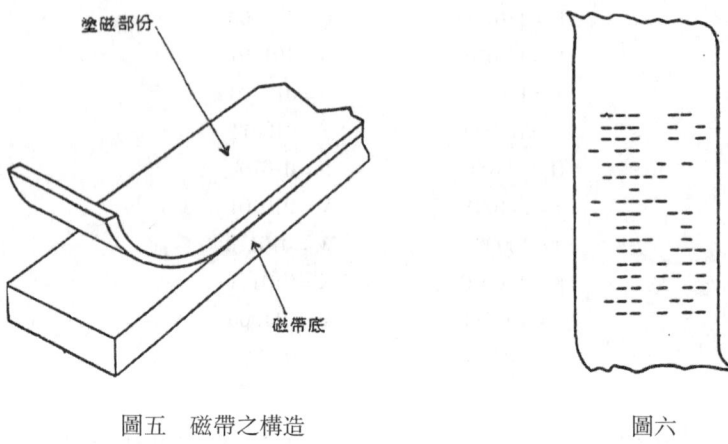

圖五　磁帶之構造　　　　　　　圖六

圖六顯示磁化的 8 個二進位之符號如何組合代替資訊。此圖在顯微鏡下，可看見磁帶上 ELEMENTARY SCHOOL 文字之組成。

因為磁帶較卡片、紙帶能記錄更多的資訊，所以磁帶是目前最常用有效的機器可閱讀形式用來轉存資訊於電子計算機中。當參觀電子計算機中心時，通常都能看到許多盤狀磁帶。圖七是二千四百尺盤狀磁帶，圖八是處理磁帶的機器，圖九是磁帶的貯存庫。

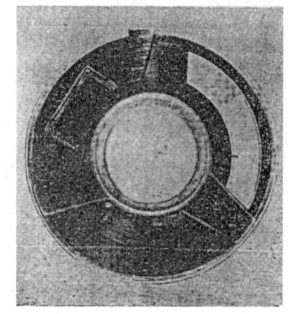

圖七

圖八　　　　　　　　圖九

打資訊在磁帶上必須用一種特殊機器。如同打字一樣，按機器鍵盤上的鍵則使磁帶上某點磁化,而此磁點即代替所要記錄的字,它是由輸送來的電訊(Signals of electricity)至某點,然後磁化此點的。這些電訊包有足夠的電流使磁帶中層氧化亞鐵微粒重新排列而轉變方向,促使由未磁化的狀態轉爲磁化的狀態。

磁帶可保持很多年,而且所佔空間很少,它的舊資訊可以被洗掉並可重新再用來記錄新資訊。它不但可以用來輸送資料入電子計算機中,並可將電子計算機輸出的資訊和所計算的結果記錄貯存起來備用。

有時電子計算機必須讀全部二千四百尺磁帶,方能找到所需的資訊,比較浪費時間和不便。爲了克服此困難,有時也採用磁碟(Magnetic disks)來貯存資訊的,它可使電子計算機直接的更快速找到之前存入的數據資料。磁碟如高度傳真的唱片(Hi-Fi records),每片磁碟的上下兩面的表層皆塗有和磁帶相同的氧化亞鐵化學物。磁碟每一面上又含有用來記錄資訊的圓型軌道,每一軌道預先定明其住址(Addresses),因此電子計算機可以很容易在磁碟上由特定住址直接找到其所需某種資訊,所以用電子計算機由磁碟中直接找資料較由碟帶中更快地獲得資料。

資訊獲得的快速要仰賴電子計算機是否能直接找到資料或是要依次找遍整個資料檔,當然是直接找到較爲快速。在電子計算機中,使用磁碟去找資料即如同利用字典來找字一樣,可直接找到所需的字,是比較快速方便的。

四、辨認文字機器 (Character Recognition Machines)

資訊科學家同時亦在實驗研究其他新的方法,不用打字或字鍵,即可將印刷的資料轉換爲機器可閱讀型式。目前已製造了這種機器,可將印刷的文字如我們肉眼一樣的閱讀後,即能自動將閱讀過的資料轉變成磁帶上的磁點,這種機器稱爲"光學辨認字"(Optical-Character Recognition──簡稱 OCR)機器"或"辨認磁字"(Magnetic Ink Character Recognitions──簡稱 MICR)機器。

圖十可看到銀行支票左下角的賬號數字,這些數字,是可用讀磁字機閱讀的。

本章中,我們已討論了一些電子計算機可操作的各種資訊轉換成機器可閱讀形式的不同方法。目前已有千百萬的儲存資訊的磁帶存在,並用電子計算機來處理它們。將來將會有更多的資訊利用此方法來記錄的。

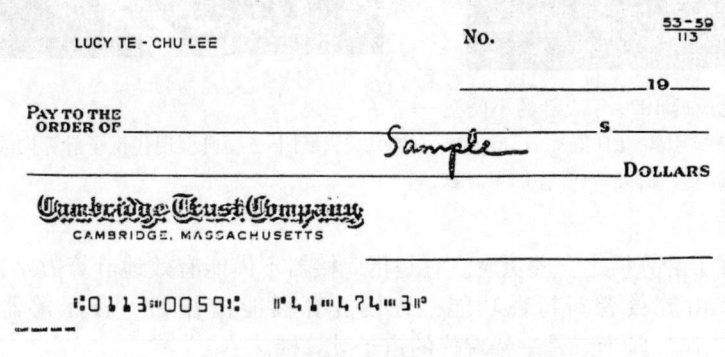

圖十　銀行支票上 MICR 可辨認的數字

當大量資料成爲有價值的電子計算機處理過的輸入資訊時,資訊科學家下一步又將作何種研究呢？下一章將討論此問題。

伍、電子計算機中取出資訊

漸漸地，當更多機器可閱讀形式的資訊問世而富有非常利用價值時，圖書館必會和圖書一樣的購進磁帶的。實際上，圖書館也已在收集影片、錄音帶等資訊，以適應大眾的興趣和使用。不久之後，圖書館將成為社區中供應大眾任何各科資訊主要機構。

人人皆知，看電影必要用放映機才可看到，聽音樂要利用唱機才能聽到播放出的立體音樂，所以同樣的也需電子計算機來協助我們利用儲存在磁帶上的資訊。電子計算機是什麼？它如何操作？能做些什麼？它又將如何能幫助我們找尋資料呢？

一八二二年，英國數學家巴氏（Charles Babbage）撰成有關設計電子計算機執行的功能大綱的論文，可惜的是，到一九四四年，工程師才能將此機器完成，第一部電子計算機設置在哈佛大學，其主要的工作是處理和計算複雜的數學問題。在過去二十五年中，電子計算機的設計進步神速，每次的都比前次的電子計算機速度更快，更便宜，更小而更有效能。一九七〇年，美國已有約 80000 部電子計算機處理各種不同性質的工作。"計算"（Compute）一詞的意思是將數目字總加一起而提供答案，電子計算機亦能做數字的加、減、乘、除之運算及其他算術運算。初期的電子計算機僅能處理數字而已。

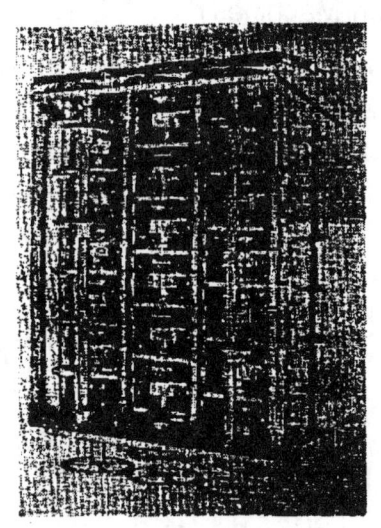

圖十一　巴氏於 1820 年設計的小模型——一架稱為階差引擎（Difference Engine）的機械，係為一引擎，能自動作簡單計算。

圖十二　典型現代電子計算機設備

現在，電子計算機之含義更廣。它是指此機器不僅能有效地計算數字，同時亦能處理文字字母。由於後者新特性功能，致使計算機能擔任如一資訊機器（Information Machine）的工作。圖十二是一架現代的電子計算機。

一、如何寫程式（How to program）

要使電子計算機當做資訊機器（Information Machine）一樣的工作的話，兩件事情是必備的:(一)機器可讀的資訊(Machine Readable Information)和(二)電子計算機程式(Computer programs)。前面已討論過機器可讀的資訊是如何製作的,尚未解釋計算機程式是什麼?很多電子計算機公司如 IBM、UNIVAC、General Electric 和 Central Data 等皆製造電子計算機。向其中任何一公司購買或租借計算機,該公司即會講解和教授機器的使用方法,為此必要學習一種新的語言——即是程式語言(Programming Language)。

程式語言是用來寫程式的,程式含有多組指令(Instructions),命令計算機去做指定的事。學習程式語言要比學德文、法文等語言容易得多。程式語言的字彙(Vocabularies)很少,皆用英文來學習和書寫,現在很多高中和大專學校已開設電子計算機程式語言課程,供學生學習如何寫作電子計算機程式。

雖然電子計算機對人類幫助很大,但它仍不能如人一樣的有學習和思考的能力。記得前面曾提過,只有人類才有思考和創造新概念的獨特能力!單靠電子計算機本身是不能做甚麼的,必須有人來命令它去做些甚麼;能指揮電子計算機去做些甚麼的,就是程式語言。

一旦學會程式語言,即可寫指令給計算機依照所要的方式去做。舉例來說,可以用程式命令電子計算機為老師將學生們的名字按字順排列印出名單。假如一些名字混亂不規則的貯入機器可讀的媒介物中——如磁帶——計算機程式可將之接字順重新編排整理好,然後用另一程式將名單用自動打字機印出或輸出。這只是利用電子計算機處理資訊的一個例子而已。同樣的資料,用程式也可以命令計算機選出六年級十歲女生的名字。由此兩個例子看來,電子計算機依照指令可做貯存、重新編排、挑選和印出資訊的工作——電子計算機可當做資訊器機使用!圖十三是電子計算機程式的一個例子。

```
100 PRINT "THIS PROGRAM CALCULATES THE AREA OF A"
110 PRINT "CIRCLE IF YOU SUPPLY THE RADIUS."
120 PRINT "WHAT IS THE RADIUS"
130 INPUT R
140 LET A = 3.1416*R↑2
150 PRINT "THE AREA IS "; A ;" SQUARE UNITS."
160 PRINT "WOULD YOU LIKE TO GIVE THE COMPUTER"
170 PRINT "ANOTHER RADIUS (TYPE YES OR NO)"
180 INPUT X$
190 IF X$ = "YES" THEN 120
200 END
```

圖十三　電子計算機程式,用 Basic 程式語言寫的

資訊科學家最感興趣的是利用電子計算機執行許多不同資訊功能。電子計算機程式已能做的有:文件和書籍的索引,語文的翻譯工作,圖書館藏書的查詢,語詞的比絞,製曲,回答諮詢,印出字典和根據學生和老師的需求傳遞有關的資訊等等。

另有程式亦可做:保險記錄檔案徹底查看工作,找尋自動發動機方面的資料,為中毒者找出正確解毒劑資料,挑選有關化學藥品的資料,檢查醫院病人的記錄和為律師查得適當的法律條文等等工作。但仍有其他程式,寫來是為了能幫助學生學習某種學科,幫助醫生找尋正確的醫療病人的方法,和提供管理人員最好的商業知識等等。

有些大型公司,如使用一種程式專做檢查新到科技期刊文章的題目。根據該公司工程師或研究人員的興趣,將這些有關興趣的專門學科字句(Profile)列入程式中,以此程式自動校對這些學科專有詞句是否包含在新到科技文章題目中,每逢有相同的字產

生,計算機程式令計算機印出記錄,將此文章之存在通知有關的人,此稱爲資訊選擇的傳播(Sclectric Dissemination of Information——簡稱 SDI)。

實驗性的語文翻譯程式也已存在,多數的機器翻譯(Machine Translation)的研究偏向於俄文譯英文,當然也有其他語文翻譯研究,包括中文在內,也被試驗過的。逐字(Word by word)的翻譯程式比較容易寫,但是,要根據文法的條理翻譯成恰當字句的程式是相當困難的事,這方面,目前尚未有最適當可靠的程式存在。然而,資訊科學家仍繼續在這方面努力研究,因爲他們知道,一旦國與國間語言隔閡如能減低的話,人類的極大的潛在裨益將自然增加。語言處理(Language Processing)這個專有名詞是資訊科學家用來形容與字和觀念有關的電子計算機程式。

二、電告電子計算機(Telephoning the computer)

幾年前,如要使用電子計算機就必要到電子計算機中心(Computer center)不可,最近已進步到可以在別的地方亦能使用計算機中心的計算機了。其方法是用自動打字機(Automatic Typewriter)接連在家裏或學校裏的電話機上,然後再電告位於他方的電子計算機,正如打電話一樣。只要電話接通了,電子計算機立即準備接受指令(Instructions),此即是所謂"線上"(On-line)作業,並能與其他使用者同時共用電子計算機時間和貯存資訊。"分時"(Time sharing)即是允許許多在不同地方的使用者在同時使用貯存在電子計算機內的資料訊息的意思。見圖十四。

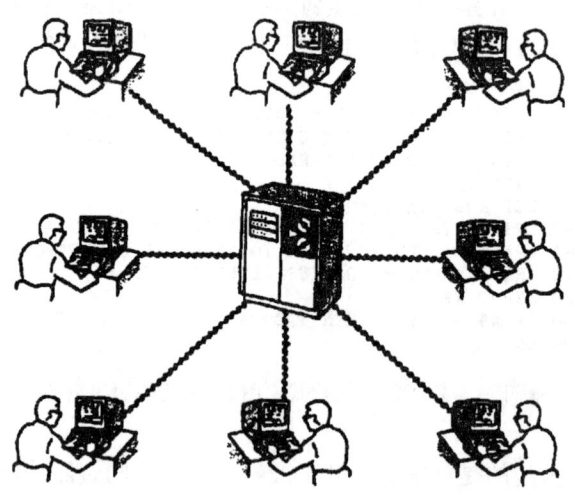

圖十四 分時系統(Time Sharing System)允許許多使用者同時使用電子計算機

以資訊科學而言,利用電話線和電子計算機聯繫的這種技術很是重要。即是無論資訊貯存或置放在何處,如有電話,皆可立即利用到它。一旦資訊貯存在機器可讀的形式媒介物上,它不僅可以用電子計算機處理,也可借電話式無線電通訊系統傳遞資訊的。

"通信"(Telecommunication)這個名詞是資訊科學家用來形容不同種類的資訊由遠距離的地方的發送傳遞方式而言。"通信"(Telecommunication)是一複合字(Compound word)。"Tele"意思是指距離,而"Communication"意思是消息的送遞,所以"Telecommunication"

即是遠距離的來回傳遞消息的意思。

由於此種發展，影響到商業、政府、教育和研究等方面對使用資訊的方法之改變和因此而置設大型資料庫（Data Bank），而充份地允許任何人皆能享用從未能利用到的大量貯存資訊。顯然地看來，各種資料訊息可以傳遞給任何地方的人們。因此，資訊科學是特別關切到改進人類使用資訊的方式，尤其是要用電子計算機方式索取資訊。

陸、資訊通訊（Communication Information）

一、電話方式（By telephone）

人類有史以來，最偉大的發明即是"電話"。一八七六年，亞歷山大·葛瑞翰·貝爾（Alexander Graham Bell）發明的。雖然有時想打電話時會有忙的信號，電話仍是個奇妙的通訊工具。不過，單獨電話本身並無多大用處，其價值是在能與其他電話相通連。電話能與其他通訊裝置互相連接愈多，其價值亦愈大。電話機間之連接並非是直接接線相通，所有的電話線皆先連接到各地所設置的中央站（Central stations）。中央站的作用是做通訊轉接的工作，將電話叫號（Calls）轉接到正確的另一電話機上，美國的電話網路系統（Telephone Network）包括約一億座電話，這些電話是和美國本土上約七億廻哩長的各種電線、電纜和無線電中繼系統交叉相互連接的。普通每天此電話網路系統可迅速正確的處理約三億以上不同形式的通訊叫號——如口信、電視信號（又稱見像"Video"信號）和電子計算機資訊等。

無疑地，電話是最佳口傳資訊的通訊方法。它能與世界上任何地方的人通話，並可用同一電線來送遞圖像（Pictures）和傳遞機器可讀的電子計算機資訊。同時亦可越洋通話，這種作法是將電話線密緊包在不透水電纜裏，由電纜佈設船（Cable ship）將之謹慎小心地放置在海底才接連通話的。夏威夷（Hawaii）與美國加州間的兩個橫跨太平洋（Trans-Pacific）海底電話纜即是一個例子。

現在資訊科學家利用電話線做口信通訊，電傳打字信號之發受，電子計算機線上作業和圖像的傳真傳送工作。雖然這些名詞比較陌生，每一名詞皆列入資訊科學家的字彙中。

電報打字機（Teletype Machine）機能很像電話，不同之處是發受之資訊不是口傳的而是打字的。美國有很多圖書館都採用電報打字方式向其他圖書館要資料，電話公司爲便於大家利用，也編印出黃皮書（Yellow page book）列出各電報打字機器的號碼。

利用電話線而使用電子計算機線上作業已很普遍，在家或教室裏必須備有電話和電子計算機終端機（Terminal）才可這樣使用電子計算機的。計算機可能在距離很遠的地方，甚至於在其他的州或城市內。

終端機這種機器，看來很像一個打字機或電視銀幕（TV Screen）。因爲計算機自有電話號碼，可打此號碼如打電話一樣，嘗聽到"嗶"（Beep）聲時，即是告知已與電子計算機連接上，自此以後，使用計算機情況正如在同一房間一樣。

一旦"在線上"，即可做很多的事。如用程式語言解決數學上的問題、學習新科目，或查尋貯存計算機內的舊資料等。資訊科學家研究很多方法協助醫生、律師、工程師和其他的人習慣的利用電子計算機線上作業。電子計算機是一種新的資訊工具，然而，必經過一段時期的演變，資訊科學才會發現其所有可能的用處的。

利用電話線來回傳送計算機貯存資料是可能的，因為電話公司的系統能將計算機的磁碼（Magnetic codes）轉換成音調（Tones）並能再轉換復原，便於雙方作業。同樣的道理可用在圖像資訊（Picture Information）傳遞。電視攝影機掃描一面印刷文件後，送出的是無數微小的黑白點組成的各型線條。舉例而言，用放大鏡仔細觀察電視銀幕上的圖片，即會發現這些圖片是由很多小點組合而成的。接受電臺（Receiving station）收到的是原始印刷文件傳真或複製品（Facsimile or duplicate）而已，這種情形是因電視攝影機掃描或被另一類似機器稱為傳真複製掃描機（Facsimile scanner）所致。Facsimile 來自拉丁字"Factum"和"Simile"，是精確複製的意思。

很多圖書館對傳真複製很注重，因為可令他們利用電報線與其他圖書館交換圖片和他種記錄的資訊。當然，每個圖書館要有一個傳真複製掃描機和一個傳真複製接受機方可處理此種工作。

資訊家正在與許多公司研究起用電話傳真複製服務（Telefacsimile services），此與美國郵局相競爭有所牴觸。此方式能供應更快的遠距離的私人通信的發受。圖十五是傳真複製掃描機。

圖十五　傳真複製掃描機（Facsimile Scanner）

另一重要的裝置物是 Touch-Tone Telephone。很多特性與自動撥號電話相同。可是，主要不同之處是它能使用者直接與電子計算機傳輸資訊。所以如此，是由於每一號碼的按鈕代表不同的音波（Frequency of Sound）發射的原因。利用 Touch-Tone Telephone 連接遠方的計算機時，它可以傳輸數字方面的資訊。當這些數字資訊被電子計算機接受後，即能遙控其作業。Touch-Tone 的發展激起資訊家考慮去研究新的方法，以建立使用者和遠方圖書館或資料庫間之聯繫。

打電話時可以看到對方的研究早已開始。一九六五年紐約世界博覽會中，電話公司曾示範一種新的電話器具稱做電視電話機（Picture phone），當打電話時可看到對方。將來總有一天，每一家、每一個學校和每一個辦公室皆裝置電視電話（Picture phone），同時因此亦將會擴大資訊傳播方法。圖十六即是電視電話機（Picture phone）。

圖十六　電視電話服務（Picture phone services）包括與電子計算機通訊，使用者可自動撥號詢問計算機顯示某種資訊在銀幕上

二、電纜方式（By Cable）

雖然電話線可以傳遞有聲會話，資訊家相信將來我們會需要更多的電話線傳送大量機器可讀的資料的。如將大量的電子計算機或電視信息擠入電話線，這些信息將會需很久時間才被傳遞到目的地。現在已發展新的通信線，它的容量遠過於狹窄的電話線所能供應的，更具有寬闊通信線，能使信息來回傳遞更快。

同軸電纜（Coaxial cable）即是一個很好的例子，它所傳遞信息的容量大於電話線幾倍以上。圖十七是同軸電纜的內部構造情形，可以看出來一些銅線（Copper wires）放置在絕緣管（Insulated tube）內。拉丁字首"Co"意思是相同"The same" "Axial"是指軸線的意思。

同軸電纜的銅線和絕緣管是平行的，所以是同軸線的；此電纜之名稱即由此而來。因爲這些銅線可以傳遞較電線更多的資訊，而每一電纜又有很多的線。由此可想而知，同軸電纜傳遞資訊容量和速度必會超過電話線的。

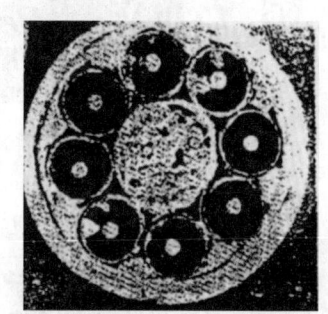

圖十七　同軸電纜內部圖

電纜有線電視臺（Cable Television Station，簡稱 CATV）能利用同軸電纜很快地傳送電視信號至每一家去。電纜電視臺有強而大的天線，可以從很多遠方的電視發射機接收電視信號，然後再發射信號經過地下電纜至各家各戶去。一般的電視只能收到當地節目，CATV 使用者則可以收到遠方的電視節目，而 CATV 傳遞的錄影信號非常清晰，明確而沒有模糊影子（Ghost）。正如電話線已進入每個家庭，同軸電纜幾年內亦會如此的。美國聯邦政府通訊委員會（Federal Communication Commission）期望能保留一個或兩個專爲傳播教育目的訊息的通訊線，可能將來透過這些教育通訊線，CATV 同軸電纜能直接傳遞圖像答案，至每一家庭電視臺上回答有關的資訊問題。

三、微波方式（By Microwave）

另一種接發資訊方式是用微波（Microwave）。工程師所指的微波是利用無線波譜（Radio spectrum）的高頻率波帶（High Frequency Bands）來傳輸的資訊系統。高頻率波帶遠超出家庭無線電收音機收到的範圍。現美國已有很多微波發送和接受電臺，還有些正在設置中。

圖十八　微波天線鐵塔　　　　圖十九　電視天線鐵塔

很容易認出在家的附近找到一個粗鼻形上面以圓盤狀的天線鐵塔（Antenna Tower），見圖。粗鼻形狀說明了微波天線塔和尖形電視天線塔（Television Antenna Tower）不同之處，見圖）。微波天線鐵塔（Microwave Antenna Tower）間之隔距約三十哩，塔的頂端必要能看到另一塔的頂端，而兩塔間不許有其他障礙物存在，此謂在視線距離內（Line of sight）。為此微波塔多設置在高建築物或高山上。微波塔的連接情形正如空中的廣闊通訊公路一樣，因為它替代了幾千個同軸電纜（Coaxial cables）。

四、人造衛星方式（By satellite）

最新而最有發展希望的發送和接受資訊方式是用通信衛星（Communication satellite）。假若能在寬闊的海洋上架設微波天線塔的話，也就不需要通信衛星了。實際上是不能設置一連串相隔三十哩的微波塔橫跨海洋的。這是由於地球的曲度原因。如試在大西洋中設置微波天線塔的話，這些微波塔必要與紐約市自由神像（Statue of Liberty）和倫敦大鵬鐘（Big Ben Clock）之高度相當才能在視線距離內，那麼這些微波塔至少要高達四百七十五哩以上。由於此種限制才引起通信衛星的發展。

 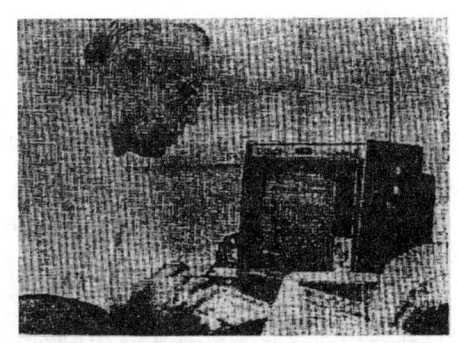

圖二十　左圖為1971年，在瑞士日內瓦召開第四次聯合國原子能和平使用會議，訪問者經過人造衛星通訊查尋美國田納西州美國原子能委員會資料庫的情形，查得資料顯示在面前的終端機上。右圖為美國田納西州的原子能委員會內部一終端機。

通信衛星是一個被放置在地球上空軌道中的物體，由地球上任何地方接受機轉送信息，真可稱為空中通訊交換臺（Switchboard in the sky）。火箭將通信衛星發射至距離赤道（Equator）很高的位置並以圓形軌道環繞而行。以此距離通信偉星的環行速度與地球旋轉時間保持相等。表面上看來猶如定位不動，由於通信衛星永遠是在視線距離內，故信息的傳播常由同一地方發出接受的。

通信衛星並不很大，該模型陳列在華盛頓通信衛星公司（Communication Satellite Corporation）的大廳內，供人參觀。它高有十公尺，寬有八公尺，有一些突出的天線，看來類似家用電視上的天線。內部有一個接受機（Receiver），可接受由地球發出的信息，一個放大器（Amplifier）用來加強信號，還有一個發射機（Transmitter）發射信息到地球上去。衛星的外面裝有一層細小的太陽電池（Solar Batteries），它可以將太陽能轉變成供衛星操作所需的電力。一個衛星使用期限約六年，然後再換新的。

南北極（South and North Pole）除外，地球上所需通訊傳送以三個衛星已敷應用了。通信衛星取代了數千個微波天線塔。現在，通信衛星用來做：國家間電視節目的發送，國際間電話之聯繫，不同國家、不同地方電子計算機間的機器可閱讀的資訊之交換，和圖像傳真的接受發送工作等。因為通信衛星，世界各地的人皆能收到一九七二年美國尼克森總統訪問中國大陸的實況轉播和德國慕尼黑世界運動會之報導。

前面曾提及，資訊的存在方式很多：它可以是錄音帶（Audio Tape）形式，印刷書本式，電視或微粒影片（Film）的錄影圖片形式，也可能是貯存在磁帶上的機器可閱讀資訊形式，或其他種種混合資訊形式等。資訊科學家特別對人造衛星發生濃厚的興趣和熱愛，因為通信衛星能用同一通訊路線（Channel）發送接受各種形式的資訊。

發\收兩用的通訊系統，能將音樂、數位和傳真信號等合而為一體整系統，通信衛星是可以做到這些的！

柒、縮影資訊（Finding Information in Microfilm）

中國有句諺語："百聞不如一見"，圖片包含太多資訊，能顯示出一般非語言文字所能全部形容的各種細節，特別是拍攝影片中的資訊。影片是一種相當有效能的資訊媒介物，它可隨時隨地錄影各種事物。影片經曝光冲洗後，可一次又一次的重覆放映使用。有書、記錄或圖表資料的微小影片稱作"微粒影片"（Microfilm）。

美國太空人——尼爾・阿姆斯壯（Neil Armstrong）和布茲・奧爾俊（Bugg Aldrin）登陸月球時，曾拍攝許多珍貴的照片，同時他們利用無線電口述形容所見的一切。這些拍攝的影片經他們帶回地球，供專家們研究影片的內容。每一影片置放在立體顯微鏡（Stereomicroscope）下，由科學家研究、驗看、測量和評估月球表面各細小部份，然後將此研究結論印製成冊，描述影片包含之多量資訊的內容。

"微粒影片"是種特別重要的資訊媒介物，不僅能將資訊的很多詳細細節攝入鏡頭，而其所佔之空間又非常少。普通一般照相機所用之影片之寬度是二英吋，然而它可將一架波音七四七（Boeing 747）飛機全圖，或整個帝國大廈（Empire State Building）建築，或美國國都（U. S. Capital）全貌拍攝在一面小的照片上。由此原因，影片有時可用來拍攝書、文字紀錄或圖表式的資訊，如一本書中某幾頁資料，商業信件檔案，報章雜誌中蒐集的資料等等。這些經微縮的資訊，並非因此而改變或更換其原始文件原有的內容，即是保存其原件的一切，這稱為縮影製作法（Microfilming）。

縮影製做允許將大量的資料縮緊成很小面積。例如，紐約時報（New York Times）按時將每日報紙製成縮影片，全月報紙只需製成一捲影片，每一捲影片中的每一"片面"（Frame）即是所謂的顯微鏡縮影照片（Microphotographs）或稱微小影像（Microimages）。

一、顯微縮影（Microphotography）之由來

一八三九年，英國人約翰・賓傑明・但塞（John Benjamin Dancer）將攝影術（Photography）與顯微鏡（Microscope）合併一起使用而製做成顯微鏡縮影片。他是使用顯微鏡鏡頭（Microscope Lens）在他的實驗中，因此能將一頁資料縮小成非常小的面積。從此以後，其他的科學家亦嘗試製做比較更小更小的微小影片和照片。一八六〇年，英國大衛・布魯斯特爵士（Sir David Brewester）發表一篇科技論文，形容如何能將很多極小的照片資料隱藏在如同墨點（Ink Dot）大小的面積內。

法普魯士戰爭時，法國政府利用顯微縮影照片與被圍攻的巴黎駐軍聯繫。大約三千頁的軍事情報被縮小成約幾吋長的影片，這些輕量的影片成捲裝入容器內縛在鴿子尾部羽毛上，當傳信鴿飛至巴黎，影片即被取出，用放映機顯示出來，內含的情報將由人工抄寫在紙上，以供閱看。

第二次大戰時，德軍為了處理自己情報間諜工作，亦發明了一種攝影法叫做"微點"（Microdot）。數頁的機密情報被縮小拍攝成極小面積——微小到可以將之隱藏在一本書的一句中之標點符號（Punctuation Marks）上！只有德國間諜工作人員才知某書的某一句點或點上藏有情報。"微點"即是一九四〇年代顯微縮影技術進步情形的一個很好的例子。從那時起到現在，在這方面亦有更多更突出的進步與改變。

二、縮影膠片的種類（Types of Films）

用做顯微縮影的膠片有四種，其中以銀鹵素化合物（Silver Halides）膠片最為普遍，這種膠片也就是一般家庭照相使用的一樣。膠片的表面塗有微小銀粒（Microscopic grains of Silver），拍攝時，光線進入相機，觸及"銀鹵素化合物"塗成的膠片表層，這即是膠

片的曝光（Exposing the film）。這種銀鹵素化合物對一般光線非常敏感，任何時候，光線觸及膠片表層即能"移去"（Uncover）銀粒而拍照。

然後，將膠片置於暗房（Darkroom）內冲洗，用化學藥品（Chemicals）洗去未曝光銀粒，冲洗後的膠片即是底片（Negative）；上面顯出深色和灰色和透明部份，這是由於利用感光乳劑（Emulsion）而致，底片可用來印製照片。

"達索"（Diazo）膠片爲第二種。這種膠片表層塗有一種染色顏料（Dye），對紫外光線（Ultraviole Light）特別敏感。紫外線和一般白日光（White Lignt）不同，它有不同的波長（Wavelength），肉眼看來是紫色的光彩。"達索"膠片遇紫外光線而曝光，部份的染色顏料即被破壞。此種膠片是置放在充滿氨氣即是阿姆尼亞蒸氣（Ammonia Vapor）貯器內冲洗的。結果顯出有深色和灰色部份。膠片上面影像清晰可見。

第三種膠片，商用名稱是"卡瓦"（Kalvar）。Kalvar 膠片塗有一層微小氣泡（Bubbles of Gas）的塑狀表層，遇紫外光線曝光就擴脹氣泡的氣體而攝照。冲洗膠片是將膠片經過有溫度滾軸（Warm-Rollers）之間而成；並不需要液狀的化學藥品來冲洗的。熱度導致氣泡脹裂呈現下面透明膠片，膠片上餘有的塑層顯示攝得的影像。此種"乾式"（Dry Developing）Kalvar 膠片冲洗特性，對商業界用的攝影特別重要有用，因爲商業上時有急需拍照之必要。

另一種是"Photochromics"膠片，此種微縮影片攝製方法與他種不同。此種膠片塗有微粒分子可變換色彩，此現象是因接觸紫外光線而致。紫外線曝光使微粒分子由有色狀態（Color State），變爲無色狀態（Colorles State），此種"轉變"不需任何熱或化學藥品的幫助。

用日光曝光亦可將照好的 Photochromics Film 膠片轉變恢復其原有的狀態（Original State）的。有此特性，拍攝成此種膠片上之縮影資料可被洗去（Erased），如磁帶（Magnetic Tape）上的資訊一樣。

以上四種不同的膠片，拍攝之資料影像的縮小面積大小是依據其使用的鏡頭而定。然而，其中以 Photochromic Film 最能用做攝製高密度的貯存縮影片的。如圖二十一是 2 吋見方（2 by 2 inches）的膠片由 Photochromic 底片製成，上面包括 2000 頁 Photochromic Microimages（PCMI）聖經（King James Version of the Holy Bible），甚至於還可攝製比此更小的縮影片。

圖二十一　2000 頁 Photochromic Microimages（PCMI）聖經

三、立體照相（Holography）

另一新技術的部份，它更使人們對縮影發生強烈興趣的是雷射（Laser）和它能用來製造立體照相（Holograms）的特性。

雷射（Laser）這個字是代表 Light Amplification by Stimulated Emission of Radiation（輻射激射的放大光波）。一九五一年，美國物理學家查理士·唐納斯（Charles H. Townes）發明一種方法能將自然平衡的一種低能量（Low Energy）分子轉變爲高能量狀態（High Energy State），甚至於使這些分子更具有活力而放出更多的能量。此種放射形態成為一強大窄狹的光柱可縮小成十萬分之一吋的寬度,這即是雷射(Laser)。

立體照相(Holograms)這個詞始於但尼斯‧嘉賓博士(Dr. Dennis Gabor),一位匈牙利科學家。在一九四〇年代的後期間,當嘉賓博士實驗着發明一種新的顯微鏡時,利用一束密緊的光源,稱為"同調光源"(Coherent Light)製成一種特殊的照相來,他稱之為立體照相(Hologram);此字源自希臘文字,是"完面照相"(Whole Picture)的意思。嘉賓博士因發明此立體照相術,於一九七一獲得諾貝爾物理獎。

此奇特的光源具有特殊功能。同調光源的光波(Waves)能一貫而不變的保持其相互間之距離,此意謂用此光源照射一物體至另一物體上知其光的波長(Wavelength of the Light),即可很正確地計量出其間的距離。一部份是因光波具此間隔固定之特性,致能用之製作立體照相。

標準攝影底版(Normal Photographic Plates)攝製成深色和淺色的影片部份,是依據目標物體(Objects)在被攝時之照明光度而定,雷射照相亦如此一般。除此之外,還加上攝錄了有關目標物體距離的資料。此法是將雷射光柱分裂(Splitting)成兩部份而致。一部份光柱照射在底版上做"查照"(reference)用;另一部份光柱放射至目標物體上和其反射光波同樣的射至底版上。此兩組相似的光波是說因為反射光柱和目標物體之輪廓和外表是在相依之外(Out of phase)之故,而發生光波干擾衝突(Interfere)。由於這些光波波長之不同,產生陰影在底版上而能攝製到目標物體的第三面(Third Dimension)部份。底版的沖洗可用一般的方法處理之。處理後的底版,肉眼看來是灰色而無光彩。然而,如用同調光源(Coherent Light)如雷射光來看的話,所攝目標物體的全部份皆可在底版上看到,包括深色、淺色和遠距離部份,顯示出完整的三面立體縮影影像(Three-Dimensional Image),見圖二十二,雷射立體照相過程圖表。

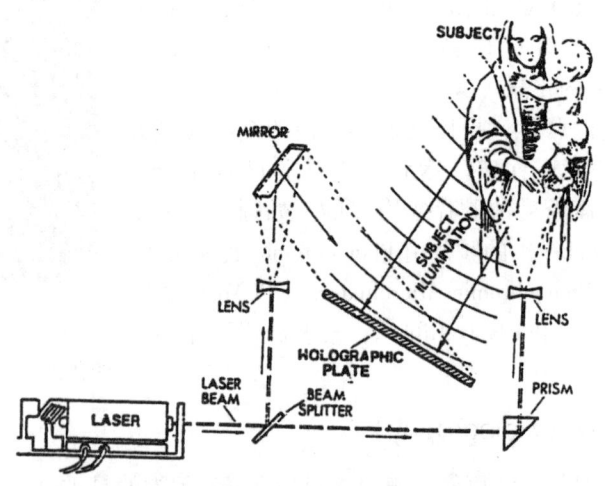

圖二十二 雷射(Laser)立體照相過程圖表

其實,這不僅是三面立體照相;遠距部份也完全徹底的攝製出來,看上去可實際見到目標物體的四週部份,如同我們平時看物一樣。這即是立體照相的新技術。事實上,將三面立體攝製的資料以顯微形式貯存在縮影片上,創開了另一種使用縮影的新境界。

四、縮影的形式（Forms of Microfilm）

很明顯的，縮影是一種非常有用的方法，可供我們用來貯存大量的資訊。一般來說，縮小的影像資料可以兩種形式來貯存——連續式和單獨式。

連續式貯存方式是將縮小的資料影像攝製在一百呎的三十五米厘或十六米厘縮影片盤（Microfilm Spools）上。一米厘等於0.04吋，所以35米厘是1.4吋寬，16米厘影片是0.64吋寬，片盤式縮影片可用人工片處理或將之放入匣式（Cartridges）中，利用自動閱讀機器（Automatic Viewing Machines）閱讀。見圖二十三，縮影片盤和匣式縮影。

圖二十三　縮影片盤（Microfilm spools）和匣式縮影

除縮影片盤形式外，影片亦可以單獨個別方式貯存。例如：一個縮影夾檔（Microfilm Jacket）可放條狀縮影片（Strips of Microfilm），孔卡縮影片（Aperture card），可包括一個或多個縮小的資料影片，是裝框在有框窗片夾（Gummed Window Frames）IBM或他種卡片上；縮影單片（Microfiche）是一面縮影片上很多縮小的資料影片；以橫（Rows）縱（Columns）式排列成行，（法文"Fiche"是薄片"Sheet"的意思）；縮影紙帶（Microtape），將縮影資料印在膠背紙（Adhesive Backed Paper）上，便於剪貼在檔卡（Card Files）上；最後，如縮影卡片（Microcards），類似縮影單片，不同的地方是它的縮影印製在紙卡上而非影片上。見圖二十四，各種縮影形式的圖片。

圖廿四　縮影單片（Microfiche）、縮影夾檔（Microfilm Jacket）、孔卡縮影（Aperture Card）、縮影片盤（Spools）、匣式縮影（Cartridge）和條狀縮影（Strip）

五、閱讀和複製（Viewing & Copying）

資訊科學家和出版家合作將圖書館全部藏書製成縮影，這樣即使成千冊的書也能貯藏在如鞋盒大小的貯藏器內！目前，美國政府是最多的縮影生產單位。

一九七〇年，美國國防部（Department of Denfense）、原子能委員會（Atomic Energy Commission）、太空總署（National Aeronautics & Space Administration）和"教育部"（Office of Education）將他們的研究和技術報告皆製成縮影單片（Microfiche），與其他總共發行了約二千萬件縮影單片。同時美國政府出版處（U. S. Government Printing Office）於一九七一年發表通告計劃將所有美國政府文件資料製成縮影。因此，縮影在所有處理資訊方式中，很快成為資訊發行的非常重要的方法，雖然最初製作縮影的目的僅是為了節省貯存空間。

為了能使人利用這些縮影資料，必須要將它放大後才能閱讀，目前市面上已有些機器不但可以用來閱讀縮影資料，同時亦可立即放大複製印出所需要的資料部份，這種機器稱為"縮影閱讀複製機"（Microfilm Reader-Printer），見圖二十五。

圖二十五　縮影閱讀複製機（Microfilm Reader-Printer）

假若您附近當地學校圖書館並沒有閱讀複製機的話，在圖書館內可能有另一種閱讀縮影的機器。資訊科學家正在研究設計一種便宜的，小型可攜帶的"手提縮影閱讀機"（Portable Microfilm Reader）便於學生在家或課室內攜帶使用。有了輕便手提縮影閱讀機，一定可以更增多學生們對各式縮影資料的使用，無論在家或校內。設計家覺得這種縮影閱讀機應是輕便的，如一本書樣大小，內部具有非常好的光源（Light source）和清晰的對光焦距（Sharp focusing）。除此之外，最重要是令人一見就喜愛，於是使用人可以舒服地利用它來閱讀縮影資料，正如他們蜷曲在沙發上看書一樣。這即是所謂的"人的因素"（Human factors）方面之考慮。資訊科學家知道盡量使人與機器（Man and Machine）間關係自然而不複雜。故在設計任何資訊機器（Information Machine）時都特別注意到"人的因素"。基於此原因，加入資訊科學研究的行列中，有很多是心理學家（Psychologists）。

六、電子計算機和縮影

當越來越多資訊製成縮影時，縮影索引也一定要編印，以便於查尋資訊之所在。美國物理學家范納佛‧布希博士（Dr. Vannevar Bush）見此需要，於一九四六年建議設計一種稱為 MEMEX 的機器，這種機器可自動地由一卷縮影中檢索資訊。現在，電子計算機不但用來做索引和查書所需的資料，同時亦可做由大量縮影檔中尋找或選擇所需的縮影照片工作。圖二十六為布希博士在麻省理工學院設計的差作用分析機（Differential Analyzer）的一部份。該分析機即是現代類比計算機（Analog Computers）之前身。

圖二十六　范納佛‧布希博士（Dr. Vannevar Bush）在麻省理工學院（M. I. T.）設計的差作用分析機（Differential Analyzer）之一部份。此分析機即是現代類比計算機（Analog Computers）之前身。

在其他方面。電子計算機也對縮影的發展影響甚大。如電子計算機可用製作微小照片上縮影上。另外為了代替電子計算機輸出結果印在報表紙上做法，即是利用程式（Programs）設計操作一種特殊具有尖銳光筆（Sharp Pencil of Light）的機器——稱為電子光柱（Electronic Beam）——來構造形成如文字和數字樣的形態，並將之放射至縮影影片上，此法就是用縮影輸出來代替報表紙的輸出方法。這種做法非常快速，每秒鐘可制約百頁的底片，這些特別的機器稱為孔姆（COM）。它的全名是 Computer Output Microfilm，意思是電子計算機管制縮影系統，也可以說是電子計算機輸出縮影資料。

電子計算機又可用來做電子印刷（Electronic Printing）排版工作。用設計的程式來控制電子計算機，使之能自動的做選用某種和某號字號，排定每頁的寬度和長度，標題插入，並能將每頁製成縮影底片，和其他等等事項。電子印刷術在資訊科學中仍在發展階段。

　　以上種種，在資訊科學界僅僅是很多發展方面的一小部份而已。主要的目的是尋求新的方法來調配電子計算機的電子能源和縮影錄影能力，以期產生創新的和有效的應用。很明顯的，縮影在資訊科學中居於非常重要的地位，除用做保留記錄外，另外很多其他的用途。不久的將來"縮小照相複製的書籍"、縮影書籍圖書館（Microbook Libraries）將會存在的。一本數百頁的書將可拍攝成一片 4×6 英吋的縮影單片（Microfiche）上。因此，成千本圖書將很容易的貯存在如鞋盒大小的貯藏器具內。明日的圖書館將不再流通借出製成縮影單片的書籍，代替是其複製品，便於使用者帶回去利用輕便手提縮影閱讀機來閱讀！

　　縮影技術為資訊科學開啓了一個新時代，聯同電子計算機和通信（Telecommunication）技術，無疑地聚成一股強大的力量可促進世界各國資訊科學之發展工作。

捌、資訊科學的展望

　　前面幾章討論到資訊科學的工具——電子計算機、通訊、縮影，用這些工具可能發展和建立資訊系統（Information Systems），以多種新方法服務大衆。例如，有很多圖書館相互合作設立資訊網（Information Networks），即是各將圖書館的資訊、圖書、視聽資料等連結一環組成一大型的圖書系統（Library System）。利用通訊系統，將資訊網內所有資訊資源供應給任何地方的人使用，使在偏僻地區的學生同樣能和住在大城市的學生一樣有權享受豐富的知識資源。由資訊網的各圖書館相互以通訊方式聯繫，將會很快的達到我們的願望。

　　僅能做到提供他人可用資訊這一點是不够的；有用的資訊，必是切題的（Relevent）、有時效性的（Timely），而對接受資訊的使用者有其特殊的價值的。為此，很多資訊科學家皆從事一些研究工作，研究不同個別的人，他使用"資訊的習慣"（Information Habits），如醫生們、律師們、商人們等等其他的人，試求瞭解他們對資訊的吸收、利用和需求等等。這些研究工作對發展更完善的資訊系統是極為重要的！

　　雖然資訊科學是一門新興學科，但很多大學已在大學部或研究所開設資訊科學課程。如一個人選擇以資訊科學為其事業的話，他可做一位研究人員，專門研究探討有關資訊科學的最基本理論問題，或為一從業人員利用資訊科學和其技術工具解決滿足某些特殊資訊的需求問題，或者從事教授青年學生學習此新興學科的基本原理等工作。

玖、結　語

　　很多年前，在空中運輸和電訊尚未發明以前，世界上資訊量尚能管理控制，而其生產量的使用率亦比較緩慢。自一九五〇年以後，整個情形完全改變了。

　　工藝技術演變的速度、人口爆發、視聽資料和電視的發展，綜合顯微縮影和通訊影響壓力以更快的速度為更多的人們生產大量的資訊。它的生產速度非常驚人！當今，人們受到資訊交換的影響程度遠過於以往他們過去的經驗。事實上，資訊速度起昇如此捷速，我們都已不能領悟到它對人類的現在和未來各方面生活之影響將有多大！

現代的各種形式資訊大量增加是很明顯的。然而，次要明顯的是，實事上任何人都不可能學習和記憶他所想知道的資料訊息。

這些問題要仰賴資訊科學家研究出方法，不但能保留人類過去成就的記錄文字和圖片等資訊，同時並能提供新的資訊給任何需要的人，新進未來的資訊家將面臨此挑戰。

任何人如接受此挑戰，選擇資訊科學為其職業的話，他們將從事刺激而定有意義的工作受到不同報酬代價和滿足個人願望的收穫，知道他們的努力貢獻能幫助傳遞舊知識給願學的人，協助他們為人類努力建立一個更完善的未來世界。

參考文獻

一、書籍部份

The Analytical Engine: Computers—Past, Present, and Future, Jeremy Bernstein, Random House, Inc., New York, 1964, 113 pp., ＄2.95 (hardback); ＄1.45 (paperback).

Annual Review of Information Science and Technology, Carlos Cuadra (Editor), American Society for Information Science Washington, D.C., 1966 to date.

Careers and Opportunities in Computer Science, John M. Carrol, E.P. Dutton and Company Inc., New York, 1967, 191 pp., ＄4.50.

The Computerized Society, James and Norman Martin, R.D. Adrian, Prentice-Hall, Inc., Englewood Cliffs, New Jersey, 1970, 560 pp., ＄10.95.

Handbook of Data Processing for Libraries, Robert M. Hayes and Joseph Becker, John Wiley and Sons, Inc., New York, 1970, 885 pp., ＄19.95.

The Information Machines, Ben H. Bagdikian, Harber and Row, Publishers, New York, 1971 359 pp., ＄8.95.

Information Storage and Retrieval, Joseph Becket and Robert M. Hayes, John Wiley and Sons, Inc., New York, 1963, 448 pp., ＄13.50.

Key Papers in Information Science, Arthur W. Elias (Editor), American Society for Information Science, Washington, D.C., 1971, 223 pp., ＄6.00.

Modern Data Processing, Robert Arnold, Harold C. Hill, and Alymer V. Nicholas, John Wiley and Sons, Inc., New York, 1973, 496 pp., ＄10.95.

二、論文部份

As We May Think, Vannevar Bush, Atlantic Monthly, 176: 101 (August, 1945). Annual Review of Information Science and Technology, Encyclopaedia Britannica, volume 1.

Behoid the Computer Revolution, Peter T. White, National Geographic Magazine, 138: 593 (November, 1970).

Communication, John R. Pierce, Scientific American, 227: 31 (September, 1972).

Information Network Prospects in the United States, Joseph Becker, Library Trends, 17: 306 (January, 1969).

Information Storage and Retrieval, Ben-Ami Lipitz, Scientific American, 215: 224 (September, 1966).

Information Technology: Its Social Potential, Edwin B. Parker and Donald A. Dunn,

Science 176: 1932 (June 30, 1972).

Microfilm Emerges from Its Dusty Corner, Lawrence Lessing, Fortune, 86: 140 (August, 1972).

Telecommunications Primer, Joseph Becker, Journal of Library Automation, 2: 148 (September, 1969).

Trends in Library Technology, Joseph Becker, Special Libraries, 62: 429 (October, 1971).

泛論資訊科學[*]

最初，人類以"記憶力"爲紀錄的實體。由於羣居的關係，人類社會趨於繁複；事物的增加，消息的演遞，"記憶力"的功能，已不敷使用，乃有圓形、記號、文字等等的發明。紀事於黏土石、石塊、紙草紙（Papyrus）或羊皮紙（Vellum）的媒體上，此爲消息儲存的雛型。迨至十五世紀，印刷術的發明，人類的文化紀錄得以大量傳遞給他人和後人參考，作爲謀求人類文化改進與發展之依據。十二世紀英國作家培根曾說："知識本身即是力量"。知識即是有系統地整理和評估資料和訊息（今日簡稱資訊——Information）之累積。"資訊"一詞，至今雖尚無適當與中肯的定義，但歸納共通的注釋，資訊爲可傳遞、可追尋或可利用的紀錄媒介，資訊亦是處理過的數據（Date）、知識或情報。它可得自經驗、觀察、交往和閱讀的途徑。人際間的關係趨於複雜，乃是由於浩如瀚海般的資訊增產與存在所致，它在人類的各種活動過程中，因而佔有一席非常重要的地位。

資訊科學（Information Science）是一門二十世紀六十年代的新興科學。由於近代的知識爆發，科技資料急劇的生產，處理資料的技術不斷的改進，導致此一新名詞的誕生。資訊科學主要的是研究資訊本身的特性、動態和傳播；資訊的產生、蒐集、處理、儲存及檢索；和資訊的通訊方法和利用等情形。其要點在於研究、處理與運用資訊的各種問題。

吾人不斷地藉着找尋資訊、交換資訊、運用資訊作爲學術研究、處理事務和行政決策的參考依據，同時也創造新的資訊供他人參考。今日過量的資訊已造成不能完全利用和處理的嚴重問題。傳統式的服務和資訊系統，不能應付目前對資訊服務的需要。各機構爲了此一緣故？紛紛設立特殊資訊中心。如美國原子能委員會即是一例，它設有二十五個專門性的資訊中心；再如"國家科學委員會"科學技術資科中心以及"國立政治大學"人文社會科學資料中心等，皆爲處理與運用科技暨人文社會科學方面的資料而設立。

近年來，資訊科學已普遍受到歐美人士的重視，認爲資訊是推動國家一切發展的基本"能源"。由於其範圍甚爲廣泛，並具有科際（Interdisciplinary）的特性，故至目前在學科方面仍未定型。美國於一九六八年將原來的美國資料學會（American Documentation Institute—ADI）擴充其組織，更名爲美國資訊科學學會（American Society of Information Science），目前擁有會員二千餘人，團體會員七十七個，遍及世界四十六個國家，分會有廿五個，另設十六個"專門興趣部門"（Special Interests Groups），以供會員按自己專長興趣加入，作爲交換意見及專門問題之探討，已成爲國際間最具領導地位的資訊科學專業組織。

在教育方面，美國近年來已正式在大學或研究所開授資訊科學課程，授予的學位亦分爲學士、碩士和博士三種。如前所述，因其範圍廣泛，故授課內容因之而異，端視其所強調的要點而定。在臺灣，各大學開授此類課程尚屬萌芽階段，與資訊科學相關的課

---

[*] 本文曾發表在《教育資料科學月刊》8 卷 2–3 期（1975 年 9 月），第 2—3 頁。

程已在圖書館學系、教育資料科學系、電機系、電子計算機科學系、應用數學系以及淡江管理科學研究所管理資訊組、系統分析組等開授。據悉，"國立政治大學"正籌備於近一、二年內成立圖書館學與資訊科學系，如屬確實，則深值得吾人稱許。

電子計算機科學與資訊科學幾乎於同時期誕生。爲了解決大量資訊處理且能提供迅速有效地答詢問題服務，必仰賴電子計算機的技術以建立資訊系統。時勢所趨，在臺灣近幾年已開始重視資訊建檔和圖書館資料之自動化。如中山科學院使用 CDC-Cyber-70 電子計算機處理圖書館的技術資料、新書通報、資料登錄和目錄卡之製作等工作；"國科會"科技資料中心亦已於最近完成全國西文科學期刊資料自動化作業，除可印出《科學期刊聯合目錄》外，還可做線上查詢（On-line Search）期刊有關資料，該中心正計劃將海內外科技人員資料輸進電子計算機建立檔案，及圖書期刊聯合採購作業自動化事宜；淡江覺生紀念圖書館也正準備利用該院電子計算機的設備增進作業效率，進而加強服務功能。當今吾人所期待者，乃是中文電子計算機輸入、輸出系統的改善務期趨於完美，則今後對於中文資訊處理所遭遇的困擾問題，將可迎刃而解。

基於臺灣各界對資訊科學逐漸重視，"中央研究院"業已於一九七四年公佈，籌設"資訊科學研究所"，"教育部"也從今年開始，於公費留學考試中增設資訊科學及系統分析兩個學門，雖然這兩種學門稍偏向於電子計算機科學，但也直接顯示政府對這一學科已在重視，從事培植人才的工作。

前已述及，資訊科學具有科際的特性，它可運用於各類學門，亦可供各行各業的人士所利用。因而對於資訊科學一門就存有不同的看法與見解。就以運用於圖書館學爲例，它不但可充實與擴大圖書館學的內容與範圍，同時亦推動圖書館學界向時代的前端邁進了一大步。同樣地，它用於其他部門，或將有助於整個社會與國家早日實現全面現代化的理想。

中美科學資料運用發展研討會*

一、前言

"中美科學合作委員會"於一九六四年成立,其目的是雙方合作共同研究及解決臺灣地區科學發展上的各種有關問題,故每年召集各項發展科學之研討會。近年來,由於"中美科學合作委員會"及"國家科學委員會",國際科學合作有關人士,以及美國總統特派前任科技特別助理畢林士博士(Dr. Bruce Billings)皆深深感到科學資料對科學發展進行,有着極不可忽視的重要性。不幸的是,臺灣各方機構人士對科學資料不但根本缺乏認識,而且亦缺乏對科學資料蒐集處理,運用及發展的制度之設立,又正當"國家科學委員會"附屬之科學資料及儀器即將分設,科學資料中心計劃成立之際,該中心之業務計劃及今後工作方針皆迫切需要訂定與研究,故決定將一九七三年"中美科學合作委員會"在華盛頓舉行研討會之討論專題爲:科學資料運用發展問題。並在亞洲協會及"國家科學委員會"資助及畢林士博士熱誠協助下邀請美國加州大學洛杉磯分校圖書管理及服務系教授海斯博士(Dr. Robert M. Hayes)於1973年八月間專程來臺灣作爲期兩星期之訪問我有關科學資料問題。海斯博士來華任務有三:(一)視察臺灣目前科學與技術資料之蒐集,尋求及傳佈的實際情況及需要。(二)建議如何加強並提高"國家科學委員會"科學資料中心之組織、業務與工作效能。(三)協助"中美科學合作委員會",計劃"中美科學資料,運用發展研討會"之召開。海斯博士於視察完畢後曾發表書面報告──科學資料在臺灣 Science Information in Taiwan──對臺灣科學資料現況作詳細分析報導,並提供各種建議,此報告爲此次"中美科學資料運用研討會"之藍本。

會議的籌劃及代表團之組成,由我方"中美科學合作委員會"負責,曾多次集會,討論參觀訪問、行程、研討議題代表發言人等事項。我方代表團由"國家科學委員會"主任委員吳大猷博士爲代表團團長,代表共計十人,分由"國家科學委員會"、科學資料中心、"中央標準局"、"中國石油公司"、農業發展復興委員會、聯合工業研究所、中山科學研究院及大同公司等單位選派,另由我駐美科學參事及臺灣留美圖書館學者九人,爲會議觀察員(Observers)共十五位。美方代表者團團長爲海斯博士,代表分由美國國家科學院、國家科學基金會、美國標準局、美國物理學會、史密史松尼協會、伯泰爾研究所、太空公司、美國喬治華盛頓大學、杜拜公司單位員責人,或圖書資料專家擔任,共十一位。另有亞洲基金會、國務院、國際發展總署、國家科學基金會、全國圖書館及資料科學委員會,馬里蘭大學及資料工業協會等單位派遣專家爲會議觀察員。同時由大會邀請美國國會圖書館及美國原子能委員會資料專家專題演講者二位,出席會議人員總數爲四十五人,研討會日程自一九七三年四月二十五日起至四月二十七日止,共計三天。

二、會前會後之參觀訪問

爲使我方代表瞭解美國科技資料之處理及運用之現況,特計劃此次行程中,在正式

---

* 本文曾發表在《"國立中央圖書館"館刊》新 6 卷第 2 期(1973 年 9 月),第 43—46 頁。

研討會舉行前後，由美國國家科學院安排下參觀訪問美國各地重要有名的大學、學術研究機構，生產單位之重要研究中心，各種圖書館、資料處理系統及中心，各地所訪問參觀之單位有：
舊金山：
　　史坦福大學圖書館（Stanford University）及其資料檢索系統（Ballots/SPIRES Systems）
洛杉磯：
　　加州大學洛杉磯分校（UCLA）之研究圖書館、工程及數學圖書館、教育及心理圖書館、化學圖書館、生物醫學圖書館資料服務中心（Center for Information Services）。
　　太空公司之研究圖書館（AEROSPACE Cooperation Library）。
　　系統發展公司（System Development Corp.）及其資料處理部門。
支加哥：
　　伊里諾伊理工學院之研究院（IITRI）及其電腦中心（Computer Search Center），該機構對美國工業界及研究機構提供各項研究及設計服務，並與韓國國家科學技術研究院（KIST）有密切之聯繫與合作。
　　約翰奈瑞爾圖書館（John Crerar Library），該館歷史悠久，爲世界有名之科技專門性之公共圖書館，又附設有 National Translation Center 收集海內外翻譯文件，出版 Translation Register Index，研究圖書館中心（Center for Research Libraries），該中心圖書館之特色是專門搜藏不常用之各種資料圖書等，並支援供應美國十六個著名大學圖書館所需之研究資料，此十六個圖書館爲該中心之基本會員圖書館及經費來源。
哥倫布士：
　　伯泰爾紀念研究所（Battele Memorial Institute）之 Information Systems Section，該所爲科學研究機構，規模龐大，該研究所曾於一九六五年協助韓國政府成立韓國科學及技術研究院（KIST）建立其工作目標及方針，現雙方仍保持密切聯繫與合作。
　　化學摘要社（Chemical Abstracts Service），該社爲美國化學學會所屬單位，專門從事化學文獻摘要工作，其出版之 *Chemical Abstracts* 爲世界最具權威性之化學參考文獻。
　　俄亥俄大專圖書館中心（Ohio College Library Center），此爲一區域性圖書館合作組織，現有會員圖書館四十八個，該中心負責將圖書目錄作業自動化。利用美國國會圖書館之 MARC Tape 及各合作院校自編之圖書目錄爲基本目錄目前完成（On-line Union Catalog 及 Shared Cataloguing System，供各館之間利用通信網以查詢聯合目錄資料，可助以選購圖書，編目分類及各單位圖書收藏情況之用，簡便迅速。
華盛頓：
　　此地值得參觀之單位甚多，由於時間有限，不能全部一一訪問，各代表以自己單位之需要及興趣分頭參觀訪問有關機構共參觀之機構有：
　　國立農業圖書館（National Agricultural Library）
　　國立醫學圖書館（National Library of Medicine）
　　國會圖書館之科學及技術部門（Science & Technology Division of Library of Congress）及 Science & Technology Reference Center
　　國防文件中心（Defense Documentation Center）

航空及太空總署資料資料中心（NASA）
國立標準局（US National Bureau of Standards）
國家技術資料中心（National Technical Information Service）
美國資料科學學會（American Society for Information Science）
美國州組織（American Organization of State）
史密史松尼科學資料交換處（Smithsonian Science Information Exchange）
美國圖書交換公司（U. S. Books Exchange Inc.）

費　城：

杜拜化學公司（Du Pont & Co）之資料處理部門，僅此部門用二百人，且從每年二億美元的研究發展經費中，以八百萬元（佔4％）來投資用於資料收集、運用及處理的工作。

科學資料所（Institute for Scientific Information）爲一營利機構，該中心出版有 *Science Citation Index Current Contents* 及 *Index Chemicus* 等重要科技參考資料。

生物摘要社（BIOSIS），該社爲著名 Biological Abstracts 出版地。

美國國立摘要及索引服務中心（National Federation of Abstracting & Indexinge Service）。

紐約市：

工程索引公司（Engineering Index Inc.）爲一私營非營利之機構，專門負責工程方面文獻資料之摘要及索引之編印工作，爲工程研究所需技術文獻主要來源。該公司定期出版 Engineering Index Card-A-Lert. COMPENDEX（Computerized Engineering Index）等，舊有之工程索引已製成微縮影片（Microfilm），另編印 Publicationed Index for Engineering, Subject Heading for Engineering（SHE）

工程學會圖書館（Engineering Societies Library）爲各工程師學會共同所組織的，各工程師學會會員免費贈送該圖書館出版物，故該館之工程方面資料收藏極爲豐富。

波士頓：

麻省理工學院（M. I. T.）之工程圖書館科學圖書館及電機系電子系統研究所之 Project INTREX。該院爲世界聞名之理工學府，其科技資料之收藏豐富並研究各種電子系統對資料檢索體系之操作與設計方面貢獻甚大。另該科學圖書館之圖書分類書目工作，是用 Micrographic Catalog Retrieval System—The National Union Catalog on Microfiche，用法簡便迅速。

三、會議情形及重要結構

研討會由四月二十五日正式開始，中心議題共分：

（一）科學及技術資料之國家政策（National Politics for Scientific Technical Information）。

（二）人力及教育需求（Manpower and Educational Needs）。

（三）技術——傳統式及革新式（Technologies-Traiditional and Innovative）。

（四）臺灣科學及技術資料系統及服務現況；美方現況與建議（Scientifc and Technical Information Systems and Services, Curient Status, Taiwan; U. S. Pespectives）。

（五）科學及技術資料系統設計與利用之情況（Aspects of Scientific and Technical Information Systems Design and Use）。

（六）國家的、雙邊的、區域性的及國際間合作之現況及新的合作可能性（Current Status and New Possibilities for National, Bilateral, Regional and International Cooperation）。

（七）未來可能性的新行動（Possibilities for Future Activities）。

（八）總論及結論（General Summary and Conclusions）第八項進行討論及報告。會議主席由中美雙方代表團團長擔任。

研討會進行方式；會中每一議案，先由中美雙方報告本方對此問題之現況、做法及問題後共同討論，其間又加美方專家專題演講，使我方代表收益不少。第三天由主席指定人選，分組研討有關問題，最後由主席綜合所有意見在大會中研討，作成決議，以供雙方參考。

雙方代表建議甚多，因時間關係無法一一決議，現僅簡述幾項重點，詳細情況尚待美方正式報告內獲知。

我方代表團團長建議兩點：

（一）成立一政策小組，對我方科學資料基本政策，進行研討並完成實施計劃。

（二）近期成立可行計劃並積極推行。

美方代表建議甚多，綜合如下：

（一）組織一十八情報小組，作爲推動科資工作之核心，接受最新知識訓練，參與臺灣科學資料一切計劃之推行。

（二）保持建立國際間非政府階層合作關係。

（三）提高圖書資料人員工作地位，並建立政策，以促進此類人員之培育。

（四）建立政策，鼓勵充分利用資料資源，確定用於科技資料經費在研究發展預算中之百分比。

（五）成立一顧問委員會，以反應使用單位之意見。

（六）在美成立採購單位或接洽書商，以集中採購所需圖書、期刊、報告等資料。

（七）充分利用美、英、日現有資料服務系統。

（八）建立發展完整科技資料體系。

（九）科技資料獲得時限以二十四小時以內爲目標，充份利用各種通信及交通工具，以利分配作業。

（十）科技報情蒐集方面，選派最有才能青年男女在科技資料蒐集工作方面作爲一線工作人員，並對上述人選予以特殊教育與訓練。

簡介"行政院國家科學委員會"科學資料及儀器中心[*]

一、創始與任務

科學資料及儀器中心爲配合科學發展及經濟建設需要,先經"國家安全會議"裁定置設,嗣奉"行政院國家科學委員會"令於一九六八年九月一日成立,以"國立清華大學"圖書館、科儀館現有規模爲基礎,暫設於新竹工業及科學研究園區"國立清華大學"內,直屬"國家科學委員會"。依據發展科學計劃,主要任務爲:

(1) 蒐集並彙編海內外有關科學與技術文獻及人才等資料,並提供各項資料技術參考。

(2) 調查並聯繫海內外科資有關機構,建立資料交換交流,相互交換合作制度。

(3) 加強科學教育,發展各級學校所需之標準基本科學儀器,協助解決有關科儀供應與技術問題。

(4) 配合學術研究與工業發展需要,研制高級精密科學儀器,提供技術服務與諮詢,以改善科學技術研究環境。

科學資料及儀器中心工作計劃共分三期完成:

第一期指會計年度 1969 年至 1972 年。
第二期指會計年度 1973 年至 1976 年。
第三期指會計年度 1977 年至 1980 年。

二、目前編制及組織

科資儀器中心現設中心主任一人,副主任一人,下設科學資料、科學儀器、技術服務、技術發展及行政管理五組,全中心員工共八十五人,今後將隨業務發展需要隨時增添人員。

三、目前進行之工作項目

(一) 科學儀器研制方面:

1. 儀器研制:接受委託,代各界研制各種精密儀器,現已制有成品者:放射線偵測儀 (Survey Meter)、脈波產生器 (Pulse Generator)、直線放大器 (Linear Amplifier)、雙直流電源供給器、高壓供給器、集體電路 (HC) 計數器及超微電流計等。

2. 電子教學示範儀器。

3. 大學物理試驗設備。

4. 正進行研制中之科學儀器有:示波器、標準機架電源器,多階脈波高度分析器等。

(二) 科學資料方面:

定期出版物爲:

1. 西文科學期刊聯合目錄:此項目錄係以全臺各大專院校、研究機構及生產單位之

---

[*] 本文曾發在《"中國圖書館學會"會報》24 期 (1972 年 12 月),第 38—40 頁。

圖書館爲對象，收錄其現藏有關科學技術方面之西文期刊，經由系統之整編而成，現暫定每二年出版一次，隔一期出版一次彙集本，第一期已於一九七〇年出版，收錄六十五個單位資料，第二期一九七二年出版爲第一期之補增版（Supplement），單位增至八十五個，西文科技期刊總共約六千餘種。現着手編彙第三期，預定於一九七三年底付印。

2. 中文報章雜誌科技論文索引：此索引刊登之資料包括中文科技期刊之論著、研究報告，及中文報章刊出之科技論文，其內容以理、工、農、醫科爲主，於一九六八年開始蒐集。中文科技期刊現已有三百多種。索引已先後出版了三輯，第一輯一九六二——一九六七；第二輯一九六八——一九六九；第三輯一九六九——一九七一；目前正積極從事第四輯（補遺輯）之彙編，預定於一九七三年六月複印。爲便利研究者資料之收集，科資儀中心提供原論文之複印服務。

3. 科技論文摘要月刊：發行科技論文中譯摘要之主要目的，是爲介紹海外重要必讀之科技論文予科學研究機構及工業單位，以激勵臺灣之科學研究，促進工業技術之發展。資料來源爲日本科學技術情報中心出版之《科學技術文獻速報》，並敦聘各科學研究機構之專門教授及工業界專家卅餘位分別擔任審稿及選譯委員，集中物理、核工、化工、食品、機械、電機、化學等七科目之摘要。每卷出版卷索引，內容包括作者索引、論文標題索引、標題分類索引、期刊索引及審譯委員通訊錄，以便讀者查尋資料。此刊發行半年之後，本中心曾發問卷並與有關方面開會商討此刊物內容等問題，決定今後此刊之內容與形式作部份調整，內容將偏於工業技術方面。資料來源儘量改用英文摘要，如：Food Science & Technology Abstracts, Electrical & Electronics Abstracts, Chemical Abstracts, etc....。於明年元月起將陸續發行食品工業、化學工業、電子電機工業、金屬機械工業等四大類雙月刊單行本，篇幅增加爲原來之三倍，以期更適合讀者之需要。

4. 專利索引：本索引係精選美國之專利公報（Official Gazette）中，適合臺灣學術界及工業界之專利項目摘錄、分類彙編而成，以供國人參考之用，從一九七一年一月開始出版，每月一期，並由本年十一月份起，增加日、加之專利，以擴大其範圍及內容。

5. 新竹工業及研究園區科技圖書聯合目錄：本目錄配合新竹工業及研究園區之發展，特將園區內所藏之科技圖書彙編成冊，全套共四冊，於一九七〇年出版，俾便讀者迅速查詢，及時運用。

6. 全臺科技圖書聯合目錄：本目錄於一九六八年十二月即開始調查，迄一九七一年三月截稿止計蒐集九十二個學術及研究機構之科技圖書，經製成卡片者約十萬餘張，經有系統之整理彙編，於一九七二年十月底付印，統計所蒐科技圖書四萬九千餘種。本目錄之製作在臺灣可謂首創，工作艱鉅，費人費時，歷時數載，始克完成。出版此目錄之目的，旨在推廣館際互借、計劃典藏、聯合採購及供作書目研究報導之用，約於一九七三年三月出版，全套約十冊左右。

7. 全臺科技人才資料：此科技人才調查資料，由開始至印出總共費時三個月，由於受時間限制，收到資料有限，總共包括二十四個單位，四百餘人。於一九七一年印出一套二冊。

8. 科學儀器聯合目錄：本目錄係將大專院校、學術研究單位及工業界研究機構之貴重且富有研究價值之儀器設備調查後，分類編目成冊，並附照片說明，每年出版一次，第一版已於一九七〇年出版，第二版一九七一年出版爲補充版，現正着手調查第三版，大約一九七三年出版。

9. 科技簡報：此簡報於一九七一年一月一日開始，其目的爲報導海內外最新之科技消息及介紹新產品、新技術，現將於今年十二月改爲"科技與工業"，篇幅增加，雙月刊出。

四、服務項目

（一）科儀方面：

1. 專業技術短期訓練：每年暑期舉辦一次放射線測量儀器訓練班，並代訓有關電子儀器及控制系統等之技術人員。

2. 儀器修護。

（二）科資方面：

1. 影印及製版服務。

2. 翻譯服務：爲配合科技發展，特提供有關科技方面之論文、報告等之翻譯服務，語文包括英、日、法、德等。

3. 諮詢服務：免費提供有關科技資料方面之服務，必要時可代向海外購買資料。去年委託本中心辦理此項服務信件有 841 封之多。

（二）特種業務：

1. 西文標準圖書目錄卡片服務：目錄整理的好壞，直接影響資料之使用，本中心成立之初，會派員至各單位進行圖書資料的調查，發現若干單位疏於目錄工作，而使寶貴資源凍結，因此爲提倡及改進目錄作業的方法，乃推展此項目錄卡片服務。一九七一年六月起，本中心先從科學及工程兩方面爲範圍實施卡片服務的工作，後由於各委託單位寄來的受編資料往往超越範圍而要求更廣更多的代編工作，基於這種實際的需要，自一九七一年八月份起改爲全數之西文卡片服務。至目前爲止，大量或經常利用此項服務的單位有大同工學院、師大、三軍總醫院、清華大學、"經濟部"聯合工業研究所、物理研究中心、中正理工學院、"中國石油探勘處"、臺灣機械公司及金屬工業研究所。

2. 館際合作：爲擴大服務範圍與中山科學研究院、"國立清華大學"、"國立交通大學"、"國立成功大學"、"經濟部"聯合工業研究所、中正理工學院、聯勤兵工技術發展中心、空軍航空發展中心、食品工業研究所等建立館際互借，以支援爲研究工作所需參閱之圖書資料，充份並有效利用雙方之圖書資源。

3. 亞太理事會科技服務登記處技術顧問委員會通訊業務：

（1）本中心爲亞太理事會科學技術服務登記處技術顧問委員會臺灣通訊處負責聯絡工作。

（2）依亞太理事會科技服務登記處所需，本中心辦理蒐集、貯藏、交換、供應及解決亞太會員國有關科技資料問題。

（3）擷取亞太科技服務登記處刊出各亞太國家科技資料、目錄，以備臺灣科技機構之需，並加強海內外科技方面交換聯繫，以有易無。

（4）協助亞太會員國及臺灣科技研究者能迅速且最適當處獲得研究用之特殊資料。

五、科學資料及科學儀器中心分設計劃

本中心在創始之初，因科學資料儀器性質完全不同，即有分別單獨成立科學資料中

心及科學儀器中心之計劃，但因當時經費困難，而合併成立科資及科儀中心。在一九六九年五月清華大學閻振興校長、"國科會"張明哲先生、"中美科學委員會"執行秘書郝履成先生，及本中心主任鄭振華先生等赴韓國考察韓國之科資中心及科儀中心，經呈遞"總統"報告分別成立科資中心及科儀中心之建議，"國家科學委員會"即著手辦理。於一九七一年向"中央研究院"購地興建科資大樓，於一九七二年四月動工，預定一九七三年初完成，科儀中心及科資中心可能於一九七三年七月正式單獨成立，決定科儀中心仍留於清華大學，現科資部份遷往南港科資大樓，成立"行政院國家科學委員會"科學資料中心。

六、科學資料中心之展望

科學資料中心之成立，不但支援學術研究及提供工業機構所需科技資料，成為臺灣科學資料資源地，進而促進科學發展與經濟建設。由於臺灣科學資料中心成立較晚，無法與歐美先進各國相比，但比亞洲地區之韓國、日本等國亦遙遙落後數年，現應積極迎頭趕上。

科資中心成立在即，"國家科學委員會"於一九七二年八月，經亞洲基金會之協助，聘請美國洛杉磯加州大學資料專家赫斯（Robert M. Hayes）博士來華考察科學資料現況，加以分析，並貢獻改進方法，同時建議計劃科資中心組織及工作事宜，以配合我方之科技方面需要。

科學資料中心之業務項目大約如下：

（一）蒐集海內外最新科技資料消息、技術雜誌及有關科學研究發展資料，予以儲存、管理、分析、摘要、彙編、出版、報導事項。

（二）繼續彙編現出版各種科技資料月刊、期刊、年刊、目錄等事項。

（三）加強聯繫海內外科資有關機構，相互支援合作，資料交換交流事項。

（四）調查登記海內外科技人才、文獻、研究專題，避免工作重複事項。

七、結論

總之，科資科儀包羅廣泛，其性質不同，合併為一實欠恰當，分設是必須最佳之決策。以後中心工作業務常盡量配合各研究機構及專業發展需要，提供有效技術及資料服務，但仍賴各界合作協助、支援及指教，以達到發展現代專業技術，支援科學發展研究之目的。

美國報導科學*

"Information explosions" 來源於第二次大戰大家對科學及技術研究工作之擴展，因而產生了如潮水般的新資料，並造成收集、處理、傳遞及運用之困難，在一九四五年 The Atlantic Monthly 期刊中，Dr. Vannevar Bush 發表的 "As We May Think" 一文中警告大家說："The difficulty seems to be, not so much that we publish unduly in view of the extent and variety of present day interest, but rather that publication has been extended far beyond our present ability to make real use of the record...." 這段的大意是說：困難之處並非 Information 過量之生產，而在於如何能利用這些記錄的 Information。此時 Information 已成爲衆人註目的一個問題。

我們都知道人類科學愈進步，工商業愈發達，社會亦愈繁榮，人們對迅速而準備的 Information 需要愈增加。一九五七年俄人造衛星 Sputnik 發射而引起美國政府對科學及技術之發展及研究加強重視，所需與產生的 Information 問題更日趨複雜。至一九六五年已視爲美國全國性的問題，舊式的處理方法已失去其效能，迫切急需新的管理技術，以解決其困難，乃有 Information Science 之產生。

Information Science 是甚麼？中文譯名不一，可譯爲消息科學、資料科學、情報科學或報導科學，爲了與本題目符合起見在此用報導科學爲其譯名。

報導科學之存在已很久了，其正統的歷史演變很難明顯的分析。可能即是由 Documentation 或 Information Retrieval 之演進而來；亦可說是其綜合所有與其有關科目的歷史而爲其演變之經過歷史，因此其包括項目很廣，有科學、技術、文藝、實際應用科目等方面，其主要的機構是報導之傳送、分析交換、儲存、檢索及應用。總之，報導科學之範圍、特性、由來及它將來發展趨勢難於定型，皆由於各人見解不同而異；正如其定義一樣。

由當今美國各大學紛紛成立之報導科學中，顯然看出各對報導科學之解釋不一，一部份人士認爲報導科學是種新的圖書管理實施方法；一部份以電腦或計算機爲操作基礎的人士認爲報導科學是運用機器來操縱語言、圖案或數目的資料學科；另一部份人士自稱爲資料學家 Documentalists 視此科目既非圖書管理學又非電腦操縱學而是一門獨立的科目，足以專門處理及分析大量科學技術方面之文件和資料爲主的科目；另有一小部份人士認爲報導科學是研究人與人間活動的互相傳播的學科；還有一部份人士認爲報導科學是與以上所說的完全無關，現在仍是門無定型的學科，孰是孰非，很難斷定。

最近發表的報導科學定義甚多，計有：1961 和 1962 年喬治亞理工學院會議中報導科學定義；1965 年 American Documentation Institute Symposium（美國資料學會的報導科學教育研討會）之定義；和 Ohio State University 宣佈報導科學系成立報告中之定義。現分述如下：

（一）喬治亞理工學院和會議議定報導科學定義是 "報導科學是一門用來研究報導

---

* 本文係 1972 年 3 月在 "美國圖書館業務專題研討會" 上的講稿。曾刊於李志鍾編著：《美國圖書館業務》，臺北遠東公司 1972 年版。

之特性和動態,具控制報導資料之流動力;和處理報導資料使能達到最佳的儲取、流通、廣泛利用的目的之最好的方法之科學。其處理程序包括:創作、傳播、收集、儲存、檢索、分析和運用;此科目之由來或關連與數學、邏輯學、語言學、心理學、電子計算機技術、運用研究學、平面藝術學、圖書管理學、工商管理學等項目"。

(二) ADI American Documentation Institute Symposium 討論會中,並未議定報導科學之定義。只解釋說:"報導科學特別是與儲存或記錄的資料、它們之產生、它們的傳播及運用有關。其特性有理論與應用科學兩方面"。

(三) Ohio State University 簡介中說明 "報導科學涉及知識的量的關係、概念、理論和方法論,是和一般科目的報導之處理及運用相同"。

(四) 一九七〇年出版的 R. Hayes & J Becker 著的 *Handbook of Data Processing for Libraries*,書中報導科學之定義是:"報導科學是研究任何報導系統 Information Systems 中可能發生報導產生程序"。

其他有關報導科學之定義甚多,不能一一論之,姑從略。由於各人對報導科學見解不同,而造成了報導科學教育科目之不統一,大約可分為下列幾種學系:以圖書管理系為主的學系是將報導科學合併於圖書管理系,認為報導科學是運用電腦來處理圖書業務,故在教材中增添如 Data Processing in the Library 之課程,亦有圖書館學系認為報導科學是專門處理科技方面報導資料,因此增添索引法和摘要法 Indexing & Abstracting 和資料中心的管理等科目。以工程為主的學系,認為報導科學與應用電子計算機科學有關,其課目注重於用電子計算機來處理語言或詢答方面問題之學科,因之而設立所謂電子計算機和報導科學系 Department of Computer and Information Sciences。以專門研究為主的學系,認為報導科學是以研究如何設計專門學科的報導系統為主,通常其課程中有系統設計學 System Design 和專門科目報導系統學,如醫學報導系統或圖書學報導系統 Medical Information System,或 Library Information System。還有學系認為報導科學應是一專門學科,應單獨成系,如李海 Lehigh 大學的 Division of Information Science。近年來由於對報導科學之重視,圖書管理系開始增多報導科學方面之課程,有的圖書研究甚至於分為圖書管理學及報導科學兩大部份,如匹茲堡大學圖書學和報導科學研究院 Graduate School of Library of Information Science。

報導科學方面的文獻和具新技術者同時不斷的增加中,根據最近的統計,在一九四〇年報導科學文獻幾乎沒有,一九五〇年約有四十篇,一九六〇年增為 300～400 篇,一九六一年是 700～800 篇,在一九六五年的 *Annual Review for Information Science of Technology* 美國報導科學和技術年論書中用的文獻為兩千一百五十七篇。由於美國聯邦政府為主要的科學及技術發展研究機構的資援者,故亦是發表報導科學文獻最多者,一九六二年有二百五十個研究計劃是由美國政府支持的,一九六四年根據 Panel of the Committee on Scientific Technical Information of the Federal Council for Science of Technology (COSATI) 估計一千三百研究計劃是由美政府資助的,是研究有關於(一)報導儲存及檢索,(二)光學或制圖學報導的處理,(三)語言與語言學,(四)電子計算機,(五)電子計算機協助的邏輯處理法,其發表之報告與文獻之多寡可想而知。

主要有關報導科學文獻期刊有:

Journal of the American Society for Information Science (formerly, *American Documentation*).

Journal of Documentation.

Journal of Chemical Documentation.

Programs:*News of Computers in Libraries.*

FID News Bulletin.

Journal of Library Automation.

Library & Information Science Abstracts.

Information:*News*,*Sources*,*Profiles*(formerly,*Scientific Information Notes*).

Documentation Abstracts.

Information Storage & Retrieval.

以圖書管理學為主的期刊有：

Library Resources & Technical Services.

Special Libraries.

和硬體（Hardware）為主的期刊有：

IBM Journal of Research & Development.

Communication of the ACM.

一般科學期刊中包括報導科學文獻的有：

Science.

Scientific American.

Science & Technology.

Physics Today.

Chemical & Engineering News.

報導科學學會或社團有：

American Society for Information Science & Technology.

Federation International de Documentation（FID）.

Special Library Association.

Medical Library Association.

American Chemical Society.

American Federation of Information Processing Society.

　　無論報導科學定義為何，其最主要的部份是 Information 和 Information System。甚麼是 Information？定義很多，Information 可說是經過處理的資料，Information 是供給決定事項的資料，又可說 Information 是與質的概念或觀念有關的知識。而 Information System 是個有組織的程序系統用來收集、處理、儲存和檢索記錄的報導以滿足不同尋求資料的需要。Information System 與一般圖書館系統很多相似之處，圖書館亦是報導系統 Information System 之一種。報導科學並非完全以電子計算機或機器為主的，運用機器不過是方法之一而已。

　　普通一般系統 System 包括組織成分有輸入、處理、儲存和輸出，如下圖：

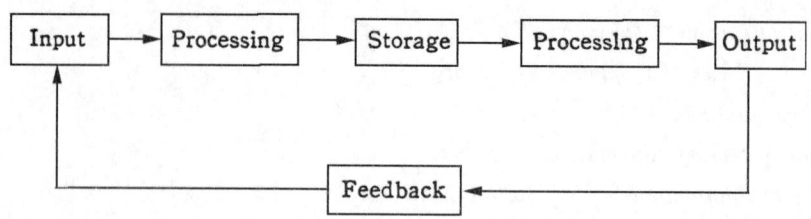

Information System 的分析和設計是根據報導科學和系統分析的原理為基礎，最主要的決策操於 System Analyst 或 System Designers 系統分析家手中。基本 Information System 構造，以略圖示之：

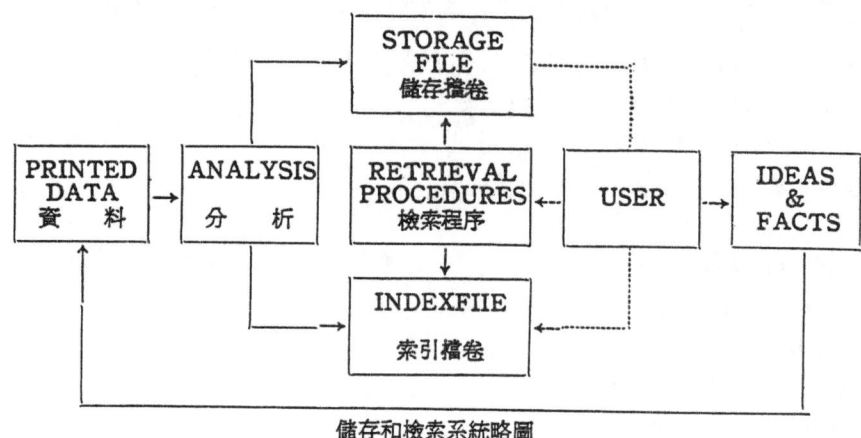

儲存和撿索系統略圖

虛線部份代表 Information System 主要部份——用者檢索資料之步驟，和一般用圖書館找尋資料方法相同。Information System 分下列部份：

（一）選擇和採購資料：報導系統多是以專門學科使用者而設，其選擇和採購資料之政策與一般圖書館或資料中心相似。

（二）分析方法：有索引法 Indexing，摘要法 Abstracting，分類法 Classifying，翻譯法 Translating 等。

（三）儲存：如何以最好的方法將資料儲入系統內，應注意資料編排法和分類法，更應注意服務方法，經濟情況和容易操作等條件。

（四）尋求和檢索資料：系統設計時應注意的事項有：（A）使用者與系統間之交互作用 Interaction。（B）各種檢索要求如：By Subject, Exhaustive Search, Browsing, Current Awareness, SDI 等。（C）決定用者的需要，有四種方式來測量用者的需要：①Field Study，②Case Study，③Survey，④Experimentation。

以上簡單解釋 Information System 設計及內容，詳細內容在此不能盡述，另外最值得研究的是 Selective Dissemination of Information（SDI）譯為選擇的傳送報導，根據最近的統計每年美國印出的資料：書——大約五十萬本，期刊——六萬多種，各種科技期刊論文達一百二十萬件，專利方面新專利有三十萬多種。學者或研究人員想能保持不斷讀到與自己研究有關之最新知識是不可能的事。據另一統計，科技資料二十四小時內有二千萬個字產生，如一個人能在一分鐘閱讀千字，以每天八小時工作計算，亦需一個半月時間才能把一天生產之資料讀完的。SDI 即是一個好的處理辦法。SDI 是一種服務，是代表任何程序用人工或機器方法選擇並供給與個人研究有關的最新文獻的服務，一般圖書館已做了很久 SDI 服務。在一九五九年 IBM 公司的 H. P. Luhn 利用電子計算機設計了第一個 SDI-Ⅰ（用 IBM 550），一九六一年設計了 SDI-Ⅱ system 現已有 SDI-Ⅴ system。1966 年統計用 SDI System 有：NASA，NLM，DDC（Defense Documentation Center），和 Chemical Abstracts。SDI 是用相配標準 Match Criteria 選出各種資料，此種相配標準方法不一，可分爲：

（一）Weighted Terms：一般採取此法。
（二）Boolean Logic：用布爾邏輯的連接詞 "And"，"OR"。
（三）"Must"，&"Not"，"May" Terms.
（四）"MiSS"&"Trash" terms.

不論是用人工或機器方法，SDI Service 對專門研究人員而言是種很重要而不可缺少的服務。

今日美國的較大型的、特殊的而有代表性的報導儲存及檢索系統 Information storage and retrieval system 有：

一、美國國立醫學圖書館 National Library and Medicine 之 MEDLARS（Medical Literature Analysis and Retrieval System）系統：美國國立醫學圖書館是目前美國及世界各國主要的醫學圖書館，設於美馬利蘭州，遠在一九六四年一月即開始，MED-LARS 系統，是一種高速索引機，每月出版一本醫學文獻月刊稱 *Index Medicus*，此期刊始於一八九七年。由於近年來改用電腦化的 MEDLARS 系統，*Index Medicus* 編排準備出版之工作由二十二天減爲五天內完成。每年並印行一本索引彙編 *Cumulative Index Medicus*。MEDLARS 包括兩千四百多種世界各地重要生物醫學文獻和引用文 Citation 一九六九年 MEDLARS 檔卷已有百萬篇以上的醫學參考文獻資料。

系統索引法是按照 Mesh（Medical Subject Heading）而編排。Mesh 是由一些編生物醫學文獻索引專家 *Index Medicus* 常用者和 MEDLARS 顧問組的醫生及生物學家共同研究而編成的，並時時改進中。

MEDLARS 系統可分成三部份：

（一）輸入系統 Input system：文件或資料被分析，依科分類及編有作者、主題、內容、書名等，製成紙帶後轉製成磁帶 Magnetic tape，以做儲存及檢索之用。

（二）檢索系統 Retrieval system：此系統專用於由計算機來索取所詢之資料。

（三）出版系統 Publication system：用計算機 GRACE（Graphic Art Composing Equipment 照片凸版裝制法）將計算機磁帶所儲備之文獻資料製成底片後影印成真出版物。

爲了廣播其效用，MEDLARS 在美國主要的大學和醫學圖書館紛紛設立分站外，並在歐洲瑞士、英國、亞洲日本設立 MEDLARS 研究中心，普遍供應與醫學方面有關的報導資料。

二、麻省理工學院 M. I. T. INTREX Project（Information Transfer Experiments）：一九六五年一部份學者和專家們在麻省 Woods Hole 五個星期會議中產生 INTREX Project。決

定設在麻省理工學院電機系的電子系統實驗所 Electronics Systems Laboratory。INTREX Project 目的是：

（一）運用最新的電子資料處理方法儲存原文及複製原文的技術來現代化一般大型圖書館作業問題。

（二）在美國政府資援下能建立全國性的圖書館網 Library Net-work 和其他資料中心。

（三）擴充高速發展電子計算機技能組織到圖書館及資料中心範圍內。

INTREX 是試驗以機器儲存圖書系統之基本模型，於一九六九年四月一日開始作業。INTREX 系統包括四部份：

（一）Augmented Computer-Stored Catalog：用計算機儲存大約 12,000 篇由教授和研究員選出的論文，期刊文獻或報告等用 Key Words 或 Key Phrases（鍵語或鍵句）索引法摘要分析資料，資料是以材料科學和工程學之報導爲主。

（二）Information Storage & Retrieval Program：利用 M. I. T. 之 IBM 7094 CTSS（分時制）計算機系統，可有十人在同時運用計算機來尋找資料，此種系統是種對話式的，用者與計算機互相對話，計算機並能幫助用者找尋所需之資料，此部份內設有監聽系統 Monitor System 用來研究人與機器相互影響的作用，Man-Machine Interaction 和用者與 INTREX 系統間發生的問題，以便用做改進 INTREX 系統之參考。

（三）User Console with Cathode-Ray-tube Display：特殊裝備的陰極射線管展示的用者控操臺，這種控制臺由 M. I. T. 電子系統所自製的，另一種控操臺是 IBM 2741 如打字機。

（四）Text Access Program（原文儲取程式部份）：12,000 期刊論文儲存在 COSAT 標準 Microfiche 上，每張 Microfiche（4×6）可存 60 頁資料，原文經過文字數字的控操臺後由 CRT 用者控操上展示出來，或複製成 35mm 底片，再經過特殊顯微膠片印字機 Microfilm Pinter 複印出原文來。

近來 Project INTREX 計劃利用現有的電子計算機儲存的論文磁帶，作爲增加 INTREX Project 現有的資料 Data Base。

除 INTREX Project 外，M. I. T. 圖書館並分別計劃用電子計算機處理一些業務：如整個 Acquisition Program 自動化的系統，在設計制目錄卡片系統和電子計算機控制期刊及雜誌目錄系統等，美國存有的報導儲存及檢索系統爲數甚多，無法一一在此述之。

總之，一般來說，報導科學的特性似乎趨向於下列幾點：

（一）科學及技術文獻爲其主要報導資料。

（二）科學家和工程師爲其最多的使用者。

（三）報導檢索系統爲主。

（四）計算機爲其處理方法。

（五）報導只代表報導系統中之一功能而已。

報導科學雖是個未定型的學科，可推猜其可能在一九九〇年左右達到成熟階段，由於其包括範圍廣泛，其將成爲一門 Interdisciplinary 的學科，其非 Science，而是所謂 Meta-Science 的學科，如下一簡圖示之：

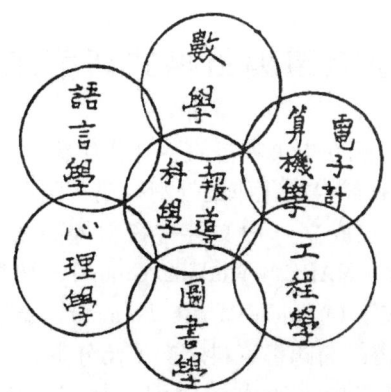

報導科學是一新的學科,僅於此向大家簡單的介紹一二,海內外對報導科學有研究的學人專家很多,筆者所知有限還請諸位專家學人多多指教。

參考圖書

1. Susan Artandi. *An Introduction to Computers in Information Science.*

2. Jack Belzer (ed). *Information Science Education: Curriculum Development and Evaluation; a Conference Proceeding.* American Documentation, 20: 327–376 (1969).

3. Vannevar Bush. "As We May Think". *Atlantic Monthly*, 174 (No. 1): 101–108 (1945).

4. Verner W. Clap. *The Future of the Research Library.* Urbana, University of Illinois Press, 1964.

5. Carlo A. Cuadra (ed.). *American Review of Information Science & Technology.* Chicago, Encyclopedia Britannica, 1966–1970. 5vos.

6. A. W. Elias, (ed). *Key Papers in Information Science.* Washington, D. C., American Society for Information Science, 1971.

7. R. Hayes and J Becker. *Handbook of Data Processing for Libraries.* New York, Becker & Hayes Inc., 1970.

8. L. B. Heilprin, (ed.). *Education for Information Science.* Washington, D. C., Spartan, 1965.

9. Bart E., Holm. *How to Manage Your Information.* New York, Reinhold, 1968.

10. *Information; A Scientific American Book.* San Francisco, Freeman, 1966.

11. *Journal of the American Society for Information Science.* 1971.

12. F. Wilfred Lancaster, *Information Retrieval Systems: Characteristics, Testing & Evaluation.* New York, Wiley, 1968.

13. Charles A. Meyers. *Computers in Knowledge-Based Fields.* Cambridge, M. I. T. Press, 1970.

14. Tefko, Saracevic, (ed.). *Introduction to Information Science.* New York, Bowker, 1970.

中文圖書機讀編目格式研訂工作報告

"中國圖書館學會"及"國立中央圖書館"合作組織之"全國圖書館自動化作業規劃委員會"為推展全國"圖書館自動化作業計劃"第一階段計劃：中文圖書資料自動化作業，於一九八〇年五月正式成立"中文圖書資料機讀式目錄工作小組"（Chinese Machine Readable Cataloguing（MARC）Working Group），研製設計國際標準統一化之"中文圖書資料機讀編目格式"（Chinese MARC Format），適用於電子計算機處理中文圖書資料，以便於國際間、圖書館間圖書資料之交流及分享。

本小組目前已設計完成"中文圖書機讀編目格式"（Chinese MARC Format for Books）。該格式是參考國際機讀編目格式（UNIMARC-1980 版及美國國會圖書館圖書資料機讀編目格式第二型（L. C. MARC II Format）之結構設計而成，磁帶上之書目著錄格式採用國際標準組織第 2709 號標準（ISO 2709）之格式，並以中文資訊交換碼（Chinese Character Code for Information Interchange—簡稱 CCCII）之中文字集為基準，書目著錄格式依據國際標準書目著錄（ISBDS）及英美編目規則第二版（AACR II）所新編訂之中國圖書資料編目規則，並採用"韋傑士羅馬拼音系統"（Wade-Giles Romanizations System）之拼音方式，考慮到海內外中文圖書編目所需之項目，該格式設計含蓋所有圖書項目欄，力求此格式國際標準化及通用化。

為測試此格式之可行性，已選 1,100 筆中文圖書資料以此格式輸入電子計算機，目前已完成部份程式設計可做下列：1）印製海內外圖書館所使用之中文圖書目錄卡片及 2）書本式圖書目錄（見附件 3），建立 Chinese MARC 資料庫。至於設計及建立終端機線上檢索查詢系統及印製各種報表等，預計將於本年十二月底完成。未來的下一步，將著手研究設計"中文非書資料機讀編目格式"。

本人謹代表中文機讀式目錄工作小組向諸位海內外圖書館界先進和專家提出之簡單報告，本小組成員有胡歐蘭、黃鴻珠、吳明德、黃克東、張鼎鍾、林蘭惠、林孟真、黃淵泉等先生女士，對其熱心研究的精神至為感佩。此項研究仍屬試驗性質，待改進之處甚多，希諸位專家學者以你們豐富之經驗多多給予我們指正並請提供寶貴之意見。

ERIC 索引典與索引典之結構*

今天很榮幸能參加這個研習會並爲諸位介紹 ERIC 索引典及其結構。講解的大綱是：
（一）索引典來源及定義
（二）索引典功能及特性
（三）索引典設計與術語或叙述語之選擇
（四）術語關聯與表示符號
（五）索引典構造及其內容
（六）索引典與標題之異同
（七）教育資料庫索引典（Thesaurus of ERIC Descriptors）
（八）ERIC 結構
（九）ERIC 與他種索引典之比較
（十）結論

（一）索引典來源及定義

索引典此專有名詞之來源是希臘字（Greek）Thēsaurós，意思是 A storehouse of treasury 倉庫、寶藏之意。*The Shorter English Dictionary* 記載 Thesaurus 最早被使用的日期是一七三六年，當時解釋 Thesaurus 是 "A treasury of storehouse of knowledge, as a dictionary, encyclopedia or the like" 是知識的寶藏和倉庫，似字典或百科全書類之參考資料。美國 *Webster Dictionary* 定義是 "Thesaurus is a book of words or of information about a particular field or set of concepts, specifically a dictionary of synonyms" 是關於某些特殊學科的字彙，是一種同義字字典。現在再以資訊貯存及檢索系統（Information Storage and Retrieval System）來看它的定義，又可說：

1. 索引典是指一系列用來做索引及檢索資料用的叙述語（Descriptors）。叙述語亦有譯爲"描述語"。索引典通常又稱爲索引語言（Indexing Language），分類設計（Classification Scheme）或系統字彙（System Vocabulary），故索引典常被特別用在資訊貯存及檢索系統中。

2. 索引典亦可解釋爲依字義編輯、劃分、類別的辭庫。它可供索引者（Indexer）與使用者（User）對索引用語（Index terms）作一有系統性的指示與控制。這就是我們在使用索引典的時候，這些有關的索引用語對我們會有什麼樣的幫助。因此索引典中採用的"叙述語"皆做標準的解釋。對於叙述語同義字（Synonyms）、半同義字（Quasi-synonyms）、異義字（Homonym）等皆作明顯的互見與參照。索引典內容多依字母順序排列一些認可的索引名詞（Terms, descriptors, keywords, uniterms, etc.），每一名詞附帶著該系統中相關名詞的記載，用多種符號（Notations）表明其間之關係。這些符號是：

　　　　USE

---

* 本文曾發表在《教育資料研討會記錄》（臺北市："國立臺灣師範大學" 1980 年），第 65—70 頁。

USE FOR（UF）
Related Term（RT）
Broader Term（BT）
Narrower Term（NT）

此種編排形式的用意是在幫助索引編製者，以及使用索引查尋資料的人選擇適當的術語。所以索引典是現代 Information Storage & Retrieval System 詞彙控制的主要工具。

索引典內容是什麼？一般索引典的內容包括兩種術語（Terms）：一種是 Descriptors，另一種是 Non-descriptors。後者又可以說是 Use References，亦卽是一般圖書館所常用之 See，See also，See references 卽是 Cross references 做法、用法相同。Descriptors 亦可稱之是認可術語（Preferred Terms），Non-descriptors 亦可稱之爲不認可術語（Non-preferred Terms）。不認可術語用 Use References 將 Descriptors 和 Non-descriptors 連結起來以便索引者與檢索者參考選用。現在來解釋一下什麼是叙述語（Descriptor）？什麼是 Use Reference？

1. 叙述語（Descriptor）是一些認可的術語，它代表某一概念（Concept）。它可能是一個字（Word），一個 Keyword，phrase，一個符號（Notation），也可能是很多字（Multiwords），就是很多字在一起代表一種術語，用術語來尋找所需的資料，故叙述語在索引典中非常重要。

2. Use Reference：對叙述語而言，就是非叙述語（Non-descriptors）。它們是不被認可的字或術語，但多是同義字（Synonyms），或半或近似同義字（Quasi-or Near-synonyms）早期有名的索引典是 Dr. Peter Roget's 在一八五二年出版的 *Thesaurus of English Words & Phrases*。它是將一些字根據其意思類集一起（The grouping of words according to their ideas）。此做法的基本原理是：當我們在用字時，選用哪一個字較爲恰當，這正是 Roget's Thesaurus 主要的作用。因此它的基本原理成爲現代資訊檢索系統的索引典的依據！索引典正式起步被使用是一九五〇年代的後期與一九六〇年代初期。首先提到使用索引典的是 IBM 的 H. P. Luhn 於一九五七年。此外杜邦（Dupont）公司一九五九年擬用索引典在化學工程、工業方面做字彙控制。在美國政府方面，如美國防部一九六〇年亦開始使用 *Thesaurus of ASTIA Descriptors*。

（二）索引典功能及特性

主要功能是：

1. 字彙控制（Vocabulary Control；As authority guide for the indexer & index user）

2. 索引編製與資詞檢索（Indexing and Searching）

3. 組合或後組合系統（Coordinated of Post-coordinate Indexing Information Retrieval Systems）

它是選擇字彙的最佳工具與指南。術語不受階層的限制，運用邏輯的方式與單一字彙組合成索引並用於檢索資料。

索引典的特性是：

1. 索引典內容是放射性的。也就是說它包括很多相關的術語，狹窄的及不用的術語。此外，索引典又是聯繫性的，連接認可的和不認可的術語。所以我們又稱索引典是一種 Association Scheme。索引典又是多面的（Many Facets）、詳細的。索引典內容之層次分得愈細愈好。內容非常明確化,所以用很多符號(Notations)來表示各術語間之關係以及每一術語的內容、使用範圍等等。

2. 索引典多以某專一學術而設計的。所謂某專一學術是指 highly specialized subject field。如:科技、工程、教育、太空、物理、農業等。

3. 現有的索引典(Thesauri)以科技方面爲最多。

4. 社會科學學科方面的索引典較少。*Thesaurus of ERIC Descriptors* 是社會科學方面的索引典,但較難設計。

5. 索引典所用語文現多以英文爲主。但亦有多種語文的(Multilingual Thesauri),但多以英文開始再譯成其他語文的。

(三) 索引典設計與術語或叙述語之選擇

設計索引典時考慮要點:

1. 檢索系統的目的與內容(Purpose & Scope of the Retrieval System)。
2. 使用對象(Users)。

索引典是檢索系統中組成部份,故必配合及依照系統之目的,應與系統之內容相關,它的設計是爲了指定的使用對象(User)而做的,否則索引典之設計與術語選擇將會有所偏差不適用的。如設計 Medical Thesaurus 一定要知道其使用對象是醫生或護士。雖然同爲醫學方面,但仍會影響到概念 Concepts 的選擇問題。不同學科、不同使用者,在設計索引典時所選之叙述語亦因之而異。例如化學家與食品工業方面即不同,所採用之概念 Concept 亦不同,以"糖"的術語來看:

a. 化學家採用的索引典中"糖"之術語有:

　　Term:Sugar(蔗糖)

　　Generic Term:Disaccharides(糖之一種)

b. 食品工業之索引典中"糖"之術語有:

　　Term:Sugar(糖)

　　Generic Term:Sweetner(甜物)

由上例可見兩者採用之術語不一樣,故在設計索引典時,要選擇適當的術語,注意使用對象爲何人,學科是什麼?這樣選擇術語才會適用。

I. 索引典的設計

一般來說,索引典的設計非常複雜,設計方法可由不同角度來著手,因此方法亦不一,可歸納下列幾種做法供參考:

(1) 實用原始索引法(Empirical, Original Indexing Approach):這是一種實用試驗性的做法,做法就如石筍狀般的,由下而上,由小而大的做法,故又稱爲 Stalagmitic Approach。做法是將有關此學科的代表性文章收集選來,由其中實際去選擇 Index Terms,採無字彙控制 Free Indexing 做法,待初期工作完成,即由索引典之設計者(Thesaurus Designer)多爲一些科學專家,將適當之術語加以評判、組織、結構起來,加以測試(Testing),決定是否實用,以後可根據需要和資料的增加,把它擴大之。此法缺點是:由於索引典之設計是根據一些代表性樣本文章,故常常會感覺到不夠完整,不容易發現和辨識出所有的問題所在。但由於此法不受字彙控制之限，亦可用完全自動方式（Fully Automatic Method）來做，即是由電子計算機做 Automatic Indexing 方式。

（2）綜合統一法（Consolidation Approach），又可稱為 Stalactitic Approach（如鐘乳石狀）：由上而下，大處來做。首先蒐集很多相關已存在之索引典，邀請學科專家，成立一委員會，各專家根據學科所長分別進行，構想設計大而周全，Macrostructure Type 做法。這些專家仍可能並不直接接觸 Documents 本身或用 Documents 中之術語，Member Experts 分別用已存在之術語（List of Terms）分擔工作，使它能更完整。所採用選擇之術語，可能現有系統之資料庫（Data Base）中尚無此資料存在！此法剛好與前一種方法做法是相反的。此種做法工程浩大，其主要的目的是建立一完整的索引典（Comprehensive Thesaurus）。最好的例子是 Engineering Joint Council 之 Thesaurus TEST（Thesaurus of Scientific & Engineering Terms）。當初設計 TEST 時：

①收集將近三百五十種各科科技詞彙、標題、索引典等。
②三百多位專家。
③建立 Data Bank，有 150000 個術語，1250000 個款目。過濾挑選後 TEST 內容包括：
　①二三、三六四 Main Entries
　②一七、八一八 Descriptors
　③五、五五四 Use References
一直被很多資訊檢索系統採用，但自一九六七年出版後，即不再修正之。

索引典之好壞，Quality 是與所花費之精力多少有關，EJC'S TEST 是相當不錯的索引典。

（3）Microthesauri Approach：此種做法是以精確訂定某一學科中之細類科目 Subfields 著手，學科只需 100～500 術語。術語由此細類之報告、文章或索引中選出，將之列成草稿，送至此類作者專家們審核，限時完成，非常迅速。然後綜合成一整體索引典。此法類似第（2）種做法，但較實際。

（4）混合式做法（Amalgam Approach）：將以上三種形式混合使用來設計索引典，它做法內容包括：
　a. 選擇某一學科重要的摘要刊物三年來的出版資料中之術語。
　b. 由專家從其他標題、字彙表中選出術語以補 a. 中之不足。
　c. 以這些字彙做索引和檢索用。
　d. 評估：使留每一術語有關款目數量（Postings）之記錄，需要時加以修改。

Ⅱ．術語的選擇

設計索引典時，術語選擇非常重要，另外有術語的維持或更新工作亦如此，這些都是繼續作業。根據什麼標準和規則來選擇術語（Criteria for Term Selection）？早期的索引典是根據美國 U. S. Office of Naval Research's Project LEX 之做法。選擇索引典術語根據他們是否在通訊、索引法和檢索中有用（Usefulness in Communications, Indexing & Retrieval）。選擇術語可以下列數點為考慮決定與否：
　a. The relative frequency of the term's occurrence is the literature of the field.
　b. The relative frequency of the term's use in the operating system.

c. Relations to descriptors already in the system.

d. Scientific or technical precisions and acceptability.

e. A maximum number of characters per terms. （如採電子計算機作業，訂定每一術語之最大長度時要考慮）

選擇叙述語可根據 UNESCO – ISO/TC46 訂定 *Guidelines for the Establishment and Development of Monolinqual Thesauri*（1973）*Guidline* 提出選擇之四步驟：

1. Collections　蒐集術語
2. Verification　請專家鑑定
3. Evaluation　評估
4. Choice　選擇

在選擇"叙述語"時要考慮到它的效果與實用價值（effectiveness of practicality for retrieval & indexing）及重要性（singnificance in the material to be indexed）。所選叙述語是否可代表某概念（concept），它們對索引製作及檢索方面之關係影響，是否最新時用語（current usage），是否常用語（Frequency of use）等等皆為考慮選擇之條件。

（四）術語關聯與表示符號（**Term Relations & Notations**）

Thesaurus 術語關聯，根據 UNESCO，1973 年 *Guidelines for the Established Development of Monolingual Science & Technology Thesauri for Information Retrieval* 解釋，一般 Thesaurus 術語關聯有三種：

Ⅰ．認可代表關聯（Preferential Relations）：認可與不認可術語關連，卽術語中哪些被認可可代表某術語被採用，而哪些不被認可的術語，他們間又如何連接！

Ⅱ．相關關聯（Affinitive Relations）：相關的關聯，是認可術語與認可術語間關連。

Ⅲ．層次關聯（Hierarchical Relations）：層次的關聯，是術語之間的種屬或全部與部份的關聯（genus—species；whole—part relations），以下各舉例子說明之：

Ⅰ．認可聯聯（Preferential Relations）的關聯，如：

①同義字（synonyms）：同義字可能採用一種而不採用另外一種，要聯結 descriptors 就用 *see*，例：Hallways *see* Corridors，兩者皆為"走廊"的意思，在有的 Thesaurus 中用 use，也有的 Thesaurus 用 *see* 這個 Notation。

②反義字（Antonyms）：如 Instability 和 Stability 如何聯結起來，可用 Instability *see* Stability.

③拼法不同（Spelling variant）：color 有兩種拼法，採用認可的，可表示如下 Colour *see* Color.

④縮寫（Abbreviations）：例如 DEP *see* Electronic Data Processing，不用縮寫的字。

⑤不採用細目（Specific to general）：如 FORTRAN 是一種 Computer Language 電子計算機的語言。在此也許 Thesaurus 不用這麼詳細的術語，就把它併入一般性的 descriptors 裏面，以 FORTRAN *see* Programming Language 表示其關聯。

⑥兩個或二個以上的關聯（Two or more terms used than one）：如術語 Social Science Methodology 不用而用 Research Methodology 和 Social Science Research 兩個術語來代表。在 Thesaurus 中是以 Social Science Methodology *see* Research Methodology & Social Science Research 示之。

⑦採用細目（Generic to specific）：這和⑤相反。如 Programming Language *see* FORTRAN；COBOL；PL/1

⑧含糊不清術語（Ambiguous terms）：如 Homographs 同字異義。對於含糊不清的術語我們加上另一個字或形容詞來代。如：Lead 不是一般所講的領導的意思而是"鉛"的意思。爲識明其意義而用右列方式示之：Lead *see* Metallic Lead。

Ⅱ．相關相聯（Affinitive Relations）：例如

①Library Science *see also* Information Science

②ERIC 的 Reading difficulty，在此又可參看其他相關的 terms。Thesaurus 中可列爲：

   Reading difficulty *RT* Reading failures
        RT Learning disabilities
  ＊*RT*（*Related Terms*）

Ⅲ．層次關聯（Hierarchical Relations）：可以下列方式表示

①更廣泛的類別術語 *Broader Term*（*BT*）：其旨在說明術語的用法中還有更大的類別。例如 Geometry *BT* Mathematics（Geometry 更大的一類是 Mathematics）。

②更狹義的類別術語 Narrower Term（*NT*）：

   Geometry *NT* Analytical Geometry（分析幾何）
      NT Plane Geometry（平面幾何）

這些在檢索時都是可以參考的。

代表符號（Notations）：有兩種。一般採用 Cross Referencing 和 Notational Systems. 由美國醫學圖書館和美國科技資訊委員會（Committee on Scientific & Technical Information——簡稱 COSATI）發展的。這些連接詞的結構（Syndetic structure）很多且它們的用法和內容是一樣的，但所用的代表符號則不同：

MeSH（NLM）**	COSATI*
See	USE
X（See from）	UF（use for）
See under	BT（Broader Term）
See also specific	NT（Narrower Term）
See also related	RT（Related Term）

  ＊COSATI 之 Notations 被很多 Thesaurus 所採用。

  ＊＊NLM（美國醫學圖書館）MeSH Notations 則爲一般圖書館用之標題（Subject Headings）所採用。

（五）索引典構造及其內容

設計任何索引典的構造（Thesaurus Structure）都一定要定明索引典的：

1. 目標、2. 主題範圍、3. 包括術語、4. 術語間關聯、5. 術語展示方式、6. 更新、編改、修正、重組、增減術語的作業程序及方法、7. 更重要的是訂定 Rules &

Conventions for Thesaurus Preparation（索引典規則）。

索引典內容的編排結構有下列幾種形式展示：

1. Alphabetic display（依字母順序排）：

一般 Thesaurus 內容主要部份多以此形式排：

  如：A
  Abaca fibers   每一個索引典術語下列就是它有關的 Terms
  USE Manile hamp
  A bandonment 1407（1407 是代表類號，所有術語皆有類號可供參考用）
  RT Depletion
   —Escape（abandonment）
   —Life
    ⋮

2. Hierarchical（層次的）display，或 Two-ways Hierarchical（ERIC）Display（雙邊層次的展示）：

  例如：Education 這個 descriptor 分類的情況是
   ・Engineering education
   ・Individual education
   ・・Flight engineer training
   ・・Pilot training
   ・Individual Training

一點・代表一層，二點・・代表再細分的層次

3. Categorized（類）display：

把所有的術語分成很多類，把它 group 在一起，然後在 Thesaurus 中就有部份以此排表，這部份也可以查用參考，例如：

  140 EDUCATION
  Acadmic Education
  Academic Freedom
  Administrator Education
   ⋮   ⋮

4. Permuted（Rotated），交換式的 display，如 KWIC index 的做法，例如：

    Automatic indexing
    Coordinate indexing
     KWIC indexing
       Indexing theory
        ⋮

在這種 display 中，可以找到 indexing 這個字，它的上下關聯叙述語，同時在 Automatic 方面，又可再見到術語（Automatic indexing），此做法是將每個 descriptors 中每個字按其字母順序排出，而皆會再出現一次，便於檢索。

5. Graphic display（圖A）：用圖來解說 Thesaurus 中有關的關連方式，例如下圖B是 BA，生物摘要，它有一個 subject profile，圖A是 Doyle's 它的做法是術語的更新：

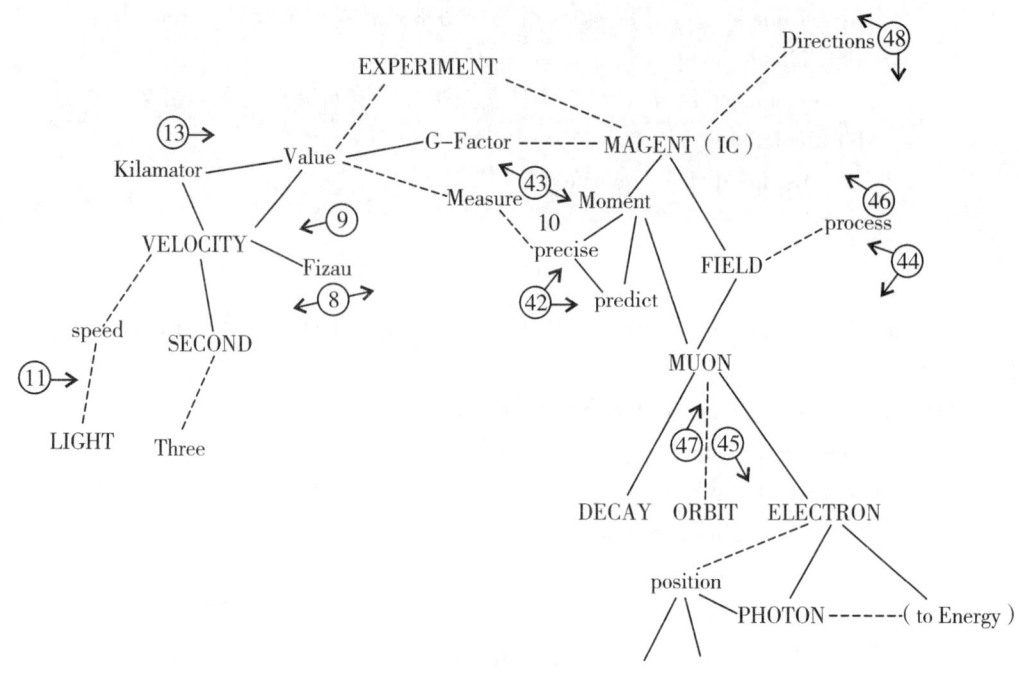

圖A　Doyle's "Semantic Road Maps"

更新的方法是指新術語和過時術語該怎麼辦？新的術語問題不大，但過時的術語則要多考慮，有二種做法可參考：

1. 把這方面的 documents 重新 index（Reindex all documents）——這個花費很大。

2. To set a cut of date，把中間怎樣用時間、日期來代表，等會將在 ERIC 索引典中會加以講解。

（六）索引典與標題之異同

索引典與標題是否相同，常會混淆不清，甚至會被認爲索引典本身就是標題。雖然索引典與標題在結構和組織很多相似地方，但實際上兩者是不同的。

標題的定義：標題卽是主題標目，英文是 Subject Heading（SH），標題是尋找特定主題範圍的有效工具，它多是由單字、片語或名詞組成的，其排列方式係按照字順排列，因爲他不受分類系統之牽制與知識層次的限定，所以使用者在尋找資料中某一款目時，可以直接從主題單字之字母順序中尋求。

標題非索引典，二者之間異同之處如下：

1. 索引典發展較 subject heading 晚。

2. 表示術語同關係之規定不同。

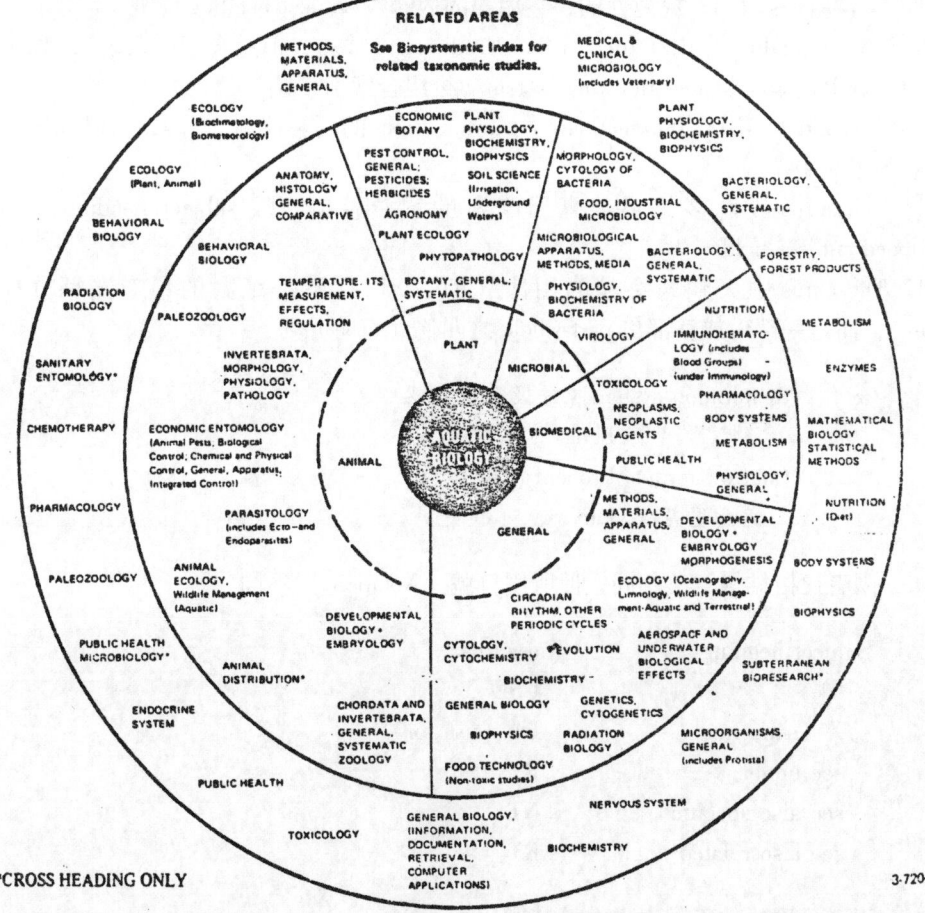

圖 B　*BA Subject profile showing broad fields, grouping of headings, and crossreferenced terms from Biological Abstracts.*

3. Subject heading 的每一個標題是有意義的（Meaningful），而 Thesaurus 之叙述語（Descriptors）有些並不是有意義的，需要與其他叙述語連用才會有意義。如索引典中的叙述語 EFFECTIVENESS 卽是。

4. Thesaurus 中術語意思較 subject heading 明確化，而且較狹義。
5. Thesaurus 中術語較 Subject heading 標題爲短。
6. Subject heading 排法是 Alphabetical，Thesaurus 也是。

除此之外 Thesaurus 附加幾種排列表：如層次表（Hierarchical Listing），叙述語字交換表（Descriptors Rotated Display），或叙述語類表（Descriptors Groups Display）等，有益於編製索引與檢索，加強其使用效果。

7. Thesaurus 中的術語採用直述式（Direct Entry），Subject heading 中採用直述式和倒述式（Inverted Entry）都有。
8. Subject heading 的款目多是由一般大類標題向下分，Thesaurus 則可列出多種多面的關係，可稱爲多面的，放射性的，它用語的內涵較 subject heading 詳細。
9. Subject heading 多用在 precoordinate indexing system（前組合索引系統），Thesaurus 則多用在於 Post-coordinated indexing system（後組合索引系統）。
10. Thesaurus 多用於 Informational retrieval system 的詞彙控制，而 subject heading 多用在一般圖書館中。
11. Thesaurus 設計多是爲某專門學科的詞彙控制，較 subject heading 爲 highly Specialized subject field。
12. Thesaurus 中大類與小類的用法（BT，NT），不是絕對的種屬關係（Genus-species），而是一部份或整部份 part-whole 之關係（有時），

例如：Respiration system（呼吸系統）裏
NT
（narrow term）
的意思是
Lung （肺部）
Bronchi （支氣管）
Larynx （喉炎）

13. 兩者連接結構意義相同，但所用符號（Notations）不同，

Subject heading	Thesaurus
see	USE
X（seen from）	UF（use for）
see under	BT
see also specific	NT
see also related	RT

14. 兩者最重要的不同之處在於其應用方面。

（七）教育資料庫索引典：**Thesaurus of ERIC Descriptors.**

許多資訊系統因檢索方式的需要，備有 subject vocabulary 的使用標準，使許多意義相近或相同的用語得以控制。

Ⅰ．教育學科（社會科學）方面用語是：
1. 細分的科目繁多，相互關係密切，所以增加其複雜性。
2. 許多基本概念常用片語或句子來表達，較理工科長。

3. 又許多教育學用語與日常用語相同，但其內容並非一般所指的，遂造成辭語控制困擾，較難。

4. ERIC 出版品 *RIE* 及 *CIJE*，無論人工或機器查尋都須用 *Thesaurus of ERIC Descriptors* 來做主題，用語的指引媒介可見其在 ERIC 系統中之地位。

Ⅱ．ERIC Thesaurus 的發展及其控制：

1. ERIC Thesaurus 的目標是提供一套教育學適用的控制辭語。

2. 1965 年 9 月，美國教育部成立 Panel on Educational Terminology（PET）專門負責索引典的發展。

3. 委員會組成份子是：教育專家、資訊專家、各教育團體的負責人等，在各主題範圍的學者提出他們的需要及問題，由教育學及索引典編纂專家來設計出適合於各種應用的一套辭語。

4. 初期會議決定採用 Free indexing 方式，來做主題分析及所有處理過程的原則。

5. 同時 "Control ERIC" 已經以 1700 件有關殘障兒童的文獻來做 Free indexing 的工作，製出 2300 個辭語送交一些教育學者，圖書館學者，及資訊專家評鑑，使這些辭語在 word form 及參見結構上做了很大的改善，作為日後索引典的基礎。

6. PET 參考 Engineers Joint Council（EJC）及 project LEX 所制定的規則，於 1966 年出版 *Rules for Thesaurus Preparations*，作為選擇標準辭語的依據，1969 年又修訂過。

7. PET 除索引典原有 Format 以外，又設計了 Rotated Descriptor Display（類似 KWIC 索引），Descriptors Groups Display Hierarchical Display 改為 Two-way Hierarchical Terms Display，來加強索引典的使用效果。

8. 這個 Two-way Hierarchical Terms Display 是第七版，1977 年版，出版銷售由 Macmillan Information Co. 承辦。

由於時間的關係剩下的一部份內容沒有時間加以說明。（此文將會在圖書館學與資訊科學期刊中發表）總之：

1. 索引典是現代資料檢索系統詞彙控制之主要工具。

2. 索引典結構設計非常複雜較難做到完善的地步。

3. 我們如建立中文學科資料庫一定要設計 subject heading，或中國語式的索引典，如何做法，要考慮週密！以上淺見僅供參考。

（八）**ERIC** 結構

（九）**ERIC** 與他種索引典之比較

（十）結論

LIBRARY NETWORKS*

OUTLINE

Ⅰ. Introduction
1. Definitions
2. Basic Network Objectives
3. Major Conferences on Library Networks

Ⅱ. History & Development
1. Origin of Library Network Concepts: Ideas and Events
2. Network Characteristics

Ⅲ. Networks
1. Structures & Configurations:
star, distributed, distributed
centralized, hierarchical and ring.
2. Types: Physical and Logical
3. Levels: Local, state (provincial), national, international
4. Functions:
  Types: Single and Multiple functions
  Services: Patron oriented
  Library oriented
  Network support
5. Limitations and Barriers:
  Geographic
  Staff
  Psychological
  Political & Legal
  Funding
  Communications
  Planning

Ⅳ. Network Participation
1. Methodology
2. Advantages & Disadvantages
3. Costs
4. Problems

Ⅴ. Network Applications
1. Acquisitions/collection Development
2. Cataloging/Technical Services
3. Circulation/ILL
4. Reference/Bibliographic searching
5. Serial Control
6. User Service/Continuing Education
7. Control
8. Other Support:
  Document delivery
  Storage/preservation

---

* 本文曾發表在《圖書館自動化專題研習會綱要》(臺北市: 臺大圖書館學系, 1984 年)。

Communication/publicity
Ⅵ. **Network Governance**:
Top-down
Bottom-up
Ⅶ. **Current Scene & Trend**:
1. Library of Congress
2. Bibliographic Utilities
3. Cooperative Projects
4. Service Centers
5. Local Systems
Ⅷ. **National Networks**:
1. U. S. A.
2. TaiWan.
Ⅸ. **Problems and Prospects**
Ⅹ. **Conclusions**
Network Bibliographies
Network Glossary

INTRODUCTION TO LIBRARY AUTOMATION*

OUTLING

Ⅰ. **Introduction**
—Definition
—Why Automate?
　　　Automation or Computerization
—Elements of Computer-based Library Systems
—Advantages & Disadvantages of Using Computer-based Systems
—The Growth of Library Automation：
　　　Electronic Library & Paperless Society

Ⅱ. **Constraints on Use of Technology**
—Technical Limitations
—Economics
—Marketing Priorities
—Copyright Restrictions
—Government Regulations
—Personal Attitudes （human factors）

Ⅲ. **Options for Automating**
—Acquiring a Turnkey Stand-alone System
—Purchasing a Software Package & Using a Stand-alone Minior Mainframe Computer
—Developing a System in-house
—Contracting for a Commercial Service
—Contracting with a Bibliographic Utility
—Relying on the Data Processing Facilaties & Staff of the Library's Parent Organization

Ⅳ. **Library Applications**
—Computerized Circulation Control Systems
—Automated Cataloguing
—Automated Reference Service
—Automated Acquisitions and Serials Control

Ⅴ. **The Data Base**
—Standard
—Level of Detail
—Retrospective Conversion
—Using the Records in a Local System
—Data-entry

Ⅵ. **Planning & Implementation**
—Risks in Automating
　　　Loss of Commitment
　　　Inadequate Resources
　　　Organizational Changes
　　　Staff Resistance
　　　Patron Attitudes
　　　Fear of Failure
—The Value of Planning

＊ 本文曾發表在《圖書館自動化專題研習會綱要》（臺北市：臺大圖書館學系，1984 年）。

—The Planning Process
    Problem Definition
    Analysis
    Synthesis
    Evaluation
    Iteration
—Cooperative Planning
—Using Consultants
—Implementation
—Selling the Program to Staff and Users

VII. **Future Trends**
—Automation Trends
—Bibliographic Utilities
—State and Regional Networks
—Computer-to-computer Communications
—Acceptance of Terminals by Library Patrons
—Record Conversion
—Automating Office Procedures
—Remote Data Base Searching
—Video and Optical Discs
—Videotext
—Electronic Mail Systems
—Telefacsimile
—Telecommunications
—The Automated Library in 1990

IX. **Conclusions**
Bibliography
Glossary

PRESENT STATUS OF LIBRARY & INFORMATION SCIENCE EDUCATION IN TAIWAN AREA*

Presently, there are six library science programs in Taiwan, including one M. A. program at "National Taiwan University"; four Bachelor's programs at "National Taiwan University", "National Taiwan Normal University", Fu Jen Catholic University, and Tamkang University, respectively, and a 3-year non-degree program in the junior World College of Journalism. Total student enrollment in these programs as of May 1988 numbered 1710, of whom 31 were M. A. candidates, 1321 B. A. candidates, and 358 non-degree students in the junior college program.

For the purpose of presentation, a brief account of these programs as to their general profile and curricula is represented in tabular forms in the following pages. Materials used in this paper are primarily based upon a survey conducted in April 1988. The paper is divided into three parts:

Ⅰ. Undergraduate Programs
   1. General profile of parent institutions of 5 library science programs.
   2. General profile of the 5 library science programs in Taiwan.
   3. Basic library science courses required by the MOE.
   4. Courses required by the individual programs.
   5. Elective courses offered by the individual programs.
   6. Information science courses offered by the individual programs.

Ⅱ. Graduate Program
   As of today, "NTU" is the only university in Taiwan to have a graduate program in library science leading to the Master's degree.

Ⅲ. Summary

Ⅰ. UNDERGRADUATE PROGRAMS

1. GENERAL PROFILE OF PARENT INSTITUTIONS OF THE 5 LS PROGRAMS

"NTU" = "NATIONAL TAIWAN UNIVERSITY"
"NTNT" = "NATIONAL TAIWAN NORMAL UNIVERSITY"
FJCU = FU JEN CATHOLIC UNIVERSITY (private)
TKU = TAMKANG UNIVERSITY (private)
WCJ = WORLD COLLEGE OF JOURNALISM (private, junior college)

---

* 李德竹, 胡述兆合著 (1988 年 6 月). Seminar on Library Automation and Information Networks. Present Status of Library & Information Science Education in the Taiwan Area. June 8 - 9, 1988, "National Central Library", Taipei, Taiwan.

ENTRIES	INSTITUTIONS				
	"NTU"	"NTNU"	FJCU	TKU	WCJ
YEAR FOUNDED	1945	1946	1950	1950	1955
ACADEMIC STATUS	UNIV.	UNIV.	UNIV.	UNIV.	JR. COLL.
NO. OF COLLEGE	7	4	6	6	0
NO. OF DEPT.	47	21	33	32	8
NO. OF DOCTORAL PROG.	45	4	1	3	0
NO. OF MASTER'S PROG.	55	19	18	18	0
NO. OF FACULTY	2252	784	1582	1483	530
FULL-TIME	1664		658	588	202
PART-TIME	588		924	895	328
NO. OF STUDENTS	17623	7438	15537	17031	5781
MALE	10898	3345	5757	8898	2866
FEMALE	6725	4093	9780	8133	2915
BACHELOR'S	14370	6791	15103	16547	0
MASTER'S	2468	535	417	456	0
DOCTORAL	785	112	17	28	0
LIBRARY HOLDINGS (VOLS)	1647184	650575	442951	400000	56285

2. GENERAL PROFILE OF THE 5 LS PROGRAMS IN THE TAIWAN.

INSTITUTIONS	NAME	YEAR ESTABLISHED	DEGREE AWARDED	PRESENT ENROLLMENT	NO. OF FACULTY
"NTU"	DEPT. OF LIBRARY SCIENCE	1961	B. A.	229	25
"NTNU"	DIV. OF LIBRARY SCIENCE, DEPT. OF SOCIAL EDUCATION	1955	B. ED.	47	10
FJCU	DEPT. OF LIBRARY SCIENCE	1970	B. A.	566	30
TKU	DEPT. OF EDUCATIONAL MEDIA AND LIBRARY SCIENCE	1971	B. A.	480	35
WCJ	DEPT. OF LIBRARY SCIENCE	1964	Non-degree program	358	(a)

(a) This program is primarily taught by part-time teachers

3. BASIC LS COURSES REQUIRED BY THE MOE

COURSE TITLE	CREDITS	"NTU" CR.	"NTNU" CR.	FJCU CR.	TKU CR.	WCJ CR.
INTRO. TO LIBRARY SCIENCE	2	X 2	X 2	X 2	X 2	X
INTRO. TO INFORMATION SCIENCE	2	X 2	X 2	X 2	X 4	X
CHINESE CAT. AND CLASS.	6	X 6	X 4	X 6	X 6	X

(續上表)

COURSE TITLE	CREDITS	"NTU"	CR.	"NTNU"	CR.	FJCU	CR.	TKU	CR.	WCJ	CR.
WESTERN CAT. AND CLASS.	6	X	6	X	4	X	6	X	6	X	
CHINESE BIBLIOGRAPHY	4	X	4	X	3	X	4	X	4	X	
NON-BOOK MATERIALS	2	X	2	X	2	X	2	X	2		
A-V MATERIALS	4	X	4			X	4	X	4		
CHINESE REFERENCE SOURCE	4	X	4	X	4	X	4	X	4	X	
WESTERN REFERENCE SOURCE	4	X	4	X	4	X	4	X	4	X	
BUILDING LIBRARY COLLECTIONS	4	X	4	X	3	X	4	X	4	X	
LIBRARY AUTOMATION	4	X	4	X	2	X	4	X	2	X	
LIBRARY ADMINISTRATION	4	X	4	X	2	X	4	X	4	X	
LIBRARY FIELD WORK	0	X	0	X	3	X	0	X	0		
INTRO. TO COMPUTER SCIENCE	4	X	4	X	2	X	4	X	4		
TOTAL	50		50		37		50		50		

4. REQUIRED COURSES BY THE INDIVIDUAL PROGRAMS

COURSE TITLE	"NTU"	CR.	"NTNU"	CR.	FJCU	CR.	TKU	CR.	WCJ	CR.
HISTORY OF LIBRARY	X	2								
SPECIAL TOPICS IN LIB. SCI.	X	2								
MASS COMMUNICATION	X	2							X	2
RES. METHODS & THESIS WRITING	X	2								
LIT. OF THE HUMANITIES		4			X	4	X	4		
LIT. OF SOCIAL SICENCES		4			X	4	X	4		
LIT. OF SCI. & TECH.		4			X	4	X	4		
COLLEGE & UNIV. LIBRARIES		2			X	2	X	2		
PUBLIC LIBRARIES		2			X	2	X	2		
SCHOOL LIBRARIES		2			X	2	X	2		
SPECIAL LIBRARIES		2			X	2	X	2		
MEDICAL LIBRARIANSHIP					X	2	X	2		
MUSIC LIBRARIES					X	2	X	2		
CHILDREN'S LIBRARIES					X	2				
SCHOOL LIBRARY ADMINISTRATION			X	2						
GOVERNMENT PUBLICATIONS							X	2		
COMPUTER PROGRAMMING							X	4		
INFO. CENTER & SERVICES							X	4		
INDEXING & ABSTRACTING							X	2		
A-V EDUCATION							X	2		
PHOTOGRAPHY							X	3		

(續上表)

COURSE TITLE	"NTU" CR.	"NTNU" CR.	FJCU CR.	TKU CR.	WCJ CR.
HISTORY OF BOOK PRINTING					X 2
PRACTICAL COMPUTER SCIENCE					X 2
APPLICATION OF MICROFORMS					X 1
MANAGEMENT OF MATERIALS					X 4
MANAGEMENT OF ARCHIVES					X 4
FIELD WORK IN LIB. ADMINISTRATION					X 2
FIELD WORK IN CHINESE CAT. & CLASS.					X 4
FIELD WORK IN WESTERN CAT. & CLASS.					X 4
FIELD WORK IN CHINESE REF. SOURCES					X 1
FIELD WORK IN WESTERN REF. SOURCES					X 1
FIELD WORK IN MANAGE. OF MATERIAL					X 4
FIELD WORK IN MANAGE. OF ARCHIVES					X 2
FIELD WORK IN BOOK SELECT. & ACQUIS.					X 2
FIELD WORK IN COMPUTER					X 2
FIELD WORK IN APPLI. OF MICROFORMS					X 1

"NTU"; FJCU: 1 of the 3 is required by the dept.
TKU: elect 2 of the 3
"NTNU": 1 of the first 4 is required by the dept.
TKU: elect 3 of the 5
FJCU: 2 of the 7 are required by the dept.

5. ELECTIVE COURSES OFFERED BY THE INDIVIDUAL PROGRAMS

COURSE TITLE	"NTU" CR.	"NTNU" CR.	FJCU CR.	TKU CR.
HISTORY OF BOOKS	X 2			
INTRO. TO REFERENCE SERVICE	X 2			
LIBRARY SERV. FOR SPECIAL READERS	X 2		X 2	
LIT. FOR YOUNG ADULTS AND CHILDREN	X 4	X 3	X 4	X 4
WESTERN LIT. FOR CHILDERN	X 4			
APPLI. OF COMPUTER IN LIB.	X 3			
APPLICATION OF FILE DESIGN	X 2			
APPLI. OF MICROCOMPUTER IN LIB.	X 3		X 2	
CATALOGING & CLASSIFICATION OF MATERIAL IN JAPANESE LANGUAGE	X 2			
CHILDREN'S LIBRARIES	X 2		X 2	
CHINESE COLLECTANEA	X 4			
COMPUTER PROGRAMMING	X 3			
ENGLISH FOR LIBRARIANS	X 2			

（續上表）

COURSE TITLE	"NTU"	CR.	"NTNU"	CR.	FJCU	CR.	TKU	CR.
GOVERNMENT DOCUMENTS	X	3						
INTRO. TO A-V MATERIALS	X	3						
INTRO. TO DATA PROCESSING FOR LIB.	X	3			X	3		
INTRO. TO FILE DESIGN	X	2			X	2		
JAPANESE REF. SOURCES	X	3						
LIBRARY STATISTICS	X	6						
PLANNING & PRODUCING A-V MATERIALS	X	3						
PRINTING & PUBLISHING	X	2						
SELECTED READING ON LIBRARY SCIENCE IN ENGLISH	X	2						
STUDY OF CLASSIFICATION SYSTEMS	X	2						
SYSTEM ANALYSIS	X	3			X	2		
REFERENCE WORK					X	2		
COLLECTION DEVELOPMENT	X	2						
DATA COMMUNICATIONS	X	2						
EVALUATION OF LIBRARY OPERATIONS	X	2						
INDEXING & ABSTRACTING	X	3			X	2		
INFORMATION STORAGE & RETRIEVAL	X	2			X	4		
INFORMATION POLICY	X	3						
INFORMATION SYSTEMS (a)	X	3						
INTRO. TO DATABASE MANAGEMENT	X	2			X	3		
ISSUES IN MODERN LIBRARIANSHIP	X	2	X	2				
LIBRARY RESOURCE SHARING	X	2						
ONLINE INFORMATION SEARCHING	X	3						
SEMINAR ON LIBRARY INFO. SYSTEMS	X	2						
STATISTICS FOR LIBRARIES	X	3			X	4		
THESAURUS CONSTRUCTION	X	3			(Cont.)			

(a) "NTU": graduate courses open to under-graduate students

| COURSE TITLE | (Cont. from p. 196) | | | | | | | |
	"NTU"	CR.	"NTNU"	CR.	FJCU	CR.	TKU	CR.
LIBRARY HISTORY			X	2			X	3
ORGANIZATION OF DOC. & ARCHIVES			X	4				
MANAGEMENT OF ARCHIVES					X	2	X	2
MUSEUM ORGANIZATION & ADMINISTRATION			X	3				
PUBLIC SERVICE IN LIBRARIES			X	2				

(續上表)

COURSE TITLE	"NTU"	CR.	"NTNU"	CR.	FJCU	CR.	TKU	CR.
	(Cont. from p. 196)							
LIT. IN SOCIAL SCIENCES			X	3	X	4		
LIT. IN SCIENCE & TECHNOLOGY			X	3	X	4		
LIT. IN HUMANITIES			X	3	X	4		
PUBLIC LIB. ADMINISTRATION			X	2				
COLLEGE & UNIV. LIB. ADMINISTRATION			X	2				
SERIAL PUBLICATIONS			X	2	X	2		
SEMINAR IN SPECIAL TOPICS			X	2	X	2		
INFORMATION SERVICES			X	4				
LIBRARY EXTENSION SERVICE			X	2	X	2		
INFORMATION PROCESSING			X	2				
DATA STRUCTURE (a)	X	2			X	2		
OPERATIONS SYSTEM (a)	X	2			X	3		
COMPARATIVE LIBRARIANSHIP (a)	X	2					X	4
BASIC TV							X	2
TV PROGRAM							X	2
MOTION PICTURE							X	2

(a) "NTU": graduate courses open to under-graduate students

6. INFORMATION SCIENCE COURSES OFFERED BY INDIVIDUAL PROGRAMS

COURSE TITLE	"NTU"	"NTNU"	FJCU	TKU	WCT
APPLI. OF COMPUTERS IN LIB.	X				X
APPLI. OF MICROCOMPUTERS IN LIB.	X				
COMPUTER PROGRAMMING	X			X	
DATA COMMUNICATIONS	X				
DATA STRUCTURE	X		X		
INDEXING & ABSTRACTING	X			X	X
INFO. CENTER & SERVICES				X	
INFORMATION MANAGEMENT	X			X	
INFORMATION NETWORKS				X	
INFORMATION POLICY	X				
INFORMATION STORAGE & RETRIEVAL	X			X	X
INFORMATION SYSTEMS	X				
INTRO. TO COMPUTER SCIENCE	X	X	X	X	
INTRO. TO DATA PROCESSING	X	X	X		

(續上表)

COURSE TITLE	"NTU"	"NTNU"	FJCU	TKU	WCT
INTRO. TO DATABASE	X		X	X	
INTRO. TO INFORMATION SCIENCE	X	X	X	X	X
LIBRARY AUTOMATION	X	X	X	X	X
MANAGEMENT OF COMPUTER CENTER	X				
ONLINE INFORMATION SEARCHING	X			X	
OPERATIONS RESEARCH	X			X	
SEMINAR OF LIB. INFO. SYSTEMS	X				
SYSTEM ANALYSIS	X		X	X	
THESAURUS CONSTRUCTION	X				
CHINESE COMPUTERS OF APPLICATIONS				X	
FIELD WORK IN COMPUTERS				X	

II. Graduate Program

Graduate Institute of Library Science at "National Taiwan University"

Year established:	1980.
Degree awarded:	M. A.
Present enrollment:	31 graduate students (11M, 20F) are currently enrolled in the program, of whom 2 are foreign students.
Faculty:	19 (10 full time, 9 part time).
Admission requirement:	Pass the entrance examination for graduate students conducted by the University which is highly competitive. (According to the records of the past few years, less than one tenth of those who took the examination passed it.)
Graduation requirements:	Requirements for the M. A. degree include:

1) 2 to 4 years of residence.
2) Completion of a minimum of 24 graduate credits. Those students who possess a B. A. degree in a subject other than library science must take an additional six remedial courses of 20 credits: Chinese Cataloguing and Classification (4 credits), Western Cataloguing and Classification. (4), Chinese Reference Sources (4), Western Reference Sources (4), Book Selection and Acquisitions (2), and Library Administration (2). These credits cannot be counted toward the 24 graduate credits required for the M. A. degree.
3) Fulfill second foreign language requirement.
4) Pass graduate examination.
5) Pass oral examination on thesis.

Curriculum: 5 courses of 10 credits are required of all grduate students. 14 of the required 24 credits for graduation may be taken from the electives. 3 courses are offered for both graduate and undergraduate students. 10 of the information science courses are primarily offered for graduate classes, but are open to senior undergraduate students.

List of Courses Offered by the "NTU" Graduate Institute of Library Science

COURSE TITLE	CREDITS	REQUIRED	ELECTIVE	REMARKS
RESEARCH METHODS	2	X		
SEMINAR IN LIBRARY ADMINISTRATION	2	X		
SEMINAR IN READER SERVICES	2	X		
SEMINAR IN TECHNICAL SERVICES	2	X		
SEMINAR IN INFORMATION SCIENCE	2	X		
LIBRARY EDUCATION	2		X	
COMPARATIVE LIBRARIANSHIP	2		X	
SPECIAL TOPICS IN CHINESE BIBLIO.	2		X	
STUDY OF CHINESE BLOCK EDITIONS	2		X	
HISTORY OF CHINESE PRINTING	2		X	
CHINESE BIBLIO. LITERATURE	2		X	
STUDY OF CHINESE RARE BOOKS	2		X	
CHINESE CLASSICAL REFERENCE	2		X	
CATALOGING FOR CHINESE CLASSICS	2		X	
THEORY OF CLASSIFICATIONS	2		X	
SEMINAR IN PUBLIC LIBRARIES	2		X	
SEMINAR IN ACADEMIC LIBRARIES	2		X	
THESIS WRITING	2		X	
OPERATIONS RESEARCH	4		X	
STUDY OF CHINESE COMPUTERS	2		X	
SEMINAR IN COMPUTER SCIENCE	2		X	
COMPUTER DATA STRUCTURE	2		X	
MANAGEMENT OF COMPUTER CENTERS	2		X	
INFORMATION SCIENCE EDUCATION	2		X	
STUDY OF A-V EDUCATION	2		X	
COLLECTION DEVELOPMENT	2		X	OFFERED FOR BOTH GRAD. & UNDER-GRADUATE STUDENTS
EVALUATION OF LIB. OPERATIONS	2		X	
ISSUES IN MODERN LIBRARIANSHIP	2		X	
INDEXING & ABSTRACTING	2		X	
INTRO. TO DATABASE MANAGEMENT	3		X	
INFORMATION STORAGE & RETRIEVAL	3		X	
THESAURUS CONSTRUCTION	2		X	
INFORMATION MANAGEMENT	3		X	
INFORMATION POLICY	3		X	
LIBRARY RESOURCE SHARING	2		X	
DATA COMMUNICATIONS	2		X	
SYSTEM ANALYSIS	2		X	
SEMINAR IN LIB. INFO. SYSTEMS	2		X	

III. Summary

1. As of today, there are six library science programs in Taiwan, including one M. A. program at the "National Taiwan University", four Bachelor's programs located in "NTU", "NTNU", Fu Jen Catholic and Tamkang universities, and a 3-year non-degree program at the junior World College of Journalism.

2. Like library and information science programs in most other developing countries, the Bachelor's degree in library science is at present the professional library degree recognized in the Taiwan not only by the Government but by the library profession as well.

3. Each of the four Bachelor's programs carries a set of core courses in library and information science required by the "Ministry of Education". They are: Introduction to Library Science, Introduction to Information Science, Chinese Cataloguing and Classification, Western Cataloguing and Classification, Chinese Reference Sources, Western Reference Sources, Building Library Collections, Bibliography, Introduction to Computer Science, Non-Book Materials, A-V Materials, Library Management, Library Automation, and Library Field Work. As far as contents of these courses are concerned, most of them are rather traditional, particularly in terms of technical services and reference services.

4. Some 23 courses in information science are currently offered in these programs, three of which, namely, Introduction to Information Science, Introduction to Computer Science, and Library Automation, are required by the "Ministry of Education". Presently, "National Taiwan University" has the largest number of courses in information science (21), about half of them offered for both graduate and undergraduate students.

5. Only a few courses in special librarianship are currently available. "NTU" has a course for special readers, Fu Jen Catholic University offers a course in music librarianship, and medical librarianship is being taught at both Tamkang and FJCU.

6. With regard to student enrollment, Fu Jen Catholic University has the largest number (566), followed by Tamkang (480), "NTU" (260, 229 undergraduate students and 31 graduate students), and "NTNU" (47). Similar to the situation in other countries throughout the world, library science students here are also predominantly female.

7. Due to the fact that over 60% of the teaching faculty in these programs received their professional library education in the United States, it is no surprise to find that many aspects of these programs, such as curriculum structure, course contents, teaching methods, etc., are patterned after American library schools.

8. While Tamkang and FJCU are planning to establish Master's programs in librarianship, "National Taiwan University" will have a Ph. D. program in its Graduate Institute of Library Science in 1989.

9. Although the library program at the junior World College of Journalism is a non-degree program, its students are regarded as library professionals. To operate properly and to maintain professional standards, the entire program needs to be improved and strengthened.

圖書館自動化概論[*]

一、導言

談到圖書館自動化，在目前這個所謂的資訊時代，自動化已變成圖書館正常的業務之一，而不再是新奇的事。因此，我們必需瞭解一下圖書館自動化方面基本的專有名詞，如 Library Automation、Library Mechanization、Data Process in Library、Computerized Library System、Computer-based Library System 等這些專有名詞在文獻中常出現，皆可代表圖書館自動化。

(一) 定義、功能、目的

圖書館自動化的定義是什麼呢？就是以機器代替機械，以機械代替人工，執行圖書館各項作業，而目前我們所指的機器是什麼呢？指的就是 Computer，我們可以用電腦來處理圖書館的業務，例如採購、編目、期刊管理、參考服務等等。

圖書館自動化有哪些功能？能幫我們做些什麼？為什麼要圖書館自動化？

1. 提高服務品質、增進生產量、減低工作成本：

以往，我們作業需花很長的時間，但在自動化之後，便可節省這些時間。以參考服務為例，以往，在從事某一主題方面的資料查詢，需花費較長的時間，自動化作業以後，便可在很短的時間內，查詢到所有需要的相關資料。換句話說，自動化可以增加我們的生產量，並可降低工作成本。

2. 減少人力及成本負擔：

在作業方面，假使我們採用出納自動化，或許僅需兩名工作人員即可，而以往可能需要較多的工作人員，因為一些重複性的工作，例如編目、採購、出納等都要做，但採用自動化以後，這些人力就可以減少了。

3. 加強館藏的控制：

這是採用自動化的一個重要原因，自動化可以將資料管理方面的效能提高。

4. 減少錯誤：

作業時，有時會有錯誤產生，但是自動化以後，可以利用電腦減少人為所造成的疏失。

5. 可加速資源的分享：

利用自動化作業方式，可以跟其他的圖書館連線，以利資源分享。

6. 減少重複的工作：

重複工作是什麼？就是有些比較 Routine 的工作，便可以利用電腦來處理。

7. 提高圖書館的聲譽：

有些圖書館也許不需要自動化，但為了聲譽而採用自動化，使其覺得好像走在時代的尖端，也就是為自動化而自動化。

---

* 本文曾發表在《圖書館自動化研討會演講專輯》(1989 年) (臺中市：臺中市立文化中心)，第 1—23 頁。

圖書館自動化的目的：
1. 希望讀者能充份利用圖書館的資源，不必花太多的時間，就能查詢到所需的資料，知道圖書館的館藏情況。
2. 希望能夠充份發揮圖書館的功能。
3. 提高圖書館管理的功能和服務品質，以往，很多事情我們做不到，自動化以後，諸如管理方面的效能便可以增高，服務品質也比以往提昇些，並且也擴充了整個服務的層面。

以上三個目的，可以使我們圖書館的業務，達到經濟化、快速化、正確化及現代化。

（二）圖書館作業自動化系統的要素：由設備方面和作業情形來看
1. 從設備方面來看
（1）硬體：
也就是我們所說的 Computer，即電腦本身。
（2）軟體：
一般來說還可分為：
（A）應用軟體：為了圖書館自動化作業而設計的軟體，也就是做事的程式軟體。
（B）系統軟體：是隨同電腦的軟體。由電腦公司提供，負責控制電腦硬體資源的分配和指派，使應用軟體與硬體之間有人擔保介面工作。
（3）資源、資料以及數據：
即使有好的硬體與軟體設備，以及良好的系統，但系統內卻是空的，就好比我們建立文化中心，從外表看起來很漂亮，設備也很好，但是卻沒有資料一樣。沒有資源，這就是最大缺點。因此，一套圖書館自動化系統，要有 Resources 和各種 Database，自動化就是把這些資料放在系統裡供大家利用。
（4）通訊設備：
通訊設備是為了遠近距離的連線，我們建立了一套系統，一定希望能將所有相關的部門都予以連線、來運用這套系統，此時，就可以利用通訊設備。例如，文化中心之下，有許多的鄉鎮圖書館，這些鄉鎮圖書館都可以查詢利用這個系統，這便是遠距離的連線。將這些通訊系統以及設備互相串聯，也就是所謂的建立"網路"。
（5）人員：
前面所提各項，都需要不同的人員來支援、操作及設計，所以需要各種相關的專業人員，這些人員是關鍵。1987 年，本人曾做過一次調查，調查在圖書館自動化方面面臨哪些困境，主要是調查圖書館人員的背景、態度及其對自動化有哪些問題。結果發現，圖書館人員的自動化背景普遍都不是很好，其專業知識也較為缺乏，但是大家對圖書館自動化的意願很高。他們認為自動化有兩個較大的問題，一是經費問題，一是人員的問題。適當且有經驗的圖書館自動化方面的人才，非常難找。工作人員具有 Computer，或設計系統方面的背景，同時也是圖書館方面的專業人才，在海內外皆少有的。因此，圖書館自動化就需仰賴電腦界的人員來幫忙，因為，我們對這方面較為陌生，所以，兩方面的人員需同心協力來作業。

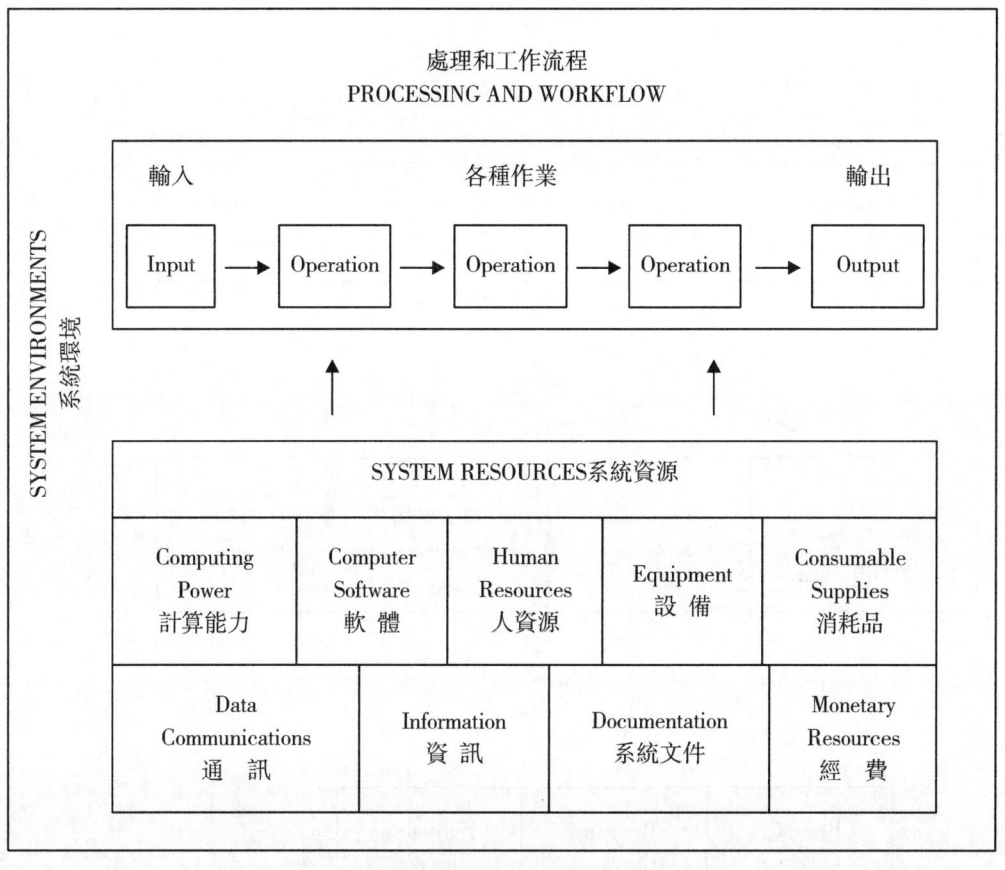

圖一　圖書館自動化系統的要素
A Block Diagram Depicting the Elements of an Automatod Library System

(6) 環境：
我們將一個系統放在文化中心，地點的選擇與設計、環境配置等皆很重要，應該要有一個良好的系統環境。

2. 從作業情形來看：（參看圖二）

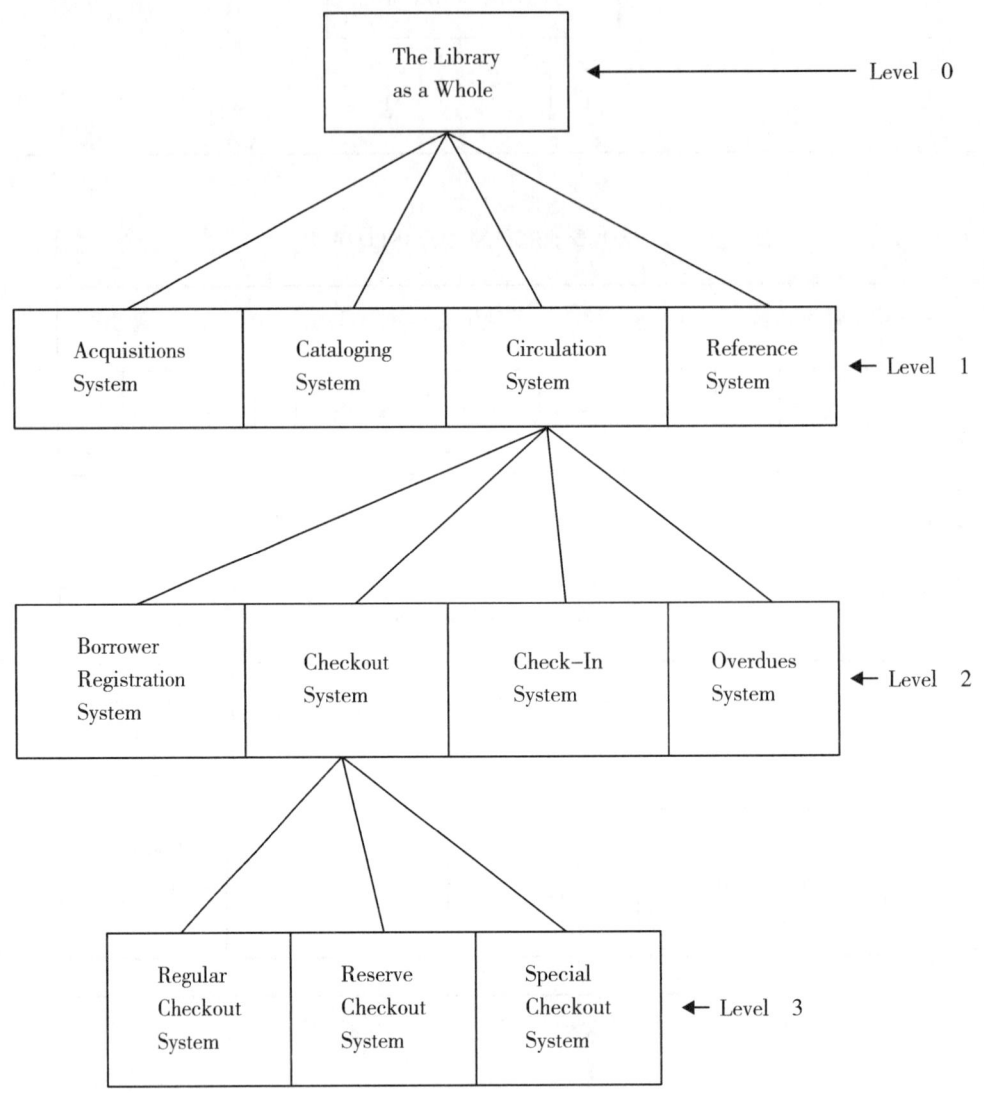

圖二　圖書館系統與子系統
Systems and Subsystems of a Library

(1) 首先應確立建立系統的目標為何？
(2) 系統處理和工作流程為何？
可以處理各種資料和事物，在輸入的時候要特別注意。
(3) 系統管理（System Management and Leadership）
要注意有多少 System Resource 才能做 Input，再做各個不同的作業，然後再輸出（Output）所要的東西。

（A）電腦硬體的資源（Computer Power）
　　（B）電腦軟體的資源
　（4）人力的支援（Human Resource）
　（5）週邊設備
　（6）日常消耗品（Consumer Supply）如紙張等。
　（7）通訊設備（Data Communication），即資訊傳輸的管道。
　（8）系統文件（Documentation）
　　指一個系統的文件，包括硬體與軟體方面的文件及操作方面的文件，這些文件可以提供館員或讀者參考用、教育訓練，或自我學習如何使用系統的各部份。一般較易為我們所忽略，但卻又非常重要的，特別是購買軟體時，一定要索取系統文件，因為系統程式有任何更改時，都應立即記錄在 documentation 中，而且經常更新的（up-to-date）。
　（9）備用資料
　（10）系統本身的環境（System environment）：空間、配置等。
　　以上，是我們從兩個不同的角度來看，建立圖書館自動化所應具備的要素。

二、圖書館作業自動化之範圍與類別

　（一）範圍：圖書館自動化可以幫助我們做：
　1. 圖書館的內部作業（House Keeping）
　　早期的圖書館自動化都是為館員處理事情，可以處理各種語言，各種型態的資料等等。
　2. 文獻檢索（Information Retrieval）也可稱為資訊自動化（Information Automation），也就是利用各種百科資料庫連線，做到文獻檢索，這些資料庫有些是書目性資料庫，例如書目、摘要、索引等，有些是非書目性資料庫，如全文性資料、法律判例數據、股票指南等等。目前，在非書目性資料庫方面是愈來愈多。另外，還有很多全是數據，如股票方面。
　3. 行政管理自動化（Office Automation）：處理辦公室內的各種行政事務。
　　如果各系統能和其他網路相連接的話，則自動化的範圍可以說是無限的。
　（二）自動化類別
　1. 依業務類型來分
　（1）記錄服務
　（2）參考服務
　（3）讀者服務
　（4）行政管理
　2. 依作業性質來分
　（1）管理性：管理圖書館
　（2）資訊性：提供良好的資料給讀者
　3. 依作業方式來分
　（1）線上作業（On-line）
　（2）離線作業（Off-line）
　4. 依系統的性質來分

(1) 單一系統（Stand alone or Single Function）
(2) 整合系統（Total Integrated System）

1980 年以後，圖書館界常常講到 Integrated Library System，Total Integrated Library System，或 Online Integrated System 這些都是講到整合系統，這些系統所有的功能在一個系統裡，並提供所有自動化的服務，其個別功能共用同一個資料庫（參見圖三），任何一個部門有所行動，在線上目錄就可以查詢到。目前的發展趨勢，便是以整合性自動化系統為主。

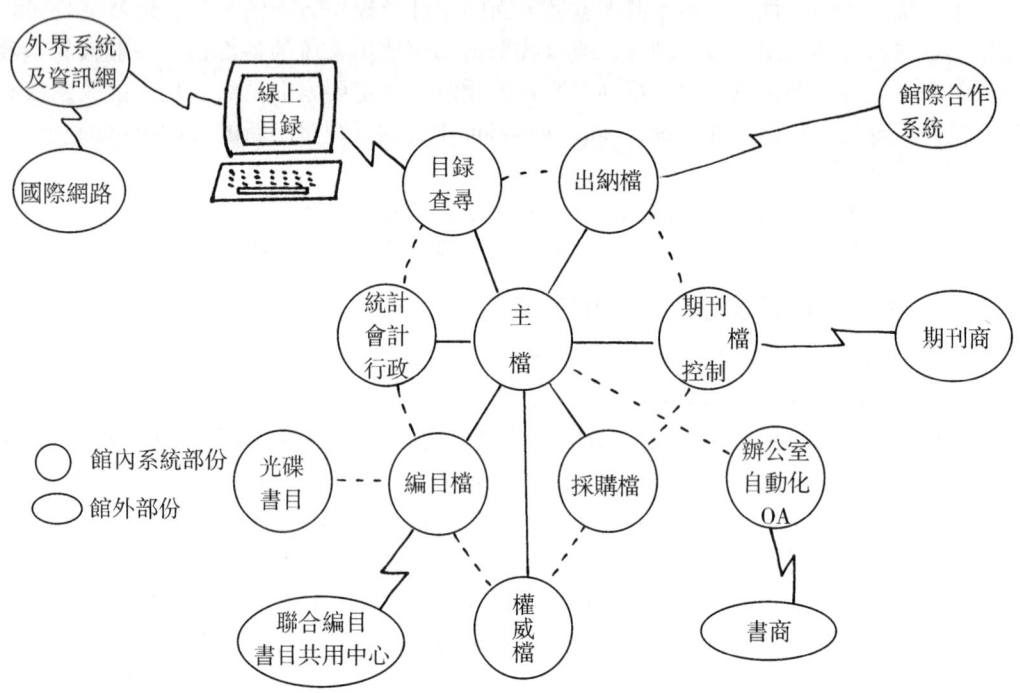

圖三　整合圖書館自動化系統概念（IOLS/AILS Concept）

5. 依系統來源分：
(1) 購買
(A) 啟鎖式或轉鍵式（Turn Key System）
現成的套裝軟體，這種軟體就像一部車，所有設備都齊全，只要 key 一開，就可以用了。
(B) 改裝（adapt）現有系統，以適合本館使用。
(2) 自行發展或本地發展的系統（In-House Development）
在臺灣，大家似乎很喜歡自行發展，但不見得能發展成功，因為太花時間、人力及金錢，所以，目前盡量不要採用自行發展的方式。
(3) 與他人合作
即與其他單位合作，例如與電腦公司合作。目前臺灣圖書館界喜歡與電腦公司合作，這是臺灣的特色，因為我們的中文處理有問題，無法找到海外適合我們使用的系統，因此，在以處理中文資料的主要情況下，要先解決中文處理的問題。目前，臺灣的電腦公司，最大的缺點是缺乏經驗，有些公司很樂意與我們合作，但合作之後，其重點卻在賣硬體。

三、圖書館作業自動化系統之規劃、選擇與實施（裝置與作業）

（一）考慮的因素
1. 人員：自動化最大的瓶頸是適當且有經驗的自動化人員非常少。
2. 設備：完整。
3. 組織：健全。
4. 經費：目前經費已不再是一個很大的問題。
5. 高階主管的決心及支持：這是自動化成功與否的最大前提。
6. 足夠、適當的人力。

（二）注意事項
1. 整體規劃
以整體的觀點考慮各種問題，並分析其瓶頸，再提出計劃，也就是從大處著眼，小處著手，花愈多的時間在規劃上，則系統會愈完整。
2. 建立各種標準
使制度合理化、作業標準化、工作精簡化，講求簡單、好用，合乎標準。
3. 週詳的計劃是非常重要的。

（三）館員的經驗談：大部份是他們失敗的經驗
1. 自動化是非常累的一件工作且是相當花錢的工作，但並不難。
2. 館員電腦方面的專業知識不足，故難以與電腦專業人員溝通。
3. 若買現成的軟體，則和 Vendor 建立的關係，不要只是口頭傳述，應該要有正式的公文，避免日後發生誤解，甚至互相攻擊失和！但應注意軟體較硬體重要！
4. 注意系統代理商或賣主的整個經濟情況和發展情形，以免日後發生對方宣布破產而遭殃。
5. 裝置時間及經費的控制都應注意。
6. 資料轉換花時間又花錢，因此資料轉換的時間、花費及其他細節都應即早設計。資料轉換時，要特別注意品質控制，我們可以透過如 OCLC 來轉換資料，也可以利用光碟或其他方式來轉換，但都是花錢又費時間。
7. 機器運轉及維修的時間或當機問題也都應考慮。
8. 自動化並不能做所有的事情，有些事情可由人工來處理即可，所以目前並未有一個真正整合的自動化系統，也就是沒有一個最理想的系統，也因此任何系統都要不斷地修改。
9. 新的機器和系統會時常更新，終端機的設計是否能與之相容？是否需花時間等待更好的系統出現？尤其是公共圖書館，終端機的設計及讀者都要特別注意，因為有很多讀者並不喜歡使用電腦亦不會打字，美國的公共圖書館也考慮到這個問題，因此他們發展一套軟體 CLS II，針對公共圖書館的需要來設計，他們的終端機且採用觸摸式（Touch Panel）讀者不必打鍵盤。
10. 系統規劃時，應該由大多數人來參與，而不要變成少數人的工作，如此才可以提各種的不同意見——集思廣益。

11. 成立自動化委員會，包括有經驗的館員、決策人員、採購部門有關人員、顧問，如法律顧問，凡牽涉到法律問題，如簽合約書等，法律顧問都可提供意見。

（四）規劃的原則

1. 要先訂定目標。
2. 分析讀者與圖書館的需求，並做系統分析：

系統分析在自動化作業規劃上是最重要的一環，將系統各種作業的流程、工作量一一列出，也就是對現況的瞭解。之後，人的需求、各種系統規格、功能需求也都應列出，這對將來寫 RFP（系統說明書）很有幫助。系統分析一定要自己分析，不要找別人分析。

3. 考慮可行的方案，根據自己的需求，選擇可行的方案。
（1）自行發展。
（2）採用改裝系統。
（3）購買套裝軟體。
（4）鄉鎮圖書館可與大圖書館連線。
（5）與電腦公司合作。
（6）與書商連線，可處理期刊或圖書等。

4. 提出需求說明書（RFP: Request for Proposal）（參看附錄）

圖書館提出系統需求，希望廠商能根據需求提出計劃，圖書館再根據計劃書選擇與哪一廠商簽約。在提出 RFP 之後，也可向各廠商提 RFI（Request for Information），即希望廠商提供本身現有系統的有關資料，以便圖書館選擇參考。

RFP 包含的內容包括：
（1）圖書館的目的、功能、工作量。
（2）投標須知，何時送標、聯絡人、投標時間、地點、方式、建議書的分類等等。
（3）系統規格（System Sepecification）需求，包括軟體、硬體及硬體裝置的環境。
（4）輸入項目。
（5）價格。
（6）維護費用。
（7）人員訓練：訓練方式、人數、次數、時間、費用。
（8）廠商參與此系統的人員的背景。
（9）付款方式、驗收、裝置方式等等。

5. 館員訓練

6. 系統評估
（1）是否能滿足需求？
（2）正確率的高低
（3）反應時間的快慢（Response Time）
（4）安全性如何？是否易被更改或破壞？
（5）彈性如何？將來若要擴大，是否能更改？

7. 標準：有了標準之後才能達到統一化
（1）一般描述書目的標準，如 AACR Ⅱ、CCR、LC Subject Heading、Sears Subject

Heading 等。

（2）機讀編目格式的標準，如 Chinese MARC：MARC 是組織書目資料的規格，也是資料結構化的規則。一般 MARC 都是根據 ISO 2709 的標準原則而訂定。

（3）資訊交換碼：便利電子計算機處理資料，以達到資料交流、交換和共享的重要工具。換言之，資訊交換碼是電子計算機共通的語言。臺灣有中文資訊交換碼（CCCII），就是處理中文的標準資訊碼、美國則有 ASCII Code，是美國國家的標準資訊交換碼，另外 IBM 有 EBCDIC 增訂的二進制資訊交換碼。

8. 人的因素：對圖書館自動化的影響很大

（1）館員不喜歡新的作業方式，不願去學習，因此，較老的館員不願接受訓練，造成館員不願接受自動化。

（2）館員除了要自我訓練外，還需要訓練讀者，因此使館員害怕而不願意接受。

（3）很多讀者只習慣舊式的服務方式。

（4）決策者對自動化的支持是由於政治因素或者人情壓力，而並非真正需要或是想接受自動化。

（5）電腦中心人員有控制自動化方向的趨勢。

（A）若先有硬體，則軟體的使用便常受製於硬體的設備。

（B）排順位的問題：若圖書館本身沒有自己單獨的系統，則將來會受到很大的限制，例如排順位時，可能是被排在最後面。

（C）有些電腦中心人員不瞭解，但又要替你做決定，甚至提出不正確的建議，甚至堅持己見，不易溝通。

四、圖書館自動化的未來發展趨勢

目前資訊的發展，諸如光碟與即將問世的第五代電腦。第五代電腦最大的特點便是具有"人工智慧"的功能，還有一些錄影的文件、電傳視訊及影像處理系統、專家系統、人工智慧等因資訊技術的發展，造成 hyper 系統的產生，如 hyper text、hyper-media 及 hyper card 等。例如教學生有關老虎的主題，就可以在 hyper 這個系統中找到，也可以看到老虎和聽到老虎的聲音，即視聽各方面甚至有關的參考資料都可一併查出。這是最近幾年的發展，由於這些新發展，使圖書館自動化變得多元化，而館員也面對更多的挑戰，因此，館員的工作變得更專業化。

圖書館自動化在未來會更普及化、個人化，所謂個人化，就是可在家裡使用自己的 PC 來查詢資料，因此可將人類的知識帶向超時間、超空間的境界。

五、結論

（一）有美國電腦專家 Richard Boss 曾預測，在 1990 年以後，美國除了學校的圖書館沒有自動化以外，其他各類型的圖書館會全面自動化。（請參看圖四"國際間圖書館自動化市場現況"及圖五"1988 年國際圖書館自動化系統市場統計"）。

由圖中統計資料得知，多數美國圖書館在 1990 年以後，會有更好的圖書館自動化系統。

（二）線上目錄的轉變使其內容更豐富、更為讀者喜愛。

（三）未來會出現"無紙"圖書館？是個問號？但讀者在自動化之後會有更多的

選擇。

（四）未來的圖書館，是朝向網路方向發展，世界是一個大網路！
（五）未來自動化系統應非常好用、方便、速度快。
（六）未來自動化的服務，可能會收費。
（七）館員的地位愈重要，將扮演資訊專家的角色！

有上述的優點和好處，相對地，會有一些問頻產生，例如，我們享受資訊的效益，也應該多注意個人的隱私權及版權的問題。

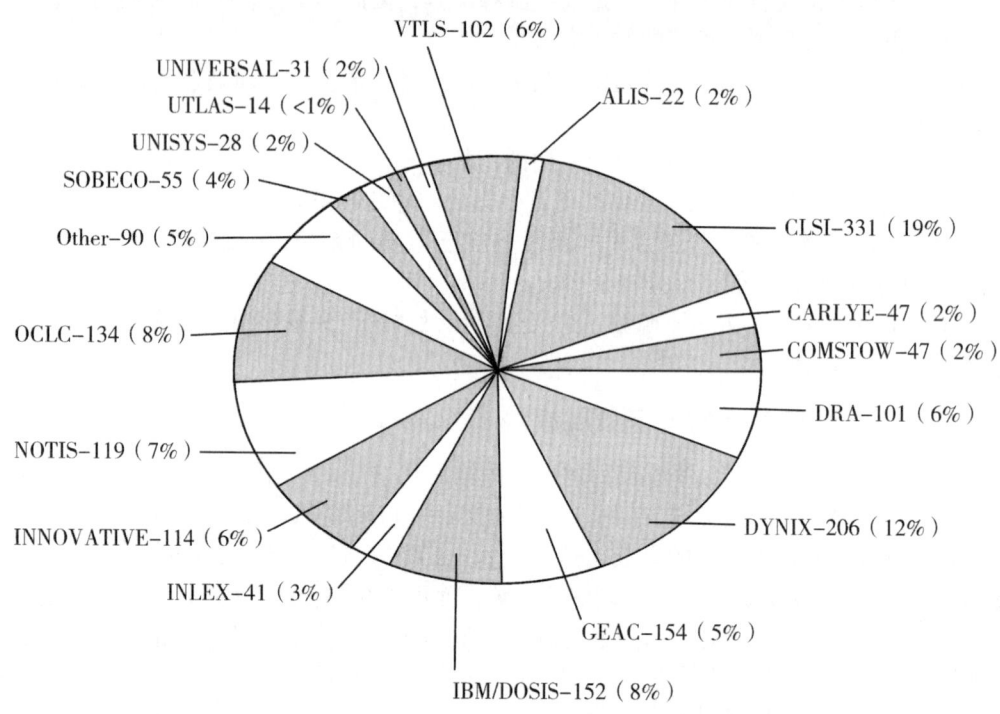

圖四　國際間圖書館自動化市場現況（約 1600 ± Installations）

資料來源：Walton, R. A. & F. R. Bridge "Automated System Marketplace 1988: Focused on Fulfilling Commitments" Library Journal 114 (6) (April 1, 1989) pp. 41-52.

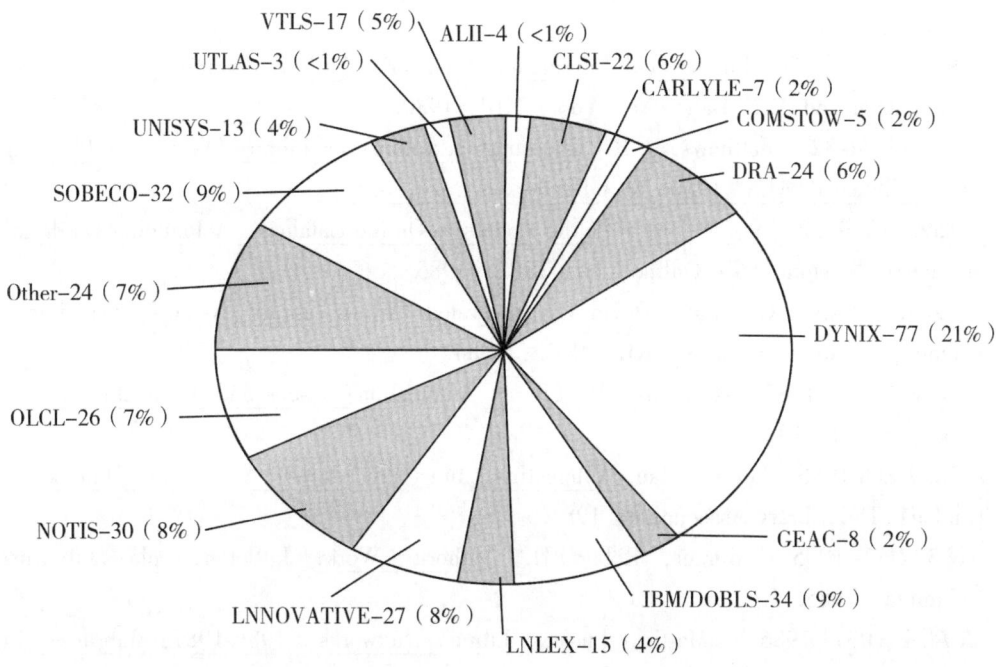

圖五　1988年國際圖書館自動化系統市場統計

參考書目

1. QA76 A844　Atwood, J. W. <u>The systems Analyst: How to Design Computer-Based</u> Systems. Rochelle Park, NJ: Hayden, 1977.

2. Z678.9 B66 1982　Boss, Richard. <u>Automating Library Acquisitions: Issues</u> and Outlook. White Plains, NY: KIP, 1982.

3. ＊Z678.9 B66 1983　　　　　　. <u>The Library Manager's Guide to Automation.</u> 2nd, ed. White Plains, NY: KIP, 1983.

4. Z699 C38　Carter, R. C. <u>Data Conversion.</u> White Plains, NY: KIP, 1983.

5. Z678.9 A1C499　University of Illionis, Graduate School, of Library Science. <u>Clinice on Library Applications of Data Processings</u>, 1966.

6. ＊Z678.9 C811　Corbin, J. B. <u>Developing Computer-Based Library Systems.</u> Rochelle Park, NJ: Hayden, 1977.

7. Z678 D6 1981　Dougherty, R. M. <u>Scientific Management of Library Operations.</u> Metuchen,

NJ: Scarecrow, 1981.
8. Z678.9 H328 1974   Hayes, R. M. and J. Becker. Handbook of Data Processing for Libraries. LA: Wiley, 1974.
9. Z699 L221   Lancaster, F. W. Libraries and Librarians in an Age of Electronics. Arlington, VA: IRP, 1982.
10. Z699.3 L616   The Library and Information Manager's Guide to Online Services. Eds. R. E. Hoover and A. H. Bahr. New York: KIP, 1980.
11. *Z678.9 M432   Matthews, J. R. Choosing an Automating Library System: A Planning Guide. Chicago: ALA. 1980. & A Reader on ..., 1983.
12. *Z699.22 M432   _____. Public Access to Online Catalogs: A Planning Guide for Managers. Weston, CT: Online, Inc. 1982; 1985.
13. *Z678.9 G45   Genaway, David C. Integrated Online Library Systems: Principles, Planning and Implementation. KIP. INC., 1984.
14. *Z678.9 R38 1985   Reynolds, D. Library Automation: Issues and Applications. New York: Bowker, 1985.
15. Z678.9 L68 1986   Lovecy, Ian. Automating Library Procedures: A Survivor's Handbook. London: The Library Association, 1984.
16. Z693 B37 1985   Burger, Robert H. Authority Work. Littleton, colo: Libraries Unlimited, 1985.
17. Z674.7 M37 1986   Martin, Susan. Library Networks, 1986-1987; Libraries in Partnership. White Plain, N. Y.: KIP, 1986.
18. Z695 C647 1985   Cochrane, Pauline A. Redesign of Catalogs and Indexes for Improved Online Subject Access: Selected Papers of Pauline A. Cochrane. Phoenix, Ar: The Oryx Press, 1985.
19. *Z678.9 C635 1985   Corbin, J. Managing the Library Automation Project. Oryx Press, 1985.
20. *Z678.9 S25 1983   Saffady, W. Introduction to Automation for Librarians. Chicago: ALA, 1983.
21. *Z678.9 T261   Tedd, L. A. An Introduction to Computer-based Library Systems. Londond: Heyden, 1980; 1984.
22. Z699.3 O538   Online Search Strategies. Eds. M. A. Plamer and R. E. Hoover. New York: KIP, 1982.
23. Z692.S5 S476   Serial Automation for Acquisitions and Inventory Control. Eds. W. G. Potter and A. F. Sirkin. Chicago: ALA, 1981.
24. Z699 U74 1983   Using Online Catalogs: A Nationwide Survey. Eds. J. R. Matthews, G. S. Lawarence, and D. K. Douglas. New York: Neal-Schuman, 1983.
25. Z674.4 D43 1987   De Gennaro, Richard. Libraries, Technology, and the Information Marketplace. Boston.; G. K. Hall, 1987.
26. Z678.L54 1987   Clayton, Marlence. Managing Library Automation. Aldershot:

Gower, 1986.
27. Lee, Lucy Te-Chu. Library Automation and Information Science: A Collection of Essays. Taipei: Sino-American, 1985.
28. 李德竹　圖書館作業自動化及資訊網路建立因素之探討，"行政院文建會"，1986年.
29. 李德竹　"圖書館自動化資訊系統發展之探討"。"中國圖書館學會"會報，43期，1988年12月：面107—123.
30. 張鼎鐘編著. 圖書館自動化導論. 學生書局, 1987年。

附　錄

DRAFTING THE RFP

The RFP is the library's primary vehicle for the procurement of automated library systems and services. As the process for acquiring an automated library system progresses, the library will become increasingly dependent on the RFP as a reference tool for understanding and evaluating vendor bids, and for monitoring time schedules and procurement strategies. As a reference tool, one of the first considerations in preparing the RFP is a comprehensive "Table of Contents" to facilitate its use. Figure 3.1 is an example of a table of contents taken from an actual RFP.

Figure 3.1
Table of Contents for a Typical RFP

1.0	Introduction
1.1	Background Information
1.2	General Rules and Conditions for Submission
1.2.1	Overview of RFP
1.2.1.	Schedule of Activities
1.2.3	Address of Contact Person
1.2.4	Date of Submission
1.3	Proposal Format
1.3.1	Arrangement
1.3.2	Number of Copies
1.3.3	Standardized Description of Development Status
2.0	Technical Proposal
2.1	Instructions to Vendors
2.2	Cover Letter
2.3	Table of Contents
2.4	Management Summary
2.5	References
2.6	Signature on Proposals
2.7	Evaluation of Proposals
2.8	Rejection of Proposals
2.9	Withdrawal of Proposals

2.10	Reguest for Clarification/Bidder's Conference
2.11	Protests
3.0	Special Requirements
3.2	Proposal Guarantee
3.2	Vendor's Cost to Develop Proposal
3.3	Performance Bond/Payments Schedule
3.4	News Release
3.5	Communication Between Library and Vendor
3.6	Performance Requirements
3.7	Warranty
3.8	Starting Date
3.9	Site Preparation
3.10	Delivery and Installation
3.11	Training Program
3.12.1	Length and Method
3.11.2	Target Group
3.11.3	Documentation
4.0	System Specifications (Functional and Technical)
4.1	General Requirements
4.1.1	Language Conventions for Mandatory and Desired Specifications
4.1.2	Background Information
4.1.3	Goals
4.1.4	Future Growth
4.2	Functional Specifications
4.2.1	General Requirements
4.2.2	Specific Requirements
4.2.3	Management Reports
4.3	Technical Specifications
4.3.1	Hardware
4.3.2	General Requirments
4.3.3	Specific Requirements (each component of every piece of equipment)
4.3.4	Formulas for Calculating Terminal Support and Storage Capacities
4.3.5	Telecommunications
4.4	Software
4.4.1	General Requirements
4.4.2	System Software
4.4.3	Applications Software
4.4.4	Utility Software
4.4.5	Data Security and Recovery
4.4.6	Provisions for Downtime
5.0	Maintenance
5.0.1	Standards

5.0.2 Mean-Time-to-Repair
5.0.3 Third Party Maintenance
5.0.4 Extended Maintenance
6.0 Financial Proposal
6.0.1 General Instructions
6.0.1.1 Spearate Proposal for Purchase and Maintenance
6.0.1.2 Format (use of specific forms, itemized price list, etc.)
6.0.1.3 Tax Computations
6.1 Financial Alternatives
6.1.1 Outright Purchase
6.1.2 Lease Option
6.1.3 Lease-Purchase Option
6.2 Maintenance
6.2.1 Options and Prices
6.2.2 Cost for Extended Maintenance (Itemized)
6.2.3 Annual Rate of Increase (maximum)
6.3 Additional cost
6.3.1 Barcodes
6.3.2 Site Preparation
6.3.3 Performance Bond
6.3.4 Delivery and Installation
6.3.5 Database Loading
6.3.6 Telecommunications
7.0 Contract Provisions
7.0.1 Vendor Responsibility
7.0.2 Library Responsibility
7.1 Specific Provisions
7.1.1 Standard Contract Legalese (e.g., indemnity, governing law, etc.)
7.1.2 Subcontractors
7.1.3 Advance Payment and Payment Schedule
7.1.4 Acceptance Test
7.1.5 Failure to Perform
7.1.6 Installation Security
7.1.7 Vendor Commitments/Warrantees
7.1.8 Maintenance Documentation (e.g., source code ownership)
7.1.9 Patent/Copyright Clause
7.1.10 Equipment Condition
7.1.11 Installation/Delivery Dates
7.1.12 Liquidated Damages (e.g., escrow for software)
7.1.13 Standard Performance
7.1.14 Engineering Changes

PLANNING AN INTEGRATED LIBRARY INFORMATION NETWORK SYSTEM: THE TAIWAN EXPERIENCE*

The purpose of this paper is to suggest a program for the development of a national library information network on Taiwan in order to facilitate the sharing of national information resources. The author has adopted a goal-oriented approach in drawing up an overall strategic plan which forms the basis for a suggested prototype system.

The overall strategic plan is as follows:

Overall goal to develop a national library information network in order to promote information exchange and information sharing.

Goal 1 to formulate a system for library information sharing.

Goal 2 to install the appropriate computer and communications equipment.

Goal 3 to design software and set standards for a library information network.

Goal 4 to establish the administrative and management systems necessary for information sharing.

Goal 5 to develop an application system for library information.

The author futhur explains these goals, deseribes the short-term plan and development of a prototype system.

In conclusion, the author makes the following suggestions:

1. The "Ministry of Education" should implement the suggestions contained in the above plan of action as soon as possible.

2. The "Ministry of Education" should set up a library information network promotion task force.

3. The national library automation and network plan should be directed by the "Ministry of Education" Computer Center. The center should allocate personnel and funds for this purpose and direct the implementation of the task force's various projects.

4. Personnel training.

5. The "Ministry of Education" should promote the Provisional Standards for the Automation of "National University Libraries".

6. The "Ministry of Education" should set up an: "academic information policy group" responsible for drafting a national information policy, and studying information sharing and the allocation policy for information resources.

7. The "Ministry of Education" should continue to support the drafting of this committee's medium-and long-term plans.

---

* Lucy Te-Chu Lee (1992, May). *Planning an Integrated library Information Network System: the Taiwan Experience.* International Seminar on Collection Development & Resources Sharing in Modern Libraries. Xi'an, China, May 17-20, 1992.

專題演講
NII 對圖書館事業的衝擊[*]
（題綱）

何謂 NII?
何謂資訊高速公路?
NII 源起
NII 的理念
NII 的構成要件
臺灣資訊通信基本建設（NII）
 臺灣 NII 推動小組組織架構及成員
 臺灣 NII 推動小組任務及工作重點
 臺灣 NII 推動現況與未來發展
海外 NII 現況與未來發展
海外 NII 現況簡介
NII 和 Information superhighway 對圖書館事業的衝擊
 1. 圖書館專業
 2. 圖書館的角色定位及重要性
 3. 圖書館員的角色定位及重要性
 4. 圖書館學教育
 5. NII 與圖書館未來發展之推動
 6. 圖書館白皮書
結論

---

[*] 李德竹（1995 年 3 月）。NII 對圖書館事業之衝擊。"全國大學校院圖書館自動化規劃第十一次研討會"（臺中市："國立中興大學" 1995 年 3 月 21 日）。

海峽兩岸第四屆圖書資訊學術研討會紀要*

1998 年"第四屆海峽兩岸圖書館資訊學術研討會"由"中華圖書資訊學教育學會"與廣州中山大學信息管理系合作舉辦，會議於本年（1998）三月三十一日至四月二日在廣州中山大學舉行。大會代表由兩岸四地（含臺灣、大陸、香港、澳門）一百十一位學者專家與會，我方代表三十人；大會論文發表共五十三篇，我方代表發表十六篇。此次爲海峽兩岸圖書資訊學學術研討會舉辦以來盛況空前的一次會議。

"圖書館自動化與網路"爲 1998 年"第四屆海峽兩岸圖書資訊學學術研討會"會議主題，其內容分爲：
1. 圖書館自動化與網路之現狀與展望
2. 資訊系統規劃的設計與管理
3. 圖書館學教育與培訓
4. 圖書館服務與資訊共享
5. 兩岸圖書資訊合作與交流

大會議程按大會主題分別舉行：

一、主持人：宋玉、黃俊貴
　　發言人：周文駿：網路化是圖書館事業建設的必由之路
　　　　　　袁名敦：臺灣大陸圖書館自動化網絡建設的進展
　　　　　　胡歐蘭、林呈潢：臺灣地區圖書館自動化與網絡發展現狀與未來展望
　　　　　　李德竹、王美鴻：臺灣地區圖書館自動化與網絡人才培訓之現況與發展
二、主題人：圖書館自動化與網絡：現狀、趨勢與策略
　　召集人：胡歐蘭、喬好勤
　　發言人：孟廣均、霍國慶：關於發展中國大陸圖書情報事業的幾點建議
　　　　　　蔡明月：從文獻分析看臺灣地區圖書館自動化與網絡化之發展過程
　　　　　　王國強：澳門資訊服務網絡概況
　　　　　　喬好勤：中國圖書館電子信息網路建設策略研究
　　　　　　吳慰慈、許貴菊：圖書館自動化與網路之現狀與展望
　　　　　　蘇倫伸：臺灣地區圖書館自動化問題分析與發展策略
　　　　　　程亞男：網路化趨勢與圖書館發展觀
　　　　　　甘　琳：思考與探索——論中國圖書館自動化與網路建設
三、主題二：信息資源建設與數字圖書館
　　召集人：陳文生、吳慰慈

---

* 李德竹、童敏惠（1998 年 6 月）。"海峽兩岸第四屆圖書資訊學術研討會紀要"。"中華圖書資訊學會"會訊，第 9 期，第 1—6 頁。

發言人：歐陽崇榮：電子圖書館：無所不在的網路圖書館
莫少強：加強數字化資源建設——迎接21世紀新挑戰
余光鎮：數字圖書館體系結構的探討
宋雪芳：網路上科技會議資訊之探討
童敏惠：從VOD看媒體資料的自動化
陳光祚：論"中國圖書情報學書目數據庫"的設計與實現
鄭恒雄：合作編目與書目共享：臺灣經驗的回顧與展望
周升恒：文獻編目工作中的規範控制

四、主題三：圖書資訊教育／規範控制
召集人：鄭恒雄、鄒志仁
發言人：王淑惠：迎接信息社會的挑戰——面向21世紀的信息管理教育
詹德優：關於圖書情報學教育改革的實踐與思考
莊道明：臺灣學術網路（Tanet）教學人員與教學內容現狀分析
曹樹金：論圖書情報學教育的"信息化"和"自動化"
楊沛超、初景利：論文獻信息普及教育
許晶華：信息管理學教育改革：課程建設的原則及體系重構
駱　偉：版本研究的時空延伸——應重視現代新型文獻的版本研究
侯漢清：評《中文圖書標題表》——兼談標題表的敘詞化改造

五、主題四：圖書資訊系統與網路技術
召集人：蘇倫伸、張曉林
發言人：沈　英：中國科學技術網（CSTnet）文獻信息系統的建設
劉洪輝：圖書館自動化網路分析
黃　儉、周志農：應用LOTUS NOTES建設多媒體網路——數據庫系統的實踐與思考
李曉紅：圖書館編目專家系統的初探
馬自衛：面向21世紀的高校地區文獻資源共享服務網路建設
張曉林：四川高校文獻信息資源共享系統分析與設計
譚祥金：圖書館自動化網路的管理
謝寶媛：網路資源評估準則之探討
王大可：圖書館自動化集成系統與網路模式——從ILAS系統的研製、應用與發展談起
顧　敏：中文資訊系統使用計量分析
尚家堯：圖書館集成管理系統對輔助決策的數據需求分析

六、主題五：資源共享與區域合作
召集人：蔡明月、張曉林
發言人：宋　玉：兩岸圖書資訊合作交流思考的問題
鐘守眞、李培：天津信息港工程——信息資源建設：機遇、挑戰、對策
施冠慨：臺灣師範學院圖書資訊服務與資源共享

　　　　　鄧小夏：信息資源共享中的電子版權問題
七、主題六：網路信息利用與服務
　　召集人：顧　敏、孟廣均
　　發言人：鄭雪玫、朱碧靜：全球資訊網在臺灣地區圖書館之應用探討
　　　　　潘華棟：四種中文搜索引擎之評估
　　　　　黃曉斌：論網路化信息資源的發展利用
　　　　　羅春榮：Internet 在館藏發展中的應用
　　　　　趙　熊：清華大學圖書館在網路環境下的信息服務實踐
　　　　　陳文生：校園圖書資訊服務規則與管理之研究
　　　　　陳昭珍：網路化的參考服務
　　　　　富　平：適應信息社會　滿足讀者需求
八、分組討論（自由發言）
　　主題一：兩岸圖書資訊合作與交流
　　召集人：宋　玉、顧　敏
　　主題二：圖書館自動化與網路
　　召集人：胡歐蘭、馬自衛
　　主題三：圖書資訊學教育
　　召集人：胡述兆、鐘守真

　　大會會場是在位於景色秀麗而具有歷史意義的廣州中山大學小禮堂和嶺南堂舉行。中山大學校園廣闊優雅，花樹叢立，形成碧海一片，環境寧靜舒暢，又學術氣息濃厚，令人有心曠神怡之感，不愧為大陸著名之重點學府之一。此次研討會在廣州中山大學信息管理系譚祥金教授、圖書館趙燕羣館長和信息管理系程煥文主任之精心籌備策劃下，各方面之招待及考量細心又週全，致使此次會議係圓滿成功，在此特致萬分之謝意。大會閉幕時，大陸中國科學院建議2000年時願與"中華圖書資訊學教育學會"共同舉辦"第五屆海峽兩岸圖書館資訊學術研討會"。

　　研討會結束後，臺灣代表分不同路線返臺。十位代表直接返臺，其餘二十位代表赴張家界等地參觀遊覽。沿途遊玩張家界、黃龍洞、桃花源等地，又至湖南長沙參觀歷史博物館、馬王堆古墓及其文物以及有中國四大書院之冠之"嶽麓書院"等。雖此次大陸之行僅九天，但收穫良多，特撰此文述之。

圖書資訊學教育西文書目（1991—1997 年）

凡　例

一、本索引係自 LISA 光碟版的資料庫中查檢出的英文書目。

二、收錄的範圍以圖書館學與資訊科學教育有關的論題，書目的年代自 1991 年至 1997 年 12 月。

三、編排依內容性質分為：壹、圖書資訊學教育；貳、圖書資訊學學校；叁、圖書資訊學課程；肆、圖書館員繼續教育；伍、圖書館利用教育；陸、隔空教育；柒、圖書館與終身教育七類。

四、在各類之下，再依作者之姓名字順排列。

壹、圖書資訊學教育

1. Ahern, T. C. & Repman, J. "The effects of technology on online education." Journal of Research on Computing in Education 26：4（Summer, 1994）：537－546.

2. Ahmad, N. "Problems and prospects of library education in Bangladesh." Herald of Library Science 30：1－2（Jan－Apr., 1991）：46－50.

3. Aina, L. O. "Directions of the information professions in Africa as reflected in the literature." International Library Review 23：4（Dec., 1991）：365－380.

4. Ainscough, P. J. "A library and information certificate course in the Seychelles." Library Review. 42：4（1993）：27－38.

5. Aiyepeku, W. O. "The challenge of implementing an African programme in information science：TRARECON." Journal of Information Science 17：5（1991）：315－320.

6. Alemna, A. A. "Libraries and librarianship in Ghana：a brief review." COMLA Newsletter 71（Mar., 1991）：2－4, 10.

7. Alemna, A. A. "Library education and rural provision in Ghana." Information Development 7（3）July 1991, 147－150.

8. Alemna, A. A. "Persistent issues in library and information science education in Africa." Education for Information 12：4（Dec., 1994）：429－436.

9. Ali, S. N. & Tikku, U. K. "Postdoctoral research in library and information science：is there a need?" Journal of Education for Library and Information Science. 31：4（Spring, 1991）：362－364.

10. Alston, R. C. "Library history：a place in the education of librarians?" Library History 9：1/2（1991）：37－51.

11. Aman, M. M. "The global information superhighway and its impact on libraries and education." Journal of Information, Communication, and Library Science. 1：4（Summer,

1995): 17-31.

12. Apeji, E. A. "Developments in education, libraries and book publishing in Nigeria." Education Libraries Journal. 40: 1 (Spring, 1997): 9-15.

13. Asundi, A. Y. "Asundi, A. Y. Specialisation in library and information science education: IATLIS National Seminar (Bangalore) 1991." Herald of Library Science. 30: 3-4 (Jul-Oct, 1991): 249-251.

14. Auster, E., Meikle, S. & Devakos, R. "Individualized instruction for undergraduates: Term Paper Clinic staffed by MLS students." College & Research Libraries 55: 6 (Nov., 1994): 550-561.

15. Barchilon, M. G. & Kelley, D. G. "A flexible technical communication education model for the year 2000." Technical Communication. 42: 4 (Nov., 1995): 590-598.

16. Bearman, D. "CONFU Digital Image Discussion Group: Educational fair use guidelines for digital images, discussion draft of July 1, 1996." Archives and Museum Informatics 10: 2 (1996): 173-179.

臺灣地區圖書館自動化人才之教育與訓練[*]

摘 要

圖書館自動化欲達到最大的效益，自動化人才的教育與訓練是關鍵的因素之一。本文的目的，在探討臺灣地區圖書館自動化人才教育與訓練課程發展的歷程。綜合分析圖書館自動化人才的教育課程與訓練內容，如：正規教育、繼續教育及臺灣主辦的國際研討會等，並與圖書館自動化的發展趨勢比較。研究結果發現，臺灣地區圖書館自動化人才教育與訓練的方式是多管道的，課程內容亦隨自動化的發展趨勢而調整，因此而使得臺灣地區圖書館的基層館員具有自動化基本的知識和操作能力、中階主管多具自動化系統規劃和評估的知能，以及圖書館高階主管對自動化趨勢的認同並能全力支持與積極推展。

一、前言

臺灣地區圖書館自動化，肇始於中山科學院引進美國機讀編目磁帶印製西文圖書目錄卡片，至今已有二十多年的歷史。圖書館自動化的發展，由早期各館的自我摸索，自行設計單一模組的自動化系統，進而引進與修改海外整合性系統，至整體規劃圖書館自動化系統，及到現今的網路化整合性資訊服務系統。為配合圖書館自動化系統的發展與自動化人才的迫切需求，臺灣地區採多種管道進行自動化人才的教育與訓練活動；於正規教育方面，各圖書館學系自1971年起陸續規劃、開授自動化相關課程；於繼續教育方面，"中國圖書館學會"自1979年起在暑期舉辦圖書館自動化專題研習會。而臺灣舉辦的國際性學術研討會自1974年起陸續討論圖書館自動化的議題，也具潛在性的教育效果。此外，館際間基於業務需要所舉行的研討會、講習會，圖書館學系舉辦的研習會，自動化廠商舉辦的產品說明會，及各圖書館於館內舉行的各種在職訓練，也都具有人才培訓的功能。本文僅就正規教育的圖書館學系、"中國圖書館學會"主辦的圖書館自動化研習會及臺灣地區舉辦的國際性研討會的內容與發展，以探討二十多年來臺灣地區圖書館自動化人才教育與訓練的歷程。

二、臺灣地區圖書館自動化的發展過程

臺灣地區圖書館自動化的發展，主要可分為五個階段：

(一) 1961年至1971年間的啟蒙時期（註1）

臺灣首次引進電腦，係於1961年底，交通大學在聯合國的資助下，採用IBM電腦支援教學研究工作。工商界利用電腦處理資料，啟於1965年臺糖公司於租用IBM電腦，應用於存量管制與處理會計薪資。圖書館使用電腦處理館務，則啟於中山科學院引進美國國會圖書館機讀編目磁帶，測試印製西文圖書卡片目錄；而淡江大學也應用該校原有

---

[*] 李德竹、王美鴻（1998年3—4月），"臺灣地區圖書館自動化人才之教育訓練"。海峽兩岸第四屆圖書資訊學術研討會（B輯）（廣州市：中山大學，1998年3月29日至4月2日），第1—20頁。

的IBM電腦上，測試印製西文館藏目錄。

此時，不但電腦技術不完備，而且軟體功能不強，圖書館人員對於電腦功能不甚清楚，而電腦人員不瞭解圖書館的作業。電腦在圖書館裡僅運用於印表工作。這個階段，圖書館自動化僅以實驗性的測試為主。

（二）1972年至1977年間的萌芽時期（註2、3）

在這個時期，電腦技術較以前改善很多，電腦的應用也日益普遍；圖書館人員與電腦人員間的溝通也較為順暢，因此多所圖書館利用電腦改進其業務。1972年，清華大學物理圖書館，利用該校原有的電腦印製書本式的西文圖書目錄；中山科學院圖書館也利用該院的電腦，整理館藏技術報告。1973年，"國科會"科資中心以電腦印製《"中華民國"西文科學期刊聯合目錄》，開啟電腦編目之先河。1974年，中山科學院圖書館，正式由美國國會圖書館機讀編目磁帶，印製西文卡片目錄。1977年淡江大學也利用該校的電腦，印製期刊目錄與西文書刊採購作業之訂單及登錄簿。

在此圖書館自動化的啟萌時期，電腦主要用於科學的運算，欠缺處理中文的能力，僅能處理西文的資料。雖然此時的圖書館自動化僅止於電腦列印，不過，整體而言，圖書館界已逐漸體認電腦在圖書館可能的應用。

（三）1978年至1984年間的基礎時期（註4）

在此階段，電腦技術有重大的進展，使得圖書館較便於利用電腦。臺灣地區於此時，推出八位元的個人電腦，而且可處理中文資料的電腦。1978年，"國立師範大學"圖書館利用神通電腦建立中文教育資料庫，並於1980年，利用該檔直接列印出版《教育論文摘要》；同年，並引進海外的ORBIT與DIALOG線上資料庫系統，首創圖書館界連線海外資料庫檢索系統的記錄。1979年，清華大學自行設計發展西文期刊編目系統。1981年，臺灣大學也自行設計期刊控制系統。1982年，政治大學發展圖書出納控制系統。1984年，交通大學在校內師生的協助下發展出西文期刊自動化系統。

1980年，"中國圖書館學會"與"國立中央圖書館"為改進圖書資料管理作業，考量圖書館自動化作業的整體發展，組織"圖書館自動化作業規劃委員會"。此委員會於1981年公佈"中文圖書資料機讀編目格式"，統一化與標準化機讀編目格式，奠下中文圖書編目作業的基礎。1983年，"國立中央圖書館"開始著手中文圖書建檔工作，同時也向OCLC採購LC MARC磁帶，進行西文圖書資料轉檔工作。

在這階段，圖書館自動化系統皆由各圖書館獨立設計，並以單一模組的目的發展，主要應用於西文期刊的目錄查詢與管理；至於中文編目功能，仍處於嘗試階段。因為作業缺乏一致性與標準化，館內各部門及館際間的作業均多重複，未能達成自動化的效益。（註5）

（四）1985年至1993年間的整合時期（註6）

從1985年起，臺灣地區電腦技術突飛猛進。除電腦公司相繼成立外，電腦處理中文的能力也大幅提昇。由於臺灣地區多家電腦公司發展圖書館自動化系統，海外的系統也相繼的被引進，使得圖書館自動化系統有更多的選擇。在此階段，圖書館自動化大多朝整合性的功能設計及採用海外的套裝軟體發展。

1988年淡江大學採用TALIS系統，首先完成整體性圖書館自動化系統，具備採購、中西文編目、出納、期刊管理、參考服務、行政管理及線上公用目錄的功能。同時，受到"教育部"委託的"整體規劃全國圖書館資訊網路計劃"研究報告的影響，各紛紛採購自動化系統主機，朝整體性網路化發展，以提昇資訊服務的水準及達成資源共享的目的，如：1990年成功大學採用UTLAS系統、1991年"中央研究院"採用INNOPAC圖書館自動化系統、1991年清華大學採用傳技公司發展的TOTALS整合性系統等。

1987年間，臺灣地區引進書目光碟片（Biblio File），用於協助西文圖書的編目工作。因為書目光碟片簡便易用，可減輕館員原始編目的負擔，於短短幾年內使用單位遽增。（註7）在資訊檢索服務方面，1980年代引進的DIALOG及ORBIT線上資料檢索系統，由於通訊費用昂貴，"國科會"的科資中心，購進常用的資料庫，提供線上檢索服務，以節省使用者的花費。再者，光碟資料庫的興起，許多線上資料庫紛紛發行光碟版，光碟資料庫又可於區域內設立光碟網路系統，方便使用者查詢，也提昇圖書館的服務品質。

（五）1994年至今的網路期

自1992年臺灣連上網際網路後，圖書館逐漸應用網際網路的各種功能與資源，於館內的業務與讀者服務上。圖書館首先推出遠距查詢公用目錄的功能，隨著網際網路的發展，尤其是1995年起，具展現多媒體與超連結的全球資訊網（World Wide Web）更是被圖書館廣泛地應用，使得圖書館能提供原文傳送的遠距資訊服務，並朝顯現全文與多媒體資訊數位化圖書館的境界邁進。

三、圖書館自動化人才的教育與訓練

為提昇館員對於圖書館自動化的瞭解與執行能力，圖書館學系、"中國圖書館學會"及相關機構等，均致力推廣圖書館自動化的理論與實務。茲就各類圖書館自動化有關的教育與訓練活動，介紹於下：

（一）圖書館學系所的圖書館自動化課程

臺灣地區圖書館學正規教育以大學部為主。由於圖書館事業的發展，有鑑於專業圖書館員的需求，爰於1955、1960、1964、1970、1971年，先後設置臺灣師範大學社會教育系圖書館組、臺灣大學圖書館學系、世界新聞專科學校圖書資料科、輔仁大學圖書館學系及淡江大學教育資料科學系。為提昇圖書館專業人員的素質，加強圖書館學的研究，於1964、1980、1985、1991、1994、1996年，分別在文化大學史學研究所、臺灣大學、臺灣師範大學社會教育系、淡江大學、輔仁大學及政治大學，設立圖書館學或相關的研究所；此外，臺灣大學並於1988年設立博士班。有關圖書館自動化課程的發展與特色，敘述於下：

1. 圖書館自動化課程的緣起

淡江大學於1970年成立教育資料學系，即將"電子計算機概論"列為必修科目，首創臺灣地區文學院開設電子計算機科目。（註8）在1983年，"教育部"訂定"電子計算機概論"與"圖書館自動化"為圖書館學系的必修科目。

2. 課程發展

依據1976年臺灣地區各圖書館學系的現況報告（註9），當時開授圖書館自動化的相關科目的情形列於表一，在淡江大學"電子計算機概論"、"電腦程式寫作"及"圖書館自動化作業"為必修科目，"索引與摘要"及"資訊中心與服務"為選修科目；臺灣大學有"計算機程式設計"、"電子計算機資料處理"、"圖書館自動化"、"系統分析與計劃"，但均為選修科目；師範大學列"電子計算機概論"為選修科目。當時正值圖書館自動化的萌芽期，圖書館自動化相關課程的目的，對文學院的學生而言，僅於介紹認識計算機的基本功能與圖書館自動化的功能、實施方法；倘若學校有相當的設備，才再施以電腦程式寫作的訓練。至於師資方面，"電子計算機概論"與"程式設計"的授課教師，主要由校內電子計算機學系的教師支援，或聘請校外的學者專家兼任之，例如當時臺灣大學圖書館學系，則聘有三位電子計算機學者任教。

在1983年，"電子計算機概論"與"圖書館自動化"已列入"教育部"公佈的圖書館學系的共同必修科目中，如表二所示。(註10) 當時 DIALOG 與 ORBIT 資料庫系統剛引進臺灣，大家也嘗試建立中文資料庫，因此多所圖書館學系也規劃開授資訊儲存與檢索類的課程。此時雖然清華大學、臺灣大學及政治大學等自行設計具單一功能的自動化系統已開始運作，但圖書館館員並未能全面掌握圖書館自動化的功能與實施方法，因此在圖書館自動化發展的基礎期，將"圖書館自動化"列為必修科目，有其階段性的功能。

1988年，根據臺灣地區圖書館學教育現況調查結果顯示，各圖書館學系提供了多樣的圖書館自動化的課程（註11），列於表三。在此時期，光碟資料庫於臺灣盛行，各資料服務中心也開始建置資料庫，因此"資訊儲存與檢索"與"系統分析設計"的課程，也相對地增加。在此整合期，所討論的圖書館自動化不再限於技術性的議題，欲達到自動化的效益，也須由管理政策面著手，因此也開授"電腦中心管理"與"資訊政策"等科目。

在1995年"教育部"於"大學法"通過後，取消部定必修科目的規定，改由各校自主。各圖書館學系依據該系的教學目標、配合圖書館資訊服務的發展趨勢及現有的師資，規劃各具特色的新課程。於新規劃的課程中，圖書館自動化課程，仍列為各校必修的核心科目，並有多種的選修科目與之配合，如表四所列。(註12) 由於圖書館廣泛地應用網際網路，通訊技術與網路資源的課程，也成為圖書館學系的核心科目。圖書館自動化管理決策層面的課程，亦受到更多學校的重視。

3. 圖書館學系圖書館自動化課程的特色

回顧臺灣地區圖書館學系所近三十年的發展，圖書館自動化人才的正規教育，具有四點特色，分別說明如下：

(1) 培育圖書館自動化基礎的人才

自1976年起，臺灣地區的圖書館學系已開授"電子計算機概論"與"圖書館自動化"科目，在1983年並明訂為必修科目，此後並開設多門的選修科目，傳授學生自動化基本的理論與知識，使得學生畢業後能順利的從事自動化的圖書館業務。

(2) 涵蓋圖書館自動化的各個層面

由歷年來圖書館自動化相關科目的成長，可發現臺灣地區圖書館學系開授的圖書館自動化課程，涵蓋的層面頗廣。電腦技術層面的課程有：電腦與程式設計、系統分析與設計；資訊處理層面的課程有：資訊儲存與檢索、圖書館自動化；管理層面的課程有：資訊管理與政策。

表一　1976年臺灣地區圖書館學系圖書館自動化相關課程

階段	學校	電腦與程式設計	資訊儲存與檢索	系統分析、設計與評估	圖書館自動化	通訊與網路	資訊管理與政策
萌芽期	師大	電子計算機概論（選, 4）					
	臺大	電子計算機程式設計（選, 3） 電子計算機資料處理（選, 3）	索引學（選, 2）	系統分析與計劃（選, 3）	圖書館自動化（選, 2）		
	輔仁						
	淡江	電子計算機概論（必, 4） 電腦程式寫作（必, 4）	索引與摘要（選, 2）		圖書館自動化作業（必, 4）		資訊中心與服務（選, 4）

課程資料來源：周駿富等，"圖書館教育現況"，圖書館學與資訊科學 2卷1期（1976年4月），頁45–73。

表二　1983年臺灣地區圖書館學系圖書館自動化與網路相關課程

階段	學校	電腦與程式設計	資訊儲存與檢索	系統分析、設計與評估	圖書館自動化	通訊與網路	資訊管理與政策
基礎期	師大	電子計算機概論（選, 2）	資訊檢索（選, 2）				
	臺大	電子計算機概論（必, 4） 電子計算機資料處理（選, 3） 電子計算機程式設計（選, 3） 電子計算機研究（研, 2）	摘要及摘要法（研, 2） 索引及索引法（研, 2）	系統分析（研, 2） 資訊系統（研, 2）	圖書館自動化（必, 4）		
	輔仁	電腦概論（選, 6）					
	淡江	電子計算機概論（必, 4） 電子計算機程式寫作（必, 4）	索引與摘要（必, 2）		圖書館自動化（必, 4） 微電腦在圖書館的應用（選, 3）		資訊中心與服務（必, 4）

課程資料來源：王振鵠，"三十年來的臺灣圖書館教育"，"中國圖書館學會"會報35期（Dec. 18, 1983），頁9–17。

表三 1988年臺灣地區圖書館學系圖書館自動化與網路相關課程

階段	學校	電腦與程式設計	資訊儲存與檢索	系統分析、設計與評估	圖書館自動化	通訊與網路	資訊管理與政策
整合期	師大	電子計算機概論（必，2）	資訊檢索（選，2）		圖書館自動化作業（必，2）		
	臺大	電子計算機概論（必，4） 中國電子計算機研究（研，2） 電子計算機專題（研，2）	資料庫概論（研，2）* 索引與摘要（研，3）* 資訊儲存與檢索（研，3）* 線上資訊檢索（研，3）* 索引典結構（研，2）*	系統分析（選，3） 檔案設計原理（選，2） 檔案設計應用（選，2） 電子計算機資料結構（研，2）	圖書館自動化（必，4） 電子計算機在圖書館的應用（選，3） 微電腦在圖書館的應用（選，3）		電腦中心管理（研，2）* 資訊政策（研，3）*
	輔仁	電子計算機概論（必，4）	資料庫（選，3） 索引與摘要（選，4） 資訊儲存與檢索（選，4）	作業系統（選，3）	圖書館自動化（必，4）		
	淡江	電子計算機概論（必，4） 中英文電腦文書處理（必，2） 電子計算機程式寫作（必，4） CAI課程原理與設計（選，2）	資料庫概論（必，2） 索引與摘要（必，2） 資訊儲存與檢索（必，2） 線上資訊檢索（必，2）	資訊管理系統（必，4） 圖書館系統分析（選，2）	圖書館自動化（必，4） 自動化專題研究（選，2） 電腦在圖書館的應用（選，2）	資訊網路（選，2）	資訊中心與服務（必，4）

*大四學生可選修

課程資料來源：宋建成，"圖書館教育"，第二次圖書館年鑑（臺北："國立中央圖書館"，1988年），頁47—66。

表四 1998 年臺灣地區圖書館學系圖書館自動化與網路相關課程

階段	學校	電腦與程式設計	資訊儲存與檢索	系統分析、設計與評估	圖書館自動化	通訊與網路	資訊管理與政策
網路期	師大	電子計算機概論（必, 2） 程式語言（選, 2）		系統分析與系統管理（選, 2） 資料庫管理（選, 2）	圖書館自動化（必, 3） 個人電腦與圖書館（選, 2） 資訊科技與圖書館（選, 2）	電腦網路與通訊（必, 2） 網路資源徵集與利用（選, 2）	個人資訊管理（選, 2）
網路期	臺大	電子計算機概論（必, 3） 文書處理（選, 2） 程式語言（選, 3）	資訊檢索（必, 3） 索引與摘要（選, 2） 自動分類與索引（選, 3） 索引典結構（研, 2） 索引及摘要（研, 2） 中文資訊處理檢索（研, 2） 資訊儲存與檢索（研, 3） 線上資訊檢索（研, 3） 中文資訊處理專題研討（研, 博, 3） 資訊尋求行為（研, 2）	資料結構（選, 3） 作業系統（選, 3） 資料庫系統（選, 3） 系統分析（選, 2） 管理資訊系統（研, 3） 光碟資料庫系統（研, 2） 電子計算機資料結構（研, 3） 資料庫管理系統（研, 3） 作業研究（研, 3）	圖書館自動化（必, 4） 圖書館自動化（研, 4） 圖書資訊系統專題（研, 博, 2）	電腦網路與通訊（必, 2） 網路資源（研, 2） 電腦網路與通訊（研, 2） 圖書館數據通信專題研究（研, 3）	圖書資訊標準（研, 2） 資訊管理（研, 博, 3） 資訊管理研討（研, 博, 2） 電腦中心管理（研, 2） 圖書館與資訊社會（研, 博, 3） 資訊政策（研, 2）

(續上表)

階段	學校	電腦與程式設計	資訊儲存與檢索	系統分析、設計與評估	圖書館自動化	通訊與網路	資訊管理與政策
網路期	輔仁	電子計算機概論（必,8） 物件導向語言（必,2） 程式語言原理（選,4） UNIX導論（必,4） CAI/多媒體與讀者專題（研,2）	資料庫檢索原理（選,4） 資訊尋求行為（選,4） 主題分析（必,4） 自動文獻處理（研,2） 多媒體資訊檢索（研,2） 資料庫檢索服務（研,2） 元資料（研,2）	資料結構（必,2） 系統分析（必,4） 資料庫系統導論（必,4） 作業系統（選,4） 資訊系統發展與評估（研,2）	圖書資訊系統（選,4） 數位化圖書館導論（研,2）	電腦網路概論（必,4） 網路資源（必,2） 網路資源與利用（選,4） 開放系統應用協定（研,2）	
網路期	淡江	資訊概論（必,4） 科技傳播概論（必,2） 中英文電腦輸入法（必,1） 電子計算機程式寫作（必,4） 多媒體技術與應用（必,2） 電子文件處理專題（研,2） 電子傳播科技（研,2）	索引及摘要（必,2） 資訊儲存與檢索（選,2） 資訊儲存與檢索專題（研,2）	資料庫結構（選,2） 管理資訊系統（選,2）	圖書館自動化作業（必,4） 自動化專題研究（選,2） 電腦在圖書館的應用（選,2） 線上目錄（研,2） 圖書館自動化專題（研,2）	網路概論（選,2） 網路專題（選,2） 網路資源與應用（必,4） 資訊網路（研,2） 學術網路與圖書館（研,2）	資訊中心與服務（選,2） 資訊政策專題（研,2）

(續上表)

階段	學校	電腦與程式設計	資訊儲存與檢索	系統分析、設計與評估	圖書館自動化	通訊與網路	資訊管理與政策
網路期	世新	電子計算機概論（必, 2） 電腦文書處理（必, 3） 程式設計（必, 3） 電子計算機應用（必, 2）	索引與摘要（必, 3） 資訊儲存與檢索（必, 3） 資訊檢索系統專題（選, 3）	資料庫管理系統（必, 3） 圖書館系統分析（研, 2） 資料庫結構（研, 2） 資訊管理系統（研, 2）	圖書館自動化（必, 4）	網路與通訊（必, 3） 網路資源檢索與應用（選, 3）	
	政大	多媒體資源研究（研, 2）	資訊組織與主題分析（研, 2） 資訊儲存與檢索（研, 2）	系統分析（研, 2） 資料庫管理系統（研, 2） 管理資訊系統（研, 2）		電腦網路與通訊（研, 2） 網路資源管理研究（研, 2）	檔案自動化專題（研, 2） 資訊政策研究（研, 2）

資料來源："中華圖書資訊教育學會"編，臺灣圖書資訊學系所現況暨教育文獻書目，（臺北：編者，1998年3月）。

(3) 依據圖書館自動化趨勢修訂課程

圖書館學系所開設的課程,皆配合圖書館自動化發展的趨勢而調整。於自動化的萌芽期,圖書館自動化已列入課程;於基礎期,圖書館自動化則列為必修科目;至整合期,圖書館自動化課程則涵蓋電腦技術、資料處理及管理等多層面;旋至網路化時期,通訊技術與網路資源也成為圖書館自動化課程的重點之一。

(4) 延聘資訊科技背景的教師

早期圖書館自動化的課程,主要邀請資訊技術相關科系的師資支援。近年來,由於圖書館自動化相關科目數量的成長,有多所圖書館學系聘請具有資訊技術背景的專任教師,如:臺灣大學聘有一位專任的助理教授,輔仁大學聘有二位專任副教授,淡江大學聘有一位專任教授與一位專任講師,及世新大學聘有一位專任的助理教授。(註13)

(二)"中國圖書館學會"主辦圖書館自動化專題研習會

"中國圖書館學會"成立於1953年,是臺灣地區成立最早的圖書館專業學會,四十多年來,對於臺灣地區的圖書館教育,具有承先啟後之角色,尤其於圖書館員在職教育的舉行,更是不遺餘力。該學會於1956年起,開授"圖書館工作人員講習班",招收圖書館工作人員做短期的講習訓練。1979年為確實符合學員的需求,也增開各類專題的研習班。

1. 緣起與發展

為增進圖書館與資料單位在職人員對圖書館自動化的認識,"中國圖書館學會"自1979年起,委託臺灣大學圖書館學系舉辦"圖書館自動化專題研習會",對圖書館學相關科系畢業現職圖書館與資料單位、並大學畢業於圖書館或資料單位服務滿兩年者,由任職單位保送接受兩週的訓練。

圖書館自動化專題研習會自1979年至1989年,共舉行11年,共有907人參加;1986年至1988年4年期間,由於報名人數激增,每年各分兩梯次舉行。1990年起,為配合資訊網路於圖書館的應用,改名為圖書館自動化及網路專題研習會,至1995年共有354人參加。1996年,再改名為圖書館與電腦網路應用專題研習班,並分基礎與進階兩班,1997年轉由世新大學承辦,兩年共有314人參加。1997年臺灣大學則承辦電子圖書館與資訊檢索專題研習班,有99人參加。總計十九年來,由"中國圖書館學會"主辦的圖書館自動化相關的研習會,參加人數共達1674人,其主題及歷年參加的人數,詳見表五。

表五 "中國圖書館學會"暑期圖書館自動化專題研習會之沿革

階段	年代	參加人數	承辦單位	重點
基礎期	1979	42	臺大	圖書館自動化專題研習會
	1980	40	臺大	圖書館自動比專題研習會
	1981	44	臺大	圖書館自動化專題研習會
	1982	67	臺大	圖書館自動化專題研習會
	1983	79	臺大	圖書館自動化專題研習會
	1984	58	臺大	圖書館自動化專題研習會
整合期	1985	61	臺大	圖書館自動化專題研習會
	1986	128	臺大	圖書館自動化專題研習會、分2梯次舉行
	1987	127	臺大	圖書館自動化專題研習會、分2梯次舉行
	1988	133	臺大	圖書館自動化專題研習會、分2梯次舉行
	1989	128	臺大	圖書館自動化專題研習會、分2梯次舉行
	1990	55	臺大	改名為"圖書館自動化及網路專題研習會"
	1991	69	臺大	圖書館自動化及網路專題研習會
	1992	64	臺大	圖書館自動化及網路專題研習會
	1993	53	臺大	圖書館自動化及網路專題研習會
網路期	1994	52	臺大	圖書館自動化及網路專題研習會
	1995	61	臺大	圖書館自動化及網路專題研習會
	1996	163	臺大	改名為"圖書館與電腦網路專題研習",基礎班與進階班
	1997	99	臺大	電子圖書館與資訊檢索專題研習班
	1997	151	世新	圖書館與電腦網路應用專題研習班,基礎班與進階班

2. 自動化專題研習會課程內容（註 14－35）

自動化專題研習會的目的,是為提昇各圖書館與資料單位在職館員的自動化或專業知識,以促進圖書館的自動化作業。課程安排以理論與實務並重,其內容包含:課堂講授、實際上機、參觀訪問、學員座談及學習考核。

臺灣地區圖書館自動化的萌芽期間,在1972年的暑期圖書館工作人員研習會中,列有十二小時的"電子計算機常識"（註36）,在1974年首次開授"圖書館自動化"科目（註37）。茲將歷年來圖書館自動化專題研習會講授的科目,分類統計列於表六,以發現各時期研習會的特色。

圖書館自動化專題研習會始於1979年,正臨圖書館自動化的基礎期。當時,中文電腦剛上市,有數所圖書館自行設計單一模組的自動化系統,中文圖書資料機讀編目格式剛發行,而DIALOG線上資料庫也新引進。研習會中課堂講授的主題,涵蓋:電腦應用與程式設計、中文資料的處理、圖書館各單位的自動化作業、中文機讀編目格式及線上資料庫的檢索。參觀訪問的機構有：臺灣大學的計算機中心、榮電公司、出產中文電腦的神通電腦公司及進行期刊自動化作業的淡江大學等。

於 1985 年至 1989 年，圖書館自動化的整合時期的早期，各圖書館處於學習圖書館業務的自動化與光碟資料庫的應用階段。研習會的講授內容，則以圖書館業務的自動化與資料庫檢索為主。至整合時期的中、後期，各圖書館考慮採購海內外發展的整合性自動化系統，"中央圖書館"的資訊網路及學術網路也開始運作，因此設計的課程類別，以系統分析評估、網路通訊及通訊標準為主，包含：圖書館自動化需求書、自動化系統評估與選擇、ISDN、ISO 標準等。

表六　歷屆"中國圖書館學會"圖書館自動化專題研習班講授科目類別統計表

階段	年度	科目類別							
		電腦與程式設計	資訊儲存與檢索	系統分析與評估3	圖書館自動化	通訊與網路	資訊管理	中文資訊處理	圖書資訊標準
基礎期	1979	3			2			2	
	1980	3	1	3	2			4	
	1981	2		1	4			3	3
	1982	1	1	3	7	1		4	1
	1983	1	4	1	9		1	3	1
	1984	2	3	3	4	3		2	1
整合期	1985	1	3	2	5			1	
	1986	2	2	2	6	2	1	1	
	1987		1	4	9				
	1988		3	3	4				
	1989	1	2	3	4	2			
	1990	2		4	2	7			
	1991			3	3	5			
	1992	3		1		7		1	9
	1993	1		4	2	7			1
網路期	1994		3	1	2	7		2	1
	1995	2		2	3	6		1	2
	1996	5	1	2	4	4			1
	1997	5	5	1	4	10	1		4

到了 1994 年以後，網際網路的廣泛應用，研習會講授內容則有：網路資源、通訊標準、網路資訊的檢索及網路資訊的整理技術等。由於大多數的圖書館已自動化，並且新進的館員在學校裡已習得自動化的基本知識，因此，圖書館業務自動化的課程單元即相

對地減少,研習會名稱改為"圖書館與電腦網路研習會"。在 1997 年由於電子圖書館的觀念盛行,旋增加"電子圖書館與資訊檢索專題研習班"。

3. 自動化專題研習班的特色

從上述的緣起、發展與課程設計,可發現圖書館自動化專題研習會具有下列的特點:

(1) 學員多為中層階級的館員

依據研習會招收學員的規定,參加的學員必須大學以上畢業,並有兩年的實際工作經驗。再依據歷年來的研習會工作報告,參加學員平均年齡為三十歲左右,因此可發現參加圖書館自動化專題研習會的學員,大多為中階的館員,往後將可能參與或主導圖書館自動化系統的設計與發展。

(2) 授課內容理論與實務並重

研習會的性質係屬在職館員的再教育,在授課的內容除理論的傳授外,並安排參觀訪問以實際瞭解資訊技術的應用。

(3) 授課方式聽講與實作並重

為讓學員有實際的操作經驗,體會自動化的效益,課程的設計中包含實際的上機操作。早期實習的內容有:中文電腦操作、DIALOG 線上資料庫的實作;近年來則有網際網路的上線實習與 HomePage 的實際設計。

(4) 課程內容隨自動化的發展而調整

將研習會的授課內容與自動化發展過程相比對,如表六顯示,研習會的授課主題,皆能及時的配合臺灣地區自動化的發展而調整。

(三) 國際會議

臺灣地區為瞭解海外圖書館事業的發展,"中央圖書館"、"中國圖書館學會"及圖書館學系,曾舉辦國際性的學術研討會,邀請海外的學者專家與會。研討會中,海外與臺灣地區的圖書館界的學者專家發表論文,介紹圖書館事業的發展趨勢、報告各國的圖書館事業現況及分享研究的成果。曾討論到圖書館自動化議題的國際性研討會有二十多場,其中規模較大的十四場研討會其論文類別統計列於表七,並且將八場較具階段性意義的研討會介紹於后:

1. 具階段意義的國際性會議

(1) 第一次亞洲圖書館合作會議(The First Conference On Asian Library Cooperation)

1974 年,"中國圖書館學會"、淡江大學教育資料系及"中央圖書館",為促進圖書館事業的發展與謀求國際間的合作,希望由人力、智慧、知識、工作經驗及資源利用等方面彼此支援合作,以達合作發展的理想,因此,由淡江大學提供經費,於該校園內舉行第一次亞洲圖書館合作會議,共有海外學者專家 50 人及臺灣地區 76 人參加。會中,分東方資源組、圖書館教育組及媒介與工藝組,進行研討,發表的論文與圖書館自動化相關的有四篇,並請"國科會"邀請來臺的圖書館與資訊科學顧問 Robert M. Hayes 專題演講圖書館自動化的問題。此次會議中乃是臺灣地區首次介紹圖書館自動化的議題。會中決議亞洲各國共同發展適用於亞洲的書目機讀記錄標準,並分享電腦應用的經驗。(註 38) 此次會議正值臺灣地區圖書館自動化的萌芽期,在圖書館裡電腦僅用於列印資料,會中介紹海外圖書館自動化的發展與問題,為萌芽中的圖書館自動化注入成長的泉水。

(2) 中文圖書資料自動化國際研討會

1981年，為推行中文圖書資訊自動化作業，以利中華文化的保存與傳播，並拓展國際間的文化與學術合作，由"中央研究院中美科學學術合作委員會"、美國學術團體聯合會及"中國圖書館學會"，共同舉辦中文圖書資料自動化國際研討會。與會的海外專家，分別來自美國研究圖書館組織（RLG, Research Libraries Group）、華聖頓州圖書館網路（WLN, Washington Libraries Network）、OCLC、美國國會圖書館、UCLA及日本韓國等地，共有兩百多人參加。該研討會的主題有：中國文字與電腦、中文資訊交換碼、中文圖書編目格式、中文圖書資料自動化及圖書館自動化國際合作。會中，WLN代表現場示範經由國際電信局專線連線查詢WLN資料庫，會場並安排十四家電腦廠商展示中文電腦。此次會議的成果有：中文資訊交換碼（CCCII）獲得海外人士的認同、中文圖書機讀編目格式符合標準與需求及傳技公司已與RLG簽訂共同發展中日韓文終端機等。（註39）此時正逢臺灣地區圖書館自動化的基礎期，除有自動化的經驗報告外，尚有現場展示，讓與會的二百多位人員有實際觀摩互換心得的機會，並對電腦處理中文資訊的技術有進一步的認識。

(3) 亞太地區第一屆圖書館學研討會

為與亞太地區的圖書館，討論圖書館自動化與資源分享事宜，"中央圖書館"與亞太理事會，聯合舉辦亞太地區第一屆圖書館學研討會，邀請亞洲地區十七個國家的圖書資訊界學者專家參加，總共有150位與會，發表44篇論文。美國資訊科學學會會長Charles Davis，於開幕時發表專題演講，介紹整合性讀書館系統與套裝軟體的功能。發表的論文主要交換各國圖書館自動化、東方語文儲存與檢索技術及建立圖書資訊網路的經驗。（註40）此次會議除讓臺灣的與會者，瞭解各國圖書館自動化的發展現況，同時也聆聽到圖書資訊網與整合性自動化系統的概念，為往後圖書館自動化整合期的發展奠下發展的脈絡。

(4) 圖書館事業合作發展研討會1986（1986 Library Cooperation of Development Seminar）

為掌握資訊科技的發展與瞭解圖書館可能的應用，於1986年8月，由"國立中央圖書館"主辦圖書館事業合作發展研討會。邀請海內外圖書館界及資訊界學者專家約160人參加，並由陳欽智女士、ALA會長Beverly P. Lynch、ASIS會長Julie Carroll Virgo擔任主講人。會中分別就國家圖書館與資訊服務政策、圖書館技術服務與讀者服務的發展、資訊傳輸與資訊系統及國際資訊合作交流進行研討，發表論文二十多篇。（註41，42）1986年，正值臺灣地區圖書館自動化整合的初期，圖書館界正在評估整體性圖書館自動化系統的可行性，及考慮建構全臺灣地區的圖書資訊系統，在此會議論文中，有國外與淡江大學報告整合性自動化系統的使用經驗報告，給予與會人士及時的學習機會。此次會議中，於臺灣首次討論到資訊服務政策的問題，也引起大家開始對此議題的重視。

(5) "中美圖書館與資訊技術研討會（Sino-American Conference on Library & Information Technology）"

為促進中美兩國在圖書館與資訊技術的交流，共同交換學術研究成果與實際經驗，由"國立中央圖書館"、臺灣大學及"中國圖書館學會",共同主辦"中美圖書館與資訊技術研討會",1987年8月於"中央圖書館"舉行。美方的代表,主要是美國圖書館與資訊科學委員會(NCLIS)的委員,與美國亞洲文化中心的學者專家。此次會議共有120人出席,發表論文14篇,主要討論的議題,在整合性的圖書館自動化系統、資訊網及資訊服務政策。(註43)

(6) 圖書館自動化與資訊網研討會

1988年6月,由"中央圖書館"、"行政院"顧問室主辦的圖書館自動化與資訊網路研討會,於"國立中央圖書館"舉行。研討的主題分為:1. 圖書館與資訊系統政策,2. 圖書館與資訊系統技術與交換碼,3. 圖書館與資訊網路,4. 圖書館與資訊專家教育與訓練。來自美國的學者有:Harold Borko,David Kaser,F. Wilfrid Lancaster,James G. Williams,及陳欽智女士。(註44,45)

(7) 圖書館與資訊服務新境界國際研討會

為促進圖書館事業的發展,加強國際間的合作,"國立中央圖書館"與"中國圖書館學會",於1991年5月聯合主辦圖書館與資訊服務新境界國際研討會,來自16個國家180名學者專家參加。討論的主題分別為:資訊與技術、新科技與資訊服務。會中討論主題有:各國圖書館事業新發展、資訊與技術、資訊媒體與服務、圖書館與資訊教育及漢學圖書館與資源等。(註46)1991年正值臺灣地區圖書館自動化發展的整合期之末期,即將進入、網路時期,此次國際會議的舉行,具有承先啟後的功能。發表的論文中,除報告資訊技術應用於圖書館的現況外,對於圖書館應用資訊技術的限制也有較多的反省;新資訊技術的應用,如光碟網路、資訊網路、全文檢索及多媒體資訊系統等,則有試驗性的研究成果報告。

(8) 21世紀資訊科學與技術的展望國際學術研討會

最近一次的國際性研討會,由世新大學與"國家圖書館"聯合主辦,名稱為21世紀資訊科學與技術的展望國際學術研討會,於1996年11月舉行。此次研討會探討資訊科學與技術的多元面向,包括:資訊研究的典範與方向、資訊使用者研究的方法論、網際網路的應用、資訊檢索技術、電子圖書館及資訊倫理與政策等。參與的海外學者有F. W. Lancaster、Debora Shaw、Betty J. Turock及中國大陸學者王崇德與孟連生。(註47) 此次研討會的主題,除討論的資訊學研究的方向、資訊倫理、資訊政策,以拓展圖書館自動化關懷的層面外,對於資訊技術的發展與應用,如:電子圖書館、資訊網路及電子出版等方面,也有多篇論文的報告。

表七 歷屆圖書館自動化相關的國際性研討會發表論文統計表

階段	日期	會議名稱	參加人數	電腦與程式設計	資訊儲存與檢索	系統分析設計與評估	圖書館自動化	通訊與網路	資訊管理與政策	中文資訊處理	圖書資訊標準
萌芽	1974	第一次亞洲圖書館合作會議	126				2				
基礎	1980	圖書館事業合作與發展研討會	80		1		9		1	1	1
	1981	中文圖書資料自動化國際研討會	220	4			5	2	1	3	5
	1983	亞太地區第一屆圖書館學研討會	150		1		8	6		8	3
	1985	亞太地區資訊與縮影管理會議	207	4	1	5	2		1	5	
	1985	圖書館學及資訊科學教育國際研討會	100		1		1		1		
	1986	圖書館事業合作發展研討會	160	1	1		6	5	4	3	1
	1987	"中美圖書與資訊技術研討會"	120	3	1	1	3	3	3		
整合	1988	圖書館自動化與資訊網研討會	170		5	1		6	3	1	1
	1988	漢學研究資源國際研討會	120		1		1				
	1990	亞太地區國會圖書館臺北國際會議	150	1	3		3	7	2	2	1
	1991	圖書館與資訊服務新境界國際研討會	180	4	1		1	4	1		
	1993	邁向21世紀的國家圖書館國際學術研討會	134	2			2				
網路	1996	21世紀資訊科學與技術的展望國際學術研討會	200	3	6	2	2	5			2

2. 國際性學術研討會的特點

就國際會議討論的議題、圖書館發展的階段、與會的代表背景分析，可發現臺灣地區舉行圖書館自動化相關的國際性研討會，具有下列的特點：

(1) 影響層級高

十四場國際性學術研討會參加的人數，如表七中所列，高達二千人次以上。由於臺灣地區參加的代表，多為圖書館自動化的學者、實務界的專家及圖書館館長與高階層的館員，會議內容所影響的層級頗高。會議中所報告的實務經驗與未來趨勢的預測，皆能引起臺灣地區學術界與實務界的注意。

(2) 引介圖書館自動化新知

來自海外尤其是自歐美先進國家的學者專家，在國際會議中報告該國的圖書館自動化經驗，使得人們得以瞭解自動化的趨勢。在圖書館自動化發展的基礎期間所舉行的國際會議中，已有多篇論文報告整合性圖書館自動化系統的功能及圖書資訊網的架構，這些議題的報告的時間，至少比臺灣的發展早五年以上。在整合時期，由於邀請美國ALA、NCLIS委員來臺，演講資訊政策的議題，亦引起臺灣地區探討資訊服務政策。

(3) 展示資訊科技的新產品

在國際會議的會場中時常展示來自海內外的資訊技術產品。早期展示的中文電腦，即獲取海外專家的肯定；後來展示的光碟資料庫系統、整合性自動化系統，及最近經常展示的數位化圖書館系統，都可讓與會人士趁機瞭解新資訊產品的內容與功能。

四、結論與建議

由以上的分析結果可知，臺灣圖書館圖書館自動化人才教育與訓練的內容，配合著圖書館自動化的發展而調整。圖書館學系以培育圖書館自動化的基礎人才為主，學生於學習自動化的基本理論與技能之外，亦可隨個人的能力與興趣，選修相關的科目。"中國圖書館學會"主辦的圖書館自動化專題研習會，以培訓在職的中階層館員為主，傳授自動化基本的知識與技術，並進行實務經驗的交流。國際性的研討會提供圖書館學系的教師、圖書館與資訊界的專家及圖書館的高階主管，再學習、再教育的機會。來自海外的經驗與論點，也影響了臺灣地區圖書館自動化發展的腳步與方向。這些正式的或潛在的教育與訓練課程，使臺灣地區的圖書館館員，不但能從容地接受自動化作業方式外，且也具自動化系統分析、評估的能力，進而能參與自動化系統的開發設計。

圖書館學是一成長的有機體，隨著資訊科技的發展，資訊傳播媒體的多元化，及資訊使用者獲取資訊行為的改變，圖書館學教育的方式與內容的變革是必然的趨勢。在教導自動化新知識與技能外，尚需培養迎接改變、接受改變及願意改變的心態。此外，更需培育自我學習的能力、掌握新知的來源及建立諮詢的管道。唯有顧及教育內容與方法及學習態度，在當前圖書館求變的呼聲下，圖書館員才能掌握先機，不致在資訊科技的潮流中迷失。

註　釋

註1：胡歐蘭，"四十年來的圖書館自動化作業"，"中國圖書館學會"四十年：1953年—1993年，(臺北："中國圖書館學會")，頁49。

註2：同註1。
註3：李德竹、莊道明，"臺灣地區'國立大學'校院圖書館自動化之經驗與問題研究"，資訊傳播與圖書館學 第1卷第2期（1994年12月），頁25。
註4：同註3。
註5：同註1，頁50。
註6：同註3。
註7：同註1，頁64。
註8：方同生，"淡江文理學院教育資料科學系"，圖書館學與資訊科學 2卷1期（1976年4月），頁64—69。
註9：周駿富等，"臺灣圖書館教育現況"，圖書館學與資訊科學 2卷1期（1976年4月），頁45—73。
註10：王振鵠，"三十年來的臺灣圖書館教育"，"中國圖書館學會"會報 35期（1983年12月），頁9—17。
註11：宋建成，"圖書館教育"，第二次圖書館年鑑（臺北："國立中央圖書館"，1988年），頁47—66。
註12："中華圖書資訊教育學會"編，圖書資訊學系所現況暨教育文獻書目，（臺北：編者，1998年3月）。
註13：同註12。
註14：周駿富，"'中國圖書館學會'1979年暑期專題研習會圖書館自動化組工作報告"，"中國圖書館學會"會報 31期（1979年12月），頁168—171。
註15：李德竹，"'中國圖書館學會'1980年暑期專題研習會圖書館自動化組工作報告"，"中國圖書館學會"會報 32期（1980年12月），頁111—114。
註16：莊芳榮，"'中國圖書館學會'1981年暑期圖書館自動化專題研習會工作報告"，"中國圖書館學會"會報 33期（1981年12月），頁176—178。
註17：吳明德，"'中國圖書館學會'1982年暑期圖書館自動化專題研習會工作報告"，"中國圖書館學會"會報 34期（1982年12月），頁150—152。
註18：王梅文，"'中國圖書館學會'1983年圖書館自動化專題研習會報告"，"中國圖書館學會"會務通訊 34期（1983年7月15日），頁4—6。
註19："1984年圖書館自動化專題研習會課程表"，圖書館自動化專題研習會綱要，（臺北："中國圖書館學會"、臺灣大學圖書館學系，1984年8月6日至18日）。
註20："1985年圖書館自動化專題研習會課程表"，圖書館自動化專題研習會綱要，（臺北："中國圖書館學會"、臺灣大學圖書館學系，1985年8月12日至24日）。
註21："1986年圖書館自動化專題研習會課程表"，圖書館自動化專題研習會綱要，（臺北："中國圖書館學會"、臺灣大學圖書館學系，1986年7月21日至8月2日，8月4日至8月16日）。
註22："1987年圖書館自動化專題研習會課程表"，圖書館自動化專題研習會綱要，（臺北："中國圖書館學會"、臺灣大學圖書館學系，1987年7月20日至8月1日，8月3日至8月15日）。
註23："1988年圖書館自動化專題研習會課程表"，圖書館自動化專題研習會綱要，（臺

北："中國圖書館學會"、臺灣大學圖書館學系，1988 年 7 月 18 日至 7 月 30 日，8 月 1 日至 8 月 13 日）。

註 24："1989 年圖書館自動化專題研習會課程表"，圖書館自動化專題研習會綱要，（臺北："中國圖書館學會"、臺灣大學圖書館學系，1989 年 7 月 17 日至 7 月 21 日，7 月 31 日至 8 月 12 日）。

註 25："1990 年圖書館自動化專題研習會課程表"，圖書館自動化專題研習會綱要，（臺北："中國圖書館學會"、臺灣大學圖書館學系，1990 年 7 月 16 日至 28 日）。

註 26："1991 年圖書館自動化與網路專題研習會課程表"，圖書館自動化與網路專題研習會綱要，（臺北："中國圖書館學會"、臺灣大學圖書館學系，1991 年 7 月 29 日至 8 月 10 日）。

註 27："1992 年圖書館自動化與網路專題研習會課程表"，圖書館自動化與網路專題研習會綱要，（臺北："中國圖書館學會"、臺灣大學圖書館學系，1992 年 7 月 20 日至 8 月 1 日）。

註 28："1993 年圖書館自動化與網路專題研習會課程表"，圖書館自動化與網路專題研習會綱要，（臺北："中國圖書館學會"、臺灣大學圖書館學系，1993 年 7 月 26 日至 8 月 7 日）。

註 29："1994 年圖書館自動化與網路專題研習班課程表"，圖書館自動化與網路專題研習班會，（臺北："中國圖書館學會"、臺灣大學圖書館學系，1994 年 7 月 10 日至 7 月 23 日）。

註 30："1995 圖書館自動化與網路專題研習會課程表"，圖書館自動化與網路專題研習會，（臺北："中國圖書館學會"、臺灣大學圖書館學系，1995 年 7 月 10 日至 22 日）。

註 31："1996 圖書館與電腦網路專題研習班基礎班課程表"，圖書館與電腦網路專題研習班基礎班，（臺北："中國圖書館學會"、臺灣大學圖書館學系，1996 年 7 月 8 日至 13 日）。

註 32："1996 圖書館與電腦網路專題研習班進階班課程表"，圖書館與電腦網路專題研習班進階班，（臺北："中國圖書館學會"、臺灣大學圖書館學系，1996 年 7 月 15 日至 20 日）。

註 33："1997 年電子圖書館與資訊檢索專題研習班"，電子圖書館與資訊檢索專題研習會，（臺北："中國圖書館學會"、臺灣大學圖書館學系，1997 年 7 月 15 日至 20 日）。

註 34："1997 圖書館與電腦網路應用研習班基礎班課程表"，圖書館與電腦網路專題研習會基礎班，（臺北："中國圖書館學會"、世界新聞傳播學院圖書資訊學系，1997 年 7 月 7 日至 12 日）。

註 35："1997 圖書館與電腦網路應用研習會進階班課程表"，圖書館與電腦網路專題研習會進階班，（臺北："中國圖書館學會"、世界新聞傳播學院圖書資訊學系，1997 年 7 月 14 日至 19 日）。

註 36：周駿富，"'中國圖書館學會' 1972 年暑期圖書館工作人員研習會簡報" "中國圖書館學會" 會報　24 期（1972 年 12 月），頁 76—80。

註37：胡安彝，"'中國圖書館學會'1974年圖書館工作人員研習會簡報"，<u>"中國圖書館學會"會報</u> 26期（1974年12月），頁153—156。

註38：方同生，"第一次亞洲圖書館合作會議"，<u>"中國圖書館學會"會報</u> 26期，（1974年12月），頁15—19。

註39：辜瑞蘭，"記'中文圖書資料自動化國際研討會'"，<u>"中國圖書館學會"會報</u> 33期（1981年12月），頁127—131。

註40：亞太地區第一屆圖書館學研討會專輯，<u>"中國圖書館學會"會訊</u> 33期（1983年4月15日），頁17—21。

註41：<u>圖書館事業合作發展研討會論文集</u>，（臺北："國立中央圖書館"，1986年）。

註42：汪雁秋、黃麗虹，"圖書館界學術合作與交流"，<u>第二次圖書館年鑑</u>（臺北："國立中央圖書館"，1988年），頁157。

註43："館務簡訊——圖書館資訊研討會加強中美技術連繫"，<u>"國立中央圖書館"館訊</u>，（1987年11月），頁20。

註44：圖書館自動化與資訊網研討會會議資料。

註45："國立中央圖書館"編，<u>"國立中央圖書館"六十六年大事記</u>（初稿），（臺北：編者，1983年），頁127—128。

註46：薛吉雄，"圖書館與資訊服務新境界國際研討會"，<u>"中國圖書館學會"會務通訊</u> 78期（1991年3月），頁53—57。

註47："21世紀資訊科學與技術的展望"國際學術研討會議程表，<u>"21世紀資訊科學與技術的展望"國際學術研討會論文集</u>，（臺北：世新傳播學院，1996年）。

E 時代圖書館自動化、網路化之注意事項[*]

摘 要

本文目的是探討圖書館作業自動化、網路化時之基本觀念和注意事項,分別以行政管理、溝通協調、心理建設、館員訓練、撰寫 RFP 和執行等六方面列條簡要說明。

Abstract

This paper intends to explore the basic concepts and fundamental issues of planning for integrated library information systems. It includes six major parts, such as, administration and management, communication and negotiations, psychological matters, staff and user training, preparing RFP, and system implementation.

關鍵詞:圖書館自動化;圖書館作業網路化;整合圖書館資訊系統
Keywords:Library Automation;Integrated Library Information Systems;Planning

前 言

21 世紀 e 時代,資訊科技之急速開發與應用,已成為人類生存之重要元素,自動化與網路化更是促使人類生活環境現代化和多元化之動力。對圖書館而言,圖書館自動化和網路化已不再是新潮流、新趨勢,而是圖書館業務之正規發展,是圖書館經營之基礎與核心,其目的是追求圖書館作業效率和效益之提高,服務品質及層面之改善。進一步地建立圖書館間之連線及全國圖書館資訊網路,並與世界各國系統接軌,以期擴增各種媒體資源之互惠互享,提高使用者滿意度,達到資訊地球村之理想目標。

規劃設計理想而實用的圖書館自動化系統是必要的,也是圖書館追求的目標。開發任何自動化系統,皆首先應對系統本身有深刻的認知,此包括現有人工系統及將開發的自動化系統,以樹立正確的觀念,建立正確的方向目標,並作有計劃、有系統的規劃,才能獲得預期之效果。因此,圖書館業務自動化網路化之觀念及注意事項應事先考量是必要的,以下分別對行政管理、溝通協調、心理建設、館員訓練、撰寫 RFP 和執行等方面之注意事項簡要說明。

一、行政管理方面(包含人事、政策、經費等)

1. 嚴忌將自動化計劃視為圖書館行政部門之"最高機密",而只限少數人參與

嚴忌將自動化計劃視為圖書館行政部門之"最高機密",而限少數人參與。相反的,圖書館自動化關係到全館事務,圖書館自動化計劃開始即應公開讓全體同仁知曉與參

---

[*] 李德竹(2004 年 7 月),"E 時代圖書館自動化、網路化注意事項"。《王振鵠教授八秩榮慶論文集》(臺北市:臺灣學生書局),第 189—200 頁。

與，集思廣益，並時常告知全體同仁進展的情形。讓大家有參與感、興奮感，同仁在心理上有認同感，在推展作業上將會得到同仁之支持與協助。早期有些圖書館在設計自動化系統時常會將其視為最高機密，這常與主管心態有關，因此使館員除熟知自己工作範圍的狀況外，對於其他的自動化業務情形都不甚瞭解，是不正確的做法。

2. 成立圖書館自動化工作小組

一般情形，圖書館會成立自動化工作小組，由該小組負責規劃自動化相關業務。小組的成員多由各部門主管組成，主要原因是圖書館自動化是全面性的，如採訪、編目、期刊、出納等，因此自動化工作牽涉各組主管業務內的工作項目，需要主管們的支持，不但各主管可藉機對其組內業務作全面的分析和考量，且經過主管們的相互討論，進而加強對全館的工作有全面的相互瞭解。必要時，亦可邀館內對自動化知識較強、有經驗的、有研究的館員加入小組。由於圖書館資訊系已將電腦網路與通訊、網路資源、圖書館自動化等課程列為必修科目，新進之館員接受自動化教育和機會甚多，也比較具有自動化、網路化之知識、興趣和概念，也不妨藉助於他們對自動化之新知與幹勁共同為圖書館自動化業務效力。

3. 指派自動化計劃負責人

自動化計劃負責人非常重要，計劃推展成功與否皆繫於此人。負責人應具有圖書館作業自動化及網路之知識與經驗、科學管理之技術與方法，以及處事嚴謹、頭腦清晰；其人格特質更應具有胸懷豁達開朗、易於接受他人之建議與批評，主動積極地廣徵意見，立即糾正錯誤及系統不當之處，以求協助達到自動化系統設計之完美與實用。

4. 圖書館自動化所用時間常常超出預定計劃的時間

圖書館自動化系統是一個龐大複雜而耗時的工程，過程中不易控制進度。自動化從設計開始到完成，需要很長的時間，而常會超出預定的計劃時間。

5. 踏踏實實的整體規劃

圖書館自動化之成敗，關鍵在於嚴謹的整體規劃/紮實計劃（solid planning）。美國圖書館自動化專家 Richard Boss 曾說："Planning is time consuming, but more time spend on planning, the better."，規劃時間花的越多越好，要踏踏實實地規劃。

規劃時應以整體考量為原則，以整體觀點考慮各項問題，分析可能的瓶頸，再以長期性的眼光擬定解決方案，不但避免流於頭痛醫頭，腳痛醫腳的毛病，更可避免因修正一項作業卻使另一項作業產生新的瓶頸。切記，整體規劃就是由大處著眼，小處著手的具體表現。首先找出並建立系統內各項功能及其間關係，整體考慮週密，建立整體觀念，對圖書館自動化業務擴展將更能得心應手。

6. 圖書館自動化費用常常超出預算

根據多人經驗而言，自動化預算無論計算的如何週密，費用多會超出原估計費用。在工作進度中常有些意外的費用而還需增加經費。特別是在早期自動化時，因經驗不足而錯估或少估經費。

7. 錢的問題（Cost）

自動化是很花費金錢（costly）的事。費用項目很多，應考慮軟體費、硬體費、資料轉換費、訓練費、裝置費、維護費、繼續開發費等。繼續開發是不可忽略的，圖書館自動化並非完成後就不再需要經費，隨著時代技術的進步，自動化系統會有繼續新增項目之必要。維護費是每年例行費用，佔所有經費的 8%～12%，可以說五年的維護費用就可以買一套新的自動化系統，如 Innopac 的維護費用每年 14%，很高；而維護費用並不包括購買新軟體或更新軟體，兩者皆需額外付費。

8. 切忌將圖書館業務自動化系統當作"研究計劃"

早期常有其他科系教授們對圖書館自動化有興趣，便著手研究並設計圖書館自動化系統中某一模組，他們在研究中發現，圖書館自動化系統是自動化系統中最複雜的一種系統。因為圖書館業務自動化系統是"長期"的繼續發展計劃，要不斷發展、改進和多方面考量的"長期發展"的業務，而"研究計劃"則多是"短期的"。由於研究者常是資訊工程、電機或電子計算機方面學者專家，缺乏圖書館業務自動化方向的經驗，又非專職，時間與進度很難掌握，其結果與做法更不易控制，更重要的是研究結束即不再繼續負責研究開發，後續如何解決接管卻是問題，也是很冒險的做法。

9. 訂定各種標準

訂定標準是相當重要的。選擇採用何種標準，傳統圖書館採用之標準：如編目規則、標題、MARC Formats、各種編碼（codes）、字集等；網路上的標準：如傳輸標準、轉換標準、Z39.50、command language 等；數位化標準：如影音、圖片、器物、拓片、文件檔等標準，對網路化及數位化趨勢都是非常重要的。目前圖書館使用的標準在自動化以後，可能發現需要再修改。圖書館要採用大家共同認定的標準而達成統一化，一致化，而不要標新立異。在決定採用何種標準時應考慮自己館內需要，同時亦應考慮到建立網路，與他館連線的互通共享的功能。臺灣訂立"國家標準"的機構是"經濟部標準檢驗局"（"Bureau of Standards, Metrology and Inspection, M. O. E. A", http://www.bsmi.gov.tw），其前身是"中央標準局"，其所訂之國家標準業已建立國家標準資料庫，已放上網路，名稱為國家標準查詢系統（http://www.cnsppa.com.tw），並有 CD-ROM 可供全文瀏覽。海外重要之標準如：國際標準組織（International Standards Organization，簡稱 ISO），美國國家資訊標準組織（National Information Standards Organization，簡稱 NISO），美國國家標準協會（American National Standards Institute，簡稱 ANSI）和 ISO MPEG 委員會（Motion Picture Expert Group，簡稱 MPEG）等。

10. 資料轉換與品質控制（Data Conversion and Quality Control）

在自動化過程中，資料轉換和品質控制（Data/Retrospective Conversion and Quality control）所花費的時間、金錢和精力是相當大的，要有心理準備。裝置新自動化系統時資料轉入系統內，還需一些前置手續。圖書館必須盡量在自動化前去除一些不需要的資料，首先要對館藏作盤點（清查）（inventory）工作，然後註銷（weeding），才能使轉換工作迅速有效率，少用的資料可以暫緩轉換的腳步，待有人使用時再將這筆資料轉入系統中，也就是明定資料轉換之先後順序。至於淘汰政策（Weeding Policy）則隨圖書館之大小和種類不同而定，通常 80% 館藏可利用一般的註銷原則，20% 則需要專業館員來判斷是否註銷。根據調查，臺灣圖書館甚少明定註銷政策。資料轉換時，同時應注意每筆資料轉換的資料品質，一般而言，資料轉換工作圖書館僅作一次，故品質控制特別重要。

11. 釐清與電算中心間之資源管理問題

曾有一段時期兩者管理問題很混亂，圖書館很依賴電算中心的設備、人力和技術支援圖書館自動化工作。目前多由圖書館自己處理自動化相關事宜，惟在各種資源上仍需釐清採購和管理上的問題，但彼此保持良好關係。

12. 聘請圖書館自動化顧問（Library Automation Consultant）和法律顧問（Legal adviser）

圖書館自動化進行中可聘請顧問，亦可不聘請。若聘請則要記得時時請益，邀請顧問參與所有活動，千萬不要當成裝飾品。聘請經驗豐富的顧問，他/她們是無盡的寶藏，善加利用顧問的專長，可以節省圖書館很多時間，對圖書館自動化之發展受益無窮。圖書館常有許多法律問題需要幫忙，圖書館購買資料亦常有版權、侵權、簽約等問題，故聘請法律顧問也是必要的。

13. 注意圖書館自動化最新發展

看到圖書館系統的新功能新技術出現，而館內系統沒有，視需要而請廠商增加功能。且館員也要隨時注意自動化系統發展動向，並隨時學習。

二、溝通協調方面

1. 單位主管之支持、態度及魄力是推展自動化成功之重要關鍵

無論是圖書館組長、館長或更高層機構首長，都是相當重要的關鍵人物。首先要注意及考慮的是主管決策者的決心。自動化是一個持續的工作，並不是現在安裝好就結束，而是要持續多年的工作。圖書館館長的決心常來自於更高層主管的重視和支持，也就是需要母機構主管的支持。主管若瞭解自動化的重要性，在觀念上能支持，就會撥出經費，圖書館便可有充足的支援。特別是館長，他/她們的支持、積極態度，以及做事的魄力及決心是圖書館業務自動化成功與否之重要關鍵。

2. 溝通（Communication）與同心合作

圖書館自動化的意見和消息的傳播、交換與溝通是必要的，並要時時注意到館員的反應。全體館員應共同合作努力、目標一致才是重要的成功要素。

3. 善用人際關係/廣交朋友

廣交朋友，與館內外的相關人士保持良好關係，尤其與決策者，請教他們，請他們支持、協調事情應助益良多。

4. 與電算中心建立良好關係

圖書館與電算中心應建立良好關係。不論是軟體、硬體及撰寫 RFP 時，皆需要電算中心的支援。一般圖書館館員對硬體網路設置等之認識較為欠缺，故在規劃自動化硬體及圖書館網路與未來校園或組織內網路融合的程度，甚至於自動化系統相關技術上處理問題，需要電算中心大力協助。

5. 與廠商建立良好的溝通管道及關係

自動化系統開始啟用後，問題才開始。系統維護及功能換新皆需要與廠商密切合作，合作關係良好才能把系統問題降到最低。有許多系統本身設計不錯，但圖書館卻用不好，多因為與廠商關係與互動不夠密切。有時有些使用海外自動化系統的圖書館常抱怨廠商服務不好，有可能是因為館員英文表達能力欠佳致使溝通不良之故。

6. 加強圖書館各部門間之溝通合作

圖書館內部組織間應互動互助同心推展自動化系統，如採訪、流通、編目、期刊、參考等工作皆息息相關。在撰寫圖書館自動化需求書時，必須將各部門間關係界定清

楚，廠商才能清楚各模組間關係，做好系統軟體在各部門間之連結，將不浪費多餘的時間去溝通。圖書館各組間不合作和相互關係不溝通的情況會造成很多不必要的問題。

　　7. 加強與其他圖書館間之溝通合作

　　現代圖書館強調無牆圖書館，任何圖書館皆不可能蒐藏所有的出版品（圖書、期刊、多媒體、資料庫等），必需仰賴他館的資源來支援讀者的需求，他館亦需要本館的協助，特別是館際互借（Inter-library loan）。因此館與館間之溝通合作是必要的。在不違背版權的狀況下，許多資源都可以放上網路，提供大家分享，成為資源的後盾。在資訊社會下，圖書館已不可能獨立存在，必須仰賴他館，達成館際合作，互通有無，以擴大資源的目的。例子如：師大、政大、中央三所大學圖書館聯合整理最新期刊目次，並配合全文（full text）連結，建立查詢系統，即是很好的例子。

三、心理建設方面

　　1. 圖書館業務自動化並不"難"，視為正規之業務

　　一般人對圖書館自動化想像中是一件很"難"與"可怕"的過程，這是由於對自動化不熟悉，會感到恐慌而排斥。1990年以來，在政府大力鼓勵支持下，積極推動各類型圖書館自動化，目前圖書館自動化已經成為正規之業務了。館員經過多年的圖書館自動化熟悉工作，已不再感到圖書館自動化業務是很難的事，但在系統技術方面仍需加強。

　　2. 切勿"閉門造車"

　　閉門造車心態最要不得，也行不通，應廣蒐意見，請教他人。館與館之間對於自動化業務最好能互相交流激盪，研擬出更好的方案。

　　3. 自動化的早期，館員的工作是會增加

　　圖書館作業自動化早期進行中，因為很多業務是雙軌進行方式，應對館員多加疏導、鼓勵、溝通。此階段僅是一過渡時期，大家應有共識、合作和意願，一起渡過難關，但這也是館員排斥自動化的原因之一，因為工作加重。要使館員能迅速進入狀況，館員常需再教育，學習新科技和新事物，雖工作負擔會加大，但學習卻是好事，也可增加館員新知、新技術和新觀念。

　　4. 軟體比硬體重要

　　瞭解自己的需求，知道所要的軟體是什麼。先決定軟體再考慮硬體。早期軟體只能專用於某一種硬體上，雖然現在的軟體甚多可以用在不同的硬體上（Transportable），但還是要先考慮軟體，然後再購買適切的硬體配備。在購買時經常會設定軟硬體功能各佔百分比，作為購買的預算。選擇軟體時要考慮：好用（User Friendly），適用性（Adaptability），活潑，有彈性（Flexibility），擴充性（Expandability）等特點。在選系統時要注意3S：（1）Specification（規格），一定要符合自己特別的需求、規格。（2）Support（Support Service）指買了圖書館系統之後，廠商的支援、售後服務，系統支援一定要好，否則後患無窮。（3）Site visit（現場展示），要實際操作系統，過去要到廠商系統展示處才能看到系統，而現在透過網路或直接使用該系統的圖書館參觀訪談。

　　5. 圖書館業務自動化是持續不斷改進之工作

　　圖書館作業自動化是一項長期工作，如一個活靶（moving target），隨時有新的功能、新的科技，甚至新的系統出現，不斷更新變動，自動化業務也因此需隨時改進，希

望能命中目標，但很難。要切忌頭痛醫頭，腳痛醫腳的情況，若只針對問題解決，經常會出現這個問題解決了卻又引發出另一個問題，絕對要全面考量問題之關連性。

    6. 無十全十美的自動化系統

    圖書館系統需求是相當理想化的（ideal），但事實上，甚少系統能達到圖書館百分之百的需求。因此圖書館則依照需求書上所註明需求功能"必要"、"次要"，以及"可有可無"的等級，作為選擇自動化系統時的參考。事實上並沒有一個十全十美的自動化系統。

    7. 好的不一定合適，適合的才是最好的

    Library Journal 期刊常有作系統市場評估，並為系統作排名，但第一名的系統未必適合所有的圖書館，應選擇最適合自己圖書館的系統，才是最好的系統，千萬不要跟著別館走。

    8. 保持幽默感

    圖書館的任何的工作，不論是自動化，或是普通的工作，都要保持一定的幽默感；因自動化事務比較瑣碎，圖書館需要花費很多時間與人力才能完成，在冗長的過程中，問題很多，容易心生倦怠、急躁，所以館員要保持適當的幽默感，才不致使問題更僵化而導致更大的危機。

    9. 具有"變"的觀念

    圖書館作業自動化不是一成不變的。尤其現在網路時代，任何事務都在快速的變動，因此要接受變的觀念，才能跟上時代，圖書館自動化系統亦如此。

四、館員訓練方面

    1. 多學、多聽、多讀、多看、多問

    館員訓練部份，除了由館內安排的訓練外，最重要的是需要靠館員自己多學、多聽、多看、多問。早期圖書館自動化作業是在摸索中學習的，館員幾乎都沒有經驗，也無處請教；只能靠館員自己多學、多讀、多看、多聽。多看書或是查看別館的自動化系統，或和有經驗的人交換意見、收集別館的資料，互相切磋，交換心得。目前，圖書館自動化系統已用之多年，館員已具有甚多經驗，何況網路上也可開放討論羣，討論相關問題並切磋經驗，受益甚多，這些皆有利於圖書館自動化業務之順利推展。

    2. 加強館員自動化觀念及訓練

    多給予館員機會學習和熟悉自動化作業之各種知識與技術，並不斷地讓他們知道最新自動化方面的發展趨勢，以健全館員的心理準備。"Keep Current is important, and must！"可添購自動化系統方面之書籍及期刊，鼓勵館員參加圖書館自動化研討會及演講、參觀、訪問等。館員的訓練是相當重要的，同時也可讓他們明瞭自動化給他們帶來的好處及限制。

    3. 館員對讀者服務角色改變——Navigator, Cyberian, KM manager

    自動化系統會影響圖書館服務性質，所以館員更需要接受訓練。因為圖書館自動化網路化後，館員的服務性質會是一個資訊導航者、網路館員和知識管理者的角色，要教導讀者如何利用網路、自動化系統蒐集和查尋所需資料等。

    4. 讀者教育訓練之重要性

    選系統時，可參考讀者的意見。系統到館安裝後，要對讀者作教育訓練。在海外，圖書館自動化系統在正式啟用時，常會邀請圖書館相關人員來參加系統啟用雞尾酒會，並有館員指導如何使用新系統。此後還會定期或不定期指導讀者使用系統，如參考館員隨時準備指導讀者，並在線上目錄（OPAC）終端機附近準備使用系統的小手冊。讀者教育訓練也是一種行銷方式，一個好系統若無人使用，也是一個失敗的系統。

5. 館員對專業的使命感

圖書館對館員而言，不只是一個工作，而是一個專業。館員不同於一般的工作人員，必需具備專業素養及使命感。若視其為一個專業，使命感才會油然而生，不但以身為圖書館之一員為榮，儘量對自己專業多做努力，熱誠地服務讀者。

五、撰寫自動化系統需求書（Request for Proposal，簡稱 RFP）方面

1. 廣蒐資料，全館參與，多提供意見

自動化系統需求書（RFP）是圖書館在自動化時對欲購系統提出之功能需求項目之計劃書，希望能根據需求書選購適切的圖書館自動化系統。要廣蒐資料，無論由文獻中，或蒐集他館自動化需求書，（Requirements for Automated System）、RFP（Request for Proposal）、系統手冊（System Manuals）、系統需求資訊（RFI）等等，已出版之需求書有政治大學和"中央研究院"圖書館的 RFP。系統手冊詳細說明每個步驟，正好能瞭解系統詳細功能，亦可作為撰寫需求書時之參考。切記所蒐集之資料僅供參考，不能照單全抄，因為每個圖書館皆有自己的特色與需求。自動化是全館的工作，需要全館同仁共同參與，提供意見。

2. 瞭解自己，瞭解自己的需求，瞭解自動化的目的及未來發展趨勢

圖書館先要能瞭解自己的需求，才能明定圖書館系統的需求。系統需求書是一個法定文件，步驟要詳細，廠商才有所依據，而且系統需求書也是簽約中的一份重要附件。因此要對圖書館本身有所瞭解，才能依此訂定一個符合需求的計劃書。

3. 圖書館工作流程的審視與檢討（系統分析）

圖書館工作流程可籍由自動化作業做全面審視與檢討，重復的工作流程可借此機會予以修改。圖書館的各工作片段都是有相關性的，在撰寫需求書時將圖書館各工作流程圖串連起來，比較人工流程與自動化流程之異同，才能真正檢討工作流程。除簡省人工重複例行性的工作由自動化代勞外，更可以借由自動化作業增加許多工作項目及功能。

4. 網路功能之重要性

早期談及圖書館自動化時，幾乎忽略網路功能。早期圖書館自動化系統是一個處理內部作業的系統，隨著時代的演進，網際網路產生，資訊共享成為潮流，由 OPAC 發展成 WebPac，可在網頁上查到圖書館資訊，亦可連絡他館資料等，查尋功能擴大，故在RFP 上要考量這項功能。在現代資訊時代，網路功能是圖書館自動化作業必備的要項。

5. 考量與其他資源之連接

考量不同媒體與不同型態資源間的連結問題，這些皆可以網路方式呈現。館內各種資訊透過網路傳輸，依 MARC 856、Search Engines、IOD 等方式連結。所有連結軟體與功能應在需求書中說明。MARC 856 的 subfield 欄位已有 30 多項，現在還定有 URL，作為資訊銜接的標準。根據 Library Jouranl 2003 年 Automated System Marketplace 的報導，目前在圖書館界的趨勢將由多使用者系統（multi-user system）到數位圖書館系統（digital library system），對於圖書館資訊系統的要求則強調應具備 reference linking, matasearching、federated searching tools，以及支援多功能 web-based library portals 等，此外，還要有能支援聯盟式（consortia）的系統。因此，在選擇圖書館自動化系統時必須考量自動化系統是否具備這些發展趨勢的潛力。

六、執行方面

1. 自動化作業內容與程序應週知全館

圖書館可透過布告欄、發 e-mail 電子郵件或以 newsletter 方式，將圖書館自動化作業程序、工作進行項目、進度等週知全館，讓全館皆有參與感。

2. 測試驗收的重要性

圖書館自動化需求書上列入的每一項目在自動化系統完成後必要接受測試與驗收，才能檢驗其缺失及是否依圖書館所提出之需求書而完成設計的自動化系統。並由各組驗收 RFP 所有項目，是否符合各項功能及反應速度。在資料轉換後，須檢驗資料庫是否沒有遺漏，並在尖峯時間測試，察看系統是否能負荷。在完整的測試後才能切實看出自動化系統的問題所在。關於測試出現的問題，應立即要求廠商修改。至於付費的問題亦應在簽約時明定其條件，何時館方應付，所以在系統問題未完全測試和驗收結束滿意後，館方絕對不應全部付清款項，逾期未能完成系統所需條件應在合約書上明訂罰則。

3. 對外宣傳及訓練

圖書館應對外宣傳已裝置圖書館自動化系統，若在校內，可在校訊通知上說明，並發文給各系所及單位，可舉辦啟用典禮、雞尾酒會等，邀請館內外人士參與；應讓多人知道，宣傳和廣告是不能缺少的，同時可定期或隨時訓練讀者系統使用方法與技巧，儘量讓讀者上手利用新的查尋資料途徑。

4. 加強資訊倫理之觀念

為加強讀者使用圖書館自動化系統、網際網路、各種資料庫、資訊檢索方法等之正確行為，圖書館有必要建立讀者資訊倫理之觀念，除書面說明使用系統需知外，並可參考網路十誡、網路禮節或資訊相關法令，避免資訊犯罪之發生。

總之，圖書館業務自動化和網路化時所注意事項，最重要者莫過於主管之決心與全力支持、圖書館現有人力和館員自動化網路化的知識與能力，以掌握整體規劃之重要性、圖書館自動化網路化之工作重點及工作重心、考量圖書館全面性作業狀況、問題、瓶頸所在，系統之重要順序及未來發展，建立合理化之制度、行事規範、簡化作業流程，以及建立圖書館業務自動化網路化之標準作業基礎。圖書館業務自動化、網路化系統雖工程浩大，耗時耗錢，但以目前海內外圖書館自動化系統之狀況和圖書館館員對自動化網路化之認知、態度和經驗而言，已不如想像中那麼難為。因此，館長、館員、使用者和系統廠商之共同合作、決心、共識和努力，才是圖書館作業自動化系統成功之重要動力。

參考書目

1. 李德竹，"圖書館業務自動化基本注意事項"，《"中國圖書館學會"會務通訊》。63期（1988年7月）：頁3—5。
2. 李德竹教授"圖書館自動化"課程講義（2000年）。

3. Marshall Breeding & Carol Roddy, "Automated System Marketplace 2003: The Competition Heats Ups", *Library Journal* 128 (6) (April 2003): 52-64.
4. Marshall Breeding, "Automated System Marketplace 2004: Migration Down Innovation Up", *Library Journal* 129 (6) (April 2004): 46-58.

《資訊科學先驅》序言[①]

　　資訊科學家多年來對資訊科學的學科名稱、定義、起源、屬性、定位、研究方法和研究客體，以及學科之理論基礎有甚多的研究與詮釋。顯然地，資訊科學似乎仍是呈現其多元化（Diversified）和科際化（Interdisciplinary）的獨特現象，近來甚至於有多科化（Multidisciplinary）之趨勢。雖然資訊科學研究學者的學術專長和背景不同，對資訊科學研究方向與主題在認知和立場上有其差異性，但整體而論，仍可推析資訊科學學科的特質與範疇，進而認識資訊科學實際上是以"資訊"（Information）為核心研究主題的學科，"資訊科技"（Information Technology）是驅使資訊科學應用與發展的重要技術工具。邁入二十一世紀以來，資訊科技的蓬勃發展與突飛猛進之勢，對深受資訊科技影響的資訊科學而言，未來資訊科學的發展會更導向實用性與技術性的特質。

　　資訊科學在臺灣，由始至今重要記事如下：

1971年　"中國圖書館學會"年會小組座談會首次介紹Information Science（當時無正式中譯名）。

1972年　"美國圖書館業務專題研討會"專題演講介紹"美國報導科學"（Information Science在該研討會中之中譯名）。

1973年　李德竹教授在美國華盛頓接受美國資訊科學學會（American Society for Information Science，簡稱ASIS，現稱ASIS & T）執行長之邀請至ASIS總部參觀。李教授是當時臺灣唯一的ASIS會員，雖談及在臺灣成立ASIS臺北分會之事，實因當時臺灣ASIS會員太少而暫緩。至1981年李教授在美進修時，曾多次函請臺灣圖書館界領導人士考慮在臺灣增多ASIS會員並成立ASIS臺北分會，至1983年，ASIS臺北分會方正式成立。

1973年　私立淡江大學教育資料科學系首先開設"資訊中心與服務"課程，課程重點在介紹資訊科學。

1974年　《圖書館學》（"中國圖書館學會"出版委員會編）出版，其中《消息中心與消息科學》（消息科學為作者之Information Science中譯名稱）一文詳介資訊科學是什麼。

1975年　《圖書館學與資訊科學》創刊。

1976年　《資訊科學概論》（The First Book of Information Science，Joseph Becker著，1974年）中譯書出版。

1979年　財團法人資訊工業策進會成立。

1983年　"國立臺灣大學"圖書館學系暨研究所，分別開設"資訊科學導論"和"資訊學研討"（研究所）課程，之後臺灣其他圖書館學系所跟進。

1983年　ASIS臺北分會成立。

1984年　ASIS臺北學生分會成立。

　　[①]　李德竹（2005年10月）。資訊科學先驅（Pioneers of information science）序言。資訊科學先驅（臺北市：文華圖書館管理資訊公司）。

1984 年	《資訊科學概論》（Guide to Information Science，Charles H. Davis & James E. Rush 著，1979 年）中譯書出版。
1988 年	《美國資訊科學學會臺北學生分會會訊》創刊。
1990 年	"臺灣學術網路"（Taiwan Academic Network，簡稱 TANet）建立。
1992 年	"中華圖書資訊學教育學會"（"Chinese Association of Library & Information Science Education，簡稱 CALISE"）成立。
1992 年	私立輔仁大學圖書館學系更名為圖書資訊學系（Department of Library and Information Science），之後，臺灣各校之圖書館學系陸續更名，"國立臺灣大學"於 1997 年更名。
1994 年	"行政院"成立國家資訊基礎建設（National Information Infrastructure，簡稱 NII）推動小組。
1994 年	《美國、中國大陸和臺灣圖書館學系所資訊科學課程之研究》（"行政院國家科學委員會"研究報告）。
1995 年	中文圖書資訊學文獻摘要資料庫（CLISA）問世。
1995 年	臺灣資訊學會（IICM）成立。
1999 年	《資訊科學的思考》出版。
2001 年	《資訊巨人：Vannevar Bush，1890—1974》出版。
2001 年	"國立政治大學"圖書資訊研究所開設"資訊科學理論"課程。
2002 年	"數位典藏國家型科技計劃"（"National Digital Archives Program，Taiwan"）開始，該計劃承襲"行政院國家科學委員會""國際數位圖書館合作計劃"（1998）、"數位博物館計劃"（1998—2000）和"數位典藏計劃"（2001）三個計劃，依據整體發展重新規劃而成。
2002—2007 年	"數位學習國家型科技計劃"（"National Science and Technology Program for e-Learning"）開始，該計劃為"行政院經濟建設委員會""挑戰2008：國家發展重點計劃"之一項。
2003 年	"中華資訊素養學會"（"Chinese Information Literacy Association"）成立。
2005 年	《資訊科學先趨》（Pioneers of Information Science）出版。

以上記事，因部份資料時日已久，或資料蒐集不易，定有疏忽遺漏之處。

資訊科學或任何一門學科之創始與演進，皆有一羣具前瞻性、領導風格的有識之士，以他們的睿智、專才、卓越理念所作的貢獻促使而成。由於他們持續不斷地研究、發明以及努力奉獻，致使資訊科學與技術之神速開發和成長。二十一世紀資訊科學與技術之應用所及已深入人們生活的每一部份，資訊科學與技術之力量對造福人類、推動全球之發展與進步，影響甚鉅。

《資訊科學先驅》之出版旨在介紹推動資訊科學與技術的先導人物，企希望讓後人瞭解他/她們對資訊科學界所作之貢獻。本書"籌備小組"決定選用美國資訊科學與技術學會（American Society for Information Science & Technology，簡稱 ASIS & T）在1987年該會創立五十週年慶年會上表揚的二十四位資訊科學先驅（Pioneers of Information Science）為撰寫對象。美國資訊科學與技術學會成立於1938年，當時學會名稱為美國文獻學會（American Documentation Institute，簡稱 ADI），1973年改名為美國資訊科學學會（ASIS），2000 年又改名為 ASIS & T。該會於 1964 年開始頒發"最佳貢獻獎"（Award of Merit）為該會最高榮譽獎，每年頒給對資訊科學界最有貢獻者，包括最佳新構想、開創新裝置、發展最佳技術，或資訊科學專業服務傑出者。歷年來從 1964—2004 年已獲獎者有四十位，《資訊科學先驅》書中將嘗試撰寫 1938—1987 年五十年間二十四位資訊科學先驅之貢獻事蹟。得獎者是：Hans Peter Luhn（1964），Charles P. Bourne（1965），Mortimer Taube（1966），Robert A. Fairthorne（1967），Carlos A. Cuadra（1968），Cyril W. Cleverdon（1970），Jerold Orne（1971），Phyllis A. Richmond（1972），Jesse H. Shera（1973），Manfred Kochen（1974），Eugene Garfield（1975），Laurence B. Heilprin（1976），Allen Kent（1977），Calvin N. Mooers（1978），Frederick Kilgour（1979），Claire K. SchultZ（1980），Herbert S. White（1981），Andrew A. Aines（1982），Dale B. Baker（1983），Joseph Becker（1984），Martha E. Williams（1984），Robert Lee Chartrand（1985），Bernard M. Fry（1986），Donald W. King（1987）等。

因預定今（2005）年十月舉辦"資訊科學先趨研討會"，故《資訊科學先驅》出版迫切，本書"籌備小組"（小組成員：陳昭珍、傅雅秀、蔡明月、王梅玲、曾淑賢、林呈潢、莊道明、謝寶煖、陳文生和歐陽崇榮）僅邀請"國立臺灣大學"圖書資訊學系博友會成員（含畢業已獲得博士學位者和博士生）撰稿，可喜的是反應非常熱烈，會友們積極認領想撰寫的對象。同時，蔡明月教授和藍文欽教授亦表示願意撰稿，非常感激。本書撰稿者共二十六位，他/她們是：張郁蔚、邱子恆、洪淑芬、傅雅秀、林呈潢、賴麗香、莊道明、陳淑君、呂春嬌、鄭惠珍、楊曉雯、張嘉彬、吳紹羣、張慧銖、林巧敏、藍文欽、葉乃静、王梅玲、陳昭珍、羅思嘉、張瀚文、王美鴻、蔡明月、林素甘、趙文心和林雯瑤。（依本書目次順序排列）撰稿者的資料蒐集詳盡、齊全，撰寫內容生動活潑，惟恐有遺漏之處，非常用心。因此本書之頁數超出五百頁，一本巨作！

《資訊科學先驅》得以順利出版，首先歸功於"籌備小組"的構思與規劃，和《資訊科學先驅》撰稿人的努力，最辛苦的是蔡明月和王梅玲兩位教授，整個暑假期間皆在忙碌審稿、校稿工作，非常辛勞。很幸運地，美國資訊科學與技術學會會長 Michael Leach 和執行長 Richard Hill 提供先驅者的照片，以及陳昭珍教授和陳教授的研究助理古敏君同學和賴穎臻小姐之辛苦居間連繫和催稿工作。總之，《資訊科學先驅》之出版，得到大家熱誠地支持與合作，該書不但提供學人對資訊科學與技術發展之先導人士和起源有進一步的認識與瞭解，同時也能為資訊科學重要理論的傳播奠基，當然更盼望《資訊科學先驅》續集之出版。

李德竹

2005 年 10 月於臺北

傳記及訪談

International Biographical Centre Cambridge CB2 3 QP England Telephone +44 (0) 1355 646600 Facsimile: +44 (0) 1353646601

5th November 1999
Professor Lucy Te-Chu Lee
"National Taiwan University"
Taipei 10764
Taiwan
China

Ref: DIB27/28

DICTIONARY OF INTERNATIONAL BIOGRAPHY, LANDMARK, MILLENNIUM TWENTY-EIGHTH EDITION PUBLICATION: MARCH/APRIL 2000

Dear Professor Lee

Please find the clipping of your entry that appeared in Dictionary of International Biography, Twenty-Seventh Edition, attached alongside. The book sold extremely well and we are proud to tell you that your achievements are now available for reference in municipal and university libraries around the world.

I now have great pleasure in inviting you to update your entry for inclusion in the Twenty-Eighth Edition, due for publication in March/April 2000.

If you wish to amend or add to your entry, please include corrections in the relevant sections overleaf. Complete your name, current address and signature and return this form by the date shown. We will then send you a typescript for approval prior to publication.

If, however, you have no new information or alterations, simply return the form on which you need only enter your name, address and signature and write "no change".

As you are aware, there has never been a charge for listing in our titles. However, we know from previous editions that biographies want their own copies so we have prepared special pre-publication prices on all bindings.

...Over

> LEE Lucy Te-Chu, b. 11 Oct 1935, China. Library and Information Science Executive. Education: BS, Chem. 1959; MLS, 1964; Adv Ctf, 1965; PhD, 1988. Appointments: Prof, Grad Inst & Dept of Lib Sci, Natl Taiwan Univ, 1985-; Chair, Lib Stands Cttee, Lib Assn of China, 1990-; Lib Devel Cttee, Min of Educ, China, 1990-; Pres, CALISE, 1994-. Publications include: Library Automation & Information Science: A Collection of Essays, 1985; Online Public Access Catalog Display Formats in Encyclopedia of Library & Information Science, 1985; Comparative Study of Information Science Curriculum in Taiwan, Mainland China and USA, 1994; Western Science Literature: Abstracts & Indexes, 1996; Information Science and Technology: A Collection of Essays, 1997; English-Chinese Terminology of Library & Information Science, 2nd ed, 1997. Honours: China Natl Sci Cncl Rsch Awd; China Min of Educ Disting Tchng Awd; Lib Assn of China Disting Contbn Awd. Memberships: Bd Dir, Supvrs, CALISE; Chair, ASIS, Taipei Chapt; Stndng Cttee, Bd of Supvrs, Bd Dir, Lib Assn of China; Lib Devel Cttee, Min of Educ, China. Hobbies: Music; Travel; Reading; Sports. Address: 5 Alley 1, Lane 29, Pei-Hsing Road, Sector 2, Hsingtien, Taiwan, China.

  While the regular price of the Library Edition is £ 135.00 Sterlintg or US $ 245.00, you may reserve copies at the greatly reduced pre-publication price ot just £ 100.00 Sterling or US $ 195.00 including postage and packing You may also wish to order a copy of the elegant Deluxe Edition at the pre-publication price of £ 195.00 Sterling or US $ 350.00. or the most exclusive Royal Edition fully bound in leather and embossed in Gold with the recipient's name on the front cover and supplied in a matching slip case. at £ 395.00 Sterling or US $ 675.00 Further details and an order form are enclosed.

  I look forward to hearing from you and hope that we may include your updated biography in the Twenty Eighth Edition of this, our flagship publication.

  Yours sincerely

Jon Gifford
Editor in Chief
Enc

  Please correct your entry shown overleaf using the headings provided. Further corrections may be written on a separate sheet of paper. If there are no alterations, write "No Change" against the entry. Include your name, address and signature and return this form by the date shown.

EDUCATION

CAREER

PUBLICATIONS

HONOURS AND AWARDS

MEMBERSHIPS OF ASSOCIATIONS, INSTITUTES, ETC

OTHER WHO'S WHOS IN WHICH YOU ARE LISTED

NAME

FULL ADDRESS (For Publication)

I certify that the above information is correct and may be published.

SIGNATURE............................   DATE...
TO ASSIST OUR ADMINISTRATION STAFF, PLEASE RETURN THIS FORM BY:

德　竹　論*

　　李德竹女士，爲臺灣大學圖書館學系資深教授，並兼任"中華圖書資訊學教育學會"理事長、臺灣地區的圖書館學會常務理事、圖書館標準委員會主任委員。她多年來一直熱忱促進海峽兩岸圖書資訊學術交流，深受兩岸學者與同仁的尊敬。

一

　　李德竹教授，1935年10月11日出生於河南省汝南縣。1956年6月畢業於美國山慈學院化學系，同年7月至1965年6月服務於美國卡內基·米倫大學（CMU）冶金實驗室，任冶金工程師。其間，1964年獲得美國匹茲堡大學圖書館學與資訊科學碩士學位，1965年5月獲得該校圖書館學與資訊科學超碩士學位。同年7月至1967年4月服務於卡內基·米倫大學韓特圖書館，任科技館員，1967年7月至1971年5月服務於美國麻省理工學院電視系電子系統實驗室，任專案研究員。1971年9月至1975年10月服務於"國科會"科學技術中心第三組，任副研究員兼組長。1976年9月至1978年7月歸臺後執教於私立淡江大學文學院教育資料科學系，任副教授。自1978年8月起任臺灣大學圖書館學系教授。1988年12月又獲得匹茲堡大學圖書館學與資訊科學博士學位。自1988年8月至1992年7月，任臺灣大學圖書館學系系主任，圖書館學研究所所長。現仍爲臺灣大學圖書館學系教授。

　　不難看出，其知識結構既完備又合理，既廣博又專深，涉及文、理、工諸領域的化學、冶金學、物理學、圖書館學、資訊學等學科。其學業遵循着由理論——實踐——再理論提高——再實踐，不斷螺旋上昇的法則：她在攻讀碩士、超碩士、博士學位期間，是在邊工作邊學習，可算是"在職"學習的典型。她23歲本科畢業，28歲碩士畢業，53歲獲博士學位，這一不平凡的經歷，充分說明了她的學風樸實、治學嚴謹、對自我知識重塑的執著追求；更反映出在教學中她爲了"要給學生一杯水，自己至少要有一桶水，甚至一缸水"的強烈渴望。

　　若從其發表的學術成果來看，至少具有以下幾個特點：

　　一是著作等身，據筆者所讀到的和所能檢索到的李德竹教授著述僅以有關圖書資訊內容爲限約有58種之多，其中專書、研究報告約有24種，約佔全部著述的44%。論文與專書這兩者近乎各佔一半，對於一個從事繁重教學與科研任務的教授來說是多麼不易！

　　二是從論著的發表時間來看，迄今爲止呈加速前進態勢。所能見到的李德竹教授最早的一種是"美國報導科學"，發表於1972年的《美國圖書館業務》（編者李志鍾），計172頁。整個七十年代集中於1972、1976、1978年三年，約佔7%。八十年代前期，約佔9%；八十年代後期，約佔21%。九十年代前期，約佔43%。而1996年、1997年上半年僅在一年半時間內，約佔14%。這是何等的驚人毅力，更顯示出她那學術青春潛力。就高等院校而言，只有在科學研究上能佔學術制高點的人，其教學上才會內容充

---

*　本文作者倪波，單位為南京大學信息管理系。

實、先進、屬於上乘。反之，則會落後。不難想象，她的教學成就正是得益於她的這份勤奮的學術耕耘。學術推動教學，技術促進學科發展，這是她孜孜的奉獻與追求。

三是縱觀這些論著所屬課題可以歸納爲五大範圍：1. 資訊科學，2. 圖書館系統自動化，3. 科技文獻及資訊服務，4. 圖書館學，5. 圖書館標準。這也就是李德竹教授五大學術專長，其中更爲突出的應當是資訊科學和圖書館自動化兩個方面。

四是論著所用文種，著述中的約佔 20% 是使用英文寫作的，這還不包括中文論著中所用及引用英文。這既便於學術研究瞭解世界，也便於世界瞭解我們。

二

作爲圖書資訊學專家學者的李德竹教授，在圖書館學和資訊科學方面碩果累累。李德竹教授在資訊科學方面，先後發表了許多真知灼見。這裏僅從有關資訊科學的興趣的特定角度切入，觀察、分析其學術見解的真諦。

被臺灣學者所理解的"資訊科學"，有時相當於大學者稱作的"情報學"，更多的是相當於"信息學"與"信息技術"。"Information Science"，作爲一個名詞的出現顯然是滯後於社會實踐的，最初是用於如何記錄知識及傳遞知識等來加以研究的，直到 1962 年，才正式出現於相關學術研討會的科學殿堂；自 1967 年，方出現於獨立系科名稱。對於資訊科學的定義，正如（ALA World Encyclopaedia of Library and information Services）（圖書館與資訊服務世界百科全書）所載："資訊是資訊經過處理後所產生的所有物，這處理的過程可以是簡單的資料傳輸、篩選組織或資料分析，資訊系統是一個普通系統視爲資訊生產的各種面貌，如自然現象、物理性或邏輯性架構等；資訊科學是研究在資訊系統上可發生的資訊生產過程之學問。"當然，資訊科學的發展決不是一蹴而就的。隨着 1940 年第一代電腦 ENLAC（Electrical Integrater and Calculator）在賓州大學被製造出來，亦即拉開了現代資訊發展的序幕，布希（V. Bush）、溫能（N. Wiener, 1894—1964）、布萊福德（S. C. Bradford, 1878—1948）、克拉克（A. C. Clarke, 1917—），申儂（C. E. Shannon）等對於基礎理論的建立與基本工具架構的設想，爲後人留下了許多啓迪。由於電腦工具的日益成熟（如電腦已由第一代真空管發展到第三代集成電路），人們已開始運用電腦從事包括文字自動索引摘要等在內的非數學運算的處理。這一時期非傳統資訊系統的先驅者有：圖伯（M. Taube, 1910—1965）、魯恩（H. P. Luh 1896—1964）、加菲德（E. Garfield, 1925—）。改革的浪潮衝擊與震撼着圖書館界，致使美國文獻學會（American Documentation Institute, ADI）終於 1963 年改名爲美國資訊科學會（American Society for Information Science, ASIS），當資訊科學應用於圖書館時，不僅有助於圖書館業務的發展，更有利於讀者服務工作的開展，不僅爲圖書館學所吸納及拓展，更爲圖書資訊學的融合夯實了牢固的基礎。如艾芬蓉（H. D. Avram）設計 MARCl、MARCII 和 RECON，蓋雷諾（R. De Gennaro）研究圖書館網絡化，蓋格樂（F. G. Kilgour）創立 OCLC 書目中心，都是將資訊技術引進到圖書館服務中來。戴維斯（R. M. Davis）、黎克賴德（J. C. Licklider）等分別提出聯機交互共生理論，夏米特（R. K. Summit）建立 Dialog 系統。蔻卓拉（C. A. Cuadra）就網絡及電子出版物的研究，威廉斯（M. E. Williams）對數據庫及專家系統的研究，賀金斯（D. T. Hawkins）聯機書目系統研究，以及布格曼（C. L. Borgman）、坦椰波（C. Tenopir）、海德倫斯

（C. R. Hidreth）等人的研究成果，使資訊科學逐漸脫離傳統圖書館借閱服務模式，而逐步利用電腦數據庫，ORBIT、DIALOG、BRS 等公司，成爲圖書館聯機檢索的對象，以彌補本身文獻之不足。貝克（J. Becker）、伊文斯（G. T. Evans）、馬庫（S. K. Markusen）、馬丁（S. K. Martin）等學者推進現代網絡化的發展。

資訊科學的獨特形成過程，以及從事資訊科學研究者的諸多學科背景，這就鑄就了資訊科學在進入常態科學階段過程中必然會引起百家爭鳴的狀態。李德竹教授認爲，對資訊科學最有貢獻的八個學科領域，分別是電腦科學（即電子計算機科學）、圖書館學、一般科學、心理學、管理學、化學、數學及統計學。換一個視角若從資訊科學引文率來看，它與電腦科學更爲密切，而與圖書館學則次之。

三

有關課程設置，往往是一個專業建設與學科發展的最敏感問題之一。這是因爲：一是培養專業人才所必備專的業知識基本架構。二是學科建設與發展的基本格局。三是關於某學科的基本理論、基本知識與基本技能、基本方法的基本展示。四是體現學科發展前沿的基本路向。五是反映該學科在現實社會實踐中最具有應用價值的基本範疇。六是雖不可能也沒有必要是其學科分類體系的全部羅列，但卻是其精華所在。李德竹教授多年前就着手這一課題的研究，試圖將臺灣地區圖書資訊教育與資訊科學本身發展都推向一個新臺階。此外，李德竹教授還分別與莊道明、蔡明月等合作，發表《圖書館學與資訊科學課程革新之探討》、《核心課程理念：資訊科學》（載《海峽兩岸第三屆圖書資訊學學術研討會論文集：B 集》武漢大學圖書情報學院，1997.3）等。他們認爲有關資訊科學課程設置可分爲八類：

第一類：電腦與程式（Computer and Programming）內容包括：1. 電子計算機概論（含電子計算機程式寫作電子計算機應用）；2. 文書處理（含電腦文書處理、電腦排版、中英文電子輸入、中文電腦檢字、中文檢字法）；3. 程式設計（含程式語言原理、Unix 導論、物件導向語言資料結構）；4. 電腦輔助教學（含 CAI 課程原理與設計電腦輔助多媒體）；5. 個人電腦與圖書館、電腦在圖書館的應用。以電子計算機概論和文書處理兩科目爲核心。

第二類：資訊需求與尋求行爲（Information Needs and Seeking Behavior）。目的是"以認清人類基本行爲並應用至資訊溝通上。"內容包括：資訊心理學（含認知心理學、資訊尋求行爲、資訊蒐集行爲）。

第三類：資訊儲存與檢索（Information Storage and Retrieval）。內容包括：1. 資訊儲存與檢索（含資訊儲存與檢索系統、資訊檢索、資訊檢索系統專題、資料庫檢索）；2. 線上資訊檢索（即聯機檢索）；3. 索引與摘要，檢索索引典結構、自動分類與檢索、資料庫概論。

第四類：資訊系統分析、設計與評估（Information and Systems Analysis, Design and Evaluation），1. 內容包括：系統分析（含系統分析與管理）；2. 資料庫管理系統（含資料庫管理、資料庫系統概論）；3. 作業系統；4. 資料系統、光碟（光盤）資訊系統。

第五類：資訊科學與技術（Information Science and Technology）。內容包括：1. 資訊科學導論（含圖書館與資訊科學導論、圖書資訊學概論）；2. 資訊科技與圖書館、傳播科技與資訊社會；3. 資訊中心與服務、圖書館資訊系統專題。

第六類：圖書館自動化、網絡與通訊（Library Automation, Networks and Communication）。內容包括：圖書館自動化、網絡與通訊、網絡資源（含網絡資源與利用、學術網絡資源應用、電腦網絡概論、電腦網絡與通訊）。

第七類：資源政策與管理（Information Policy and Management）。內容包括：資訊管理、管理資訊系統、電腦中心管理。

第八類：其他包括：1. 圖書館統計學（含教育資料統計、統計套裝軟體運用）；2. 離散數學、演算法。

四

資訊網絡時代的到來，是科技進步及社會發展的必然結果。資訊網絡，是由計算機、通訊線路和用户的終端設備相結合而成的向讀者或用户提供信息的系統。網絡的建立，實際上是增加了各圖書館、情報部門、計算機存儲信息的容量，提高了信息資源的使用效率，有利於資源共享，從全局來看也必然節省了財力與物力。現代信息技術，包括計算機技術、微電子技術（即集成電路技術）、通訊技術等。李德竹教授是臺灣地區圖書資訊學界積極倡導者，勇於實踐者與著名奠基人之一。

發展資訊網絡已成爲世界各國的共識。美國以 Internet 爲骨干網等，其重點以建立寬帶無縫網。日本則以光纖網爲主幹網，試圖至 2010 年覆蓋全國人口。韓國，已於今年實現主要城市互連，本世紀末光纖到路邊，至 2015 年實現光纖到户。而新加坡今年已實現光纖到路邊，將於 2005 年光纖到户。資訊傳遞貴在迅速，因而資訊業的飛快發展勢不可擋。

資訊網絡對社會的影響將是全方位、多角度、深層次的，增強競爭能力、促進科學技術、經濟、文化與教育等的發展，增加就業機會、改善人們生活質量，提高社會運作效率。與此同時，李德竹教授指出，資訊網絡對圖書館事業產生難以估量的影響，甚至"任何資訊技術的改變，對於圖書館均會產生一定的影響力"。主要表現在：

（一）對圖書館環境的影響：主要表現在拓寬獲取資訊的渠道，迎接電子圖書館（electronic library）、虛擬圖書館（Virtual library）時代的到來，提高圖書館的地位，增强圖書館的功能等。

（二）對圖書館館藏的影響：主要表現在館藏發現觀念的改變，使用權比擁有權更重要，館藏特色及特藏的建設發展更加重要，館際合作的可行性增加等。

（三）對圖書館從業人員的影響：主要表現在資訊檢索中間人（Intermediary）的檢索服務將逐漸減少，服務方式的變化，職責的加重等。

（四）對讀者的影響：主要表現在網絡教育盛行，對傳統圖書館的依賴淡化，資訊素養蔚然成風等。

正因爲如此，圖書館界將應採取怎樣的對策呢？李德竹教授等認爲：首先，必須加速圖書館聯網建設，掌握網上資源的內容與發展趨勢，以便於更好地利用。其次，要發展具有特色的反映臺灣情況的中文數據庫，利用網絡加速有關學校課程與社會教育建設。再次，瞭解讀者與用户對資訊網絡的需求、改進服務方式，重視對讀者與用户的教育與培訓。

五

　　李德竹教授是臺灣圖書館學界著名的圖書資訊學專家，在圖書館自動化、機讀目錄、圖書館標準與資訊網絡諸領域內的研究都有着很深的造詣。可以這樣說，她始終站在臺灣地區圖書館現代技術理論研究與實施的前列。她是一位熱忱、和藹並具有淵博學識的學者，爲促進海峽兩岸圖書資訊業的合作與繁榮而奔走。在她的許多論著中，都誠摯地闡明有關圖書資訊業務現代技術運用的真知灼見。她認爲，圖書館如何經濟有效地收集與利用各種文獻信息資源，以及如何讓讀者與用戶能及時、準確地獲得各自所需要的信息，通常是其兩大重要使命。爲此，圖書館除了加大現代化技術設備與實施投資力度、加緊圖書館科學管理、加強圖書館工作者職業道德與行風建設等之外，必需全面推行圖書館自動化，並通過網絡連接其他信息自動化系統。特別值得一提的是：EDI（Electronic Data Interechange，即電子資料交換）技術，不僅適應金融、貿易、海關、商業、圖書出版業，同時也是圖書館自動化重要參考與選擇。

　　EDI 技術的優點可以概括爲：節約作業成本，信息交換過程中很少出現錯誤，改善資料庫之間與信息中心之間的信息流，資料不需要重複輸入，通訊溝通迅速等；EDI 系統的組成要素，主要包括四個方面：

　　（1）EDI 標準的選擇。EDI 用於電腦傳輸可由電腦自行處理的格式，無需再用人爲介入。使用者可以根據自身的特性與需求，來進行選擇較爲適當的標準，其標準一般可分爲兩類：即技術上的傳送標準和業務上的格示標準。

　　（2）EDI 軟件的整合。主要是指進行資料的收集與利用，包括翻譯軟件，以及連通軟件。

　　（3）EDI 網絡。EDI 資料傳送主要有兩種方法：一是點對點的直接傳送方式，這種方式適用於傳送對象比較固定、傳送距離比較近，彼此之間所採用的軟件又比較一致等。二是通過第三者的網絡系統的間接傳送 EDI 可以通過加值網絡的加值服務來實現 EDI 的目的。

　　（4）電腦硬件。通常個人電腦可以運行 EDI 系統的成本不是很高。

六

　　李德竹教授主要研究成果介紹於下，供研究者參考：

（一）論文及著述

1. 圖書館學教師研究趨勢及資訊需求. 李德竹. 當代圖書館事業論集. 臺北：正中，1994：627－664

2. EDI 與圖書館應用. 李德竹. 圖書館與資訊研究論文集. 臺北：漢美，1996.9：123－156

3. 臺灣地區"國立大學"院校圖書館自動化之經驗與問題. 李德竹、莊道明. 海峽兩岸第二屆圖書資訊學術研討會論文. 1994.8. 北京大學

4. 美國書目計量學博士論文評析. 李德竹.（臺北）"中國圖書館學會"會訊，1993（51）：231－241

5. 資訊網絡時代臺灣地區圖書資訊服務的新方向. 海峽兩岸首屆圖書資訊學術研討會論文集. 上海：華東師範大學，1993.12：114－131

6. 圖書館學與資訊科學課程革新之探討．李德竹、莊道明．海峽兩岸第三屆圖書資訊學術研討會論文集：B集．武漢大學圖書情報學院，1997.3：1-4

7. 臺灣地區圖書館自動化人才之教育與訓練．李德竹、王美鴻．海峽兩岸第四屆圖書資訊學學術研討會論文集：B集．廣州：中山大學，1998.3：1-21

8. 臺灣科技資訊網絡．李德竹．書府，1991（12）：4-10

9. 加值與圖書館作業．李德竹．書府，1990（11）：7-8

10. 圖書館自動化概論．李德竹．臺中市立文化中心，1989：1-13

11. 資訊與電腦．李德竹．書府，1989（10）：8-9

12. 臺灣學術研究圖書館館員對圖書館自動化認識的態度．李德竹．（臺灣大學）圖書館學刊．1987（5）：13-36

13. 圖書館作業自動化基本注意事項．李德竹．書府，1987（8）：15-17

14. "中華圖書資訊學教育學會"．李德竹．書府，1992（13）

15. 李德竹，1985，On-line Public Access Catalog Display Formats. Encyclopedia of Library and Information Science. vol. 38. 3. pp. 325-338

16. 李德竹，1983. Non-bibliographic Database of Library and Information Science. vol. 9 (1). pp. 74-93

17. 李德竹，1984. Early use Study Journal of Library and Infornation Science vol. 10 (2). pp. 163-183

18. 資料庫與線上檢索服務．李德竹．圖書館學與資訊科學，1981. vol, 5（1）pp. 79-103

19. 技術報告分析．李德竹．教育資料科學月刊．1976（11：4），（12：1）p. 18

20. 臺灣圖書館自動化系統線上目錄及其顯示格式之研究．李德竹．（臺灣大學）圖書館學刊，1991，11（7）：1-64

21. 資訊高速公路——邁向21世紀圖書館服務的契機．李德竹．建構資訊高速公路圖書館扮演的角色學術研討會，臺北，1994

22. 李德竹，1992，Planning An Integrated Library Information Network System：the Taiwan Experience International Seminar on Collection Development & Resources Sharing in Modern Libraries. May 17-20，1992. xi'an，China

23. 李德竹、胡述兆，1989，Present Status of Library & information Science Education in Taiwan Seminar on Library Automation and Information Networks 1988，June 8-9，Nationl Central Library，Taipei.

24. 李德竹 ed. 1989，Library Automation and Information Networke 1988，Proceedings the Taiwan. Commitee for Scientific and Scholarly. Cooperation with the U. S. A. cademia Sinica，National Central Library，Taipei，247P

25. 李德竹，1985，Education and Training for On-line Use of Database in Taiwan. Internation Conference on Library and Information Science Education，Nov. 29-30，National Taiwan University，Taipei.

26. 李德竹，1981. Chinese MARC：Its Present Status and Future Development，International confence on Chines Library Automation Proceedings，April 1981，"National Taiwan Technology

Institute".

(二) 專書及其他

1. 西文科學文獻摘要與索引. 李德竹. 臺北：文華, 1996. 8. 646 頁

2. 圖書館學與資訊科學大辭典. 胡述兆總編, 李德竹、盧荷生副總編. 臺北：漢美, 1995. 12；2988 頁（三冊）

3. 重要科技文獻指南：摘要與索引. 李德竹. 臺北：文華, 1994. 418 頁

4. 圖書館學暨資訊科學詞彙. 李德竹. 臺北：文華, 1993. 3. 674 頁

5. 圖書館學與資訊科學字彙. 李德竹. 臺北：漢美, 1985. 418 頁

6. 資訊科學概論. 李德竹譯. 臺北：楓城, 1978. 132 頁

7. 李德竹. 1985. Library and Information Science Collection of Essays Taipei, Sino-American 210P.

8. 美國、中國大陸和臺灣圖書館學系所資訊課程之研究. 李德竹. 臺北, 210 頁

實事求是，開朗豁達*

——專訪臺大圖書館學系暨研究所教授李德竹博士

李老師留影於蘇州拙政園

　　文學院的冬晨，彌漫著蕭瑟的美意。踏上文學院的小徑，腦海中逐漸浮現李老師講授圖書館自動化課程時那樣投入忘我的神采，還有擔任系主任時無時無刻為學生和系務忙碌的身影。輕敲著李老師研究室的門，掩不住興奮而期待的心情。老師親切的招呼，伴著紫花茶杯泛起的茶香，一步步引領我們一同分享她邁向成功的歷程與慧心獨具的生活哲學。

堅強刻苦的留學生涯

　　在高中畢業之後，李老師通過了重重資格的限制及甄試，爭取到一份極為難得的全額獎學金，漂洋過海到當時中國人，尤其是女性不多的新大陸展開了刻苦堅毅的留學生活。雖然年少時期就離家求學，但由於虔誠的信仰與堅毅不拔的個性，李老師很快地適應了美國生活與學習的環境。

　　位於匹茲堡的母校——山慈學院，是一所教會辦的女校，學校中修女和同學共聚一堂，校風相當樸實。剛進入山慈學院就讀時，李老師曾考慮主修教育方面的課程，但性向測驗的結果顯示李老師在理工方面優異的資質，就選擇化學為主修，同時也選擇了數學與物理為副主修。

---

* 本文由黃倩如、朱慧敏採訪整理，曾發表在《圖書館資訊學刊》13期（1995年5月），第72—76頁。

二位化學領域的啓蒙恩師

課餘時間因爲領有全額獎學金的關係，必須爲學校做一些服務工作，其中以協助教授作實驗最爲頻繁。除了幫忙配化學藥品外，到了三、四年級時，導師——Sister Constance 也會請李老師帶領學校裏的護校學生實習護士做化學實驗。Sister Constance 是一位學識相當豐富、擁有化學博士學位的老師，除了生活給李老師相當多的關懷與照顧，其本身對於學問的追求相當努力，到了晚年還親自動手做實驗，其治學的嚴謹態度深深地影響了學生時代的李老師。

同時李老師也擔任當時系主任 Dr. Kreke 的研究助理，Dr. Kreke 是研究生化科學領域、並從事癌症研究的知名學者。在這樣的背景熏陶下，李老師在美國化學學會匹茲堡分會開會期間發表了一篇令人贊賞的研究論文，因而榮獲學生獎。李老師雖然輕描淡寫地提起這段當時表現極佳的往事，不過相信這個獎一定對當時隻身在外求學的她起了莫大的鼓舞作用，引導她繼續向前行。

工作不忘學習

在化學領域初露頭角後的她，理所當然地贏得了二所知名大學所提供的獎學金，但因顧及經濟的因素，李老師決定先開始工作。第一份工作就是在卡內基・米倫大學（Carnegie-Mellon University）內的冶金實驗室中擔任冶金工程師（冶金也就是材料科學的前身），卡內基・米倫大學是所高科技著稱的學校，聲譽卓著，多年來爲工業界儲備相當多的科技人才。工作雖然辛苦，李老師仍不忘進修，即使因爲工作上種種限制不能進修正式的化學碩士學位，還是持續地旁聽現代數學、以及若干西方文學方面的課程。

"相當有趣的是，講授現代數學的教授居然每堂課都叫我上臺去示範演算，而忘了我只是工作之餘的旁聽生。"她認真的學習態度與傑出的數理能力可見一斑。

爲了把演算的機會留給課堂上正式修習的學生，李老師開始找尋另外的進修課程，在好朋友熱心的建議和不斷的自我要求之下，她踏入陌生的一門新興科學，成爲一位帶動新觀念、新思想的傑出人才。

無心插柳柳成蔭

"説起念圖書館學，其實是始料未及的。"李老師笑著説。她提到畢業後工作的歲月，在匹茲堡中國同學會擔任秘書，與當時的中國同學會會長李華偉教授熟識，李華偉教授認爲李老師有科技學科的背景，正是圖書館界所缺乏的人才，大力説服李老師攻讀圖書館學與資訊科學。

李老師自此開始白天工作，晚上在匹茲堡大學進修圖書館學與資訊科學。第一學期是圖書館學導論與分類編目的入門課程，好學不倦的她順利地修習完成，從此培養了濃厚的興趣而無法自拔。

匹茲堡是美國重工業的代表重鎮，有相當多科技方面的專門圖書館，所以母校匹茲堡大學延聘了許多附近專門圖書館從事實務的專家來校授課，李老師研究所指導老師是著名的資訊學家 Dr. Allen Kent 教授，深受其熏陶，因此在資訊科學與圖書館自動化領域中奠立了豐富而厚實的基礎。

在學期間，李老師對於第二手或舊書目錄如何採購產生興趣，在授課教授亦是著名分類編目專家 Dr. Andrew Osborn 的鼓勵下，與圖書館界許多實際負責珍善本採購的專家展開訪談，這豐碩的成果讓她認識了不少圖書館界的前輩，不但完成了此一論題為"The Second-Hand Catalog"的碩士論文，對於傳統圖書館學理論與實務方面的精心研究，更成為她未來成功的源泉。

從實驗室走入圖書館
(From laboratory to librarry)

"想回家了，是我唸完書的頭一個"念頭。然而當時因熱心幫一位學姊到卡內基‧米倫大學圖書館應徵圖書館館員的工作，因為她的文史背景不符合館方的需求，沒有成功，圖書館館長在應徵過程中得知我在數理及圖書館學方面都有涉獵，就說服我加入圖書館專業的行列。後來就負責科技方面圖書的採購編目處理等管理工作。"

這第一份圖書館員的工作，李老師學以致用，由於數理背景契合，終於使得多年來卡內基‧米倫大學韓特圖書館與化學系、數學系的老師的緊張關係得以緩和。而擔任李老師助手的三名資深非專業的事務員，即使已有數十年的工作經驗，每次排卡片時，一旁還放著卡片排檢規則，遇到一些小小的疑慮，總是不斷查考，這樣虛心及嚴謹的態度，著實使李老師印象深刻而佩服。"其實專業和非專業的區別，主要是對於工作執著與否與投入精神的多寡，而不能單以學歷為標準。"

INTREX 專案研究

由於赴美之後一直待在匹茲堡，也興起了換換環境的念頭。在一次旅行之中，李老師找到了麻省理工學院（MIT）電機系電子系統實驗室專案研究員的工作。這份工作是負責一個資訊系統的專案——INTREX（Information Transfer Experiment）。"INTREX 可以說是早期最著名的資訊儲存檢索系統，主要希望能在幾年之內將 MIT 轉變為電子圖書館的形態。計劃先從近六個月的科技期刊論文開始進行深入的主題分析，找出關鍵詞做成索引，根據索引可找出全文，還可以隨著讀者的需要放大部份文章中的附圖，雖然儲存的媒體是縮影型式，但後來這個系統的許多細膩的觀念與做法，都影響後來許多資訊系統的設計與發展。此專案因為成效不錯，也吸引了世界各國許多資訊學的學者來參觀研討。INTREX 這項專案，即使因為考慮的太週詳，而耗費太多的人力與金錢，但其貢獻之深遠的確是不容忽視的。"

教學之樂樂無窮

INTREX 正式上線啟用後，李老師收到家信及全家照片，深感父親即將八十大壽，親情的召喚讓她暫時打消了重回匹茲堡攻讀博士學位的念頭，回到臺灣加入資訊發展生力軍的行列。

"國科會"科學資料中心第三組組長的工作是以行政工作為主，與原先李老師想從事研究的心意有些差距，但抱著"只要想去做、肯去做，任何事情都可以成功的信念"，也圓滿完成許多階段性的任務。

對於教育有濃厚的興趣的她，因為有教書的機會，就轉為專業教學與研究的工作，沉浸其中至今已達二十多年之久。"教書的工作，的確是一項良心的事業。"

談到教學的理念，"因材施教"是李老師從早期到淡江教書，一直到臺灣大學任教秉持的一貫信念。"得天下英才而教之固然喜悅，但有時候遇到有潛力的學生，一時徬徨失措，方向未定，如果給予不斷的鼓勵與關懷，就可以讓他們適時的發展，而有所貢獻和成就，這就是當老師最大的安慰。教書的辛苦也隨之煙消雲散了。"

愛之深、責之切

"愛之深，責之切"是多年來無數受益的同學們對李老師最深刻的印象，因為她平日對於課業與生活中的嚴格要求，一開始往往讓同學們望之卻步，而萌生打退堂鼓的念頭。其實只要能夠通過她嚴格的訓練，日後在面對人生種種的挑戰時，更能有面對問題的智慧與耐力。

偶有學生不聽她善意的勸告，執意而為犯下錯誤，她總是在失望之餘，竭盡所能地為他們設想，幫助學生解決問題。也就是因為如此，小小的研究室常常擠滿了造訪的學生，從畢業十幾年已踏出社會工作的到大一新生，李老師總是不厭其煩地為他們提出最中肯的建言。

追求學問的高峯

有感於圖書館學與資訊科學的日新月異，於1988年間李老師又重回母校取得博士學位，此時正是臺灣圖書館自動化系統發展的重要關鍵時刻，從發展機讀編目格式一直到各大學院校圖書館自動化系統建構，無一不見李老師忙碌的身影，她不斷將海外圖書館自動化系統發展的趨勢與脈動引進，為圖書館界人士建立了相當務實的正確觀念。

"人的因素，是圖書館自動化發展成功與否的要件。""圖書館自動化並不是萬靈丹，而是帶動圖書館服務品質與工作效率的提昇，並不能完全解決積弊已久的各種問題。"這簡單的二則話，正是她多年細心觀察的心血結晶。

精益求精

身為臺灣大學文學院第一位女性系主任，李老師必於開學選課時一一仔細地查看每位同學的選課單，熱心地推薦新開的課程，還特別注意同學的成績單，一一垂詢。"其實同學有時是需要督促的，也許這樣的督促讓同學感覺有壓力，這卻是我必須為同學們盡的一份心力。既然要做，就要全力投入。"

因為這樣投入的精神，四年任期內，她曾邀請各學院優秀的教師為同學授課，延聘旅美知名圖書館學專家擔任客座教授，將海外圖書館學最新的發展與趨勢傳達回來。研究開立更多更新而符合未來潮流需要的課程，讓圖書館學系在文學院中扮演帶動電腦與資訊發展應用的角色，更在全系老師共同努力下，成立了臺灣第一所圖書館學博士班，為培養圖書館界更高層的管理與研究人才而努力。

"從事行政的工作也許比較能夠成就大事，不過教學與研究卻是我更想努力的方向。"在卸下繁忙的系主任職務後，李老師專心地作研究以及計劃，其研究的方向既深且廣。從最早期的為"教育部"圖書館事業委員會主持"整體規劃圖書館資訊網路系統"，後又受"國科會"委託負責"圖書資訊事業之規劃案"，研擬出臺灣目前急需研究的二十二個課題，到美國、中國大陸和臺灣圖書館學系所資訊課程之研究，一直到圖書館服務與資訊素養之研究等，內容廣被資訊科學、圖書館系統自動化，圖書館標準、以及圖書館學與資訊科學教育。

同時李老師也不忘著書,除了過去出版的許多學術專著外,最近也準備重新整理出版一重要科技文獻指南,爲更多的圖書館員與讀者指引利用科技方面專有的工具書,其他尚有兩本著作正在撰寫中。

從容中道,冷靜客觀

近年來,李老師致力於圖書館標準的訂定,唯有標準的確立,才是建立圖書館網的基礎,減少不必要人力、物力的浪費。更常常受邀爲許多進行中的計劃或專案擔任分析與協調的角色,因爲專注嚴謹的治學態度,能夠站在客觀公平的立場分析事理,往往能夠直言不諱,不偏不倚地贏得衆人的信服。"實事求是這四個字可以代表我個人做人處世的原則,從不強求任何一項職位與名銜,免除了這些心理上的負擔,自然立場超然,能夠以不同的角度觀察事物,心靈的空間才能無限地拓展。"

對於剛剛進入圖書館界學習的我們,李老師也提出她多年的經驗與心得:"多謙虛學習,不宜躁進,努力的成果到成熟的時候就會顯現出來,多關心別人,不強求任何事情與名利,除了專業方面的精進,對整個世界許許多多的學問保持好奇的心,廣泛地涉獵,整個人沉浸在無垠的學海中,對人生才有多層次、多角度的體驗。還有,就是"事在人爲",沒有做不到的事,重點是要不要去做。

欣見兩岸交流

近年來在兩岸圖書館界的交流中,李老師認爲兩岸圖書館界的溝通與共識正在逐步地建立當中。對於大陸近來許多圖書館學系改爲"信息管理學系"的情形感到些許遺憾,她認爲最重要的不是名稱的修改,而是兩岸把圖書館學的課程做一番整理,希望明年(1996)"第三次海峽兩岸圖書資訊學研討會"研討圖書館學核心課程問題,藉此能夠訂立標準,建立共識,並能將傳統的圖書館學與資訊科學整合在一起,在傳統中賦予自動化與資訊科學的新意,同時鼓勵與培養專業師資不斷地精進,避免跟不上時代的發展與進步,這也是李老師擔任"中華圖書資訊學教育學會"理事長職務正在努力的目標。

未來展望

學生時期就積極參與學會活動的李老師,自1957年美國化學學會匹茲堡分會,一直持續不斷地活躍於各個學會中,包括美國資訊科學學會臺北分會、美國圖書館學會圖書館資訊科技學會、美國圖書館學會、美國圖書館學與資訊科學教育學會、"中國圖書館學會"、"中華圖書資訊學教育學會",其中在"中國圖書館學會"還擔任過圖書館自動化規劃委員會的召集人,以及圖書館標準委員會的主任委員,對於"中國圖書館學會"的支持與成長不遺餘力,因而在1993年榮獲特殊貢獻獎。

於1994年7月李老師開始擔任"中華圖書資訊學教育學會"理事長,全力爲建立圖書館課程之標準與培育圖書館界師資而努力。"圖書館學研究所一一設立之後,就有一個隱憂,如果師資培育跟不上時代的進步,要求現有的師資教授新興的課程,往往因爲老師們的志趣實在與必須講授的課程不合,而產生反效果。因此如果在設立課程標準之後,依據需要遴選專長符合的老師,就可確保師資的專業品質,鼓勵現有師資儘量地重新充實自我，接受時代潮流的考驗，圖書館學的未來才能有長足的進步與突破。

最近，李老師又見海內外皆積極推展"國家資訊基礎建設（NII）"，曾兩次發表專題演講，說明 NII 對圖書館之衝擊及重要性是不能忽視的。另計劃由中華圖書資訊學教育學會於今年十月舉辦"資訊基礎建設研討會"，呼籲圖書館界對 NII 的重視，激勵大家自我檢討，努力準備資訊社會之來臨。

結　語

驚見時光的流逝，在享用了她盛情招待的可口午餐之後，李老師也透露她閑暇之餘的休閑生活，"參觀畫廊、美術館是早期留學美國就養成的嗜好，還經常購買博物館、交響樂團發行的套票，觀賞展覽、戲劇表演、芭蕾舞蹈、音樂演奏會，也愛中國的京劇，這或許是受到父母親的影響。"而隨時隨地注意新的藝文活動訊息，下課後繞個彎到附近的畫廊看看，或在家聆聽古典音樂，都帶給她無窮的樂趣和風雅細緻的人文素養。

是的，一步一腳印，在專業的執著上，李老師秉持戰戰兢兢、好學不倦的糟神在圖書館學與資訊科學的領域中不斷地開創新局，在生活中，她豁然開朗的生活態度、清亮不屈的氣度，使其永遠保持神采奕奕的風度與氣質。這的的確確為身為圖書館後輩的我們，樹立最佳的典範。

（黃倩如、朱慧敏採訪整理）

李德竹：臺灣資訊科學教育的領導者*

[摘要 Abstract]

　　本文介紹"國立臺灣大學"圖書館學系李德竹教授之傑出成就，文中分別就其研究者、作者、教育者及學會領導者不同角色敘述其學術成就。李教授係美國匹茲堡大學圖書館學與新資訊科學博士，專長資訊科學、圖書館系統自動化、科技文獻、圖書館資訊標準及資訊服務等。現任"教育部"圖書館事業發展委員會委員、"中華圖書資訊學教育學會"理事長與"中國圖書館學會"常務理事等職務。李教授研究成果豐碩，共發表論文及著作四十餘種，曾獲"國科會"優等研究獎及"教育部"優良教師獎等學術榮譽。

　　Abstract：From different roles as researcher/author, educator, and professional leader, this article presents the outstanding achievements of Professor Lucy Te-Chu Lee of "National Taiwan University" Department of Library Science. Professor Lee received her Ph. D. degree from University of Pittsburgh School of Library and Information Science. Her specialized research fields are information sciences, Library automation, science and technology literature, and library information standards. Professor Lee is Currently Member of Library Development Committee of the "Ministry of Education", the President of "Chinese Association of Library and Information Science Education (CALISE)" and also serves in the Standing "Committee of Library Association of China". Professor Lee is a prolific author of over forty scholarly articles and books. She has received the Excellent Research Awards from the "National Science Council", Outstanding Teacher Award from the "Ministry of Education", and other honors.

---

　　* 本文由傅雅秀、陳昭珍合作撰寫，曾發表在《資訊傳播與圖書館學》1卷3期（1985年3月），第71—77頁。

照片一（Picture 1）："國立臺灣大學"圖書館學系李德竹教授
（Professor Lucy Te-Chu Lee, Department of Library Science, "National Taiwan University"）

照片二（Picture 2）：李德竹教授與艾倫‧肯特教授（Professor Lucy Te-Chu Lee and Distinguished Professor Allen Kent of University of Pittsburgh）

照片三（Picture 3）：李德竹教授與北京大學周文駿教授（右二）、王萬宗主任（左一）及臺灣大學胡述兆教授（右一）(Director Wang Wan-Zong of Peking University, Professor Lucy Te-Chu Lee, Professor Zhou Wen-Jun of Peking University, and Professor James S. C. Hu of National Taiwan University) (from left to right).

一、前言

　　承蒙"資訊傳播與圖書館學"總編輯沈師寶環教授指定我二人介紹臺灣大學圖書館學系李德竹教授，使我們既感榮幸卻又惶恐。榮幸的是，李教授是我二人的博士論文指導教授，有機會介紹恩師，理應當仁不讓。惶恐的是，李教授研究成果豐碩，學術活動積極活躍，唯恐禿筆無法盡述老師之成就與貢獻。一來由於才拙，二來亦限於篇幅，但又不敢輕乎，故以下即簡短的試就李教授之學習經歷、學術成就、教育貢獻、學會活動、特殊榮譽等多元的角度來描述這位當代圖書館學暨資訊科學大師。

二、主要學經歷

　　李教授高中畢業後即赴美就讀，於山慈學院主修化學，並取得學士學位，深厚的數理基礎對於其後資訊科學方面之研究助益甚大。大學畢業後李教授又進入極負盛名的匹茲堡大學圖書館與資訊科學研究所深造，並於此取得圖書館學暨資訊科學碩士、超碩士及博士學位，其指導教授即是大名鼎鼎的資訊科學大師肯特教授（Dr. Allen Kent）《圖書館學與資訊科學百科全書》（*Encyclopedia of Library and Information Science*）總編輯。

　　李教授在完成超碩士學位後，曾接受麻省理工學院電機系電子系統實驗室之聘約，參與著名的 INTREX Project（Information Transfer Experiments Project），此計劃是資訊貯存與檢索系統之開拓先鋒計劃，首先選擇重要的科技期刊論文，經深度分析及處理後，輸入電腦建立資料庫及系統，李教授當時便是負責分析選擇期刊論文的專家之一。回臺後，李教授在"國科會"科學技術資料中心任組長職務，策劃編輯多種科技參考工具書。之後，亦曾應聘於淡江大學教育資料科學系授課，一九七八年轉任臺灣大學圖書館學系任教。[1]

三、研究成果

智慧與努力是李教授成功的因素，授課之餘，李教授勤於閱讀論著、參加研討會，是以能掌握最新學術發展趨勢。此外，李教授研究與治學並進，曾數度獲得"國科會"優等研究獎之殊榮。著有學術論文二十七篇，專書及研究報告計十五冊，成果甚為豐碩且驚人。

李教授之著作以資訊科學及圖書館自動化為主要研究領域，其多篇相關課題之皇皇巨著，不但是最早將資訊科學之重要概念由海外引進臺灣者，更一路帶領著臺灣圖書館自動化走上整合時代、網路時代，並且也以其一貫具前瞻性的眼光，勾勒出21世紀圖書館資訊服務的新方向。尤其李教授與淡江大學黃世雄教授於1991年6月完成的"整體規劃圖書館資訊網路系統"研究計劃案，更是奠立今日大學校院圖書自動化發展的重要基礎。該計劃是結合圖書館專家，電腦、資訊及通信界學者，共同研議完成，整份報告最後提交"教育部"電算中心執行推動。而計劃書中的六項暫行規範，亦成為大學校院圖書館自動化的基本共同需求。因為有了這個基礎的建立，使得各"國立大學"校院圖書館的自動化系統，不但順利推展，同時可連接上臺灣學術網路系統。因此，今日"國立大學"校院圖書館自動化系統能有此成就，李教授的研究貢獻，實功不可沒。

除了資訊科學及圖書館自動化方面之著作外，李教授研究之觸角也延及圖書館事業的源頭——圖書館學暨資訊科學教育問題，一心希望為臺灣圖書館教育事業奠下百年深基，她以本土需要為主，參酌西方及大陸地區之圖書館學教育現況為輔，希望找出在資訊科技日新月異的現代，臺灣圖書館學教育的改革之道。

人民之資訊素養是衡量社會是否已邁入資訊社會的重要指標，當我們的眼光還迷戀於科技的光環之際，李教授已得其機先的研究有關資訊素養相關問題，其真知灼見，實在令我輩敬佩。

四、教育貢獻

李教授一直不倦不侮地為圖書館界作育英才，至今已桃李滿天下，並曾得到"教育部"大學校院特等優良教師獎。"外表高大漂亮、意志堅定、教學認真嚴謹"是第一期書府"學人畫像"一欄中本系大學部學生對李教授的描述，此一對李教授教學態度的描述可謂相當中肯。[2]李教授之授課方式相當靈活生動，除了親自細心講解外，更會嚴格要求學生上臺報告，臺下聽報告的同學則須於同學報告完畢後提出問題及不同之見解。是以修課學生無不戰戰兢兢，不敢心存僥幸，過程雖然辛苦，但是經此磨練後，無不認為穫益良多。李教授修改學生作業及論文時，更是字斟句酌，一遍又一遍，不厭其煩。有問題到研究室請教時，老師雖在百忙中，仍以親切之態度一一為學生解惑。

在系主任兼所長任內，李教授開設系統分析、微電腦、資料庫和通訊、光碟多媒體等資訊科學方面的課程，努力爭取合適的教師，使課程多元化與層次化。一九八八年，公私立大學"文學院必修科目修訂委員會"推定臺大圖書館學系為"圖書館學系修訂小組"召集學系，李老師為召集人，邀請相關校系主任共同參與，先後召開兩次圖書館學系必修科目修訂小組會議，討論修改圖書館學系必修課程有關事宜，最後訂定臺灣圖書館學系共同遵循的標準必修課程，貢獻良多。[3]

一九八九年，臺大圖書館學研究所增設博士班，為臺灣圖書館學教育寫下新的一頁。博士班的開設不僅為臺灣圖書館界培育更多圖書館學暨資訊科學師資及高級管理人才，同時也提昇圖書館學之學術地位與研究水準。就此，胡述兆教授與李德竹教授兩位前後任所長的努力實在功不可沒。1994年，李教授又應大陸南開大學信息資源管理學系之邀赴該系講學，開創了兩岸教師學術交流之始。

五、學會活動

李教授認為學會是一個獲得新知及志同道合的朋友之管道，而圖書館事業尤其需要藉由學會的協調與同業的通力合作，才能解決共通的問題，所以她對於學會的投注可謂不遺餘力。從早期主持中國機讀編目格式的訂定開始，李教授在"中國圖書館學會"中曾擔任圖書館自動化規劃委員會主任委員、首屆標準委員會主任委員，常務理事等職務。無論那一個角色，李教授無不盡心盡力，尤其在短短三年的標準委員會主任委員任內，帶領圖書館界同仁完成了三十多種圖書館暨資訊科學相關標準，最是為人稱道。此外，李教授雖人在美國從事學術研究工作，但仍寫信給臺灣圖書館界人士發起成立美國資訊科學臺北分會，回國後李教授亦曾擔任美國資訊科學學會臺北分會會長，並於任內成功地舉辦多次叫好又叫座的研討會。同時她也是美國資訊科學學會臺北學生分會的顧問。該會之"美國資訊科學學會臺北學生分會會訊"在李老師及歷任顧問老師的精心指導下無論刊物內容、組織、或版面格式設計，一年比一年美觀、充實、專業，在臺灣已深獲圖書資訊界之重視並廣為參考利用。

一九九一年李教授結合圖書館同道申請成立"中華圖書資訊學教育學會"，並擔任最為艱苦的籌備會主任，就學會章程、徵收會員、申請"內政部"、準備成立大會、年度工作計劃及歲出入預算表等加以規劃擬定，備極辛勞。

六、特殊榮譽

李教授多次獲得海內外學術獎狀，除上述之"國科會"優等研究獎，"教育部"大學院校特等優良教師獎外，亦曾獲得多種海外學術榮譽，例如 Beta Phi Mu International Library Science Honor Society Member, Phi Tai Phi Scholastic Honor Society of American Member，以及美國化學學會的優良學生獎。

"中國圖書館學會"有鑑於李教授會主持機讀編目格式之研訂及圖書館自動化作業規劃及網路系統之研究，近年來並主持圖書資訊標準化工作，完成各項重要國家標準等貢獻，於一九九三年會員大會上頒與"中國圖書館學會"特殊貢獻獎。

七、結語

對於這樣一位經常一心多用、身兼數職卻又精力充沛，力求完美的老師，我們實在望塵莫及；其治學之用心、研究態度之嚴謹是吾輩當起而效法者；而最為我們尊崇的則為其對圖書館界的犧牲奉獻，與在資訊科學方面真知灼見的帶領。

八、李德竹教授著作目錄

(一) 論文及著述

李德竹，莊道明（1994）"臺灣地區'國立大學'院校圖書館自動化之經驗與問题",资讯传播与图书馆学,第一卷第二期(1995年),页24—33。

李德竹(1994)"图书馆学教师研究趋势及资讯需求",当代图书馆专业论集,页627—664。

李德竹,庄道明(1994)"资讯网路时代台湾地区图书资讯服务的新方向"。"中国图书馆学会"会报,第52期(1994年),页51—62。

李德竹,傅雅秀(1993)"美国书目计量学博士论文评析","中国图书馆学会"会讯,第51期(1993年),页231—241。

李德竹(1992)"中华图书资讯学教育学会"。书府,第13期。

李德竹(1991)"科技资讯网路"。书府,第12期,页4—10。

李德竹(1990)"加值与图书馆作业"。书府,第11期,页7—8。

李德竹(1989)"图书馆自动化概论"。图书馆自动化研讨会演讲专辑(台中市文化中心:台中市),页1—23。

李德竹(1989)"资讯与电脑",书府,第10期,页8—9。

李德竹(1988)"图书馆自动化资讯系统发展之研究"。中华图书馆学会会报,第43期,页107—123。

李德竹(1987)"学术研究图书馆馆员对图书馆自动化认识与态度。"图书馆学刊,第5期,页13—36。

李德竹(1987)"图书馆作业自动化基本注意事项"。书府,第8期,页15—17。

李德竹(1986)"图书馆作业自动化及资讯网路建立因素探讨"。文建会,页134。

李德竹(1985)"On-line Public Access Catalog Display Formats"Encyclopedia of Library and Information Science VoL 38,Suppl. 3,pp. 325–338.

李德竹(1984)"WEBNET Circulation System:An Early Use Study"Journal of Library and Information Science Vol. 10(2),pp. 163–183.

李德竹(1983)"Non-bibliographic Database"Journal of Library and Information Science Vol. 9(1),pp. 74–93.

李德竹(1981)"资料库与线上检索服务"。图书馆学与资讯科学,5(1)页79—103。

李德竹(1976)"技术报告的分析"。教育资料科学月刊,11(4),12(1),页18。

(二)会议论文

李德竹(1994)"资讯高速公路——迈向21世纪图书馆服务的契机"。建构资讯高速公路图书馆扮演的角色学术研讨会,1994年10月1日,"国立中央图书馆",台北市。

李德竹,庄道明(1994)"台湾地区'国立大学'院校图书馆自动化之经验与问题"。海峡两岸第二届图书资讯学研讨会,1994年8月,北京大学,北京市。

李德竹,庄道明(1993)"资讯网路时代台湾地区图书馆资讯服务的新方向"。海峡两岸首届图书资讯学术研讨会,1993年12月,上海华东师范大学,上海市。

李德竹(1993)"图书资讯事业之规划"。"行政院国家科学委员会"专题研究计划,1993年10月1日,"国科会",台北。

李德竹(1992)"Planning an Integrated Library Information Network System:the Taiwan Experience."International Seminar on Collection Development & Resources Sharing in Modem

Libraries, May 17 – 20, 1992. Xi'an, China.

李德竹, 胡述兆 (1989) "Present Status of Library & Information Science Education in the Taiwan," Seminar on Library Automation and Information Networks 1988, June 8 – 9, 1988, "National Central Library", Taipei.

李德竹 ed., (1989) "Library Automation and Information Networks, 1988". Proceedings of Taiwan Committee for Scientific and Scholarly Cooperation with the U.S., Academia Sinica, "National Central Library", Taipei, p. 247

李德竹 (1985) "Education and Training for On-line Use of Database in Taiwan", International Conference on Library and Information Science Education, Nov. 29 – 30, National Taiwan University, Taipei.

李德竹 (1981) "Chinese MARC: Its Present Status and Future Development". International Conference on Chinese Library Automation Proceedings, April 1981, National Taiwan Technology Institute, Taipei.

(三) 專書、研究報告及其他

李德竹 (1995) 重要科技文獻指南:摘要與索引。臺北:文華, 印刷中。

李德竹 (1994) 美國資訊基礎建設——NII。南開大學信息資源管理系十週年慶祝大會專題學術演講, 1994年9月16日, 南開大學天津市。

李德竹 (1994) 美國、中國大陸和臺灣圖書館學系所資訊課程之研究。臺北:"國科會", 210頁。

李德竹 (1994) 由資訊素養研究圖書館資訊服務之意義與內涵。臺北:"國科會", 110頁。

李德竹 (1993) 圖書館學暨資訊科學詞彙。臺北市:文華, 674頁。

李德竹 (1992) 圖書館教師研究趨勢及資訊需求之研究。臺北:"國科會", 160頁。

李德竹 (計劃主持人) (1992) 科學工藝博物館附設圖書館方案:營運部份規劃報告。臺北市:"國立臺灣大學"圖書館學研究所, 87頁。

李德竹 (計劃主持人) (1991) 交通資訊分類表。臺北市:"交通部"。

李德竹 (1991) 圖書館自動化系統線上目錄及其顯示格式之探討。臺北:"國科會"。

李德竹 (計劃主持人) (1991) 整體規劃圖書館資訊網路系統。臺北市:"教育部"。

李德竹 ed., (1989) Library Automation and Information Networks, 1988. Proceedings of the Taiwan Committee for Scientific and Scholarly Cooperation with the U.S., Academia Sinica, "National Central Library", Taipei, 247p.

李德竹 (1988) The Effect of Knowledge & Attitudes of Library Directors and Professional Librarians Toward Library Automation on Automated Programs in Academic and Research Libraries in Taiwan. Ph. D. Dissertation, University of Pittsburgh.

李德竹 (1985) Library Automation and Information Science: A Collection of Essays. Taipei: "Sino-American", 210p.

李德竹（1985）圖書館學與資訊科學字彙。臺北市：漢美，418 面。
李德竹（1978）重要科技文獻指南：摘要與索引。臺北市：自然科學，418 面。
李德竹（1978）資訊科學概論。新竹市：楓城，132 面。
李德竹（1972）"美國報導科學"。美國圖書館業務（編者李志鍾），臺北市：遠東，172 面。

附　註

1. 學人畫像，書府 1 期（1978 年），頁 7。
2. 同上。
3. 李德竹，"'教育部'和本系新修訂之圖書館學系必修課程"，書府 11 期（1990 年月），頁 7。
4. 李德竹，"中華圖書資訊學教育學會"，書府 13 期（1992 年 6 月），頁 4—5。

本會李德竹教授爲資訊科學專家，親自主持"中文機讀編目格式"小組*

本會會員李德竹，爲資訊科學專家，現任"國立臺灣大學"圖書館學系教授，擔任資訊科學概論及科技文獻等科目教學，頗受學生歡迎。

"中國圖書館學會"與"國立中央圖書館"爲推動圖書館自動化作業，於一九八〇年五月成立工作小組擔任研訂"中文機讀編目格式"（Chinese MARC Format），該小組成員共八人，皆爲大學教授或專業圖書館員，由李德竹教授主持，小組工作目的在發展中文電腦之中文圖書目錄，建立中文資料庫進而建立臺灣資訊網。該小組在李教授領導下，日夜工作，任勞任怨，於一九八一年元月完成設計。一九八一年二月十四日至十九日，"中國圖書館學會"，"中央研究院"中美科學學術合作委員會及美國學術團體聯合會（American council of Learned Societies）在臺北舉行"中文圖書資料自動化國際研討會"，出席者中外專家達二百二十人。李教授曾在研討會上宣讀"Chinese MARC Format for Books"論文，引起熱烈討論，頗爲轟動。中文圖書機讀編目格式設計之完成，即可利用電腦將中文圖書，以線上（On line）作業推廣全世界，對發揚中華文化實爲一極大之貢獻。李教授成功不居，認爲此乃光榮天主之事。

一九八一年八月十七日至二十三日圖書館學會國際聯合會（IFLA）在東德舉行，"教育部"資助李教授率領該工作小組成員三人前往參加，李教授在會中宣讀中文圖書機讀編目格式之論文，頗引起各國代表之興趣，會畢，李教授返國，隨即接受"國家科學會"之資助，前往美國進修一年，專門研究"資料庫"（Data Base）。現就讀匹茲堡大學（University of Pittsburgh）圖書館及資料科學研究所，李教授曾在該所獲得碩士學位，今日舊地重遊，再逢昔日同學好友，倍感愉快，生活極爲愜意云云。

---

* 本文由趙來龍撰寫，曾發表在《中國天主教文化協進會會訊》第 3 期（1982 年 1 月），第 8 頁。

談圖書館發展趨勢[*]

我們懷著惶恐的心情踏進老師的辦公室，老師正在通電話，示意我們坐下，隨著老師親切的笑容和手勢，才化開了我們心頭的緊張；在新文學院大樓內伴著陣陣濃郁的咖啡香，我們開始了訪問：

問：首先想請問老師的是圖書館未來新的進一步發展是什麼？

答：最新的發展嘛……不外圖書館趨向自動化館際合作（Interlibrary Loan），建立資訊網（Library of Information Network）等等！

問：是什麼原因促成圖書館走向自動化，館際合作和建立資訊網？

答：原因很多，主要還是資料的急速膨脹，尤其是在海外，就美國而言，一年之內光是科學家所發表的研究論文就為數甚多，更何況還有其他學科之研究出版品呢！資料增加的快速已非人力所能負擔得了！一方面是經費問題，圖書館的經費無法隨著資料同比例的增加，使圖書館感到資料不夠充實，另一方面則是貯存，整理及充分有效利用的問題，再者，也為了避免不必要的重複購置的浪費。為瞭解決這些問題，利用館際合作可以彌補資料之不足，電子計算機——新的工具，可幫助迅速處理龐大煩亂的資料，建立資訊網系統，以期更擴大發揮資料之"互通有無"的效果。

問：可否請老師談一談海內外館際合作的情形？

答：館際合作種類很多，有合作採購、合作編目、合作處理等等。美國早期最有名的如：1948 年之 Farmington plan，EDUCOM，近年來 Ohio College Library Center（O. C. L. C.），Center for Research Libraries（CRL）之成立類，皆是。另外一種 Consortia（合作團）方式也是，它不但由很多機構組成，還有經費支持！資訊網則有地區性的，全國性的或世界性的！如 WLN（Washington Library Network），Regional Madical Library Network 等皆是。

臺灣館際合作方面："中央圖書館"曾擬定"公共圖書館館際圖書互借合作辦法"，又於一九七四年成立"科技圖書館及資料單位館際合作組織"，現會員有將近四十個單位，每年開大會一次。

問：可否再請老師談談最近圖書館很熱門的問題——圖書館自動化現在發展的狀況。

答：自從電腦問世以來，確實給人類生活帶來了不少的衝擊，但也使人類邁進了另一個新的生活形態。不可諱言地，電腦確實有許多好處，它可以記憶許多人腦無法記憶的那麼多東西，它可以代替人類操作許多枯燥重複的工作，並使錯誤減至最低。海外圖書館自動化已經非常普遍。一九七八年，我在舊金山特別去坐了一次地下火車，從進口買票，找錢，到整列火車進站、出站、停車、開門、關門，一切都是由電腦控制，火車頭只有一個人坐在一組電腦前面，兩手叉在口袋裡，只盯著面前之終端機，他的工作不是操作而在監視，不用操心其他，電腦會完全控制所有的過程。電腦已發展到這種地步。就圖書館使用電腦情形來說，目前也只是達到選擇性的做些某方面的工作，譬如出

---

[*] 本文係吳寬、陳玉蘭採訪稿，曾發表在《書府》2 期（1980 年），第 6—9 頁。

納、採購期刊、分類編目等。參考服務方面已採用檢索各種書目資料庫（Data Base）。這些資料庫是由公營或民營之代理商（Vendors）或出版商（Publishers）出租供應，如 SDC, LOCKHEED, BRS 等代理商，非常方便經濟。

　　圖書館自動化可以節省許多不必要的人力浪費，而且可以免去許多枯燥、無味且重複操作的工作，將這些人力加以再訓練，分配去做其他更有意義的工作。記得我以前負責編的《西文期刊聯合目錄》，每次都要三個人花三個月的時間去校對、改正、再出版。其實這些機械化的工作都可以交給電腦去處理的。另一方面電腦的記憶儲存量相當可觀，磁帶、磁碟檔、磁鼓等記憶裝置，對於儲存圖書館龐大且急速發展的資料是非常有利的。

　　問：那不是在發展電腦後圖書館都要裁員了！

　　答：初期在建立整個系統時，仍然需要相當多的人力，在系統完成以後會減少些！

　　問：可否請老師說明一下什麼是 On-line Time Sharing System（線上分時系統）？

　　答：實際是這樣的，在中央有一個中央控制系統，貯存有大量資料，使用者在各個地方，如分館、教室，都可以共同享有中央控制系統內的資料，只要擁有一架 Terminal（終端機）或電報打字機（Teletype writer）或陰極射線管（Cathode Ray Tube），透過通信系統，如電話線，連接於中央控制系統，本身圖書館即可利用 Terminal 與中央控制系統接通，進行資料輸入或輸出的工作了。（如附圖）

　　這看似同時使用，其實是一種 Time Sharing System（分時系統），電子計算機處理有先後次序，速度快，感覺不到的！

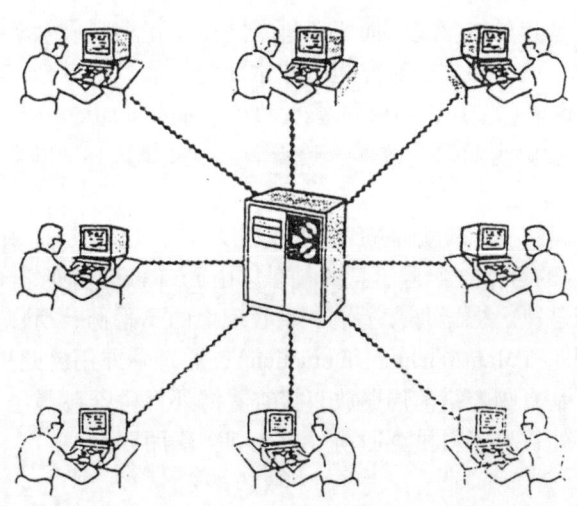

附圖　分時系統（Time Sharing System）允許許多使用者同時使用電子計算機

　　問：中山科學研究院和"國科會"科學技術資料中心不是也有電子計算機，他們自動化的情形如何？

　　答：中山科學研究院有電子計算機，他們早已用之制出卡片來，最近即將完成期刊自動化作業；目前正在計劃技術報告和圖書的自動化問題。科技中心方面，他們自己沒有機器，但使用"行政院"科計處之電子計算機。科技中心早在一九七五年已開始用電子計算機製作"西文期刊聯合目錄"，近年來開始著手各種資料庫（Data Base）之建立，以期建立臺灣資訊網。

問：也有很多人對圖書館現在自動化不以為然，認為我們普遍還未建立起各鄉鎮的基本圖書館形態，不宜過早談圖書館自動化，老師依您意見呢？

答：我覺得他們錯了，電腦已經在人們日常生活中廣泛的被應用了，諸如我們現在家裡收的電費、水費就是利用電腦處理的；我們現實生活中已或多或少和電腦發生了密切的關係；為什麼電腦它這麼快的邁向生活化，正如我前面提過的，使用電腦可以節省很多人力，省去許多不需要再去重複的工作。如果我們建立起"中央資料系統"，則在任何偏僻的鄉鎮地區，只要有一架 Terminal，插上電源，即可予求予取，甚為方便，不需要再花大量的人力，經費重複工作了。

圖書館最主要的功用就是能夠對一羣龐大的資料加以完善的控制並且有效的利用，提供需要的人最適當的資料，而電腦呢，正可以幫助我們有效地控制及迅速地處理這日益增多且繁雜的資料，在使用時亦可以立即地檢索到，以提供讀者完整、快速的資料。不過，倒是有一點需要特別強調的是，我們在趨向自動化的同時，希望也能教育大眾，普遍養成多閱讀、多參考、多利用圖書館的習慣；需要雙方面配合，才能使圖書館發展更有意義。

臺灣圖書館自動化作業，起步已很晚了，還待何時？

問：老師，最近似乎 Information Science，（資訊科學）非常熱門，報上也常提到，老師可否談談它的內容及發展。

答：一國重要的是其科技發展，而資訊科學之產生正與科技發展有密切的關係。目前資訊科學尚未定型，但已知它的研究範圍非常廣泛，而且和其他許多學科亦有密切關係，如 Computer Science（電子計算機科學）、Telecommunication（通信）、Micrographies（縮影學）、管理科學、圖書館學、數學、邏輯學、語文學、心理學等。

問：心理學？

答：對！顧名思義，資訊就是資料和訊息之意，也就是研究人與人之間如何Communicate（通訊）的科學，傳遞訊息的科學。由於資訊科學與電子計算機關係密切，故在人類面對這反應迅速之機器，會產生一些心理上的不平衡，所以我們必需要研究人與機器之交互作用問題（Man-Machine Interaction），心理學即用於此！

問：昨天報上不是有國際電信局開放直接查尋海外百科資料嗎？

答：電信局的海外百科資料供應服務，首先與美國開放。

問：實際情形如何？

答：你們來時我剛和電信局通電話，就是在問這件事情。實際情況是這樣的：臺灣用戶可利用數據終端設備，經由數據電路與海內外數據機構交換機系統連接，可立即連接到美國臺灣收容有大電腦資料庫系統的 TYMNET 及 TELENET 兩個數據資料網路，並由此接入其他供應百科資料或電腦處理服務公司，如 SDC, LOCKHEED, 提取所需之百科資料或資料處理服務之業務。

問：老師覺得它的效果會如何？

答：應該不錯的，不過我覺得我們目前最迫切的還是應先建立起我們自己的資訊網,其實很多資料我們都有,但是使用者卻不知它們的存在,也不知它們的所在,反而花錢向海外尋找、購買,這種捨近求遠的方式並不能說很好。所以圖書館界應檢討我們的服務效果!

問:老師,圖書館學和資訊科學有關連嗎?

答:它們不同,但關係密切,它們之間不是競爭而是互相支持的,資訊科學注意整個資料傳遞的過程,不看重外表形式是否為書。目前圖書館研究所方面有關資訊科學課程的有五大類:圖書館自動化作業、資訊儲存與檢索、系統分析、交互作用的電腦系統、程式設計。以後的圖書館可能是一種資訊中心的形態。

問:前一陣報上還提到要全力發展資訊工業。

答:是的,我們已成立一個資訊工業策進委員會,是一財團法人的組織。美國現在全國最大的工業是資訊工業!

你們有沒有修電子計算機資料處理,圖書館自動化和資訊方面的課?

問:修了一門電子計算機程式寫作。

答:太少了!基本瞭解電子計算機是怎麼回事?它能為我們做些什麼?在將來走向自動化時,至少還能與程式師和系統分析師交談溝通;如果一竅不通,如何協調?應再去選點這方面的課才是,將來趨勢是如此,否則如何應付得了呢?我說的對嗎?

(相視而笑)

踏出文學院,夜暮已低垂,天空中飄著雨絲還透著幾許的涼意,但是我們心中都有一種溫暖踏實的感覺。古人云:"秀才不出門,能知天下事",未來的時代,我們只要擁有一架終端機,在任何地方,電源一插,世界各地的資料也就呈現在我們的眼前,古人的理想不也就成真了!

參考書籍:

資訊科學概論　李德竹譯

書　評

Retrieve data otherwise located only after laboriously paging through the multiple volumes of the printed directories.

Puzzling surprises, however, await the more experienced searcher. For example, not one but three different function keys are available to select and group items to be searched, such as the variants of a truncated term. The resulting sets must be named in order to be viewed on the screen (for example, after typing the truncated "environment?," and selecting the variants to be searched, a set name is requested; the variants are then combined with the Boolean "OR"; what appears on screen is the set name but not the terms selected). When viewing the records of a retrieved set, the system automatically moves from one record to the next unless the user cancels this function (this is not a bad feature, but it is disconcerting at first and inadequately explained). And the list of retrieved sets is often maddeningly obscured by the various windows that open on the screen.

Gale Global Access: *Associations*'s real power becomes evident only through greater familiarity with the system, more complex searching, and use of the advanced features. The ability to free-text search, in addition to using keywords and defined subjects, is a great improvement over the more limited access of the print directories. And the advanced features, which include the ability to add notes to records, an autodialer that allows immediate contact with an association, and the analysis of sets through the creation of cross-tabulated, tables, will be a boon to association staff and fundraisers.

The suitability of *Gale Global Access*: *Associations* depends on its function as either a ready reference or a research tool, and the search expertise or patience of the user. Individuals with little computer experience will have to spend a fair amount of time reading through the documentation, accessing the help screens, or consulting with a librarian before they can use the system. For repeated use this may be worth it, but to find out about one or two organization, it most likely is not. Therefore, *Gale Global Access*: *Associations* is not recommended as a CD-ROM ready reference tool for the untrained patron. It is more valuable as a resource for trained staff or in a setting where the staff has time to train patrons who will use it repeatedly. But it is best suited for a development or association office where its quite powerful and flexible capabilities will be fully utilized and will be worth the time invested in training.

Catholic University of America　　　　　　　　　　　　　　　　　　　　　　　DEBORAH OZGA
Washington, D. C.

Introduction to Automation for Librarians. Second Ed. W. SAFFADY. American Library Association, Chicago (1989). $40.00. viii +363 pp. ISBN 0 - 8389 - 0503 - x.

This book is a substantial revision of Saffady's earlier edition, published in 1984. With similar content, format, and style, the author once again has done an excellent job in this introductory text on library automation, which is intended for librarians, information specialists, library school students, and interested audiences.

Like its predecessor, it is intended as a survey of automated library systems and technologies. This volume comprises eight chapters and is divided into two equal parts: the fundamentals of data processing and library applications. The first part of this book/discusses the basic concepts and definitions of the latest advances in computer hardware, software, data processing and related technologies. The reader is made aware of the increasing importance of microcomputers-and optical storage media used in libraries, the popular software packages, machine readable databases, the trends in distributed system concepts, the topology of computer network design, and telecommunication devices for libraries. In addition, a comprehensive survey of current computer-and non-computer-based technologies, such as micrographics, facsimile, video-based information systems, and optical filing systems for document storage and retrieval are described.

The second half of the book concentrates on the historical details, problems, and current state of the art in specific automated library functions: the circulation control systems, catalogs and cataloguing activities, automated reference services, and acquisitions and serials control systems. In comparison with the first edition, there is expanded coverage of the above functions. This section describes prewritten software and turnkey systems for automation of circulation control and the various aspects and approaches to automation of descriptive cataloguing and the production of library catalogs (including MARC-derivative products and online catalog access systems) The major bibliographic utilities and their products and services, such as the authority records, CD-ROM products, CJK (Chinese, Japanese, and Korea) workstations, and local systems are also covered in detail.

For automated reference services, this volume provides a more detailed treatment of machine readable data bases and online searching services, including European multidisciplinary search services for special clientele, CD-ROM reference products as possible alternatives to online services, and considerable development of various document delivery systems. Finally, the last chapter of this book concludes with an overview of various automation alternatives for acquisitions and serials control functions.

As a whole, this is an excellent book of technology for library automation, and it has 72 more pages than its first edition. There are additional information technologies and extensive illustrations led to clarify the text, and a considerable number of current references listed at the end of each Chapter.

One area that the author has overlooked is REACC (RLIN East Asian Character Code), a rently designed standard for CJK bibliographic usage, adopted by OCLC, RLG, LC, and others in the U. S. and Asian bibliographic communities (it has become an important standard for processing Chinese, Japanese, and Korea language materials).

Overall, Saffady has given us a well-organized text in a clear, concise, and readable style, which indeed an achievement. This book is a valuable basic textbook for library students and working professionals as well.

Sept & Graduate Institute of Library Science   LUCY TE-CHU LEE
"National Taiwan University"
Taiwan.

Handbook of Effective Disaster Recovery Planning: A Seminar/Workshop Approach. A. ARNELL, McGraw Hill, New York (1990). $89.50. xxix + 333 pp. ISBN 0-07-002394-8.

take records management programs, disaster recovery planning is gaining more acceptance as a necessary element of conducting business. Unfortunately, previous to the publication of this handbook, there was no one best text to consult for assistance in conducting such planning. However, by thousands of pages of documentation prepared for use in seminars and workshops, the author was prepared a comprehensive and well-written guide to effective disaster recovery planning. In the introduction that "the primary objective of this handbook is to provide the supporting material—the tools—to make the process work" (p. xi). It appears that objective has been met through the presentation of disaster recovery planning basics in ten parts.

DALE A. STIRLING

EDITOR: SHIRLEY HAVENS

Communication Overview

Conroy, Barbara & Barbara Schindler Jones. Improving Communication in the Library.
   Oryx. 1986. 195p. index, bibliog. LC 84 - 42815. ISBN 0 - 89774 - 172 - 2. pap. $25.

Because personnel management is generally regarded as one of the most problematic and time-consuming areas of administration, there can be little disagreement that skill in communication is one that any modern manager must acquire.

The treatment in this volume, while not purporting to be either research or original thinking on the subject of communication, is rather an overview in the context of the library setting, stemming apparently from the authors' reading and experience.

Divided into three major sections, the work addresses "Organizational Communication in Libraries," "People Working and Communicating Together," and "Communication and Change." The first two sections are a useful and succinct practical review of such issues and problems as organizational structure, conflict, the decision-making process, listening skills, and barriers to communication, among others. The third section, however, is too slight to satisfy the authors' ambitious assertion that it "prepares the librarian for their evitable changes ahead, especially those brought about by our society's shift from an industrial to an information base."

While this volume may not meet the needs of the experienced manager or those seeking an in-depth treat ment of the subject, it may raise the consciousness of the neophyte library administrator or students of library administration. Moreover, the bibliographies that are included can lead those interested to some of the extensive literature on the subject outside the field of librarianship. —*Larry Earl Bone, Mercy College Libraries, Dobbs Ferry, New York*

Electronic Publishing

Gurnsey, John. The Information Professions in the Electronic Age.
   Clive Bingley; dist. by Shoe String. (Looking Forward in Librarianship Series:). 1986. 206p. index, bibliog. ISBN 085157 - 380 - 0. $25.

There are three parts to this book: electronic publishing, the various electronic technologies, and their impact upon the profession. The first part is an extremely useful survey of the impact and growth of electronic publishing on a worldwide basis. The author provides excellent insight to the economics and the legal and social issues. Copyright problems are often cited as an example of how society continues to use 19th Century laws to deal with 20th Century problems. There is also an excellent chapter on electronic archiving, and the techniques which the profession will need to master.

The second section on the technologies is a valuable overview of online serices, videotext, CATV and satellites, video and optical storage, computer software, the electronic journal, document delivery, and electronic mail. Gurnsey has done creditable work in compressing information on the development, application, and potential of these technologies to libraries. He has provided useful comparisons between European and North American applications.

Gurnsey indicates the book is not about electronic publishing, however, but about the profession's response to technological change. He approaches that in the third section, and is less successful in this effort, at least from an American viewpoint. He reviews the current status of library, education and the incorporation of information science primarily in the context of the

United Kingdom. The same is true in his review of the role of the professional societies. His conclusions, nonetheless, mirror those made by others who have studied professional preparation in the United States. Namely, more progress is needed.

This is a useful overview of electronic publishing and new technologies. —*Donald J. Sager, Milwaukee Public Library*

Cartographic Reference Lit

Guide to U. S. Map Resources. comp. by David A. Cobb.
American Library Assn. 1986. 196p. index. LC 85 - 22958. ISBN 0 - 8389 - 0439 - 4. $25.

Several years ago a handful of the young map librarians staged a quiet revolt by seceding from the geography and map division of SLA and forming a fledgling round table within ALA. Despite SLA's attractions (chiefly its venetable *Bulletin*), the upstarts argued that map librarians belong in ALA because most map collections are in the public rather than the private sector. Their bimonthly newsletter, *baseline*, was born in 1979 and since then MAGERT has generated excellent programs and much irreverent discussion at ALA conferences. Now they have produced a volume by which we can judge them, Cobb's *Guide to U. S. Map Resources*.

Since it is blatant competition for SLA's well-known *Map Collections in the U. S. and Canada* (1954; 4th ed. 1985), a dispassionate comparison of the two seems in order. In quantity the SLA directory lists only 804 collections while Cobb lists 919 (a 14 percent increase). Each gives roughly the same information per entry, with the SLA list emphasizing subject content and Cobb physical and statistical data. Each is arranged geographically, but the layout of the SLA volume is easier to read. It also has a comprehensive index while Cobb does not (a major drawback).

The main advantage of Cobb's guide over its predecessor is the appendix, "Sources for Cartographic Information," a directory of 1000 agencies and officials who create control, or publish cartographic data. His book is also hardbound, printed on acid-free paper, and contains a statistical account of U. S. map collections (all lacking in the SLA volume). In sum, it is a fine first effort for MAGERT and a welcome addition to cartographic reference literature. —*Michael Edmonds, State Historical Society of Wisconsin, Madison*

Lee Essays

Lee, Lucy Te-Chu. Library Automation & Information Science: A Collection of Essays by Lucy Te-Chu Lee.
1985. "Sino-American Publishing Co. Ltd. "; dist. by Department of Library Science, "National Taiwan University". Taipei, 219p. $15.

Professor Lucy Lee, "National Taiwan University", presents eight essays covering many aspects of library automation: MARC formats, automated circulation systems, online public access catalogs, nonbibliographic databases, training, and online searching. Despite a number of small but irritating grammatical lapses. The papers provide good introduction with the mature reviews being particularly useful. —*Lindy Siegert School of Library Service, Dalhousie University, Halifax, Nova Scotia.*

"圖書館學暨資訊科學常用字彙" 評介[*]

圖書館學暨資訊科學常用字彙（*English-Chinese Library & Information Science Terminology*） 李德竹編著 1981年9月 新竹市 楓城出版社 291面（楓城學術叢書） 精裝NT$250元 平裝200元

如衆所知，自從圖書館自動化成爲今日圖書館學主要的課題之一後，與其有關的資訊科學也已納入圖書館學研究的範疇之內，而受到圖書館界人士相當的重視。任何一門學科，如欲作登堂入室的瞭解，必先對其所使用之"語言"有一正確基本的認識，圖書館學及資訊科學自也不例外。臺灣大學圖書館學系李德竹教授有鑑於此需要以及學人對英文專有名詞見解不同致使譯名分歧而造成教學或使用上的困擾問題，乃毅然於一九八〇年暑假展開字彙之蒐集翻譯工作，並於一九八一年九月編就《圖書館學暨資訊科學常用字彙》一書，以供圖書館學界及資訊科學界人士作相互的對照及參考之用。

此書共收錄約5480個圖書館學及資訊科學常用字彙，並於附錄中列有韋傑士羅馬拼音系統，圖書館學常用縮寫字、特殊符號表、照相排字技術、鉛字及照相字體、字體級數及轉換表與中西文參考文獻等七部份參考資料，資料之收集不可謂不廣不豐。全書體例採用字典方式，將所選英文字彙按逐字排列法（Word by Word）依次排列，每一字彙後賦予中文譯名，惟不作任何內容上的解釋，故讀者若對某名詞欲作更進一步的瞭解，則尚需自他處求得之。另外本書中有許多譯名是採直譯式，讀來不免有生硬的感覺，且因缺少彈性的解釋，而降低了活用的價值；而其部份譯名之正確性也有不少尚待商榷之處，例如：

Anamorphic map 據臺大地理學系所提供之譯名爲"示意圖"，而本書譯爲"歪像地圖"；

Centralized & cooperative acqquisition 之譯爲"合作購書計劃"，而忽略了前面Centralized "集中式"一字；

Cheapbook 之譯爲"廉價傳奇文物"，在此傳奇文物一辭顯有不妥；

Communication 之廣泛被譯爲"通訊"不若"傳訊"或"傳播"一詞來得妥當適合；

Communication Science 之譯爲"大衆傳播科學"實爲"傳播科學"之誤，大衆傳播科學應爲 Mass Communication Science，祇係傳播科學中的一種；

Film developer、Film duplicattor 及 Film slitter 中之"Film"一字均譯爲"縮影"或"縮影底片"，實與原意不合；

Video recordings 之譯爲"錄影帶"不若"錄影資料"之將影碟包括進去較爲適當。筆者因曾在美攻讀傳播科學，故所舉之例較偏重視聽資料方面，由於譯名之是否合適正確，其影響後學者甚大，若非筆者專精之處，實不敢獨力妄自加以論斷，惟心中存疑之處除上述所舉例子外尚有很多，相信其他學者專家在閱過本書後，可能也會有與筆者相同之感。最後在此應該一提的是本書因倉促間出版，故難免會有一些打字上的錯誤，如

---

[*] 本書評撰寫人爲陸毓興，曾發表在《"中國圖書館學會"會報》33期（1981年12月），第150—151頁。

"Additional record definition"之誤爲"Additimal record definition","Audiodisc"之誤爲"Andiodisc","Catalog reisonne"之誤爲"Cataly reisonne"等，在此不便加以一一列舉出，惟望本書在出第二版時能予以修正。

此書雖或有以上所述之瑕疵，然在圖書館學及資訊科學缺乏此類對英文專有名詞給予適當中文譯名之今日，仍有相當重要及廣泛的參考價值，而李女士爲統一圖書館學及資訊科學字彙上所做的努力及貢獻，此書本身即爲最好的明證。

評介"重要科技文獻指南"第一輯*

重要科技文獻指南第一輯摘要與索引　李德竹編著　一九七八年
自然科學文化公司印行　〔8〕；383 面　定價 180 元

今日科技人員正面臨兩種主要力量所形的技術趨勢（Technical Climate）的衝擊。其一為科技的進步率大得驚人，目前的最新標準方法至明日可能即已過時。換言之，從理論研究發展到實用階段及商用產品的時間正在縮短。幾年前，雷射（Laser）還是昂貴的實驗工具，僅有一些零散的研究報導；曾幾何時今天已投入生產線，因此，成千上萬關於 Laser 的描述在各種型式的文獻中都可找到。其二為社會複雜性大大地增加，使得科技人員單獨在一個領域中從事研究成為不太可能的事；科學技術間各個部門之界限更為含糊不清。科技人員必須具備多方面相關的知識領域，才足以應付目前社會複雜性之挑戰。例如物理學者在太空計劃中對其物理學有關的生物學感到興趣；同時海洋工程師必須有多種才能，包括海洋學、結構工程及電子學；而且由於科技對社會愈來愈重要，因此每項科技計劃必須以社會及經濟情況為考慮的主要依據；即使是從事現場工作的工程師或科技人員，也必須具備多方面經營才幹，才可以在團隊工作中領導統禦部屬或其同事合羣相處。這種種力量反映到科技文獻的結果，變得連最近刊行的資料亦被更新的成果迅速的取代。文獻本身導致科技改變率的增加，也因而製造更多的文獻，這就是所謂的自給系統（Self-feeding System）。（註一）

據專家估計：1750 至 1900 年的 150 年間，人類知識總量增加一倍；由 1900 至 1950 年，五十年之內，又增加了一倍；而從 1950 年至 1960 年，短短的十年時間，知識總量也增加了一倍。再根據 1968 年的統計顯示：單是美國一個國家每年出版的科學書籍就有 68 萬冊；各種研究報告將近百萬件；科學期刊論文更多達 120 萬冊（註二）。這還是幾年前的統計數字，若再加上全世界的出版品一併計算，其數量就更龐大驚人了。再依據另一位專家 Derek J. de Solla Price 指出：在最近兩個世紀中，技術期刊的數目呈指數率（Exponential Rate）地增加。1750 年大約僅有 10 種科學期刊，1850 年增加到 1,000 種，至 1950 年大約 80,000 種之多。期刊索引及摘要專刊以相似形態，每 50 年成長 10 倍（註三）。"資料爆炸"（Information Explosion）的另外一個例子是：Chemical Abstracts 是化學領域中摘要的主要資料來源，每年索引的論文數目至 1960 年代每年摘要 14 萬 5 千個款目，到 1970 年增加到大約 30 萬個，1970 年代中葉已增加到 30 萬個。1960—1970 年間論文的增加率約每年 8.4%，等於每九年增加總數的一倍。包含在 CA 的專利資料增加率為 10.9%（註四）。顯然地，文獻的膨脹速度如此之快，使得科技人員即使窮畢生之力，亦無法趕得上其速率。那麼科技研究及工作人員如何在如此浩繁的科技資料中，找尋該用合用的文獻，以掌握新知研究發展，繼續開創新機造福人羣？科技參考圖資的有效利用，殆為科技人員系統應用科技新知，以拓展學科研究創造成果的不二法門。

過去臺灣出版了許多有關參考書的指南，如何多源君的《中文參考書指南》（文史

---

* 本書評撰寫人為陳善捷，曾發表在《"中國圖書館學會"會報》30 期（1978 年 12 月），第 175—176 頁。

哲出版，1972年影印本）；李志鍾及汪引蘭兩君的《中文參考用書指南》（正中書局，1972年）；應裕康與謝雲飛兩君的《中文工具書指引》（蘭臺書店，1975年）；及沈寶環君的《西文參考書指南》（東海大學，1966年）等，各書內容雖或多或少討論到科技參考工具，惟上列各書的收錄面有一定限制，不合科技研究需要。所幸，臺灣有關科學與技術的第一本參考工具專書業已最近出版，即李德竹女士編著的《重要科技文獻指南》第一輯《摘要與索引》（自然科學文化事業公司，1978年）。（註五）

《摘要與索引》一書，詳細介紹廿二種臺灣館藏以英文發行的世界各國重要科技摘要及索引，全書分正文及附錄兩部份：正文係按（1）一般性；（2）化學、物理及核子科學；（3）農業及生物科學；（4）工程及技術；（5）醫學等五大類編排的22種摘要及索引論析。每個類目按下列項目介紹：（一）主題簡介，包括中英文名稱及簡稱；刊別、創刊年及刊行演變史；出版機構名稱、地址及簡介；訂購地址、價格及原始文件訂購辦法等。（二）出版機構的組織及宗旨，說明出版機構成立年代及其組織目的。（三）學科範圍，說明刊物包括之主題範圍。（四）收錄範圍，說明刊物收錄資料的語文、形態（期刊論文、書籍、專利、技術報告、會議記錄等）及種數等。（五）內容簡介，提示各該刊物的目次內容。（六）編排方法，說明刊物編排方式，舉例詳細介紹之。（七）檢索方法，舉例說明檢索要領。（八）優缺點，分別列出各該刊物的優劣點。（九）相關出版品，分別列出同一機構出版之重要相關出版品及其他機構出版之相關出版品。（十）館藏單位，概略說明各該刊物在臺灣之館藏單位名稱及所藏年代。末附參考書目，列出所有參考文獻。附錄則包括（一）海外重要科技及其相關之 Data Bases。（二）臺灣出版的重要科技摘要及索引之簡要介紹。（三）參考書目。（四）相關出版品書目等（註六）。此書編排體例完善，內容詳實深入，舉例盡求週到，特別是概略刊出廿二種摘要及索引的館藏單位，雖然在真正利用時還需要借重於"國科會"科學技術資料中心編印的《科學期刊聯合目錄》的協助，但已頗具實用性。惟由於收編項目繁多，舉例編排往往令人目不暇接的感覺，尤其是項目太多太雜，一般認為僅合適相當科技背景的研究及工作人員和專業圖書館員之應用。誠如姚朋（彭歌）先生在《三三草》中對該書所作評語"對於科技人員，這本文獻指南當然是極有價值；我覺得特別應指出來的是，非有科技知識，大概看不懂、也不需要去看"。（註七）

一般理工科系學生，學習程序以由淺入深為優，因為基礎研究必須有起步，這本內容深入詳盡的參考工具書恐不易引起初學研究者的興趣及利用。圖書館科系同學課程研究，旨在學習日後指導讀者如何利用此等工具書，因此更須廣泛接受各種參考資源的實習，以配合將來從事專業之需。該書列舉22摘要及索引，作為教學或參考資料雖精，但種數則嫌太少。就其收錄項目內容而言，主題簡介一項，只要涵蓋刊名及其簡稱，刊別、創刊年及出版機構即可。刊物演變及訂購程序及費用，因手續經常變動，價格由於通貨膨脹的壓力亦常調整，且為負責採錄工作的專業圖書館員所關心的事，對讀者利用顯然沒有重大的意義；出版機構組織及宗旨實可與主題簡介項內出版機構合併介紹，藉以避免重複並節省參見款目；又學科範圍既在說明刊物包括的主題範圍，即亦應合併於主題簡介內闡述。要言之，此種參考工具指南應以闡述各種收錄刊物內容及其編排檢索方法為主要目的，餘者應儘量精簡以配合一般初學研究者的興趣及圖書館科系學生之應用，庶幾合乎編撰者在序言中所表明的"對象"及"目的"～對象是（一）圖書館學及教育資料科學系學生，（二）圖書館工作現職人員，（三）從事科學技術研究者；目的是（一）便利讀者對重要科技摘要及索引文獻之認識瞭解，（二）幫助讀者自我學習摘要及索引之使用方法，進而自我檢索使用。（註八）

參考圖書及資料範圍相當廣泛，本書僅說明摘要及索引，然若以其編輯體例及規模，收錄其他各種型式的參考圖資，一併出版時，恐非數十巨冊無法容納。因為除英文部份外，為使科技生根，就必須加強中文科技參考圖資的翔實介紹，同時鼓勵編製並指導讀者利用。

總之，此書內容精闢編製體例完善，雖略有瑕疵，仍不失為目前具有高度水準的科技參考工具書指引之一，是文教及圖書館界的一大幸事。

附錄：李德竹教授主要著作目錄及學術貢獻

專書【含學術獎勵】

資訊巨人，Vannevar Bush（1890—1974），文華（臺北），2001，194 頁。
中文圖書資訊學文獻摘要資料庫書目，漢珍（臺北），2000，312 頁。
資訊科學與圖書館學專題論輯，文華（臺北），2000，511 頁。
資訊科學與技術專題論輯。文華（臺北），1997，397 頁。
圖書館學暨資訊科學詞彙。第二版，文華（臺北），1997，800 頁。第一版，1993，674 頁。
西文科學文獻摘要與索引。文華（臺北），1996，650 頁。
圖書館學與資訊科學大辭典（副總編輯）。漢美（臺北），1995，3 冊（2988 頁）。
Library Automation and Information Networks, ed. 1988, Proceedings of the Taiwan. Committee for Scientific and Scholarly Cooperation with the U. S., Academia Sinica, "National Central Library", Taipei, 1989 247p.
The Effect of Knowledge & Attitudes of Library Directors and Professional Librarians toward Library Automation on Automated Programs in Academic and Research Libraries in Taiwan, Ph. D. Dissertation. University of Pittsburgh, 1988, 248p.
Library Automation and Information Science: A Collection of Essays. Taipei. "Sino-American", 1985, 210p.［甲種］
圖書館學與資訊科學字彙。漢美圖書公司（臺北），1985，418 面。
重要科技文獻指南：第一輯 摘要與索引。自然科學文化事業公司（臺北），1978，380 面。
資訊科學概論。楓城（臺北），1978，132 面。（譯本）。

研究報告【含學術獎勵】

（一）個別研究報告
海峽兩岸圖書資訊相關國家標準之比較研究。專題研究報告，2001。
以書目計量學方法探討資訊科學之父 Vannevar Bush 對資訊時代的重要影響與貢獻。"國科會"（臺北），1999。
大學圖書館館員學習利用網際網路態度之研究。"國科會"，1998。［甲種］
由圖書館資訊服務規劃圖書館資訊素養之培育方針與評量指標。"國科會"，1997。［甲種］
大學圖書館資訊倫理認知與問題之研究。"國科會"，1996。［甲種］
評析"國立大學"校院圖書館自動化系統線上公用目錄功能與介面特性。"國科會"，1996。

電子資料交換（EDI）應用於圖書館之研究（Ⅰ）（Ⅱ）。"國科會"，1994，1995。〔甲種〕

圖書資訊事業之規劃。"國科會"，1994。

由資訊素養研究圖書館資訊服務之意義與內涵。"國科會"，1994。〔甲種〕

美國、中國大陸和臺灣圖書館學系所資訊課程之研究。"國科會"，1993。〔優等〕

圖書館學教師研究趨勢及資訊需求之研究。"國科會"，1992。〔甲種〕

圖書館自動化系統線上目錄及其顯示格式之探討。"國科會"，1991。〔甲種〕

圖書館作業自動化及資訊網路建立因素探討。"文建會"，1986。

學術圖書館館員對圖書館自動化認識與態度之研究。"國科會"，1986。〔甲種〕

（二）整體（大）型計劃主持人

中文圖書資訊學文獻摘要資料庫（Chinese Library & Information Science Abstracts，簡稱 CLISA）。漢珍，1997—。

圖書館相關國家標準草案研擬。"中國圖書館學會"，"經濟部"中央標準局委託，1997，1996，1995，1994，1993。

科學工藝博物館附設圖書館方案：營運部份規劃報告。"教育部"，1992。

整體規劃圖書館資訊網路系統。"教育部"，1991。

交通資訊分類表。"交通部"，1991。

中國機讀編目格式。第一版，第二版，"中國圖書館學會"，"國立中央圖書館"，1981，1982。

論文（期刊、會議及其他著述）【合學術獎勵】

"圖書館員資訊素養之培育方針與評量指標"。圖書與資訊學刊。

"資訊素養的意義、內涵與演變"。圖書與資訊學刊, Vol. 35（Nov. 2000）：1—25,

"從 Vannevar Bush "As We May Think" 談資訊科學與技術之演進與發展"。圖書與資訊學刊, Vol. 32（Feb. 2000）：1—16.

"海峽兩岸圖書館相關國家標準現況之研究"，海峽兩岸第五屆圖書資訊學研討會（B 輯），中國科學院（成都），頁9—36，9月1-3日，2000。

"資訊巨人 Vannevar Bush（1890 - 1974）"，臺北市立圖書館館訊, Vol. 16（4）（Dec. 1999）：55—67。

"圖書館相關國家標準"。圖書與資訊學刊, Vol. 28（Feb 1999）：1—22。

"海峽兩岸第四屆圖書資訊學學術研討會紀要"。"中華圖書資訊學教育學會"會訊, Vol 9（June 1998）：1—6。

"臺灣與美國圖書資訊學系所資訊科學課程之比較研究"。圖書與資訊學刊, Vol. 26（Aug. 1998），頁1—27。

"臺灣地區圖書館自動化人才之教育訓練"，海峽兩岸第四屆圖書資訊學學術研討會（B 輯）中山大學（廣州）頁1—20，1998。

"圖書館學與資訊科學課程革新之探討"，海峽兩岸第三屆圖書資訊學學術研討會，武漢大學（武昌市），1997。

"評析'國立大學'校院圖書館自動化系統線上公用目錄功能與介面特性"。Proceedings of the National Science Council：Part C：Humanities and Social Sciences Vol. 7 (3)（July 1997）：334－351。

"臺灣大學圖書館資訊倫理認知與問題之研究"。臺北市立圖書館館訊，Vol. 13 (5)（1996）：頁1—17。

"EDI與圖書館應用"，圖書館與資訊科學研究論集：胡述兆教授七秩榮慶論文集。漢美（臺北市），頁115—147，1996。

"NII對圖書館之衝擊"，技術學院暨專科學校圖書館事業研討會，"教育部"技職司，崑山工商專科學校（臺南），5月19—22日，1995。

"NII對圖書館事業之衝擊"，全國大學校院圖書館自動化規劃第十一次研討會，"國立中興大學"（臺中），3月21日，1995，。

"資訊高速公路——邁向21世紀圖書館服務的契機"，建構資訊高速公路圖書館扮演的角色學術研討會，"國立中央圖書館"（臺北），10月1日，1994。

"資訊高速公路"，南開大學信息資源管理學系十週年慶祝大會，南開大學（天津市），9月16日，1994。

"臺灣地區'國立大學'院校圖書館自動化之經驗與問題"，海峽兩岸第二屆圖書資訊學術研討會，北京大學（北京市），8月21—24日，1994。

"圖書館學教師研究趨勢及資訊需求"，當代圖書館事業論集，漢美（臺北市），頁627—664，1994。

"資訊網路時代臺灣地區圖書資訊服務的新方向"，"中國圖書館學會"會報第52期（1994）：51—62。

"我對改進圖書資訊學教育的淺見"，上海高校圖書情報季刊，13期（1994）：7。

"美國書目計量學博士論文評析"，"中國圖書館學會"會訊第51期（1993）：231—241。

"資訊網路時代臺灣地區圖書館資訊服務的新方向"，海峽兩岸首屆圖書資訊學術研討會，上海市，12月，1993。

"Planning An Integrated Library Information Network System：the Taiwan Experience" International Seminar on Collection Development & Resources Sharing in Modern Libraries，Xi'an，China，May 17－20，1992.

"科技資訊網路"，書府第12期（1991）：4—10。

"加值與圖書館作業"，書府第11期（1990）：4—6。

"圖書館自動化概論"，圖書館自動化研討會演講專輯（臺中市：臺中市立文化中心），頁1—23，1989。

"資訊與電腦"，書府第10期（1989）：8—9。

"Present Status of Library & Information Science Education in Taiwan，"Seminar on Library Automation and Information Networks，"National Central Library"（Taipei，Taiwan.）June 8－9，1988.

Library Automation and Information Networks 1988，Proceedings the Taiwan Committee for

Scientific and Scholarly Cooperation with the U.S., Academic Sinica, "National Central Library", Taipei., 247 p, 1989.

"圖書館自動化資訊系統發展之研究","中國圖書館學會"會報,第 43 期 (1988):107—123。[優等]

"學術研究圖書館館員對圖書館自動化認識與態度",圖書館學刊第 5 期(1987): 13—36。

"On-line Public Access Catalog Display Formats", Encyclopedia of Library and Information Science Vol. 38, Suppl. 3 (1985): 325-338.

"Education and Training for On-line Use of Database in Taiwan", International Conference on Library and Information Science Education, Nov. 29-30, National Taiwan University, Taipei, 1985. [甲種]

"WEBNET Circulation System: An Early Use Study", Journal of Library and Information Science Vol. 10 (2) (1984): 163-183.

"Non-bibliographic Database", Journal of Library and Information Science Vol. 9 (1) (1983): 74-93.

"資料庫與線上檢索服務",圖書館學與資訊科學 5 (1) (1981):79—103.

"Chinese MARC: Its Present Status and Future Development", Journal of Library & Information Science Vol. 7 (1) (1981): 1-18.

"Chinese MARC: Its Present Status and Future Development", International Conference on Chinese Library Automation Proceedings, April 1981, National Taiwan Technology Institute, Taipei. And also presented at International Federation of Library Associations and Institutions (IFLA) Conference, 1981.

"Chinese MARC Format for Books", Paper presented at IFLA Annual Meeting, Leipzig, East Germany, Oct., 1981.

"ERIC 索引典與索引典之結構",教育資料研討會記錄,"國立師範大學",1980: 65—70。

"'教育部'和本系新修訂之圖書館專業必修課程",書府 1 期(1980):7—8。

"美國報導科學"。美國圖書館業務(編者李志鍾),臺北市:遠東,1972:172。

海內外學術獎及其他學術活動

(一)貢獻與學術獎

"中國圖書館學會"特殊貢獻獎(1993 年)

"教育部"大學校院教學特優教師獎(1991 年)

"國科會"甲、優等研究獎(十一次)

Beta Phi Mu, International Library Science Honor Society Member (1990-)

Phi Tai Phi Scholastic Honor Society of America Member (1991-)

American Chemical Society, Pittsburgh Section, Student Affiliate Chapters Award (1958)

(二)講學

北京大學信息管理系講座(北京,1998 年)

南開大學信息資源管理系講座（天津，1996 年）

University of Pittsburgh, School of Library & Information Science 訪問學者（U.S.A., Pittsburgh, 1993 年）

（三）應邀為國際著名期刊編輯委員

Annals of Information Technology and Librarianship（AITL）, Penn State Harrisburg, Idea Group Publishing（美國）

Asian Libraries, Library Marketing Services Ltd.（泰國）

The Third World Libraries, Rosary College（美國）

The Library Quarterly, The University of Chicago Press（美國）

（四）應邀列入國際名人錄

Who's Who in the World, Marquis Who's Who（美國），2002.

Dictionary of International Biography（DIB）, Melrose Press Ltd.（英國），2000.

International Who's Who of Professional and Business Women, IBC, Cambridge（英國），1989.

世界名人錄（北京）

世界華人英才名錄（北京）(http://www.worldperson.com)

世界華人精英大典（中國國際名人名家研究院，北京）

發光的女人：她們為什麼提早成功（文經社，臺北），1992。